A few decades after the tried and tested commentaries by F. F. Bruce and by C. K. Barrett, Walton provides an excellent, fresh commentary on the book of Acts in the best British tradition: detailed and erudite explanation of the Greek text (that is, commentary on the actual text rather than on research old and new) and a balanced focus on history and theology in Acts. Walton stresses the way in which God acted in all of the events and the responses he sought (and still seeks!) from people In addition, the commentary possesses a clarity in style, a warm faith perspective, and inspiring reflections on the meaning of the text for our day and age. Read, learn, enjoy, and serve!

—***Christoph W. Stenschke,*** Department of New Testament and Related Literature, Faculty of Theology and Religion, University of Pretoria, South Africa

The first volume of Steve Walton's Word commentary on Acts is a long-awaited publishing achievement. With his accustomed clarity and charity, Walton invites us to sit around the table with the Greek text of Acts in the center, engaging in conversation with a wealth of scholarship old and new. Walton explains the Greek text clearly (with "intermediate" Greek students in mind), threading his way expertly through the intricacies of Acts interpretation but never losing sight of the message of the text about the way God acts in the world and its importance for readers today.

—***Loveday Alexander,*** professor emerita, University of Sheffield

Steve Walton's commentary is a long-awaited event in the study of Acts of the Apostles. Walton is rightly known for his mastery of the scholarly literature, and he puts that knowledge to admirable use in his reading of the text. Scholars, pastors, teachers, and students will all benefit from Walton's exposition.

—***C. Kavin Rowe,*** George Washington Ivey Distinguished Professor of New Testament, Duke University

With critical attention to history and theology and to literary and cultural contexts alike, Steve Walton invites us to read Acts in all its complexity so that Luke's storytelling can continue to nurture faithful communities today. This commentary will quickly become a vital resource on Acts for both scholars and preachers.

—***Eric Barreto,*** Weyerhaeuser Associate Professor of New Testament, Princeton Theological Seminary

Steve Walton is one of the leading scholars of the Acts of the Apostles of this generation. With this thorough commentary, we have the benefit of sitting at the feet of a master interpreter of Acts and learning what he has to say about the entire corpus of Acts. You are in for a feast!

—***Osvaldo Padilla,*** professor of divinity and New Testament, Beeson Divinity School

This wonderful commentary reflects decades of detailed study of the text of the Acts of the Apostles. It is a remarkable achievement: a commentary on the Greek text, fully informed by recent scholarship, which discusses all the important dimensions of the text of Acts and is rich in theological depth and insight. It will be a treasured resource for decades to come, assisting scholars and students alike to interpret the message of Acts.

—***Paul Trebilco,*** professor of New Testament studies, University of Otago, New Zealand

Steve Walton has dedicated decades to studying Acts and scholarship about this intriguing piece of scripture. His detailed exposition of Acts consistently keeps the biblical text in the center of the discussion. A storehouse loaded with knowledge and insight to feed scholars, ministry leaders, and students, Walton's commentary is no small achievement!

—***Matthew L. Skinner,*** Asher O. and Carrie Nasby Professor of New Testament, Luther Seminary

I welcome this eclectic, traditional, and conservative reading of this commentary based on the Greek text of Acts (1–9). The variety of reading approaches allows the reader to gain a better understanding of the overall salvific message for all, rather than just the opinions of scholars. Expectantly, I await the culmination of the project. I plan to use the commentary in my classes.

— ***Ruben Muñoz-Larrondo,*** associate professor of biblical studies, Andrews University

In this first volume of three, Steve Walton's expertise on the book of Acts is supremely evident. Careful and thorough, Walton's commentary keeps our eyes firmly fixed on the text of Acts, while illuminating key historical and theological matters, as well as the text's richly Jewish context. In doing so, Walton has provided an invaluable resource to students, scholars, and pastors alike for many years to come.

—***Brittany E. Wilson,*** associate professor of New Testament, Duke University

Steve Walton is a master of exegetical conversation with rich detail and a teacher's voice. This volume is a valuable contribution to Luke-Acts scholarship and will be needed on the shelves of pastors, teachers, scholars, and students.

—***Sarah Harris,*** research fellow, Carey Baptist College, New Zealand

WORD BIBLICAL COMMENTARY

Volumes

1 Genesis 1–15 . . . Gordon J. Wenham
2 Genesis 16–50 . . . Gordon J. Wenham
3 Exodus . . . John I. Durham
4 Leviticus . . . John E. Hartley
5 Numbers** . . . Philip J. Budd
6a Deuteronomy 1:1–21:9, Second Edition . . . Duane L. Christensen
6b Deuteronomy 21:10–34:12 . . . Duane L. Christensen
7a Joshua 1–12, Second Edition . . . Trent C. Butler
7b Joshua 13–24, Second Edition . . . Trent C. Butler
8 Judges . . . Trent C. Butler
9 Ruth–Esther . . . Frederic W. Bush
10 1 Samuel, Second Edition . . . Ralph W. Klein
11 2 Samuel . . . A. A. Anderson
12 1 Kings, Second Edition . . . Simon J. Devries
13 2 Kings . . . T. R. Hobbs
14 1 Chronicles** . . . Roddy Braun
15 2 Chronicles** . . . Raymond B. Dillard
16 Ezra–Nehemiah** . . . H. G. M. Williamson
17 Job 1–20 . . . David J. A. Clines
18a Job 21–37 . . . David J. A. Clines
18b Job 38–42 . . . David J. A. Clines
19 Psalms 1–50, Second Edition** . . . Peter C. Craigie, with Marvin E. Tate
20 Psalms 51–100** . . . Marvin E. Tate
21 Psalms 101–150, Revised Edition** . . . Leslie C. Allen
22 Proverbs . . . Roland Murphy
23a Ecclesiastes . . . Roland Murphy
23b Song of Songs/Lamentations . . . Duane Garrett and Paul House
24 Isaiah 1–33, Revised Edition . . . John D. W. Watts
25 Isaiah 34–66, Revised Edition . . . John D. W. Watts
26 Jeremiah 1–25 . . . Peter C. Craigie, Page H. Kelley, and Joel F. Drinkard Jr.
27 Jeremiah 26–52 . . . Gerald L. Keown, Pamela J. Scalise, and Thomas G. Smothers
28 Ezekiel 1–19 . . . Leslie C. Allen
29 Ezekiel 20–48 . . . Leslie C. Allen
30 Daniel, Revised Edition . . . John Goldingay
31 Hosea–Jonah** . . . Douglas Stuart
32 Micah–Malachi** . . . Ralph L. Smith
33a Matthew 1–13** . . . Donald A. Hagner
33b Matthew 14–28** . . . Donald A. Hagner
34a Mark 1–8:26** . . . Robert A. Guelich
34b Mark 8:27–16:20** . . . Craig A. Evans
35a Luke 1–9:20** . . . John Nolland
35b Luke 9:21–18:34** . . . John Nolland
35c Luke 18:35–24:53** . . . John Nolland
36 John, Second Edition** . . . George R. Beasley-Murray
37a Acts 1–9:42* . . . Steve Walton
37b Acts 9:43–19* . . . Steve Walton
37c Acts 20–28* . . . Steve Walton
38a Romans 1–8** . . . James D. G. Dunn
38b Romans 9–16** . . . James D. G. Dunn
39 1 Corinthians* . . . TBA
40 2 Corinthians, Second Edition . . . Ralph P. Martin
41 Galatians** . . . Richard N. Longenecker
42 Ephesians** . . . Andrew T. Lincoln
43 Philippians . . . Ralph P. Martin and Gerald F. Hawthorne
44a Colossians* . . . Clinton E. Arnold
44b Philemon* . . . Clinton E. Arnold and Daniel K. Darko
45 1 & 2 Thessalonians, Revised Edition . . . Seyoon Kim and F. F. Bruce
46 Pastoral Epistles . . . William D. Mounce
47a Hebrews 1–8** . . . William L. Lane
47b Hebrews 9–13** . . . William L. Lane
48 James** . . . Ralph P. Martin
49 1 Peter** . . . J. Ramsey Michaels
50 Jude, 2 Peter** . . . Richard J. Bauckham
51 1, 2, 3, John, Revised** . . . Stephen S. Smalley
52a Revelation 1–5** . . . David E. Aune
52b Revelation 6–16** . . . David E. Aune
52c Revelation 17–22** . . . David E. Aune

**Forthcoming as of 2024*
***Revised/new edition forthcoming as of 2024*

37A WORD BIBLICAL COMMENTARY

Acts 1–9:42

STEVE WALTON

Old Testament Editor: Nancy L. deClaissé-Walford

New Testament Editor: David B. Capes

ZONDERVAN ACADEMIC

Acts 1–9:42, Volume 37A

Published in Grand Rapids, Michigan, by Zondervan. Zondervan is a registered trademark of HarperCollins Christian Publishing, Inc.

Requests for information should be addressed to customercare@harpercollins.com.

Zondervan titles may be purchased in bulk for educational, business, fundraising, or sales promotional use. For information, please email SpecialMarkets@Zondervan.com.

Library of Congress Cataloging-in-Publication Data

Names: Walton, Steve, 1955- author.
Title: Acts 1:1-9:42 / Steve Walton.
Description: Grand Rapids, Michigan : Zondervan Academic, [2024] | Series: Word biblical commentary ; volume 37A | Includes bibliographical references and index.
Identifiers: LCCN 2023057919 (print) | LCCN 2023057920 (ebook) | ISBN 9780310599388 (hardcover) | ISBN 9780310599401 (ebook)
Subjects: LCSH: Bible. Acts, I, 1-IX, 42--Commentaries.
Classification: LCC BS2625.53 .W35 2024 (print) | LCC BS2625.53 (ebook) | DDC 226.6/07--dc23/eng/20240408
LC record available at https://lccn.loc.gov/2023057919
LC ebook record available at https://lccn.loc.gov/2023057920

Unless otherwise noted, all Scripture translations are those of the author.

Printed in the United States of America

25 26 27 28 29 30 31 32 33 34 35 /TRM/ 15 14 13 12 11 10 9 8 7 6 5 4 3

Contents

Editors' Preface

The launching of the Word Biblical Commentary in 1977 brought to fulfillment the dream of a new commentary series on the books of the Bible. The founding editorial board determined to include a number of features in the commentary series that were distinctive at the time and remain essential features of a trustworthy commentary in the twenty-first century.

The original editorial board sought authors from around the world who, while broadly identified as evangelical in its positive, historic sense, represented a rich diversity of denominational allegiances and who could offer the best in biblical scholarship. It was important for the editors that while these authors were scholars actively engaged in teaching in university and seminary settings, they were also involved in church ministry. That commitment continues today as revisions and updates are undertaken on various volumes in the series.

The board determined that the layout of the commentary series would follow a format consciously designed to assist readers at different levels. First, authors were to use their own *Translations* of the texts as the basis of their comments and exegesis, examining carefully the textual, linguistic, and structural evidence and providing ample explanatory *Notes*. Thus, in the words of the original editorial board, while the series is based on the biblical languages, "it seeks to make the technical and scholarly approach to a theological understanding of Scripture understandable by—and useful to—the fledging student, the working minister, and colleagues in the guild of professional scholars and teachers as well." As revisions and updates are produced, the same careful attention to translation has been maintained. Secondly, an extensive *Bibliography* at the beginning of each section provided the reader with ample information on the then state of scholarship and an opportunity to dig deeper. That continues in the revisions and updates with only slight changes to the format of the bibliographies. Thirdly, the section titled *Form/Structure/Setting* discussed the redaction, genre, sources, and tradition. They concern the origin of the text, its canonical form, and its relation to the biblical and extrabiblical contexts in order to illuminate the structure and character of the text. And finally, the *Comment* and *Explanation* sections first offered a verse-by-verse interpretation of the text and dialogue with interpreters, engaging with current opinion and scholarly research and then discussing its relevance to the ongoing life of faith communities today. These two important sections are maintained in the revised and updated volumes, and to aid in reading, footnotes are now employed in place of in-text citations. The ongoing revisions and updates also extensively incorporate new scholarship and provide insights into the relevance of the biblical texts for faith communities in the twenty-first century.

The current editorial board, in the spirit of the founding editorial board, pray that "if these aims come anywhere near realization, the intention of the editors will have been met, and the labor of our team of contributors rewarded."

Old Testament Editor: Nancy L. deClaissé-Walford
New Testament Editor: David B. Capes

Author's Preface

It is a risky thing to write a commentary, for it involves decisions about where to focus at almost every point. It is particularly so with Acts, for it is a unique book in the New Testament in telling the story of the beginnings and growth of the earliest believing communities and has a wide range of questions and issues worthy of discussion in almost every passage. Many reviews of academic books go along the lines of: "This is interesting, but it isn't what I would have done." This goes double for biblical commentaries, and so I am acutely aware of the many questions I have chosen not to pursue and the likelihood that I shall receive the same kinds of reviews. Nevertheless, I have written what I have written, and I offer this study to my fellow scholars and to students and pastors who study the book of Acts as a contribution to further study that will, I am sure, quarry more ideas and material than I have been able to do.

In studying a biblical book, I am deeply aware of standing on the shoulders of others whose research and insights have enabled me to see the book more clearly. My scholarly debts will be apparent in the sectional bibliographies and footnotes (whose introduction is a wise change made by the series editors from earlier volumes). A number of others have encouraged and helped me in various ways. Julie Robb acted as my research assistant for a substantial period and contributed much. The late Geoffrey Williams cast his classicist's eye over my *Translation* and *Notes* sections, and they are much better for his comments. Julie and Geoffrey were two members of my summer Acts reading weeks, along with (at different times) Andy Bannister, Jane McLarty, Christy Sunman, Dave Sunman, Jody Barnard, and Simon Marchant, and I gained much from conversations about Acts with them. People too numerous to list have kindly read drafts of sections, and I am immensely grateful for their comments.

I have had extended research leave periods in which I have worked on this commentary, notably at the Center for Theological Inquiry, Princeton, NJ, and in Cambridge at Tyndale House, and as visiting fellow at Clare Hall and visiting scholar at the Faculty of Divinity. I am thankful for colleagues in these places who have facilitated my research, and particularly for the wonderful library resources available.

Over the period of writing this commentary, since the initial invitation to work on it from Ralph P. Martin, then the NT series editor, I have worked in different colleges and universities, and I am glad to have had some encouraging and supportive colleagues, particularly in New Testament, in those places. I am also very grateful to Ralph's successors as NT editors of the series, Peter Davids and now David Capes, as well as my editors at Zondervan Academic, Katya Covrett and Lee Fields.

Seventy-two people have kindly received a monthly email from me and prayed regularly for me during the writing of this commentary. This group of people have been faithful in encouraging me and praying, and I'm immensely glad to have them praying on my behalf.

Finally, throughout the whole process, my wife Ali has patiently experienced the presence of "the commentary" in our marriage and home. I cannot repay the time and effort that has gone into this book, but I can and do express my deep thanks to her.

Steve Walton, April 2022

Abbreviations

A. General Abbreviations

abs.	absolute
acc.	accusative
act.	active
adj.	adjective/adjectival
ad loc.	*ad locum* "at the place"
adv.	adverb/adverbial
al.	*alia* "other (witnesses)"
aor.	aorist
art.	article, articular
ca.	circa
ch., chs.	chapter, chapters
conj.	conjunction
dat.	dative
dem.	demonstrative
esp.	especially
ET	English translation
EVV	English versions
f.	feminine
frg./frgs	fragment(s)
FS	Festschrift
fut.	future
gen.	genitive
Gk.	Greek
Heb.	Hebrew
impf.	imperfect
impv.	imperative
inart.	inarticular
indef.	indefinite
indic.	indicative
inf.	infinitive
lit.	literal/literally
m.	masculine
mid.	middle
MS, MSS	manuscript, manuscripts
Mt	Mount(ain)
n, nn	note, notes
neut.	neuter
nom.	nominative
ns	new series
obj.	object/objective
par./pars	parallel passage(s)
pass.	passive
per.	person, personal
periph.	periphrastic
pf.	perfect
pl.	plural
plpf.	pluperfect
prep.	preposition
pres.	present
pron.	pronoun
ptc.	participle
rdg.	reading
R.	Rabbi
rel.	relative
repr.	reprinted
rev.	revised
sg.	singular
subj.	subject/subjective
supp.	supplement
s.v.	*sub verbo* ("under the word")
trans.	translator, translated by
UBS	United Bible Societies
UP	University Press
usu.	usually
voc.	vocative
v.l.	*varia lectio* (variant reading)

B. Texts, Translations, and Paraphrases

CEB	Common English Bible
CEV	Contemporary English Version
CSB	Christian Standard Bible
ECM	Editio Critica Maior III. Edited by H. Strutwolf, G. Gäbel, A. Hüffmeier, G. Mink, and K. Wachtel. *Apostelgeschichte.* 4 vols. Stuttgart: Deutsche Bibelgesellschaft, 2017
GNB	Good News Bible
HCSB	Holman Christian Standard Bible
KJV	King James (Authorised) Version
LXX	Septuagint (normally A. Rahlfs and R. Hanhart, eds. *Septuaginta: id est Vetus Testamentum graece iuxta LXX interpretes.* Editio altera. Stuttgart: Deutsche Bibelgesellschaft, 2006
MESSAGE	E. Peterson, *The Message*
MT	Masoretic Text
$NA^{27/28}$	*Novum Testamentum Graece.* 27th/28th corrected eds. 2001, 2012
NASB	New American Standard Bible
NEB	New English Bible
NET	New English Translation (http://www.bible.org/netbible/index.htm)
NETS	New English Translation of the Septuagint
NIV84	New International Version (1984 ed.)
NIV	New International Version (2011 ed.)
NLT	New Living Translation
NRSV	New Revised Standard Version
NRSVue	New Revised Standard Version, updated edition
NTE	*The New Testament for Everyone.* T. Wright. London: SPCK, 2011 = *The Kingdom New Testament.* New York: HarperOne, 2011
PHILLIPS	J. B. Phillips, *The New Testament in Modern English*
REB	Revised English Bible
RSV	Revised Standard Version
SP	Samaritan Pentateuch
THGNT	[Tyndale House Greek New Testament.] *The Greek New Testament: Produced at Tyndale House, Cambridge.* Edited by Dirk Jongkind. Wheaton, IL: Crossway; Cambridge: Cambridge University Press, 2017
TNIV	Today's New International Version
TO^2	*Le texte occidental des Actes des Apôtres.* Boismard, M.-É. 2nd ed. Ebib ns 40. Paris: Gabalda, 2000

UBS[4/5] United Bible Societies. *The Greek New Testament*. 4th (corrected)/5th ed. 1993, 2014
WH Westcott, B. F., and F. J. A. Hort, eds. *The Greek New Testament*. Peabody, MA: Hendrickson, 2007 (original ed. 1881)
α′ Aquila
θ′ Theodotion
σ′ Symmachus

C. Commonly Used Periodicals, Reference Works, and Serials

ABD *Anchor Bible Dictionary*. Edited by D. N. Freedman. 6 vols. New York: Doubleday, 1992
AcBib Academica Biblica
AGJU Arbeiten zur Geschichte des antiken Judentums und des Urchristentums
AnGr Analecta gregoriana
ANRW *Aufstieg und Niedergang der römischen Welt: Geschichte und Kultur Roms im Spiegel der neueren Forschung*. Edited by H. Temporini and W. Haase. Part 2, Principat. Berlin: de Gruyter, 1972
ANTF Arbeiten zur neutestamentlichen Textforschung
ArBib The Aramaic Bible
ASMS American Society of Missiology Series
AThR *Anglican Theological Review*
AYBRL Anchor Yale Bible Reference Library
BAFCS The Book of Acts in Its First Century Setting
BAGD Bauer, W., W. F. Arndt, F. W. Gingrich, and F. W. Danker, eds. *A Greek-English Lexicon of the New Testament and Other Early Christian Literature*. 2nd ed. Chicago: University of Chicago Press, 1979
BDB Brown, Francis, S. R. Driver, and Charles A. Briggs. *A Hebrew and English Lexicon of the Old Testament*
BegC *The Beginnings of Christianity, Part I: The Acts of the Apostles*. Edited by F. J. Foakes Jackson and K. Lake. 5 vols. London: Macmillan, 1920–33. Repr., Grand Rapids: Baker, 1977.
BDAG Bauer, W., F. W. Danker, W. F. Arndt, and F. W. Gingrich, eds. *A Greek-English Lexicon of the New Testament and Other Early Christian Literature*. 3rd ed. Chicago: University of Chicago Press, 2000
BDF Blass, F., A. Debrunner, and R. W. Funk. *A Greek Grammar of the New Testament and Other Early Christian Literature*. Cambridge: Cambridge University Press, 1961.
BHGNT Baylor Handbook on the Greek New Testament

Bib	*Biblica*
BibInt	Biblical Interpretation Series
BibInt	*Biblical Interpretation*
BiTS	Biblical Tools and Studies
BNP	*Brill's New Pauly: Encyclopaedia of the Ancient World.* Edited by H. Cancik. 22 vols. Leiden: Brill: 2002–2011
BSem	The Biblical Seminar
BT	*Bible Translator*
BTB	*Biblical Theology Bulletin*
BTCB	Brazos Theological Commentary on the Bible
BU	Biblische Untersuchungen
Burton	Burton, Ernest de W. *Syntax of the Moods and Tenses in New Testament Greek.* 3rd ed. Edinburgh: T&T Clark, 1898. Repr., 1973
BZ	*Biblische Zeitschrift*
CBGM	Coherence-Based Genealogical Method
CBQ	*Catholic Biblical Quarterly*
CBSC	Cambridge Bible for Schools and Colleges
CC	Continental Commentaries
CD	*Church Dogmatics.* K. Barth. Translated and edited by G. W. Bromiley and T. F. Torrance. 14 vols. Logos Research ed. London: T&T Clark, 1963–2011
CGCG	*Cambridge Grammar of Classical Greek.* E. van Boas, A. Rijksbaron, L. Huitink, and M. de Bakker. Cambridge: Cambridge University Press, 2019
CGL	*Cambridge Greek Lexicon.* Edited by J. Diggle, B. L. James, P. J. Fraser, O. B. Simkin, A. A. Thompson, and S. J. Westripp. 2 vols. Cambridge: Cambridge University Press, 2021
CHJ	*The Cambridge History of Judaism.* Edited by W. D. Davies, L. Finkelstein, W. Horbury, J. Sturdy, S. T. Katz, P. I. Lieberman, R. Chazan, J. Karp, A. Sutcliffe, M. B. Hart, and T. Michels. 8 vols. Cambridge: Cambridge University Press, 1984–97.
ChrT	*Christianity Today*
CIG	*Corpus Inscriptionum Graecarum.* Edited by A. Boeckh. 4 vols. Berlin: Ex officina Academica, 1828–1877
CIJ	*Corpus Inscriptionum Iudaicarum.* Edited by J. B. Frey. 2 vols. Rome: Pontificio istituto di archeologia cristiana, 1936, 1952
CIJ^{2}	*Corpus of Jewish Inscriptions: Jewish Inscriptions from the Third Century BC to the Seventh Century AD.* Edited by J. B. Frey. 2nd ed. Library of Biblical Studies. New York: Ktav, 1975

CIL — *Corpus Inscriptionum Latinarum*. Berlin-Brandenburgischen Akadmie der Wissenschaften. 17 vols. Berlin: Reimerum, 1862–

CJA — Christianity and Judaism in Antiquity

CJOD — Contraversions: Jews and Other Differences

CMRDM — *Corpus monumentorum religionis dei Menis*. Edited by E. N. Lane. 4 vols. Etudes préliminaires aux religions orientales dans l'Empire romain 19. Leiden: Brill, 1971–1978

Comfort — Comfort, P. W. *New Testament Text and Translation Commentary*. Carol Stream, IL: Tyndale House, 2008

ConcJ — *Concordia Journal*

CPJ — *Corpus Papyrorum Judaicarum*. Edited by V. A. Tcherikover, A. Fuks, and M. Stern. 3 vols. Cambridge, MA: Magnes/Harvard University Press, 1957–1963

CR — *Classical Review*

CWHS — *Cambridge World History of Slavery*. Edited by K. Bradley, P. Cartledge, D. Eltis, and S. L. Engerman. 4 vols. Cambridge: Cambridge University Press, 2011–2017

D&M — Dana, H. E., and J. R. Mantey. *A Manual Grammar of the Greek New Testament*. New York: Macmillan, 1957

DBIm — *Dictionary of Biblical Imagery*. Edited by L. Ryken, J. C. Wilhoit, and T. Longman III. Leicester: Inter-Varsity Press; Downers Grove, IL: InterVarsity Press, 1998

DFNTG[2] — *Discourse Features of New Testament Greek*. S. H. Levinsohn, 2nd ed. Dallas: SIL International, 2000

DJG — *Dictionary of Jesus and the Gospels*. Edited by J. B. Green, S. McKnight, and I. H. Marshall. Leicester: Inter-Varsity Press, 1992

DJG[2] — *Dictionary of Jesus and the Gospels*. Edited by J. B. Green, J. K. Brown and N. Perrin. 2nd ed. Downers Grove, IL: IVP Academic, 2013

DLNTD — *Dictionary of the Later New Testament and Its Developments*. Edited by R. P. Martin and P. H. Davids. Leicester: Inter-Varsity Press; Downers Grove, IL: IVP Academic, 1997

DNTB — *Dictionary of New Testament Background*. Edited by C. A. Evans and S. E. Porter. Downers Grove, IL: IVP Academic; Leicester: Inter-Varsity Press, 2000

DOCD — Digital *Oxford Classical Dictionary*, online: https://oxfordre.com/classics

EBC — *The Expositor's Bible Commentary*. Edited by F. E. Gaebelein. 12 vols. Grand Rapids: Zondervan, 1976–88

EC — Epworth Commentaries

EDNT	*Exegetical Dictionary of the New Testament.* Edited by H. Balz and G. Schneider. 3 vols. Grand Rapids: Eerdmans, 1990–1993
EDG	*Etymological Dictionary of Greek.* R. Beekes and L. van Beek. 2 vols. Leiden Indo-European Etymological Dictionary Series 10. Leiden: Brill, 2010
EH	Europäische Hochschulschriften
EHPR	Etudes d'histoire et de philosophie religieuses
ESEC	Emory Studies in Early Christianity
ETR	*Études theologiques et religieuses*
EvQ	*Evangelical Quarterly*
EvRT	*Evangelical Review of Theology*
ExpTim	*Expository Times*
FCNT	Feminist Companion to the New Testament and Early Christian Writings
GE	*Brill Dictionary of Ancient Greek.* Edited by F. Montanari, M. Goh, and C. M. Schroeder. Leiden: Brill, 2015
GELS	Muraoka, T. *A Greek-English Lexicon of the Septuagint.* Leuven: Peeters, 2009
HNT	Handbuch zum Neuen Testament
IBMR	*International Bulletin for Missionary Research*
IBRB	Institute for Biblical Research Bibliographies
IDB	*The Interpreter's Dictionary of the Bible.* Edited by G. A. Buttrick. 4 vols. Nashville: Abingdon, 1962.
IGRR	*Inscriptiones Graecae ad res romanas pertinentes.* Edited by R. Cagnet. 3 vols. Paris: Leroux, 1906–1927.
ILS	*Inscriptiones Latinae Selectae.* Edited by H. Dessau. 3 vols. Berlin: Weidmann, 1892–1916
Int	Interpretation (commentary series)
Int	*Interpretation* (journal)
JASCG	*Journal of the American Society for Church Growth*
JBLMS	Journal of Biblical Literature Monograph Series
JPT	*Journal of Pentecostal Theology*
JPTSup	Journal of Pentecostal Theology Supplement Series
JRT	*Journal of Religious Thought*
JSJSup	Journal for the Study of Judaism Supplement Series
JSNT	*Journal for the Study of the New Testament*
JSNTSup	Journal for the Study of the New Testament Supplement Series
JSPSup	Journal for the Study of the Pseudepigrapha Supplement Series
JSS	*Journal of Semitic Studies*

L&N	Louw, J. P., and E. A. Nida, eds. *Greek-English Lexicon of the New Testament Based on Semantic Domains.* 2 vols. 2nd ed. New York: United Bible Societies, 1988
LCL	Loeb Classical Library
LD	Lectio Divina
LDGNT	*Lexham Discourse Greek New Testament.* S. E. Runge. Logos ed. Bellingham, WA: Lexham, 2008–2014
LEH^2	Lust, J., E. Eynikel, and K. Hauspie, eds. *A Greek-English Lexicon of the Septuagint.* Revised ed. Stuttgart: Deutsche Bibelgesellschaft, 2003
LGPN	*Lexicon of Greek Personal Names.* P. M. Fraser, E. Matthews, M. J. Osborne, S. G. Byrne, T. Corsten, J.-S. Balzat, R. W. V. Catling, É. Chiricat and F. Marchand. 5 vols. Oxford: Clarendon, 1987–2018
LMM	*Lutheran Mission Matters*
LNTS	Library of New Testament Studies
LSJ	Liddell, Henry George, Robert Scott, Henry Stuart Jones, eds. *A Greek-English Lexicon.* 9th ed. 2 vols. Oxford: Clarendon, 1940. Repr., 1951
LSJ (1996)	Liddell, Henry George, Robert Scott, Henry Stuart Jones, Roderick McKenzie, P. G. W. Glare, and A. Anne Thompson. *A Greek-English Lexicon.* 9th ed. With revised supplement. Oxford: Clarendon, 1996
McKay	McKay, K. L. *A New Syntax of the Verb in New Testament Greek: An Aspectual Approach.* Studies in Biblical Greek 5. New York: Peter Lang, 1994
Moule	Moule, C. F. D. *An Idiom-Book of New Testament Greek.* 2nd ed. Cambridge: Cambridge University Press, 1959
MHT	Moulton, J. H., W. F. Howard and N. Turner. *Grammar of New Testament Greek.* 4 vols. Edinburgh: T&T Clark, 1906–76
Miss	*Missiology*
MNTS	McMaster New Testament Studies
MTL	Marshall's Theological Library
Neot	*Neotestamentica*
NewDocs	*New Documents Illustrating Earliest Christianity.* Edited by G. H. R. Horsley and S. R. Llewelyn. 10 vols. North Ryde, NSW: Ancient History Documentary Research Centre, Macquarie University; Grand Rapids: Eerdmans, 1981–2012
NIDNTT	*The New International Dictionary of New Testament Theology.* Edited by C. Brown. 4 vols. Exeter: Paternoster; Grand Rapids: Zondervan, 1975–1978

NIDNTTE	*New International Dictionary of New Testament Theology and Exegesis*. Edited by M. Silva. 2nd ed. 5 vols. Grand Rapids: Zondervan, 2014
NovT	*Novum Testamentum*
NovTSup	Novum Testamentum Supplement Series
NTDH	Neukirchener theologische Dissertationen und Habilitationen
NTM	New Testament Monographs
NTS	*New Testament Studies*
NTSI	The New Testament and the Scriptures of Israel
NTTS	New Testament Tools and Studies
NVBS	New Voices in Biblical Studies
OCD[3]	*Oxford Classical Dictionary*. Edited by S. Hornblower and A. Spawforth. 3rd ed. Oxford: Oxford University Press, 1996
OCP	*Online Critical Pseudepigrapha* https://pseudepigrapha.org
OGIS	*Orientis Graeci Inscriptiones Selectae*. Edited by W. Dittenberger. 2 vols. Leipzig: Hirzel, 1903–1905
OHAGR	*Oxford Handbook of Ancient Greek Religion*. Edited by E. Eidinow and J. Kindt. Oxford: Oxford University Press, 2015
OTL	Old Testament Library
OTP	*The Old Testament Pseudepigrapha*. Edited by J. H. Charlesworth. 2 vols. New York: Doubleday, 1983, 1985
OxPap	*The Oxyrhynchus Papyri*. Edited by S. Hunt. London: British Academy/Egypt Exploration Society, 1898–
PBA	*Proceedings of the British Academy*
PBM	Paternoster Biblical Monographs
PBTM	Paternoster Biblical and Theological Monographs
PC	Proclamation Commentaries
PGM	*Papyri Graecae Magicae: die griechischen Zauberpapyri*. Edited by K. Preisendanz. 2 vols. Leipzig: Teubner, 1928; ET: H. D Betz, ed. *The Greek Magical Papyri in Translation: Including the Demotic Spells, vol. 1: Text*. 2nd ed. Chicago: University of Chicago Press, 1992
PJBR	*Polish Journal of Biblical Research*
PLAL	Perspectives on Linguistics and Ancient Languages
PNTC	Pillar New Testament Commentary
Poet. Today	*Poetics Today*
Porter	Porter, S. E. *Idioms of the Greek New Testament*. 2nd ed. Biblical Languages: Greek 2. Sheffield: JSOT, 1994.
PRSt	*Perspectives in Religious Studies*
POLTTS	Pittsburgh Original Language Texts and Translations Series
PTMS	Princeton Theological Monograph Series

Radermacher	Radermacher, L. *Neutestamentliche Grammatik: das Griechisch des Neuen Testaments im Zusammenhang mit der Volkssprache.* 2nd ed. HNT 1. Tübingen: Mohr Siebeck, 1925
RelSRev	*Religious Studies Review*
ResQ	*Restoration Quarterly*
RevQ	*Revue de Qumran*
Robertson	Robertson, A. T. *A Grammar of the Greek New Testament in the Light of Historical Research.* London: Hodder & Stoughton, 1914
RTR	*Reformed Theological Review*
SAIS	Studies in the Aramaic Interpretation of Scripture
SBLDS	Society of Biblical Literature Dissertation Series
SBLMS	Society of Biblical Literature Monograph Series
SBLSP	Society of Biblical Literature Seminar Papers
SBT	Studies in Biblical Theology
Schneemelcher	Schneemelcher, W., and R. M. Wilson, eds. *New Testament Apocrypha.* Revised ed. 2 vols. Cambridge: James Clarke, 1991
Schürer	Schürer, E., G. Vermes, and F. Millar. *The History of the Jewish People in the Age of Jesus Christ (175 BC–AD 135).* Revised ed. 4 vols. Edinburgh: T&T Clark, 1973–1986
SCI	*Scripta Classica Israelica*
SCJ	Studies in Christianity and Judaism
SEG	Supplementum epigraphicum gracecum
SHBC	Smith and Helwys Bible Commentary
SIG	*Sylloge Inscriptionum Graecarum.* Edited by W. Dittenberger. 3rd ed. 4 vols. Leipzig: Hirzel, 1915–1924
SJLA	Studies in Judaism in Late Antiquity
SNTSMS	Society for New Testament Studies Monograph Series
SNTSU	Studien zum Neuen Testament und seiner Umwelt
SNTW	Studies in the New Testament and its World
STDJ	Studies on the Texts of the Desert of Judea
Str-B	Strack, H., and P. Billerbeck, eds. *Kommentar zum Neuen Testament aus Talmud und Midrasch.* 7 vols. München: Beck, 1922
TANZ	Texte und Arbeiten zum neutestamentlichen Zeitalter
TCGNT	*A Textual Commentary on the Greek New Testament.* B. M. Metzger. Corrected ed. London: United Bible Societies, 1975
TCGNT[2]	*A Textual Commentary on the Greek New Testament.* B. M. Metzger, 2nd ed. Stuttgart: Deutsche Bibelgesellschaft/United Bible Societies, 1994
TDNT	*Theological Dictionary of the New Testament.* Edited by G. Kittel and G. Friedrich. Translated by G. W. Bromiley. 10 vols. Grand Rapids: Eerdmans, 1964–1976

Them	*Themelios*
Thrall, *Particles*	Thrall, M. E. *Greek Particles in the New Testament.* NTTS 3. Leiden: Brill, 1962
TUGAL	Texte und Untersuchungen zur Geschichte der altchristlichen Literatur
TynBul	*Tyndale Bulletin*
TZ	*Theologische Zeitschrift*
USQR	*Union Seminary Quarterly Review*
VL	Denaux, A., R. Corstjens and H. Margada. *The Vocabulary of Luke: An Alphabetical Presentation and a Survey of Characteristic and Noteworthy Words and Word Groups in Luke's Gospel.* BiTS 10. Leuven: Peeters, 2009
von Siebenthal	von Siebenthal, H. *Ancient Greek Grammar for the Study of the New Testament.* New York: Peter Lang, 2020
VTSup	Supplements to Vetus Testamentum
Wallace	Wallace, D. B. *Greek Grammar beyond the Basics: An Exegetical Syntax of the New Testament.* Grand Rapids: Zondervan Academic, 1996
WBC	Word Biblical Commentary
WestBC	Westminster Bible Companion
WMANT	Wissenschaftliche Monographien zum Alten und Neuen Testament
WUNT	Wissenschaftliche Untersuchungen zum Neuen Testament
ZCINT	Zondervan Critical Introduction to the New Testament
Zerwick	Zerwick, M. *Biblical Greek Illustrated by Examples.* Rome: Pontifical Biblical Institute, 1963, repr. 1979

D. Books of the Bible with Apocrypha

Gen	Genesis	Neh	Nehemiah
Exod	Exodus	Esth	Esther
Lev	Leviticus	Job	Job
Num	Numbers	Ps(s)	Psalms
Deut	Deuteronomy	Prov	Proverbs
Josh	Joshua	Eccl (or Qoh)	Ecclesiastes
Judg	Judges	Song (or Cant)	Song of Songs
Ruth	Ruth	Isa	Isaiah
1–2 Sam	1–2 Samuel	Jer	Jeremiah
1–2 Kgs	1–2 Kings	Lam	Lamentations
1–4 Kgdms	1–4 Kingdoms (LXX of 1 Sam–2 Kgs)	Ezek	Ezekiel
		Dan	Daniel
1–2 Chr	1–2 Chronicles	Hos	Hosea
Ezra	Ezra	Joel	Joel

Amos	Amos	Tob	Tobit
Obad	Obadiah	Wis	Wisdom of Solomon
Jonah	Jonah		
Mic	Micah	Matt	Matthew
Nah	Nahum	Mark	Mark
Hab	Habakkuk	Luke	Luke
Zeph	Zephaniah	John	John
Hag	Haggai	Acts	Acts
Zech	Zechariah	Rom	Romans
Mal	Malachi	1–2 Cor	1–2 Corinthians
Bar	Baruch	Gal	Galatians
Add Dan	Additions to Daniel	Eph	Ephesians
Pr Azar	Prayer of Azariah	Phil	Philippians
Bel	Bel and the Dragon	Col	Colossians
Sg Three	Song of the Three	1–2 Thess	1–2 Thessalonians
Sus	Susanna	1–2 Tim	1–2 Timothy
1–2 Esd	1–2 Esdras	Titus	Titus
Add Esth	Additions to Esther	Phlm	Philemon
Ep Jer	Epistle of Jeremiah	Heb	Hebrews
Jdt	Judith	Jas	James
1–4 Macc	1–4 Maccabees	1–2 Pet	1–2 Peter
Pr Man	Prayer of Manasseh	1–3 John	1–3 John
Ps 151	Psalm 151	Jude	Jude
Sir	Sirach	Rev	Revelation

E. Pseudepigrapha and Early Jewish Literature

1 En.	1 Enoch	Midr.	Midrash (followed by the usual abbreviation for the biblical book)
2 Bar.	2 Baruch		
4 Bar.	4 Baruch		
4 Ezra	4 Ezra	Pesiq. Rab.	Pesiqta Rabbati
Apoc. Ab.	Apocalypse of Abraham	Pirq. R. El.	Pirqe de Rabbi Eliezer
		Pss. Sol.	Psalms of Solomon
Apoc. Mos.	Apocalypse of Moses	*Ord. Levi*	*Ordinances of Levi*
As. Mos.	Assumption of Moses	Rab.	Midrash Rabbah (preceded by the usual abbreviation for the biblical book)
Ascen. Isa.	Ascension of Isaiah		
Exor. A	*Exorcism fragment A*		
Jos. Asen.	Joseph and Aseneth		
Jub.	Jubilees	Sib. Or.	Sybilline Oracles
LAB	Liber antiquitatum biblicarum (Pseudo-Philo)	T. Ab.	Testament of Abraham
		T. Job	Testament of Job
		T. Jos.	Testament of Joseph
Let. Aris.	Letter of Aristeas	T. Jud.	Testament of Judah

T. Mos.	Testament of Moses	T. Sim.	Testament of Simeon
T. Reu.	Testament of Reuben		

F. Dead Sea Scrolls

1QH	Thanksgiving Hymns	4QpNah/169	Pesher on Nahum
		4QFlor/174	Florilegium
1QM	War Scroll	4QTest/175	Testimonia
1QpHab	Pesher on Habakkuk	4Q266	Damascus[a]
		4Q284	Purification Liturgy
1QS	Community Rule		
1QSa	Rule of the Congregation	4Q379	Psalms of Joshua[b]
		4QMMT/394	Miqṣat Maʿaśê ha-Toraha
CD	Damascus Document		
		4Q503	Daily Prayers
4QGen-Exod[a]/1	Genesis-Exodus	11Q5/Ps[a]	Psalms Scroll[a]
4QExod[b]/13	Exodus[b]	11QTemple/19	Temple
4Q158	Biblical Paraphrases		

G. Philo

Abraham	*On the Life of Abraham*	*Joseph*	*On the Life of Joseph*
Alleg. Interp.	*Allegorical Interpretation*	*Migration*	*On the Migration of Abraham*
Creation	*On the Creation of the World*		
		Moses	*On the Life of Moses*
Decal.	*Decalogue*	*Names*	*On the Change of Names*
Dreams	*On Dreams* [=*De somniis*]	*Posterity*	*On the Posterity of Cain*
Embassy	*On the Embassy to Gaius* [= *Legatio ad Gaium*]	*QE* 1, 2	*Questions and Answers in Exodus* 1, 2
Heir	*Who Is the Heir?*	*Spec. Laws*	*On the Special Laws*
Hypoth.	*Hypothetica*	*Virtues*	*On the Virtues*

H. Josephus

Ag. Ap.	*Against Apion*	*J.W.*	*Jewish War*
Ant.	*Antiquities of the Jews*	*Life*	*The Life*

I. Early Christian and Greco-Roman Literature

1–2 Clem.	1–2 Clement
Acts Andr.	Acts of Andrew
Acts Paul	Acts of Paul

Aeschylus, *Cho.*	Aeschylus, *Choephori* [= *Libation-Bearers*]
Apoc. Pet.	Apocalypse of Peter
Apollonius Rhodius, *Argon.*	Apollonius of Rhodes, *Argonautica*
Appian, *Bell. civ.*	Appian, *Civil Wars*
Apuleis, *Metam.*	Apuleis, *Metamorphoses* [= *The Golden Ass*]
Aristotle, *Eth. nic.*	Aristotle, *Nicomachean Ethics*
Aristotle, *Pol.*	Aristotle, *Politics*
Arrian, *Anab.*	Arrian, *Anabasis*
Augustine, *Bapt.*	Augustine, *Baptism* [= *De baptismo contra Donatistas*]
Augustine, *Conf.*	Augustine, *Confessions*
Augustine, *Spir. et litt.*	Augustine, *De spiritu et littera* [= *The Spirit and the Letter*]
Barn.	Barnabas
Chariton, *Chaer.*	Chariton, *Chaereas and Callirhoe*
Chrysostom, *Hom. Act.*	John Chrysostom, *Homilies on the Acts of the Apostles* [= *Homiliae in Acta apostolorum*]
Cicero, *De or.*	Cicero, *De oratore*
Cicero, *Div.*	Cicero, *De divinatione*
Cicero, *Flac.*	Cicero, *Pro Flacco*
Cicero, *Inv.*	Cicero, *De Inventione rhetorica*
Cicero, *Phil.*	Cicero, *Orationes philippicae*
Demosthenes, *1–3 Olynth.*	Demosthenes, *1–3 Olynthiac*
Did.	Didache
Dio Cass.	Dio Cassius, *History of Rome*
Diodorus Siculus, *Hist.*	Diodorus Siculus, *Histories*
Diog. Laert.	Diogenes Laertius, *Lives and Opinions of Eminent Philosophers*
Ephrem, *Comm. Diatess.*	Ephrem the Syrian, *Commentary on the Diatessaron*
Epictetus, *Disc.*	Epictetus, *Discourses*
Euripides, *Bacch.*	Euripides, *Bacchae*
Eusebius, *Hist. eccl.*	Eusebius, *Ecclesiastical History*
Eusebius, *Praep. ev.*	Eusebius, *Praeparatio evangelica*
Galen, *Atr. Bil.*	Galen, *Atra Bile*
Gos. Pet.	Gospel of Peter
Gregory Nazianzus, *Or.*	Gregory of Nazianzus, *Oratio in laudum Basilii*
Herm. Mand.	Shepherd of Hermas, Mandate(s)
Herm. Vis.	Shepherd of Hermas, Vision(s)
Herodianus, *Hist.*	Herodianus, *Roman History since the Death of the Divine Marcus*
Herodotus, *Hist.*	Herodotus, *Histories*
Hippolytus, *Haer.*	Hippolytus, *Refutation of All Heresies*

Hist. Aug.	*Historia Augusta* [= *Augustan History*]
Homer, *Il.*	Homer, *Iliad*
Homer, *Od.*	Homer, *Odyssey*
Iamblichus, *Myst.*	Iamblichus, *On the Mysteries of Egypt* [= *De Mysteriis*]
Iamblichus, *Vit. Pyth.*	Iamblichus, *Life of Pythagoras*
Ign. *Magn.*	Ignatius, *To the Magnesians*
Ign. *Phld.*	Ignatius, *To the Philadelphians*
Ign. *Pol.*	Ignatius, *To Polycarp*
Ign. *Rom.*	Ignatius, *To the Romans*
Ign. *Smyrn.*	Ignatius, *To the Smyrnaeans*
Ign. *Trall.*	Ignatius, *To the Trallians*
Irenaeus, *Haer.*	Irenaeus, *Against Heresies*
Isocrates, *Areop.*	Isocrates, *Areopagatica* (= *Or.* 7)
Isocrates, *Ep.*	Isocrates, *Epistles*
Isocrates, *Or.*	Isocrates, *Speeches*
Jerome, *Helv.*	Jerome, *Adversus Helvidium de Mariae virginitate perpetua* [= *Against Helvidius concerning the perpetual virginity of Mary*]
Jerome, *Vir. ill.*	Jerome, *De viris illustribus* [= *On the Lives of Illustrious Men.*]
Jerome, *Epist.*	Jerome, *Epistles (Epistulae)*
Julian, *Galileans*	Julian (the Apostate), *Against the Galileans*
Justin, *1 Apol.*	Justin, *First Apology*
Justin, *Dial.*	Justin, *Dialogue with Trypho*
Juvenal, *Sat.*	Juvenal, *Satires*
Livy, *Ab urbe cond.*	Livy, *Ab urbe condita* [= *History of Rome*]
Lucan, *Bell.*	Lucan, *On the Civil War* [= *De Bello Civili*; also known as *Pharsalia*]
Lucian, *Alex.*	Lucian, *Alexander the False Prophet*
Lucian, *Eunuch.*	Lucian, *The Eunuch*
Lucian, *Jupp. trag.*	Lucian, *Zeus Rants* [= *Juppiter confutatus*]
Lucian, *Philops.*	Lucian, *The Lover of Lies* [= *Philopseudes*]
Longus, *Daph. Chl.*	Longus, *the Story of Daphis and Chloe*
Origen, *Cels.*	Origen, *Against Celsus*
Origen, *Philoc.*	Origen, *Philocalia*
Ovid, *Fast.*	Ovid, *Fasti*
Ovid, *Metam.*	Ovid, *Metamorphes*
Mart. Pol.	Martyrdom of Polycarp
Pausanius, *Descr.*	Pausanius, *Description of Greece*
Philostratus, *Vit. Apoll.*	Philostratus, *Life of Apollonius*
Plato, *Euthyphr.*	Plato, *Euthyphro*
Plato, *Leg.*	Plato, *Laws*

Plato, *Prot.*	Plato, *Protagoras*
Plato, *Resp.*	Plato, *Republic*
Plato, *Symp.*	Plato, *Symposium*
Plato, *Tim.*	Plato, *Timaeus*
Pliny, *Nat.*	Pliny the Elder, *Natural History* [= *Naturalis historia*]
Pliny, *Ep.*	Pliny the Younger, *Epistles* [= *Epistulae*]
Plutarch, *Alc.*	Plutarch, *Alcibiades*
Plutarch, *Cic.*	Plutarch, *Cicero*
Plutarch, *Dem.*	Plutarch, *Demosthenes*
Plutarch, *Mor.*	Plutarch, *Moralia*
Polybius, *Hist.*	Polybius, *Histories* [= *Historiae*]
P.Oxy.	*Oxyrhynchus Papyrus*
P. Ryl.	Rylands Papyri
P.Tebt.	Tebtunis Papyri
Pol. *Phil*	Polycarp, *To the Philippians*
Polyaenus, *Strat.*	Polyaenus, *Strategemata*
Polybius, *Hist.*	Polybius, *Universal History*
Prudentius, *Ditt.*	Prudentius, *Dittochaeon*
Quintilian, *Inst.*	Quintilian, *Institutio oratoria*
Res. gest. divi Aug.	Res gestae divi Augusti
Seneca, *Ep.*	Seneca, *Epistles*
Seneca, *Nat.*	Seneca, *Naturales Quaestiones*
Sophocles, *Ant.*	Sophocles, *Antigone*
Strabo, *Geog.*	Strabo, *Geography*
Suetonius, *Claud.*	Suetonius, *The Divine Claudius* [= *Divus Claudius*]
Suetonius, *Dom.*	Suetonius, *Domitian* [= *Domitianus*]
Suetonius, *Nero*	Suetonius, *Nero*
Suetonius, *Vesp.*	Suetonius, *Vespasian*
Tacitus, *Ann.*	Tacitus, *Annals*
Tacitus, *Hist.*	Tactitus, *Histories*
Tertullian, *Apol.*	Tertullian, *Apology* [= *Apologeticus*]
Tertullian, *Bapt.*	Tertullian, *Of Baptism* [= *De baptismo*]
Tertullian, *Spect.*	Tertullian, *Of the Shows* [= *De spectaculis*]
Theon, *Prog.*	Theon, *Progymnasmata*
Theophrastus, *Char.*	Theophrastus, *Characters*
Thucydides, *P.W.*	Thucydides, *History of the Peloponnesian War*
Virgil, *Aen.*	Virgil, *Aeneid*
Xenophon, *Anab.*	Xenophon of Athens, *Anabasis*
Xenophon, *Cyr.*	Xenophon of Athens, *Cyropaedia*
Xenophon, *Ant. Hab.*	Xenophon of Ephesus, *The Story of Anthia and Habracomes*

J. Mishnah, Talmud, and Other Jewish Texts

y.	Jerusalem Talmud	ʿOr.	ʿOrlah
b.	Babylonian Talmud	Roš Haš.	Roš Haššanah
t.	Tosefta	S. ʿOlam Rab.	Seder ʿOlam Rabbah
m.	Mishnah		
ʾAbot	ʾAbot	Šabb.	Šabbat
Bik.	Bikkurim	Sem.	Semaḥot
Ketub.	Kettubot	Sanh.	Sanhedrin
Mek.	Mekilta	Soṭah	Soṭah
Mid.	Middot	Yebam.	Yebamot
Nid.	Niddah		

K. Targumic Material

Tg. Isa.	Targum of Isaiah
Tg. Neof.	Targum Neofiti
Tg. Ps-J.	Targum Pseudo-Jonathan
Tg. Song	Targum Song of Songs (Canticles)
Tg. Yer. I	Targum Yerušalmi I

General Bibliography

Aarflot, C. H. *God (in) Acts: The Characterization of God in the Acts of the Apostles.* Eugene, OR: Pickwick, 2020.

Abegg, M. G., P. W. Flint and E. Ulrich. *The Dead Sea Scrolls Bible.* Edinburgh: T&T Clark; New York: HarperOne, 1999.

Adams, E. *The Stars Will Fall from Heaven: Cosmic Catastrophe in the New Testament and its World.* LNTS 347. London: T&T Clark, 2007.

Adler, N. *Taufe und Handauflegung: eine exegetisch-theologische Untersuchung von Apg 8, 14–17.* NTAbh 19.3. Münster Weste: Aschendorff, 1951.

Agnew, F. H. "On the Origin of the Term *Apostolos.*" *CBQ* 38 (1976): 49–53.

Aland, B. "Entstehung, Charakter und Herkunft des sog. westlichen Textes untersucht an der Apostelgeschichte." *ETL* 62 (1986): 5–65.

Aland, K. *Kurzgefasste Liste der griechischen Handschriften des Neuen Testaments.* 2nd ed. ANTF 1. Berlin: de Gruyter, 1994.

———. *Text und Textwert der griechischen Handschriften des Neuen Testaments:* III *Die Apostelgeschichte.* 2 vols. ANTF 20/21. Berlin: de Gruyter, 1993.

Alexander, L. *Acts.* People's Bible. Oxford: Bible Reading Fellowship, 2006.

———. *Acts in its Ancient Literary Context: A Classicist Looks at the Acts of the Apostles.* LNTS 298. London: T&T Clark, 2005.

———. "Ancient Book Production and the Circulation of the Gospels." Pages 71–111 in *The Gospels for All Christians.* Edited by R. Bauckham. Edinburgh: T&T Clark; Grand Rapids: Eerdmans, 1997.

———. "Fact, Fiction and the Genre of Acts." *NTS* 44 (1998): 380–99.

———. "The Preface to Acts and the Historians." Pages 73–103 in *History, Literature and Society in the Book of Acts.* Edited by B. Witherington III. Cambridge: Cambridge University Press, 1996.

———. *The Preface to Luke's Gospel: Literary Convention and Social Context in Luke 1.1–4 and Acts 1.1.* SNTSMS 78. Cambridge: Cambridge University Press, 1993.

———. "Reading Luke-Acts from Back to Front." Pages 419–46 in *The Unity of Luke-Acts.* Edited by J. Verheyden. BETL 142. Leuven: Leuven University Press/Peeters, 1999.

———. "Review Article." *JTS* ns 52 (2001): 691–703.

Alexander, P. S. "Retelling the Old Testament." Pages 99–121 in *It is Written: Scripture Citing Scripture. Essays in Honour of Barnabas Lindars.* Edited by D. A. Carson and H. G. M. Williamson. Cambridge: Cambridge University Press, 1988.

———, ed. *The Targum of Canticles.* Aramaic Bible 17A. London: T&T Clark, 2003.

Allen, L. C. *The Books of Joel, Obadiah, Jonah and Micah.* NICOT. London: Hodder & Stoughton, 1976.

———. "The Old Testament Background of (προ)ὁρίζειν in the New Testament." *NTS* 17 (1970): 104–8.

———. *Psalms 101–150.* WBC 21. Waco, TX: Word, 1983.

Allison, D. C., Jr. "Acts 9:1–9, 22:6–11, 26:12–18: Paul and Ezekiel." *JBL* 135 (2016): 807–26.

Andersen, T. D. "The Meaning of ἔχοντες χάριν πρός in Acts 2:47." *NTS* 34 (1988): 604–10.

Anderson, A. A. *The Book of Psalms.* 2 vols. NCB. London: Oliphants, 1972.

Anderson, K. L. *"But God Raised Him from the Dead": The Theology of Jesus's Resurrection in Luke-Acts.* PBM. Milton Keynes: Paternoster, 2006.

Anderson, P. N. "Acts 4:19–20—An Overlooked First-Century Clue to Johannine Authorship and Luke's Dependence upon the Johannine Tradition." On Bible and Interpretation. https://bibleinterp.arizona.edu/opeds/acts357920. 2010.

Angel, A. R. *Chaos and the Son of Man: The Hebrew Chaoskampf Tradition in the Period 515 BCE to 200 CE.* LSTS 60. London: T&T Clark, 2006.

Argyle, A. W. "O. Cullmann's Theory concerning κωλύειν." *ExpTim* 67 (1955): 17.

Ascough, R. S. "Benefaction Gone Wrong: The 'Sin' of Ananias and Sapphira in Context." Pages 91–110 in *Text and Artifact in the Religions of Mediterranean Antiquity.* Edited by S. G. Wilson and M. Desjardins. Ontario: Wilfrid Laurier University Press, 2000.

Atkinson, W. *Baptism in the Spirit: Luke-Acts and the Dunn Debate.* Eugene, OR: Pickwick, 2011.

Aune, D. E. *The New Testament in its Literary Environment.* Cambridge: James Clarke, 1988.

———. *Revelation.* 3 vols. WBC 52A–C. Dallas, TX: Word, 1997–98.

Avemarie, F. *Die Tauferzählungen der Apostelgeschichte: Theologie und Geschichte.* WUNT 139. Tübingen: Mohr Siebeck, 2002.

Baban, O. D. *On the Road Encounters in Luke-Acts: Hellenistic Mimesis and Luke's Theology of the Way.* PBM. Milton Keynes: Paternoster, 2006.

Bachmann, M. "Die Stephanusepisode (Apg 6,1–8,3): ihre Bedeutung für die lukanische Sicht des jerusalemischen Tempels und des Judentums." Pages 545–62 in *The Unity of Luke-Acts.* Edited by J. Verheyden. Leuven: Peeters, 1999.

Bailey, K. E. *Finding the Lost: Cultural Keys to Luke 15.* St. Louis: Concordia, 1992.

———. "Informal Controlled Oral Tradition and the Synoptic Gospels." *Them* 20 (1995): 4–11.

Bammel, E. "Jewish Activity against Christians in Palestine according to Acts." Pages 357–64 in *The Book of Acts in Its Palestinian Setting.* Edited by R. Bauckham. BAFCS 4. Carlisle: Paternoster; Grand Rapids: Eerdmans, 1995.

Barbi, A. *Il Cristo celeste presente nella Chiesa: Tradizione e radazione in Atti 3, 19–21.* AnBib 64. Rome: Biblical Institute, 1979.

Barclay, J. M. G. *Jews in the Mediterranean Diaspora from Alexander to Trajan (323 BCE–117 CE).* Edinburgh: T&T Clark, 1996.

———. "Manipulating Moses: Exodus 2:10–15 in Egyptian Judaism and the New Testament." Pages 28–46 in *Text as Pretext: Essays in Honour of Robert Davidson.* Edited by R. P. Carroll. JSOTSup 138. Sheffield: JSOT, 1992.

———. *Paul and the Gift.* Grand Rapids: Eerdmans, 2015.

Barnett, P. W. *The Birth of Christianity: The First Twenty Years.* After Jesus 1. Grand Rapids: Eerdmans, 2005.

———. "The Jewish Sign Prophets—AD 40–70: Their Intentions and Origin." *NTS* 27 (1981): 679–97.

Barr, J. *The Semantics of Biblical Language.* Oxford: Oxford University Press, 1961.

Barrett, C. K. "Attitudes to the Temple in the Acts of the Apostles." Pages 345–67 in *Templum Amicitiae.* Edited by W. Horbury. JSNTSup 48. Sheffield: JSOT, 1991.

———. *A Critical and Exegetical Commentary on the Acts of the Apostles.* 2 vols. ICC. Edinburgh: T&T Clark, 1994, 1998.

———. "Faith and Eschatology in Acts 3." Pages 1–17 in *Glaube und Eschatologie: Festschrift für Werner Georg Kümmel zum 80. Geburtstag.* Edited by E. Grässer and O. Merk. Tubingen: Mohr, 1985.

———. "The Historicity of Acts." *JTS* ns 50 (1999): 515–34.

———. "Light on the Holy Spirit from Simon Magus (Acts 8:4–25)." Pages 281–95 in *Les Actes des Apôtres: traditions, rédaction, théologie.* Edited by J. Kremer. BETL 48. Gembloux: Duculot; Leuven: Leuven University Press, 1979.

———. *Luke the Historian in Recent Study*. London: Epworth, 1961.

———. "Old Testament History according to Stephen and Paul." Pages 57–69 in *Studien zum Text und zur Ethik des Neuen Testaments: Festschrift zum 80. Geburtstag von Heinrich Greeven*. Edited by W. Schrage. BZNW 47. Berlin: de Gruyter, 1986.

———. "Salvation Proclaimed, XII: Acts 4:8–12." *ExpTim* 94 (1982): 68–71.

———. "*Shaliaḥ* and Apostle." Pages 88–102 in *Donum Gentilicium: New Testament Studies in Honour of David Daube*. Edited by E. Bammel, C. K. Barrett and W. D. Davies. Oxford: Clarendon, 1978.

———. "Stephen and the Son of Man." Pages 32–38 in *Apophoreta*. Edited by W. Eltester and F. H. Kettler. BZNW 30. Berlin: Topelmann, 1964.

Bartchy, S. S. "Community of Goods in Acts: Idealization or Social Reality?" Pages 309–18 in *The Future of Early Christianity*. Edited by B. A. Pearson. Minneapolis: Fortress, 1991.

Barton, S. C. *The Spirituality of the Gospels*. London: SPCK, 1992.

Bassler, J. M. *God and Mammon: Asking for Money in the New Testament*. Nashville: Abingdon, 1991.

Batibuka, P. N. "Baptism: Passivity or Action? A New Understanding of Baptism as a Rite of Entry in Romans 6." PhD diss., London School of Theology/Middlesex University, 2012.

Bauckham, R., ed. *The Book of Acts in Its Palestinian Setting*. BAFCS 4. Carlisle: Paternoster; Grand Rapids: Eerdmans, 1995.

———. "The Early Jerusalem Church, Qumran, and the Essenes." Pages 63–89 in *The Dead Sea Scrolls as Background to Postbiblical Judaism and Early Christianity: Papers from an International Conference at St Andrews in 2001*. Edited by J. R. Davila. STDJ 46. Leiden: Brill, 2003.

———. *The Fate of the Dead: Studies on the Jewish and Christian Apocalypses*. NovTSup 93. Leiden: Brill, 1998.

———. "For Whom Were the Gospels Written?" Pages 9–48 in *The Gospels for All Christians*. Edited by R. Bauckham. Edinburgh: T&T Clark; Grand Rapids: Eerdmans, 1997.

———. *God Crucified: Monotheism and Christology in the New Testament*. Didsbury Lectures 1996. Carlisle: Paternoster, 1998.

———. *Gospel Women: Studies of the Named Women in the Gospels*. London: T&T Clark, 2002.

———. "James and the Jerusalem Church." Pages 415–80 in *The Book of Acts in Its Palestinian Setting*. Edited by R. Bauckham. BAFCS 4. Carlisle: Paternoster; Grand Rapids: Eerdmans, 1995.

———. *The Jewish World around the New Testament: Collected Essays I*. WUNT 233. Tübingen: Mohr Siebeck, 2008.

———. *Jude and the Relatives of Jesus in the Early Church*. Edinburgh: T&T Clark, 1990.

———. "The Restoration of Israel in Luke-Acts." Pages 435–87 in *Restoration: Old Testament, Jewish and Christian Perspectives*. Edited by J. M. Scott. JSJSup 72. Leiden: Brill, 2001.

Bauer, D. R. *The Book of Acts as Story: A Narrative-Critical Study*. Grand Rapids: Baker Academic, 2021.

Bauer, J. B. "Καρδιογνώστης, ein unbeachteter Aspekt (Apg 1,24; 15,8)." *BZ* 32 (1988): 114–17.

Bauernfeind, O. *Die Apostelgeschichte*. THKNT 5. Leipzig: Deichert, 1939.

———. "Tradition und Komposition in dem Apotakatastasisspruch Apostelgeschichte 3,20f." Pages 13–23 in *Abraham unser Vater: Juden und Christen im Gespäch über die Bible: Festschrift für Otto Michel zum 60. Geburtstag*. Edited by O. Betz, M. Hengel and P. Schmidt. Leiden: Brill, 1963.

Baur, F. C. *Das Christentum und die christliche Kirche der drei ersten Jahrhunderte.* Tübingen: Fues, 1853.

———. *Paul the Apostle of Jesus Christ: His Life and Works, His Epistles and Teachings.* 2 vols. 2nd ed. London: Williams & Norgate, 1876.

Bayer, H. F. "Christ-Centred Eschatology in Acts 3:17–26." Pages 236–50 in *Jesus of Nazareth, Lord and Christ: Essays on the Historical Jesus and New Testament Christology.* Edited by J. B. Green and M. Turner. Carlisle: Paternoster; Grand Rapids: Eerdmans, 1994.

Beale, G. K. "The Descent of the Eschatological Temple in the Form of the Spirit at Pentecost: Part I: The Clearest Evidence." *TynBul* 56 (2005): 73–102.

———. *The Temple and the Church's Mission: A Biblical Theology of the Dwelling Place of God.* NSBT. Leicester: Inter-Varsity Press, 2005.

Beardslee, W. A. "The Casting of Lots at Qumran in the Book of Acts." *NovT* 4 (1960): 245–52.

Beasley-Murray, G. R. *Baptism in the New Testament.* Exeter: Paternoster, 1973.

Béchard, D. P. *Paul outside the Walls: A Study of Luke's Socio-Geographical Universalism in Acts 14:8–20.* AnBib 143. Rome: Pontifical Biblical Institute, 2000.

Bede, The Venerable. *Commentary on the Acts of the Apostles.* ed. L. T. Martin. Cistercian Studies 117. Kalamazoo, MI: Cistercian, 1989.

Beers, H. *The Followers of Jesus as the Servant: Luke's Model from Isaiah for the Disciples in Luke-Acts.* LNTS 535. London: Bloomsbury T&T Clark, 2015.

Bellinger, W. H., and W. R. Farmer, eds. *Jesus and the Suffering Servant: Isaiah 53 and Christian Origins.* Harrisburg, PA: Trinity Press International, 1998.

Bengel, J. A. *Gnomon Novi Testamenti.* 4 vols. 3rd ed. Stuttgart: Steinkopf, 1860.

Benoit, P. *Jesus and the Gospel.* 2 vols. London: Darton Longman & Todd, 1974.

———. "Some Notes on the 'Summaries' in Acts 2, 4 and 5." Pages 94–103 in vol. 2 of *Jesus and the Gospel.* Edited by P. Benoit. 2 vols. London: Darton Longman & Todd, 1974.

Berger, P. L., and T. Luckmann. *The Social Construction of Reality: A Treatise in the Sociology of Knowledge.* London: Allen Lane/Penguin, 1967 repr. 1991.

Bergmeier, R. "Die Gestalt des Simon Magus in Apg 8 und in der simonianischen Gnosis—Aporien einer Gesamtdeutung." *ZNW* 77 (1986): 267–75.

Bernhard, L. "Das frühchristliche Verständnis der Formel ΙΗΣΟΥΣ ΠΑΙΣ ΘΕΟΥ aufgrund der alten Bibelübersetzungen." Pages 21–29 in *Lingua Restituta Orientalis: Festgabe für Julius Assfalg.* Edited by R. Schulz and M. Görg. Ägypten und Altes Testament: Studien zu Geschichte, Kultur und Religion Ägyptens und des Alten Testaments 20. Wiesbaden: Otto Harrassowitz, 1990.

Betz, H. D., ed. *The Greek Magical Papyri in Translation: Including the Demotic Spells, vol. 1: Text.* 2nd ed. Chicago: University of Chicago Press, 1992.

Beyschlag, K. *Simon Magus und die christliche Gnosis.* WUNT 16. Tübingen: Mohr, 1974.

Biggar, N. "Showing the Gospel in Social Praxis." *Anvil* 8 (1991): 7–18.

Biguzzi, G. "Witnessing Two by Two in the Acts of the Apostles." *Bib* 92 (2011): 1–20.

Bihler, J. *Die Stephanusgeschichte.* Münchener Theologische Studien 1, Historische Abteilung 16. München: Max Hübner, 1963.

Bird, M. F. *Jesus and the Origins of the Gentile Mission.* LNTS 331. London: T&T Clark, 2006.

Bishop, E. F. F. "Guide to Those Who Arrested Jesus." *EvQ* 40 (1968): 41–42.

Black, A. "'Your Sons and Your Daughters Will Prophesy. . . .': Pairings of Men and Women in Luke-Acts." Pages 193–206 in *Scripture and Traditions: Essays on Early Judaism and Christianity in Honor of Carl R. Holladay.* Edited by P. Gray and G. R. O'Day. NovTSup 129. Leiden: Brill, 2008.

Black, M. *An Aramaic Approach to the Gospels and Acts*. 3rd ed. Oxford: Clarendon, 1967.

———. "The Holy Spirit in the Western Text of Acts." Pages 159–70 in *New Testament Textual Criticism: Its Significance for Exegesis. Essays in Honour of Bruce M. Metzger.* Edited by E. J. Epp and G. D. Fee. Oxford: Clarendon, 1981.

———. "Judas of Galilee and Josephus's 'Fourth Philosophy.'" Pages 45–54 in *Josephus-Studien: Untersuchungen zu Josephus, dem antiken Judentum and dem Neuen Testament*. Edited by O. Betz, K. Haacker and M. Hengel. Göttingen: Vandenhoeck & Ruprecht, 1974.

Blackman, E. C. "The Hellenists of Acts iv.1." *ExpTim* 48 (1937): 524–25.

Blass, F. *Acta apostolorum sive Lucae ad Theophilum liber alter: editio philologica apparatu critico, commentario perpetuo, indice verborum illustrata*. Göttingen: Vandenhoeck & Ruprecht, 1895.

———. *Philology of the Gospels*. London: Macmillan, 1898.

Blinzer, J. "The Jewish Punishment of Stoning in the New Testament Period." Pages 147–61 in *The Trial of Jesus: Cambridge Studies in Honour of C. F. D. Moule*. Edited by E. Bammel. SBT 2.13. London: SCM, 1970.

Blomberg, C. L. *Neither Poverty nor Riches: A Biblical Theology of Material Possessions*. NSBT 7. Nottingham: Apollos, 1999.

Bock, D. L. *Acts*. BECNT 5. Grand Rapids: Baker, 2007.

———. *Proclamation from Prophecy and Pattern: Lucan Old Testament Christology*. JSNTSup 12. Sheffield: JSOT, 1987.

Boesenberg, D. "Retelling Moses's Killing of the Egyptian: Acts 7 in Its Jewish Context." *BTB* 48 (2018): 148–56.

Böhm, M. *Samarien und die Samaritai bei Lukas: Eine Studie zum religionshistorischen und traditionsgeschichtlichen Hintergrund der lukanischen Samarientexte und zu deren topographischer Verhaftung*. WUNT II/111. Tübingen: Mohr Siebeck, 1999.

Boismard, M.-É. *Le texte occidental des Actes des Apôtres*. 2nd ed. EBib ns 40. Paris: Gabalda, 2000.

Boismard, M.-É., and A. Lamouille. *Les Actes des Deux Apôtres*. 3 vols. EBib ns 12–14. Paris: Librairie Lecoffre/Gabalda, 1990.

———. *Le texte occidental des Actes des Apôtres: Recontruction et réhabilitation*. 2 vols. Synthèse 17. Paris: Éditions Recherche sur les Civilisations, 1984.

Bolt, P. "Mission and Witness." Pages 191–214 in *Witness to the Gospel: The Theology of Acts*. Edited by I. H. Marshall and D. Peterson. Grand Rapids/Cambridge: Eerdmans, 1998.

Bond, H. K. "Acts 4:12 and its First Century Setting." *ThSc* 10 (2003): 7–17.

———. *Caiaphas: Friend of Rome and Judge of Jesus?* Louisville: Westminster John Knox, 2004.

Booth, W. C. *The Rhetoric of Fiction*. Chicago: University of Chicago Press, 1961.

Borg, M. J. *Conflict, Holiness, and Politics in the Teachings of Jesus*. Revised ed. Harrisburg: Trinity Press International, 1998.

Bousset, W. *Kyrios Christos: A History of the Belief in Christ from the Beginnings of Christianity to Irenaeus*. Nashville, TN: Abingdon, 1970.

Bovon, F. *Luke the Theologian: Fifty-five Years of Research (1950–2005)*. 2nd revised ed. Waco, TX: Baylor University Press, 2006.

Bowen, C. R. "The Meaning of συναλιζόμενος in Ac 1,4." *ZNW* 13 (1912): 254–55.

Bowker, J. W. "'Merkabah' Visions and the Vision of Paul." *JSS* 16 (1971): 157–73.

———. "Speeches in Acts: A Study in Proem and Yelammedenu Form." *NTS* 14 (1967): 96–111.

Bowman, J. *Samaritan Documents: Relating to Their History, Religion, and Life*. POLTTS 2. Pittsburgh: Pickwick, 1977.

———. *The Samaritan Problem: Studies in the Relationships of Samaritanism, Judaism, and Early Christianity*. PTMS 4. Pittsburgh: Pickwick, 1975.

Bratcher, R. G. "Having Loosed the Pangs of Death." *BT* 10 (1959): 18–20.

———. "ἀκούω in Acts 9:7 and 22:9." *ExpTim* 71 (1960): 243–45.

Braun, H. *Qumran und das Neue Testament*. 2 vols. Tübingen: J. C. B. Mohr (Paul Siebeck), 1966.

Brawley, R. L. "Abrahamic Covenant Traditions and the Characterization of God in Luke-Acts." Pages 109–32 in *The Unity of Luke-Acts*. Edited by J. Verheyden. BETL 142. Leuven: Leuven University Press/Peeters, 1999.

———. *Centering on God: Method and Message in Luke-Acts*. Louisville: Westminster John Knox, 1990.

———. *Luke-Acts and the Jews: Conflict, Apology, and Conciliation*. SBLMS 33. Atlanta: Scholars, 1987.

———. *Text to Text Pours Forth Speech: Voices of Scripture in Luke-Acts*. Bloomington & Indianapolis: Indiana University Press, 1995.

Brehm, H. A. "The Meaning of Ἑλληνιστής in Acts in Light of a Diachronic Analysis of ἑλληνίζειν." Pages 180–99 in *Discourse Analysis and Other Topics in Biblical Greek*. Edited by S. E. Porter and D. A. Carson. JSNTSup 113. Sheffield: Sheffield Academic, 1995.

———. "Vindicating the Rejected One: Stephen's Speech as a Critique of the Jewish Leaders." Pages 266–97 in *Early Christian Interpretation of the Scriptures of Israel: Investigations and Proposals*. Edited by C. A. Evans and J. A. Sanders. JSNTSup 148/SSEJC 5. Sheffield: Sheffield Academic, 1997.

Brinkhof, J. H. A. "Philip, One of the Seven in Acts (6:1–6; 8:4–40; 21:8)." Pages 79–90 in *Deacons and Diakonia in Early Christianity*. Edited by B. J. Koet, E. Murphy and E. Ryökäs. WUNT II/479. Tübingen: Mohr Siebeck, 2018.

Brinkman, J. A. "The Literary Background of the 'Catalogue of the Nations' (Acts 2:9–11)." *CBQ* 25 (1963): 418–27.

Brock, S. P. "ΒΑΡΝΑΒΑΣ, ΥΙΟΣ ΠΑΡΑΚΛΗΣΕΩΣ." *JTS* ns 25 (1974): 93–98.

Brodie, T. L. "Towards Unraveling the Rhetorical Imitation of Sources in Acts: 2 Kgs 5 as One Component of Acts 8:9–40." *Bib* 67 (1986): 41–67.

Brooten, B. J. *Women Leaders in the Ancient Synagogue: Inscriptional Evidence and Background Issues*. BJS 36. Chico, CA: Scholars, 1982.

Broshi, M. "Estimating the Population of Ancient Jerusalem." Pages 110–20 in *Bread, Wine, Walls and Scrolls*. Edited by M. Broshi. JSPSup 36. Sheffield: Sheffield Academic, 2001.

Brown, J. K. *The Gospels as Stories: A Narrative Approach to Matthew, Mark, Luke, and John*. Grand Rapids: Baker Academic, 2020.

Brown, R. E. *The Death of the Messiah*. 2 vols. ABRL. London: Geoffrey Chapman, 1994.

———, **K. P. Donfried, J. A. Fitzmyer, and J. Reumann**, eds. *Mary in the New Testament: A Collaborative Assessment by Protestant and Roman Catholic Scholars*. Philadelphia: Fortress; New York: Paulist, 1978.

Brown, S. *Apostasy and Perseverance in the Theology of Luke*. AnBib 36. Rome: Pontifical Biblical Institute, 1969.

Bruce, F. F. *The Acts of the Apostles*. 3rd ed. Leicester: Apollos, 1990.

———. *The Book of Acts*. revised ed. NICNT. Grand Rapids: Eerdmans, 1988.

———. "The Church of Jerusalem in the Acts of the Apostles." *BJRL* 67 (1985): 641–61.

———. *Commentary on the Book of Acts*. NICNT. Grand Rapids: Eerdmans, 1954.

———. *The Epistle of Paul to the Galatians: A Commentary on the Greek Text*. NIGTC. Exeter: Paternoster, 1982.

———. "Philip and the Ethiopian." *JSS* 34 (1989): 377–86.

Brueggemann, W. *Isaiah.* 2 vols. WestBC. Louisville: Westminster John Knox, 1998.

Brug, J. F. "Acts 1:26—Lottery or Election?" *WLQ* 95 (1998): 212–214.

Buckwalter, D. *The Character and Purpose of Luke's Christology.* SNTSMS 89. Cambridge: Cambridge University Press, 1996.

Buitenwerf, R. "Acts 9:1–25. Narrative History Based on the Letters of Paul." Pages 61–88 in *Jesus, Paul, and Early Christianity: Studies in Honour of Henk Jan de Jonge.* Edited by R. Buitenwerf, H. W. Hollander and J. Tromp. NovTSup 130. Leiden: Brill, 2008.

Bultmann, R. *The History of the Synoptic Tradition.* Translated by J. Marsh. 2nd ed. Oxford: Blackwell, 1968.

———. *Theology of the New Testament.* 2 vols. Translated by K. Grobel. London: SCM, 1952, 1955.

Bunine, A. "La date de la première visit de Paul à Jérusalem." *RB* 113 (2006): 436–56, 601–22.

Burchard, C. "Fussnoten zum neutestamentlichen Griechisch." *ZNW* 61 (1970): 157–71.

Burke, S. D. "Queering Early Christian Discourse: The Ethiopian Eunuch." Pages 175–89 in *Bible Trouble: Queer Reading at the Boundaries of Biblical Scholarship.* Edited by T. Hornsby and K. Stone. SBLSem 67. Atlanta, GA: SBL, 2011.

Burkitt, F. C. "Acts 2:47." *JBL* 37 (1918): 234.

Burridge, R. A. *What are the Gospels? A Comparison with Graeco-Roman Biography.* 3rd ed. Waco, TX: Baylor University Press, 2018.

Burton, E. D. W. *A Critical and Exegetical Commentary on the Epistle to the Galatians.* ICC. Edinburgh: T&T Clark, 1920.

Busch, A. "Presence Deferred: The Name of Jesus and Self-Referential Eschatological Prophecy in Acts 3." *BibInt* 17 (2009): 521–53.

Buth, R. and R. S. Notley, eds. *The Language Environment of First Century Judaea: Jerusalem Studies in the Synoptic Gospels.* Jewish and Christian Perspectives 26. Leiden: Brill, 2014.

Butticaz, S. "'Has God Rejected His People?' (Romans 11.1). The Salvation of Israel in Acts: Narrative Claim of a Pauline Legacy." Pages 148–64 in *Paul and the Heritage of Israel: Luke's Narrative Claim upon Paul and Israel's Legacy.* Edited by D. P. Moessner, D. Marguerat, M. C. Parsons and M. Wolter. LNTS 452. London: T&T Clark, 2012.

———. "Actes 3,1–26: le relèvement de l'infirme comme paradigme de la restauration d'Israël." *ETR* 84 (2009): 177–88.

———. "The Church in Acts: Universality of Salvation, Ethnicity, and Philanthropy." *ASE* 36 (2019): 433–52.

Byron, G. L. *Symbolic Blackness and Ethnic Difference in Early Christian Literature.* London: Routledge, 2002.

Cadbury, H. J. "Acts and Eschatology." Pages 300–321 in *The Background of the New Testament and its Eschatology.* Edited by W. D. Davies and D. Daube. Cambridge: Cambridge University Press, 1956.

———. "Commentary on the Preface of Luke." Pages 488–510 in vol. 2 of *The Beginnings of Christianity, Part I.* Edited by F. J. Foakes Jackson and K. Lake. 5 vols. London: Macmillan, 1933.

———. "Some Semitic Personal Names in Luke-Acts." Pages 45–56 in *Amicitiae Corolla. A Volume of Essays Presented to James Rendel Harris, D.Litt. on the Occasion of his Eightieth Birthday.* Edited by H. G. Wood. London: University of London Press, 1933.

Caink, D. M. "Acts 4:32–37 in the NIV." *ExpTim* 113 (2001): 50.

Caird, G. B. *The Apostolic Age.* 2nd ed. London: Duckworth, 1975.

Callan, T. "Pauline Midrash: The Exegetical Background of Gal 3:19b." *JBL* 99 (1980): 549–567.

———. "The Preface of Luke-Acts and Historiography." *NTS* 31 (1985): 576–81.

Calvin, J. *The Acts of the Apostles.* 2 vols. Translated by C. Featherstone. Edinburgh: St Andrew's Press, 1966.

Camp, A. L. "Reexamining the Rule of Concord in Acts 2:38." *ResQ* 39 (1997): 37–42.

Campbell, C. R. *Paul and Union with Christ: An Exegetical and Theological Study.* Grand Rapids: Zondervan Academic, 2012.

———. *Verbal Aspect, the Indicative Mood, and Narrative: Soundings in the Greek of the New Testament.* SBG. 13. New York: Peter Lang, 2007.

Campbell, D. A. "An Anchor for Pauline Chronology: Paul's Flight from 'the Ethnarch of King Aretas' (2 Corinthians 11:32–33)." *JBL* 121 (2002): 279–302.

Campbell, J. Y. "ΚΟΙΝΩΝΙΑ and its Cognates in the New Testament." *JBL* 51 (1932): 352–80.

Capper, B. J. "Community of Goods in the Early Jerusalem Church." *ANRW* 26.2:1730–74. Part 2, *Principat* 26.2. Edited by H. Temporini and W. Haase. Berlin: de Gruyter, 1995.

———. "Holy Community of Life and Property amongst the Poor: A Response to Steve Walton." *EvQ* 80 (2008): 113–27.

———. "The Interpretation of Acts 5.4." *JSNT* 19 (1983): 117–31.

———. "The Palestinian Cultural Context of Earliest Christian Community of Goods." Pages 323–56 in *The Book of Acts in Its Palestinian Setting.* Edited by R. Bauckham. BAFCS 4. Carlisle: Paternoster; Grand Rapids: Eerdmans, 1995.

Carroll, J. T. *Response to the End of History: Eschatology and Situation in Luke-Acts.* SBLDS 92. Atlanta, GA: Scholars, 1988.

Carson, C. R. "Acts 8:37—A Textual Reexamination." *USQR* 51 (1997): 57–78.

———. "'Do You Understand What You Are Reading?' A Reading of the Ethiopian Eunuch Story (Acts 8.26–40) from a Site of Cultural Marronage." PhD diss., Union Theological Seminary, 1999.

Carson, D. A. *The Difficult Doctrine of the Love of God.* Leicester: Inter-Varsity Press, 2000.

———. "Matthew." Pages 3–599 in vol. 8 of *Expositor's Bible Commentary.* Edited by Frank E. Gaebelein. 12 vols. Grand Rapids: Zondervan, 1984.

———. "The Purpose of the Fourth Gospel: John 20:31 Reconsidered." *JBL* 106 (1987): 639–51.

Carter, T. *The Forgiveness of Sins.* Cambridge: James Clarke, 2016.

Catto, S. K. *Reconstructing the First-Century Synagogue: A Critical Analysis of Current Research.* LNTS 363. London: T&T Clark, 2007.

Cerfaux, L. "La première communauté Chretienne à Jerusalem (Act., II,41–V,42)." *ETL* 16 (1939): 5–31.

———. *Recueil Lucien Cerfaux: Études d'exégèse et d'histoire religieuse de Monseigneur Cerfaux, réunies à l'occasion de son soixante-dixième anniversaire.* 2 vols. BETL 6-7. Gembloux: Duculot, 1954.

Chance, J. B. *Jerusalem, the Temple and the New Age in Luke-Acts.* Macon, GA: Mercer University Press, 1978.

Chapman, D. W. *Ancient Jewish and Christian Perceptions of Crucifixion.* WUNT II/244. Tübingen: Mohr Siebeck, 2008.

Chase, F. H. "On πρηνὴς γενόμενος in Acts 1.18." *JTS* 12 (1911): 278–85.

Chatman, S. *Story and Discourse: Narrative Structure in Fiction and Film.* Ithaca, NY: Cornell University Press, 1978.

Cheetham, F. P. "Acts 2:47: ἔχοντες χάριν πρὸς ὅλον τὸν λαόν." *ExpTim* 74 (1963): 214–15.
Cheng, L. *The Characterisation of God in Acts: The Indirect Portrayal of an Invisible Character.* PBM. Milton Keynes: Paternoster, 2011.
Chilton, B., ed. *The Isaiah Targum: Introduction, Translation, Apparatus and Notes.* Aramaic Bible 11. Edinburgh: T&T Clark, 1987.
Christiansen, E. J. "Taufe als Initiation in der Apostelgeschichte." *ST* 40 (1986): 55–79.
Churchill, T. W. R. *Divine Initiative and the Christology of the Damascus Road Encounter.* Eugene, OR: Pickwick, 2010.
Clark, Albert C. *The Acts of the Apostles: A Critical Edition.* Oxford: Clarendon, 1933.
Clark, Andrew C. "Apostleship: Evidence from the New Testament and Early Christian Literature." *VE* 19 (1989): 49–82.
———. *Parallel Lives: The Relation of Paul to the Apostles in the Lucan Perspective.* PBTM. Carlisle: Paternoster, 2001.
———. "The Role of the Apostles." Pages 169–90 in *Witness to the Gospel: The Theology of Acts.* Edited by I. H. Marshall and D. Peterson. Grand Rapids/Cambridge: Eerdmans, 1998.
Co, M. A. "The Major Summaries in Acts: Acts 2:42–47; 4:32–35; 5:12–16: Linguistic and Literary Relationship." *ETL* 68 (1992): 49–85.
Coggan, D. *The Prayers of the New Testament.* London: Hodder & Stoughton, 1967.
Coggins, R. J. "The Samaritans and Acts." *NTS* 28 (1982): 423–34.
Cohen, S. J. D. *Josephus in Galilee and Rome: His Vita and Development as a Historian.* Columbia Studies in the Classical Tradition 8. Leiden: Brill, 1979.
Cohick, L. H. *Women in the World of the Earliest Christians: Illuminating Ancient Ways of Life.* Grand Rapids: Baker Academic, 2009.
Collins, J. J. *Daniel.* Hermeneia. Minneapolis: Fortress, 1993.
Collins, J. N. *Diakonia: Re-Interpreting the Ancient Resources.* New York: Oxford University Press, 1990.
———. *Diakonia Studies: Critical Issues in Ministry.* New York: Oxford University Press, 2014.
Collins, R. F. "Paul's Damascus Experience: Reflections on the Lukan Account." *LS* 11 (1986): 99–118.
Conzelmann, H. *Acts of the Apostles.* Translated by J. Limburg, A. T. Kraabel and D. H. Juel. Hermeneia. Philadelphia: Fortress, 1987.
———. *The Theology of St Luke.* Translated by G. Buswell. London: Faber & Faber, 1960.
Coppens, J. "L'imposition des mains dans les Actes des Apôtres." Pages 405–38 in *Les Actes des Apôtres: tradition, rédaction, théologie.* Edited by J. Kremer. BETL 48. Leuven: Leuven University Press, 1979.
Cosgrove, C. H. "The Divine ΔEI in Luke-Acts: Investigations into the Lukan Understanding of God's Providence." *NovT* 26 (1984): 168–90.
Cowton, C. J. "The Alms Trade: A Note on Identifying the Beautiful Gate of Acts 3.2." *NTS* 42 (1996): 475–76.
Crabbe, K. "Being Found Fighting against God: Luke's Gamaliel and Josephus on Human Responses to Divine Providence." *ZNW* 106 (2015): 21–39.
———. *Luke/Acts and the End of History.* BZNW 238. Berlin: de Gruyter, 2019.
Craigie, P. C. *Psalms 1–50.* WBC 19. Waco, TX: Word, 1983.
Creamer, J. M., A. B. Spencer and F. P. Viljoen. "Who is Theophilus? Discovering the Original Reader of Luke-Acts." *In die Skriflig* 48 (2014): 1–7.
Creed, J. M. "The Text and Interpretation of Acts i.1–2." *JTS* ns 35 (1934): 176–82.
Crisler, B. C. "The Acoustics and Crowd Capacity of Natural Theaters in Palestine." *BA* 39 (1976): 128–41.

Crown, A. D., ed. *The Samaritans.* Tübingen: Mohr Siebeck, 1989.

Crump, D. *Jesus the Intercessor: Prayer and Christology in Luke-Acts.* WUNT II/49. Tübingen: J. C. B. Mohr (Paul Siebeck), 1992.

Cullmann, O. *Baptism in the New Testament.* SBT 1. London: SCM, 1951.

———. *The Christology of the New Testament.* 2nd ed. London: SCM, 1963.

———. *The Early Church.* London: SCM, 1956.

Culpepper, H. H. "Acts 4:12." *RevExp* 89 (1992): 85–87.

Culy, M. M. "The Clue is in the Case: Distinguishing Adjectival and Adverbial Participles." *PRSt* 30 (2004): 441–54.

Culy, M. M., and M. C. Parsons. *Acts: A Handbook on the Greek Text.* BHGNT. Waco, TX: Baylor University Press, 2003.

Cunningham, S. *'Through Many Tribulations': The Theology of Persecution in Luke-Acts.* JSNTSup 142. Sheffield: Sheffield Academic, 1997.

Czachesz, I. *Commission Narratives: A Comparative Study of the Canonical and Apocryphal Acts.* Studies on Early Christian Apocrypha 8. Leuven: Peeters, 2007.

———. "Socio-Rhetorical Exegesis of Acts 9:1–30." *CV* 37 (1995): 5–32.

Dahl, N. A. "The Story of Abraham in Luke-Acts." Pages 139–58 in *Studies in Luke-Acts.* Edited by L. E. Keck and J. L. Martyn. London: SPCK, 1968.

Dana, H. E. "Where Did Paul Persecute the Church?" *AThR* 20 (1938): 16–26.

Danker, F. W. *Benefactor: Epigraphic Study of a Graeco-Roman and New Testament Semantic Field.* St. Louis: Clayton, 1982.

Darr, J. A. "Irenic or Ironic: Another Look at Gamaliel before the Sandhedrin (Acts 5:33–42)." Pages 121–39 in *Literary Studies in Luke-Acts.* Edited by R. P. Thompson and T. E. Phillips. Macon, GA: Mercer University Press, 1998.

———. *On Character Building: The Reader and the Rhetoric of Characterization in Luke-Acts.* Louisville: Westminster John Knox, 1992.

Das, A. A. "Acts 8: Water, Baptism, and the Spirit." *ConcJ* 19 (1993): 108–34.

Daube, D. *The New Testament and Rabbinic Judaism.* Jordan Lectures in Comparative Religion 1952. London: Athlone, 1956.

———. "A Reform in Acts and its Models." Pages 151–63 in *Jews, Greeks, and Christians: Religious Cultures in Late Antiquity.* Edited by R. Hamerton-Kelly and R. Scroggs. Leiden: Brill, 1976.

Davies, J. G. *He Ascended into Heaven: A Study in the History of Doctrine.* Bampton Lectures 1958. London: Lutterworth, 1958.

———. "Pentecost and Glossolalia." *JTS* ns 3 (1952): 228–31.

———. "The Prefigurement of the Ascension in the Third Gospel." *JTS* ns 6 (1955): 229–33.

Davies, W. D. "Jerusalem and the Land in the Christian Tradition." Pages 115–54 in *The Jerusalem Colloquium on Religion, Peoplehood, Nation, and Land, Jerusalem, Oct 30–Nov 8, 1970.* Edited by M. H. Tanenbaum and R. J. Z. Werblowsky. Jerusalem: H. S. Truman Research Institute of the Hebrew University, 1972.

Davis, J. C. "Another Look at the Relationship between Baptism and Forgiveness of Sins in Acts 2:38." *ResQ* 24 (1981): 80–88.

Dawsey, J. M. "The Literary Unity of Luke-Acts: Questions of Style—A Task for Literary Critics." *NTS* 35 (1989): 48–66.

Dawson, A. *Healing, Weakness and Power: Perspectives on Healing in the Writings of Mark, Luke and Paul.* PBM. Milton Keynes: Paternoster, 2008.

de Jonge, H. J. "The Chronology of the Ascension Stories in Luke and Acts." *NTS* 59 (2013): 151–71.

de la Potterie, I. "Les deux noms de Jérusalem dans les Actes des Apôtres." *Bib* 63 (1982): 153–87.

de Ste. Croix, G. E. M. *The Class Struggle in the Ancient Greek World: From the Archaic Age to the Arab Conquests.* London: Duckworth, 1981.

de Villiers, P. "The Medium is the Message: Luke and the Language of the New Testament against a Graeco-Roman Background." *Neot* 24 (1990): 247–56.

de Waard, J. "The Quotation from Deuteronomy in Acts 3,22.23 and the Palestinian Text: Additional Arguments." *Bib* 52 (1971): 537–40.

Dean-Otting, M. *Heavenly Journeys: A Study of the Motif in Hellenistic Jewish Literature.* Judentum und Umwelt 8. Frankfurt am Main: Peter Lang, 1984.

Decock, P. B. "The Understanding of Isaiah 53:7–8 in Acts 8:32, 33." *Neot* 14 (1981): 111–33.

Degenhardt, H. J. *Lukas, Evangelist der Armen.* Stuttgart: Katholisches Bibelwerk, 1965.

Deissmann, G. A. *Bible Studies.* Translated by A. Grieve. Edinburgh: T&T Clark, 1901.

———. *Light from the Ancient East: The New Testament Illustrated by Recently Discovered Texts of the Graeco-Roman World.* 4th ed. Translated by L. R. M. Strachan. London: Hodder & Stoughton, 1927.

del Agua, A. "The Evangelization of the Kingdom of God." Pages 639–61 in *The Unity of Luke-Acts.* Edited by J. Verheyden. BETL 142. Leuven: Leuven University Press/Peeters, 1999.

Delling, G. *Die Zueignung des Heils in der Taufe: Eine Untersuchung zum neutestamentlichen "taufen auf den Namen."* Berlin: Evangelische Verlagsanstalt, 1961.

Delobel, J. "The Text of Luke-Acts: A Confrontation of Recent Theories." Pages 83–107 in *The Unity of Luke-Acts.* Edited by J. Verheyden. BETL 142. Leuven: Leuven University Press/Peeters, 1999.

Denaux, A., R. Corstjens, and H. Margada. *The Vocabulary of Luke: An Alphabetical Presentation and a Survey of Characteristic and Noteworthy Words and Word Groups in Luke's Gospel.* BiTS 10. Leuven: Peeters, 2009.

Dennison, C. G. "How is Jesus the Son of God? Luke's Baptism Narrative and Christology." *CTJ* 17 (1982): 6–25.

Derrett, J. D. M. "Akeldama (Acts 1:19)." *Bijdr* 56 (1995): 122–32.

———. "Ananias, Sapphira, and the Right of Property." Pages 193–201 in vol. 1 of *Studies in the New Testament.* Edited by J. D. M. Derrett. 6 vols. Leiden: Brill, 1977.

———. "Simon Magus (Acts 8:9–24)." *ZNW* 73 (1982): 52–68.

Dibelius, D. O. *Die Werdende Kirche: Eine Einführung in die Apostelgeschichte.* Hamburg: Furche, 1951.

Dibelius, M. "Herodes und Pilatus." *ZNW* 16 (1915): 113–26.

———. *Studies in the Acts of the Apostles.* London: SCM, 1956.

Dickerson, P. L. "The Sources of the Account of the Mission to Samaria in Acts 8:5–25." *NovT* 39 (1997): 210–34.

Dillon, R. J. *From Eye-Witnesses to Ministers of the Word: Tradition and Composition in Luke 24.* AnBib 82. Rome: Biblical Institute Press, 1978.

———. "The Prophecy of Christ and His Witnesses according to the Discourses of Acts." *NTS* 32 (1986): 544–56.

Dinkler, E. "Philippus und der ANHP AIΘIOΨ (Apg 8,26–40): Historische und geographische Bemerkungen zum Missionsablauf nach Lukas." Pages 85–95 in *Jesus und Paulus.* Edited by E. E. Ellis and E. Grässer. Göttingen: Vandenhoeck & Ruprecht, 1975.

Dinkler, M. B. "The Politics of Stephen's Storytelling: Narrative Rhetoric and Reflexivity in Acts 7:2–53." *ZNW* 111 (2020): 33–64.

Đỗ, M. Y. T. *The Lucan Journey: A Study of Luke 9:28–36 and Acts 1:6–11 as an Architectural Pair.* European University Studies: Theology, Series XXIII vol. 895. Bern: Peter Lang, 2010.

Doble, P. *The Paradox of Salvation: Luke's Theology of the Cross.* SNTSMS 87. Cambridge: Cambridge University Press, 1996.

———. "The Psalms in Luke-Acts." Pages 83–117 in *The Psalms in the New Testament.* Edited by S. Moyise and M. J. J. Menken. NTSI. London: T&T Clark, 2004.

———. "The Son of Man Saying in Stephen's Witnessing: Acts 6.8–8.2." *NTS* 31 (1985): 68–84.

Dodd, C. H. *According to the Scriptures: The Sub-Structure of New Testament Theology.* London: Nisbet, 1952.

———. *The Apostolic Preaching and its Development.* London: Hodder & Stoughton, 1936.

———. *The Interpretation of the Fourth Gospel.* Cambridge: Cambridge University Press, 1953.

———. "The Mind of Paul: A Psychological Approach." *BJRL* 17 (1933): 91–105.

Domagalski, B. "Waren die 'Sieben' (Apg 6,1–7) Diakone?" *BZ* 26 (1982): 21–33.

Dombrowski, B. W. "*hyḥd* in 1QS and τὸ κοινόν: An Instance of Early Greek and Jewish Synthesis." *HTR* 59 (1966): 293–307.

Dömer, M. *Das Heil Gottes: Studien zur Theologie des lukanischen Doppelwerkes.* BBB 51. Köln-Bonn: Peter Hanstein, 1978.

Donaldson, T. L. "Moses Typology and the Sectarian Nature of Early Christian Anti-Judaism: A Study in Acts 7." *JSNT* 4 (1981): 27–52.

Dowd, W. A. "Exegetical Notes: Breaking Bread (Acts 2:46)." *CBQ* 1 (1939): 358–62.

Downing, F. G. "Common Ground with Paganism in Luke and in Josephus." *NTS* 28 (1982): 546–59.

Dozeman, T. B. "The Book of Numbers." Pages 1–268 in vol. 2 of *The New Interpreter's Bible.* Edited by L. E. Keck. 12 vols. Nashville, TN: Abingdon, 1994.

Drane, J. "Simon the Samaritan and the Lukan Concept of Salvation History." *EvQ* 47 (1975): 131–37.

Dunn, J. D. G. *The Acts of the Apostles.* EC. London: Epworth, 1996.

———. "The Ascension of Jesus: A Test Case for Hermeneutics." Pages 301–22 in *Auferstehung—Resurrection: The Fourth Durham-Tübingen Research Symposium: Resurrection, Transfiguration, and Exaltation in Old Testament, Ancient Judaism, and Early Christianity (Tübingen, September 1999).* Edited by F. Avemarie and H. Lichtenberger. WUNT 135. Tübingen: Mohr Siebeck, 2001.

———. *Baptism in the Holy Spirit.* London: SCM, 1970.

———. "Baptism in the Spirit: A Response to Pentecostal Scholarship on Luke-Acts." *JPT* 3 (1993): 3–27.

———. "'Baptized' as Metaphor." Pages 294–310 in *Dimensions of Baptism: Biblical and Theological Studies.* Edited by S. E. Porter and A. R. Cross. JSNTSup 234. London: Sheffield Academic, 2002.

———. *Beginning from Jerusalem.* Cambridge/Grand Rapids: Eerdmans, 2009.

———. *The Christ and the Spirit: Collected Essays of James D. G. Dunn.* 2 vols. Edinburgh: T&T Clark; Grand Rapids: Eerdmans, 1998.

———. *The Epistle to the Galatians.* BNTC. Peabody, MA: Hendrickson, 1993.

———. *Jesus and the Spirit: A Study of the Religious and Charismatic Experience of Jesus and the First Christians as Reflected in the New Testament.* London: SCM, 1975.

———. *Jesus Remembered.* Christianity in the Making 1. Grand Rapids: Eerdmans, 2003.

———. *The Partings of the Ways: Between Christianity and Judaism and Their Significance for the Character of Christianity.* London: SCM, 1991.

———. *Romans.* 2 vols. WBC 38A-B. Dallas: Word, 1988.

———. "ΚΥΡΙΟΣ in Acts." Pages 241–53 in vol. 1 of *The Christ and the Spirit: Collected Essays of James D. G. Dunn.* Edited by J. D. G. Dunn. 2 vols. Edinburgh: T&T Clark; Grand Rapids: Eerdmans, 1998.

Dupont, J. *Études sur les Actes des Apôtres.* LD 45. Paris: Cerf, 1967.

———. "La destinee de Judas prophetisée par David (Actes 1:16–20)." *CBQ* 23 (1961): 41–51.

———. "La Structure Oratoire du Discours d'Etienne (Actes 7)." *Bib* 66 (1985): 153–67.

———. "Le douzieme apôtre (Acts 1:15–26): à propos d'une explication recente." Pages 139–45 in vol. 1 of *The New Testament Age: Essays in Honor of Bo Reicke.* Edited by W. C. Weinrich. 2 vols. Macon, GA: Mercer University Press, 1984.

———. "Les discours de Pierre dans les Actes et le chapitre XXIV de l'évangile de Luc." Pages 329–72 in *L'évangile de Luc.* Edited by F. Neirynck. 2nd ed. BETL 32. Leuven: Leuven University Press, 1973.

———. *Nouvelles études sur les Actes des Apôtres.* LD 118. Paris: Cerf, 1984.

———. *The Salvation of the Gentiles: Studies in the Acts of the Apostles.* New York: Paulist, 1979.

———. *The Sources of Acts: The Present Position.* London: Darton, Longman & Todd, 1964.

———. "ἈΝΕΛΗΜΦΘΗ (Act. I. 2)." *NTS* 8 (1962): 154–57.

Eckey, W. *Die Apostelgeschichte: Der Weg des Evangeliums von Jerusalem nach Rom.* 2 vols. Neukirchen-Vluyn: Neukirchener, 2000.

Edwards, J. R. "Parallels and Patterns between Luke and Acts." *BBR* 27 (2017): 485–501.

Edwards, M. "Simon Magus, the Bad Samaritan." Pages 69–91 in *Portraits: Biographical Representation in the Greek and Latin Literature of the Roman Empire.* Edited by M. Edwards and S. Swain. Oxford: Clarendon, 1997.

Ehrhardt, A. *The Acts of the Apostles: Ten Lectures.* Manchester: Manchester University Press, 1969.

Eisen, U. E. *Die Poetik der Apostelgeschichte: eine narratologische Studie.* NTOA 58. Göttingen: Vandenhoeck & Ruprecht; Fribourg: Academic, 2006.

Ellingworth, P. "'Men and Brethren . . .' (Acts 1.16)." *BT* 55 (2004): 153–55.

Elliott, J. K. *Essays and Studies in New Testament Textual Criticism.* Estudios de Filolgía Neotestamentaria 3. Cordoba: Ediciones el Almendro, 1990.

———. "The Greek Manuscript Heritage of the Book of Acts." *FilNT* 9 (1997): 37–50.

———. "Jerusalem in Acts and the Gospels." *NTS* 23 (1977): 462–469.

———. "The Text of Acts in the Light of Two Recent Studies." *NTS* 34 (1988): 250–58.

Elliott, M. *Faithful Feelings: Rethinking Emotion in the New Testament.* Nottingham: Inter-Varsity Press, 2005.

Ellis, E. E. "'The End of the Earth' (Acts 1:8)." *BBR* 1 (1991): 123–32.

Emerton, J. A. Review of M. Wilcox, *The Semitisms of Acts. JSS* 13 (1968): 282–97.

Epp, E. J. "Coptic Manuscript G67 and the Rôle of Codex Bezae as a Western Witness in Acts." *JBL* 85 (1966): 197–212.

———. "The 'Ignorance Motif' in Acts and Anti-Judaic Tendencies in Codex Bezae." *HTR* 55 (1962): 51–62.

———. "Text-Critical Witnesses and Methodology for Isolating a Distinctive D-Text in Acts." *NovT* 59 (2017): 225–96.

———. *The Theological Tendency of Codex Bezae Cantabrigiensis in Acts.* SNTSMS 3. Cambridge: Cambridge University Press, 1966.

Erichsen-Wendt, F. "Tabitha—Leben an der Grenze: ein Beitrag zum Verständnis von Apg 9,36–43." *BN* 127 (2005): 67–90.

Ervin, H. M. *Conversion-initiation and the Baptism in the Holy Spirit: A Critique of James D.G. Dunn, Baptism in the Holy Spirit.* Peabody, MA: Hendrickson, 1984.

Esler, P. F. *Community and Gospel in Luke-Acts: The Social and Political Motivations of Lucan Theology.* SNTSMS 57. Cambridge: Cambridge University Press, 1987.

———. "Glossolalia and the Admission of Gentiles into the Early Christian Community." *BTB* 22 (1992): 136–42.

Estrada, N. P. *From Followers to Leaders: The Apostles in the Ritual of Status Transformation in Acts 1–2.* JSNTSup 255. London: T&T Clark, 2004.

Evans, C. A. "Luke and the Rewritten Bible: Aspects of Lukan Hagiography." Pages 170–201 in *The Pseudepigrapha and Early Biblical Interpretation.* Edited by J. H. Charlesworth and C. A. Evans. JSPSup 14. Sheffield: JSOT, 1993.

———. "Prophecy and Polemic: Jews in Luke's Scriptural Apologetic." Pages 171–211 in *Luke and Scripture: The Function of Sacred Tradition in Luke-Acts.* Edited by C. A. Evans and J. A. Sanders. Minneapolis: Fortress, 1993.

———. "The Prophetic Setting of the Pentecost Sermon." Pages 212–24 in *Luke and Scripture: The Function of Sacred Tradition in Luke-Acts.* Edited by C. A. Evans and J. A. Sanders. Minneapolis: Fortress, 1993.

Everts, J. "Tongues or Languages? Contextual Consistency in the Translation of Acts 2." *JPT* 2 (1994): 71–80.

Fackre, G. J., R. H. Nash, and J. Sanders. *What about Those Who Have Never Heard? Three Views on the Destiny of the Unevangelized.* Downers Grove, IL: IVP Academic, 1995.

Fanning, B. M. *Verbal Aspect in New Testament Greek.* Oxford Theological Monographs. Oxford: Clarendon, 1990.

Farrow, D. *Ascension and Ecclesia: On the Significance of the Doctrine of the Ascension for Ecclesiology and Christian Cosmology.* Edinburgh: T&T Clark, 1999.

Fee, G. D. "Baptism in the Holy Spirit: The Issue of Separability and Subsequence." *Pneuma* 7 (1985): 87–99.

Feldkämper, L. *Der betende Jesus als Heilsmittler nach Lukas.* Veröffentlichungen des Missionspriesterseminars St Augustin bei Bonn 29. St Augustin: Steyler Verlag, 1978.

Ferguson, E. *Baptism in the Early Church: History, Theology, and Liturgy in the First Five Centuries.* Grand Rapids/Cambridge: Eerdmans, 2009.

———. "The Hellenists in the Book of Acts." *ResQ* 12 (1969): 159–80.

———. "Laying on of Hands in Acts 6:6 and 13:3." *ResQ* 4 (1960): 250–52.

———. "Qumran and Codex D." *RevQ* 8 (1972): 75–80.

Field, F. *Notes on the Translation of the New Testament.* Cambridge: Cambridge University Press, 1899.

Finger, R. H. "'Mary, Please Pass the Bread': Social Implications of the Lord's Supper in the Early Church." Pages 250–55, 330 in *The Lord's Supper: Believers' Church Perspectives.* Edited by D. R. Stoffer. Scottsdale: Herald, 1997.

———. *Of Widows and Meals: Communal Meals in the Book of Acts.* Grand Rapids: Eerdmans, 2007.

Fiorenza, E. S. *In Memory of Her: A Feminist Theological Reconstruction of Christian Origins.* London: SCM, 1983.

Fitzmyer, J. A. *The Acts of the Apostles: A New Translation and Commentary.* AB 31. New York: Doubleday, 1998.

———. "The Ascension of Christ and Pentecost." Pages 265–94 in *To Advance the Gospel: New Testament Studies.* Edited by J. A. Fitzmyer. 2nd ed. Grand Rapids: Eerdmans; Livonia, MI: Dove, 1998.

———. "David, 'Being Therefore a Prophet' (Acts 2:30)." *CBQ* 34 (1972): 332–39.

———. "The Designations of Christians in Acts and Their Significance." Pages 223–36 in *Unité et diversité dans l'Église.* Edited by Pontifical Biblical Commission. Teologia e filosofia 15. Vatican City: Libreria Editrice Vaticana, 1989.

———. *Essays on the Semitic Background of the New Testament.* London: Geoffrey Chapman, 1971.

———. "Jewish Christianity in Acts in Light of the Qumran Scrolls." Pages 233–57 in *Studies in Luke-Acts*. Edited by L. E. Keck. and J. L. Martyn. London: SPCK, 1968.

———. *Luke*. 2 vols. AB 28A–B. Garden City, NY: Doubleday, 1981, 1985.

———. *The Semitic Background of the New Testament*. Biblical Resource series. Grand Rapids: Eerdmans; Livonia, MI: Dove, 1997.

Fletcher-Louis, C. H. T. *Luke-Acts: Angels, Christology and Soteriology*. WUNT II/94. Tübingen: Mohr Siebeck, 1997.

Flesher, P. V. M. and B. D. Chilton. *The Targums: A Critical Introduction*. SAIS 12. Leiden: Brill, 2011.

Flusser, D. *Entdeckungen im Neuen Testament 1: Jesusworte und ihre Überlieferung*. Neukirchen-Vluyn: Neukirchener Verlag, 1987.

———. "Two Notes on the Midrash on 2 Sam 7." *IEJ* 9 (1959): 99–109.

Forbes, C. *Prophecy and Inspired Speech in Early Christianity and Its Hellenistic Environment*. WUNT II/75. Tübingen: Mohr Siebeck, 1995.

Forbes, G. W., and S. D. Harrower. *Raised from Obscurity: A Narratival and Theological Study of the Characterization of Women in Luke-Acts*. Eugene, OR: Pickwick, 2015.

Förster, N. *Das gemeinschaftliche Gebet in der Sicht des Lukas*. BTS 4. Leuven: Peeters, 2007.

Foulkes, I. W. "Two Semantic Problems in the Translation of Acts 4:5–20." *BT* 29 (1978): 121–25.

France, D. "Barnabas—Son of Encouragement." *Them* 4 (1978–79): 3–6.

France, R. T. *The Gospel of Mark*. NIGTC. Carlisle: Paternoster, 2002.

———. "The Servant of the Lord in the Teaching of Jesus." *TynBul* 19 (1968): 26–52.

Franklin, B. *The Autobiography of Benjamin Franklin*. Bedford, MA: Applewood, 1793; repr. 2008.

Franklin, E. "The Ascension and the Eschatology of Luke-Acts." *SJT* 23 (1970): 191–200.

———. *Christ the Lord: A Study in the Purpose and Theology of Luke-Acts*. London: SPCK, 1975.

Fraser, R. "Office of Deacon." *Presb* 11 (1985): 13–19.

Freedman, H., and M. Simon, eds. *Midrash Rabbah*. 10 vols. London: Soncino, 1939.

Fresch, C. J. "Is There an Emphatic μέν?: A Consideration of the Particle's Development and Its Function in Koine." *NTS* 63 (2017): 261–78.

Friedrich, G. "Die Gegner des Paulus im 2. Korintherbrief." Pages 181–215 in *Abraham unser Vater: Juden und Christen im Gespräch über die Bibel*. Edited by O. Betz, M. Hengel and P. Schmidt. AGJU 5. Leiden: Brill, 1963.

Fuller, R. H. "The Choice of Matthias." Pages 140–46 in vol. 6 of *Studia Evangelica*. Edited by E. A. Livingstone. TUGAL 112. 7 vols. Berlin: Akademie, 1973.

———. *The Foundations of New Testament Christology*. London: Collins, 1969.

Fung, R. Y. K. *The Epistle to the Galatians*. NICNT. Grand Rapids: Eerdmans, 1982.

Funk, R. W. *The Poetics of Biblical Narrative*. FF. Sonoma, CA: Polebridge, 1988.

Gallagher, R. L. "From 'Doingness' to 'Beingness': A Missiological Interpretation: Acts 4:23–31." Pages 45–58 in *Mission in Acts: Ancient Narratives in Contemporary Context*. Edited by R. L. Gallagher and P. Hertig. ASMS 34. Maryknoll, NY: Orbis, 2004.

Garrett, S. R. *The Demise of the Devil: Magic and the Demonic in Luke's Writings*. Minneapolis: Fortress, 1989.

———. "The Meaning of Jesus' Death in Luke." *WW* 12 (1992): 11–16.

Garrison, R. *The Significance of Theophilus as Luke's Reader*. Studies in the Bible and Early Christianity 62. Lewiston, NY: Edwin Mellen, 2004.

Gasque, W. W. "The Book of Acts and History." Pages 54–72 in *Unity and Diversity in New Testament Theology*. Edited by R. A. Guelich. Grand Rapids: Eerdmans, 1978.

———. *A History of the Criticism of the Acts of the Apostles.* Grand Rapids: Eerdmans, 1975.

———. "The Speeches of Acts: Dibelius Reconsidered." Pages 232–50 in *New Dimensions in New Testament Study.* Edited by R. N. Longenecker and M. C. Tenney. Grand Rapids: Zondervan, 1974.

Gaventa, B. R. *Acts.* ANTC. Nashville: Abingdon, 2003.

———. "Acts of the Apostles." Pages 33–47 in vol. 1 of *New Interpreter's Dictionary of the Bible.* Edited by K. D. Sakenfeld. 5 vols. Nashville: Abingdon, 2006.

———. *From Darkness to Light: Aspects of Conversion in the New Testament.* OBT 20. Philadelphia: Fortress, 1986.

———. *Mary: Glimpses of the Mother of Jesus.* Personalities of the New Testament. Edinburgh: T&T Clark, 1999.

———. "The Overthrown Enemy: Luke's Portrait of Paul." Pages 439–50 in *Society of Biblical Literature 1985 Seminar Papers.* SBLSP 24. Atlanta: Scholars, 1985.

———. "To Speak Thy Word with All Boldness: Acts 4:23–31." *FM* 3 (1985–86): 76–82.

Geer, T. C., Jr. "The Two Faces of Codex 33 in Acts." *NovT* 31 (1989): 39–47.

Gempf, C. H. "Public Speaking and Published Accounts." Pages 259–303 in *The Book of Acts in Its Ancient Literary Setting.* Edited by B. W. Winter and A. D. Clarke. BAFCS 1. Carlisle: Paternoster; Grand Rapids: Eerdmans, 1993.

Gen, R. M. "The Phenomena of Miracles and Divine Infliction in Luke-Acts: Their Theological Significance." *Pneuma* 11 (1989): 3–19.

George, A. "L'emploi chez Luc du vocabulaire de salut." *NTS* 23 (1976): 308–20.

Gerhardsson, B. "Einige Bemerkungen zu Apg 4:32." *ST* 24 (1970): 142–49.

Gilbert, G. "The List of Nations in Acts 2: Roman Propaganda and the Lukan Response." *JBL* 121 (2002): 497–529.

Giles, K. "Apostles before and after Paul." *Chm* 99 (1985): 241–56.

Giles, K. N. "Luke's Use of the Term ἐκκλησία with Special Reference to Acts 20:28 and 9:31." *NTS* 31 (1985): 135–42.

Gill, D. H. "Structure of Acts 9." *Bib* 55 (1974): 546–48.

Gill, D. W. J. "Behind the Classical Façade: Local Religions of the Roman Empire." Pages 85–100 in *One God, One Lord: Christianity in a World of Religious Pluralism.* Edited by A. D. Clarke and B. W. Winter. 2nd ed. Grand Rapids: Baker, 1992.

Gill, D. W. J. and C. H. Gempf, eds. *The Book of Acts in Its Graeco-Roman Setting.* BAFCS 2. Carlisle: Paternoster; Grand Rapids: Eerdmans, 1994.

Glombitza, O. "Zur Charakterisierung des Stephanus in Act 6 und 7." *ZNW* 53 (1962): 238–44.

Goguel, M. "Les premières réalisations du christianisme." Pages 211–36 in vol. 3 of *Histoire générale des religions.* Edited by M. Gorce and R. Mortier. 5 vols. Paris: Quillet, 1952.

Goldingay, J. "Are They Comic Acts?" *EvQ* 69 (1997): 99–107.

González, J. L. "Reading from My Bicultural Place: Acts 6:1–7." Pages 139–47 in vol. 1 of *Reading from This Place.* Edited by F. F. Segovia and M. A. Tolbert. 2 vols. Minneapolis: Fortress, 1995.

Gooding, D. W. *True to the Faith: A Fresh Approach to the Acts of the Apostles.* London: Hodder & Stoughton, 1990.

Goodspeed, E. J. "Some Greek Notes." *JBL* 73 (1954): 84–92.

Goulder, M. D. *Luke: A New Paradigm.* 2 vols. JSNTSup 20. Sheffield: JSOT, 1989.

———. *Type and History in Acts.* London: SPCK, 1964.

Gourgues, M. "Esprit des commencements et esprit des prolongements dans les *Actes*: Note sur la 'pentecôte des Samaritains' (*Act.*, viii, 5–25)." *RB* 93 (1986): 376–85.

———. "'Exalté à la droite de Dieu': (Actes 2:33; 5:31)." *ScEs* 27 (1975): 303–27.

Gowler, D. B. *Host, Guest, Enemy and Friend: Portraits of the Pharisees in Luke and Acts.* ESEC 2. New York: Peter Lang, 1991.

Grant, J. A. "Singing the Cover Versions: Psalms, Reinterpretation and Biblical Theology in Acts 1–4." *SBET* 25 (2007): 27–49.

Grassi, J. A. "Emmaus Revisited (Luke 24:13–35 and Acts 8:26–40)." *CBQ* 26 (1964): 463–67.

Greehy, J. G. "Community of Goods—Qumran and Acts." *ITQ* 32 (1965): 230–40.

Green, E. M. B. *The Meaning of Salvation.* London: Hodder & Stoughton, 1965.

Green, J. B. *Conversion in Luke-Acts: Divine Action, Human Cognition, and the People of God.* Grand Rapids: Baker Academic, 2015.

———. "From 'John's Baptism' to 'Baptism in the Name of the Lord Jesus': The Significance of Baptism in Luke-Acts." Pages 157–72 in *Baptism in the New Testament and the Church: Historical and Contemporary Studies in Honour of R. E. O. White.* Edited by S. E. Porter and A. R. Cross. JSNTSup 171. Sheffield: Sheffield Academic, 1999.

———. "Good News to Whom? Jesus and the 'Poor' in the Gospel of Luke." Pages 59–74 in *Jesus of Nazareth: Lord and Christ. Essays on the Historical Jesus and New Testament Christology.* Edited by J. B. Green and M. Turner. Carlisle: Paternoster; Grand Rapids: Eerdmans, 1994.

———. *The Gospel of Luke.* NICNT. Grand Rapids/Cambridge: Eerdmans, 1997.

———. "Happiness in the Topsy-Turvy World of Luke-Acts." Pages 169–85 in *The Bible and the Pursuit of Happiness.* Edited by B. A. Strawn. New York: Oxford University Press, 2012.

———. "'He Ascended into Heaven': Jesus' Ascension in Lukan Perspective, and Beyond." Pages 130–50 in *Ears that Hear: Explorations in Theological Interpretation of the Bible.* Edited by J. B. Green and T. Meadowcroft. Sheffield: Sheffield Phoenix, 2013.

———. "'In Our Own Languages': Pentecost, Babel, and the Shaping of Christian Community in Acts 2:1–13." Pages 198–213 in *The Word Leaps the Gap: Essays on Scripture and Theology in Honor of Richard B. Hays.* Edited by J. R. Wagner, C. K. Rowe and A. K. Grieb. Grand Rapids: Eerdmans, 2008.

———. *Luke as Narrative Theologian: Texts and Topics.* WUNT 446. Tübingen: Mohr Siebeck, 2020.

———. "Persevering Together in Prayer: The Significance of Prayer in the Acts of the Apostles." Pages 183–202 in *Into God's Presence: Prayer in the New Testament.* Edited by R. N. Longenecker. MNTS. Grand Rapids: Eerdmans, 2001.

———. *Practicing Theological Interpretation: Engaging Biblical Texts for Faith and Formation.* Grand Rapids: Baker Academic, 2011.

———. *The Theology of the Gospel of Luke.* NT Theology. Cambridge: Cambridge University Press, 1995.

———. "What You See Depends on What You are Looking for: Jesus's Ascension as a Test Case for Thinking about Biblical Theology and Theological Interpretation of Scripture." *Int* 70 (2016): 445–57.

———. "'Witnesses of His Resurrection': Resurrection, Salvation, Discipleship, and Mission in the Acts of the Apostles." Pages 228–46 in *Life in the Face of Death.* Edited by R. N. Longenecker. Grand Rapids: Eerdmans, 1998.

Greenhut, Z. "Burial Cave of the Caiaphas Family." *BAR* 18 (1992): 28–36, 76.

Gregson, F. J. R. *Everything in Common? The Theology and Practice of the Sharing of Possessions in Community in the New Testament.* Eugene, OR: Pickwick, 2017.

Grider, J. K. "Predestination as Temporal Only." *WesTJ* 22 (1987): 56–64.

Griffiths, J. D. "The Spirit as Gift: The Influence of the Gift of the Spirit on the Community Life as Described by the Summary Statements in Acts." PhD diss., Flinders University, Adelaide, 2020.

Guggenheimer, H. W. *Seder Olam: The Rabbinic View of Biblical Chronology*. Northvale, NJ: Jason Aronson, 1998.

Gunderson, J. "Stones and Screams: Emotion and Masculinity in Acts 7:54–8:1." Paper presented in the Book of Acts Section, Society of Biblical Literature, 2019.

Haar, S. *Simon Magus: The First Gnostic?* BZNW 119. Berlin: de Gruyter, 2003.

Hacking, K. J. *Signs and Wonders Then and Now: Miracle-Working, Commissioning and Discipleship*. Nottingham: Apollos, 2006.

Haenchen, E. *The Acts of the Apostles*. Translated by R. McL. Wilson. Oxford: Blackwell, 1971.

———. "The Book of Acts as Source Material for the History of Early Christianity." Pages 258–78 in *Studies in Luke-Acts*. Edited by L. E. Keck and J. L. Martyn. London: SPCK, 1968.

———. "Simon Magus in der Apostelgeschichte." Pages 267–79 in *Gnosis und Neues Testament*. Edited by K. W. Tröger. Gütersloh: Mohn, 1973.

Hahn, F. "Das Problem alter christologischer Überlieferungen in der Apostelgeschichte unter besonderer Berücksichtung von Acta 3,19–21." Pages 129–54 in *Les Actes des Apôtres: tradition, rédaction, théologie*. Edited by J. Kremer. BETL 48. Gembloux: Duculot; Leuven Univeristy Press, 1979.

Hall, R. G. *Revealed Histories: Techniques for Ancient Jewish and Christian Historiography*. JSPSup 6. Sheffield: JSOT, 1991.

Hamm, D., SJ. "You are Precious in My Sight." *Way* 18 (1978): 193–203.

———. "Acts 3,1–10: The Healing of the Temple Beggar as Lucan Theology." *Bib* 67 (1986): 305–19.

———. "Acts 3:12–26: Peter's Speech and the Healing of the Man Born Lame." *PRSt* 11 (1984): 199–217.

———. "Paul's Blindness and Its Healing: Clue to Symbolic Intent (Acts 9, 22 and 26)." *Bib* 71 (1990): 63–72.

———. "The Tamid Service in Luke-Acts: The Cultic Background behind Luke's Theology of Worship (Luke 1:5–25; 18:9–14; 24:50–53; Acts 3:1; 10:3, 30)." *CBQ* 65 (2003): 215–31.

Hamman, A. "La nouvelle Pentecôte (Actes 4,24–30)." *BVC* 14 (1956): 82–90.

Hanson, J. S. "Dreams and Visions in the Graeco-Roman World and Early Christianity." *ANRW* 23.2:1395–1427. Part 2, *Principat* 23.2. Edited by H. Temporini and W. Haase. Berlin: de Gruyter, 1980.

Hanson, R. P. C. *The Acts*. New Clarendon Bible. Oxford: Clarendon, 1967.

Haraguchi, T. "A Call for Repentance to the Whole Israel—A Rhetorical Study of Acts 3:12–26." *AJT* 18 (2004): 267–82.

Harnack, A. von. *The Acts of the Apostles*. Translated by J. R. Wilkinson. London: Williams & Norgate, 1909.

———. *The Date of the Acts and of the Synoptic Gospels*. London: Williams & Norgate, 1911.

Harrill, J. A. "Divine Judgement against Ananias and Sapphira (Acts 5:1–11): A Stock Scene of Perjury and Death." *JBL* 130 (2011): 351–69.

Harris, J. R. "Did Judas Really Commit Suicide?" *AJT* 4 (1900): 490–513.

———. *Four Lectures on the Western Text of the New Testament*. London: Cambridge University Press, 1894.

Harris, M. J. *Jesus as God: The New Testament Use of Theos in Reference to Jesus*. Grand Rapids: Baker, 1992.

———. *Raised Immortal: Resurrection and Immortality in the New Testament.* MTL. London: Marshall Morgan & Scott, 1983.

Hartman, L. *'Into the Name of the Lord Jesus': Baptism in the Early Church.* SNTW. Edinburgh: T&T Clark, 1997.

———. "La formule baptismale dans les Actes des Apôtres: quelques observations relatives au style de Luc." Pages 727–38 in *À Cause de l'Évangile: Études sur les Synoptiques et les Actes offertes au P. Jacques Dupont, OSB à l'occasion de son 70e anniversaire.* Edited by F. Refoulé. LD 123. Paris: Cerf, 1985.

Hastings, A. *Prophet and Witness in Jerusalem: A Study of the Teaching of Saint Luke.* London: Longmans, Green, 1958.

Havelaar, H. "Hellenistic Parallels to Acts 5:1–11 and the Problem of Conflicting Interpretations." *JSNT* 67 (1997): 63–82.

Hay, D. M. *Glory at the Right Hand: Psalm 110 in Early Christianity.* SBLMS 18. Nashville: Abingdon, 1973.

Haya-Prats, G., SJ. *Empowered Believers: The Holy Spirit in the Book of Acts.* Translated by S. A. Ellington. Eugene, OR: Cascade, 2011.

Hays, C. M. *Luke's Wealth Ethics: A Study in Their Coherence and Character.* WUNT II/275. Tübingen: Mohr Siebeck, 2010.

———. "What is the Place of My Rest? Being Migrant People(s) of the God of All the Earth." *OpenTh* 7 (2021): 150–68.

Hays, R. B. "Figural Exegesis and the Retrospective Re-cognition of Israel's Story." *BBR* 29 (2019): 32–48.

———. *The Moral Vision of the New Testament: Community, Cross, New Creation: A Contemporary Introduction to New Testament Ethics.* San Francisco: HarperSanFrancisco, 1996.

Head, P. M. "Acts and the Problem of Its Texts." Pages 415–44 in *The Book of Acts in Its Ancient Literary Setting.* Edited by B. W. Winter and A. D. Clarke. BAFCS 1. Carlisle: Paternoster; Grand Rapids: Eerdmans, 1993.

Hedrick, C. W. "Paul's Conversion/Call: A Comparative Analysis of the Three Reports in Acts." *JBL* 100 (1981): 415–32.

Heiligenthal, R. "Werke der Barmherzigkeit oder Almosen: zur Bedeutung von ἐλεημοσύνη." *NovT* 25 (1983): 289–301.

Heintz, F. *Simon 'Le magicien': Actes 8, 5–25 et l'accusation de magie contre les prophètes thaumaturges dans l'antiquité.* CahRB 39. Paris: Gabalda, 1997.

Heitmüller, W. *"Im Namen Jesu." Eine sprach.- u. religionsgeschichtliche Untersuchung zum Neuen Testament, speziell zur altchristlichen Taufe.* FRLANT I/2. Göttingen: Vandenhoeck & Ruprecht, 1903.

Hemer, C. J. "Acts and Galatians Reconsidered." *Them* 2 (1977): 81–88.

———. *The Book of Acts in the Setting of Hellenistic History.* Edited by C. H. Gempf. WUNT 49. Tübingen: Mohr Siebeck, 1989.

Hengel, M. *Acts and the History of Earliest Christianity.* London: SCM, 1979.

———. *Between Jesus and Paul.* London: SCM, 1983.

———. *The Charismatic Leader and His Followers.* SNTW. Edinburgh: T&T Clark, 1981.

———. "The Geography of Palestine." Pages 27–78 in *The Book of Acts in Its Palestinian Setting.* Edited by R. Bauckham. BAFCS 4. Grand Rapids: Eerdmans, 1995.

———. "Ioudaia in der geographischen Liste Apg 2,9–11 und Syrien als 'Grossjudäa.'" *RHPR* 80 (2000): 51–68.

———. "Jerusalem als jüdische und hellenistische Stadt." Pages 115–56 in vol. 2 of *Kleine Schriften.* Edited by M. Hengel. 2 vols. WUNT 90, 109. Tübingen: Mohr Siebeck, 1996.

———. *Judaism and Hellenism: Studies in Their Encounter in Palestine during the Early Hellenistic Period.* Translated by J. Bowden. 2 vols. London: SCM, 1974.

———. *Property and Riches in the Early Church.* London: SCM, 1974.

———. *Saint Peter: The Underestimated Apostle.* Translated by T. H. Trapp. Grand Rapids: Eerdmans, 2010.

———. *The Son of God: The Origin of Christology and the History of Jewish-Hellenistic Religion.* Translated by J. Bowden. London: SCM, 1976.

———. "Ἰουδαία in the Geographical List of Acts 2:9–11 and Syria as 'Greater Judea.'" *BBR* 10 (2000): 161–80.

Hengel, M., and D. P. Bailey. "The Effective History of Isaiah 53 in the Pre-Christian Period." Pages 75–146 in *The Suffering Servant: Isaiah 53 in Jewish and Christian Sources.* Edited by B. Janowski and P. Stuhlmacher. Grand Rapids: Eerdmans, 2004.

Hengel, M., and R. Deines. *The Pre-Christian Paul.* London: SCM, 1991.

Hengel, M., and R. Deines. *The Septuagint as Christian Scripture: Its Prehistory and the Problem of Its Canon.* OT Studies. Edinburgh: T&T Clark, 2002.

Hengel, M., and A. M. Schwemer. *Paul between Damascus and Antioch: The Unknown Years.* London: SCM, 1997.

Henrichs-Tarasenkova, N. "Good News about Resurrection." *JTI* 15 (2021): 262–76.

Hertig, P. "The Magical Mystery Tour: Philip Encounters Magic and Materialism in Samaria." Pages 103–13 in *Mission in Acts: Ancient Narratives in Contemporary Context.* Edited by R. L. Gallagher and P. Hertig. ASMS 34. Maryknoll, NY: Orbis, 2004.

Higbie, C. "Divide and Edit: A Brief History of Book Divisions." *HSCP* 105 (2010): 1–31.

Hill, C. C. *Hellenists and Hebrews: Reappraising Division within the Earliest Church.* Minneapolis: Fortress, 1992.

Hilton, A. R. *Illiterate Apostles: Uneducated Early Christians and the Literates Who Loved Them.* LNTS 541. London: T&T Clark, 2018.

Hirzel, R. *Die Strafe der Steinigung.* Darmstadt: Wissenschaftliche Buchgesellschaft, 1967.

Hjelm, I. "Simon Magus in Patristic and Samaritan Sources: The Growth of a Tradition." Pages 263–84 in *Die Samaritaner und die Bibel: Historische und literarische Wechselwirkungen zwischen biblischen und samaritanischen Traditionen = The Samaritans and the Bible: Historical and Literary Interactions between Biblical and Samaritan Traditions.* Edited by J. Frey, U. Schattner-Rieser and K. Schmid. Studia Judaica 70/Studia Samaritana 7. Berlin: de Gruyter, 2012.

Hobart, W. K. *The Medical Language of St Luke.* Dublin University Press series. Dublin: Hodges, Figgis & Co., 1882.

Hock, R. F. *The Social Context of Paul's Ministry: Tentmaking and Apostleship.* Philadelphia: Fortress, 1980.

Holladay, C. R. *Acts: A Commentary.* NTL. Louisville: Westminster John Knox, 2016.

Holmås, G. O. *Prayer and Vindication in Luke-Acts: The Theme of Prayer within the Context of the Legitimating and Edifying Objective of the Lukan Narrative.* LNTS 433. London: T&T Clark, 2011.

Holmes, M. W., ed. *The Apostolic Fathers: Greek Texts and English Translations.* 3rd ed. Grand Rapids: Baker Academic, 2007.

Holtz, T. *Untersuchungen über die alttestamentlichen Zitate bei Lukas.* TUGAL 104. Berlin: Akademie-Verlag, 1968.

Hooker, M. D. *Jesus and the Servant: The Influence of the Servant Concept of Deutero-Isaiah in the New Testament.* London: SPCK, 1959.

Horbury, W. "The 'Caiaphas' Ossuaries and Joseph Caiaphas." *PEQ* 126 (1994): 32–48.

———. "Septuagintal and New Testament Conceptions of the Church." Pages 1–17 in *A Vision for the Church: Studies in Early Christian Ecclesiology in Honour of J. P. M. Sweet.* Edited by M. Bockmuehl and M. B. Thompson. Edinburgh: T&T Clark, 1997.

Horn, F. W. *Glaube und Handeln in der Theologie des Lukas.* GTA 26. Göttingen: Vandenhoeck & Ruprecht, 1983.

Horrell, D. G., ed. *Social-Scientific Approaches to New Testament Interpretation.* Edinburgh: T&T Clark, 1999.

Horsley, G. H. R. "The Inscriptions of Ephesos and the New Testament." *NovT* 34 (1992): 105–68.

Hort, F. J. A. *The Christian Ecclesia: A Course of Lectures on the Early History and Early Conceptions of the Ecclesia and Four Sermons.* London: Macmillan, 1897.

Hötzinger, H. "Schriftgebrauch in der Stephanusepisode: Apg 6,1–8,3." Pages 305–45 in *Scriptural Authority in Early Judaism and Ancient Christianity.* Edited by G. G. Xeravits, T. Nicklas and I. Kalimi. DCLS 16. Berlin: de Gruyter, 2013.

Houlden, L. "Beyond Belief: Preaching the Ascension." *Theology* 94 (1991): 173–80.

Hovenden, G. *Speaking in Tongues: The New Testament Evidence in Context.* JPTSup 22. London: Sheffield Academic, 2002.

Hubbard, B. J. "Commissioning Stories in Luke-Acts: A Study of Their Antecedents, Form and Content." *Semeia* 8 (1977): 103–26.

Hübner, H. *Biblische Theologie des Neuen Testaments.* 3 vols. Göttingen: Vandenhoek & Ruprecht, 1990–95.

Huebner, S. R. *Papyri and the Social World of the New Testament.* Cambridge: Cambridge University Press, 2019.

Hull, J. H. E. *The Holy Spirit in the Acts of the Apostles.* London: Lutterworth, 1967.

Hultgren, A. J. "Paul's Pre-Christian Persecutions of the Church. Their Purpose, Locale, and Nature." *JBL* 95 (1976): 97–111.

Hume, D. A. *The Early Christian Community: A Narrative Analysis of Acts 2:41–47 and 4:32–35.* WUNT II/298. Tübingen: Mohr Siebeck, 2011.

Humphrey, E. M. *And I Turned to See the Voice: The Rhetoric of Vision in the New Testament.* Grand Rapids: Baker Academic, 2007.

Hur, J. *A Dynamic Reading of the Holy Spirit in Luke-Acts.* JSNTSup 211. Sheffield: Sheffield Academic, 2001.

Hurtado, L. W. *Lord Jesus Christ: Devotion to Jesus in Earliest Christianity.* Grand Rapids/Cambridge: Eerdmans, 2003.

Hyytiäinen, P. "The Changing Text of Acts: A Phylogenetic Approach." *TC* 26 (2021): 1–28.

———. "Evolving Gamaliel Tradition in Codex Bezae Cantabrigiensis, Acts 5:38–39: A Novel Application of Coherence-Based Genealogical Method (CBGM)." *TC* 24 (2019): 1–22.

James, W. *The Varieties of Religious Experience: A Study in Human Nature. The Gifford Lectures 1901–1902.* London: Longmans, Green, 1902.

Janowitz, N. *Magic in the Roman World: Pagans, Jews, and Christians.* Religion in the First Christian Centuries. London: Routledge, 2001.

Jantsch, T. "The God of Glory: Explicit References to God in Discourses in the Acts of the Apostles (7:2–53; 14:15–18; 17:22–31)." *StTJ* 4 (2018): 197–222.

Jeremias, J. "Das Gebetsleben Jesu." *ZNW* 25 (1926): 123–40.

———. *The Eucharistic Words of Jesus.* London: SCM, 1966.

———. *Heiligengräber in Jesu Umwelt (Mt. 23, 29; Lk. 11, 47): Eine Untersuchung zur Volksreligion der Zeit Jesu.* Göttingen: Vandenhoeck & Ruprecht, 1958.

———. *Infant Baptism in the First Four Centuries.* Translated by D. Cairns. London: SCM, 1960.

———. *Jerusalem in the Time of Jesus.* Translated by F. H. and C. H. Cave. London: SCM, 1969.

———. *The Origins of Infant Baptism: A Further Study in Reply to Kurt Aland.* Translated by D. M. Barton. London: SCM, 1963.

———. "Untersuchungen zum Quellenproblem der Apostelgeschichte." *ZNW* 36 (1937): 205–21.

Jervell, J. *Die Apostelgeschichte.* 17th ed. KEK. Göttingen: Vandenhoeck & Ruprecht, 1998.

———. *Luke and the People of God.* Minneapolis: Augsburg, 1972.

———. *The Theology of the Acts of the Apostles.* NT Theology. Cambridge: Cambridge University Press, 1996.

Jeska, J. *Die Geschichte Israels in der Sicht des Lukas: Apg 7,25b–53 und 13,17–25 im Kontext antik-jüdischer Summarien der Geschichte Israels.* FRLANT 195. Göttingen: Vandenhoeck & Ruprecht, 2001.

Jipp, J. W. "The Acts of the Apostles." Pages 350–67 in *The State of New Testament Studies: A Survey of Recent Research.* Edited by S. McKnight and N. K. Gupta. Grand Rapids: Baker Academic, 2019.

Johnson, A. "Resurrection, Ascension and the Developing Portrait of the God of Israel in Acts." *SJT* 57 (2004): 146–62.

Johnson, D. E. "Jesus against the Idols: The Use of Isaianic Servant Songs in the Missiology of Acts." *WTJ* 52 (1990): 343–53.

Johnson, E. A. *Truly our Sister: A Theology of Mary in the Communion of Saints.* London/New York: Continuum, 2003.

Johnson, L. T. *The Acts of the Apostles.* SP 5. Collegeville, MN: Liturgical, 1992.

———. *The Literary Function of Possessions in Luke-Acts.* SBLDS 39. Missoula, MT: Scholars, 1977.

———. *Septuagintal Midrash in the Speeches of Acts.* The Père Marquette Lecture in Theology 2002. Milwaukee, WI: Marquette University Press, 2002.

Johnson, S. E. "The Dead Sea Manual of Discipline and the Jerusalem Church of Acts." *ZAW* 66 (1954): 106–20.

Jones, B. C. "The Meaning of the Phrase, 'And the Witnesses Laid Down Their Cloaks' in Acts 7:58." *ExpTim* 123 (2011): 113–18.

Jones, D. L. "The Title 'Author of Life (Leader)' in the Acts of the Apostles." Pages 627–36 in *Society of Biblical Literature 1994 Seminar Papers.* SBLSP 33. Atlanta: SBL, 1994.

Jongkind, D. *An Introduction to the Greek New Testament Produced at Tyndale House, Cambridge.* Wheaton, IL: Crossway, 2019.

Judd, A. "Gadamer, *wirkungsgeschichtliches Bewusstsein,* and What to Do about Judas (Acts 1:12–22)." *AusBR* 66 (2018): 43–58.

Judge, E. A. *Social Distinctives of the Christians in the First Century: Pivotal Essays.* Edited by D. M. Scholer. Peabody, MA: Hendrickson, 2008.

Juel, D. *Messianic Exegesis: Christological Interpretation of the Old Testament in Early Christianity.* Philadelphia: Fortress, 1987.

Kaiser, O. *Isaiah 13–39: A Commentary.* OTL. Philadelphia: Westminster, 1974.

Karmon, Y. "Geographical Influences on the Historical Routes in the Sharon Plain." *PEQ* 93 (1961): 43–60.

Karris, R. J. *Prayer and the New Testament.* Companions to the New Testament. New York: Crossroad, 2000.

Kato, T. "Le caractère lucanien de l'image de la communauté primitive de Jérusalem en Act 4,32–35." *AJBI* 20 (1994): 79–95.

Katz, P. "ἐν πυρί φλογός." *ZNW* 46 (1955): 133–38.

Kauppi, L. A. *Foreign but Familiar Gods: Greco-Romans Read Religion in Acts.* LNTS 277. London: T&T Clark, 2006.

Keener, C. S. *Acts: An Exegetical Commentary.* 4 vols. Grand Rapids: Baker Academic, 2012–2015.

———. "Interethnic Marriages in the New Testament (Matt 1:3–6; Acts 7:29; 16:1–3; cf. 1 Cor 7:14)." *CrisThR* 6 (2009): 25–43.

———. *Miracles: The Credibility of the New Testament Accounts.* 2 vols. Grand Rapids: Baker Academic, 2011.

———. *Miracles Today: The Supernatural Work of God in the Modern World.* Grand Rapids: Baker Academic, 2021.

———. "The Plausibility of Luke's Growth Figures in Acts 2.41; 4.4; 21.20." *JGRChJ* 7 (2010): 140–63.

———. "Three Notes on Figurative Language: Invented Guilt in Acts 7.55–60, Paul's Figurative Vote in Acts 26.10, Figurate Eyes in Galatians 2.15." *JGRChJ* 5 (2008): 42–50.

Keith, C. "The Oddity of the Reference to Jesus in Acts 4:13b." *JBL* 134 (2015): 791–811.

Kellum, L. S. *Acts.* EGGNT. Nashville: B&H Academic, 2020.

Kelly, J. G. "Lucan Christology and the Jewish-Christian Dialogue." *JES* 21 (1984): 688–708.

Kennedy, G. A. *New Testament Interpretation through Rhetorical Criticism.* Chapel Hill: University of North Carolina Press, 1984.

Kenyon, F. G. "The Western Text in the Gospels and Acts." *PBA* 24 (1938): 287–315.

Kern, P. H. "Paul's Conversion and Luke's Portayal of Character in Acts 8–10." *TynBul* 54 (2003): 63–80.

Kilgallen, J. J. "'The Apostles Whom He Chose Because of the Holy Spirit': A Suggestion Regarding Acts 1,2." *Bib* 81 (2000): 414–17.

———. "The Function of Stephen's Speech (Acts 7,2–53)." *Bib* 70 (1989): 173–93.

———. "Persecution in the Acts of the Apostles." Pages 143–60, 245–50 in *Luke and Acts.* Edited by G. O'Collins and G. Marconi. New York: Paulist, 1991.

———. "A Rhetorical and Source-Traditions Study of Acts 2,33." *Bib* 77 (1996): 178–96.

———. *The Stephen Speech: A Literary and Redactional Study of Acts 7,2–53.* AnBib 67. Rome: Biblical Institute Press, 1976.

———. "The Use of Psalm 16:8–11 in Peter's Pentecost Speech." *ExpTim* 113 (2001): 47–50.

———. "'With Many Other Words' (Acts 2,40): Theological Assumptions in Peter's Pentecost Speech." *Bib* 83 (2001): 71–87.

Kilpatrick, G. D. "An Eclectic Study of the Text of Acts." Pages 64–77 in *Biblical and Patristic Studies in Memory of Robert Pierce Casey.* Edited by J. N. Birdsall and R. W. Thomson. Freiburg: Herder, 1963.

———. "Some Quotations in Acts." Pages 81–97 in *Les Actes des Apôtres: traditions, rédaction, théologie.* Edited by J. Kremer. BETL 48. Gembloux: Duculot; Leuven: Leuven University Press, 1979.

———. "ΛAOI at Luke 2:31 and Acts 4:25, 27." *JTS* ns 16 (1965): 127.

Kim, J.-W. "Explicit Quotations from Genesis within the Context of Stephen's Speech in Acts." *Neot* 41 (2007): 341–60.

Kim, K.-J. *Stewardship and Almsgiving in Luke's Theology.* JSNTSup 155. Sheffield: Sheffield Academic, 1998.

Kim, S. *The Origin of Paul's Gospel.* 2nd ed. WUNT II/4. Tübingen: J. C. B. Mohr (Paul Siebeck), 1984.

King, F. J. "'Pointing the Bone': Sorcery Syndrome and Uncanny Death in Acts 5:1–11." *IBS* 30 (2012): 12–37.

King, F. J., and S. Selvendran. "Rhubarb, Rhubarb, Alleluia, Amen: Xenolalia, Glossolalia, and Neurophysiology." *BTB* 49 (2019): 88–95.

Kirk, J. A. "Apostleship since Rengstorf: Towards a Synthesis." *NTS* 21 (1975): 249–64.
Klauck, H.-J. "Gütergemeinschaft in der klassischen Antike, im Qumran und im Neuen Testament." *RevQ* 11 (1982): 47–79.
———. *Magic and Paganism in Early Christianity: The World of the Acts of the Apostles.* Edinburgh: T&T Clark, 2000.
Klein, G. *Die zwölf Apostel: Ursprung und Gehalt einer Idee.* FRLANT 77. Göttingen: Vandenhoeck & Ruprecht, 1961.
Klijn, A. F. J. "Stephen's Speech—Acts VII. 2–53." *NTS* 4 (1957): 25–31.
———. *A Survey of the Researches into the Western Text of the Gospels and Acts.* Utrecht: Kemnik en Zoom, 1949.
———. "A Survey of the Researches into the Western Text of the Gospels and Acts (1949–1959)." *NovT* 3 (1959): 1–27, 161–73.
———. *A Survey of the Researches into the Western Text of the Gospels and Acts, Part Two, 1949–1969.* NovTSup 21. Leiden: Brill, 1969.
Kloppenborg, J. S. *Christ's Associations: Connecting and Belonging in the Ancient City.* New Haven: Yale University Press, 2019.
Klutz, T. *The Exorcism Stories in Luke-Acts: A Sociostylistic Reading.* SNTSMS 129. Cambridge: Cambridge University Press, 2004.
Knopf, R., and G. Hollman. *Die Schriften des Neuen Testaments, Band 3: Die Apostelgeschichte, der Heräerbrief und die katholischen Briefe.* Göttingen: Vandenhoek & Ruprecht, 1917.
Knowling, R. J. "The Acts of the Apostles." Pages 1–554 in vol. 2 of *The Expositor's Greek Testament.* Edited by W. R. Nicoll. 4th ed. 5 vols. London: Hodder & Stoughton, 1900.
Koch, D. A. "Geistbesitz, Geistverleihung und Wundermacht: Erwägungen zur Tradition und zur lukanischen Redaktion in Apg 8:5–25." *ZNW* 77 (1986): 64–82.
Kochenash, M. "Political Correction: Luke's Tabitha (Acts 9:36–43), Virgil's Dido, and Cleopatra." *NovT* 60 (2018): 1–13.
———. "You Can't Hear 'Aeneas' without Thinking of Rome." *JBL* 136 (2017): 667–685.
Kodell, J. "Luke's Use of ΛΑΟΣ, 'People', Especially in the Jerusalem Narrative." *CBQ* 31 (1969): 327–43.
———. "'The Word of God Grew.' The Ecclesial Tendency of Λόγος in Acts 6:7; 12:24; 19:20." *Bib* 55 (1974): 505–19.
Koester, H. *Introduction to the New Testament, vol. 1: History, Culture, and Religion of the Hellenistic Age.* 2nd ed. Berlin: de Gruyter, 1995.
Koet, B. J. "Isaiah in Luke-Acts." Pages 79–100 in *Isaiah in the New Testament.* Edited by S. Moyise and M. J. J. Menken. New Testament and the Scriptures of Israel. London: T&T Clark, 2005.
———. "Luke 10:38–42 and Acts 6:1–7: A Lukan Diptych on Diakonia." Pages 163–85 in *Studies in the Greek Bible: Essays in Honor of Francis T. Gignac, SJ.* Edited by J. Corley and V. Kemp. Washington, DC: Catholic Biblical Association of America, 2008.
Koivisto, R. A. "Stephen's Speech: A Theology of Errors?" *GTJ* 8 (1987): 101–14.
Kollmann, B. *Joseph Barnabas: Leben und Wirkungsgeschichte.* SBS 175. Stuttgart: Katholisches Bibelwerk, 1998.
Koperski, V. "Luke 10,38–42 and Acts 6,1–7: Women and Discipleship in the Literary Context of Luke-Acts." Pages 517–44 in *The Unity of Luke Acts.* Edited by J. Verheyden. BETL 142. Leuven: Leuven University Press/Peeters, 1999.
Kränkl, E. *Jesus, der Knecht Gottes: Die heilsgeschichtliche Stellung Jesu in den Reden der Apostelgeschichte.* BU 8. Regensburg: Pustet, 1972.
Kraus, T. J. "'Uneducated,' 'Ignorant,' or Even 'Illiterate'? Aspects and Background for an Understanding of Agrammatoi (and Idiotai) in Acts 4.13." *NTS* 45 (1999): 434–49.

Kremer, J. *Pfingstbericht und Pfingstgeschehen: Eine exegetische Untersuchung zur Apg 2,1–13.* SBS 63/64. Stuttgart: KBW, 1973.

Kretschmar, G. "Himmelfahrt und Pfingsten." *ZKG* 66 (1955): 209–53.

Krodel, G. *Acts.* PC. Philadelphia: Fortress, 1981.

Kuecker, A. J. "The Spirit and the 'Other,' Satan and the 'Self': Economic Ethics as a Consequence of Identity Transformation in Luke-Acts." Pages 81–103 in *Engaging Economics: New Testament Scenarios and Early Christian Reception.* Edited by B. W. Longenecker and K. D. Liebengood. Grand Rapids: Eerdmans, 2009.

Kurz, W. S. "Acts 3:19–26 as a Test of the Role of Eschatology in Lukan Christology." Pages 309–23 in *Society of Biblical Literature 1977 Seminar Papers.* SBLSP 16. Atlanta: SBL, 1977.

———. "Effects of Variant Narrators in Acts 10–11." *NTS* 43 (1997): 570–86.

———. *Reading Luke-Acts: Dynamics of Biblical Narrative.* Louisville, KY: Westminster John Knox, 1993.

Lamoreaux, J. T. "Social Identity, Boundary Breaking, and Ritual: Saul's Recruitment on the Road to Damascus." *BTB* 38 (2008): 122–34.

Lampe, G. W. H. *The Seal of the Spirit: A Study in the Doctrine of Baptism and Confirmation in the New Testament and the Fathers.* London: Longmans Green, 1951.

Lane, W. L. "Times of Refreshment: A Study in Eschatological Periodization in Judaism and Christianity." PhD diss., Harvard Divinity School, 1962.

Lang, M. *Die Kunst des christlichen Lebens: rezeptionsästhetische Studien zum lukanischen Paulusbild.* AGB 29. Leipzig: Evangelische Verlagsanstalt, 2008.

Larsson, E. "Die Hellenisten und die Urgemeinde." *NTS* 33 (1987): 205–25.

Lauterbach, J. Z. *Mekilta De-Rabbi Ishmael.* 3 vols. Philadelphia: Jewish Publication Society, 1976.

Le Donne, A. "The Improper Temple Offering of Ananias and Sapphira." *NTS* 59 (2013): 346–64.

Le Roux, L. V. "Style and the Text of Acts 4:25(a)." *Neot* 25 (1991): 29–32.

Leaney, A. R. C. "Why There were Forty Days between the Resurrection and the Ascension in Acts 1,3." Pages 417–19 in vol. 4 of *Studia Evangelica.* Edited by F. L. Cross. 7 vols. TUGAL 102. Berlin: Akademie, 1968.

Lee, D. *Luke-Acts and 'Tragic History': Communicating Gospel with the World.* WUNT II/346. Tübingen: Mohr Siebeck, 2013.

Lee, J. J. "On Distracting and Disappearing Joy: An Exegetical Comparison of the Ethiopian Eunuch and the Slave-Girl Rhoda in Acts." *HBT* 40 (2018): 65–77.

Lee, S.-I. *Jesus and Gospel Traditions in Bilingual Context: A Study in the Interdirectionality of Language.* BZNW 186. Berlin: de Gruyter, 2012.

Leivestad, R. "ταπεινός—ταπεινόφρων." *NovT* 8 (1966): 36–47.

Lennartsson, G. *Refreshing and Restoration: Two Eschatological Motifs in Acts 3:19–21.* Lund: Lund University, Centre for Theology and Religious Studies, 2007.

Léonas, A. "A Note on Acts 3,25–26: The Meaning of Peter's Genesis Quotation." *ETL* 76 (2000): 149–61.

Levine, L. I. *The Ancient Synagogue: The First Thousand Years.* New Haven: Yale University Press, 2000.

Levinskaya, I. *The Book of Acts in Its Diaspora Setting.* BAFCS 5. Carlisle: Paternoster; Grand Rapids: Eerdmans, 1996.

Levinsohn, S. H. *Textual Connections in Acts.* SBLMS 31. Atlanta: Scholars, 1987.

Lewis, C. S. *Miracles: A Preliminary Study.* London: Bles, 1947.

Lienhard, J. T. "Acts 6:1–6: A Redactional View." *CBQ* 37 (1975): 228–36.

Lightfoot, J. B. *The Acts of the Apostles.* Lightfoot Legacy 1. Downers Grove, IL: IVP Academic, 2014.

———. *St Paul's Epistle to the Galatians.* 10th ed. Peabody, MA: Hendricksen, 1890 repr. 1993.

Lincoln, A. T. "Theology and History in the Interpretation of Luke's Pentecost." *ExpTim* 96 (1985): 204–9.

Lindars, B. *John.* NT Guides. Sheffield: JSOT, 1990.

———. *New Testament Apologetic: The Doctrinal Significance of the Old Testament Quotations.* London: SCM, 1961.

Lindemann, A. "The Beginnings of Christian Life in Jerusalem according to the Summaries in the Acts of the Apostles (Acts 2:42–47; 4:32–37; 5:12–16)." Pages 202–18 in *Common Life in the Early Church: Essays Honoring Graydon F. Snyder.* Edited by J. V. Hills. Harrisburg, PA: Trinity Press International, 1998.

———. "Der 'Äthiopische Eunuch' und die Anfange der Mission under den Völkern nach Apg 8–11." Pages 109–33 in *Die Apostelgeschichte und die hellenistische Geschichtsschreibung: Festschrift für Eckhard Plümacher zu seinem 65. Geburtstag.* Edited by C. Breytenbach and J. Schröter. AGJU 57. Leiden: Brill, 2004.

Lindjier, C. H. "Two Creative Encounters in the Work of Luke: Luke xxiv 13–15 and Acts viii 26–40." Pages 77–85 in *Miscellanea Neotestamentica.* Edited by T. Baarda, A. F. J. Klijn, and W. C. van Unnik. 2 vols. NovTSup 48. Leiden: Brill, 1987.

Litwak, K. D. *Echoes of Scripture in Luke-Acts: Telling the History of God's People Intertextually.* JSNTSup 282. London: T&T Clark, 2005.

Lodge, D. "Analysis and Interpretation of the Realist Text: A Pluralistic Approach to Ernest Hemingway's 'Cat in the Rain.'" *Poet. Today* 1 (1980): 5–22.

Lohfink, G. "Christologie und Geschichtsbild in Apg 3:19–21." *BZ* ns 13 (1969): 223–41.

———. *The Conversion of St Paul: Narrative and History in Acts.* Translated by B. J. Malina. Herald Scriptural Library. Chicago: Franciscan Herald, 1976.

———. *Die Himmelfahrt Jesu: Untersuchungen zu den Himmelfahrts- und Erhöhungstexten bei Lukas.* SANT 26. München: Kösel, 1971.

———. *Die Sammlung Israels: Eine Untersuchung zur lukanischen Ekklesiologie.* SANT 39. München: Kösel, 1975.

Lohse, E. *Colossians and Philemon: A Commentary.* Translated by W. R. Pohlemann and R. J. Karris. Hermeneia. Philadelphia: Fortress, 1971.

Loisy, A. *Les Actes des Apôtres.* Paris: Nourry, 1920.

Longenecker, B. W. *Rhetoric at the Boundaries: The Art and Theology of the New Testament Chain-Link Transitions.* Waco, TX: Baylor University Press, 2005.

Longenecker, R. N. "Acts." Pages 663–1102 in vol. 10 of *Expositor's Bible Commentary.* Edited by T. Longman III and D. E. Garland. Revised ed. 13 vols. Grand Rapids: Zondervan Academic, 2007.

———. *Acts.* Expositor's Bible Commentary. Grand Rapids: Zondervan, 1995.

———. "The Acts of the Apostles." Pages 207–573 in vol. 9 of *The Expositor's Bible Commentary.* Edited by F. E. Gaebelein. 12 vols. Grand Rapids: Zondervan, 1981.

———. *Biblical Exegesis in the Apostolic Period.* Grand Rapids: Eerdmans, 1975.

———. *The Christology of Early Jewish Christianity.* SBT 2/17. London: SCM, 1970.

———. *Galatians.* WBC 41. Dallas, TX: Word, 1990.

———, ed. *The Road from Damascus: The Impact of Paul's Conversion on His Life, Thought and Ministry.* MNTS. Grand Rapids/Cambridge: Eerdmans, 1997.

Löning, K. *Die Saulustradition in der Apostelgeschichte.* NTAbh 2/9. Münster: Aschendorff, 1973.

Lövestam, E. "Der Rettungsappel in Ag 2, 40." *ASTI* 12 (1983): 85–92.

Lüdemann, G. "The Acts of the Apostles and the Beginnings of Simonian Gnosis." *NTS* 33 (1987): 420–26.

———. *Early Christianity according to the Traditions in Acts: A Commentary*. London: SCM, 1989.

———. *Untersuchungen zur simonianischen Gnosis*. GTA 1. Göttingen: Vandenhoeck & Ruprecht, 1975.

Lumby, J. R. *The Acts of the Apostles*. CBSC. Cambridge: Cambridge University Press, 1893.

Lyall, F. *Slaves, Citizens, Sons: Legal Metaphors in the Epistles*. Grand Rapids: Academie, 1984.

Lyons, G. *Pauline Autobiography: Towards a New Understanding*. SBLDS 73. Atlanta: Scholars, 1985.

Lyons, W. J. "The Words of Gamaliel (Acts 5.38–39) and the Irony of Indeterminacy." *JSNT* 68 (1997): 23–49.

Macaskill, G. *Union with Christ in the New Testament*. Oxford: Oxford University Press, 2018.

MacDonald, D. R. *Does the New Testament Imitate Homer? Four Cases from the Acts of the Apostles*. New Haven: Yale University Press, 2003.

———. *The Gospels and Homer: Imitations of Greek Epic in Mark and Luke-Acts*. Lanham, MD: Rowman & Littlefield, 2015.

———. "Luke's Use of Papias for Narrating the Death of Judas." Pages 43–62 in *Reading Acts Today: Essays in Honour of Loveday C. A. Alexander*. Edited by S. Walton, T. E. Phillips, L. K. Pietersen and F. S. Spencer. LNTS 427. London: T&T Clark, 2011.

MacDonald, J. *The Theology of the Samaritans*. NTL. London: SCM, 1964.

MacDonald, W. G. "Christology and 'The Angel of the Lord.'" Pages 324–55 in *Current Issues in Biblical and Patristic Interpretation: Studies in Honor of Merrill C. Tenney Presented by His Former Students*. Edited by G. F. Hawthorne. Grand Rapids: Eerdmans, 1975.

———. "Glossolalia in the New Testament." Pages 127–40 in *Speaking in Tongues: A Guide to Research on Glossolalia*. Edited by W. E. Mills. Grand Rapids: Eerdmans, 1986.

MacKay, D. *The Clockwork Image: A Christian Perspective on Science*. London: Inter-Varsity Press, 1974.

Macnamara, L. *My Chosen Instrument: The Characterisation of Paul in Acts 7:58–15:41*. AnBib 215. Rome: Gregorian & Biblical, 2016.

MacRae, G. W. "'Whom Heaven Must Receive until the Time': Reflections on the Christology of Acts." *Int* 27 (1973): 151–65.

Maddox, R. *The Purpose of Luke-Acts*. SNTW. Edinburgh: T&T Clark, 1982.

Maiburg, U. "Christus der Eckstein: Ps 118:22 und Jes 28:16 im Neuen Testament und bei den lateinischen Vatern." Pages 247–56 in *Vivarium: Festchrift Theodor Klauser zum 90. Geburtstag*. Edited by E. Dassmann and K. Thraede. JACErg 11. Münster: Aschendorff, 1984.

Maile, J. F. "The Ascension in Luke-Acts." *TynBul* 37 (1986): 29–59.

Mainville, O. "Le Messianimse de Jésus: Le repoport annonce/accomplissement entre Lc 1,35 et Ac 2,33." Pages 313–27 in *The Unity of Luke-Acts*. Edited by J. Verheyden. BETL 142. Leuven: Leuven University Press/Peeters, 1999.

———. "Le péché contre l'Esprit annoncé en Lc 12.10, commis en Ac 4.16–18: Une illustration de l'unité de Luc et Actes." *NTS* 45 (1999): 38–50.

———. *The Spirit in Luke-Acts*. Translated by S. Spolarich. Eugene, OR: Wipf & Stock, 2016.

Malina, B. J. *The New Testament World: Insights from Cultural Anthropology*. 3rd ed. Louisville: Westminster John Knox, 2001.

Malina, B. J., and J. J. Pilch. *Social-Science Commentary on the Book of Acts.* Minneapolis: Fortress, 2008.

Mallen, P. *The Reading and Transformation of Isaiah in Luke-Acts.* LNTS 367. London: T&T Clark, 2008.

Maloney, L. *All That God Had Done with Them: The Narration of the Works of God in the Early Christian Community as Described in the Acts of the Apostles.* American University Studies, series VII, Theology and Religion 91. New York: Peter Lang, 1991.

Manns, F. "Un midrash chretien: Le recit de la mort de Judas." *RevScRel* 54 (1980): 197–203.

Mansell, P. W. "The Rise and Fall of the Twelve." PhD diss., St Mary's University, Twickenham, 2017.

Mantey, J. R. "The Causal Use of εἰς in the New Testament." *JBL* 70 (1951): 45–48.

———. "On Causal εἰς Again." *JBL* 70 (1951): 309–11.

Marconi, G. "History as a Hermeneutical Interpretation of the Difference between Acts 3:1–10 and 4:8–12." Pages 167–80, 252–57 in *Luke and Acts.* Edited by G. O'Collins and G. Marconi. New York: Paulist, 1991.

Marcus, R. "The Elusive Causal εἰς." *JBL* 71 (1952): 43–44.

———. "On Causal εἰς." *JBL* 70 (1951): 129–30.

Mare, W. H. "Acts 7: Jewish or Samaritan in Character?" *WTJ* 34 (1971): 1–21.

Marguerat, D. *The First Christian Historian: Writing the "Acts of the Apostles".* SNTSMS 121. Cambridge: Cambridge University Press, 2002.

———. *Les Actes des apôtres.* 2 vols. CNT 5. Genève: Labor et Fides, 2007, 2015.

———. "Magic and Miracle in the Acts of the Apostles." Pages 100–124 in *Magic in the Biblical World: From the Rod of Aaron to the Ring of Solomon.* Edited by T. Klutz. JSNTSup 245. London: T&T Clark, 2003.

Marguerat, D., and Y. Bourquin. *How to Read Bible Stories.* London: SCM, 1999.

Marrow, S. B. "Παρρησία and the New Testament." *CBQ* 44 (1982): 431–46.

Marshall, I. H. "Acts." Pages 513–606 in *Commentary on the New Testament Use of the Old Testament.* Edited by G. K. Beale and D. A. Carson. Nottingham: Apollos; Grand Rapids: Baker Academic, 2007.

———. *The Acts of the Apostles: An Introduction and Commentary.* TNTC. Leicester: Inter-Varsity Press, 1980.

———. "The Christology of Luke's Gospel and Acts." Pages 122–47 in *Contours of Christology in the New Testament.* Edited by R. N. Longenecker. MNTS. Grand Rapids: Eerdmans, 2005.

———. *The Gospel of Luke: A Commentary on the Greek Text.* NIGTC. Exeter: Paternoster, 1978.

———. "How Far Did the Early Christians *Worship* God?" *Chm* 99 (1985): 216–29.

———. *Last Supper and Lord's Supper.* Exeter: Paternoster, 1980.

———. *Luke: Historian and Theologian.* Exeter: Paternoster, 1970.

———. "The Meaning of the Verb 'Baptize.'" Pages 8–24 in *Dimensions of Baptism: Biblical and Theological Studies.* Edited by S. E. Porter and A. R. Cross. JSNTSup 234. London: Sheffield Academic, 2002.

———. "Palestinian and Hellenistic Christianity: Some Critical Comments." *NTS* 19 (1972): 271–87.

———. "The Place of Acts 20.28 in Luke's Theology of the Cross." in *Reading Acts Today: Essays in Honour of Loveday C. A. Alexander.* Edited by S. Walton, T. E. Phillips, L. K. Pietersen and F. S. Spencer. LNTS 427. London: T&T Clark, 2011.

———. "The Significance of Pentecost." *SJT* 30 (1977): 347–69.

Marshall, I. H., and P. H. Towner. *A Critical and Exegetical Commentary on the Pastoral Epistles.* ICC. Edinburgh: T&T Clark, 1999.

Marshall, M. *The Portrayals of the Pharisees in the Gospels and Acts.* FRLANT 254. Göttingen: Vandenhoeck & Ruprecht, 2015.

Martin, C. J. "A Chamberlain's Journey and the Challenge of Interpretation for Liberation." *Semeia* 47 (1989): 105–35.

Martin, R. P. *2 Corinthians.* WBC 40. Dallas, TX: Word, 1986.

———. *2 Corinthians.* 2nd ed. WBC 40. Dallas, TX: Word, 2014.

Martín-Asensio, G. "Participant Reference and Foregrounded Syntax in the Stephen Episode." Pages 235–57 in *Discourse Analysis and the New Testament.* Edited by S. E. Porter and J. T. Reed. JSNTSup 170. Sheffield: Sheffield Academic, 1999.

Mason, S. "Chief Priests, Sadducees, Pharisees and Sanhedrin in Acts." Pages 115–77 in *The Book of Acts in Its Palestinian Setting.* Edited by R. Bauckham. BAFCS 4. Carlisle: Paternoster; Grand Rapids: Eerdmans, 1995.

———. *Josephus and the New Testament.* 2nd ed. Peabody, MA: Hendrickson, 2003.

Masson, C. "La reconstitution du collège des Douze d'après Actes 1,15–26." *RTP* 5 (1955): 193–201.

Maston, J. "How Wrong Were the Disciples about the Kingdom? Thoughts on Acts 1:6." *ExpTim* 126 (2015): 169–78.

Matera, F. J. "Responsibility for the Death of Jesus according to the Acts of the Apostles." *JSNT* 39 (1990): 77–93.

Matthews, C. R. "Philip and Simon, Luke and Peter: A Lukan Sequel and Its Intertextual Success." Pages 133–46 in *Society of Biblical Literature 1992 Seminar Papers.* SBLSP 31. Atlanta: SBL, 1992.

———. *Philip: Apostle and Evangelist: Configurations of a Tradition.* NovTSup 105. Leiden: Brill, 2002.

Matthews, S. *Perfect Martyr: The Stoning of Stephen and the Construction of Christian Identity.* New York: Oxford University Press, 2010.

Maxwell, K. R. *Hearing between the Lines: The Audience as Fellow-Worker in Luke-Acts and Its Literary Milieu.* LNTS 425. London: T&T Clark, 2010.

McCabe, D. R. *How to Kill Things with Words: Ananias and Sapphira under the Prophetic Speech-Act of Divine Judgement (Acts 4.32–5.11).* LNTS 454. London: T&T Clark, 2011.

McCane, B. R. *Roll Back the Stone: Death and Burial in the World of Jesus.* Harrisburg, PA: Trinity Press International, 2003.

McCaughey, J. D. "The Intention of the Author: Some Questions about the Exegesis of Acts 6:1–6." *AusBR* 7 (1959): 27–36.

McCollough, D. J. *Ritual Water, Ritual Spirit: An Analysis of the Timing, Mechanism and Manifestation of Spirit-Reception in Luke-Acts.* PBM. Bletchley: Paternoster, 2017.

McDermott, J. M. "The Biblical Doctrine of KOINΩNIA, Part II." *BZ* 19 (1975): 219–33.

McIntyre, L. B., Jr. "Baptism and Forgiveness in Acts 2:38." *BSac* 153 (1996): 53–62.

Mealand, D. L. "Community of Goods and Utopian Allusions in Acts II–IV." *JTS* ns 28 (1977): 96–99.

———. "The Phrase 'Many Proofs' in Acts 1,3 and in Hellenistic Writers." *ZNW* 80 (1989): 134–35.

Meek, J. A. *The Gentile Mission in Old Testament Citations in Acts: Text, Hermeneutic, and Purpose.* LNTS 385. London: T&T Clark, 2008.

Meeks, W. A. "Simon Magus in Recent Research." *RelSRev* 3 (1977): 137–42.

Meier, J. P. "The Circle of the Twelve: Did It Exist during Jesus' Public Ministry?" *JBL* 116 (1997): 635–72.

———. *A Marginal Jew: Rethinking the Historical Jesus.* 4 vols. AYBRL. New York: Doubleday; New Haven: Yale University Press, 1991–2009.

Melbourne, B. L. "Acts 1:8 re-examined: is Acts 8 its fulfillment?" *JRT* 57 (2005): 1–18.

Ménard, J. E. "*Pais Theou* as Messianic Title in the Book of Acts." *CBQ* 19 (1957): 83–92.

Menoud, P. H. *Jesus Christ and the Faith: A Collection of Studies.* Translated by E. M. Paul. PTMS 18. Pittsburgh: Pickwick, 1978.

Menzies, G. W. "Pre-Lucan Occurrences of the Phrase 'Tongue(s) of Fire.'" *Pneuma* 22 (2000): 27–60.

Menzies, R. P. *Empowered for Witness: The Spirit in Luke-Acts.* JPTSup 6. Sheffield: Sheffield Academic, 1994.

Metzger, B. M. "Ancient Astrological Geography and Acts 2:9–11." Pages 123–33 in *Apostolic History and the Gospel: Biblical and Historical Essays Presented to F. F. Bruce on His 60th Birthday.* Edited by W. W. Gasque and R. P. Martin. Exeter: Paternoster, 1970.

———. *Historical and Literary Studies: Pagan, Jewish, and Christian.* NTTS 8. Leiden: Brill, 1968.

———. *The Text of the New Testament: Its Transmission, Corruption and Restoration.* 3rd ed. Oxford: Oxford University Press, 1992.

Metzger, B. M., and B. D. Ehrman. *The Text of the New Testament: Its Transmission, Corruption and Restoration.* 4th ed. Oxford: Oxford University Press, 2005.

Meyer, B. F. "The Initial Self-Understanding of the Church." *CBQ* 27 (1965): 35–42.

Millard, A. R. *Reading and Writing in the Time of Jesus.* BSem 69. Sheffield: Sheffield Academic, 2001.

Miller, J. B. F. *Convinced That God Had Called Us: Dreams, Visions, and the Perception of God's Will in Luke-Acts.* BibInt 85. Leiden: Brill, 2007.

Mitchell, A. C. "The Social Function of Friendship in Acts 2:44–47 and 4:32–37." *JBL* 111 (1992): 255–72.

Mittelstadt, M. W. *The Spirit and Suffering in Luke-Acts: Implications for a Pentecostal Pneumatology.* JPTSup 26. London: T&T Clark, 2004.

Miura, Y. *David in Luke-Acts: His Portrayal in the Light of Early Judaism.* WUNT II/232. Tübingen: Mohr Siebeck, 2007.

Moberly, R. W. L. *At the Mountain of God: Story and Theology in Exodus 32–34.* JSOTSup 33. Sheffield: JSOT, 1983.

Moehring, H. R. "The Verb *akouein* in Acts 9:7 and Acts 22:9." *NovT* 3 (1959): 80–99.

Moessner, D. P. "'The Christ Must Suffer': New Light on the Jesus-Peter, Stephen, Paul Parallels in Acts." *NovT* 28 (1986): 220–56.

———. "Suffering, Intercession and Eschatological Atonement: An Uncommon Common View in the Testament of Moses and in Luke-Acts." Pages 202–27 in *The Pseudepigrapha and Early Biblical Interpretation.* Edited by J. H. Charlesworth and C. A. Evans. JSPSup 14. Sheffield: JSOT, 1993.

———. "*Two* Lords 'at the Right Hand'? The Psalms and an Intertextual Reading of Peter's Pentecost Speech (Acts 2:14–36)." Pages 215–32 in *Literary Studies in Luke-Acts.* Edited by R. P. Thompson and T. E. Phillips. Macon, Ga: Mercer University Press, 1998.

Monloubou, L. *La prière selon Saint Luc: recherche d'une structure.* LD 89. Paris: Cerf, 1976.

Moo, D. J. "Tradition and the Old Testament in Matt. 27:3–10." Pages 157–75 in *Studies in Midrash and Historiography.* Edited by R. T. France and D. Wenham. Gospel Perspectives 3. Sheffield: JSOT, 1983.

Moore, G. F. *Judaism in the First Centuries of the Christian Era, the Age of the Tannaim.* 3 vols. Cambridge, MA: Harvard University Press, 1927.

Moore, T. S. "The Lukan Great Commission and the Isaianic Servant." *BSac* 154 (1997): 47–60.

———. "'To the End of the Earth': The Geographic and Ethnic Universalism of Acts 1:8 in Light of Isaianic Influence on Luke." *JETS* 40 (1997): 389–99.

Morgan, T. *Roman Faith and Christian Faith.* Oxford: Oxford University Press, 2015.

Morlan, D. S. *Conversion in Luke and Paul: An Exegetical and Theological Exploration.* LNTS 464. London: Bloomsbury, 2013.

Morrice, W. G. *Joy in the New Testament.* Exeter: Paternoster, 1984.

Moule, C. F. D. "The Ascension—Acts 1.9." *ExpTim* 68 (1957): 205–9.

———. "The Christology of Acts." Pages 159–85 in *Studies in Luke-Acts.* Edited by L. E. Keck and J. L. Martyn. London: SPCK, 1968.

———. "H. W. Moule on Acts iv.25." *ExpTim* 65 (1954): 220–21.

———. "Once More: Who Were the Hellenists?" *ExpTim* 70 (1959): 100–102.

———. *The Origin of Christology.* Cambridge: Cambridge University Press, 1977.

———. *The Phenomenon of the New Testament.* London: SCM, 1967.

———. "Sanctuary and Sacrifice in the Church of the New Testament." *JTS* ns 1 (1950): 29–41.

Moule, H. W. "ὁ τοῦ πατρὸς ἡμῶν διὰ πνεύματος ἁγίου στόματος Δαυὶδ παιδός σου εἰπών· ἱνατί κ.τ.λ.—Acts iv.25." *ExpTim* 51 (1940): 396.

Müller, P.-G. *ΧΡΙΣΤΟΣ ΑΡΧΗΓΟΣ: Der religionsgeschichtliche und theologische Hintergrund einer neutestamentlichen Christusprädikation.* EH 23/28. Frankfurt-am-Main: Peter Lang, 1973.

Munck, J., W. F. Albright, and C. S. Mann. *The Acts of the Apostles.* AB 31. New York: Doubleday, 1967.

Mundle, W. "Die Stephanusrede Apg. 7: Eine Martyrerapologie." *ZNW* 20 (1921): 133–47.

Murphy, S. J. "The Role of Barnabas in the Book of Acts." *BSac* 167 (2010): 319–41.

Murphy-O'Connor, J. "The Cenacle: Topographical Setting for Acts 2:44–45." Pages 303–21 in *The Book of Acts in Its Palestinian Setting.* Edited by R. Bauckham. BAFCS 4. Carlisle: Paternoster; Grand Rapids: Eerdmans, 1995.

———. *The Holy Land.* 5th ed. Oxford: Oxford University Press, 2008.

Myllykoski, M. "Being There: The Function of the Supernatural in Acts 1–12." Pages 146–79 in *Wonders Never Cease: The Purpose of Narrating Miracle Stories in the New Testament and Its Religious Environment.* Edited by M. Labahn and B. J. Lietaert Peerbolte. LNTS 288. London: T&T Clark, 2006.

Nagel, N. E. "The Twelve and the Seven in Acts 6 and the Needy." *ConcJ* 31 (2005): 113–26.

Naiden, F. S. *Ancient Supplication.* Oxford: Oxford University Press, 2006.

Nave, G. D. *The Role and Function of Repentance in Luke-Acts.* SBLAcBib 4. Leiden: Brill, 2002.

Neagoe, A. *The Trial of the Gospel: An Apologetic Reading of Luke's Trial Narratives.* SNTSMS 116. Cambridge: Cambridge University Press, 2002.

Nellessen, E. "Tradition und Schrift in der Perikope von der Erwahlung des Mattias (Apg 1,15–26)." *BZ* ns 19 (1975): 205–18.

Neudorfer, H.-W. "The Speech of Stephen." Pages 275–94 in *Witness to the Gospel: The Theology of Acts.* Edited by I. H. Marshall and D. Peterson. Grand Rapids/Cambridge: Eerdmans, 1998.

Neusner, J. *The Rabbinic Traditions about the Pharisees before 70.* 3 vols. Leiden: Brill, 1971.

Newbigin, L. "Witness in a Biblical Perspective." *MisSt* 3 (1986): 80–84.

Newman, B. M., Jr., and E. A. Nida. *A Translator's Handbook on the Acts of the Apostles.* Helps for Translators 12. London: United Bible Societies, 1972.

Niccum, C. "A Note on Acts 1:14." *NovT* 36 (1994): 196–99.

Noble, J. *Common Property, the Golden Age, and Empire in Acts 2:42–47 and 4:32–35.* LNTS 636. London: Bloomsbury T&T Clark, 2020.

Nock, A. D. *Conversion: The Old and the New in Religion from Alexander the Great to Augustine of Hippo.* Oxford: Clarendon, 1933.

Nolland, J. *Luke.* 3 vols. WBC 35A–C. Dallas, TX: Word, 1989–93.

———. "Luke's Use of χάρις." *NTS* 32 (1986): 614–20.

Noorda, S. J. "Scene and Summary. A Proposal for Reading Acts 4,32–5,16." Pages 475–83 in *Les Actes des Apôtres: traditions, rédaction, théologie.* Edited by J. Kremer. BETL 48. Gembloux: Duculot; Leuven: Leuven University Press, 1979.

Novick, T. "Succeeding Judas: Exegesis in Acts 1:15–26." *JBL* 129 (2010): 795–99.

O'Brien, P. T. "The Church as a Heavenly and Eschatological Entity." Pages 88–105 in *The Church in the Bible and the World.* Edited by D. A. Carson. Exeter: Paternoster, 1987.

———. "Prayer in Luke-Acts." *TynBul* 24 (1973): 111–27.

O'Neill, J. C. "The Connection between Baptism and the Gift of the Spirit in Acts." *JSNT* 63 (1996): 87–103.

———. *The Theology of Acts in Its Historical Setting.* London: SPCK, 1961.

———. *The Theology of Acts in Its Historical Setting.* 2nd ed. London: SPCK, 1970.

O'Reilly, L. *Word and Sign in the Acts of the Apostles: A Study in Lucan Theology.* AnGr 243. Rome: Editrice Pontificia Università Gregoriana, 1987.

O'Toole, R. F. "Acts 2:30 and the Davidic Covenant of Pentecost." *JBL* 102 (1983): 245–58.

———. "The Kingdom of God in Luke-Acts." Pages 147–62 in *The Kingdom of God in Twentieth-Century Interpretation.* Peabody, MA: Hendrickson, 1987.

———. "Luke's Understanding of Jesus' Resurrection-Ascension-Exaltation." *BTB* 9 (1979): 106–14.

———. "Parallels between Jesus and His Disciples in Luke-Acts: A Further Study." *BZ* 27 (1983): 195–212.

———. "Philip and the Ethiopian Eunuch (Acts VIII 25–40)." *JSNT* 17 (1983): 25–34.

———. "Some Observations on *anistēmi*, 'I Raise', in Acts 3:22, 26." *ScEs* 31 (1979): 85–92.

———. "You Did Not Lie to Us (Human Beings) But to God (Acts 5,4c)." *Bib* 76 (1995): 182–209.

Oh, D. W. "The Name, the Temple, and the People of the Lord: The Connection between the Name of the Lord and the Temple of the Lord." PhD diss., Australian College of Theology/Ridley College, Melbourne, 2018.

Öhler, M. *Barnabas: die historische Person und ihre Rezeption in der Apostelgeschichte.* WUNT 156. Tübingen: Mohr Siebeck, 2003.

———. "Die Jerusalemer Urgemeinde im Spiegel des antiken Vereinswesens." *NTS* 51 (2005): 393–415.

Okholm, D. L., and T. R. Phillips, eds. *More than One Way? Four Views on Salvation in a Pluralistic World.* Grand Rapids: Zondervan Academic, 1995.

Olyan, S. M. "'Anyone Blind or Lame Shall Not Enter the House': On the Interpretation of Second Samuel 5:8b." *CBQ* 60 (1998): 218–27.

Omanson, R. L. "How Does it All Fit Together? Thoughts on Translating Acts 1:15–22 and 15:19–21." *BT* 41 (1990): 416–21.

Osburn, C. D. "The Search for the Original Text of Acts: The International Project on the Text of Acts." *JSNT* 44 (1991): 39–55.

———. "The Third Person Imperative in Acts 2:38." *ResQ* 26 (1983): 81–84.

Oulton, J. E. L. "The Holy Spirit, Baptism, and Laying on of Hands in Acts." *ExpTim* 66 (1955): 236–40.

Ovey, M. J. *The Feasts of Repentance: From Luke-Acts to Systematic and Pastoral Theology.* NSBT 49. Nottingham: Apollos, 2019.

Owen, H. P. "Stephen's Vision in Acts vii. 55–6." *NTS* 1 (1955): 224–26.

Page, T. E. Review of F. Blass, *Acta Apostolorum. CR* 11 (1897): 317–20.

Palmer, D. W. "The Literary Background of Acts 1.1–14." *NTS* 33 (1987): 427–38.

Panten, K. E. "A History of Research on Codex Bezæ." *TynBul* 47 (1996): 185–87.

Pao, D. W. *Acts and the Isaianic New Exodus.* BibStL. Grand Rapids: Baker Academic, 2002.

———. "Waiters or Preachers: Acts 6:1–7 and the Lukan Table Fellowship Motif." *JBL* 130 (2011): 127–44.

Park, H. D. *Finding Herem? A Study of Luke-Acts in the Light of Herem.* LNTS 357. London: T&T Clark, 2007.

Park, S. *Pentecost and Sinai: The Festival of Weeks as a Celebration of the Sinai Event.* LHBOTS 342. London: T&T Clark, 2008.

Parker, D. C. *Codex Bezae An Early Christian Manuscript and Its Text.* Cambridge: Cambridge University Press, 1992.

———. *An Introduction to the New Testament Manuscripts and Their Texts.* Cambridge: Cambridge University Press, 2008.

Parker, D. C., and S. R. Pickering. "4698. Acta Apostolorum 10–12, 15–17." Pages 1–45 in *The Oxyrhynchus Papyri, vol. LXXIV.* Edited by D. Leith, D. C. Parker, S. R. Pickering, N. Gonis and M. Malouta. Graeco-Roman Memoirs 95. London: Egypt Explortation Society, 2009.

Parker, P. "Once More, Acts and Galatians." *JBL* 86 (1967): 175–82.

Parsons, M. C. *Acts.* Paideia. Grand Rapids: Baker Academic, 2008.

———. *Body and Character in Luke and Acts: The Subversion of Physiognomy in Early Christianity.* Grand Rapids: Baker Academic, 2006.

———. "The Character of the Lame Man in Acts 3–4." *JBL* 124 (2005): 295–312.

———. *The Departure of Jesus in Luke-Acts: The Ascension Narratives in Context.* JSNTSup 21. Sheffield: JSOT, 1987.

———. "Isaiah 53 in Acts 8: A Reply to Professor Morna Hooker." Pages 104–19 in *Jesus and the Suffering Servant: Isaiah 53 and Christian Origins.* Edited by W. Bellinger and W. R. Farmer. Harrisburg, PA: Trinity Press International, 1998.

———. "The Text of Acts 1:2 Reconsidered." *CBQ* 50 (1988): 58–71.

Paschke, B. "Prayer to Jesus in the Canonical and in the Apocryphal Acts of the Apostles." *ETL* 89 (2013): 49–71.

Payne, D. F. "Semitisms in the Book of Acts." Pages 134–50 in *Apostolic History and the Gospel: Biblical and Historical Essays Presented to F. F. Bruce on His 60th Birthday.* Edited by W. W. Gasque and R. P. Martin. Exeter: Paternoster, 1970.

Peace, R. V. *Conversion in the New Testament: Paul and the Twelve.* Grand Rapids/Cambridge: Eerdmans, 1999.

Pelikan, J. *Acts.* BTCB. Grand Rapids: Brazos, 2005.

Penner, T. C. *In Praise of Christian Origins: Stephen and the Hellenists in Lukan Apologetic Historiography.* ESEC 10. London: T&T Clark, 2004.

———. "Narrative as Persuasion: Epideictic Rhetoric and Scribal Amplification in the Stephen Episode in Acts." Pages 352–67 in *Society of Biblical Literature 1996 Seminar Papers.* SBLSP 35. Atlanta: Scholars, 1996.

Penney, J. M. *The Missionary Emphasis of Lukan Pneumatology.* JPTSup 12. Sheffield: Sheffield Academic, 1997.

Pervo, R. I. *Acts.* Hermeneia. Minneapolis: Fortress, 2009.

———. *Dating Acts: Between the Evangelists and the Apologists.* Santa Rosa, CA: Polebridge, 2006.

———. *Profit with Delight.* Philadelphia: Fortress, 1987.

———. "ΠΑΝΤΑ ΚΟΙΝΑ: The Feeding Stories in the Light of Economic Data and Social Practice." Pages 164–94 in *Religious Propaganda and Missionary Competition in the New Testament World: Essays Honoring Dieter Georgi.* Edited by L. Bormann, K. Del Tredici and A. Standhartinger. NovTSup 74. Leiden: Brill, 1994.

Pesch, R. *Die Apostelgeschichte.* 2 vols. EKKNT. Zürich: Benzinger, 1986.

———. *Die Vision des Stephanus: Apg 7,55–56 im Rahmen der Apostelgeschichte.* SBS 12. Stuttgart: Katholisches Bibelwerk, 1967.

Peterson, B. K. "Stephen's Speech as a Modified Prophetic *rîḇ* Formula." *JETS* 57 (2014): 351–69.

Peterson, D. *The Acts of the Apostles.* PNTC. Nottingham: Apollos; Grand Rapids: Eerdmans, 2009.

———. *Engaging with God: A Biblical Theology of Worship.* Leicester: Apollos, 1992.

———. "The Motif of Fulfilment and the Purpose of Luke-Acts." Pages 83–104 in *The Book of Acts in Its Ancient Literary Setting.* Edited by B. W. Winter and A. D. Clarke. BAFCS 1. Carlisle: Paternoster; Grand Rapids: Eerdmans, 1993.

Petterson, C. *Acts of Empire: The Acts of the Apostles and Imperial Ideology.* 2nd ed. Critical Theory & Biblical Studies. Eugene, OR: Cascade, 2020.

Pfitzner, V. C. "'Pneumatic' Apostleship? Apostle and Spirit in the Acts of the Apostles." Pages 210–35 in *Wort in der Zeit: neutestamentliche Studien: Festgabe für Karl Heinrich Rengstorf zum 75. Geburtstag.* Edited by W. Haubeck and M. Bachmann. Leiden: Brill, 1980.

Philo. *The Works of Philo: Complete and Unabridged.* Translated by C. D. Yonge. New updated edn. Peabody, MA: Hendrickson, 1995.

Pilch, J. J. "Paul's Ecstatic Trance Experience near Damascus in Acts of the Apostles." *HvTSt* 58 (2002): 690–707.

———. *Visions and Healing in the Acts of the Apostles: How the Early Believers Experienced God.* Collegeville, MN: Liturgical, 2004.

Pinnock, C. H. "Acts 4:12: No Other Name under Heaven." *ThSc* 10 (2003): 19–28.

Platner, S. B., and T. Ashby. *A Topographical Dictionary of Ancient Rome.* London: Oxford University Press, 1929.

Plümacher, E. *Lukas als hellenistischer Schriftsteller: Studien zur Apostelgeschichte.* Göttingen: Vandenhoeck & Ruprecht, 1972.

Plymale, S. F. *The Prayer Texts of Luke-Acts.* American University Studies: Series VII: Theology & Religion 118. New York: Peter Lang, 1991.

Porter, R. J. "What Did Philip Say to the Eunuch?" *ExpTim* 100 (1988): 54–55.

Porter, S. E. "Magic in the Book of Acts." Pages 107–21 in *A Kind of Magic: Understanding Magic in the New Testament and Its Religious Environment.* Edited by M. Labahn and B. J. Lietaert Peerbolte. LNTS 306. London: T&T Clark, 2007.

———. "The Unity of Luke-Acts and the Ascension." Pages 111–36 in *Ascent into Heaven in Luke-Acts: New Explorations of Luke's Narrative Hinge.* Edited by D. W. Pao and D. Bryan. Minneapolis: Fortress, 2016.

———. *Verbal Aspect in the Greek of the New Testament, with Reference to Tense and Mood.* SBG 1. New York: Peter Lang, 1989.

Powell, M. A. *What is Narrative Criticism?* London: SPCK, 1993.

Praeder, S. M. "Jesus-Paul, Peter-Paul, and Jesus-Peter Parallelisms in Luke-Acts: A History of Reader Response." Pages 23–39 in *Society of Biblical Literature 1984 Seminar Papers.* SBLSP 23. Chico, CA: Scholars, 1984.

Price, R. M. *The Widow Traditions in Luke-Acts: A Feminist-Critical Scrutiny.* SBLDS 155. Atlanta: Scholars, 1997.

Price, T. L. *Structural Lexicology and the Greek New Testament: Applying Corpus Linguistics for Word Sense Possibility Delimitation using Collocational Indicators.* PLAL 6. Piscataway, NJ: Gorgias, 2015.

Pulleyn, S. *Prayer in Greek Religion* Oxford: Clarendon, 1997.

Pummer, R. *Early Christian Authors on Samaritans and Samaritanism: Texts, Translations and Commentary.* TSAJ 92. Tübingen: Mohr Siebeck, 2002.

———. “The Present State of Samaritan Studies I.” *JSS* 21 (1976): 39–61.
———. “The Present State of Samaritan Studies II.” *JSS* 22 (1977): 27–47.
———. *The Samaritans.* Leiden: Brill, 1987.
———. *The Samaritans: A Profile.* Grand Rapids: Eerdmans, 2015.

Quesnel, M. *Baptisés dans l’esprit: baptême et Esprit Saint dans les Actes des Apôtres.* LD 120. Paris: Cerf, 1985.

Quesnell, Q. “The Women at Luke’s Supper.” Pages 59–79 in *Political Issues in Luke-Acts.* Edited by R. J. Cassidy and P. J. Scharper. Maryknoll, NY: Orbis, 1983.

Rackham, R. B. *The Acts of the Apostles.* 2nd ed. Westminster Commentaries. London: Methuen, 1904.
———. “The Acts of the Apostles II: A Plea for an Early Date.” *JTS* 1 (1899): 76–87.

Radin, M. “Freedom of Speech in Ancient Athens.” *AJP* 48 (1927): 215–30.

Rambo, L. R., and C. E. Farhadian, eds. *The Oxford Handbook of Religious Conversion.* Oxford: Oxford University Press, 2014.

Ramsay, W. M. *St Paul the Traveller and Roman Citizen.* London: Hodder & Stoughton, 1895.

Rapske, B. M. “Acts, Travel and Shipwreck.” Pages 1–47 in *The Book of Acts in Its Graeco-Roman Setting.* Edited by D. W. J. Gill and C. H. Gempf. BAFCS 2. Carlisle: Paternoster; Grand Rapids: Eerdmans, 1994.
———. *The Book of Acts and Paul in Roman Custody.* BAFCS 3. Carlisle: Paternoster; Grand Rapids: Eerdmans, 1994.

Ravens, D. *Luke and the Restoration of Israel.* JSNTSup 119. Sheffield: Sheffield Academic, 1995.

Read-Heimerdinger, J. “Barnabas in Acts: A Study of His Role in the Text of Codex Bezae.” *JSNT* 72 (1998): 23–66.
———. *The Bezan Text of Acts: A Contribution of Discourse Analysis to Textual Criticism.* JSNTSup 236. London: Sheffield Academic, 2002.
———. “The «Long» and the «Short» Texts of Acts: A Closer Look at the Quantity and Types of Variation.” *RCatT* 22 (1997): 245–61.

Reardon, T. W. “‘Hanging on a Tree’: Deuteronomy 21.22–23 and the Rhetoric of Jesus’ Crucifixion in Acts 5.12–42.” *JSNT* 37 (2015): 407–31.

Reece, S. “Jesus as Healer: Etymologizing of Proper Names in Luke-Acts.” *ZNW* 110 (2019): 186–201.

Reich, R. “Caiaphas Name Inscribed on Bone Boxes.” *BAR* 18 (1992): 38–44, 76.

Reicke, B. I. *Glaube und Leben der Urgemeinde: Bemerkungen zu Apg. 1–7.* ATANT 32. Zürich: Zwingli, 1957.

Reimer, A. M. *Miracle and Magic: A Study in the Acts of the Apostles and the Life of Apollonius of Tyana.* JSNTSup 235. London: Sheffield Academic, 2002.

Reimer, I. R. *Women in the Acts of the Apostles: A Feminist Liberation Perspective.* Minneapolis: Fortress, 1995.

Reinhardt, W. “The Population Size of Jerusalem and the Numerical Growth of the Christian Church.” Pages 237–65 in *The Book of Acts in Its Palestinian Setting.* Edited by R. Bauckham. BAFCS 4. Carlisle: Paternoster; Grand Rapids: Eerdmans, 1995.

Rengstorf, K. H. “The Election of Matthias.” Pages 178–87 in *Current Issues in New Testament Interpretation: Essays in Honour of O. Piper.* Edited by W. Klassen and G. F. Synder. London: SCM, 1962.

Renié, J. “L’élection de Mathias (Act. I, 15–26): Authenticité du Récit.” *RB* 55 (1948): 43–53.

Rese, M. *Alttestamentliche Motive in der Christologie des Lukas.* SNT 1. Gütersloh: Mohn, 1969.

———. "Die Funktion der alttestamentlichen Zitate und der Anspielungen in den Reden der Apostelgeschichte." Pages 61–79 in *Les Actes des Apôtres: tradition, rédaction, théologie*. Edited by J. Kremer. BETL 48. Gembloux: Duculot; Leuven: Leuven University Press, 1979.

Resseguie, J. L. *Narrative Criticism of the New Testament: An Introduction*. Grand Rapids: Baker Academic, 2005.

Rhamie, G. C. A. "Whiteness, Conviviality and Agency: The Ethiopian Eunuch (Acts 8:26–40) and Conceptuality in the Imperial Imagination of Biblical Studies." PhD diss., Canterbury Christ Church University, 2019.

Richard, E. J. *Acts 6:1–8:4: The Author's Method of Composition*. SBLDS 41. Missoula, MT: Scholars, 1978.

———. "Acts 7: An Investigation of the Samaritan Evidence." *CBQ* 39 (1977): 190–208.

———. "The Creative Use of Amos by the Author of Acts." *NovT* 24 (1982): 37–53.

———. "The Polemical Character of the Joseph Episode in Acts 7." *JBL* 98 (1979): 255–67.

Richards, E. R. *Paul and First-Century Letter-Writing: Secretaries, Composition and Collection*. Downers Grove, IL: IVP Academic, 2004.

Riesner, R. "Jesus, the Primitive Community, and the Essene Quarter of Jerusalem." Pages 198–234 in *Jesus and the Dead Sea Scrolls*. Edited by J. H. Charlesworth. ABRL. New York: Doubleday, 1992.

———. *Paul's Early Period: Chronology, Mission Strategy, Theology*. Translated by D. Stott. Grand Rapids/Cambridge: Eerdmans, 1998.

———. "Synagogues in Jerusalem." Pages 179–211 in *The Book of Acts in Its Palestinian Setting*. Edited by R. Bauckham. BAFCS 4. Carlisle: Paternoster; Grand Rapids: Eerdmans, 1995.

Rimaud, D. "La première prière liturgique dans le livre des Actes (Actes, 4, 23–31 cf. Ps. 2 et 145)." *La Maison-Dieu* 51 (1957): 99–115.

Ritmeyer, L. and K. Ritmeyer. *Jerusalem in the Year 30 AD*. Jerusalem: Carta, 2004.

———. *The Ritual of the Temple in the Time of Christ*. Jerusalem: Carta, 2002.

Rius-Camps, J. and J. Read-Heimerdinger. *The Message of Acts in Codex Bezae: A Comparison with the Alexandrian Tradition*. 4 vols. JSNTSup/LNTS 257, 302, 365, 415. London: T&T Clark, 2004–2009.

Robb, J. E. "The Prophet Like Moses: Its Jewish Context and Use in the Early Christian Tradition." PhD diss., King's College London, 2003.

Robertson, J. *The Death of Judas: The Characterization of Judas Iscariot in Three Early Christian Accounts of his Death*. Sheffield: Sheffield Phoenix, 2012.

Robinson, B. P. "The Place of the Emmaus Story in Luke-Acts." *NTS* 30 (1984): 481–97.

Robinson, J. A. T. "The Most Primitive Christology of All?" *JTS* ns 7 (1956): 177–89.

Roloff, J. *Die Apostelgeschichte*. NTD 5. Göttingen: Vandenhoeck & Ruprecht, 1981.

Romm, J. S. *The Edges of the Earth in Ancient Thought: Geography, Exploration, and Fiction*. Princeton: Princeton University Press, 1992.

Røsæg, N. A. "The Blinding of Paul: Observations to a Theme." *SEÅ* 71 (2006): 159–85.

Rosen, A. P. "The Ascension and Exaltation of Jesus in Lukan Theology." *AJPS* 19 (2016): 179–206.

Rosica, T. M. "The Road to Emmaus and the Road to Gaza: Luke 24:13–35 and Acts 8:26–40." *Worship* 68 (1994): 117–31.

Rosner, B. S. "Acts and Biblical History." Pages 65–82 in *The Book of Acts in Its Ancient Literary Setting*. Edited by B. W. Winter and A. D. Clarke. BAFCS 1. Carlisle: Paternoster; Grand Rapids: Eerdmans, 1993.

———. "The Progress of the Word." Pages 215–33 in *Witness to the Gospel: The Theology of Acts*. Edited by I. H. Marshall and D. Peterson. Grand Rapids/Cambridge: Eerdmans, 1998.

Rostovtzeff, M. I., and P. M. Fraser (reviser). *The Social and Economic History of the Roman Empire.* 2 vols. 2nd ed. Oxford: Oxford University Press, 1957.

Roth, S. J. *The Blind, the Lame and the Poor: Character Types in Luke-Acts.* JSNTSup 144. Sheffield: Sheffield Academic, 1997.

Rowe, C. K. "Acts 2.36 and the Continuity of Lukan Christology." *NTS* 53 (2007): 37–56.

———. *Early Narrative Christology: The Lord in the Gospel of Luke.* Grand Rapids: Baker Academic, 2009.

Rudolph, K. "Simon—Magus oder Gnosticus? Zur Stand der Debatte." *TRu* 42 (1977): 278–359.

Runge, S. E. *Discourse Grammar of the Greek New Testament: A Practical Introduction for Teaching and Exegesis.* Lexham Bible Reference. Peabody, MA: Hendrickson, 2010.

Rusam, D. *Das Alte Testament bei Lukas.* BZNW 112. Berlin: de Gruyter, 2003.

Safrai, S. "Relations between the Diaspora and the Land of Israel." Pages 184–215 in vol. 1 of *The Jewish People in the First Century: Historical Geography, Political History, Social, Cultural and Religious Life and Institutions.* Edited by S. Shemuel and M. Stern. 2 vols. CRINT 1/1&2. Assen: Van Gorcum, 1976.

———. "The Synagogue." Pages 908–44 in vol. 2 of *The Jewish People in the First Century: Historical Geography, Political History, Social, Cultural and Religious Life and Institutions.* Edited by S. Shemuel and M. Stern. 2 vols. CRINT 1/1&2. Assen: Van Gorcum, 1976.

Saller, R. P. *Personal Patronage under the Early Empire.* Cambridge: Cambridge University Press, 1982.

Samkutty, V. J. *The Samaritan Mission in Acts.* LNTS 328. London: T&T Clark, 2006.

Sanders, E. P. *Jesus and Judaism.* London: SCM, 1984.

———. *Jewish Law from Jesus to the Mishnah: Five Studies.* London: SCM, 1990.

———. *Judaism: Practice and Belief 63 BCE–66 CE.* London: SCM, 1992.

Sanders, J. T. *The Jews in Luke-Acts.* London: SCM, 1987.

Sandmel, S. "Parallelomania." *JBL* 81 (1962): 1–13.

Sandnes, K. O. "Beyond 'Love Language': A Critical Examination of Krister Stendahl's Exegesis of Acts 4:12." *ST* 52 (1998): 43–56.

Scharlemann, M. H. *Stephen: A Singular Saint.* AnBib 34. Rome: Pontifical Biblical Institute, 1968.

Schenke, L. "Die Kontrastformel Apg 4,10b." *BZ* ns 26 (1982): 1–20.

Schille, G. "Das Leiden des Herrn: Die evangelische Passionstradition und ihr ‚Sitz im Leben.'" *ZTK* 52 (1955): 161–205.

———. *Die Apostelgeschichte des Lukas.* THKNT. Berlin: Evangelische Verlagsanstalt, 1983.

Schmidt, F. "Élection et tirage au sort (1QS VI,13–23 et Ac 1,15–26)." *RHPR* 80 (2000): 105–17.

Schmithals, W. *Die Apostelgeschichte des Lukas.* ZBK NT 3.2. Zürich: Theologischer Verlag, 1982.

Schmitt, J. "L'église de Jérusalem, ou la 'restoration' d'Israel." *RevScRel* 27 (1953): 209–18.

Schnabel, E. J. *Acts.* ZECNT 5. Grand Rapids: Zondervan Academic, 2012.

———. *Early Christian Mission.* 2 vols. Downers Grove, IL: IVP Academic, 2004.

Schnackenburg, R. "Die lukanische Eschatologie im Lichte von Aussagen der Apostelgeschichte." Pages 249–65 in *Glaube und Eschatologie: Festschrift für Werner Georg Kümmel zum 80. Geburtstag.* Edited by E. Grässer and O. Merk. Tübingen: J. C. B. Mohr, 1985.

Schneider, G. *Die Apostelgeschichte.* 2 vols. HTKNT. Freiburg: Herder, 1980, 1982.

———. "Gott und Christus als ΚΥΡΙΟΣ nach der Apostelgeschichte." Pages 161–74 in *Begegnung mit dem Wort.* Edited by J. Zmijewski and E. Nellessen. BBB 53. Bonn: Hanstein, 1979.

———. "Stephanus, die Hellenisten und Samaria." Pages 215–40 in *Les Actes des Apôtres: traditions, rédaction, théologie.* Edited by J. Kremer. BETL 48. Gembloux: Duculot; Leuven: Leuven University Press, 1979.

Schofield, C. "Linking Prayer and Hold Proclamation: An Exegetical Study of Acts 4:23–31 and Ephesians 6:18–20 with Implications for Contemporary Church Growth." *JASCG* 8 (1997): 63–76.

Schottroff, L., and W. Stegemann. *Jesus von Nazareth, Hoffnung der Armen.* Urban-Taschenbücher Bd 639: T-Reihe. Stuttgart: Kohlhammer, 1978.

Schröter, J. "Die Taufe in der Apostelgeschichte." Pages 557–86 in vol. 1 of *Ablution, Initiation, and Baptism: Late Antiquity, Early Judaism, and Early Christianity = Waschungen, Initiation und Taufe: Spätantike, frühes Judentum und frühes Christentum.* Edited by D. Hellholm, R. Vegge, Ø. Norderval and C. Hellholm. 3 vols. BZNW 176. Berlin: de Gruyter, 2011.

Schwartz, D. R. "Non-joining Sympathisers (Acts 5.13–14)." *Bib* 64 (1983): 550–55.

Schwartz, J. "Peter and Ben Stada in Lydda." Pages 391–414 in *The Book of Acts in Its Palestinian Setting.* Edited by R. Bauckham. BAFCS 4. Carlisle: Paternoster; Grand Rapids: Eerdmans, 1995.

Schweizer, E. *Church Order in the New Testament.* London: SCM, 1961.

Schwemer, A. M. "Lukas as Kenner der Septuaginta und die Rede des Stephanus (Apg 7,2–53)." Pages 301–28 in *Die Septuaginta und das frühe Christentum = The Septuagint and Christian Origins.* Edited by T. S. Caulley and H. Lichtenberger. WUNT 277. Tübingen: Mohr Siebeck, 2011.

Scobie, C. H. H. "The Origins and Development of Samaritan Christianity." *NTS* 19 (1973): 390–414.

———. "The Use of Source Material in the Speeches of Acts III and VII." *NTS* 25 (1979): 399–421.

Scott, J. M. *Geography in Early Judaism and Christianity: The Book of Jubilees.* SNTSMS 113. Cambridge: Cambridge University Press, 2002.

———. "Luke's Geographical Horizon." Pages 483–544 in *The Book of Acts in Its Graeco-Roman Setting.* D. W. J. Gill and C. H. Gempf. BAFCS 2. Carlisle: Paternoster; Grand Rapids: Eerdmans, 1994.

Scrivener, F. H. A. *Bezae Codex Cantabrigiensis.* Cambridge: Deighton Bell, 1864; Pittsburgh Reprint Series 5. Pittsburgh: Pickwick, 1978.

Scroggs, R. "Earliest Hellenistic Christianity." Pages 176–206 in *Religions in Antiquity: Essays in Memory of Erwin Ramsdell Goodenough.* Edited by J. Neusner. SHR 14. Leiden: Brill, 1968.

Seccombe, D. P. "Luke and Isaiah." *NTS* 27 (1981): 252–59.

———. *Possessions and the Poor in Luke-Acts.* SNTSU B/6. Linz: A. Fuchs, 1982.

———. "Was There Organised Charity in Jerusalem before the Christians?" *JTS* ns 29 (1978): 140–43.

Segal, A. F. *Paul the Convert: The Apostolate and Apostasy of Saul the Pharisee.* New Haven: Yale University Press, 1990.

Seim, T. K. *The Double Message: Patterns of Gender in Luke-Acts.* SNTW. Edinburgh: T&T Clark, 1994.

Seitz, C. R. *Isaiah 1–39.* Int. Louisville: John Knox, 1993.

Seland, T. *Establishment Violence in Philo and Luke: A Study of Non-Conformity to the Torah and Jewish Vigilante Reactions.* BibInt 15. Leiden: Brill, 1995.

Sell, P. "The Seven in Acts 6 as a Ministry Team." *BSac* 167 (2010): 58–67.

Sheeley, S. M. *Narrative Asides in Luke-Acts.* JSNTSup 72. Sheffield: JSOT, 1992.

Shepherd, W. H., Jr. *The Narrative Function of the Holy Spirit as a Character in Luke-Acts.* SBLDS 147. Atlanta: Scholars, 1994.

Sherwin-White, A. N. *Roman Society and Roman Law in the New Testament.* Grand Rapids: Baker, 1963; repr., 1981.

Shin, W. G. "Integrated Stories and Israel's Contested Worship Space: Exod 15.17 and Stephen's Retelling of *Heilsgeschichte* (Acts 7)." *NTS* 64 (2018): 495–513.

Shulam, J., and H. Le Cornu. *A Commentary on the Jewish Roots of Acts.* 2 vols. Jerusalem: Academon, 2003.

Simon, M. "Saint Stephen and the Jerusalem Temple." *JEH* 2 (1951): 127–42.

Simon, M. *St Stephen and the Hellenists in the Primitive Church: The Haskell Lectures 1956.* London: Longmans, Green & Co., 1958.

Skeat, T. C. "The Codex Sinaiticus and the Codex Vaticanus and Constantine." *JTS* ns 50 (1999): 583–625.

Skinner, M. L. *The Trial Narratives: Conflict, Power, and Identity in the New Testament.* Louisville: Westminster John Knox, 2010.

Sleeman, M. *Geography and the Ascension Narrative in Acts.* SNTSMS 146. Cambridge: Cambridge University Press, 2009.

Smalley, S. S. "The Christology of Acts." *ExpTim* 73 (1962): 358–62.

———. "Spirit, Kingdom and Prayer in Luke-Acts." *NovT* 15 (1973): 59–71.

Smallwood, E. M. "High Priests and Politics in Roman Palestine." *JTS* ns 13 (1962): 14–34.

Smit, P.-B. "Negotiating a New World View in Acts 1.8? A Note on the Expression ἕως ἐσχάτου τῆς γῆς." *NTS* 63 (2017): 1–22.

Smith, A. "'Full of Spirit and Wisdom': Luke's Portrait of Stephen (Acts 6:1–8:1a) as a Man of Self-Mastery." Pages 97–114 in *Asceticism and the New Testament.* Edited by L. E. Vaage. New York: Routledge, 1999.

———. "A Second Step in African Biblical Interpretation: A Generic Reading Analysis of Acts 8:26–40." Pages 213–28 in vol. 1 of *Reading from this Place.* Edited by F. F. Segovia and M. A. Tolbert. 2 vols. Minneapolis: Fortress, 1995.

Smith, G. A. *The Historical Geography of the Holy Land.* 25th ed. London: Hodder & Stoughton, 1931.

Smith, M. "The Account of Simon Magus in Acts 8." Pages 735–49 in vol. 2 of *Harry Austryn Wolfson: Jubilee Volume on the Occasion of His Seventy-Fifth Birthday.* 3 vols. Jerusalem: American Academy for Jewish Research, 1965.

Smith, S. *The Fate of the Jerusalem Temple in Luke-Acts: An Intertextual Approach to Jesus' Laments over Jerusalem and Stephen's Speech.* LNTS 553. London: Bloomsbury T&T Clark, 2017.

Smith, T. C. "The Significance of the Stephen Episode in Acts." Pages 15–26 in vol. 2 of *Society of Biblical Literature 1975 Seminar Papers.* 2 vols. SBLSP 14. Atlanta: SBL, 1975.

Snowden, F. M., Jr. *Before Color Prejudice: The Ancient View of Blacks.* Cambridge, MA: Harvard University Press, 1983.

———. *Blacks in Antiquity: Ethiopians in the Greco-Roman Experience.* Cambridge, MA: Harvard University Press, 1970.

Soards, M. L. *The Speeches in Acts: Their Content, Context, and Concerns.* Louisville: Westminster John Knox, 1994.

Sparks, H. F. D. "The Semitisms of the Acts." *JTS* ns 1 (1950): 16–28.

Speckman, M. T. "Healing and Wholeness in Luke-Acts as Foundation for Economic Development: A Particular Reference to 'ΟΛΟΚΛΗΡΙΑ in Acts 3:16." *Neot* 36 (2002): 97–109.

Spencer, F. S. *Acts.* Readings. Sheffield: Sheffield Academic, 1997.

———. "The Ethiopian Eunuch and his Bible: A Social-Science Analysis." *BTB* 22 (1992): 155–65.

———. *Journeying through Acts: A Literary-Cultural Reading*. Peabody, MA: Hendrickson, 2004.

———. "Neglected Widows in Acts 6:1–7." *CBQ* 56 (1994): 715–33.

———. *The Portrait of Philip in Acts: A Study of Roles and Relations*. JSNTSup 67. Sheffield: JSOT, 1992.

Squires, J. T. "The Function of Acts 8:4–12:25." *NTS* 44 (1998): 608–17.

———. *The Plan of God in Luke-Acts*. SNTSMS 76. Cambridge: Cambridge University Press, 1993.

———. "The Plan of God in the Acts of the Apostles." Pages 19–39 in *Witness to the Gospel: The Theology of Acts*. Edited by I. H. Marshall and D. Peterson. Grand Rapids: Eerdmans, 1998.

Stählin, G. "Das Bild der Witwe: ein Beitrag zur Bildersprache der Bibel und zum Phänomen der Personifikation in der Antike." *JAC* 17 (1974): 5–20.

———. *Die Apostelgeschichte*. 10th ed. NTD 5. Göttingen: Vandenhoeck & Ruprecht, 1962.

Stanley, D. M. "Paul's Conversion in Acts." *CBQ* 15 (1953): 315–38.

Stanton, G. N. "Stephen in Lucan Perspective." Pages 345–60 in *Studia Biblica 1978*. III. *Papers on Paul and Other New Testament Authors*. Edited by E. A. Livingstone. JSNTSup 3. Sheffield: JSOT, 1980.

Stark, R. *The Rise of Christianity: A Sociologist Reconsiders History*. Princeton: Princeton University Press, 1996.

Stemberger, G. "Die Stephanusrede (Apg 7) und die jüdische Tradition." Pages 154–74 in *Jesus in der Verkündigung der Kirche*. Edited by A. Fuchs. Linz: SNTSU, 1976.

Stendahl, K. "Christ's Lordship and Religious Pluralism." Pages 7–18 in *Christ's Lordship and Religious Pluralism*. Edited by G. H. Anderson and T. F. Stransky. Maryknoll, NY: Orbis, 1981.

———. *Paul among Jews and Gentiles, and Other Essays*. London: SCM, 1977.

Stenschke, C. W. *Luke's Portrait of Gentiles Prior to Their Coming to Faith*. WUNT II/108. Tübingen: Mohr Siebeck, 1999.

———. "The Need for Salvation." Pages 125–44 in *Witness to the Gospel: The Theology of Acts*. Edited by I. H. Marshall and D. Peterson. Grand Rapids/Cambridge: Eerdmans, 1998.

Sterling, G. E. "'Athletes of Virtue': An Analysis of the Summaries in Acts (2:41–47; 4:32–35; 5:12–16)." *JBL* 113 (1994): 679–96.

———. *Historiography and Self Definition: Josephos, Luke-Acts and Apologetic Historiography*. NovTSup 64. Leiden: Brill, 1992.

———. "'Opening the Scriptures': The Legitimation of the Jewish Diaspora and the Early Christian Mission." Pages 199–217 in *Jesus and the Heritage of Israel: Luke's Narrative Claim upon Israel's Legacy*. Edited by D. P. Moessner. Harrisburg, PA: Trinity Press International, 1999.

Steyn, G. J. *Septuagint Quotations in the Context of the Petrine and Pauline Speeches of the Acta Apostolorum*. CBET 12. Kampen: Kok Pharos, 1995.

Stier, R. *The Words of the Apostles*. 2nd ed. Edinburgh: T&T Clark, 1869.

Stolle, V. *Der Zeuge als Angeklagter: Untersuchungen zum Paulusbild des Lukas*. Stuttgart: Kohlhammer, 1973.

Stott, J. R. W. *The Message of Acts: To the Ends of the Earth*. Bible Speaks Today. Leicester: Inter-Varsity Press, 1990.

Strange, D. *The Possibility of Salvation among the Unevangelised: An Analysis of Inclusivism in Recent Evangelical Theology*. PBTM. Carlisle: Paternoster, 2002.

Strange, W. A. *The Problem of the Text of Acts.* SNTSMS 71. Cambridge: Cambridge University Press, 1992.

Strauss, D. F. *The Life of Jesus Critically Examined.* Translated by G. Eliot. Lives of Jesus. London: SCM, 1973.

Strauss, M. L. *The Davidic Messiah in Luke-Acts: The Promise and Its Fulfillment in Lukan Christology.* JSNTSup 110. Sheffield: Sheffield Academic, 1995.

Strelan, R. "Gamaliel's Hunch." *AusBR* 47 (1999): 53–69.

———. "The Running Prophet (Acts 8:30)." *NovT* 43 (2001): 31–38.

———. *Strange Acts: Studies in the Cultural World of the Acts of the Apostles.* BZNW 126. Berlin: de Gruyter, 2004.

———. "Strange Stares: ἀτενίζειν in Acts." *NovT* 41 (1999): 235–55.

———. "Tabitha: the Gazelle of Joppa (Acts 9:36–41)." *BTB* 39 (2009): 77–86.

———. "Who Was Bar Jesus (Acts 13,6–12)?" *Bib* 85 (2004): 65–81.

Stroup, C. *The Christians Who Became Jews: Acts of the Apostles and Ethnicity in the Roman City.* New Haven: Yale University Press, 2020.

Stuhlmacher, P. "Isaiah 53 in the Gospels and Acts." Pages 147–62 in *The Suffering Servant: Isaiah 53 in Jewish and Christian Sources.* Edited by B. Janowski and P. Stuhlmacher. Grand Rapids: Eerdmans, 2004.

Swain, J. W. "Gamaliel's Speech and Caligula's Statue." *HTR* 37 (1944): 341–49.

Swanson, R. J., ed. *New Testament Greek Manuscripts, Variant Readings Arranged in Horizontal Lines against Codex Vaticanus: The Acts of the Apostles.* Pasadena, CA: William Carey International University Press; Sheffield: Sheffield Academic, 1998.

Sweeney, J. P. "Stephen's Speech (Acts 7:2–53): Is it as 'Anti-Temple' as Is Frequently Alleged?" *TrinJ* ns 23 (2002): 185–210.

Sylva, D. D. "The Meaning and Function of Acts 7:46–50." *JBL* 106 (1987): 261–75.

Tabb, B. J. "Is the Lucan Jesus a 'Martyr'? A Critical Assessment of a Scholarly Consensus." *CBQ* 77 (2015): 280–301.

———. *Suffering in Ancient Worldview: Luke, Seneca and 4 Maccabees in Dialogue.* LNTS 569. London: Bloomsbury T&T Clark, 2017.

Tabb, B. J., and S. Walton. "Exodus in Luke-Acts." Pages 61–87 in *Exodus in the New Testament.* Edited by S. Ehorn. LNTS 663. London: Bloomsbury T&T Clark, 2022.

Talbert, C. H. *Acts.* Knox Preaching Guides. Atlanta: John Knox, 1984.

———. Review of H.-J. Michel, *Die Abschiedsrede des Paulus an die Kirche: Apg. 20,17–38.* *JBL* 94 (1975): 145.

———. *Literary Patterns, Theological Themes, and the Genre of Luke-Acts.* SBLMS 20. Missoula, MT: Scholars, 1974.

———. *Luke and the Gnostics: An Examination of Lucan Purpose.* Nashville: Abingdon, 1966.

———. *Reading Acts: A Literary and Theological Commentary on the Acts of the Apostles.* Revised ed. Macon, GA: Smyth & Helwys, 2005.

———. *Reading Luke-Acts in Its Mediterranean Milieu.* NovTSup 107. Leiden: Brill, 2003.

Tannehill, R. C. "The Functions of Peter's Mission Speeches in the Narrative of Acts." *NTS* 37 (1991): 400–414.

———. *Luke.* ANTC. Nashville: Abingdon, 1996.

———. *The Narrative Unity of Luke-Acts: A Literary Interpretation.* 2 vols. Minneapolis: Fortress, 1986, 1990.

———. *The Shape of Luke's Story: Essays on Luke-Acts.* Eugene, OR: Cascade, 2005.

Taylor, J. "La Fraction du Pain en Luc-Actes." Pages 281–95 in *The Unity of Luke-Acts.* Edited by J. Verheyden. BETL 142. Leuven: Leuven University Press/Peeters, 1999.

Taylor, J. E. "Paul's Caesarea." Pages 42–67 in *The Urban World and the First Christians.* Edited by S. Walton, P. R. Trebilco and D. W. J. Gill. Grand Rapids: Eerdmans, 2017.

Taylor, N. H. "Luke-Acts and the Temple." Pages 709–21 in *The Unity of Luke-Acts*. Edited by J. Verheyden. BETL 142. Leuven: Leuven University Press/Peeters, 1999.

Teeple, H. M. *The Mosaic Eschatological Prophet*. JBLMS 10. Philadelphia: SBL, 1957.

Theissen, G. "Hellenisten und Hebraer (Apg 6,1–6): Gab es eine Spaltung der Urgemeinde?" Pages 323–43 in vol. 3 of *Geschichte—Tradition—Reflexion: Festschrift für Martin Hengel zum 70. Geburtstag*. Edited by H. Cancik, H. Lichtenberger and P. Schäfer. 3 vols. Tubingen: Mohr Siebeck, 1996.

———. *The Miracle Stories of the Early Christian Tradition*. Translated by J. K. Riches. Philadelphia: Fortress, 1983.

———. "Urchristlicher Liebeskommunismus: Zum 'Sitz im Leben' des Topos ἅπαντα κοινά." Pages 689–712 in *Texts and Contexts: Biblical Texts in Their Textual and Situational Contexts: Essays in Honor of Lars Hartman*. Edited by T. Fornberg and D. Hellholm. Oslo: Scandinavian University Press, 1995.

Thiede, C. P. *Simon Peter: From Galilee to Rome*. Exeter: Paternoster, 1988.

Thiele, W. "Eine Bemerkung zu Act 1:14." *ZNW* 53 (1962): 110–11.

Thiering, B. "Qumran Initiation and New Testament Baptism." *NTS* 27 (1981): 615–31.

Thiselton, A. C. *The First Epistle to the Corinthians*. NIGTC. Carlisle: Paternoster; Grand Rapids: Eerdmans, 2000.

Thomas, J. C. *The Devil, Disease and Deliverance: Origins of Illness in New Testament Thought*. JPTSup 13. Sheffield: Sheffield Academic, 1998.

Thompson, A. J. *One Lord, One People: The Unity of the Church in Acts in Its Literary Setting*. LNTS 359. London: T&T Clark, 2008.

———. "Unity in Acts: Idealization or Reality?" *JETS* 51 (2008): 523–42.

Thompson, M. B. "The Holy Internet: Communication between Churches in the First Christian Generation." Pages 49–70 in *The Gospels for All Christians: Rethinking the Gospel Audiences*. Edited by R. Bauckham. Edinburgh: T&T Clark; Grand Rapids: Eerdmans, 1998.

Thompson, R. "Diaspora Jewish Freedmen: Stephen's Deadly Opponents." *BSac* 173 (2016): 166–81.

Thompson, R. P. *Keeping the Church in Its Place: The Church as Narrative Character in Acts*. London: T&T Clark, 2006.

Thornton, L. S. *The Common Life in the Body of Christ*. 2nd ed. Westminster: Dacre, 1944.

Thornton, T. C. G. "Continuing Steadfast in Prayer: New Light on a New Testament Phrase." *ExpTim* 83 (1971): 23–24.

———. "Stephen's Use of Isaiah LXVI,1." *JTS* ns 25 (1974): 432–34.

———. "To The End of the Earth: Acts 1:8." *ExpTim* 89 (1978): 374–75.

Thrall, M. E. *Greek Particles in the New Testament*. NTTS 3. Leiden: Brill, 1962.

Thurston, B. *Spiritual Life in the Early Church: The Witness of Acts and Ephesians*. Minneapolis: Fortress, 1993.

———. "τὸ ὑπερῷον in Acts 1:13." *ExpTim* 80 (1968): 21–22.

Tidball, D. *The Social Context of the New Testament*. Carlisle: Paternoster, 1983; Grand Rapids: Academic Books, Zondervan, 1984. Repr., 1997.

Tiede, D. L. "The Exaltation of Jesus and the Restoration of Israel in Acts 1." Pages 278–86 in *Christians among Jews and Gentiles: Essays in Honor of Krister Stendahl on His Sixty-Fifth Birthday*. Edited by G. W. E. Nickelsburg and G. MacRae. Philadelphia: Fortress, 1986.

Tiessen, T. L. *Who Can Be Saved? Reassessing Salvation in Christ and World Religions*. Downers Grove, IL: IVP Academic, 2004.

Tomson, P. J. "Gamaliel's Counsel and the Apologetic Strategy of Luke-Acts." Pages 585–604 in *The Unity of Luke-Acts*. Edited by J. Verheyden. Leuven: Peeters, 1999.

Toner, J. P. *Popular Culture in Ancient Rome*. Cambridge: Polity, 2009.

Torrance, T. F. *Space, Time, and Resurrection.* Edinburgh: Handsel, 1976.

Torrey, C. C. *The Composition and Date of Acts.* HTS 1. Cambridge, MA: Harvard University Press, 1916.

Tov, E. "Biblical Texts as Reworked in Some Qumran Manuscripts with Special Attention to 4QRP and 4QParaGen-Exod." Pages 111–34 in *The Community of the Renewed Covenant: The Notre Dame Symposium on the Dead Sea Scrolls.* Edited by E. Ulrich and J. C. VanderKam. CJA 10. Notre Dame: University of Notre Dame Press, 1994.

Townsend, J. T. "Acts 9:1–29 and Early Church Tradition." Pages 119–31 in *Society of Biblical Literature 1988 Seminar Papers.* SBLSP 27. 1988.

Trebilco, P. R. "Asia." Pages 291–362 in *The Book of Acts in Its Graeco-Roman Setting.* Edited by D. W. J. Gill and C. H. Gempf. BAFCS 2. Carlisle: Paternoster; Grand Rapids: Eerdmans, 1994.

———. *Self-designations and Group Identity in the New Testament.* Cambridge: Cambridge University Press, 2012.

Trites, A. A. "The Importance of Legal Scenes and Language in the Book of Acts." *NovT* 16 (1974): 278–84.

———. *The New Testament Concept of Witness.* SNTSMS 31. Cambridge: Cambridge University Press, 1977.

Trocmé, É. *Le 'Livre des Actes' et l'histoire.* EHPR 45. Paris: Presses universitaires de France, 1957.

Trudinger, P. "Stephen and the Life of the Primitive Church." *BTB* 14 (1984): 18–22.

Trull, G. V. "An Exegesis of Psalm 16:10." *BSac* 161 (2004): 304–21.

———. "Peter's Interpretation of Psalm 16:8–11 in Acts 2:25–32." *BSac* 161 (2004): 432–48.

———. "Views on Peter's Use of Psalm 16:8–11 in Acts 2:25–32." *BSac* 161 (2004): 194–214.

Trumbower, J. A. "The Historical Jesus and the Speech of Gamaliel (Acts 5.35–39)." *NTS* 39 (1993): 500–517.

Turner, M. *The Holy Spirit and Spiritual Gifts Then and Now.* Carlisle: Paternoster, 1996.

———. "Interpreting the Samaritans of Acts 8: The Waterloo of Pentecostal Soteriology and Pneumatology?" *Pneuma* 23 (2001): 265–86.

———. *Power from on High: The Spirit in Israel's Restoration and Witness in Luke-Acts.* JPTSup 9. Sheffield: Sheffield Academic, 1996.

———. "The Spirit of Christ and Christology." Pages 168–90 in *Christ the Lord: Studies in Christology Presented to Donald Guthrie.* Edited by H. H. Rowdon. Leicester: Inter-Varsity Press, 1982.

———. "The Spirit of Christ and 'Divine' Christology." Pages 413–36 in *Jesus of Nazareth: Lord and Christ. Essays on the Historical Jesus and New Testament Christology.* Edited by J. B. Green and M. Turner. Carlisle: Paternoster; Grand Rapids: Eerdmans, 1994.

———. "The Spirit of Prophecy and the Power of Authoritative Preaching in Luke-Acts: A Question of Origins." *NTS* 38 (1992): 66–88.

Twelftree, G. H. *People of the Spirit: Exploring Luke's View of the Church.* London: SPCK; Grand Rapids: Baker Academic, 2009.

———. "Prayer and the Coming of the Spirit in Acts." *ExpTim* 117 (2006): 271–76.

Tyson, J. B. "Acts 6:1–7 and Dietary Regulations in Early Christianity." *PRSt* 10 (1983): 145–61.

———. "The Gentile Mission and the Authority of Scripture in Acts." *NTS* 33 (1987): 619–31.

Ulrich, E. C., ed. *The Biblical Qumran Scrolls: Transcriptions and Textual Variants.* VTSup 134. Leiden: Brill, 2010.

van den Eynde, S. "Children of the Promise: On the ΔΙΑΘΗΚΗ-Promise to Abraham in Lk 1,72 and Acts 3,25." Pages 469–82 in *The Unity of Luke Acts*. Edited by J. Verheyden. Leuven: Peeters, 1999.

van der Horst, P. W. "Hellenistic Parallels to Acts (Chapters 3 and 4)." *JSNT* 35 (1989): 37–46.

———. "Hellenistic Parallels to the Acts of the Apostles: 1,1–26." *ZNW* 74 (1983): 17–26.

———. "Hellenistic Parallels to the Acts of the Apostles (2.1–47)." *JSNT* 25 (1985): 49–60.

———. "Peter's Shadow." *NTS* 23 (1977): 204–12.

van Stempvoort, P. A. "The Interpretation of the Ascension in Luke and Acts." *NTS* 5 (1958): 30–42.

van Unnik, W. C. "Der Befehl an Philippus." *ZNW* 47 (1956): 181–91.

———. "Die Apostelgeschichte und die Häresien." Pages 402–9 in vol. 1 of *Sparsa Collecta: The Collected Essays of W. C. van Unnik*. Edited by W. C. van Unnik. 3 vols. NovTSup 29–31. Leiden: Brill, 1973.

———. *Sparsa Collecta: The Collected Essays of W. C. van Unnik*. 4 vols. NovTSup 29–31, 156. Leiden: Brill, 1973–2014.

VanderKam, J. C. "Covenant and Pentecost." *CTJ* 37 (2002): 239–54.

———. *The Dead Sea Scrolls Today*. London: SPCK; Grand Rapids: Eerdmans, 1994.

Vanlaningham, M. G. "Should the Church Evangelize Israel? A Response to Franz Mussner and Other Sonderweg Proponents." *TrinJ* 22 (2001): 197–217.

Vazakas, A. A. "Is Acts I–XV.35 a Literal Translation from an Aramaic Original?" *JBL* 37 (1918): 105–10.

Vermes, G. *Jesus the Jew: A Historian's Reading of the Gospels*. London: Fontana/Collins, 1973.

Via, E. J. "An Interpretation of Acts 7:35–37 from the Perspective of Major Themes in Luke-Acts." Pages 209–23 in vol. 2 of *Society of Biblical Literature 1978 Seminar Papers*. 2 vols. SBLSP 18. Atlanta: SBL, 1978.

Vielhauer, P. "On the Paulinism of Acts." Pages 33–50 in *Studies in Luke-Acts*. Edited by L. E. Keck and J. L. Martyn. London: SPCK, 1968.

Vögeli, A. "Lukas und Euripides." *TZ* 9 (1953): 415–38.

Volf, M. *Free of Charge: Giving and Forgiving in a Culture Stripped of Grace*. Grand Rapids: Zondervan, 2006.

von Baer, H. *Der Heilige Geist in den Lukasschriften*. BWANT 3.3. Stuttgart: Kohlhammer, 1926.

von der Goltz, E. F. *Das Gebet in der ältesten Christenheit: eine geschichtliche Untersuchung*. Leipzig: Hinrichs, 1901.

von Dobbeler, A. *Der Evangelist Philippus in der Geschichte des Urchristentums: Eine prosopographische Skizze*. TANZ 30. Tübingen: Francke, 2000.

von Wahlde, U. C. "Acts 4,24–31: The Prayer of the Apostles in Response to the Persecution of Peter and John—and Its Consequences." *Bib* 77 (1996): 237–44.

———. "The Theological Assessment of the First Christian Persecution: The Apostles' Prayer and Its Consequences in Acts 4,24–31." *Bib* 76 (1995): 523–31.

Wainwright, A. W. "Luke and the Restoration of the Kingdom to Israel." *ExpTim* 89 (1977): 76–79.

Walker, P. W. L. *Jesus and the Holy City: New Testament Perspectives on Jerusalem*. Grand Rapids/Cambridge: Eerdmans, 1996.

Wall, R. W. "The Acts of the Apostles." Pages 1–368 in vol. 10 of *The New Interpreter's Bible*. Edited by L. E. Keck. 12 vols. Nashville: Abingdon, 2002.

Wallace, J. B. "Benefactor and Paradigm: Viewing Jesus's Ascension in Luke-Acts through Greco-Roman Ascension Traditions." Pages 83–107 in *Ascent into Heaven in Luke-Acts: New Explorations of Luke's Narrative Hinge.* Edited by D. W. Pao and D. Bryan. Minneapolis: Fortress, 2016.

Walter, N. "Apostelgeschichte 6.1 und die Anfänge der Urgemeinde in Jerusalem." *NTS* 29 (1983): 370–93.

Walton, S. "Acts as Biblical History?" Pages 51–68 in *Le corpus lucanien (Luc-Actes) et l'historiographie ancienne: quels rapports?* Edited by S. Butticaz, L. Devillers, J. M. Morgan and S. Walton. Théologie biblique 2. Zürich: Lit, 2019.

———. "The Acts—of God? What is the 'Acts of the Apostles' All About?" *EvQ* 80 (2008): 291–306.

———. "Acts, Book of." Pages 27–31 in *Dictionary for Theological Interpretation of the Bible.* Edited by K. J. Vanhoozer, C. G. Bartholomew, D. J. Treier, and N. T. Wright. London: SPCK; Grand Rapids: Baker Academic, 2005.

———. "Acts: Many Questions, Many Answers." Pages 229–50 in *The Face of New Testament Studies.* Edited by S. McKnight and G. R. Osborne. Leicester: Apollos; Grand Rapids: Baker Academic, 2004.

———. "Calling the Church Names: Learning about Christian Identity from Acts." *PRSt* 41 (2014): 223–41.

———. "The End: What and When? Eschatology in Luke-Acts." Pages 383–95 in *Eschatology in Antiquity: Forms and Functions.* Edited by H. Marlow, K. Pollman, and H. Van Noorden. Abingdon: Routledge, 2021.

———. "'The Heavens Opened': Cosmological and Theological Transformation in Luke and Acts." Pages 60–73 in *Cosmology and New Testament Theology.* Edited by J. T. Pennington and S. M. McDonough. LNTS 355. London: T&T Clark, 2008.

———. "How Mighty a Minority Were the Hellenists?" Pages 305–27 in *Earliest Christian History: History, Literature, and Theology. Essays from the Tyndale Fellowship in Honor of Martin Hengel.* Edited by M. F. Bird and J. Maston. WUNT 2/320. Tübingen: Mohr Siebeck, 2012.

———. "Identity and Christology: The Ascended Jesus in the Book of Acts." Pages 130–48 in *The Earliest Perceptions of Jesus in Context: Essays in Honour of John Nolland.* Edited by A. W. White, D. Wenham and C. A. Evans. LNTS 566. London: Bloomsbury T&T Clark, 2018.

———. "Jesus, Present and/or Absent? The Presence and Presentation of Jesus as a Character in the Book of Acts." Pages 123–40 in *Characters and Characterization in Luke-Acts.* Edited by F. Dicken and J. A. Snyder. LNTS 548. London: Bloomsbury T&T Clark, 2016.

———. "Jesus's Ascension through Old Testament Narrative Traditions." Pages 29–39 in *Ascent into Heaven in Luke-Acts: New Explorations of Luke's Narrative Hinge.* Edited by D. W. Pao and D. Bryan. Minneapolis: Fortress, 2016.

———. "Leadership and Lifestyle: Luke's Paul, Luke's Jesus and the Paul of 1 Thessalonians." *TynBul* 48 (1997): 377–80.

———. *Leadership and Lifestyle: The Portrait of Paul in the Miletus Speech and 1 Thessalonians.* SNTSMS 108. Cambridge: Cambridge University Press, 2000.

———. "Paul, Patronage and Pay: What Do We Know about the Apostle's Financial Support?" Pages 220–33 in *Paul as Missionary: Identity, Activity, Theology, and Practice.* Edited by T. J. Burke and B. S. Rosner. LNTS 420. London: T&T Clark, 2011.

———. "Primitive Communism in Acts? Does Acts Present the Community of Goods (2:44–45; 4:32–35) as Mistaken?" *EvQ* 80 (2008): 99–111.

———. "Rhetorical Criticism: An Introduction." *Them* 21 (1995): 4–9.

———. "The State They Were In: Luke's View of the Roman Empire." Pages 1–41 in *Rome in the Bible and the Early Church*. Edited by P. Oakes. Carlisle: Paternoster; Grand Rapids: Baker Academic, 2002.

———. "A Tale of Two Perspectives? The Temple in Acts." Pages 135–49 in *Heaven on Earth: The Temple in Biblical Theology*. Edited by T. D. Alexander and S. J. Gathercole. Carlisle: Paternoster, 2004.

———. "Turning Anthropology Right Side Up: Seeing Human Life and Existence Lukewise." Pages 99–119 in *Anthropology and New Testament Theology*. Edited by J. S. Maston and B. E. Reynolds. LNTS 529. London: Bloomsbury T&T Clark, 2018.

———. "Ὁμοθυμαδόν in Acts: Co-location, Common Action or 'Of One Heart and Mind'?" Pages 89–105 in *The New Testament in Its First Century Setting: Essays on Context and Background in Honour of B. W. Winter on His 65th Birthday*. Edited by P. J. Williams, A. D. Clarke, P. M. Head, and D. Instone-Brewer. Grand Rapids/Cambridge: Eerdmans, 2004.

Wanke, J. "'. . . wie sie ihn beim Brotbrechen erkannten': Zur Auslegung der Emmauserzählung Lk 24,13–35." *BZ* 18 (1974): 180–92.

Warrington, K. "Acts and the Healing Narratives: Why?" *JPT* 14 (2006): 189–217.

Wasserman, T., and P. J. Gurry. *A New Approach to Textual Criticism: An Introduction to the Coherence-Based Genealogical Method*. RBS 80. Atlanta: SBL; Stuttgart: Deutsche Bibelgesellschaft, 2017.

Weatherly, J. A. *Jewish Responsibility for the Death of Jesus in Luke-Acts*. JSNTSup 106. Sheffield: Sheffield Academic, 1994.

———. "The Jews in Luke-Acts." *TynBul* 40 (1989): 107–17.

Weaver, J. B. *Plots of Epiphany: Prison-Escape in Acts of the Apostles*. BZNW 131. Berlin: de Gruyter, 2004.

Webber, R. C. "'Why Were the Heathen So Arrogant?' The Socio-Rhetorical Strategy of Acts 3–4." *BTB* 22 (1992): 19–25.

Wedderburn, A. J. M. "Traditions and Redaction in Acts 2:1–13." *JSNT* 55 (1994): 27–54.

Weinert, F. D. "Luke, Stephen and the Temple in Luke-Acts." *BTB* 17 (1987): 88–90.

Weinstock, S. "The Geographical Catalogue in Acts 2, 9–11." *JRS* 38 (1948): 43–46.

Weiser, Alfons. *Die Apostelgeschichte*. 2 vols. ÖTK. Gütersloh: Mohn, 1981, 1985.

———. "Die Nachwahl des Mattias (Apg 1,15–26): Zur Rezeption und Deutung urchristlicher Geschichte durch Lukas." Pages 97–110 in *Zur Geschichte des Urchristentums*. Edited by G. Dautzenberg. Freiburg: Herder, 1979.

Weiser, Artur. *The Psalms: A Commentary*. OTL. London: SCM, 1962.

Weissenrieder, A. "Searching for the Middle Ground from the End of the Earth: The Embodiment of Space in Acts 8:26–40." *Neot* 48 (2014): 115–61.

Wendel, U. *Gemeinde in Kraft: Das Gemeindeverständnis in den Summarien der Apostelgeschichte*. NTDH 20. Neukirchen-Vluyn: Neukirchener, 1998.

Wenham, D. "Acts and the Pauline Corpus II. The Evidence of Parallels." Pages 215–58 in *The Book of Acts in Its Ancient Literary Setting*. Edited by B. W. Winter and A. D. Clarke. BAFCS 1. Carlisle: Paternoster; Grand Rapids: Eerdmans, 1993.

———. *From Good News to Gospels: What Did the First Christians Say about Jesus?* Grand Rapids: Eerdmans, 2018.

Wenham, D., and S. Walton. *Exploring the New Testament, Volume 1: A Guide to the Gospels and Acts*. 2nd ed. London: SPCK; Downers Grove, IL: IVP Academic, 2011.

Wenham, G. J. *The Book of Leviticus*. NICOT. Grand Rapids: Eerdmans, 1979.

———. "Contemporary Bible Commentary: The Primacy of Exegesis and the Religious Dimension." Pages 1–12 in *Proceedings of the Tenth World Congress of Jewish Studies, Division A: The Bible and Its World*. Edited by D. Assaf. Jerusalem: World Union of Jewish Studies, 1990.

Wenk, M. *Community-Forming Power: The Socio-Ethical Role of the Spirit in Luke-Acts.* JPTSup 19. Sheffield: Sheffield Academic, 2000.

Westcott, B. F., and F. J. A. Hort. *The New Testament in the Original Greek: Introduction and Appendix.* 2nd ed. London: Macmillan, 1896.

White, A. W. *The Prophets Agree: The Function of the Book of the Twelve Prophets in Acts.* BibInt 184. Leiden: Brill, 2020.

———. "Revisiting the 'Creative' Use of Amos in Acts and What It Tells Us About Luke." *BTB* 46 (2016): 79–90.

Whitenton, M. R. "Rewriting Abraham and Joseph: Stephen's speech (Acts 7:2–16) and Jewish Exegetical Traditions." *NovT* 54 (2012): 149–67.

Whitlock, M. G. "Acts 1:15–26 and the Craft of New Testament Poetry." *CBQ* 77 (2015): 87–106.

Whittaker, M. "'Signs and Wonders': The Pagan Background." Pages 155–58 in vol. 5 of *Studia Evangelica.* Edited by F. L. Cross. 7 vols. TUGAL 5/47. Berlin: Akademie-Verlag, 1968.

Wieser, T. "Community: Its Unity, Diversity and Universality." *Semeia* 33 (1985): 83–95.

Wikenhauser, A. "Doppleträume." *Bib* 29 (1948): 100–111.

Wilckens, U. *Die Missionsreden der Apostelgeschichte: Form- und traditionsgechichtliche Untersuchungen.* 3rd ed. WMANT 5. Neukirchen: Neukirchener, 1974.

Wilcox, M. "The Judas-Tradition in Acts 1:15–26." *NTS* 19 (1973): 438–52.

———. *The Semitisms of Acts.* Oxford: Clarendon, 1965.

———. "Upon the Tree: Deut 21:22–23 in the New Testament." *JBL* 96 (1977): 85–99.

Wildberger, H. *Isaiah 28–39: A Commentary.* CC. Minneapolis: Fortress, 1991.

Williams, B. E. *Miracle Stories in the Biblical Book Acts of the Apostles.* Mellen Biblical Press 59. Lewiston, NY: Edwin Mellen, 2001.

Williams, D. J. *Acts.* Good News Commentaries. San Francisco: Harper & Row, 1985.

Williams, M. H. "Palestinian Jewish Personal Names in Acts." Pages 79–113 in *The Book of Acts in Its Palestinian Setting.* Edited by R. Bauckham. BAFCS 4. Carlisle: Paternoster; Grand Rapids: Eerdmans, 1995.

Williams, P. "Where Two or Three Are Gathered Together: Evaluating Agreements between Two or More Early Versions." Pages 239–58 in *The Early Text of the New Testament.* Edited by C. Hill and M. Kruger. Oxford: Oxford University Press, 2012.

Wills, L. "The Form of the Sermon in Hellenistic Judaism and Early Christianity." *HTR* 77 (1984): 277–99.

Wilson, B. E. "The Blinding of Paul and the Power of God: Masculinity, Sight, and Self-Control in Acts 9." *JBL* 133 (2014): 367–87.

———. "Hearing the Word and Seeing the Light: Voice and Vision in Acts." *JSNT* 38 (2016): 456–81.

———. *Unmanly Men: Refigurations of Masculinity in Luke-Acts.* New York: Oxford University Press, 2015.

Wilson, J. M. *The Acts of the Apostles Translated from the Codex Bezae with an Introduction on Its Lucan Origin and Importance.* London: SPCK; New York: Macmillan, 1923.

Wilson, R. McL. "Simon and Gnostic Origins." Pages 485–91 in *Les Actes des Apôtres: traditions, rédaction, théologie.* Edited by J. Kremer. BETL 48. Gembloux: Duculot; Leuven: Leuven University Press, 1979.

Wilson, S. G. *The Gentiles and the Gentile Mission in Luke-Acts.* SNTSMS 23. Cambridge: Cambridge University Press, 1973.

Winter, B. W., and A. D. Clarke, eds. *The Book of Acts in Its Ancient Literary Setting.* BAFCS 1. Carlisle: Paternoster; Grand Rapids: Eerdmans, 1993.

Wise, M. O. *Language and Literacy in Roman Judaea: A Study of the Bar Kokhba Documents.* AYBRL. New Haven: Yale University Press, 2015.

Witherington, B., III. *The Acts of the Apostles: A Socio-Rhetorical Commentary.* Carlisle: Paternoster; Grand Rapids: Eerdmans, 1998.

———. "The Anti-Feminist Tendencies of the 'Western' Text in Acts." *JBL* 103 (1984): 82–84.

———. "Editing the Good News: Some Synoptic Lessons for the Study of Acts." Pages 324–47 in *History, Literature and Society in the Book of Acts.* Edited by B. Witherington III. Cambridge: Cambridge University Press, 1996.

———. "Salvation and Health in Christian Antiquity: The Soteriology of Luke-Acts in its First Century Setting." Pages 145–66 in *Witness to the Gospel: The Theology of Acts.* Edited by I. H. Marshall and D. Peterson. Grand Rapids/Cambridge: Eerdmans, 1998.

Witherup, R. D. "Functional Redundancy in the Acts of the Apostles: A Case Study." *JSNT* 48 (1992): 67–86.

Wolff, C. "Λαλεῖν γλῶσσαι in the Acts of the Apostles." Pages 189–99 in *Paul, Luke and the Graeco-Roman World.* Edited by A. Christophersen, C. Claussen, J. Frey and B. Longenecker. FS A. J. M. Wedderburn. JSNTSup 217. London: Sheffield Academic, 2002.

Wolff, H. W. *Joel and Amos.* Translated by W. Janzen, S. D. McBride, Jr., and C. A. Muenchow. Hermeneia. Philadelphia: Fortress, 1977.

Woods, E. J. *The 'Finger of God' and Pneumatology in Luke-Acts.* JSNTSup 205. Sheffield: Sheffield Academic, 2001.

Wright, D. F. "Mary in the New Testament." Pages 15–33 in *Chosen by God: Mary in Evangelical Perspective.* Edited by D. F. Wright. London: Marshall Pickering, 1989.

Wright, N. T. "Hope Deferred? Against the Dogma of Delay." *EC* 9 (2018): 37–82.

———. *Jesus and the Victory of God.* Christian Origins & the Question of God 2. London: SPCK, 1996.

———. "The Letter to the Romans." Pages 395–770 in vol. 10 of *The New Interpreter's Bible.* Edited by L. E. Keck. 12 vols. Nashville: Abingdon, 2002.

———. *New Heavens, New Earth: The Biblical Picture of Christian Hope.* Grove Biblical 11. Cambridge: Grove, 1999.

———. *The New Testament and the People of God.* Christian Origins & the Question of God 1. London: SPCK, 1992.

———. *The Resurrection of the Son of God.* Christian Origins & the Question of God 3. London: SPCK, 2003.

———. *Who was Jesus?* London: SPCK; Grand Rapids: Eerdmans, 1992.

Wright, T. *Paul: A Biography.* London: SPCK, 2017.

Wynn, K. H. "Disability in Biblical Translation." *BT* 52 (2001): 402–14.

Yamauchi, E. M. "Why the Ethiopian Eunuch Was Not from Ethiopia." Pages 351–65 in *Interpreting the New Testament Text: Introduction to the Art and Science of Exegesis.* Edited by D. L. Bock and B. M. Fanning. Wheaton, IL: Crossway, 2006.

Yao, S. "Dismantling Social Barriers through Table Fellowship: Acts 2:42–47." Pages 29–36 in *Mission in Acts.* Edited by R. L. Gallagher and P. Hertig. ASMS 34. Maryknoll, NY: Orbis, 2004.

York, J. O. *The Last Shall Be First: The Rhetoric of Reversal in Luke.* JSNTSup 46. Sheffield: JSOT, 1991.

Zangenberg, J. *Frühes Christentum in Samarien: topographische und traditionsgeschichtliche Studien zu den Samarientexten im Johannesevangelium.* TANZ 27. Tübingen: Francke, 1998.

Zehnle, R. F. *Peter's Pentecost Discourse: Tradition and Lukan Reinterpretation in Peter's Speeches in Acts 2 and 3.* SBLMS 15. Nashville: Abingdon, 1971.

Zeichmann, C. B. "Οἱ στρατηγοὶ τοῦ ἱεροῦ and the Location of Luke-Acts' Composition." *EC* 3 (2012): 172–87.

Ziesler, J. A. "Luke and the Pharisees." *NTS* 25 (1979): 146–57.

———. "The Name of Jesus in the Acts of the Apostles." *JSNT* 2 (1979): 28–41.

Zimmermann, H. "Die Sammelberichte der Apostelgeschichte." *BZ* ns 5 (1961): 71–82.

Zwiep, A. W. *The Ascension of the Messiah in Lukan Christology*. NovTSup 87. Leiden: Brill, 1997.

———. *Judas and the Choice of Matthias: A Study on Context and Concern of Acts 1:15–26*. WUNT II/187. Tübingen: Mohr Siebeck, 2004.

———. "The Text of the Ascension Narratives (Luke 24.50–3; Acts 1.1–2, 9–11)." *NTS* 42 (1996): 219–44.

Introduction

A. *What Kind of Commentary Is This?*

Bibliography

Alexander, L. "Fact." ———. "Review Article." **Best, E.** "Reading." **Gasque, W. W.** *History*. **Hagner, D. A.** "Writing." **Jipp, J.** "Acts." **Walton, S.** "Acts, Book of." ———. "Acts of God." ———. "Many Questions." **Wenham, G. J.** "Commentary."

An Invitation to Acts

Acts is an exciting book, for it tells the story of the growth of the earliest Christian movement from Jesus's ascension to Paul's arrival in Rome, a period of about thirty years of rapid development. During that period the earliest believers' understanding of God and his purposes grew in directions that they did not anticipate: from its beginnings as a Jewish messianic renewal movement, "the Way" (Acts 9:2; 19:23), within a generation the believing community included gentiles without requiring them to be circumcised or keep the whole torah. Acts ranges over this period, highlighting key moments and people in the overall story to show how Jesus went on acting and teaching—note 1:1, "the things which Jesus *began* (ἤρξατο) both to do and to teach."

More than this, Acts is fundamentally a book about *God*, for its author presents the key moments in the story first and foremost as God's actions.[1] Acts is not a story of human planning and strategy—rather the reverse, for regularly God does something new and the believing community is swept along by God's purposes, even to the extent of being dragged along behind kicking and screaming! The story begins with the believers waiting for God in response to Jesus's call to wait for the Father's promise, power from on high (1:4–5; Luke 24:49), a promise fulfilled on the day of Pentecost (2:1–4). In response to Peter's explanation of events, many join the community by responding to God in repentance and water baptism (2:37–41). The story presents God as personally active in the new community, such as in its growth through the Lord's word (4:31; 6:7; 8:4, 14), the judgment visited on Ananias and Sapphira (5:1–11), Peter's deliverance from prison twice (5:19–21; 12:3–11), Peter and John's wisdom in speaking boldly to the Sanhedrin twice (4:5–12; 5:29–32), and God sustaining and empowering the believers in persecution (note the answer to prayer in 4:23–31).

The key moments toward the inclusion of gentiles occur at God's initiative: God does miracles among the Samaritans when Philip preaches to them (8:6–7), and the Spirit falls on the same people when Peter and John pray for them (8:14–17); God sends Philip to the Ethiopian on the desert road (8:26),

1 Walton, "Acts of God," with, e.g., Gaventa, *Acts*, esp. 25–39; Brawley, *Centering*; Squires, *Plan*.

where Philip finds the man reading Isaiah's prophecy of the suffering servant (8:30–34); Jesus appears to Saul of Tarsus on the way to Damascus and turns him from persecutor of believers to preacher of faith in Jesus (9:3–6, 17–22); God engineers a meeting of the God-fearing Roman soldier Cornelius and the reluctant Peter (10:1–24) and has the temerity to interrupt Peter's address by sending the Holy Spirit on Cornelius and his relatives and friends, an event which leads both to these gentiles being baptized (10:44–48) and to the skeptical Jerusalem believers recognizing that God has accepted them (11:15–18); God uses persecution to cause a mixed Jew-gentile believing community to come into being in Antioch, a development which the Jerusalem church verifies through Barnabas (11:19–26); God speaks through Agabus the prophet to make provision from this ethnically mixed community for the Jewish believers (11:27–30); and God speaks again by the Spirit to send Barnabas and Saul to a wider mission (13:1–3).

Paul's ministry, which forms the focus of the second half of the book (Acts 13–28), is a ministry which depends on God's action and is at times driven by divine action to prevent Paul going in some directions in order to point him in new directions (16:6–10). Thus, for example: Barnabas and Paul are sent out by the Spirit from Syrian Antioch (13:1–4); Paul is filled with the Spirit when facing opposition (13:9–11); God testifies to Paul and Barnabas's preaching by signs and wonders (14:3; 19:11–12), including healing a man with a congenital disability (14:8–10); Luke repeats the phrase "all that God had done" concerning their work (14:27; 15:4, 12); Peter stresses God's action in his speech in Jerusalem (15:7–11); the Lord opens Lydia's heart to the gospel (16:14–15); the Lord appears to Paul to encourage him in Corinth (18:9–10); Luke attributes the transformation of believers who formerly practised magic to the Lord's word (19:20); the Spirit is the one who appoints overseers for the Ephesian community (20:28); God is the one who will sustain the elders' ministry (20:32); the Lord encourages Paul under arrest in Jerusalem (23:11)—indeed, Paul's whole ministry is enabled by God (26:22–23).

Acts offers readers today a unique window into the life of the earliest believers: no other early Christian document covers this period in this way, and no other early Christian document gives such a view of how the earliest communities developed. Acts complements the picture(s) provided by the NT letters in offering a narrative concerning the communities' establishment and growth and the issues they faced in those processes.

For Christian readers today, Acts also presents key resources for Christian reflection and action concerning, for example, the nature of God and God's action in the world; the nature and message of Christian mission and the respective roles of evangelism and social transformation; the work of the Holy Spirit; the understanding of how believers (Jewish and gentile) relate to non-believing Jews and their wider implications for Christian-Jewish relations today; and Christian engagement with the "powers that be," locally, nationally, and internationally.

Engaging with Acts

Acts is an inviting book, but it is challenging too.[2] Acts invites comment and elucidation at a number of different levels: textual, lexical/grammatical/syntactical, historical, literary, social-scientific, and theological. In what follows I shall sketch a number of these issues by way of locating the work of both past scholarship—especially past commentaries—and this commentary. William Ramsay remarked in 1895 that "It is impossible to find anything to say about *Acts* that has not been said before by somebody"[3]—that applies several times over today! However, by the end of this section I hope you, as my reader, will be clearer on what I am hoping to achieve in this commentary.

Textual questions. First, Acts invites discussion at a *textual* level, for there are two major early manuscript traditions for Acts which differ in numerous places. The so-called Western text, represented chiefly in Codex Bezae, varies significantly from the Alexandrian text, represented chiefly in Codices Sinaiticus and Vaticanus (see fuller discussion below). Some have presented valuable page by page comparisons of the two textual traditions[4] or explanations for the textual decisions taken in a printed edition.[5] It would be easy for a commentator to fill a commentary by focusing only on such differences—indeed, Metzger spends 224 pages (almost a third) of *TCGNT*[2] on Acts alone. Rius-Camps and Read-Heimerdinger published a four-volume, textually focused commentary: they seek to compare and contrast the presentation of Acts in Codex Bezae (on the one hand) and Codices Sinaiticus and Vaticanus (on the other) and argue that there are significant differences of emphasis, ideology, and theology between them. Their textual apparatus is particularly full and helpful and has been valuable to me in preparing this commentary.[6]

To declare my hand at this point, I shall be commenting essentially on the Alexandrian text, which I consider (for reasons set out below) to be nearest, in the main, to the original text of Acts. I shall refer to discussions regarding variant readings found among the manuscripts. In a few places I come to different conclusions to the editors of NA$^{27/28}$/UBS$^{4/5}$, and I shall explain my reasons in those places. In places readings found in the so-called Western text are of interest (for a variety of reasons) and I shall mention them (in the *Notes*) and in some cases explore them briefly (in the *Comment*). But those seeking very full discussion of variants will need to look elsewhere.

---

2 For overviews of scholarship, see Walton, "Many Questions"; Jipp, "Acts."

3 Ramsay, *St Paul*, viii (his italics).

4 Ropes in *BegC*, vol. 3.

5 Metzger in, successively, *TCGNT* and *TCGNT*[2].

6 Rius-Camps and Read-Heimerdinger, *Message*. I am grateful to Dr. Read-Heimerdinger, who kindly allowed me access to the text of vol. 2 prior to publication.

Vocabulary, grammar, and syntax. Secondly, Acts's Greek *lexical choices, grammar, and syntax* are worthy of comment. In general, Luke writes some of the most literary Greek in the NT, and he communicates lucidly and stylishly. His choices of words are often striking and particularly apposite, and he has quite a high proportion of NT *hapax legomena*, as well as a number of words which seem to be favorites of his.[7] The standard lexica (esp. BDAG, LSJ, L&N, *EDNT*, and now *CGL*) are helpful in tracking these uses, and I have made extensive use of them. However, in places Luke's form of expression is less than clear; some sentences are difficult to construe. Culy and Parsons particularly provide good help for intermediate Greek students (or those whose Greek is not as sharp as it once was) verse-by-verse in disentangling the syntax and grammar of Acts.[8] Barrett and Bruce also discuss numerous grammatical/syntactical points in some depth.[9] I have made extensive use of these resources, along with the grammars (notably Wallace, whom I have often cited because he is so helpful for intermediate students). In general, I comment where such issues affect the meaning of the text or where the Greek construction needs explanation or discussion, given that others have dealt with such issues so thoroughly. In the *Notes* on my translation and discussions of particular words and phrases in the *Comment*, I have those with intermediate knowledge of Greek in mind.

It is frequently suggested that Semitic influence lies behind some of the grammatical infelicities in Acts, especially in the earlier chapters, which are describing events which take place in a Semitic environment.[10] However, Semitic influences on word order are hard to assess because of our limited knowledge of typical Semitic sentence and clause structures.[11] Further, and most significantly, it is widely recognized that Luke's Greek is strongly influenced by the LXX (Haenchen estimates between 80 and 90% of Luke's vocabulary is found in the LXX[12]), which is itself Greek translated from Hebrew and Aramaic, and this has inclined more recent scholarship to use the category of "Semitism" sparingly concerning phrases and words in Acts, if at all.[13]

Historical questions. Thirdly, because Acts touches so frequently on historical events, places, and people, past scholarship has frequently focused on assessing *the accuracy of Luke's portrait* of the ancient world in general, and the earliest Christians in particular. During the twentieth century perhaps the majority view of scholarship, especially in Germany, was negative concerning

---

7 See the helpful lists of Lukanisms in Goulder, *Luke*, 2:800–809; *VL*.

8 Culy and Parsons, *Acts*; also Kellum, *Acts*.

9 Barrett, *Acts*; Bruce, *Acts* (1990).

10 Argued most significantly by Blass, *Philology*, 193–95, 201; Torrey, *Composition*, esp. 1–41; Wilcox, *Semitisms*; MHT, 4:45–63.

11 Read-Heimerdinger, *Bezan Text*, 67; Wilcox, *Semitisms*, 112–13.

12 Haenchen, *Acts*, 72.

13 Note esp. Fitzmyer, *Acts*, 114–18 (with full bibliography), and the cautious conclusions of Wilcox, *Semitisms*, 180–85.

the historicity of the events in Acts, and this view surfaces most notably in the commentaries of Conzelmann, Haenchen, and Lüdemann and certain major monographs and essays.[14] Following Dibelius's epoch-making work, scholarship focuses on asking what Luke was saying in Acts, frequently on the seeming assumption that events had not taken place as Luke had reported them (in Dibelius's case, while also holding that Luke was Paul's travel companion). A wedge is frequently driven between "history" and "theology" as categories—if Acts was theologically motivated, it could not also be historically reliable. Pervo later proposes that Luke's literary model was the ancient novel and suggests that to classify Acts in this way shows that Luke aims to profit his readers while delighting them with his storytelling, to the neglect of presenting events accurately. Alexander shows that a strict dichotomy of "fact" and "fiction" in terms of literary genre is overly simple: the situation is more complex than Pervo allows.[15]

English-speaking (and particularly British) scholarship of the same period, by contrast, notes Luke's painstaking accuracy over many details of places, titles and names of rulers, and the general historical and topographical context of the stories of Acts, as well as the evident "undesigned coincidences" of material in Acts and the Pauline letters, and thus regards Luke as being given what we might call "the benefit of the doubt" where events or details could not be corroborated from non-Christian sources. Such an approach characterizes the commentaries of Bruce and Marshall (the latter in constant dialogue with Haenchen), and Marshall's important and influential monograph, *Luke: Historian and Theologian*.[16] Hemer's posthumous monograph documents in great detail the vast amount of historical information in Acts which "meshes" well with other ancient sources, especially epigraphy, where Hemer's knowledge is vast.[17]

Methodologically, this series of debates engages with source criticism and redaction criticism because scholars have sought sources which took them nearer to the historical events which lie behind Luke's narrative. Thus, they attempted to separate "source" from "redaction" passage by passage. Lüdemann's commentary is a more recent attempt to do this in order to isolate an historical core of events which may be affirmed with confidence as having taken place (a rather slim core, it must be said!).[18]

However, while there seems to be widespread agreement that Luke used sources, there is virtually no agreement on the nature of the sources (written

14 Notably Dibelius, *Studies*; Vielhauer, "Paulinism."

15 Alexander, "Fact," 380–99.

16 Bruce, *Acts* (1990) (1st ed. 1951); Marshall, *Acts* (TNTC); Marshall, *Historian*. They reflect, and frequently cite, the earlier work of Ramsay, *St Paul*; Sherwin-White, *Society*; Gasque, "Speeches"; Gasque, *History*; Gasque, "Book."

17 Hemer, *Book*.

18 Lüdemann, *Early Christianity*.

or oral) or their precise contents.[19] The difficulty in identifying source contents is acute, for we lack Luke's *Vorlage* to compare with his finished product. This feature distinguishes source criticism of Acts from source criticism of Luke's Gospel, for in the latter (assuming Markan priority) we have at least one of Luke's sources available. The likeliest "source" to be identified in Acts is the so-called "we" passages (16:10–17; 20:5–15; 21:1–18; 27:1–28:16), which are set apart by their use of first-person plural verbs and the personal pronoun ἡμεῖς ("we"). However, Luke has everywhere made any sources his own, for there are not obvious changes in Greek style in different sections of Acts—Luke's own style dominates throughout.[20]

In more recent scholarship there seems to have been more of a meeting of minds on historical questions. Thus, for example, from the English-speaking world, the commentaries of Barrett and Fitzmyer, and the series *The Book of Acts in Its First Century Setting*, treat Acts as a valuable source for the history of earliest Christianity, as do the commentary of Jervell and Hengel's monographs from the German-speaking world.[21]

Literary approaches. Luke Johnson is the first to bring literary approaches, now known under the banner of "narrative criticism," to (Luke-)Acts in his PhD dissertation.[22] This groundbreaking work approaches Luke-Acts by asking about the literary function of sharing possessions, rather than (for example) the historical value of Luke's accounts of this phenomenon, or the sources Luke uses and how he edits them. Johnson brought the work of literary critics such as Booth and Chatman into the field, engaging with plot, characters, settings and point of view.[23] His commentary works this programme out passage by passage.[24]

Around the same period, Tannehill's studies of the narrative unity of Luke-Acts provide a thoughtful and engaging reading of the two books.[25] His volume on Acts was the first to apply narrative criticism to the whole book and is full of insights, particularly in finding interconnections within the double work as he reads the texts holistically. He highlights previews and reviews, as Luke introduces an idea he later develops more fully, or later summarizes a theme which he narrates at length.[26]

Tannehill and Johnson's work opens the door to a number of subsequent

---

19 See Fitzmyer, *Acts*, 80–85, for a judicious survey of the discussion over the twentieth century.

20 Dupont, *Sources*, 166; Fitzmyer, *Acts*, 81.

21 Barrett, *Acts*, 2:xxxiii–lxxxi; see also Barrett, "Historicity"; Fitzmyer, *Acts*, 124–28 (with useful bibliography); Winter and Clarke, eds., *Literary Setting*; Gill and Gempf, eds., *Graeco-Roman Setting*; Rapske, *Paul*; Bauckham, ed. *Palestinian*; Levinskaya, *Diaspora Setting*; Jervell, *Apostelgeschichte*; Hengel, *Acts*; Hengel, *Between*.

22 Johnson, *Function*. For helpful introductions to such approaches, see Powell, *Narrative Criticism*; Marguerat and Bourquin, *How to Read*; Brown, *Gospels*; Resseguie, *Narrative Criticism*.

23 Booth, *Rhetoric*; Chatman, *Story and Discourse*.

24 Johnson, *Acts*.

25 Tannehill, *Unity*; see also Tannehill, *Luke*.

26 E.g., Tannehill, *Unity*, 2:252, 255–61.

monographs and commentaries working with a literary approach.[27] Such approaches properly insist that reading and understanding what Luke says logically precedes asking questions about sources, redaction, historicity. Interestingly, the work of such scholars also allows conversation about Luke's message and communication irrespective of whether the scholar agrees with Luke's message. Tannehill makes clear that he does not accept Luke's view that Christians should seek to persuade Jewish people to become followers of Jesus while being clear that this is Luke's view.[28]

Social-scientific approaches. The impact and expression of the social setting of earliest Christianity becomes a significant concern in scholarship from the 1980s.[29] Philip Esler is one of the first to seek the social and political concerns which shape Luke's thinking.[30] He regards apparently theological concerns as encoded political/social concerns[31] and argues that Luke's central concern is legitimating the Christian faith of his (believing) readers. He develops his argument by considering table fellowship, the Jewish law, the temple, poor and rich people, and the Roman Empire. The value of such approaches lies in the insistence that Luke's social setting(s) must have influenced his writing and presentation, even if unconsciously. It is not necessary to accept Esler's assertion that theology is just coded sociology or politics to make use of social-scientific data and interpretive methods. In terms of commentaries, Witherington perhaps comes closest to this approach in his socio-rhetorical study of Acts.[32]

Theological approaches. Older commentaries back to Chrysostom and Bede approach Acts primarily as a theological document, that is, as a text which speaks of God and his ways.[33] While theological concerns never disappear entirely from view through the eras of redaction criticism and literary approaches, they tend to be subordinated to reconstruction of the history behind the text (redaction criticism) and study of how Luke communicates, sometimes at the expense of what he communicates (literary approaches). More recently, the question of God is back on the agenda of Acts scholarship. This door was pushed ajar by the work of Brawley and developed in a fine theocentric commentary by Gaventa.[34] Both are drawing on narrative criticism and use its tools to interrogate the text for the understanding of God

27 Among the commentaries, see Spencer, *Acts* (republished as Spencer, *Journeying*); Gooding, *True*; Bauer, *Acts*; Marguerat, *Actes*. Example monographs include Spencer, *Portrait*; Darr, *Character*; Hur, *Reading*; Shepherd, *Function*; Marguerat, *Historian*.

28 Tannehill, *Unity*, 2:3.

29 For surveys, see Tidball, *Social Context*, and the valuable collection of key essays, Horrell, ed. *Social-Scientific Approaches to New Testament Interpretation*.

30 Esler, *Community*.

31 Esler, *Community*, 1–16.

32 Witherington, *Acts*.

33 Chrysostom, *Hom. Act.*; Bede, *Acts*.

34 Brawley, *Centering*; Gaventa, *Acts*.

which it instantiates. Necessarily, this involves asking about the place of Jesus and the Holy Spirit.[35]

Wall develops his theological approach using canonical criticism, reading Acts in the wider context of the NT and biblical canons, an approach for which he is justly well-known.[36] Those interested in thinking about Acts in the context of biblical theology will find his work of considerable interest, for he places Acts in dialogue with the perspectives of other scriptural authors, and thereby teases out its commonalities and distinctives in relation to them.

Key Features of This Commentary

It is clear from the above that a number of different approaches can be, and are, taken to writing a commentary on Acts. What approach does this commentary adopt? Part of the answer is given by the format of the Word Biblical Commentary,[37] which first provides a *Bibliography* of works relevant to the pericope. Here I have not listed all works cited in the section but those with substantive contribution to interpreting the pericope in question; some other works relevant on a particular point are mentioned only in footnotes. The format then (rightly) walks the reader through the *Translation* of the text with *Notes* on specific points, including brief comment on key textual variants. I have aimed at those with intermediate knowledge of Greek in this section, seeking to be aware of the kinds of constructions and issues which such people may need reminding of. *Form/Structure/Setting* then considers the delimitation of the pericope under consideration, what might be said about sources and historicity of the section, the form and structure of the section and any subsections, and the setting of the pericope in the immediate and wider literary contexts. *Comment* goes on to sentence-by-sentence discussion of the text, seeking to paint in key social, cultural, and literary settings that are important for understanding the text in its ancient contexts and offering exegesis of the pericope. Here is where I locate detailed discussion of the interpretation of the pericope, although I have not sought to catalog different interpretations exhaustively—that would have made the commentary far longer and would be in danger of hiding the wood for the trees. The picture I have in my mind is of myself and the various scholars I engage with sitting around a table with the Greek text of Acts in the middle of the table. The text is the focus of our discussion, not the scholars and their opinions. Kingsley Barrett wisely observes that a time comes when, reversing Pilate's dictum, an author must say: "What I have read, I have read."[38] Put more prosaically, it could be said that commentaries are

35 On Jesus, see, e.g., Hurtado, *Lord*, 177–216; Walton, "Jesus." On the Holy Spirit, see, e.g., Dunn, *Baptism*; Menzies, *Empowered*; Turner, *Power*; Atkinson, *Baptism*.

36 Wall, "Acts."

37 For a similar account of commentating, see Wenham, "Commentary." He is the author of the two-volume WBC on Genesis.

38 Barrett, *Acts*, 1:ix.

never finished but only abandoned, for "of the making of many books there is no end" (Eccl 12:12). I prefer to think of drawing such a line under scholarship as a virtue for, to adapt a phrase from my friend Dick France, I intend that this is a commentary on Acts, not a commentary on the commentaries on Acts.[39] Those who wish for a telephone directory of opinions will need to look elsewhere. *Explanation* then pulls the threads of the discussion together to offer an interpretation of the whole pericope. I often say to students and pastors that this is the section of the Word Biblical Commentary to read first, for it gives readers an overview of the passage and its key emphases and puts them in a position then to dive into the detail in the other parts of the discussion. In places I have provided *Excurses* on particular points and have cross-referred to them at relevant places in the discussion. I have also used cross-referencing to fuller discussions elsewhere to avoid needless repetition and to attempt to keep the length of the commentary within reasonable bounds.

Focus on the Message

Another reason for beginning reading with the *Explanation* on a passage is that my focus in writing is on the interpretation of the message of Acts. I am interested in other things as they contribute to this question.

Issues of the most likely original text clearly affect the message of the book in significant ways, although I shall not attempt to redo the fine work others have done in this regard. The social and cultural settings of the book and its stories are also highly relevant to understanding Luke's work in its ancient setting, both in the ostensible location of the events and in the way Luke uses language, key words, and technical terms. I seek to highlight these as they affect the message Luke communicates through his text. Likewise, I discuss the historical settings of events, including our knowledge of people, places, and events from other ancient sources, as they contribute to our interpretation of the text rather than as of interest in their own right. That is not to say such study is not interesting or valuable—it simply is not what I am attempting to do.

To read Acts aright, it is important to engage with both Jewish and Greco-Roman settings, not least because both are evident in the book, as the early chapters in Jerusalem and Paul's evangelism in the Greco-Roman world respectively bear witness. More broadly, Luke is communicating about a movement whose origins are within Judaism and yet that embraces gentiles, finally without requiring them to submit to keeping the torah and being circumcised (if men). Luke is writing for a community of believers strongly rooted in Judaism—the sheer volume of quotations, echoes, and allusions to Scripture show this. He is also writing for a community of believers who include many from Greek and Roman heritage: the fact that he writes in Greek, the *lingua franca* of the Roman Empire, particularly in the east, alone

39 France, *Mark*, 1.

shows this. He is thus communicating from Jewish roots into this world. This commentary seeks to be sensitive to this double context.

My conviction after studying Acts for some years is that Luke is communicating about God and what God is doing in the world.[40] Gaventa and Sleeman have helped me see the way that the exalted Jesus is active in the events of Acts, but in a different way to the Third Gospel.[41] Jesus is now active from heaven, where he has been exalted to the Father's right side and from where he pours out the Spirit (2:33). Jesus's actions and location place him, remarkably, alongside the God of Israel as deserving worship and begin the process of reflection that will lead eventually to Trinitarian theology. The Holy Spirit's role among the believers is not, thus, merely as Jesus's "alter ego" but as an active agent carrying forward God's will. Many have undertaken to review the Spirit's work in Acts, and I draw on their work (see n35 above). Readers will find my comments focusing on the way in which this God acts and the response he seeks from people, and believers in particular, particularly in the *Explanation* sections.

What about . . . ?

Some readers will reach this point and wonder where my discussions of authorship, date, theology, etc. are. I share Barrett's conviction that one should discuss such things after reading through the text of the book rather than in advance.[42] Of course, there is a necessary hermeneutical spiral in reading a text, where a reader's initial understanding is modified as she reads the text carefully, reconstructs that understanding, reads further, and so on. Nevertheless, theories about these questions should be constructed in the light of careful exegesis of the text, for only then can all the data be considered, as far as one mind is able to do so. This means I shall engage with such questions at the end of my third volume on Acts, rather than here.[43]

B. The Text of Acts

Bibliography

Aland, B. "Entstehung." **Aland, K.** *Textwert.* ———. *Kurzgefasste Liste* (2nd ed.). **Aland, K. and B. Aland.** *Text* (2nd ed.), 54–55. **Barrett, C. K.** *Acts,* 1:2–29; 2:xix–xxiii. **Black, M.** *Aramaic,* 28–34, 277–80. ———. "Spirit." **Blass, F.** *Acta.* ———. *Philology,* 96–137. **Boismard, M.-E., OP.** *Texte occidental* (2nd ed.). **Bosimard, M.-E. and A. Lamouille.** *Texte* (1984). ———. *Actes, vols I–III.* **Clark, A. C.** *Acts.* **Delobel, J.** "Text." **Dibelius, M.** *Studies,* 84–92. **Elliott, J. K.** *Essays.* ———. "Greek Manuscript Heritage." ———. Review of Boismard and Lamouille, *Texte occidental.* ———. "Text of Acts." **Epp, E. J.** "Coptic Manuscript G67." ———. "Text-Critical Witnesses." ———. *Theological Tendency.* **Fitzmyer, J. B.** *Acts,* 66–79 (with good bibliography). **Geer, T. C., Jr.** "Two

40 See Walton, "Acts, Book of"; Walton, "Acts of God."
41 Gaventa, "Acts"; Sleeman, *Geography.*
42 Barrett, *Acts,* 1:1.
43 I shall also address them in a forthcoming ZICNT volume on Acts.

Faces." **Haenchen, E.** *Acts,* 50–60. **Harris, J. R.** *Codex Bezae,* 191–225. ———. *Four Lectures.* **Head, P.** "Acts." **Hyytiäinen, P.** "Changing Text." **Jongkind, D.** *Introduction.* **Kenyon, F. G.** "Western Text." **Kilpatrick, G. D.** "Eclectic Study." **Klijn, A. F. J.** *Survey* (1949). ———. "Survey." ———. *Survey, Part 2.* **Metzger, B. M.** *Text* (3rd ed.). ———, ed. *Textual Commentary* (2nd ed.) [= *TCGNT*²], 222–445, esp. 222–36. **Metzger, B. M., and B. D. Ehrman.** *Text* (4th ed.). **Osburn, C. D.** "Search." **Page, T. E.** Review of Blass, *Acta.* **Panten, K. E.** "History." **Parker, D. C.** *Codex Bezae.* ———. *Introduction,* 286–98. **Parker, D. C., and S. R. Pickering.** "4698." **Read-Heimerdinger, J.** *Bezan Text.* **Rius-Camps, J., and J. Read-Heimerdinger.** *Message.* **Ropes, J. H.** *Text* [= *BegC,* vol. 3]. **Scrivener, F. H. A.** *Bezae.* **Strange, W. A.** *Problem.* **Strutwolf, H., G. Gäbel, A. Hüffmeier, G. Mink, and K. Wachtel, eds.** *Acts/Apostelgeschichte* [= ECM]. **Swanson, R. J.** *NT Greek Manuscripts: Acts.* **Wasserman, T., and P. J. Gurry.** *New Approach.* **Wilson, J. M.** *Acts.* **Witherington, Ben, III.** "Anti-feminist Tendencies."

The Manuscript Tradition of Acts

No book of the NT has as complex a textual tradition as Acts;[44] in particular, scholars frequently identify two early forms of the text which differ markedly at a number of points, traditionally known as Alexandrian and Western (see further on text types, below). There are some 612 Greek manuscript witnesses to Acts,[45] plus versions in various languages and quotations and allusions in patristic writers.[46]

(1) *The major witnesses.* The Greek *papyri,* which are generally the oldest manuscripts available, are of great value in establishing the text of Acts, and there are some fifteen papyri which contain parts of the book. They range from around AD 300 to the eighth century.[47] However, the vast majority contain only fragments of a few verses; only 𝔓[45, 74] have a substantial amount of the book.

The next oldest group are the Greek *majuscule (or uncial) manuscripts.* We are fortunate to have thirty-two, ranging from the fourth to the tenth century, and including a number of earlier copies which have the whole of Acts (notably ℵ A B C). Other important majuscules include the bilingual Greek-Latin manuscripts D/d and E 08/e, which are both relatively early (fifth to sixth century) and provide evidence for Western readings (see below on text clusters).

The Greek *minuscule manuscripts* are, as for the rest of the NT, very numerous,[48] but mostly not of great antiquity or value for establishing the original text of the NT (see below on the Byzantine text cluster). Some are of particular value, notably 614 and 1739, both fairly late (thirteenth and tenth century, respectively), but both witnessing to a text from an earlier era—in the case of

44 For an alternative review of the topic to 1991, see Osburn, "Search."

45 Elliott, "Heritage," 38–44, lists them exhaustively. See also Aland, *Liste* and the updated version online: https://ntvmr.uni-muenster.de/liste.

46 Barrett, *Acts,* 1:8–20, enumerates main versions and patristic citations; Strange, *Problem,* 193–204, provides a full list.

47 See the list including contents, ECM, 2:5.

48 Elliott, "Heritage," 39–44, lists 567.

1739, quite possibly from the late fourth century.[49] Manuscript 33 is interesting in that in Acts 1:1–11:25 the text generally agrees with other Byzantine manuscripts, but in 11:16–28:31 it generally agrees with Alexandrian manuscripts, probably indicating a change of the exemplar being copied.[50]

There are almost six hundred Greek *lectionaries* that contain parts of Acts, dating from the tenth to the sixteenth centuries,[51] but these have not yet been widely studied by scholars.

The *versions* in other languages also preserve the text of Acts, although in the case of individual readings it is, of course, necessary to translate into Greek to reconstruct the text used by those who created the version. Most important are copies of Acts in Latin (both the Old Latin and the Vulgate), Coptic (Sahidic, Middle Egyptian, and Bohairic dialects), Syriac (Peshitta and Harklean), and Ethiopic.[52] The Coptic manuscript G67 is dated between the fourth and sixth centuries and witnesses to a Western text.[53] The text of the Harklean Syriac dates from AD 616 and includes a critical apparatus and marginal notes that highlight a number of Western readings.

Citations in the patristic writers are also important.[54] The earliest explicit citation of Acts is from a Latin translation (rather than the original Greek) of the second-century writer Irenaeus. When Irenaeus quotes from Acts he frequently—but by no means always—agrees with D, Old Latin manuscripts, and readings found in the Harklean Syriac margins, in such places witnessing to Western readings.[55]

In the third century Clement of Alexandria, Tertullian, Origen, and Cyprian quote Acts; in the fourth century Eusebius of Caesarea, Lucifer of Cagliari, Athanasius of Alexandria, and Cyril of Jerusalem; in the fifth century Chrysostom (the first to write a commentary, in the form of a series of homilies, on Acts), Jerome, Augustine, Cyril of Alexandria, Bede, and Speculum (or Pseudo-Augustine).

(2) The main clusters of texts. I am writing when the *Editio Critica Maior* of Acts is available,[56] and that, along with the claims of its editors about the manuscript tradition of Acts, has generated a debate concerning traditional text clusters (often called "text types") of those manuscripts. I shall first sketch the approach which was widely accepted for a century, before outlining the present debate.

Among the wide range of witnesses to the text of Acts, while there is broad

49 Metzger, *Text* (3rd ed.), 65.
50 Hyytiäinen, "Changing Text," 11; Geer, "Two Faces," esp. 47.
51 ECM, 2:15. Strangely, the German here gives an upper date of sixteenth century, but the English fifteenth century.
52 See the lists in ECM, 2:136–44 (Latin), 145–67 (Coptic), 168–75 (Syriac), 175–76 (Ethiopic).
53 Epp, "Coptic Manuscript G67."
54 For a full list, see ECM, 2:52–126.
55 Barrett, *Acts,* 1:16–17, lists examples of Irenean readings of both sorts.
56 In many respects this now supersedes the earlier valuable work of Swanson, ed., *Acts.* The collations of MSS in Aland, *Textwert,* continue to be valuable.

agreement on the story told by the text, there is considerable variety on the details. Traditionally, scholars identify three main clusters of manuscripts of Acts. The first and the largest group is that of the Byzantine manuscripts, which contain a text that seems to have been created by conflating the variant readings found in the other two clusters, at or before the time of Chrysostom in the fourth/early fifth century (for his text is of this type).[57] Those who first edit this text include all readings found in the manuscripts available, so as to lose nothing that might be original. Typical examples include the majuscules H L P Ψ, and the majority of minuscules. The two clusters of manuscripts used by the Byzantine conflator(s) are traditionally known as the Alexandrian (or Old Uncial) and the Western.

The Alexandrian cluster is so-called because it is associated with the city of Alexandria in Egypt. Typical examples include the papyri $\mathfrak{P}^{45, 74}$, the majuscules ℵ A B C, and the minuscule 81;[58] this text is also found in the Sahidic version and the quotations found in Clement of Alexandria[59] and Origen. Some differentiate an early ("Neutral" [Westcott and Hort's term] or "primary Alexandrian") and a later ("Alexandrian" [Westcott and Hort] or "secondary Alexandrian") form of this text, the early form being found in $\mathfrak{P}^{45, 50, 74}$ ℵ B Sahidic Clement of Alexandria Origen, and the later in $\mathfrak{P}^{50}$ A C Ψ 33 81 104 326 (and probably 1739[60]).[61]

This cluster's text forms the basis of modern critical editions of Acts, particularly that found in NA$^{27/28}$ and UBS$^{4/5}$, in line with the view of Westcott and Hort that this text is very close to the autographs. Although the editors of NA$^{27/28}$ and UBS$^{4/5}$ say that they follow an eclectic approach, taking each reading on its merits,[62] in practice they follow the Alexandrian text the vast majority of the time.

The Western witnesses are so called because the first examples of this text to be identified (in the nineteenth century) were thought to originate in the western part of the Mediterranean basin (North Africa, Italy, and France). Later scholarship has identified manuscripts and versions from other geographical regions, particularly Egypt and Syria,[63] as part of this group, although the name Western has remained. Key Western witnesses for Acts are the majuscule D,[64] the papyri $\mathfrak{P}^{38, 48}$ and perhaps $\mathfrak{P}^{29}$ (although it contains no distinctively Western

---

57 Barrett, *Acts*, 1:21, suggests at the time of Lucian, early in the fourth century.

58 Parker, *Introduction*, 290.

59 Metzger and Ehrman, *Text* (4th ed.), 277n10.

60 So Metzger and Ehrman, *Text* (4th ed), 88.

61 Metzger and Ehrman, *Text* (4th ed.), 278.

62 *TCGNT*^{2}, 235.

63 Harris, *Four Lectures*, esp. 213–14, argues for a North African provenance. Aland, "Entstehung," esp. 57–62, makes a cogent case for the origins of this text cluster in Syria. Parker, *Codex Bezae*, argues for Berytus (Beirut) as the origin of D.

64 D lacks 8:29–10:14; 22:10–20; 22:29–28:31. See Parker, *Codex Bezae*; Panten, "History." Wilson, *Acts*, provides an accessible English translation of Codex Bezae's text of Acts.

readings[65]), the minuscules 383 614, the African Old Latin manuscript h, the Harklean Syriac, including readings written it its margins,[66] the Coptic (Middle Egyptian) manuscript G67, and at least some citations in Irenaeus, Cyprian, and Augustine. It is generally accepted in scholarship that D alone is not *the* Western text, for it contains scribal errors and amendments that are not attributable to a "Western tendency" (and other witnesses in this group are similarly mixed in the text they attest);[67] thus, as with the Alexandrian text, scholars have endeavoured to reconstruct the "original" Western text from the later witnesses.[68]

Western readings are usually characterized as having greater length: the overall length of the Western text is often quoted as about 8.5% greater than classic Alexandrian manuscripts, based on Kenyon's comparison of Clark's (Western) text and that of Westcott and Hort (Alexandrian).[69] Read-Heimerdinger claims the difference is only 6.6% when D and B are compared as specific representatives of those text clusters.[70] Westcott and Hort identified strong paraphrasing and harmonising tendencies in Western manuscripts.[71]

Strange sees the distinctively longer Western readings as "commentary."[72] In terms of the narrative, Western readings provide small scenes that help move the story along or explain its development more fully (e.g., at Acts 14:2; 16:30; 18:12; 21:16–17; 27:15), make entrances and exits of characters from the story explicit (e.g., 5:18, 21, 22; 11:28; 12:23; 14:18; 16:35; 28:29), give other details that fill out changes of scene (e.g., 3:11; 19:28), and provide information about characters' movements (e.g., 8:1; 14:7; 15:34; 18:2; 20:15) or motives (e.g., 13:8; 18:21; 19:1; 23:25; 24:24; 26:14). In terms of theology, Western readings often add fuller titles of the person of Jesus (e.g., D reads ὁ κύριος Ἰησοῦς Χριστός, "the Lord Jesus Messiah," sixteen times[73] by contrast with only two in the Alexandrian text at 11:17; 28:31), stress the act of believing as crucial to entering the Christian community (e.g., 2:41; 4:31; 8:37; 11:17; 18:8), and generally provide "edifying" material (e.g., 4:32; 5:15; 9:22, 40).

Strange stresses that the Western readings are not offering a different message to the Alexandrian; rather, "All Western readings in Acts are related to the non-Western text. They clarify and smooth the other text, they recast certain scenes, they add details, they explain, and sometimes they correct. But they do not add wholly new material."[74] In particular, he argues that the Western portrayal of the apostles does not elevate them as might be expected

65 Barrett, *Acts*, 1:2.
66 Parker, *Introduction*, 291.
67 Epp, "Text-Critical Witnesses," 228–29; Blass, *Philology*, 107–8.
68 See esp. Clark, *Acts*; Boismard, *Texte occidental* (2nd ed.).
69 Kenyon, "Western Text," 310.
70 Read-Heimerdinger, "Long and Short," 247.
71 *NT in Greek*, 120–26.
72 *Problem*, 40–56.
73 Strange, *Problem*, 214n44, gives references.
74 *Problem*, 52.

when compared with the apocryphal Acts, nor does it anachronistically use apostolic figures in direct relation to the debates of the early second century, such as concerning Gnosticism.

That said, it must be added that the Western witnesses do not only provide additions but can substitute alternative wordings, change word order, or omit words found in the Alexandrian manuscripts. Read-Heimerdinger compares D and B, and finds that, of 3642 differences, 39.7% have words added in D, 37.1% are places where D provides an alternative wording, 7.2% have a different word order, and 16% have words omitted in D.[75] Further, she notes that the spread of variation is not even in the whole book: there is a greater proportion of "alternative" readings in D from ch. 14 onwards, and there is more "alternative" material in direct speech compared with narrative, and more "additional" material in narrative compared with direct speech. Thus, the picture is more complex than the Western manuscripts simply being longer than the Alexandrian: the Western text represents a different stream of text entirely.

Recently, however, this "two streams" approach has been challenged, notably by Parker and Pickering, and Gäbel and Wachtel. Parker and Pickering's work on the fifth-century $\mathfrak{P}^{127}$, which contains fragments of the text of Acts 10–12 and 15–17, suggests that it cannot easily be assigned to either the Alexandrian or Western cluster, for the text is at times closer to B and at times closer to D/d.[76] Gäbel and Wachtel argue there is no evidence for a single early Western text of Acts, and thus the idea should be abandoned.[77] This is because they do not find real coherence among witnesses usually labeled "Western."[78] They thus agree with Parker's observation: "The main thing that the manuscripts of this type (sc. Western) have in common is that while they differ from those of other types, they differ from each other almost as much."[79] Wachtel observes, "If there are agreements between Irenaeus' citations and variants in 05, this does not mean that the 'Western text' goes back to the second century, but rather that these particular variants do. Thus, the notion of a second century 'Western text' should be abandoned once and for all."[80] Parker further notes the small number of manuscripts understood to belong to the Alexandrian cluster (he estimates twelve) and regards this as "claiming a great deal from very little."[81] These scholars prefer to consider the relationship of texts and

75 "Long and Short," 250–51.

76 Parker and Pickering, "4698," esp. 8. Gäbel, drawing on findings from the CBGM, suggests that $\mathfrak{P}^{127}$ is a potential descendant of D (ECM, 3:88), as does Epp, "Text-Critical Witnesses," 240, 257–64.

77 ECM, 3:83–136 (esp. 133–34); 137–48 (esp. 147–48). They disagree on the process by which Western readings came into being.

78 Wachtel, ECM, 3:138–48.

79 Parker, *Introduction*, 171. Contrast Epp's claim that the D-cluster of texts agree with each other 88% of the time for readings in 425 units of variation and that 97% of such readings disagree with both ℵ and B; Epp, "Text-Critical Witnesses."

80 ECM, 3:147.

81 Parker, *Introduction*, 171.

readings rather than manuscripts.[82] Parker claims, "[T]he textual criticism of Acts is in essence not very different from any other kind of textual criticism, in that it involves the study of individual witnesses to remove error, followed by the comparison of different forms of text in order to recover the oldest possible form, for which all witnesses potentially provide evidence."[83]

However, the debate is not over, for Hyytiäinen argues that computer-based phylogenetic analysis used in plant genetics, when applied to Acts, does suggest there are two major text clusters.[84] Nuancing traditional approaches, Hyytiäinen argues for thinking in terms of networks of texts and clustering rather than strict "types."[85] Such an approach allows for greater consideration of the contamination of texts that happens when scribes have access to more than one manuscript when copying. His work thus far only samples Acts 5 but is suggestive for the wider debate. Epp, too, samples a range of readings from the D-cluster of texts and argues that there is considerable coherence among them over against the Alexandrian cluster.[86] In what follows, I consider how scholarly discussion of the varying texts of Acts has developed and outline the working approach taken in this commentary.

Theories[87]

Given two differing early forms of the text of Acts, we face a problem more acute than elsewhere in the NT, for in the other books the Western readings do not affect the length so significantly or provide so many variations. We turn, then, to consider the explanations scholars have offered for these differences among the manuscript traditions.

Broadly, there have been four major approaches to the manuscript traditions of Acts: to view the Alexandrian text as an abbreviated form of the more primitive Western text (a significant minority view in current scholarship), to view the Western text as a later development from a more primitive Alexandrian form (the majority view in scholarship of the last one hundred years), to view neither as more primitive but to adopt an eclectic approach to variant readings, and to study the two traditions as of interest in their own right.

(1) The Western text as more primitive. Blass argues that Luke himself produced two editions of Acts, a first draft, written in Rome, which was rougher in style and included many unnecessary details, and a second, written in

---

82 On the Coherence-Based Genealogical Method (CBGM) developed by Gerd Mink and now used by the Text Institut in Münster, see the helpful introduction, Wasserman and Gurry, *New Approach*.

83 Parker, *Introduction*, 298.

84 Hyytiäinen, "Changing Text," esp. 17–28.

85 Cf. Epp, "Text-Critical Witnesses," 226, preferring "clusters" to "types."

86 Epp, "Text-Critical Witnesses," summary: 246.

87 For accounts of the history of research, see Strange, *Problem*, 1–33; Barrett, *Acts*, 1:22–26; *TCGNT*², 225–35; Klijn, *Survey* (1949); Klijn, "Survey" (1949–59); Klijn, *Survey, Part 2*; Head, "Acts," 417–28; Delobel, "Text," 84–96; Parker, *Introduction*, 293–301.

Antioch, which was better in style and shorter.[88] The Western text originates from Luke's first draft, and the Alexandrian from his second. Blass sees the Western readings as much in Lukan style as the Alexandrian.[89]

Blass is both supported and criticized in the years following his publication of this proposal. His critics argue that the heightened Christology of the Western witnesses, shown by their use of expanded titles for Jesus, is more likely to be later, for it is unlikely that later scribes and editors would "lower" the Christology of Western texts to produce the Alexandrian.[90] Further, the apparent inconsistencies of theology, history, and geography between the Alexandrian and Western texts suggest that it is unlikely that one author produced two contradictory text forms; Haenchen cites the varying forms of the Apostolic Decree (Acts 15:20, 29) as an example.[91]

Clark accepts the latter criticism of Blass's view but nevertheless believes, on the unusual principle that the longer reading is weightier (*lectio longior potior*), that the Western text is both Lukan and more primitive and the Alexandrian text a later edition.[92] He notes that D is set out in sense lines or *stichoi*, and it would be easy for the eye of a scribe to jump from a similar end/beginning on one line to the end/beginning of the line below and thus omit a line by homoioarcton or homoioteleuteon (an example of the latter is 4:32).[93] He earlier proposed that this had happened in error but, following Ropes's criticism that this view fails to account for apparently deliberate and rational differences between the two text types,[94] in Clark's edition of the text of Acts he argues that this abbreviating was done deliberately by an editor but in fact botching the resultant text by this means.[95]

Boismard and Lamouille's major edition of the Western text aims "to rehabilitate the Western text of the Acts of the Apostles by showing that it could not have been written except by Luke himself."[96] Their work includes a very full study of Lukan style in Acts, and they use this analysis to enable them to reconstruct the Western text from the varying forms found in the extant witnesses. They claim, on the basis of their study of Lukan style, that the Western text is "an authentically Lukan text, in certain passages more Lukan than the Alexandrian text."[97]

---

88 *Acta*; *Philology*, 96–137.

89 *Philology*, 118.

90 Esp. Page, review of Blass, *Acta*; Ropes, *BegC*, 3:ccxxvii–ccxxxii; Harris, *Four Lectures*, 62–66.

91 Haenchen, *Acts*, 51.

92 *Acts*.

93 See the edition of Scrivener, *Bezae*, here 341. Following a line ending ψυχὴ μία "one soul," D reads καὶ οὐκ ἦν διάκρισις ἐν αὐτοῖς οὐδεμία "and there was no distinction among them"; the latter is absent from Alexandrian MSS such as ℵ B. See discussion *TCGNT*², 283.

94 *BegC*, 3:ccxxvi–ccxxvii.

95 *Acts*, xxiv–xxxii, xlv–lii.

96 *Texte* (1984); *Actes* I; *Actes* II; *Actes* III; Boismard, *Texte occidental*, 2nd ed. The quotation is from *Texte* (1984), 1:ix (my translation).

97 *Texte* (1984), 1:97 (my translation).

They postulate three editions of Acts: (1) an original draft, Acts I, written by an unknown Jewish-Christian author around AD 60–62 using three sources, document P (concerning Peter), a "voyage journal" (concerning Paul's travels), and document J (drawn from the circle of John the baptizer); (2) a revised and expanded text, Acts II (or TO = "Texte occidental" = Western text), produced by Luke, the companion of Paul, around AD 80; (3) a further revised text, Acts III, made with reference to some of the original sources and produced by an unknown author for a gentile audience in Rome in the 90s AD. They identify Acts II as the "true" Western text, of which D is a corrupt version (which they refer to as TO^2). Few have been persuaded by Boismard and Lamouille's full hypothesis, although the textual apparatus and evidence on Lukan style which they provide has put scholars hugely in their debt.

Read-Heimerdinger, later in collaboration with Rius-Camps, interprets D on the basis that it is Lukan and earlier than the text of B.[98] She particularly uses discourse analysis to offer an account of the "inner coherence" of word choice and narrative in the Bezan text of Acts.[99]

(2) The Alexandrian text as more primitive. This is the majority view in scholarship in recent times. Notably, it is the view of Westcott and Hort, whose text has been highly influential in all subsequent editions of the Greek NT. They explain the Western text as due to the free handling of the text by scribes prior to Acts being recognized as sacred Scripture.[100] Subsequently this becomes the mainstream view through Ropes, by both his critique of Blass and his arguments that the Western text evidenced a consistent revision by someone other than the author rather than numerous individual amendments.[101] Ropes presents the Western text as including many stylistic improvements, elaborations, and expansions.[102] He also argues that the Western reviser sometimes stresses Jewish opposition to the gospel message (e.g., in 14:5; 24:5[103]) but on the whole does not see a strong theological motivation behind this revision.

Epp's work on the theological tendency of the D-text, which he identifies as anti-Jewish (see above), is compatible with this text being later, for it is hard to imagine the earliest believers, who were all Jewish, producing a text that is markedly anti-Jewish. Similarly, Witherington argues that the D-text downplays the role of women in earliest Christianity, such as the addition of καὶ τέκνοις, "and the children," of the women (1:14), the identification of women in Thessalonica as γυναῖκες τῶν πρώτων, "wives of prominent men," instead of γυναικῶν ... τῶν

98 Read-Heimerdinger, *Bezan Text*; Rius-Camps and Read-Heimerdinger, *Message*. The latter presents an outstanding textual apparatus along with commentary assuming the priority of the Bezan text.

99 Rius-Camps and Read-Heimerdinger, *Message*, 1:9.

100 As later did Dibelius, *Studies*, 89–90.

101 *BegC*, 3:viii.

102 *BegC*, 3:ccxxxi–ccxxxiii.

103 See *BegC*, 3:ccxxxiii. Epp, *Tendency*, esp. 41–164, argues that D exhibits a consistent anti-Jewish bias.

πρώτων, "women of prominence" (17:4), the omission of Damaris (17:34), and the switch of the sequence of Priscilla and Aquila to name him first (18:26). Head adds arguments based on the D-text's heightened use of christological designations for Jesus, fuller mentions of the work of the Spirit, greater focus on the authority of the apostles, and shaping of the apostolic decree.[104]

(3) Eclectic approaches. After the Second World War a trend which had precursors in the work of Lake and Cadbury[105] came to full flower in an eclectic approach to the text of Acts—and, indeed, to the whole NT. Kilpatrick advocates this approach, arguing that the best criterion to use in textual criticism is the author's own usage and style.[106]

An influential statement of this view is that of Metzger, who argues that the lack of a generally accepted hypothesis of the relation of the Alexandrian and Western texts of Acts means that the only real option is to take the evidence on its merits in each individual reading, not privileging one set of texts over the other.[107] However, as Metzger admits, in practice the UBS Committee, which edited the NA$^{27/28}$/UBS$^{4/5}$ text, generally accepted Alexandrian readings in preference to Western ones. Elliott, who advocates "radical eclecticism"—the view that no set of manuscripts should be privileged over others in establishing the text—argues that this means that the UBS Committee in practice privileges the Alexandrian witnesses.[108] Elliott thus seeks the starting text (*Ausgangstext*) in any manuscript, no matter what ostensible date it has.[109]

One result of eclectic approaches is the search for Semitisms in Acts, for if either tradition might preserve Lukan material, it was argued that wording which reflected a Semitic style or source was likely to be more primitive. A key study is that of Black, a book that went through three editions over twenty-one years, in which he identifies Semitic turns of phrase in Western witnesses in places.[110] He thus argues that at these points the Western tradition is closer to the original than the Alexandrian. Wilcox takes Black's work further and applies it more fully to Acts, arguing for similar conclusions.[111]

(4) Studying the texts in their own right. Parker is a primary advocate of this approach, rejecting the view that there are two distinct and identifiable textual streams. He detects in D not one major editing process but "stages of growth."[112] Similarly, his work with Pickering on 𝔓^{127} identifies this manuscript's text as at times closer to B and at times closer to D/d. Thus, Parker sees the text of D as not the work of one mind but as reflecting the developing beliefs of

104 Head, "Acts," esp. 429–42, and see below for more detail.
105 *BegC*, vols. 4–5.
106 E.g., Kilpatrick, "Eclectic Study," 69–70.
107 *TCGNT*², 235–56.
108 For a brief statement of Elliott's approach, see *Essays*, 17–43.
109 Elliott, "Text of Acts."
110 *Aramaic*, summary: 277–80.
111 *Semitisms*.
112 Parker, *Introduction*, 298.

groups of believers. Hence, with Epp and Witherington, he sees anti-Jewish tendencies, a greater focus on the Spirit's work, stronger interest in one of more apostles, and a tendency to limit the contribution of women.[113] That said, Parker considers the text of the Alexandrian witnesses, particularly ℵ and B, to be a more primitive form, while accepting that the Alexandrian texts can err.[114] He thus wishes to study the text forms of manuscripts as witnesses to how early believers read and interpreted Acts.[115]

Key Questions

Several factors combined support the NA$^{27/28}$/UBS$^{4/5}$ editors' decision to treat the Alexandrian tradition as older, and the Western as representing various states of revision of this older text.[116]

First, there is christological expansion. Titles of Jesus are frequently added or expanded, in adding χριστός (e.g., 1:21; 4:33; 8:16; 11:20; 15:11; 16:31; 19:5; 21:13) or κύριος (e.g., 2:38; 5:42; 7:55; 10:48; 18:5) or both (13:33). The Ethiopian eunuch's confession of faith underlines a high view of Jesus: πιστεύω τὸν υἱὸν τοῦ θεοῦ εἶναι τὸν Ἰησοῦν Χριστόν, "I believe the son of God to be Jesus the Messiah" (8:37).[117]

Secondly, a number of Western readings give local color and details, e.g., the eunuch's declaration of faith (8:37), the introduction of the negative version of the Golden Rule in the apostolic decree (15:20, 29), the use of details found in later accounts of Paul's Damascus Road experience (9:4–6; 22:10; 26:14),[118] the "seven steps" (12:10), specification of the hours of work in the school of Tyrannus (19:9), details of Paul's journey to Jerusalem (21:16), and identifying Paul's guard as τῷ στρατοπεδάρχῳ, "the captain of the guard" (28:16).[119] It would be difficult to explain a later scribe deleting such details if they were originally present.

Thirdly, Western readings frequently smooth transitions in the text, such as[120] the move from the temple into Solomon's Portico (3:11), Cornelius's slave announcing Peter's arrival prior to Peter's meeting Cornelius (10:25), a statement that Paul and Barnabas stay in Lystra, providing clarification of location after a prior statement that they went on to Lystra and Derbe (14:6–7), explanation of the otherwise abrupt appearance of Jewish opponents in Lystra

---

113 Parker, *Introduction*, 299; Epp, *Tendency*; Witherington, "Anti-feminist Tendencies," 82–84.

114 Parker, *Introduction*, 298.

115 Parker, *Introduction*, 301; so also Witherington, "Anti-feminist Tendencies," 83–84.

116 See Head, "Acts," 429–42, for much of what follows.

117 Head, "Acts," 433–34, provides details, compares other baptismal expansions in D and other Western witnesses (2:41; 18:8; 19:5), and rightly critiques Strange's view that 8:37 was removed to hide Christian initiation rites—if so, the Western expansions at other baptisms are surprising; Strange, *Problem*, 69–70.

118 *TCGNT*², 317–18.

119 Kenyon, "Western Text," 310–11.

120 Dibelius, *Studies*, 85–87. See the relevant discussions in *TCGNT*² in each case.

(14:18–19), clarification that the earthquake in Philippi causes the magistrates' change of mind about releasing Paul and Silas (16:35), and the statement that Paul was saying farewell as he returned Eutychus alive to the Troas believers, smoothing the transition to Paul's departure (20:12). As with the local-color examples, it is hard to understand why a later scribe might remove such details and easy to see why they might be introduced to clarify the flow of the story.

Fourthly, there are a number of further references to the Holy Spirit or clarifications (6:10; 11:17; 15:7, 29, 32; 19:1; 20:3). These emphasize the Spirit's empowerment of believers[121] and develop a Lukan theme.[122]

Fifthly, the authority and power of the apostles is more marked in a number of Western readings, notably 5:15; 6:10–11; 9:22; 13:8, 43; 14:7; 16:4.[123] Nevertheless, these readings do not go as far as the later apocryphal Acts in, for example, refuting Gnosticism, encouraging martyrdom, or encouraging delay of baptism (see Acts Paul, passim). They thus do not directly address the issues of the second century, although they mark a staging point along the way there.[124]

Finally, the wording of the apostolic decree, in which the negative form of the Golden Rule is twice present in Western witnesses (15:20, 29), again looks like an addition. If originally present, it is difficult to explain why it might be removed, particularly given other Western readings such as 21:25, where Paul is told concerning the gentiles who have believed that the Jewish believers οὐδὲν ἔχουσιν λέγειν πρός σε ἡμεῖς γάρ . . . κρίναντες μηδὲν τοιοῦτον τηρεῖν αὐτοὺς εἰ μή . . . , "have nothing to say against you, for . . . we have given judgment that they should keep nothing of the sort except . . . " The reference is to (not) keeping the Jewish law as a whole, which reflects the Western reading including the negative Golden Rule in 15:29.[125]

This is a strong cumulative case, and in the commentary which follows I shall work with the text edited in NA[28]/UBS[5] as modified in ECM, although without slavishly following those editions where I consider the combination of external and internal evidence points to a different reading. In particular, where the D-cluster offers local color that has reasonable claim to be historical, I shall consider these readings carefully. I shall also take into account the recent THGNT, since this adopts a different method in arriving at the text, drawing particularly on our oldest extant manuscripts (all papyri, majuscules prior to the fifth century, and a selection of eleven further majuscules and two minuscules that provide important later support or variations).[126]

121 See Black, "Spirit," observing that in these passages the Spirit inspires speech, directs the believers, or is related to baptism.

122 See Turner, *Power.*

123 For details, see Head, "Acts," 436–37.

124 Head, "Acts"; with Strange, *Problem,* 55.

125 Head, "Acts," 441–42.

126 See Jongkind, *Introduction,* for the manuscripts used and the principles adopted.

The Roman World in the Times of Acts

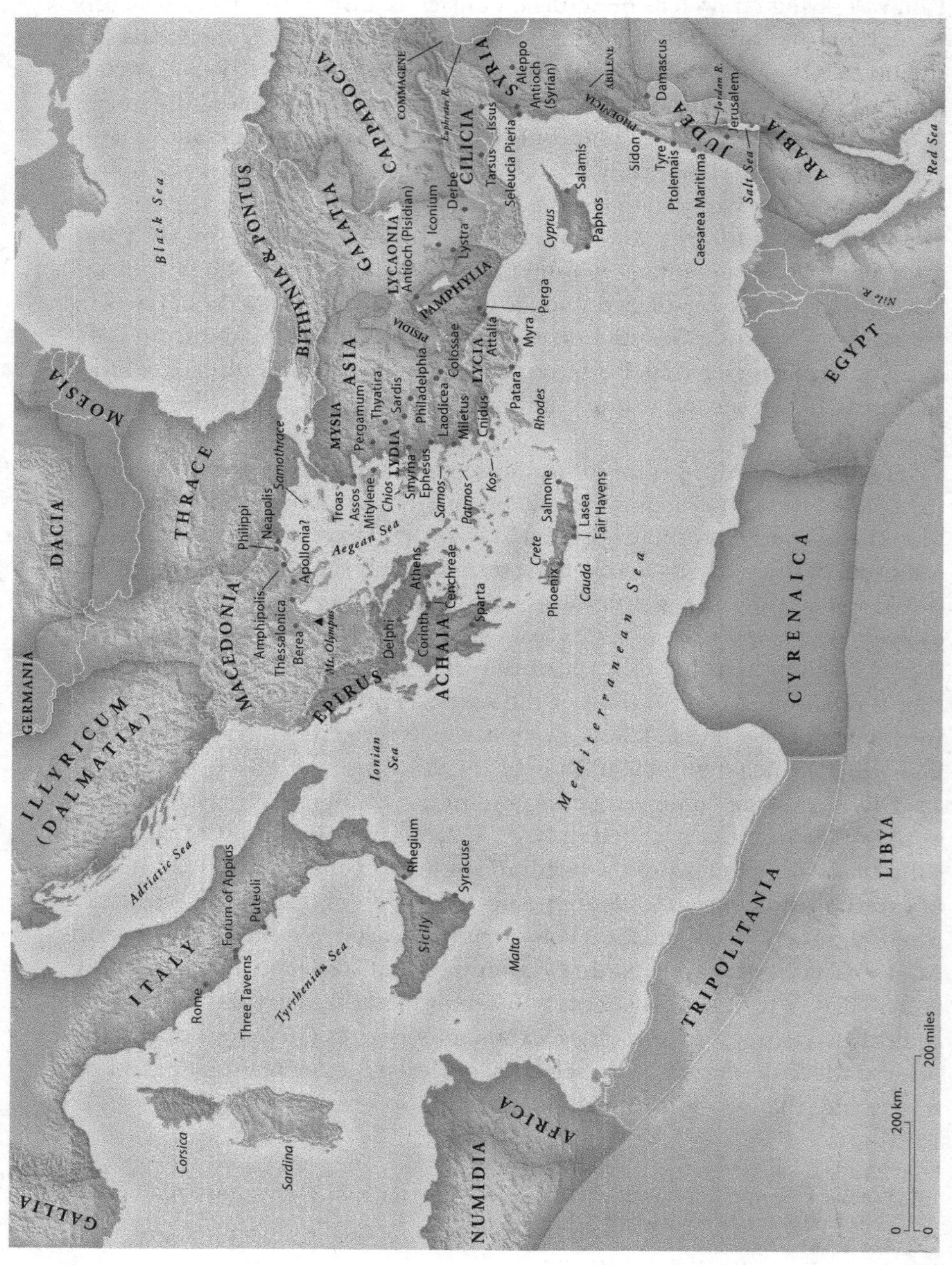

I. Beginning at the Beginnings (1–2)

A. Superscription (1:1–2)

Bibliography

Agnew, F. H. "Origin." **Alexander, L. C. A.** "Ancient Book." ———. *Preface.* ———. "Preface to Acts." **Barrett, C. K.** "*Shaliah.*" **Brown, S.** "Role." **Cadbury, H. J.** "Commentary," *BegC,* 2:488–510. **Callan, T.** "Preface." **Clark, A. C.** "Role." **Creamer, J. M., A. B. Spencer and F. P. Viljoen.** "Who." **Creed, J. M.** "Text." **de Jonge, H. J.** "Chronology." **Dunn, J. D. G.** *Beginning,* 138–45. **Dupont, J.** "ἈΝΕΛΗΜΦΘΗ." **Epp, E. J.** "Ascension." **Fresch, C. J.** "Is There." **Garrison, R.** *Significance.* **Gaventa, B. R.** "Acts." **Goodspeed, E. J.** "Some Greek Notes." **Higbie, C.** "Divide." **Kilgallen, J. J.** "'Apostles." **Kim, K.-J.** *Stewardship,* 37–44. **Kirk, J. A.** "Apostleship." **Lake, K.** "Preface." **Marshall, I. H.** "Former." **Meier, J. P.** "Circle." **Palmer, D. W.** "Literary Background." **Parsons, M. C.** "Text." **Pfitzner, V. C.** "Pneumatic Apostleship." **Robbins, V. K.** "Prefaces." **Rosner, B. S.** "Acts." **Sleeman, M.** *Geography.* **Sterling, G. E.** *Historiography,* 325–63. **Turner, M.** *Power,* 335–37. **van Stempvoort, P. A.** "Interpretation." **Walton, S.** "Biblical History." **Zwiep, A. W.** "Text."

Translation

1 In the first book, Theophilus, I wrote[a] about everything which Jesus[b] began both[c] to do and to teach, 2 until the day when[d] he was taken up[e] after giving instructions, through the Holy Spirit,[f] to the apostles[g] whom he had chosen.

Notes

a. ἐποιησάμην is loosely rendered "wrote"; more precisely it means "produced" ("ποιέω," BDAG 839, §1.a) or "composed" (*EDNT* 3:124); cf. Isocrates, *Ep.* 2.2; "ποιέω," BDAG 840, §7.a.

b. B D (alone) omit ὁ before Ἰησοῦς. Attic usage allows that the definite article be omitted for the first use in the book, and this may explain that omission. However, the article may be anaphoric, referring back to the Jesus introduced in Luke's Gospel, and this, with the weight of MSS supporting its presence, suggests the article is original; with *TCGNT*², 236, contra Clark, *Acts,* 2; WH.

c. The enclitic particle τέ is widely used in Acts (151 of 215 NT uses); see Levinsohn, *Connections,* 121–36.

d. ἄχρι ἧς ἡμέρας, "until the day when," is gen. by rel. attraction (Wallace, 338–39); the phrase in full would be τῆς ἡμέρας ἐν ᾗ, "the day upon which" (Bruce, *Acts* [1990], 98), although Bruce wrongly has a smooth breathing on the dat. rel. pn.; cf. 7:18.

e. D it$^{gig, t}$ syr^{hmg} Augustine Varimadum place ἀνελήμφθη, "he was taken up" (or its Latin equivalent), immediately after ἡμέρας, "day," whereas other MSS place ἀνελήμφθη at the end of the sentence; they also have καὶ ἐκέλευσεν κηρύσσειν τὸ εὐαγγέλιον, "and he commanded [them] to preach the gospel," at the end of the sentence. (See the helpful table of other minor variants in Parsons, "Text," 63.) The presence of the latter phrase should be understood as a scribe seeking to clarify the content of the instructions given earlier in the verse (ἐντειλάμενος, "after giving instructions") and thus is likely to be secondary. Clark and Ropes's proposal, that the Old Latin provides a route to a conjectural emendation that excludes ἀνελήμφθη (*BegC*, 3:256–61), predates the discovery of $\mathfrak{P}^{75}$ in 1961, a MS which has the majority reading. See *TCGNT*², 236–41 (thorough discussion); Zwiep, "Text", 234–38; Parsons, "Text"; Creed, "Text"; contra Lake, *BegC*, 5:1–3; Clark, *Acts*, 336–37.

f. This slightly awkward English word order clarifies that διὰ πνεύματος ἁγίου, "through the Holy Spirit," is to be taken with ἐντειλάμενος, "having commanded."

g. ἐντέλλομαι, "give instructions to," takes dat. of the one(s) being instructed, here τοῖς ἀποστόλοις, "the apostles," ("ἐντέλλω," BDAG 339).

Form/Structure/Setting

Form. Luke here sets the scene for his book by linking this book back to his previous book, Luke's Gospel, very briefly summarising the Gospel's contents and directing the reader's attention to what is to come, which is, by implication, what Jesus *continued* to do and to teach (see *Comment*). These two verses thus introduce the whole book, rather than merely setting the scene for Acts 1:3–11 or vv. 3–26.[1]

These two verses recapitulate Luke's previous book in the manner of other ancient authors, most commonly in the "scientific" authors who wrote technical treatises,[2] but also in some historians.[3] In particular, Josephus, *Ag. Ap.* 2.1–2, forms an interesting parallel to Acts 1:1–2, including reference to and summary of a previous book, vocative address to a dedicatee, and outline of what is to follow (the latter is explicit in Josephus, implicit in Acts):

> In the first volume of this work (Διὰ μὲν οὖν τοῦ προτέρου βιβλίου), my most esteemed Epaphroditus (τιμιώτατε . . . Ἐπαφρόδιτε), I demonstrated the antiquity of our race, corroborating my statements by the writings of Phoenicians, Chaldaeans, and Egyptians, besides citing as witnesses numerous Greek historians; I also challenged the statements of Manetho, Chaeremon, and some others. I shall now proceed to refute the rest of the authors who have attacked us. (Thackeray, LCL)

It is sometimes claimed that the elements in the prefaces of Acts and the Gospel point to (Luke-)Acts being an historical work in the tradition of Greco-Roman historiography.[4] However, Alexander argues cogently that the features of authorial first person, dedication, recapitulation, (lack of) mention of subject matter, and (abrupt) transition into narrative are not distinctive

1 With Fitzmyer, *Acts*, 191.
2 Alexander, *Preface*, 143–44, for discussion and references; cf. Palmer, "Literary Background," 427.
3 Alexander, "Preface to Acts," 84.
4 See Callan, "Preface," who focuses on the Gospel preface; Witherington, *Acts*, 11.

features of a preface to a historical work in antiquity.[5] This is not to say that Acts is not an historical work but simply to say that the preface alone does not demonstrate that it is in the style of Greco-Roman historiography. Rosner thus takes a broader view of the language, themes, models, literary techniques, and theological understanding of history in the *whole* book in arguing that Acts is modelled on biblical history and that Luke is seeking to place the Acts story in continuity with the salvation history told in Scripture.[6]

Structure/Setting. Verses 1–2 present a series of elements setting the scene for Acts: (i) reference back to Luke's first book (v. 1a), (ii) dedication (v. 1b), (iii) recapitulation of the contents of the first book (v. 1c), and (iv) delimitation of the first book (v. 2). There is then a rather abrupt transition into the narrative, which reviews and elucidates material from Luke 24 (vv. 3–8).[7]

Parsons argues that the sequence of 1:1–3 should be seen as follows:[8]

v. 1	A	Jesus acts (ποιεῖν)
		B Jesus teaches (διδάσκειν)
v. 2		B Jesus teaches (ἐντειλάμενος)
	A	Jesus acts (ἀνελήμφθη)
v. 3	A	Jesus acts (παρέστησεν . . . ὀπτανόμενος)
		B Jesus teaches (λέγων τὰ περὶ τῆς βασιλείας τοῦ θεοῦ)

However, this misunderstands the relationship between vv. 1–2 and 3–11, as well as marginalizing much of the contents of these verses. Rather, as well as setting the scene for what immediately follow, vv. 1–2 function as the introduction, summarizing the contents of the Gospel and preparing the reader for the period now to be described in Acts.

Comment

1 μέν (untranslated) in combination with the fronted Τὸν . . . πρῶτον λόγον, "the first book," identifies the focus of this clause as Luke's previous book and implies an (unstated) contrast with "in the second book."[9] μέν frequently has an answering δέ, and some consider the solitary use of μέν an anacoluthon.[10] Alexander notes that Luke's use here is not generally found in scientific prefaces (although she notes a partial parallel in Vettius Valens, p. 294 line

5 Alexander, "Preface to Acts."

6 Rosner, "Acts"; similarly, Walton, "Biblical History"; Sterling, *Historiography*, 325–63.

7 With Alexander, "Preface to Acts," 94–95; contra Witherington, *Acts*, 106.

8 Parsons, "Text," 68–69.

9 Levinsohn, *Connections*, 26–27.

10 Alexander, *Preface*, 143. If so, the corresponding clause δεύτερον (δέ) λόγον, "second book," is implied, referring to the present work; Robertson, 1152. I owe this suggestion to Chris Fresch: see his article Fresch, "Is There," esp. 272n38.

4, and cites other examples of anacoluthon[11]), and that μέν without δέ is not uncommon in the NT (e.g., Acts 21:39; 27:21; cf. Rom 1:8).[12]

Τὸν . . . πρῶτον λόγον, "the . . . first book," signals that this book is the continuation of the story begun in the Gospel, and Luke will go on to repeat the closing scene of the Gospel (Luke 22:24–53; Acts 1:6–11). Thus, to read Acts necessitates taking account of Luke's Gospel: Acts is not a "closed," independent narrative, for there are people, ideas, and major themes from the Gospel which are presupposed in Acts.

The superlative form πρῶτον, "first," is used, as often in Koine, for the earlier comparative form πρότερος, "previous."[13] Thus it need not have the sense "first" of a series of more than two and imply a third volume in view.[14]

λόγον here is "book" or "treatise," which extends the senses of λόγος found in earlier writers such as "tale, narrative" (e.g., Herodotus, Hist. 5.36 ὁ πρῶτος λόγος = "the earlier part of my tale"), "discussion, debate" (e.g., Aristotle, *Pol.* 1264b39), and hence it can be used of a section of a dialogue or treatise.[15] The medical writer Galen (second century AD) uses λόγος to mean βιβλίον, "book," and that is the sense here—it is the book containing Luke's narrative;[16] cf. uses in 2:22, 40, of the "words" of Peter's speech and his "arguments," "message."[17]

ἐποιησάμην, "I wrote." Here is Luke's authorial fingerprint in the first-person singular. Some ancient historians use first-person (singular or plural) in their prefaces,[18] but it is far from universal—historians often write of themselves in the third person.[19] Thus we cannot conclude from the first-person verb alone that this is an historical writing.

Luke does not mention any literary predecessors to this volume, by contrast with his Gospel (Luke 1:1), which perhaps suggests that Luke was the first to write a "church history" that followed on from the life and ministry of Jesus.[20]

ὦ Θεόφιλε, "Theophilus." Luke's use of the vocative with ὦ, "O," in Acts is similar to that found in classical authors and signifies the normal polite form of address.[21] In classical usage, the vocative with ὦ is usually located in mid-sentence, rather than at the beginning, and thus lacks emphasis (cf. Acts

---

11 Alexander, *Preface,* 143n46.
12 Alexander, *Preface,* 143, 144.
13 Bruce, *Acts* (1990), 97; Alexander, *Preface,* 144.
14 Alexander, *Preface,* 145.
15 Alexander, *Preface,* 144–45.
16 Alexander, *Preface,* 145; cf. "λόγος," BDAG 600, §1.b; "λόγος," LSJ. Higbie, "Divide," 16–24 gives a number of examples of λόγος meaning "book," and the whole article helpfully discusses ancient authors' and editors' practice in dividing a work into books.
17 See the useful summary of ancient book production in Shulam and Le Cornu, *Acts,* 1:4–5.
18 Herodotus, *Hist.* 1.1; Thucydides 1.3.1–2; 1.22.1–2; 5.26.4–6; Polybius 6.2.1–7; 9.1.1–2.7; 9.1.1–5; Diodorus Siculus 1.3.1, 5; 1.4.1–53; 1.42.2; 2.1.2–3; 3.1.3—the latter two are resumptive prefaces akin to Acts 1:1–2.
19 E.g., Thucydides 1.1.1; 5.26.1; Diodorus Siculus 2.1.1; 3.1.1–2; see Alexander, "Preface to Acts," 85, to whom I owe most references to the historians.
20 Witherington, *Acts,* 9.
21 Wallace, 69; BDF, §146; Barrett, *Acts,* 1:65; Alexander, *Preface,* 132.

18:14; 27:21). Luke's use of the articular vocative in Acts contrasts with other NT books (including Luke's Gospel), which follow Hellenistic usage whereby the articular vocative is emphatic and used in contexts where significant emotion is present (e.g., Matt 15:28). Contrast Acts 13:10 and κράτιστε Θεόφιλε, "most excellent Theophilus" (Luke 1:3), there with the common post-classical lack of ὦ.

The name Θεόφιλος, "Theophilus," was not Roman but Greek in origin and was commonly used by hellenized Jews.[22] It means "lover of God" or "loved by God" and Bede plays on this meaning: "Theophilus means 'lover of God' or 'beloved of God'. Therefore, anyone who is a lover of God may therefore believe that this [work] was written for him."[23] The presence of κράτιστε, "most excellent," with the name in Luke 1:3 suggests that the name corresponds to a real, historical individual rather than being a cipher for a God-loving (or God-loved) reader.[24] Further, ancient dedications (which are relatively rare in historical writers) commonly name the addressee of the book, and the dedicatees very rarely appear to be fictional.[25]

In the preface to the Gospel, Luke has addressed Theophilus as "most excellent," κράτιστε, a form of address used elsewhere in Acts only for the governors Felix (Acts 23:26; 24:3) and Festus (26:25), and so a reader of Acts might assume that Theophilus had similar social standing.[26] While the term "most excellent" was applied to those of equestrian rank in some periods and contexts, it had wider use to those holding public office.[27] We thus cannot be sure whether Theophilus was Luke's social superior, although this is a strong possibility. If Theophilus did have such social standing, it is unlikely that he was Jewish,[28] and it is reasonable to see him as providing some form of patronage for an assembly of Jesus followers, such as by hosting the meetings, or gathering a library of early Christian writings for the community to use, or enabling Luke's work to gain a wider audience.[29] Goodspeed suggests that Theophilus might provide for the publication of the Gospel and Acts,[30] although "publish" would mean something very different in the

22 E.g., *Let. Aris.* 49; *CPJ* 1, No. 21 line 9 (p 157); *NewDocs* 2:58–60 §18; 3:38 §9; other examples: Cadbury, "Commentary," 507; MM 288; Hemer, *Book*, 221n1.

23 Bede, *Acts*, ad. loc.

24 Barrett, *Acts*, 1:66; Kim, *Stewardship*, 37–39.

25 Alexander, *Preface*, 27–29, 188; Creamer, Spencer, and Viljoen, "Who." Garrison, *Significance*, probably goes too far in identifying Theophilus as an outright non-believer who needs persuading that the gospel was not a threat to the Roman Empire: much of Luke-Acts is not germane to such a focused argument, as Barrett, *Luke the Historian*, 63, notes. See also Walton, "State," 2–5.

26 Cf. also Josephus's use of κράτιστος for his patron Epaphroditus, *Life* 76 §430; *Ag. Ap.* 1.1 §1.

27 "κράτιστος," BDAG 565; Cadbury, "Commentary," 505–7; e.g., Josephus uses it for Vitellius, the governor of Syria, *Ant.* 20.1.2 §12; cf. 15.11.4 §405.

28 Creamer, Spencer, and Viljoen, "Who," 3.

29 Alexander, "Ancient Book," 98–99.

30 Goodspeed, "Some Greek Notes," 84.

ancient context than today, being first about oral performance and only secondarily about making physical copies of a work, and so may not be a helpful category to use.[31]

The evidence of the Gospel's preface (Luke 1:1–4, especially v. 4[32]) suggests that Theophilus is not being given an initial introduction to the Christian faith, for it is too imprecise about its subject for a complete outsider. Acts should similarly be considered as addressed to a readership at least open to the Christian faith and, more probably, professing that faith.[33]

πάντων . . . ὧν ἤρξατο ὁ Ἰησοῦς ποιεῖν τε καὶ διδάσκειν, "everything . . . which Jesus began both to do and to teach." Luke here summarizes his previous book and hints at the focus of this second book. The clause's subject, ὁ Ἰησοῦς, "Jesus," is itself the focus of the first book, as Burridge has cogently argued concerning all of the Gospels.[34] In particular, the previous book related both the deeds and teaching of Jesus, for Jesus's significance rests on both: his deeds are interpreted by his teaching, and his teaching is exemplified and carried out in his deeds. διδάσκειν, "to teach," also anticipates the key activities of the apostles and Paul (Acts 4:2, 18; 5:21, 25, 27–28, 41–42; 11:26; 15:35; 18:11; 20:20; 21:21, 28; and note that Acts closes with a reference to Paul teaching about Jesus, 28:31). πάντων, "everything," has the rhetorical force of indicating that the Gospel is sufficient for its purpose, to instruct Theophilus (Luke 1:4).[35]

ἤρξατο, "began," could be Semitic redundancy,[36] or could denote the beginning of Jesus's ministry in the Gospel (taking it to mean "from the beginning," usually based on the claimed parallel usage in Acts 1:22[37]), or could imply that Luke's second volume contains what Jesus *continues* to do and teach by the Spirit.[38] It is noticeable that the exalted Jesus himself continues to act within the ongoing story of Acts; although physically absent, he is powerfully present: Jesus pours out the Spirit (2:33), Jesus appears to Saul (9:5) and tells Saul that it is Jesus he has been persecuting (9:4), Jesus orchestrates events in Damascus (9:10–19a), Jesus heals (9:34), Jesus appears to Paul in the temple (22:17–18), and Jesus himself is active in announcing light to Israel and the gentiles (26:23).[39] Certainly Luke considers that Jesus acts through the Spirit (v. 2), but Acts goes further than that in presenting the exalted Jesus *himself* acting from heaven.[40] Thus it is likely that ἤρξατο has its full force of "began"

31 Alexander, "Ancient Book," 86–87; Alexander, *Preface*, 193–94.

32 Nolland, *Luke*, 1:11; Alexander, *Preface*, ch. 6, esp. 139, 141–42; Creamer, Spencer, and Viljoen, "Who," 3–4.

33 Kim, *Stewardship*, 39–41.

34 Burridge, *What*, 3rd ed.

35 Marguerat, *Actes*, 1:37.

36 *BegC*, 4:3; Witherington, *Acts*, 10.

37 So, Conzelmann, *Acts*, 3; Fitzmyer, *Acts*, 195; Marguerat, *Actes*, 1:37n7.

38 Barrett, *Acts*, 1:66–67.

39 See Gaventa, "Acts," esp. 43.

40 See Sleeman, *Geography*; summaries: 77–81, 256–58.

here, implying that Acts will be the story of how Jesus continues to act, both in person from heaven and through his varied agents.

2 Luke enumerates four key themes he will develop in the retelling of the ascension story which follows: (i) Jesus's command to witness to him, (ii) the role of the apostles, (iii) the Holy Spirit, and (iv) Jesus's ascension and exaltation.[41]

ἄχρι ἧς ἡμέρας . . . ἀνελήμφθη, "until the day when . . . he was taken up," is the core of this clause, wrapped around a subclause, producing somewhat awkward syntax. The passive verb ἀνελήμφθη, "he was taken up," indicates that Jesus did not take himself up but suggests that he was taken up by God. Peter's Pentecost speech will draw the implications that God has vindicated Jesus and exalted him to the place of rule (2:32–36). Van Stempvoort argues that ἀνελήμφθη should be seen as having the sense "pass away, be removed from this world," noting the usage of the noun ἀνάλημψις in this sense.[42] He therefore argues that ἀνελήμφθη does not refer to the ascension here, by contrast with v. 11. Delling takes the reference here as to the ascension, while seeing the reference in Luke 9:51 to the death of Jesus but adding, "[p]ossibly it also refers to the taking up, or taking back to God which begins with death and which is completed with the Lucan ascension."[43] The context, including the ending of Luke (24:51, *si vera lectio*[44]) and 1:9–11, speak of the ascension, the latter using this verb, which means that a technical sense of "ascend" is appropriate (cf. ἀνελήμφθη ἐν δόξῃ, "he was taken up in glory," 1 Tim 3:16). ἀναλαμβάνω is also used in the LXX for the departures of Elijah (e.g., 2 Kgs 2:9, 10, 11; 1 Macc 2:58 "Elijah, because of great zeal for the law, was taken up into heaven [ἀνελήμφθη εἰς τὸν οὐρανόν]"; Sir 48:9 "the one who was taken up [ὁ ἀναλημφθείς] in a whirlwind of fire") and Enoch (Sir 49:14 "No one was created upon the earth of such a kind as Enoch, for he was taken up from the earth [αὐτὸς ἀνελήμφθη ἀπὸ τῆς γῆς]"). The key Lukan parallel is Acts 1:22, ἕως τῆς ἡμέρας ἧς ἀνελήμφθη ἀφ ἡμῶν, "until the day when he was taken up from us," which corresponds very closely to this verse: "it is difficult to understand the same words in 1:2 and 1:22 differently."[45]

In both vv. 2 and 22 it is a singular "day" which is mentioned, and Parsons claims that Luke can use the singular "day" to describe a whole process.[46] He cites Luke 1:20 in support, where the angel tells Zechariah that he will be silent ἄχρι ἧς ἡμέρας γένηται ταῦτα, "until the day that these things are come

41 With Longenecker, "Acts," 49.

42 van Stempvoort, "Interpretation," 32–33. "ἀνάλημψις," BDAG 67, cites *Pss. Sol.* 4:18, *Ps.-Clem.* 3:47, and a Christian inscription from Aphrodisias; to these van Stempvoort adds other references, notably Luke 9:51.

43 *TDNT* 4:8–9, quoting 9; cf. Dupont, "ἈΝΕΛΗΜΦΘΗ," 156; Fitzmyer, *Luke,* 1:828; Marshall, *Gospel of Luke,* 405; Parsons, "Text," 70.

44 For an argument that it was in the original text of Luke, see Williams, "Where Two," 255–56.

45 Dupont, "ἈΝΕΛΗΜΦΘΗ," 156 (my translation).

46 Parsons, "Text," 68.

to pass," and 1:57–64, indicating that the fulfillment of the angel's word in the birth and naming of John took some eight days, and thus argues that the singular nature of ἡμέρας, "day," here is inconclusive. However, it seems more natural to understand the singular ἡμέρας, "day," in v. 22 here as indicating a particular day—and thus that the usage in v. 2 denotes a particular day.[47]

ἐντειλάμενος . . . διὰ πνεύματος ἁγίου, "after giving instructions . . . through the Holy Spirit." διὰ πνεύματος ἁγίου belongs with the participle ἐντειλάμενος, "after giving instructions," rather than ἐξελέξατο, "he had chosen," so that Luke emphasizes that Jesus taught by the Spirit's enabling (cf. Luke 3:21–22; 4:14, 18) and specifically that Jesus's call to witness was connected with the Spirit (Luke 24:48–49; Acts 1:8). As well as the latter point, this is probable because of (i) the location of the prepositional phrase before the relative pronoun οὕς, "whom," and (ii) the parallel in Luke 6:13, which does not mention the Spirit in connection with Jesus's choice of the Twelve.[48] Which instructions does Luke mean here? He certainly includes the specific instruction to wait in the city for power from on high (Luke 24:44–49; Acts 1:4–5).[49] He probably also includes the instructions given by Jesus during his post-resurrection ministry (1:3). It may also be that Luke is here signaling that the apostles experienced Jesus's Spirit-enabled teaching during his whole ministry from his baptism onwards.[50]

διά, "through," + genitive πνεύματος ἁγίου, "the Holy Spirit," denotes agency or means, portraying Jesus's post-resurrection instructions to the apostles as in continuity with his pre-resurrection, Spirit-empowered teaching ministry (note again Luke 3:21–11; 4:14, 18), contra Kilgallen, who argues that διά + genitive here should be understood as causal, "because of."[51] However, although this use is known, it is rare[52] and otherwise unknown for Luke. "[T]o come under the influence of a man's charismatically empowered teaching is to open oneself up to the spiritual power that expresses itself therein"[53]—Jesus's Spirit-enabled teaching equips the apostles for their future ministry in his name. Dunn suggests there is also a hint that during the forty days Jesus is not yet exalted to the place from whence he can give the Spirit (Acts 2:33).[54]

τοῖς ἀποστόλοις . . . οὓς ἐξελέξατο, "to the apostles . . . whom he had chosen," highlights the group who form the heart of the renewed Israel which

---

47 Fitzmyer, *Acts*, 196. de Jonge, "Chronology," argues, against the mainstream of scholarship, that this phrase locates Jesus's ascension on the day of his resurrection, claiming that this is also seen in Luke 24:51–53, and thus that the forty days of appearances (1:3) follow Jesus's ascension rather than precede it.

48 With NRSVue, NIV; Culy and Parsons, *Acts*, 3; Barrett, *Acts*, 1:69; Turner, *Power*, 335n47; contra Marshall, *Acts* (TNTC), 57n1; Haenchen, *Acts*, 139; Kilgallen, "Apostles."

49 Pfitzner, "Pneumatic Apostleship," 215.

50 Turner, *Power*, 337.

51 Kilgallen, "Apostles."

52 "διά," BDAG 225, §A.5, lists only Rom 8:3; 2 Cor 9:13 as NT examples.

53 Turner, *Power*, 336.

54 Dunn, *Beginning*, 143n46.

Jesus is bringing into being. ἐξελέξατο (ἐκλέγομαι) is a Lukan favorite (eleven of twenty-two NT uses are in Luke-Acts); the verb is found only in the middle voice in the NT, a voice which suggests that Jesus chose them for himself.[55] Luke tells the story of their choice in his Gospel (Luke 6:12–16) as following a night of prayer by Jesus—a unique period of prolonged prayer by Jesus in Luke—a model which becomes normative for later choices for particular roles in the believing community (Acts 1:24; 6:6; 13:2–3; 14:23). This group are Jesus's provision for continuity between his pre- and post-ascension ministry.[56]

ἀπόστολος, "apostle," is used frequently by Luke (6x in Luke; 28x in Acts; contrast once each in Matt, Mark and John).[57] Its first use in Luke (Luke 6:13) identifies the Twelve as apostles, and Jesus identifies these twelve as those who will judge the twelve tribes of Israel (Luke 22:24–30, esp. v. 30), thus underlining that his choice of them is to form the core of his renewed Israel. The choice of twelve in Luke 6:13 prepares for the necessity to add a replacement for Judas (Acts 1:15–26), and apostles are mentioned frequently in Acts 1–16 but not after 16:4. Luke's use is mostly concerning the Twelve (so that the group can be identified simply as οἱ δώδεκα, "the Twelve," 6:2), although Luke's designation of Barnabas and Paul as οἱ ἀπόστολοι, "the apostles" (14:4, 14), shows his knowledge of wider early Christian usage (cf. Paul's insistence that he is an apostle, e.g., Gal 1:1, 17; 1 Cor 9:1–2; 2 Cor 11:12). Early Christian use of the term ἀπόστολος is probably derived from the verb ἀποστέλλω, "send," which is used widely in the Gospels and Acts but is rare in the Greek OT (only 1 Kgs 14:6 LXX [also in α′]; Isa 18:2 σ′). In classical sources, ἀπόστολος could denote a person or thing sent, such as a naval expedition or its commander, an order for dispatch of a vessel, and—much more rarely in pre-Christian usage—an envoy (Herodotus, *Hist.* 1.21) or group of representatives (Josephus, *Ant.* 17.11.1 §300). The NT use echoes this minority of uses. The Christian use of the term may parallel the (later) rabbinic concept of the שָׁלוּחַ (*šālûaḥ*), the "sent one" commissioned to act (and speak) for another (cf. m. Ber. 5:5),[58] or may be a Christian innovation based on the verb ἀποστέλλω.[59] The latter view seems less likely if Jesus himself used an Aramaic equivalent in designating the Twelve, and their sending out by Jesus with power to deliver from demons, to announce the kingdom, and to heal (Luke 9:1–6) implies that they act and speak for him.[60] On the former view, the Christian and

55 "ἐκλέγομαι," BDAG 305.
56 Nolland, *Luke*, 1:270.
57 See valuable discussion in Clark, "Role."
58 Rengstorf, *TDNT* 1:407–45; Barrett, "*Shaliaḥ*," nuances Rengstorf's view; see critical responses in Kirk, "Apostleship"; O. Becker, *NIDNTT* 1:369–74.
59 See useful reviews of scholarship in Agnew, "Origin"; O. Becker, *NIDNTT* 1:365–74.
60 For a cogent defence of the existence of the twelve during Jesus's ministry, see Meier, "Circle."

rabbinic parallel concepts are suggested to be rooted in a common OT/Jewish sending convention, although the rabbinic usage is entirely concerning a human sender, by contrast with the Christian usage where God is frequently (though not always) the sender (e.g., Luke 11:49; 1 Cor 1:1; 12:28; 2 Cor 1:1; Gal 1:1). (On apostleship, see *Comment* on 1:21–22, 26; 2:42; 4:35; 14:4, 14.)

Explanation

Luke sets the scene for his book in these verses by introducing key themes. He links Acts to his Gospel as a "volume two," dedicated to the same Theophilus, probably a man of some social standing who hosted and supported a Jesus-community and who may have a role in making Luke's writings known. The Gospel focused on Jesus's acts and teaching. What has changed is that Jesus is no longer present on earth, for he has been "taken up" to his place in heaven at God's right hand (Acts 1:2, 11; 2:33). Acts will focus throughout on what Jesus does and teaches, both in his own person from heaven and through his agents the Spirit and the Spirit-taught (and soon to be Spirit-empowered) apostles (note that the book ends with Paul "teaching about the Lord Jesus Christ," 28:31). Luke will next explain the instructions given to the apostles and present Jesus speaking of the Spirit's enabling power for them (1:3–8) before being taken up to heaven (1:9–11), so as well as introducing the whole of Acts, these verses prepare for the immediately following paragraphs.

B. Jesus Ascends to Heaven (1:3–11)

Bibliography

Alexander, L. C. A. *Context.* ———. "Reading." **Anderson, K. L.** *But God,* 6–10, 41–47. **Bauckham, R.** "James." ———. "Restoration." **Beers, H.** *Followers,* 131–33. **Biguzzi, G.** "Witnessing." **Bolt, P.** "Mission." **Bowen, C. R.** "Meaning." **Buckwalter, D.** *Character,* 173–92. **Buzzard, A.** "Acts 1:6." **Carroll, J. T.** *Response,* 123–28. **Chance, J. B.** *Jerusalem.* **Conzelmann, H.** *Theology.* **Davies, J. G.** *He Ascended,* 27–58. ———. "Prefigurement." **de Jonge, H. J.** "Chronology." **de la Potterie, I., SJ.** "Les deux noms." **Dean-Otting, M.** *Heavenly Journeys.* **del Agua, A.** "Evangelization." **Dillon, R. J.** *Eye-witnesses.* **Đỗ, M. Y. T.** *Lucan Journey,* esp. 135–75. **Donne, B. K.** *Christ Ascended.* **Dunn, J. D. G.** "Ascension of Jesus." ———. *Baptism,* 38–54. ———. "'Baptized' as Metaphor." ———. *Beginning.* 138–49. **Eisen, U. E.** *Poetik,* 146–57. **Elliott, J. K.** "Jerusalem." **Ellis, E. E.** "End." **Estrada, N. P.** *Followers,* 46–102. **Farrow, D.** *Ascension and Ecclesia,* 15–40. **Fitzmyer, J. A.** "Ascension." **Franklin, E.** "Ascension and Eschatology." ———. *Christ,* 29–41. **Gaventa, B. R.** "Acts." **Goulder, M. D.** *Type,* 146–49. **Green, J. B.** "He Ascended." ———. "What You See." **Harris, M. J.** *Raised Immortal,* 86–94. **Hastings, A.** *Prophet.* **Houlden, L.** "Beyond Belief." **Johnson, A.** "Resurrection." **Johnson, D. E.** "Jesus." **Kurz, W. S.** *Reading,* 74–76. **Leaney, A. R. C.** "Why." **Lewis, C. S.** *Miracles,* ch. 16. **Lohfink, G.** *Himmelfahrt.* **Longenecker, B. W.** *Rhetoric,* 166–70. **Maddox, R.** *Purpose,* 106–8. **Maile, J. F.** "Ascension." **Mallen, P.** *Reading,* 78–93. **Marshall, I. H.** "Meaning". **Maston, J.** "How Wrong." **Mealand, D. L.** "Phrase." **Melbourne, B. L.** "Acts 1:8." **Menzies, R. P.** *Empowered,* 128–31, 168–72. **Metzger, B. M.** *Studies,* 77–87. **Moore, T. S.** "To the End." **Moule, C. F. D.** "Ascension." **Myllykowski, M.** "Being," 162–64. **Newbigin, L.** "Witness." **O'Toole, R. F.** "Kingdom." ———. "Luke's Understanding." **Oulton, J. E. L.** "Spirit." **Pao, D. W.** *Acts,* 91–96. **Parsons, M. C.** *Departure,* esp. 115–99. **Pilch, J. J.** *Visions,* 14–22. **Platner, S. B. and T. Ashby.** *Dictionary,* 342. **Porter, S. E.** "Unity." **Poythress, V. S.** "Translating." **Rengstorf, K. H.** "Election." **Romm, J. S.** *Edges.* **Rosen, A. P.** "Ascension." **Rosner, B. S.** "Progress," 217–19. **Sanders, E. P.** *Jesus.* **Schnabel, E. J.** *Mission,* 1:371–76. **Schnackenburg, R.** "Eschatologie," esp. 252–56. **Scott, J. M.** *Geography,* 56–62. **Sleeman, M.** *Geography,* 64–81. **Smit, P.-B.** "Negotiating." **Strange, W. A.** *Problem,* 113–15. **Strauss, D. F.** *Life,* 745–56. **Strelan, R.** *Strange,* 33–49. **Talbert, C. H.** *Patterns,* 112–16. **Thornton, T. C. G.** "To The End." **Tiede, D. L.** "Exaltation." **Torrance, T. F.** *Space,* 106–93. **Torrey, C. C.** *Composition,* 23–24. **Trites, A. A.** *Concept,* 128–53. ———. "Importance." **Turner, M.** *Power,* esp. 294–303. **van Stempvoort, P. A.** "Interpretation." **van Unnik, W. C.** *Sparsa,* 1:386–401. **Wainwright, A. W.** "Luke." **Walker, P. W. L.** *Jesus.* **Wallace, J. B.** "Benefactor." **Walton, S.** "Heavens." ———. "Jesus's Ascension." ———. "State," esp. 64–71. ———. "Tale," esp. 144–48. **Wilcox, M.** *Semitisms,* 106–9. **Wilson, S. G.** *Gentiles,* 78–107. **Wright, N. T.** *Jesus.* ———. *New Heavens.* ———. *New Testament.* ———. *Resurrection.* **Zehnle, R. F.** *Discourse,* 95–104. **Zwiep, A. W.** *Ascension.* ———. *Judas.*

Translation

3 After he had suffered,[a] he also presented himself to them[b] alive by many convincing proofs, by appearing to them during forty days and speaking about matters

concerning the kingdom of God. 4 While eating with them,[c] he commanded them not to leave[d] Jerusalem but to wait for the promise of the Father, "which[e] you heard from me, 5 for John baptized with water, but you shall be baptized with [the] Holy Spirit before many days are past." 6 In consequence, those who had gathered began asking him, "Lord,[f] are you at this time restoring the kingdom to Israel?" 7 He said to them, "It is not for you to know the times and seasons which the Father has laid down by his own authority, 8 but you shall receive power when the Holy Spirit has come[g] upon you, and you shall be my witnesses not only in Jerusalem but also in all Judea and Samaria and to the end of the earth.

9 After he had said these things, as they were watching,[h] he was lifted up and a cloud took him up, out of their sight.[i] 10 While[j] he was going[k] and they were gazing intently into heaven,[l] suddenly two men in white clothes were standing[m] by them, 11 and they said, "Men of Galilee, why are you standing staring[n] into heaven? This Jesus who has been taken up from you into heaven[o] will come in the same way[p] in which you saw him going into heaven.

Notes

a. μετὰ τὸ παθεῖν αὐτόν, "after he had suffered," prep. + art. inf. (+ acc. "subject" αὐτόν) portraying action prior to main verb παρέστησεν, "he presented."

b. i.e., the apostles; the antecedent of dat. rel. pn. οἷς, "to whom," is τοῖς ἀποστόλοις, "the apostles" (v. 2).

c. συναλίζω occurs only here in NT and LXX. It is singular, which is a little surprising given its sense of "meet together," although it modifies sg. παρήγγειλεν, "he commanded" (Culy and Parsons, *Acts*, 5). συναλίζω is common elsewhere ("συναλίζω," LSJ 1694, §A; "συναλίζω," BDAG 964, §2). Early versions (it vg syr[h, p] arm geo aeth cop) translate it as "eat with" (*TCGNT*^{2}, 241), as does Chrysostom, noting the parallel in 10:41 (*Hom. Act.* I.4). Wilcox, *Semitisms*, 106–9, suggests a Semitic derivation, although it appears to be a natural Greek translation of the key Heb. term לחם (*lḥm*) found in Ps 141:4 (LXX 140:4) (see critique in Emerton, *Semitisms*, 293–94). More likely, its derivation is "eat salt with"; "συναλίζω," LSJ 1694, §B; "συναλίζω," BDAG 964, §1; Torrey, *Composition*, 23–24; Bruce, *Acts* (1990), 101. Metzger claims that this meaning is not extant elsewhere until the second century AD (*TCGNT*^{2}, 242), although note Manetho, *Apotelsmatica* 5.339 (deriving from third century BC). The reading συναυλιζόμενος, "staying with," in the sense "spending the night with," found in a number of minuscules (including 323 614 1241 1739), is more likely to have arisen to clarify the majority reading than the reverse (Barrett, *Acts*, 1:71). See full discussion in Anderson, *But God*, 192–93; Bowen, "Meaning."

d. μὴ χωρίζεσθαι ἀλλὰ περιμένειν, "not to leave but to wait": infs. express the content of the command Jesus gave in indirect speech.

e. Change from indirect to direct speech, as is common in the NT, signaled by 2 pl. verb ἠκούσατε, "you heard"; BDF, §470.2.

f. εἰ introduces a direct question and is thus untranslated; BDF, §440.

g. ἐπελθόντος τοῦ ἁγίου πνεύματος, "when the Holy Spirit has come," gen. abs., unusually *following* the main clause.

h. βλεπόντων αὐτῶν, "as they were watching," temporal gen. abs.

i. Metonymy: ἀπὸ τῶν ὀφθαλμῶν αὐτῶν, "from their eyes"; Culy and Parsons, *Acts*, 9–10. NIV translates well: "before their very eyes."

j. Temporal ὡς, as frequently in Luke-Acts; "ὡς," BDAG 1105, §8.

k. πορευομένου αὐτοῦ, "As he was going," temporal gen. abs.

l. Or perhaps "the sky," here and in v. 11 (thrice).

m. παρειστήκεισαν plpf. ind. act. παρίστημι. Intransitive plpf. of this verb has force of impf.; "παρίστημι," BDAG 778, §2.b.α; "ἵστημι," BDAG 428, §C.1.

n. The witnesses divide fairly evenly between βλέποντες, "looking" (ℵ* B E 33 81 180 218 440 522 614 630 642 945 1245 1642 1704 1739 1831 1875 1884 1891 2298 2495 *al*), and the intensified form ἐμβλέποντες, "looking at, staring" ($\mathfrak{P}^{56}$ ℵ^{c} A C [D ἐνβλέποντες] most minuscules). If ἐμβλέποντες were original, copyists could have changed it to the simple form to conform to βλεπόντων (v. 9) or simply in error; equally, if βλέποντες were original, copyists could have changed it to the compound form for variety in words referring to sight, which are many in this context.

o. εἰς τὸν οὐρανόν, "into heaven," is absent from D 33^{c} 242 326* gig t* some vg and bo MSS and Augustine and Vigilius. Given otherwise strong support for the phrase's presence, and three other undisputed uses in vv. 10–11, it seems more likely that it was omitted in error than that a fourth use was introduced by copyists; *TCGNT*^{2}, 245; Haenchen, *Acts*, 150n8.

p. The rel. pn. ὅν, "which," precedes the noun τρόπον, "way," to which it refers, perhaps suggesting intensity of expression "in the *very same* way"; Culy and Parsons, *Acts*, 11.

Form/Structure/Setting

Delimitation of pericope. Following the preface (vv. 1–2), Luke first relates the activities of the risen Jesus over a forty-day period before his ascension. The forty days form the frame for this section, mentioned in the first sentence (v. 3) and closed by the ascension (vv. 9–11). From here on Jesus will be active from his exalted place in heaven. The return to Jerusalem (v. 12), changing location, is then picked up in v. 13 and thus v. 12 opens a new section.[1]

Sources/historicity. The ascension of Jesus marks the close of the forty-day period of resurrection appearances (v. 3) and vividly shows the risen Jesus entering heaven; εἰς τὸν οὐρανόν, "into heaven," comes three times in vv. 10–11. The account in Luke 24:50–53 appears to be of the same event but with no time frame provided: v. 50 is linked to v. 49 only by the vague δέ, which can be used as a marker of change of temporal setting.[2] There is thus no basis for the categorical assertion that Luke's Gospel presents the departure as happening on the day of Jesus's resurrection in contradiction of Acts.[3] This account contains the same note of Jesus entering heaven (v. 51). Given this strong note in both tellings of the event, the ascension should be seen as Jesus's final exaltation to heaven.

1 With Đỗ, *Journey*, 138.

2 Levinsohn, *Connections*, 87.

3 Davies, *Ascended*, 48–49; Haenchen, *Acts*, 141, among others; for fuller critique, see Harris, *Raised*, 89–91.

The parallels between the two accounts are significant and strongly suggest that these are two accounts of the same event.[4]

	Luke 24	**Acts 1**
Apostles as Jesus's witnesses	v. 48	v. 8b
Witness begins in Jerusalem	v. 47c	v. 8b
Witness to go everywhere	"all nations," v. 47b	"the end of the earth," v. 8b
Jesus's command to stay in Jerusalem	v. 49b	v. 4a
Wait for the Father's promise	v. 49a	v. 4b
Apostles will have power	"clothed," v. 49a	"receive," v. 8b
Jesus ascends	v. 51	v. 9

There are differences, too, notably that the Gospel account lacks the cloud, the disciples' inability to see Jesus as he ascends (v. 9), the appearance of the two men (v. 10), and their message (v. 11); and Acts lacks Jesus's act of blessing (Luke 24:50). Eisen acutely observes, concerning the parallel accounts of Jesus's ascension in vv. 9–11 and Luke 24:50–51: "The essential differences can be explained by the fact that the story of exaltation in the Gospel of Luke has the function of leading the reader or listener out of the story, whereas in the Acts it has the function of taking the reader or listener into the story."[5]

How, then, does Luke see the relationship of Jesus's resurrection, exaltation, and ascension? Anderson lists five positions but notes that three—those we consider below—enjoy greatest scholarly support.[6]

First, Lohfink and others propose that Luke distinguishes the ascension, which is Jesus's exaltation, from his resurrection. Lohfink in particular argues that Luke models the ascension on "rapture" stories (*Entrückung*), such as the departure of Elijah (2 Kgs 2:11–12) and similar Greco-Roman stories.[7] On this view, Luke introduces a new element into early Christian reflection on Jesus, for previous authors (notably Hebrews) regarded resurrection and exaltation as of one piece and had no ascension story.[8]

---

4 The table is based on Estrada, *Followers*, 84–84. For full discussion, see Parsons, *Departure*, esp. 189–98; Porter, "Unity"; Đỗ, *Journey* 142–47.
5 Eisen, *Poetik*, 154 (my translation); so also Parsons, *Departure*, 198.
6 Anderson, *But God*, 41–47; see also the valuable earlier survey of O'Toole, "Understanding."
7 Lohfink, *Himmelfahrt*, 270. Strelan, *Strange Acts*, 42–46, discusses the Greco-Roman sources.
8 Lohfink, *Himmelfahrt*, 80–98.

However, Luke also seems to link Jesus's resurrection to exaltation, notably in Luke 24:26; Acts 2:30–31; 13:33, where kingly or coronation psalms (especially Pss 2; 16) are interpreted as speaking of Jesus's resurrection. Acts 2:33; 5:31 certainly link Jesus's exaltation to his heavenly session, but this need not exclude the clear link of exaltation and resurrection too. Further, Parsons makes a good case that in 1:9–11 Luke is utilising a traditional account of the ascension in his telling of the story, and this makes it unlikely that Luke is the inventor of the ascension[9] (cf. Heb 4:14, speaking of Jesus "having passed through [διεληλυθότα] the heavens"; Phil 2:5–11; 1 Tim 3:16; Heb 1:3; 2:9). Indeed, Parsons shows that the terminology of "assumption" found in Greco-Roman writers is not found in the Acts ascension account, although some (but only *some*) of the features of the Greco-Roman stories are in the Acts account (clouds, angels, mountains).[10] In sum, Lohfink appears to be oversimplifying Luke's view.

Secondly, Fitzmyer and Zwiep argue that the resurrection and the ascension should be identified.[11] Jesus ascends to heaven at his resurrection and then appears from heaven to his followers.[12] Thus the appearance of Luke 24:50–53; Acts 1:6–11 is simply Jesus's final resurrection appearance and has no other significance. So Fitzmyer argues that Luke 24:26 presents Jesus rebuking the Emmaus pair for not realising that he has already ascended to heaven.[13]

However, the accounts of Jesus's resurrection in the Acts speeches do not portray events this way.[14] In Acts 10:34–43 Jesus's death (v. 39) is followed by God raising him and the appearances (v. 40) with no hint of an ascension to heaven before Jesus appears. Similarly, in Acts 13:16–41 Jesus's death (v. 29) is followed by God raising him (v. 30) and Jesus appearing (v. 31), again with no ascension to heaven interposed.

Further, Luke 24 consistently portrays Jesus having been raised using ἐγείρω (in the passive voice to indicate that God did the raising, vv. 6, 34), whereas Jesus's ascension into heaven is described using ἀνεφέρετο, "he was carried up" (v. 51). Similarly, Acts 1 uses ἀνελήμφθη, "he was taken up" (v. 2), and ἐπήρθη, "he was lifted up" (v. 9), for the ascension, whereas the speeches of Acts consistently use ἐγείρω or ἀνίστημι for Jesus's resurrection (e.g., 2:24, 32; 3:15; 4:10; 10:40; 13:30, 33, 34, 37; 17:3, 31). In both books, Jesus's exaltation εἰς τὸν οὐρανόν, "into heaven," is never expressed using the latter two verbs.[15] Similarly, Luke does not use "glorification" language in connection

9 Parsons, *Departure*, 140–49.
10 Parsons, *Departure*, 136–40.
11 Fitzmyer, "Ascension," esp. 265–77; Zwiep, *Ascension*.
12 Cf. Maile, "Ascension," esp. 45–46.
13 Fitzmyer, "Ascension," 275.
14 Anderson, *But God*, 46.
15 Davies, *Ascended*, 30–34.

with Jesus's resurrection but reserves it for Jesus's ascension.[16] These clear differentiations of vocabulary strongly suggest a differentiation of the events described; it is thus a mistake to identify ascension and resurrection.[17]

Thirdly, the resurrection and ascension are seen as particular moments in the process of Jesus's exaltation, which includes them both:[18] they have a "functional unity."[19] Luke uses exaltation language for both events throughout his *Doppelwerk*, and even within one speech—for in Acts 2:30–32 Jesus's resurrection is spoken of as his exaltation to the Davidic throne, and in 2:33–34 it is Jesus's raising to the right hand of God, which is his exaltation. Thus the ascension may be seen as the culmination of the process of Jesus's exaltation and the point at which Jesus is visually exalted to heaven, thus providing the disciples with a visual demonstration of the truth of Jesus's exalted status.[20] Hence, Acts 1:9–10 uses a rich visual vocabulary that stresses the reality of the event: βλεπόντων, "as they were watching," τῶν ὀφθαλμῶν αὐτῶν, "their sight," ἀτενίζοντες, "gazing intently," [ἐμ]βλέποντες, "staring," ἐθεάσασθε, "you saw." This third view is convincing and connects well with Luke's primary focus in the speeches of Acts being on the resurrection of Jesus, while noting Luke's readiness to speak of the heavenly session or ascension of Jesus in other (fewer) places.

Criticism of the historical value of Luke's ascension account has centered on two main areas:[21] that it assumes an outdated three (or more) "tier" model of the universe;[22] and that it is a Christianized version of Jewish and Greco-Roman stories, notably the apotheosis of emperors; e.g., Dio Cass. 56.46.2 reports that Senator Numerius Atticus was rewarded with one million sesterces for swearing that he saw Augustus ascending into heaven.[23]

While Luke is using a pictorial way of writing, as many ancient (and modern) writers do, it seems unlikely that he (or other NT writers) envisaged Jesus dwelling a few miles above earth—speaking of heaven as "above" the earth need not imply this assumption, any more than people today speaking of the sun "rising" necessarily entails the view that the earth is static and the sun moves around the earth.[24] More likely, Luke draws on tradition in telling this story, for the "forty days" (Acts 1:3) and the use of visual vocabulary (see above) bespeak an event in space-time that clarifies how the apostolic band came to understand that Jesus was now exalted in heaven at the Father's right

16 Franklin, *Christ*, 21.
17 So also Porter, "Unity," 120–24.
18 van Stempvoort, "Interpretation"; Metzger, *Studies*, 77–82.
19 Anderson, *But God*, 46.
20 Cf. Franklin, *Christ*, 36.
21 Cf. also Pilch, *Visions*, 14–22, asserting the ascension account to be a collective visionary experience, with thin evidence.
22 Davies, *Ascended*, 56–58; Houlden, "Beyond Belief," 174.
23 Wright, *Resurrection*, 55–60, discusses this claimed similarity critically.
24 Moule, "Ascension," 208; cf. Wright, *Resurrection*, 653–56; Metzger, *Studies*, 84–85.

hand.[25] The claimed silence of Luke 24 and John 20 on this matter does not override the voice of Acts 1.[26]

Ancient stories of entering heaven can be analyzed into two kinds:[27] those involving a journey of the soul to heaven, sometimes to return to earth with revelation from God and sometimes after death (both found frequently in Second Temple Jewish apocalyptic writings, e.g., T. Ab. 7.19–8.3; 14:6–7[28]), and those involving a "rapture" tradition (such as the Elijah story, 2 Kgs 2:1–18, or the departure of Romulus).[29] Luke's ascension accounts include more elements of the latter but nevertheless present Jesus's ascension as unique, rather than simply modeled on other accounts, for Jesus's ascension marks the end of his sequence of post-resurrection appearances to his disciples.[30] Although Christian tradition centuries later could tell the story of Christ's exaltation in terms that echo the apotheosis of emperors, Luke's stories show little such connection, since they are not about a "soul" departing to a higher plane but about a physical departure of a re-embodied and transformed Jesus. That said, it is likely that to speak of Jesus entering heaven implicitly challenged imperial rule, for it placed Jesus where deceased emperors were supposed to be.[31]

Structure. Some prefer to divide the text after v. 5 on the basis that vv. 1–5 review the past and then vv. 6–11 begin the story of Acts proper.[32] Certainly there is a step in the narrative at v. 6, marked by μὲν οὖν, "in consequence," and the location changes, but this connective strongly links v. 5 with what follows (see *Comment*). Similarly, although there is a shift in v. 9 to the description of the ascension, vv. 9–11 are closely tied to vv. 6–8 through Καὶ ταῦτα εἰπών, "and having said these things" (v. 9).[33]

The story is told from the disciples' earth-bound perspective:[34] once Jesus is hidden by the cloud (v. 9), they are left looking into the sky (v. 10). The implicit rebuke of the two men in white (v. 11) is that their perspective *is* earth-bound and thus limited, as their question in v. 6 was. Jesus's response (vv. 7–8), Jesus's ascension at God's hands (v. 9), and the two men's words (v. 11) point to a heavenly perspective, focused on what God is doing and will do.[35]

Setting. A key function of the ascension narrative is to introduce the story of Acts.[36] This section works at several levels. (i) It focuses on the kingdom of

25 Torrance, *Resurrection*, esp. ch. 6.
26 Harris, *Raised*, 89–91; note John 20:17, which implies Jesus's ascension to heaven.
27 Lohfink, *Himmelfahrt*, 32–50; cf. Metzger, *Studies*, 80n1.
28 Further references: Lohfink, *Himmelfahrt*, 51–53.
29 Lohfink, *Himmelfahrt*, 55–70; Zwiep, *Ascension*, 36–79.
30 For a comparison with Elijah's departure which recognizes similarities and differences, see Walton, "Jesus's Ascension."
31 On proposed Greco-Roman parallels, see Wallace, "Benefactor."
32 E.g., Bock, *Acts*, 58; Đỗ, *Journey*, 136–38.
33 Đỗ, *Journey*, 139.
34 Franklin, *Christ*, 39; Eisen, *Poetik*, 156.
35 Cf. Parsons, *Departure*, 178–79, characterizing the story as having "internal focalization."
36 Parsons, *Departure*, 151; Sleeman, *Geography*, esp. 77–81.

God, which is a key theme in the Gospel and signaled at key points in Acts (vv. 3, 6; 28:23, 31; see *Comment* on v. 3). (ii) It sets the scene for the gospel mission in Acts (v. 8). Thus, "[t]hroughout the narrative, the reader is preoccupied not with the question of *whether* or not the mission will be completed, but *how* that fulfillment will be achieved."[37] (iii) It prepares for the coming of the Spirit who will be the power of the believers' mission throughout the known world (v. 8). (iv) It indicates that Jesus now reigns alongside God and thus contributes to what Johnson calls "the developing portrait of the God of Israel" (vv. 9–11, cf. 2:33).[38] (v) It delimits the period of the church's life by the two men's words that Jesus will return in the same way (v. 11).

Comment

3 Luke stresses the reality of both Jesus's death and resurrection: his aliveness-again was as real as his death: Jesus's resurrection appearances are described here using the same wording as Tabitha's return from death (Acts 9:41: παρέστησεν αὐτὴν ζῶσαν, "he presented her alive"[39]). Jesus offered πολλοῖς τεκμηρίοις, "many convincing proofs." τεκμήριον is a NT *hapax legomenon*, although used frequently by Josephus (e.g., *Ant* 3.15.3 §318 πολλὰ . . . καὶ ἄλλα τεκμήρια, "and many other proofs," 17.5.6 §128; 5.1.13 §39[40]). Aristotle, *Rhet.* 1.2.16 defines τεκμήριον as a "necessary (ἀναγκαῖον) sign."

These proofs were given by two means: Jesus's appearing to them ὀπτανόμενος αὐτοῖς, "by appearing to them," and λέγων, "speaking," with them over a period of forty days.[41] Luke here presents the disciples' experience of encountering Jesus in sight and speech as a key ground for belief in Jesus's resurrection. The verb ὀπτάνομαι simply denotes being seen;[42] it is found only here in the NT (cf. LXX 1 Kgs 8:8; Tob 12:19; Eup. 2:18; *Ord. Levi* 1:26–29; *Exor. A* 1:32–37[43]). The disciples' personal encounter with the risen Jesus was a key piece of evidence of his resurrection, as 1 Cor 15:5–8 makes clear. Their experience also qualifies them as witnesses to Jesus (v. 8; cf. vv. 21–22). Further, Luke 24:39 denies that the risen Jesus is a "spirit," πνεῦμα, but rather has σάρκα καὶ ὀστέα, "flesh and bones." The resurrection stories in the Gospels are not simply a later "concretizing" of the belief in the (spiritual, non-corporeal) risen-ness of Jesus.[44] Luke-Acts does not address the question where Jesus "was" during the forty days of appearances, although it seems unlikely that

37 Parsons, *Departure*, 155 (his italics).
38 Johnson, "Resurrection."
39 Anderson, *But God*, 189.
40 Mealand, "Phrase," gives other Hellenistic uses of the phrase.
41 Dillon, *Eye-witnesses*, 198–99; contra Anderson, *But God*, 189–90.
42 "ὀπτάνομαι," BDAG 717; "ὀπτάζομαι," LSJ (an earlier form).
43 Deissmann, *Light*, 83, cites second-century BC Ptolemaic papyri using this word, which may explain the LXX use (since found in Egypt, traditionally the home of LXX).
44 See, very fully, Wright, *Resurrection*, esp. chs 1–4, 9, 18–19.

he intends readers to think of Jesus as living on earth in one of the villages around Jerusalem.

Luke alone mentions that Jesus's appearances went on δἰ ἡμερῶν τεσσεράκοντα, "during forty days," and this period's clear symbolic value (cf. Luke 4:1–2 and the resonances of the forty year wilderness period after the exodus[45]) suggests to some that it is either not historical[46] or misunderstood by Luke.[47] There is a parallel forty-day waiting period before Ezra's and Baruch's ascensions (4 Ezra 16:23, 36, 43, 44, 45, 49; 2 Bar. 76:4). However, Pentecost is the only date canvassed in the NT for the public "outing" of the believing community, and it would be natural for the Galilean disciples to return north after Passover with a view to returning to Jerusalem for the next great pilgrim festival, Pentecost. There is a good fit between Luke's Jerusalem resurrection appearances in the immediate aftermath of Passover (Luke 24:13–43), the later the Galilean resurrection appearances (Matt 28:16–20; John 21), the ascension of Jesus from Olivet (Acts 1:12), and the disciples then remaining in the city at Jesus's explicit command (v. 4) for the relatively short period of ten days.[48]

λέγων τὰ περὶ τῆς βασιλείας τοῦ θεοῦ, "speaking about matters concerning the kingdom of God." The kingdom of God is the core of Jesus's teaching in Luke's Gospel, mentioned some thirty-three times, notably in the summaries of Luke 4:43; 8:1; 9:2, 60; 10:9, 11, which identify the kingdom as the central topic of both Jesus's and his disciples' proclamation. Thus, the risen Jesus teaches the same themes as he did prior to his death. While mentioned less frequently mentioned in Acts, the kingdom of God continues to be central, as can be seen by its mention at strategic points: Acts 8:12, summarising Philip's preaching in Samaria, and 19:8; 20:25; 28:23, 31, summarising Paul's teaching in Ephesus and Rome. Jesus's teaching his disciples here prepares for the key role of the apostles' teaching in the believing community (2:42; 4:33; 6:2, 4). Indeed, Acts is "bookended" by τὰ περὶ τῆς βασιλείας τοῦ θεοῦ, "matters concerning the kingdom of God," here and κηρύσσων τὴν βασιλείαν τοῦ θεοῦ καὶ διδάσκων τὰ περὶ τοῦ κυρίου Ἰησοῦ Χριστοῦ, "preaching the kingdom of God and teaching matters concerning the Lord Jesus" (28:31), which also echoes τὰ περὶ Ἰησοῦ τοῦ Ναζαρηνοῦ, "matters concerning Jesus of Nazareth" (Luke 24:19). These phrases interpret one another and clarify that the focus of the kingdom is its king, who is Jesus.[49]

4–5 συναλιζόμενος, "while eating with," echoes the resurrection meal scenes in Luke 24:30, 31, 35, 41–43; Acts 10:41.[50] Those stories both underline the

45 Jervell, *Apostelgeschichte*, 111.

46 E.g., Haenchen, *Acts*, 141n1; Conzelmann, *Acts*, 5–6; Wilson, *Gentiles*, 98; Dunn, *Beginning*, 139–42.

47 Leaney, "Forty."

48 See also Moule, "Ascension," 206–7; Maile, "Ascension," 48–54.

49 del Agua, "Evangelization," 655; for helpful discussion, see Turner, *Power*, 290–97, 319–41; O'Toole, "Kingdom."

50 It is not necessary, as de Jonge, "Chronology," 161, suggests, to identify "eating with" (v. 4)

physicality of Jesus's resurrection body and the significance of a shared meal as an important setting for meeting the risen one and thus prepare for the important role of meals in the life of the believing community (2:42, 46; 20:7, 11). Culturally, to share food is a key means of expressing hospitality and welcome—hence the indignation of some Jewish believers at Peter sharing meals with gentiles (11:3; cf. Gal 2:11–21).

Jesus tells his disciples to wait in the city for the Father's promise (as in Luke 24:49). This promise, echoing OT passages such as Isa 32:15; Joel 2:28–32 LXX (quoted in Acts 2:17–21; MT 3:1–5), has the same content as the baptizer's promise of the Spirit,[51] but it is now imminent. The absence of "fire" here (contrast Luke 3:16) suggests to Dunn that Jesus has absorbed the "fire" of God's wrath in his death, and thus that the Spirit is the fruit of the cross.[52] While this may be theologically appropriate, it must be doubted whether it is Luke's view of the baptizer's promise, since there are tongues ὡσεὶ πυρός, "like those of fire," at Pentecost at the Spirit's coming (Acts 2:3), suggesting that Pentecost itself is to be seen as the disciples being baptized "with Spirit and fire."[53]

This brief mention of the Father's promise is designed to recall the expectations of Israel's restoration and renewal that are prominent in Luke 1–2[54] and that will now be fulfilled in consequence of the Spirit's Pentecostal coming (Acts 2). The focus of Israel, and thus the focus of Israel's restoration, is Jerusalem, and that is why the disciples must wait there (cf. "in Jerusalem," 1:8; Isa 40:1–2; 65:18–25; Zech 8).[55]

Jesus contrasts John's cleansing baptism ὕδατι, "in water," with the forthcoming baptism ἐν πνεύματι . . . ἁγίῳ, "with the Holy Spirit." βαπτίζω, "baptize," used twice in this verse, signifies drowning or immersion in an element; it is derived from βάπτω, "dip," and can be used literally concerning people being immersed or washed or drowned[56] and ships being sunk,[57] as well as metaphorically for (e.g.) a city being "flooded" with people.[58] Marshall argues cogently that a good English translation of the verb is "drench with a liquid," used literally with water and metaphorically with fire and Spirit, for which liquid metaphors were used, combined with verbs

---

with the meal of Luke 24:36–49; it is more likely that Luke here indicates a number of occasions of eating together after Jesus was raised.

51 With Menzies, *Empowered*, 1771.

52 *Baptism*, 44.

53 For further critique of Dunn, see Turner, *Power*, 298n87.

54 Bauckham, "Restoration," 439–66.

55 See Fitzmyer, *Acts*, 199; Chance, *Jerusalem*, ch. 1, on Jerusalem as source of salvation in Jewish thought.

56 LXX 2 Kgs 5:14; Jdt 12:7; Sir 34:26 [EVV 31]; Josephus, *J.W.* 1.22.2. §437; *Ant.* 15.3.3. §55.

57 Josephus, *J.W.* 2.20.1 §556; 3.8.5 §368; 3.9.3 §423; 3.10.9 §§525, 527; *Ant.* 9.10.2 §212; *Life* 3 §15.

58 Josephus, *J.W.* 4.3.3 §137. For further examples of all uses, see "βαπτίζω," LSJ, and the judicious discussions of Marshall, "Meaning"; Dunn, "Baptized."

such as "pour" or "drink."[59] Thus one mode of water baptism in the earliest churches was probably affusion, although the most widely used mode of baptism was immersion. That said, the metaphor's focus is on the state of being drenched—that the person is soaked in the element poured—rather than the mode of drenching.[60] The noun βάπτισμα, "baptism," appears to be a Christian coinage, since it is found only in Christian literature.[61] Early Christians knew baptism in water both as a rite signifying repentance used by John the baptizer, as the Christian initiation rite,[62] and being baptized in the Holy Spirit (Luke 3:16b; Acts 11:16). There is no record in the NT of the apostles being baptized in water. Oulton offers two possible explanations: (i) that their water baptism by John sufficed, and (ii) that their time with Jesus during his ministry, especially during the post-resurrection forty days, served in place of water baptism (cf. Tertullian, *Bapt.* 12).[63]

To be "baptized in [the] Holy Spirit," ἐν πνεύματι βαπτισθήσεσθε ἁγίῳ, signifies being drenched by the Spirit and probably denotes cleansing. As John's water baptism pointed to forgiveness of sins and called the people to repentance in preparation for the Messiah's coming (Luke 3:3, 16–17), so the coming Spirit baptism will bring that cleansing-forgiveness into effect and make it available to many. Menzies reads Acts 1:5 as denoting *only* the early church's Spirit-empowered witness as the means by which the cleansing-forgiveness takes place and thus understands being baptized in the Spirit as *entirely* about empowerment for witness.[64] However, here it is the disciples themselves who are baptized by the Spirit (βαπτισθήσεσθε, "you will be baptized," is passive), rather than them being the means by which others are baptized, and thus the Spirit's work here is a cleansing with soteriological effects on the disciples;[65] v. 8 will go on to speak of the Spirit empowering the disciples for witness. (On the relationship of water and Spirit baptism, see "Theological Themes" in vol. 3.)

6 μὲν οὖν, "In consequence," signals that what follows is a development from what precedes, not necessarily in total continuity with it and often implying a second—more appropriate—response that follows.[66] Here, at a later meeting with the risen Jesus, the disciples' initial response to Jesus's words in vv. 4–5

---

59 E.g., *fire*: Ps 11:6; Dan 7:10; 4 Ezra 13:10–11; Sib. Or. 3:54; 2:196–205, 252–54; 1QH[a] XI, 29–32; *Spirit*: Isa 32:15; 44:3–4; Zech 12:10; Ezek 39:29; Joel 2:28–32; 1QS III, 7–9; IV, 20–21; T. Jud. 24.2–3; John 7:38–39; 1 Cor 12:13; Acts 2:33; 10:45.

60 Marshall, "Meaning," 22–23.

61 "βάπτισμα," BDAG 165.

62 See *Comment* on 2:38; cf. Luke 3:3, 7, 12, 16a; 7:29–30; Acts 2:38, 41; 8:12, 16, 36, 38; 9:18; 10:47–48; 16:15, 33; 18:8; 19:3–5; 22:16.

63 Oulton, "Spirit," 237.

64 Menzies, *Empowered*, 128–31.

65 Turner, *Power*, 345.

66 The expression is found 27x in Acts (of 39 NT uses), and signals both continuation (οὖν) and looking forward prospectively (μέν); it thus comes at key transition points in the narrative of Acts. Full discussion: Levinsohn, *Connections*, 141–50.

is to ask about the restoration of the kingdom to Israel, and their second response will be to wait obediently (1:12–14; 2:1). Given the restoration of Israel resonances of vv. 4–5, their question is a natural one.[67] The question's assumptions nevertheless reflect the Gospels' portrait of the disciples as not fully grasping the nature of Jesus's restoration agenda for Israel.[68]

εἰ ἐν τῷ χρόνῳ τούτῳ ἀποκαθιστάνεις τὴν βασιλείαν τῷ Ἰσραήλ;, "Are you at this time restoring the kingdom to Israel?" This question is predicated on two assumptions: that Israel will rule over the nations, a common expectation in Jewish eschatology (e.g., Isa 60:12; Zech 8:20–23; Pss Sol. 17:23–24; Luke 1: 71, 74);[69] and that Jesus will bring about this rule. Restoration is a key Jewish theme (Hos 11:11; Jer 23:8 LXX; 24:6; Mal 3:23 LXX [MT 24; EVV 4:6]; Sir 48:10); the Eighteen Benedictions (Amidah) pray for Israel's restoration (notably 10, 11, 14, 15, 17). Jesus does not reject either of their presuppositions but reshapes them in his response (Acts 1:7–8). The angels' words further reshape their expectations (vv. 10–11): Jesus is the key, and Israel will be restored, but not as (and when) the disciples assume.[70] ἀποκαθιστάνεις, "restoring," is cognate with ἀποκατάστασις, "restoration" (3:21), and the fact that the "restoration of all things (πάντων)" is in view also signals the reshaping of the disciples' expectations. Jesus is renewing and restoring Israel, for sure, but with the restoration of all things at the end in view, via the gospel going through the whole earth, as 1:8 will signal and as Luke 2:32 has hinted in speaking of "a light for revelation to the gentiles, and glory to your people Israel."[71]

7–8 Jesus has already promised the apostles that they will rule Israel (Luke 22:30) and will be given the kingdom (Luke 12:32), and so their question in Acts 1:6 is implicitly about the apostles' rule. Jesus's answer (vv. 7–8) provides a startlingly different means to that end. οὐχ ὑμῶν ἐστιν γνῶναι χρόνους ἢ καιρούς, "It is not for you to know the times and seasons," indicates that timing is not the key issue, or even a very important issue. The collocation of χρόνους, "times," and καιρούς, "seasons," is found elsewhere in the NT only at 1 Thess 5:1, also a passage with an eschatological focus.[72] Since ὁ πατὴρ ἔθετο ἐν τῇ ἰδίᾳ ἐξουσίᾳ, "the Father has set [them] by his own authority," the disciples are to submit to God's ruling authority over such matters. This does not mean that Luke has given up "all expectation of an imminent end."[73] Rather, "Jesus' response to the disciples' question is not formulated to correct the readers'

---

67 Turner, *Power,* 299; contra Calvin, *Acts,* ad. loc.: "There are as many errors in this question as words," also Sanders, *Jesus,* 116; for fuller response, see Maston, "How Wrong."

68 Wright, *Jesus,* 463n71.

69 Đỗ, *Journey,* 159, 164; Wainwright, "Luke," 76–77.

70 Sleeman, *Geography,* 68–70.

71 See Nolland, *Luke,* 1:120. For a fine, brief exposition of the restoration of Israel in Luke-Acts, see Eisen, *Poetik,* 150–51.

72 Kurz, *Reading,* 75, also notes an echo of Jesus's eschatological discourse in Luke 21, although the words used here are not found there.

73 Haenchen, *Acts,* 143.

'christology' or 'eschatology,' but to introduce the whole narrative of Acts as a testimony to the reign of God's Messiah through his twelve apostles who declare repentance and forgiveness to Israel."[74] Thus, "Luke's concern is not *when* the kingdom of God will come (as is generally assumed) but *who* will qualify to be admitted to it."[75] The timing of Jesus's return (v. 11) is neither knowable nor relevant to the apostles—or, thus, Luke's readers.

Several Isaianic echoes reverberate through vv. 7–8.[76] Luke reads Isa 32:15 LXX ἕως ἂν ἐπέλθῃ ἐφ' ὑμᾶς πνεῦμα ἀφ' ὑψηλοῦ, "until a spirit from on high comes upon you," located in a passage about Israel's new exodus restoration, in terms of the Spirit's coming to empower for witness. Isaiah 43:10–12 sits in a passage about the role of God's servant, Israel (43:1), and proclaims "you are my witnesses" (MT: LXX has "be [γένεσθε, imperative] my witnesses"; cf. also 44:8). Isaiah 49:6 speaks of the role of God's servant not only as restoring Israel, but also as "a light to the nations (LXX ἕως ἐσχάτου τῆς γῆς, "to the end of the earth," echoed verbatim in v. 8), that my salvation may reach to the end of the earth." Isa 49:6 will be directly quoted in Acts 13:47, in the context of the mission turning toward gentiles. These Isaianic echoes signal that the disciples are to take part in God's restoration of Israel (which is the Isaianic servant's ministry) in order to bring light to the nations, in conjunction with Jesus the Messiah (cf. 3:19–21), and following his example and lead (Luke 2:32).[77] Empowered by the Spirit, they will reach beyond and through the restored Israel to the world, a servant ministry in which Paul, too, will participate.[78]

Jesus's response thus reshapes the disciples' assumptions in Acts 1:6. There is an eschatological hope of Israel's restoration, but the restoration's shape will not be Israel's *ruling over* the nations but the *incorporation of* the nations into Israel's hope through Israel's Messiah. The restored and reshaped Israel will *serve* the nations as light bringer, rather than ruling them.[79] It is not, however, that the disciples' Spirit-empowered witness ἕως ἐσχάτου τῆς γῆς, "to the end of the earth," is the substance of the restoration of Israel but rather that this witness is the means by which the way is prepared for what will become ἀποκαταστάσεως πάντων, "the restoration *of all things*" (3:21).[80] Acts 1:7 clarifies (in similar vein to 3:20–21) that the timing of this (final) restoration is in the Father's hands. The need for witness "to the end of the earth" implies that the promised return of Jesus (v. 11) will not be immediate. Carroll notes that the parallel questions in Luke 19:11 (implied) and 21:7 receive a similar answer that suggests a period of

74 Tiede, "Exaltation," 286.
75 Maddox, *Purpose*, 106.
76 Turner, *Power*, 300–301; Pao, *Acts*, 91–96; Mallen, *Reading*, 78–84; Moore, "End"; Johnson, "Jesus," 346–49; Beers, *Followers*, 131–33.
77 Mallen, *Reading*, 81–82.
78 Mallen, *Reading*, 84–93.
79 Bauckham, "Restoration," 477.
80 Bauckham, "Restoration," 476–77; Turner, *Power*, 299–300.

time before the end.[81] (There is considerable debate over the nature and timing of the restoration of Israel: see *Comment* on 3:21.)

By contrast (ἀλλά "but") with the lack of clarity over the timing of restoration, Jesus expresses confidence over what will happen next. λήμψεσθε δύναμιν ἐπελθόντος τοῦ ἁγίου πνεύματος ἐφ ὑμᾶς καὶ ἔσεσθέ μου μάρτυρες, "you will receive power when the Spirit comes upon you and you will be my witnesses." The heart of Luke's understanding of the Spirit's role is empowerment for witness, although it is not the *only* facet of the Spirit's work in Acts.[82] That the Spirit enables inspired speech is a commonplace in Jewish expectation of this period.[83]

The disciples' vocation as witnesses flows from the coming of the Spirit: ἔσεσθε is indicative, "you shall be," rather than imperative "be!"[84] Jesus makes a promise that the disciples will be witnesses as a result of divine enabling rather than giving a direct exhortation to witness (contrast Jesus's command in Matt 28:19–20). For Luke's readers this saying certainly signals that the heartbeat of the believing community is witness to the gospel and also that with this great responsibility comes the promise of great power and divine enabling: to this extent Jesus's words contain "at once gift and obligation."[85]

μου μάρτυρες, "my witnesses," portrays the group (Οἱ . . . συνελθόντες, "those who had gathered" in Acts 1:6, is vague in reference) both as witnesses who belong to Jesus (and are thus sent and authorized by him) and as witnesses whose testimony concerns Jesus—we need not torture the genitive μου, "my," to choose one or other alternative (cf. the same double entendre in Isa 43:12). "Witness" is a judicial term, used metaphorically concerning testimony that these disciples will offer in order to persuade people to come to the right verdict concerning Jesus. The word group is widespread in Acts: the noun μάρτυς "witness" at Acts 1:8, 22; 2:32; 3:15; 5:32; 6:13; 7:58; 10:39, 41; 13:31; 22:15, 20; 26:16; the nouns μαρτυρία and μαρτύριον, "testimony," at 4:33; 7:44; 22:18; the verb μαρτυρέω, "testify," at 6:3; 10:22, 43; 13:22; 14:3; 15:8; 16:2; 22:5, 12; 23:11; 26:5; and the verb μαρτύρομαι, "testify," at 20:26; 26:22.[86] There are a number of courtroom or quasi-judicial scenes in Acts where such testimony takes place,[87] but "witness" terminology is not restricted to these places.[88] This term's use signals Luke's wider purpose of providing apostolic testimony in writing Acts:[89]

81 Carroll, *Response*, 124.
82 I thus agree with what Menzies, *Empowered*, passim, affirms but reject his denial that the Spirit has other roles in Luke-Acts, with Turner, *Power*, esp. 431–33.
83 Excellent summary, with references, in Turner, *Power*, 92–103.
84 Contra Schnabel, *Mission*, 1:371n240, who treats the future as having "imperatival meaning."
85 Haenchen, *Acts*, 144.
86 See Trites, *Concept*, 128; Bolt, "Mission," 192–94, for helpful analyses of this word group, and Newbigin, "Witness," for a valuable overview of biblical usage.
87 Acts 4:5–22; 5:27–41; 6:12–7:60; 16:16–40; 17:6–9; 18:12–17; 21:27–26:32; cf. Luke 12:9–12; 21:12–15; see Trites, "Importance"; Johnson, "Jesus," 347–48.
88 Trites, *Concept*, 128–53.
89 See further Trites, *Concept*, 140.

Luke does not use "witness" language of the believing community at large but uses it as a technical term for ear- and eyewitness testimony to Jesus by people qualified to offer such testimony, principally the apostles (2:32; 3:15; 4:33; 5:32; 10:39, 41; 13:31) but also Paul (13:30; 22:15; 26:16) and Stephen (22:20).[90] Hence, the qualifications for the one to replace Judas include the experience which will allow them to give eyewitness testimony (1:21–22), and the preface to Luke's Gospel signals the importance of eyewitness testimony, evidently including the apostolic band (Luke 1:1–4). However, Jesus's commission in Luke 24:44–49 does not distinguish between the apostles and those with them (αὐτοί, "them," in vv. 36, 44 includes "the eleven and their companions" and the two who walked to Emmaus, v. 33[91]). Further, the group being addressed here, Οἱ μὲν οὖν συνελθόντες, "those who had come together" (v. 6), may include the larger group mentioned in vv. 14, 21.[92]

Their testimony in Acts concerns Jesus in at least three senses.[93] They witness to (i) the facts of Jesus's ministry, death, and resurrection (1:21–22; 2:22–24; 10:36–42); (ii) Jesus's character of holiness and righteousness that gave rise to his deeds of power and healing (3:14; 10:38); and (iii) Jesus's status following his death and resurrection (and soon to include his exaltation), which calls for repentance and trust in Jesus (2:38; 3:22–23; 10:43; Luke 24:46–47). Their witness to Jesus is also interpreted in Acts as witness to the kingdom of God (Acts 28:23) in continuity with the Gospel (cf. 1:3).[94] However they do not "take on Jesus's mantle" in the way that Elisha did after Elijah—the apostles are not Jesus's successors but his witnesses.[95]

The testimony will spread in a series of growing circles that are widely understood to signal the structure of Acts.[96] First, they will testify in Jerusalem (Acts 1–7); then persecution will drive them into Judea and Samaria (Acts 8), before the call of the key witness who will go to the end of the earth, Saul (Acts 9), and the beginnings of including gentiles (Acts 10:1–11:18). It is noticeable that it is not those present who accomplish the later parts of the mission, to gentiles.[97] However, the book does not follow such a structure tidily, since it returns on several occasions to Jerusalem (9:26–30; 11:2–18; 15:4–29; 19:21; 21:15–23:24). This statement, rather, reorders the disciples' perception of space,[98] for the land of Israel—and Jerusalem, and its temple in particular—is no longer central to God's ordering of the world: instead, the whole of the

90 Bolt, "Mission," esp. 196–210.
91 Nolland, *Luke*, 3:1220.
92 Haenchen, *Acts*, 142–43; contra Estrada, *Followers*, 47, who maintains that Acts 1 has an exclusive focus on the apostles. For fuller critique of Bolt's view, see Mallen, *Reading*, 191–93.
93 Trites, *Concept*, 144; cf, Đỗ, *Journey*, 166–67.
94 del Agua, "Evangelization," 655.
95 Contra Estrada, *Followers*, 96.
96 E.g., Conzelmann, *Acts*, 7; Dunn, *Beginning*, 145.
97 Biguzzi, "Witnessing," 3–6.
98 With Sleeman, *Geography*, 70–72.

inhabited world becomes "sacred space," for God meets people in the whole world and Jesus sends his disciples into the whole world (see *Comment* on "the end of the earth," below).[99]

Jerusalem is a key location in Acts; the story returns there several times (Acts 9; 11; 15; 21–26). It was commonly expected to be a center of renewal in the prophets.[100] A key difference from the expectation of passages such as Isa 60:3–16; 66:18–24; Zech 8:20–23 is that the proclamation of the messengers in Acts who go to the nations is not that the nations come to Jerusalem (Isa 66:20), but rather that the community of believers will spread out worldwide.[101] Access to God will now be through Jesus, not the temple and its ceremonies.[102]

There are two spellings of "Jerusalem" in (Luke-)Acts, the Hellenistic Ἰεροσόλυμα (22x) and the "Hebrew" form Ἰερουσαλήμ (37x), which is found in LXX except in apocryphal books known only in Greek (1 Esd; Tob; 1 Mac; 2 Macc). There are textual variants at a number of places.[103] Luke is the only evangelist who uses both forms widely.[104] The latter is used here; the former in v. 4. There is some debate over the significance of the variation in spelling. (i) Elliott observes that Ἰερουσαλήμ is used predominantly in Acts 1–7, and when a Jew speaks to Jews, or when the setting is Palestinian.[105] (ii) Walker argues that Luke's use of Ἰερουσαλήμ indicates "his endorsement of the way Jewish people saw the city as different from others," i.e., it highlights the city's theological significance.[106] (iii) Hastings suggests that Ἰερουσαλήμ is used in texts of particular theological significance, although he concedes there is no "rigid pattern."[107] (iv) de la Potterie observes that, after the predominance of Ἰερουσαλήμ in Acts 1–7, in chs. 8–19 the two forms alternate; in chs. 20–24 the "Hebrew" form predominates, and this during Paul's stay in the city; and from 25:7 to the end, the Hellenistic form alone is used;[108] he considers that the Hellenistic form is used in contexts of apostolic mission or the dispersion, whereas the "Hebrew" form is used when the focus is on what Jesus did in the city or on the role of the apostles (including Paul) in the city, especially in Acts

---

99 Smit, "Negotiating," unpersuasively argues that Acts is Jerusalem-centric, placing other places as peripheral.

100 E.g., Isa 2:2–3; 40:2, 9; 41:27; 44:26, 28; 62:6–7; 65:18–19; 66:10, 13, 20; Jer 3:17; Joel 3:1, 16–17, 20; Mic 4:2; Zech 8:3–8, 20–23; 14:1–11; see Bauckham, "Jerusalem Church," 425–26.

101 Cf. Alexander, *Context*, 109; contra Scott, *Geography*, 57. Cf. Riesner, *Period*, 245–53, arguing that Isa 66:18–21 was influential on Paul's understanding of the geographical spread of his mission.

102 Walton, "Tale," esp. 144–48.

103 De la Potterie, "Les deux," 154–55, considers that only six are in serious doubt (2:43; 11:2; 15:4; 19:21; 20:16; 21:4); cf. Elliott, "Jerusalem," 464–67, who discusses all the variant readings.

104 The only exception is Matt 23:37, which uses the "Hebrew" form; de la Potterie, "Les deux," 153.

105 Elliott, "Jerusalem," 462–67.

106 Walker, *Jesus*, 69n48.

107 Hastings, *Prophet*, 103–6.

108 See his table of the distribution of uses, de la Potterie, "Les deux," 156.

8–19.[109] There is something to be said for de la Potterie's nuanced analysis, for it suggests that the significance of the city is as the place where Jesus died, rose, and ascended to accomplish salvation;[110] this qualifies Walker's claim that Luke endorsed the Jewish view of the city as *in itself* holy. The theological center of the believing community is not an earthly city but the heavenly Jesus.[111]

Luke portrays the gospel's initial expansion into Judea as the result of persecution in Jerusalem (8:1 with *Comment* there); beyond the summary in 9:31, little is said about the believing communities in the Judean countryside. It is interesting that, other than 9:31, nothing is said of believing communities in Galilee, the place of Jesus's and the disciples' origin.

Samaria is the focus of Acts 8:5–25, and the gospel's reception there represents a key further stage in the restoration of Israel, for Luke probably sees the Samaritans as representing the ten lost northern tribes reunited with the Judeans through Jesus Christ (Ezek 37:15–24; see *Comment* on 8:5 for discussion and references).

Three main identifications of "the end of the earth" have been proposed:[112] (i) *Rome*,[113] since Acts ends there, it was the greatest city of the world, and Pompey was said to have come ἀπ' ἐσχάτου τῆς γῆς, "from the end of the earth" (Pss. Sol. 8:15). However, Pss. Sol. probably refers to Pompey coming from Spain, rather than Rome, to the east in 67 BC, and thus does not present Rome as "the end of the earth."[114] Rome was seen as the *center* of the earth, for there stood a golden milepost, the *Millarium Aureum*, from which distances were measured through the Roman Empire; it was engraved with distances to major cities throughout the empire (Dio Cass. 54.8.4).[115] (ii) *Spain*, for it was the furthest point west in the Roman Empire, and Paul planned to travel there (Rom 15:28).[116] Strabo refers to Gades, on the west coast of Spain, as "the end of the earth" (*Geog.* 3.1.8), and Silius Italicus says Gades lies "at the end of the world" (*Punica* 17.637).[117] It is unlikely that this is Luke's view, for Spain is not mentioned in Acts. (iii) *The whole world*,[118] ἕως ἐσχάτου τῆς γῆς, "to the end of the earth," echoes Isa 49:6 LXX (as also in 13:47), and LXX use suggests that the

109 De la Potterie, "Les deux," 161–62.

110 De la Potterie, "Les deux," 185–86.

111 Walton, "Tale," 144–48; so also Davies, "Jerusalem," 153.

112 For others, see Schnabel, *Mission*, 1:372; for documentation of scholarly views up to 1966, see van Unnik, *Sparsa*, 1:387–90.

113 E.g., Jervell, *Apostelgeschichte*, 116; Barrett, *Acts*, 1:80.

114 Rosner, "Progress," 218.

115 Discussion: Platner and Ashby, *Dictionary*, 342; Alexander, "Reading," 472n29; cf. Strabo, *Geog.* 17.3.24, discussed in Scott, *Geography*, 17.

116 Ellis, "End."

117 Riesner, *Period*, 305; concerning Spain or Gades, he also cites Juvenal *Sat.* 10.1–2; Lucan *Bell.* 3.454.

118 van Unnik, *Sparsa*, 1:386–401; Schnabel, *Mission*, 1:372–73; Rosner, "Progress," 218–19; Scott, *Geography*, 58–61; Alexander, "Reading," 427–27.

phrase simply means "the whole world," without having a particular place in mind as *the* end of the earth (Isa 8:9; 14:22; 48:20; 49:6; 62:11; Jer 10:13; 28:16 [LXX 35:16]; 32:32 [LXX 39:32]; 38:8 [LXX 45:8]; 1 Macc 3:9; Pss. Sol. 1:4).[119]

The latter view is persuasive: it echoes the mission εἰς πάντα τὰ ἔθνη, "to all the nations," given to the disciples in Luke 24:47, a verse that goes on to say that this mission is ἀρξάμενοι ἀπὸ Ἰερουσαλήμ, "beginning from Jerusalem," and for which the disciples will be Jesus's witnesses, further resonating with this verse in Acts. The lack of the explicit phrase "to all the nations" here maintains the suspense in the narrative as Luke's readers engage with the developing story of the worldwide mission from the disciples' point of view.[120] This interpretation fits well with Luke's well-known use of Isaianic echoes,[121] and, as in Isa 49:6, implies that gentiles are in mind without excluding a widespread mission to the Jewish diaspora.[122] Thus in Acts, when Paul goes to a new city, his normal pattern is to go to the synagogue first and then to the gentiles (e.g., Antioch, 13:13–49; Corinth, 18:1–11; Ephesus, 19:1–10). A mission to the Jewish diaspora would be the disciples' probable initial understanding of Jesus's words.[123] Psalm 2:8 LXX, addressing Israel's king, offers an interesting parallel: "I will give you the nations (ἔθνη) as your inheritance and as your possession the furthest points of the earth (τὰ πέρατα τῆς γῆς)" (my translation). The psalm uses a partial synonym of ἔσχατος, "end," πέρας, "furthest point," and Ps 2:7 is cited elsewhere in connection with Jesus's exaltation as Messiah, notably in Acts 13:33, where D has Ps 2:8 in addition to v. 7 (see *Comment* on 13:33). This parallel reinforces the sense of Jesus's authority over the whole earth and thus the disciples' mission to announce his rule worldwide. The primary reference of the phrase "the end of the earth" is thus *geographical* rather than focused on a variety of people groups, although by the end of Acts readers will recognize the double entendre of the phrase as embracing gentiles across the Roman world. The whole inhabited earth was known to stretch to Spain in the west, the Arctic in the north (the Scythians lived in this area), Ethiopia in the south,[124] and China (the Seres, the "silk people") in the east.[125] The claim that the apostolic witness will encompass the whole world carries an implicit challenge to the universalizing claims of the Roman Empire, which

---

119 Smit, "Negotiating," 20–21, suggests that everywhere outside Jerusalem, Judea, and Samaria is considered "the end of the earth" and thus peripheral. However, the activity and presence of God, Jesus, and the Spirit in diverse places relativizes any sense of Jerusalem as central—it is simply the starting point (Luke 24:47). More fully: Walton, "Tale," 144–49.

120 Zehnle, *Discourse,* 99.

121 Mallen, *Reading.*

122 Butticaz, "Has God," 161, notes the Pauline parallel in Rom 10:18: εἰς τὰ πέρατα τῆς οἰκουμένης, "to the corners/ends of the inhabited world," itself a quotation from Ps 18:5 LXX [MT 19:4]. Gentiles: Wilson, *Gentiles,* 94n1; diaspora: Moore, "Commission," 397–98.

123 Cf. Rengstorf, "Election," 186–87.

124 See *Comment* on 8:27 and Thornton, "End." Melbourne, "Acts 1:8," unpersuasively suggests that Philip's mission in Acts 8 fulfills 1:8.

125 Schnabel, *Mission,* 1:373–74.

considers itself to rule the known world, exemplified in Augustus's claim that he had subjected "the whole world" (*orbem terrarum*) to the Romans (Preface, Res. gest. divi Aug.), or Ovid's statement, "The land of other nations has a fixed boundary: the circuit of Rome is the circuit of the world" (*Fasti* 2.684 [Frazer/Goold, LCL]).[126]

9–11 Repetition (5x) of phrases denoting sight and εἰς τὸν οὐρανόν, "into heaven," marks these verses. The former signal that Luke portrays an event that is neither a vision or dream[127]—for the terms used are not the usual terms for such phenomena—nor simply a retrojected explanation of Jesus's exalted status, arrived at by other means.[128] Rather, Luke portrays the ascension as an event that was the means by which the disciples came to understand Jesus's exalted status in heaven[129]—hence the repetition of "into heaven."[130] The "sight" terms also invite Luke's readers to "see" this account aright.[131] Jesus now reigns and acts from heaven: "heaven now becomes the reality that structures and maps the life of Jesus's followers."[132] Just as Luke stresses the physical nature of Jesus's resurrection by Jesus eating with the disciples (Luke 24:36–43; see *Comment* on vv. 4–5), so Luke locates the risen human body of Jesus in heaven.[133] It is a false antithesis (as well as a caricature) to write, "For Luke what is significant is not that Jesus was lifted off the ground into space, but, as all scholars agree, that he has been elevated to the status of heavenly Lord."[134]

9 Καὶ ταῦτα εἰπών, "After he had said these things," is a vague time notice; it most probably means that Jesus's words in vv. 7–8 were spoken not long prior to his ascension,[135] with the possibility of a change of location between the events of vv. 6–8 and 9–11 (note v. 12, which specifies the location as the Mount of Olives; so also Luke 24:50, "Bethany"). It is also possible, but less likely, that the events of Acts 1:9–11 happen on a different occasion (cf. the same expression in Luke 19:28).

βλεπόντων αὐτῶν, "as they were watching" (Acts 1:9a), is the first of five "sight" phrases in vv. 9–11; this present genitive absolute portrays the disciples

---

126 See *Comment* on Acts 10:36; Walton, "State," 26–28; Romm, *Edges*, 121–27.
127 As Dunn, "Ascension," 304, concedes.
128 Contra, e.g., Lohfink, *Himmelfahrt*; see *Form/Structure/Setting*.
129 With Strauss, *Life*, 750: he is clear that this is Luke's understanding but goes on to regard such an event as incredible; contrast Lewis, *Miracles*, ch. 16.
130 Strelan, *Strange Acts*, 39 compares Ps 102 19 LXX [MT 103:19]; Isa 66:1 LXX.
131 Green, "What You See," 446.
132 Green, "He Ascended," 139; see also Sleeman, *Geography*, passim.
133 See also a valuable discussion of second-century writers on the significance of the ascension, pointing to this conclusion, in Green, "He Ascended," 142–50; cf. Talbert, *Patterns*, 112–16, also highlights the bodily nature of the one who ascended and the continuity between Jesus as the one who dies and rises in Jerusalem and as the one who ascends. Talbert asserts that Luke's stress on these points is challenging alternative views, but such mirror reading is unnecessary—Luke is more probably reproducing the tradition he received.
134 Strelan, *Strange Acts*, 35.
135 de Jonge, "Chronology," 158n25. Đỗ, *Journey*, 139 considers this a strong link.

as continuing to look as Jesus was lifted up. This verb choice "places the Ascension in the same category of events as any other happening in the story of Jesus."[136] It may also allude to the departure of Elijah, where Elisha is told that he will receive a double portion of Elijah's spirit if he *sees* Elijah depart, and that is what happens (2 Kgs 2:9–15).[137] If so, the disciples' reception of the Holy Spirit—and thus their reception of Jesus's prophetic mantle—is some days later (Acts 2:1–4).[138]

ἐπήρθη καὶ νεφέλη ὑπέλαβεν αὐτὸν ἀπὸ τῶν ὀφθαλμῶν αὐτῶν, "he was lifted up and a cloud took him up, out of their sight" (v. 9b), the second "sight" phrase, has Jesus as passive, being lifted by another (presumably God[139]). He is then taken up (not "hidden") on a cloud:[140] "the cloud is not a fog cloud hiding a mystery but a royal chariot showing the reality of the disappearance of Christ."[141] ἐπήρθη, "he was lifted up," is an unusual word for exaltation, echoing Ps 8:2 LXX, which speaks of God, whose greatness is ἐπήρθη . . . ὑπεράνω τῶν οὐρανῶν, "exalted above the heavens," and thus signals Jesus's place in heaven.[142] Jesus's passivity indicates that the ascension is both God's recognition of him and God's bestowal of an exalted status upon him. The reason for the disciples to venerate Jesus will be that the God of Israel has vindicated and exalted him (cf. 2:32–33, also using a passive verb ὑψωθείς, "having been exalted").

νεφέλη, "a cloud," symbolizes God's presence, as frequently in Scripture (e.g., Exod 9:16; 13:21–22; 40:33–38; Pss 67:35 LXX; 88:7 LXX). The singular echoes Luke 21:27, where a singular cloud at the "coming"[143] of the Son of Man stands in place of the plural "clouds" in Mark 13:26; Matt 24:30. This dominical saying itself echoes Dan 7:13, where both MT and LXX have the plural; the echo of Dan 7:13 very probably comes from primitive Christian tradition.[144] The Dan 7:13 echo points to Jesus now exercising the universal rule and authority afforded the son of man there. There may also be an echo of the singular cloud in Luke's transfiguration (Luke 9:34–35, although there Luke does not differ from Mark 9:7; Matt 17:5). Davies proposes a wealth of parallels between Acts 1:1–12 and Luke 9:1–34.[145] Luke's phrasing in Luke 21:27 prepares for this use in Acts and thus connects Jesus's ascension to both to his anticipatory glorification in the transfiguration and also his return, as Acts 1:11 makes explicit (cf. 1 Thess 4:17; Rev 1:7; 14:14–16).

---

136 Barrett, *Acts*, 1:81; cf. Metzger, *Studies*, 82; Đỗ, *Journey*, 156–57.
137 Johnson, *Acts*, 31.
138 Rosen, "Ascension," 196.
139 So Strelan, *Strange Acts*, 35.
140 "ὑπολαμβάνω," LSJ gives "take up by getting under."
141 van Stempvoort, "Interpretation," 38.
142 Strelan, *Strange Acts*, 36.
143 Probably "going," so Wright, *Jesus*, 361.
144 With Parsons, *Departure*, 144.
145 Davies, "Prefigurement," 229–31; cf. Talbert, review of Michel, *Die Abschiedsrede des Paulus*, 61–62.

Jesus has now penetrated the barrier between the earthly and heavenly realms, and as a result unprecedented traffic will flow between the two: angelic activity marks the early chapters of Acts (1:10–11; 5:19; 8:26; 10:3; 12:7–11, 23; cf. 27:23–24), as do the coming and activity of the Spirit (e.g., 2:1–4; 4:8, 31; 6:10; 7:55; 8:17; 9:17; 10:44; 11:28; 13:2, 9, 52) and consequent "signs and wonders" (e.g., 2:22, 43; 4:30; 5:12; 6:8; 14:3; 15:12). Healings by the exalted Jesus (note 3:6, 16; 4:10; 9:34) liberate, and exorcisms in his name deliver (e.g., 5:16; 8:7; 16:16–18; 19:12).[146]

The ascension therefore does not mark Jesus's *departure*, as though he is now inactive in the world but rather his exaltation to the place of power over the world. "The ascension, for Luke, indicates that Jesus is Lord, that is, he is active in the affairs of the world and especially in the affairs of Israel. He is engaged in a work that will culminate in making his enemies his footstool. No one can or should oppose him."[147] The heavenly dimension of the universe is vital to understanding the development of the story of Acts, for Jesus's followers will witness between Jesus's ascension and his return (1:11) in a space that is open to heaven's involvement, as has been the case in Luke's Gospel.[148]

10 ὡς ἀτενίζοντες ἦσαν εἰς τὸν οὐρανὸν πορευομένου αὐτοῦ, "While he was going and they were gazing intently into heaven," includes the third "sight" phrase and the first mention of heaven. The verb is a Lukan favorite, here in a periphrastic construction ἀτενίζοντες ἦσαν, "they were gazing intently."[149] Strelan claims that ἀτενίζοντες, "gazing intently," implies entering into a "hypnotic-like vision."[150] However, the verb here, as elsewhere, simply denotes intent looking or staring at something or someone,[151] which suggests that Luke is using a verb of sight to signal the disciples' eyewitness role,[152] a role that includes them having seen the ascension (1:22; 5:31–32).[153] In any case, Luke uses other visual words here that carry no visionary implication. Although εἰς τὸν οὐρανόν could be translated "into the sky" in the three uses in 1:10–11, "into heaven" is better, for it announces Jesus's entry into God's realm (v. 11; cf. 2:33). πορευομένου αὐτοῦ, "while he was going," denotes "a natural and visible movement . . . a physical transfer from one place to another,"[154] underlining that this is not a visionary non-physical event.

---

146 More fully, see Walton, "Heavens."

147 Strelan, *Strange Acts*, 47. So also Gaventa, "Acts"; Buckwalter, *Character*, 182–84; contra Fitzmyer, *Acts*, 194: "The ascension . . . functions as the end of the Period of Jesus"; and Zwiep, *Ascension*, 182: "Luke advocates an 'absentee christology, i.e., a christology that is dominated by the (physical) absence *and present inactivity* of the exalted Lord" (his italics).

148 Walton, "Heavens," esp. 64–71; Sleeman, *Geography*, 79.

149 MHT, 4:52; the verb occurs in Luke 4:20; 22:56; Acts 1:10; 3:4, 12; 6:15; 7:55; 10:4; 11:6; 13:9; 14:9; 23:1; only 2 Cor 3:7, 13 elsewhere in NT.

150 Strelan, *Strange Acts*, 38–39.

151 "ἀτενίζω," BDAG 148.

152 Fitzmyer, *Acts*, 210.

153 With Strelan, *Strange Acts*, 41.

154 Đỗ, *Journey*, 154–55, quoting 155; her discussion of this phrase is very helpful.

ἰδού, "suddenly," signals to the reader that something surprising or significant is happening or is about to happen (cf. 8:27; 10:17; 12:7; 16:1), here the arrival of two new characters who prove to be heavenly messengers.[155] Luke also uses it in speech to signal the same thing to a hearer within the text, with the reader "overhearing."[156] This is the first of twenty-three uses in Acts, following on fifty-seven occurrences in Luke.[157]

ἄνδρες δύο . . . ἐν ἐσθήσεσι λευκαῖς, "two men . . . in white clothes," echoes the transfiguration (Luke 9:30, where the two are Moses and Elijah) and Jesus's resurrection (Luke 24:4, the two angels at the tomb, strikingly also using the Lukanism ἐσθής, "clothing"[158]). Here, as in Luke 24:4, heavenly, angelic figures are identified as such by their white clothes (cf. 2 Macc 11:8; Mark 16:5; John 20:12; Herm. *Vis.* 1.2.2; *Sim.* 8.2.3) and provide divine commentary on events for the earth-bound disciples, as in, for example, Dan 9:20–27, and also elsewhere in Luke-Acts.[159] In the transfiguration, it is Jesus whose clothes are white; the two present are Moses and Elijah, but it is not necessary to suppose that Moses and Elijah are present here.[160]

ἄγγελος (which is not used here but occurs regularly in Acts and Luke) denotes a messenger or envoy who may be human or heavenly in origin,[161] although the large majority in the NT are heavenly.[162] LXX uses this term 300x and, particularly after the Babylonian exile, it has the sense of a divine messenger sent from heaven, notably in Daniel (3:92, 95 [MT 3:25, 28]). Some angels there are named (e.g., Dan 8:16; 9:21; 10:13). Later Judaism has a developed angelology, such as at Qumran, where the community understand themselves to live in communion with angels.[163] In Luke-Acts, angelic appearances are clustered around the birth stories (Luke 1:8–20, 26–38; 2:8–15, 21); Jesus's death and resurrection (Luke 22:43 *si vera lectio*; 24:4–8, 23); in relation to the believers in Jerusalem, moving the mission outward (Acts 8:26), particularly in bringing Cornelius to contact Peter (10:3, 7, 22; 11:13); freeing believers from prison (5:19; 12:7–11); in causing Herod's death (12:23); and in reassuring Paul of the safety of the ship in the storm (27:23). In many respects, they function similarly to the Spirit (cf. 8:26, 29, 39), as agents of YHWH and the exalted Jesus, carrying the *missio Dei* forward by speech and actions, positively directing the believers, and negatively by protecting and guarding the

155 Đỗ, *Journey*, 170.
156 E.g., Acts 5:9, 25; 7:56; 8:36; 10:19, 21, 30; 11:11; 13:11, 25, 46; 20:22, 25; 27:24.
157 In total, 193 NT occurrences, including sixty-two in Matthew, and twenty-six in Revelation; no other book has above seven.
158 *VL* 251.
159 Luke 1:8–20, 26–38; 2:9–15, 21; 24:1–9, 23; Acts 8:26; 10:3–8, 30–33; 11:13; 12:7–11, 23; 27:23.
160 As Goulder, *Type*, 147–48 claims.
161 "ἄγγελος," BDAG 8–9.
162 G. Kittel, "ἄγγελος," *TDNT* 1:83 at §D.1. On the roles of angels, see M. J. Davidson, "Angel," *NIDB* 1:148–55; C. A. Newsom and D. F. Watson, "Angels," *ABD* 1:248–56.
163 E.g., 1QS XI, 7–8; 1QSa II, 8–9. "ἄγγελος," *NIDNTTE* 1:122 at JL §3.

believers. Luke, in common with other NT authors, does not speculate about the origin or nature of angels—they are mentioned rather matter-of-factly.

11 ἄνδρες Γαλιλαῖοι, "men of Galilee," reiterates the origins of the disciple group as craftworkers and fishermen from the north (cf. Luke 5:1–11; 22:59; 23:5, 49, 55, including several references in the latter part of Luke[164]), a point that Luke develops when portraying the Pentecost crowd's surprise at the Galilean disciples' tongues-speech (Acts 2:7) and the Sanhedrin's surprise at their eloquence (5:37). This is the first example of a number of double vocatives in Acts, including ἄνδρες ἀδελφοί, "men, brothers" (e.g., 1:16; 2:29), ἄνδρες Ἰουδαῖοι, "men, Jews" (e.g., 2:14; 13:15), ἄνδρες Ἰσραηλῖται, "men, Israelites" (e.g., 2:22; 3:12; 5:34; 13:16; 21:27; cf. Josephus, *Ant.* 3.8.1 §189). They are found in Jewish settings apart from ἄνδρες Ἀθηναῖοι, "men, Athenians" (Acts 17:22; cf. Demosthenes, *1 Olynth.* 1), and ἄνδρες Ἐφέσιοι, "men, Ephesians" (Acts 19:35). This is a Greek, not a Semitic, idiom,[165] and introduces words seeking to win over the named group to the speaker's view.[166]

τί ἑστήκατε ἐμβλέποντες εἰς τὸν οὐρανόν;, "Why are you standing staring into heaven?" This fourth "seeing" phrase concerning Jesus's ascension offers a corrective and reorientation to the disciples: rather than being sky scanners, focused on Jesus's place in heaven,[167] they have a job they will be equipped to do (v. 8). This contrasts with Second Temple Jewish writings that portray a journey to heaven; rather than making such a journey, the disciples will travel through the inhabited earth. Sleeman observes that the main form-critical markers of heavenly journeys are absent even from the story of Jesus's ascension.[168] The disciples' vocation "was to be witnesses not stargazers."[169]

οὗτος ὁ Ἰησοῦς ὁ ἀναλημφθεὶς ἀφ ὑμῶν εἰς τὸν οὐρανὸν οὕτως ἐλεύσεται ὃν τρόπον ἐθεάσασθε αὐτὸν πορευόμενον εἰς τὸν οὐρανόν, "This Jesus, who has been taken up from you into heaven, will come in the same way in which you saw him going into heaven." This saying, including the fifth "sight" phrase in vv. 9–11, mentions Jesus's return for the first time in Acts; it will become a theme of the apostolic preaching as the time of universal restoration (3:21) and judgment when the master returns (10:42; 17:31; cf. Luke 12: 35–48; 19:11–27). οὕτως . . . ὃν τρόπον, "likewise . . . in the same way," indicates that Jesus will come from heaven to earth (cf. 1 Thess 4:16) accompanied by the same "stage props," namely the cloud (v. 9; cf. Luke 21:7; Matt 24:30; 26:64; Mark 13:26; 14:62; Dan 7:13)—but his return will not be a private event for disciples, as the ascension was: his return will be public (Luke 17:25; cf. Rev 1:7). The reality of Jesus's reign, presently beyond the sight of mortals, for he is in heaven, will

---

164 So Johnson, *Acts*, 27.
165 Barrett, *Acts*, 1:83; van der Horst, "Parallels 1,1–26," 22; Zwiep, *Judas*, 85n38.
166 Cf. Calvin, *Acts*, ad loc.
167 Contra Haenchen, *Acts*, 150, who asserts they are focused on his return.
168 Sleeman, *Geography*, 77. For the markers of such journeys, see Dean-Otting, *Journeys*, 4–5.
169 Stott, *Message of Acts*, 51.

then be universally seen and experienced. οὕτως also implies "so really and so certainly," and underlines that the disciples may be confident in the promise of Jesus's return, even if they do not know its timing.[170] "Paradoxically, his departure from the world is the guarantee of a return."[171]

Wright interprets the apocalyptic passages in the Synoptics (esp. Mark 13; Matt 24; Luke 21) as speaking of the forthcoming vindication of Jesus in his resurrection and in the fall of Jerusalem and thus considers that this is the first time anyone speaks to the disciples about Jesus's return.[172] He believes Jesus did not speak of his return to earth prior to his death, on the ground that the disciples could not possibly, at that time, have understood him. This is as much a discussion about the interpretation of the Gospels as of v. 11; suffice to say here that Wright is correct in affirming that early Christian expectation was of the return of Jesus as the time when the universe would be restored and renewed and Jesus would rule as king on the renewed earth.[173]

This saying highlights the reality of Jesus's return while saying nothing about its timing (cf. v. 7; 1 Thess 5:1–2). Conzelmann reads Acts, and this saying in particular, as addressing a situation where immediate expectation of the return of Jesus has been disappointed.[174] On this view, this passage "delimits" the expectation to the indefinite future, and the church and a process of "salvation history" produce a new eschatology to replace imminent expectation; cf. the misleading characterisation, "The end is *postponed* to much later times."[175] However, if anything, this saying seems to address a concern that Jesus may be gone for good (cf. 2 Pet 3:3–4) and reinforces the promise of his return.[176] Franklin observes that Luke "was not necessarily expecting [Jesus's return] to be long delayed,"[177] rightly identifying the openness in timing found here. That said, it is hazardous to "mirror-read" this text to reconstruct Luke's own situation, for it is likely that Luke (in common with the other evangelists) writes for a wide audience rather than a particular believing community.[178] Further, we lack evidence of early Christian disappointment at the "failure" of a hope for Jesus's return within a short period, not least in the early fathers, where the hope of Jesus's return is still lively.[179] Gaventa observes that Luke-Acts contains numerous examples of promises fulfilled (from OT

170 Fitzmyer, *Acts*, 211; Eisen, *Poetik*, 155: ". . . the beginning of the narrative refers to the end of the story that is not now being told" (my translation); cf. Schnackenburg, "Eschatologie," 255–56.

171 Marguerat, *Actes*, 1:49 (my translation).

172 Wright, *New Testament*, 459–64; Wright, *Jesus*, ch. 8, esp. 339–68.

173 For a fine short exposition of this theme, see Wright, *New Heavens*.

174 Conzelmann, *Theology*, passim.

175 Myllykoski, "Being," 163 (my italics).

176 Wilson, *Gentiles*, 106.

177 Franklin, "Ascension," 200.

178 Bauckham, "For Whom."

179 E.g., 1 Clem. 23:4–5; Justin, *1 Apol.* 51; Tertullian, *Spect.* 30; see also Wright, *New Testament*, 462–64.

to NT or within Luke's two-volume work) that would bolster early Christian expectation that the promise of Jesus's return would be kept.[180]

Explanation

Luke continues and completes his transition from the Gospel to Acts in these verses, summarising the latter part of his Gospel and setting the scene for the story of the church's growth.

Verses 3–5 provide a very compact summary of the latter part of Luke's Gospel: Jesus's death ("after he had suffered," v. 3; cf. Luke 23), resurrection ("he presented himself to them alive," Acts 1:3; cf. vv. 4–8; Luke 24), his command to stay in Jerusalem (Acts 1:4, cf. v. 2; Luke 24:49), and his promise of the Spirit (Acts 1:4; cf. v. 8; Luke 24:49). This section also refers to John the baptizer (Acts 1:5), and thus vv. 3–5 with vv. 1–2 summarize the whole of Luke's Gospel. Such deep connectedness shows that Luke intends Acts to be read as the continuation of the story of Jesus.

To assert that Acts continues the story of Jesus immediately raises the question of the nature of his involvement in the story after his death and resurrection. The latter part of this passage (vv. 6–11) answers that question in several important ways.

First, Jesus is still restoring Israel after his resurrection, but not in the way the disciples' question presupposes (v. 6). Jesus is the one who will restore Israel, but rather than Israel reigning over the nations, Israel will open up to embrace and welcome the nations "to the end of the earth" (v. 8). The timing of the restoration is unclear (v. 7), but Luke's readers can be confident in it, for the promise of Jesus (v. 8) does not deny it. The means of Israel's restoration will be the witness of the believing community and the work of the Spirit (v. 8) rather than military might—Jesus's reign is announced by witnesses, not soldiers, contrasting with the world-ruling ambitions of the Roman Empire.

Secondly, Jesus will thus be represented by his witnesses, the believing community, who are both sent *by* him as his witnesses and sent to witness *to and about* him (v. 8)—"My witnesses" encompasses both senses. Their Spirit-empowered testimony will be focused on Jesus in order to persuade hearers to come to a right verdict about Jesus, a verdict that reverses the mistaken human verdict of those who crucified Jesus, as God reversed that verdict in Jesus's resurrection—this is the burden of the early evangelistic speeches (2:23–24; 3:13–15).

Thirdly, Jesus will be present through the Spirit's enabling of the witnesses (1:8). The promised Holy Spirit will bring the presence and power of God, now known in and through Jesus the Messiah, to the world through God's people. Later, Simon will offer money to gain the power to hand on the Spirit, but

180 Gaventa, *Acts*, 67.

the Spirit is sheer gift (8:20) from a generous God who honors the promise of his Messiah.

Fourthly, Jesus is present in heaven alongside God and thus in the position of power and rule in the universe (1:9–11; cf. Dan 7:13–14). He is not an absentee from the story—rather, this story expands anthropocentric and geocentric conceptions of geography to include the heavenly dimension. In the chapters to come Luke's readers will see how his rule plays out—in Jesus's ability to send the Spirit (Acts 2:33), to heal and perform "signs and wonders" (3:6–7, 16; 4:10, 30; 8:5–8; 9:34), to empower and embolden his witnesses (4:13, 19–20, 29–31, 33; 5:29–32), to rescue his followers or enable them to endure suffering and injustice (4:18–21; 5:19–20, 21; 7:55–60), and even to turn around the life direction of Jesus's arch-opponent, Saul (9:3–6, 17–22). Jesus's rule will extend throughout the inhabited world, "to the end of the earth" (1:8), hinting toward the inclusion of gentiles in the believing community. Jesus's rule necessarily relativizes the claims of the emperor to universal jurisdiction, as YHWH's rule in the OT had done against the empires of its day.

Fifthly, Jesus will not stay in heaven forever but will return to earth (v. 11). The first of a cluster of angelic appearances in Acts provides divine interpretation of Jesus's ascension, directing the believers' attention into God's future when Jesus will return to wrap up history and bring God's universal restoration to its goal and climax (3:21). This firm hope—a hope without timetable—governs and undergirds the believing community's response to suffering and discouragement, for it points to the day when the present, invisible rule of Jesus over the cosmos will become visible and apparent to all.

C. Between Jesus's Ascension and the Spirit's Coming (1:12–26)

Bibliography

Bauckham, R. *Jude,* 19–32. ———. "Restoration." **Bauer, J. B.** "Καρδιογνώστης." **Beardslee, W. A.** "Casting." **Benoit, P.** *Jesus,* 1:189–207. **Bishop, E. F. F.** "Guide." **Brawley, R. L.** *Text,* 61–74. **Brooten, B. J.** *Women Leaders.* **Brown, R. E.** *Death,* 1: 565–67 [with fuller bibliography on the death of Judas], 636–59; 2:1404–10. **Brown, R. E., K. P. Donfried, J. A. Fitzmyer and J. Reumann, eds.** *Mary,* 105–77. **Brug, J. F.** "Acts 1:26." **Chase, F. H.** "Acts 1.18." **Cohick, L. H.** *Women,* 195–224. **Cosgrove, C. H.** "Divine." **Derrett, J. D. M.** "Akeldama." **Doble, P.** "Psalms." **Dodd, C. H.** *According,* esp. 57–60. **Dunn, J. D. G.** *Beginning,* 149–55. **Dupont, J.** "Destinee." ———. "Douxieme Apôtre." ———. *Nouvelles,* 296–318. **Eisen, U. E.** *Poetik,* 157–61. **Ellingworth, P.** "Men." **Estrada, N. P.** *Followers,* 104–88. **Ferguson, E.** "Qumran." **Fuller, R. H.** "Choice." **Gaventa, B. R.** *Mary,* esp. 49–78. **Gordon, A. B.** "Fate." **Grant, J. A.** "Singing," esp. 38–44. **Green, J. B.** "Persevering," esp. 185, 189–90. ———. *Theology.* **Harris, J. R.** "Did Judas." **Jervell, J.** *Luke,* 75–112. **Johnson, E. A.** *Truly.* **Johnson, L. T.** *Function,* 174–83. ———. *Decision,* 60–62. ———. *Midrash,* 14–15. **Judd, A.** "Gadamer." **Kauppi, L. A.** *Gods,* 19–27. **Kilpatrick, G. D.** "Quotations." **Kurz, W. S.** *Reading,* 76–77. **Lake, K.** "Death," *BegC,* 5:22–30. **Lee, D.** *Luke-Acts,* 220–26. **Levine, L. I.** *Ancient Synagogue,* 470–90. **Lindars, B., SSF.** *Apologetic,* 99–109. **Litwak, K. D.** *Echoes.* **MacDonald, D. R.** *Gospels and Homer,* 60–65. ———. "Luke's Use." ———. *Testament,* 105–19. **Manns, F.** "Midrash." **Masson, C.** "Reconstitution." **McCabe, D. R.** *Kill,* 200–208. **Meier, J. P.** "Circle." ———. *Marginal Jew,* 1:318–32. **Moo, D.** "Tradition," 157–75. **Murphy-O'Connor, J.** "Cenacle." ———. *Land,* 136–37. **Nellessen, E.** "Tradition." **Niccum, C.** "Note." **Novick, T.** "Succeeding." **Omanson, R. L.** "How." **Pfitzner, V. C.** "Pneumatic Apostleship," 216–19. **Quesnell, Q.** "Women." **Read-Heimerdinger, J.** "Barnabas." **Rengstorf, K. H.** "Election." **Renié, J.** "L'élection." **Riesner, R.** "Jesus, the Primitive Community." **Robertson, J.** *Death.* **Schmidt, F.** "Élection." **Sleeman, M.** *Geography,* 81–91. **Steyn, G. J.** *Quotations,* 38–63. **Talbert, C. H.** *Reading Luke-Acts,* 19–55. **Thiele, W.** "Bemerkung." **Thornton, T. C. G.** "Continuing." **Thurston, B. B.** "τὸ ὑπερῷον." **Torrey, C. C.** *Composition,* 10–14. **Trebilco, P. R.** *Self-designations,* 38–46. **Twelftree, G. H.** "Prayer," 271–72. **Vazakas, A. A.** "Is Acts." **Walton, S.** "Ὁμοθυμαδόν," 101, 104–5. **Weiser, A.** "Nachwahl." **Whitlock, M. G.** "Acts 1:15–26." **Wilcox, M.** "Judas-tradition." **Wilcox, M.** "Judas-tradition." ———. *Semitisms,* 93–100. **Wilson, S. G.** *Gentiles,* 107–20. **Zehnle, R. F.** *Pentecost Discourse,* 104–11. **Zwiep, A. W.** *Judas.*

Translation

12 Then they returned to Jerusalem from the Mount of Olives, which is about a
Sabbath's journey from Jerusalem. 13 When they entered Jerusalem,[a] they went up
into the upper room where they were staying, Peter and John and James[b] and Andrew,
Philip and Thomas, Bartholomew and Matthew, James the son of Alphaeus and Simon

the Zealot and Judas the son of James. [14] These all were persistently devoting themselves with one mind to prayer,[c] together with the women[d] and Mary the mother of Jesus and[e] his brothers.

[15] In those days Peter stood up among the brothers[f] and sisters[g] (there was a crowd of about[h] one hundred and twenty people[i] together) and said, [16] "People, brothers and sisters, it was necessary for the Scripture to be fulfilled which the Holy Spirit spoke ahead of time through the mouth of David concerning Judas, who became a guide to those who arrested Jesus— [17] for he was counted among us and he was given a share in this ministry. [18] Indeed, this very man acquired a plot of land from the reward for his wickedness and, after falling head first, he burst open in the middle and all his bowels[j] were poured out.[k] [19] This became known to everyone living in Jerusalem, so that that plot was called in their own[l] language "Hakeldamach,"[m] which means "place of blood." [20] For as it is written in the book of Psalms, "Let his[n] residence become deserted,[o] and let there be no dweller in it," and, "let another take his position of responsibility." [21] Therefore it is necessary for one of the men who went about with us for the entire period during which[p] the Lord Jesus went in and out among us, [22] beginning from John's baptism until the day when[q] he was taken up from us—one of these must become a witness of his resurrection with us." [23] And they proposed[r] two, Joseph called Barsabbas,[s] who was known as Justus, and Matthias. [24] And they prayed, "You Lord, the one who knows everyone's hearts, show which one of these two you have chosen [25] to take the position[t] of this apostolic ministry from which Judas turned aside to go to his own position."[u] [26] And they cast lots for them,[v] and the lot fell for Matthias and he was added[w] to the eleven apostles.

Notes

a. "Jerusalem" is not named here but is clearly implied by v. 12.

b. Later MSS (E and many minuscules) have varying orders for the first three apostles, frequently adopting the more usual order "Peter and James and John" (cf. Matt 17:1; Mark 5:37; 13:3—contrast Luke 8:51; 9:28, which both have "Peter and John and James"); D has "Peter and John, James (spelled Ἐιάκωβος) and Andrew."

c. C[3] and many minuscules add καὶ τῇ δεήσει, "and to supplication," probably under the influence of Phil 4:6; *TCGNT*[2], 246.

d. D reads καὶ τέκνοις, "and children," suggesting that the women present were the wives of the Eleven, a typical "anti-feminist" reading of D; Seim, *Message*, 22; Rius-Camps and Read-Heimerdinger, *Message*, 1:56. Cf. 21:5 σὺν γυναιξὶν καὶ τέκνοις, "with women and children"; *TCGNT*[2], 246; Niccum, "Note"; Thiele, "Bemerkung"; Witherington, "Anti-feminist Tendencies."

e. σύν, "with," is found here in B C[3] E 33 81 326 and most minuscules, putting a greater distance between Jesus and his "brothers" by paralleling σὺν γυναιξίν, "with the women," and σὺν τοῖς ἀδελφοῖς αὐτοῦ, "with his brothers." σύν was probably added to support the perpetual virginity of Mary; it is missing from ℵ A C* D 88 104 134 241 464[c] 468 547 876 915 1175 1311 1758 1765 1838 etc.; *TCGNT*[2], 246–47.

f. A number of Western witnesses (D E 1739[s] it[e, gig, p] Cyprian Augustine) read μαθητῶν, "disciples," rather than ἀδελφῶν, "brothers," probably to avoid confusion with the "brothers" of v. 14; *TCGNT*^{2}, 247.

g. τῶν ἀδελφῶν includes the women mentioned in v. 14, and I therefore translate inclusively, "brothers and sisters."

h. ὡσεί, "about," is used for approximate numbers (2:41; 19:7; "ὡσεί," BDAG 1106, §2), as is the simpler form ὡς (4:4; 5:7, 36; 13:18; 19:34; "ὡς," BDAG 1103, §6).

i. ὀνομάτων, "names," here standing for "persons" ("ὄνομα," BDAG 713, §2); cf. Rev 3:4; 11:13.

j. σπλάγχνα, "bowels," denotes the inner parts of the body, especially the entrails; "σπλάγχνον," BDAG 938.

k. ἐξεχύθη, "were poured out," aor. pass. ind. ἐκχύννω, Hellenistic form of ἐκχέω; see "ἐκχέω," BDAG 312, §1.b.

l. ἰδίᾳ, "their own," is absent from ℵ 𝔓^{74vid} B* D, probably by haplogr.; *TCGNT*^{2}, 248.

m. Most Greek MSS spell this word Ἀκελδαμά, equivalent to Aramaic) חקלדם *ḥqldm*), "field of blood." However, earlier majuscules (ℵ A B D E) spell the word with a final χ or κ, representing a transliteration of the Aramaic ℵ, which is silent; *TCGNT*^{2}, 248–49; MHT, 2:108; Zwiep, *Judas*, 91.

n. 81 326 2495 vg$^{cl, ww}$ syr^{hmg} read αὐτῶν, "their," in place of αὐτοῦ, "his," harmonising the quotation with Ps 68:26 LXX (MT 69:26; EVV 69:25).

o. Taking ἔρημος adjectivally, "deserted"; BDAG 391 s.v., §1.a.

p. ἐν παντὶ χρόνῳ, "for the entire period during which," dat. rel. pn. ᾧ, would usually mean "at which" when speaking of time but here clearly denotes time during which (usually denoted by gen.). It is possibly dat. by rel. attraction (MHT, 3:324; Porter, 251–52) or because the dat. functions like a gen. of time (Wallace, 156 with n45).

q. τῆς ἡμέρας ἧς, "the day when," rel. attraction: τῆς ἡμέρας ᾗ, "the day on which," would be better Greek style.

r. D* it^{gig} Augustine read sg. ἔστησεν, "*he* proposed," entailing the later view that Peter ruled the church with the authority of monepiscopate; *TCGNT*^{2}, 249. A corrector has amended D to ἔστησαν, "they proposed."

s. D 6^s it vg^{mss} read Βαρναβᾶν, "Barnabas," leading Read-Heimerdinger, "Barnabas", 50–53, to identify this Joseph with the one in 4:36. However the solid support of 𝔓^{47vid} ℵ A B E Ψ 81 and most other MSS, and the possibility of an easy slip of memory by a scribe, suggest the reading Βαρσαββᾶν, "Barsabbas," is secure.

t. τόπον, "position," in the sense of task or role; "τόπος," BDAG 1011, §3. ℵ C^3 E 33 1739 𝔐 read κλῆρον, "share," probably under the influence of τὸν κλῆρον τῆς διακονίας ταύτης, "the share of this ministry," in v. 17. There is strong support for τόπον from 𝔓^{74} and Alexandrian (A B C* Ψ cop$^{sa, bo}$) and Western (D it$^{d, gig}$ syr^{hmg} Augustine) witnesses.

u. The repetition of τόπος, "position," in v. 25 is shown by translating the word the same way in each case (cf. NRSVue, GNB). REB hides the echo: "to receive this *office* . . . which Judas abandoned to go *where he belonged.*"

v. D* E Ψ and most minuscules read gen. αὐτῶν, "of them," rather than dat. (of advantage) αὐτοῖς, "for them"—but dat. is strongly supported by ℵ A B C 33 81 1739 vg cop$^{sa, bo}$; *TCGNT*^{2}, 250. Ferguson, "Qumran," discusses the intriguing possibility that the D reading indicates a process of community decision making akin to that at Qumran (see *Comment* on v. 27).

w. Rather than the rare συγκατεψηφίσθη, "he was added," read by most witnesses, D* reads συψηφίσθη, "he was counted," and a corrector has amended to the more correct συνεψηφίσθη (cf. 19:19). D also reads "twelve," ιβ′, rather than "eleven," ἕνδεκα, taking μετά in the sense "among," rather than "to"; *TCGNT*^{2}, 250.

Form/Structure/Setting

Delimitation of pericope. This section narrates key events in the transitional period between the ascension of Jesus (1:9–11) and the coming of the Spirit (2:1–4). During this time the life of the followers of Jesus is about waiting, in accordance with the dominical instruction (1:4). The believers remain in Jerusalem and focus their waiting in prayer (v. 14), a characteristic of the Christian community throughout Acts (and a Lukan theme in the Gospel[1]).

After a general characterization of the period (vv. 12–14), Luke focuses on a particular moment: Peter calls the community to replace Judas among the apostles (vv. 15–22), citing Scripture in support of his call. The community responds by proposing two, Joseph Barsabbas and Matthias (v. 23), and by praying that God will show them which one God wishes to take this role (v. 25). The divine will is ascertained by casting lots, and Matthias is chosen (v. 26). Both subsections end with the mention of prayer (vv. 14, 24–25).

Sources/historicity. We may be confident of the existence of the group of twelve during Jesus's ministry; note particularly 1 Cor 15:5, found in our earliest literary testimony to the resurrection of Jesus.[2]

Judas's death (vv. 18–19) is also attested by Matt 27:3–10 and fragment 18 of Papias, preserved by Apollinaris of Laodicea.[3] There are common elements to the three versions: (i) money from Judas is used to acquire a plot of land near Jerusalem, (ii) the name of the plot was "field of blood," (iii) Scripture interprets the death of Judas, and (iv) Judas dies in tragic circumstances. These commonalities suggest the death of Judas is rooted in historical tradition.[4] There are also differences: (i) Matthew has the priests "buy" (ἀγοράζω) the field, whereas Acts has Judas himself "acquire" (κτάομαι) the field (which does not necessarily mean that he himself purchased the field; see *Comment*), and (ii) Matthew says that Judas was remorseful and hanged himself (not mentioned by Luke or Papias), whereas Acts attributes Judas's death to a fall. The Acts account is very brief, and it is not at all straightforward to reconstruct events: Acts does not say whether Judas hanged himself or not.[5] Since

---

1 Fitzmyer, *Luke*, 1:244–47.

2 For a defence of the historicity of Jesus's choice of a band of twelve during his ministry, see Meier, "Circle." Lüdemann, *Early Christianity*, 31, 36, similarly agrees that the existence of the group of twelve and the list of their names are based on historical tradition.

3 Greek text and ET: Holmes, ed. *Fathers*, 754–57. For speculative arguments that Luke is dependent on Papias and the *Iliad* for his account and that Matthew created his account from various passages in Scripture, see MacDonald, "Luke's Use"; MacDonald, *Gospels and Homer*, 60–65; MacDonald, *Does the New Testament*, 105–19.

4 Benoit, *Jesus*, 1:206–7; Zehnle, *Discourse*, 106; Weiser, "Nachwahl," 99. Cf. Nellessen, "Tradition," arguing that the story is rooted in historical tradition.

5 Lightfoot, *Acts*, 80–84, highlights that Acts mentions Judas's death only allusively and thus is lacking in detail. He considers "that St. Peter evidently supposes his hearers to be acquainted with the main facts, and therefore . . . selects those facts *only* that have a bearing on his immediate purpose" (82, emphasis original).

at least Ephrem, *Comm. Diatess.* XX.18, it has been suggested that the two versions could be harmonized by supposing that Judas hanged himself and the rope broke, with the outcome that he fell and his innards spilled out.[6] Such attempts at historical reconstruction are at best possible; the difficulty is not that the three accounts are necessarily contradictory but simply that the information provided by each of them is too limited to enable a reconstruction that commands confidence.[7]

It is hard to imagine why Luke might create the story of the election of Matthias to replace Judas. The Jewish names of the candidates and the Jewish process of election by casting lots speak for its historicity.[8] The appropriation of Scripture (vv. 20–21) is similar to some pesher interpretation at Qumran, where the focus was not so much interpreting Scripture per se, but interpreting recent events in terms drawn from Scripture, which makes creation of events unlikely.[9] Lüdemann observes that "we have no means of checking anything,"[10] but lack of corroboration from other sources is far from uncommon in ancient history. Were Luke to invent a story to authenticate Matthias, it would be much more likely that he would have the risen Jesus choose a replacement or hold back an appointment until after the Spirit comes at Pentecost.[11] "[N]o *Sitz im Leben* for such a piece of tradition is so natural or likely as the early days of perplexity."[12] It is notable that Luke does not continue to present the Twelve as having a decisive leadership role in the believing communities later in Acts—thus, for example, James is not replaced when he is killed (12:2). These reasons, and the lack of any further role for Matthias in Acts (or elsewhere in early Christian tradition) speak for the historicity of this story.[13]

Luke, of course, tells the story in his own style,[14] bringing out links with the preceding section in the mention of the Spirit (v. 16; cf. vv. 4, 8) and use of ἀνελήμφθη, "he was taken up," for Jesus's ascension (v. 22; cf. vv. 2, 11).[15]

Structure. The structure of the section is straightforward:

---

6 For other harmonizing interpretations, see Harris, "Did Judas," 493–96.

7 Carson, "Matthew," 562.

8 Weiser, "Nachwahl," 99, who considers Luke's source to be a written tradition.

9 With Moo, "Tradition," 167, discussing the Matthean account of Judas's death. Weiser, "Nachwahl," 100–101, thinks it likely that the Ps 68 (MT 69) quotations were linked in tradition with Judas's death.

10 *Acts*, 37.

11 With Dunn, *Beginning*, 154.

12 Dodd, *According*, 59.

13 Wilson, *Gentiles*, 108.

14 Also vocabulary: see Renié, "L'élection," estimating that 72% of the 56 most significant words are Lukanisms. Cf. Manns's attempt to argue that Luke is telling vv. 16–20 by reading Aramaic scriptural texts midrashically, while being clear that he regards the event as historical (Manns, "Midrash"). This is not a strong argument, for it depends on much later Targums as claimed sources for Luke's writing.

15 Zehnle, *Discourse*, 105.

vv. 12–14 Return from the Mount of Olives and waiting

A general description of the life of group during this transitional period. Its role is to move the reader's attention from the ascension of Jesus (vv. 6–11) toward the detailed account of the community's action in replacing Judas (vv. 15–26) via the group's united prayer in obedience to Jesus.

vv. 15–26 The replacement of Judas
 vv. 15–22 Peter calls the community to replace Judas
  vv. 15–20a Judas's death interpreted with Scripture
  vv. 20b–22 The need to replace Judas interpreted with Scripture
 vv. 23–26 The process of choosing the new apostle

Talbert suggests that the structure of the passage corresponds to the OT "choice of supplementary leadership" after the manner of the appointment of leaders to assist Moses (Exod 18:14–25) or Joshua's appointment to succeed Moses (Num 27:12–23).[16] There are four elements to this *Gattung*: (i) the problem stated (vv. 15–20; cf. Exod 18:14–18; Num 27:12–14); (ii) the proposed solution (vv. 21a, 22b; cf. Exod 18:19–23; Num 27:15–17); (iii) the qualifications of the new leader(s) (vv. 21b–22; cf. Exod 18:21; Num 27:18–21); and (iv) setting apart of the new leader(s) (vv. 23–26; cf. Exod 18:25; Num 27:22–23). While there are broad parallels (although lacking specific echoes of vocabulary[17]), there is no mention of the laying on of hands, which is key in the OT stories (and which Luke mentions elsewhere, e.g., Acts 6:6; 13:3). This analysis adds little which could not be seen from reading Acts on its own terms.

Setting. A key role of this section is as a bridge from the ascension of Jesus to the coming of the Spirit at Pentecost. Other than the two candidates for apostleship, the other characters named are all known from Luke's Gospel.[18] Matthias is never mentioned again in Acts (along with most of the apostolic band), and the Twelve as a group are only mentioned at 6:2. When James is killed, he is not replaced (12:2). This section is evidently important for its preparatory role and has no wider significance.[19] Because the restoration of Israel is central to what God is now doing, it is vital for the body of believers to be seen as seeking God in prayer (vv. 12–14) and restoring the number of the apostolic band to twelve (Luke 22:28–30; see *Comment* on vv. 21–22).[20] It is

16 Talbert, *Acts*, 22; and his fuller discussion of Greco-Roman parallels in Talbert, *Reading Luke-Acts*, esp. 19–55.
17 Zwiep, *Judas*, 61.
18 Eisen, *Poetik*, 159–60.
19 Pfitzner, "Pneumatic Apostleship," 216–18.
20 With Pfitzner, "Pneumatic Apostleship," 218.

to the group of about 120, who form the restored-Israel-in-miniature, that the Spirit will come in order to renew and equip them for witness to Israel (1:8, 22, 25).

Estrada proposes that the apostolic band is in process of being transformed from followers of Jesus to leaders of the community in this passage,[21] and there is truth in that view. However, he runs beyond the evidence in assuming that the apostles share collectively in the guilt of Judas's betrayal of Jesus.[22] Thus his reading of the text through this lens, asserting that there is a transformation ritual going on and that the apostles must establish their credibility with the wider disciple group of 120 before the Spirit can come,[23] is doubtful—if anyone's honor needs defending, it is Jesus's, for he chose Judas to be part of the apostolic band, and vv. 16–20 establish Judas's responsibility and guilt.[24]

Comment

12 moves the action from Olivet to the city, as the group return. This group is the same as those who witnessed the ascension and probably includes at least some of those mentioned in vv. 14, 15 (see *Comment* on vv. 7–8). Luke adds that the mount is σαββάτου ἔχον ὁδόν, "a Sabbath's day journey," from the city; there is no reason to think this necessarily means that Jesus's ascension took place on a Sabbath, particularly given the forty-day timetable that Luke specifies (v. 3; contra Chrysostom, *Hom. Act.* 3). This distance was the maximum a devout Jew should walk on the Sabbath; m. Sotah 5:3 specifies 2,000 cubits (0.57 miles/0.91 km)—from Olivet to the city was about 0.4 miles/0.7 km. This is the first indication of the location of Jesus's ascension, for Τότε, "then," suggests that the departure to Jerusalem is the next action to take place after Jesus's ascension. The location on a mountain echoes the location of another significant encounter with the glorified Jesus—the transfiguration (Luke 9:28).

13 τὸ ὑπερῷον, "the upper room," is used only in Acts in the NT (here; 9:37, 39; 20:8). Luke specifies this room with the article, which suggests that it was well-known to his readers. He uses a different term for the room where the last supper was held (Luke 22:12, ἀνάγαιον, "upstairs room"); the article here may be anaphoric, indicating that this is the same room.[25] In the Gospel Luke is following Mark 14:15, whereas here he writes independently or has a different source. If the two rooms are one and the same, the likely site is the Cenacle.[26] The term itself simply refers to an upstairs room, frequently built

21 Estrada, *Followers*.
22 Estrada, *Followers*, 6–7.
23 Estrada, *Followers*, 151–88.
24 Sleeman, *Geography*, 87–88.
25 Barrett, *Acts*, 1:86.
26 Murphy-O'Connor, "Cenacle"; Riesner, "Jesus, the Primitive Community," 201–6.

on top of a flat-roofed house.[27] It was clearly a substantial room if the meeting of 120 people portrayed in v. 15 took place there[28] and may have been the place where James and the other believers met (12:17).[29] It is unlikely that a room in the temple courts is meant here—that view mistakenly identifies the location in Luke 24:52–53 with this location.[30]

οὗ ἦσαν καταμένοντες, "where they were staying." The participle of this periphrastic imperfect is an NT *hapax legomenon* (unless 1 Cor 6:16 v.l. καταμενῶ is original) and means "stay, live," often on a temporary basis,[31] implying that the eleven were lodging in this room. Luke also portrays the 120 as meeting there on a regular basis (Acts 1:14).

The list of the eleven agrees in content with Luke 6:14–16, with some differences in sequence.[32] Judas is missing, of course, and this gap prepares for the narrative of his betrayal (Acts 1:18–19).[33] Peter is prominent in the first half of Acts as a key protagonist in the church's growth and development, often as spokesman for the apostolic band, as here (vv. 15–22).[34] Peter is referred to in the Cornelius story (and only there in Acts) as "Simon, known as Peter" or similar.[35] John is second here (fourth in Luke), reflecting his prominence as Peter's partner in key stories to follow (3:1, 3, 11; 4:13, 19; 8:14—John only appears as Peter's partner in Acts, separating Peter from his brother Andrew).[36] James appears in Acts only to be executed (12:2). The others are not mentioned in Acts.

Luke elsewhere identifies this group as οἱ ἀπόστολοι, "the apostles," as he will do in v. 26.[37] He also refers to them as οἱ δώδεκα, "the Twelve" (6:2; cf. 2:14). As a group, they are not mentioned after 16:4, reflecting both Luke's focus on Paul's ministry thereafter and the growing role of a wider group in the leadership of the believing community in Jerusalem (21:18; cf. 15:2, 4, 6, 22), referred to as οἱ πρεσβύτεροι, "the elders" (see *Comment* on 11:30), including James (cf. 15:12–21), who exercises a presiding role.

14 Luke introduces a key theme, prayer, and thereby demonstrates that

27 E.g., LXX Judg 3:20, 23, 24, 25; 2 Kgs 1:2; 4:10, 11; 23:12; see "ὑπερῷον," BDAG 1034.

28 Shulam and Le Cornu, *Acts*, 1:30, cite rabbinic evidence for such rooms being rented out for meetings.

29 Riesner, "Jesus, the Primitive Community," 201.

30 With Haenchen, *Acts*, 153n2; contra Thurston, "τὸ ὑπερῷον," who proposes that a room in the temple's outer courts is meant.

31 "καταμένω," BDAG 522; "καταμένω," MM 329–30; contra Haenchen, *Acts*, 153n3.

32 With Nolland, *Luke*, 1:270–71; Marshall, *Gospel of Luke*, 239–41; Fitzmyer, *Luke*, 1:614–16, 618–20.

33 Johnson, *Acts*, 34; cf. Estrada, *Followers*, 121–25.

34 See Acts 2:14, 37–38; 3:1, 3, 6, 11, 12; 4:8, 13, 19; 5:3, 8–9, 15, 29; 8:14, 20; 9:32, 34, 38–40; 10:5, 9, 13–14, 17–19, 21, 25, 32, 34, 44–46; 11:2, 4, 7, 13; 12:3, 5, 6–7, 11, 14, 16, 18; 15:7.

35 Acts 10:5, 18, 32; 11:13; cf. Luke 5:8; 6:14.

36 Cf. Luke 6:14, where the pairs of brothers are listed together in the first four places in the list, Mark 3:16, where Andrew is fourth, and Matt 10:2, where Andrew is second.

37 See Luke 6:13; Acts 2:37, 42, 43, 35; 4:35, 37; 5:2, 12, 18, 29, 40; 6:6; 8:1, 18; 9:27; 11:1; 15:2, 6, 22–23; 16:4; cf. 14:4, 14.

the group are obedient to Jesus's instruction to "wait" (v. 4). This is the first mention of προσευχή, "prayer," in the book (although previously used in Luke 6:12; 19:46; 22:45) and, indeed, the first time in Luke-Acts when the disciples actually pray.[38] Green acutely observes that the disciples have been taught to pray, called to pray and—we might add—have seen Jesus modeling prayer, and yet do not themselves pray until this point.[39] In the Gospel, Luke focuses on prayer more strongly than the other Synoptics, mentioning prayer where Mark and Matthew do not, notably concerning Jesus praying.[40] In Acts, prayer is the heartbeat of the believing community, indicating at key stages their readiness to engage with God.[41] Luke uses multiple terms here to portray their focus on prayer: they "persistently devoted themselves," ἦσαν προσκαρτεροῦντες; οὗτοι πάντες, "they all," i.e., all those named in v. 13, were involved, plus others; and the Lukanism ὁμοθυμαδόν, "with one mind," signals that the group was deeply united in this action.[42] The latter word is found ten times in Acts (here; 2:46; 4:24; 5:12; 7:57; 8:6; 12:20; 15:25; 18:12; 19:29; only elsewhere in NT at Rom 15:6); it generally denotes shared action stemming from a shared commitment.[43] This is likely to be primarily corporate, rather than individual, prayer.[44] A feature of this persistent prayer is probably that God would send the promised Holy Spirit in line with Jesus's words (1:4–5) and Jesus's own promise that the Father will give the Holy Spirit to those who ask (Luke 11:13).[45] The believers' persistent devotion and unity of mind contrast with the disciples' failure to pray in Gethsemane (Luke 22:40, 45–46); the collocation of προσκαρτερέω and ὁμοθυμαδόν notably recurs in 2:46, characterizing the believers,[46] and persistent devotion to prayer and the ministry of the word is a key feature of the apostles' ministry (6:4).

σὺν γυναιξίν, "together with the women." Luke presents the group meeting to pray as wider than the apostolic band: v. 15 specifies that this group were part of a larger circle of 120, and 2:1 portrays this wider group as those upon whom the Spirit comes. The presence of women with the eleven reflects the picture in Luke of Jesus's followers, where some women take prominent roles

---

38 The noun προσευχή, "prayer," is found at Acts 2:42; 3:1; 6:4; 10:4, 31; 12:5; 16:13, 16; Luke 6:12; 19:46; 22:45; and the verb προσεύχομαι, "pray," at Acts 1:24; 6:6; 8:15; 9:11, 40; 10:9, 30; 11:5; 12:12; 13:3; 14:23; 16:25; 20:36; 21:5; 22:17; 28:8; Luke 1:10; 3:21; 5:16; 6:12, 28; 9:18, 28, 29; 11:1, 2; 18:1, 10, 11; 20:47; 22:40, 41, 44, 46.

39 Green, "Persevering," 185.

40 Luke 3:21; 5:16; 6:12; 9:18, 28–29; 11:1; 22: 31–32; 23:46; see Fitzmyer, *Luke*, 1:244–47; Green, *Theology*, 58–60, 111–12; Barton, *Spirituality*, 87–91.

41 Thus Twelftree, "Prayer," 271, argues that in Acts the Spirit is given by God to "devoted or prayerful people."

42 Walton, "Ὁμοθυμαδόν," 101.

43 Walton, "Ὁμοθυμαδόν," esp. 104–5.

44 Thornton, "Continuing." Twelftree, "Prayer," 271, observes the presence of the article here, τῇ προσευχῇ, "prayer," and suggests it may denote specific prayer, such as the temple prayers (cf. 3:1).

45 Brawley, *Text*, 76.

46 As here, with dative of the thing persisted in; "προσκαρτερέω," BDAG 881, §2.a.

(Luke 8:1–3; 10:38–42; 23:49, 55–56; 24:1–11).[47] It may be that wealthy women continued to provide for the group's needs at this time.[48] To suggest that σύν, "together with," signals that the apostles now have the backing and support of the women and Jesus's family is to ask the preposition to bear more weight than is reasonable.[49]

καὶ Μαριὰμ τῇ μητρὶ τοῦ Ἰησοῦ καὶ τοῖς ἀδελφοῖς αὐτοῦ, "and Mary the mother of Jesus and his brothers," makes it clear that members of Jesus's family are now part of the company of his followers. There are a number of women called "Mary" among the early followers of Jesus (Luke 10:39; Matt 27:61; John 11:2), and so Luke specifies that this one is Jesus's mother. Here, Mary is a believer, echoing her initial presentation in Luke 1:38 and resolving her uncertainties in intervening years.[50] Given that Luke does not mention her in his passion narrative among the women at the cross, it is reasonable to see her presence among the believing community here as historical tradition.[51] Luke's infancy story is told from Mary's perspective (Luke 1:26–56; 2:1–52; note 2:19, 34, 51b), and his portrait of Mary is perhaps the fullest in any (canonical) Gospel.[52] However, this is her only named appearance in Acts, consistent with the fact that Jesus's adopted family, the believing community, has far greater significance than blood ties to Jesus. τοῖς ἀδελφοῖς αὐτοῦ, "his brothers," most probably refers to Jesus's siblings; it is very unlikely to mean "cousins," as some maintain, for there is no clear instance of ἀδελφός meaning "cousin" in the NT.[53] Jesus's mother and brothers were marginalized by Jesus during his ministry according to Luke 8:19–21, although this should not be overstated as Jesus rejecting his family[54] (cf. Luke 14:26; note the more negative view in Mark 3:21—unparalleled in Luke—which portrays Jesus's family as seeking to restrain Jesus forcibly).

15 Although there is a clear change of scene, marked by a vague time notice, ἐν ταῖς ἡμέραις ταύταις, "in those days" (a Lukan signal of change of scene, Luke 1:39; 6:12; Acts 6:1; 11:27[55]), the location is unchanged, in the upper room.[56] This room now holds about 120, rather than simply being the eleven's sleeping quarters (v. 13). Luke's aside about the number provides a

47 Lüdemann, *Early Christianity*, 31, accepts the historicity of this point.

48 Bruce, *Acts* (1990), 106; Peterson, *Acts*, 117; contra Barrett, *Acts*, 1:89.

49 *Pace* Estrada, *Followers*, 149–50.

50 Gaventa, *Mary*, 71–72; Wright, "Mary in the NT," 18; cf. Brown, Donfried, Fitzmyer and Reumann, eds., *Mary*, 176–77.

51 Johnson, *Truly*, 298.

52 Gaventa, *Mary*, 49–78; Brown, Donfried, Fitzmyer and Reumann, eds., *Mary*, 105–77.

53 Meier, *Marginal Jew*, 1:318–32; Wright, "Mary in the NT," 19–22; Bauckham, *Jude*, 19–32. Jerome, *Helv.* 16-17 seeks to argue that the meaning of ἀδελφός can be "nephew," based on Gen 13:8, 11. Each of the cases he cites are examples of uses of ἀδελφός for "relative," and none refers to a cousin; to refer to a nephew as ἀδελφός, i.e., "relative," does not indicate that ἀδελφός can mean "nephew."

54 Dunn, *Jesus*, 595–99.

55 Cf. Jervell, *Apostelgeschichte*, 123; Weiser, "Nachwahl," 102.

56 Quesnell, "Women," 62.

baseline for the subsequent growth of the believing community (note 2:41; 4:4; 6:1, 7).[57] The group is τῶν ἀδελφῶν, "of the brothers and sisters," including at least the eleven and the women and relatives of Jesus (vv. 13, 14). This term is widely used in Acts for members of the believing communities, indicating that they saw themselves as bound together by family ties through their shared relationship with God through Jesus.[58] This phrasing most probably stems from Jesus's own diction (Mark 3:31–35), and the fact that this term was used for fellow Jews (in Acts and elsewhere) places its origins in a Jewish milieu.[59] ἔστησαν, "*they* put forward," denotes the action of this wider group, who now act at Peter's prompting to replace Judas.

ἀναστὰς Πέτρος, "Peter stood up." Standing is a common posture for addressing a group in antiquity.[60] It is fruitless to discuss whether Peter speaks as leader or spokesman of the group or of the apostles, since Luke gives no indication of this[61]—only textual variants (see *Notes* on v. 23) suggest Peter has "primacy" in this decision. It is striking, however, that Peter now fulfills the promise of Jesus that he will "strengthen your brothers" (Luke 22:32) after he turns back from his own threefold denial of Jesus (Luke 22:54–62). Peter contrasts with Judas, showing that an act of betrayal is not necessarily final.

ἐπὶ τὸ αὐτό, "together," is a Lukanism (6x in Luke-Acts of 10x in NT[62]). Bruce suggests that the phrase may have acquired a semi-technical sense in Acts of "in church fellowship,"[63] and that fits with its use in 2:47. This is thus a further marker of the unity of the believing community. In LXX this phrase renders the Heb. יחד (*yḥd*), "together," in the senses "in the same place, at the same time, in community,"[64] drawing it close to the sense of ὁμοθυμαδόν, "with one mind" (v. 14).[65] However, it is unlikely to be a Semitism here,[66] for it is also used in the Greco-Roman topos of friendship.[67]

16–17 ἄνδρες ἀδελφοί, "People, brothers and sisters." (On the idiom, see *Comment* on v. 11.) Some consider that ἄνδρες indicates that, out of the mixed group present (v. 14), the men are the primary audience of Peter's speech, since the one to be added to the apostolic band is to be a man (v. 21).[68] However, our earliest Greek interpreter of Acts, Chrysostom (*Hom. Act.* 3), takes this

57 See Sheeley, *Asides*, 120.

58 Acts 6:3; 9:17, 30; 10:23; 11:1, 12, 29; 12:17; 14:42; 15:1, 3, 7, 13, 22, 23, 32, 33, 36, 40; 16:2, 40; 17:6, 10, 14; 18:18, 27; 21:7, 20; 22:13; 28:14.

59 Trebilco, *Self-designations*, 38–46.

60 Xenophon, *Anab.* 5.1.2, 5; Plutarch, *Cic.* 16.3; cf. 1 Cor 14:30.

61 Estrada, *Followers*, 152–53.

62 Luke 17:35; Acts 1:15; 2:1, 44, 47; 4:26; cf. Matt 22:34; 1 Cor 7:5; 11:20; 14:23.

63 *Acts* (1990), 108; also Barrett, *Acts*, 1:173.

64 E.g., 2 Sam 10:15; Pss 2:2; 49:11 [LXX 48:11]; 98:8 [LXX 97:8]; 133:1 [LXX 132:1].

65 Dupont, *Nouvelles*, 308.

66 Vazakas, "Is Acts," 106–8, contra Torrey, *Composition*, 10–14; Wilcox, *Semitisms*, 93–100.

67 Iamblichus, *Vit. Pyth.* 30.167–69; Plato, *Rep.* 5.462C, both of whom use ἐπὶ τὸ αὐτό "together"; Cerfaux, *Recueil*, 2:150–51.

68 Ellingworth, "Men."

phrase to refer to both men and women: "See the dignity of the church, the angelic condition! No distinction there, 'neither male nor female.' I would that the churches were such now!" Further, Acts 17:34 shows that ἄνδρες can include women.[69] Acts elsewhere highlights the place of women (5:14; 8:3, 12; 9:2; 17:12; 22:4). Peter may be treating the gathering as analogous to a synagogue holding an election, and there is evidence that women could hold synagogue offices.[70] Seim, among others, notes that 120 men is the minimum required for a Jewish Sanhedrin (cf. m. Sanh. 1:6) and thus argues that only men were present at this time and that the group called πάντες, "all" (Acts 1:14; 2:1), is a wider group.[71] However, the Mishnah (ca. AD 200) is not necessarily good evidence for first-century practice, and there is no indication that Luke intends the 120 here to be different from "all" (v. 14); it is most likely that Peter addresses both men and women in the believing community.[72]

ἔδει πληρωθῆναι τὴν γραφὴν ἣν προεῖπεν τὸ πνεῦμα τὸ ἅγιον διὰ στόματος Δαυὶδ, "it was necessary for the Scripture to be fulfilled which the Holy Spirit spoke ahead of time through the mouth of David." Peter reflects theologically with Scripture on the death of Judas, who is now named after his omission in the list in v. 13. Peter both sees God's purposes in Scripture being worked out through Judas's death and reads Scripture to interpret the meaning of Judas's death.[73] Scripture is understood as having divine origin, "the Holy Spirit," τὸ πνεῦμα τὸ ἅγιον, through a human agent, "by the mouth of David," διὰ στόματος Δαυίδ, and contemporary relevance, "spoke ahead of time . . . concerning Judas," προεῖπεν . . . περὶ Ἰούδα. Thus Peter speaks of necessity, ἔδει, "it was necessary" (imperfect, implying that events have already fulfilled God's purpose[74]), and fulfillment, πληρωθῆναι τὴν γραφήν, "the Scripture to be fulfilled." These themes are prefigured in Luke's Gospel, where the necessary elements of Jesus's life, ministry, and death are rooted in the divine will,[75] a divine will expressed in Scripture.[76] Peter has learned from Jesus how to read Scripture, for Luke implies that such learning was a key element of Jesus's instruction during his post-resurrection appearances (Luke 24:26–27, 32, 45–47). Luke uses terminology found in Greco-Roman sources concerning oracles and prophecy,[77] and a reader familiar with such usage would recog-

---

69 "ἀνήρ," BDAG 79, §2.

70 Levine, *Ancient Synagogue*, 470–90; Brooten, *Women Leaders*; Cohick, *Women*, 195–224, esp. 209–14.

71 Seim, *Message*, 136–37.

72 Barrett, *Acts*, 1:96; Reimer, *Women*, 228–29; Pesch, *Apostelgeschichte*, 1:87.

73 Kurz, *Reading*, 77, suggests that Peter's interpretation of Scripture is derived from Jesus's teaching during his post-resurrection appearances (1:2; Luke 24:44).

74 *BegC*, 4:12.

75 Note δεῖ, "it is necessary," Luke 2:49; 4:43; 9:22; 13:16, 33; 17:25; 22:37; 24:7, 26, 44; see Cosgrove, "Divine."

76 Luke 3:4; 4:4, 8, 21; 18:31; 22:37; 24:27, 32, 44–46.

77 πληρόω, "fulfill": Polyaenus, *Strat.* 1.18; Plutarch, *Cic.* 17.4; προλέγω, "foretell": Plato, *Euthyphr.* 3C; Kauppi, *Gods*, 20–21.

nize both similarities with and differences from Luke's usage and theological framework[78] (see also *Comment* on vv. 25–26).

τὴν γραφήν, "the Scripture," probably implies a specific passage of Scripture, with the article acting as a specifier.[79] The obvious candidates are the passages cited in v. 20, although some have seen an echo of Ps 41:9 (LXX 40:10), "Even my close friend in whom I trusted, who ate of my bread, has lifted the heel against me" (NRSVue), connected at the level of ideas (v. 17) rather than including a verbal parallel to the Luke-Acts accounts of Judas's betrayal. However, there is little contact with what Peter says: he does not speak of Judas's intimacy with Jesus here but of Judas's presence among the apostles.[80] The imperfect tense of ἔδει, "it was necessary," is a difficulty for understanding the passages cited in v. 20 as "the Scripture" here, if understood to suggest that events have already happened to fulfill "the Scripture," for the second passage cited in v. 20 concerns an event yet to happen, the replacement of Judas. Thus, it is most probable that it is v. 20a (Ps 69:25 [68:26 LXX]) alone that Peter has in mind here as "the Scripture."[81] (See also *Comment* on Acts 1:20.)

Peter's portrait of Judas focuses on his betrayal of trust. Judas changed from being "numbered among us," κατηριθμημένος . . . ἐν ἡμῖν,[82] and allocated a share in the ministry of the apostolic band (τὸν κλῆρον τῆς διακονίας ταύτης, cf. v. 25) to being the one who guided those who arrested Jesus (Luke 22:3–6, 21–23, 47–48).[83] This is not an excommunication, as Estrada proposes,[84] for it is hardly possible to excommunicate a dead person! Two striking echoes underline Luke's point: Luke 22:3, Ἰούδαν τὸν καλούμενον Ἰσκαριώτην, ὄντα ἐκ τοῦ *ἀριθμοῦ* τῶν δώδεκα, "Judas called Iscariot, being from the *number* of the Twelve" (contrast Mark 14:10; Matt 26:14), highlights Judas's privileged position; and it is notable that "the allocation," τὸν κλῆρον, of the ministry to Judas prepares for the choice of his replacement by lot (ὁ κλῆρος, v. 26)—Luke's play on words drives the point home. Luke's passion narrative stresses that Judas, as he leads the arresting group to Jesus, is "one of the Twelve," εἷς τῶν δώδεκα (Luke 22:47). Although the Spirit announced the betrayal in advance, there is no suggestion or implication that Judas is merely a puppet of the divine will: he bears responsibility for his decision to hand Jesus over.

---

78 Kauppi, *Gods*, 25.

79 For discussion of the options, see Dupont, "Destinee."

80 Dupont, "Destinee," 42–43, with references.

81 With Dupont, "Destinee," 47–50.

82 Cf. Tg. Neof. Gen 44:18 in Cairo Genizah MS D, which specifies that Benjamin was "numbered" among the twelve patriarchs; discussion: Wilcox, "Judas-tradition," 447–48. It is unlikely that Acts is here dependent on the Targum, *pace* Wilcox; for critique, see Dupont, "Douxieme Apôtre."

83 Bishop, "Guide," plausibly suggests that "who became a guide to those who arrested Jesus" is parenthetical, rather than part of Peter's speech, since it reflects knowledge that Peter's audience already had and does not designate Jesus as "Lord." For a helpful overview of Judas in Luke's Gospel, see Robertson, *Death*, 86–92.

84 Estrada, *Followers*, 182–84.

18–19 may be a parenthetical comment by Luke.[85] These verses are introduced by a transitional phrase, μὲν οὖν, "indeed," and it seems strange for Peter to refer to Aramaic as τῇ ἰδίᾳ διαλέκτῳ *αὐτῶν*, "*their* own language" since it was also his own mother tongue.[86] For Luke, by contrast, it would be natural to write this phrase, since his mother tongue was probably Greek, and so vv. 18–19 may well be Lukan comment rather than Petrine speech, designed to help his readers.[87] However, v. 20 does not flow smoothly from v. 17, since it assumes the content of vv. 18–19, and "their" refers to the Jerusalem dwellers rather than Jewish people or Palestine dwellers in general. Thus, it is also possible that Luke presents vv. 18–19 as an aside in Peter's speech, explaining the background to his request for nominations for a "successor" to Judas, and so we consider vv. 18–19 to be part of Peter's speech.

Judas's reward for betraying Jesus enabled him to acquire (ἐκτήσατο) a plot of land (χωρίον)—χωρίον does not necessarily mean "field," i.e., a cultivated place; it simply denotes a location.[88] ἐκτήσατο is middle voice with the force "he acquired for himself," which Wallace identifies as causative, i.e., that although the chief priests do the handing over of money after Judas's death (Matt 27:7), Judas is the ultimate source of the purchase, since it was his "blood money" used to buy it.[89] Judas's purchase contrasts with believers who sold fields (Acts 4:34); they give out of their desire to serve, but Judas purchases out of his guilt. There may also be an echo of tragic histories, where greed for more is a symptom of intruding on divine space.[90] Luke 22:4–5 presents the agreement of the chief priests to give Judas money following his offer of betraying Jesus, rather than conditional upon his betrayal. In combination with Satan entering Judas (22:3), Judas's greed leads to the reversal of his fortune in the purchase of this land where he dies tragically.[91] His avarice and purchase of a plot of land contrasts sharply with Barnabas's generosity in selling a plot of land and giving the proceeds to the believing community (Acts 4:36–37).[92]

πρηνὴς γενόμενος ἐλάκησεν μέσος καὶ ἐξεχύθη πάντα τὰ σπλάγχνα αὐτοῦ, "after falling head first, he burst open in the middle and all his bowels were poured

85 Omanson, "How," 416–18; Witherington, *Acts*, 171; Zwiep, *Judas*, 88; so GNB, NIV, NEB, NRSVue, NET, ESV.

86 Some propose that Hebrew was a living spoken language in Palestine at this time (e.g., Buth and Notley, eds., *Language Environment*, propose that Hebrew was the spoken language in use in Palestine this period). If so, the version of Hebrew in use would be closer to Mishnaic Hebrew than biblical Hebrew. Biblical Hebrew was, of course, known among educated rabbis and the like. However, there is evidence for widespread use of Aramaic in first-century Palestine, particular as the language of less literate people, and thus it is most likely that (here and elsewhere) the language in use is Aramaic (see, e.g., Wise, *Language and Literacy*; Flessher and Chilton, *Targums*, 267–83).

87 Zwiep, *Judas*, 146; Weiser, "Nachwahl," 103.

88 "χωρίον," BDAG 1095; "χωρίον," LSJ; contra L&N §1.95.

89 Wallace, 434–25; "κτάομαι," LSJ, §I.1, giving classical examples.

90 Lee, *Luke-Acts*, 224–26.

91 Lee, *Luke-Acts*, 225.

92 Robertson, *Death*, 101.

out." πρηνής denotes falling "headlong."[93] Judas's gruesome death is described briefly and rather vaguely in terms partially echoed in Papias's later account, which may be independent of Luke's account[94] (see *Form/Structure/Setting*). Such a form of death characterizes wicked people (e.g., Wis 4:19; 2 Sam 10:10; cf. Acts 12:23), and thus "the death of Judas is not an accident or a tragic mishap . . . but an act of divine punishment."[95] b. Ḥul. 56a tells of a man who fell from a roof to his death in such a way that his entrails protruded from his body cavity and indicates that the man's father drew the entrails into the body. This suggests that the spilling of the innards is dishonorable.[96]

Luke gives no indication of the location of Judas's death (nor does Matt 27:5); Luke's comment about the place's name is thus not the result of Judas's death being there but rather the result of Judas's association with that plot of land. The place is called "Hakeldamach," Ἁκελδαμάχ, a transliteration of an Aramaic name that Luke translates accurately as "place of blood," χωρίον αἵματος, in common with Matt 27:8.[97] Luke's general tendency is to eliminate Semitic words, by contrast with Mark, who retains and explains them.[98] The presence of this Aramaic term thus suggests that Luke is drawing on Palestinian tradition.[99] Hakeldamach is traditionally located in the Hinnom valley, southwest of Jerusalem.[100] The name could be a result of the Jerusalemites' hearing of the means of Judas's death, which would involve copious amounts of blood being spilled (v. 18b), or it could be that the subject of γνωστὸν ἐγένετο, "this became known," refers to Judas's acceptance of "blood money" for handing over Jesus (v. 18a; cf. Matt 27:6–8), or some combination of the two.

20 contains quotations from Pss 68:26 LXX (MT 69:26; EVV 69:25); 108:8 LXX (MT 109:8), using the lens of Scripture to interpret Judas's apostasy, and concluding that they need to replace Judas.[101] The first quotation interprets the past event of Judas's death, which creates a vacancy in the apostolic band, and concludes the first part of the speech (Acts 1:16–20a)—hence ἔδει "it *was* necessary" (v. 16[102]). The second quotation shows that it is now scripturally appropriate to replace Judas and leads into the requirements for his successor

93 *BegC*, 5:27–29, contra Chase, "Acts 1.18," who argues that the term denotes a disease.
94 Brown, *Death*, 2:1409–10.
95 Zwiep, *Judas*, 76.
96 For other examples, see Robertson, *Death*, 105–8.
97 On the derivation of the name, see Derrett, "Akeldama," 129–31.
98 E.g., Mark 3:17 (cf. Luke 6:14); 5:41 (cf. Luke 8:54); 7:11, 34 (no Lukan parallels); 15:22 (cf. Luke 23:33).
99 Wilcox, *Semitisms*, 87–89; Zwiep, *Judas*, 91.
100 R. W. Smith, "Akeldama," *ABD* 1:134; Murphy-O'Connor, *Land*, 136–37.
101 For a helpful hermeneutical discussion in conversation with Gadamer, see Judd, "Gadamer." Whitlock, "Acts 1:15–26," offers a thoughtful discussion of the MT, targumic, and LXX renderings of these psalm extracts.
102 Cf. John 17:12; see Lindars, *Apologetic*, 109.

(vv. 20b–22)—hence δεῖ "it *is* necessary" (v. 21).[103] The source of the quotations is specified as "the book of Psalms," βίβλῳ ψαλμῶν, unusually in the NT (cf. Luke 20:42). Both cited psalms are traditionally attributed to David, who was widely seen as a prophet (cf. Acts 2:30), and both quotations are close to LXX. Psalm 68:26 has been made singular rather than plural, identifying Judas as its fulfillment;[104] ἐν τοῖς σκηνώμασιν αὐτῶν, "in their tents," is not included, leaving ἡ ἔπαυλις αὐτῶν, "their dwelling place," able to refer both to the field Judas obtained and (when read with Ps 108:8) to τὴν ἐπισκοπὴν αὐτοῦ, "his position of responsibility," which Judas abandoned (cf. the play on τόπος "position" in v. 25).[105] ἐν αὐτῇ, "in it," is added to the end of the quotation and clarifies that a singular "place" is in mind. In Ps 108:8 only λαβέτω, "let him take," is different—the original is the optative of the same verb, λάβοι (Ps 108:8 LXX), which has similar force,[106] or the difference of mood could be for consistency with the imperative γενηθήτω, "let . . . become," in the first quotation.[107] MT is not substantially different in sense in either passage, and so we cannot be confident whether Luke is drawing on the Greek or Hebrew OT here.[108] The two quotations thus, on the surface, appear to say contradictory things: Judas's place should be abandoned, and his place should be filled; Peter's resolution is that the one who replaces Judas must be qualified in similar ways to Judas (Acts 1:21–22).[109]

In content, Ps 68 LXX is an individual lament ascribed to David, with a major theme of a godly person being oppressed by the ungodly, and was read by early Christians to speak of the suffering of Jesus as the anointed Messiah,[110] thus (for Luke) providing a link with his passion narrative.[111] It was also read concerning those who rejected Jesus (Rom 11:9–10).[112] Psalm 108 LXX speaks from a similar situation of suffering and includes a section of curses upon the psalmist's enemies, from which v. 8 comes. Verse 8a might have been quoted, γενηθήτωσαν αἱ ἡμέραι αὐτοῦ ὀλίγαι, "Let his days be few," since it would be appropriate for Judas's death. Kilpatrick suggests that Luke is now interpreting v. 8b in a way different from its original use,[113] a speculation that lacks

103 Dodd, *According*, 58n1; for this analysis, cf. Zehnle, *Discourse*, 104.

104 Lindars, *Apologetic*, 102–3; Steyn, *Quotations*, 53. Bock, *Acts*, 86, postulates that Luke has access to a different textual tradition, but MT and LXX agree in using the plural, and no text using the singular is extant. It looks more likely that this is a deliberate rereading of the psalm by Peter (with Judd, "Gadamer," 52).

105 Judd, "Gadamer," 55, with Whitlock, "Acts 1:15–26," 97–99; also Novick, "Succeeding," 799.

106 BDF, §384, notes that, in the Hellenistic period, the imperative is taking over the optative's function of expressing a wish.

107 Marshall, "Acts," 530; Steyn, *Quotations*, 58–59.

108 Steyn, *Quotations*, 49; contra Fuller, "Choice," 141, who considers the use of ἔπαυλις and ἐπισκοπήν to show that Luke used LXX without offering supporting evidence.

109 So Novick, "Succeeding," 797–99.

110 Matt 27:34, 48; Mark 15:23, 36; Luke 23:36; John 2:17; 15:25; 19:29; Rom 15:3.

111 Doble, "Psalms," 115–16; Dunn, *Beginning*, 153.

112 Lindars, *Apologetic*, 99–108.

113 Kilpatrick, "Quotations," 86–87.

evidence—the fact is that v. 8b is being quoted, not v. 8a.[114] These psalms are being mined for apologetic explanation of the apostasy of Judas, one of the apostolic band chosen by Jesus himself,[115] and the use is the recognized Jewish interpretive technique *qal waḥomer*, moving from what is said in these psalms about David's suffering at the hands of wicked people to Jesus's suffering caused by Judas, whose actions were "uniquely false and evil."[116] There is no reason to think that the earliest believers—in this period before Pentecost—could not have made this link themselves, particularly given that the risen Jesus had been educating them in how to read Scripture (Luke 24:44–47).[117]

21–22 Luke stresses Judas's membership of the Twelve when writing of his betrayal of Jesus (Acts 1:17; Luke 22:3, 47). Since Judas's betrayal has left a gap in the number of the Twelve, he needs to be replaced—there is a divine necessity (indicated, as often in Luke-Acts, by δεῖ, "it is necessary"), for his replacement restores the symbolism of the Twelve representing the twelve tribes of Israel and fulfills Jesus's promise that the apostles will judge the twelve tribes of Israel (Luke 22:28–30[118]). The fact that Luke does not specify twelve apostles in Luke 22:30 is irrelevant, for he specifies twelve *tribes*, making the restoration-of-Israel symbolism clear; cf. 1 Esd 5:8, where the return from the Babylonian exile is led by a group of twelve.[119] It is thus no accident that Luke will speak of Peter standing "with the eleven" (σὺν τοῖς ἕνδεκα) at Pentecost (Acts 2:14). In their role the Twelve will replace the failed Jerusalem leadership (Luke 20:9–19; cf. Acts 3:27). Restoration of Israel themes continue to undergird developments in the early community: in the first half of Acts through to the apostles' final appearance as a group in 15:2, 6, 22, the Twelve are witnesses to *Israel*, seeking Israel's renewal and restoration in responding to their testimony to Jesus's exalted status as Israel's Messiah and the world's Lord (cf. 2:36). The Twelve will form the core of the renewed Israel, which will expand to include gentiles,[120] but not to the exclusion of mission among Jews—even in Acts 28 Paul is found among Jews in Rome expounding the gospel message. However, when James is later killed (12:2) he is not replaced in the circle of twelve apostles, which suggests that the symbolism of twelve is particularly significant for this early period when the focus is on Israel; notably, especially from Acts 13 onwards, the gospel's reach extends to include gentiles in the renewed and restored Israel.[121]

The one to replace Judas will be a man—ἀνδρῶν specifically indicates "men"

114 Steyn, *Quotations*, 59. Whitlock, "Acts 1:15–26," 99–100, plausibly suggests that the line is excluded because Peter's subject is the fate of Judas's *place*, not the fate of Judas himself.

115 Fuller discussion: Brawley, *Text*, 61–74.

116 Longenecker, *Exegesis*, 97; cf. Grant, "Singing," 41–43.

117 Fuller, "Choice," 146; Dunn, *Beginning*, 153.

118 Bauckham, "Restoration," 469, there prefers the translation "ruling" to "judging" understood in a narrow sense.

119 *Pace* Estrada, *Followers*, 172–76.

120 Jervell, *Luke*, 93.

121 Zwiep, *Judas*, 52, suggests that it is Judas's apostasy which necessitates his replacement.

here, by contrast with 1:16.[122] The leadership of the new community is at this point still in male hands. The coming of the Spirit will accelerate change begun in Jesus's own ministry in his inclusion of women (e.g., Luke 8:1–3; 10:39), and we shall read of women taking significant roles in the believing communities.[123]

The role of the apostles is here defined in terms of μάρτυς, "witness" (see *Comment* on Acts 1:8). Their witness, or testimony, focuses on the resurrection of Jesus (v. 22b) but also includes the life, ministry, and ascension of Jesus—hence the requirement that the new apostle should have been present throughout that period (vv. 21–22b). The Semitism εἰσῆλθεν καὶ ἐξῆλθεν, "come in and go out," expresses intimate engagement (see *Comment* on 9:28). ἀνελήμφθη, "he was taken up," echoes 1:2, 11 (see *Comment* on v. 2). This testimony is illustrated in the evangelistic speeches in Jerusalem, which focus on Jesus's life, ministry, death, resurrection, and exaltation (2:22–36; 3:12–26). These speech summaries include only brief details of Jesus's life, for much was already public knowledge, at least in Jerusalem (e.g., 2:22). Luke's readers already had the stories of Jesus's life and ministry, as well as his death, resurrection, and exaltation in the Gospel: Luke's readers are represented by the wider audiences in the diaspora portrayed in the later chapters of Acts.

23–26 The process of decision making has three phases: an initial selection of a shortlist of two (v. 23) on the basis of Peter's criteria (vv. 21–22), prayer for God's guidance (vv. 24–25), and the casting of lots to decide between the two proposed (v. 26). The process shows a fascinating combination of God's sovereignty and human engagement with God's purposes. The failure of Judas has shown that humans can reject God's purposes; by contrast, the believing group submits to God's will and seeks to cooperate with God's desires.

23 Luke says nothing of the method by which ἔστησαν, "they proposed," the two men, nor whether it was the eleven or the wider group who proposed them. We know little of Joseph Barsabbas and Matthias outside this brief mention. Papias (*apud* Eusebius, *Hist. eccl.* 3.39.9; cf. Mark 16:18) reports that the daughters of Philip the evangelist (Acts 21:9) told the story of Joseph Barsabbas drinking poison without harm. Eusebius (*Hist. eccl.* 1.12.3) reports a tradition that Matthias was one of the seventy (Luke 10:1) and also that Clement of Alexandria said that Matthias fell into heresy (*Hist. eccl.* 3.29.4). Joseph and Matthias/Matthew are common Jewish names, especially in Palestine, in this period.[124] Our lack of solid information about these two is no different from our lack of information concerning most of the Twelve, and thus "the NT is much more interested in the fact *that* they existed than in *what* they did."[125] The symbolism of the number twelve, especially in corresponding

122 *Pace* Zwiep, *Judas*, 155.
123 Note v. 14 and see *Comment* on 2:17, 18; 5:14; 8:12; 9:2; 16:13–14; 17:4, 12, 24; 18:2, 18, 26.
124 Williams, "Names," 89–90, 91–92.
125 Barrett, *Acts*, 1:102 (his italics).

to the number of tribes of Israel, is more important than the identities and activities of the twelve individuals.

24–25 The decision is made in prayer and through casting lots. For the first time, we overhear the nascent community praying (cf. 4:24–30), and their prayer focuses on God and his purposes.

They address the Lord as καρδιογνῶστα, "the one who knows everyone's hearts," a word found only at Acts 1:24; 15:8 in NT, never in LXX, and only elsewhere in Christian authors.[126] It is most likely God who is addressed, for he is the knower of hearts in 15:8.[127] There are three nuances to this word: knowing the innermost aspects of a person (e.g., 1 Sam 16:7; cf. Luke 5:22); foreknowledge of events (Herm. Mand. 4.3.4 [31]); and being the one who ultimately determines a person's destiny, for which "heart" may stand.[128] This word is in apposition to κύριε, "Lord," and the combination of the two characterizes the one addressed as both all-knowing (for he knows what others cannot know) and all-powerful (for he does what others cannot do). The words pick up the earlier emphasis on God's knowledge of events to come (vv. 16, 20) and God's purposes not being frustrated (vv. 20, 21).

The believers submit the decision about Judas's replacement to the divine will and purpose by requesting ἀνάδειξον ὃν ἐξελέξω ἐκ τούτων τῶν δύο ἕνα, "show which one of these two you have chosen." The divine choice of the twelfth member echoes Jesus's original choice of the Twelve, using the same verb, ἐκλέγομαι, "choose" (Luke 6:13), and also being grounded in prayer (Luke 6:12). Moreover, it is a choice that contrasts strikingly with the normal process of becoming a disciple, by which a person sought out a rabbi/teacher rather than the teacher seeking his own students/disciples.[129] It is thus probable that the "Lord" addressed here is Jesus, also called "Lord" in Acts 1:6, 21.[130] The exalted Jesus is being asked to indicate his will for his apostolic band[131]—Luke portrays a remarkable shift in the understanding of Jesus as one to whom it is now appropriate to address prayer, i.e., Jesus is being identified as sharing the divinity of the God of Israel, who is the only appropriate one to whom Jews would address prayer and worship (Deut 6:4; 10:20; 13:4).[132]

τὸν τόπον τῆς διακονίας ταύτης καὶ ἀποστολῆς combines διακονία, "ministry," and ἀποστολή, "apostleship," as a hendiadys—the two terms form one idea,

126 "καρδιογνώστης," BDAG 509; Haenchen, *Acts*, 162n8; cf. Luke 16:15 (unparalleled in Matthew, Mark).

127 Contra Sleeman, *Geography*, 90, who thinks a reference to the exalted Jesus is most likely because Jesus is identified as κύριος, "Lord," in the context (1:6, 21).

128 Bauer, "Καρδιογνώστης," 114–16.

129 Hengel, *Leader*, 50–51, with references.

130 Harris, *Jesus as God*, 316.

131 Talbert, *Acts*, 21; Barrett, *Acts*, 1:103; Sleeman, *Geography*, 90; Rengstorf, "Election," 184.

132 See the exposition of this theme in Bauckham, *God*.

"apostolic ministry"[133] or "service consisting of apostleship";[134] "office" (REB) is anachronistic at this stage of the early church's life. The use of τόπος, "position," is no mere redundancy, for *this* position, assigned by God, is contrasted with Judas's decision to turn to "*his own* position," τὸν τόπον τὸν ἴδιον, later in the sentence. Judas's sin consists in turning away (παρέβη) from God's place of *service* for him, and wanting his own place, his own possession—and, ironically, he dies in his own place—the place he now possesses—the field of blood.[135]

26 ἔδωκαν κλήρους αὐτοῖς, "and they cast lots for them."[136] Casting lots has the effect of excluding human interference in the choice and leaving the decision in God's hands:[137] it is not understood in ancient times as arbitrary. Lots are used in Scripture as a means for seeking God's will (Prov 16:33): the distribution of the land was by lot (Num 26:55–56; 33:54; Josh 18:6; cf. Neh 11:1); lots were used in a judicial context to find a guilty person, such as the discovery of Achan (Josh 7:10–21) or the choice between David and Jonathan (1 Sam 14:40–42); lots decided which goat was spared on the Day of Atonement (Lev 16:7–10) or which priest would offer sacrifice and prayer on a particular day (Luke 1:8–9). Josephus reports that the choice of high priest was made by lot in this period (*J.W.* 4.3.7–8 §§151–57, AD 67). Greco-Roman societies also used lots to seek the will of the gods, such as in the selection of the Council of the Five Hundred in classical Athens (e.g., Aristotle, *Ath. pol.* 8.1).[138] The Qumran community used "lot" (גורל, *gwrl*) for decisions made by the community, apparently to indicate that the decision made was considered to have divine sanction (1QS V, 3; VI, 16, 18, 22).[139]

The choice of Matthias re-completes the Twelve as he is added to the eleven (cf. Luke 24:9, 33).[140] All is now ready for the Spirit's coming. That this is so is suggested by the failure to replace James on his death (Acts 12:2)—the

133 Bruce, *Acts* (1990), 112.

134 Barrett, *Acts*, 1:103; cf. Wallace, 288.

135 Johnson, *Function*, 181–82. Zwiep, *Judas*, 166–68, discusses other possible referents for "his own position," preferring the view that it is a euphemism for Judas's place after death in Gehenna; Weiser, "Nachwahl," 107, thinks similarly.

136 Brug, "Acts 1:26," argues that the verb ἔδωκαν properly means "give," different from the more usual βάλλω, "cast, throw" (e.g., Matt 27:35; Mark 15:24; Luke 23:34; John 19:24; LXX Ps 21:19 [MT 22:19]) and suggests that the phrase here may denote an election, not a lottery. However, κλῆρος does not mean "vote" (typically, ψῆφος, is used for the pebble with which people voted), and ἔπεσεν ὁ κλῆρος is most naturally translated "the lot fell," as in LXX Esth 3:7; Jonah 1:7; Ezek 24:6; 1 Chr 26:14 (Ferguson, "Qumran," 79n27; Barrett, *Acts*, 1:104–5; Schmidt, "Élection"). 1 Sam 14:41 LXX combines δίδωμι, "give," and the cognate verb of κλῆρος, κληρόω, "choose by lot" (Ferguson, "Qumran," 78).

137 E.g., in 1 Chr 24:5, 31, the organization of priests and Levites took place by lot (cf. 1 Chr 26:13 for the gatekeepers). The phrase אֵלֶּה עִם־אֵלֶּה (*ʾēllê ʿim-ʾēllê*), "all alike" (NRSVue), indicates the impartiality of the process (cf. NIV).

138 "Sortition," *OCD*[3] 1426; Kauppi, *Gods*, 21–24, 25–26.

139 Beardslee, "Casting," 247–48.

140 Masson, "Reconsitution highlights the significance of the number twelve as signaling a continuing mission to Israel"; see also *Comment* on vv. 21–22.

symbolic number of twelve is crucial at this stage, since it signals that God is restoring and renewing Israel in preparation for the Spirit's coming. Peter's departure from Jerusalem for his own safety further reduces the number still in the city (12:17, see *Comment*). The functions of the Twelve are taken up by a wider group of "elders" at a later date (11:30; see *Comment*).

It is sometimes suggested that the group should have waited for the coming of the Spirit before choosing a twelfth apostle and that they would then have recognized Paul as such.[141] However, Paul lacked the qualification of accompanying Jesus throughout his earthly ministry (v. 21; note 1 Cor 15:3–5, where he says that he received such stories from others), and it was crucial to have twelve apostles at this stage of Israel's renewal and reconstitution, a stage at which Paul was not available.[142] While this is the only occasion in Acts where lots are used to facilitate a decision—here between two apparently well-qualified candidates—the use of Scripture to justify the need to replace Judas (Acts 1:16, 20), the community's prayer (vv. 24–25), and the submission to God's choice (v. 24b) through lots (v. 26) all portray this as an appointment in tune with God's purposes. Luke offers no criticism of this approach, by contrast with Philo, who explicitly opposes the use of lots to appoint magistrates and rulers (*Spec. Laws* 4.29–30 §§151–57).

Explanation

Luke paints a vivid picture of the believing community at a time of transition between Jesus's ascension and the coming of the Spirit. The believers are obedient to the command of Jesus to wait in Jerusalem (Acts 1:4, 12) and carry this out in united and fervent prayer (v. 14). The community depends on Jesus for its life, and prayer, which demonstrates that dependence, will be a key feature of its life throughout Acts (see *Comment* on v. 14).

The submission of the community to God and God's purposes is also seen in their attention to Scripture, understood as spoken by the Spirit (v. 16), to interpret events. Judas's betrayal of Jesus, hinted at by his absence from the list of eleven (v. 13) and a piece of "unfinished business" from Luke's Gospel (Luke 22:3–6, 21–23, 47–48), is now tackled head on. Peter reads Pss 68:26 LXX (MT 69:25) and 108:8 LXX (MT 109:8) as speaking of Judas's betrayal. Both come from psalms of lament in a situation where a godly person suffers at the hand of ungodly people, and Ps 108 LXX was understood by early Christians to speak of Jesus's unjust suffering (Matt 27:34, 48; Mark 15:23, 36; Luke 23:36; John 2:17; 15:25; 19:29; Rom 15:3). Here, Peter interprets them as applicable to Judas who is an ungodly man par excellence who betrayed Jesus into the hands of other ungodly people. The story of Judas's gruesome death

141 E.g., Stier, *Words*, 12–15.
142 Cf. Longenecker, "Acts," 63.

(vv. 18–19) is laid alongside these verses (v. 20) to draw the conclusion that Judas must be replaced by another (vv. 21–22).

Judas's tragic loss to the apostolic band contrasts with Peter's rehabilitation. Peter also betrays Jesus, by denying his association with Jesus (Luke 22:54–62). However, in Peter's case the Gospel records Jesus's promise of his return after Satan has "sifted" him (Luke 22:31–34), by contrast with Satan's "entering" Judas (Luke 22:3). Peter visits the empty tomb and is "amazed" (Luke 24:12), the last mention of him by name in the Gospel. Peter's appearance here is his first mention by name in Acts, heading the list of the eleven (Acts 1:13) and then leading the community in its reflection and action (vv. 15–22). He will also be the spokesman at Pentecost (2:14).

Peter's rehabilitation and Judas's loss both fall within the sovereign purpose of God. God's control of history is stressed at both beginning and end of Peter's speech with "it is/was necessary" (vv. 16, 21), indicating divine necessity, and throughout the story of the choice of Judas's replacement: (i) the divine mission was not stopped by Judas's loss, for he was to be replaced; (ii) Scripture (understood as God's voice) announced Judas's actions in advance (vv. 16, 20), and so his betrayal did not thwart God's plan; (iii) the believing community did what was required to replace Judas and be ready for the coming of the Spirit, in submission to God's will through prayer and casting lots (vv. 21–26); and (iv) the Twelve was thus complete before Pentecost, prepared to be the leaders of the restored Israel.

The sovereign Lord, Jesus himself, to whom the believers pray, knows everyone's heart and is asked to make his choice known (v. 24). It is to the Lord's choice that the community submits two candidates to replace Judas through prayer (v. 25) and casting lots (v. 26). Luke commends glad submission to the Lord (God and Jesus) and active participation in the Lord's purposes rather than an attitude of resigned inevitability about what will happen.

The Lord's purposes are focused on Israel's renewal and restoration (cf. 1:6–8; 3:21), hence the need to complete the number of twelve apostles, a number symbolic of the twelve tribes (Luke 22:28–30). These Twelve are to give themselves to witnessing to Jesus's ministry, death, and resurrection (hence the "person specification" in Acts 1:21–22), echoing Jesus's promise (1:8) and preparing for the centrality of the apostolic teaching (2:42) and testimony (6:2, 4) later in Acts. The Petrine evangelistic speeches center on Jesus and his resurrection (2:22–36; 3:12–26), as will Paul's testimony later (esp. 17:18).

In sum, Luke presents a body of people who are open to God but do not yet know how God's purposes will happen. What they are being invited to do by Peter is to submit gladly to these purposes, which center on witness to Jesus, the Lord.

D. The Spirit Comes at Pentecost (2:1–41)

Bibliography

Adams, E. *Stars.* **Anderson, K. L.** *But God,* 200–219. **Avemarie, F.** *Tauferzählungen,* 177–213. **Barrett, C. K.** "Faith." **Bauckham, R.** *Fate,* 269–89. ———. "James." ———. "Restoration." **Beale, G. K.** "Descent I." ———. "Descent II." ———. *Temple,* 201–16. **Beasley-Murray, G. R.** *Baptism,* 93–125. **Béchard, D. P., SJ.** *Paul,* 211–24. **Bird, M. F.** *Origins,* 26–29. **Black, A.** "Sons." **Bock, D. L.** *Proclamation,* 128–32, 156–87. **Bratcher, R. G.** "Loosed." **Brawley, R. L.** *Text,* 75–90, 158–62. **Brinkman, J. A.** "Background." **Broshi, M.** "Estimating." **Buckwalter, D.** *Character,* 194–96. **Camp, A. L.** "Reexamining." **Carroll, J. T.** *Response,* 128–36. **Christiansen, E. J.** "Taufe." **Crabbe, K.** *Luke/Acts,* esp. 193–96. **Crisler, B. C.** "Acoustics." **Davies, J. G.** "Pentecost." **Davis, J. C.** "Look." **Delling, G.** *Zueignung,* pages. **Dillon, R. J.** "Prophecy." **Dinkler, M. B.** "Politics." **Dodd, C. H.** *According,* 46–48. **Dunn, J. D. G.** *Baptism.* ch. 4. ———. *Beginning,* §22.3 (156–71). **Dupont, J.** "Discours de Pierre." ———. *Nouvelles,* 193–295. ———. *Salvation,* 35–59. **Esler, P. F.** "Glossolalia." **Evans, C. A.** "Setting." **Everts, J.** "Tongues." **Farrow, D.** *Ascension and Ecclesia,* 22–26. **Fee, G. D.** "Baptism." **Ferguson, E.** *Baptism,* 166–70. **Fitzmyer, J. A.** "Ascension." ———. "David." **Flusser, D.** "Two Notes." **Gaventa, B. R.** "Acts." **Gempf, C. H.** "Speaking." **George, A.** "L'emploi." **Gilbert, G.** "List." **Gourgues, M., OP.** "Exalté." **Green, E. M. B.** *Meaning,* 136–51. **Green, J. B.** "Baptism." ———. "In Our Own." **Hacking, K. J.** *Signs,* 244–49. **Hartman, L.** *Name,* 37–50, 129–33. ———. "Formule." **Hay, D. M.** *Glory,* 19–373, 70–72. **Haya-Prats, G.** *Believers.* **Hays, R. B.** "Figural Exegesis," 40–41. **Heitmüller, W.** *Namen.* **Hengel, M.** "Ἰουδαία." ———. "Ioudaia." ———. "Jerusalem." **Henrichs-Tarasenkova, N.** "Good News." **Horsley, G. H. R.** "Inscriptions." **Hur, J.** *Reading,* 221–35. **Jeremias, J.** *Infant,* 19–24. ———. *Jerusalem,* 58–84. ———. *Origins.* **Johnson, A.** "Resurrection." **Johnson, L. T.** *Function,* 183–90. ———. *Midrash,* 5–17. **Kaiser, W. C., Jr.** "Promise." **Keener, C. S.** "Plausibility." **Kilgallen, J. J.** "Rhetorical." ———. "Use." ———. "With Many." **Kilpatrick, G. D.** "Quotations," 81–83. **King, F. J., and S. Selvendran.** "Rhubarb." **Kremer, J.** *Pfingstbericht.* **Kretschmar, G.** "Himmelfahrt." **Kurz, W. S.** *Reading,* 77–80. **Lennartsson, G.** *Refreshing.* **Lincoln, A. T.** "Theology." **Lindars, B.** *Apologetic,* 36–59. **Litwak, K. D.** Echoes. 155–79. **Lövestam, E.** "Rettungsappel." **MacDonald, W. G.** "Glossolalia." **MacRae, G. W.** "Heaven." **Mainville, O.** "Messianimse." ———. *Spirit* [ET of *L'Espirit*]. **Mantey, J. R.** "Again." ———. "Causal." **Marcus, R.** "Elusive." ———. "On Causal." **Marrow, S. B.** "Παρρησία." **Marshall, I. H.** "Christology." ———. *Historian,* 94–102, 175–78. ———. "Meaning." ———. "Significance." **McCollough, D. J.** *Ritual,* 97–136. **McIntyre, L. B., Jr.** "Baptism." **Meek, J. A.** *Gentile Mission,* 95–113. **Menzies, G. W.** "Occurrences." **Menzies, R. P.** *Empowered,* 173–201. **Metzger, B. M.** "Geography." ———. *Studies,* 77–87. **Moessner, D. P.** "Lords." **Morlan, D. S.** *Conversion,* 108–34. **Nagel, P.** "*Schechina.*" **Nave, G. D.** *Role,* 199–202. **O'Toole, R. F.** "Acts 2:30." **Osburn, C. D.** "Imperative." **Ovey, M. J.** *Feasts,* 39–43. **Pao, D. W.** *Acts,* 156–59. **Park, S.** *Pentecost,* esp. 176–238. **Pfitzner, V. C.** "Pneumatic Apostleship," 219–21. **Ravens, D.** *Luke,* 150–52. **Reinhardt, W.** "Population." **Rese, M.** "Funktion," 73–76. ———. *Motive,* 45–66. **Rowe, C. K.** "Acts 2.36." ———. *Christology.*

Safrai, S. "Relations." **Sanders, E. P.** *Jesus*, 212–18. ———. *Judaism*, 125–27. **Schnabel, E. J.** *Mission*, 1:398–405. **Schröter, J.** "Taufe," 562–67. **Scott, J. M.** *Geography*, 62–84. ———. "Horizon." **Shepherd, W. H., Jr.** *Function*, 159–67. **Sleeman, M.** *Geography*, 94–104. **Smalley, S. S.** "Christology." **Squires, J. T.** *Plan*, 64–65. **Stenschke, C.** "Need." **Steyn, G. J.** *Quotations*, 64–128. **Strauss, M. L.** *Davidic*, 131–47. **Stroup, C.** *Christians*, 41–69. **Tannehill, R. C.** "Functions," 401–4. **Torrey, C. C.** *Composition*, 28–29. **Trebilco, P. R.** "Asia." **Trull, G. V.** "Exegesis." ———. "Interpretation." ———. "Views." **Turner, M.** "Divine." ———. "Christology." ———. *Holy Spirit*, 222–23. ———. *Power*, 266–315. **Twelftree, G. H.** *People*. 65–87. **van der Horst, P. W.** "Parallels 2.1–47." **VanderKam, J. C.** "Covenant." **von Baer, H.** *Geist*, esp. 86–94. **Walton, S.** "Heavens." **Weatherly, J. A.** *Responsibility*, esp. 50–98. **Wedderburn, A. J. M.** "Traditions." **Weinstock, S.** "Geographical." **White, A. W.** *Prophets*, 54–100. **Whittaker, M.** "Signs." **Wilcox, M.** *Semitisms*, 46–48. **Wolff, C.** "Λαλεῖν." **Wright, N. T.** *Jesus*, 208–9. ———. *New Testament*, 280–86. ———. *Resurrection*, 129–206, 451–57. **Zehnle, R. F.** *Pentecost Discourse*. **Ziesler, J. A.** "Name."

Translation

1 When the day of Pentecost arrived[a] they were all[b] together in the same place. 2 Suddenly a sound came from heaven like the rushing of a mighty wind and it filled the whole house where they were sitting. 3 Divided tongues, like those of fire, appeared to them, and [the fire] rested[c] on each one of them, 4 and all of them were filled with the Holy Spirit and they began to speak in other languages as the Spirit gave them the ability to express themselves.

5 Now devout Jews from every nation under heaven were living in Jerusalem. 6 At this sound,[d] a crowd gathered in a state of agitation,[e] because each one was hearing[f] them speak in their own language. 7 They were astonished and amazed, saying, "Surely all these who are speaking are Galileans? 8 How, then, do we each hear them in our own mother tongue? 9 Parthians and Medes and Elamites and those who live in Mesopotamia, Judea[g] and Cappadocia, Pontus and Asia, 10 Phrygia and Pamphylia, Egypt and the districts of Libya near[h] Cyrene, and Roman visitors, 11 both [native] Jews and proselytes, Cretans and Arabs—we hear them proclaiming God's mighty deeds *in our own languages*!"[i]

12 All of them were astonished and perplexed, saying to each other, "What's going on here?" 13 However, others jeered at them, "They are full of new wine!"

14 Peter stood with the eleven, raised his voice and addressed them, "Judeans[j] and all who live in Jerusalem, let this be known to you and pay careful attention to my words. 15 These people are not drunk, as you suppose, for it is only the third hour of the day. 16 Rather, this is what was announced through the prophet Joel:

> 17 And it shall be in the last days,[k] says God,
> I will pour out my Spirit on all flesh.
> And your sons and daughters are going to prophesy
> and your young men are going to see visions
> and your old people are going to dream dreams;

18 and even on my male and female slaves in those days
I will pour out my Spirit,
and they are going to prophesy.
19 And I will give wonders in the heaven above
and signs on the earth below,
blood and fire and smoky vapors.
20 The sun is going to be transformed into darkness
and the moon into blood,
before the great and glorious day of the Lord comes.
21 And whoever calls on the name of the Lord is going to be saved.

22 People of Israel, listen[l] to these words! Jesus of Nazareth, a man marked out by God to you by means of deeds of power and wonders and signs which[m] God did through him among you, as you yourselves know— 23 this man, given up in line with the predetermined plan and foreknowledge of God, you nailed to a cross and killed through the hand of lawless people— 24 this man[n] God raised, freeing [him] from the agonies of death,[o] since it was not possible for him to be held by it. 25 For David says about[p] him:

I saw the Lord before me at all times,
because he is at my right side so that I will not be shaken.
26 Therefore my heart was glad and my tongue rejoiced.
Moreover my flesh will live in hope,
27 because you will not abandon my life to Hades
nor will you hand over your godly one to experience decay.
28 You have made known to me the paths of life.
You have filled me with gladness[q] in your presence.

29 Brothers and sisters, I can confidently tell you that our ancestor David died and was buried, and his tomb is among us to this day. 30 So,[r] because he was a prophet and knew that God had sworn an oath to him that one from the fruit of his loins would sit upon his throne, 31 he foresaw and spoke about the resurrection of the Messiah:

He was neither abandoned in Hades, nor did his flesh experience[s] decay.

32 This Jesus God raised up, of which fact we ourselves are all witnesses; 33 therefore, after being exalted to[t] the right side of God, and having received the promise which is the Holy Spirit[u] from the Father, he has poured out what[v] you yourselves are seeing and hearing. 34 For it was not David who went up into the heavens, but he himself says:

The Lord said to my Lord: 'Sit at my right side, 35 until I place your enemies as a footstool for your feet.'

36 So then, let the whole house of Israel know beyond a doubt that God has appointed him both Lord and Messiah—this Jesus whom you crucified."

37 When they heard, they were cut to the heart and said to Peter and the rest of the apostles, "What must we do, brothers and sisters?" 38 Peter said to them,[w] "Repent and

be baptized, each one of you, in[x] the name of Jesus Messiah for the forgiveness of your sins, and you shall receive the gift of the Holy Spirit. [39] For the promise is for you and your children and all those far away, whoever the Lord our God calls."

[40] He went on testifying and exhorting them with many other words, "Be saved from this crooked generation!"

[41] So then, those who accepted his message were baptized, and on that day about[y] three thousand were added.

Notes

a. ἐν τῷ συμπληροῦσθαι can be rendered "was fulfilled," which could be understood as marking the end of the day. However, v. 15 makes clear that this is not Luke's meaning, and he uses the cognate verb πίμπλημι, "fulfill," in the same way in Luke 1:57, portraying Elizabeth as reaching the time to give birth, not the time when she had already given birth; Dupont, *Salvation*, 36–37.

b. D (and the facing Latin, d) reads Καὶ ἐγένετο ἐν ταῖς ἡμέραις ἐκείναις τοῦ συμπληροῦσθαι τὴν ἡμέραν τῆς πεντηκοστῆς ὄντων αὐτῶν πάντων, "It happened in those days that the day of Pentecost arrived, they were all . . ." This links this story more closely to the preceding episodes; Rius-Camps and Read-Heimerdinger, *Message*, 1:141, 143–44.

c. The change from plural ὤφθησαν, "they appeared," to singular ἐκάθισεν, "it rested," implies that the fire (πυρός) is the subject of the second verb.

d. γενομένης . . . τῆς φωνῆς ταύτης, gen. abs., "having come . . . this sound."

e. καὶ συνεχύθη, "and it was agitated," sc. the crowd.

f. εἷς ἕκαστος, "each one," sg. takes pl. verb ἤκουον, "they were hearing"; MHT, 3:312 states that ἕκαστος is found with sg. verb 25x in NT and pl. verb 11x; in LXX sg. verb 56x; pl. verb 89x.

g. Although Ἰουδαίαν, "Judea," has overwhelming support among Greek MSS, versions, and patristic citations, it is replaced by some ancient and modern writers, since it is somewhat surprising that Judeans should express amazement that they can understand Galileans; for details, see *TCGNT*², 253–54.

h. "κατά," BDAG 511, §B.1.b, "toward," in the sense "near."

i. I follow NTE in using italics to show emphasis.

j. Since all of those present were Jewish, the distinction between Ἰουδαῖοί and οἱ κατοικοῦντες Ἰερουσαλὴμ πάντες, "all who live in Jerusalem," suggests that the first should here be rendered "Judeans," denoting those born in the area, and the second denotes Jewish people living in the city—either permanently or temporarily for the feast—who did not originate in Judea.

k. The reading μετὰ ταῦτα found in B 076 and a small number of other sources (see ECM, ad loc.) is an assimilation to Joel 3:1 LXX. The overwhelming weight of ancient MSS read ἐν ταῖς ἐσχάταις ἡμέραις, "in the last days." Haenchen, *Acts*, 179 cannot believe that Luke would write the latter: "In Lucan theology the last days do not begin as soon as the Spirit has been outpoured!" Haenchen is working from his construct of Lukan theology rather than allowing text-critical principles to guide him.

l. The aor. impv. ἀκούσατε suggests a call to give focused auditory attention, "listen!"

m. οἷς, "which," rel. pn. attracted into dative by its antecedents, δυνάμεσιν καὶ τέρασιν καὶ σημείοις, "deeds of power and wonders and signs"; the acc. pl. rel. pn. οὕς, "which," might be used here, but this is a classical construction (*CGCG*, §50.13).

n. ὅν, "whom," resumptive rel. pn. Referring back to τοῦτον, "this man," (v. 23) and thence to Ἰησοῦν, "Jesus" (v. 22).

o. ὠδῖνας, "agonies," is normally used in connection with the pains of childbirth (e.g., 1 Thess 5:3) and is here used metaphorically for great pains; "ὠδίν," BDAG 1102, §b.α (see *Comment*). In place of θανάτου, "death," D, with some patristic sources, reads ᾅδου, "Hades," which fits with some cultures' lack of a word for "death," using a word for "the realm of the dead" as an equivalent (Newman and Nida, *Acts*, 49). θανάτου, "death," has overwhelming MS support; ECM, ad loc.

p. The combination of λέγω, "say," with εἰς, "about," is very unusual in the NT (cf. Luke 22:65; John 8:26; Eph 5:32). Similar passages suggest that the preposition identifies the referent of the speech, which need not imply that Peter is treating the Messiah as the *sole* referent of Ps 15:8–11a LXX (cited in vv. 25–28); Kaiser, "Promise," 228; Trull, "Views," 438–39.

q. εὐφροσύνης, "with gladness," gen. of the thing filling a space, as usual following πληρόω; "εὐφροσύνη," BDAG 828, §1.b.

r. οὖν, "so," is resumptive, rather than indicating an inference; "οὖν," BDAG 736, §2.a.

s. εἶδεν, lit. "saw," used metaphorically here; "ὁράω," BDAG 719 §A.3.

t. Taking the dat. τῇ δεξιᾷ as locative, "to the right," rather than instrumental "by the right"; see BDF, §199, noting that the locative use is rare in the NT, contra Barrett, *Acts*, 1:149.

u. τοῦ πνεύματος τοῦ ἁγίου, epexegetical gen., "which is the Holy Spirit."

v. ἐξέχεεν τοῦτο ὅ, "he has poured out this, which," referring to the Pentecost phenomena of tongues, wind, and fire.

w. Of the variety of readings, the most important are: (i) Πέτρος δὲ πρὸς αὐτούς· Μετανοήσατε, "And Peter to them, 'Repent,'" B 218 606 630 1835 *al*; (ii) Πέτρος δὲ αὐτούς· Μετανοήσατε, φησίν, "And Peter to them, 'Repent,' he said," 𝔓[74vid] א A C 81 630 945 1175 1642* 1704 1739 1891 vg *al*; (iii) Πέτρος δὲ πρὸς αὐτούς φησίν, Μετανοήσατε, "And Peter said to them, 'Repent,'" D it[d, p, r] Irenaeus[lat vid]. (iv) Πέτρος δὲ ἔφη πρὸς αὐτούς· Μετανοήσατε, "And Peter said to them, 'Repent,'" E P Ψ Byz(-i) it[gig] vg[mss]. Reading (ii) has the strongest early support, save B. The most probable explanation of the absence of φησίν, "he said," in MSS supporting (i) is that it was thought to interrupt the flow of Peter's speech (Barrett, *Acts*, 1:153), although see Metzger's dissenting note (*TCGNT*², 261), arguing that only (i) explains the introduction of verbs of speech into the other variants.

x. ἐπί, v.l. ἐν, B C D 429 522 1739 2298 etc. Both have the sense "in": the introduction of ἐν seems to be a change to produce consistency with other uses in Acts (cf. 10:48); *TCGNT*², 261.

y. ὡσεί, "about," with the number τρισχίλιαι, "three thousand": see n. h on 1:15.

Form/Structure/Setting

Delimitation of pericope and structure. The temporal marker ἐν τῷ συμπληροῦσθαι τὴν ἡμέραν, "when the day . . . arrived" (v. 1a; prepositional infinitival phrase with accusative), signals the beginning of a new story, and the central event is described from the narrator's perspective in vv. 1–4 (this phrase shows that Pentecost is the fulfillment of 1:8[1]). The remainder of this story

1 Lüdemann, *Early Christianity*, 39.

alternates between the crowd and Peter:[2] vv. 5–13 focus on the crowd and its (varying) responses to the phenomena of vv. 1–4; vv. 14–36 are Peter's speech, which first interprets the phenomena as signs of the Spirit being poured out (vv. 15–21, citing Joel 3:1–5 LXX) and then focuses on Jesus, the one who pours out the Spirit (Acts 2:22–36); v. 37 presents the crowd's response to Peter's speech, wanting to know what to do; vv. 38–40 present Peter spelling out the required response (vv. 38–39) and continuing to speak to call the crowd to make that response (v. 40); v. 41 then presents the crowd's acceptance of Peter's terms (see *Comment* on whether v. 41 belongs here or with vv. 42–47). Dupont observes a pattern to the Petrine speeches in Acts of an exordium (here vv. 14–21), a description of Jesus's earthly ministry (v. 22), the crucifixion (v. 23); the resurrection (v. 24a), the messianic significance of the resurrection (vv. 24b–36), and the announcement of the forgiveness of sins (vv. 37–40).[3]

Sources/historicity. Luke's Pentecost story asserts that the church originated in a "big bang" rather than a slower evolutionary development over a longer period. All of our sources portray the inception and initial growth of the Jesus movement happening over a short period, focused in Jerusalem; we lack any evidence that the disciples gradually came to believe in Jesus's "risenness" and then created stories of his resurrection and exaltation to express that belief. This passage encapsulates and expounds this "big bang" understanding of both Christian origins and the origins of Christology (see *Comment* on v. 33). This is not to suggest that there are no difficulties in interpreting the nature of the event; these difficulties have led some to argue that the story is at least partially—and sometimes wholly—a Lukan creation.[4] The following are the main points discussed.

First, there is no other account of this event elsewhere in the NT. However—the ascension aside—there are also few accounts of events in Acts found elsewhere in the NT; indeed, Jesus's birth and baptism are unattested outside the Gospels.[5] Further, there is widespread evidence that the Spirit's coming is a key foundational event for the church and was promised beforehand: the sayings of John the baptizer (Matt 3:11; Mark 1:8; Luke 3:16; John 1:33), Jesus's promise of the Spirit's aid for the disciples (Matt 10:20; Mark 13:11; Luke 12:12), Jesus's specific promise that the Spirit will come (Luke 24:49; John 7:39; 14:15–17, 26; 15:26; 16:13; 20:22), and Paul's stress on the foundational nature of the Spirit for Christian life and experience (Rom 8:9; Gal 3:2; 1 Cor 3:16–17; cf. Heb 2:4; Rom 15:19; 2 Cor 12:12).

Secondly, there is debate over the location of the event, some suggesting

2 Dunn, *Beginning*, 158, suggests the crowd functions like a chorus in a Greek play.
3 Dupont, "Discours de Pierre," 242–55.
4 For discussion, see Lincoln, "Theology"; Marshall, "Significance"; Dunn, *Beginning*, 164–71; Haenchen, *Acts*, 173–75; Zehnle, *Discourse*, esp. 111–23.
5 Kremer, *Pfingsbericht*, 237.

that it may not have taken place in Jerusalem. There are resurrection appearances located in Galilee (Mark 14:28; 16:7; Matt 28:16–20; John 21), and thus some propose that such encounters with the risen Christ may have led to believing communities forming in Galilee. Lincoln cites the church in Damascus (Acts 9) as one example of a church beginning independently of Jerusalem,[6] but Damascus is not located in Galilee and Luke does not suggest that all churches were planted from Jerusalem directly—the wandering groups of Acts 8:4; 11:19 are examples of disciples who plant churches without being formally "sent" from Jerusalem. Granted, Luke does not mention Galilean resurrection appearances (although to describe Luke as "suppressing" them is too strong[7]) and records Jesus instructing the disciples to remain in Jerusalem (Luke 24:49; Acts 1:4). However, in both cases there is no precise note of time, and it may be that the disciples did not obey Jesus and did return to Galilee.[8] (See further Dunn's third point below.)

Thirdly, the dating of the event at Pentecost is questioned. Some propose that the resurrection appearance to "more than five hundred" (1 Cor 15:6) is likely to have taken place after the coming of the Spirit on a group of about 120 (Acts 1:15; 2:1). If so, Luke has schematized a forty-day period of appearances and the coming of the Spirit at Pentecost in a way that is tidier than the historical reality. Until the fourth century, the East Syrian and Palestinian churches celebrated the ascension fifty days after Easter, which suggests Luke's timetable of forty days plus ten after Easter was not universally known.[9] However, the Lukan timetable may have been widely known, and it is possible that these churches celebrated the ascension and the coming of the Spirit on the same day (cf. Eph 4:7–8).[10]

Fourthly, it is suggested that Luke's presentation connects the believers' mission with the coming of the Spirit in a way that is in tension with other accounts of the origin of the mission that connect it with resurrection appearances (Matt 28:18–20; cf. Paul's view that an apostle is one who has seen the risen Christ, 1 Cor 9:1). However, this unnecessarily divides what Luke unites: Luke relates Jesus's call to mission during resurrection appearances (Luke 24:45–48; Acts 1:8) as well as connecting it firmly with the empowerment of the Spirit (Luke 24:29; Acts 1:8).

Fifthly, there are features of the account that cause difficulties. (i) Luke's account echoes John the baptizer's prophecy (Luke 3:16) and perhaps Sinai accounts and thus may be created from them. (ii) The relationship of the tongues-speech here, which appears to be in known languages (Acts 2:4, 6), with that found elsewhere in Acts (10:45, 46; 19:6) and in Paul (1 Cor 12,

---

6 Lincoln, "Theology," 206.
7 Contra Lincoln, "Theology," 206.
8 Marshall, *Acts* (TNTC), 58.
9 Kretschmar, "Himmelfahrt."
10 Marshall, "Significance," 363.

14), where it seems to be unknown languages. Further, when Peter spoke (Acts 2:14–36), he spoke in Greek (or perhaps Aramaic), so tongues-speech appears superfluous. The criticism that the disciples were drunk (v. 13) fits better with ecstatic glossolalia than speech in known languages. (iii) The people of vv. 5–13 are from *every* nation (παντὸς ἔθνους, v. 5), which fits very conveniently with Luke's theology of mission (cf. 1:8), and they are able to list all the nations from which they come (vv. 9–11), which is somewhat surprising. (iv) Peter's speech is, in common with other speeches in Acts, a composition of the author.[11] It would not have been recorded at the time and uses a Greek text close to the LXX, and this seems unlikely in Jerusalem. (v) How would it be possible to baptize three thousand by immersion during the dry season? It is frequently suggested that Luke exaggerates his numbers here and elsewhere. (For responses to these detailed points, see *Comment*.)

By contrast, Dunn identifies six lines of evidence that form a powerful case for the essential historicity of the Spirit's coming at Pentecost.[12]

First, the Jesus movement originated as an "enthusiastic sect" within Judaism, as Paul testifies (e.g., 1 Cor 14, concerning tongues-speech; 1 Thess 5:19, warning against quenching the Spirit; 2 Cor 12:1, 7, speaking of Paul's own visions and revelations; Rom 15:19; Gal 3:5, claiming signs and wonders performed by the Spirit's power). Similarly, Eph 5:18 contrasts drunkenness and being filled with the Spirit in a way suggestive of Pentecost; Heb 2:4 attributes signs and wonders to the Spirit; and John 4:23–24 with 4:14; 7:38–39 portrays worship as "in Spirit." These recorded phenomena most probably can be traced back to a first "outbreak of inspired mass ecstasy,"[13] and Pentecost is the only candidate in our sources for such an event.

Secondly, our sources are unanimous in seeing experiences of the Spirit as the "fulfillment of prophetic hope,"[14] notably in Paul (Gal 3:14; Eph 1:13; 2 Cor 3:3 echoing Ezek 11:19; 1 Thess 4:8, echoing Ezek 36:26–27; cf. Rev 11:11, echoing Ezek 37:5, 10; 1 Pet 4:14 drawing on Isa 11:2). The image of the Spirit being "poured out" (taken from Joel) found here (Acts 2:17–18) is also found in Rom 5:5; Titus 3:6. Paul understands believers to have been "baptized in one Spirit" (1 Cor 12:13), and John draws on distinctively biblical language in portraying the coming of the Spirit (John 20:22 echoing Gen 2:7; Ezek 37:9).

Thirdly, no location other than Jerusalem is mentioned as the possible center or place of origin of the Jesus movement.[15] Paul acknowledges the special place Jerusalem has (Gal 2:1–10; Rom 15:25–27), and if there had been another such place Paul, of all people, would surely have mentioned

11 For Lukan vocabulary throughout the section, see Avemarie, *Tauferzählungen*, 183–86. See general discussion of the speeches in vol. 3, and my forthcoming ZICNT volume on Acts.
12 *Beginning*, 164–71.
13 Lohse, *TDNT* 6:51.
14 Dunn, *Beginning*, 165.
15 Cf. Lincoln, "Theology," 206–7.

it, given the tensions between Paul and the Jerusalem leadership to which Acts 15 bears witness. Further, most key leaders in the early Jesus movement were Galileans, not Jerusalemites, notably the apostles Peter, James, John, and James the brother of Jesus. These Galileans also considered Jerusalem as the hub of earliest Christianity. The likely explanation of these features is that Luke (with the other evangelists) is right in portraying the central events of the death, resurrection, and ascension of Jesus and the coming of the Spirit as taking place in Jerusalem.

Fourthly, the likely timescale of events necessitates a short period between the death of Jesus and the beginnings of the Jesus movement. Saul/Paul's Damascus Road experience most probably took place within two or three years of Jesus's death (see *Form/Structure/Setting* on 9:1–31) and thus was preceded by the events of Acts 2–8, including Saul's persecution of believers (see the next paragraph). The earliest believers only mention two Jewish festivals—Passover and Pentecost (Acts 20:16; 1 Cor 16:8)—which suggests that something of significance was attached to each of them. The death and resurrection of Jesus (Passover) and the coming of the Spirit (Pentecost) are precisely such events.[16] Dunn also notes that Pentecost would provide a natural time for Galilean disciples to return to Jerusalem after spending time back in Galilee where some resurrection appearances took place (see *Comment* on 1:3).[17]

Fifthly, the speedy growth of the Jesus movement—sufficient to require persecution by Saul—is best explained by a "big bang" rather than a gradual development. Luke's portrait of the crowd at Pentecost as including numerous diaspora Jews who had settled in Jerusalem (Acts 2:5) is probably historical, for we meet Barnabas (4:36–37) and Mnason (21:16), who are both diaspora Jews who own property in or near the city. The "Hellenist" synagogues (e.g., 6:9) further illustrate the presence of such people.

Sixthly, *religionsgeschichtliche* parallels suggest that the tongues-speech portrayed by Luke is plausible. Such stories tend to be passed on orally, and it is frequently difficult to find written sources for them that command confidence. It is probable that Luke obtained the story of Pentecost orally at first- or secondhand and that he trusted those who told him of tongues-speech. In sum, it is unlikely that Luke invented the Pentecost story; it is most probably rooted in historical tradition.

However, beyond the probability that Luke used sources, it is hard to identify the shape of the sources he used in composing this account.[18] Tensions

16 Jervell, *Apostelgeschichte*, 138, with further references.

17 *Beginning*, 168–69.

18 Contra the confident assertions of Lüdemann, *Early Christianity*, 40–42; Wedderburn, "Traditions," 53.

that we, as moderns, perceive in the narrative may not have been seen as tensions by ancients.

Setting. There is significant debate concerning the most important biblical background(s) for the coming of the Spirit at Pentecost. Pentecost was the Jewish Feast of Weeks (Shavu'ot) or Firstfruits (see *Comment* on v. 1). Some argue that Pentecost is associated with the giving of the law at Sinai in the first century. In addition, some see a reversal of the Babel story (Gen 11). How far can we be confident that these are significant for Luke's presentation and understanding of the coming of the Spirit?

Three key arguments support the *link with Sinai.* (i) Pentecost was regarded as a feast of the giving of the law. In the mid-second century AD, R. Jose ben Ḥalafta regards the Feast of Weeks as also a feast of the giving of the torah at Sinai (S. ʿOlam Rab. 5;[19] cf. b. Pes. 68b; y. Meg. 26a), but we lack earlier extant explicit statements of this connection. However, Deut 16:21 associates the Feast of Weeks with deliverance from Egypt, and calculation based on Exod 19:1 also places this feast at the same time, relative to the exodus, as the giving of the law at Sinai.[20] Second Chronicles 15:10–12 also times Asa's renewal of the covenant to coincide with this feast. In the second century BC, Jubilees associates the timing of this feast, in the middle of the third month, with the covenants with Noah (6:17–20), Abraham (15:1) and Moses (1:1).[21] The Qumran community hold a festival of the renewal of the covenant annually and seem to follow the same calendar as Jubilees (1QS I, 8–II, 18; 4Q266 frg. 11, 17–18).[22] Philo, *Decal.* 33, presents the giving of the law at Sinai as an invisible sound which "changed into flaming fire" (πρὸς πῦρ φλογοειδὲς μεταβαλοῦσα), although Philo himself associates the giving of the law with the Feast of Trumpets (*Spec. Laws* 2.188–89), which may suggest that the link between Pentecost and the giving of the law was not yet established in mainstream Judaism. These sources together suggest that an association of Pentecost and the giving of the law was at least being discussed in some Jewish circles at the time of the first Christian Pentecost,[23] and it is likely that the rabbis after AD 70 developed an already existing understanding of Pentecost rather than creating a new view.[24]

(ii) Elements in Luke's telling of the Pentecost story echo Sinai traditions. This does not mean that Acts 2 shows literary dependence on such traditions (e.g., in Philo or Tg. Ps-J.) but rather that a reader familiar with the Sinai traditions would recognize the Pentecost account as sounding similar to their

19 Text and discussion: Guggenheimer, *Seder,* 59, 67–70.
20 Beale, "Descent I," 79.
21 With Mainville, *Spirit,* 183.
22 VanderKam, "Covenant," 241–46. For the connection, see more fully Park, *Pentecost,* 78–175.
23 See Turner, *Power,* 280–81; contra Menzies, *Empowered,* 190–93.
24 Dunn, *Baptism,* 49; Dunn, *NIDNTT* 2:784–85; contra Lohse, *TDNT* 6:48–50.

knowledge of Sinai.[25] Philo's accounts of the giving of the law (*Decal.* 33; *Spec. Leg.* 2.189[26]) speak of the law as like fire and including a loud sound and include other vocabulary used in Acts 2. Philo's and Luke's accounts are similar in picturing a theophany before God's people, describing a key event in redemptive history that marks a new beginning for God's people of that day, including a miraculous sound and something like fire from heaven dividing among those present and resulting in miraculous speech that touches people of many languages.[27] While there are some similarities with other biblical events,[28] principally in vocabulary, they lack the key structural features noted.

(iii) There are specific Mosaic echoes in the Pentecost story.[29] Turner notes:[30] the quotation from Joel 3:1–5 LXX (Acts 2:17–21) looks forward to the fulfillment of Moses's longing that all of God's people should have the Spirit (Num 11:29);[31] the apocalyptic language of Joel 3 echoes that of the exodus events and Sinai; and Joel's fire and clouds of smoke echo Sinai traditions (Exod 19:16–19). In addition, Luke parallels Jesus and Moses elsewhere as those who perform signs and wonders (Acts 2:22; 7:36), and such a link seems likely here between 2:19 and 22; and Peter's choice of "this crooked generation" (v. 40) parallels the wilderness generation (Deut 32:5). Most significantly, the implicit story of Acts 2:33–34a echoes Ps 68:19 [LXX 67:19] and should be seen through the lens of the psalm. Thus Jesus—paralleling Moses, not David—is the one who has "gone up" to receive a gift from YHWH and who then "comes down" to give the gift to people (cf. Tg. Ps 68:19, a Pentecost psalm that may stand behind the interpretation of this verse in Eph 4:8) (see *Comment* on vv. 33–34).[32] Instead of Moses going up the mountain and coming down with *the law*, Jesus ascends to the Father and receives and pours out *the Spirit*. O'Toole criticizes this view,[33] but his argument seems predicated on the view that Luke could only be alluding to one biblical promise, which is most clearly that to David. However, a clear echo of David in the psalms cited in the speech need not preclude a Mosaic echo too.

The link with Sinai thus seems probable, and the Spirit has the same role and location in the story of earliest Christianity as the torah does in Israel's story, a theme that Paul develops fully (e.g., Rom 8; 2 Cor 3). The Spirit is the one who guides God's people in God's ways, and this new covenant goes beyond the torah by providing power for God's people to live God's way, in conformity with his purposes revealed in Scripture (cf. Ezek 36:26–27;

25 Turner, *Power*, 283; Wedderburn, "Traditions," 29–39.
26 For English translations, see Turner, *Power*, 283–84.
27 Turner, *Power*, 284–85.
28 As Menzies, *Empowered*, 193–98, notes.
29 See the survey of Moses typology in Luke-Acts in Park, *Pentecost*, 184–97.
30 *Power*, 285–86; see also Park, *Pentecost*, 208–33.
31 Beale, "Descent I," 74–76.
32 See also VanderKam, *Scrolls*, 248–29.
33 O'Toole, "Acts 2:30."

Jer 31:33).[34] As Acts develops, there is no indication that Jewish believers are *required* to give up torah observance, but it is clear that the role of the torah is relativized by the admission of gentiles to the believing community without them being required to be circumcised or to keep the torah (esp. Acts 15:19–29).

Bede (on 2:4) makes a link with *the tower of Babel* (Gen 11:1–9).[35] There are also a number of linguistic echoes of Gen 11 LXX: φωνή, "sounds, language" (v. 6; Gen 11:1, 7); οὐρανός, "heaven" (v. 2; Gen 11:4); πῦρ, "fire" (v. 3; Gen 11:3); γλῶσσα, "language" (v. 4; Gen 11:7); and συγχέω, "confuse" (v. 6; Gen 11:7).[36] Pentecost is not a simple reversal of Babel, for there confusion occurs through the multiplication of languages (Gen 11:7, 9) after people had had only one shared language, whereas at Pentecost clarity comes through the *multiplication* of languages that the apostles can speak—but Peter then speaks in Greek (or perhaps Aramaic) to explain about Jesus (vv. 14–36). However, the verbal echoes of Babel are limited, and Luke does not seem to have gone out of his way to enable his readers to see the link.[37] Perhaps Pentecost may be seen, from our readerly perspective, as a parody of Babel that signals the universal claim of Israel's God upon the whole of humanity through Jesus: "At Babel, God hindered universal communication to save humanity from itself. At Pentecost, God now enables universal communication in a diversity of languages for the proclamation of the gospel in God's name."[38] The difference between "make a name for ourselves" (Gen 11:4) and proclaiming God's mighty deeds (v. 11) supports such a parodic contrast.[39]

In relation to Luke's Gospel, parallels have been drawn with Jesus's experience of the Spirit at his baptism (Luke 3:21–22): "What Jordan was to Jesus, Pentecost was to the disciples."[40] This leads both Dunn and Menzies, in different ways, to see the experience as normative for Christian believers. For Dunn, both events are about entry into the new age and covenant—at Jordan, Jesus entered into new covenant life, and at Pentecost the disciples became true new covenant believers by receiving the Spirit: "there were no Christians (properly speaking) prior to Pentecost."[41] For Menzies, both experiences are about empowerment for mission: at Jordan, Jesus is being empowered for his teaching mission, and at Pentecost, the believers are being empowered to

34 On the Spirit in Acts as empowering ethical living, see Turner, *Power*, 404–18.

35 Twelftree, *People*, 78, notes a number of vocabulary parallels in the Greek text of the stories; cf. Gregory Nazianzus, *Or.* 41.16; Beale, *Temple*, 201–3.

36 Davies, "Pentecost," 228–29.

37 Barrett, *Acts*, 1:112; Marshall, *Acts* (TNTC), 68.

38 King and Selvendran, "Rhubarb," 90.

39 For other valuable reflections on the Babel parallels, see Green, "Our Own," 207–13.

40 Dunn, *Baptism*, 40; cf. Menzies, *Empowered*, 174.

41 Dunn, *Baptism*, 42–54, quoting 51.

proclaim the gospel—the Spirit comes on both Jesus and the believers as the prophetic Spirit who enables proclamation.[42]

However, Jesus's Jordan experience is a private vision to Jesus and is not named as his receiving or being baptized with the Spirit: ἀνεῳχθῆναι τὸν οὐρανόν, "the heaven was opened" (Luke 3:21), is standard apocalyptic language for a vision (cf. Acts 7:56; 10:11; Rev 19:11) and introduces a private experience of Jesus (seen also, according to John 1:32, by John the baptizer). Jesus was conceived by the Spirit (Luke 1:35) and so does not "receive" the Spirit here. Further, the heavenly voice echoes Ps 2:7 and Isa 42:1–2 and thus tells Jesus of his Davidic (messianic) and servant-herald roles, and the descent of the Spirit in dove-form is to signal Jesus's equipping for his unique messianic ministry: Jesus is being empowered "as the messianic son and servant to commence the promised cleansing/restoration of Zion."[43] It is thus an experience *unique* to Jesus and does not parallel believers' experience at Pentecost.

Seen in this light, Pentecost is primarily empowering the believers for witness rather than their entry into new covenant life.[44] Moreover, the disciples were already experiencing that new life, at least in part, during Jesus's ministry through his teaching, miracles, healing, and—not least—the power they received to participate in Jesus's mission (Luke 9:1–6, 10; cf. 10:1–24).[45]

Pentecost is rightly seen as pivotal to the narrative of Acts (and Luke-Acts), for the Spirit's coming both highlights who Jesus is (note especially vv. 33, 36) and enables the believers to bear witness to Jesus. The apostles' speeches in the rest of Acts give the same focus to Jesus (3:13–16; 4:8–12; 5:30–31; 8:5, 35; 10:36–43; 13:26–41; 17:18, 30–31; 19:4; 20:21; 22:8, 18; 26:15; 28:23), and to become a follower of Jesus is to be transformed by the Spirit, expressed programmatically in 2:38 (cf. 8:15, 17; 9:17; 10:44–45, 47; 11:15–16; 15:8; 19:2, 6). The Spirit is the power of the apostolic testimony, enabling and equipping the witnesses to speak and persuading those who hear.[46]

Comment

1 Καὶ ἐν τῷ συμπληροῦσθαι τὴν ἡμέραν τῆς πεντηκοστῆς, "When the day of Pentecost arrived," marks a major transition in the story, echoing Luke's phrasing at the moment when Jesus "set his face to go to Jerusalem": Ἐγένετο δὲ ἐν τῷ συμπληροῦσθαι τὰς ἡμέρας τῆς ἀναλήμψεως αὐτοῦ, "It happened when the day of his being taken up arrived" (Luke 9:51). There is also an echo of Jer 25:11–12 LXX, which prophesies the return from exile ἐν τῷ πληρωθῆναι [A reads συμπληροῦσθαι] τὰ ἑβδομήκοντα ἔτη, "after seventy years have been

42 Menzies, *Empowered*, 171–89.

43 Turner, *Power*, 200; for this paragraph, see 188–201.

44 Menzies, *Empowered*, 174–75.

45 Contra Dunn, *Baptism*; on this theme, see Turner, *Power*, 318–41.

46 Schnabel, *Mission*, 1:402–3.

fulfilled," hinting at restoration of Israel themes.[47] "Pentecost," πεντηκοστή, was the Greek name for the one-day Jewish festival Shavu'ot, the feast of weeks, celebrated fifty days after Passover, around the middle of the third month of the year (Tob 2:1; Josephus, *J.W.* 6.5.3. §299). It originated as an agricultural holiday, marking the end of the barley harvest and the beginning of the wheat harvest (Exod 34:22; Lev 23:15–16; Deut 16:10, 16; 2 Chr 8:13; Philo, *Spec. Laws* 2:176–187; cf. m. Bik. 3:2–8).[48] In the first century AD it continued to be a harvest celebration but also seems to have developed an association with covenant renewal and the giving of the law on Sinai (see *Form/Structure/Setting*).

ἦσαν πάντες ὁμοῦ ἐπὶ τὸ αὐτό, "they were all together in one place," most naturally refers back to those gathered in the previous incident, i.e., the 120 of 1:15 (a group including women, see *Comment* on 1:15, 16–17), rather than the group listed in 1:13–14.[49] Their togetherness is more than physical colocation, for Luke uses both ὁμοῦ, "together," and ἐπὶ τὸ αὐτό, "in one place." ὁμοῦ, "together," echoes the unity denoted by ὁμοθυμαδόν in 1:14, a term that in turn echoes the united commitment of the people to the law at Sinai (Exod 19:8 LXX; cf. Mek. Exod 19:2, 98; 20:2).[50]

2–4 Luke records the key event as a series of phenomena: a sound (v. 2), the "tongues like fire" (v. 3), the group being filled with the Spirit and speaking in other languages (v. 4).

2 ἐκ τοῦ οὐρανοῦ ἦχος ὥσπερ φερομένης πνοῆς βιαίας καὶ ἐπλήρωσεν ὅλον τὸν οἶκον, "a sound came from heaven like the rushing of a mighty wind and it filled the whole house," echoes biblical passages that portray the coming of God as a noisy event (Sir 46:17; Joel 4:14 LXX [different from EVV 3:14]; cf. the use of "breath" [Heb. רוּחַ (*rûaḥ*)], which can mean "wind" or "S/spirit" in 2 Sam 22:16; Job 37:10; Ezek 13:13). In the NT outside Luke-Acts, ἦχος, "sound," is found only at Heb 12:19, where it describes the trumpet sound at Sinai. The noise ἐκ τοῦ οὐρανοῦ, "from heaven," recalls the heavenly vision of Jesus at his baptism (Luke 3:21–22) and that Jesus himself is now located in heaven (Acts 1:10–11)—thus Luke begins to point to Jesus as the one who pours out the Spirit (see 2:33). This phrase prepares for Saul's encounter with a heavenly light (9:3; 22:6) and Peter's heaven-sent vision (10:11, 16; 11:5, 9–10), highlighting the divine origin of what is taking place. It also hints at God's self-revelation (Deut 4:36 LXX, referring also to the fire at Sinai).[51] The heavenly session of Jesus increases traffic between heaven and earth (cf. Acts 2:33).[52]

47 Kurz, *Reading*, 77–78.
48 More fully, Shulam and Le Cornu, *Acts*, 1:53–58.
49 With Dunn, *Baptism*, 40; contra Dupont, *Salvation*, 37–38; Pfitzner, "Pneumatic Apostleship," 220, who identify the group as the Twelve on the basis of the references in 1:26; 2:14.
50 Dupont, *Salvation*, 38–39; Beale, "Descent I," 79.
51 Nagel, "Twelve," 115, relates this manifestation of God to the later rabbinic concept of the *Shekinah* (which he spells *Schechina*), God being present in a place or among a group of people.
52 Walton, "Heavens," 68.

The location is a "house" (οἶκος). It is most likely that the initial event took place in the upper room where the believers had been gathering (1:13), but the commotion led to crowds gathering and the apostles (at least) moving into the streets to engage with the crowds (see *Comment* on 2:6). Some suggest the "house" is the temple,[53] but the posture of sitting (καθήμενοι) probably rules this out, since people did not *sit* in the temple.[54] Beale's examples of individuals sitting in the temple courts (Matt 26:55; John 8:2; Luke 2:46; John 2:14) do not show that groups did this, and Ezra 10:9—which represents a unique occasion—is not good evidence for first-century practice.[55] Luke does not mention the temple until later (Acts 2:46).

3 ὤφθησαν αὐτοῖς διαμεριζόμεναι γλῶσσαι ὡσεὶ πυρός, "Divided tongues, like those of fire, appeared to them." The visual phenomenon accompanies the sound: ὤφθησαν, "appeared" (or "were seen"), is a Lukan expression (13 of 23 NT uses of the aorist passive of ὁράω are in Luke-Acts), most frequently used for visual experiences where the viewer meets God or a heavenly agent (Luke 1:11; 9:31; 22:43; 24:23; Acts 7:2, 30, 35; 9:17; 13:31; 16:9; 26:16). This is a so-called "divine passive," signaling that the visual experience is given by God: a divine revelation is taking place. The "tongues" are "divided" (διαμεριζόμεναι); the participle is probably middle voice, "dividing themselves," portraying the fire-like tongues as subdividing so as to settle on each of those present. Later rabbinic writings portray the word given by God at Sinai as dividing into seventy tongues (i.e., languages)—corresponding to the number of nations in Gen 10—so that people of all nations might understand the torah (b. Shab. 88b; Midr. Ps 92:3). Fire is a common feature of biblical theophanies,[56] notably in connection with the Sinai experience (Exod 19:18; 24:17; Deut 4:5; 5:22; 9:15).[57] The expression ὡσεὶ πυρός, "like those of fire," may draw on Exod 24:17; 19:18, concerning Sinai.[58] The coming of fire pictures this event as fulfilling the baptizer's promise that Jesus would baptize with Spirit *and fire* (Luke 3:16), and there the fire metaphor concerns cleansing and purging Israel.[59] The coming of the Spirit is the purging fire that produces a group of people ready to be witnesses to Jesus (1:8).

ἐκάθισεν ἐφ᾽ ἕνα ἕκαστον αὐτῶν, "[the fire] rested on each one of them." The connotation of καθίζω, "rest," is of staying, in parallel with Jesus's experience of the Spirit coming upon and staying upon him (Luke 3:21–22; 4:1, 14, 18),

53 E.g., Bruce, *Book* (1954), 55–56.

54 Marshall, "Significance," 353. Bruce, *Acts* (1990), 114, later recognizes this.

55 "Descent I," 65n6.

56 E.g., Gen 19:24; Exod 3:2; 9:23–24; 13:21; 14:24; Judg 6:21; 1 Kgs 18:23–25, 36–38; 2 Kgs 1:12, 14; 2:11; 6:17; 2 Chr 7:1, 3; Ps 97:3 [LXX 96:3]; cf. 4 Ezra 13:8–11.

57 Fire is associated with divine presence in Greco-Roman writers, e.g., Homer, *Il.* 18.255–27; Euripides, *Bacch.* 757–58; Cicero, *Div.* 1.53.121; for these and other sources, see van der Horst, "Parallels, 2.1–47," 49–50.

58 Menzies, "Occurrences," 55.

59 Turner, *Power,* 170–87; discussion: Brawley, *Text,* 76–77.

thus portraying the believers in parallel with their Lord. The verb playfully echoes the group's seated position (Acts 2:2, using the same verb), as well as resonating with the Fourth Gospel's description of the Spirit resting on Jesus (John 1:32–33, although using a different verb).

4 ἐπλήσθησαν πάντες πνεύματος ἁγίου, "all of them were filled with the Holy Spirit," explains the content of the phenomena.[60] This event fulfills Jesus's promise (1:8; Luke 24:49): the believers are being baptized in the Holy Spirit. The metaphor "baptize" has often been seen as about *immersion* in the Spirit,[61] and thus a filling by that means, but is more likely about the Spirit being poured on the believers *from above* (cf. ἐξέχεεν, "poured out," Acts 2:33),[62] with the outcome that the believers are filled by the Spirit. Luke's Gospel includes key people filled with the Spirit in the opening chapters: John the baptizer (Luke 1:15), Elizabeth and Zechariah (1:41, 67), and Jesus (Luke 4:1; cf. 1:35), and Acts will go on to characterize others this way, including some present at Pentecost: Peter and the other apostles (Acts 4:8, 31), Stephen (6:5; 7:55), Paul (9:17; 13:9), Barnabas (11:24), and the Antiochene disciples (13:52).

ἤρξαντο λαλεῖν ἑτέραις γλώσσαις καθὼς τὸ πνεῦμα ἐδίδου ἀποφθέγγεσθαι αὐτοῖς, "they began to speak in other languages as the Spirit gave them ability to speak." Pentecost is the fulfillment of Jesus's promise of empowerment for the task of witness, and so it is no surprise that Spirit-enabled testimony follows, as with other fillings with the Spirit (4:8, 31; 9:17 with 20).[63] We learn from the crowd that they speak of God's mighty acts (2:11), which suggests they speak of the coming, life, death, resurrection, and exaltation of Jesus (see *Comment* on v. 11). Peter's speech that follows (vv. 14–36) focuses strongly on those themes.

What kind of speech is this tongues-speech? Paul reports that believers in Corinth (and he himself) speak in tongues (1 Cor 12:10, 28; 13:8; 14:2, etc.) and contrasts such speech with intelligible prophecy (1 Cor 14:2, 4–6, 9, 13–14, 18–19, 23, 27). Paul's references might suggest that the Spirit-inspired speech at Pentecost is similar, and the crowd's accusation of drunkenness (Acts 2:13) could support that view. When tongues-speech occurs elsewhere in Acts, it also appears to be unintelligible: at 19:6 the parallel phrases, "they both spoke in tongues and prophesied," ἐλάλουν τε γλώσσαις καὶ ἐπροφήτευον, suggest two different activities, like the Spirit-inspired speech at Cornelius's house, which is "speaking in tongues and magnifying God," λαλούντων γλώσσαις καὶ μεγαλυνόντων τὸν θεόν (10:46). Cornelius's experience is interpreted as similar to Pentecost (10:47; 11:15; 15:8), and thus some argue that Pentecost involves unintelligible speech. (See *Comment* on 2:6 for the suggestion that the miracle was one of hearing, not speech.) However, the speech here is *ἑτέραις γλώσσαις*,

60 On the metaphor of filling, see Turner, *Power*, 165–69.
61 E.g., Dupont, *Salvation*, 44.
62 Marshall, "Meaning"; see also *Comment* n on 1:5.
63 Hur, *Reading*, 224–25; Turner, *Power*, 167–68.

"in *other* languages," a phrase that denotes foreign languages (cf. Sir 1:22; Isa 28:11 LXX), an observation supported by people from diverse linguistic groups both understanding (Acts 2:6) and remarking on the speakers all being Galileans (v. 7). Further, the verb ἀποφθέγγομαι, "express oneself," is unusual; it recurs in the NT only in v. 14, where it refers to Peter's (intelligible) speech, and in 26:25, where it signals the solemnity of Paul's (intelligible) speech to Festus, by contrast with Festus's suggestion that Paul is out of his mind. Thus, the phenomenon at Pentecost is xenolalia (i.e., speech in known foreign languages) rather than glossolalia (i.e., speech in unknown languages).[64] Forbes shows that glossolalia and xenolalia were unknown elsewhere in Jewish or Greco-Roman cultures.[65] It is no wonder that this unprecedented event quickly drew a crowd.

5–11 Now the focus shifts to others' reactions to the event, and Luke here identifies an initial reaction and its basis (v. 6b), the development into amazement and questioning, again with its basis (v. 7), and a fuller expression of their amazement (v. 8), before the breadth of membership of the crowd is described (vv. 9–11).

5 εὐλαβεῖς, "devout," portrays the Jews present as people devoted to God and concerned to live God's way: they are "honestly seeking God" and thus "real candidates for conversion."[66] Their devotion is further signaled by the fact that they are living in Jerusalem, even though they come from "every nation under heaven." Luke-Acts has all four NT uses of εὐλαβής: Luke 2:25 (Simeon), here, Acts 8:2 (those who buried Stephen), and 22:12 (Ananias). Devout Jews moved to live in Jerusalem from the diaspora,[67] especially as they became older and wanted to be buried there.[68] The city was central to Judaism, seen as the heart of the land, it was there that the Messiah was expected to appear, and it was there that many of the most important Torah schools were:[69] the evidence of Greek names in tombs that are evidently Jewish suggests that a good proportion of the population were such.[70] Josephus also notes the presence of non-Palestinians in the city (*J.W.* 1.20.3 §397; 1.22.2 §437; 1.33.9 §672)—the Cypriot Joseph Barnabas may well have been such a person (4:36–37).

κατοικοῦντες, "living," should not be understood to include only those permanently resident in Jerusalem, for among the crowds in 2:9 are οἱ *κατοικοῦντες* τὴν Μεσοποταμίαν Ἰουδαίαν τε καὶ Καππαδοκίαν, "those who *live* in Mesopotamia,

64 With Turner, *Holy Spirit*, 222–23; Dupont, *Salvation*, 45–52; Wolff, "Λαλεῖν," 190; contra Esler, "Glossolalia," 141. King and Selvendran, "Rhubarb," cautiously suggest that neuroscience may point to different cognitive and neural processes at work in xenolalia and glossolalia.
65 Forbes, *Prophecy*, esp. chs 2–7; summary: Turner, *Holy Spirit*, 235–37.
66 Morlan, *Conversion*, 120.
67 Jeremias, *Jerusalem*, 58–71; Safrai, "Relations," 195, 198.
68 Safrai, "Relations," 193–94, citing, inter alia, *CIJ* II, nos. 1233, 1284.
69 Hengel, "Jerusalem," 148.
70 Hengel, *Between*, 17–18, 175n53.

Judea and Cappadocia."[71] This is an unusual use of this verb, but to assert that Luke uses κατοικέω in its usual sense of permanent residence both here and in v. 9, and thus is using different sources that he has not resolved, is to assume incoherence in Luke's writing.[72] Pilgrims came to the feast in vast numbers from the land and the diaspora, swelling the population by up to fivefold.[73] These pilgrims are also included, although Luke says nothing about the proportions of residents and pilgrims in the crowd or among those who became believers.

ἀπὸ παντὸς ἔθνους τῶν ὑπὸ τὸν οὐρανόν, "every nation under heaven," assumes the conventional wisdom that Jewish people could be found among every nation (Josephus, *Ant.* 14.7.2 §115, citing Strabo).[74] This is return-from-exile language (Deut 30:4–5 LXX; cf. Neh 1:8–9; 2 Macc 2:18),[75] and the list of nations from which the Jewish people present come (vv. 9–11) makes this more explicit. There are echoes here of Simeon (Luke 1:30–32) and Jesus's words in Acts 1:8; this language prepares for the mission to all nations (cf. 2:21, 39; 3:25; 4:12). Luke does not anachronistically have gentiles present at Pentecost, but this phrase gives a clear hint of outreach to all peoples.[76] Von Baer rightly comments, "The Pentecostal Spirit is the missionary Spirit."[77] It is no accident that Luke speaks of the nations "under heaven," echoing the universal claims of YHWH implied in Deut 2:25; 4:19, for Jesus's heavenly location and reign (Acts 1:9–11) mean that the nations are under his sway.[78] The list of nations (vv. 9–11) should be read in this light.

ἤκουον εἷς ἕκαστος τῇ ἰδίᾳ διαλέκτῳ λαλούντων αὐτῶν, "each one was hearing them speak in their own language." The puzzlement of the crowd is explained by further elucidation of the phenomenon of speech. People from many places (vv. 9–11) recognized their mother tongues in the believers' speech. τῇ ἰδίᾳ διαλέκτῳ, "in their own language," here and v. 8 is clearly coreferential with ταῖς ἡμετέραις γλώσσαις, "in our own languages" (v. 11), underlining that the phenomenon is xenolalia (see *Comment* on v. 4).[79]

6 γενομένης δὲ τῆς φωνῆς ταύτης, "at this sound." φωνή is a more general word for "sound" that can embrace all the auditory phenomena—wind and tongues-speech—mentioned here.[80] It is found twice in the Sinai account (Exod 19:16 LXX) and in other theophanic accounts (2 Sam 22:14 LXX).[81]

---

71 Marshall, "Significance," 357.
72 Pesch, *Apostelgeschichte*, 1:105.
73 Jeremias, *Jerusalem*, 79–83.
74 See further P. R. Trebilco, "Diaspora Judaism," *DLNTD* 287–91.
75 Bauckham, "Restoration," 471–72.
76 Hur, *Reading*, 224; contra Jervell, *Apostelgeschichte*, 134–35, who claims "the list of nations also shows clearly that it concerns world *Judaism*, not the world" (my translation and italics).
77 *Geist*, 103 (my translation).
78 Sleeman, *Geography*, 96–98.
79 MacDonald, "Glossolalia," 129.
80 Contra Lightfoot, *Acts*, 87, who regards it as referring only to the voice(s) of the tongues-speakers.
81 Menzies, *Empowered*, 195–96, discusses occurrences of the cluster of words found in this

συνῆλθεν τὸ πλῆθος, "a crowd gathered." If the initial event took place in the upper room (see *Comment* on v. 2), this moves the story into public space, perhaps the streets surrounding the upper room (the apostles could have stood on part of the roof of the house on which the upper room was built) or a space elsewhere in the city to which the crowds moved (which could be the temple courts, for that would be a natural gathering point in the city if there was a commotion—although the main street of the city was ten metres (33 feet) wide, so a substantial crowd could gather there[82]).

ἤκουον εἷς ἕκαστος τῇ ἰδίᾳ διαλέκτῳ λαλούντων αὐτῶν, "each one was hearing them speak in their own language." The most natural way to take Luke's language here and in v. 11, ἀκούομεν λαλούντων αὐτῶν *ταῖς ἡμετέραις γλώσσαις*, "we hear them proclaiming . . . *in our own languages*," is that the miracle was one of speech rather than hearing, since the terms διάλεκτος, "mother tongue," and γλῶσσα, "language," both denote different languages, especially when combined with ἕτερος, "other," as they are in vv. 4, 11.[83] If the miracle were one of hearing, we should expect Luke to mention that the Spirit fell on the *hearers*, and there is no suggestion of that.[84]

7–8 The crowd's initial reaction is a mixture of wonder (ἐξίσταντο . . . καὶ ἐθαύμαζον, "they were astonished . . . and amazed") and agitation and confusion (συνεχύθη); what is happening is beyond their experience (see *Comment* on v. 4). Luke characteristically uses ἐξίστημι, "be astonished," in response to God's action in Acts (2:12; 8:9, 11, 13; 9:21; 10:45; 12:16): his word choice here indicates his understanding of the event. The crowd, by contrast, express confusion in two questions: "Surely all these who are speaking are Galileans?" οὐχ ἰδοὺ ἅπαντες οὗτοί εἰσιν οἱ λαλοῦντες Γαλιλαῖοι; a question expecting the answer, "Yes, of course!" and, "How then do we each hear them in our own mother tongue?" (v. 8). Luke may assume that some in the crowd recognized them as Jesus's followers (for they had been in Jerusalem during Jesus's last week, Luke 19–24), and that information spread quickly among the crowd. The most prominent members of the 120 were Galileans, the apostles, and members of Jesus's family (1:13–14), but the group could have included others who were not. The crowd's questions underline the significance of the xenolalia for Luke's readers: the believers are being enabled by God the Spirit to speak languages they have never learned. The crowd's response goes on to be divided (vv. 12–13).

9–11 The list of places from which the Jews present come is probably not intended to be comprehensive, but exemplary, unlike the list of seventy

---

account and other Second Temple Jewish sources.

82 Schnabel, *Mission*, 1:419.

83 Kremer, *Pfingsbericht*, 135–36; Dunn, *Beginning*, 159–60; contra Bruce, *Acts* (1990), 115; the "hearing" view is defended by Everts, "Tongues," 74–75, and mentioned by Bede, *Acts*, ad loc., citing Gregory of Nazianzus.

84 Green, "Our Own," 200–201n9.

nations in Gen 10, traditionally considered by Jews to be complete.[85] The structure of the list is in three (or perhaps four) parts: (i) Parthians and Medes and Elamites (three plural nouns joined by καί); (ii) those dwelling in Mesopotamia, Judea and Cappadocia, Pontus and Asia, Phrygia and Pamphylia, Egypt and the part of Libya near Cyrene (οἱ κατοικοῦντες + a series of accusative place-names); (iii) Roman visitors (οἱ ἐπιδημοῦντες Ῥωμαῖοι), who are both Jews and proselytes (Ἰουδαῖοί τε καὶ προσήλυτοι is in apposition to οἱ ἐπιδημοῦντες Ῥωμαῖοι), and in addition Cretans and Arabs (or the latter two could be considered to be a fourth grouping).[86] "Roman visitors" denotes people who are Roman citizens (not necessarily people who live in Rome), for "Roman citizen" is the meaning of Ῥωμαῖος elsewhere in Acts (16:21, 37, 38; 22:25, 26, 27, 29; 23:37; 25:16; 28:17).[87] The subdivision of these Roman visitors (or perhaps the whole list) is into native Jews (Ἰουδαῖοι) and proselytes (προσήλυτοι); the latter were people who were born gentile but had become Jewish: men would be circumcised, and both men and women underwent a ceremonial washing or baptism and offered sacrifice.[88] Philo has a parallel list of places where Jewish communities live that has a similar wide spread of such places around the Mediterranean basin:

> Concerning the holy city I must now say what is necessary. It, as I have already stated, is my native country, and the metropolis, not only of the one country of Judea, but also of many, by reason of the colonies which it has sent out from time to time into the bordering districts of Egypt, Phoenicia, Syria in general, and especially that part of it which is called Coelo-Syria, and also with those more distant regions of Pamphylia, Cilicia, the greater part of Asia Minor as far as Bithynia, and the furthermost corners of Pontus. And in the same manner into Europe, into Thessaly, and Boeotia, and Macedonia, and Aetolia, and Attica, and Argos, and Corinth and all the most fertile and wealthiest districts of Peloponnesus. And not only are the continents full of Jewish colonies, but also all the most celebrated islands are so too; such as Euboea, and Cyprus, and Crete. (Philo *Leg.* 281–82 [Yonge])

It is noticeable that "Medes" and "those who live in Mesopotamia" probably refer to members of the "lost" northern Israelite tribes exiled in 722 BC who had continued to worship YHWH (cf. Anna from the tribe of Asher, Luke 2:36),

85 Scott, "Horizon," 499–522.

86 For Jewish communities in these places, see Fitzmyer, *Acts*, 240–43; Hemer, *Book*, 222–23; Jeremias, *Jerusalem*, 62–71; Trebilco, "Diaspora Judaism," *DLNTD* 287-99, §3.

87 With Barrett, *Acts*, 1:123; Béchard, *Paul*, 214n117; *BegC*, 4:20.

88 See S. McKnight, "Proselytism and Godfearers," *DNTB* 835–47. Stroup, *Christians*, 67, observes, "For Luke proselytes are Jews," even though he recognizes this distinction which Jewish people make among themselves.

and thus the restoration-of-Israel theme present in the early chapters of Acts (especially in the restoration of a twelfth apostle, 1:15–26) is again present,[89] echoing prophetic promises of the restoration of the twelve tribes (e.g., Ezek 37:15–23).

The list, along with the clear statement that they are Ἰουδαῖοι . . . ἀπὸ παντὸς ἔθνους τῶν ὑπὸ τὸν οὐρανόν, "Jews . . . from every nation under heaven" (v. 5), highlights the hybrid ethnic identity of many first-century diaspora Jews. They are Jewish, but they are also Parthian, Median, etc. Stroup shows that this is not unusual in the Roman Empire, for hybrid identities were common, not least for those who were Roman citizens and yet from a particular nation (e.g., Saul of Tarsus).[90]

Notable gaps in the list, looking from the perspective of the rest of Acts, are Achaia and Macedonia, which are major centers of the Pauline mission (much of Acts 16–19 is set there), Syria, Ethiopia, Cyprus, Cicilia, and Galatia. This shows that Luke has not composed this list as a "table of contents" for Acts but suggests that he received the list from tradition: it reflected the home locations of a number who became believers at Pentecost.[91] The list provides a first glimpse of what witness "to the end of the earth" (1:8) will look like, and the heavenly perspective identified in v. 5 ("nations *under heaven*") signals that the claims of the gospel extend to cover the whole world—an interesting and pertinent contrast with Roman claims to dominate the whole world, e.g., Res. gest. divi Aug., Preface: "[Augustus] brought the world under the empire of the Roman people" (cf. the list of victories over nations, lines 25–33).[92] Strikingly, the list here includes both Roman citizens and people from Parthia, which was outside the Roman Empire.

Bauckham sees the list as hinging around Judea as a center:[93] the first group moves from the east (Parthia, southeast of the Caspian Sea) through Media (southwest of the Caspian Sea), Elam (north of the Persian Gulf) and Mesopotamia (between the Tigris and Euphrates rivers) into Judea (which may include Syria[94] and might then explain why "Judeans" could express surprise at understanding Galileans, vv. 7–8); the second group moves northwest through Cappadocia (part of eastern Asia Minor) to Pontus (on the shores of the Black Sea), and swings back through Asia (the western part of Asia Minor),

---

89 Bauckham, "Restoration," 471.

90 Stroup, *Christians*, 61–64. In his wider argument, he proposes that such hybrid identities open up a space in Jewish identity for later gentile believers to be integrated into God's people and regarded as, in some sense, Jewish.

91 Dunn, *Beginning*, 158; Fitzmyer, *Acts*, 240; Kremer, *Pfingsbericht*, 156, 164. For cogent critique of Weinstock and Brinkman's proposal that the list derives from an ancient zodiac list, see Metzger, "Geography," with Weinstock, "Catalogue"; Brinkman, "Background."

92 See Scott, "Horizon," 490–91; Gilbert, "List," 509–24. For examples of Greco-Roman geographical catalogues, see van der Horst, "Parallels, 2.1–47," 53–54.

93 "Jerusalem Church," 418–23; cf. Marguerat, *Actes*, 1:79.

94 So Hengel, "Ioudaia" (ET: Hengel, "Ἰουδαία"); *pace* Haenchen, *Acts*, 170.

Phrygia (in central Asia Minor), and Pamphylia (on the southern coast of Asia Minor) on a trajectory toward Judea; the third group goes south into north Africa (Egypt and Libya) before moving across the Mediterranean to Rome and then toward Judea through Crete and then south again to Arabia. However, it is unlikely that we should translate "visitors from Rome," i.e., people living in that city (see above); it is more likely that the "Roman visitors" (who are Jewish) are members of the Pentecost crowd who have Roman citizenship. Further, although Judea, centered in Jerusalem, has an honored place in Acts (which undermines Scott's objection that this structure is different from the syntactical structure[95]), the heavenly claim to the whole earth (1:8; 2:5) relativizes the city's place theologically—to see Judea, and Jerusalem in particular, as in some sense the "center" of the believing community is to miss that the community's true center is in heaven, where its Lord is at God's right side (2:33–34).[96] This change of center from a physical location to heaven will precipitate a major shift in the place that the temple—seen as the earthly dwelling of YHWH—has.

Scott suggests that the list echoes the Gen 10 table of nations, as part of his case that the whole of Acts is shaped by mission to the descendants of Noah's three sons,[97] but his case is not strong. The fact that only two names here are found in Gen 10 (Medes and Elamites), and only nine recur in Josephus's table of nations (*Ant.* 1.6.1–4 §§122–47), is hardly strong evidence, particularly given that Josephus's list is more comprehensive than Luke's. Further, the apparent lack of structure as a feature common to other tables of nations is unremarkable (whereas a shared structure could be evidence for a shared tradition). Finally, the fact that the list is "part for whole" (*pars pro toto*), like some other lists of nations that are understood to be dependent on Gen 10, is insufficient evidence that the Gen 10 table is specifically in mind.[98]

τὰ μεγαλεῖα τοῦ θεοῦ, "God's mighty deeds," is the content of the tongues-speech. The phrase is unique in the NT, but either the phrase "his/God's mighty deeds" or the statement that God has done mighty deeds is found in LXX generally referring to God's deeds in saving his people (Deut 11:2; 3 Macc 7:22; Ps 70:19 [MT 71:19]; Sir 18:4; 36:10; 42:21; cf. τὰ δυναστεία τοῦ κυρίου, "the powerful acts of the Lord" LXX Ps 105:2 [MT 106:2]; 150:2). In Luke's infancy narrative, Mary similarly proclaims God's mighty deeds (μεγάλα, Luke 1:49) in the birth of Jesus. The phrase denotes "invasive charismatic praise," in which the believers, inspired by the Spirit, give praise to God for his deeds in salvation through Jesus (cf. 10:46; 19:6)[99] and/or proclamation

95 Scott, *Geography*, 71–72.
96 Sleeman, *Geography*, 97.
97 "Horizon," 527–41; *Geography*, 77–84; also Béchard, *Paul*, 211–24.
98 For critique of Scott's wider argument, see Schnabel, *Mission*, 1:498–99; Gilbert, "List," 503–5.
99 Turner, *Power*, 271–72; *BegC*, 4:20; Haya-Prats, *Believers*, 174, 198; Wolff, "Λαλεῖν," 195–97.

directed to the crowds of what God has done in Jesus.[100] Given the broader biblical setting, the context nearby (1:8) and more widely in Luke-Acts (Luke 1:41, 67), where being filling with the Spirit results in testimony to Jesus in praise or prophecy, it seems more probable that the crowds are overhearing the believers praising God and thereby indirectly hearing proclamation of what God has done in Jesus. Were they hearing direct proclamation we might expect Luke's more usual verbs denoting such proclamation (ἀναγγέλλω, "announce," διαγγέλλω, "proclaim," εὐαγγελίζομαι, "proclaim good news," or κηρύσσω, "preach"),[101] and it would be harder to understand the accusation of drunkenness (v. 13). Peter's following speech then elucidates and explains more fully in a common language, once the tongues-speech has gained the crowd's attention.

12–13 After the (syntactically) background description of the crowd, the main storyline resumes, again focusing on the crowd's reaction. Luke now makes the divided response explicit, typifying response to the believers throughout Acts, where there is an "interplay between rejection and acceptance of the gospel."[102] Thus, following the healing of the man at the Beautiful Gate (3:1–10), Peter's speech (3:11–26) leads to both persecution (4:1–3) and many believing (4:4). Similarly, the second Sanhedrin hearing (5:17–41) follows a summary statement of the church's growth (5:14); Stephen's trial and death (6:8–7:60) follows a further summary of the church's growth (6:7); and in the diaspora, Paul and his colleagues regularly meet both conversions and opposition in Antioch (13:42–43, 45), Iconium (14:1–2), Thessalonica (17:4–9), and Beroea (17:10–11, 13). Here, some respond with amazement (ἐξίσταντο) combined with perplexity (διηπόρουν; cf. Herod's perplexity at Jesus, Luke 9:7), expressing their question aloud, "What's going on here?" τί θέλει τοῦτο εἶναι;, suggesting an openness to learn more. Others "jeered," διαχλευάζοντες (a NT *hapax legomenon*; the simple verb is found only in Acts 17:32, again portraying a negative reaction to the gospel message; cf. Festus's reaction to Paul, 26:24), accusing them of having had their fill (the probable force of the periphrastic perfect μεμεστωμένοι εἰσίν, "they are full"[103]) with γλεῦκος, a word denoting unfermented or partly fermented wine that tasted sweet and was not expensive (cf. Job 32:19 LXX; Josephus, *Ant.* 2.5.2 §64)—thus the believers were not just being mocked for drunkenness but for being drunk on *cheap* wine.[104] Such sweet wine could be kept for up to a year, so it could be available at the season of Pentecost. The criticism could be a natural reaction to hearing languages other than one's own spoken or to the cacophony of multiple languages. Either way, it was a good way for opponents

100 Menzies, *Empowered*, 177.
101 Turner, *Power*, 272.
102 Jervell, *Theology*, 37.
103 Barrett, *Acts*, 1:125.
104 Barrett, *Acts*, 1:125.

to attack the believers.[105] It constitutes a challenge to the believers' honor, and Peter will be the agent of their riposte.[106] It need not imply that the believers spoke unknown languages of the kind known in Corinthian glossolalia.

14–36 The subject switches to Peter and we hear his speech, in which he interprets what happens through the lens of Scripture, first to identify that the Pentecost phenomena are in tune with Scripture (vv. 16–21) and then to explain the recent events concerning Jesus (vv. 22–36). The sections both begin with a double vocative and a call to listen (vv. 14, 22). Peter's speech centers on the role of God in Jesus's life, ministry, death, resurrection, exaltation, and pouring out of the Spirit, interpreting these events through the lens of Scripture to show that Jesus is now to be recognized as both Davidic Messiah and as Lord. The prophetic gift of the Spirit announced by Joel is at work through Jesus's prophetic ministry (vv. 22–23) and David's prophetic announcement of the Messiah (vv. 24–36).[107]

14–15 set the scene for the speech by providing an interim rebuttal of the charge of drunkenness. Peter stands σὺν τοῖς ἕνδεκα, "with the eleven": the core of the renewed Israel (Luke 22:30), reconstituted in Acts 1:15–26, stands to invite others to join with them in responding to the work of God in and through Jesus, now experienced by the Spirit. ἀπεφθέγξατο, "he addressed," by contrast with the accusation of drunkenness, denotes sober speech in Paul's speech to Festus (26:25)—there responding to Festus's claim that Paul is crazy (26:24).[108]

Peter identifies two parts of the crowd, native Judeans (Ἰουδαῖοι) and others who live in Jerusalem (οἱ κατοικοῦντες Ἰερουσαλὴμ πάντες), and speaks in a language all understand—most probably Greek, since it was the common language of diaspora Jews, but possibly Aramaic. ἀπεφθέγξατο, "addressed" does not denote the tongues-speech.[109] The importance of Peter's words is underlined by his twofold call to listen carefully (v. 14b), a call that will be renewed when he moves to focus on Jesus (v. 22).

ὥρα τρίτη τῆς ἡμέρας, "the third hour of the day," assumes that day begins at 6 a.m., so this event takes place at 9 a.m. Peter's reasoning assumes that drunkenness is a feature of the night (cf. 1 Thess 5:7), and thus it is too early in the day to have drunk sufficient to be intoxicated.[110]

16–21 Peter now begins the body of the speech by quoting Scripture, in

---

105 Kremer, *Pfingsbericht*, 162; Marshall, "Significance," 361.

106 Brawley, *Text*, 78.

107 White, *Prophets*, 70–83. White's claim that the crowd plays a prophetic role is unconvincing.

108 Green, "Our Own," 204, speculates from this parallel that the speech in v. 11 is "charismatic interpretation of Scripture," but this is to blur the two passages.

109 With Dunn, *Beginning*, 160n114; Haenchen, *Acts*, 168n3, the latter noting that the verb means "to speak in a solemn or inspired way, but not ecstatic speech"; contra Jervell, *Apostelgeschichte*, 134.

110 Cf. mockery of drinking at 8 a.m. in Cicero, *Phil.* 2.41.104; van der Horst, "Parallels, 2.1–47," 56.

similar manner to Jesus programmatically reading Scripture at the start of his public ministry and interpreting it concerning the present event of his work (Luke 4:16–21). The quotation is from Joel 3:1–5a LXX (EVV 2:28–32a) and it interprets the events that take place: τοῦτό ἐστιν τὸ εἰρημένον διὰ τοῦ προφήτου Ἰωήλ, "this is what was announced through the prophet Joel."[111] The prophecy in Joel speaks of a coming time when God will act and echoes Moses's longing that all of God's people would have the Spirit and were prophets (Num 11:29; Midr. Ps 14:6 claims that the fulfillment of Moses's longing, as prophesied by Joel, will take place in the world to come). The elements of the Spirit's work in Joel are typical of the gifts the Spirit was expected to bring in first-century Judaism: dreams and visions were means of charismatic revelation, as was prophetic speech inspired by the Spirit. Within the Pentecost narrative, it is likely that the xenolalic tongues-speech was seen as invasive charismatic praise, also an expected manifestation of the Spirit (see *Comment* on 2:9–11 above).[112] Thus Joel 3:1–2 is cited as explaining the events of vv. 1–4: this is God pouring out the Spirit. The quotation goes on, and it is also clear that Acts 2:21 (= Joel 3:5a LXX) gives the basis for the following section of the speech, where Jesus is identified as the one who pours out the Spirit (Acts 2:33) and the Lord upon whom people must call to be saved (vv. 36, 38).

It is relatively unusual in the NT for the book of Scripture cited to be named;[113] it is much commoner for the author either simply to quote or to use a formula such as "it is written," γέγραπται, to introduce a quotation. In addition to this quotation, Joel 3:5c LXX is alluded to in Acts 2:39.[114] Here is a biblical text known elsewhere in the NT (Rom 10:13 quotes, and Luke 21:25; Mark 13:24; Rev 9:2 allude to, Joel 3:5 LXX; cf. also Rev 6:12), which suggests that it was known reasonably widely in the early church, and thus that this citation is probably primitive.[115]

The principal differences from LXX Joel 3:1–5a are: (i) the use of ἐν ταῖς ἐσχάταις ἡμέραις, λέγει ὁ θεός, "in the last days, says God" (v. 17), in place of Joel's μετὰ ταῦτα, "after these things" (which B reads, probably a harmonization with LXX[116]): ἐν ταῖς ἐσχάταις ἡμέραις probably echoes Isa 2:2 LXX (the only use of that phrase in LXX); (ii) the reversal of the clauses about dreams and visions (v. 17b; cf. Joel 3:1b LXX); (iii) some expansion in v. 18, adding μου, "my," twice, and καὶ προφητεύσουσιν, "and they shall prophesy"; (iv) some expansions in v. 19, adding ἄνω, "above," σημεῖα, "signs," and κάτω, "below"; cf. Joel 3:3

111 See the full and helpful discussion of Luke's appropriation of the Joel citation in White, *Prophets*, 54–100, including a valuable comparison with the way T. Jud. 24 reads the Joel passage.

112 Turner, *Power*, 271.

113 Cf. Luke 3:4; 4:17; 20:42; Acts 1:20; 8:28; 13:33; Matt 3:3; 4:14; 8:17; 13:14; 15:7; 24:15; 27:9; Mark 1:2; 7:6; 10:4; 11:17; John 1:23; 12:38; Rom 9:27, 29; 10:16, 20; 15:12.

114 Dodd, *According*, 47.

115 Marshall, "Significance," 362; Dodd, *According*, 46–48.

116 Bock, *Proclamation*, 160–61.

LXX.[117] Of these, (i) is most significant and frames the quotation as God speaking, in tune with the phrase "*through* (διά) the prophet Joel," portraying the prophet as God's spokesman, speaking accurately his Lord's message (cf. on 1:16–17). See below on the other differences.

There are strong connections between the Pentecost story and both Joel 3:1–5a and the whole book of Joel, suggesting that Luke invites his readers to see the event through the lens of Joel's prophecy.[118] Nagel highlights that the immediate context has God saying, "I am in Israel's midst, and I am the Lord your God," ἐν μέσῳ τοῦ Ισραηλ ἐγώ εἰμι, καὶ ἐγὼ κύριος ὁ θεὸς ὑμῶν (Joel 2:27 LXX), which is clearly relevant to this Pentecostal manifestation of God's presence.[119] Evans identifies some twenty words in the Pentecost story outside the quotation in Acts 2:17–21 that occur in LXX Joel, often providing "essential details."[120] Notable are: πῦρ, "fire" (Acts 2:3; Joel 3:3; cf. Luke 3:16); the dispersion of the Jewish people among πάντα τὰ ἔθνη, "all the nations" (Acts 2:5, 9–11; Joel 3:2); the call to attention using ἐνωτίσασθε, "pay careful attention" (Acts 2:14; Joel 1:2; NT *hapax legomenon*); the accusation of drunkenness using μεθύω (Acts 2:15; Joel 1:5; only six other times in NT); and συγχέω (Acts 2:6; Joel 2:1, 10; only three other times in NT, all in Acts: 9:22; 21:27, 31).

Luke has not simply taken over Joel's ideas, however; he has reshaped them around the Pentecost event, and he uses such ideas to link backwards and forwards in the overall story of Luke-Acts.[121] Peter's speech will interpret Joel's words as showing that Jesus is now enthroned as Lord of all by the Father, and the outpouring of the Spirit is the sign that the eschatological age announced by Joel has begun.[122] By this means, Luke underlines Peter's initial statement that "[t]his is what was announced through the prophet Joel" and implies that it applies to the whole of God's work in the believing community in Acts. Luke links backwards to John the baptizer's ministry, both in his baptism of repentance leading to forgiveness (Luke 3:3; cf. Acts 2:38) and his prophecy of one who will baptize with the Spirit and fire (Luke 3:16; cf. Acts 2:3, 4). The pouring out of the Spirit on πᾶσαν σάρκα, "all flesh" (v. 17; Joel 3:1), echoes the quotation of Isa 40:5 in Luke 3:6. Luke picks up the "wonders" (τέρατα, Acts 2:19; Joel 3:3)—adding "signs" (σημεῖα, Acts 2:19)—both in reference to Jesus (v. 22) and in the report to the Jerusalem gathering that such things happen among gentiles (15:12). A further link with the Jerusalem gathering is the use of the "name" (2:21; Joel 3:5; Amos 9:12 cited in Acts 15:17): God is taking from among the gentiles "a people for his name" (τῷ ὀνόματι αὐτοῦ,

117 See Turner, *Power*, 269–70; in more detail, Kilpatrick, "Quotations," 81–83.
118 For what follows, see Evans, "Setting."
119 Nagel, "Twelve," 116.
120 "Setting," 216 with n11.
121 With Litwak, *Echoes*, 157: "Joel 3.1–5 has been recontextualized . . . One would not understand Joel 3 the way that Acts 2 uses it simply by reading Joel on its own."
122 White, *Prophets*, 57.

15:14). The coming of the Spirit announced by Joel and narrated by Luke will be repeated at strategic moments in Luke's ongoing story, notably upon Cornelius's household (10:44; 11:15) and the twelve disciples of John the baptizer (19:6). Visions and dreams are features of the progress of witness to Jesus at key points, including in the development of the gentile mission (2:17; Joel 3:1; cf. Acts 9:10; 10:3, 17; 11:5; 16:9, 10; 18:9). The theme of calling on the Lord's name (τὸ ὄνομα κυρίου, 2:21; Joel 3:5) is important, for baptism/conversion involves calling on Jesus's name (Acts 2:38; 4:12; 8:12; 10:43, 48; 19:5; 22:16), as is the language of being "saved" (σωθήσεται, 2:21; Joel 3:5; cf. Acts 2:40, 47; 4:9, 12; 11:14; 14:9; 15:1, 11; 16:30, 31; note also Luke's fourfold ἡ πίστις σου σέσωκέν σε, "your faith has saved you," Luke 7:50; 8:36; 17:19; 18:42).

17–18 Joel's eschatology is being realized in the events of Pentecost and the life and growth of the believing community. That is why it is appropriate for Peter to speak of "the last days," ταῖς ἐσχάταις ἡμέραις (Acts 2:17; Isa 2:2): the ministry, death, resurrection, and exaltation of Jesus have inaugurated the final (messianic) period of history in which the Spirit is given to all God's people.[123] This is "not the end of time, but the time of the end."[124] Peter's speech will go on to argue the coming of the Spirit shows that Jesus is the Messiah (Acts 2:36). The phrase from Isa 2:2 LXX renders Heb. באחרית הימים (*b̠ʾḥryt̠ hymym*), "in the latter days," and comes in the context of a prophecy of people coming from gentile nations to God's mountain to know God (Isa 2:1–4). The prophecy goes on to say ἐκ γὰρ Σιων ἐξελεύσεται νόμος καὶ λόγος κυρίου ἐξ Ιερουσαλημ, "for the law shall go out from Zion and the word of the Lord from Jerusalem" (v. 3b), mapping the shape of the gospel mission in Acts.[125]

λέγει ὁ θεός, "God says," identifies God as speaker, which means that YHWH is the "Lord" (κύριος) who pours out the Spirit and on whom people are to call to be saved (Acts 2:21). However, it will become clear in v. 33 that Jesus is the one who pours out "what you see and hear" and in v. 36 that Jesus is now Lord, so that Peter calls on people to be baptized in *Jesus's* name (v. 38; cf. Rom 10:13, also citing Joel 3:5). Thus, this insertion into the quotation is highly significant in preparing for the christological point toward which Peter's speech drives.

The metaphor ἐκχεῶ, "I will pour out," is not widely used for God giving the Spirit in the Greek Bible outside Joel and this citation (although see Zech 12:10; Titus 3:6), but it links with the probable sense of "baptize" as "drench with a liquid" (see *Comment* on 1:5). Thus, this metaphor strengthens the likelihood that Pentecost is the believers' being baptized in the Spirit.

ἐπὶ πᾶσαν σάρκα, "on all flesh," echoes Isa 40:5 LXX, quoted in Luke 3:6 (Luke 3:4–6 is a longer quotation from Isa 40 than Mark 1:3, which lacks

123 White, *Prophets*, 68, sees "in the last days" as turning "a significant page in God's redemptive-historical plan."

124 Brawley, *Text*, 80; similarly, Carroll, *Response*, 133.

125 Pao, *Acts*, 156–59.

Isa 40:4–5), and hints at the Spirit's availability to all people, a theme that will be developed later in Acts when the Spirit falls on Cornelius's gentile household (Acts 10:44, 45, 47; 11:15, 16). While the focus in the Pentecost story is on the universal availability of the Spirit to all *Jews*, the connection with Isa 40, as well as the reference to "all who are far away" (Acts 2:39, see *Comment* there), points to the Spirit-enabled restoration of Israel being the means of blessing for the nations.[126] This universality, opening direct access to God for his people by the Spirit, has elements of a return to Eden, where the first humans had direct access to God (Gen 1:28–29; 2:16, 19–20; 3:8a; cf. Joel 2:3, mentioning Eden).[127]

The comprehensiveness of God's pouring out of the Spirit is further expressed by its inclusion of both men and women: οἱ υἱοὶ ὑμῶν καὶ αἱ θυγατέρες ὑμῶν, "your sons and daughters," and τοὺς δούλους μου καὶ ἐπὶ τὰς δούλας μου, "my male and female slaves" (cf. 5:14; 8:12; 17:2);[128] and older and younger people: οἱ νεανίσκοι ὑμῶν . . . καὶ οἱ πρεσβύτεροι ὑμῶν, "your young and your old." Each will manifest the Spirit's empowering in prototypical gifts: prophecy, visions, and dreams.[129]

προφητεύσουσιν, "they shall prophesy," quoted from Joel in Acts 2:17 and added in v. 18, here denotes comprehensible speech that may be immediately inspired by God or that reports an experience of charismatic revelation or wisdom.[130] Thus Peter's speech is not to be understood as prophecy: within the speech, David and Joel are prophets (vv. 16, 30), and male and female believers will later prophesy (11:27–28; 13:1; 15:32; 19:6; 21:9, 10–11; cf. Anna, Luke 2:36–38).[131] The latter prophesying is how Luke most probably interprets this prophecy within the horizon of Acts. The universality of this gift of prophecy echoes Moses's longing that all the Lord's people would prophesy (Num 11:29).

τοὺς δούλους μου καὶ ἐπὶ τὰς δούλας μου, "my male and female slaves," points back in the Gospel to Simeon (Luke 2:29), Jesus's parables about the delayed master (12:35–38, 42–28), the invitations to the banquet (14:16–24), the pounds ("minas," 19:11–27), and the wicked tenants (20:9–19). Each of these use slavery language to portray relationship to God/Jesus, and this image is rooted in Scripture, where the patriarchs, prophets, kings, and the people of Israel are called YHWH's slaves (e.g., Exod 32:13; Lev 25:55; 1 Sam 3:9; Ezra 9:11; Neh 1:6, 11; 2:20; Heb. עֶבֶד [*ʿebed*]; LXX has either δοῦλος, "slave," or οἰκέτης, "household member [usually, slave]"). The inclusion of both female

126 See also Meek, *Gentile Mission*, 107–8.
127 White, *Prophets*, 60.
128 See Black, "Sons," 201–3; Seim, *Message*, 51.
129 On the prototypical gifts of the Spirit in early Judaism, see Turner, *Power*, 92–101.
130 Turner, *Power*, 98–99.
131 Contra White, *Prophets*, 70.

and male slaves echoes the mixed nature of the group on whom the Spirit falls (see *Comment* on 2:1).

19–20 τέρατα . . . καὶ σημεῖα, "wonders . . . and signs," will be a feature of the church's ministry, empowered by the Spirit (2:43; 4:30; 5:12; 6:8; 14:3; 15:12; cf. Rom 15:19; 2 Cor 12:12; Heb 2:4), as well as being a marker of God working through an individual in the past (Jesus: Acts 2:22; Moses: 7:36). The combination of terms indicates both the miraculous nature of the events (τέρας, "wonder") and that the events pointed to the greatness of the God who did them (σημεῖον, "sign"). Bock also considers a reference to the signs that accompanied the crucifixion (cf. Luke 23:44–45) or future cosmic signs at the coming day of the Lord (in tune with Acts 2:20),[132] which is possible, although the phrase "wonders and signs" is not used in Luke's apocalyptic discourse (Luke 21; contrast Matt 24:24; Mark 13:22). The variation in word order of the two within Acts does not seem significant.[133] The phrase derives from the exodus story,[134] and thus Joel's prophecy (and Luke's citation of it) lays God's new action in pouring out the Spirit alongside God's saving work in the past and connects to the "new exodus" theme that Luke develops in his Gospel (see also *Comment* on 2:17–18, 22)[135] and also to Luke's theme of Jesus as the "prophet like Moses" (see *Comment* on 3:22). Pagan readers would hear echoes of stories about "wonders and signs" done by the gods.[136] Luke (or his source) expands Joel by adding ἄνω, "above," and σημεῖα . . . κάτω, "signs . . . below," again providing a note of comprehensiveness: the whole of the created order will be impacted by the work of the Spirit.

The cosmic phenomena (Acts 2:20a) echo Jesus's apocalyptic teaching (Luke 21:25; cf. Mark 13:24; Matt 24:29; Rev 6:12) and most probably refer to the same things.[137] It is debated whether the phenomena are used to indicate the cosmic significance of the fall of political and other earthly powers[138] or to refer to the destruction of the known universe.[139] Here, these cosmic phenomena presage God's judgment: the "day of the Lord" is a day when God will act to vindicate his people (and sometimes the nations too) and bring judgment on those who reject him—including among Israel—in both OT and NT.[140] The darkness recalls that at Jesus's crucifixion (Luke 23:44–45). The day is called

132 *Proclamation,* 167.

133 Contra Rengstorf, *TDNT* 7:242–43.

134 LXX Exod 7:3, 9; 11:9, 10; Deut 4:34; 6:22; 7:19; 11:3; 26:8; 29:3; 34:11; Pss 77:43 [MT 78:43]; 134:9 [MT 135:9]; Jer 39:20, 21 [MT 32:20, 21]; Bar 2:11.

135 Turner, *Power,* 244–50; Pao, *Acts,* passim. Dillon, "Prophecy," 546–47, considers the Deuteronomy parallels particularly significant in showing that the "wonders and signs" validate the prophetic ministry of the apostolic witnesses.

136 Whittaker, "Signs."

137 Adams, *Stars,* 177n219.

138 Wright, *Jesus,* 208–9; Wright, *New Testament,* 280–86.

139 Adams, *Stars,* passim.

140 E.g., Isa 13:6, 9; 58:13; Jer 46:10; Ezek 30:3; Joel 1:15; 2:1, 11; 3:4 (EVV 2:31); 4:14 (EVV 3:14); 1 Cor 5:5; 2 Cor 1:14; 1 Thess 5:2; 2 Thess 2:2; 2 Pet 3:10.

μεγάλην καὶ ἐπιφανῆ, "great and glorious"; the latter term's cognate ἐπιφάνεια, "manifestation," is used in the NT with reference to Jesus's return (2 Thess 2:8; 1 Tim 6:14; 2 Tim 4:1, 8; Titus 2:13) and in Greek literature with reference to the appearance of a god or the accession of a ruler.[141] These phenomena appear, then, to look to the end of the age when Acts 1:11 is carried out.[142]

21 For Joel, to "call on the Lord's name," ἐπικαλέσηται τὸ ὄνομα κυρίου, is to call on YHWH, that is, to worship him, and "will be saved," σωθήσεται, in Joel's setting refers to being kept safe amidst coming physical threat and disaster summarized as "the day of the Lord."[143] Peter's speech "bursts its [sc. Joel's promise's] original wrappings"[144] and relates the promise to calling on the name of *Jesus* via the interpretation of Pss 16 and 110 (LXX Pss 15 and 109) that follows (Acts 2:22–36), with the implication that the nature of being "saved" is now centered on what Jesus does in saving people (thus v. 38).[145] Hence (v. 33) the exalted Jesus is also the one who enacts the prophecy: he pours out the Spirit. The "name" of Jesus will be a major theme in the following chapters, for it brings forgiveness and the Spirit (2:38), healing (3:6, 16; 4:10; 16:18), and "signs and wonders" (4:30). To be a believer is to be one who calls on Jesus's name (9:14, 21; 22:16). To be "saved" in this setting thus focuses on deliverance from God's future judgment (in continuity with Joel's meaning) and knowing in the present that one will be "saved" on that day (see *Comment* on 2:40 and 3:16).[146]

Peter's citation from Joel ends at Joel 3:5a, and thus does not include v. 5b, which would tie the promised salvation to Jews. When Acts 2:39 alludes to Joel 3:5, an echo of Isa 57:19 expands Joel's reference to include "those who are far off" (see *Comment* on 2:39).[147] Thus this citation's limitation prepares the way for the inclusion of gentiles.[148]

22–36 Peter's speech transitions from quoting Joel to focus firmly on Jesus, beginning with the thematic accusative Ἰησοῦν τὸν Ναζωραῖον, "Jesus the Nazarene," echoed in ἄνδρα, "a man" (v. 22), τοῦτον, "this man" (v. 23), ὅν, "this man" (v. 24, lit. "whom"), αὐτόν, "him" (v. 25), τοῦ Χριστοῦ, "of the Messiah" (v. 31), τοῦτον τὸν Ἰησοῦν, "this Jesus" (v. 32), αὐτόν, "him" (v. 36), and τοῦτον τὸν Ἰησοῦν, "this Jesus" (v. 36). The burden of Peter's words concerns Jesus, for he is now the Lord on whom people must call to be saved, and to understand the coming of the Spirit rightly is to recognize that Jesus is the Lord (see *Comment* on vv. 33, 36), and now is the moment to call on Jesus

141 "ἐπιφάνεια," LSJ 669, §§I.2, 4; Barrett, *Acts*, 1:138.
142 Shepherd, *Function*, 164, observes that πρίν, "before," makes clear that the day of the Lord has not yet come.
143 Wolff, *Joel and Amos*, 68; Allen, *Joel*, 101–2.
144 Allen, *Joel*, 102.
145 Buckwalter, *Character*, 196.
146 Marshall, *Historian*, 96.
147 Carroll, *Response*, 131.
148 See also Meek, *Gentile Mission*, 108–9.

to be saved (vv. 21, 38).[149] Peter's emphasis is on Jesus's attestation by God throughout.[150] Peter's key claims about Jesus are: (i) God worked through him, and this is public knowledge (v. 22); (ii) according to God's purpose, the people of Jerusalem killed Jesus (v. 23); (iii) God raised Jesus from the dead (v. 24); (iv) Scripture testifies to and interprets the death and resurrection of Jesus (vv. 25–31); (v) the risen and exalted Jesus is now at God's right hand and has poured out the Spirit, as Scripture also testifies (vv. 32–36).

22 The double vocative Ἄνδρες Ἰσραηλῖται, lit. "men, Israelites," addresses the crowd afresh, echoing v. 14 but this time as "people of Israel." This term suggests that the crowd symbolizes Israel as a whole being offered the chance to repent and turn to follow Jesus. It is little used in the NT outside Acts (also in Acts 3:12; 5:35; 13:16; 21:28, always in the same double vocative; cf. John 1:47; Rom 9:4; 11:1; 2 Cor 11:22). The rest of the speech will interpret Scripture with reference to Jesus, and this address begins to draw the hearers into this process by engaging them as people who share this inheritance. They are called to give attention to what follows: ἀκούσατε τοὺς λόγους τούτους, "listen to these words"; here Peter signals that what follows is crucial. This is the first of five imperative uses of ἀκούω, "listen," each addressed by believers to not-yet-believers (Acts 7:2; 13:16; 15:13; 22:1).[151]

The thematic accusative Ἰησοῦν τὸν Ναζωραῖον, "Jesus the Nazarene," is given prominence by its fronted location in the sentence (it is the direct object of ἀνείλατε, "you killed," 2:23). Jesus is the topic of the speech, although he is not the subject of the main verbs (hence the continuing references to Jesus in the accusative in vv. 23, 24, 32, 36)—that role is reserved for God; it is God's testimony to Jesus and action in, through, and concerning Jesus that sets Jesus apart.

Jesus is ἀποδεδειγμένον, "marked out," by God by means of "deeds of power and wonders and signs," δυνάμεσιν καὶ τέρασιν καὶ σημείοις. As in v. 19, this cluster echoes biblical language about God's action in the exodus and the adapted quotation from Joel. Jesus's own healings and exorcisms reported in the Third Gospel are interpreted by this phrase as this kind of (divine) action (although note that Jesus refuses to do signs, Luke 11:16, 29; 23:8, but acts with power 4:36; 6:19; 8:46; 9:1; 10:13, 19; 19:37), and such deeds will become a marker of what God is now doing through the believing community (Acts 2:43; 8:13; 14:3; 15:12). The use of σημείοις, "signs," also echoes Jesus's words about signs in the heavenly bodies (Luke 21:25), further indicating the eschatological significance of the Pentecost events.[152] These remarkable events

149 Kilgallen, "With Many," 75–76.

150 Squires, *Plan*, 64–65.

151 Dinkler, "Politics," 36, overstates when she claims the eighty-five uses of the verb in any mood in Acts as support of the claim that the apostles often call others to listen; most uses are in narrative describing the act of listening or hearing.

152 White, *Prophets*, 76.

are public, for they were done "among you," ἐν μέσῳ ὑμῶν, and Peter claims that the audience are aware of these events: "as you yourselves know," αὐτοὶ οἴδατε, they signify that God is active, and they identify the person(s) through whom God is active. The message is that the hearers need to pay attention to the one through whom God works, whether in himself (in the case of Jesus) or as a witness to Israel's God and Jesus (in the case of the believers).[153]

23 The focus on Jesus continues, reignited by a further thematic accusative τοῦτον, "this man," highlighting that Jesus is no divine visitor like the gods of Olympus, but truly human. If Jesus truly was a man through whom God worked in remarkable ways, Peter must explain why he was crucified, a common theme of early Christian apologetics, especially among Jews, for whom a crucified Messiah was a contradiction in terms.[154] Peter's explanation begins by asserting that Jesus was handed over to people as part of God's "plan and foreknowledge"[155] and that his death happened by the actions of the people to whom Peter speaks.[156] διὰ χειρὸς ἀνόμων, "by the hands of lawless people," points to the Roman authorities as cooperating in Jesus's death (Acts 4:27). Though God purposed to present Jesus to them, God's people rejected him.[157] The combination of divine purpose and human responsibility is found elsewhere in Acts (notably 4:27–28). The key evidence that Jesus's death was in God's plan is found in Scripture (which will be expounded to that end in 2:25–35) and Jesus's resurrection (v. 24).

24 Peter turns to Jesus's resurrection as key evidence that God was at work in Jesus's death, a point that will be a central focus of early Christian preaching (2:32; 3:22, 26; 13:33).[158] The continuing focus on Jesus is signaled by ὅν, "whom," before Peter emphasizes that God acted in raising Jesus, and not merely resuscitating him (contrast Lazarus in John 11, who presumably died again), freeing him from death's "agonies," ὠδῖνας, so that death lost its grip on Jesus. κρατεῖσθαι, "to be held," is widely used for physical holding or restraint in Matthew and Mark (it is absent from Luke), and in Acts 24:6 for seizing in arrest. ἀνέστησεν, "he raised," is much used by Luke when speaking of the

153 Luke may also be pointing his readers to the Third Gospel, which records the words and deeds of Jesus; White, *Prophets*, 73, 75.

154 E.g., Deut 21:22–23 asserts that anyone hanged on a tree is under God's curse; cf. Acts 5:30; 10:39; Gal 3:13; LXX Gen 40:19; Josh 8:29; 10:26; Esth 5:14; 6:4; 7:10; 8:7; 1 Esdr 6:31 (EVV 6:32).

155 Squires, *Plan*, 57; Dupont, *Nouvelles*, 68–69.

156 Weatherly, *Responsibility*, 82–85, shows that Peter's accusation is focused on the Jerusalemites and their leaders rather than all Jews.

157 Crabbe, *Luke/Acts*, 193–96, argues that Jesus's death is not asserted to be part of God's plan here; rather, it is the responsibility of Peter's audience of Jerusalemites to whom Jesus was handed by God. This seems a false antithesis: Jesus's death is part of God's plan, and the people who caused it bear responsibility for it. In Luke's Gospel, responsibility for Jesus's death is shared by the chief priests and other Jews in authority (Luke 22:52, 63–71; 23:1–2, 5), Pilate (Luke 23:3–4, 13–16, 20, 24–25), Herod (Luke 23:6–12), and the "rent-a-mob" at Pilate's palace early in the morning (Luke 23:13–23).

158 See Anderson, *But God*, chs 7–9.

resurrection of Jesus (8x in Acts; 4x in Luke; the cognate noun ἀνάστασις, "resurrection," occurs 9x in Acts), whereas Paul prefers ἐγείρω, "raise" (21x in undisputed Paulines + 3x in disputed Paulines; Acts 7x; Luke 3x).[159] Luke stresses, with other NT writers, that God raised Jesus: rather than "Jesus rose," Luke prefers "God raised Jesus" (active voice of ἀνίστημι or ἐγείρω, Acts 2:24, 32; 3:15; 4:10; 5:30; 10:40; 13:30, 33, 37; 17:31) or "Jesus was raised" (passive voice of ἐγείρω, Luke 24:6, 34).

τὰς ὠδῖνας τοῦ θανάτου, "the agonies of death," uses the pains of childbirth metaphorically. ὠδίν generally means "birth pangs" (e.g., 1 Thess 5:3), although it can be used in a broader sense of intense pain (e.g., LXX Exod 15:14; Deut 2:25; Job 21:17);[160] the phrase is found in LXX 2 Sam 22:6; Pss 17:5 [MT 18:5; EVV 18:4]; 114:3 [MT 116:3], where in each case ὠδῖνας corresponds to Heb. חבל (*ḥbl*), which means "cords" or "pains" (depending on how it is vocalized).[161] Thus Bratcher, arguing that Greek readers would have seen the expression as unnatural, interprets the phrase as indicating that "God raised Jesus by untying the cords with which death held him fast."[162] However, it seems unlikely that Luke's readers would have made this series of associations.[163] Bock agrees with Bratcher about the echoes but suggests there is a conscious wordplay on the ambiguity, resulting in a mixed metaphor, where the pains associated with death are portrayed as surrounding and taking a person captive.[164] The main alternative is to see the childbirth metaphor as dominant, indicating the cessation of death's birth pangs,[165] placing Jesus's resurrection in an eschatological context where death hands back those it holds.[166] Anderson demonstrates that the expression is a natural Greek idiom, used in classical and Hellenistic sources, and thus that Luke's audience would have grasped that the metaphor used was childbirth.[167] Other NT authors use birth pangs as a metaphor in eschatological contexts (Matt 24:8; Rom 8:22; 1 Thess 5:3; Rev 12:2) and thus here the point seems to be that death's "pregnancy" is coming to an end and it must give up those it holds in its grasp, a metaphor that would resonate particularly with mothers who heard this story.[168] This is a unique sense in biblical Greek but not thereby impossible.

159 Fuller statistics: Anderson, *But God*, 32.
160 See Schneider, *Apostelgeschichte*, 1:272n77; Strauss, *Davidic*, 135–36.
161 BDB 286.
162 "Loosed," 20; cf. Torrey, *Composition*, 28–29; Wilcox, *Semitisms*, 46–48.
163 Anderson, *But God*, 204–5.
164 *Proclamation*, 171–72; cf. Johnson, *Midrash*, 15–17.
165 Field, *Notes*, 112.
166 Cf. Isa 26:19–20 LXX—which uses the metaphor of childbirth—with 1 Clem. 50:4; 1 En. 51:1; 4 Ezra 4:41b–43a; 7:32; Rev 20:13; LAB 3:10; 33:3; 2 Bar. 21:23; 42:8; 50:2; Apoc. Pet. 4:3–4, 10–12; Midr. Pss 1:20; Song Rab. 2:1 §2 (citing Isa 26:19); Pirq. R. El. 34; Pesiq. Rab. 21:4; b. Sanh. 92a; I owe these references to Bauckham, *Fate*, 271–75; see his valuable discussion, 275–88.
167 Anderson, *But God*, 205–6.
168 Anderson, *But God*, 207; cf. Henrichs-Tarasenkova, "Good News," 272–75.

Jewish expectation of the resurrection of the dead was comprehended within a "two ages" framework, in which the resurrection of the dead ushered in the "new age." By contrast, for Luke (and other Christian writers), Jesus as an individual has been raised from the dead and "this age" continues, but with the recognition that the "age to come" has invaded "this age," and thus that the last day will come when the general resurrection takes place, guaranteed by Jesus's resurrection. The resurrection of Jesus thus reshapes Jewish eschatology into a "now and not yet" Christian perspective (see *Comment* on 3:20–21; 4:2[169]). Here Peter's expression connotes the defeat of death's restraining power: Jesus's resurrection is a rebirth that anticipates and enables the ultimate rebirth of creation.[170] This point here contrasts sharply with George Bernard Shaw's observation that death is the ultimate statistic: one out of one dies—Jesus, being raised from the dead never to die again, is the single and singular exception to this.

καθότι οὐκ ἦν δυνατὸν κρατεῖσθαι αὐτὸν ὑπ' αὐτοῦ, "since it was not possible for him to be held by [death]," indicates that God did not merely raise Jesus, but there was a divine *necessity* about Jesus's resurrection. Since the speech will go on (vv. 25–29) to interpret Ps 15:8–11a LXX (MT 16:8–11a) as prophesying Jesus's resurrection, the probable content of the divine necessity here is fulfillment of biblical prophecy.[171]

25–28 Peter interprets the (exact) quotation from Ps 15:8–11a LXX (MT 16:8–11a) as being David speaking about another, the Messiah (Acts 2:25, 29–30). In its OT setting, the psalm is widely understood to be the psalmist's cry for preservation from death.[172] The superscription, "A *miktam* of David," shows that King David was seen as its author (also v. 29 below). Anderson identifies several features of Peter's use of the quotation that point to a "prophetic" resurrection interpretation of the psalm:[173] (i) the introductory Δαυὶδ γὰρ λέγει εἰς αὐτόν, "For David says about him" (v. 25), which assumes a pesher-style exegesis that will support and explain (γάρ, "for") the nature and inevitability of Jesus's resurrection (v. 24);[174] (ii) the use of προοράω in the sense "foresaw" rather than a spatial sense; (iii) the use of ἐπ' ἐλπίδι, "in hope" in connection with "flesh" (v. 26) points to resurrection; (iv) the interpretation offered in v. 31 (see *Comment* there); (v) ὁδοὺς ζωῆς, "paths of life" (v. 28), connotes aliveness, a key component of resurrection for Luke (cf. Acts 1:3; 9:41; 20:12; 25:19; Luke 20:38; 24:5, 23); and (vi) gladness and rejoicing (Acts 2:26, 28) are characteristic of those living in the resurrection age (cf. Isa 26:19; 1 En.

169 More fully, Wright, *Resurrection*, 451–57.
170 Cf. Henrichs-Tarasenkova, "Good News," 269–70.
171 Trull, "Interpretation," 437.
172 E.g., Weiser, *Psalms*, 178; for the view that David spoke of resurrection, see Trull, "Exegesis."
173 *But God*, 208–9; cf. Bock, *Proclamation*, 173–77, arguing that MT could also lead to a "resurrection" interpretation.
174 Longenecker, *Exegesis*, 100; Kilgallen, "Use," 47–49.

51:4–5). The quotation's focus is on deliverance from the decay involved in death ("decay" is διαφθορά, Acts 2:27, an apparent difference between MT and LXX; MT has "the pit," שַׁחַת [*šaḥat*] although this is regularly translated by διαφθορά in LXX[175])—and for Jewish minds this would necessarily mean *physical* decay, for resurrection was indubitably physical.[176] Indeed, experience of physical decay after death was widespread among first-century Jews because they practised secondary burial (i.e., later burial of a person's bones after the flesh had rotted away).[177] The fact that Luke here (as elsewhere) cites the Greek Bible means it is likely that Luke is here "writing up" the tradition of the speech available to him for his Greek-speaking audience.

29–31 David himself, Peter argues, cannot be the referent of the psalm, even though he is its author, for he experienced the bodily decay involved in death—indeed, his tomb was a well-known landmark in Jerusalem (v. 29; cf. Neh 3:16; Josephus, *Ant.* 13.8.4 §249; *J.W.* 1.2.5 §61). David is not speaking of a general resurrection but of the resurrection of a specific person ("your godly one," Acts 2:27), and that before the person's corpse decayed (v. 27). Thus, David must have been speaking of the Messiah to come (v. 30). The force of the argument is not to prove the resurrection of Jesus but to claim that the resurrection of Jesus demonstrates him to be the Messiah of whom the psalm is understood to speak.[178] The strength of Peter's defense of this interpretation suggests that it was novel. It involves a series of key points expressed in causal participial phrases: because David was (ὑπάρχων) a prophet, and because David knew that (εἰδὼς ὅτι) God had sworn an oath, expressing a covenant relationship with him, that one of his descendants would sit on his throne (echoing Ps 131:11 [MT 132:11]; 2 Sam 7:12–16). The combination of these two things meant that David foresaw (προϊδών) and therefore spoke of the Messiah's resurrection.

The Christian messianic reading of this psalm is a good example of "reading backwards," since we know of no other Jewish readers of Scripture who understood the psalm as prophetic of the Messiah.[179] This interpretation may stem from the covenant theme, which connected the psalm to God's oath to David, and from the description of the one delivered as τὸν ὅσιόν σου, "your godly one" (v. 27).[180] The only hint that Luke may give of this interpretation's origins is the conversations between the risen Jesus and the disciples (Acts 1:2–3; Luke 24:27, 44—note the specific mention of Psalms in the latter verse).

---

175 Steyn, *Quotations,* 107; discussion: Bock, *Proclamation,* 175–76; Rese, *Motive,* 57–58.
176 Wright, *Resurrection,* 200–206, summarizing his full discussion.
177 Anderson, *But God,* 211n57, with further references.
178 Somewhat surprisingly, Rese considers this use of Scripture to be "typological," since he claims that David embodies the person of the Messiah, which is the opposite of what Peter argues; Rese, "Funktion," 76.
179 Hays, "Figural Exegesis," 41.
180 Bock, *Proclamation,* 178–80; Trull, "Exegesis," 313–15; for other approaches see Trull, "Views."

29 This is the first use of παρρησία—here "confidence"; more generally "boldness"—in Acts, which is characteristic of apostolic speech in Acts, including in contexts where danger results from such bold speech (the noun or verb are found in Acts 4:13, 28, 31; 9:27, 28–29; 13:46; 14:3; 19:8; 26:26). The echo in 28:31, presenting Paul as speaking boldly, completes an *inclusio*, suggesting that this is how Luke portrays the earliest believers and how he wants the church of his day to be too; it forms "a program for the future task of the church."[181] Marrow shows that NT usage is tightly connected to Christian gospel proclamation (Eph 6:19; Phil 1:20) and bold access to God (Heb 4:16; 10:19; 1 John 5:14), whereas it was previously used in political contexts, denoting the right to speak openly and freely, a right restricted to free citizens.[182]

30 προφήτης . . . ὑπάρχων, "being . . . a prophet." Luke assumes that the psalmists were prophets, even though the OT itself never says that David is called a prophet (e.g., Luke 20:41–42; 24:44; Acts 1:16, 20; 4:25; 13:33–36[183]). Specifically, in first-century Palestine (but not in the OT), David was considered to be a prophet: 11Q Ps[a] 27.2–11, esp. 11, says that David "composed [the Psalms] through prophecy given him by the Most High" (Wise et al.); Josephus, *Ant.* 6.8.2 §166, writes that David began to prophesy when the divine power left Saul and came to David.[184] David is portrayed here as exercising the prophetic ministry which is a marker of the Spirit's work (Acts 2:17, 18, citing Joel; see *Comment* there).[185]

εἰδὼς ὅτι ὅρκῳ ὤμοσεν αὐτῷ ὁ θεὸς ἐκ καρποῦ τῆς ὀσφύος αὐτοῦ καθίσαι ἐπὶ τὸν θρόνον αὐτοῦ, "[he] knew that God had sworn an oath to him that one from the fruit of his loins would sit upon his throne," alludes to Ps 132:11 (LXX 131:11), a passage that itself echoes God's promise through Nathan that a descendant of David would always sit on the throne (2 Sam 7:12–16).[186]

31 προϊδὼν ἐλάλησεν περὶ τῆς ἀναστάσεως τοῦ Χριστοῦ, "he foresaw and spoke about the resurrection of the Messiah." Peter reads Ps 15:8–11a LXX (MT 16:8–11a) as focusing on the Messiah and regards David as knowing this. Luke's presentation here coheres with the widespread early Christian understanding of Scripture as pointing to and focusing on Jesus (cf. 1 Pet 1:10–12[187]).

Peter then quotes Ps 15:10 LXX, again with two amendments: the verb tenses are changed from future to aorist: οὔτε ἐγκατελείφθη . . . οὔτε . . . εἶδεν, "he was neither abandoned . . . nor . . . did . . . he experience," indicating that the prophecy was fulfilled in Jesus's resurrection; and ἡ σὰρξ αὐτοῦ, "his

181 Marrow, "Παρρησία," 442.
182 "Παρρησία."
183 Johnson, *Acts*, 51.
184 Fitzmyer, "David"; Trull, "Interpretation," 441–42.
185 White, *Prophets*, 78–79.
186 O'Toole, "Acts 2:30," esp. 252–54.
187 Discussion: Trull, "Interpretation," 445–46.

flesh," replaces τὸν ὅσιόν σου, "your godly one," clarifying that physical decay is in mind. Peter thus focuses his audience's attention on a particular part of the psalm quotation, v. 10b, and reads it in the context of eschatological messianic hope which, for the majority of first-century Jews, included physical resurrection.[188]

32–36 Now comes the key connection: Jesus has been raised from the dead by God (v. 32) and thus is demonstrated to be Messiah (Acts 2:36). Not only that, but God has now acted to exalt Jesus to God's right hand—and Jesus is the one who now pours out the Spirit. Jesus's pouring out the Spirit identifies him as Lord (v. 36), that is, as one in the same category as YHWH.

32 Introduced by another thematic accusative, τοῦτον τὸν Ἰησοῦν, "this Jesus," Peter re-announces Jesus's resurrection (cf. v. 24) and exaltation (v. 33) in order to interpret them through the biblical passages he has quoted. ἀνέστησεν ὁ θεός, "God raised," here is most likely to refer to Jesus's resurrection, using the same language as v. 24; Jesus's ascension is described in v. 33 using language never used in the NT for Jesus's resurrection. It is the apostolic band and their associates (πάντες ἡμεῖς, "we ourselves . . . all"; see *Comment* on v. 1) who testify to the event of Jesus's resurrection, for they alone can offer eyewitness testimony, and this is how they continue to be portrayed: the core of their testimony concerns Jesus and his resurrection (see *Comment* on 1:8, 22).

33 This sentence, which answers the crowd's question, "What's going on here?" (v. 12), is crucial for understanding Luke's Christology.[189] It is vital to recognize the sequence of events and the actants for each event. Jesus is exalted to God's right side; Jesus then receives the Holy Spirit from the Father; and Jesus then pours out the Spirit with the effects of τοῦτο ὃ ὑμεῖς βλέπετε καὶ ἀκούετε, "what you yourselves are seeing and hearing." The discourse here, as elsewhere in Acts, "is centered on Yahweh, the *one* God of Israel, whose eschatological identity is constituted by the narrated activities of *three* separate centers of action, viz. Father, risen Son, and poured out Holy Spirit."[190] The shift from "God" earlier in the speech to τοῦ πατρός, "the Father," recalls that the Spirit is τὴν ἐπαγγελίαν τοῦ πατρός μου, "the promise of my Father" (Luke 24:49; Acts 1:4; cf. John 14:14, 25–26).[191] It also implicitly identifies Jesus as God's Son, recalling the angel's announcement (Luke 1:35; cf. 2:49 τοῦ πατρός μου, "my Father").

Jesus's exaltation, narrated in the ascension (Acts 1:9–11), is the first step:

---

188 The Sadducees are the obvious exception, 23:8; Luke 20:27.

189 See the fine discussion of Mainville, *Spirit,* who locates this verse as the hinge of the whole of Luke-Acts, identifying v. 33a as looking back and completing the story of Luke's Gospel and v. 33b as looking forward to the story Acts tells, providing an explanation of later events.

190 Johnson, "Resurrection," 160.

191 Kilgallen, "Rhetorical," 192–95, argues that the parallel language in Luke and John concerning the Father sending the Spirit in Jesus's name points to a traditional source "which reflects the way Jesus spoke about the Spirit" (193).

Jesus has been "exalted," ὑψωθείς, a passive that affirms that God did this.[192] Jesus's ascension, with his resurrection,[193] demonstrates God's vindication of Jesus against the mistaken human verdict of his execution (cf. 2:23–24). Not only that, but God now has placed Jesus at his right side, a place of recognition (v. 34) and authority over those who rejected him (v. 35).[194] This phrase prepares the way for the quotation from Ps 110:1 (LXX 109:1) that follows (Acts 2:34–35), and it is not necessary to seek a further source for the verb ὑψόω, "exalt," than Ps 88.[195] Metzger rightly observes, "To sit . . . at the right hand of God does not mean that Christ is resting; it affirms that he is reigning as king, wielding the power of divine omnipotence."[196] Similarly, Farrow: "News of his coronation in heaven (still hidden from view) has reached earth in the pandemonium of Pentecost."[197] Jesus is not absent from the narrative but will continue to be active, reigning from heaven.[198]

The exalted Jesus has received "the promise which is the Holy Spirit," τὴν . . . ἐπαγγελίαν τοῦ πνεύματος τοῦ ἁγίου, from the Father, in a sense that is new, while fulfilling his own promise of the Spirit as the Father's gift (Luke 24:47; Acts 1:4–5, 8). Jesus's conception and empowerment by the Spirit is a key theme of Luke's Gospel (note Luke 1:35; 3:21–22; 4:1, 14, 18), and John the baptizer has promised that Jesus will baptize with the Holy Spirit (3:16; cf. Acts 1:8), but in none of these passages is Jesus said to "receive" the Spirit. The new element here is that the Spirit is given to Jesus in such a way that he can now give the Spirit to others, fulfilling the baptizer's promise. The death, resurrection, and exaltation of Jesus are preconditions to the Spirit's availability through Jesus, now recognized as Israel's Messiah and Lord (cf. John 7:39).

Thus Jesus now "has poured out," ἐξέχεεν, the Spirit—evinced by the phenomena of sight and sound (Acts 2:2–4), "what you yourselves are seeing and hearing," ὃ ὑμεῖς βλέπετε καὶ ἀκούετε[199]—upon people on earth, echoing the (archaic[200]) language of the Joel quotation (ἐκχέω, vv. 17, 18 = Joel 3:1, 2 LXX [MT 2:28, 29]) and Jesus's own promise, ἐγὼ ἀποστέλλω τὴν ἐπαγγελίαν τοῦ πατρός μου ἐφ' ὑμᾶς, "I myself am sending the promise of my Father upon you" (Luke 24:49). This is the answer to the crowd's question (v. 12),[201] and the

192 On the verb choice, see Mainville, *Spirit*, 51–59.
193 Anderson, *But God*, 213–18.
194 It is more likely that τῇ δεξιᾷ is local ("at the right side") rather than instrumental ("by means of the right [hand]"), since that illuminates and supports the quotation from Ps 110:1 (Acts 2:34–35); for discussion and full references, see Mainville, *Spirit*, 30–34; Gourgues, "Exalté." More fully on the significance of the "right side," see Mainville, *Spirit*, 60–95.
195 See Ps 88:14, 17, 18, 20, 25, 28, 43; contra O'Toole, "Acts 2:30," 249–50.
196 *Studies*, 87; cf. Calvin, *Inst.* 2.16.15.
197 Farrow, *Ascension*, 25.
198 Sleeman, *Geography*, 101; Gaventa, "Acts," 42–43; contrast MacRae, "Heaven."
199 The reference to what ὑμεῖς βλέπετε, "you yourselves see," indicates that more than speech in other languages is included, contra McCollough, *Ritual*, 117.
200 On ἐκχέω, see *Comment* on 10:45.
201 Well recognized by Kilgallen, "Rhetorical."

remarkable point is that, whereas in Joel it is YHWH who pours out the Spirit, here *Jesus* does this—hence the Spirit, normally in the OT the Spirit of *God* (e.g., Gen 41:38; Num 24:2; Judg 6:34; 1 Sam 10:10; 2 Chr 24:20; Ezek 11:24) may now properly be designated "the Spirit of Jesus" (Acts 16:7). Peter's speech gives Jesus a role that YHWH, and YHWH alone (see Isa 44:3; Ezek 36:26–27; 39:29), has in first-century Judaism, and thus Jesus is now appropriately given a designation that YHWH alone deserves, κύριος, "Lord" (Acts 2:36). "Nothing in Jewish religion and theology prepared us for such a development."[202] Turner proposes that this verse provides the origin of Christian worship of Jesus, for it is Jesus's pouring out of the Spirit that clarifies his identity as one standing uniquely alongside the God of Israel.[203] Thus Jesus properly deserves the worship that Israel's God alone should receive, a development seen in prayer addressed to Jesus (e.g., 7:59; cf. Luke 23:42).

This verse may allude to Ps 67:19 LXX [MT 68:19; EVV 68:18], echoing its language of exaltation (ἀνέβης εἰς ὕψος, "you ascended on high") and receiving (ἔλαβες δόματα, "you received gifts").[204] This psalm was associated with Pentecost in the first century, and it is interesting that Tg. Ps 68:19 says, "You have ascended to heaven, that is Moses the prophet. You have taken captivity captive, you have learned the words of the torah, you have given them as gifts to men." Turner argues that the Targum, although later than the NT, includes earlier traditional material that may also be reflected in Eph 4:8.[205] Luke's interpretation of the psalm contrasts with that of the rabbis: they regard Moses as the ascender and as receiving the torah he gave to God's people, whereas for Luke Jesus is the ascender who receives the Spirit and then gives the Spirit to God's renewed people.[206] If so, Jesus is like and greater than both David and Moses.[207]

34–35 οὐ γὰρ Δαυὶδ ἀνέβη εἰς τοὺς οὐρανούς, "For it was not David who went up into the heavens." Peter now makes the same interpretive move as earlier in the speech (vv. 29–30), arguing that a passage attributed to David cannot be about David. The negative οὐ, "not," is fronted to emphasize that it was not David who ascended (cf. v. 15; 16:37; Luke 6:43; 8:17).[208]

Here, the passage cited is Ps 110:1 (LXX 109:1), a royal psalm possibly used for a coronation.[209] This quotation enriches the understanding of Ps 15:6–11 LXX (MT 16:6–11) in Acts 2:25–28, for it now indicates that the one about whom David prophesied (v. 30) would not experience bodily decay in death

202 Dunn, *Beginning*, 222.
203 "Christology"; "Divine."
204 Lindars, *Apologetic*, 44.
205 *Power*, 286–87.
206 Dupont, *Nouvelles*, 208–9.
207 Turner, *Power*, 286–89; contra O'Toole, "Acts 2:30; Menzies, *Empowered*, 199–201.
208 Barrett, *Acts*, 1:150.
209 So, e.g., Weiser, *Psalms*, 694–94; Anderson, *Psalms*, 2:767; Allen, *Psalms 101–150*, 111–13; Hay, *Glory*, 19–33.

is the one who stands as "Lord" over all.[210] Peter argues that David himself did not ascend to sit at the Lord's right hand, and so he cannot be the "my Lord" whom "the Lord" (i.e., YHWH) addresses. The quotation corresponds to LXX and thus also to the citation in Luke 20:42–43. LXX differs from MT in its double use of κύριος, "Lord"; in MT the first is יהוה, YHWH, and the second is אָדוֹן (*ʾādôn*), distinguishing YHWH from a human figure. Jesus's argument in Luke 20 does not hinge upon the LXX, for in Greek or Hebrew the point is that one being addressed by YHWH is David's Lord, although as Messiah he would necessarily be David's descendant.[211] Thus, Jesus uses this psalm to argue that the Messiah is superior to David, the psalm's author, and the psalm by implication asserts that the Messiah will sit at God's right hand, a claim made directly by Jesus on trial (Luke 22:69) and recognized as blasphemous from the Sanhedrin's perspective (Luke 22:71). Here, Peter asserts that the Sanhedrin were wrong, and Jesus was right, for Jesus was vindicated by God and raised to sit at God's right hand to "co-regency" with the Father (thus assuming the ascension story from Acts 1:9–11).[212] Because David himself was a prophet (2:30), this use of Scripture should be seen as prophetic fulfillment.[213]

ἕως ἄν, "until." This reading of Ps 110:1 locates Jesus followers in the period between the exaltation of Jesus, through his resurrection and ascension, and his ultimate triumph, when his enemies are made his footstool—the time of his promised return (Acts 1:11). In that period they know the security of Jesus's exalted reign, the experience of the Spirit poured out by Jesus, and the promise of his return.

36 The speech comes to its conclusion (οὖν, "so then") with an affirmation of the present status of Jesus, contrasted with how the hearers had treated him. This conclusion is expressed with great confidence (ἀσφαλῶς, "beyond a doubt," found elsewhere in NT only at 16:23; Mark 14:44, although note the echo of ἀσφάλεια, "certainty," from Luke 1:1, and πολλοῖς τεκμηρίοις, "many convincing proofs," from Acts 1:3[214]).

πᾶς οἶκος Ἰσραήλ, "the whole house of Israel," is suggestive of the restoration of the twelve tribes prophesied in Scripture (e.g., Ezek 37:15–28; 48:1–7).[215] The restoration of the ten lost tribes is hinted at by the presence of Anna of the tribe of Asher (Luke 2:36) and by Jesus's promise that the apostles will judge the *twelve* tribes (Luke 22:30). (See *Comment* on the "Medes," 2:9–11.)

καὶ κύριον αὐτὸν καὶ χριστὸν ἐποίησεν ὁ θεός, "God has appointed him both

210 Cf. Moessner, "Lords."
211 Bock, *Proclamation*, 130.
212 Bock, *Proclamation*, 184; Hay, *Glory*, 70–71. Cf. use of this verse in 7:55–56; Rom 8:34; Eph 1:20; Col 3:1; Heb 1:3, 13; 8:1; 10:12–13; 12:2; 1 Pet 3:22.
213 Bock, *Proclamation*, 186; contra Rese, *Motive*, 62.
214 White, *Prophets*, 79.
215 See Bauckham, "Restoration," 473.

Lord and Messiah." The unusual location of αὐτόν, "him," between the epithets κύριον, "Lord," and χριστόν, "Messiah," suggests a particular emphasis on the designation of Jesus as "Lord,"[216] which in the setting of v. 33 places Jesus in the same category as YHWH, Israel's Lord.[217] The terms chosen point back to Peter's interpretations of Scripture: Jesus is the Lord on whom people must call to be saved (v. 21; cf. v. 38); Jesus is the one whose body did not rot in the decay of death, and is thus Messiah, Israel's true king (vv. 27, 31[218]); and Jesus is the reigning Lord who gives the Spirit and has the right to judge his enemies (vv. 33–35). But what is the sense of ἐποίησεν, "appointed," here?[219] Is Peter suggesting that something has changed about Jesus through the resurrection? Mainville argues that the climax of the Pentecost speech indicates that Jesus became Messiah at the resurrection.[220] If so, this verse is in tension with the picture in Luke's Gospel that Jesus was Lord and Messiah already, and thus some suggest that this verse represents pre-Lukan tradition that Luke has inserted, rather unreflectively, into this speech.[221] However, Luke 1:35 indicates that Jesus was "Son of God" from his conception, and this title has a messianic sense in Jewish settings.[222] Luke 1:43 has Jesus enter the story while in Mary's womb as "Lord."[223] Luke 2:11 proclaims Jesus at his birth as Savior, Messiah, and Lord in the present (ἐστιν, "is"), not the future. Rowe goes on to map the use of κύριος, "Lord," in Luke's Gospel and argues cogently that "Luke creates a narrative christology in which Jesus's identity as κύριος stands at the center."[224] After the resurrection, the disciples can say, "The Lord (ὁ κύριος) has risen" (Luke 24:34) implying that the one they already know as "the Lord" has risen, rather than "the risen one is Lord," which would suggest that Jesus *became* Lord through the resurrection. Thus "[h]e who shares the throne of God shares his deity; and he who is God is what he is from and to eternity—otherwise he is not God,"[225] although Barrett believes this statement represents the later, reflective view found in Paul rather than the view expressed here. However, it seems more likely that the view expressed here represents Luke's view—for why would Luke introduce a statement that contradicted the christological portrait built up so carefully through his

---

216 Bock, *Proclamation*, 184.

217 Contra Hay, *Glory*, 72–73, asserting that Jesus only rules the church until the parousia.

218 Cf. LXX 1 Sam 16:6; 24:6, 10; 26:9, 11, 16, 23; 2 Sam 1:14, 16; 2:5; 19:21; 22:51; 23:1; Pss 2:2; 17:51 (MT 18:51; EVV 18:50); 19:7 (MT 20:7; EVV 20:6); 131:10, 17 (MT 132:10, 17); Pss Sol. 17:32; 18:0, 5, 7.

219 For a valuable history of interpretation, see Rowe, "Acts 2.36," 38–46.

220 Mainville, "Messianisme"; also Barrett, *Acts*, 1:151–52, and numerous others whom he cites; see critique in Marshall, "Christology," 139–41.

221 E.g., Haenchen, *Acts*, 187; for further references, see Rowe, "Acts 2.36," 42–46.

222 D. R. Bauer, "Son of God," *DJG* 770. Kilgallen, "With Many," highlights the role of Luke 1:35 as a presupposition of the speech.

223 Rowe, "Acts 2.36," 51.

224 Rowe, "Acts 2.36," 51–53, quoting 52; more fully, see his *Christology*.

225 Barrett, *Acts*, 1:152.

Gospel? Peter's argument is that it is through Jesus's resurrection, ascension, and pouring out of the Spirit that he is now *known* to be Messiah and Lord, and he now exercises the full prerogatives that go with this status; hence Peter and John later appeal to the exalted Jesus's lordship as the justification and foundation of their ministry (Acts 4:11).[226] Thus ἐποίησεν, "appointed," should be understood from the angle of human perception: the house of Israel is to change its perception of Jesus because God has raised him from the dead—the fronted, emphatic position of ἀσφαλῶς, "beyond a doubt," shows that this change of perception is the focus of the sentence.[227]

Regarding the designation of Jesus as χριστός, "Messiah," it is noteworthy that the Gospels' motif that Jesus does not proclaim himself to be Messiah and discourages others from openly doing so is paralleled by two other figures from around the same period: the Teacher of Righteousness and Simeon ben Kosebah.[228] In each case there is the combination of external acclamation of the person as Messiah, reticence by the individual to speak of himself in such terms, and nevertheless evidence of the person's own belief in the validity of messianic claims being made about him.[229] Behind this combination of phenomena stands a common Jewish belief that "no man can be defined as a messiah before he has accomplished the task of the anointed."[230] The understanding of what that task was varied considerably between Jesus, Simeon ben Kosebah, and the Teacher of Righteousness, but they seem to share this presupposition. Such an understanding makes sense of Peter's proclamation here, for it is only after Jesus's death, in which he carries out the redeeming messianic task, that God declares Jesus to have accomplished the task (and therefore to be recognized as Messiah) by the act of raising him from the dead. Similarly, in Luke's Gospel, it is only post-resurrection that Jesus initiates a conversation about himself as Messiah (Luke 24:26, 46). Such a view also explains the verdict of blasphemy at the Jewish trial, for in affirming that he was Messiah in his answer to the high priest's question, Jesus was doing something it was believed that God alone could do—declaring a person to be Messiah—and thus he was claiming a divine prerogative and blaspheming (Mark 14:58–64; cf. Luke 22:66–71).

τοῦτον τὸν Ἰησοῦν ὃν ὑμεῖς ἐσταυρώσατε, "this Jesus whom you crucified," prepares for the call to repentance that will follow. Peter juxtaposes the status of Jesus with the deeply mistaken way that the people of Jerusalem and their leaders have treated him: Jesus's exaltation is simultaneously an announcement of his greatness and of the audience's guilt, stressed by the emphatic

226 Smalley, "Christology," 361.
227 Rowe, "Acts 2.36," 55.
228 Flusser, "Two Notes," 107–9.
229 Longenecker, *Christology*, 71–74.
230 Flusser, "Two Notes," 107.

ὑμεῖς, "you."[231] Jesus's lordship is not a private matter of individual choice but a statement of public truth that calls everyone to respond in repentance and submission to Jesus, similar to the announcement of a new emperor: to announce that Augustus, for example, was emperor was to call those who heard to submit to his rule.

37 κατενύγησαν τὴν καρδίαν, "they were cut to the heart." The metaphor expresses sharp pain, here remorse for the crowd's part in Jesus's death.[232] The crowd's response to the Pentecostal events has changed from 2:12–13, where they focused on the phenomena and the believers. When the crowd ask a question now, it is about themselves, how to respond: their attention has been shifted to Jesus by Peter's speech. Ἀκούσαντες, "When they heard," is thus both temporal and causal.

The deliberative question τί ποιήσωμεν, ἄνδρες ἀδελφοί;, "What must we do, brothers and sisters?," echoes the questions to John the baptizer (Luke 3:10, 12, 14 τί . . . ποιήσωμεν; "What . . . must we do?"[233]) and thus locates this passage as part of separating from "this wayward generation" (Acts 2:40) in similar manner to the response to John by the crowds.[234] The double vocative ἄνδρες ἀδελφοί, "brothers and sisters," echoes Peter's address to the crowd (v. 29) and reflects a positive attitude to the believers: "their hearts are already won over."[235]

38–39 paradigmatically lay out the response required, which is both personal and corporate: the verbs include a corporate call to repentance (μετανοήσατε, plural), a call to submit individually to baptism (βαπτισθήτω *ἕκαστος* ὑμῶν, "be baptized *each one* of you," singular), and an assurance that this promise is for many (ὑμῖν . . . καὶ τοῖς τέκνοις ὑμῶν καὶ πᾶσιν τοῖς εἰς μακράν, "for you . . . and your children and all those far away").[236]

38 μετανοήσατε, "repent," is the first element of response and calls on the hearers both to change their minds about Jesus and to change the direction of their lives in consequence.[237] This call is addressed to the Jerusalemites corporately, for it was their corporate demand that led to Jesus's death (Luke 23:13–23). Remarkably, the door to repentance is open even to those responsible for the Messiah's death.[238] Such turning is a characteristic response to the gospel message, in both Jewish and gentile settings.[239] Luke also uses ἐπιστρέφω + ἐπὶ

231 Ovey, *Feasts*, 40–41.

232 κατανύσσομαι, "cut," is a NT *hapax legomenon*, but cf. LXX Gen 27:38; 34:7; 1 Kgs 20:27, 29; Ps 108:16 (MT 109:16); Isa 6:5; 47:5; Sir 14:1.

233 Cf. Ravens, *Luke*, 150–51, providing a convenient table of parallels between this passage and Luke 3.

234 Johnson, *Function*, 184.

235 Haenchen, *Acts*, 184.

236 Avemarie, *Tauferzählungen*, 177–81, regards this as a paradigm of Lukan baptismal theology.

237 With Nave, *Role*, 199.

238 Ovey, *Feasts*, 42.

239 Jewish: here; 3:19; 5:31; cf. Luke 3:3, 8; 5:32; 10:13; 13:3, 5; 15:7, 10; 16:30; 17:3, 4; gentile: Acts 11:18; 17:30; cf. 20:21; 26:20; Luke 24:47; cf. Paul: Rom 2:4; 2 Cor 7:9, 10; 12:21.

τὸν κύριον or ἐπὶ τὸν θεόν, "turn" + "to the Lord" or "to God," in both Jewish and gentile settings.[240]

βαπτισθήτω ἕκαστος ὑμῶν, "be baptized, each one of you," calls on the hearers to submit individually to water baptism as their response to God's call in Jesus to belong to him, both portraying and expressing their repentance.[241] Baptism is the appropriate response to the call to repentance.[242] The passive verb βαπτισθήτω, "be baptized," indicates that another baptizes each one—baptism, thus understood, presents forgiveness from God as a gift received (as is the Spirit, see below). Household baptisms elsewhere in Acts make it clear that each member of the household was baptized rather than the head of the house being baptized on behalf of the group (e.g., 16:15, 33)—water baptism enacts the individual's response.[243] Initiation into the Jesus community thus contrasts with initiation into the Jewish community, for both women and men (ἕκαστος ὑμῶν "each one of you") are baptized in similar manner (e.g. 5:14; 8:12), by contrast with circumcisison, which was a male-only rite. The image of water baptism connects with John the baptizer's ministry, and his baptism also expresses repentance and leads to cleansing-forgiveness (Luke 3:3). (On the imagery and probable mode of water baptism, see *Comment* on 1:5.)

ἐπὶ τῷ ὀνόματι Ἰησοῦ Χριστοῦ, "in the name of Jesus Messiah." This is the first use of the "name" of Jesus [Messiah] in Acts, and it will become a key expression, denoting the power of Jesus at work: through this name healing, deliverance, and signs and wonders occur (3:6, 16; 4:10, 30; 16:18; 19:13), salvation is found uniquely in this name (4:12), the believers speak in this name (4:17, 18; 5:28, 40), the apostles suffer for Jesus's name (5:40; 15:26; 21:13; 26:9), the name is the substance of evangelistic proclamation (8:12; 9:15, 27, 28), believers call upon the name (9:21), baptism is in the name (here; 8:16; 10:48; 19:5; 22:16), forgiveness comes through the name (here; 10:43), and gentiles who are believers are "a people for [God's] name" (15:14, 17).[244]

The association of Jesus's name with baptism has been suggested to denote ownership of the baptized by Jesus, based on business documents found in Egypt that use "into the name of X" to mean "into the possession of X."[245] This view, once widely accepted,[246] is now doubted, since the vagueness of this expression means that it may take on different senses in different contexts

240 Jewish: Acts 11:21; cf. Luke 1:16, 17; 22:32; gentile: Acts 14:15; 15:19; 17:30; cf. Paul: 2 Cor 3:16; 1 Thess 1:9.

241 Cf. Wallace, 370–71; 1 Pet 3:21.

242 Christiansen, "Taufe," 62.

243 For other places where second-person-plural imperatives are collocated with third-person singulars that individualize the response called for, see LXX Exod 16:29; Josh 6:10; 2 Kgs 10:19; Zech 7:10; 1 Macc 10:63; Did. 15:3; Ign. *Mag.* 6:2; discussion: Camp, "Reexamining" (responding to McIntyre, "Baptism"); Osburn, "Imperative."

244 See helpful discussion, Hacking, *Signs*, 244–49.

245 Heitmüller, *Namen*; summaries: 109, 127, 331, 332–33. Critique: Hartman, *Name*, 39–40.

246 E.g., Haenchen, *Acts*, 184; further sources: Hartman, *Name*, 40n16.

and the meaning may not transfer straightforwardly from a commercial to a religious setting.[247] More probably the expression represents Heb. לשם (*lšm*) meaning "having in mind" or "with regard to," and when used in the context of a religious rite such as baptism denotes either the one whom the baptizand "has in mind" or the one "with regard to" whom the rite is enacted.[248] This view fits well with Acts's use of this expression with ἐπικαλέω, "call upon" (2:21; 9:14, 21; 15:17; 22:16).[249] Acts 22:16 is a particularly helpful parallel, suggesting that in baptism the baptizand calls upon the name of Jesus for forgiveness.[250] The echo of 2:21, where it is by calling on the Lord's name (there, YHWH) that people are saved, strikingly portrays Jesus as the one whom people are to call upon (see *Comment* on v. 21[251]). Fitzmyer accurately observes, "For Luke the 'name of Jesus' connotes the real and effective representation of Jesus himself."[252] Calling on his name is calling on the one who sits alongside God on the throne of the universe, the one with whom authority and power rest, and such calling will result in God's power, the Spirit, sent by Jesus (v. 33), coming upon the baptized. The baptized person comes under the protection of Jesus.[253]

The association of Jesus's name with baptism is expressed in Acts using ἐπί, "upon" (here; 4:18; cf. Luke 24:47), ἐν, "in" (2:38 v.l.; 10:48), and εἰς, "into" (8:16; 19:5). Other NT authors use different prepositions with mention of Jesus's name.[254] The forms with ἐπί and ἐν reflect LXX usage in worship contexts: people call, pray, or serve ἐπί God's name[255] and sing praise, bless people, call, or give thanks ἐν God's name.[256] εἰς τὸ ὄνομα, "into the name," is found only in Acts in baptismal contexts. There seems little, if any, difference in substance between the use of the three prepositions.[257] Likewise, there does not seem particular significance in the variations in the genitive expressions used with "the name": Ἰησοῦ Χριστοῦ, "Jesus Messiah" (here; 4:10; 8:12; 10:48; 16:18), [τοῦ] Ἰησοῦ, "Jesus" (4:18, 30; 5:40; 9:27; 26:9), τοῦ κυρίου Ἰησοῦ, "the Lord Jesus" (8:16; 19:5, 13, 17; 21:13), τοῦ κυρίου ἡμῶν Ἰησοῦ Χριστοῦ, "our Lord Jesus Messiah" (15:26).[258]

εἰς ἄφεσιν τῶν ἁμαρτιῶν ὑμῶν, "for the forgiveness of your sins," echoes Luke

247 Hartman, *Name*, 40; Delling, *Zueignung*, 32–36; Ziesler, "Name," 30.
248 Hartman, *Name*, 42–43, citing m. Nid 5.6; m. Zeb 4.6.
249 See further Barrett, "Faith," 7–8.
250 With Ferguson, *Baptism*, 183.
251 Cf. Ferguson, *Baptism*, 168–69; Ziesler, "Name," 29; Beasley-Murray, *Baptism*, 100–101.
252 Fitzmyer, *Acts*, 266.
253 Jervell, *Apostelgeschichte*, 153.
254 Mark 9:41; 1 Cor 1:10; 5:4; 6:11; Eph 5:20; Phil 2:10; Col 3:17; 2 Thess 3:6; 1 Pet 4:14; 1 John 3:23; cf. 1 Cor 1:13, 15.
255 LXX Gen 12:8; Deut 10:8; 17:12.
256 LXX 2 Sam 6:18; 22:50; 1 Kgs 18:24; 1 Chr 16:2, 10; Pss 18:49; 44:8; 104:3 (MT 105:3); 128:8 (MT 129:8).
257 Hartman, "Formule"; Ferguson, *Baptism*, 182–83; Ziesler, "Name," 29–30.
258 Although see Hartman, *Name*, 39; Schröter, "Taufe," 566, for the suggestion that the choice may reflect the speaker in the story.

3:3—although that verse lacks the personal pronoun ὑμῶν, "your"—and the collocation of baptism and repentance there. Thus, Green argues that John's baptism provides a template for baptism here.[259] This phrase also appears in Luke 24:47, which similarly lacks mention of baptism. The preposition εἰς has been asserted to be causal, meaning "because of,"[260] but more probably expresses purpose. Thus, εἰς here suggests that it is what precedes that leads to a person receiving the forgiveness of sins. So is it repentance alone that leads to forgiveness[261] (on the basis of concord between the plural verb μετανοήσατε and the plural ὑμῶν, "your," qualifying τῶν ἁμαρτιῶν, "of sins") or both baptism and repentance?[262] Significantly, the singular ἕκαστος, "each one," is used as the antecedent of a noun with the genitive ὑμῶν in 3:26, also in the context of turning from evil, which suggests that repentance and baptism *together* lead to forgiveness: baptism both expresses repentance and assures of forgiveness.[263] It is also noteworthy that when baptism and/or repentance are mentioned with forgiveness or salvation in the NT, the sequence is always that forgiveness/salvation follows whichever of baptism and repentance is mentioned.[264] Although repentance can be mentioned with forgiveness but without baptism (Luke 24:47; Acts 5:30; cf. Acts 3:19), the present verse appears to be presenting a "norm" that will be replicated in other stories in Acts—hence, for example, the requirement that Cornelius's glossalalic household be baptized in water, to catch up with what God has already done (10:47–48), and Luke's evident surprise that the baptized Samaritan believers had not received the Spirit (8:16). Paul certainly expected that every Christian would have been baptized and thus alluded to baptism in his letters on this basis (Rom 6:1–4, written to a church he had not visited and thus betraying Paul's assumptions; 1 Cor 6:11; 12:13).[265] Given that the repentance here appears to be corporate (see above) and thus relates to the Jerusalemites' corporate failure of crucifying Jesus, the forgiveness offered probably focuses on the same corporate action (cf. 3:17–19 for a similar sequence) rather than being a more general offer of forgiveness.

καὶ λήμψεσθε τὴν δωρεὰν τοῦ ἁγίου πνεύματος, "and you shall receive the gift of the Holy Spirit," promises the same divine enabling to those who respond as the apostolic band has received; the genitive τοῦ ἁγίου πνεύματος is epexegetical, meaning "which is the Holy Spirit."[266] This gift is the second

259 "John's Baptism," 160–61, 162–65.

260 So Mantey, "Causal"; Mantey, "Again." However, the extrabiblical passages cited for a causal sense more probably use εἰς to express purpose: Marcus, "On Causal"; Marcus, "Elusive"; Davis, "Look."

261 So McIntyre, "Baptism."

262 So Camp, "Reexamining."

263 Cf. Green, "John's Baptism," 167.

264 Davis, "Look," 86–87, notes Mark 1:4; 16:15, 16 (although the latter two verses are widely recognized as textually secondary, *TCGNT*², 102–7); Luke 3:3; Acts 2:38; 22:16; 1 Pet 3:20, 21.

265 See Beasley-Murray, *Baptism*, 94–95.

266 E.g., Barrett, *Acts*, 1:155.

part of the divine action: καί, "and," is consecutive, indicating a further result flowing from repentance and baptism.[267] This is where baptism in Jesus's name advances on John's baptism, which was only preparatory for the coming of Jesus (see 19:4–6 with *Comment* there).[268] Baptism now initiates the baptized into the community of Jesus followers, which is the eschatological Israel, through the renewing and enlivening gift of the Spirit. That said, Gaventa rightly argues that καί cannot be taken as indicating that the Spirit flows mechanically from baptism;[269] rather, the Spirit is God's gift (δωρεά) with his timing.[270] The requirement of repentance also signals this. On λήμψεσθε, "receive," see *Comment* on 10:47. A reader's expectation might be that those who repent and are baptized will experience a similar enabling to bear witness (1:8) and/or to prophesy (vv. 17–19, quoting Joel 3:1–2 LXX [EVV 2:28–29]),[271] although it is striking that Luke does not record any examples of individuals who were baptized in water at Pentecost bearing witness or prophesying.[272] It is unlikely that the xenolalia of v. 4 would be seen as a normal accompaniment of receiving the gift of the Spirit, for invasive charismatic praise expressed in known languages was previously unknown in Judaism and is not explicitly mentioned elsewhere in Acts when the Spirit is given—other stories do not say that the hearers understood Spirit-speech (see *Comment* on 10:46; 19:6).[273]

A pattern is being portrayed here: God will now give the Spirit to those who repent and are baptized in Jesus's name, normally without any expectation of delay in either the baptism following the repentance or in the forgiveness or the giving of the Spirit following the baptism: "The Spirit is not a special gift to some, but will be given to every church member, and thus belongs to the church and will be given in baptism."[274] Hence (as noted above) the surprise in 8:16 that the Spirit has not yet fallen on the Samaritan believers, and Paul's instinctive question to the "disciples" in Ephesus, "Did you receive the Holy Spirit when you believed?" (19:2).[275] Thus in 2:41 Luke does not need to state that those baptized received the Spirit or forgiveness, for v. 38 establishes on the lips of a reliable character that this is the normal way events happen.[276] Where this pattern is not followed, there are good reasons for the apparent exceptions (see *Comment* on 8:12–17; 9:17–18; 10:44–48; 19:1–7).

---

267 BDF, §142(2); "καί," BDAG 495, §1.b.ζ.
268 With Christiansen, "Taufe," 63.
269 Gaventa, *Acts*, 80.
270 Twelftree, *People*, 85–86.
271 Menzies, *Empowered*, 171–72, 186–89.
272 Turner, *Power*, 359.
273 Turner, *Power*, 357.
274 Jervell, *Apostelgeschichte*, 150 (my translation); so also Turner, *Power*, 358; Haenchen, *Acts*, 184.
275 Cf. Fee, "Baptism," 94.
276 McCollough, *Ritual*, 123, calls Peter Luke's "normative spokesperson."

The Spirit's effects in ethical transformation and the formation of the believing community will be seen in the next paragraph (vv. 42–47).[277]

39 γάρ, "for," introduces an explanation of the last part of the previous sentence, receiving the gift of the Spirit, the connection being made clear by ἡ ἐπαγγελία, "the promise." The anaphoric article ἡ, which we could translate "this," points to the previous mention of "the promise," there of the Spirit (v. 33; cf. Luke 24:49), which itself points to the promise of John the baptizer (Luke 3:16; see *Comment* on v. 33). The use of ἐπαγγελία elsewhere in Acts and Paul[278] suggests that "the promise" is wider than the outpouring of the Spirit, extending to the covenant to which God has committed himself,[279] and, if so, the reference to the Spirit encapsulates and represents the blessings of the covenant: the Spirit is "the new covenant fulfillment of the ancient covenant promise."[280]

This sentence explains the breadth of those who may receive the promised Spirit. A Jewish audience (indeed, any ancient audience) would think in terms of family solidarity.[281] Thus they would understand τοῖς τέκνοις ὑμῶν, "your children," to be included in the promise (cf. ἡμῖν καὶ τοῖς τέκνοις ἡμῶν, "to us and our children," Pss. Sol. 8:33). (Male) circumcision signaled the inclusion of children in the covenant promises (Gen 17:9–14; cf. 1 Macc 1:15, 48). Joel's prophecy indicated that young children and old people were included in the promise (Acts 2:17), portraying the whole family in miniature. Jeremias infers that the hearers' children were to be baptized too, which is reasonable,[282] although it is goes too far to suggest that this necessarily entails infant baptism—we simply do not know the ages of the hearers' children.

πᾶσιν τοῖς εἰς μακράν, "all who are far away," echoes Isa 57:19 LXX, εἰρήνην ἐπ᾽ εἰρήνην τοῖς μακρὰν καὶ τοῖς ἐγγὺς οὖσιν, "peace upon peace to those far away and to those near," and Isa 43:6 LXX parallels μακράν with ἄκρων τῆς γῆς, "ends of the earth." μακράν here refers primarily to distance in space rather than time. The final phrase ὅσους ἂν προσκαλέσηται κύριος ὁ θεὸς ἡμῶν, "whoever the Lord our God calls to himself," echoes Joel 3:5b (EVV 2:32b), οὓς κύριος προσκέκληται, "whom the Lord has called," a phrase not quoted in vv. 17–21.[283] προσκαλέω, "call," indicates a summons, not merely an invitation (cf. 5:40; 6:2; 13:2, 7; 16:10; 23:23; LXX Gen 28:1; Exod 3:18; 5:3; Esth 8:1; Ps 49:4 [MT 50:4]; Amos 5:8; 9:6; Ign. *Trall.* 11:2)—those who come to God and

277 Turner, *Power,* 406, 412–15.

278 Acts 7:17; 13:23, 32; 26:6; Rom 4:13, 14, 16, 20; 9:4, 8, 9; 15:8; Gal 3:14, 16–18, 21–22; Eph 2:12.

279 Barrett, *Acts,* 1:155; Schröter, "Taufe," 563; contra MacDonald, "Glossolalia," 130.

280 Dunn, *Baptism,* 47.

281 Jeremias, *Infant,* 22–23; cf. Gen 9:9; 13:15; 17:7–9; Josh 24:15; Pss 18:50; 89:34–37; 123:11–12; note also the "household" formula that Jeremias, *Infant,* 19–24, identifies with Acts 11:14; 16:15, 31–33; 18:8.

282 *Infant,* 40.

283 Jeremias, *Origins,* 26; White, *Prophets,* 84.

receive the promised Spirit are those whom God has drawn. The picture in Joel 3:5 is of an eschatological pilgrimage to Jerusalem in response to God's summons, and thus "all who are far away" would most naturally be understood at the time of Peter's speech as diaspora Jews, and perhaps some gentiles, for some versions of the eschatological pilgrimage included gentiles (e.g., Zech 8:20–23; Isa 2:1–3; 56:6–8; cf. Isa 49:6; Sib. Or. 3:616–617, 772–773; Pss. Sol. 17:34–35).[284] However, the way Luke's story will develop expands this category dramatically in tune with Joel's promise that the Spirit will be poured out on πᾶσαν σάρκα, "all flesh" (v. 17, citing Joel 3:1 [EVV 2:28] and echoing the quotation of Isa 40:3 in Luke 3:6).[285] The Samaritans were certainly "far away," geographically and in other ways (8:5–25). The Ethiopian eunuch is another example of one from "far away" due to deformity (Deut 23:1–2) who joins the believing community (8:26–40, see *Comment* on vv. 27–28), and ultimately the conversion of Cornelius and his household points clearly to the inclusion of gentiles (11:18). Hence, μακράν, "far away," is found in the context of Paul's mission to the gentiles among diaspora Jews (22:21; cf. Eph 2:13, 17).[286]

40 ἑτέροις τε λόγοις πλείοσιν διεμαρτύρατο καὶ παρεκάλει αὐτούς, "He went on testifying and exhorting them with many other words." By the use of the imperfects διεμαρτύρατο . . . παρεκάλει, "he went on testifying . . . exhorting," Luke shows that he is presenting a summary of Peter's words at Pentecost, as Luke does in other speeches.[287] Peter both informs (διεμαρτύρατο), a term signaling the seriousness of the content,[288] and calls on (παρεκάλει) his audience to respond, engaging with them intellectually, emotionally, and volitionally: the message they are hearing is aimed at changing the way they live and think and perceive the world—it is not mere rearrangement of their intellectual furniture.

σώθητε ἀπὸ τῆς γενεᾶς τῆς σκολιᾶς ταύτης, "Be saved from this crooked generation!" Peter now applies the language of the Joel quotation (πᾶς ὃς ἂν ἐπικαλέσηται τὸ ὄνομα κυρίου σωθήσεται, "whoever calls on the name of the Lord will be saved," Acts 2:21) to his audience. Salvation is escape from danger, here by dissociation from peers responsible for the death of Jesus (for repentance is focused on this responsibility in vv. 23, 36–38).[289] It is noteworthy that the verb σώθητε, "be saved," is passive, as we noted βαπτισθήτω, "be baptized" (v. 38), is. In this first use of "salvation" language in Acts, Luke signals that salvation—like the baptism that pictures and effects it—is God's action, received by humans; cf. v. 47, where τοὺς σῳζομένους, "those who were being saved," is

284 See Sanders, *Jesus*, 212–18; Bird, *Origins*, 26–29, both with further ancient references.
285 With Litwak, *Echoes*, 158–59; cf. Meek, *Gentile Mission*, 109–10.
286 Bauckham, "Restoration," 474.
287 Kilgallen, "With Many," proposes that "many other words" were part of the call to response. See helpful discussions of the Acts speeches as précis in relation to the practice of other ancient authors in Hemer, *Book*, 75–79, 415–27; Gempf, "Speaking."
288 "διαμαρτύρομαι," BDAG 233.
289 Weatherly, *Responsibility*, 107.

also passive. It is thus mistaken to translate σώθητε, "save yourselves" (as if the verb were middle voice), as many EVV do, e.g., NIV, NRSVue, ESV, KJV; contrast CSB, CEB, NKJV, NTE. Acts 4:12 will further clarify both that this salvation comes through Jesus alone, and that salvation is a rich term, including the physical healing of the disabled man at the Beautiful Gate (note 4:9). Salvation for Luke is deliverance from the judgment coming on this crooked generation, and is seen by membership of the believing community who have been saved (this verse; cf. Luke 7:50; 8:48; 17:19; 18:42), are in process of being saved (2:47), and will be saved at the last day (for the salvation spoken of in Joel is on the day of the Lord, vv. 20–21; cf. 17:31; 15:1, 11).[290] The blessings of salvation include forgiveness of sins and the gift of the Spirit through repentance and baptism (2:38; 5:31).

τῆς γενεᾶς τῆς σκολιᾶς ταύτης, "this crooked generation," echoes Jesus's criticisms of "this generation" in Luke 7:31; 9:41; 11:29–32; 11:50–51; 17:25 and the OT characterization of the desert generation at the time of the exodus as "crooked" (Deut 32:5; Ps 77:8 [LXX; MT 78:8]; cf. Heb 3:10); these uses focus on a particular group of people, not the whole Jewish race. Josephus uses γενεά, "generation," for a specific Jewish faction led by John of Giscala without including all others in Jerusalem, let alone all other Jews of the day (*J.W.* 5.10.5 §442; 5.13.6 §566; 6.8.5 §408).[291] Similarly, rabbinic authors and the targums both identify specific generations as evil or corrupt, but without treating every individual of that period of Jewish history as evil or corrupt: Noah, Caleb, and Joshua are examples of godly people excluded from this condemnation.[292] Thus Luke is not suggesting that all Jews everywhere are directly guilty of the death of Jesus, for Peter could not say to every Jew that "you crucified and killed [Jesus]" (v. 23; contrast "they" as responsible in 10:39; 13:27–29)—it was the Jerusalemites and their leaders, in particular, who bore this responsibility.[293] Paul uses γενεᾶς σκολιᾶς, "crooked generation," for people who live outside Christ (Phil 2:15), a wider referent than Jewish people alone, which may suggest that Luke intends the use here to show his readers that the call to be saved is addressed to many more than the audience at Pentecost—indeed, that it applies to all who read Peter's address.[294]

41 is transitional; the combination μὲν οὖν, "so then," combines continuation (οὖν) and a prospective marker (μέν).[295] This sentence belongs most naturally with vv. 1–40 rather than vv. 42–47, since it echoes v. 38, presenting

---

290 For the breadth of salvation in Luke-Acts, see Marshall, *Historian*, 94–102, 176–78; Green, *Meaning*, 136–51; George, "L'emploi."

291 Weatherly, *Responsibility*, 102–3; his whole discussion of "this generation," 100–107, is illuminating.

292 References and discussion: Lövestam, "Rettungsappel," 85–87.

293 Weatherly, *Responsibility*, esp. ch. 2; for connections between the speech and the surrounding narrative, see Tannehill, "Functions," 401–4.

294 Cf. Stenschke, "Need," 135–40.

295 Levinsohn, *Connections*, 137–50.

the response the crowd make as baptism; and ἐν τῇ ἡμέρᾳ ἐκείνῃ, "on that day," locates this sentence as part of the Pentecost event, whereas vv. 42–47 provide a generalizing summary of the believing community's life beyond Pentecost. Further, the verb tense choices suggest a break at the end of the sentence, where aorist main verbs (ἐβαπτίσθησαν . . . προσετέθησαν, "they were baptized . . . they were added") are replaced by imperfects (vv. 42–47), contrasting the summary (vv. 42–47) with the specific actions here.

Verse 41 echoes v. 38, showing that people responded as called. It identifies key characteristics of the responsive Israel: they "accepted his message" (implying repentance) and were baptized, with the implication (from v. 38) that they then received forgiveness and the Spirit.[296] προσετέθησαν, "were added," probably signifies that *God* added (as v. 47, same verb). It implies that they join an existing entity, and the assembly, ἐκκλησία, of Jesus followers is not mentioned until 5:11. They join "those who came to believe" (v. 44), which grows around the original 120 (1:15), a group in continuity with Israel, now being reshaped around Jesus as Messiah.[297]

Some consider the approximate[298] number of three thousand converts to be an exaggeration, objecting that such a large crowd could not hear one person speak,[299] that such a high proportion of the Jerusalem population responding is implausible,[300] and that the lack of a river nearby and the timing of the event in the dry season imply that baptisms could not have happened as v. 41 asserts. No significant suggestions appear to have been made of a symbolic or theological significance to the number (about) three thousand, however, and so there is good reason to regard this figure as coming from early tradition.[301] However, there is evidence that speakers could be heard by large groups in the ancient and modern worlds—the size of some ancient theatres suggests that large crowds could hear clearly (Ephesus had a theatre seating twenty thousand[302]), and the ministries of George Whitefield, John Wesley, and others were conducted to large outdoor crowds.[303] Further, Jeremias's estimate of Jerusalem's population is probably a significant underestimate: an estimate of sixty thousand to one hundred twenty thousand is more likely, particularly because the population density in ancient times was much greater

296 Johnson, *Function*, 184–85.

297 Lennartsson, *Refreshing*, 111–12.

298 ὡσεί, "about," indicates a rounded, rather than exact, figure.

299 Haenchen, *Acts*, 188.

300 Haenchen, *Acts*, 215n2, depends on Jeremias's (under)estimate of Jerusalem's population as 25,000 in *Jerusalem*, 83n24. Keener, "Plausibility," 151–58, gives examples of rapid early growth in modern religious movements.

301 Pesch, *Apostelgeschichte*, 1:126; Reinhardt, "Population," 265.

302 Horsley, "Inscriptions," 110n15; Trebilco, "Asia," 348; cf. Crisler, "Acoustics," who uses modern acoustic measuring instruments to assess some biblical speech scenes, concluding that they are plausible.

303 Benjamin Franklin calculated that Whitefield could be heard by thirty thousand people: Franklin, *Autobiography*, 163–64; I owe the reference to Lee Gatiss.

than the nineteenth-century figures Jeremias uses.[304] During festivals, the city swelled in numbers because of visitors, and the Temple Mount could hold as many as four hundred thousand.[305] Barrett suggests that "the reference to baptism may arise out of Luke's familiarity with the practice of his own day."[306] This assumes that baptism was by immersion, which Luke does not say. Marshall argues cogently that the verb βαπτίζω most probably means to be deluged or sprinkled with a liquid poured from above (see *Comment* on 1:4–5), and this at least allows the possibility of affusion or sprinkling as the mode of baptism[307]—if so, baptizing three thousand is possible with a limited water supply.[308] The further objection that Pilate would have put such a mass event to a stop as politically and socially disruptive assumes that Pilate was in the city, which was frequently not the case.[309]

Explanation

The coming of the Spirit at Pentecost is a key moment in the story of Acts, for here key divine promises are fulfilled and the believing community is empowered for its task of witness to Jesus (1:8). These promises are rooted in Scripture (Joel 2:28–32a EVV, quoted in Acts 2:17–21) and run through John the baptizer (Luke 3:16) and Jesus himself—both his own baptismal vision of the Spirit (Luke 3:21–22) and his promise (Luke 24:49; Acts 1:8). This strong thread of continuity furthers the emphasis in Acts 1 on the restoration and renewal of Israel, as the Spirit comes to enable the believing community to live in harmony with God's purposes (cf. Ezek 26:25–27 with Jer 31:31–34).

The event is described briefly (Acts 2:1–4), and the remainder of the section is a kind of dialogue between various sections of the crowd (vv. 5–13, 37, 41) and Peter (vv. 14–36, 38–40). The crowd's main role is to provide a foil to Peter's exposition, leading to their generally positive response to Peter's call to repent (v. 37, 41).

The Spirit's coming is illuminated by a comparison with the giving of the torah at Sinai and the ministry of Moses. While our earliest sources explicitly linking the Jewish festival of Pentecost with the giving of the torah are second century AD, there seems to have been debate among earlier Jewish authors about such a link. Luke echoes Sinai traditions in the coming of the Spirit/

---

304 Broshi, "Estimating"; Reinhardt, "Population," 238–59, 263.

305 See discussion of festival numbers in Sanders, *Judaism*, 125–27. Sanders also notes there that the Sacred Mosque in Mecca holds five hundred thousand for prayer, and it is only 7% larger than the Jerusalem temple mount.

306 Barrett, *Acts*, 1:160.

307 "Meaning."

308 Keener, "Plausibility," 143–46, assuming immersion as the mode of baptism, argues that there were sufficient *miqvaot* pools near the temple to allow thousands of visitors each day to bathe, and cites archaeological evidence for at least 150 such pools.

309 Marshall, "Significance," 361.

torah with fire and a loud noise, a theophany, and marking a new beginning in redemptive history (cf. Philo, *Dec.* 33; *Spec. Leg.* 2.189). Moreover, the Joel quotation (vv. 17–21) looks to the fulfillment of Moses's longing that all of God's people should have the Spirit (Num 11:29); the apocalyptic language of Joel echoes that of the exodus events and Sinai; and Joel's fire and clouds of smoke echo Sinai traditions (Exod 19:16–19). Instead of the "story" of the Pentecost Psalm 68:19 MT of Moses going up to receive the torah and then coming down to give the torah to God's people, Jesus has gone up to the Father and now pours out the Spirit (cf. Eph 4:8). The Spirit has the same role and location in the Christian story as the torah has in Israel's story, as guide for life with God, but with the new dimension of power to live this life (cf. Rom 8; 2 Cor 3).

The crowd's reactions (Acts 2:5–13) suggest that the phenomena described in vv. 1–4 were visible and audible to a large group. The most probable scenario is that the initial event took place in a private place (such as the upper room of 1:13, which seems to be the location of the prayers of 1:14), and the noise, wind, and speech drew a crowd (v. 6) and led to at least the Twelve moving into the wider Jerusalem main street, and perhaps to the temple courts.

The phenomena (vv. 1–4) recall biblical theophanies and are sourced in heaven—thus the ascended Jesus is now acting from heaven (v. 33). The tongues of fire link to Scripture and Luke's Gospel: they recall Sinai (Exod 24:17; 19:18); they echo John the baptizer's promise of a baptism with Spirit *and fire* (Luke 3:16), a promise of Israel's cleansing to prepare for witness to Jesus; and, like their Lord, the disciples are being equipped for ministry (cf. Acts 1:8; Luke 3:21–22; 4:1, 14, 18). Speech in known foreign, but unlearned, languages (xenolalia) then announces the meaning of the event to the crowds, as the believers declare praise for God's mighty acts (Acts 2:11), probably focused in the recent events of Jesus's life, ministry, death and resurrection. Xenolalic speech is unprecedented in Jewish or Greco-Roman cultures, so it is no surprise that it draws a crowd. These events show that the Spirit is filling the believers (v. 4a) and enabling them to speak in this way.

The crowd's reaction (vv. 5–13) is divided. The blend of Jerusalem dwellers and Passover pilgrims from around the diaspora (vv. 5, 9–11) symbolically portray and look forward to the wide geographical reach the gospel will have by the end of Acts—although at this point, the audience are all Jewish. Most wonder (vv. 7–8) and are puzzled (v. 12), but others are scornful (v. 13): this combination of reactions will be repeated elsewhere in Acts as the gospel divides Jewish communities—some respond positively (as they will here, v. 41), and some reject the gospel message (e.g., 13:42–43, 45).

Peter's response to the crowd's divided reaction is to offer an explanation rooted in Scripture of the phenomena, which becomes the vehicle for telling the story of Jesus, a story that runs beyond his death to his resurrection and ascension to the Father's right hand (vv. 14–36). After an initial call to listen

(v. 14) and a brief explanation of why the group are not drunk (v. 15), Peter turns to Joel 2:28–32a EVV and quotes it at length. This is the explanation of what is happening: God is fulfilling his promise through Joel to pour out the Spirit upon all kinds of people (vv. 17–18), and that is why Peter can interpret the time as "the last days" (v. 17). The use of Scripture here is not simply repetition of what Joel says: the speech uses Joel (the whole book seems to be alluded to in places here and elsewhere in Acts; see *Comment* on vv. 16–21) and the events of Pentecost and the early community's life to interpret each other. Thus, the later Joel quotation also prepares for what Peter goes on to say about Jesus, whom Peter will identify as the one who pours out the Spirit (v. 33) and who is now the Lord on whom people must call to be saved (vv. 36, 38).

Scripture is key, too, to the development of Peter's argument, as Peter cites Pss 16:8–11 (vv. 25–27, 31) and 110:1 (vv. 34–35). In both cases Peter asserts that David speaks prophetically (v. 30) and that David is not speaking about himself (vv. 29–31, 34). Thus, David must be speaking of the Messiah, Jesus, raised from the dead (vv. 31, 32, 24) and given an exalted place (v. 34). Scripture again interprets contemporary events, here Jesus's death, resurrection, and exaltation. Luke presents Peter as engaging in scriptural interpretation in similar manner to other NT writers, not least the author of 1 Peter (e.g., 1 Pet 1:10–12, 23–25; 2:4–10).

The heart and focus of Peter's speech is Jesus: he is the one concerning whom Peter speaks. Although Jesus is the topical (and syntactical) focus of the speech, the grammatical subject is generally God, for Peter's point is about what God has done in and for Jesus. Thus God acted in and through Jesus's ministry (Acts 1:22), God's purposes were accomplished in Jesus's death at the hands of the people of Jerusalem and their leaders (v. 23), God raised Jesus from death (v. 24), God spoke in Scripture to announce these events (vv. 25–31, 34–35), and God exalted Jesus to his right hand and gave Jesus the Spirit to pour out (v. 33). This divine testimony to Jesus leads to two key declarations: that Jesus is the one who pours out the Spirit (v. 33) and is thus to be identified with God who pours out the Spirit (v. 17; Joel 3:1); and that Jesus is both Lord (identified with YHWH) and Messiah (YHWH's emissary). Peter is not announcing that Jesus has become something that he was not before, for the Christology here builds on the portrait of Jesus in Luke's Gospel, where Jesus is "Son of God" from conception (Luke 1:35), "Lord" while in Mary's womb (Luke 1:43), and is announced to the shepherds as Savior, Messiah, and Lord (Luke 2:11). Rather, "made" (v. 36) should be seen as a human perception: Israel is to change its view of Jesus because of God's action in raising and exalting him and giving him the Spirit to pour out.

To make such declarations about Jesus demands response, and members of the crowd engage both emotionally—they are "cut to the heart"—and volitionally—they wish to know how to act (v. 37). Their response has shifted from asking about the disciples (vv. 12–13) to asking about themselves.

The required response (vv. 38–39) is paradigmatic for response to the gospel message throughout Acts, although elements of the response have particular poignancy for the Jerusalemites. They are to repent—to change their minds about Jesus and change the direction of their lives in consequence, and the Jerusalemites' role in Jesus's death makes this demand acute. They are to be baptized in water to portray and express their repentance, and the passive "be baptized" focuses on the baptizand receiving a gift from God. God's gift requires a response, and this baptism is "in the name of Jesus Messiah," portraying those baptized as responding by calling on the name of Jesus (cf. v. 21), that is, on Jesus himself, the one now known to sit at YHWH's right hand, ruling the universe. From these two actions flow consequences: the baptized person receives forgiveness (echoing John's baptism, Luke 3:3) and the Spirit as a gift. These consequences are the normal expectation of Christian initiation. Not only that, but this promise is open to the children of the hearers, as would be normal for Jews who thought in terms of family solidarity, and others "far away." The latter phrase in its setting refers to diaspora Jews, but in Luke's wider context hints at the ultimate inclusion of gentiles (cf. Acts 22:21). Peter's call on them to respond in this way is not brief, for v. 40 hints that he went on speaking with the crowd for some time.

The passage closes with a transition (v. 41) that declares that there was such a response, and it was substantial—three thousand people were added in one day. For this number to be added suggests that baptism was not necessarily by immersion, for there was not a river near to the temple courts.

Luke thus presents his readers with a "launch" story for the believing community, but not a "new launch" (nor "the birthday of the church"), for *the undergirding of Scripture shows that the believers are in continuity with the ancient faith of Judaism.* Outside the framework of Judaism, none of what Peter says, none of the events that take place, makes sense—the restoration of Israel is fully in process now that the exalted Jesus has poured out the Spirit, and Luke hints that there is more to that restoration than meets the eye, for eventually gentiles ("those who are far away," v. 39) will be drawn in too.

E. The Life of the Early Community (2:42–47)

Bibliography

Andersen, T. D. "Meaning." **Barrett, C. K.** "Attitudes." **Bauckham, R.** "Early." **Benoit, P.** "Notes." **Black, M.** *Aramaic,* 10. **Blomberg, C. L.** *Neither,* 161–63. **Braun, H.** *Qumran.* **Burkitt, F. C.** "Acts 2:47." **Cadbury, H. J.** "Summaries," *BegC,* 5:392–402. **Campbell, J. Y.** "ΚΟΙΝΩΝΙΑ." **Capper, B. J.** "Community," esp. 1734–41. ———. "Context." **Cerfaux, L.** "Communauté." **Cheetham, F. P.** "Acts 2:47." **Clark, A. C.** "Apostleship." ———. "Role." **Co, M. A.** "Summaries." **Crump, D.** *Jesus,* 101–7. **Daniélou, J.** "Communauté." **Degenhardt, H. J.** *Lukas,* 163–68. **Dibelius, M.** *Studies,* 8–10. **Dombrowski, B. W.** "1QS." **Dowd, W. A.** "Notes." **Downing, F. G.** "Common Ground." **Dunn, J. D. G.** "ΚΥΡΙΟΣ." **Dupont, J.** *Salvation,* 85–102 [= *Études,* 503–19]. ———. *Nouvelles,* 296–318. **Emerton, J. A.** Review of Wilcox, *Semitisms,* 282–97. **Finger, R. H.** *Widows,* 220–45. **Fitzmyer, J.** *Background,* 271–303. ———. "Designations." ———. "Jewish," 241–44. **Fuller, R. H.** *Foundations,* 157. **Giles, K. N.** "Apostles," 244–46. **Greehy, J. G.** "Community." **Green, J. B.** "Persevering," esp. 185–86. **Gregson, F. J. R.** *Everything,* 46–50, 66–78. **Griffiths, J. D.** "Spirit." **Hays, C. M.** *Ethics,* 190–211. **Hengel, M.** *Acts,* 8–13. ———. *Property,* 31–34. **Hume, D. A.** *Community,* 87–118. **Jeremias, J.** *Jerusalem,* 126–34. ———. *Words,* 118–21. **Jervell, J.** *Theology,* 13–15. **Johnson, L. T.** *Function,* 183–90. **Johnson, S. E.** "Manual." **Kim, K.-J.** *Stewardship,* 218–83. **Klauck, H.-J.** "Gütergemeinschaft." **Lake, K.** "Communism." *BegC,* 5:140–51. **Lindemann, A.** "Beginnings," 203–9. **Marshall, I. H.** *Supper,* 123–33. ———. "Worship." **McDermott, J. M., SJ,** "Doctrine II," 230–31. **Mealand, D. L.** "Community." **Menoud, P. H.** *Jesus,* 84–101. **Meyer, B. F.** "Self-Understanding." **Monloubou, L.** *Prière,* 35–40. **Moule, C. F. D.** *Worship,* 13–24. **Murphy-O'Connor, J.** "Cenacle." **Noble, J.** *Common Property.* **Öhler, M.** "Urgemeinde." **Payne, D. F.** "Semitisms." **Peterson, D.** *Engaging,* 152–65. **Pfitzner, V. C.** "Pneumatic," 221–22. **Reicke, B. I.** *Diakonie,* 202–6. **Ritmeyer, L. & K. Ritmeyer** *Ritual.* **Sanders, E. P.** *Judaism,* 51–72. **Schnabel, E.** *Mission,* 1:407–20. **Schneider, G.** "Gott," 168. **Schottroff, L. and W. Stegemann.** *Jesus.* **Seccombe, D. P.** "Charity." ———. *Possessions,* 200–218. **Sterling, G. E.** "Athletes." **Taylor, J.** "Fraction." **Theissen, G.** "Liebeskommunismus." **Thompson, R. P.** *Keeping,* 45–61. **Thornton, L. S.** *Life,* esp. 5–33. **Torrey, C. C.** *Composition,* 10–14. **Trebilco, P. R.** *Self-designations,* 72–99, 103–11. **Turner, M.** *Power,* 412–14. **van der Horst, P. W.** "Parallels, 2.1–47." **Walton, S.** "Calling," 234–36. ———. "Communism." ———. "Ὁμοθυμαδόν," 99. ———. "Tale," 135–36. **Wendel, U.** *Gemeinde.* **Wenk, M.** *Power,* 259–73. **Wieser, T.** "Community," 87–88. **Wilcox, M.** *Semitisms,* 93–100. **Yao, S.** "Dismantling." **Zimmermann, H.** "Sammelberichte."

Translation

[42] They were devoting[a] themselves to the apostles' teaching and the fellowship, the
breaking of bread, and the prayers. [43] Fear kept coming on everyone, and many wonders and signs were taking place through the apostles.[b] [44] All those who had come to
believe[c] were together, and they used to hold everything as common; [45] they used to sell

their[d] possessions and belongings and distribute the proceeds[e] to all, as anyone had need.[f] 46 Day by day, both spending much time together in the temple and breaking bread in homes, they shared food with joy and singleness of heart, 47 praising God and having favor with[g] the whole people. Every day the Lord was adding to their group[h] those being saved.

Notes

a. Ἦσαν . . . προσκαρτεροῦντες, periph. Impf. Denoting habitual activity, "they were devoting themselves"; cf. Johnson, *Acts*, 56: "[t]hey were constant in their attention."

b. There is some confusion in the text in vv. 43–44. 𝔓[74vid] (which has a gap here) ℵ A C E Ψ 88 1611 1837 2147 2344 2495 lat (mae) bo read φόβος τε ἦν μέγας ἐπὶ πάντας (αὐτούς Ψ 2147), "and great fear was upon (them) all" (v. 43a), and ἐν Ἰερουσαλήμ, "in Jerusalem" (v. 43b). The text translated is read by B D 1739 𝔐 it[d, gig, p*, r] syr[h] sa and this represents solid early Alexandrian and Western support. The various longer readings smooth the somewhat harsh transition to v. 44; *TCGNT*², 262; Haenchen, *Acts*, 192n3; Barrett, *Acts*, 1:167.

c. οἱ πιστεύσαντες, aor. ptc., "those who had come to believe," is read by ℵ B H² 056 0142 28 36 104 2495 *pc* cop; οἱ πιστεύοντες, pres. ptc., "the believers," is read by 𝔓[75vid] (although the crucial letters are missing from the MS) A C D E P Ψ 049 33 81 1175 1739 2412 2495 𝔐, and adopted by ECM, UBS⁵/NA²⁸. The aor. parallels the undisputed reading in 4:32 (and D's reading in 2:41), and the solid support of ℵ B, along with a context where many have recently come to faith (2:41) suggest the aor. is the original reading, contra *TCGNT*², 263.

d. The articles τά and τάς function as possessive pronouns; the possessions and belongings are those of the believers; cf. Wallace, 215–16.

e. D reads καθ' ἡμέραν, "daily."

f. ἄν + impf. εἶχεν, "had," is iterative, suggesting a sequence of separate, but regular, events of having need; MHT, 1:167; "ἄν," BDAG 56, §I.a.α; Barrett, *Acts*, 1:169; Bruce, *Acts* (1990), 133, 160. Cf. 4:35; 1 Cor 12:2, the only other places where this classical usage is found in NT.

g. πρός denotes "with" (s.v., BDAG 874, §3.e); for the view that it has its commoner sense "toward," and thus portrays the outward attitudes of the believers, see Cheetham, "Acts 2:47"; Andersen, "Meaning." Co, "Summaries," 75n67, provides a valuable discussion, concluding that whichever view is taken, the central point is that "a favorable relationship existed between the believers and the people."

h. Some scribes clearly found the use of ἐπὶ τὸ αὐτό, "their group," unusual, for E H² I P Ψ 049 056, a number of minuscules, *Byz*, and syr take ἐπὶ τὸ αὐτό with 3:1, denoting that Peter and John went "together" to the temple. Others include (ἐν) τῇ ἐκκλησίᾳ, "(in) the assembly," as well as or instead of ἐπὶ τὸ αὐτό, including D E H² P Ψ 104 1739 *Byz* Chrysostom.

Form/Structure/Setting

Delimitation of pericope. Verse 42 begins with an undefined subject "they," referring back to those who respond to the message by being baptized (v. 41). In addition, v. 41 begins with μὲν οὖν, which can be the marker of a new section (cf. 1:6; 8:4). Thus, some take 2:41 as the beginning of the summary.[1] However, the shift to imperfect verbs in vv. 42–47 highlights this section's summary character, following the aorists that predominate in vv. 37–41 (where ten of fourteen indicatives are aorist). It is thus appropriate to see v. 42 as beginning a new paragraph, though clearly linked to the previous paragraph. In addition, the four points in v. 42 are developed in vv. 43–47 (see *Structure* below), tying v. 42 strongly to the rest of the paragraph.

Sources/historicity. This passage is often identified as the first of three summaries of the life of the early community in Jerusalem, the others being 4:32–35 and 5:12–16.[2] All three summaries are characterized by imperfect verbs portraying ongoing, typical actions. Some scholars see the summaries as Lukan free compositions with no basis in tradition because they have a generalizing character and appear to be easily detached from their literary setting.[3] Dibelius notes that the summaries connect with surrounding stories: the signs (2:43–47) lead into the healing (3:1–10); the sale of possessions (4:32–35) leads to the example of Barnabas (4:36–37); the tension between 5:13, 14 is resolved by the imprisonment that follows (5:17–18).[4] Thus, in line with the episodic style of Acts, Schmithals suggests that the summaries have been composed by Luke as generalized versions of these specific incidents.[5] Cadbury draws attention to Luke's editing of Markan material in his Gospel to include summaries (e.g., Luke 7:21).[6]

Certainly there is evidence of Lukanisms in the summaries,[7] and these imply that Luke's hand is evident in the presentation of the material. However, Luke's writing suggests that he certainly knows more than he includes in Acts, particularly given the constraints of space in a typical papyrus roll (Luke 1:1).[8] Lukan *phrasing* need not imply Lukan *creation* of the material; equally, the presence of words that are not Lukan favorites need not imply the work of an editor later than Luke, as Benoit proposes.[9] Further, Theissen notes the relative isolation of the topos of sharing possessions in Luke-Acts, for Luke provides no saying of Jesus that instructs his followers to share their goods with each other; rather, Luke's Jesus tells his followers to give all that they have to *the poor* (Luke 18:22; cf. 19:8).[10] Had Luke wished to create material

---

1 E.g., Sterling, "Athletes," 680n7; Barrett, *Acts*, 1:159.

2 E.g., Cadbury, "Summaries"; for helpful surveys of scholarship, see Co, "Summaries," 49–55; Theissen, "Liebeskommunismus," 689–91.

3 E.g., Lüdemann, *Early Christianity*, 47.

4 *Studies*, 9–10.

5 *Apostelgeschichte*, 37; so also Zimmermann, "Sammelberichte," 72–77, who speculates that vv. 41, 44, 46–47 are "original" and the rest are generalizing statements drawn from these sentences.

6 "Summaries," 392–95.

7 See the list in Barrett, *Acts*, 1:161.

8 Cadbury, "Summaries," 401; Hengel, *Acts*, 8–13.

9 "Notes"; cf. criticisms by Haenchen, *Acts*, 194–95.

10 "Liebeskommunismus," 699–700.

teaching the sharing of goods, he would have been likely to spread it more widely in his two books; thus, Theissen cogently argues, this material is most probably traditional.[11] The summaries present the early community's united, shared life as normative, as can be seen from Luke's negative portrayal of later threats to the unity of the believers (e.g., 5:1–11; 6:1–7).[12]

The Greco-Roman topos of friendship is frequently noted as parallel to the shared life, and especially the shared goods, of the early community, here and in 4:32–5:11; 6:1–7.[13] In addition, Greco-Roman writers also looked back to an ideal utopian situation where people held goods in common (see *Comment* on vv. 44–45[14]). While there are certainly parallels of thought, and the Greco-Roman ideals were widely known (and thus likely to have been known by Luke), it is notable that the group are called οἱ πιστεύσαντες, "those who had come to believe" (v. 44), rather than "the friends" (see *Comment* on 4:34).[15] This implies that it is their faith—their friendship with God in Christ, we might say—that is the defining characteristic of their shared life.[16] Further, the Platonic sharing of possessions was only practised by the "guardians" of the community, that is, the élite, whereas Luke portrays the early believers' sharing as including both rich and poor, not least widows (6:1).[17] It is thus unlikely that this Greco-Roman theme is the source of Luke's phrasing, although the parallels of thought suggest that Luke may have written in dialogue with the Greco-Roman tradition at this point and thus presented the early community apologetically as fulfilling the highest ideals of the Greco-Roman world.[18]

Öhler makes an interesting argument that there are conceptual parallels between the early Jesus community and ancient associations:[19] (i) the relative equality of members, (ii) the expression of friendship ideals among non-elite people, (iii) the sharing of goods that was practiced by some associations, particularly based on benefactions from wealthy members, and (iv) shared meals and (for some associations) meeting in homes. He also notes some differences, notably that the standing of believers grew through gospel proclamation rather than benefaction, the lack of entry or membership fees payable among Jesus followers, and daily meetings (much more frequent than associations). The combination of similarities and differences (rightly)

---

11 This argument speaks against the claim that Luke includes this material because he advocates sharing possessions for the church of his day, which did not practise sharing in the way depicted here; so Schottroff and Stegemann, *Jesus*, 153.

12 Wenk, *Power*, 263–65.

13 E.g., Talbert, *Reading Acts*, 48; Sterling, "Athletes," 689–70, both with useful references.

14 See also Hengel, *Property*, 8–9; Mealand, "Community," 97–98; Noble, *Common Property*, passim.

15 Theissen, "Liebeskommunismus," 699.

16 Hume, *Community*, 97–99.

17 For a valuable review of the Greco-Roman sources, see Klauck, "Gütergemeinschaft," 48–57.

18 Sterling, "Athletes," 695–96; Thompson, *Keeping*, 52–55.

19 Öhler, "Urgemeinde"; see also the very full treatment of associations in relation to the Jesus communities in Kloppenborg, *Christ's Associations*.

leads him to conclude, "Although Luke's account takes up elements that were also important for associations, it tells of a new form of community. Luke understands it as a model for the balance between rich and poor, daily fellowship through the breaking of bread, and access to power based on spiritual competence."[20]

Structure. Verse 42 sets the agenda for the rest of the paragraph, where each element of this sentence is unpacked.[21] The apostles who teach also do wonders and signs (v. 43b), and new members are added to the group (v. 47b), at least partly through the favourable impression created (v. 47aβ) by the apostolic teaching and the apostolic wonders and signs (cf. 5:12, 14; 6:2, 4, 7). The "fellowship" of the believers is spelled out in being ἐπὶ τὸ αὐτό, "together" (2:44a), and in their sharing of possessions (vv. 44b–45)—again, this is probably a factor in the growth in numbers of believers (v. 47b). The "breaking of bread" is repeated and expanded to include shared meals in homes (v. 46b), and "the prayers" includes their participation in temple worship (v. 46a) and praising God (v. 47aα).

Setting. Luke locates the community's lifestyle as an outcome of the gift of the Spirit (v. 38) by linking this summary backwards to the events of Pentecost through continuity of participants: οἱ . . . ἀποδεξάμενοι τὸν λόγον αὐτοῦ, "those who received his message" (v. 41), are those who Ἦσαν . . . προσκαρτεροῦντες, "were devoting themselves" (v. 42[22]).[23] In addition, the references to "wonders and signs" (v. 43) and the temple (v. 46) prepare the way for the healing at the temple gate (3:1–10). Bruce also highlights the eschatological context set by the phrase ἐν ταῖς ἐσχάταις ἡμέραις, "in the last days" (v. 17), inserted into the Joel quotation—Luke portrays the life of the believers as that of the restored Israel, indwelt by the Spirit.[24]

Comment

42 Four features characterize the life of the earliest community; each one recurs in later descriptions of the life of the believers in Acts, strongly suggesting that Luke wishes these features to be seen in the church life of his day. Jeremias proposes that these delineate the sequence of early Christian meetings;[25] if so, Luke has chosen a rather obscure way of communicating this sequence and has not reproduced it in the small number of descriptions

20 Öhler, "Urgemeinde," 415 (my translation).
21 Cf. Roloff, *Apostelgeschichte*, 65–66.
22 With Schneider, *Apostelgeschichte*, 1:239.
23 Turner, *Power*, 412–14; Johnson, *Function*, 183–84; Wenk, *Power*, 261–63.
24 Bruce, *Acts* (1990), 132.
25 Jeremias, *Words*, 118–21. Thompson, *Keeping*, 47–49, suggests they form two pairs, relating to worship (breaking bread, prayers) and social interaction (teaching, fellowship). This rather divides what Luke unites in engagement with God and each other in community.

of believers' meetings elsewhere in Acts (e.g., Acts 20:7–12).[26] Marshall more plausibly sees these as typical features of early Christian meetings without necessarily implying that they all occurred at every meeting or that they always occurred in the same order.[27]

Luke introduces the features by writing that the believers ἦσαν . . . προσκαρτεροῦντες, "were . . . devoting themselves," focusing (by the lexical choice) on the persistence and (by the choice of imperfect) on the regularity of the believers' activities. The verb echoes the description of the pre-Pentecost community (see *Comment* on 1:14, also periphrastic imperfect) and will recur in v. 46, where it is combined with locative ἐν, "in," and thus has the sense "spend much time in."[28]

τῇ διδαχῇ τῶν ἀποστόλων, "to the apostles' teaching," is the first-named feature, suggesting it may have priority, at least logically, over the others. The particular knowledge of the apostles, since they had been with Jesus from the beginning of his public ministry (1:21–22; cf. Luke 6:12–13), along with their commission to be witnesses (Acts 1:2, 8, 22b), uniquely fitted them for this task. Their teaching ministry echoes that of Jesus, whom Luke characterizes as "Teacher" and speaks of him teaching often (about forty uses: Luke 3:12; 4:15, 31, 32; 5:3, 17, etc.). Notably, they continue Jesus's own teaching to them (Acts 1:1), rooted in Scripture (Luke 24:27, 45). The Jerusalem apostles will continue to be central throughout the first half of Acts, acting as validators for divinely initiated activities.[29] Apostolic authority is seen elsewhere in 1 Cor 12:28; 14:37; Eph 2:20; 3:5.[30]

τῇ κοινωνίᾳ, "the fellowship," is the only use of this term in Luke-Acts. General Greek usage is in the sense of an association or partnership, including a marriage partnership.[31] Campbell suggests that it simply denotes financial contributions (cf. Acts 2:44–45), along the lines of the use in Rom 15:26; 2 Cor 8:4; 9:13; Heb 13:16.[32] Luke's use of the cognate adjective κοινός, "common," in Acts 2:44 and 4:32 concerning the sharing of possessions suggests financial sharing is included.[33] However, there is no contextual signal here to alert Luke's readers to a semi-technical use of the term concerning finances, and so a more general sense seems likely, embracing the shared life of the new community, which itself derives from a shared engagement with God known in Jesus

26 More fully, Haenchen, *Acts*, 191.
27 Marshall, *Supper*, 127. For a valuable discussion on the unity shown in the early believing community, see Dupont, *Nouvelles*, 296–318.
28 "προσκαρτερέω," BDAG 881, §2.a.
29 See *Comment* on 1:2, 26; 4:35; 6:2, 4; 8:14, 18; 9:27; 14:4; 15:2. In 15:2, 4, 6, 22, they meet with οἱ πρεσβύτεροι, "the elders," and are not mentioned after 16:4.
30 On apostles, see Clark, "Apostleship," esp. 66–69; Giles, "Apostles"; and literature they cite.
31 "κοινωνία," LSJ; "κοινωνία," BDAG 552, §1.
32 "ΚΟΙΝΩΝΙΑ," 374–75.
33 Dupont, *Nouvelles*, 299.

(2:38–39; see *Comment* there).[34] This "common life"[35] is expressed in the sharing of money and goods (vv. 44–45) as well as meals (v. 46[36]). Fitzmyer suggests that this usage may be illuminated by Qumran use of יחד (*yḥd*), "together," as a technical term for the community that shared in communal study and observance of the torah, as well as possessions.[37] While κοινωνία, "fellowship," may not be used here as a name for the group, it conveys the sense of shared *life*.[38]

τῇ κλάσει τοῦ ἄρτου, "the breaking of bread," is a particular expression of the fellowship of the new community; this metonymic reference signals a larger whole by one characteristic gesture.[39] Two main referents are proposed. (i) A broad reference to shared meals, both here and in v. 46.[40] Kim proposes that these shared meals met the poor members' need for food, such as the widows of 6:1.[41] Shared meals also constitute the believing community as a "fictive kinship group," that is, a group that function like a family.[42] However, the location of the phrase "the breaking of bread" between "the fellowship" and "the prayers" rather suggests that "the breaking of bread" was at least in the context of corporate worship.[43] (ii) A specific reference to the Eucharist, perhaps treating this phrase as a technical term for a Eucharist separate from a shared meal.[44] Jeremias further argues that rabbinic usage of the expression always refers to the ceremonial opening of a shared meal.[45] However, such a usage here seems unlikely since it would isolate one element of a shared meal—it seems much more likely that the whole of the shared meal is in view. Didache 10:1 indicates that a shared meal continued to be a feature of the eucharistic celebration and, if Luke has such a situation in mind, it is plausible to see this reference as a meal that included a eucharistic remembrance, a use in tune with Acts 2:46 (see below, and cf. 20:7, 11).[46] This expression echoes usage in Luke's Gospel, notably Jesus's institution of the Eucharist (Luke 22:19, where the cognate verb κλάω, "break," is used; cf. 1 Cor 10:16;

---

34 McDermott, "Doctrine II," 231, argues that the unity of spirit here is further portrayed throughout the early chapters of Acts (1:14; 2:46; 4:32). Thornton, *Life*, 41–43, shows how this theme resonates with Phil 1 and Gal 6:6.

35 The helpful translation of Thornton, *Life*, 5–6.

36 With Seccombe, *Possessions*, 203–7, including a helpful brief survey of Philo's use of κοινωνία.

37 Fitzmyer, *Background*, 284–85; cf. Capper, "Context," 336; Dombrowski, "1QS"; Braun, *Qumran*, 1:143.

38 Note also Bauckham's cogent criticisms of the argument that κοινωνία is a name for the group: "Early," 85–88.

39 Taylor, "Fraction," 282; Menoud, *Jesus*, 86–87.

40 Haenchen, *Acts*, 191.

41 *Stewardship*, 250–51.

42 Finger, *Widows*, 230. Yao, "Dismantling," 29–30, cites Douglas's anthropological observation about the significance of meals and relates this to his experience as a Filipino Chinese arriving in the USA.

43 Menoud, *Jesus*, 86.

44 Jeremias, *Words*, 120–21; Taylor, "Fraction"; Dowd, "Notes."

45 *Words*, 109, 174nn3, 4.

46 With Menoud, *Jesus*, 86–89.

11:23–24) and his post-resurrection meals with his disciples (Luke 24:28–35, 36–43), particularly the mentions of "the breaking of bread" in 24:30, 35, as the means by which Jesus was known; thus some reference to the Eucharist, and that as a way the presence of Jesus was known, is probable within the context of a shared meal.[47] This theme is in tune with the known practice of the Corinthian believers (1 Cor 11:17–34) and thus likely to be historical.[48]

ταῖς προσευχαῖς, "the prayers," is unique in the NT in specifying *the* prayers and being plural;[49] other uses of this noun in Acts regularly have the genitive of a person or group attached (e.g., 10:4, the only other plural use). This uniqueness suggests that the article may be denoting specific prayers,[50] and these could be the temple prayers[51] (see *Comment* on 3:1) or the new community's prayers—in light of v. 46, both may be included in this expression, thus portraying the believers at this stage as a messianic Jewish sect rather than a group separate from Judaism. Luke seems likely to be pointing his readers to his Gospel, where prayer is a prominent motif, not least in the temple (Luke 1:8–22; 2:22–38).[52] The strong likelihood is that the believers' community prayers were addressed to the Lord Jesus, for it was on his name that people called to be saved (Acts 2:38; cf. 1:24; 7:59; 9:14, 21; 22:16).[53]

43 ἐγίνετο δὲ πάσῃ ψυχῇ φόβος, "Fear kept coming on everyone." φόβος, "fear," here denotes reverential awe toward God (cf. Luke 1:12, 65; 5:26; Acts 5:5, 11; 19:17) resulting from the power seen in the "wonders and signs" done through the apostles. The imperfect ἐγίνετο, "kept coming," highlights that such fear was characteristic of the period rather than mere short-term panic.[54] The continuing work of God among them led to a continuing response of awe. πάσῃ ψυχῇ, "on everyone," a Septuagintal expression, could denote those who are the subject of v. 42, the believers, or have a wider reference to those who had contact with the believers.[55] The parallel expression ὅλον τὸν λαόν, "the whole people" (v. 46), forms an *inclusio* with this and thus suggests that the wider Jewish community is in view.[56]

πολλά τε τέρατα καὶ σημεῖα, "and many wonders and signs," echoes the same phrase in 2:19, 22 in the same sequence (by contrast with other uses, which speak consistently of σημεῖα καὶ τέρατα, "signs and wonders": 4:30; 5:12; 6:8; 7:36; 14:3; 15:12). Thus, Luke underlines that the Spirit is at work among

---

47 Hume, *Community*, 107–8; Tannehill, *Unity*, 2:190; Gregson, *Everything*, 50.
48 Marshall, *Supper*, 127; Pesch, *Apostelgeschichte*, 1:130.
49 Col 4:12 is only a partial parallel, for there the article indicates that the referent is Epaphras's prayers.
50 Barrett, *Acts*, 1:166; contra NIV, "to prayer."
51 Barrett, "Attitudes," 347; Thornton, *Life*, 6; Monloubou, *Prière*, 36.
52 See Hume, *Community*, 104–6.
53 Green, "Persevering," 186–88; Hurtado, *Lord*, 198.
54 Fitzmyer, *Acts*, 268; Barrett, *Acts*, 1:166; Bruce, *Acts* (1990), 132.
55 E.g., Haenchen, *Acts*, 191–92.
56 With Hume, *Community*, 128.

the believers, both in fulfillment of the prophecy of Joel quoted in 2:19 and in continuity with the Spirit's work through Jesus (2:22). In light of 3:1–10; 5:1–11, the phrase most probably denotes healings, exorcisms, and other "deeds of power." Luke thus demonstrates that the events now taking place fulfill OT prophecy (2:19 echoes Joel 2:28–32 [LXX 3:1–5]), as already seen in the ministry of Jesus (Acts 2:22) and the apostles' activities when sent out by Jesus (Luke 9:1–2, 6). The fulfillment theme underlines that God is now acting to restore Israel in Spirit-enabled deeds of power.

διὰ τῶν ἀποστόλων ἐγίνετο, "were taking place *through* the apostles," clarifies that that apostles are not the source of the power producing the "wonders and signs"—they are merely the agents διά, "through," whom God works. Hence Peter and John will bring healing ἐν τῷ ὀνόματι Ἰησοῦ Χριστοῦ τοῦ Ναζωραίου, "in the name of Jesus the Messiah of Nazareth" (3:6).

44 πάντες δὲ οἱ πιστεύσαντες ἦσαν ἐπὶ τὸ αὐτό, "All those who had come to believe were together." The group are designated as πάντες . . . οἱ πιστεύσαντες, "all those . . . who had come to believe," the first time the group are so named in Acts.[57] "The believers" becomes a key expression describing the groups of Jesus followers, used twelve times in Acts.[58] The aorist participle here signifies entry into the community (cf. other similar aorists: 4:4; 9:42; 13:12; 14:1; 16:31; 18:8); other places utilize present or perfect participles.[59] It is striking that this term became so prominent among Jesus followers and was used primarily of relationships between humans and God/Jesus, for it characterizes them as people who trust in God through Jesus.[60] Faith as trust in a god was known in classical sources, although not widely.[61] The participle form was also rare in Scripture (LXX Prov 30:1; Isa 28:16). The Jesus followers' use probably stems from Jesus himself, for the Synoptic Gospels record him seeing πίστις, "faith, trust," as a key response to his ministry (e.g., Luke 7:50; 8:12–13, 25, 48, 50; 17:5–6, 19; 18:42; 22:32).[62] It becomes a prominent theme in Paul's writings,[63] and the Pauline tradition may well have been influential on Luke—although the widespread use of "faith, trust" language in the NT suggests that it was common coin among the earliest Jesus followers. Not for nothing do we today speak of "Christian *faith*" as the primary designation of following Jesus. ἐπὶ τὸ αὐτό, "together," expresses both that the believers met together and the unity of the community (see *Comment* on 1:15, and cf. 1 Cor 11:18, 20, where Paul speaks of meeting ἐν ἐκκλησίᾳ, "in assembly," and then repeats to the point

57 On this designation, see Walton, "Calling," 234–36; Trebilco, *Self-designations*, 103–11; Fitzmyer, "Designations," 225–26.

58 Here; 4:32; 5:14; 10:43; 11:21; 13:39; 15:5; 18:27; 21:20, 25; 22:19.

59 Present: 2:44; 5:14; 10:43; 13:39; 22:19; perfect: 15:5; 18:27; 19:18; 21:20, 25.

60 Morgan, *Faith*, 235.

61 G. Barth, "πίστις, πιστεύω," *EDNT* 3:92; "πιστεύω," BDAG 816, §2; Morgan, *Faith*, 123–24, 137–41.

62 Wright, *Jesus*, 259–63; Trebilco, *Self-designations*, 90–99; Morgan, *Faith*, 350–52.

63 Trebilco, *Self-designations*, 72–90; Morgan, *Faith*, esp. 212–306.

with ἐπὶ τὸ αὐτό, "together," indicating that ἐν ἐκκλησίᾳ denotes the community rather than the place where the community meets).[64] Bruce suggests that they may have formed themselves into a messianic synagogue.[65]

εἶχον ἅπαντα κοινά, "they used to hold all things as common," and the following clause (v. 46) implies that the handling of possessions was emblematic of the earliest believers' fellowship.[66] Luke does not portray a primitive "communism" among the first believers, for this statement simply portrays them holding their possessions loosely, as in trust from God, echoing the biblical view that everything is truly owned by God and held in stewardship by God's human vicegerents (e.g., Ps 24:1; Gen 1:26–28).[67] The believers' attitude was that their possessions were not their own but available to others as needed. There is no evidence in Acts that believers were *required* to contribute all of their possessions to a common pool;[68] rather, owners regularly sold property (v. 45), and some continued to own homes (e.g., 12:12).[69] Thus the believers contrast with the Essenes, who practised compulsory common ownership of possessions as part of a two-stage membership (Josephus, *J.W.* 2.8.3 §122; 1QS VI, 19–25; IX, 8–9).[70] The believers' community life involves a reversal of normal human rivalry for resources and avoids the way that "legislated sharing" generally produces a division of "insiders" and "outsiders."[71]

45 τὰ κτήματα καὶ τὰς ὑπάρξεις ἐπίπρασκον, "they used to sell possessions and belongings." The distinction between τὰ κτήματα "possessions" and τὰς ὑπάρξεις "belongings" may be between land or houses (cf. 5:1, 3; LXX Prov 31:16; Sir 28:24; 36:25; 51:21; Hos 2:17; Joel 1:11) and personal possessions (cf. LXX 2 Chr 35:7; Ezra 10:8; Ps 77:48; Prov 8:21; 13:11; 18:11; 19:14; 1 Macc 12:23), although the vagueness of the words and the fact that they met in homes (Acts 2:46) may suggest that Luke portrays the believers selling non-essentials that did not include their homes.[72] Luke does not write that they sold *all* their possessions, either here or in the parallel 4:34–35.[73] The portrait is not, as Hengel asserts, of an enthusiastic group who expect the end of the world at any time and thus treat property with complete abandon;[74] rather, members sold

64 Dupont, *Nouvelles*, 309. See also Bauckham, "Early."
65 *Acts* (1990), 132.
66 Johnson, *Function*, 184.
67 Walton, "Communism."
68 Haenchen, *Acts*, 192, contra Capper, "Context," 335–41.
69 Murphy-O'Connor, "Cenacle," 320, argues cogently that the Cenacle is the likely site of one such large home.
70 See Capper, "Community," 1744–51; Johnson, "Manual," 108–9. Greehy, "Community," offers a detailed comparison of practices of sharing possessions at Qumran and here, concluding that there is "a great difference" between them, such that Essene influence on the early believers is unlikely.
71 Wieser, "Community," 88.
72 Alexander, *Acts* (People's Bible), 37.
73 Theissen, "Liebeskommunismus," 698.
74 Hengel, *Property*, 32.

their possessions to meet specific needs, portrayed by the habitual imperfects ἐπίπρασκον, "they used to sell," and διεμέριζον, "they used to distribute."[75] This tense choice speaks against Capper's proposal that those joining the community were required to give all their possessions into the community's control.[76] The verb διεμέριζον, "they used to distribute," echoes God's distribution of the tongues of fire at Pentecost (2:3, same verb), thus portraying the community's generosity and gift giving as in line with God's.[77] In response to God's generosity to them in Jesus, they held their possessions loosely as stewards of the gifts of God and thus were ready and willing to share them with those in need.[78] These specific needs were most likely within the believing community and may have arisen from three sources: first, the apostles themselves were mostly Galilean and thus lacked immediate family members in Jerusalem, who would have been their normal support network; secondly, those who became believers may have been abandoned by their family, thus losing their main means of support; and thirdly, widows and orphans who became believers may have been rejected by non-believing Jews and thus rendered ineligible for charitable support from synagogues and other Jewish bodies.

The readiness to share with others in need is a theme of Greco-Roman writers: κοινὰ τὰ φίλων, "friends have all things common," was proverbial;[79] the ancient ideal of the city included common ownership;[80] and the Pythagoreans were known for their sharing of goods[81] (see *Comment* on 4:32).[82] However, Kim notes that benefaction systems in Greco-Roman society were based on reciprocity and took place only among élites, whereas the believers' sharing came from altruism and took place between wealthy and poor members of the community.[83] Luke thus portrays the believers as fulfilling and exceeding the highest ideals of Greco-Roman societies through the enabling of God's Holy Spirit (cf. Tertullian, *Apol.* 39.5–6, 11a).

In a Jewish setting, καθότι ἄν τις χρείαν εἶχεν, "as anyone had need," echoes Deut 15:4, "There shall not be a needy person among you," an echo that becomes clearer and louder in 4:34. The Qumran community practised compulsory sharing of possessions,[84] and also considered themselves a community

---

75 Lake, *BegC*, 5:140; Peterson, *Engaging*, 154.
76 With Hays, *Ethics*, 198–99; contra Capper, "Context," 337–41.
77 Griffiths, "Spirit," 177.
78 Walton, "Communism," 105.
79 E.g., Aristotle, *Eth. nic.* 9.8.2; *Pol.* 1263A; Plato, *Resp.* 449C; Plutarch, *Mor.* 767E; Philo, *Abraham* 235.
80 E.g., Plato, *Resp.* 420C–422D; 462B–464A; Seneca, *Ep.* 90.38.
81 Iamblichus, *Vit. Pyth.* 30.168; see Gregson, *Everything*, 75–77.
82 See the sources discussed in Hume, *Community*, 44–77; Mealand, "Community," 97–98; Talbert, *Reading Acts*, 48; Dupont, *Salvation*, 87–91; Johnson, *Acts*, 62.
83 Kim, *Stewardship*, 282; see 253–77 for helpful survey of Greco-Roman practices.
84 1QS V, 1–3, 14–16, 20; VI, 17–22, 24–25; VII, 24–25; VIII, 22–23; IX, 3–11; CD IX, 10–15; X, 18–20; XII, 6–7; XIII, 14–15; XIV, 20; XX, 7.

of the Spirit.[85] By contrast, rabbinic Judaism seems not to have seen sharing possessions as something to aim at (e.g., m. ʾAbot 5:10) (see *Comment* on 4:34–35).[86] Similarly, in the Greco-Roman world, people were highly selective in those they shared possessions with, focusing on those who were worthy or deserving and who could repay them in some way.[87]

46 The daily (καθ' ἡμέραν) meetings of the believers take two forms: they meet ὁμοθυμαδόν ἐν τῷ ἱερῷ, "together in the temple," where there was enough space for everyone to be present, and κατ' οἶκον, "in homes" (cf. Rom 16:5; 1 Cor 16:19; Col 4:15; Phlm 2), for more intimate gatherings.[88] ὁμοθυμαδόν, here "together," can have a fuller sense that denotes the inner unity of the group (e.g., 1:14; 4:24; 5:12), but the contrast with κατ' οἶκον, "in homes," suggests that it denotes shared location here.[89] Wendel proposes that the structure of the Greek implies that the meals took place both in the temple and in homes: the two forms of meeting are both denoted by participial clauses connected by τε . . . τε, "both . . . and," thus both participial clauses are dependent on μετελάμβανον τροφῆς, "they shared food."[90] Such an inclusive "open table" policy echoes Jesus's willingness to welcome sinners to shared meals, scandalizing the Pharisees and other Jewish authorities (e.g., Luke 15:1–2; 7:37–39; 14:12–14).[91] If so, the "public" meals would have an evangelistic impact, as non-believing Jews could join in the meals and begin to experience the life of the new community (cf. m. Bek. 4:1, citing Deut 15:20; m. Pesaḥ 10:6).[92] Elkanah and his family eating at the shrine (1 Sam 1:3–5) models eating the sacrificer's portion of a sacrificial animal at the place of sacrifice (see also the rule about consuming the meat from the purification and reparation offerings within a short time, Lev 7:15–18[93]).

The denotation of ἱερόν, "temple," is the temple courts, as opposed to ναός, which Luke uses for the shrine within the temple (Luke 1:9, 21, 22; 23:45).[94] Luke repeatedly reports the believers' presence in the temple courts in the early chapters of Acts (3:1–3, 8, 10, 11; 5:12, 20–21, 25, 42; also Luke 24:53) before the persecution that arose because of Stephen (Acts 8:1). The temple gatherings almost certainly included participation in the temple worship;[95] the temple would be a natural center for those who believed Jesus to be Israel's Messiah (see *Comment* on 3:1). The fact that the believers regularly met in

85 1QS IX, 3–4; Wenk, *Power*, 105, 265–68.
86 Johnson, *Acts*, 59.
87 See the full discussion of Barclay, *Gift*, 24–51.
88 Barrett, *Acts*, 1:170; contra Jeremias, *Jerusalem*, 131n20, who proposes that κατ' οἶκον indicates that the believers had their own meeting house.
89 Walton, "Ὁμοθυμαδόν," 99; contra Johnson, *Acts*, 59.
90 Wendel, *Gemeinde*, 183–86.
91 Helpful discussion of meals in Jesus's ministry: Borg, *Conflict* (rev. ed.), 98–109.
92 Wendel, *Gemeinde*, 219–20.
93 Discussion: Wenham, *Leviticus*, 124.
94 Walton, "Tale," 135–36.
95 Degenhardt, *Lukas*, 167.

Solomon's Portico (5:12; cf. 3:11), a large, covered area, suggests that they also had their own gatherings within the temple courts and that these were an occasion for the apostles to teach the whole group in ways that were not possible in private homes. In their presence in and use of the temple, they imitate Jesus (Luke 2:46; 20:1; 21:5, 37, 38; 22:52–53). Johnson may be right to see the temple's "last authentic role" as being the place where the apostles proclaim the message about Jesus.[96]

κλῶντές . . . ἄρτον . . . μετελάμβανον τροφῆς, "breaking . . . bread . . . they shared in food." The meetings included actual meals, not merely symbolic eating of small amounts; τροφῆς denotes "meals."[97] It was in that context that the symbolic action of breaking bread to remember the Lord took place (see *Comment* on v. 42). Houses become a critically important location for the believers' meetings throughout Acts, thus contrasting with the requirement of special buildings such as the temple (e.g., 9:39–41; 10:1–48; 12:12; 20:7–12).[98]

As they eat and drink together, they are characterized by "joy," ἀγαλλιάσει—not a Lukan retrojection from his own day to the earliest period[99] but evidence that the resurrection and the coming of the Spirit were bringing the believers the firstfruits of the messianic age, "an anticipated experience of the parousia,"[100] and resulting in this joy (cf. joy resulting from the Philippian jailer's conversion, 16:34). Joy is also a fascinating contrast with the tensions apparent at the apostles' meal gathering for the Last Supper (Luke 22:24).[101]

ἀφελότητι, "singleness," is a rare word; this is its only NT use. The cognate ἁπλότης, "simplicity, sincerity," is found in Paul,[102] and that is likely the sense here, denoting the unmixed (and hence, "simple" or "pure") desires of the believers.

47 αἰνοῦντες τὸν θεόν, "praising God," is a characteristic Lukan response to God's action (Luke 2:13, 20; 18:43; 19:37; Acts 3:8, 9), although it is relatively rare for Luke to report praise and thanks to God in Christian meetings. More typically, Luke speaks of teaching, fellowship, and prayer.[103]

τὸν λαόν, "the people," here, as normally in LXX, means the people of Israel, as opposed to other nations (e.g., Exod 12:33). Jervell highlights the way Luke uses this term to indicate the continuity of the believing community with Israel and that there continue to be large numbers of Jewish people who become

96 Johnson, *Function*, 188–89. On the temple, see the helpful discussions of the structure of the buildings in Schnabel, *Mission*, 1:418–19; Sanders, *Judaism*, 51–72; Ritmeyer and Ritmeyer, *Ritual*, 10–28 (with illustrations).

97 Haenchen, *Acts*, 192.

98 See Walton, "Tale," 146–48.

99 Contra Barrett, *Acts*, 1:171.

100 Fuller, *Foundations*, 157. Cf. 13:52; Luke 1:14, 44, 47; and LXX Pss 9:3 (EVV 2); 13:7 (MT 14:7); 19:6 (MT 20:6; EVV 20:5); 20:2 (MT 21:2; EVV 21:1); 30:8 (MT 31:8; EVV 31:7); 47:12 (MT 48:12; EVV 48:11); 52:7 (MT 53:7; EVV 53:6); 125:2, 5, 6 (MT/EVV 126:2, 5, 6).

101 Hume, *Community*, 108, 117

102 Rom 12:8; 2 Cor 1:12; 8:2; 9:11,13; 11:3; Eph 6:5; Col 3:22; cf. LXX 1 Chr 29:17; Wis 1:1.

103 Marshall, *Acts* (TNTC), 85–86; cf. Marshall, "Worship," 220–23.

believers throughout Acts (2:41; 4:4; 5:14; 6:1, 7; 9:42; 12:24; 13:43; 14:1; 17:10–12; 21:20).[104] It is not until later that opposition from Jewish people occurs.

ὁ δὲ κύριος προσετίθει τοὺς σῳζομένους καθ' ἡμέραν, "Every day the Lord was adding . . . those being saved." The designation as τοὺς σῳζομένους, "those being saved," recalls the Joel quotation in Peter's speech—these are the people who call on the Lord's name (2:21)[105]—and also Peter's call to respond: they are being saved from "this crooked generation" (v. 40). As the believers meet daily with one another (v. 46), so the Lord daily meets with people and brings them into the community of salvation. The divine initiative in sending the Spirit is here reflected in the divine initiative in expanding the community of salvation—a major Lukan theme that will be seen repeatedly in the rest of Acts (e.g., 8:26, 29; 10:3–6, 9–16, 19–20; 11:12, 15–18; 13:2, 48; 15:7–9). Luke's use of ὁ . . . κύριος, "the . . . Lord," is flexible; in 2:21–22 "the Lord" of Joel 2 is identified as Jesus, and Acts 2:36 speaks of Jesus as Lord. In this context, where Luke twice speaks of "God" and "the Lord" in the same sentence as apparently different figures (2:36, 47; cf. 5:14; 11:24), it is most likely that Jesus is in mind as the Lord who produces the growth in numbers.[106]

ἐπὶ τὸ αὐτό, "their group," rather than "to their number,"[107] for it is more likely to hear the echo of the expression ἐπὶ τὸ αὐτό from v. 44, where it denotes the togetherness of the body of believers.[108] The parallel between συνερχομένων ὑμῶν ἐν ἐκκλησίᾳ, "when you meet as an assembly," and συνερχομένων . . . ὑμῶν ἐπὶ τὸ αὐτό, "when you meet together," (1 Cor 11:18, 20) suggests that ἐπὶ τὸ αὐτό there and here refers to the believers' togetherness as a group. ἐπὶ τὸ αὐτό appropriately closes the summary by reiterating the note of the unity of the group, a central theme of this section.

Explanation

The believers' life following the tumultuous event of Pentecost is presented in glowing and dynamic terms, highlighting seven key features, which present the community's life as a norm for Luke's (believing) readers.

First and foremost, *the believers are bound together into a community,* described uniquely in Acts as "fellowship" (v. 42), denoting both that their life is shared together in daily meetings (v. 46) and that it involved sharing material resources. This sharing is not unnatural within Middle Eastern culture, but Luke presents

---

104 E.g., Jervell, *Theology*, 13–15.

105 With Meyer, "Self-Understanding," 38.

106 Cf. Dunn, "ΚΥΡΙΟΣ," 250; contrast Schneider, "Gott," 168, arguing that the "Lord" is God.

107 "ἐπί," BDAG 91, §1.c.β.

108 Discussion: Wilcox, *Semitisms*, 93–100; Payne, "Semitisms," 142; Black, *Aramaic*, 10; MHT, 2:473; Bauckham, "Early," 85–88; Burkitt, "Acts 2:47"; all contra Torrey, *Composition*, 10–14, who suggests that the phrase here represents a mistranslation of an Aramaic original meaning "strongly."

it in terms that echo the highest aspirations of both Jewish Scripture and Greco-Roman writings (vv. 44–45 with 4:32–35). The believers include diaspora Jews who remained in Jerusalem after Pentecost (2:9–11), Galilean disciples and apostles, and urban Jerusalemites, both wealthy and poor. This diversity highlights a contrast with Greco-Roman approaches to sharing possessions, for the latter were limited to those of equal (normally high) social status—here the poor's needs are met through their wealthier sisters and brothers.

Secondly, *the teaching of the risen Jesus's authorized representatives, the apostles* (v. 42), binds their life together. This teaching probably takes place when the larger company of believers meets in the temple courts (v. 46). The apostles formed the core of the "waiting" group before Pentecost (1:13) and are restored to their full, highly symbolic, number of twelve (1:15–26), portraying the new community as Israel renewed and restored, and now their teaching is a core activity of this community. Through their teaching the new believers, who may not have known or heard Jesus in person, are able to learn the teaching of the one whose death has been overturned by God (2:22–24, 33) and to be instructed in what it means to live with him as Messiah and Lord (2:36) in the community of the Spirit (2:33, 38). The apostles' assessment, as the divinely appointed leaders, will be crucial to future developments in the life of the believing community (e.g., 4:35; 6:2–6; 8:14; 9:26–27; 15:2, 6); they will be the bedrock of the restored Israel (cf. Luke 22:28–30).

Thirdly, *joyful shared meals* are an expression of the common life of the believers, particularly in homes (v. 46) and probably including meals in the temple courts (see *Comment* on v. 46); if so, this echoes the open table practised by Jesus during his earthly ministry (cf. Luke 15:1–2) and has an evangelistic impact, especially if not-yet-believers are welcomed to share such public meals. These meals include the symbolic action of "breaking bread" (Acts 2:42, 46), an action that recalls Jesus's reinterpretation of the Passover meal concerning his death (Luke 22:14–20) and is thus most likely to be eucharistic. At this stage of the community's development the eucharistic actions are not separated from an actual meal, a situation that continues in the Pauline communities (1 Cor 11:17–34).

Fourthly, *sharing possessions* is emblematic of the community's life (vv. 44–45). The believers show a radical readiness to share their possessions with other believers who are in need. They hold their possessions lightly as stewards of God's good gifts. There is no trace here of a dualistic rejection of the material world; rather, the way believers handle material objects and money reflects their understanding of the generosity of God toward them in Christ and by the Spirit. In this the believers provide for those in need, as opposed to the Greco-Roman model, where possessions were shared only among those of high social status. To share in this way fulfills the aspirations of Scripture, that among God's people no one should be in need (Deut 15:4).

Fifthly, *the believers pray*, both in the regular temple prayers (Acts 2:46; cf.

3:1) and their own community prayers, the two being summed up as "the prayers" (2:42). They are a messianic renewal movement within Judaism, not a separate body, for they do not withdraw from temple worship—their self-perception would be as Israel renewed or reconstituted rather than a new Israel. Nevertheless, their prayers may well be addressed to Jesus as Lord (cf. 2:36), the one on whom people call in baptism (see *Comment* on 2:38), and this represents a dramatic new development in Jewish engagement with YHWH. Prayer will continue to be the first resort of the believers and a key way of seeking God's purpose and will (e.g., 3:1; 4:24–31; 7:59; 12:5, 12).

Sixthly, *the fellowship of the believers embraces others* rather than excluding them. Acts 2:47 notes both the high regard in which the believers are held and the associated (and doubtless causally connected) growth of the community. Verse 46 suggests that the believers held meals in the temple courts as well as in homes; such meals were inclusive after the model of Jesus's own practice and communicated the central beliefs of the community concerning Jesus, not least as the action of "breaking bread" was performed and explained.

Finally, and crucially, *the whole is the work of God.* The believers have come to faith and received the gift of the Spirit (2:38), and the Spirit's power is doubtless to be seen in the community's life—a life that fulfills the divine aspirations of Scripture that none among God's people will be in need (e.g., Deut 15:4, alluded to in Acts 2:45 and echoed more explicitly in 4:34). The growth of the community is explicitly stated to be the work of God (2:47), a work of "the Lord," who (in light of 2:21–22, 36) may well be Jesus—he is continuing to act and teach as he had done in his earthly ministry (cf. 1:1).

Reflecting on this passage and 4:34–35 in commenting on John 8:26–27, Augustine makes the link of the life and unity of the community with the life and unity of God more explicit:

> If, as they drew near to God, those many souls became, in the power of love, but one soul and these many hearts but one heart, what must the very source of love effect between the Father and the Son? Is not the Trinity for even greater reasons, but one God? . . . If the love of God poured forth in our hearts by the Holy Spirit, who is given to us, is able to make of many souls but one soul and of many hearts but one heart, how much more are the Father and the Son and Holy Spirit but one God, one Light, one Principle?" (*Tract. Ev. Jo.* 39.5 [Martin & Smith])

II. The Mission in Jerusalem (3:1–8:3)

A. Jesus Heals—And Its Consequences (3:1–4:31)

1. Jesus Heals the Man at the Beautiful Gate (3:1–10)

Bibliography

Bauckham, R. "Restoration." **Busch, A.** 'Presence." **Butticaz, S. D.** "Actes 3,1–26." **Conzelmann, H.** *Theology*, 170–206. **Cowton, C. J.** "Alms." **Funk, R. W.** *Poetics*, 59–74. **Hamm, D., SJ.** "Acts 3,1–10." ———. "Acts 3:12–26." ———. "Sign." ———. "Tamid." **Jervell, J.** *Theology*, 23–25. **Johnson, L. T.** *Function*, 190–91. **Lake, K.** "The Beautiful Gate," *BegC*, 5:479–86. **Marconi, G.** "History." **Myllykowski, M.** "Being," 166. **O'Reilly, L.** *Word*, 122–60. **Olyan, S. M.** "Anyone." **Parsons, M. C.** "Character." ———. *Body*, 109–22. **Pilch, J. J.** *Visions*, 39–43. **Roth, S. J.** *Blind*. **Sanders, E. P.** *Judaism*, 308–13. **Speckman, M. T.** "Healing," esp. 102–6. **Strelan, R.** "Stares." **Warrington, K.** "Acts." **Williams, B. E.** *Miracle*, 56–61. **Wynn, K. H.** "Disability."

Translation

1 Peter and John were going up to the temple at the hour of prayer,[a] the ninth hour.
2 A man who suffered from a congenital disability of his legs[b] used to be carried and placed[c] day by day by the temple gate known as "Beautiful"[d] in order to ask[e] for alms from those entering the temple.[f]
3 When he saw[g] Peter and John about to enter[h] the temple, he began asking to receive alms.
4 Peter, together with John, looked intently[i] at him and said, "Look[j] at us."
5 He[k] focused his attention[l] on them, expecting to receive something from them.
6 Peter said, "Silver and gold I do not possess;[m] but what I do have, this I give to you: in the name of Jesus Messiah the Nazarene,[n] walk!"
7 Taking him by the right hand,[o] he lifted him up. Immediately[p] his feet and ankles were made strong;
8 he leapt up, stood, and began walking, and entered the temple with them while walking and leaping and[q] praising God.
9 All the people saw him walking and praising God,
10 and they kept recognizing[r] him as the one who sat asking for alms at the Beautiful Gate of the temple—and they were filled with wonder and amazement[s] at what had happened to him.

Notes

a. D is clearer on the timing of events: it begins the sentence Ἐν δὲ ταῖς ἡμέραις ταύταις, "in those days," and has τὸ δειλινόν, "the afternoon," before ἐπὶ τὴν ὥραν, "at the hour," underlining that it is the time of the afternoon sacrifice.

b. τις ἀνὴρ χωλὸς ἐκ κοιλίας μητρὸς αὐτοῦ ὑπάρχων, "a certain man, being lame from his mother's womb"; the translation reflects a concern to portray people with disabilities as *people* first (rather as Luke distinguishes the man from his disability, Williams, *Miracle*, 57) instead of using terms such as "a cripple," which are seen as derogatory; Wynn, "Disability", esp. 406.

c. ἐβαστάζετο . . . ἐτίθουν, "he used to be carried . . . they used to place," impf. for habitual actions (in the case of ἐβαστάζετο, *pace* Haenchen, *Acts*, 198n11; Wallace, 544); ἐτίθουν is impersonal.

d. Ὡραίαν, "Beautiful," is a meaning only attested in biblical Greek; cf., e.g., LXX Gen 2:9; 3:6; 26:7, where it translates Heb. words for "pleasant to the senses." For other meanings, see "ὡραία," LSJ.

e. Gen. art. inf. τοῦ αἰτεῖν expressing purpose, "in order to ask."

f. D* reads παρ' αὐτῶν, "from them," thus portraying the man as waiting specifically for Peter and John; Rius-Camps and Read-Heimerdinger, *Message*, 1:206.

g. D reads οὗτος ἀτενίσας τοῖς ὀφθαλμοῖς αὐτοῦ καὶ ἰδών, "this man fixed his eyes and saw." In this story D uses ἀτενίζω only for the man and never for Peter and John, and has it three times (vv. 3, 4, 5), by contrast with only once in 𝔓[74] ℵ B.

h. μέλλοντας εἰσιέναι, "being about to enter"; ptc. of μέλλω, "be about to," + inf., a Lukanism; Schneider, *Apostelgeschichte*, 1:300n33.

i. D reads ἐμβλέψας, "they saw"; perhaps "they considered"; Rius-Camps and Read-Heimerdinger, *Message*, 1:207.

j. D reads ἀτένισον, "look intently."

k. Art. ὁ with δέ acting as per. pron., "he" (Wallace, 211–12); δέ signals switch of subject; Levinsohn, *Connections*, 87–89.

l. ἐπεῖχεν, impf., "he focused his attention," "ἐπέχω," BDAG 362, §2; D reads ἀτενίσας, "he fixed his eyes."

m. οὐχ ὑπάρχει μοι, lit., "do not belong to me"; cf. "ὑπάρχω," BDAG, 1029, §1.

n. NA[28]/UBS[5] include ἔγειρε καί, "rise and," in square brackets, indicating some doubt about their place in the text (the reading is graded C in UBS[5]). These words are not found in ℵ B D sa, normally reckoned to be a powerful combination of primary Alexandrian (ℵ B) and Western (D) witnesses; they are read by A C E Ψ 095 33 1739 𝔐 lat syr mae bo Ir[lat] Cyp (Eus) Lcf. Given the weight of MSS that lack these words, it seems less likely that they were omitted—for Peter goes on to take the man's hand and raise him up (v. 7), rendering these words rather superfluous—and more likely that they were added under the influence of Luke 5:23, where Jesus heals a man with a similar illness; *pace* Johnson, Acts, 66.

o. τῆς δεξιᾶς χειρός, "by the right hand," gen. with πιάζω, "take hold of"; Wallace, 131–32; "πιάζω," BDAG 812, §1.

p. παραχρῆμα, "immediately," a Lukan favorite (16x Luke-Acts; in NT otherwise only at Matt 21:19, 20); note its use in the parallel healing in Luke 5:25.

q. D mae lack περιπατῶν καὶ ἁλλόμενος καί, "walking and leaping and," with the effect that the focus is on the fact that the man can now enter the temple for worship; Rius-Camps and Read-Heimerdinger, *Message*, 1:208.

r. ἐπεγίνωσκον, distributive impf. for various people performing the same action, "they kept recognizing"; Wallace, 547; McKay, §4.3.3.

s. θάμβους καὶ ἐκστάσεως, "wonder and amazement," both Lukanisms; former found only in Luke-Acts; Acts has 5 of 7 NT uses in Luke-Acts.

Form/Structure/Setting

Form. The healing story utilizes a pattern familiar from form criticism of the Gospels,[1] first introducing the agents of healing (v. 1, Peter and John), then the sick person, together with a description of the illness (v. 2). The circumstances of the healing follow, including a description of the means of

1 Conzelmann, *Acts*, 25.

healing—Peter's words in response to his request for help—and Peter helping him to his feet (vv. 3–7). Luke then highlights the results, for the man who was healed, as he walks and leaps and praises God (v. 8), and for the onlookers, who characteristically respond with amazement (vv. 9–10).

O'Reilly observes that much of the vocabulary of the story is Lukan, although agreeing with Schneider that the story has a traditional basis.[2] Unless one adopts the radical skepticism of Lüdemann ("Those who are lame from their childhood are [unfortunately] not made whole again"),[3] there is no good reason to doubt that this kind of remarkable event could and did occur among the earliest Christians.[4]

Some think the mention of John, especially in v. 4, suggests he has been added to a story that did not originally contain him.[5] However, the earliest Jesus followers seem to have worked in twos (Luke 10:1), and John is elsewhere associated in this way with Peter (22:8; Acts 4:13, 19; 8:14). Thus, the basis for the inclusion of John is most probably traditional.

Structure. The participants and temporal markers in each sub-scene highlight the structure of this story.[6]

The story is introduced (2:1–2) by bringing the participants together (Peter and John, the man) at the same time (the hour of prayer, the ninth hour) in the same place (the Beautiful Gate of the temple).

A series of actions mark the heart of the story (vv. 3–7), the grammatical subject bouncing between the participants to highlight interaction and exchange between them:

v. 3 *the man* saw (ἰδών) and began asking (ἠρώτα)
    v. 4 *Peter and John* looked (ἀτενίσας) and spoke (εἶπεν)
v. 5 *the man* looked (ἐπεῖχεν) and expected (προσδοκῶν)
    vv. 6–7a *Peter* spoke (εἶπεν), took hold (πιάσας), and lifted (ἤγειρεν)
v. 7b *the man's* feet and ankles were made strong (ἐστερεώθησαν)

The story concludes (vv. 8–10) with the man rising (with recapitulation of his healing—not for nothing does Conzelmann find v. 8 "overloaded"![7]) and entering the temple (shift of scene) with Peter and John (v. 8), where they encounter new participants (πᾶς ὁ λαός, "all the people," v. 9) who recognize and validate his healing. The healing is summarized, now as a completed event of the past (v. 10, note the perfect tense of τῷ συμβεβηκότι, "the thing

2 O'Reilly, *Word*, 125–26; Schneider, *Apostelgeschichte*, 1:297.
3 Lüdemann, *Early Christianity*, 54.
4 With Dunn, *Acts*, 38.
5 E.g., Barrett, *Acts*, 1:175; Haenchen, *Acts*, 198n1, 199.
6 For what follows, see the helpful formalist analysis in Funk, *Poetics*, 59–74.
7 Conzelmann, *Acts*, 26.

which had happened"). Verse 11 then begins the next development in a new location, τῇ στοᾷ τῇ καλουμένῃ Σολομῶντος, "Solomon's portico."

Luke here frequently uses verb tenses that tell a vivid story that carries us along as readers and draws us in, rather like watching a video recording of an event. There is a predominance of continuous verb tenses: of the nineteen indicative verbs, three are present and eight imperfect (63%), and of the fifteen participles, twelve are present (80%)—in both cases a higher proportion are "continuous" by comparison with NT narrative more generally (45% of indicatives are present or imperfect; 48% of participles are present) and Luke-Acts in particular (respectively 40% and 48%). The proportion of imperfect indicatives is particularly high (in NT narrative 14% of indicatives; in Luke-Acts 18%; here 42%). The imperfect is used to describe habitual events (e.g., ἐτίθουν, "he used to be put," v. 2), events that begin and then continue for some time (the inceptive imperfect, e.g., περιεπάτει, "he began to walk," v. 8), events in process of happening (e.g., ἀνέβαινον, "they were going up," v. 1), and repeated events (e.g., the distributive imperfect ἐπεγίνωσκον, "they kept recognizing," v. 10).

Luke clearly focuses attention on this story, telling it in greater detail than most other healings in Acts (cf., e.g., 6:8; 8:7; 9:17–18, 33–34). In some ways it is presented as typical, in parallel fashion to Peter's speech in Acts 2.[8] However, it is certainly not that Luke knows of few such healings, as 5:16 (οἵτινες ἐθεραπεύοντο ἅπαντες, "they were all being healed") makes clear—by that phrase Luke indicates that he sees such healings as a natural outflow of the coming of the Spirit. It seems most likely that Luke focuses attention on this healing because it indicates that the prophesied restoration of Israel is in process of happening: it happens at the very heart of Judaism, the temple (the Beautiful Gate is mentioned twice, vv. 2, 10, and τὸ ἱερόν, "the temple," itself six times, vv. 1, 2 [twice], 3, 8, 10), and there are several significant pieces of symbolism in the way Luke presents the story.[9]

Setting. As to connections with the previous section, this story gives a specific example of believers going to the temple to pray (2:46), and the healing of the man is an example of the "signs and wonders" announced in the Pentecost speech and narrative (2:19, 43).[10]

The story also has links both forwards within Acts and backwards to the Gospel.[11] In Acts 14:8–11, a man whose disability is described in the same terms as the man here (he is τις ἀνὴρ . . . χωλὸς ἐκ κοιλίας μητρὸς αὐτοῦ, "a certain man . . . lame from his mother's womb," 14:8, exactly the same phrase as in 3:2) is healed in a gentile (indeed, pagan) setting in Lystra through Paul.

8 O'Reilly, *Word*, 124–25.
9 See below and Hamm, "Acts 3,1–10."
10 With Tannehill, *Unity*, 2:48, among many others.
11 O'Reilly, *Word*, 129–34.

It has frequently been suggested that Luke deliberately parallels Peter and Paul by providing similar healings.[12] The specific parallel of these Petrine and Pauline healings in (respectively) Jewish and gentile contexts may be part of Luke's pattern of the gospel message going first to Jews and then to gentiles. Luke 5:17–26 provides a further parallel, where Jesus heals a man with a similar disability: he is paralyzed and carried by friends (v. 18, cf. Acts 3:2; 14:8). There are a number of parallels of language (sometimes using synonyms) among these three stories,[13] although a significant major difference is that both Peter and Paul deny that the power derives from them (3:6, 12; 14:15), whereas Jesus heals on his own authority (Luke 5:24). The triple parallelism thus suggests that Luke is presenting both Peter and Paul as imitating the model provided by their Master, from whom the power to heal is derived.[14]

A further forward link, although more significant for the apostles' appearance before the Sanhedrin (4:1–22), is to 5:12–16, where further "signs and wonders" are done through the apostles (5:12, 14–16), with the believers meeting in Solomon's Portico (5:12); arrest and a further appearance before the Sanhedrin result (5:17–41). Luke is presenting a pattern of God acting among and through the believing community, with a consistent response of persecution by the Jewish authorities. (See on 4:1–22; 5:12–16, 17–42.)

Comment

1 Luke presents his "cast" in vv. 1–2: first come Peter and John, who are named and then are the subject of the first main verb, ἀνέβαινον, "they were going up." This verb is a natural choice here, since the Temple Mount is significantly higher than other parts of the city. On the temple, see *Comment* on 2:46.

ἐπὶ τὴν ὥραν τῆς προσευχῆς τὴν ἐνάτην, "at the hour of prayer, the ninth [hour]," indicates a precise time for this incident: the ninth hour in Jewish reckoning—3 p.m. in our reckoning—was a time of sacrifice (Dan 9:21; Jdt 9:1; Josephus, *Ant.* 14.4.3 §65), and this indicates that the early community participate in the temple rites[15]—a hint that Luke has not imposed on his material a later view that the temple was redundant in the light of the death of Jesus (contrast, e.g., Heb 10:1–18). Indeed, this burnt offering was an atoning sacrifice, one of two daily sacrifices of a lamb, collectively known as the *Tamid*, the other being offered in the morning.[16] At this stage of the Jesus-community's history there was not an expectation of a separation from Judaism, although Luke's appellation "the hour *of prayer* (τῆς προσευχῆς)" may show his Christian

12 E.g., Rackham, *Acts*, 48, xlvii–l; for discussion of the general issue of parallelism, see Walton, *Leadership*, 34–51.
13 See table, Schneider, *Apostelgeschichte*, 1:307.
14 Rackham, *Acts*, xlix.
15 *Pace* Calvin, *Acts*, 1:92.
16 Exod 29:38–42; Num 28:1–8; Josephus, *Ant.* 14.4.3 §65; m. Tamid; Schürer 2:300–307.

perspective on the temple as a place where valid prayer can take place, but not valid sacrifice.[17] The Jewish practices of the Jesus-community chime in with Luke's focus on the debate about who reads Scripture correctly, the Jesus followers or the Jewish Jerusalem leadership (e.g., note use of Scripture in 2:17–21; 25–28, 31, 34; 4:11, 25–26). Luke's underlining of the Jewish credentials of the apostles through their participation in temple worship shows them to be the true Jews who are experiencing the fulfillment of the Scriptures and, indeed, the reality to which the temple itself points (cf. 7:44–53). The inability of temple practice to bring healing to the man—and his exclusion from the temple because of his disability (see below)—hints at the debate over the temple that will emerge fully in Stephen's speech (7:2–53).[18] Myllykoski acutely observes, "From among many miracles that could open the public activity of the apostles, Luke has chosen this one that takes place as a challenging intrusion into the domain of the temple authorities who become the enemies of the believers."[19]

2 Although χωλός, "lame," can also be used for upper limb disabilities;[20] the fact that the man had to be carried to his place each day shows that it here denotes a disability of the lower limb(s). The man's passivity is emphasized by this word and the ongoing aspect of the imperfect tenses of ἐβαστάζετο, "he used to be carried," and ετίθουν, "they used to place."[21] The choice of χωλός, "lame," is notable for two reasons.

First, people with such disabilities were not permitted to take part as priests in Israel's worship (Lev 21:16–23) and may not have been allowed to enter the shrine of the temple (so 2 Sam 5:8 LXX;[22] cf. Deut 23:2 LXX [EVV 23:1]). Matthew 21:14 indicates that people with visual impairment or lameness were permitted into some areas of the temple courts, although the later rabbinic source m. Menaḥ. 9:8 does not include men who are lame among those not permitted to lay hands on a sacrificial animal,[23] and m. Ḥag. 1:1 lists people who are lame as those excused from the requirement to appear before the Lord; cf. the exclusion of people with disabilities from full membership of the Qumran community (e.g., 1QSa II, 5–6; 11Q19 [Temple] XLV, 12–14). Similarly, animals with disabilities were not acceptable as offerings (Deut 15:21).

However, people who were lame were proverbially weak (2 Sam 5:6; 9:3, 8), and to help them was considered commendable (Job 29:15). A key scriptural promise, relevant here, was that a time would come when God would restore people with such disabilities so that they would "leap like a deer" (Isa 35:6, where LXX has χωλός, "lame").[24] Cf. Mic 4:6, 7, also prophesying that the

17 Schneider, *Apostelgeschichte*, 1:299.
18 Cf. Gaventa, *Acts*, 119.
19 Myllykoski, "Being," 166.
20 "χωλός," BDAG 1093.
21 Marconi, "History," 171–72.
22 Discussion: Olyan, "Anyone."
23 Discussion: Jeremias, *Jerusalem*, 117–18.
24 See further Roth, *Blind*, 107–8.

Lord will assemble people who are lame as his faithful remnant; there, LXX has τὴν συντετριμμένην, "people who are crushed," rather than χωλός, "lame"; MT has הַצֹּלֵעָה (*hassōlēʿâ*), "people who limp." The link to the restoration of Israel theme here is thus made through the Heb. text rather than LXX, as Bauckham argues regularly happens in Luke 1–2.[25]

Secondly, in Luke 7:22 the expression χωλοὶ περιπατοῦσιν, "people who are lame walk," is part of Jesus's answer to the question from John's disciples as to whether Jesus is the coming one. The expression is part of a paraphrase of Isa 35:5–6 and recalls Luke 4:18. Luke 7:22 follows Jesus healing a man who is παραλελυμένος, "paralyzed," and thus unable to walk (Luke 5:17–26, quoting v. 18); so, Jesus's messianic restoration work includes healing people like this man. Further, in Luke 14:13 people who are lame are specified as part of a group who are to be invited to banquets, just as, in the immediately following parable, the master of the house replaces his reluctant dinner guests with (among others) people who are lame (Luke 14:21).[26] Roth observes that people who are lame, along with people who are visually impaired or poor, are stereotypical characters whose role is to highlight who Jesus is.[27] He argues that this passage utilizes the man who was lame similarly in order to present the apostles as prophets announcing Jesus's resurrection and demonstrating the power of God's Spirit and Jesus's name.[28] While this is true, the background of people with such disabilities being unable to take a full part in worship suggests that there is a strong "restoration of Israel" dimension to this story (see further *Comment* on v. 8).

ἐκ κοιλίας μητρὸς αὐτοῦ, "from his mother's womb," underlines the depth of the man's need, as do the facts that he has to come καθ' ἡμέραν, "day by day," to seek the worshipers' gifts and that he has to be carried—this is a person who cannot support himself and who is an outsider to Israel's worship, sitting on the outer limits of the temple at the hour of sacrifice.

The view that three in the afternoon would be unusually late for a beggar to arrive at the temple[29] misunderstands the way the habitual imperfects ἐβαστάζετο . . . ἐτίθουν, "he used to be carried . . . they used to place" (v. 2), are used.[30] Verses 2–3 are one sentence in Greek, and the central verb ἠρώτα, "he began to ask," does not appear until v. 3: the description in v. 2 is setting the scene for the man's request in v. 3. Further, Luke clearly presents the man as sitting (rather than being carried) when Peter helps him up (v. 7).[31] However, even if ἐβαστάζετο is to be taken as ongoing action, "he was being carried,"

25 Bauckham, "Restoration," 481–82.
26 See Green, *Luke*, 561.
27 Roth, *Blind*, 172–77, 179–83.
28 Roth, *Blind*, 210–11.
29 Haenchen, *Acts*, 198n11.
30 See *Note* c.
31 With Barrett, *Acts*, 1:179.

it would be natural for the man's friends to bring him at the time of peak "traffic," just before the afternoon sacrifice, so Haenchen's view of the tense need not lead to his skepticism about the timing.

τὴν θύραν τοῦ ἱεροῦ τὴν λεγομένην Ὡραίαν, "the gate of the temple known as 'Beautiful,'" is unique to this passage among our ancient sources about the temple. Two main possibilities have been suggested for identifying this gate. (i) The "Shushan" Gate, one of three gates on the east side of the outer wall of the temple area. On this gate there was a carving of the Persian city of Susa (m. Mid. 1.3), hence the name. Lake claims that this abbreviation stems at least from Prudentius in the fifth century AD (*Ditt.* 44).[32] However, Prudentius only says, "The gate of the Temple which men called the Beautiful still stands. It is the illustrious work of Solomon, but at that gate a greater work of Christ shone forth. For a lame man bidden by Peter's lips to rise was amazed to find his feet loosened and able to run" (Thomson, LCL), which is not strong support for the identification that Lake suggests. (ii) A brass gate called the Corinthian Gate by Josephus (*J.W.* 5.5.3 §§201–5) and the Nicanor Gate by the Mishnah (m. Mid. 1:4; 2:3, 5). Josephus (*J.W.* 5.5.3 §201) comments that this gate was finer than those covered in silver or gold, and the Mishnah (m. Mid. 2:3) record that a miracle had caused its brass to appear like gold. Our sources are not completely clear as to whether the brass gate stood between the Court of the Gentiles and the Court of the Women, or between the Court of the Women and the Court of Israel.[33]

Option (ii) is the view adopted by many scholars,[34] principally because the east side of the temple had a steep climb toward the temple mount and would thus be less likely to be used by those who came from much of the city (it would have been the natural route for those coming from the direction of the Mount of Olives). Hence (it is argued) a beggar would not choose to sit by the eastern gates but would sit near gates where the mass of people would enter. However, Cowton cogently observes that the distribution of likely entrants would affect the *distribution* of beggars at different gates (those where more entered would be likely to have more beggars) but not necessarily whether beggars gathered at a given gate or not.[35] Rather, the temple would be a natural place for beggars to beg (since giving alms is commendable in Judaism and those visiting the temple are likely to be relatively devout), and competition among beggars would mean that they spread themselves around the various gates: "a quieter gate might be economically attractive to an individual beggar, who might prosper by gaining a proportionately larger 'slice' of a smaller 'cake.'"[36] Thus the standard economic argument is flawed.

32 Lake, *BegC*, 5:480.
33 See Sanders, *Judaism*, 308–13, for plans.
34 Notably Schürer, 2:296; Jeremias, *Jerusalem*, 23n43; and the full discussion in *BegC*, 5:479–86.
35 Cowton, "Alms."
36 Cowton, "Alms," 476.

When Peter and John enter the temple with the man, the people run to them in Solomon's Portico (v. 11), which stands just within the eastern wall of the temple complex (Josephus, *J.W.* 5.5.1 §184); thus, to take the gate to be the Shushan Gate makes better sense of the movements presented here. Further, Luke's use of τὸ ἱερόν, "the temple," refers consistently to the wider temple complex (Luke 4:9; 19:45; Acts 2:46; 5:12); Luke reserves τὸ ναός, "the shrine," for the temple shrine proper (Luke 1:9, 21, 22; 23:45), again suggesting that he is presenting the gate as an entrance to the temple complex.[37] To take the gate to be the Nicanor/Corinthian Gate (on either view of its location) means that Peter, John, and the man must have doubled back to go to Solomon's Portico after the healing. The Western text has Peter and John leaving the temple in v. 11a and reentering (see *Notes* on v. 11), thus resolving this issue. That reading bears testimony to the natural understanding of v. 2 as presenting a gate on the outer wall of the temple complex. Thus, the most probable reading of Luke's presentation suggests that the "Beautiful Gate" is the Shushan Gate.

3 The beggar seeks ἐλεημοσύνην, "alms," from Peter and John. Contributing to the needy was considered commendable in Judaism and a duty for the faithful: almsgiving was reckoned one of the three pillars of Judaism.[38] However, the man's economic dependence on almsgiving was a denial of the Jubilee vision of Deut 15:4, where there were to be no needy people among God's people (cf. Acts 4:34 and *Comment* there)—indeed, Luke's Gospel presents Jesus as critical of: the merchants who, ironically, used the temple as a means of making money (Luke 19:45–46); those who impoverished widows while appearing outwardly devout (Luke 20:47); and the builders of the temple, who took from the poor to build a magnificent spectacle (Luke 21:1–6).[39] Hamm notes that the regular LXX sense of ἐλεημοσύνη is "mercy," particularly as a characteristic of YHWH (e.g., Pss 23:5 [MT 24:5]; 102:6 [MT 103:6]; Isa 1:27; 28:17; 59:16).[40] This word choice thus has a double entendre, presenting the man as seeking "alms" but instead receiving "mercy" from God who saves/heals him, restores him to Israel, and thereby removes him from the economic misery of begging. In particular, Isa 1:27[41] has a context of restoration-of-Israel imagery, thus suggesting strongly that the renewed community, represented by Peter and John, is the true people of God (see further on v. 8).

4 σὺν τῷ Ἰωάννῃ, "with John": see *Form/Structure/Setting.*

ἀτενίσας, "fixing their eyes," is a suggestive phrase. First, it seems likely that most visitors to the temple would not look *at* the beggars in this focused way; even if they gave them money, they would be unlikely to make eye contact

37 With Hamm, "Acts 3,1–10," 309–10; Schneider, *Apostelgeschichte,* 1:303.
38 Tobit 1:3, 16; 4:7, 10–11, 16; 12:8–9; 14:10–11; Sir 7:10; 12:3; 17:22; 29:12; 40:17, 24; cf. Acts 9:36; 10:2, 4, 31; 20:35; 24:17; m. ʾAbot 1:2.
39 With Spencer, *Acts,* 46.
40 Hamm, "Acts 3,1–10," 316.
41 Mistakenly cited by Hamm as 8:27.

with them. Thus, when Peter and John focus attention on the man in response to his request, they engage him as a person, a fellow human being, after the compassionate manner of Jesus engaging with those he healed (e.g., Luke 5:12–13; 7:13–14, 37–38, 44–50; 8:44–48; 13:10–13).[42]

Secondly, we can recognize that Peter has God-given insight before he speaks (Acts 3:4, 6) and acts (v. 7), but the results (v. 8) show that, not the choice of verb here (cf. the parallel Pauline healing in 14:9, where Luke is explicit about Paul's perception that the man had faith to be healed). The word does not imply entering an "altered state of consciousness" through a self-induced trance.[43] Strelan appears to confuse sense and reference in arguing that, because ἀτενίζω, "fix my eyes on," frequently *appears* in co-texts where divine epiphanies or power are being experienced, it *denotes* a particular form of "seeing." Rather than presenting the divine as being at the disposal of humans who enter the divine realm through trance or the like, Luke presents the divine as invading the human realm at God's initiative, sometimes—as here—through a human agent, but not always (e.g., 9:3–6; 10:3–6, 10–16).

βλέψον εἰς ἡμᾶς, "Look at us!," commands Peter, by contrast with Moses's reaction on YHWH appearing to him at the burning bush, of averting his eyes (Exod 3:6)—perhaps a significant non-echo given the clear echo of this appearance in Acts 3:13 (see *Comment* there). Peter invites the beggar to be expectant rather than fearful.[44]

5 Luke rings the changes on his verbs of sight, using ἀτενίσας, "fixing his eyes," and βλέψον, "look!" (v. 4), and now ἐπεῖχεν, "he focused his attention." The latter is a partial synonym of the first;[45] the change appears to be simply stylistic variation, highlighting the man's expectancy, although his hope is for money or something of value. Hamm notes the prevalence of words to do with visual attention in this passage (vv. 3, 4, 5, 12) and argues that, while ἰδών, "seeing" (v. 3), is a conventional Lukan way of introducing a story (e.g., Luke 1:12; 5:8, 12; 7:13; 11:38), the request to the man to look at Peter and John and his obedient response focus our attention on the apostles as the mediators of the healing.[46] Verses 6, 12–13 will go on to present Peter clarifying that the source of the healing is the powerful name of Jesus.

6 Some are puzzled by Peter's statement that ἀργύριον καὶ χρυσίον οὐχ ὑπάρχει μοι, "silver and gold are not at my disposal," since he had the community resources laid at his feet (4:34–35).[47] However, the communal resources were primarily for needy people within the believing community rather than

42 I owe this suggestion to Conrad Gempf.
43 *Pace* Pilch, *Visions*, 40–1; Strelan, "Stares."
44 It is doubtful that this contrast indicates the absence of Jesus, contra Busch, "Presence," 539.
45 L&N §§24.33, 49.
46 "Acts 3,1–10," 311.
47 E.g., Haenchen, *Acts*, 199n7.

beggars (cf. 6:1).[48] Hamm argues that the combination of ἀργύριον, "silver," and χρυσίον, "gold," can be associated with idolatry in the OT and claims that the healing's symbolism of end-time restoration of Israel is reinforced by "silver and gold" alluding to idolatry that led to spiritual paralysis.[49] However, "silver and gold" is a standard OT image for great wealth (found over two hundred times in LXX), and the point in most of the passages cited by Hamm is not that silver and gold are inevitably associated with idolatry but rather that it is an abuse of wealth to use them in service of idols. Further, this expression is used for coinage (e.g., Josephus, *Ant.* 15.1.2 §5; cf. 1 Pet 3:18). So, it seems more likely that the image is simply a straightforward denial of personal wealth by Peter, used as an antithesis to what he can and does give in healing.[50]

Peter's words to the beggar hold back the statement of what he is giving until the very end, with dramatic effect: περιπάτει, "walk!," is the last word of the sentence. Before this terse command comes a buildup in which Peter describes what he cannot give the man—for he does not have ἀργύριον καὶ χρυσίον, "silver and gold"—and then says he will give him what he can, before clarifying that this will come ἐν τῷ ὀνόματι Ἰησοῦ Χριστοῦ τοῦ Ναζωραίου, "in the name of Jesus Messiah the Nazarene" (see discussion of "the name" in *Comment* on 2:38). The name of Jesus will become a central issue as this story develops (3:13, 16 [twice], 20; 4:2, 10, 13, 18, 27, 30, 33), and thus the central focus of the story is christological.[51] In the light of the previous use of this dative phrase in 2:38 (where the preposition is ἐπί but with no significant difference in meaning) and the emphasis in Peter's previous speech that God has made the risen Jesus Messiah (2:31, 36), it seems likely that Χριστοῦ is here a titular use as "Messiah" rather than simply a "surname" for Jesus—Jesus's identity as Messiah is the reason that his name has power to heal, for as Messiah he is bringing about the restoration of Israel hinted at in Luke 4:18; 7:22 (see *Comment* on v. 2). Therefore the apostles, while they are mediators of the healing (v. 5), are only mediators—the source of power is elsewhere.[52] It seems highly unlikely that this use of "the name" for healing should be paralleled with magical practices, for v. 16 clarifies that human faith is required, and Luke is clearly against magical practices (e.g., 8:9–24; 13:6–12; 19:18–20).[53] Rather, "the name" denotes that "Jesus himself is the miracle worker,"[54] and thus Jesus is not to be regarded as absent from his people after his ascension

48 Barrett, *Acts*, 1:176.

49 Hamm, "Acts 3,1–10," 314; he cites LXX Exod 20:23; Deut 7:25; 29:16; Pss 113:12–16 (MT 115:4–6); 134:15 (MT 135:15); Hos 8:4; Bar 6:3, 9, 10, 39, 57.

50 Johnson, *Function*, 190–91.

51 Warrington, "Acts," 199–207.

52 Hamm, "Acts 3,1–10," 311.

53 With Barrett, *Acts*, 1:176–77.

54 Jervell, *Apostelgeschichte*, 160 (my translation); cf. 3:16; 4:10.

to heaven in 1:10 and only to be seen as a figure of the past—he is present and active (cf. 9:34).[55]

7 Peter gives effect to his command by helping the man to his feet. Warrington suggests that the use of touch parallels the healing ministry of Jesus, identifying it as symbolic of prophetic power, the hand of the healer representing the power of God, as in the OT phrase "the hand of God/the Lord" (e.g., Num 11:23; 1 Sam 5:6–7; 1 Chr 29:12; Ps 21:8 [LXX 20:9]; Isa 1:25; Jer 16:21; Dan 5:23; Zech 13:7).[56] However, the "hand" here is the man's, not Peter's, and so it is unlikely that such divine symbolism is intended.

Luke highlights the immediacy of the healing with παραχρῆμα, "immediately," in similar vein to Jesus's own healing ministry (cf. Luke 4:39; 5:25; 8:44, 55; 13:13; 18:43[57])—as Peter helps him up, αἱ βάσεις αὐτοῦ καὶ τὰ σφυδρά, "his feet and ankles," are "made strong." The passive verb ἐστερεώθησαν, "were made strong," highlights that the healing is a divine action,[58] particularly in the light of the qualification ἐν τῷ ὀνόματι Ἰησοῦ Χριστοῦ τοῦ Ναζωραίου, "in the name of Jesus Messiah the Nazarene" (v. 6), and Peter's denial in v. 12. Indeed, this verb is used in LXX for creation (LXX Pss 74:4 [MT 75:4; EVV 75:3]; 92:1 [MT 93:1]; 135:6 [MT 136:6]; Isa 42:5; 44:24), suggesting that "The raising of the lame man is a re-creative gesture, restoring in its fullness a vitiated identity and reinstalling the human in the covenant sealed by God with his people."[59] My structural analysis (see *Form/Structure/Setting* above) indicates that ἐστερεώθησαν, "they were made strong," is the key moment of the story—this is the moment where God-in-Jesus steps into the narrative and acts—all that follows through to 4:31 results from this divine action.

O'Reilly is rightly cautious of the suggestion, which dates back to Chrysostom, *Hom. Act.* VIII, that ἤγειρεν, "he raised," is a conscious parallel to the use of this verb in v. 15 in relation to the resurrection of Jesus, not least because the latter event has a place of significance and uniqueness in Luke's thought denied to the former.[60]

βάσεις, "feet," is a NT *hapax legomenon* (the more usual NT term for foot being πούς, e.g., 14:8, 10), but βάσις is found seventy times in LXX, frequently for the foot of an inanimate object such as the bases for the posts that supported the tent of meeting (Exod 26:19, 21, 25, 32, 37).[61]

8 Hamm feels a tension between Peter raising the man (v. 7, where the man is passive) and ἐξαλλόμενος ἔστη, "he leapt up, stood," here (where the man is active), although we are probably simply seeing two moments of action

55 Warrington, "Acts," 203, 207; *pace* Conzelmann, *Theology*, 170–206.
56 Warrington, "Acts," 204–5.
57 A Lukan favorite: *VL* 480–81, with further references.
58 With Fitzmyer, *Acts*, 279.
59 Butticaz, "Actes 3,1–26," 182 (my translation); I owe the LXX references to Butticaz.
60 O'Reilly, *Word*, 126–27; contra Hamm, "Acts 3:12–26," 203.
61 See the helpful lexical note in *BegC*, 4:33.

in sequence.[62] The restoration of the man's legs leads to mobility, for he now stands to walk. Hamm goes on to suggest that the balance of passive and active is likely to be echoing the balance of divine activity (ἐν τῷ ὀνόματι Ἰησοῦ Χριστοῦ τοῦ Ναζωραίου, "in the name of Jesus Messiah the Nazarene," v. 6; cf. v. 16) and human faith in that name (twice in v. 16). This suggestion is rather more artistic preaching than careful exegesis.

Luke here provides three clues that the restoration of Israel is in process (see further, *Comment* on v. 21). First, the first steps of the man's life (he was "lame from his mother's womb," v. 2) take him into the temple, accompanying Peter and John. This is precisely the area where he could not previously participate fully in worship because of his disability. Hamm argues that the entry into the temple as a worshiper is the "deepest meaning" of this account;[63] this applies whatever the solution to the question of his location in v. 2. He moves from being a passive recipient of almsgiving (v. 2, see *Comment* on the verb tenses) to an active participant in the life of Israel and its worship: the verbs used concerning the man in vv. 6, 7, 8, 9—especially the fourfold repetition of περιπατέω, "walk"—denote active movement and stress the completeness of his healing.[64] As he enters he is αἰνῶν τὸν θεόν, "praising God." Thus, he represents an outsider to the worship of Israel becoming an insider—for him the temple is now a "house of prayer" (Luke 19:46).[65] He is being restored to Israel, and in that action Israel is being restored to God's purposes for her.[66] The healing is thus not an event offering "extrinsic" demonstration of Israel's restoration but is an intrinsic part of the restoration itself.[67]

Secondly, the man's entry σὺν αὐτοῖς, "with them," hints at his restoration to the community of Israel and, because "them" is Peter and John, points to his inclusion in the restored and renewed people of God constituted around the exalted Jesus. The people rushing toward "them" (v. 11a) underlines this point.[68]

Thirdly, Luke records the actions of the man as ἐξαλλόμενος, "leaping up," and ἁλλόμενος, "leaping," both unusual verbs in biblical usage. Both represent an appropriately exuberant response to God's grace in healing rather than the measured, slow gait considered as manly.[69] More than that, the former verb is found in Mic 2:12 LXX of the remnant of Israel who ἐξαλοῦνται, "shall leap forth," in exultation at their release from suffering, part of a passage concerning the restoration of Israel.[70] The latter verb is used in Isa 35:6 LXX

62 Hamm, "Acts 3,1–10," 315.
63 Hamm, "Acts 3,1–10," 310–11.
64 Marconi, "History," 177–78.
65 Johnson, *Acts*, 72.
66 Butticaz, "Church," esp. 181.
67 For the extrinsic/intrinsic distinction in relation to healing, see Turner, *Holy Spirit*, 247–51.
68 Butticaz, "Church," 181.
69 Parsons, "Character," 310–11 with references to primary sources.
70 Hamm, "Acts 3,1–10," 312–13.

of the restoration of Israel envisaged by the prophet (τότε ἁλεῖται ὡς ἔλαφος ὁ χωλός, "then the person who is lame will leap like a deer"), expecting physical healing as its fulfillment.[71] The setting in Isa 35 is full of language of the restoration of Zion in the end time (note Isa 34, strongly linked with Isa 35[72]), when God will return and restore the fortunes of his people: in this time those redeemed will rejoice in Zion (Isa 35:10), an event of which this healed man's rejoicing is redolent. "Salvation is more than just being delivered from one's enemies; it includes Israel's being formed into a people once again and being renewed."[73] As we noted on Acts 3:2, Isa 35:5–6 is the passage cited in Luke 7:22 by Jesus concerning his ministry in response to the question from John's disciples whether he is the Messiah. Brueggemann astutely observes, "The claim is made that in the ministry of Jesus, God's new governance is effected, the new governance for which Judaism has long waited."[74] We might add that "God's new governance" is now being effected among the believing community through the apostles. Thus, the connection with Luke 7:22 both underlines the theme of Israel's restoration and clarifies that this restoration comes through the exalted Messiah Jesus,[75] as Peter's speech will explain (vv. 16, 18–21).

9 Assuming that the beggar sat outside the Shushan Gate (see *Comment* on v. 2), the people would see him entering the temple through the eastern wall into the court of the gentiles, near Solomon's Portico (see v. 11).

πᾶς ὁ λαός, "all the people," naturally refers to all the people in the temple courts at that time (as in Luke 1:21), and the expression lacks a specifier such as Ἰσραήλ, "Israel" (found in Acts 4:10). In the context of the strong restoration-of-Israel theme in this passage (a theme continued in Peter's speech, esp. 3:18–26), it may also be suggestive of the whole people *of Israel*, for Luke regularly uses ὁ λαός, "the people," in "Israel" contexts (e.g., 4:10; 5:13; 7:17).[76]

10 ἐπεγίνωσκον δὲ αὐτόν, "and they recognized him," suggests that some in the crowd who regularly walked past him identified the man; it would be natural for the story of his former disability to spread rapidly among the crowd in the temple complex.

Luke pictures their response as θάμβους καὶ ἐκστάσεως, "wonder and amazement," both words found predominantly in Luke-Acts in the NT. θάμβος, "wonder," occurs in the NT three times: here, Luke 4:36, and 5:9 (note the compound ἔκθαμβοι, "utterly astonished," in v. 11); ἔκστασις, "amazement," occurs here, Luke 5:26; Acts 10:10; 11:5; 22:7 and elsewhere in the NT only at Mark 5:42; 16:8. ἔκστασις, "amazement," is particularly striking and is frequently used for ecstatic visions (10:10; 11:5; 22:17), thus picturing the people as beside

71 Kaiser, *Isaiah 13–39*, 362.
72 Seitz, *Isaiah 1–39*, 236; Speckman, "Healing," 103.
73 Wildberger, *Isaiah 28–39*, 357, on Isa 35:6.
74 Brueggemann, *Isaiah*, 1:278.
75 O'Reilly, *Word*, 128.
76 Jervell, *Theology*, 23–25.

themselves in amazement. These two words are found in Luke's Gospel in co-texts of exorcism (4:36), healing (5:26), and miracle (5:9), thus suggesting that Luke here portrays the apostles continuing the ministry of Jesus (cf. Acts 1:1 with *Comment* there). Luke wants his readers to recognize how striking this healing is, and he will continue to hammer this point home—note how 4:22, at the end of the Sanhedrin hearing, again highlights the remarkable nature of the healing.

Explanation

The two on the walk to Emmaus had hoped that Jesus was the one to redeem Israel (Luke 24:21). The disciples had asked the Lord, "Is this the time when you will restore the kingdom to Israel?" (Acts 1:6), and received what seemed to be a somewhat evasive answer (1:7–8). This story demonstrates that Israel's restoration *is* in progress and clarifies the nature of the restoration which God is accomplishing by means of the powerful name of Jesus and through the believers (here Peter and John).

Luke has shown us that the Spirit-endowed believing community is prayerful, both in their homes and in the temple (2:42, 46, 47). They are a community where amazing "wonders and signs" are performed by the apostles (v. 43). The themes of prayer, the temple, and wonders and signs are now exemplified in a specific event.

Peter and John are presented as loyal Jews who attend the temple at the time of the afternoon sacrifice (3:1). As they arrive at the entrance gate, they meet a man in dire straits (v. 2): he has a congenital disability that both compels him to beg and marks him as unable to participate fully in the worshiping life of the temple—indeed, it is outside the temple where he sits begging, a location with not a little irony, for there he offers those attending the temple the chance to fulfill their obligation of almsgiving to the needy. This is a man needy—physically, socially, economically—and in exclusion from worshiping God.

However, what happens brings him radical change. Peter dramatically, almost teasingly, announces that he has no money to give him, but gives him something of far greater value—the ability to walk (vv. 6–7). This gift comes "in the name of Jesus Messiah the Nazarene" and is expressed using a passive verb, "his feet and ankles were made strong" (v. 7), highlighting that it is Jesus who does this—his status and power as Israel's Messiah (cf. 2:36) bring restoration to the man. The healing of people who are lame is a key element of prophetic expectation at the time when God acts to restore his people (Isa 35:6), and Jesus the Messiah is now bringing this restoration through his people, the believers.

We learned at Pentecost that the move of God now taking place fulfills his ancient promises (see on Acts 2:16–36); so now this healing demonstrates that restoration—truly, "this is that which was spoken by the prophet" (2:16). The healing is not an event offering "extrinsic" demonstration of Israel's restoration but is an intrinsic part of the restoration itself. Peter's speech which follows (3:12–26) explains the nature of the restoration more fully and invites hearers to participate in it.

Jesus's ministry through Peter and John demonstrates his powerful presence among his people, a presence all the more real since the coming of the Spirit at Pentecost in the previous chapter. It is thus appropriate that Luke tells this story in similar colors to Jesus's healing of a man who had a disability of the legs such that he had to be carried too (Luke 5:17–26), for the apostles are continuing Jesus's own restoration mission. Jesus's healing prepares readers of Luke's Gospel to recognize Jesus as the fulfiller of Isa 35:5–6 in his response to John's disciples' question whether he is "the one who is to come," the Messiah (Luke 7:19).

The restoration of the man moves him—literally!—and he shifts from passive recipient of charity to active worshiper. A sequence of active verbs has him as subject: "he sprang to his feet and began to walk and went . . . into the temple walking and leaping and praising God . . . walking and praising God" (Acts 3:8–9). His first destination is not to return to his home but to offer thanksgiving to God in the temple—he is a fully restored Israelite who will no longer be economically and physically dependent; instead, he will be able to support others as an expression of his praise to the Lord who has healed him (cf. Luke 19:8–9).

The demonstration of Israel's restoration in the man's healing leads into an explanation, as Peter will take the opportunity to speak to the "rubbernecking" crowd, whose knowledge of the man as "the one sitting for alms at the Beautiful Gate of the temple" (Acts 3:10) confirms that this is a real, tangible healing that cannot be gainsaid. In such a situation, preaching offers positive explanation of what God is doing, as Peter will do (vv. 12–26), rather than defensive apologetic.

Thus, the answer to the disciples' question of 1:6 is emerging: Israel *is* being restored, but not to worldly, political power; rather, Israel is becoming inclusive of those previously excluded from its company (cf. Luke 13:16; 19:9, where the woman bent over and Zaccheus the tax collector are both declared to be full members of Israel as respectively daughter and son of Abraham). The healing of the man does not merely *point to* the restoration of Israel but is itself *an integral part of* the restoration process, as Peter's speech will go on to explain (Acts 3:12–26).

2. Peter's Speech and Differing Responses (3:11–4:4)

Bibliography

Anderson, K. L. *But God,* 219–33, 281–84. **Barbi, A.** *Cristo.* **Bammel, E.** "Activity." **Barrett, C. K.** "Faith." **Bauckham, R.** "Restoration," 477–82. **Bauernfeind, O.** "Tradition." **Bayer, H. F.** "Eschatology." **Bock, D. L.** *Proclamation,* 187–98. **Brawley,**

R. L. "Covenant." ———. *Text*, 91–107. **Busch, A.** "Presence." **Butticaz, S. D.** "Actes 3,1–26." **Cadbury, H. J.** "Acts and Eschatology." **Carroll, J. T.** *Response*, 137–54. **Cerfaux, L.** "Communauté." **Culy, M. M.** "Clue." **Cunningham, S.** *Tribulations*, ch. 3. **de Waard, J.** "Quotation." **Dillon, R. J.** "Prophecy." **Doble, P.** *Paradox*, 151–60, 219–20. **Dodd, C. H.** *According*, 54–60. ———. *Preaching*, 37–47. **Dunn, J. D. G.** *Beginning*, 214–16. **Dupont, J.** "Discours de Pierre." **Epp, E. J.** "Ignorance." **Hahn, F.** "Problem." **Hamm, D.** "Acts 3:12–26." **Haraguchi, T.** "Call." **Hobart, W. K.** *Language*, 193–94. **Holtz, T.** *Untersuchungen*, 71–81. **Jeremias, J.** *Jerusalem* 160–62, 228–32. **Jervell, J.** *Luke*, 58–60. ———. *Theology*, 34–43. **Jones, D. L.** "Title." **Kelly, J. G.** "Christology." **Kilgallen, J. J.** "Persecution." **Kilpatrick, G. D.** "Quotations," 86. **Kodell, J.** "Use." **Kränkl, E.** *Jesus*, 125–29 **Kurz, W. S.** "Acts 3:19–26." **Lane, W. L.** "Times." **Lennartsson, G.** *Refreshing.* **Léonas, A.** "Note." **Lohfink, G.** "Christologie." **Mallen, P.** *Reading*, 125–27. **Marconi, G.** "History." **Marshall, I. H.** "Place." **Matera, F. J.** "Responsibility." **Ménard, J. E.** "*Pais Theou.*" **Moule, C. F. D.** "Acts iv.25." ———. "Christology." ———. *Origin*, 11–22. **O'Neill, J. C.** *Theology* (1961), 133–39. **O'Toole, R. F., SJ.** "Observations." **Ovey, M. J.** *Feasts*, 43–45. **Reicke, B. I.** *Glaube*, 44–45, 66–71. **Reinhardt, W.** "Population." **Rese, M.** *Motive*, 66–77. **Robb, J. E.** "Prophet." **Robinson, J. A. T.** "Christology." **Schmitt, J.** "L'église." **Schnackenburg, R.** "Eschatologie," esp. 256–58. **Scobie, C. H. H.** "Use." **Scott, J. M.** *Geography*, 84–85. **Seccombe, D. P.** "Luke and Isaiah." **Smalley, S. S.** "Christology." **Speckman, M. T.** "Healing." **Squires, J. T.** *Plan*, 65–66, 97–98. **Steyn, G. J.** *Quotations*, 129–58. **Strange, W. A.** *Problem*, 115–22. **Strauss, M. L.** *Davidic*, 247–49. **Tannehill, R. C.** "Functions," 404–6. **Teeple, H. M.** *Prophet.* **Turner, M.** *Power*, 308–12. **van den Eynde, S.** "Children." **Vanlaningham, M. G.** "Should." **Vermes, G.** *Jesus*, 69–78. **Wainwright, A. W.** "Luke." **Walton, S.** *Leadership.* **Weatherly, J. A.** *Responsibility.* **Wenham, D.** *Good News*, 13–26. **Wilckens, U.** *Missionsreden*, esp. 37–44, 60–61. **Wills, L.** "Form." **Wilson, S. G.** *Gentiles*, 219–22. **Zehnle, R. F.** *Pentecost Discourse.* **Zeichmann, C. B.** "στρατηγοί." **Ziesler, J. A.** "Name." **Zwiep, A. W.** *Ascension*, 109–15.

Translation

3[11] While he was holding on[a] to Peter and John, all the people ran together toward them in the Portico named after Solomon,[b] absolutely amazed. [12] On seeing them, Peter addressed the people, "People of Israel, why are you amazed about this or why are you staring at us, as if by our own power or godliness we had made him walk? [13] The God of Abraham and Isaac and Jacob, the God of our ancestors, glorified his servant Jesus. You people handed over and denied him before Pilate, who had decided to release[c] him; [14] you yourselves denied the holy and righteous one and asked for a murderer to be given to you. [15] Indeed, you killed the one who leads the way to life, whom God raised from the dead—we ourselves are witnesses of this fact.[d] [16] On the basis of faith in his name[e]—that name has made this man strong, whom you observe and recognize; the faith which comes through Jesus[f] gave him this full health before you all.

[17] And now, brothers and sisters, I realize that you acted from ignorance, as your rulers did too; [18] but in this way God fulfilled what he had announced in advance by the mouth of all the prophets, that his Messiah would suffer.[g] [19] So then, repent and turn in order to have your sins blotted out, [20] so that times of refreshing may come from the Lord[h] and that he may send the Messiah appointed for you, Jesus, [21] whom heaven must receive[i] until the times of restoration of all things,[j] of which God spoke by

the mouth of his holy prophets ages ago. 22 Moses said, "The Lord our God will raise up a prophet like me from among your own people;[k] pay careful attention to whatever he says to you. 23 And it shall be that anyone who does not pay careful attention[l] to that prophet shall be cut off from the people." 24 Indeed, all the prophets from Samuel onwards[m] who spoke also announced[n] these days. 25 You yourselves are the inheritors[o] of the prophets and the covenant which God made with your ancestors when he said to Abraham, "In your seed all the families of the earth shall be blessed."[p] 26 It was for your benefit, first of all,[q] that God raised up his servant and sent him, the one who blesses[r] you by turning each one from your evil ways.

4:1 While the apostles[s] were speaking[t] to the people, the priests[u] and the captain of the temple guard[v] and the Sadducees came upon them. 2 They were deeply offended[w] because the apostles[x] were teaching[y] the people and proclaiming in Jesus the resurrection from the dead, 3 and they arrested[z] them and placed[aa] them in overnight custody,[bb] since it was already evening. 4 Many of those who had heard the word came to believe,[cc] and the number of men[dd] was about five thousand.

Notes

a. Κρατοῦντος . . . αὐτοῦ, "as he held on," gen. abs. The acc. dir. obj. τὸν Πέτρον καὶ τὸν Ἰωάννην, "Peter and John," suggests a firm grasp rather than a gentle touch, which a gen. obj. would generally denote; Wallace, 132; cf. "κρατέω," BDAG 564, §2.a.

b. D presents a different picture from Alexandrian and Byzantine witnesses: ἐκπορευομένου δὲ τοῦ Πέτρου καὶ Ἰωάνου συνεξεπορευέτο κρατῶν αὐτοὺς· οἱ δὲ θαμβηθέντες ἔστησαν ἐν τῇ στοᾷ ἡ καλουμένη Σολομῶνος ἔκθαμβοι, "As Peter and John were coming out, he came out with them, holding onto them; those who had been amazed were standing absolutely amazed in the portico named after Solomon." D thus resolves the ambiguity in other witnesses over who αὐτούς, "them," is, although it contains the error of qualifying the dat. noun στοᾷ, "portico," with the nom. ptc. καλουμένη, "called," and for this reason is unlikely to be original; with *TCGNT*², 269, contra Rius-Camps and Read-Heimerdinger, *Message,* 1:220; Strange, *Problem,* 115–19, cf. 223n50, who both attempt to explain the error. Bruce, *Acts* (1990), 139, suggests the error may be a result of Semitic influence, also found in Revelation.

c. Inf. ἀπολύειν, "to release," used in indirect (or reported) speech following the verb of perception, κρίναντος, "judging"; Wallace, 603–4. D adds αὐτὸν θέλοντος, giving the whole the meaning "Pilate, who gave judgment of him, wanted to release him." D's sentence is overloaded and may reflect a marginal note being incorporated in the text of D; Strange, *Problem,* 120–22.

d. Rel. pron. οὗ could be (i) masc., in which case it refers to τὸν . . . ἀρχηγόν, "the author," and we should translate "we ourselves are his witnesses"; or (ii) neut., in which case it refers to the fact previously mentioned, that God had raised him from the dead, and we should translate "we ourselves are witnesses to this fact." Either implies the other, so Barrett, *Acts,* 1:198.

e. τοῦ ὀνόματος, obj. gen., "in [his] name," contra Culy and Parsons, *Acts,* 58, who take it as subj. gen.

f. αὐτοῦ, "him"; the translation clarifies the referent of each of the pronouns.

g. Inf. παθεῖν, "to suffer," is appositional, defining the content of προκατήγγειλεν, "he announced in advance."

h. ἀπὸ προσώπου τοῦ κυρίου, lit., "from the face of the Lord," synecdoche for the Lord himself; "πρόσωπον," BDAG 888, §1.b.β.ℵ; cf. LXX Gen 3:8; 35:1; Exod 10:11; 14:25.

i. δέξασθαι, "to receive," aor. inf. combined with the temporal deictic marker ἄχρι, "until," to show that the action of receiving will continue for a period; Wallace, 568n4.

j. Taking πάντων as neut., "all things," rather than masc. "all people"; cf. Barrett, *Acts*, 1:207.

k. τῶν ἀδελφῶν ὑμῶν, "your brothers," denoting the Israelite community; "ἀδελφός," BDAG 18, §2b.

l. (μὴ) ἀκούσῃ, "(does not) pay attention," aor. subj.; subj. in indef. rel. clause following ἥτις ἐάν, "whoever."

m. καὶ τῶν καθεξῆς, "and those in order," i.e., those who followed after Samuel; Culy and Parsons, *Acts*, 61.

n. Taking ὅσοι, "who," as the subject of ἐλάλησαν, and καί as adverbial "also"; cf. Barrett, *Acts*, 1:211.

o. οἱ υἱοί, "the sons," those who inherit from their ancestors; cf. "υἱός," BDAG 1024–25, §2.

p. The probable LXX sources of this quotation (see *Comment* on 3:25) read ἐνευλογηθήσονται, "shall be blessed in," with 𝔓[74] ℵ A[c] D E 0165 33 𝔐, whereas A* B Ψ 323 945 1739 *pc* Ir[lat vid] read εὐλογηθήσονται "shall be blessed"; C alone reads ἐπευλογηθήσονται, "shall be blessed upon" (and C's sole attestation suggests this is unlikely to be original). If ἐνευλογηθήσονται is read, this would be the only use of this compound in the NT and, if this were original, it is just possible that scribes might remove the preposition ἐν to make the verb consistent with εὐλογοῦντα, "blessing" (v. 26). However, if the preposition were absent, it would be natural for a scribe who knew LXX to introduce it, and that argument tips the balance toward regarding εὐλογηθήσονται as original.

q. Taking πρῶτον, "first of all," with ὑμῖν, "for your benefit," and thus as an adverb qualifying ἀπέστειλεν, "sent," rather than as qualifying the ptc. ἀναστήσας, "raised up"; Barrett, *Acts*, 1:213; Culy and Parsons, *Acts*, 62; see *Comment* on 3:26.

r. Adj. ptc. εὐλογοῦντα, "blessing," modifying αὐτόν, "him," both masc. acc. sg., expressing what the servant does; Culy, "Clue", esp. 449–50; Culy and Parsons, *Acts*, 62–63; contra Wallace, 635–37.

s. αὐτῶν, "they" (see next note on gen. case); translation clarifies who is being written about here.

t. Λαλούντων . . . αὐτῶν, "while they were speaking," gen. abs.; pres. ptc., suggests action contemporaneous with the arrival of the priests, etc.

u. B C read ἀρχιερεῖς, "high priests," a reading adopted by WH.

v. D lacks ὁ στρατηγὸς τοῦ ἱεροῦ, "the captain of the temple guard."

w. διαπονούμενοι pres. ptc. διαπονέομαι, "being deeply offended"; ptc. expressing reason for the action, reinforced by the following clause.

x. αὐτούς, "they"; translation clarifies who is being written about here.

y. διδάσκειν, "to teach," pres. inf., functioning causally (as is καταγγέλλειν, "to proclaim") with preposition and article διὰ τό, "because they were teaching the people."

z. ἐπέβαλον . . . τὰς χεῖρας, "they laid hands" in the sense "arrest"; L&N §37.110. Cf. re Jesus: Matt 16:50; Mark 14:46; Luke 20:19; John 7:30, 44; and re believers: Luke 21:12; Acts 5:18; 12:1; 21:27.

aa. ἔθεντο, aor. mid. from τίθημι, but with no significant difference in meaning from act.; "τίθημι," BDAG 1003.

bb. εἰς τήρησιν εἰς τὴν αὔριον, lit., "in custody until the following day."

cc. ἐπίστευσαν, inceptive aor., "they came to believe"; Wallace, 558–59.

dd. τῶν ἀνδρῶν probably refers specifically to "men," as it most frequently does, especially throughout Acts, where it is often paired with γυναῖκες, "women," e.g., 5:14; 8:12; 9:2; 17:12, 34; 22:4; cf. Matt 14:21; with Barrett, *Acts*, 1:222; Bruce, *Acts* (1990), 148; NIV; HCSB; contra TNIV "believers"; NRSVue "they."

Form/Structure/Setting

Delimitation of pericope. A linking section (3:11–12a) bridges from the healing itself and sets the scene for Peter's speech (3:12b–26), which is itself followed by a divided response (4:1–4). The response could be treated as a separate section; however, 4:5–22 also centers on a Petrine speech and ends with a divided response (vv. 21–22), which suggests that we may see the two scenes as parallel and include the response in both cases.

Sources/historicity. There is a longstanding debate over Luke's sources for this speech, with some arguing that the theology is primitive,[77] mainly on the grounds that language found here is rare elsewhere in the NT, particularly concerning God (ὁ θεὸς Ἀβραὰμ και Ἰσαὰκ καὶ Ἰακώβ, "the God of Abraham and Isaac and Jacob"; ὁ θεὸς τῶν πατέρων ἡμῶν, "the God of our ancestors"), Jesus (e.g., παῖς, "servant"; ὁ ἅγιος καὶ δίκαιος, "the holy and righteous one"; ὁ ἀρχηγὸς τῆς ζωῆς, "the one who leads the way to life"), the audience (οἱ υἱοὶ τῶν προφητῶν καὶ τῆς διαθήκης, "the inheritors of the prophets and the covenant"), forgiveness (ἐξαλειφθῆναι, "to blot out") and eschatology (καιροὶ ἀναψύξεως, "times of refreshing"; χρόνοι ἀποκαταστάσεως, "times of restoration"). Building on the work of Bailey on Luke's Gospel, Lennartsson plausibly proposes that the Jerusalem believing community preserved traditions about their own history, including this speech.[78] Others consider the language largely Lukan composition, often with the claim that Luke is deliberately using "archaic" language to characterize this speech as coming from the earliest period.[79] Such questions are not easy to decide, since Luke has generally integrated his sources well into his book.[80] Hence, there is wide agreement that Luke uses sources but little agreement on the nature and content of those sources. We shall consider the background of key terms below, but without optimism that we can recover a source underlying the speech.

Structure. The link from the healing story (3:1–10) is made by shifting the scene to inside the temple complex, in Solomon's portico (v. 11), and by Peter beginning his speech with reference to the healing in order to deny that he and John had the power to accomplish the healing (v. 12). Peter's negative statement prepares for his positive statement of the power of Jesus (v. 16). Barrett is mistaken, however, in suggesting that the only links are found in vv. 12, 16.[81] Hamm identifies a number of other links between the developing story and the healing that lead him to suggest that "the speech *interprets* the

77 E.g., Zehnle, *Discourse.*
78 Lennartsson, *Refreshing,* 39–40, 41–45; Bailey, *Finding,* 41–45. See also Bailey, "Informal"; Wenham, *Good News,* 13–26; Jervell, *Luke,* 19–39.
79 E.g., Lohfink, "Christologie"; O'Neill, *Theology* (1961), 117–45.
80 Carroll, *Response,* 151–54.
81 Barrett, "Faith," 2–3.

healing story":[82] (i) the play on the dual meaning of σῴζω as "heal" or "save" (4:9, 12); (ii) the "dynamic of attention" produced by the range of verbs of seeing (3:3, 4, 5, 10) which draws attention to the role of the apostles as mediators of Jesus's authority as prophet like Moses (3:13, 19–26); (iii) the combination of passivity and activity by the beggar (3:7, 8), echoed in the explanation that both the name of Jesus and faith are involved in the healing (3:16); (iv) the strong emphasis on the healed man walking, leaping, and praising, especially the echo of Isa 35:6 LXX (see *Comment* on 3:8), re-echoed in the choice of ὁλοκληρία, "wholeness" (3:16).[83]

There are a number of similarities between this speech and the Pentecost speech, which are listed in the chart on p. 256.[84]

While there are strong similarities, there are also significant differences, not least the sequence of these points, as is clear above.[85] In addition, there are gaps in each of the two speeches relative to the other.

The Pentecost speech lacks the ignorance of the hearers in their actions against Jesus (3:17); "remnant" theology (3:19–21);[86] explicit mention of Pilate's role (3:13); Jesus as παῖς, "servant" (3:13), ὁ ἅγιος καὶ δίκαιος, "the holy and righteous one" (3:14), ὁ ἀρχηγὸς τῆς ζωῆς, "the one who leads the way to life," and prophet like Moses (3:22–23); the necessity for *the Messiah* to suffer (3:18); particular eschatological imagery and teaching, including Jesus coming from heaven in the future (3:20–21); the warning against exclusion by failing to respond (3:23).

The Acts 3 speech lacks mention of: the Holy Spirit (2:33, 38); baptism (2:38); and a community to join (2:39, 41–32). Thus, although there is a broad similarity,[87] there are significant differences. The combination of similarities and differences suggests that each speech is tailored to its situation.[88] We have seen that this is so with the Pentecost speech, and the *Comment* will explore that issue for this speech.

In terms of content, Peter's speech centers on God; God is the initiator of what has taken place and what will take place: ὁ θεός, "God," is a grammatical subject in vv. 13, 15, 18, 20, 21, 22, 25, 26.[89] Peter focuses on the accreditation which God has given to Jesus through his resurrection (vv. 13, 15), by contrast with the human verdict of the Jerusalemite Jews and their leaders who handed Jesus over to Pilate to be executed (vv. 13–14, 17).[90]

82 Hamm, "Acts 3:12–26," 199 (his italics); see also Butticaz, "Actes 3,1–26."
83 Bauckham, "Restoration," 481–82.
84 Largely following Zehnle, *Discourse*, 19–23.
85 Contra Reicke, *Glaube*, 44–45, 66–71; for critique, see Zehnle, *Discourse*, 23–24.
86 Longenecker, *Acts (1996)*, 91–92.
87 Wilckens, *Missionsreden*, 54; Reicke, *Glaube*, 44–45; cf. Dodd, *Preaching*, 37–47.
88 With Tannehill, "Functions," 404–6.
89 Bayer, "Eschatology," 241.
90 See further Squires, *Plan*, 65–66.

Feature	Acts 2	Acts 3
Salutation ἄνδρες Ἰσραηλῖται lit. "men, Israelites"	vv. 14, 22, 29	v. 12b
Beginning with correction of a false impression	vv. 14–15	v. 12b
God has glorified Jesus, whom the hearers rejected	v. 36	vv. 13–14
Contrast of the hearers killing Jesus and God raising him; the speaker and colleagues as witnesses of this	vv. 22–24, 32	v. 15
The startling event the hearers witness is linked to Jesus	vv. 16–21, 33, 38	v. 16
Everything happened according to God's will and plan	v. 23	v. 18
Call to repentance and offer of forgiveness of sins	v. 38	v. 19
Reference to Jesus, now in heaven, and his relation to the hearers	vv. 33, 34–35	vv. 20–21
Explaining God's action, which has led to Jesus's eminent role, with reference to Scripture	vv. 25–28, 29–31	vv. 22–24
Privileged role of hearers, but not for their benefit alone	v. 39	v. 25
Jesus's ministry and his preaching of repentance	vv. 22, 40	v. 26
Shortly after the speech: the number who responded	v. 41	4:4

The divine focus is combined with a strong thrust toward "you": emphatic ὑμεῖς appears in vv. 13, 14, 25, "you" is a grammatical subject in vv. 13, 14, 15, 16, 17, 19, 22, 25, and the speech concludes with a threefold flourish: "*To you* (ὑμῖν) first . . . blessing *you* (ὑμᾶς) by turning each one from *your* (ὑμῶν) evil ways" (v. 26).

The speech is organized around an interplay between these twin foci: in the first part, vv. 12b–16 (with the opening marked by the double vocative ἄνδρες Ἰσραηλῖται, "people, Israelites"):

The Jewish ancestral God has glorified Jesus
You handed him over and denied him
You denied him and asked for a murderer instead
God raised him from the dead
We are witnesses
You see and recognize this healing
which happened by faith in Jesus's name

The long sentence in vv. 13–15 hinges around a series of intensifying contrasts between God's actions (glorifying Jesus, raising him from the dead) and the actions of the Jerusalemite Jews and their leaders, which were the polar opposite (handing him over, denying him, asking for a murderer).[91] In the midst of this series of contrasts, the emphatic "of this *we ourselves* (ἡμεῖς) are witnesses" stands out—the apostolic testimony to the resurrection of Jesus is as crucial here as it is in 2:32.

The second part of the speech (beginning 3:17, marked by καὶ νῦν, "and now," and the vocative ἀδελφοί, "brothers and sisters") sets out the response required to God's action in vindicating Jesus after the hearers' rejection and the blessings that follow such a response:

You and your leaders acted in ignorance
God fulfilled his pre-announced plan through these events
You should repent and turn
so that *God* may wipe out *your* sins [passive verb implying God's action]
so that times of refreshing may come from *God*
so that *God* may send Jesus
heaven [*God's* realm] must receive him
until the time *God* announced through the holy prophets.

Scripture is then invoked as testifying both to the need for appropriate response (v. 22) and the consequences of ignoring what Jesus, the prophet like Moses, says (v. 23). Scripture's testimony is invoked both specifically (vv. 22–23, 25) and in more general terms (v. 24). The same divine/human interplay can be seen in vv. 22–25:

Through Moses, *God* said he would send a prophet like Moses
You should listen to everything he says
if *you* don't, *you* will be cut off from the people.
Samuel and all the prophets [*God's* messengers] spoke about these days
You are the inheritors of the prophets and covenant
which *God* gave to your ancestors

91 Wilckens, *Missionsreden*, 39.

Finally, Peter concludes by summarizing, returning the focus to Jesus, the servant sent by God for blessing each one who turns from their evil ways (v. 26), again with a divine/human mixture of actions:

For you, first,
God raised his servant up and sent him
so that *he [Jesus]* might bless *you*
by turning *you* from your evil ways.

The speech is an indictment for the hearers' wrongdoing, but it is not only that. Its divine focus means there is the possibility for change. Because Jesus has been exalted by God in his resurrection, Jesus now has power to heal the man (v. 15) and to bring forgiveness and heavenly refreshment to the hearers (vv. 19–20). These blessings depend on the hearers repenting and turning to God (v. 19a). It is noticeable that, while "you" is prominent in v. 26, it is never a grammatical subject, as it regularly is in the rest of the speech—rather, we find dative, accusative and genitive (ὑμῖν, ὑμᾶς, ὑμῶν), each highlighting that "you" are recipients of something done by another, whether God or his servant Jesus. The hearers' repenting and turning opens the door for change, but it is God-in-Jesus who first makes the possibility of change available and then brings about the change.

Setting. It is appropriate that we then learn of a twofold response to this offer. On one hand, the priests, the temple captain, and the Sadducees will hear nothing of this and throw Peter and John in jail (4:1–3); on the other hand, many respond by believing (4:4). This divided response to the message echoes the divided response to the Pentecost events (2:6, 12–13) and will be characteristic throughout the remainder of Acts (e.g., 13:42–45). A crisis will develop around this twofold response to Jesus the Messiah of Israel, for it will ultimately redefine the people of God:[92] those who believe in the name of Jesus will be YHWH's people and inherit all the blessings that God gives (13:19–22), and those who reject Jesus will be excluded (13:23).

The opposition first seen here will grow in Jerusalem, in the apostles being forbidden to speak in the name of Jesus (4:18), a second arrest and hearing resulting in a flogging (5:17–41), opposition to Stephen resulting in a hearing (6:9–14) and Stephen's death (7:54–60), a growing persecution that drives believers from the city (8:1–3; 11:19), Saul's plan to attack believers in Damascus (9:1–2), a plot to kill the converted Saul (9:23), and Herod killing James and arresting Peter (12:1–4). Thus, the major theme of the believers' response to suffering and persecution is introduced here.[93]

---

92 Cf. Jervell, *Theology*, 34–43.
93 See full discussion of the theme in Cunningham, *Tribulations*, ch. 3.

Comment

11 Κρατοῦντος δὲ αὐτοῦ τὸν Πέτρον καὶ τὸν Ἰωάννην, "While he was holding on to Peter and John," portrays the man holding fast to them (see *Note* a). As in vv. 4–5, there is a contrast with YHWH's appearance to Moses at the burning bush. There, God tells Moses to stay at a distance and remove his sandals because he stands on holy ground (Exod 3:5). Here, the man has already entered the temple in an undignified manner (vv. 8–9), and now he holds tight to God's spokesmen. The danger of intimate engagement with YHWH is of no concern here, as God's people pave the way to God.[94]

The people in the temple courts ran toward them ἐπὶ τῇ στοᾷ τῇ καλουμένῃ Σολομῶντος, "in the Portico named after Solomon," a covered colonnade[95] whose building was traditionally attributed to Solomon, located inside the eastern wall of the temple court.[96] Thus if the Beautiful Gate were within the temple shrine (see *Comment* on v. 2), the apostles and the man must have left the shrine and gone toward Solomon's Portico, which is the scenario in Codex Bezae (D), where the apostles leave the shrine with the man holding onto them and the people who had been amazed (v. 10) standing in Solomon's Portico.[97] The translation, by contrast, reflects the reading of the overwhelming majority of manuscripts and reinforces the likelihood that Luke pictures the healing taking place outside the outer wall of the temple courts (see *Comment* on v. 2), and then the man entering with the apostles and standing in Solomon's Portico, just inside the temple's outer wall. John 10:23 notes Solomon's Portico as a place where Jesus walked with his disciples, and the presence of such an incidental detail in John is likely to be historical. Acts presents this portico as subsequently (perhaps consequently) a key meeting place for the earliest believers (Acts 5:12), for their numbers were such that a private house was not large enough for them all—a deficiency already hinted at by 2:46, which contrasts meeting ὁμοθυμαδὸν ἐν τῷ ἱερῷ, "together in the temple," and breaking bread κατ' οἶκον, "from house to house."

ἔκθαμβοι, "absolutely amazed," is a compound form of θάμβους, "amazed" (v. 10); this repetition underlines the remarkable nature of the healing and opens the way for Peter to interpret it through his speech.[98] The prefixing of the preposition ἐκ suggests an intensification of the amazement and perhaps echoes ἐκστάσεως in v. 10.[99] The compound is an NT *hapax legomeonon*, found

---

94 Contra Busch, "Presence," 540, who interprets the contrast with Moses as implying that Jesus is not present with Peter and John.

95 "Stoa," *OCD*[3] 1445.

96 Josephus, *J.W.* 5.5.1 §§184–85; *Ant.* 15.11.3 §§396–401; 20.9.7 §§220–21; it is not mentioned in the Mishnah.

97 Rius-Camps and Read-Heimerdinger, *Message*, 1:226–27.

98 Butticaz, "Actes 3,1–26," 178.

99 Hamm, "Acts 3:12–26," 201.

in the second-century BC writer Polybius 20.10.9: οἱ μὲν οὖν περὶ τὸν Φαινέαν ἔκθαμβοι γεγονότες ἔστασαν ἄφωνοι πάντες, "Phaeneas and all those with him stood in speechless amazement."[100]

12 ἰδὼν δὲ ὁ Πέτρος ἀπεκρίνατο πρὸς τὸν λαόν, "On seeing them, Peter addressed the people." The speech begins from the people's response to the healing. ἀπεκρίνατο, "he addressed," is aor. mid. of ἀποκρίνομαι, "answer," and connotes "a solemn or legal utterance" in this voice.[101] Luke's choice of λαός, "people," rather than ὄχλος, "crowd," may be significant, for he often uses λαός for the whole people of Israel (e.g., Luke 3:15; 19:47; 20:6; 22:22; Acts 2:47; 3:9, 23).[102] Haraguchi therefore suggests this speech may be presented as addressing the people *as a whole* in the temple with the offer of forgiveness.[103] However, the charge of responsibility for Jesus's death (vv. 13–15) applies specifically to the Jerusalemite Jews and their leaders (note the contrast of "you" here with "they" in 13:27–29). Further, λαός is used by Luke without necessarily implying that the whole Jewish people is the referent, especially in the early chapters of Acts, where the people are differentiated from their leaders—see v. 17; cf. Luke 23:13; and note the way that λαός is differentiated from the leaders throughout the present sequence in 4:1–4, 17, 21; 5:13–17, 26.[104] Thus Haraguchi's claim goes too far, although there is clearly a symbolic significance in proclaiming the gospel at the heart of Judaism in the temple.

ἄνδρες Ἰσραηλῖται, "People of Israel"; see *Comment* on 2:22.

θαυμάζετε, "you are amazed," and ἀτενίζετε, "you are staring," echo the description of the healing (vv. 10, 4 respectively) and lead into the key question of the source of the power for the healing, expressed through a rhetorical question (which will become an actual question in 4:7). Peter strenuously denies that he and John themselves have δυνάμει ἢ εὐσεβείᾳ, "power or godliness," sufficient to perform such a healing; rather, δύναμις, "power," comes from God by the Spirit (the use of δύναμις in 1:8 is programmatic for the whole book), and it is because of the relation of *Jesus* to God—not Peter or John's godliness—that the healing has taken place (vv. 12, 16). Barnabas and Paul will make a similar point in Lystra when a pagan crowd assumes their power has produced healing (14:15). This point provides an interesting contrast with other first-century figures whose godliness was said to lead to miraculous events, whether a Jewish teacher or a Hellenistic θεῖος ἀνήρ, "divine man." Jewish examples include Honi the Circle Drawer/Onias (m. Taʿan. 3:8; Gen. Rab. 13:7; Josephus, *Ant.* 14.2.1 §§22–24) and Hanina ben Dosa

---

100 "ἔκθαμβος," BDAG 303; L&N §§25.208, 211.

101 By contrast with the more usual aor. pass. in the NT; so Wallace, 421, citing "ἀποκρίνομαι," BAGD 93.

102 Jervell, *Theology*, 23.

103 "Call," 271; also Butticaz, "Actes 3,1–26," 183.

104 More fully, Weatherly, *Responsibility*, 70–71; Kodell, "Use," esp. 327–28.

(m. Soṭah 9:15).[105] On the alleged Hellenistic "divine man," Philostratus (*Vit. Apoll.* 3.18; 8.5, 7) reports examples of humans considered to be gods and discusses the appropriateness of such an identification.[106] Peter and John's modesty here contrasts with previous conduct among the disciples, who had disputed who was greatest (Luke 9:46; 22:24) and had repeatedly been taught by Jesus about the importance of humility (Luke 9:48; 14:11; 18:14; 22:26)—Luke thus suggests that the lesson has finally gone home following the coming of the Spirit.[107] This contrast highlights Luke's emphasis throughout Acts that power is derived from God through Jesus and thus that God's messengers are mere humans (cf. 10:25–26; 14:15, and the correction of misunderstanding which begins the Pentecost speech, 2:12–16).

13 The sonorous title ὁ θεὸς Ἀβραὰμ και Ἰσαὰκ και Ἰακώβ, ὁ θεὸς τῶν πατέρων ἡμῶν, "the God of Abraham and Isaac and Jacob, the God of our ancestors," recalls Exod 3:6, 15, 16 (the only LXX passages where all three patriarchs are named together in genitive relation to God) and thus evokes both YHWH's covenant faithfulness in the deliverance of his people in the exodus and YHWH's call of Moses to be his prophet—the latter is a note that will return in vv. 22–23. The assertion about Jesus that follows on the heels of this title places Jesus firmly within a theme of the fulfillment of God's purposes in and through Israel, a theme that will bring the speech to a close (v. 26). In the historic setting of the temple, that embodies the promises and faithfulness of YHWH, such a focus is vital to any Jesus apologetic that is likely to convince.

ἐδόξασεν τὸν παῖδα αὐτοῦ Ἰησοῦν, "he glorified his servant Jesus." Peter's speech shifts focus to Jesus, for he is showing that the healing is deeply christological and is emblematic of what God is now doing in restoring Israel.[108] In Luke-Acts the verb δοξάζω, "glorify," is normally used with humans as subject and God as object,[109] in line with the predominant use in LXX (e.g., Exod 15:1, 2). But here Jesus, rather than God, is the object being glorified, and—even more remarkably—he is being glorified by *God*, a usage more familiar from John (e.g., John 8:54; 13:31–32; 16:14; 17:1). How has God glorified his servant? In the light of Acts 2:32–36 and the explicit references to Jesus's resurrection (v. 15) and place in heaven (v. 21) here, it is natural to think of the resurrection and exaltation of Jesus, and they are likely referents here: "the miracles of Acts, of which the restoration of the beggar at the Beautiful Gate is the archetype, are the present traces of the resurrection of Christ, the permanent effects of Easter."[110] In addition, in this particular co-text, where

105 See Vermes, *Jesus*, 69–78, for helpful discussion and references.
106 See also B. L. Blackburn, "Divine Man/Theios Aner," *DJG* 189–91.
107 Tannehill, *Unity*, 1:53.
108 Butticaz, "Actes 3,1–26," esp. 183–84.
109 Acts 4:21; 11:18; 21:20; cf. 13:48 ἐδόξαζον τὸν λόγον τοῦ κυρίου, "they glorified the word of the Lord"; Luke 2:20; 5:25; 7:16; 13:13; 17:15; 18:43; 23:47.
110 Butticaz, "Actes 3,1–26," 183, (my translation).

Peter has brought healing in the name of Jesus (v. 6) and highlights that it is Jesus's name which has produced the healing (v. 16), it seems natural to see some reference to Jesus being glorified through the healing of the man.[111] Bock combines these two thoughts: "The Servant Jesus is glorified in that he sits in heaven, despite his having suffered on the cross, and exercizes his authority in this healing."[112] Jesus is no mere figure of the past but one who continues to act from heaven as God's agent in healing.

Jesus is τὸν παῖδα αὐτοῦ, "his servant," a description that is rare in the NT (only here; 4:27, 30; Matt 12:18—the latter citing Isa 42:1). παῖς is never found in the NT outside the Gospels and Acts, although it occurs in Did. 9:2; 10:2; 1 Clem. 59:2–4; Barn. 6:1; 9:2; Mart. Pol. 14:1; 20:2—Did. 9:2 concerns David; others concern Jesus. Luke has described both Israel and David as God's παῖς (Luke 1:54, 69). Two OT allusions can be identified here.

First, Isa 52:13 LXX ὁ παῖς μου . . . ὑψωθήσεται καὶ δοξασθήσεται σφόδρα, "my servant . . . shall be exalted and greatly glorified," uniquely in LXX combines the same verb and noun as here. Cerfaux observes that the two key verbs used to express the exaltation of Jesus as Messiah in the early chapters of Acts are δοξάζω, "glorify" (Acts 3:13), and ὑψόω, "exalt" (2:33; 5:31),[113] and they are collocated in Isa 52:13 LXX.[114] This link suggests that we should see the echo of Isa 52:13 as bringing with it the OT co-text of the servant's suffering, death, and exaltation. Strauss rightly argues that Luke's alleged reduced emphasis (compared to Mark) on the atoning significance of Jesus's death does not exclude a link with Isaiah's suffering servant, since Luke elsewhere shows an understanding of the death of Jesus as atoning (see *Comment* on 3:14).[115] The link with Isaiah's servant is made more probable by Peter going on to speak of Jesus's rejection, suffering, death, and exaltation—Jesus is painted using the colors of the servant of Isaiah. The effect is to offer an apologetic for the believers' claim that Jesus who has been crucified is exalted, for he fulfills the servant's role as one who suffers for others and is then vindicated.[116] (See *Comment* on 8:34.)

Secondly, Luke uses παῖς, "servant," for Israel (Luke 1:54; cf. Isa 42:1; 44:1–2, 21; 45:4) and David (Luke 1:69; Acts 4:25; cf. Isa 37:35) in settings that emphasize that Jesus is the fulfillment of the promises of YHWH. Kränkl agrees that Luke does not use παῖς in a technical sense and that the earliest Christians did not use παῖς exclusively for the Isaianic servant.[117]

111 Hamm, "Acts 3:12–26," 202, contra Anderson, *But God*, 223.
112 *Proclamation*, 189.
113 Cerfaux, "Communauté," 20.
114 Mallen, *Reading*, 125–26; Kränkl, *Jesus*, 125–26; Anderson, *But God*, 223; contra Doble, *Paradox*, 153, who sees the reference to δόξα, "glory," relating to the whole of Jesus's life; but this is not apparent in this co-text and misses the point concerning the collocation.
115 Strauss, *Davidic*, 247–49.
116 Moule, "Christology," 169–70.
117 *Jesus*, 172.

Thus it can be a term used for anyone who carries out God's will.[118] Further, behind the uses for Israel and David we should probably see OT identification (especially in Isa 40–55) of both the nation and the king as Yahweh's servant (Heb. עֶבֶד [*ʿebed*] consistently translated παῖς in LXX), and thus παῖς here connotes and fills out the nature of the messianic-kingly character and role of Jesus.[119] This identification is confirmed by subsequent references to Jesus as the Messiah or God's Messiah (Acts 3:18, 20): Jesus's messianic mission has been carried out through humble, suffering, servant obedience to YHWH.[120]

We are here encountering an early, strongly Jewish, christological description that gradually fell into disuse, perhaps predictably, as the believing communities became more gentile in their character—although note use of "servant" in the apostolic fathers, cited above. Noting the location of "servant" in prayer contexts in the apostolic fathers, Kränkl suggests its origins are liturgical, which is somewhat speculative.[121] Ménard suggests that the application of "servant of the Lord" to Jesus is an original point in the Christology of Acts and believes its application to Jesus resulted from post-resurrection reflection on Scripture by the believers.[122] However, France cogently argues that Jesus himself used and reflected on the Isaianic servant passages in relation to his own mission, particularly in Luke 22:37; Mark 10:45; 14:24.[123] The double OT echo detected above suggests that "the servant of the Lord" is a category like "the son of man," with both individual and corporate aspects (cf. Dan 7:13–14, 18, where the son of man is an individual but is also the saints of the Most High[124]). If so, this connection parallels Paul's understanding of the believing community as entering into Jesus's sufferings (e.g., Rom 8:17; Gal 2:19–20; Phil 3:10; Col 1:24).

ὃν ὑμεῖς . . . παρεδώκατε, "whom you people handed over." By contrast with God glorifying Jesus, Peter's hearers are guilty of dishonoring Jesus. The emphatic ὑμεῖς, "you people," makes it difficult to claim that Luke is hereby condemning the Jewish people as a whole, for it puts the focus on the Jerusalemites to whom Peter speaks.[125] Luke's phrasing echoes both Jesus's predictions of his suffering (Luke 9:44; 18:32) and the passion story itself

118 Strauss, *Davidic*, 247.

119 Hurtado, *Lord*, 190–93.

120 Cf. the later Tg. Isa. 52:13, which adds "Messiah" to explain "my servant"—as do some MSS of Tg. Isa. 42:1—and may represent an earlier exegetical tradition; Bruce, *Acts* (1990), 139; Chilton, ed., *Isaiah Targum*, xxvi; for fuller discussion of identification of the "servant" as the Messiah, see J. Jeremias & W. Zimmerli, "παῖς θεοῦ," *TDNT* 5:681–82, 686–700.

121 *Jesus*, 129; cf. Robinson, "Christology," 179.

122 Ménard, "*Pais Theou*," 88–91.

123 France, "Servant"; with Jeremias & Zimmerli, "παῖς θεοῦ," *TDNT* 5:712–17; O. Michel & I. H. Marshall, "παῖς θεοῦ," *NIDNTT* 3:611–12; *pace* Hooker, *Jesus*; O'Neill, *Theology* (1961), 133–39.

124 See the judicious discussion in Moule, *Origin*, 11–22.

125 Matera, "Responsibility," 86–87, observes this point more widely in Acts.

(Luke 20:20; 22:4, 6, 21, 22, 48; 23:25; 24:7, 20).[126] Pilate κρίναντος ἐκείνου ἀπολύειν, "had decided to release him," echoes Pilate's threefold declaration of Jesus's innocence (Luke 23:4, 16, 22), a feature highlighted in Luke's passion narrative. This focus on Pilate's decision to release Jesus is not incompatible with Acts 4:27,[127] where Pilate is held jointly responsible for Jesus's death, for Pilate took the final decision to hand Jesus over (Luke 23:24, using a technical term for giving judgment, ἐπικρίνω; cf. 2 Macc 4:47; 3 Macc 4:2[128]).

14 Jesus is characterized as τὸν ἅγιον καὶ δίκαιον, "the holy and righteous one," a unique combination in the NT (not found in LXX either, although note that YHWH is both holy and righteous in 1 Sam 2:2 = Ode 3:2; cf. Isa 5:16; 33:5–6 LXX). Zehnle proposes a "prophet like Moses" background for this description on the basis of Moses's description as προφήτης ἁγίος, "a holy prophet" (Wis 11:1), with the parallel usage for Jesus as ὁ ἅγιος τοῦ θεοῦ, "the holy one of God," in John 6:69, and reference to Moses as "the just" in rabbinic literature.[129] However, unless John is earlier than Acts, it cannot necessarily be used as evidence for how *Luke* understood this double descriptor, and later rabbinic sources (alas, Zehnle does not cite primary sources in support of this claim) equally are unreliable as a guide to Luke's thought.[130]

"The Holy One" is properly a title of YHWH, especially as "the Holy One of Israel" (e.g., Pss 70:22 [MT 71:22]; 77:41 [MT 78:41]; 88:19 [MT 89:19; EVV 89:18]; Isa 1:4; 5:19; 12:6; 17:7; 30:11, 12; 40:5; 41:20; 43:3, 14; 45:11; 48:17; 49:7; 55:5; 60:9; Jer 27:29 [MT 50:29]). Before Jesus's birth, the angel announced that Jesus would be holy (Luke 1:35), and the context of Luke 2:23 suggests the focus is Jesus being "set apart" for God's purposes as Messiah—hence the reference to him as "the son of God" in Luke 1:35[131]—as well as exhibiting outstanding ethical quality arising from his relationship with YHWH.[132] Later the Capernaum demoniac calls Jesus ὁ ἅγιος τοῦ θεοῦ, "the Holy One of God" (Luke 4:34; cf. Mark 1:24; John 6:69), showing a recognition of Jesus's true nature by spiritual opposition.[133] Seccombe proposes Ps 15:10 LXX (MT 16:10) as source, given that this psalm was used as a messianic testimonium (Acts 2:27; 13:35), and this is certainly possible, particularly in the light of the possible echo of Ps 15:11 LXX in the next verse.[134]

Jesus is spoken of as ὁ δίκαιος, "the righteous one," in Acts 7:52; 22:14 by Jewish Jesus followers, as in this co-text (cf. 1 Pet 3:18; 1 John 2:1, 29; 3:7—both in Jewish-Christian settings). This description of Jesus is found

126 Johnson, *Acts*, 67.
127 Contra Barrett, *Acts*, 1:195.
128 See "ἐπικρίνω," MM 240 ; "ἐπικρίνω," LSJ.
129 Zehnle, *Discourse*, 49–52.
130 With Robb, "Prophet," 92.
131 Cf. Green, *Luke*, 91.
132 Turner, *Power*, 158–59.
133 Green, *Luke*, 223.
134 Seccombe, "Luke and Isaiah," 257.

primarily in co-texts about his death and may have resulted from the application of Hab 2:4; Isa 53:11 LXX to him in similar manner to the description of an eschatological figure as "the righteous one" in 1 En. 38:2–3; 53:6.[135] Alternatively (or perhaps in addition), there may be a messianic flavor, given that the messianic king can be called "the righteous one" (Zech 9:9, cited in Matt 21:5; John 12:15; Pss. Sol. 17:32). The term probably has overtones of devoted loyalty to God (cf. Luke 2:25; 25:30; Acts 10:22[136]). In this passage it underlines the innocence of Jesus already declared by Pilate (3:13b) in language that echoes the centurion's declaration of Jesus's innocence, an expression unique to Luke's passion narrative (Luke 23:47; contrast Mark 15:39; Matt 27:54).

The exchange of the innocent Jesus for the guilty Barabbas is a particular focus of Luke's passion narrative (Luke 23:25, where the word order both emphasizes Barabbas's guilt and parallels the two men), and it reappears here. This phrasing hints that Luke has an understanding of Jesus's death as redemptive, illustrated by Jesus dying in Barabbas's place. While Luke does not theologize about the death of Jesus in the same way as other NT writers, the presence of explicit redemptive language elsewhere in Luke-Acts (Luke 22:19–20; Acts 20:28) alerts us to its more allusive presence here.[137]

15 ἀρχηγός can mean "pioneer/hero" or "author/founder,"[138] but its widespread use for "leader" in LXX (and elsewhere) is the probable reason for its application to Jesus by the earliest Christians.[139] Zehnle's proposal that a Moses parallel is being invoked, on the ground that Moses is called ἄρχων, "ruler" (7:35, quoting Exod 2:14 LXX), a word related to ἀρχηγός, "leader," is implausible.[140] The genitive τῆς ζωῆς is a genitive of direction, "to life."[141] The earliest believers understand Jesus to have this role because he himself was the first to rise from the dead (26:23; 1 Cor 15:20)[142] rather than this phrase simply being equivalent to "firstborn from among the dead."[143] Hebrews 2:10 uses an equivalent expression, ἀρχηγός τῆς σωτηρίας, for *ḥayyē* in Aramaic can mean either "life" or "salvation."[144] The choice of the descriptor τὸν . . . ἀρχηγὸν τῆς ζωῆς, "the one who leads the way to life," both signals that Jesus's

135 Hurtado, *Lord*, 189–90; cf. Mallen, *Reading*, 127.

136 See further Doble, *Paradox*, 158–59, 136–42.

137 Walton, *Leadership*, 91–98, 107–10, 137–39; Marshall, "Place."

138 For examples, see Jones, "Title," 627nn3–6.

139 Acts 5:31; Heb 2:10; 12:2. In LXX, see Exod 6.14; Num 10.4; 13.2, 3 (MT 3,4); 14.4; 24.17; Deut 32.21; 1 Chr 5.24; Neh 2.9; 7.70, 71; Isa 3.6, 7; 30.4; Jdt 14.2; 1 Macc 9.61. Discussion: "ἀρχηγός," *EDNT* 1:163–64; more fully Müller, ΧΡΙΣΤΟΣ, 249–70. For extrabiblical uses, see Barrett, *Acts*, 1:197.

140 Zehnle, *Discourse*, 47–48.

141 BDF, §166; cf. Mic 1:13 LXX ἀρχηγὸς ἁμαρτίας αὐτή ἐστιν, "she is the leader of sin," i.e., the one who leads the way to sin.

142 Fitzmyer, *Acts*, 286; Conzelmann, *Acts*, 28.

143 So Smalley, "Christology," 362.

144 Bruce, *Acts* (1990), 141.

resurrection ensures that believers will be raised[145] and highlights the irony of the Jerusalemite Jews' killing one who by his resurrection leads the way to life itself. The healing of the man also demonstrates how Jesus brings fullness of life.[146] On the latter point, the echo of Acts 2:28 is noteworthy: Peter's speech presents Jesus as the fulfillment of David's announcement in Ps 16 LXX (MT 17); particularly interesting is the link to Ps 16:11 LXX (MT 17:11): ἐγνώρισάς μοι ὁδοὺς ζωῆς, "you show to me the paths of life," i.e., the paths that lead to life.[147]

ὃν ὁ θεὸς ἤγειρεν ἐκ νεκρῶν, "whom God raised from the dead," specifies how God has vindicated Jesus after the Jews of Jerusalem murdered him. Jesus's resurrection is the basis and power behind what God is now doing.[148] It is not necessary to see the verb ἤγειρεν, "raised," as making a link to Peter raising the man (Acts 3:7, same verb).[149]

The only intrusion of anyone other than God or "you" as grammatical subject into the speech is with the emphatic "of this *we ourselves* (ἡμεῖς) are witnesses." The statement performs a twofold function. First, it states who gives testimony to the resurrection of Jesus—Peter and John, as representative apostles, are the authorized witnesses (cf. 1:21–22). Throughout Acts, the themes of testimony and the resurrection are linked—God's action in vindicating Jesus is the focus of believers' testimony (1:22; 2:23–24, 32; 4:10; 5:30–32; 10:41–43; 13:30–31; 22:14–15; 26:16).[150] Thus the resurrection of Jesus opens this discourse (3:13–15).[151] Secondly, it clarifies the role of the apostles positively, following Peter's denial that they have power to heal in themselves (v. 12): they are not healers but witnesses (see further on 1:8). The "witness" motif here may assist in understanding Luke's mention of the silent presence of John throughout the sequence of events from 3:1 to 4:22, in that biblical law requires two witnesses to establish a case (Deut 19:15).

16 The Greek of this verse is far from straightforward, leading Pervo to conjecture a textual emendation that deletes τὸ ὄνομα αὐτοῦ as a redundant gloss.[152] Moule suggests that there may be here three attempts at saying the same thing:[153]

> καὶ ἐπὶ τῇ πίστει τοῦ ὀνόματος αὐτοῦ
> τοῦτον . . . ἐστερέωσεν τὸ ὄνομα αὐτοῦ,
> καὶ ἡ πίστις ἡ δι' αὐτοῦ ἔδωκεν αὐτῷ τὴν ὁλοκληρίαν ταύτην . . .

145 Anderson, *But God*, 225.
146 Hamm, "Acts 3:12–26," 203.
147 Hamm, "Acts 3:12–26," 203.
148 Anderson, *But God*, 223.
149 *Pace* Hamm, "Acts 3:12–26," 203.
150 See Anderson, *But God*, 220.
151 Cf. Anderson, *But God*, 221–24.
152 Pervo, *Acts*, 106.
153 Moule, "Acts iv.25," 220.

and by faith in his name
his name has made this person strong,
and faith in him gave to him this full health . . .

Moule goes on to suggest that Luke may have left his work unrevised with different possible wordings, and a later scribe(s) copied all the alternatives into the text that we see in our manuscripts. Be that as it may, Moule helpfully identifies that the three phrases collectively clarify the means of healing.

Schneider suggests a chiastic organisation of the sentence:[154]

v. 16a	**v. 16b**
1 τοῦτον . . .	3 ἡ πίστις ἡ δι᾽ αὐτοῦ
2 ἐστερέωσεν	2 ἔδωκεν
3 τὸ ὄνομα αὐτου	1 αὐτῷ τὴν ὁλοκληρίαν
1 this one . . .	3 faith in him
2 has made strong	2 has given
3 his name	1 to him full health

Each half of the verse is expanded by a short phrase: v. 16a with ὃν θεωρεῖτε καὶ οἴδατε, "whom you see and recognize," and v. 16b with ἀπέναντι πάντων ὑμῶν, "before you all." Schneider proposes that Luke's source contained the simpler chiastic structure and that Luke has provided the short phrases and the introductory καὶ ἐπὶ τῇ πίστει τοῦ ὀνόματος αὐτοῦ, "and by faith in his name." Such speculation about sources is rather unfruitful,[155] but Schneider's chiastic structure also identifies the three parallel descriptions recognized by Moule, although it is worth noting that the opening phrase completes the chiasm by providing a faith/name—name/faith structure.[156] The weight of the three phrases conveys the central place of both faith and "the name" in the man's healing.

Whose faith is it? Hamm notes the parallel healing in 14:8–10 (esp. v. 9b) and identifies the faith as that of the man rather than Peter and John, further noting that the faith of the agent of healing is never mentioned in Luke-Acts.[157] Further, the man's praise (vv. 8, 9) suggests he exercised faith.[158] Less persuasively, Witherington notes the silence over the man's faith (or lack of it) and suggests that Peter and John's faith in Jesus is implicit earlier (vv. 12–13) and therefore concludes that this is Peter and John's faith.[159]

154 Schneider, *Apostelgeschichte*, 1:320–21.
155 As is that of Barrett, "Faith," 5–6.
156 Spencer, *Acts*, 47.
157 Hamm, "Acts 3:12–26," 204; also Gaventa, *Acts*, 87; Haenchen, *Acts*, 207.
158 Marshall, *Acts* (TNTC), 92.
159 Witherington, *Acts*, 182.

What kind of faith is it? For Luke, πίστις, "faith," is a characteristic attitude of those wanting something (Luke 5:20; 7:9, 50; 8:25; 17:5–6, 19; Acts 14:7), *pace* Hamm, who sees Luke 7:50; 17:19 as examples of faith as response to God's gift[160]—rather, in both cases, the faith spoken of predates the healing, highlighted by the perfect tense ἡ πίστις σου *σέσωκέν* σε, "your faith *has saved* you." This faith is characterized by two phrases in Acts 3:16:

(i) τοῦ ὀνόματος is an objective genitive, "in [his] name," and this raises significant christological implications, for to say that a person has faith in Jesus's name, and that it is through faith in Jesus's name that healing has come, is to place Jesus alongside YHWH.[161] As "the name of YHWH" is a way of speaking of YHWH's authority and majesty,[162] so Jesus's name bespeaks his authority and majesty.[163] While this speech stops short of placing Jesus in the same category as God, this bold phrase certainly points in that direction (on "the name" see *Comment* on 2:38).

(ii) ἡ δι᾽ αὐτοῦ, "which comes through Jesus," could refer to faith deriving from or evoked by Jesus or the name (genitive of source; αὐτοῦ could be masculine, referring to Jesus, or neuter, referring to "the name," τὸ ὄνομα) or faith in the power of Jesus (circumstantial). It is not easy to resolve this,[164] but the sense is clear—the faith focuses on Jesus and the name does not have power in and of itself.

Thus this verse as a whole combines emphasis on the name and on faith,[165] and therefore τὸ ὄνομα αὐτοῦ, "his name," is not a freestanding entity or seen as exercising a "magical" effect on its own.[166] In the recent context in Acts, ὄνομα is used for calling on the Lord's name and for invoking Jesus's name in baptism (2:21, 38; see *Comment* there).[167] This verse, then, is consistent with the earlier uses of τὸ ὄνομα, "the name," for the name stands for the Lord himself as the object of faith. Further, the earliest believers used *only* the name of Jesus in this way, contrasting with use of a variety of names in magical spells and the like—Jesus's name is uniquely powerful and effective, further pointing to the parallel with biblical use of the "name of YHWH."[168] It is striking that Luke locates this understanding in Palestine early in the development of the

160 Hamm, "Acts 3:12–26," 205n19.

161 Ziesler, "Name," 34, observes that the whole speech fills "the name" with content focused on Jesus, crucified and now raised vindicated: "The healing by the name is thus 'gospelised.'"

162 E.g., LXX Gen 12:8; 13:4; 21:33; Deut 12:11, 21; 1 Kgs 5:17, 19 (EVV 5:3, 5); 8:17, 18, 20; 2 Kgs 21:4, 7; 23:27; Neh 1:11; Ps 33:4 (MT 34:3).

163 Ziesler, "Name," 35–37.

164 So MHT, 3:267.

165 Barrett, *Acts,* 1:200.

166 Nor is the "name" a cipher indicating that Jesus is absent following his ascension; rather, his name denotes his presence and power at work, contra Busch, "Presence," 530–32.

167 Barrett, "Faith," 7–8.

168 Hurtado, *Lord,* 204–5.

believing community, and there is no good reason to doubt that the name of Jesus was so used.[169]

ὁλοκληρίαν, "full health," is a NT *hapax legomenon* and may connote four dimensions of health. First, it is found in the LXX only at Isa 1:6 v.l., which speaks of Israel in rebellion against YHWH as being without ὁλοκληρία from the feet to the head[170]—thus, a dimension of restored relationship to God is suggested. Secondly, the physician Galen uses the cognate adjective ὁλόκληρος, "sound, whole," for bodily health,[171] and it is used thus in LXX,[172] suggesting a physical dimension. Thirdly, the cognate adjective may be cultic, used for unblemished animals that could be offered in sacrifice (e.g., Ezek 15:5 LXX).[173] This resonance makes sense in this co-text, where the man enters the temple as a full participant in the worshiping life of the people of God, whereas in 4:10 ὑγιής, a commoner word for "healthy," is used (11x NT; 9x LXX)—thus, there is a dimension of restoration to full participation in the people of God. Fourthly, the man is given the opportunity of economic productivity—he will no longer need to beg and is thus economically "healthy" too.[174] The man's restoration is comprehensive.[175]

17 Καὶ νῦν, ἀδελφοί, "And now, brothers and sisters," marks the transition to the second part of the speech (cf. 20:22, 25, 32).

οἶδα ὅτι κατὰ ἄγνοιαν ἐπράξατε ὥσπερ καὶ οἱ ἄρχοντες ὑμῶν, "I realise that you acted from ignorance, as your rulers did too." οἱ ἄρχοντες ὑμῶν, "your leaders," is a Lukan designation for the various groups named by Luke (the scribes, elders, etc.).[176] As here for the Jerusalemite Jews and their leaders, in Luke's Gospel the disciples' lack of understanding is a mitigating factor (Luke 9:45; 18:34; 24:16, 31), although they are still responsible for their actions. Chrysostom compares Joseph's words to his brothers in Gen 45:5, which make clear that God was in control of events but did not mean that the brothers were not responsible for their actions.[177] The OT makes a distinction between intentional and unintentional sin and allows forgiveness for the latter (Num 15:23–31).[178] That said, now that Peter has told them this, they are no longer ignorant; thus, if they fail to repent, they become knowing sinners

169 Hurtado, *Lord*, 205.
170 Hamm, "Acts 3:12–26," 206, proposes other connections with Isa 1.
171 Hobart, *Language*, 193–94.
172 E.g., Zech 11:16; Johnson, *Acts*, 68.
173 Dunn, *Acts*, 40.
174 Speckman, "Healing," 102.
175 Marconi, "History," 172–73.
176 See Luke 23:35; 24:20; Acts 4:5, 8, 26; 13:27; 14:5; 16:19; with Weatherly, *Responsibility*, 64–65.
177 *Hom. Act.* ix, p 56.
178 Cf. D's reading specifying that the Jerusalemites and their leaders acted πονηρόν, "in an evil way," which removes any exoneration which the ignorance motif allows; see Epp, "Ignorance," 53–57.

and the Torah makes no provision for forgiveness of deliberate sin.[179] Luke 23:34 presents Jesus praying for forgiveness those who crucify him because they do not know what they are doing, and there may be a case for regarding it as Lukan.[180] The ignorance motif will recur when Paul speaks in Pisidian Antioch (Acts 14:27) and Athens (17:30), also with the offer of the possibility of change. In the Athenian gentile setting, ignorance "levels the playing field for both Jews . . . and gentiles."[181] It is asserted elsewhere in the NT, of both Jews and gentiles (Rom 10:2–3; 1 Tim 1:12–13; Eph 4:17–18; 1 Pet 1:14; 2 Pet 2:12).

There is great irony here in Peter, of all people, speaking thus, for Peter himself denied the Lord after vehemently rejecting the idea that he might do that (Luke 22:31–34, 54–62). It is now this former denier who, after presenting his hearers' responsibility for denying Jesus (Acts 3:13, 14), offers them the possibility of change.[182] His address at this point in the speech, ἀδελφοί, "brothers and sisters," engages his audience in solidarity, and Luke's readers will recognize that this solidarity goes beyond ethnicity to shared denial of Jesus.

18 ὁ . . . θεός, "God," is fronted and separated from its verb προκατήγγειλεν, "had announced in advance" (cf. Eph 2:4, where ὁ . . . θεός [with δέ] is used to highlight the key transition in the passage). This reference to Scripture strongly echoes Jesus's interpretation of Scripture in Luke 24:26–27, 46—Peter appeals over the heads of the Jewish leaders who crucified Jesus to God, the author of Scripture, who has overturned the mistaken human verdict on Jesus.[183] God's purposes were not frustrated, but rather carried out, through Jesus's suffering; there is a clear echo of the Pentecost speech (Acts 2:23–36; cf. 17:2–3, also in a Jewish setting), and the repetition emphasizes the key theme of God's vindication of Jesus.

διὰ στόματος πάντων τῶν προφητῶν, "through the mouth of all the prophets," gives a window into the early believers' understanding of Scripture as having dual—human and divine—authorship, in similar manner to 2 Pet 1:20–21.

It is God's ("his") Messiah, τὸν χριστόν αὐτοῦ, who suffers, which is unexpected, for there are no OT passages which speak of the Messiah suffering—and the crowd would be surprised at this assertion. However, Pervo is right to see this as a primitive "early Christian presupposition to biblical exegesis,"[184] in similar terms to τοῦτό ἐστιν τὸ εἰρημένον διὰ τοῦ προφήτου, "this is the event announced through the prophet" (2:16). The expression τὸν χριστόν αὐτοῦ, "his Messiah/anointed," is found in LXX,[185] and the likeliest echo seems to be Ps 2:2, a royal/messianic psalm quoted in Acts 4:26. The earliest believers

179 Cf. Marshall, *Acts* (TNTC), 92.
180 Doble, *Paradox*, 181–82.
181 Pervo, *Acts*, 107.
182 Hamm, "Acts 3:12–26," 207.
183 Brawley, *Text*, 94.
184 *Acts*, 107.
185 Pss 2:2; 17:51 (MT 18:51; EVV 18:50); 19:7 (MT 20:7; EVV 20:6); 27:8 (MT 28:8); Amos 4:13.

reimagined messiahship in the light of their knowledge and experience of Jesus as a suffering and exalted Messiah and heard Scripture as testimony to the necessity of Jesus's messianic suffering.[186] The likeliest source for this belief is Jesus himself.[187] How was the claim made that the Messiah had to suffer? Linking the Messiah with the Isaianic servant seems the probable interpretive strategy to draw this conclusion,[188] a conclusion that reworks traditional messianic concepts (typified by Luke 23:35) around what Jesus was known to have done.

19 Now we learn about the response required.[189] The combination μετανοήσατε . . . καὶ ἐπιστρέψατε, "repent . . . and turn," is found only here and Luke 17:4; Acts 26:20 in the NT. Isaiah 46:8 LXX explains μετανοήσατε, "repent," as ἐπιστρέψατε τῇ καρδίᾳ, "turn in/with the heart," where the heart denotes the will (as throughout Scripture). Luke uses the latter verb a little more (he has fourteen of thirty-two NT uses of μετανοέω and eighteen of thirty-six NT uses of ἐπιστρέφω), and it is common in LXX as a translation of Heb. שׁוּב (*šwḇ*), "turn," particularly in contexts of turning back to God (e.g., Isa 19:22; 31:6; 45:22; 55:7; Mal 3:7). In particular, to turn is the response expected in Paul's preaching (Acts 14:15; 26:18; 26:20; cf. 1 Thess 1:9 for conversion to the living God, and Gal 4:9 for reverse conversion away from following Jesus). The combination represents a two-part movement, negatively repenting *from* sin and positively turning *to* God, and this brings forgiveness, εἰς τὸ ἐξαλειφθῆναι ὑμῶν τὰς ἁμαρτίας, "to have your sins blotted out" (cf. Acts 26:18), in similar manner to 2:38 where ἄφεσιν τῶν ἁμαρτιῶν *ὑμῶν*, "forgiveness of *your* sins," addressed to the Pentecost crowd may be connected with the Jerusalemites rejecting and murdering Jesus and failing to recognize him as Israel's Messiah.[190] Thus a corporate repentance is part of Luke's meaning here—Peter is seeking that Jerusalem's populace will turn from their recent wrongdoing to Jesus, and thereby seek renewal and restoration of the whole of Israel rather than just the formation of a messianic sect.

The parallel with 2:38–29 has interesting differences as well as similarities, for there is no mention here of baptism (nor elsewhere where there is a call to repentance, note 17:30; 26:20) and a community to join. Luke presents this speech as being interrupted (4:1) and probably expects his readers to recognize the connection with 2:38–39 and to fill in this gap from there. Such a connection would be natural if the Pentecost speech is Luke's fullest expression of evangelistic preaching in Jerusalem[191] and these key points

186 Dunn, *Beginning*, 215–16; cf. Wright, *Resurrection*, 554–63, esp. 562–63.

187 For full and persuasive defense of this view, see Wright, *Jesus*, 484–538.

188 With Mallen, *Reading*, 126; Bruce, *Acts* (1990), 143.

189 Wills, "Form," 286, notes this transition from exposition to exhortation, which he sees as typical of early Christian preaching.

190 Ovey, *Feasts*, 44.

191 Cf. Zehnle, *Discourse*, e.g., 94, and passim, who regards it as Luke's fullest theological statement.

are taken as read elsewhere, as he seems to do—at least in part—with other speeches, notably those in Antioch, among diaspora Jews (13:16–41), and in Athens, among pagans (17:22–31).

Two purpose clauses follow, expressing the outcome of repentance and turning.[192] The first (3:19b) speaks of the blotting out of sins, which is both individual and corporate, including rejecting and crucifying Jesus. The second (v. 20) goes on to wider consequences for the world. Thus, repentance and turning are not merely ways of dealing with the past but are future-facing: they open the door for what God will bring through Christ.

20 καιροὶ ἀναψύξεως, "times of refreshing," is an unusual expression. Luke uses the singular καιρός, "time," for the "absolute end-time events" in combination with the plural καιροί, "times," for events leading up the end, e.g., Acts 2:17–20a uses the plural and then v. 20b uses the singular; similarly in Luke 17:26–31 the "days," ταῖς ἡμέραις (v. 26), lead up to "the day," ᾗ ἡμέρᾳ (v. 30);[193] this strongly suggests that the plural καιροί, "times," denotes interim events before the end itself (cf. also Luke 21:24; Acts 1:7).

ἀνάψυξις, "refreshing," is found only here in the NT, and only at Exod 8:11 in LXX, MT (EVV 8:15), where it refers to the temporary respite Pharaoh saw when the plague of frogs was withdrawn. Barrett notes that Philo, *Abraham* 152, uses this word also for a temporary break.[194] He further notes that the "broadly synonymous" ἀναψυχή is used for a time or place of relief by Plato, *Symp.* 176A (a break from drinking wine after a heavy night of drinking!), and in the LXX Ps 65:12 (MT 66:12); Hos 12:9 (EVV 12:8); Jer 30:26 (MT 49:31). The cognate verb ἀναψύχω, "refresh," in LXX describes animals' rest on the Sabbath (Exod 23:12); a drink of water (Judg 15:19; 2 Sam 16:14); Saul's relief when David played his harp (1 Sam 16:23); the oppressed people's revival of spirits (2 Macc 13:11; cf. 2 Tim 1:16); recovery from weariness (Ps 38:14 [MT 39:14; EVV 39:13]). There may thus be an overtone of Israel's restoration using a metaphor portraying new life.[195]

These lines converge to suggest that καιροὶ ἀναψύξεως, "times of refreshing," denote present, temporary refreshings and revivings rather than the "final messianic deliverance," and thus this expression portrays people experiencing in the present—at least in part—the reality that the whole of creation will experience at the Messiah's return. Hence, these times come ἀπὸ προσώπου τοῦ κυρίου, "from the Lord" (cf. such blessings coming from heaven in Dan 2:28; Rev 21:2; 4 Ezra 8:52; 12:32; 13:26[196]). Pervo suggests that the phrase

192 Vanlaningham, "Should," 214.

193 See further Kurz, "Acts 3:19–26," 310 with n8; Bayer, "Eschatology," 245; Carroll, *Response*, 88, 143.

194 "Faith," 10–13.

195 Bauckham, "Restoration," 477–79. Schmitt, "L'eglise," esp. 215, stresses the Deuteronomic background to Israel's restoration and argues that the believing community is being presented as in strong continuity with Israel.

196 Zwiep, *Ascension*, 114.

"evokes . . . the leisure and abundance of the eschatological era."[197] The healing of the man and the forgiveness now offered are examples of such anticipations of the future in the present: Kurz rightly refers to this as an inaugurated eschatology.[198]

In addition, the phrase may echo two themes.[199] (i) Lohfink suggests a link to a tradition like 4 Ezra 11:46a "And so the whole earth . . . shall be refreshed again" ([R. H. Charles]; Latin: *uti refrigeret omnis terra*).[200] Lohfink proposes that the underlying Greek for *uti refrigeret* was ἵνα ἀναψύξαι, "so that it may be refreshed." If such a tradition from Jewish apocalyptic underlies καιροὶ ἀναψύξεως, "times of refreshing," and it can be no more than a possibility, it is likely that this represents the application of the Jewish term to the time of salvation now present through Jesus. (ii) Lane links this expression to the free translation of Isa 32:15 in Symmachus: ἕως ἂν ἐπέλθῃ ἐφ' ὑμᾶς ἀνάψυξις ἐξ ὕψους, "until a refreshing from on high shall come upon you."[201] The thematic parallel of this verse with Acts 2:38 supports this link, for in 2:38 repentance (with water baptism) is linked to the outpouring of the Spirit, and here repentance is linked to times of refreshing.[202] If this background is likely, again Jewish apocalyptic forms the background to the choice of term, and Luke's use relates the present experience of Jesus and the Spirit in healing, deliverance, and salvation (broadly understood) to the future expectation of the apocalypticists.[203] On either reading, this expression asserts that what was promised for the future is now available in the present through Jesus the risen and exalted Messiah.

Robinson claims that the Christology of 3:19–20 is that Jesus is yet to become Messiah and will do so at his return, and he suggests that this is a very primitive Christology.[204] However, v. 18 describes Jesus as Messiah when suffering, and Luke sees no contradiction in juxtaposing that description of Jesus's messiahship and this one.[205] Thus the choice of a perfect participle, προκεχειρισμένον, "having been appointed," in this setting suggests that Jesus has already been appointed as Messiah and continues to be so.

All of this still leaves open when the "sending" of the Messiah (v. 20b) will take place, but it clearly implies a period of time, which should not be misconstrued as a "delay"; rather, this verse suggests that such an expectation

197 *Acts*, 107n37.
198 Kurz, "Acts 3:19–26," 310; cf. Schmitt, "L'eglise," 216, seeing vv. 20–21 as portraying a two-stage eschatology; contrast Cadbury, "Acts and Eschatology," arguing that Luke has no "realized eschatology" (although he does not discuss this verse), and Butticaz, "Actes 3,1–26," 186–87.
199 Hamm, "Acts 3:12–26," 207–8.
200 "Christologie," 231–32.
201 "Times."
202 Bayer, "Eschatology," 246.
203 So Lennartsson, *Refreshing*, 261, noting Symmachus's rendering of Isa 32:15 (above).
204 "Christology," esp. 181–83.
205 Moule, "Christology," 167–69.

goes back to the earliest days of the believing community.[206] "[A] passage like Acts 3:19–21 shows that for [Luke], despite all the emphasis on the presence of salvation, the view of the future and of completion remains a constituent element."[207] Hamm argues that the Messiah being sent refers to Jesus operating "as prophet within the mission of his church," on the bases that Jesus as Anointed One is here being painted in the colors of Moses and that within Acts Jesus is identified with his church in mission (9:5; 22:8; 26:15, each featuring Jesus speaking to Saul from heaven and presenting himself as the one whom Saul is persecuting).[208] That the speech uses Mosaic categories to clarify Jesus's role is clear (3:22–23); however, it seems hard to see ἀποστείλῃ, "he may send," as anything other than a reference to the return of Jesus in the light of the promise of 1:11 (although cf. God's sending Elijah, Mal 3:22 LXX[209]). However, no further events or conditions are required before the end comes,[210] and so it could be imminent—but it could be a long time coming too. The concerns of this speech are not so much to do with an eschatological timetable but with christological clarity: the hearers need to recognize and respond to the risen Jesus as Messiah.

21 ὃν δεῖ οὐρανὸν . . . δέξασθαι, "whom heaven must . . . receive." The present location of Jesus is in the realm of God, heaven, until he returns (cf. 1:11), and δεῖ, "it is necessary," indicates that the timing of his being in heaven depends on God. However, this does not mean Jesus is entirely absent and inactive on earth. The power of his name in healing the man (3:6; cf. 3:16; 4:10, 30) and his own interventions in the story of his people (e.g., 9:5, 33) are examples of Jesus's continuing activity on earth.[211]

ἄχρι χρόνων ἀποκαταστάσεως πάντων, "until the times of restoration of all things," is a unique expression in the Greek Bible. Possible translations of ἀποκατάστασις are "restoration, re-establishment, return, reversal, recovery, renewal"; there are examples from military (return to a location or position), medical (recovery from illness), and cosmological (return of heavenly bodies to the same place in the sky) co-texts.[212] Hamm notes that the verb ἀποκαθίστημι, "restore," is found in both LXX and NT in relation to healing (Jer 15:19; Exod 4:7; Lev 13:16; Luke 6:10 and parallels; Mark 8:25), Israel's restoration to the land (Jer 16:15; 23:8; 24:6; 27:19; 29:6; Ezek 17:23; perhaps Acts 1:6), an individual being restored to the community (Heb 13:19), and Elijah's eschatological work (Mal 3:23 [MT 3:24; EVV 4:6]; Mark 9:12; Matt 17:11—see further

---

206 Zehnle, *Discourse*, 93; Marshall, *Acts* (TNTC), 94; contra Carroll, *Response*, 150.
207 Hahn, "Problem," 153 (my translation).
208 "Acts 3:12–26," 208, 212.
209 Zwiep, *Ascension*, 115.
210 Bayer, "Eschatology," 250.
211 See Gaventa, "Acts," 42–43; contra Busch, "Presence," esp. 540–41.
212 "ἀποκατάστασις," LSJ 201, and "ἀποκατάστασις," MM 63; cf. Philo, *Heir* 293, in relation to the deliverance from Egypt; Josephus, *Ant.* 11.3.8 §63; 11.4.6. §98, concerning the temple's restoration after the return from Babylonian exile.

Comment on v. 26).[213] The cognate verb is used in *OGIS* 90:18 for "establishment in the proper place" and in the papyri for payment of money due.[214] However, Acts 1:6 is of greater relevance to the sense here, where the Hellenistic form ἀποκαθιστάνω is used, and there the likeliest sense is "restore," suggesting that is the likely sense in this verse too: thus "God, through Christ, will restore his fallen world to the purity and integrity of its initial creation."[215]

The timing of the restoration is debated, although ἄχρι, "until," suggests a limit to that time (cf. similar divine limitations, 2 Bar 13:3; 25:1; 4 Ezra 12:3[216]). Hamm sees the uses of Isa 49:6 in 13:47; 26:23 and Amos 9:11–12 in Acts 15:16 as implying that Jacob's tribes and David's fallen tent have been restored, and thus the restoration of "all things" is in progress and gentile mission may begin.[217] Hamm further takes ἄχρι in the sense "until the end of," seeing Jesus's return from heaven as taking place at the end of the "times of restoration of all things"—thus this expression and "times of refreshing" (v. 20) are coreferential.[218] However, it seems unlikely that Luke regards what happens in the passages which Hamm cites as "the restoration of *all things* (πάντων)." They are a real but partial experience of God's restoration (and the healing that has taken place is an example—the speech flows naturally from the healing), but they are not the full package (cf. Luke 21:5–26).[219] More likely, Luke is expressing an eschatological tension familiar from Paul (cf., e.g., 1 Cor 10:11; 15:20), between the present "times of refreshing" and the yet-to-be "restoration of all things." Kurz helpfully compares Paul's use of μαράνα θά, "our Lord come!" (1 Cor 16:22), a prayer that makes sense only as spoken to one who is now alive but physically absent.[220]

Luke suggests the kind of restoration he has in mind by adding ὧν ἐλάλησεν ὁ θεὸς διὰ στόματος τῶν ἁγίων ἀπ᾽ αἰῶνος αὐτοῦ προφητῶν, "of which God spoke ages ago through the mouth of his holy prophets." It is more straightforward to see the antecedent of the relative pronoun ὧν, "of which," as χρόνων, "times," rather than πάντων, "all things," although Bauckham prefers to regard the phrase as elliptical, meaning, "the restoration of all things of [whose restoration] God spoke by the mouth of his holy prophets."[221] Scholars have

---

213 "Acts 3:12–26," 209–10.

214 *BegC*, 4:38, presumably depending on "ἀποκαθίστημι," MM 62–63.

215 Barrett, "Faith," 16. For the idea of the restoration or renewal of creation, see Isa 62:1–5; 65:17; 66:22; Mal 3:2–4; 2 Esd 7:75, 88–99; 1 En. 45:3–5; As. Mos. 1.18; 10.1–10. Fitzmyer, *Acts*, 289, has a helpful note concerning the later development by Origen and others of the idea that the restoration of all things would be into a purely "spiritual" state.

216 Zwiep, *Ascension*, 114, drawing on Barbi, *Cristo*.

217 "Acts 3:12–26," 210–11; also Turner, *Power*, 419–20; Jervell, *Luke*, 51–52; contrast Wainwright, "Luke," 77, who takes the restoration here to be that of Israel.

218 "Acts 3:12–26," 209n31; also Carroll, *Response*, 145.

219 So Lennartsson, *Refreshing*, 126, 266–67; Johnson, *Acts*, 74.

220 Kurz, "Acts 3:19–26," 318; see also the excursus on Luke's eschatology in Witherington, *Acts*, 184–86.

221 Bauckham, "Restoration," 479, comparing Mark 9:12.

labored to identify more precisely which passages are alluded to here,[222] but Luke himself shows us an example in citing Moses in Acts 3:22–23 and then broadens this to a reference to πάντες . . . οἱ προφῆται ἀπὸ Σαμουὴλ καὶ τῶν καθεξῆ, "all the prophets from Samuel onwards" (v. 24). The latter suggests that it is the broad sweep of divine scriptural promises of restoration for Israel and the cosmos that are in view here, rather than specific texts. It is clear, however, that this reference underlines the hints of restoration found in the narrative of the healing, notably in the allusion to Isa 35:6 LXX (see *Comment* on v. 8).

22–23 The quotation here is from Deut 18:15 with a phrase from Lev 23:29,[223] both from books traditionally attributed to Moses: hence the unusual citation formula Μωϋσῆς . . . εἶπεν, "Moses . . . said" (cf. 7:37, also citing Deut 18:15).[224] This composite quotation identifies Jesus as the prophet like Moses. Deuteronomy 18:15, 18 LXX reads (words used by Luke in the same form are underlined, and words given by Luke in paraphrase or an equivalent expression are dotted underlined—the use of singular forms for "you" reflects the singular forms in the Heb.):

> προφήτην ἐκ τῶν ἀδελφῶν σου ὡς ἐμὲ ἀναστήσει σοι κύριος ὁ θεός σου, αὐτοῦ ἀκούσεσθε . . . προφήτην ἀναστήσω αὐτοῖς ἐκ τῶν ἀδελφῶν αὐτῶν ὥσπερ σὲ καὶ δώσω τὸ ῥῆμά μου ἐν τῷ στόματι αὐτοῦ, καὶ λαλήσει αὐτοῖς καθότι ἂν ἐντείλωμαι αὐτῷ·
>
> The Lord your God will raise up for you a prophet like me from among your brothers; you shall hear him . . . I will raise up for them a prophet just like you from among their brothers, and I will give my word in his mouth, and he shall speak to them whatever I command him. (NETS)

From Lev 23:29 comes: πᾶσα ψυχή, ἥτις μὴ ταπεινωθήσεται ἐν αὐτῇ τῇ ἡμέρᾳ ταύτῃ, ἐξολεθρευθήσεται ἐκ τοῦ λαοῦ αὐτῆς, "Any soul who does not humble himself on that particular day shall be exterminated from his people" (NETS).

Luke's word order varies somewhat from his sources, notably by locating ὑμῖν, "for you," earlier than Deut 18:15 and thereby placing some emphasis on the audience's need to respond (the context in Deut 18:19 clarifies that v. 15 is a general statement by stating "the person, whoever," ὁ ἄνθρωπος, ὃς ἐάν[225]). κατὰ πάντα ὅσα ἂν λαλήσῃ πρὸς ὑμᾶς. ἔσται δέ, "to whatever he says to you. And it shall be," is not derived from Deuteronomy or Leviticus and prepares for the warning of the danger of not responding (Acts 3:23b).

---

222 E.g., Hamm, "Acts 3:12–26," 210.

223 Loisy, *Actes*, 235; Bock, *Proclamation*, 192; contra de Waard, "Quotation," who sees Deut 18:19 as the source for v. 23—but see Bock's critique.

224 In Luke, cf. προσέταξεν Μωϋσῆς, "Moses commanded" (5:14); Μωϋσῆς ἔγραψεν, "Moses wrote," and Μωϋσῆς ἐμήνυσεν, "Moses made known" (20:28, 37); see also Matt 22:24; Mark 7:10; 10:3, 4; 12:19; John 1:45; 8:5; Rom 10:15, 19; Heb 12:21.

225 Bock, *Proclamation*, 191.

How these two texts came to be combined in this way is debated; this is the only place in the NT where they are combined. Dodd suggests that these texts come from a primitive testimony collection and were associated fortuitously, although there is no obvious reason that Luke could not have drawn directly on the Greek OT without an intervening tradition.[226] Bock proposes a Jewish-Christian source.[227]

The Qumran community expected such a prophet like Moses who would divide those who paid attention to him from those who did not, so that the latter would be punished (1QS X, 11; 4QTest 5–7). There seem to have been other Jewish people who expected a second Moses figure (John 1:21, 25; 7:40).[228] This description of Jesus is relatively rare in the NT[229] and is (understandably) found only in Jewish settings, which suggests that it fell into disuse over time. Dunn suggests this was because its inadequacy as an expression of Christology was recognized;[230] it is worth noticing that here it is one of a number of descriptors for Jesus, and that neither John nor Luke use it without other descriptors being used too.

Hamm sees the citation as providing an example of the "restoration of all things" (Acts 3:21).[231] Dupont argues that the shift of word order from LXX highlights ἀναστήσει, "he will raise up," and now relates it to the resurrection of Jesus rather than the OT use for a prophet entering the stage of history (e.g., Deut 13:1; 18:18; 34:10; Sir 48:1).[232] A reference to Jesus's resurrection seems likely over his earthly ministry or his second coming.[233] (i) Jesus's earthly ministry has already been suggested by the account of him being handed over and killed (Acts 3:13b–15), and reference only to Jesus's earthly ministry would mean there was no possibility of repentance for those who rejected him then and thus Peter's offer of a way back would be futile.[234] (ii) The call to repent requires immediate response, not waiting until the prophet appears in the future.

αὐτοῦ ἀκούσεσθε κατὰ πάντα ὅσα ἂν λαλήσῃ πρὸς ὑμᾶς, "pay careful attention to whatever he says to you," uses ἀκούω not merely in the sense of "listen," but "listen and heed"—for failure to pay attention has disastrous consequences (v. 23). The addition of πρὸς ὑμᾶς, "to you," to the LXX here sharpens the point that the OT applies to Peter's hearers—Scripture is the divine voice addressing them, and it is addressing them about Jesus and their need to follow him. There is a strong echo of the divine voice addressing the disciples

226 Dodd, *According*, 54–55, 57–60; similarly, Holtz, *Untersuchungen*, 71–81.
227 Bock, *Proclamation*, 192.
228 Robb, "Prophet," 30–85; Jeremias, "Μωυσῆς," *TDNT* 4:857–64, 867–73.
229 See Robb, "Prophet" for full discussion.
230 Dunn, *Acts*, 43.
231 "Acts 3:12–26," 212.
232 Dupont, "Discours de Pierre," 262n67
233 Robb, "Prophet," 100; contra, e.g., Teeple, *Prophet*, 86; Busch, "Presence," 544–45.
234 Anderson, *But God*, 231–32; Krodel, *Acts* (ProcC), 29.

at the transfiguration, "listen to him," αὐτοῦ ἀκούετε (Luke 9:35), and this Jesus tradition may be a further source used by the early believers in this composite biblical echo.

As Peter presents the issue, it is membership in Israel that is at stake here; true Israelites are those who pay attention to Jesus, the prophet like Moses, and correspondingly, those who reject Jesus are no longer true members of the people of God.[235] The nature of the people of God is being redefined around Jesus, a theme hinted at in Luke's birth narratives, for Jesus has come "for the falling and rising of many in Israel" (Acts 2:34). The rejection of those who reject the prophet like Moses will appear again in 7:35, where Stephen will speak of Moses typologically. Acts 3:23 is a negative counterpart to 2:21[236] and 2:39.[237] However, Pervo's claim, "The contrast between the promise of 2:39 and the threat of 3:23 will be, in retrospect, a foreshadowing of the ultimate Jewish reaction to the message"[238] is overstated, for throughout Acts the gospel divides the Jewish communities it encounters, including some positive response, even in the final scene, where "some were convinced" (28:24).

24 πάντες δὲ οἱ προφῆται ἀπὸ Σαμουὴλ καὶ τῶν καθεξῆς ὅσοι, "all the prophets from Samuel onwards," is linked to vv. 22–23 by δέ answering μέν (v. 22; I have left both words untranslated), thus adding the testimony of Samuel and the prophets to that of Moses, the prophet par excellence.[239] The mention of Samuel looks like a reference to the prophetic books of the Hebrew canon, beginning with the book of Samuel (it is one book in the Hebrew canon) rather than a reference to the prophet Samuel himself,[240] although it is possible that the early believers regarded Samuel's prophecies of David's rule as fulfilled in Jesus as Messiah.[241]

κατήγγειλαν τὰς ἡμέρας ταύτας, "announced these days." κατήγγειλαν, "announced," is an Acts favourite (eleven of eighteen NT uses; not found in any other NT narrative book—other uses all in the Pauline corpus). The whole expression shows a "this is that" pesher hermeneutic being used, strongly echoing 2:16—the present events are the reality that the prophets foresaw and foretold. Thus, the healing, like the tongues-speech of 2:4, 13, functions as a sign that restoration has begun.[242]

---

235 Haenchen, *Acts*, 209; Turner, *Power*, 311.
236 Rese, *Motive*, 66.
237 Pervo, *Acts*, 109.
238 Pervo, *Acts*, 110.
239 Dillon, "Prophecy," 548.
240 Jervell, *Apostelgeschichte*, 170.
241 Marshall, *Acts* (TNTC), 95. To recognize that the "prophets" meant are the *scriptural* prophets, who testify to the coming of the one who will also be the prophet like Moses, resolves Busch's puzzling argument that, since the prophets announce an eschatological prophet like Moses, then that prophet must also announce a further eschatological prophet like Moses, etc., *ad infinitum*; Busch, "Presence," 549. Busch's logic-chopping reading is misguided.
242 Hamm, "Acts 3:12–26," 213.

25 Peter's hearers are addressed as οἱ υἱοὶ τῶν προφητῶν καὶ τῆς διαθήκης ἧς διέθετο ὁ θεὸς πρὸς τοὺς πατέρας ὑμῶν, "the inheritors [sons] of the prophets and of the covenant which God gave to your ancestors." οἱ υἱοὶ τῶν προφητῶν, "the inheritors [lit. sons] of the prophets," is more usually used in LXX for groups of prophets (e.g., 1 Kgs 20:35; 2 Kgs 2:3, 5, 7, 15), although in Tob 4:12 it refers to the whole of Israel. υἱοί, lit., "sons," here denotes the position of Peter's audience as those who may inherit what is promised by the prophets and in YHWH's covenant with Israel. It contrasts with the accusation that Jewish ancestors killed the prophets (Acts 7:52), and Luke is content to leave the two contrasting responses to the prophets—as to the gospel—side by side.[243] As at the beginning (3:13), so here at the close of the speech, Peter invokes the ancestral Jewish God, but here to call his Jerusalemite Jewish hearers (ὑμεῖς, "you yourselves," is emphatic, by presence and location) to respond by becoming followers of Jesus rather than bearing responsibility for his death. Peter invites them to identify with those who listen attentively to the prophet like Moses (v. 22) rather than those who will not listen to him and are cut off (v. 23). This link hints that the Mosaic covenant is being coalesced with the Abrahamic covenant mentioned in the following biblical citation (cf. 7:8); both are in Luke's mind.[244] Thus Peter, in the tradition of the Baptizer (Luke 3:8), invites his audience to be true Israelites who inherit the covenant and claim their inheritance—and in the new situation following Jesus's death, resurrection, and exaltation, to inherit is contingent on following Jesus as Israel's Messiah. Paul argues similarly in Gal 3, where the substance of God's promise to Abraham is Jesus and those who belong to Jesus are inheritors of the divine promise (vv. 14, 16–18. 22, 29 and note the inheritance language in 4:1–7). The parallel with the Qumran community is interesting, for they too considered themselves to be "sons of the covenant" (1QM XVII, 8; 4Q284 frg. 4, 2; 4Q503 frg. 7–9, 3) and thus the inheritors of God's promises to Israel.

The quotation which follows echoes Gen 22:18; 26:4[245] and is probably chosen over the first divine promise to Abram in Gen 12:3b because it explicitly mentions descendants, ἐν τῷ σπέρματί σου, "in your seed."[246] That expression is fronted in Luke's citation, by contrast with LXX, suggesting emphasis.[247] The co-text of Gen 22:18 is Abraham's offering of Isaac, which suggests atonement, although Luke does not make anything of this connection, but keeps the focus on the "seed" promise.[248] Luke uses σπέρμα, "seed," generally to refer to Israel

243 Weatherly, *Responsibility*, 133.
244 Brawley, "Covenant," 125.
245 Although not LXX; Bauckham, "Restoration," 480n89, notes that the word order corresponds to that of the Heb. text of Gen 12:3; 22:18.
246 Hamm, "Acts 3:12–26," 213; Bock, *Proclamation*, 195; Rese, *Motive*, 72–73; contra Witherington, *Acts*, 188.
247 Steyn, *Quotations*, 154–55.
248 Bock, *Proclamation*, 196.

and Israelites rather than Jesus or his church (Luke 1:55; Acts 7:5, 6; 13:23;[249]), by contrast with Gal 3:16, 19, which identify Jesus as the "seed." Further, the introduction to Acts 3:25 identifies the hearers as the descendants of Abraham, and thus, although it is possible that Luke plays on the ambiguity of "seed" and makes some reference to Jesus as the "seed,"[250] it is unlikely that it refers primarily or exclusively to Jesus here.[251] There are echoes of the promises of blessing for Israel in the early chapters of Luke's Gospel (notably Luke 1:32–33, 54–55, 68–79; 2:32, 38), but now it is clear that the divine purposes are not for a nationalistic, political restoration of Israel but for a restored Israel that will lead to the worldwide blessing promised to and through Abraham.[252]

The inclusion of πᾶσαι αἱ πατριαὶ τῆς γῆς, "all the families of the earth," in the statement of God's ancient promise to Abraham, although different from τὰ ἔθνη in Gen 22:18; 26:4 LXX (and perhaps drawn from Ps 21:28 LXX [MT 22:28; EVV 22:27][253]), nevertheless hints that the people of God will ultimately include gentiles. Scott sees a hint at the Table of Nations (Gen 10) in this phrasing, since synagogue-attending Jews would know that as the backcloth to God's call of Abraham.[254] Given that the plural τὰ ἔθνη in Acts normally means gentiles as opposed to Jews, the choice of αἱ πατριαί is a natural way of including the Jewish people, in line with the hearers being told that God sent his child/servant ὑμῖν *πρῶτον*, "to you [sc. Jews] *first*" (Acts 3:26),[255] which itself suggests that others will later benefit; this against the creative argument of Léonas that this verse concerns a blessing for Israel. He thus translates, "And all the families of the land who are part of your offspring shall be blessed," on the basis of reading ἐνευλογηθήσονται, "blessed in" (as LXX), rather than εὐλογηθήσονται, "blessed" (see *Note* p), and arguing that the presence of the preposition ἐν implies inclusion.[256] Léonas's argument seems unlikely for textual reasons and because at least some Jewish eschatology understood the gentiles to be beneficiaries of blessing through Israel in the end times (e.g., Zech 8:20–23). Of course, Luke's Christian readers know already that gentiles will be included—probably many of them are gentiles—so these hints can be left as hints at this stage; the full story will emerge as Acts develops.

26 The speech is summarized in this remarkably compact statement, using vocabulary which picks up its various themes.

---

249 Cf. Luke 13:16; 19:9 (Jervell, *Luke*, 58–59); and similar usage in Rom 1:3; 4:13, 16; 9:7; 11:1; 2 Cor 11:22; Gal 3:29; 2 Tim 2:8.

250 Cf. Turner, *Power*, 309–10.

251 As do van den Eynde, "Children," 472; Bock, *Proclamation*, 195; Fitzmyer, *Acts*, 290; Wilson, *Gentiles*, 219–22.

252 Bauckham, "Restoration," 481; Scott, *Geography*, 84.

253 Conzelmann, *Acts*, 30.

254 Scott, *Geography*, 85.

255 Steyn, *Quotations*, 155, 157; Rese, *Motive*, 73; Wilckens, *Missionsreden*, 43n1.

256 Léonas, "Note."

Luke is presenting Israel as the route through which the blessing of God flows to the world—hence ὑμῖν πρῶτον, "for your benefit *first*," in v. 26, identifying the recipients of the blessings brought by Jesus as *first* the Jewish people.[257] Luke's readers are hearing this at a time when they already know that gentiles will join the people of God—and many readers are likely to be gentiles. In that setting, vv. 25–26 together affirm the importance of God's work among the Jewish people as a route to gentiles receiving God's blessing too;[258] cf. Rom 1:16; 2:10; 3:29; 9:24; 10:12—it is likely that Romans is addressing a situation where gentile believers need reminding that they receive blessing through the Jewish people.[259]

ἀναστήσας ὁ θεὸς τὸν παῖδα αὐτοῦ ἀπέστειλεν αὐτόν, "God raised up his servant and sent him," echoes Acts 3:15, 20, 22, highlighting that God sent Jesus onto the stage of history, as in Luke 4:43 ἐπὶ τοῦτο ἀπεστάλην, "I was sent for this [purpose]." ἀναστήσας, "raised up," here appears not to refer to his resurrection, for it would be hard to see in what sense Jesus was "sent," ἀπέστειλεν, to the people after his resurrection.[260] Peter looks back over the life and ministry of Jesus as a divine mission: Jesus is thus the divine παῖς, "servant," a term that can be used for Moses (e.g., Josh 14:7) and echoes the allusion to the Isaianic servant of Isa 52:13. This word choice thus presents Jesus using colors from Acts 3:13 and 22.

The accusative participle εὐλογοῦντα, "blessing," modifies αὐτόν, "him"; it is thus inappropriate to treat the participle adverbially as expressing the purpose of *God* in sending his servant, as is common in English versions.[261] The construction puts the focus on αὐτόν, "him"—Jesus, the servant sent by God—*he* is the one through whom blessing comes. The choice of εὐλογέω, "bless," here also echoes the quotation from Gen 22:18 in Acts 3:25. The sentence goes on to clarify that the specific blessing offered is forgiveness, received through a turning from evil enabled by Jesus, ἐν τῷ ἀποστρέφειν ἕκαστον ἀπὸ τῶν πονηριῶν ὑμῶν, "by turning each one from your evil ways," here echoing the call ἐπιστρέψατε, "turn!" (v. 19). Thus, the conclusion of the speech keeps the focus on God acting in and through Jesus, and the blessings Jesus brings, and hammers home the need to change both attitude and lifestyle to follow him. This sentence also assumes, in common with the healing in Jesus's name (vv. 6, 16), that Jesus is not an absentee but at work in the present.

---

257 This is a more natural reading of the syntax than to take the adverb πρῶτος, "first," as speaking of the first time Jesus appeared, i.e., at his birth, contra Busch, "Presence," 548.

258 Butticaz, "Actes 3,1–26," 185; cf. Jervell, *Apostelgeschichte*, 171.

259 So, e.g., Dunn, *Romans*, 1:xliv–lviii; Wright, "Romans," 406–8.

260 With Haenchen, *Acts*, 209–10; Bruce, *Acts* (1990), 146; Barrett, *Acts*, 1:213; *pace* O'Toole, "Observations"; Hamm, "Acts 3:12–26," 214–15. Hamm suggests that, just as Moses was sent after being rejected, so Jesus is sent in present mission after the rejection of the cross, cf. 7:35—but this is a link which Luke does not make here; and Kurz, "Acts 3:19–26," 312, who proposes that Jesus is "sent to the listeners in the apostles."

261 With Culy, "Clue," esp. 449–50, *contra*, e.g., NRSVue, NIV, CEV, NLT.

A number of scholars, beginning with Bauernfeind,[262] suggest that Jesus is being presented in terms derived from the presentation of Elijah in Mal 3:22–23 LXX (EVV 4:5–6), based on (i) the use of the same verb of sending (ἀποστέλλω) and a verb of restoration (ἀποκαθιστάνω) that in the LXX translates שׁוב (*šwb*), "turn";[263] (ii) Jesus's being taken away into heaven (Acts 3:21), echoing Elijah's departure (Sir 48:9–10); and (iii) the link of Moses and Elijah in the transfiguration (Luke 9:30) would coincide with Jesus presented here as the prophet like Moses and as one like Elijah.[264] The similarities are clear, although—as with Moses—Jesus is clearly being presented as one greater than Elijah. Bauernfeind's further assertion that Luke is adapting an Elijah-tradition derived from disciples of John the Baptist and replacing Elijah with Jesus is impossible to verify, and the amount of Lukan vocabulary here makes it unlikely.[265]

4:1–4 portrays a divided response to the message which will become typical in Jewish response to the gospel in the rest of Acts:[266] some oppose and attack the gospel witnesses, and others believe and accept the message.

4:1 Λαλούντων . . . αὐτῶν, "while they were speaking," is plural, suggesting that both Peter and John were speaking. Given that events compressed here took at least two hours (see *Comment* on 4:3), this suggests that dialogue between the crowds and both Peter and John takes place over that time. There is no need to deduce that Luke's source had both Peter and John delivering the speech (3:12–26).[267] The parallel with Jesus is striking: Luke also uses a genitive absolute to show that Jesus was speaking when arrested (Luke 22:47).[268]

The arresting group has three components. οἱ ἱερεῖς, "the priests," were some of the priests on duty at the temple during this week, offering the regular morning and evening sacrifices. Luke will draw attention to priests who became believers later (6:7), so that the division in Israel also cuts through its priesthood.

ὁ στρατηγὸς τοῦ ἱεροῦ, "the captain of the temple," was perhaps a senior priest, ranking second only to the high priest, who oversaw the cultic life and the security of the temple.[269] He had power of arrest in the temple precincts. στρατηγός, "captain" is a Lukanism (8x Acts; 2x Luke; never else in NT) and echoes those who arrest Jesus in Luke 22:52.[270] The plural found in Luke (22:4,

262 Bauernfeind, *Apostelgeschichte*, 66–69.
263 Kelly, "Christology," 705–6.
264 See further Kurz, "Acts 3:19–26," 313–16, who develops fuller links to Sir 48 and argues cogently that Luke has assimilated any "early Christology" here into his own wider scheme.
265 Bauernfeind, "Tradition"; see Carroll, *Response*, 151–54.
266 5:12–42; 6:8–7:60; 9:19b–25, 27–31; 13:15–51; 14:1–6; 17:1–9, 10–14; 18:1–17; 19:1–10.
267 *Pace* Barrett, "Faith," 8–9.
268 Pervo, *Acts*, 111.
269 Josephus, *Ant.* 20.6.2 §131; Jeremias, *Jerusalem*, 160–63; Schürer 2:277–78; Hengel, *Judaism*, 1:25. Zeichmann, "στρατηγοί," is doubtful of this view and proposes that the term reflects Luke's use of a term used in his location in Ephesus.
270 Tannehill, *Unity*, 2:58–59.

52) implies a group and may be a looser use for a group overseen by a singular "captain" (cf. Josephus, *Ant.* 20.6.2 §131; *J.W.* 6.5.3 §294). Cf. Acts 5:26, where the στρατηγός oversees a group of ὑπηρέται, "attendants."

οἱ Σαδδουκαῖοι, "the Sadducees," are mentioned here for the first time in Acts.[271] This Jewish group is known from the Gospels and Josephus (*Ant.* 13.10.6 §§297–298; 18.1.4 §§16–17; *J.W.* 2.8.14 §§164–165). The Sadducees were strongest among the lay elite but had much support among priests too. They had no legal powers as such, and so we should probably think of a group supporting the arresting officers or perhaps as those who had drawn Peter's preaching to the arresting officers' attention. Mark and Luke only mention the Sadducees in the story concerning their question about the woman who married seven brothers (Mark 12:18–27; Luke 20:27–38). Matthew also reports that story (Matt 22:23–34) and often pairs the Sadducees with the Pharisees as opponents of Jesus (Matt 3:7; 16:1, 6, 11–12), whereas Luke can present Pharisees much more positively (Luke 7:36; 11:37; 13:31; 14:1; Acts 5:34–35; 23:6–9; 26:5). Bammel observes that Luke draws attention to the part of the Sadducees in persecution of the apostles (see 5:17, the only other mention of this group in Acts) and, given their rejection of the resurrection of the dead by contrast with the Pharisees (23:8; Luke 20:27), this is understandable.[272]

ἐπέστησαν αὐτοῖς, "[they] came upon them." This Lukan verb (ἐφίστημι, 18x Luke-Acts of 21x NT) here connotes a sudden appearance,[273] portraying a rapid deployment of the arresting group in order to stop Peter's preaching—the temple authorities acted in haste once they heard what was happening.

2 διὰ τὸ διδάσκειν αὐτοὺς τὸν λαόν, "because they were teaching the people." The priests, etc., would be annoyed because they would not recognize the authority of the apostles to teach (cf. the note of their jealousy in 5:17), as well as being offended by the content of their teaching.[274]

ἐν τῷ Ἰησοῦ τὴν ἀνάστασιν τὴν ἐκ νεκρῶν, "in Jesus the resurrection of the dead." Bammel recognizes that "the Jewish actions against the apostles are regarded as entirely caused by their preaching Jesus's resurrection."[275] Luke's word order focuses attention on "in Jesus" (ἐν τῷ Ἰησοῦ). In what sense is the preposition (and the case) being used? (i) Barrett notes that the generality of Jews would accept a proclamation of general resurrection at the end (Dan 12:2), but the Sadducees denied this (v. 1).[276] He takes ἐν as instrumental, expressing "by means of," giving the sense that resurrection was now available through or by means of Jesus. (ii) Moule takes it as "in the case of Jesus,"

271 On the Sadducees, see Jeremias, *Jerusalem*, 228–32; Schürer, 2:404–14; G. G. Porton, "Sadducees," *ABD* 5:892–95.

272 "Activity," 361.

273 "ἐφίστημι," BDAG 418, §1.

274 Cf. Tannehill, *Unity*, 2:59.

275 Bammel, "Activity," 358.

276 *Acts*, 1:219–20.

arguing that the definite article τὴν ἀνάστασιν τὴν ἐκ νεκρῶν, "*the* resurrection of the dead," means that the resurrection expected at the end of history *had already taken place* in the case of Jesus.[277] Thus Jesus's resurrection is the first eschatological resurrection and the guarantee of eschatological resurrection for believers.[278] Such a claim would particularly aggravate Sadducean members of the Sanhedrin, for not only did they not believe in the resurrection, but they had given judgment that Jesus must die. (iii) Kilgallen takes the statement to mean that they understood the resurrection of Jesus to support the belief that all would be raised, clearly something Sadducees would oppose.[279] Whichever interpretation is correct, this expression has significant christological implications, for it focuses God's eschatological purposes in Jesus. The implications are not fully spelled out here, which suggests that Luke is reflecting primitive beliefs rather than superimposing a later perspective. (See *Comment* on 4:7 concerning the issue at the hearing.)

3 ἐπέβαλον αὐτοῖς τὰς χεῖρας, "they laid hands upon them." Cf. other uses of this language in NT, esp. Luke 21:12 predicting that "they" will lay hands upon you; also of arrest of Jesus, potential or actual (Matt 16:50; Mark 14:46; Luke 20:19; John 7:30, 44) and of Jesus followers later (Acts 5:18; 12:1; 21:27). The echo of Luke 20:19 is particularly interesting, since Luke alone uses this phrase at that point in the arrest of Jesus (cf. Mark 12:12; Matt 21:46, both using κρατῆσαι, "to arrest"[280])—Luke is presenting the apostles' arrest in similar terms to that of Jesus.

ἔθεντο εἰς τήρησιν εἰς τὴν αὔριον· ἦν γὰρ ἑσπέρα ἤδη, "[they] placed them in overnight custody, since it was already evening." Given that Peter and John arrive at the temple about 3 p.m. (Acts 3:1), this means these events take some two hours or more, since ἑσπέρα, "evening" (in NT only here; Luke 24:27; Acts 20:15 v.l.; 28:23), is "a period from late in the afternoon until darkness."[281] That certainly underlines the impression that Peter's speech is at most a précis. The prison used is probably the same as in Acts 5:18 (see *Comment* there).

4 Now we encounter the second, more positive, response to the healing and Peter's preaching. Luke distinguishes between hearing (τῶν ἀκουσάντων τὸν λόγον, "those who had heard the word") and hearing with a response of faith (ἐπίστευσαν, "[they] came to believe"), as he does in 2:37, 41, although with different vocabulary (cf. Luke 3:8; Acts 8:22; 26:20, which link repentance and action).

Luke closes this section with his second, and final, numerical estimate of the number of (male) Jesus followers; it is not clear whether the five thousand are in addition to or include the three thousand mentioned at Pentecost

277 *Origin*, 67; also Haenchen, *Acts*, 214; Wright, *Resurrection*, 452.
278 Anderson, *But God*, 281–84.
279 "Persecution," 146.
280 Tannehill, *Unity*, 2:69.
281 L&N §67.191.

(2:41). If there were five thousand men in total, that bespeaks a community of perhaps twenty thousand members including women and children. While these figures are large, they are not out of the question in a setting where Jerusalem's population grew to as many as two hundred thousand at festival times (cf. *Comment* on 2:41).[282] ἀριθμός, "number," is a Lukanism used mainly to signal large numbers.[283]

Explanation

Peter speaks to the people to explain the basis of the healing of the man (3:1–10) and invites them to become believers themselves. This speech has both significant parallels with and differences from the Pentecost speech (2:14–36); the differences highlight that this speech is tailored to this situation. Notably, the speech begins with the healing (v. 12), identifies the healing as an event that glorifies Jesus (v. 13), and makes it clear that it is through Jesus that the man was healed (v. 16). It also advances the plot of Acts by leading into the first experience of persecution (4:1–3).

The speech is fundamentally theocentric: God—the ancestral God of the Jews (v. 13)—has glorified Jesus (v. 13), raised Jesus (vv. 15, 26), speaks through Moses and the prophets (vv. 18, 21b, 22–25), and will send "times of refreshing" (v. 20a) and ultimately Jesus himself at the times of restoration (v. 21b). Throughout, the initiative is God's.

Three major themes are intertwined in this speech, and each grows out of the divine initiative: Christology, eschatology, and the fulfillment of Scripture.

The person of Jesus is crucial to Peter's exposition, for Peter aims to reverse his hearers' understanding of Jesus. By contrast with their rejection, Peter wants the Jerusalemites to see Jesus from God's perspective. In order to do that, he uses a range of descriptions for Jesus that are unusual in the NT: Jesus is the servant of God (v. 13), the holy and righteous one (v. 14), the one who leads the way to life (v. 15), the Messiah who must suffer (v. 18), and the prophet like Moses (vv. 22–23). Each of these titles is rooted in Scripture. Not only that, but Jesus is now properly the object of faith (v. 16), and his name is powerful—both quite remarkable claims, for they implicitly place Jesus alongside YHWH—the one who is the only true God and thus the only proper object of faith for faithful Jews (cf. Deut 6:4–5; 1 Cor 8:6). The variety of the descriptions and their rarity elsewhere in early Christian writings bespeaks a period when Christology was not formulaic, centered on a small number of "titles," but rather in process of development in a distinctly Jewish context: Luke is portraying active christological reflection and expression in

282 See also Reinhardt, "Population," 264; Hanson, *Acts*, 76–77; contra Pervo, *Acts*, 86–87; Stark, *Rise*, 5–13—the latter claims a 40% per decade growth rate for the early church over its first 350 years.

283 Luke 22:3; Acts 4:4; 5:36; 6:7; 11:21; 16:5; Paul 1x; John 1x; Rev 10x.

the earliest days of the Christian movement, in response to what God is doing in reaching out through the apostles to restore people such as the man at the Beautiful Gate.

As God's servant, Jesus fills out Isaiah's portrait of God's servant who suffers for God's people (notably Isa 52:13–53:12), embodies God's purposes for Israel which is also called God's servant in Scripture (Isa 42:1; 44:1–2, 21; 45:4), and takes on the kingly role of God's servant David (Luke 1:69; Acts 4:25; cf. Isa 37:35). Like the Isaianic servant (cf. Isa 53:10–12), Jesus has gone through suffering and been vindicated ("glorified," v. 13) by God in his resurrection and exaltation to heaven (v. 21) and through his present exercise of power in healing the man (v. 16)—for Jesus is active on earth from his location in heaven.

As "the holy and righteous one" (v. 14), Jesus exhibits key characteristics of YHWH, "the Holy One of Israel" (a prominent OT designation of God, especially in Isa 40–55, e.g., 40:5; 41:20; 43:3, 14; 45:11; 48:17; 49:7; 55:5). Jesus is set apart for God and reflects in his life and character the distinctive separateness of God (Luke 1:35; 2:23). Jesus is "*the* . . . righteous one" par excellence on the lips of Jewish Christian speakers elsewhere in Acts (7:52; 22:14), and his righteousness is frequently associated with the effects of his death (cf. 1 Pet 3:18; 1 John 2:1, 29; 3:7). There may also be messianic overtones, for Zechariah's messianic king is "the righteous one" (9:9), as well as a hint of Jesus's innocence, which is a prominent theme in Luke's crucifixion narrative (Luke 23:47; note the exchange of the innocent Jesus and the guilty Barabbas in 23:25).

By being the first to pass through death to resurrection and exaltation, Jesus is now "the one who leads the way to life" (v. 15; cf. 26:23; 1 Cor 15:20)—Luke portrays the great irony that the Jerusalemite Jews *killed* this life-giver, and their mistake was undone by God raising him from the dead. This point is the heart of the apostolic testimony, stressed by Peter: "we ourselves are witnesses of this" (v. 15b), representing the only intrusion of a grammatical subject other than "God" or "you" in the speech.

Jesus's suffering is not simply a human injustice reversed by God, but he suffers *as Messiah*, as announced in Scripture (v. 18). Such a claim would have been surprising to Jewish ears, for no single OT passage speaks of the Messiah suffering, and yet this claim is fundamental to early Christian preaching and belief. Their recognition of Jesus as both the Isaianic suffering servant and the Messiah led to reworking traditional Jewish concepts of Messiah (e.g., Luke 23:35) around Jesus's life, ministry, death, and resurrection, resulting in this new understanding of a suffering Messiah—and this reworking most probably had its roots in Jesus's own teaching and understanding of his mission.

As the prophet like Moses (Acts 3:22–23), Jesus is the one who must be listened to attentively, for, like Moses before him, he speaks from God. Peter's speech draws on Deut 18:15, 18; Lev 23:29 and a stream of Jewish expectation of one like Moses to come, found also at Qumran (1QS 9.11; 4QTest/175 5–7), and points his hearers to the magnitude of the issue at stake: to reject Jesus is to reject God and to cut oneself off from God's people (Acts 3:23).

The exaltation of Jesus has now changed the way that history—past, present, and future—is seen, so that Peter's speech engages with key eschatological themes (vv. 20–21). The past, particularly the words of Scripture, is now seen as focused on what God has done in Jesus and is doing in restoring and renewing Israel, for this is God's decisive action. In the present, Jesus now resides in heaven (v. 21a), as "times of refreshing" come to God's people (v. 20a), which include forgiveness, healing, new life and, quite possibly, hint at the gift of the Spirit. "Within the story, Peter's speech . . . affords Jerusalem Jews their (final) opportunity to take their place within the covenant people who experience the salvation of God. For Luke's readers, these verses stress the importance of penitent faith, and the urgency of the church's mission . . . Eschatological expectation serves to heighten the urgency of the church's activity in the present."[284] Thus the believers' mission—both the apostles and Luke's believing readers—is to make these things known and lead others to repentance and faith in Jesus. In the future—an indefinite future that should not be misconstrued as a "delay"—Jesus the Messiah will be sent by God, at the "times of restoration of all things" (v. 21a). This picture represents an inaugurated eschatology similar to that found in Paul, where some of the blessings of the age to come are experienced now, but those blessings will be experienced in their fullness when Jesus returns. In terms of the timing of Jesus's return from heaven, "Since the parousia's arrival is not susceptible to prediction, the question about persevering faith is not just a question for the future; it is primarily a challenge to faith today."[285] In the meantime, God-in-Jesus is restoring and reconstituting Israel around her Messiah: the healing of the man is not simply a magic trick to gain attention but symbolizes and embodies the restoration of Israel—Peter highlights the place of Israel in salvation history and invites his audience to join in with what God is now doing.

Throughout the speech, Peter is interpreting Scripture through the lens of Jesus's life, death, resurrection, and exaltation, and it is crucial for this Jewish audience that he demonstrates that what has recently happened and is happening now is in accord with Scripture—only thus will his audience embrace Jesus as the fulfillment of their ancestral faith and hopes. Hence, God is introduced as the ancestral God (v. 13; Exod 3:6), and his prophets announced the Messiah's suffering (Acts 3:18), the universal restoration to come (v. 21), and the events of "these days" (v. 24). Jesus is the prophet like Moses, who was himself the model prophet (vv. 22–23; Deut 18:15, 18;

284 Carroll, *Response*, 151.
285 Carroll, *Response*, 149.

Lev 23:29), and Jesus is the means of fulfillment of God's promise to Abraham (Acts 3:25; Gen 22:18; 26:4; 12:3). "Christ is . . . presented as the one in whom the counsel of God becomes visible."[286] We here touch the theme of who speaks for God in the new situation, in the form of who interprets Scripture correctly; this will be a major issue in the conflict with the Jewish authorities which follows this incident and speech.

The counterpoint to divine initiative is human response. Peter's speech also focuses on the hearers, the Jerusalemite Jews, named regularly as "you"—the Greek is frequently emphatic, especially in Acts 3:13, 14, 25, and note the threefold "you" in v. 26. The people are differentiated from their leaders (v. 17)—both are responsible, but differently. Peter identifies the people's part in the death of Jesus, handing him over and denying him before Pilate (v. 13), asking for the murderer Barabbas in his place (v. 14), and thus bearing some responsibility for Jesus's death (v. 15). These actions were in ignorance of what God was doing (v. 17), and thus there is a way back to God through repentance (v. 19), for Scripture allows that unintentional sin can be forgiven (e.g., Num 15:23–31). This repentance leads to "times of refreshing" coming from heaven (Acts 3:20). However, to reject Jesus is to cut oneself off from the people of God, now being redefined around Jesus (v. 23), for Jesus is the substance to which Moses, the prophets, and God's covenant with Abraham testified (vv. 18, 22–25). This reconstitution is the restoration of Israel, and Luke hints that it will include gentiles (v. 26, echoing Gen 22:18; 26:24; 12:3b).

The twofold response that follows highlights a division in Israel caused by Jesus. On one hand, the Jewish leaders initiate action to suppress the apostolic preaching by arresting and jailing Peter and John (Acts 4:1–3), for they cannot accept either the apostles' authority to teach or their announcement of resurrection in the case of, and through, Jesus (v. 2). The Sadducees denied any resurrection, and the priests would object to the apostles teaching at all, for they were not properly trained (cf. 4:13). On the other hand, a large group come to believe (v. 4), so that the believing community grows in size to five thousand men (suggesting a total community of around twenty thousand, including women and children). Luke portrays a mission which meets with great success among Jews in these early days—the movement is not distinct from Judaism but a renewal movement from within.

3. God Equips Peter and John in a Sanhedrin Hearing (4:5–22)

Bibliography

Anderson, P. N. "Acts 4:19–20." **Avemarie, F.** *Tauferzählungen*, 119–20. **Bammel, E.** "Activity." **Barrett, C. K.** "Salvation." **Beale, G. K.** *Temple*, 216. **Bock, D. L.** *Proclamation*, 198–201. **Bolt, P.** "Mission." **Bond, H. K.** "Acts 4:12." ———. *Caiaphas*, 1–8. **Brawley,**

286 Bayer, "Eschatology," 245.

R. L. *Text,* 91–107. **Butticaz, S. D.** "Acts 3,1–26." **Culpepper, H. H.** "Acts 4:12." **Cunningham, S.** *Tribulations,* 188–89. **Danker, F. W.** *Benefactor,* 323–34, 339–41. **de Villiers, P.** "Medium." **Dodd, C. H.** *According,* 99–100. **Dupont, J.** *Sources,* 42–50. **Edwards, J. R.** "Parallels." **Epp, E. J.** *Tendency,* 120–29. **Foulkes, I. W.** "Problems." **Fresch, C. J.** "Is There." **Funk, R. W.** *Poetics,* 83–96. **George, A.** "L'emploi." **Green, E. M. B.** *Meaning,* 136–51. **Greenhut, Z.** "Cave." **Hamm, D.** "Acts 3,1–10." **Hilton, A. R.** *Illiterate Apostles.* **Horbury, W.** "Caiaphas." **Hull, J. H. E.** *Spirit,* 120–24. **Jeremias, J.** *Jerusalem,* 147–267. ———. "Untersuchungen." **Johnson, L. T.** *Function,* 193–96. **Keith, C.** "Oddity." **Kraus, T. J.** "Uneducated." **Lindars, B.** *Apologetic,* 169–86. **Macaskill, G.** *Union,* 164–65. **Maiburg, U.** "Christus." **Mainville, O.** "Péché." **Marconi, G.** "History." **Marrow, S. B.** "Παρρησία." **Marshall, I. H.** *Historian,* 94–102. **Mason, S.** "Priests," esp. 147–58. **Moule, C. F. D.** *Origin,* 89–94. **Parsons, M. C.** "Character." **Pinnock, C. H.** "Acts 4:12." **Radin, M.** "Freedom." **Reich, R.** "Caiaphas." **Reicke, B. I.** *Glaube,* 73–80. **Rese, M.** *Motive,* 113–15. **Ritmeyer, L., and K. Ritmeyer.** *Jerusalem,* 50–53. **Sanders, E. P.** *Judaism,* 472–81. **Sanders, J. T.** *Jews,* 238–39. **Sandnes, K. O.** "Beyond." **Schenke, L.** "Kontrastformel." **Schnabel, E. J.** *Mission,* 1:420–23. **Smallwood, E. M.** "High Priests." **Soards, M.** *Speeches,* 44–47. **Stendahl, K.** "Lordship." **Stolle, V.** *Zeuge,* 220–26. **Tannehill, R. C.** "Functions," 407–8. **Turner, M. M. B.** *Power.* ———. "Spirit of Prophecy." **van der Horst, P. W.** "Parallels, 3 and 4," 41–43. **Weatherly, J.** *Responsibility,* 69. **Webber, R. C.** "Why." **Wilckens, U.** *Missionsreden,* 44–45, 61–62. **Wilcox, M.** *Semitisms,* 90–92, 172–73. **Woods, E. J.** *Finger.* **Ziesler, J. A.** "Name."

Translation

5 The next day, their rulers, the elders, and the scribes assembled together[a] in
Jerusalem, 6 with Annas the high priest, Caiaphas, John and Alexander, and other
members[b] of the high-priestly family. 7 After they made them stand in the midst, they
began to inquire, "By what power or by what name did you people[c] do this?" 8 Then
Peter, filled with the Holy Spirit, said to them, "Rulers of the people and elders, 9 if
we ourselves[d] are being examined today about an act of kindness done for a sick man,
as to how he was healed, 10 then let it be known to all of you and to all the people of
Israel that it is by the name of Jesus the Messiah of Nazareth, whom you crucified and
God raised from the dead—it is by this one[e] that this man stands before you healthy.
11 He is the stone contemptuously rejected by you builders, which has become head
of the corner. 12 There is salvation in no one[f] else, for there is no other name under
heaven given among people by which we must be saved."

13 Now when they saw the boldness of Peter and John and understood that they
lacked formal education and scribal training,[g] they began to be amazed and to recognize them as people who[h] had been[i] with Jesus.[j] 14 Since they saw the man who had
been healed standing with them, they had nothing to say in opposition.[k] 15 After they
had ordered them to leave the Sanhedrin, they began to confer with one another:
16 "What are we to do[l] with these people? For that a publicly recognized[m] sign has been
done through them is clear to all the inhabitants of Jerusalem, and we cannot deny it.
17 However, so that it may not spread any further[n] among the people, let us warn them
no longer to speak in this name to anyone."[o]

18 They recalled[p] them and ordered them[q] neither to speak nor teach at all[r] in the
name of Jesus. 19 But Peter and John answered them, "Whether it is right before God

to listen to you rather than God,[s] you decide! [20] As for us,[t] we cannot do anything other than speak of the things which we have seen and heard."

[21] After threatening further, since they had not found any way[u] to punish them, they released them on account of the people, for everyone was glorifying God because of what had happened—[22] for the man on whom this sign of healing had been performed[v] was over forty years[w] old.

Notes

a. Inf. συναχθῆναι, "to assemble together," functions as subject of Ἐγένετο, "it happened," a favorite Lukan construction, frequently found with a temporal expression, as here (ἐπὶ τὴν αὔριον, "on the next day"), e.g., Luke 2:1; Acts 9:37; 10:25; 22:6, 17; McKay §6.1.5; Schneider, *Apostelgeschichte*, 1:344n21. This construction moves the narrative on to the next stage (Newman and Nida, *Acts*, 93) and marks this information as the specific "background" circumstances in which the events to follow take place (*DFNTG*[2], 177–79). It is found in the Greek OT some ninety times, notably sixty-one times in Genesis. The "subject" of the inf. is the acc. τοὺς ἄρχοντας καὶ τοὺς πρεσβυτέρους καὶ τοὺς γραμματεῖς, "the rulers and the elders and the scribes."

b. ὅσοι ἦσαν, "as many as were."

c. ὑμεῖς scornfully emphatic both by its presence and its location at the end of the sentence—hence, "you people"; Bruce, *Acts* (1990), 151.

d. Emphatic ἡμεῖς, "we ourselves," responding to emphatic ὑμεῖς, "you" (v. 7).

e. Taking the antecedent of τούτῳ, "by this," to be Ἰησοῦ, "Jesus," rather than ὀνόματι, "name," although the person clearly entails the name, and vice versa; with Schenke, "Kontrastformel," 12.

f. οὐδενί could be m., "no one," or neut. If neut., it would refer to ὀνόματι, "name" (v. 10), but the mention of ὄνομα later in this sentence strongly suggests the translation "no one"; Barrett, *Acts*, 1:230.

g. ἄνθρωποι ἀγράμματοί εἰσιν καὶ ἰδιῶται, lit., "they were uneducated people and untrained." See *Comment on v. 13.*

h. ἐπεγίνωσκόν τε αὐτοὺς ὅτι, "and they recognized them, that"; ὅτι, "that," introduces an indirect discourse clause that states the particular fact about Peter and John that the council members recalled to mind; Wallace, 458, 539, and see *Comment* on v. 13.

i. ἦσαν, impf. in indirect discourse requiring English perfect, "[they] had been."

j. h mae read v. 13b following v. 14, so that the authorities recognize the apostles as Jesus's followers only after noticing the healed man's presence. *TO*[2] 98 reconstructs a Western reading in Greek: τινὲς δὲ ἐξ αὐτῶν ἐπεγίνωσκον αὐτοὺς ὅτι σὺν τῷ Ἰησοῦ συνέστρεφον, "and some of them began to recognize them, that they had been associates of Jesus." Discussion: Epp, *Tendency*, 121–24.

k. aor. inf. ἀντειπεῖν means "to say in opposition" when used absolutely; "ἀντιλέγω," LSJ, §3.

l. ποιήσωμεν, deliberative subjunctive with τί, "What are we to do?"

m. Taking γνωστόν, "known" (hence "publicly recognized," Barrett, *Acts*, 1:235), as qualifying σημεῖον, "sign," because of their proximity and the word order, by contrast with other uses in Acts where γνωστόν often precedes a ὅτι, "that," clause (4:10; 13:38; 28:22, 28); Culy and Parsons, *Acts*, 71; contra Johnson, *Acts*, 79.

n. ἐπὶ πλεῖον, "any further," in distance ("πολύς," BDAG 849, §2.b.β) or time (cf. 20:9; 24:4; Haenchen, *Acts*, 219n4; Conzelmann, *Acts*, 33) or both (Barrett, *Acts*, 1:235; Jervell, *Apostelgeschichte*, 180).

o. μηκέτι . . . μηδενί, lit., "no longer . . . to no one"; double negative with emphatic force.

p. καλέσαντες, "having recalled," echoes κελεύσαντες, "having ordered" (v. 15), an assonance that would be apparent when hearing Acts read aloud.

q. αὐτούς, "them," serves as direct obj. of both ptc. καλέσαντες, "recalling," and indic. παρήγγειλαν, "they ordered."

r. καθόλου, "completely," is an NT *hapax legomenon*, formed from καθ' + ὅλου, "καθόλου," LSJ; used in LXX Amos 3:3, 4; Ezek 13:3, 22; 17:14; Dan 3:50 (EVV Prayer of Azariah 1:27). The acc. article τό marks the expression καθόλου μὴ φθέγγεσθαι μηδὲ διδάσκειν, "neither to speak or to teach at all," as the direct obj. of παρήγγειλαν, "they ordered"; cf. Barrett, *Acts*, 1:236.

s. ὑμῶν . . . τοῦ θεοῦ, both gen. as personal obj. of inf. ἀκούειν "to listen"; "ἀκούω," BDAG 38, §4.

t. Emphatic ἡμεῖς, "we."

u. D syr^{p} mae bo read μὴ εὑρίσκοντες αἰτίαν, "not having found any reason," rather than μηδὲν εὑρίσκοντες, "having found nothing," read by other MSS. D's reading echoes similar readings in Luke 23:22 (D); Acts 13:28 (most MSS) concerning the Jewish leaders finding reasons for putting Jesus to death and thus both parallels the apostles' experience with that of Jesus and adds an anti-Jewish thrust to the text; Epp, *Tendency*, 126.

v. γεγόνει, "had been performed," plpf. of γίνομαι without augment, as frequently for plpf. verbs in NT; Bruce, *Acts* (1990), 155, provides examples.

w. ἐτῶν, "years," is fronted in its clause (and thus separated from τεσσεράκοντα, "forty"), suggesting some emphasis, perhaps, "*as far as his age was concerned*, the man was over forty."

Form/Structure/Setting

Delimitation of pericope. Verse 5 begins with a temporal and spatial shift, which in combination show that the narrative is entering a new scene.[287] The scene closes with divided response to the apostles similar to that found in vv. 1–4, with the Sanhedrin seeking to silence Peter and John (v. 21a) and the people glorifying God (vv. 21b–22): the parallel suggests that vv. 1–4 belong with the previous scene and vv. 21–22 ends this scene.

Sources/historicity. Some find various historical problems with this passage: (i) Peter and John are arrested because they preach the resurrection (v. 2), but the Sanhedrin inquires about the healing (v. 7);[288] (ii) the apparent belated recognition that Peter and John had been with Jesus (v. 13) conflicts with v. 2;[289] and (iii) the Sanhedrin did not have the power of arrest.[290] These lead some to propose that this passage has been heavily redacted, if not created *ex nihilo*, by Luke.[291] Nevertheless, it is impossible to detect sources

287 Parsons, "Character," 300; Funk, *Poetics*, 85–86.

288 Barrett, *Acts*, 1:217; Roloff, *Apostelgeschichte*, 80; Haenchen, *Acts*, 221.

289 Barrett, *Acts*, 1:217; Haenchen, *Acts*, 221.

290 Haenchen, *Acts*, 220.

291 Conzelmann, *Acts*, 32; Weiser, *Apostelgeschichte*, 1:123–24; Schneider, *Apostelgeschichte*, 1:342; Haenchen, *Acts*, 223–24; Jervell, *Apostelgeschichte*, 183.

here with any confidence, not least because the passage has much Lukan language.[292]

However, given the claims which the believers were making publicly about Jesus, it is entirely understandable that the authorities should wish at least to ascertain what the apostles were saying. We have clear evidence for legal measures being taken against the believers at least by the time of Paul (e.g., 1 Thess 2:14; Gal 1:23).[293] Further, it is not unlikely that Sadducees were involved, for they were tied closely to the occupying Roman power and would thus have both the ability and the desire to suppress a movement which might lead to instability (cf. the action of the Sadducee Ananus against James in AD 62, reported in Josephus, *Ant.* 20.9.1 §§199–203). Thus, the scene is plausible. On (i) and (ii) above, see *Comment* on the relevant verses. On the question whether the hearing in Acts 5:27–41 is a "doublet" of this story, see *Form/Structure/Setting* on that passage.

Luke here reports a closed session of the Sanhedrin (vv. 15–17), and it is not possible to know whether Luke had access to information from the meeting (through a member or officer of the Sanhedrin who was sympathetic to the Jesus-community) or whether he reconstructed the kind of discussion that took place on the basis of the outcome.[294]

Schenke argues that the rather stylized "contrast formula" of v. 10b ὃν ὑμεῖς ἐσταυρώσατε, ὃν ὁ θεὸς ἤγειρεν ἐκ νεκρῶν, "whom you crucified, whom God raised from the dead," is traditional, drawn from early Christian preaching.[295] This is certainly possible and supports the antiquity of the saying. The particular phrasing here fits the narrative situation well by the inclusion of the emphatic personal pronoun ὑμεῖς, "you," which focuses attention on the Sanhedrin's part in the death of Jesus.[296] Schenke wishes to see the personal pronoun as part of the traditional formula and (wrongly) understands it to be focusing the accusation on the Jews as a race (see *Comment* on v. 10).

Structure. The passage is organized around the engagement between the Jewish leaders and Peter (and John, his silent partner). Verses 5–7 set the scene and then present the initial question: by what means was the healing performed (v. 7b)? Peter responds in similar tones to his speech in 3:12–26, again putting the focus strongly on Jesus, particularly his unjust crucifixion at the leaders' hands and God's counter-verdict in raising him from the dead (4:8–12). The leaders then bring to cognizance that the apostles are followers of Jesus and debate in private how to respond, before recalling Peter and John and instructing them not to speak or teach in Jesus's name—the

292 Wilcox, *Semitisms*, 172–73; Barrett, *Acts*, 1:217.
293 Jervell, *Apostelgeschichte*, 183.
294 Marshall, *Acts* (TNTC), 101–2.
295 Schenke, "Kontrastformel," 9–20.
296 Wilckens, *Missionsreden*, 44, observes that the speech is "entirely shaped by the situation of the interrogation" (my translation).

leaders' focus, too, is on Jesus (vv. 13–18). Three responses follow: first, Peter rejects their instruction, asserting that the believers must go on testifying to their aural and visual experience (vv. 19–20); then, the leaders find that they cannot take further steps (v. 21a); and finally, the people go on glorifying God for the healing of a man over forty years old (vv. 21b–22).

Setting. The presence of key words from previous sections show that this scene is the natural development from them: (i) ἐν ποίᾳ δυνάμει ἢ ἐν ποίῳ ὀνόματι, "by what power or what name" (v. 7), and ἐν τῷ ὀνόματι Ἰησοῦ Χριστοῦ τοῦ Ναζωραίου, "by the name of Jesus Messiah of Nazareth" v. 10, echo 3:6, 12, 16; (ii) σέσωται, "saved/whole" (v. 9), ἡ σωτηρία, "salvation," and σωθῆναι, "to be saved" (v. 12), echo 2:32, 40, 47; (iii) τοὺς ἄρχοντας, "rulers" (vv. 5, 8), echoes οἱ ἄρχοντες ὑμῶν, "your rulers" (3:17); and (iv) ὃν ὑμεῖς ἐσταυρώσατε, ὃν ὁ θεὸς ἤγειρεν ἐκ νεκρῶν, "whom you crucified, whom God raised from the dead" (v. 10), echoes the focus on the hearers' responsibility for the death of Jesus and God's counter-verdict found in 3:15—the second clause reproduces part of 3:15 verbatim. These links imply that Peter is now showing the full significance of the healing.[297]

Conflict in the city over the Messiah is far from over: it is in a new phase with the apostles testifying to Jesus as the Messiah and calling people to repent. The apostles are presented as facing the same difficulties as their Master and responding in similar vein. This connection is signalled by a number of parallels between this chapter and Luke's passion story, and in each case it seems likely that we are seeing Lukan emphasis, for at each point below his passion story is different from Matthew and Mark:[298] (i) Acts 4:5 has the examination on the morning after the arrest, as Luke 22:66; (ii) the use of συναχθῆναι, "to gather together," for the meeting of the Sanhedrin echoes Luke 22:66 and prepares for Acts 4:26, citing Ps 2:2 οἱ ἄρχοντες συνήχθησαν, "the rulers were gathered"; (iii) τοὺς ἄρχοντας, "the rulers," echoes Luke 23:13, 35; 24:20; (iv) Acts 4:7 echoes the question of the nature of Jesus's authority in Luke 20:2; (v) the use of Ps 118:22 in Acts 4:11 echoes the quotation of the psalm by Jesus (Luke 20:17), where it is used in the context of leaders killing God's messenger, an image also found in Acts 4:10; (vi) "the people" support the apostles (v. 21; cf. 5:26), as they supported Jesus (Luke 19:47–48; 20:19; 22:2), in each case delaying—but not preventing—trial and punishment to follow; (vii) there is no evidence of guilt in both cases (Acts 4:21; Luke 23:4, 14–15).[299]

Further, the parallel with Luke 5:17–26 (already noted concerning Acts 3:1–10), when seen in its wider setting is significant—in both passages the healing of a man who cannot walk is linked to "a basic proclamation of Jesus's

297 Tannehill, *Unity*, 2:61.

298 Items (i) to (vi) below are drawn from Tannehill, *Unity*, 2:68–69; see also *Form/Structure/Setting* on 4:1–4.

299 Fitzmyer, *Acts*, 297.

saving significance . . . and both provoke opposition from religious leaders" (note vv. 9–12; Luke 5:21, 24–35).[300]

This healing functions as something of a "template" for other healings in Acts performed through both Peter and Paul (5:15–16; 9:33–35, 36–42; 14:8–10; 19:11; 20:7–12; 28:8–9).[301] Hence Luke presents this story and its consequences much more fully than the subsequent healings.

Comment

5 The body before which Peter and John are brought after their overnight custody consists of αὐτῶν τοὺς ἄρχοντας καὶ τοὺς πρεσβυτέρους καὶ τοὺς γραμματεῖς, "their rulers, elders, and the scribes," the three main groups that made up the (Great) Sanhedrin, the highest Jewish court.[302] The high priest himself presided. To hold a hearing all seventy-one members were not required to be present: the Mishnah envisages different-sized groups for various kinds of hearings (m. Sanh. 1:1–6). As to location, the Mishnah pictures a large לשכת הגזית (*lškt hgzyt*), "rock-hewn," room in the form of a basilica (m. Sanh. 11:2; m. Mid. 5:4; b. Yoma 25a). Josephus seems to locate this room outside the temple precincts, near to the Xystus, a large meeting place (*J.W.* 5.4.2 §144),[303] whereas the Mishnah locates it inside the inner forecourt of the temple.[304] The Talmud suggests that the Sanhedrin's meeting place was moved around the time depicted here to the חנות (*ḥnwt*), "bazaar" (b. Šabb. 15a; b. Roš Haš. 31a; b. Sanh. 41a; b. ʿAbod. Zar. 8b), but this seems unlikely since it is not mentioned in either Josephus or the Mishnah, both earlier sources.[305]

τοὺς ἄρχοντας are the senior priests (cf. Josephus, *J.W.* 2.16.1 §333; 2.17.1 §§405, 407; 2.21.7 §627), elsewhere called ἀρχιερεῖς, "chief priests" (e.g., Acts 4:23), those who were more or less permanently on duty at the temple because they had oversight of central aspects of the temple's life.[306] τοὺς πρεσβυτέρους, "the elders," are probably the heads of the leading (wealthy) families, and thus mainly Sadducean (Josephus, *Ant.* 18.1.4 §17; 13.10.6 §298; 20.9.1 §199).[307] τοὺς γραμματεῖς, "the scribes," are men trained in the law, and mainly Pharisaic (Acts 23:9 clarifies that not all scribes were Pharisees).[308] There is no explicit mention of Pharisees at this stage, perhaps because the issue at stake is the resurrection of Jesus, and the Pharisees were known to

300 Tannehill, *Unity*, 2:51.

301 Squires, *Plan*, 98; Johnson, *Function*, 193–96.

302 Schürer 2:199–236, esp. 212–13; A. Saldarini, "Sanhedrin," *ABD* 5:975–80; Reicke, *Glaube*, 73–75; contra Sanders, *Judaism*, 472–81, who doubts that such a body existed.

303 Ritmeyer and Ritmeyer, *Jerusalem*, 50–53.

304 Discussion: Schürer 2:223–24.

305 Schürer, 2:224–25.

306 Jeremias, *Jerusalem*, 175–81.

307 Jeremias, *Jerusalem*, 222–32.

308 On the scribes, see further Jeremias, *Jerusalem*, 233–45.

believe in resurrection in general terms. Acts 5:34; 23:6–9 show that Luke knows that this body includes Pharisees.

αὐτῶν, "their," hints at the debate going on in this story and subsequent ones over who is the true people of God. The Sanhedrin members are "their" leaders—the failed and now-rejected leaders of Israel—for they crucified the Messiah (v. 10). The apostles are therefore the (human) leaders of the restored people of God which clusters around Jesus (Luke 22:28).[309]

In his earlier speech Peter has accused the Sanhedrin of wrongly killing the Messiah of Israel (Acts 3:13–15) and acting ignorantly (3:17), and these are serious charges to lay against the leading body—both religious and political—of Israel.[310] The Sanhedrin would be sensitive to the situation, for the Romans could and did replace high priests at will.[311] They would thus want to act in a way that prevented any public disorder.

6 Ἄννας ὁ ἀρχιερεύς, "Annas the high priest." Annas had served as high priest AD 6–15 (Josephus, *Ant.* 18.2.1–2 §§26–35; cf. Luke 3:2), and former high priests could retain the title.[312] It is likely that Annas was still influential—note the role he played in the trial of Jesus (John 18:13, 24).[313]

Καϊάφας, "Caiaphas," was Annas's son-in-law (John 18:13) and served as high priest ca. AD 18–36 (Josephus, *Ant.* 18.2.2 §35; 18.4.3 §95), providing a latest date for this hearing as AD 36. He was thus high priest when Jesus was tried (John 11:49; 18:13). His full name was Joseph Caiaphas (Josephus, *Ant.* 18.4.3 §95), and he was one of five of Annas's sons who held office as high priest (Josephus, *Ant.* 20.9.1 §198). In 1990 there was a remarkable find in Jerusalem of a family burial cave including two ossuaries inscribed with the family name קפא (*qf'*), whose Greek equivalent is Καϊάφας, "Caiaphas."[314] One is ornately decorated and labeled "Joseph son of Caiaphas," יהוסף בר קפא (*yhwsf br qf'*) and contains the bones of a man about sixty years old. The combination with the presence of a coin in another ossuary in this cave from the reign of Herod Agrippa (AD 37–44) suggests that this could well be the same person mentioned here.[315]

We know nothing otherwise of Ἰωάννης καὶ Ἀλέξανδρος, "John and Alexander." The reading of D, Ἰωναθᾶς, "Jonathan," may refer to a son of Annas mentioned by Josephus (*Ant.* 18.4.3 §95).[316]

---

309 Jervell, *Apostelgeschichte*, 176.
310 Contra Dunn, *Acts*, 52, who wonders why the highest court of Israel would be called together over a minor matter.
311 Reicke, *Glaube*, 76.
312 Smallwood, "High Priests," 16; Fitzmyer, *Acts*, 299; contra Conzelmann, *Acts*, 32, who sees this as a mistake by Luke.
313 For examples of the influence of other former high priests, see Jeremias, *Jerusalem*, 157–58.
314 Greenhut, "Cave"; Reich, "Caiaphas."
315 For a contrary view, see Horbury, "Caiaphas," critiqued by Bond, *Caiaphas*, 1–8, although Bond is not completely confident of the identification.
316 See Barrett, *Acts*, 1:225; Jeremias, *Jerusalem*, 197.

ὅσοι ἦσαν ἐκ γένους ἀρχιερατικοῦ, "other members of the high-priestly family," denotes some fifteen to twenty senior priests who formed the body that oversaw the life of the temple, including its cult, its order, and its finances.[317] They were frequently related to the high priest and appointments were often nepotistic, as γένους, "families," bears witness. Indeed, of the twenty-five high priests who came from ordinary priestly families (rather than Zadokite families through which the legitimate high priesthood in Jerusalem passed until 172 BC) just four families provided twenty-two.[318]

7 στήσαντες αὐτοὺς ἐν τῷ μέσῳ, "After they made them stand in the midst." The physical arrangement of Sanhedrin meetings was in a semicircle (m. Sanh. 4:3) with the accused in the center.

ἐν ποίᾳ δυνάμει ἢ ἐν ποίῳ ὀνόματι ἐποιήσατε τοῦτο ὑμεῖς;, "By what power or by what name did you people do this?" The initial question is about the healing, not the preaching, although Acts 4:1–3 suggest that they were arrested for both preaching in the temple courts and, specifically, preaching the resurrection through or in the case of Jesus. Haenchen and Bond find this line of questioning a difficulty, leading Bond to posit that Luke is (badly) combining different sources.[319] However, it seems entirely logical for the Sanhedrin's questions to take the issues one step at a time, beginning with the healing,[320] which is itself a manifestation of the resurrection and exaltation of Jesus.[321] The phrasing of this question echoes 3:6, 12, 16 and Luke 20:2—the latter a question posed to Jesus in the same place by the same authorities;[322] δυνάμει, "power," is about the source of the healing, and ὀνόματι, "name," connotes authority—the apostles are being asked whose authority they invoked to heal the man.[323] Luke does not give a full account of the proceedings (which might include, e.g., establishing the identity of the accused and clarifying the charges against them) but focuses on the salient points for his purpose, which center on the power of the name of Jesus.[324]

8 πλησθεὶς πνεύματος ἁγίου, "filled with the Holy Spirit," signals that the speaker thus filled speaks from God. The leadership of the people of God is passing from the hands of the Sanhedrin into those of the apostles, who are inspired and empowered by God—and this contrast will be sharpened as this story develops. In addition, this particular filling fulfills Jesus's promises of Luke 12:11–12, that the disciples would be given words by the Spirit when on trial,[325] and Acts 1:8, that the Spirit would equip them to witness, and

317 Jeremias, *Jerusalem*, 180.
318 Jeremias, *Jerusalem*, 193–97.
319 Haenchen, *Acts*, 222–23; Bond, "Acts 4:12," 17n1.
320 Marshall, *Acts* (TNTC), 99.
321 Jervell, *Apostelgeschichte*, 177.
322 Edwards, "Parallels," 487–88.
323 Foulkes, "Problems," 122.
324 Jervell, *Apostelgeschichte*, 177.
325 With Woods, *Finger*, 227.

prepares for further fulfillment in 4:31 in response to the believers' prayer. This, the second use of this expression in Acts (see *Comment* on 2:4), raises the question of the relationship of this "filling" with the Pentecostal one. The use here is consistent with Luke's other uses of the aorist of πίμπλημι, "fill completely" + genitive of divine Spirit as denoting "events or inspirations of short duration"—here, clearly the speech that follows.[326] Witness inspired by the Spirit is a natural extension of the Jewish understanding of the "Spirit of prophecy" as inspiring speech and bringing charismatic wisdom and revelation, and such events form a major focus of the Spirit's ministry in Acts (1:8; 2:4, 11; 4:31; 6:10; 8:29, 39; 9:17–20, 31; 10:19; 11:12; 13:2, 4; 16:6–7).[327]

ἄρχοντες τοῦ λαοῦ καὶ πρεσβύτεροι, "Rulers of the people and elders," is a respectful, but not fawning, form of address that performs the function of a *captatio benvolentiae*, an introduction designed to win the audience's goodwill.[328] This form of address shows that the believers still think of themselves as members of the Jewish community,[329] in line with Peter and John's entry to the temple at the hour of sacrifice (see *Comment* on 3:1). This form of address is unique; when Paul later addresses the Sanhedrin, he speaks to them as ἄνδρες ἀδελφοί (23:1, 6; cf. 1:16; 2:29, 37). Given that Peter will go on to cite Ps 117:22 LXX (MT 118:22) (Acts 4:11), Brawley's suggestion that Ps 117:6 LXX is salient here is plausible: "The Lord is a helper to me; I will not fear what a person may do to me" (NETS). More so, Macaskill notes that ἄρχοντες, "rulers," echoes Ps 117:9 LXX (MT 118:9), "It is better to hope in the Lord than to hope in rulers (ἄρχοντας)," identifying the source of Peter's hope and the man's healing.[330]

9 ἀνακρινόμεθα, "we are being examined," is used in Attic Greek for preliminary examination by magistrates to prepare for a trial.[331] Such a sense comports with the presentation of this hearing,[332] and the outcome is that a decision not to prosecute is taken (Acts 4:16–17 and note v. 21). However, this verb is also used in 12:19; 24:8; 28:18 for more formal trials,[333] so not too much should be built on the lexical choice alone.

εὐεργεσίᾳ, "a good deed," hints at benefaction; it is a Lukanism used in the Greco-Roman world for benefaction to (e.g.) a city by a wealthy citizen.[334] This

---

326 See Turner, *Power*, 165–69, quoting 167; thus, the contortions of Hull, *Spirit*, 120–24, over the relation of this event and Pentecost are unnecessary.

327 See Turner, *Power*, 349–50, 402–4; Turner, "Spirit of Prophecy."

328 Soards, *Speeches*, 45.

329 "The early church still understands itself as a part of the people and recognizes its authorities as a matter of course." Stählin, *Apostelgeschichte*, 72 (my translation).

330 Macaskill, *Union*, 164.

331 "ἀνακρίνω," LSJ 109, §A.II.2.

332 Wall, "Acts," 88, sees this meeting as "[having] the informality of a pre-trial hearing" met to decide whether to prosecute or not.

333 Haenchen, *Acts*, 216n6.

334 Plato, *Leg.* 850B; Aristotle, *Pol.* 1286B; cf. uses of the cognate verb in Luke 22:25 regarding such benefaction and Acts 10:38 regarding Jesus as one who does good, and see "εὐεργεσία," BDAG 405; "εὐεργεσία," *EDNT* 2:76–77; Danker, *Benefactor*, 323–24.

labeling is designed to focus on the real issue: there is no issue or debate about the healing (indeed, the man is present, vv. 14, 21); rather, the controversy is about the name and person of Jesus.

ἀνθρώπου ἀσθενοῦς, "for a sick man," uses a standard word for physical weakness (the word group is used in this sense in Luke 4:40; 5:15; 8:2; 9:2; 10:9; 13:11; Acts 5:15, 16; 9:37; 19:12; 20:35; 28:19); while it can be used for moral weakness,[335] there is no need to see it here as suggesting the view found in some writings that sees physical weakness as indicative of moral weakness.[336]

σέσωται, "he was healed." There is a pun on the verb (and the cognate noun σωτηρία, "salvation") in its use here and in 4:12, a pun that is hard to bring out in English: "made whole" in both places conveys the sense but is archaic.[337] Here it refers to physical healing, in v. 12 to "end-time salvation."[338] Luke shows that physical healing is in view by other lexical choices: ὑγιής, "healthy" (v. 10), τεθεραπευμένον, "having been healed" (v. 14), and ἴασις, "healing" (v. 22). However, the healing is more than physical: by contrast with earlier descriptions of the healing in 3:1–10, 12–16, "salvation" vocabulary here and in v. 12 (twice)[339] leads Luke's readers to a fuller notion of "salvation."[340]

10 γνωστὸν ἔστω, "let it be known," focuses the audience's attention on what Peter is about to say by way of explanation of the healing; it amounts to saying, "Pay attention: this is important!" It is a Lukan expression: it echoes 2:14, appears also in 13:38; 28:28, and is not found elsewhere in NT.[341]

The explanation is not just for the Sanhedrin, πᾶσιν ὑμῖν, "to all of you," but the real target audience is Israel as a whole, παντὶ τῷ λαῷ Ἰσραήλ, "the whole people of Israel." The mission of the believers is to call *the nation* to believe in Jesus as Messiah and Savior, and the answer in 4:10–12 centers on Jesus and makes points that echo the speeches of chs. 2–3.

ἐν τῷ ὀνόματι Ἰησοῦ Χριστοῦ τοῦ Ναζωραίου, "in the name of Jesus Messiah of Nazareth," is fronted in the ὅτι, "that," clause—Peter wants his hearers to consider Jesus, not the apostles themselves, who are merely his spokesmen. *Jesus* is the one with whom the Sanhedrin need to reckon (cf. 3:13, 16). Peter thus begins the move from the healing itself to the apostolic teaching about Jesus, which for Peter (and Luke) is the real issue.[342]

Peter states the reason Jesus is so important in a pithy antithesis: while the Sanhedrin themselves had crucified Jesus, God had reversed this human verdict by raising Jesus from the dead.

335 "ἀσθενής," BDAG 142, §2.c.
336 Contra Parsons, "Character," 303–4; see Walton, *Leadership*, 170–72, and *Comment* on 20:35.
337 Foulkes, "Problems," 125.
338 Haenchen, *Acts*, 217; more fully, Hamm, "Acts 3,1–10," 306.
339 Marconi, "History," 178–79.
340 Foulkes, "Problems," 124–25.
341 Cf. LXX Ezra 4:12; 5:8; 1 Esdr 2:18; 6:8, the only LXX uses—thus, it is hardly a Septuagintalism, contra Haenchen, *Acts*, 218n8.
342 With Tannehill, "Functions," 407.

ὃν ὑμεῖς ἐσταυρώσατε, "whom you yourselves crucified," echoes 2:23, 36; 3:13–15a, where Peter spoke to Jerusalemite Jews;[343] here he speaks to their leaders (as the co-text of 4:5–6 makes clear) and holds them personally responsible (note the emphatic personal pronoun ὑμεῖς, "you yourselves") for the death of Jesus.[344] Peter does not draw attention to the redemptive significance of the cross[345]—in this speech it is simply Jesus who brings salvation.

ὃν ὁ θεὸς ἤγειρεν ἐκ νεκρῶν, "whom God raised from the dead," echoes 2:23; 3:15. The subject ὁ θεός, "God," is fronted before the verb (by contrast with Luke's more usual practice of placing the subject after the verb), thus focusing on God's action as a contrast to that of ὑμεῖς, "you yourselves," fronted in the previous clause.[346] With this reversal cf. Gen 50:20 concerning Joseph.[347] Haenchen wrongly asserts that the issue here is resurrection per se and therefore doubts that this story is historical, since on those grounds the Sadducees involved in the apostles' arrest (v. 1) would have had to take every Pharisee to court![348] Rather, the issue for Peter is the resurrection *of Jesus*, for this establishes his identity and power to save. Peter thus places the question of what *God* is now doing front and center in the hearing—the Sanhedrin must decide whether they are going to line up with God's action in Jesus and repent of crucifying him.[349] Peter's words challenge the Sanhedrin's honor, for they are responsible for Jesus's crucifixion.[350]

ὑγιής, "healthy,"[351] is the only use of this word in Acts (see *Comment* on σέσωται, "he was healed," v. 9).

11 Having asserted who Jesus is by his resurrection, Peter now turns to Scripture, as he had earlier done (2:16–21, 25–28, 31, 34–35; 3:18, 21–25). He echoes Ps 118:22 (LXX 117:22), but this is not a precise quotation (differently from other NT citations of this verse that closely follow LXX: Luke 20:17; Matt 21:42; Mark 12:10; 1 Pet 2:7). Luke's Jesus has cited this passage in the parable of the vineyard (Luke 20:17), and the Jewish leadership there recognized that the parable was aimed at them (Luke 20:19). Luke's use here is double-edged. First, Peter claims that the death and resurrection of Jesus fulfill Scripture, and thus that the vindication of Jesus in the resurrection

343 Wilckens, *Missionsreden*, 44, notes that the contrast "you crucified . . . God raised" is a concise summary of Peter's speech (3:12–26).

344 With Weatherly, *Responsibility*, 69; contra Sanders, *Jews*, 238–39, erroneously arguing that the mention of the people of Israel earlier in this verse means that this phrase should be seen as targeted on all Jews.

345 Schenke, "Kontrastformel," 19.

346 *DFNTG*², 37–38.

347 Barrett, "Salvation," 69.

348 Haenchen, *Acts*, 221.

349 Roloff, *Apostelgeschichte*, 82, is too cautious in suggesting "at least implicitly in this a warning is spoken" (my translation).

350 Webber, "Why," 22.

351 "ὑγιής," BDAG 1023, §1.a.

following his rejection by the Jewish leaders took place under the hand of God and in order to further God's purposes.[352] Hence, submission to Jesus is now (to shift the metaphor) the touchstone of what it means to belong to Israel, further underlining that God, through Jesus, is now restoring Israel. Secondly, the scriptural citation shows the Sanhedrin to be guilty because they rejected Jesus.[353] Psalm 118:22 is a significant verse in early Christian thought, also cited in Mark 12:10; Matt 21:42 (Luke's quotation is briefer than Mark's and Matthew's: they quote v. 23 as well); 1 Pet 2:7; Barn. 6:4.[354] The force of the scriptural quotation is that, at least in theory, Scripture is shared ground between Peter and the Sanhedrin.[355]

There are two significant differences between this echo and LXX, which both bring greater focus and emphasis to the citation and make it doubtful that Luke is simply editing the LXX here.

(i) ἐξουθενηθείς, "was scornfully rejected," differs from LXX and other NT citations of Ps 118:22, which have ἀπεδοκίμασαν, "was rejected," thus presenting a stronger form of rejection which is scornful (although ἐξουθενηθείς is used elsewhere in LXX to translate MT's מאס [*mʾs*], "reject," e.g., 1 Sam 8:7; 10:19). While a stone may be rejected, the note of *scornful* rejection applies more naturally to a person, and thus focuses the interpretation of Ps 118:22 as prophetic of Jesus.[356] Luke may have chosen ἐξουθενηθείς, "was scornfully rejected," to echo Luke 18:9 and especially 23:11 (in both verses this verb appears to be Lukan choice[357]). Alternatively, it may be that Luke alone has access to a tradition in which such a shift was made and makes this shift explicit after the resurrection of Jesus, rather than in the earlier citation in Luke 20:17 (where he would have been aware of the Markan citation of Ps 118:22–23 in that setting).[358]

(ii) The addition of ὑφ' ὑμῶν, "by you," which focuses the scriptural allusion on the responsibility of the Sanhedrin—rather than the whole Jewish people—for the death of Jesus, and thus their need to repent.[359] This addition echoes the change from "you" singular to plural in Acts 3:22–23 (citing Deut 18:15, 19), also allowing the OT text to be read as aimed at Peter and John's audience (see *Comment* on 3:22–23).

---

352 Maiburg, "Christus," 249.

353 Gaventa, *Acts*, 93.

354 See discussion in Lindars, *Apologetic*, 169–86.

355 Brawley, *Text*, 95.

356 Dupont, *Sources*, 142, proposes an echo of Isa 53:3 by noting that ἐξουδενέω, "scornfully reject," used here, is found in Mark 9:12 in what seems a clear allusion to Isa 53 (so Lindars, *Apologetic*, 81; France, *Mark*, 335). As Rese, *Motive*, 113–14, notes, however, LXX does not use ἐξουδενέω: it is found in α′, σ′, and θ′ at Isa 53:3 (so also Lindars, *Apologetic*, 81). It seems to me implausible to use Mark to interpret Acts at this point, given that Luke lacks a parallel to Mark 9:12, although Luke may be building on a tradition also found in Mark.

357 Weatherly, *Responsibility*, 57n3.

358 Brawley, *Text*, 96. More fully, with other alternatives, see Bock, *Proclamation*, 199–200.

359 Jervell, *Apostelgeschichte*, 179n418; Bock, *Proclamation*, 199; Macaskill, *Union*, 165.

There are wider echoes of Ps 118, one of the Psalms of Ascents used in pilgrimage to Jerusalem, in the present complex of stories:[360] (i) the gate of the Lord that the righteous enter (Ps 118:20) and the Beautiful Gate (Acts 3:2) which the healed man enters with Peter and John (3:8); (ii) the insistence that it is God who has acted (Ps 118:23) and Peter's claim that God-in-Jesus has healed the man (Acts 3:12, 16); and (iii) the psalmist's commitment to praising God because God has become his *salvation* (Ps 118:21; LXX 117:21 ἐγένου μοι εἰς *σωτηρίαν*, "you have become *salvation* for me") and the healed man's praise (Acts 3:8, 9) for an act that Peter calls σέσωται, "he has been saved" (4:9). Green rightly notes that these echoes exemplify the phenomenon recognized by Dodd, that the earliest Christians did not pull isolated "proof texts" from the OT but cited particular verses as pointers to whole passages and saw those passages as shaping their understanding of what God had done and was doing through Jesus.[361] Further, the "plot" of the psalm, beginning with confession and praise of God for his mercy given in the face of opposition resonates with the opposition to Jesus and God's mercy in raising him from the dead. Brawley notes Jesus's use of Ps 118:5–6 (LXX 117:5–6) on the cross (Luke 23:46), which underlines this allusion. Further Ps 118:10–12 (LXX 117:10–12) speaks of the nations opposing the psalmist, which comports well with gentile involvement in Jesus's death (cf. Acts 4:27). The psalmist's defense is thrice stated as "the name of the Lord" (Ps 118:10, 11, 12 [LXX 117:10, 11, 12]), and it is the name of Jesus that has produced this man's healing (Acts 4:7, 10; 3:6). There is also a hint of resurrection in "I shall not die, but I shall live, and recount the deeds of the Lord. In disciplining the Lord disciplined me, and to death he did not surrender me" (LXX Ps 117:17–18 NETS [MT 118:17–18]). Strikingly, too, Peter and John's bold response to the Sanhedrin echoes the psalmist's confidence: "The Lord is a helper to me; I will not fear what a person may do to me" (LXX Ps 117:6 NETS [MT 118:6]; see also vv. 7–9).

κεφαλὴν γωνίας, "head of the corner," is an expression found only in Ps 117:21 LXX and literature citing or alluding to that verse. It appears to refer to a copingstone,[362] although some suggest that it refers specifically to a stone at the top of the joint of two walls in a building (cf. the related term ἀκρογωνιαῖος, "cornerstone," in Eph 2:20; 1 Pet 2:6). The precise location is not so important, since the significance of this location is clearly that this a place of honor following the earlier rejection.[363] Jesus's placing as "head of the corner" makes him the center and heart of the reconstitution of Israel now in progress through the apostles.

360 For what follows, see Green, *Meaning*, 144; Brawley, *Text*, 96–99.
361 Dodd, *According*, passim, esp. 59–110; summary, 126–27.
362 J. Jeremias, "κεφαλὴ γωνίας," *TDNT* 1:792–93; H. J. Cadbury, *BegC*, 5:373–75.
363 Barrett, *Acts*, 1:230.

In the verse as a whole, there is a hint of Luke's understanding of the temple, in that the Sanhedrin's rejection (ὑφ' *ὑμῶν* τῶν οἰκοδόμων, "by *you* builders") of the true cornerstone, Jesus himself, will lead to the destruction of the Jerusalem temple, as Jesus prophesied (Luke 19:44; 21:5–6[364]), and its replacement by a new temple consisting of the believers.[365]

12 ἡ σωτηρία, "salvation," and σωθῆναι, "to be saved," echo v. 9 but expand the meaning of "salvation" beyond physical healing: it acquires "a deeper sense."[366] This is clear because Peter's address to ἡμᾶς, "we," includes many who do not need physical healing, and the focus in the co-text is on his claims about Jesus (vv. 10–11); these features show that a wider sense of "salvation" is in view, including incorporation into the renewed people of God which is reconstituted around Jesus.[367] Luke is using "salvation" language in a similar sense to 2:40, which entails both individuals and Israel as a people being saved from the coming judgment of God (see *Comment* on 2:40).

The salvation that is available comes through Jesus alone: (i) the links back to ἐν ἄλλῳ οὐδενί . . . οὐδὲ . . . ὄνομά ἐστιν ἕτερον, "in no one else . . . there is no other name" (vv. 10–11), make this clear; and (ii) ὑπὸ τὸν οὐρανόν, "under heaven," denotes the whole universe (Eccl 1:13; 3:1)[368] and thus claims universal applicability;[369] and (iii) the passive δεδομένον ἐν ἀνθρώποις, "given among people," shows that this is God's gift, to be received by people.[370] This statement is thus "Luke's way of asserting that Christianity is absolute."[371] In particular, it claims that salvation is not available through any form of Judaism that rejects Jesus as Messiah and so carries an implicit call to the Sanhedrin to repent of their decision to have Jesus crucified and to Luke's (mainly gentile) readers to respond to Jesus and turn from any other way they follow.[372]

It may be that the mention of ὄνομα . . . ἐν ᾧ, "name . . . by which," hints at baptism as the way to enter into salvation, in line with the earlier use of ὄνομα in Acts 2:38 (see *Comment* there, and note 8:16; 10:48; 19:5).[373] In other Acts co-texts where "salvation" language is used, baptism is often not far to seek.

---

364 Cf. Spencer, *Acts*, 50.

365 Beale, *Temple*, 216; Macaskill, *Union*, 164–65; Keener, *Acts*, 2:1149. On the temple as an image for the believing community, see Moule, *Origin*, 89–94.

366 George, "L'emploi," 313 (my translation).

367 Bond, "Acts 4:12," 12–13; Wilckens, *Missionsreden*, 61–62.

368 "οὐρανός," BDAG 737, §1.b.

369 Both points with Schnabel, *Mission*, 1:422; his whole discussion of this verse is helpful, 1:420–23. Sandnes, "Beyond," 48 observes that LXX use of "under heaven" relates to: God as creator, i.e., his lordship over everything (e.g., Gen 1:9; Job 28:24; Prov 8:26, 28); the whole of humanity or created beings (e.g., Eccl 1:13; 3:1); a state—notably praise or condemnation—that is universally valid (e.g., Exod 17:14; Deut 9:14; Jer 10:11); all people on earth, esp. the nations (e.g., Deut 2:25; 4:19; Dan 9:12).

370 Fitzmyer, *Acts*, 302.

371 Haenchen, *Acts*, 217; so also Roloff, *Apostelgeschichte*, 83.

372 Marshall, *Acts* (TNTC), 100.

373 Cf. Bultmann, *Theology*, 1:136.

Of course, the healed man has not—yet—been baptized, for the apostles were arrested before they could do so.[374] This is so programmatically in 2:21 with 2:38—and keywords from the Joel 3:1–5 LXX quotation in Acts 2:17–21 are echoed here, notably ὄνομα, "name," and σῴζω, "save," both from 2:21.[375] For the collocation of baptism and salvation, see also 11:13–14 with 10:46b–48; 16:31 with 16:33. Thus it is plausible to see a baptismal hint here.[376]

Three features of Luke's phrasing keep the focus on God's action and desires. First, δεδομένον ἐν ἀνθρώποις, "is given among people," shows that human beings do not find this means of salvation; they receive it from another—the name of Jesus is the *divinely given* means of salvation. Secondly, the Lukanism δεῖ, "it is necessary," points to divine necessity—salvation through Jesus is *God's* way. Thirdly, the passive infinitive σωθῆναι," to be saved," indicates that ἡμᾶς, "we," do not save ourselves, but rather that salvation comes from outside us, from God.

Pinnock, among others, claims that Luke does not here address the situation of those who have never heard of Jesus or the status of other religions.[377] In similar vein, Culpepper accepts that this verse states the "absolute" nature of Christianity but argues that today's world of religious pluralism means that we should see Christianity as one way among many to "faith" (which he does not define).[378] Although Pinnock may be formally correct, in that the issues in Luke's day are somewhat different from those today, his arguments fail to recognize the widespread religious pluralism in the first century AD that raised precisely these issues in the most acute form, not least in the Greco-Roman world into which Luke wrote. When read within the book of Acts, which expounds the progressive expansion of the gospel "to the end of the earth" (1:8), and falls in the wider scriptural setting of the exclusive and universal claims of YHWH (e.g., Deut 6:4–5; Isa 43:10–11; 45:21–22; 46:9),"God's claim to be the only Saviour extends far beyond the Jews; it includes the ends (*sic*) of the earth. This is exactly what Acts 4:12 is claiming for Christ as well."[379] The breadth of Peter's claim here is the same as that of the OT: YHWH, now known in and through Jesus, is the one true God and the one true Savior (cf. Paul's appropriation of the Shema in 1 Cor 8:6).

---

374 Avemarie, *Tauferzählungen*, 119–20, objects that there is no mention of the man's baptism.

375 Wall, "Acts," 90.

376 Contra Barrett, *Acts*, 1:232, who appears more to be criticizing an *ex opere operato* view of the sacraments than expounding Luke's theology.

377 Pinnock, "Acts 4:12"; similarly, Stendahl, "Lordship." For cogent critique of Stendahl's claim that this sentence should be read as "love language," see Sandnes, "Beyond."

378 Culpepper, "Acts 4:12." It is impossible to address such issues in any depth within the confines of this commentary; among the vast secondary literature, the following survey the issues helpfully: Okholm and Phillips, eds., *More*; Fackre, Nash and Sanders, *What* (helpful summary table, 26); Strange, *Possibility* (response to Pinnock; Appendix 1 provides a useful taxonomy of views); Tiessen, *Who*.

379 Sandnes, "Beyond," 53. On the motifs of boldness, lack of education, and amazement here, see the full and helpful treatment of Hilton, *Illiterate Apostles*.

13 Luke here presents Peter and John filtered through the eyes of their opponents in the Sanhedrin rather than giving his own perspective.[380] The Sanhedrin find themselves divided in opinion, for the healing of the man is clear (v. 14), as is the eloquence and boldness of the apostles, and yet they wish to restrain the apostles from their claims about Jesus.[381]

παρρησίαν is "boldness" but with a sense of "confidence," perhaps "audacity," too (see *Comment* on 2:29).[382] The ability to speak freely and boldly was a quality prized among Greeks, particularly Cynics (Dio Chysostom, *Oration* 32.11; 77–78.37, 45; Lucian of Samosata, *Demonax* 3, 10–11),[383] and was a marker of being of similar social standing to the one addressed boldly (Plutarch, *Mor.* 55B-E),[384] and this may partly account for the Sanhedrin's surprise: they are taken aback at Peter's frank and direct speech to them, telling them of their responsibility for murdering the one whom God has now vindicated by resurrection (Acts 4:10–11). The Sanhedrin are powerful people and social superiors—it would be usual for a social (and religious) inferior to speak with flattery.[385] It is also a characteristic of the righteous one who is vindicated in Wis 5:1.[386] As v. 20 will clarify, their boldness comes from a sense of compulsion to speak comparable to that of Jeremiah (Jer 20:7–9) and Paul (1 Cor 9:16).[387] Acts 4:29 will further clarify that such boldness is a divine gift that here and in v. 29 flows from being filled with the Spirit (vv. 8, 31), thus fulfilling Jesus's promise that they would be equipped by the Spirit to speak before the authorities (Luke 12:11–12).[388] This boldness stops the Sanhedrin in their tracks: ἐθαύμαζον, "they began to be amazed," just as the temple crowds were at the healing (Acts 3:12, same verb).

ἄνθρωποι ἀγράμματοί εἰσιν καὶ ἰδιῶται, lit., "they were uneducated people and untrained." The two descriptions of Peter and John attributed to the Sanhedrin imply that the apostles lack formal education, here probably formal rabbinic education. ἀγράμματοι, "uneducated," can simply denote "illiterate" in the sense of not being able to read and write,[389] which should not be seen as a negative judgment in the ancient world, where many people were in this sense "illiterate."[390] More broadly, it connotes lack of education (e.g., Plato,

380 McCabe, *Kill*, 189.
381 Reicke, *Glaube*, 78.
382 "παρρησία," BDAG 781, §3.a; Hilton, *Illiterate Apostles*, 98–100.
383 Radin, "Freedom."
384 Further references: Hume, *Community*, 133n39.
385 Hume, *Community*, 133.
386 Doble, *Paradox*, 156.
387 Marrow, "Παρρησία," 442.
388 Hilton, *Illiterate Apostles*, 159, also highlights Luke 21:12–15, where it is Jesus who will equip them to speak in such circumstances, noting the echoes of ἐπιβάλλω in the sense "arrest" (Luke 21:12; Acts 4:3), and ἀντιλέγω, "say in opposition" (Luke 12:15; Acts 4:14), and the apostles' response in Acts embodying the idea of ἀπολογέομαι, "defend" (Luke 21:14).
389 For examples, see Barrett, *Acts*, 1:233.
390 Keith, "Oddity," 794–95.

Tim. 23A; Epictetus, *Disc.* 2.9.10). Here it contrasts with τοὺς γραμματεῖς, "the scribes" (v. 5), who had formal training in Jewish law.[391] ἰδιῶται, "untrained," was used in classical authors in contrast to rulers or various intellectuals to express that those so described were "laypeople" or "amateurs" in the field concerned; cf. 2 Cor 11:6; Josephus, *Ant.* 2.12.2 §271, both using the term for people inexpert in speaking, and 1 Cor 14:16, 23, 24, using the term for "outsiders" to the believing community.[392] Socially, Luke's reference to Peter and John as ἀγράμματοι καὶ ἰδιῶται suggests that the former identifies them as from the uneducated group within society, and the latter presents them as part of the "rank and file" rather than the powerful élites.[393]

From Luke's perspective, this recognition shows that the Spirit is inspiring them, cf. Luke 12:11–12.[394] Luke beautifully portrays the difference that the coming of the Spirit makes to Peter, who swore that he was ready to die or go to prison for Jesus (Luke 22:33) but denied Jesus three times (Luke 22:54–62). Indeed, what Peter denied was that he was σὺν τῷ Ἰησοῦ, "with Jesus," the phrase used here; cf. καὶ οὗτος *σὺν αὐτῷ* ἦν, "this one also was *with him*" Luke 22:56 with 58, 59.

ἐπεγίνωσκόν τε αὐτοὺς ὅτι σὺν τῷ Ἰησοῦ ἦσαν, "and they recognized them as people who had been with Jesus," does not imply that they had not previously realized that Peter and John were associates of Jesus; Acts 4:2 would make that inference surprising, although the seeming tension between vv. 2, 13 causes Barrett to propose that they come from different sources.[395] On Barrett's view, the problem is Luke's failure to edit his sources consistently. The explanation is to be sought elsewhere, for the sense of ἐπιγινώσκω here is surely "take cognizance of"[396] (cf. the same verb in 3:10)—the council members make the connection between the new information of the apostles' boldness and the already known fact that they are Jesus's followers.[397] ἐθαύμαζον, "they were amazed," echoes responses to Jesus's teaching and actions in Luke (4:22; 9:43; 11:14, 38; 20:26). This doubtless leads them to reflect that the apostles are speaking with the same effect as their Master, and by using Ps 118:22—a text used by Jesus—the students have become like their teacher, who also lacked scribal training (cf. Luke 6:40).[398] In Luke's hands this phrase is heavily ironic, for the

391 Dodd, *The Interpretation of the Fourth Gospel*, 82n1, proposes that the combination ἀγράμματοί . . . καὶ ἰδιῶται, "uneducated . . . and untrained," has its roots in Heb. technical terms for people unlearned in the torah.

392 See "ἰδιώτης," MM 299; Kraus, "Uneducated," 436nn5–6. The usual senses fit well here; it is thus unlikely that it has the sense "common" or "profane," derived from Heb. הדיוט (*hdywṭ*) as Wilcox, *Semitisms*, 101, speculates; see Emerton, review of Wilcox, *Semitisms*, 295.

393 De Villiers, "Medium," 250–55.

394 With Hilton, *Illiterate Apostles*, 156–61; Haenchen, *Acts*, 216.

395 Barrett, *Acts*, 1:234.

396 "ἐπιγινώσκω," BDAG 369, § 3.

397 With Bruce, *Acts* (1990), 153.

398 Brawley, *Text*, 98. Keith, "Oddity," 799–805, argues that this portrait of Jesus is in tension with his apparent facility in Luke (but not Mark) with reading Scripture aloud, including

Sanhedrin are about to reject the apostles just as they rejected Jesus. Readers of Luke's Gospel might think particularly of Jesus's opening of the disciples' minds to understand Scripture (Luke 24:45) as a particular "being with Jesus."[399]

14 τόν τε ἄνθρωπον βλέποντες σὺν αὐτοῖς ἑστῶτα τὸν τεθεραπευμένον, "Since they saw the man who had been healed standing with them." The healed person was living testimony that could not be gainsaid (cf. the healings in John 5, 9). Chrysostom acutely observes, "Great was the boldness of the man; that even in the judgment-hall he has not left them" (*Hom. Act.* X).

οὐδὲν εἶχον ἀντειπεῖν, "they had nothing to say in opposition," echoes Luke 21:15, where Jesus promises that in times of pressure his followers will be defended: οὐ δυνήσονται ἀντιστῆναι ἢ *ἀντειπεῖν* ἅπαντες οἱ ἀντικείμενοι ὑμῖν, "your opponents will not be able to withstand or *speak in opposition*." The verb is a Lukan favourite (nine of eleven NT uses in Luke-Acts; this is the first use in Acts; see also 13:45; 28:19, 22).

15 ἔξω τοῦ συνεδρίου ἀπελθεῖν, "to go out of the Sanhedrin," probably denotes the Sanhedrin's meeting place.[400] This is the first use of the term συνέδριον, "Sanhedrin," in Acts; it will be mentioned fourteen times in total, always as opposing the believers (5:21, 27, 34, 41; 6:12, 15; 22:30; 23:1, 6, 15, 20, 28; 24:20; otherwise in NT only once each in Luke and John, and thrice each in Matthew and Mark). See *Comment* on v. 5 on the composition and nature of the body. Sending the apostles out is in line with later rabbinic tradition that the court deliberates in private after hearing the witness (b. Sanh. 30a; so also 5:34).[401]

16–17 μὲν . . . ἀλλ', "on the one hand . . . on the other hand," sets up the quandary that the Sanhedrin face.[402] On the one hand, it is indisputable that the man has been miraculously healed; it is γνωστὸν σημεῖον, "a publicly recognized sign," nicely echoing *γνωστὸν ἔστω*, "let it be *known*" (v. 10). On the other hand, the Sanhedrin cannot concede that the name of Jesus has power to do such things and allow the apostles to continue to preach in the name of Jesus, for they condemned him as a messianic pretender (Luke 22:67–71; 23:2). The result is the heavy irony that "the leaders of God's people want to prevent the people from finding the Messiah"![403] Thus it is here that the issue of the apostles' teaching comes into clear focus in the story after the Sanhedrin's initial question about the healing (v. 7).

It is most striking that the Sanhedrin do not mention God in their deliberations, even though, ironically, σημεῖον, "sign," suggests "done by God" (cf.

---

finding a particular passage (Luke 4:17). Accordingly, Keith suggests Luke is drawing on Mark's portrait of Jesus as lacking scribal training (e.g., Mark 1:22).

399 Brawley, *Text*, 99.

400 "συνέδριον," BDAG 967, §3.

401 Reicke, *Glaube*, 76.

402 μέν is thus not emphatic but anticipates the clause in v. 17; with Fresch, "Is There," 270–71, contra (e.g.) D&M, 261.

403 Jervell, *Apostelgeschichte*, 180 (my translation).

earlier uses in 2:19, 22, 43, and see *Comment* at 2:22).[404] More, they cannot bring themselves even to use the name of Jesus, but use τῷ ὀνόματι τούτῳ, "that name," instead (although cf. v. 18). This silence forms a stark contrast with Peter's initial words and his response when he and John return. These words focus on the question of what God has done (v. 10) and what God desires (v. 19). The hearing, in other words, is presented by Luke in a way which shows that the believers are in tune with the purpose of God and the Sanhedrin are not.[405] The crucial dividing feature is what each group makes of Jesus, and Peter's two speeches in the hearing provide the opportunity for the Sanhedrin to repent of their part in the crucifixion of Jesus—an opportunity they decline to take. Further, Luke's presentation of the apostles as receiving the promise that the Spirit will inspire their speech when on trial (Luke 12:11–12; Acts 4:9) suggests that the Sanhedrin, by their categorical rejection of the Spirit-inspired testimony of the apostles, fulfill the adjacent warning for those who blaspheme against the Holy Spirit (Luke 12:10, a saying found in a different co-text in Mark 3:29; Matt 12:33, which reinforces the likelihood that Luke is hinting at this connection).[406] The parallel is reinforced by the presence in both passages of emphatic ὑμεῖς, "you" (three times in Luke 12:4, 5, 8; four times in Acts 4:10, 11). Other possible occasions of blasphemy against the Holy Spirit in Acts are 7:51; 28:25.

μὴ διανεμηθῇ, "it may not spread," has no explicit subject: it may be the news about the healing, or the message of Jesus, or the group of believers itself—the three are interconnected, of course: the first or second implies the other two, and the third would draw on the first two.

18 The Sanhedrin want to silence the apostles, and their order prepares for the further hearing and events of 5:17–18, 27–28. Their command is an attempt to save face in a situation where they are aware they on weak ground.[407] μὴ φθέγγεσθαι μηδὲ διδάσκειν, "neither to speak nor teach," uses two present infinitives, suggesting that this command is to stop doing something they are already doing.[408] φθέγγεσθαι, "to speak," cf. LXX Wis 1:8; Amos 1:2; the compound verb ἀποφθέγγεσθαι, "to speak out," is found in 2:4, 14; 26:25; otherwise in NT only in 2 Pet 2:16, 18. In combination with διδάσκειν, "to teach," which connotes public proclamation (v. 2), it is possible that φθέγγεσθαι denotes private speech to individuals or smaller groups.[409]

ἐπὶ τῷ ὀνόματι τοῦ Ἰησοῦ, "in the name of Jesus," here connotes making the assertions that Jesus is Messiah and raised from the dead (v. 10; cf. 2:32–36),

404 With Squires, *Plan*, 98.
405 Cunningham, *Tribulations*, 188–89.
406 Mainville, "Péché," 40–44.
407 Webber, "Why," 23; his stimulating article studies the sequence of events in Acts 3–4 from the social-scientific perspective of labeling theory.
408 Barrett, *Acts*, 1:236; Bruce, *Acts* (1990), 155.
409 Barrett, *Acts*, 1:236–37.

i.e., it focuses on the content of the message, although it could also signal the authorisation of Jesus and thus invoke his name as the power effective through the preaching.[410]

19 Peter and John's answer focuses on the real issue: what does God want? The sharpness of their question comes from the Sanhedrin's position as the official voice of Judaism—thus, the Sanhedrin should be those who speak for God. However, Peter has already shown that they are complicit in the crucifixion of God's Messiah, a verdict reversed by God (v. 10). Thus, they are acting illegitimately in instructing the believers to be silent about Jesus and are thereby forfeiting their leadership of the people of God.[411] This issue will return in 5:29, 38–39, when Peter will renew the point, and one of the Sanhedrin's own, Gamaliel, will observe that God is the one to be obeyed.

This answer would resonate with both Jewish and Greco-Roman readers. Peter and John's analysis of the issue at stake has biblical echoes (e.g., 1 Sam 15:22–23; Jer 7:22–23; Dan 3:16–18; 2 Macc 7:2; cf. Josephus, *Ant.* 17.6.3 §§158–59) and a close verbal parallel in Plato, *Apol.* 29d, reporting Socrates's speech at his trial in Athens: πείσομαι δὲ μᾶλλον τῷ θεῷ ἢ ὑμῖν, "I shall obey the god rather than you." It is likely that the Socrates saying was proverbial in the first century, for it is quoted or alluded to in Greek in Plutarch, *Sept. sap. conv.* 7 (152C); Epictetus, *Disc.* 1.30.1; and in Latin in Livy 39.37.17 "Indeed we respect you, Romans, and if you wish it so, we even fear you; but still more do we both respect and fear the immortal gods."[412]

ἐνώπιον τοῦ θεοῦ, "before God," denotes life lived in God's presence and thus in conscious knowledge of and submission to God. The expression echoes Scripture, e.g., Exod 22:7–8 LXX (EVV 8–9; also a judicial context); 23:17; 34:23; Judg 21:2; 1 Kgs 8:59, 65 (the dedication of the temple). It is generalized in terms of life lived "before God" in LXX 2 Chr 14:1 (EVV 2); 36:12; Ezra 8:21; Neh 1:4; Pss 55:14 (MT 56:14; EVV 56:13); 67:4 (MT 68:4; EVV 68:3).

ἀκούειν here connotes "to obey," as in Acts 3:22, 23 (quoting Deut 18:15) and perhaps Acts 28:28, although this usage appears not widespread in Acts.[413]

κρίνατε, "you judge!," is ironic, in that Peter is turning the tables on the Sanhedrin: they have Peter and John on trial, but this remark puts them on trial concerning their assessment of Jesus. More, if the Sanhedrin did judge rightly, they would find they were condemned—for that is the implication of "as did your leaders" (3:17). Implicitly, Peter is arguing that the Sanhedrin have lost the right to speak for God, and the believing community now has that position.[414]

---

410 Ziesler, "Name," 32–33.

411 Jervell, *Apostelgeschichte*, 181.

412 Barrett, *Acts*, 2:828–29, 830, further notes echoes of Socrates in Acts 17:17, 18.

413 Contra Wall, "Acts," 90; see "ἀκούω," BDAG 37.

414 Wall, "Acts," 91.

20 The apostles' sense of compulsion to speak is strong: the two negatives οὐ δυνάμεθα . . . μὴ λαλεῖν, lit., "we are not able . . . not to speak," reinforce each other to produce an emphatic statement; cf. Jer 20:7–9; Amos 3:8; 1 Cor 9:16. οὐ δυνάμεθα, "we are not able," perhaps echoes the cognate noun δύναμις, "power," from Acts 1:8 and thus underlines the divine empowering which the apostles experience.[415]

The emphatic ἡμεῖς, "as for us," following hard on the heels of the ironic κρίνατε, "you judge!" (v. 19), shows the sharpness of Peter and John's contrast between themselves and the Sanhedrin.

ἃ εἴδαμεν καὶ ἠκούσαμεν, "the things which we have seen and heard," denotes both the teaching and death of Jesus (1:21–22; cf. 10:39) and particularly the resurrection appearances of Jesus, of which they are witnesses (v. 10; 3:15; cf. 1:3, 8; 5:2).[416] Luke here uses a pair of words that speak first of the deeds of Jesus (which the apostles saw) and then of his words (which the apostles heard), echoing the classic pair of characteristics of a benefactor in the Greco-Roman world, "[n]oble action in concert with fine words."[417] This pairing builds on the statement that εὐεργεσίᾳ, "a good deed," had been done through the name of Jesus (4:9–10 with *Comment* there).

λαλεῖν, "to speak," echoes the testimony theme—it is characteristic of the apostles that they must speak in testimony to Jesus. The present tense of the infinitive λαλεῖν reinforces the sense of them *going on* speaking (cf. 6:2, 4).

21 The hands of the Sanhedrin are tied, for there is nothing they can say in response—first, they have found no ground in law to punish the apostles, and secondly, the crowd's reaction, in praising God for the healing, prevents the Sanhedrin from punishing the apostles. Indeed, Luke marks the Sanhedrin membership as dishonest in seeking to cover up Jesus's healing work.[418]

μηδὲν εὑρίσκοντες τὸ πῶς κολάσωνται αὐτούς, "since they had not found any way to punish them," Jeremias reconstructs events by suggesting that the apostles' recognized lack of education (v. 13) meant, under rabbinic law (cf. m. Sanh. 5:1; 8:4; m. Mak. 1:8–9), that they could only be warned for a first offense because they acted in ignorance.[419] Cf. the connection of Mark 2:23–28 and 3:1–6; the twofold intention of Saul in Acts 9:1 both to warn, ἀπειλῆς, "threats," and to punish, φόνου, "murder"; and 1QS V, 25–VI, 1, where a warning before witnesses precedes formal legal action. A subsequent similar offense would lead to punishment (thus 5:28 recalls this warning). While Luke

---

415 Soards, *Speeches*, 47. Stolle, *Zeuge*, 222, highlights that this divine compulsion is part of Luke's demonstration that the apostles now speak for God.

416 Anderson, "Acts 4:19–20," 11–13, highlights the parallels of "seen and heard" in 1 John 1:3; John 3:32, suggesting that this use of Johannine diction reopens the questions of Luke's access to Johannine tradition. Here, Luke functions as a "witness to the witnesses"; so Bolt, "Mission," 213.

417 Danker, *Benefactor*, 339–41.

418 Jervell, *Apostelgeschichte*, 182.

419 Jeremias, "Untersuchungen," 208–13.

has not explicitly presented events this way,[420] nevertheless Jeremias provides a plausible explanation for the sequence of events in Acts 4–5 and undermines any argument that sees the two hearings before the Sanhedrin as two tellings of the same event (see also *Form/Structure/Setting* on 5:27–42).

διὰ τὸν λαόν, "because of the people." Considering the people prevents the Sanhedrin from punishing the apostles; compare 5:26 and contrast the people's view of the believers (4:13b). Compare also vv. 14, 16 where the public nature of the healing is crucial to the Sanhedrin's deliberations, and also the role of the people in pressurizing the leaders in Luke 19:48; 20:6, 19, 26; 22:2.

ὅτι πάντες ἐδόξαζον τὸν θεὸν ἐπὶ τῷ γεγονότι, "for everyone was glorifying God because of what had happened." Ironically, the people, rather than their leaders, recognize what was truly going on, that God was acting through the apostles. The leadership of Israel is thus passing from the "old guard," who are out of tune with God, to the apostles, who are God's agents and spokesmen. The verb ἐδόξαζον, "they were glorifying," echoes responses to healings in Luke's Gospel (e.g., Acts 5:25, 26; 17:15; 18:43; cf. Mark 2:12; Matt 9:8; 15:31), and further underlines that the apostles act as Jesus's agents, doing what he did.

22 τὸ σημεῖον τοῦτο τῆς ἰάσεως, "this sign of healing," marks the event as not merely a healing but as symbolic of something bigger, namely the restoration of Israel being accomplished by Jesus (see *Comment* on 3:8).

ἐτῶν γὰρ ἦν πλειόνων τεσσεράκοντα ὁ ἄνθρωπος, "for the man was over forty years old." Barrett complains about Luke's imprecise language in appearing to allow that the people might not have glorified God if the man had been younger,[421] but Barrett's is surely a perverse reading: the stress on the healed man's age simply highlights both how amazing the healing was and how long the man had been suffering and waiting.[422] It may be, in the context of other restoration-of-Israel echoes in this sequence of stories (see *Comment* on 3:2, 6, 8, 21–25), that the forty years hints at Israel's wilderness wanderings following the exodus and thus at the "new exodus" restoration of Israel (cf. 7:36, 42; 13:18),[423] although Johnson expresses caution on the ground that stating the duration of sickness is quite common in healing stories.[424]

Explanation

As a result of the healing (3:1–10) and Peter's preaching (3:11–16), the first clash with the Jewish authorities follows. Peter and John are taken into custody, ostensibly for their preaching (4:2). The hearing before the Sanhedrin begins with the question of the healing (v. 7), thus taking events in their

420 Barrett, *Acts*, 1:238; Dupont, *Sources*, 44–45.
421 Barrett, *Acts*, 1:239.
422 Fitzmyer, *Acts*, 304.
423 Spencer, *Acts*, 52; Butticaz, "Actes 3,1–26," 181.
424 Johnson, *Acts*, 79.

chronological sequence, and concludes with the issue of their preaching, as Peter and John are forbidden to speak in the name of Jesus (vv. 17–18).

The hostility of the Sanhedrin, Judaism's highest court, stems from their prior rejection of Jesus (Luke 22:66–23:2; 23:5, 10, 13–24)—if they were not to act against the apostles, they would be implicitly admitting that they were wrong about Jesus. Thus, the leadership of Israel is at stake in this encounter: the apostles are beginning to fulfill the promise of Jesus that they will exercise delegated authority to judge (i.e., rule) the twelve tribes of Israel (Luke 22:30), and so the old leadership represented by the Sanhedrin resist them.

A key issue here is who speaks for the God of Israel, and Luke signals in various ways that Peter and John do and the Sanhedrin do not.

First, Peter's speech is empowered by the Holy Spirit (Acts 4:8); hence he speaks with boldness and a cogency that surprises the formally trained and educated membership of the Sanhedrin (v. 13). Readers of Luke's Gospel hear the fulfillment of Jesus's promise that the Holy Spirit will equip the apostles to do precisely this when on trial (Luke 12:11–12) and thus recognize that the apostles are on God's side.

Secondly, Peter focuses on God's attestation of Jesus: in raising Jesus from the dead, God has placed him as Messiah (Acts 4:10, echoing 2:36). Consequently, Jesus's name is powerfully effective in healing (v. 10), and uniquely effective in bringing salvation, understood more broadly (v. 12). Not only so, but Scripture, God's book, speaks of the role of Jesus—he is the cornerstone of God's purposes (v. 11, alluding to Ps 118:22), and so people's response to him determines their relation to Israel's God and their membership in the renewed Israel.

Thirdly, in their response to the Sanhedrin's demand for silence about Jesus, Peter and John return to the issue of God's will (Acts 4:19–20). Peter and John (and, by implication, the whole apostolic band) experience a compulsion to speak about Jesus's life, ministry, teaching, death, and resurrection (which are "the things which we have seen and heard," v. 20), a compulsion Luke's readers recognize as stemming from the divine power of the Holy Spirit (v. 8; 1:8). Haenchen notes that Luke wishes to bring "home to the reader the justice and obligation of preaching Christ, and showing from the example of the apostles . . . how the Christian, certain of divine assistance, should fearlessly bear witness for his Lord, unquelled by police, arrest or official interdict."[425]

Fourthly, the wider community is glorifying God for the man's healing (4:21–22)—and the man is standing there healed (vv. 10, 14, 22).

By contrast, first, the Sanhedrin never mention God in their questioning or deliberations at all; rather, they are concerned only with how they can suppress this new movement in spite of the incontrovertible evidence of the

425 Haenchen, *Acts*, 223–24.

man's healing (vv. 16–17). Indeed, they may be an example of what it means to blaspheme against the Holy Spirit (Luke 12:10), for they refuse to listen to the Spirit-inspired testimony of the apostles.

Secondly, Peter addresses them as responsible for the death of Jesus by sharpening the allusion to Ps 118:22 (Acts 4:11): the Sanhedrin, who should have been building the people of God ("you, the builders"), rejected Jesus with contempt and thus cut themselves out of the salvation found in him alone (v. 12). Peter's speech carries an implicit call to the Sanhedrin to repent, a call which will, tragically, be rejected by their attempt to suppress the believers (vv. 17–18).

Thirdly, the Jewish leaders try to forbid speech about Jesus that God both wishes to take place (vv. 18–19) and empowers the apostles in order to facilitate it taking place (v. 8). The Sanhedrin seek to quash a message and a movement, both of which God wishes to spread. "Religious heroism here confronts the dreary politics of expediency, which above all wants only quiet among the people."[426]

Fourthly, by contrast with the divine empowering of the apostles, the Sanhedrin are impotent in the face of God's actions, both in raising Jesus (v. 10) and in seeking to forbid the apostolic preaching, since the healed man stands in silent testimony (vv. 14, 16, 22). As they were unable to dispose of Jesus (v. 10), now they cannot prevent the message spreading, for it has the name of Jesus and the power of the Spirit behind it (vv. 8, 10, 12, 18–20).

This story further develops our understanding of what God is now doing in several ways. It underlines God's decisive action in raising Jesus from the dead, in reversal of the Sanhedrin's verdict (v. 10). It demonstrates afresh that the Holy Spirit empowers courageous testimony to God's action in Jesus and now through the believing community (vv. 8–12, 13, 19–20; Luke 12:11–12).

Perhaps most significantly, in referring to the healing this story introduces the vocabulary of salvation (Acts 4:9) and stretches that vocabulary beyond physical healing to a wider and fuller sense (v. 12, echoing 2:21, 40, 47). The healing, accomplished through the name of Jesus, is emblematic of Israel's restoration—thus Peter both initially addresses the rulers as a respectful insider, 4:8, and clarifies that his words are for "all the people of Israel," v. 10. The restored Israel is centered and clustered around the exalted Jesus, Israel's Messiah, who fulfills Scripture in taking this position (vv. 10–11, citing Ps 118:22). Thus, there can be no going back to a form of Judaism that rejects Jesus as Messiah. Further, Israel's restoration is itself part of "salvation," and there is the hint that the salvation offered by Jesus will extend to all the peoples of the earth, for there is "no other name *under heaven given among people* by which we must be saved" (Acts 4:12).

426 Knopf and Hollman, *Schriften 3*, 24 (my translation).

4. *The Believers Turn to God under Pressure and Receive Power (4:23–31)*

Bibliography

Bauckham, R. *God.* **Bernhard, L.** "Verständnis." **Bock, D. L.** *Proclamation,* 201–8. **Brawley, R. L.** *Text,* 91–107. **Carson, D. A.** *Doctrine,* esp. 53–54. **Coggan, D.** *Prayers,* 77–79. **Cosgrove, C. H.** "Divine." **Cunningham, S.** *Tribulations,* 189–90. **Dibelius, M.** "Herodes." **Dodd, C. H.** *According,* 104–10. **Dömer, M.** *Heil,* 63–68. **Downing, F. G.** "Common Ground." **Dupont, J.** *Études,* 521–22. **Feldkämper, L.** *Jesus,* 306–14, 319–20. **Flusser, D.** *Entdeckungen,* 1:32–39, esp. 34–35. **Förster, N.** *Gebet,* 382–95. **Funk, R. W.** *Poetics,* 59–97, esp. 96–97. **Gallagher, R. L.** "Doingness." **Gaventa, B. R.** "To Speak." **Green, J. B.** "Persevering," 191–92. **Grider, J. K.** "Predestination." **Hamm, D.** "Precious." **Hamman, A.** "Pentecôte." **Holmås, G. O.** *Prayer,* 179–84. **Holtz, T.** *Untersuchungen,* 53–56. **Hull, J. H. E.** *Spirit,* 121–24. **Johnson, L. T.** *Midrash,* 29–35. **Juel, D.** *Exegesis.* **Karris, R. J.** *Prayer,* 77–78. **Kilpatrick, G. D.** "ΛΑΟΙ." **Kränkl, E.** *Jesus,* 109–11, 125–29. **Kremer, J.** *Pfingstbericht,* 201–4. **Le Roux, L. V.** "Style." **Longenecker, R. N.** *Christology,* 104–7. **Mainville, O.** *Spirit,* 221–22. **Maloney, L. M.** *All,* 43–66. **Ménard, J. E.** "*Pais Theou.*" **Miura, Y.** *David,* 160–74. **Monloubou, L.** *Prière,* 212–14. **Moule, C. F. D.** "Christology," 169–70. ———. "Acts iv.25." **Moule, H. W.** "Acts iv.25." **O'Brien, P. T.** "Prayer." **Plymale, S. F.** *Prayer,* 78–88. **Reece, S.** "Jesus." **Reicke, B. I.** *Glaube,* 80–84. **Rese, M.** *Motive,* 94–97. **Rimaud, D.** "Prière." **Rusam, D.** *Testament,* 376–82. **Sanders, J. T.** *Jews,* 13–14. **Schille, G.** "Leiden." **Schnabel, E. J.** *Mission,* 1:415–16. **Schofield, C.** "Linking," 64–70. **Smalley, S. S.** "Spirit." **Sparks, H. F. D.** "Semitisms," 24. **Squires, J. T.** *Plan,* 98–99, 171. **Strauss, M. L.** *Davidic,* 202–8. **Thurston, B.** *Life,* 55–65, 105–7. **Torrey, C. C.** *Composition,* 16–18. **Twelftree, G. H.** "Prayer." **van der Horst, P.** "Parallels, 3 and 4." **von der Goltz, E. F.** *Gebet,* 235–36. **von Wahlde, U. C.** "Acts 4,23–31." **Walton, S.** "Ὁμοθυμαδόν," 101–2. **Weatherly, J. A.** *Responsibility,* 92–94. **Webber, R. C.** "Why." **Wilcox, M.** *Semitisms,* 69–72, 146–47. **Woods, E. J.** *Finger,* 224–34.

Translation

23 After they were released, they returned to their own people[a] and reported the things that the chief priests and elders had said to them. 24 Those who heard raised their voice[b] in united concern to God, "Sovereign Ruler, you[c] who made heaven and earth and the sea and everything in them; 25 you spoke[d] by the mouth of our ancestor David, your servant, through the Holy Spirit,[e] 'Why were the nations furious and why did the peoples devise[f] useless plans? 26 The kings of the earth stood with hostile intent[g] and the rulers gathered together against the Lord and against his anointed one.'[h] 27 Yes,[i] in truth they *did* gather[j] in this city against your holy servant Jesus whom you anointed—both Herod and Pontius Pilate, together with the gentiles and the peoples of Israel— 28 to do whatever things your hand and your[k] purpose had predetermined[l] to happen. 29 Now, concerning the present situation,[m] Lord, pay attention[n] to their[o] threats and grant your servants to continue speaking[p] your word with all boldness, 30 while you stretch out[q] your[r] hand for healing, and signs and wonders are done through the name of your holy servant Jesus. 31 After they had prayed,[s] the place in which they were gathered was shaken, and they were all[t] filled with the Holy Spirit and continued to speak[u] the word of God with boldness.

Notes

a. τοὺς ἰδίους, "their own people," m. pl. adj. functioning as noun in the sense "the Christian family"; with Barrett, *Acts*, 1:242, contra Johnson, *Acts*, 83, who takes the referent to be the other apostles.

b. φωνήν, lit., "a voice"; this distributive use portrays the group as speaking with one voice (but not necessarily in unison, contra Pesch, *Apostelgeschichte*, 1:175), and so it is natural in English to render "*their* voice."

c. Emphatic σύ, "you," could be voc. (as in the translation) or the subject of a clause whose complement is ὁ ποιήσας, "the one who made," giving the sense "you are the one who made"; Culy and Parsons, *Acts*, 76.

d. ὁ . . . εἰπών, articular aor. ptc., "the one who spoke," stands in apposition to σύ, "you," or ὁ ποιήσας, "the one who made," in v. 24; either way it further defines the one addressed.

e. ὁ τοῦ πατρὸς ἡμῶν διὰ πνεύματος ἁγίου στόματος Δαυὶδ παιδός σου εἰπών is an unusual word order, woodenly translated: "the one who by means of our ancestor through the Holy Spirit by means of the mouth of David your servant spoke." The MS support for this reading, which is adopted in NA[28]/UBS[5]/ECM, is very strong: 𝔓[74vid] ℵ A B E Ψ 33 323 (945) 1739 *al*, and its difficulty is reflected in variant readings: (i) ὁ διὰ στόματος Δαυὶδ παιδός σου εἰπών, "the one who through the mouth of David your servant spoke" 𝔐; (ii) ὃς διὰ πνεύματος ἁγίου διὰ τοῦ στόματος λαλήσας Δαυεὶδ παιδός σου, "who through the Holy Spirit through the mouth spoke David your servant," D; (iii) ὁ πνεύματι ἁγίῳ διὰ στόματος τοῦ πατρὸς ἡμῶν Δαυὶδ τοῦ παιδός σου εἰπών, "the one who by the Holy Spirit through the mouth of our ancestor David your servant spoke," 629 *pc*. Each of these variants represents a clear improvement over the NA[28]/UBS[5]/ECM reading (and it is unlikely that a scribe would deliberately amend a clear sentence to make it harder), and each lacks the breadth and antiquity of support for that reading—thus both internal and external evidence point to the reading adopted. The problems of the word order of this reading have led to numerous theories of primitive corruption or an Aramaic original, none entirely satisfactory. For discussion, see *TCGNT*[2], 279–81; *BegC*, 3:40–41; Barrett, *Acts*, 1:244–45; H. W. Moule, "Acts iv.25"; C. F. D. Moule, "Acts iv.25", 220; Torrey, *Composition*, 16–18; Wilcox, *Semitisms*, 146–47; Sparks, "Semitisms," 24; Rius-Camps and Read-Heimerdinger, *Message*, 1:270–71; Bock, *Proclamation*, 202–3; Rese, *Motive*, 94; Maloney, *All*, 43–45.

f. ἐμελέτησαν, "devise," aor. of μελετάω, found only here and 1 Tim 4:15 (there in the sense "practise") in NT; "μελετάω," BDAG 627. The sense "devize" or "plan" is found in a second-century BC law from Beroea; *NewDocs* 2 §82.

g. παρέστησαν, "they stood," 2nd aor. intransitive from παρίστημι; "παρίστημι," BDAG 778, §2.a.β; L&N §17.3.

h. τοῦ χριστοῦ αὐτοῦ, "his anointed one," in the setting of Acts connotes "his *Messiah*" (cf. 2:31, 36; 3:18, 20; 5:42; 8:5; 9:22; 17:3; 18:5; 26:23); the translation seeks to help English readers hear the echo in the verb ἔχρισας (from χρίω, "he anointed," v. 27).

i. γάρ, lit., "for," introduces an explanation how the present situation reflects the Ps 2:1 quotation in v. 25; "γάρ," BDAG 189, §2.

j. συνήχθησαν, "they did gather," is fronted for emphasis.

k. σου, "your," following βουλή, "purpose," is read by ℵ A[2] D E[c vid] P Ψ 𝔐 *al*; it is absent from A* B E*[vid] 945 1704 1739 it[gig] vg[mss] *al*. This represents a fine balance of MS support, and a case can be made for the inclusion or exclusion of σου by scribal error. It is in square brackets in NA[28]/UBS[5] and ECM has a split-line reading, both indicating some uncertainty.

l. ἡ χείρ σου καὶ ἡ βουλή σου προώρισεν, "your hand and your purpose had predetermined," is a zeugma: while βουλή, "purpose," makes sense as a subject of προώρισεν, "had determined," χείρ, "hand," does not (cf. Pindar, *Nem.* 8.11–12 βασιλεὺς χειρὶ καὶ βουλαῖς ἄριστος, "a king, the best in hand and purposes"). However, the sense is clear: the actions of the Lord's hand are in tune with the plans of the Lord's mind.

m. τὰ νῦν, acc. of respect, "as to where things are now"; "νῦν," BDAG 681, §2.b; Wallace, 203.

n. ἔπιδε, "pay attention," aor. impv. of ἐφοράω ("ἐπεῖδον," BDAG 360); this verb is found only here and Luke 1:25 in the NT.

o. αὐτῶν, "their," is resumptive, referring back to οἱ ἀρχιερεῖς καὶ οἱ πρεσβύτεροι, "the chief priests and the elders" (v. 23). BDF, §288.2 suggest that in Luke-Acts αὑτος can function like αὑτος οὑτος, "this one," or αὑτος ἐκεινος, "that one," citing Luke 13:1; cf. Matt 10:26, where αὑτους, "them," is resumptive from "they," the subject of διώκωσιν "persecute," Matt 10:23 (I owe this example to Geoffrey Williams).

p. λαλεῖν, pres. inf. of λαλέω, "to speak," functioning as direct object of δός, "give"; pres. tense suggests continuing an action, especially in light of Peter and John's boldness (4:13).

q. ἐν τῷ . . . ἐκτείνειν σε . . . καὶ σημεῖα καὶ τέρατα . . . γίνεσθαι, "while you stretch out . . . and signs and wonders are done," ἐν + dat. art. pres. infs. ἐκτείνειν and γίνεσθαι expressing action contemporaneous with λαλεῖν, "to speak," and thus echoing the description of Jesus's ministry in 2:22; with Fitzmyer, *Acts*, 310; contra Barrett, *Acts*, 1:249; Culy and Parsons, *Acts*, 77, 79, who see this phrase as the means by which the request in v. 29 would be carried out.

r. σου, "your," is read by 𝔓[45] ℵ D E P Ψ 𝔐, a weighty combination of Alexandrian and Western witnesses. It is absent from 𝔓[74] A B 1175 it[d, gig] Lucifer. Its absence is likely to be the work of scribes seeking to conform the style to Attic, rather than its presence being the result of scribes conforming this expression to those found in vv. 27, 29; *TCGNT*[2], 282.

s. δεηθέντων αὐτῶν, temporal (aor.) gen. abs., "after they had prayed."

t. ἅπαντες, m. pl. adj. of ἅπας, "all," a form found frequently in Luke-Acts with no significant difference in meaning from the simpler form πᾶς; Luke generally uses ἅπας following a consonant (e.g., Acts 2:44—but not invariably, e.g., Luke 1:3; Acts 2:7), in line with Attic usage, which sought euphony; Robertson, 771.

u. ἐλάλουν, impf. suggesting continuing action, "they continued to speak"; with Lumby, *Acts*, 51; Barrett, *Acts*, 1:250.

Form/Structure/Setting

Delimitation of pericope. The section begins with a location shift, as Peter and John leave the Sanhedrin meeting and return to their own group (4:23).[427] The section focuses on the believers' response to the Sanhedrin's warning (vv. 18, 21, 23) and God's response to the prayer (v. 31).

Form/Historicity. Luke provides the narrative frame of the story (vv. 23–24a, 31),[428] and debate concerning form and sources concerns the prayer (vv. 24b–30).

Thurston suggests that this prayer is modeled on that of Hezekiah (2 Kgs

427 Förster, *Gebet*, 385.
428 With Maloney, *All*, 45.

19:15–19/Isa 37:15–20), including address to God as sovereign creator (Acts 4:24–26; 2 Kgs 19:15), statement of the speakers' present situation (Acts 4:27–28; 2 Kgs 19:16–18), and request for God's help to take God's purposes forward (Acts 4:29–30; 2 Kgs 19:19).[429] While there is a parallel of godly response to an external threat (see *Comment*, 4:29), such a pattern of prayer is so broad and general as to make it unlikely that Hezekiah's prayer was the specific model used by Luke or his source—thus, von der Goltz suggests Tob 3:11–12; 8:6–7, 15 as examples of a similar prayer structure.[430] Accepting that the broad pattern is drawn from biblical traditions of prayer, we may agree that "[b]y resorting to prayer at this precise moment, the young community aligns itself with the best of Israel's history as well as with the example of Christ."[431]

Haenchen also argues for a parallel with Isa 37.[432] However, because the request (Isa 37:20) is not the same as the request here (vv. 29–30), and because there is a shift from Herod and Pilate (Acts 4:27–28) to the present threat by the Sanhedrin (v. 29), Haenchen considers there is a "seam" between vv. 28 and 29 where Luke either engages in free composition to fit with the later development of the story or combines sources.[433] Nevertheless, the believers' prayer draws a clear parallel between the persecution of Jesus (vv. 27–28) and their own persecution (vv. 29–30).[434] These threats are presented as coming from united opposition to Jesus and his people and thus are seen synoptically.[435]

The echoes of earlier parts of the story chain from 3:1 to here (see *Comment*) show that this prayer is literarily appropriate for this setting.[436] The Palestinian features of the prayer, especially the manner of interpreting Scripture (4:25–28), further reinforce the historical appropriateness of the prayer.

Dömer argues that the prayer is a Lukan composition on the grounds that the exegesis of Ps 2:1–2 is artificial in the context of prayer; the link of the prayer to the previous event (Acts 4:23 with vv. 17, 21) shows that the prayer belongs with the Lukan frame; there is much Lukan vocabulary in the prayer;[437] the connection between Ps 2:1–2 and the community's suffering, rather than Jesus's suffering, is unusual in the NT and therefore likely to be Lukan; and the prayer parallels OT prayers such as 2 Kgs 19:15–19.[438]

429 *Life*, 59; so also Förster, *Gebet*, 387.
430 *Gebet*, 235n1.
431 Plymale, *Texts*, 81.
432 *Acts*, 226.
433 *Acts*, 228; cf. Schneider, *Apostelgeschichte*, 1:355.
434 Cunningham, *Tribulations*, 189n5.
435 Tannehill, *Unity*, 2:71, notes parallels between Luke's passion narrative and Acts 3–7.
436 Contra von der Goltz, *Gebet*, 236, who asserts that the prayer could just as easily stand in other places in Acts.
437 See also Maloney, *All*, 48–50.
438 Dömer, *Heil*, 63–66; cf. Schneider, *Apostelgeschichte*, 1:354–55.

Bock critiques these arguments effectively:[439] the handling of Scripture in a prayer context is plausible on the basis of Christian practice (and, we might add, reflects other biblical prayers, e.g., Neh 1:7–9); the link to the context proves nothing either way about the origin of the material; the Lukan language shows only that Luke has reported the material in his own words—it provides no evidence of the origins of the material; the use of the OT here is unusual, but that does not demonstrate that it is Lukan or non-Lukan, precisely because it is unique; and the "fit" of the prayer with OT examples is not exact, as we noted above. Bock further notes the tension between Acts 4:27 and both the presentation of Pontius Pilate in Luke 23:1–5 as not responsible for Jesus's death and the positive elements in Luke's portrayal of Roman officialdom;[440] contrast Dibelius, who proposes that Christian use of the psalm created the scene of Herod's involvement in Luke 23.[441] Kränkl rightly notes that Dibelius's view does not account for the "harmless role" Herod plays in Luke 23, by contrast with the "active function" he has here.[442] Bock therefore suggests that this tension shows that Luke has not sought to conform the prayer to his own theological emphases and agrees with Stählin, Marshall, and Roloff in regarding the contents of the prayer as traditional.[443]

The language of the prayer certainly demonstrates Luke's ability to write in a Septuagintal style (see details in *Comment*), although without excluding the presence of Semitic sources or thought, for LXX translation Greek is heavily influenced by its Semitic sources. However, here, as elsewhere in Acts, it is very difficult to identify sources with any confidence.[444]

Structure. Structurally, vv. 23–24a prepare for the prayer by announcing the shift of setting back to the community of believers (v. 23a), Peter and John's "report back" of what was said by the Sanhedrin (v. 23b), which recapitulates the previous scene, and the believers' reaction in turning to pray (v. 24a).[445] Maloney, who identifies a "reporting scene" schema in several passages in Acts, notes the compression of her first four elements here: transition from the previous scene; arrival; assembly of the community; and report, thus placing the focus on the prayer.[446]

The prayer itself occupies the bulk of the section. It falls into two sections, each beginning with invocation of God: the believers address God as sovereign

439 *Proclamation*, 204–5, 361n159.
440 *Proclamation*, 205; see also Walton, "State," esp. 20–23.
441 Dibelius, "Herodes."
442 Kränkl, *Jesus*, 111.
443 Stählin, *Apostelgeschichte*, 78; Marshall, *Acts* (TNTC), 104; Roloff, *Apostelgeschichte*, 85–86. Cf. Reicke, *Glaube*, 81, suggesting that the form of this prayer reflects forms used in the primitive church, while noting that it is unlikely that someone wrote the prayer down or remembered it verbatim.
444 Sparks, "Semitisms," 24; contra Torrey, *Composition*, 6, 16–18; Wilcox, *Semitisms*, 69–72.
445 With Funk, *Poetics*, 97.
446 Maloney, *All*, 50. She also studies 11:1–18; 12:11–17; 14:26–28; 15:1–35; 21:15–20; see discussion at those passages.

creator (v. 24a) and "Lord" (v. 29).[447] The believers then focus on God's control of events, expressed by interpreting the opposition to Jesus, God's anointed Messiah, as both fulfilling Scripture (key words from vv. 25–26, which quotes Ps 2:1–2 LXX, are echoed in Acts 4:27) and being under God's powerful hand and purpose (v. 28). By implication, the present events are under God's control too, and the actual request (vv. 29–30) entreats the Lord both to enable the believers to respond to the Sanhedrin's threats by continuing to speak God's word boldly and to provide the reinforcement of "signs and wonders" through Jesus's powerful name.[448]

Verse 31 then reports God's action in response to the believers' prayer, in the specific events (both verbs are aorist) of the location being shaken and the Holy Spirit filling them all, as well as in a renewed, ongoing ability (imperfect verb) to speak God's word boldly, precisely fulfilling their request (v. 29b).

Setting. This prayer is not merely a model for Luke's hearers but flows out of the threats made to Peter and John (vv. 18, 21). Indeed, this is no isolated prayer in panic; rather, it grows naturally out of the prayer life of the early believers.[449] We have seen them praying as they wait for the promise of the Spirit (1:14) and as they appoint leaders (1:24–25). Prayer and praise to God are notable features of the community's life (2:42, 47), and they join in the temple prayers (2:46; 3:1 with *Comment*). We shall see them praying as they choose and appoint administrators to care for the widows (6:6), appointments that are designed to free the apostles to pray as well as preach (6:4). Thus their natural resort under pressure is to turn to God in prayer, by contrast with the disciples' failure to pray when Jesus exhorted them to do so in Gethsemane (Luke 22:40–46)—the coming of the Spirit is transforming their life with God.[450] The transformation continues in the following section, where the sharing of possessions again demonstrates the Spirit's power at work (cf. 2:41–47).[451] The reading of Ps 2 offered in this prayer interprets the situation theologically, both for the participants in the story and for Luke's hearers: God truly reigns and his mission moves forward in spite of opposition. God enables and empowers his people to persist in such circumstances.[452] O'Brien helpfully compares Hezekiah's prayer under pressure (Isa 37:16–20; 2 Kgs 19:15–19), where an historical review leads to a direct request for God to deal with enemies.[453]

447 Von Wahlde, "Acts 4,24–31"; Holmås, *Prayer*, 181.
448 For similar structures in three prayers in Josephus, *Ant.* 1.18.6 §§ 272–73; 4.3.2 §§40–50; 20.4.2 §§89–90, see the table in Downing, "Common Ground," 548–49.
449 With Thurston, *Life*, 56; Rimaud, "Prière," 100.
450 Tannehill, *Unity*, 2:71–72.
451 Dunn, *Baptism*, 51.
452 With Twelftree, "Prayer," 273.
453 O'Brien, "Prayer," 123.

Comment

23 accomplishes transition from the Sanhedrin scene to the assembly of believers.[454] Ἀπολυθέντες δέ, "After they were released," shifts the location away from the Sanhedrin; ἦλθον πρὸς τοὺς ἰδίους, "they returned to their own people," introduces the new location for this scene and implies that (at least some of) the community gathered (see further below); καὶ ἀπήγγειλαν ὅσα πρὸς αὐτοὺς οἱ ἀρχιερεῖς καὶ οἱ πρεσβύτεροι εἶπαν, "and reported the things which the chief priests and elders had said to them," shows them recounting their experience.

τοὺς ἰδίους, "their own people." Rea translates this phrase in *P.Oxy.* 3314.15 as "true friends,"[455] and this expression—used for people of the same blood family (Sir. 11:34) or race (Philo, *Mos.* 1:177)—signals the sense of mutual belonging and support in the early believing community (cf. 24:23). "Their own people" could be the believing community in general or the apostolic group in particular. In favour of the latter is the focus of the prayer on the apostolic activity of speaking God's word boldly (vv. 29–30; cf. 4:1, 4; 6:2, 4; 10:44)—the kind of speech Peter and John made to the Sanhedrin (4:13). On this view, the correlatives δέσποτα, "Sovereign Ruler" (v. 24), and τοῖς δούλοις σου, "your servants" (v. 29), refer naturally to the Master in relation to the apostolic band, and ἅπαντες, "all" (v. 31), refers to the whole apostolic group rather than the whole believing community.[456] However, the focus of the prayer on the apostolic proclamation, so that the apostles are the referents of "your servants," does not necessarily imply that the praying group is *only* the apostles. It is difficult for the view that the praying group is the whole believing community (which Acts numbers at over five thousand at this point, 4:4) that Luke says that "all" spoke the word with boldness (v. 31). This phrase suggests that everyone present spoke in this way. A possible solution is that this was a unique occasion when the whole believing community did so speak, although the imperfect ἐλάλουν, "they went on speaking" (v. 31), goes against that idea. The best solution may be to see this group as meeting in a private home, perhaps that of Mary (12:12) and consisting of the apostles and a number of others.[457]

24 ὁμοθυμαδόν has the sense "in united concern," for Luke has already noted that they were in the same physical location (v. 23)—the believers share a passion for God's mission among the Jewish people.[458] It is unlikely to mean that they spoke in unison.[459] The believers' united determination

454 Maloney, *All*, 50–52.
455 *OxPap* 46:104.
456 So Dupont, *Études*, 521–22; Johnson, *Acts*, 83; Johnson, *Midrash*, 31.
457 Cf. Barrett, *Acts*, 1:242–43.
458 Walton, "Ὁμοθυμαδόν," 101–2; Fitzmyer, *Acts*, 407.
459 Contra Gaventa, *Acts*, 95.

contrasts with the authorities' weakness and paralysis (4:14–17, 21) and leads to powerful response by God (v. 31).[460]

ἦραν φωνὴν πρὸς τὸν θεόν, "they lifted their voice to God." The phrase "lift the voice," αἴρω φωνήν, connotes intense or emotional speech.[461] The gathering's first recourse under pressure is to turn to God, contrasting with the disciples' failure to pray when urged to do so by Jesus in the Garden of Gethsemane (Luke 22:39–46). They have no other resources to leverage against the threat: their only resort is to God.[462] There is no need to assume that Luke portrays united recitation of the whole prayer by the group: if one person led the group by praying aloud, others could and would align themselves with the prayer. It is possible, of course, that they did recite Ps 2 together.[463] Brawley helpfully observes that Ps 117 LXX (MT 118), cited in the previous section (Acts 4:11), calls on its readers to acknowledge God's goodness (vv. 1–4, 19, 21, 28–29) in response to his aid in affliction (vv. 5–7).[464] Thus, the "plot" of the psalm is played out by the believers' actions in both acknowledging God's recent actions and calling on God to act again in their present afflictions. Hence on this occasion they receive power from God to meet the opposition and continue their God-given work (v. 31).[465]

δέσποτα, "Sovereign Ruler," is a relatively rare form of address to God in the NT (only elsewhere in Luke 2:29; Rev 6:10; it is also used of God in 2 Pet 2:1; Jude 4). It focuses on the power and authority of the one so addressed (Philo, *Heir* 23); it is especially apposite in praying in a situation of persecution by people who seem to have power (cf. Sir 36:1; 3 Macc 2:2;[466] Josephus, *Ant.* 2.12.2 §270; 4.3.2 §40; 20.4.2 §90). Gallagher relates this designation for God to the other parts of the prayer, which identify God's sovereignty in creation (v. 24b), over humanity (vv. 25–28), and over the present situation (vv. 29–30).[467] Other uses concern human masters of slaves (1 Tim 6:1, 2; 2 Tim 2:21; Titus 2:9; 1 Pet 2:18; Aristotle, *Pol.* 1:1254a), rulers such as the emperor (Philo, *Opif.* 83.5; Dio Cass. 55.12.2; Herodianus, *Hist.* 1.6.4), or the gods (e.g., Xenophon, *Anab.* 3.2.13).[468] When Luke uses this word here and in Simeon's song (Luke 2:29), those praying are called δοῦλοι, "servants/slaves" (v. 29, see *Comment*).

σὺ ὁ ποιήσας τὸν οὐρανὸν καὶ τὴν γῆν καὶ τὴν θάλασσαν καὶ πάντα τὰ ἐν αὐτοῖς, "you who made heaven and earth and the sea and everything in them." σύ is

460 Schnabel, *Mission*, 1:416.
461 LXX 1 Sam 11:4; 24:16; 30:4; 2 Sam 3:32; 2 Kgs 19:22; cf. Isa 13:2; 37:23, using the synonym ὑψόω, "lift up."
462 Schille, *Apostelgeschichte*, 138–39.
463 Both points with Rimaud, "Prière," 110–11.
464 *Text*, 100.
465 See the insightful discussion of Tannehill, *Unity*, 2:71–72.
466 I owe these references to Spencer, *Acts*, 54.
467 Gallagher, "Doingness," 47–48.
468 See further "δεσπότης," LSJ; "δεσπότης," *CGL* 1:332.

emphatic (and probably vocative, see *Note* c), connoting "you alone." God's unique creative ability is one of the key features distinguishing God from all created reality: "the only true God, YHWH, the God of Israel, is sole Creator of all things and sole Ruler of all things."[469] This phrase echoes LXX Exod 20:11; Neh 9:6; Ps 145:6 (MT 146:6); and Isa 37:16 but is not an exact quotation of any of these verses. Moses's prayer in Josephus, *Ant.* 4.3.2 §40, also combines reference to God as δέσποτα, "Sovereign Ruler," with God's power over creation, using "heaven and earth and sea," itself also echoing Ps 145:6 LXX.[470] It follows the sequence of the creation story in Gen 1:1–2:3, as the OT passages cited above do, thus drawing on a Jewish understanding of the world as created by God and therefore under God's sovereign control; cf. the prayer in Jdt 9:12, although it is interesting that there an appeal to God's creation power comes later in the prayer, by contrast with this prayer, where it is the believers' first theme. God's creative power also appears in Acts 14:15; 17:24, both in pagan contexts. On the basis of God's great power, the believers appeal to God to act.

25 The text is not straightforward (see *Note* e): (i) the article ὁ, "you," is ten words away from its related participle εἰπών, "said" (cf. Rom 5:17, where the article οἱ is nine words away from its participle λαμβάνοντες); (ii) the fronted phrase τοῦ πατρὸς ἡμῶν, "our ancestor," is in apposition to Δαυίδ, "David," but precedes it and is separated from it; (iii) it is unusual for biblical authors to speak of God speaking διὰ πνεύματος ἁγίου, "through the Holy Spirit" (although cf. Acts 1:2, 16; 28:25, and note Tg. Isa. 40:13a; 59:21[471]); and (iv) it would be natural to expect a second διά, "through," before στόματος, "mouth," to balance that before πνεύματος, "Spirit." However, von Wahlde, who offers the above analysis of the difficulties, notes that the whole presents an elegant chiasm that introduces the quotation from Ps 2 with a "rhetorical flourish":[472]

A: ὁ "you"
B: τοῦ πατρὸς ἡμῶν, "by our ancestor"
C: διὰ πνεύματος ἁγίου, "through the Holy Spirit"
C′: στόματος Δαυὶδ, "by the mouth of David"
B′: παιδός σου, "your servant"
A′: εἰπών, "spoke"

A and A′ clearly belong together. B and B′ nicely parallel David's relation to the Jewish people as their ancestor and his relation to God, whose servant he is. C and C′ then present the two means by which God speaks, the Spirit

469 Bauckham, *God*, 10–11, with full biblical and Second Temple Jewish references.
470 Karris, *Prayer*, 77.
471 ET in Read-Heimerdinger, *Bezan Text*, 154–55.
472 "Assessment," 266–67; similarly Le Roux, "Style," esp. 31–32. This removes the need to identify C as Lukan redaction, suggested by Schille, "Leiden," 172.

and David's mouth. While we might expect a second διά, "through," at the beginning of C′ to make the parallel complete, nevertheless this parallel is impressive.

διὰ πνεύματος ἁγίου στόματος Δαυίδ, "through the Holy Spirit by the mouth of David," identifies David as prophetic (cf. 2:30 with *Comment*), for (διὰ) στόματος, "(through) the mouth," is elsewhere used in Acts in this way (3:18, 21; cf. 1:16). The parallel noted above points to Luke's understanding of Scripture as having dual—divine and human—authorship, a theme echoed elsewhere in Acts (e.g., 1:16–17 with *Comment*) and the NT (e.g., Heb 1:1; 2 Pet 1:20–21; Mark 12:36; Matt 19:4–5). The divine voice is heard through the personality and particularity of the human author. "She [the believing community] does not first invent her prayer, she knows that only the Spirit, in her, can pray; she is aware that she is repeating what God has told her through the Scriptures and the prophets."[473] Psalm 2 is not labeled as Davidic in the Psalter, and this may be an example of "Davidicization" around the turn of the eras, whereby David is named as the representative of the entire Psalter.[474]

παιδός σου, "your servant," identifies David as one who served God well in the past (cf. Did. 9:2), in line with Luke's wider use of παῖς, "servant" (see *Comment* on Acts 3:13; 4:27, 30). 3:13 and 4:27, 30 speak of Jesus as "servant"; the application of this appellation to the human David echoes believers being named as God's servants (2:18; 4:29; 16:17, using the synonym δοῦλος; the different word may signal the unique link of Jesus to David as messianic servant fulfilling God's covenant promise of a king to follow David, 2 Sam 7:12–14).[475] By implication, the believers as God's servants would be ready to experience similar persecution and suffering to their Master, the servant par excellence (cf. Luke 21:12; John 15:20).

25b–26 quote Ps 2:1–2 LXX verbatim (MT does not differ significantly in meaning from LXX),[476] and Acts 4:27–28 apply these verses to Jesus's trial and ministry. This passage in the NT alone quotes these verses of Ps 2; Ps 2:7 is quoted elsewhere. The earliest messianic reading of this psalm seems to be Pss. Sol. 17:21–25, there focusing on the punishment of the king's opponents in Ps 2:9 (cf. Rev 2:27). The earliest Christians read the psalm as speaking of Jesus as Messiah (Ps 2:7 is cited in Acts 13:33; Heb 1:5; 5:5; Justin Martyr, *1 Apol.* 40) and to his people, the believing community (Rev 2:27 echoes Ps

473 Rimaud, "Prière," 104 (my translation).

474 Miura, *David*, 126, 161 cites 11QPs[a] XXVII; 4QMMT[d] frgs. 14–21, 10; m. Abot 6:9 as examples. Cf. Luke 24:44, where "the Psalms" stands for the Writings within the Hebrew canon.

475 Cf. Moule, "Christology," 169–70. On the parallel of David and Jesus, see Miura, *David*, 173–74. For a fascinating study of translations of vv. 25, 27 from antiquity to modern times, which regularly distinguish David as God's "servant" from Jesus as God's "son," see Bernhard, "Verständnis."

476 Holtz, *Untersuchungen*, 56, suggests this use, and the exact LXX quotation of Ps 2:7 in 13:33 may come from a testimony book of scriptural quotations seen as witnessing to Jesus.

2:9.[477] This creative use of Scripture originates in the earliest period of the believing community (see *Form/Structure/Setting*) prior to the Pauline letters, and it is easy to agree with Dodd: "To account for the beginning of this most original and fruitful process of re-thinking the Old Testament we found need to postulate a creative mind. The Gospels offer us one."[478]

ἔθνη, "nations," generally denotes "gentiles" in Acts,[479] and they are also the referent of ἔθνη in Ps 2:1 LXX, for they oppose YHWH's anointed king of Israel. Bock rightly notes that ἔθνη does not itself *mean* "gentiles"; here, the context in Ps 2 identifies the referent as gentiles.[480]

27–28 apply the quotation from Ps 2 to the present situation, as γὰρ ἐπ' ἀληθείας, "Yes, in truth," makes explicit, echoing the psalm's language: συνήχθησαν, "there were gathered together," is repeated (also echoing Acts 4:5, the narrative account of the gathering of the Jerusalem leadership against Jesus); Ἰησοῦν ὃν ἔχρισας, "Jesus whom you anointed," echoes τοῦ χριστοῦ αὐτοῦ, "your anointed one" (v. 26); ἔθνεσιν, "gentiles," and λαοῖς, "peoples" (referring to Israel[481]), echo the same words in v. 25b. Such a "this is that" form of prayer is natural for the believers, interpreting the events of Jesus's trial and death through the lens of Scripture (see 2:17–21, 25–36 with *Comment*). This use parallels pesher interpretation at Qumran in highlighting particular phrases or words as speaking about the present or future of God's people: e.g., 4Q174 frg. 1 2i.1.18–19 quotes Ps 2:1–2 and interprets it to speak of a gentile conspiracy against the elect of Israel in the last days.[482] This use of Scripture is not likely to have arisen in later, gentile Christian circles but reflects an early, Palestinian origin.[483]

τὸν ἅγιον παῖδά σου, "your holy servant," paints Jesus using colors seen in earlier speeches. παῖδα, "servant," echoes the speech following the healing (Acts 3:13, 26) and thus reinforces the narrative thread running from 3:1 to 4:31 (see *Comment* on 3:13). It echoes the description of David as παιδός σου, "your servant" (v. 25), but Jesus exceeds David, for he is also ἅγιος, "holy" (cf. v. 30), a description given to no human in LXX. Jesus is identified as ἅγιος, "holy," in Luke 1:35; 4:34; Acts 3:14, and as παῖς, "servant," in Acts 3:13, 26 (see *Comment* in those places). The covenant theme of Ps 2, emphasizing the Lord's choice of his anointed king (vv. 2, 6–9), and the strong theme of Jesus as the fulfillment of the psalm (Acts 4:25a, 27a) together imply that here David is

477 Dodd, *According*, 105; Rusam, *Testament*, 379.
478 *According*, 110.
479 9:15; 10:45; 11:1, 18; 13:46, 47, 48; 14:2, 5, 27; 15:3, 7, 12, 14, 19, 23; 18:6; 21:11, 19, 21, 25; 22:21; 26:17, 20, 23; 28:28.
480 Bock, *Proclamation*, 206.
481 Kilpatrick, "ΛΑΟΙ."
482 With Johnson, *Midrash*, 33–35. It is rather surprising that Förster, *Gebet*, 388 claims "This parallelizing and actualizing scriptural exegesis does not follow any Jewish models" (my translation).
483 With Flusser, *Entdeckungen*, 35.

being treated as a messianic type fulfilled by Jesus rather than simply a model godly person who might be labeled as God's servant.[484] Given the usage of this term in 3:13, where it alludes to Isaiah's "servant of the Lord," Luke's hearers would recognize an Isaianic echo here, because of the mention of Jesus's anointing by God and his suffering (see below, with *Comment* on 3:13).[485] It is frequently suggested that the application of παῖς, "servant," to Jesus reflects early Palestinian liturgical usage,[486] and this may be so (see *Comment* on v. 30). However, liturgy alone is an insufficient explanation of the origin of Jesus's identification as παῖς; without Jesus's prior identification as Messiah because of his resurrection and (indeed) Jesus's own use of the term "servant," such usage would not arise.[487]

ὃν ἔχρισας, "whom you anointed," clearly echoes τοῦ χριστοῦ αὐτοῦ, "your anointed one" (v. 26), which suggests that the earliest believers recognized Jesus as the fulfillment of Ps 2 once they identified him as Messiah (cf. Acts 2:36[488]). It is likely that the anointing referred to is Jesus's messianic empowerment by the Spirit at his baptism[489] (the point is made explicit in 10:38): see Luke 3:21–22 and note the use of Isa 61:1–2 in relation to Jesus's anointing by the Spirit in the following episode, Luke 4:16–30.[490]

Ἡρῴδης τε καὶ Πόντιος Πιλᾶτος σὺν ἔθνεσιν καὶ λαοῖς Ἰσραήλ, "both Herod and Pontius Pilate, together with the gentiles and the peoples of Israel," is held back until this place in the sentence with dramatic effect, for οἱ βασιλεῖς τῆς γῆς καὶ οἱ ἄρχοντες, "the kings of the earth and the rulers" (Acts 4:26; Ps 2:2), now refers to opposition against God's anointed servant Jesus by *Jewish* people, in collaboration with gentiles. The group of opponents reflects the list from Ps 2:2 (Acts 4:26: Herod = "the kings of the earth"; Pontius Pilate = "the rulers"; the Roman soldiers = "the gentiles"; the Jewish people of Jerusalem = "the peoples of Israel"), rather than the sequence portrayed in Luke 23.[491] This labeling of present people using Ps 2[492] implicitly identifies the believers with Jesus. The list also echoes the presentation in Luke 23 of the trial and crucifixion of Jesus (Herod, vv. 7–12;[493] Pilate, vv. 1–6, 13–25; the gentiles,

484 Contra Kränkl, *Jesus*, 172. Hamman's formulation reflects Luke's understanding better: "The speeches in Acts show us that Jesus is called a servant because his whole life was one of submission to the will of his Father, that he never stopped serving people by blessing them, in order to save them"; Hamman, "Pentecôte," 87 (my translation).

485 With Ménard, "*Pais Theou*," 83–92; Plymale, *Texts*, 84; contra Juel, *Exegesis*, 79, 85, 131; Doble, *Paradox*, 153.

486 E.g., Bock, *Proclamation*, 207.

487 Longenecker, *Christology*, 104–7.

488 See Bock, *Proclamation*, 206.

489 With Bock, *Proclamation*, 363n170.

490 Turner, *Power*, 188–201; Strauss, *Davidic*, 202–8 present a strong case for seeing the coming of the Spirit at Jesus's baptism in messianic terms.

491 Haenchen, *Acts*, 226–27; Rese, *Motive*, 95.

492 On labeling in Acts 3–4, see Webber, "Why," here 23.

493 Gaventa, "To Speak," 78, suggests the presence of Herod and Pilate is incongruous, since neither seeks Jesus's death. However, both are involved in Jesus's death, and their failure

vv. 32–34, 36–37; the peoples of the Jews, vv. 1–2, 5, 13, 18, 21, 23, 35, 39). In particular, in Luke 23 Pilate is a gentile who bears some responsibility for the death of Jesus: he hands over Jesus, v. 25.[494] Sanders's arguments that Pilate is not implicated in Jesus's death are exposed as special pleading by Weatherly.[495]

28 ποιῆσαι ὅσα ἡ χείρ σου καὶ ἡ βουλή σου προώρισεν γενέσθαι, "to do whatever your hand and your purpose had predetermined to happen," uses four key phrases to convey God's control of historical contingencies. Together with v. 27, this clause conveys the heavy irony that the human actors' efforts to oppose God's purposes in Jesus were outmaneuvered by God, who took hold of the darkest event of history and shaped it to bring blessing to the world.[496] Luke assumes compatibility between the divine and human levels of explanation of events: God is sovereign and people are responsible for their actions.[497] The understanding of God's working in and through Jesus's passion and thus fulfilling Scripture is a Lukan theme (e.g., Luke 24:26, 44; Acts 2:23; 3:18).[498] It echoes the theme (although not the wording) of God's rule over the contingencies of history in Ps 2:4–9.

Luke uses the infinitive ποιῆσαι, "to do," to express God's superintending purpose in the actions of his opponents. Yes, they συνήχθησαν, "gathered together," but, by contrast with normal grammatical structures where the infinitive would express the purpose of the subject of συνήχθησαν (Herod, Pontius Pilate, the gentiles, and the peoples of Israel), it was not their plans that were carried out, but God's purpose.

ἡ χείρ σου, "your hand," is a metaphor for God's power at work, both in saving and empowering his people[499] and in judgment.[500] In particular, God's hand executes God's purpose (Isa 14:24–27).[501]

ἡ βουλή σου προώρισεν, "your purpose had determined," cf. Acts 2:23. This expression strongly emphasizes the superintending purpose of God in historical contingencies. It "excludes notions of a closed, causally-connected history process,"[502] for it stresses God's active intervention to "steer" events,

to discharge Jesus after recognizing him as innocent means they are responsible for Jesus's death, even if not actively seeking it.

494 Contra Kränkl, *Jesus*, 110, who asserts that there is a tension between Luke and Acts over this point.

495 Sanders, *Jews*, 14; Weatherly, *Responsibility*, 92–93.

496 Cf. Coggan, *Prayers*, 78. Grider, "Predestination," 61–62, observes that the statement concerns divine ordering of history rather than the rulers' "eternal destiny" (as part of a less persuasive wider argument that "predestination" is only found in the NT regarding temporal events rather than concerning people's ultimate life with or without God).

497 Cf. Carson, *Doctrine*, 53–54.

498 Hamm, "Precious," 201.

499 E.g., Exod 3:19–20; 7:4–5; 13:14, 16; Deut 9:26; Ezra 8:31; Neh 2:8, 18; Eccl 2:24; Ezek 20:33–34; Wis 3:1; Luke 1:66; Acts 4:30; 11:21.

500 E.g., Deut 2:15; Isa 14:24–27; Ezek 6:14; 2 Macc 7:31; Acts 13:11; see Lohse, "χείρ," *TDNT* 9:427, 431.

501 Contra Woods, *Finger*, 230, who asserts that God's hand "is equated with" God's purpose.

502 Cosgrove, "Divine," 184.

and therefore provides encouragement to the church. Nevertheless, God's plan does not override human agency or will, as the use of βουλή, "plan," in Gamaliel's speech shows: he urges the Sanhedrin not to oppose God's plan, which is a real possibility—for they would be defeated if they did (5:38–39; see *Comment* there).[503] The conclusion in 4:28 draws on this confidence concerning God's past control of history to his control of present events. Allen suggests that the NT uses of προορίζω (here; Rom 8:29–30; 1 Cor 2:7; Eph 1:5, 11) derive from the divine decree of Ps 2:7, "You are my son."[504] However, Luke uses the simple verb ὁρίζω at Acts 2:23; 10:42; 11:29; 17:26, 31; Luke 22:22, and it is used elsewhere in relation to the decrees of Fate (Aeschylus, *Cho.* 927; Sophocles, *Ant.* 451–52, 454–55, 465; Euripides, *Frg.* 218). Thus, Luke's use of the compound verb here may draw on broader usage rather than requiring a specific reference to Ps 2:7.[505]

On the prayer to this point, which has not yet directly addressed the situation, Schille wisely observes: "The . . . praise of God . . . forgets the present in such a way that it seems to be devoted solely to the enumeration in unfolding of Christology,"[506] thereby indicating the divine and christological focus of the believers. Their view of reality, including their immediate situation, is determined by their view of God and Christ.

29 καὶ τὰ νῦν, "now, concerning the present situation," is transitional, used at the "hinge" between past and present events in speeches (cf. 5:38; 20:32; 27:22; a Lukan favorite—it occurs nowhere else in the NT). It leads from looking back to Jesus's suffering[507] and the Sanhedrin's instruction to cease speaking in the name of Jesus (v. 18) into the believers' request, which is the main point;[508] cf. the use of καὶ νῦν κύριε, "and now, Lord," at similar transition points in the prayers of Tob 3:12; 8:7; 2 Kgs 19:19 LXX. It also signals that the request is based upon the powerful works of God in creation (Acts 4:24), in Scripture seen as prophecy (vv. 25–26), and in the trial and death of Jesus (vv. 27–28); the choice of κύριε, "Lord," here is a title of power, echoing δέσποτα, "Sovereign Ruler" (v. 24).[509]

The request has four components: that God would take notice of the threats, that God would give the believers boldness to go on speaking his word, that God would accompany the speaking by healing, and that God would accompany the preaching by signs and wonders.[510] The believers do not hesitate to pray in this way because they recognize their experience of

503 Hamm, "Precious," 201.
504 "Background," 105–6.
505 Squires, *Plan*, 171n89.
506 Schille, *Apostelgeschichte*, 139 (my translation).
507 Förster, *Gebet*, 391.
508 Culy and Parsons, *Acts*, 78.
509 Green, "Persevering," 192.
510 Rimaud, "Prière," 107–8, imaginatively suggests that the fourfold request is rooted in Ps 2:8–9, where God addresses the psalmist and invites him to ask for the nations' submission.

suffering as mirroring that of Jesus and fulfilling the warnings of Jesus (Luke 6:22–23; 10:16; 12:4–10; 21:12–19; cf. John 15:20).[511] They do not pray for the cessation of the opposition or their removal from the situation but for "more of the same" in God's and their response to the opposition.[512]

ἔπιδε ἐπὶ τὰς ἀπειλὰς αὐτῶν, "pay attention to their threats," asks God to focus his attention on the present situation or (perhaps better) acknowledges that he has these threats in hand as much as he did the events of Jesus's trial and death.[513] ἔπιδε, "pay attention," is used elsewhere for God's care for creation and for his people (Job 22:12; Pss 34:17 [MT 35:17]; 112:6 [MT 113:6]; 137:6 [MT 138:6]; 2 Macc 8:2); here it has the sense of the American idiom "take care of," meaning "deal with": "the 'menaces' of the authorities are submitted to the authority of God."[514] αὐτῶν, "their," is resumptive; it refers back to οἱ ἀρχιερεῖς καὶ οἱ πρεσβύτεροι, "the chief priests and elders" (Acts 4:23). Cunningham, by contrast, argues that the antecedent is Ἡρῴδης τε καὶ Πόντιος Πιλᾶτος σὺν ἔθνεσιν καὶ λαοῖς Ἰσραήλ, "both Herod and Pontius Pilate with the gentiles and the peoples of Israel" (v. 27), while agreeing that the thought is of the present threats made in vv. 17, 21.[515] The believers do not try meet the situation themselves, in their own power, or ask God to take vengeance on those who killed Jesus and threaten them, or ask God to remove the threats, but pass on the threats to God, as is appropriate for subordinates—note their self-description as τοῖς δούλοις σου, "your servants," discussed below. Hezekiah's response to the threats of the Assyrians, by bringing the threatening letter to God in prayer (2 Kgs 18:13–19:37, esp. 19:14–19), illustrates a similar response.[516] Unlike Hezekiah, the believers do not pray for deliverance *from* the situation (2 Kgs 19:19) but for God's power *in* the situation.

δὸς τοῖς δούλοις σου μετὰ παρρησίας πάσης λαλεῖν τὸν λόγον σου, "grant your servants to continue speaking your word with all boldness," focuses on what the believers want God to do. They consider themselves to be τοῖς δούλοις σου, "your servants," echoing teaching of Jesus about discipleship (Luke 12:37; 17:10; 19:13, 15) and the prophecy of Joel 3:2 LXX (EVV 2:29) quoted in Acts 2:18. Luke's lexical choice here draws a distinction between the standing of Jesus as παῖς, "servant/child" (4:27)—a term never applied in the NT to believers in relation to God—and the position of the believers as δοῦλοι, "servants/slaves." This self-designation is appropriate in a co-text where the sovereign power of God is being strongly emphasized (v. 24; the only other

511 Green, "Persevering," 192; Monloubou, *Prière*, 213–14.
512 Hamm, "Precious," 202.
513 Coggan, *Prayers*, 78. Gaventa, "To Speak," 79, observes, "For Luke, the persecution of the apostles *corresponds* to the persecution of Jesus" (her italics).
514 Monloubou, *Prière*, 213, my translation; so also Plymale, *Texts*, 85; Schofield, "Linking," 67.
515 *Tribulations*, 189.
516 Thurston, *Life*, 59.

place in Acts where believers are described this way is 16:17, where the speaker is a demonized woman).

λαλεῖν τὸν λόγον σου, "to speak your word." The continuation of the believers' activity of speaking God's word is highlighted by the echo of μετὰ παρρησίας, "with boldness," from 4:13 and the continuous present infinitive λαλεῖν, "to speak" (see this phrase, which becomes a technical term for gospel proclamation, in v. 31; 8:25; 11:19; 14:25; 16:6, 32).[517] The boldness of speech for which the believers pray is in tune with the wider context of Ps 2, quoted earlier in Acts 4:25–26: "Happy are all who take refuge in [the Lord]" (Ps 2:12 NRSVue). The believers do not pray for a way out of the situation but for God's equipping in the situation, in line with the promise of Jesus (Luke 12:11:12; see *Comment* on 4:8) that comes in the co-text of Jesus's warning that his followers must be ready to acknowledge their allegiance to him (Luke 12:8–9).

30 Again the believers acknowledge that the power for healing comes from God, not from them, a theme running through this sequence of stories. ἐν τῷ τὴν χεῖρά σου ἐκτείνειν σε εἰς ἴασιν, "while you stretch out your hand for healing," echoes v. 28 (and closely parallels Ezek 6:14 LXX).[518] Possibly there is an allusion to Moses's characteristic gesture of stretching out his hand (Exod 4:4; 14:21; 17:11–13)[519] and thus a further signal that Jesus is the "prophet like Moses" (see *Comment* on 3:22–23). There is certainly an echo of Jesus laying hands on people for healing, with a particularly close parallel in Luke 5:13: καὶ ἐκτείνας τὴν χεῖρα ἥψατο αὐτοῦ, "and stretching out his hand, he touched him" (cf. Luke 4:40; 13:13).[520]

σημεῖα καὶ τέρατα, "signs and wonders," also echoes the description of the ministry of Jesus (2:22) and the apostles (2:43), as well as relating to this specific healing, which is a σημεῖον, "sign" (4:16, 22) (see *Comment* on 2:19–20). There is also a Mosaic echo, for the time of the exodus was a time of signs and wonders too (Exod 4:1–9, 17, 28, 30; 7:9; 10:1; 11:9–10), and Moses was rejected by the people in similar manner to Jesus and the apostles' rejection by the Sanhedrin (see Acts 7:35 with *Comment*).[521] While v. 31 does not explicitly mention such events (apart from the shaking of the building), 5:12–16 will soon enumerate the performance of many signs and wonders—not to mention 5:1–11, which shows the power of God at work in judgment (see also 6:8; 14:3; 15:12). As always in Acts, signs and wonders are not intended to draw attention to the believers involved in them, but rather they accompany and validate the proclamation of the word (cf. 8:6–7 with *Comment*).[522]

517 Haenchen, *Acts*, 227n5.

518 ἐν τῷ + infinitive is a common LXX construction which Luke also uses; Wilcox, *Semitisms*, 57, 69, 70.

519 Thurston, *Life*, 60.

520 Förster, *Gebet*, 392.

521 Johnson, *Midrash*, 30.

522 So also Schofield, "Linking," 67.

It is διὰ τοῦ ὀνόματος τοῦ ἁγίου παιδός σου Ἰησοῦ, "through the name of your holy servant Jesus," that these events will take place, as they have already taken place (3:6, 12–13, 16; 4:10; see *Comment* on 2:38). The believers ask that God will act so that their ministry will continue to display the same divine features the ministry of Jesus displayed. There may be word play between ἴασιν, "to heal," and Ἰησοῦ, "Jesus."[523] This expression is found relatively rarely in gentile Christian usage before AD 170: Jeremias notes eleven references to Jesus as παῖς θεοῦ, "servant of God," in only three books (Did. 9:2, 3; 10:2, 3, 7; 1 Clem. 59:2–4 [twice]; Mart. Pol. 14:1–3 [thrice]; 20:2).[524] Each book uses the expression διὰ Ἰησοῦ τοῦ παιδός σου, "through Jesus your servant"—very close to that found here—and each uses this phrase in liturgical settings, thus suggesting that the phrase may be a Jewish expression preserved in gentile Christian prayer[525] (cf. Aramaic αββα, an intimate term for a father, which Paul assumes that gentile believers use in prayer, Rom 8:15; Gal 4:6).

31 makes clear in a variety of ways that God answers their prayer positively and thus shows divine approval for the nascent believing community:[526] "the locus for God's redemptive presence is now the worshipping community."[527] Mainville acutely observes two key features: the Spirit is continually at work in the believing community, renewing and empowering them; and the Spirit is given only as the community dedicate themselves to prayer in order to be guided by God. "It is only in listening to the Spirit that the works of God are accomplished."[528]

δεηθέντων αὐτῶν, "when they had prayed," uses a relatively unusual word for asking, δέομαι, conveying that the request has some urgency.[529] The believers' urgency in asking is necessary and appropriate, for their situation, being threatened by the authorities, is beyond mere human ability to repair. In NT and LXX, requests labeled using δέομαι are frequently addressed to God or to Jesus. The verb appears here for the first time in Acts.[530]

ἐσαλεύθη ὁ τόπος, "the place was shaken." The passive verb ἐσαλεύθη, "was shaken," suggests a divine shaking, reflects OT theophanies,[531] and is an exercise of God's rule as δεσπότης, "Sovereign Lord" (Acts 4:24).[532] The use of such

523 Reece, "Jesus as Healer," 194.
524 "παῖς θεοῦ," *TDNT* 5:702–3.
525 Wilcox, *Semitisms*, 71–72.
526 Holmås, *Prayer*, 180.
527 Holmås, *Prayer*, 184.
528 Mainville, *Spirit*, 222.
529 L&N §33.170; "δέομαι," BDAG 218; pre-Christian usage includes for begging, "δέομαι," LSJ, §II.2.
530 It occurs also at 8:22, 24, 34; 10:2; 21:39; 26:3; Luke 5:12; 8:28, 38; 9:38,40; 10:2; 21:36; 22:32; 15 out of 22 NT uses are found in Luke-Acts; cf. LXX Exod 32:11, 31; Josh 7:7; 1 Kgs 8:33, 47; 13:6; Pss 27:2 (MT 28:2); 118:58 (MT 119:58); Mal 1:9.
531 E.g., Exod 19:18; Ps 60:2 (LXX 59:4); Isa 6:4; 64:1; cf. Josephus, *Ant.* 4.3.2 §§40–52; 7.4.1 §§76–77; 4 Ezra 6:11–34; for other sources, see van der Horst, "Parallels, 3 and 4," 44–45.
532 Rimaud, "Prière," 111.

imagery from the giving of the law at Sinai in Luke's portrayal of Pentecost (2:2–3; see *Form/Structure/Setting* on 2:1–41) is reprised in this experience of the filling of the Holy Spirit: Luke is underlining that this really is the God of Israel at work.[533]

ἐπλήσθησαν ἅπαντες τοῦ ἁγίου πνεύματος, "they were all filled with the Holy Spirit," highlights the means God uses to equip the believers to continue to speak God's word boldly, as in 4:8 (see *Comment* there), and as the Spirit had enabled David to speak (v. 25).[534] It echoes the Pentecostal filling, for 2:4b is very close in wording to this phrase and also uses the same verb λαλέω, "speak,"[535] although it is not a "new Pentecost."[536] The combination of these two connections and the shaking of the place shows that God has answered the believers' prayer even though they have not explicitly asked for the Spirit to come. The collocation of the aorist participle of filling and the verb of speech signals that the Spirit inspires the speech that follows, not that those filled enter into a long-term state: hence believers filled with the Spirit at Pentecost (2:4) can be filled again.[537] Smalley notes the collocation of Spirit, God's reign (kingdom) and prayer in this passage, in common with other places in Luke-Acts: "Where the Spirit is, there is the kingdom," and the means by which the Spirit's power is accessed is prayer (Luke 11:13).[538]

ἐλάλουν . . . μετὰ παρρησίας, "they continued to speak . . . boldly." The imperfect verb portrays the speech as ongoing,[539] echoing the continuous tense of the request λαλεῖν, "to speak," in Acts 4:29 (see *Comment* there). This boldness is gifted by God in response to prayer rather than being the kind of boldness exhibited by particular human personalities.[540] The Jesus-community is able to stand against persecution only through God's enabling.

τὸν λόγον τοῦ θεοῦ, "the word of God." This is a key expression in Acts,[541] along with the similar expressions ὁ λόγος [σου], "the/your word,"[542] ὁ λόγος τοῦ κυρίου, "the word of the Lord,"[543] ὁ λόγος τῆς σωτηρίας, "the word of salvation" (13:26), ὁ λόγος τῆς χάριτος αὐτοῦ, "the word of his grace" (14:3; 20:32), and ὁ λόγος τοῦ εὐαγγελίου, "the word of the gospel" (15:7). ὁ λόγος, "the word," denotes the gospel message and echoes LXX use for the messages of the

533 Kremer, *Pfingsbericht*, 204.
534 Rimaud, "Prière," 111–12.
535 Kremer, *Pfingsbericht*, 203.
536 Contra Hamman, "Pentecôte," 89.
537 Turner, *Power*, 167–68; contra Hull, *Spirit*, 121–24. Conzelmann, *Acts*, 35 observes, "Luke is indicating how Pentecost becomes a present reality."
538 Smalley, "Spirit," esp. 66–70; cf. Feldkämper, *Jesus*, 319–20, who argues that the Spirit given to the praying disciples equips them to act as Jesus did, but always in dependence on God's power rather than having power in themselves (and thus, by contrast with Jesus).
539 With Holmås, *Prayer*, 183.
540 Gaventa, "To Speak," 80.
541 6:2, 7; 8:14; 11:1; 12:24; 13:5, 7, 46; 17:13; 18:11.
542 4:4; 6:4; 8:4; 10:44; 11:19; 16:6; 17:11; 18:5.
543 8:25; 13:44, 38, 49; 15:35, 36; 16:32; 19:10, 20; 20:35.

prophets,[544] as well as being the message which Jesus proclaimed.[545] The genitive τοῦ θεοῦ, "of God," is probably both subjective and objective, denoting both the source and content of the message. At times Luke seems to personify "the word," for it can grow (6:7; 12:24) and change lives as it is welcomed or accepted (2:41; 8:14; 11:1; 17:11). It is notable that the various "the word" expressions frequently occur in the context of opposition (as here) or primary evangelism.[546]

Explanation

The believers respond to the threats of the Jewish leadership with prayer, and their united resort to prayer as their *first* resort in pressure demonstrates substantial progress from the apostles' failure to pray in the crisis of Gethsemane (Luke 22:39–46). We should recognize the impact of the Spirit's coming in this transformed response to opposition.

This prayer—the only record of the text of a prayer in Acts—focuses on divine action. "The primary subject of the prayer is God."[547] God is the Sovereign Ruler who acts providentially in creation (Acts 4:24). God has given earlier revelation recorded in Scripture (vv. 25–26). God's plan and control of history is seen in the trial, death, and resurrection of Jesus (v. 28). God will do healings, signs, and wonders along with empowering the believers to go on speaking boldly (vv. 29–31). God is being defined as the one who has acted in and through Jesus and who now acts in and through Jesus's followers (vv. 28, 30). This divine action is focused on the Spirit's role: the Spirit inspired David (v. 25), empowered Jesus (Luke 3:22; 4:1, 14, 18), and now empowers the believers (Acts 4:31). This new "filling" echoes Pentecost but is not a repetition of Pentecost, for it leads to ongoing intelligible speech rather than short-term tongues-speech (v. 31). Tannehill acutely observes: "The effort to control history by armies and nuclear weapons appears foolish if we believe in such a God, but it never seems foolish to fearful people. In a time of threat, prayer can be a rediscovery of the sovereign God who wins by letting our opponents win and then transforming the expected result. This rediscovery can keep God's witnesses faithful in spite of threats."[548] To pray is to act, for prayer aligns the believers' will with God's will.

The prayer demonstrates that the praying church is a hermeneutical church, for they read their experience through the lens of Scripture. Their

544 E.g., LXX 2 Sam 24:11; 1 Kgs 12:22; 13:5, 20; Isa 1:10; 2:1; 28:14; 38:4; 39:5, 8; 66:5; Jer 1:2, 4, 11, 13; 2:4, 31; 7:2; 9:12; 11:1; 27:1 (MT 50:1); 34:15; 35:7; Ezek 1:3; 7:1; 11:14; 12:1, 8, 17, 21, 26; 13:1; 36:1, 16; Hos 1:1, 2; 3:4; Amos 5 1; 8:11; Mic 1:1; 6:1; Joel 1:1; Jonah 1:1; 3:1; Zeph 1:1; 2:5; Hag 1:1, 3; 2:10, 20; Zech 1:1, 7; 4:6, 8; 6:9; 7:1, 4, 8; 8:1; Mal 1:1.

545 Luke 5:1; 8:11, 21; 11:28; cf. Luke 4:22, 32; 6:47; 7:7; 9:26, 44; 21:33; 24:19, 44.

546 Pao, *Acts*, 150–56; see his full and helpful discussion, 147–80, and *Comment* on 1:8.

547 Thurston, *Life*, 59.

548 Tannehill, *Unity*, 2:73.

prayer interprets Ps 2:1–2 as speaking of the experience of Jesus's arrest, trial, and death, shockingly identifying the Jewish leadership with those opposed to God in the psalm. Responsibility for Jesus's death sits with a wide group, including the rulers (Herod the Jewish ruler and Pilate the Roman governor) and other gentiles and Israelites (Acts 4:27). Human power does not have the last word, for what they did against Jesus was within the sovereign purpose of God (v. 28)—thus their plans to frustrate God and his purposes were "useless" (v. 25). In the light of this reading of Scripture and recent events, the believers pray to God concerning the present threat.

The prayer further demonstrates how the earliest believers interpret suffering and opposition to their message and ministry. They understand it as echoing the experience of Jesus himself and as fulfilling Jesus's warnings (see *Comment* on v. 29). Accordingly, their response is not to avoid opposition by capitulating, running away, or seeking to overcome the opposition themselves. Nor is their response to ask God to remove the opposition. Nor is their reaction to understand opposition as signifying divine disfavor. Rather, they seek God's power to continue their proclamation and to accompany their proclamation with deeds of power (vv. 29–30). "Luke in no way suggests that the community of believers is responsible for overcoming the opposition; it is God's doing and His victory."[549] Their focus stays on the purposes of God, which are centered on the progress of the word, and it is for this that they ask (vv. 29, 31; cf. 1:8). The shaking of the building and their continuing bold, Spirit-enabled proclamation (4:31) demonstrate that their understanding is in line with that of God.

Coggan summarizes finely: "The story of the Church has been an interesting commentary on the fact that, when God's servants have been humble enough to be His agents and prayerful enough to pray as did this group in Acts 4, the healing work has been continued—'signs and wonders' have been done 'through the name of Thy holy servant Jesus.'"[550]

549 Plymale, *Texts*, 87.
550 Coggan, *Prayers*, 79.

B. The Assembly Sharing (4:32–5:16)

1. The Assembly's Shared Life (4:32–35)

Bibliography

Ascough, R. S. "Benefaction." **Bassler, J. M.** *God,* 117–30. **Benoit, P.** "Notes." **Bihler, J.** *Stephanusgeschichte,* 197–202. **Blomberg, C. L.** *Neither,* 164–65. **Bovon, F.** *Luke 1950–2005,* 442–53. **Caink, D. M.** "Acts 4:32–37." **Capper, B. J.** "Context." **Cerfaux, L.** "Communauté." **Co, M. A.** "Summaries." **Degenhardt, H. J.** *Lukas,* 168–72. **Dibelius, M.** *Studies,* 1–25, esp. 9–10. **Downing, F. G.** "Common Ground." **Dupont, J.** *Salvation,* 85–102 [= *Études,* 503–19]. **Fee, G. D.** "Baptism." **Fitzmyer, J. A.** "Jewish Christianity" [= *Essays,* 271–303]. **Gerhardsson, B.** "Bemerkungen." **Greehy, J. G.** "Community." **Gregson, F. J. R.** *Everything,* 50–56. **Hays, C. M.** *Ethics,* 190–211. **Hays, R. B.** *Vision,* 122–25. **Hengel, M.** *Property,* 31–34. **Horn, F. W.** *Glaube,* 40. **Hume, D. A.** *Community,* 119–39. **Jeremias, J.** "Untersuchungen." **Johnson, L. T.** *Function,* 198–203. **Johnson, S. E.** "Manual." **Judge, E. A.** *Distinctives,* 105–7. **Kato, T.** "Caractère." **Klauck, H.-J.** "Gütergemeinschaft." **Kuecker, A. J.** "Spirit." **Lindemann, A.** "Beginnings," esp. 209–12. **Marconi, G.** "History." **Marguerat, D.** *Historian,* 155–78. **Mealand, D. L.** "Community." **Mitchell, A. C.** "Function." **Noble, J.** *Common Property.* **Nolland, J.** "Use." **Noorda, S. J.** "Scene." **Pfitzner, V. C.** "Pneumatic Apostleship." **Plümacher, E.** *Lukas,* 16–18. **Reicke, B. I.** *Glaube,* 108–10. **Seccombe, D. P.** *Possessions,* 200–209. **Smalley, S. S.** "Spirit." **Sölle, D.** "Church." **Sterling, G. E.** "Athletes." **Theissen, G.** "Liebeskommunismus." **Thompson, A. J.** *One,* 70–74, 89–93. **Thompson, R. P.** *Keeping,* 69–77. **Thornton, L. S.** *Life,* esp. 7–8. **Trites, A. A.** *Concept,* 68–71. **van der Horst, P. W.** "Parallels, 3 and 4," 46. **Walton, S.** "Communism." ———. "Patronage." **Wendel, U.** *Gemeinde,* esp. 33–83, 107–9, 278–83. **Wieser, T.** "Community," 87–88. **Zimmermann, H.** "Sammelberichte."

Translation

32 The heart and soul of the group[a] of those who had come to believe was one[b]—
not even a single person used to say that any of their possessions[c] was their own, but
all things were common for them. 33 With great power the apostles kept giving[d] their
testimony to the resurrection of the Lord Jesus, and great grace was upon them all.
34 This was seen in that[e] there was[f] no one in need among them, since those who were
owners of fields or houses used to sell them[g] and bring[h] the proceeds of what they
had sold 35 and lay them at the apostles' feet, and they were distributed[i] to each one,
as anyone had need.[j]

Notes

a. Here πλῆθος, "group," refers to the identifiable congregation of believers rather than being a general term for a "crowd." cf. *CIJ,* 2:804, for this use (an inscription from a synagogue in Apamea, Syria).

b. D E (and their Latin parallel texts d and e) also have καὶ οὐκ ἦν διακρίσις (E χωρισμός) ἐν αὐτοῖς οὐδεμία (E τις), "and there was no quarrel [E division] among them," a typical Western expansion that clarifies further; *TCGNT*², 283.

c. τῶν ὑπαρχόντων, "the possessions"; "ὑπάρχω," BDAG 1029–30, §1 notes that this is a frequent use in papyri.

d. ἀπεδίδουν, "regularly gave," iterative impf. of ἀποδίδωμι; Trites, *Concept*, 68.

e. γάρ is explanatory of the claim in the previous clause, hence "This was seen in that"; Culy and Parsons, *Acts*, 82.

f. ὑπῆρχεν, "there existed," is read by 𝔓[8] D E Ψ 33 𝔐; ἦν, "there was," is read by 𝔓[74] ℵ A (B) 323 945 1175 1505 1739 *al.* 40 of 60 NT uses of ὑπάρχω, "exist," are in Luke-Acts, and so Elliott, "Text of Acts," 255, argues that ὑπῆρχεν was original, altered in order to avoid three occurrences of this verb in three verses (cf. vv. 32, 34). However, MS support for ἦν is strong, and it is at least equally likely that a later scribe would change the verb from ἦν to be in tune with Luke's known tendency to use ὑπάρχω.

g. The implied object of πωλοῦντες, "used to sell," is some of the χωρίων ἢ οἰκιῶν, "fields or houses"; Barrett, *Acts*, 1:255. The lack of an explicit direct object is not unusual in Greek.

h. The combination of the pres. ptc. πωλοῦντες, "selling," and the impf. ἔφερον, "they used to bring," suggests a series of regular actions; NIV represents this by "From time to time," although this perhaps conveys greater irregularity than the Greek tenses suggest. Caink, "Acts 4:32–37," fails to recognize this use of the impf.

i. διεδίδετο, 3 sg. impf., lit., "it was distributed," treating the gifts as a composite object; the translation "they were distributed" reflects more natural English concord with the plural τὰς τιμάς, "the proceeds" (v. 34).

j. ἄν . . . εἶχεν, "had," see *Note* f on 2:45, using the identical phrase.

Form/Structure/Setting

Delimitation of pericope. While δέ (4:32) marks a new discourse unit concerned with the shared life of the earliest believers,[1] it is not entirely disconnected from the preceding paragraph. The powerful testimony of the apostles to the resurrection (4:33) flows from the filling with the Holy Spirit that they received in response to prayer (4:29, 31),[2] and τῆς ἀναστάσεως τοῦ κυρίου Ἰησοῦ, "the resurrection of the Lord Jesus" (4:33), defines the content of ἐλάλουν τὸν λόγον τοῦ θεοῦ, "they were speaking the word of God" (4:31). Some see the summary beginning at v. 31c, where an imperfect verb ἐλάλουν, "they continued speaking," is used.[3] However, v. 31c so clearly demonstrates God's answer to the request of v. 29 that it is unwise to separate v. 31c from the earlier verses.[4] There is also a contrast between the believers being filled with the Spirit and Ananias being filled with Satan (5:3). More broadly, the shared life of the community (4:32–35) flows from the Spirit's indwelling the community here, in similar manner to the earlier description of the community's life (2:42–47) flowing from the Spirit's coming at Pentecost (Acts 2:1–4, 14–21, 33).[5]

Sources/historicity. As with other summaries, imperfect verbs predominate,

---

1 Levinsohn, *Connections*, 109.
2 Pfitzner, "Pneumatic Apostleship," 222.
3 Wendel, *Gemeinde*, 56–57.
4 With Hume, *Community*, 120–21.
5 Smalley, "Spirit," esp. 66–67.

following a story mainly told using aorist main verbs. There is a good deal of Lukan characteristic vocabulary here, including the repetition of καθότι ἄν τις χρείαν εἶχεν, "as anyone had need" (v. 35), from 2:45.[6] As with the description in 2:42–47, there is no substantial reason to doubt that Luke bases this section on traditional material.[7] Dibelius notes that this section leads naturally into the following stories of Barnabas (vv. 46–47) and Ananias and Sapphira (5:1–11) and sees Luke as using a technique known from Mark, of using a summary to generalize individual events in Jesus's ministry.[8] This is a helpful structural observation, although it tells us little concerning the historical value of this summary. Haenchen asserts that there is a contradiction between vv. 32 and 34–35, seeing the former as portraying the believers as retaining their property and the latter as them selling it.[9] This is a doubtful reading of these verses (see *Comment*). In addition, there are echoes of the teaching of Jesus in Luke's Gospel; see *Comment* on vv. 34–35.[10] (See *Form/Structure/Setting* on 2:42–47 for discussion of proposed Greco-Roman parallels, which some see as sources here too.[11])

While there are parallels with the earlier summary in 2:42–47, it is also clear that events have moved on: there are new believers (2:47b; 4:4)[12] and the practice of sharing possessions is more developed: not only are property owners selling goods (v. 34; cf. 2:45), but also the proceeds are now laid at the apostles' feet, almost ceremonially (v. 35).[13] Further, Luke's description of the community's shared life here comes in the face of opposition (4:1–21), whereas 2:42–27 comes in the setting of joy and newness at Pentecost.[14] Some find historical tensions between this passage and the earlier summary,[15] but the developments in the community's life, necessary because of enlargement and a growing understanding of the community's needs, account naturally for

6 Co, "Summaries," 63–64, provides details.

7 Barrett, *Acts*, 1:25; Seccombe, *Possessions*, 209; Theissen, "Liebeskommunismus," 701. After a careful examination, Cerfaux, "Communauté," 28–31, concludes that Luke portrays the theology and practice of "an archaic Christianity" (29, my translation) and considers that "through [this section of Acts] we can trace the main features of the history of the first Christian community in Jerusalem" (31, my translation).

8 Dibelius, *Studies*, 9–10 with n11.

9 Haenchen, *Acts*, 233.

10 With Theissen, "Liebeskommunismus," 704, contra Reicke, *Glaube*, 108–10, who considers 2:42–27 and 4:32–35 to be describing "almost the same events" (109, my translation), although he also considers that these summaries are rooted in historical tradition.

11 In particular, Zimmermann, "Sammelberichte," 81–82, considers Greco-Roman understanding to be the source of Luke's "idealisation" of the early community's sharing of possessions; cf. Bihler, *Stephanusgeschichte*, 202. Zimmerman wrongly assumes that parallelism of ideas, or even words, requires dependence of one source on another, on which see the classic article, Sandmel, "Parallelomania."

12 Co, "Summaries," 74.

13 Rius-Camps and Read-Heimerdinger, *Message*, 1:287–88.

14 Thompson, *Keeping*, 77.

15 E.g., Jeremias, "Untersuchungen," 207, sees three "strata" of material in 4:36–37; 4:32, 34–35; and 2:44–45; 4:33, with the last being Lukan in origin.

the differences between the two accounts.[16] The development will continue, notably in the shift of responsibility for distribution away from the apostles in 6:1–7.[17]

Wendel helpfully proposes that the summaries as a whole are presenting a picture of community life in order to stimulate Luke's contemporaries to reflect on what is possible.[18] This was what God could do in the earliest community and, by implication, God can still transform people to be ready to share economically with sister and brother believers. Wendel suggests this without asserting that the passages are parenetic in the sense of advocating a particular form of economic sharing.

Structure. This paragraph develops from the initial statement of the shared life of the believers, expressed in the universal provision resulting from sharing possessions (v. 32), into the powerful testimony of the apostles to Jesus's resurrection (v. 33). Two explanatory γάρ, "for," clauses (v. 34a–b) then provide further explanation of the sharing of possessions as the ground for the great power of the apostolic testimony, with the second expanded by further clauses (vv. 34c–35). Thus, the paragraph begins and ends with the faith of those who had come to faith who lived in mutual care and unity (vv. 32, 34–35) and centers on the mainspring of their shared life, which is also the means for others to come to faith: the apostolic testimony to Jesus's resurrection (v. 33).

Setting. Acts 4:32–35 outlines the nature of the shared life of the believers in broadly similar terms to 2:42–47 but with a particular focus on the sharing of possessions (4:34–45). The sharing is the focus of the following two paragraphs, signaled by key phrases that are echoed:[19] Barnabas models the sharing positively by selling a field and giving the proceeds to the community (4:36–37), and then Ananias and Sapphira provide a negative mirror image, for their gift to the community results in their deaths (5:1–11).[20] The theme of the power of the apostolic testimony (4:33) returns in the mention of many signs and wonders Διὰ . . . τῶν χειρῶν τῶν ἀποστόλων, "through . . . the hands of the apostles" (5:12), itself unpacked in terms of healings (5:15–16).

Comment

32 The effect of the unusual word order of the first clause is to contrast the first words, Τοῦ . . . πλήθους, "of the congregation," and the last, μία, "one."

16 Cf. Lindemann, "Beginnings," 216.

17 Kato, "Carectère," 94–95, concludes that Luke is not presenting an idealised view of how believing communities should always live but the way this community in this city at this time lived.

18 *Gemeinde,* esp. 33–83, 107–9, with summary on 283.

19 Sterling, "Athletes," 682.

20 Marguerat, *Historian,* 159–60, observes that this sequence of summary (4:32–35), followed by event(s) (4:36–37; 5:1–10) and contrasted effect (5:5b, 11) reflects a wider pattern seen in relation to the summaries in 2:42–27 and 5:12–16.

Luke thus conveys that the diverse members of the believing community were united, and the second clause illustrates this oneness by their handling of material goods. Their sharing of possessions flows from and expresses their shared experience of new life in Christ.[21]

καρδία καὶ ψυχὴ μία, "heart and soul . . . one." Luke's phrasing parallels both OT and Hellenistic ideals of sharing possessions and friendship,[22] as well as echoing 2:44. The oneness of heart and soul resonates with Jer 32:29, "I will give them one heart and one way" (LXX 39:29 differs), and Ezek 11:19, "I will give them one heart." Both passages come in the setting of YHWH restoring Israel and, in Ezekiel, giving them a new spirit, suggestive in this passage of the Holy Spirit's work among the believers. The combination καρδία καὶ ψυχή, "heart and soul," expresses a total response to God (cf. LXX Deut 4:29; 6:5, 6; 10:12; 11:13, 18; 13:4 [EVV 13:3]; 26:16; 28:65; 30:2, 6, 10).[23] Gerhardsson proposes that there may also be an allusion to the Shema (Deut 6:5): there, love for God is expressed in "heart and soul and strength"—the third term may correspond to the sharing of goods.[24] He also sees a parallel with Lev 19:18, which treats love for neighbor as an outcome of YHWH's name and nature.

ψυχὴ μία, "soul one," conveys an ideal of friendship rather than an ideal of a wider society; cf. Diogenes Laertius 5.20, where Aristotle answers the question, "What is a friend?" with μία ψυχὴ δύο σώματασιν ἐνοικοῦσα, "One soul inhabiting two bodies."[25] There are numerous Greco-Roman parallels to this phrase, in both Greek and Latin, in the context of friendship.[26] Cf. Phil 1:27, elucidated by 2:2: being "one soul" is seen by united thought and action, centered on the gospel. Moreover, Plato, *Resp.* 464A–66D, and Aristotle, *Pol.* 2.1–2 locate their discussions of sharing possessions in the context of finding a form of government which enables unity rather than division, and thus when Luke goes on to write of sharing possessions, educated Greco-Roman readers would be likely to hear an implicit claim that the believers displayed the unity to which Greek and Roman governance aspired.[27] The major difference concerning the believers is that they share in this way among people of a wide variety of social standings, whereas the Greco-Roman aspirations to sharing were among elite people only.[28]

---

21 Dupont, *Salvation*, 96–102. Hengel, *Property*, 32, rightly observes (against the view that sharing possessions was under compulsion), "The decisive thing was *koinonia*, not organization."

22 For Hellenistic sources, see Hume, *Community*, 122n8; Dupont, *Salvation*, 96–97; Seccombe, *Possessions*, 200n2; Co, "Summaries," 65n50; Mealand, "Community," 97–98.

23 Thompson, *Keeping*, 71, with n187.

24 Gerhardsson, "Bermerkungen," 145.

25 Seccombe, *Possessions*, 202.

26 References: van der Horst, "Parallels, 3 and 4," 46; Plümacher, *Lukas*, 16–18; Thompson, *Keeping*, 71n185.

27 Thompson, *One*, 89–93; cf. Klauck, "Gütergemeinschaft," esp. 72–74.

28 Among others, Blomberg, *Neither*, 164; Hays, *Ethics*, 209. On the Greco-Roman parallels, see Gregson, *Everything*, 53–55; Hays, *Ethics*, 201–8.

τῶν πιστευσάντων, “of those who had come to believe.” The aorist participle suggests the focus is on their having come to faith rather than their present ongoing faith (which would more naturally be represented by a present participle, cf. 2:44).[29] Luke uses τῶν πιστευσάντων, “the believers,” and κοινωνία, “fellowship” (2:42), rather than φιλία, “friendship,” and ἰσότης, “equality” (cf. 2 Cor 8:13), and thus avoids the overtones of the Greco-Roman patronage system conveyed by those terms.[30]

This is the first use of πλῆθος, “congregation,” for the Christian community in Acts (it occurs at 2:6 for the crowd at Pentecost). The word is a Lukan favorite (twenty-six of thirty-one NT uses are in Luke-Acts). Its referent here is the believing community; the genitive τῶν πιστευσάντων, “of those who had come to believe,” provides definition of *which* congregation was meant. πλῆθος is similarly used in Jewish setting (e.g., *CIJ* 2:804); this parallels the use of רבים (*rbym*), “multitudes,” to refer to the congregation at Qumran (1QS V, 2, 9, 22; VI, 19), as well as the use of πλῆθος twice in LXX to translate קהל (*qhl*), the word regularly used for the assembly of Israel (Exod 12:6; 2 Chr 31:18).[31] Luke will use the word similarly for a Christian assembly in Acts 6:2, 5; 15:12, 30;[32] however, he also uses it for the Sanhedrin (23:7), as well as for other substantial bodies of people, in line with classical usage (e.g., 5:14; 14:1, 4; 17:4; 21:36; 25:24).[33]

οὐδὲ εἷς τι τῶν ὑπαρχόντων αὐτῷ ἔλεγεν ἴδιον εἶναι ἀλλ᾽ ἦν αὐτοῖς ἅπαντα κοινά, “not even a single person used to say that any of their possessions was their own, but all things were shared by them,” echoes 2:44–45 (see *Comment* there). This clause is joined to the previous one by a simple καί, “and,” which does not identify union of soul from the earlier clause as either cause or effect of the sharing of possessions; Dupont helpfully suggests both have truth in them.[34] As in the earlier passage, this does not mean that the earliest believers practised communism or required compulsory contribution of goods into the common fund at some stage of joining the community. To speak of τῶν ὑπαρχόντων αὐτῷ, “their possessions,” presupposes that believers had their own possessions (cf. 5:4 with *Comment* there).[35] Rather, as 4:34–35 explain and vv. 36–37 illustrate, individuals voluntarily gave from their means in order to

29 Barrett, *Acts*, 1:251.

30 With Theissen, “Liebeskommunismus,” 699. Cf. Judge, *Distinctives*, 105–7, making a similar argument for the downplaying of φιλία, “friendship,” in Paul.

31 Johnson, “Manual,” 112.

32 “πλῆθος,” BDAG 825–26, §2.b.δ.

33 “πλῆθος,” LSJ, §I.2.b; Bruce, *Acts* (1990), 159.

34 *Salvation*, 101; contrast Thornton, *Life*, 7–8, who sees all things being shared as a consequence of their united heart and soul. Thornton is contrasting this with the view that the sharing was the consequence of imminent parousia expectation, and he is certainly correct that Luke makes no connection between such expectation and the sharing of possessions. However, we may doubt the premise that the earliest believers were expecting the parousia immediately and were disappointed; see Wright, “Hope Deferred?”; Walton, “The End.”

35 Kato, “Carectère,” 282, reporting the view of Araī.

support others. The principle at work was not compulsion but an openhearted holding of possessions lightly, seeing the needs of others in the community as of greater importance than individuals or families accumulating goods for themselves.[36] The ethical ideal is not poverty but detachment from material goods.[37] Thus, "[p]rivate property remains, but the owners consider it not as private but as common property";[38] cf. Mitchell's observation that the Greco-Roman ideals did not exclude private property but advocated a similar "openhanded" approach to sharing it with friends in need.[39] In the Third Gospel, the practice of the women who supported Jesus and his disciples is comparable (Luke 8:1–3). There is no clear evidence for an inner and outer circle within the community, where the inner circle shared everything and the outer circle that had not yet entered into that state.[40] Luke clearly does not see this general statement as contradicting the Ananias and Sapphira story, where the couple fail to practise such loose holding of possessions—this passage is a summary, not an exhaustive description.

33 The presence of v. 33 between the initial statement about possessions being regarded as common (v. 32) and the description of the practice of sharing possessions (vv. 34–35) suggests that the apostles' proclamation of the resurrection of Jesus is the ground and basis of the shared life of the new community.[41] See further on γάρ (*Comment* on v. 34).

δυνάμει μεγάλῃ, "with great power," may be a dative of means,[42] manner,[43] or accompaniment. It is fronted for emphasis, highlighting the essential work of the Spirit in the early believers' shared life. The Spirit's work is not a quiet background work, but the heart and driver of what happens.[44] The reference is to both the apostles' preaching and the "signs and wonders," since vv. 29, 31 portray the believers praying for power seen in both their testimony and God doing "signs and wonders." Further, "signs and wonders" are mentioned again in 5:12–16 as a feature of the community's life and witness.[45]

ἀπεδίδουν τὸ μαρτύριον οἱ ἀπόστολοι τῆς ἀναστάσεως τοῦ κυρίου Ἰησοῦ, "the apostles kept giving their testimony to the resurrection of the Lord Jesus," portrays the apostles doing precisely what the Sanhedrin forbade them to do (4:18). It is an unusual phrase, for generally Luke prefers verbs for witness and testimony rather than nouns, notably μαρτυρέω, "testify," and εὐαγγελίζομαι,

---

36 See Noorda, "Scene," 482n31; Walton, "Communism," esp. 102–9; Kuecker, "Spirit," 84–88; Greehy, "Community," 237. Wieser, "Community," 88, observes that such sharing is "the only logical alternative" to competition over resources.

37 Bovon, *Luke 1950–2005*, 448, summarizing Dupont; cf. Kato, "Carectère," 86–89.

38 Horn, *Glaube*, 40 (my translation); also Degenhardt, *Lukas*, 170–71.

39 "Function," 262–64.

40 Ascough, "Benefaction," 95; contra Capper, "Context," 337–38.

41 Lindemann, "Beginnings," 210.

42 Bruce, *Acts* (1990), 160.

43 Culy and Parsons, *Acts*, 80.

44 Fee, "Baptism," 95.

45 Cf. Schneider, *Apostelgeschichte*, 1:365.

"proclaim good news." However, ἀπεδίδουν τὸ μαρτύριον, "they kept giving their testimony," is clearly equivalent in meaning, and the imperfect verb enables Luke to indicate regularity of testimony.[46] τό, "the," probably definitizes the noun μαρτύριον, "testimony," and the following genitive chain τῆς ἀναστάσεως τοῦ κυρίου Ἰησοῦ, "of the resurrection of the Lord Jesus," clarifies the content of the apostles' testimony on Jesus being raised, as elsewhere in Acts.[47] The article τό may well also function as a personal pronoun "their."[48] Luke alludes to Jesus's promise that the apostles will be his witnesses (1:8; cf. 1:22; 2:32, 40; 3:15),[49] and thus shows this promise's fulfillment. This verse continues to demonstrate the divine answer to the request for boldness in testimony (4:29, 31). There is also a partial link to the teaching role of the apostles in the previous summary of the community's life (2:42), but in this passage the apostolic testimony is more directed to outsiders.

χάρις τε μεγάλη ἦν ἐπὶ πάντας αὐτούς, "and great grace was upon them all," parallels δυνάμει μεγάλῃ, "great power," in the earlier clause. The close parallel in Luke 2:40, the unqualified use of χάρις, "grace," and the linked co-text (signaled by τέ, "and") of people who have responded to the apostles' evangelistic testimony, all suggest that the source of the grace, as well as the power, is God rather than the people.[50]

34 γάρ, "for," makes a clear link between the "great grace" of God upon the community and the community's provision for those in need: sharing possessions so that none were needy was an outcome of the work of God in the community (cf. the similar connection made in 6:7 with *Comment* there).[51]

Verses 34–35 (in common with vv. 32–33) have a sequence of imperfect verbs, common in summaries (cf. 2:42–47; 5:12–16; 9:31): ἦν, "was," ὑπῆρχον, "were," ἔφερον, "used to . . . bring," ἐτίθουν, "used to . . . lay," διεδίδετο, "they were distributed," and εἶχεν, "had." The imperfects are distributive, indicating that different people sold their goods at different times. The imperfects also portray such events as regular occurrences in the life of the community:[52] as need arose, it was met from the common fund provided by believers who sold possessions and brought the money to the apostles for distribution.[53]

ἐνδεής, "needy," is an NT *hapax legomenon,* although it occurs twenty-four times in LXX. The comparative form occurs in Herm. Vis. 3.1.2.[54] Deuteronomy

46 With Trites, *Concept,* 68.
47 Cf. 2:24; 3:26; 4:2, 10; 5:30; 13:30, 33, 37; 17:3, 18, 31; with Trites, *Concept,* 68; see also *Notes.*
48 Wallace, 215–16.
49 Hume, *Community,* 131.
50 Culy and Parsons, *Acts,* 81–82; Barrett, *Acts,* 1:254; Co, "Summaries," 76; Nolland, "Use," 616–17; contra Lindemann, "Beginnings," 211n42; Benoit, "Notes," 99, who considers that 2:47, where the χάρις is of the people, is closer in wording than Luke 2:40.
51 Hays, *Vision,* 123.
52 With Barrett, *Acts,* 1:255.
53 So also Dunn, *Acts,* 59.
54 "ἐνδεής," BDAG 331; the word is formed from ἐν + δέησις = "in + need."

15:4 LXX is especially close to this phrase: ὅτι οὐκ ἔσται ἐν σοὶ ἐνδεής, "for there shall not be a needy person among you." Deuteronomy 15:4 comes in the midst of laws on the remission of debts every seven years—laws which may never have been enacted—and asserts that the regular redistribution of property implied by these laws would not cause poverty or deprivation. Cf. Tg. Yer I. Deut 15:4–5: "there shall be no poor among you, for the Lord will indeed bless you in the land that the Lord your God is giving you as an inheritance to possess, if only you will indeed accept the Word of the Lord your God so as to diligently do all this commandment that I am commanding you today." The believing community is painted in the colors of the ideal Israelite community of Deut 15, although Deut 15:7–11 calls Israelites to give *loans* rather than gifts to fellow Israelites in need with the recognition that the money may never be repaid because of the sabbatical year. The contrast with the ethic of reciprocity in the Greco-Roman world is striking here, for those who are wealthy give to the community in support of those in need without evident expectation of benefit, whether in repayment or in recognition or honor or other client-type responses.[55] Isocrates's idealized description of ancient Athens where no one was in need only included τῶν πολιτῶν, "citizens": τότε μὲν οὐδεὶς ἦν τῶν πολιτῶν ἐνδης τῶν ἀναγκαίων, οὐδὲ προσαιτῶν τοὺς ἐντυγχάνοντας τὴν πόλιν κατῄσχυνε, "in that day no one of the citizens lacked the necessaries of life nor shamed the city by begging from passers-by" (*Areop.* 83 = *Or.* 7.83 [Norlin, LCL]; cf. Seneca, *Ep.* 90.38). By contrast, this social transformation portrays the believing community as bringing "good news to the poor," in fulfillment of Jesus's "Nazareth manifesto" (Luke 4:16–21; see also *Comment* on 2:44).[56]

κτήτορες, "owners," is found frequently in papyri for those who own real estate,[57] and is a further NT *hapax legomenon,* although cognate with the verb κτάομαι, "acquire/possess" (found five times in Luke-Acts from seven NT uses), and the noun κτῆμα, "property/piece of land" (two of four NT uses are in Acts). Barrett notes, "[t]he verbal statistics fit with Luke's . . . interest in property and poverty."[58]

χωρίων ἢ οἰκιῶν, "fields or houses," marks the things sold as nonessentials of life, for the evidence of 2:46 and 12:12 is that believers did not sell their own houses.[59] This phrase thus partially unpacks the vaguer statement of 2:45, that they were selling τὰ κτήματα καὶ τὰς ὑπάρξεις, "possessions and belongings." It is striking to contrast the sale of fields here with Judas's use of the proceeds of handing Jesus over to purchase a field (1:18, using κτάομαι, "acquire/possess").

πωλοῦντες, "sold," echoes the teaching of Jesus in lexical choice and

55 Mitchell, "Function," esp. 264–66; cf. Walton, "Patronage."
56 Hume, *Community,* 137–39.
57 *NewDocs* 2:89 §57.
58 Barrett, *Acts,* 1:255.
59 Lindemann, "Beginnings," 211n46; Alexander, *Acts* (People's Bible), 46–47.

co-text: Luke 12:33, *Πωλήσατε* τὰ ὑπάρχοντα ὑμῶν καὶ δότε ἐλεημοσύνην, "*Sell* your possessions and give alms," and 18:22, πάντα ὅσα ἔχεις *πώλησον* καὶ διάδος πτωχοῖς, "*Sell* all that you have and distribute to the poor" (also including διαδίδωμι, "distribute," found in διεδίδετο, "they distributed," v. 35[60]). Acts 12:33 is addressed to the disciples and 18:22 to the enquiring ruler. The latter echo points to the radical shift in lifestyle that Jesus calls the ruler to adopt, a shift now exemplified among the believers.[61] Luke portrays the believers as living out their Master's teaching. This present participle portrays ongoing action in similar manner to the imperfects in this passage.[62]

35 ἐτίθουν παρὰ τοὺς πόδας τῶν ἀποστόλων, "lay them at the apostles' feet." This is the first of three uses of this expression in Acts (also 4:37; 5:2). The apostles receive the contributions; the placement at their feet denotes the handing over of the money into the apostles' trust to dispose as they see fit, but more besides.[63] The expression "be at the feet of" another person is frequent in LXX and denotes submission to the authority and power of the other.[64] In Luke's Gospel, sitting at Jesus's feet similarly denotes submission and the authority of Jesus over demons and in teaching and healing.[65] The expression thus connotes an attitude of humility on the part of the donor,[66] a point Luke underlines in Barnabas the field owner (and therefore a person of some substance) placing his money at the feet of a fisherman (Acts 4:37). "[T]he way one disposes of one's possessions reflects the way one disposes oneself."[67] Rather than the giver being named and honored, the giving of the gift via the apostles avoided and subverted the honor expected for benefactors.[68] The unity of the believing community—the renewed Israel—under the apostles' authority is reinforced by this symbolic action and continues the theme seen in the hearing, where the central issue is whether the apostles or the Sanhedrin speak for Israel's God (see *Explanation* on 4:5–22). The distance between the believing community and the Jerusalemite Jews at large is increasing, since the believers are engaging more fully with each other materially as well as in other ways; at the same time, 4:33a and 5:12–16 show that the believers are reaching out to those of their fellow Jews who are open.

---

60 So also Hays, *Ethics*, 193–94.
61 Gregson, *Everything*, 53.
62 Gregson, *Everything*, 52.
63 For this and what follows, see the valuable discussion in Johnson, *Function*, 201–2.
64 E.g., LXX Josh 10:24; 1 Sam 25:24, 41; 2 Sam 22:39; Pss 8:7 [EVV 8:6]; 17:10 [MT 18:10, EVV 18:9]; 46:4 [MT 47:4, EVV 47:3]; 98:5 [MT 99:5]; 109:1 [MT 110:1]; 131:7 [MT 132:7]; cf. Cicero, *Flac.* 68, describing a large amount of gold being laid at the feet of Sextus Caesius, thus putting it at the Romans' disposal.
65 Luke 7:38, 44, 45, 46; 8:35, 41; 10:39; 17:16; 20:34; cf. Acts 2:35; 10:25; 22:3. These biblical and Lukan parallels are more pertinent than CD XIV, 13; 1QS VI, 19–20, cited by Fitzmyer, "Jewish," 248 [= Fitzmyer, *Essays*, 294].
66 Thompson, *Keeping*, 74.
67 Bassler, *God*, 124; cf. Johnson, *Function*, 202.
68 Kuecker, "Spirit," 90.

διεδίδετο δὲ ἑκάστῳ καθότι ἄν τις χρείαν εἶχεν, "and they were distributed to each one, as anyone had need." There is no necessary implication that the apostles themselves carry out the distribution of the donations, for διεδίδετο, "it was distributed," is impersonal. The decision as to who received what probably gives rise to the issue highlighted in 6:1–2, where the apostles decline to take responsibility for such arrangements when that task becomes a hindrance to proclamation and prayer.

ἑκάστῳ, "to each one," individualizes the statement πᾶσιν, "to all" (2:45), about the distribution, perhaps suggesting that individuals had to present evidence of their need before receiving money from the common fund.[69]

καθότι ἄν τις χρείαν εἶχεν, "as anyone had need," is also found in 2:45 (see *Comment* there).

Explanation

Luke's second summary of the community life of the believers both reiterates and develops the portrait from the first (2:42–27). The believers' request for boldness for them in speaking God's word accompanied by God acting in healing, signs, and wonders (4:29–30) continues to be granted as the Spirit who fills them (4:31) has effect in their shared life. The apostles' testimony is the bold proclamation (4:33a), accompanied by God's "great grace" (4:33b). The linkage of 4:29–30 with this passage implies that the believers' community life (4:32, 34–35) is also an expression of God's great grace and power. In 2:42–27, the community's shared life grew out of the glorious gift of the Spirit at Pentecost, and here Luke portrays that shared life being sustained in the midst of opposition (esp. 4:18, 21a).

Luke uses terms which Greco-Roman and Jewish readers would both recognize in describing the unity and support found in the community's life. Elite Greco-Roman writers looked back to a golden era when goods were shared (including even wives! Plato, *Resp.* 5.449c–d) and spoke of ideals of sharing possessions in friendships, but their aspirations stopped with those of high social status. There was no hope that such sharing would extend to those lower down the human food chain; for some, slaves in particular were not fully human. The believers' oneness and sharing fulfill these community ideals in Greco-Roman thought and go startlingly beyond them by including those in need (Acts 4:34, 35)—their needs are met by those with resources to sell, such as houses or real estate (v. 34). This picture of the Spirit's work is deeply un-egocentric; rather, it is community oriented.

Jewish hearers of Acts would recognize the allusion in v. 34 to Deut 15:4–5, "There will, however, be no one in need among you, because the LORD is sure to bless you in the land that the LORD your God is giving you as a possession

69 Lindemann, "Beginnings," 212.

to occupy, if only you will obey the LORD your God by diligently observing this entire commandment that I command you today." That passage looks to a time of God's blessing through his command of the seven-yearly remission of debts (Deut 15:1–3), blessing such that no Israelite would be in need in the promised land. "[T]here was no one in need among them" (Acts 4:34) signals that the believing community fulfills these hopes for Israel and further underlines that the believing community represents the renewed and restored Israel of prophecy to which Jewish people looked forward.

The "heart and soul" unity of which Luke writes (v. 32a) is thus not ethereal but deeply earthed in the realities of daily need by sharing possessions as required (v. 32b). Essene communities in Palestine met evening by evening, and each brought the money they had earned that day to pool in order to buy what was needed to eat together (Philo, *Hypoth.* 1.10–11). By contrast with the Qumran community, the believers are not required to contribute but give voluntarily in response to God's generosity to them in raising Jesus from the dead (signalled by the Greek translated "This was seen in that," Acts 4:34). By implication, they demonstrate that Jesus, now vindicated by God, is the gateway to God (hence baptism was in Jesus's name, 2:38).

The apostles are charged with responsibility for overseeing the distribution of the common fund, and placing the money at their feet symbolizes this (4:35). It also shows recognition of the authority given to the apostles by the exalted Jesus, an authority to be used—as here—for the community's strengthening and support rather than merely for the benefit of those in authority. At this stage of the community's life, such a role for the apostles appears feasible, but this will soon change (6:1–7).

This summary prepares for the following two scenes, which portray Barnabas as a positive example of sharing (4:36–37) and Ananias and Sapphira as a negative example (5:1–11). Luke then provides a further summary (5:12–16), which mirrors this one in some ways (although not mentioning the sharing of possessions) while expanding the portrait of the community further.

To read this passage is to be provoked to ask what happened later in the life of the believing community, since economic sharing did not continue in this form. Luke himself goes on, however, to describe other forms of economic sharing among believers, including between communities of believers. The Antiochene believers sent to the Jerusalem believers at time of famine (11:27–30). Dorcas is commended as one who contributed by making clothes for widows (9:36, 39). Paul provides for himself and his companions through his physical work (20:34; 18:3). Paul asserts that he does not desire others' goods (20:33) but rather seeks to support the weak (20:35), a practice he presents to the Ephesian elders for their imitation. As an example, Paul pays the hairdressing expenses of a group of Jewish believers who take a vow (21:23–24, 26). This variety of forms of economic sharing as expressions of response to the gospel is in tune with Paul's own teaching in 2 Cor 8–9, where his call for generous giving is rooted in God's generous giving in Christ (8:9) and his invitation to the Corinthians is that their surplus should provide for others in need (8:13–14). In sum, it seems that the principle that believers should be ready to share economically with their sisters and brothers in need underlay a "mixed economy" of expressions of that principle.

2. Barnabas: A Positive Example (4:36–37)

Bibliography

Brock, S. P. "ΒΑΡΝΑΒΑΣ." **Cadbury, H. J.** "Names," 47–48. **Danker, F. W.** *Benefactor*, 436–86. **Deissmann, G. A.** *Studies*, 307–10. **Dupont, J.** *Sources*, 62–72. **France, D.** "Barnabas." **Hays, C. M.** *Ethics*, 212–13. **Hengel, M.** *Property*, 31–34. **Hengel, M., and A. M. Schwemer.** *Damascus*, 211–14. **Hume, D. A.** *Community*, 141–42. **Jeremias, J.** *Jerusalem*, 207–13. **Johnson, L. T.** *Function*, 203–4. **Kollmann, B.** *Joseph Barnabas*, 21–24. **Kuecker, A. J.** "Spirit," 91–96. **Marguerat, D.** *Historian*, 155–78. **Mitchell, A. C.** "Function." **Murphy, S. J.** "Role," 319–22. **Myllykoski, M.** "Being There," 151–53. **Noorda, S. J.** "Scene." **Öhler, M.** *Barnabas*, 87–187. **Saller, R. P.** *Patronage*. **Sheeley, S. M.** *Asides*. **Shepherd, W. H., Jr.** *Function*, 170–73. **Thompson, R. P.** *Keeping*, 75. **Williams, M. H.** "Names," 89.

Translation

[36] Joseph (who was called Barnabas by the apostles, which means[a] "son of encouragement"), a Levite, a Cypriot by race, [37] who owned a field,[b] sold it and brought the money and laid it at[c] the apostles' feet.

Notes

a. ὅ ἐστιν μεθερμηνευόμενον is an idiom meaning, "which is, being translated" ("μεθερμηνεύω," BDAG 625; Culy and Parsons, *Acts*, 83). The neuter rel. pn. is part of the idiom, although it refers to a masc. noun, Βαρναβᾶς. The verb is periph. pres. (pres. indic. + pres. ptc. [pass.]).

b. ὑπάρχοντος αὐτῷ ἀγροῦ, lit., "a field being to him"; gen. abs. with dat. of possession αὐτῷ; Culy and Parsons, *Acts*, 84.

c. παρά 𝔓[57, 74] A B D Ψ 33 1739 𝔐; πρός ℵ E 36 *pc.* There seems to be no great difference in meaning between the two; παρά is used with the same verb in v. 35; 5:32 (where there is no variant reading). UBS[4]/NA[27] and ECM read πρός, for they consider it more likely that scribes would harmonize the readings in the three verses, but this decision is taken against the strong MS support for παρά, which THGNT reads; discussion: *TCGNT*[2], 284.

Form/Structure/Setting

This sentence introduces a new topic (signaled by δέ, untranslated),[70] Joseph Barnabas, who offers a positive model of the generosity among the community described in vv. 32–35; Ananias and Sapphira will offer a negative

70 With Öhler, *Barnabas*, 89.

model (5:1–11).[71] These vignettes condense the sharing into specific events which exemplify the principles at work.[72] Luke introduces Barnabas briefly; he will become significant later in Acts, especially in facilitating Saul's entry into the Jerusalem believing community (9:26–28), bringing Saul to Antioch (11:22–26), traveling with him (13:1–3), and taking Paul's side over the conditions of admission of gentiles to the community (15:1–4, 12), until Barnabas and Paul's dispute over John Mark led to them separating (15:36–40). Luke introduces him without a clear indication of his future significance[73] (cf. Luke's brief introduction of Saul, 7:58; 8:1a[74]). Dunn speculates that Barnabas may be singled out here as the first wealthy person who made a substantial gift to the community.[75] If so, the historical value of this story is underlined.

Hengel suggests Luke is using an Antiochene source here, presumably on the basis that Barnabas is strongly connected with Antioch (11:22–26; 13:1; 14:26; 15:22, 30, 35).[76] If there is a source in play here, Luke has—as always—incorporated the source material so well into his own style and presentation that it is impossible to be confident what is source and what is Lukan redaction.[77]

Comment

36–37 Ἰωσὴφ δὲ ὁ ἐπικληθεὶς Βαρναβᾶς ἀπὸ τῶν ἀποστόλων, "Joseph (who was called Barnabas by the apostles"). Joseph is introduced and will emerge in Acts as a significant minor character. Ἰωσήφ, "Joseph," signals his Jewish family,[78] as does his being a Levite. He is the first new character in Acts who is not an apostle or a relative of Jesus.[79] Here we learn that he received the nickname Βαρναβᾶς, "Barnabas," from the apostles, which is the "Christian" name by which he is known in the rest of the NT.[80] The apostles' naming of Barnabas is significant as a marker of his character and identity (cf. Philo, *Names* 70–71, 121): it signals his submission to them, for the giving of a name in Scripture is the prerogative of a superior (Gen 2:19; 17:5; 19:39; 25:26, 36; etc.; cf. Jos. Asen. 15:6).[81]

71 With Marguerat, *Historian*, 160–62, who observes a wider pattern of summary followed by event(s) (here vv. 36–37 and 5:1–10) and followed by contrasted effect (here 5:5b, 11).

72 Kuecker, "Spirit," 91. For my phrasing, see Marguerat, *Historian*, 161.

73 Tannehill, *Unity*, 2:78.

74 Discussion: Longenecker, *Rhetoric*, 192–98.

75 Dunn, *Acts*, 59.

76 Hengel, *Property*, 33.

77 For discussion of a possible Antiochene source, see the following, although none agree that 4:36–37 comes from an Antiochene source: Barrett, *Acts*, 1:51–56, noting that Jerome, *Vir. ill.* 7, identifies Luke as "a doctor of Antioch"; Haenchen, *Acts*, 82–84; Fitzmyer, *Acts*, 80–90; Dupont, *Sources*, 62–72; Myllykoski, "Being," 151–53, conveniently summarizes the important work of Harnack, *Acts*.

78 Murphy, "Role," 320; for examples, see Williams, "Names," 89.

79 Kuecker, "Spirit," 92.

80 Acts 9:27; 11:22, 30; 12:25; 13:1, 3, 7, 43, 46, 50; 14:12, 14, 20; 15:2, 12, 22, 25, 35, 36, 37, 39; 1 Cor 9:6; Gal 2:1, 9, 13; Col 4:10.

81 Johnson, *Acts*, 87.

Βαρναβᾶς . . . ὅ ἐστιν μεθερμηνευόμενον υἱὸς παρακλήσεως, "Barnabas . . . which means 'son of encouragement.'" The name "Barnabas" is derived from Hebrew or Aramaic, but does not actually *mean* "son of encouragement."[82] This phrase is a Hebraism for a person characterized as an encourager,[83] and this naming signals and foreshadows the way Barnabas will act as the book develops.[84] This meaning may derive from *bar-nabi* in Aramaic, "son of a prophet,"[85] a "popular etymology."[86] The name "Barnabas" probably derives from the god Nebo and means "son of Nebo" (cf. Νεβοῦς, "Nebo," Isa 46:1 σ′),[87] although Luke's interpretation as "son of encouragement" shows that it was not understood among the community as a pagan title.[88] This nickname implies he was one who regularly encouraged/exhorted the community verbally through teaching and perhaps prophecy (cf. Acts 13:1) and probably implicitly through his deeds.[89] Thus he is known as a son of encouragement among the apostles. He is John Mark's cousin (Col 4:10; cf. Acts 15:37)[90] and will emerge as a firm supporter of the emerging gentile mission (11:19–24), as well as Paul's sponsor (9:26–28; 11:25–26) and companion on his early travels (13:1–15:35), before he and Paul divide over John Mark (15:36–40).

Λευίτης . . . ὑπάρχοντος αὐτῷ ἀγροῦ, "a Levite . . . who owned a field." Levites supported the priests in their temple service, including serving as musicians, singers, and the temple police.[91] As a Levite he would be from the same social echelon as some of the Sanhedrin rather than being considered unlearned like the Galileans Peter and John (4:13). Nevertheless, he identifies with the believers rather than the Sanhedrin.[92] In Scripture, Levites were allocated no land since God was considered their "inheritance/portion" (Deut 12:12; 14:29; Josh 14:3, 4; 18:7), although there was land allocated to them by other tribes (Josh 21:1–41; cf. Lev 25:32).[93] By the first century, some Levites owned land (e.g., Josephus, see: *Life* 1 §§1–5; 14–15 §§68–83). Barnabas's field may have been ancestral land in Cyprus, although Hengel suggests that his family relationship with John Mark and Mary, who was known to have property in

82 On the name "Barnabas," see Brock, "ΒΑΡΝΑΒΑΣ"; Öhler, *Barnabas*, 141–67.

83 "υἱός," BDAG 1025, §2.c.β.

84 See below and France, "Barnabas"; Sheeley, *Asides*, 127, 171.

85 See Barrett, *Acts*, 1:258–59; Brock, "ΒΑΡΝΑΒΑΣ," for careful discussion.

86 "Βαρναβᾶς," BDAG 167.

87 Deissmann, *Bible*, 307–10; Cadbury, "Names," 47–48; Fitzmyer, *Acts*, 320–21 (with bibliography).

88 Hengel and Schwemer, *Paul between*, 211–13. Kollmann, *Joseph Barnabas*, 24, rightly observes that it is incredible that the Jerusalem apostles knowingly nicknamed Joseph as the son of a pagan god.

89 Kuecker, "Spirit," 94.

90 "ἀνεψιός," BDAG 78—not "uncle," as KJV; Lohse, *Colossians and Philemon*, 172n21.

91 Summaries with primary source references: Jeremias, *Jerusalem*, 207–13; Schürer, 2:250–56, 284–91.

92 Hume, *Community*, 141.

93 Although Schürer, 2:256, claims this was "largely a theory."

Jerusalem (Acts 12:12), makes it more likely that the field was in Palestine, perhaps in Jerusalem.[94]

Κύπριος τῷ γένει, "a Cypriot by race," denotes either that Barnabas was born in Cyprus or that his family were from there although he lived in Judea.[95] He is certainly found in Jerusalem later (9:27; 11:22). Barnabas is a diaspora Jew recognized by the apostles as an authentic "Hebrew" Jew, for as a Levite he would have spoken Aramaic and Hebrew, although his mother tongue was probably Greek, due to his Cypriot origins.[96] The apostles also recognize him as a believer who functions under their authority (see above and below);[97] his role as "mediating" between Paul and the Jerusalem leadership later (9:26–28) may grow out of this combination of factors.[98] It is notable that the first destination of Barnabas and Saul after their commissioning in Antioch was to Barnabas's home island (13:4 with *Comment*) and that Barnabas returned there with John Mark after separating from Paul (15:39).

πωλήσας ἤνεγκεν τὸ χρῆμα, "sold it and brought the money." Barnabas epitomizes the generosity of the early community in his readiness to sell land and contribute the money to the community.[99] He epitomizes a Spirit-filled lifestyle, for he should be understood to be among those filled by the Spirit in 4:31. He is not presented as a particularly generous or remarkable donor[100] but simply as a model[101] or representative example.[102] The aorist verbs with Barnabas as subject, πωλήσας, "having sold"; ἤνεγκεν, "brought"; ἔθηκεν, "laid," highlight Barnabas individually and echo the same verbs in continuous tenses for the community's actions—respectively πωλοῦντες (present participle), "used to sell," v. 34; ἔφερον (imperfect), "used to . . . bring," v. 34; ἐτίθουν (imperfect), "used to . . . lay," v. 35).[103] "As the example of Barnabas shows, the Spirit inspires a community of goods, not a community of greed."[104] χρῆμα, "money," is a Lukanism (five of six NT uses are in Luke-Acts; this is the first use in Acts). The (unusual) singular denotes a specific amount.[105] χρῆμα can have a negative connotation (Mark 10:23 par. Luke 18:24; Acts 8:18, 20; 24:26), although the use here seems neutral.

ἔθηκεν πρὸς τοὺς πόδας τῶν ἀποστόλων, "[he] laid [it] at the apostles' feet" (see *Comment* on this phrase in v. 35). It is notable that Barnabas, a person of substance as a landowner, bows before Peter, a fisherman, and thus demonstrates

94 Hengel and Schwemer, *Paul between*, 213.
95 Öhler, *Barnabas*, 97–98.
96 Kuecker, "Spirit," 92.
97 Cf. Barrett, *Acts*, 1:258.
98 Johnson, *Function*, 203–4; Öhler, *Barnabas*, 99, 184.
99 Kollmann, *Joseph Barnabas*, 21, sees no reason to doubt the historicity of this event.
100 Contra Haenchen, *Acts*, 233.
101 Noorda, "Scene," 482.
102 Marguerat, *Actes*, 1:164.
103 Thompson, *Keeping*, 79n206; Marguerat, *Actes*, 1:172n40.
104 Shepherd, *Function*, 172.
105 "χρῆμα," BDAG 1089, §2.b.

the status change within the believing community.[106] Rather than acting as a traditional benefactor, who would receive honors for his donation,[107] Barnabas humbles himself at their feet. This feature at least qualifies Hays's assertion that there is no status reversal here.[108]

Explanation

This brief story has two main functions within Luke's overall narrative: retrospectively, to provide an example of the early community's sharing of possessions (echoing 4:32–35); and prospectively, to introduce Joseph Barnabas, who will become a significant character within the plot development of Acts.

Barnabas epitomizes the early community's readiness to sell their possessions in order to meet the needs of the community. That a man of means contributes to the community's needs shows that the community's shared life in the Spirit comes at a cost (cf. 2 Sam 24:24). That Barnabas gives so generously shows that he models the generosity of God-in-Christ to Israel and the world, a generosity seen *inter alia* in the outpouring of the Spirit (Acts 2:1–41), the healing of the man at the Beautiful Gate (3:1–10), boldness of speech (4:29, 31), and "signs and wonders" (2:22, 43; 4:30–31; 5:12; 6:8) (cf. Paul's appeal for financial gifts based on God's generosity in Christ, 2 Cor 8–9, esp. 8:9).

In addition, Barnabas is being introduced by Luke as a reliable character who will grow in significance later,[109] although Luke gives no indication here that Barnabas will become so significant. Key characteristics, which become highly significant in his later roles, mark him: he is generous; he is perceived as a "son of encouragement"; he is a Levite and thus a learned "Hebrew of Hebrews" (Phil 3:5) who is acceptable to the "Hebrews" of the community; and he submits to the apostles' leadership by accepting their naming of him and by laying money at their feet. This (perhaps unusual) combination equips him well for his "mediating" role between the apostles and Saul of Tarsus (9:26–28) and then his partnership with Saul, initially in Antioch (11:25–26), in travels further afield (13:1–14:28), and in explaining and defending the incorporation of uncircumcised gentiles into the believing community (15:2, 12, 22, 25, 35).

3. Ananias and Sapphira: A Negative Example (5:1–11)

Bibliography

Ascough, R. S. "Benefaction." **Bartchy, S. S.** "Community." **Blomberg, C. L.** *Neither,* 165–67. **Brawley, R. L.** *Centering,* 176–79. **Brown, S.** *Apostasy,* 98–109. **Capper, B. J.** "Context." ———. "Community." ———. "Interpretation." **Derrett, J. D. M.** "Ananias." **Dibelius, D. O.** *Kirche,* 62–65. **Forbes, G. W., and S. D. Harrower.** *Raised,*

106 Mitchell, "Function," 269–70.
107 Saller, *Patronage,* 21, 23–29; Danker, *Benefactor,* 436–86.
108 *Ethics,* 212–13.
109 Thompson, *Keeping,* 75.

157–60. **Harrill, J. A.** "Judgement." **Havelaar, H.** "Parallels." **Hays, C. M.** *Ethics*, 214–25. **Hobart, W. K.** *Language*, 37–38. **Hume, D. A.** *Community*, 139–40, 142–47. **Hur, J.** *Reading*, esp. 175–78. **Jeremias, J.** *Jerusalem*, 130–32. **Johnson, L. T.** *Function*, 204–10. **King, F. J.** "Pointing." **Kuecker, A. J.** "Spirit," esp. 96–102. **Le Donne, A.** "Offering." **Lee, D.** *Luke-Acts*, 226–33. **Lohfink, G.** *Sammlung*. **Marguerat, D.** *Historian*, 155–78. **McCabe, D. R.** *Kill*. **McCane, B. R.** *Roll*. **Mitchell, A. C.** "Function," 270–71. **O'Brien, P. T.** "Church," esp. 91–98. **O'Toole, R. F.** "Lie." **Oh, D. W.** "Name." **Park, H. D.** *Herem*, 131–43. **Reimer, A. M.** *Miracle*, 108–10. **Reimer, I. R.** *Women*, 1–29. **Seccombe, D. P.** *Possessions*, 210–14. **Shepherd, W. H., Jr.** *Function*, 170–73. **Strelan, R.** *Strange Acts*, 199–208. **Theissen, G.** "Liebeskommunismus." ———. *Stories*. **Thomas, J. C.** *Devil*, 231–43. **Thompson, A. J.** *One*, 70–74. **Thompson, R. P.** *Keeping*, 77–83. **Trebilco, P. R.** *Self-designations*, 185–98. **Turner, M.** *Power*, 406–7. **Walton, S.** "Communism." **Wenk, M.** *Power*, 305–6. **Wieser, T.** "Community," 87–88.

Translation

[1] A certain man,[a] Ananias by name,[b] together with Sapphira his wife, sold a piece
of property[c] [2] and kept back for himself[d] some of the proceeds with his wife's full
knowledge,[e] and brought only a part,[f] which he laid at the apostles' feet. [3] Peter said,
"Ananias, why has Satan filled your heart so that you attempted to deceive[g] the Holy
Spirit by keeping something[h] back for yourself from the proceeds of the field? [4] While
the field remained yours, it remained yours to dispose of, and after it was sold, it was at
your disposal, wasn't it?[i] Why[j] did you contrive[k] this deed in your heart? You have not
lied to human beings but to God." [5] On hearing these words, Ananias fell down and
died, and great fear came upon all those who heard. [6] The young men immediately[l]
wrapped him[m] up, and they carried him out and buried him.

[7] There was an interval of about[n] three hours, and his wife entered, not being aware
of[o] what had happened. [8] Peter responded[p] to her, "Tell me, did you[q] sell the field for
such and such price?"[r] She[s] said, "Yes, for such and such price." [9] Peter said[t] to her,
"Why[u] did you agree together[v] to test the Spirit of the Lord? Look, the feet of those
who buried your husband are at the door, and they will carry[w] you out." [10] Immediately
she fell at his feet and died. The young men entered, found her dead, carried her out,
and buried her beside her husband. [11] Great fear came upon the whole assembly and
all who heard these things.

Notes

a. δέ, untranslated, marking switch of subject, introducing a new paragraph (although also signaling continuity through contrast); Levinsohn, *Connections*, 87–89; Thompson, *Keeping*, 78n215.

b. ὀνόματι, "by name," dat. of reference (Bruce, *Acts* (1990), 162; "ὄνομα," BDAG 711, §1.a) + nom. of appellation Ἁνανίας, "Ananias" (Wallace, 61); first use of this Lukan favorite construction in Acts—dat. ὀνόματι with a personal name is common in Luke-Acts (Luke 1:5; 5:27; 10:38; 16:20; 19:2; 23:50; 24:18; Acts 5:34; 8:9; 9:10, 11, 12, 33, 36; 10:1; 11:28; 12:13; 16:1, 14; 17:34; 18:2, 7, 24; 20:9; 21:10; 27:1; 28:7); elsewhere in NT only at Matt 27:32; Mark 5:22.

c. κτῆμα is a general term for a "possession" ("κτῆμα," BDAG 572, §1); vv. 3, 8 make clear that it is a field.

d. ἐνοσφίσατο, aor. indic. mid. with classical mid. reflexive sense "he kept back *for himself*"; L&N §57.246; "νοσφίζω," BDAG 679.

e. συνειδυίης καὶ τῆς γυναικός, gen. abs. "his wife also knowing."

f. μέρος τι, "a certain part."

g. ψεύσασθαι + acc.—here τὸ πνεῦμα τὸ ἅγιον, "the Holy Spirit"—normally means "deceive by lying" ("ψεύδομαι," MM 697); here it denotes Ananias's (unsuccessful) attempt to deceive the Holy Spirit; "ψεύδομαι," BDAG 1096, §2; cf. "ψεύδω," LSJ, §B.III; L&N §33.253. See *Comment* on v. 4.

h. "something" represents the unstated object of νοσφίσασθαι, "to keep back for oneself."

i. οὐχί signals a question expecting the answer, "Yes"; Culy and Parsons, *Acts*, 86.

j. τί ὅτι is either shorthand for τί γέγονεν ὅτι (Haenchen, *Acts*, 237n6; Barrett, *Acts*, 1:267, comparing John 14:22) or τί ἐστιν ὅτι (Bruce, *Acts* (1990), 163) and means, "Why?"

k. ἔθου, aor. mid. of τίθημι in sense "contrive"; "τίθημι," BDAG 1003, §1.b.ε.

l. ἀναστάντες, aor. ptc., lit., "having arisen"; this pleonastic ptc. of ἀνίστημι, used with an indic. verb (συνέστειλαν, "they wrapped"), has connotative force, suggesting that the action of the main verb is a response to the preceding event ("ἀνίστημι," BDAG 83, §10; cf. Culy and Parsons, *Acts*, 93 on 5:17) rather than focusing on the young men literally standing up. It is probably a Semitic idiom, e.g., LXX Gen 13:17; 22:3 (second use); 23:7; Josh 1:2; 8:1; Judg 8:20; 2 Sam 15:9; 1 Esd 4:47; Tob 10:10; see MHT, 2:453.

m. αὐτόν, "him," standing for "his body."

n. ὡς in characteristic Lukan sense "about" with a number; see *Note* h on 1:15.

o. (μὴ) εἰδυῖα, pf. ptc. of οἶδα with pres. force, "(not) knowing," portraying her not knowing the fact of Ananias's death as she entered the room.

p. ἀπεκρίθη more usually "answered," but Peter's speech is a response to Sapphira's arrival, not speech, hence "responded"; Barrett, *Acts*, 1:269.

q. Plural, denoting Sapphira and Ananias.

r. τοσούτου, gen. of price (Wallace, 122), a relatively rare use of gen. It denotes a limited (unspecified) amount; "τοσοῦτος," BDAG 1012, §4.

s. ἡ δέ signals switch of subject to Sapphira (fem. art.).

t. There is no verb for "said"; it is to be supplied.

u. See *Note* j above on τί ὅτι, "Why."

v. συνεφωνήθη ὑμῖν, "you agree together," combines an impersonal passive with dative following a συν- compound verb.

w. ἐξοίσουσίν, "they will carry out," 3 pl. fut. of ἐκφέρω; syntactically, "they" is the feet of those who buried her husband; it metonymically denotes the people to whom the feet belonged.

Form/Structure/Setting

Delimitation of pericope. A new story is introduced by δέ in combination with a switch of subject to new characters, Ananias and Sapphira (v. 1), although the theme of sharing of possessions, introduced in 4:32–35 and modeled by Barnabas (4:36–37), continues. Ananias and Sapphira will model what not to do in sharing possessions, contrasting with Barnabas (4:36–37) (Barrett sees this as the significance of δέ[110]).

Sources/historicity. Havelaar helpfully lists a number of potential parallel

110 *Acts*, 1:264.

Hellenistic texts[111] but notes that "sudden, divinely instigated death" is rare in such literature (73). The deaths of Ananias and Sapphira, "quickly, without time to repent and without and identifiable cause of death (like illness)" have only one parallel, from the cult of Mên.[112]

A parallel incident is recorded on a bronze plaque (which replaced an original stone inscription from 1814) on the Market Cross in Devizes, Wiltshire. It reports the death on 25 January 1753 of Mrs. Ruth Pierce, a widow who collapsed and died after twice "calling on the Almighty for witness" that she had paid her full share for a sack of grain she and three other women had bought at the market. The inquest found her cause of death as "the visitation of the great and almighty God."[113]

There is debate over the most significant context against which to see this incident, specifically what motivates Ananias and Sapphira to withhold money and then to lie (vv. 3, 9).[114] Derrett suggests that a concern about financial security on Sapphira's part led to them keeping back a part equivalent to her *ketubah* (see *Comment* on v. 2).[115] Capper considers the financial contribution by Ananias and Sapphira as a "first stage" of community membership similar to that found in the "novitiate" at Qumran (see *Comment* on v. 4).[116] Park, among numerous others, argues that the sin of Achan in keeping "devoted things" for himself (Josh 7) is a key parallel (see *Comment* on v. 2).[117] Brawley proposes a parallel with the Vaccaei, a community in Spain who practised collective farming and who executed any who took (using νοσφίζω, as in v. 2) part of the produce for themselves (Diodorus Siculus 5.34.3).[118] Ascough identifies benefaction within Greco-Roman associations as most important, and Ananias and Sapphira's deceit as an action aimed at receiving the honor normally given to generous benefactors (see *Comment* on v. 2).[119] Bartchy has a similar view to Ascough, although seeing "fictive kinship" as the context for benefaction.[120] Jeremias assesses Ananias and Sapphira's sin as withholding something vowed to God.[121] Havelaar concludes that the story is most similar to an excommunication.[122]

---

111 "Parallels," 67–73.

112 Havelaar, "Parallels," 73 (translation 70); text: *CMRDM* 1:51.

113 "Devizes Market Cross, Wiltshire," *Minerva Stone Conservation*, http://www.minervaconservation.com/projects/devizesmarketcross.html.

114 Cf. the taxonomy of Fitzmyer, *Acts*, 318–19, and the valuable summary of Harrill, "Judgement," 352–53.

115 "Ananias."

116 "Interpretation"; "Context."

117 *Herem*, 131–45.

118 *Centering*, 177; cf. Capper, "Community," 124.

119 "Benefaction."

120 Bartchy, "Community," esp. 315–18; cf. Mitchell, "Function," who sees the context as Greco-Roman ideals of friendship.

121 *Jerusalem*, 130n19; cf. Talbert, *Reading Acts*, 50; Malina and Pilch, *Acts*, 48.

122 "Parallels."

Structure. The story is organized around a brief introduction (vv. 1–2) and two units (vv. 3–6, 7–11), each containing a conversation between Peter and Ananias or Sapphira (vv. 3–4, 7–9) and startling results (vv. 5–6, 10–11). Each unit draws the conclusion that ἐγένετο φόβος μέγας, "great fear came," on people who heard as a result (vv. 5b, 11). O'Toole sees vv. 1–2 as part of the first unit,[123] but his claimed parallel introduction of husband and wife (vv. 1a, 7a) is not really parallel, since Sapphira is introduced in v. 1 too. Likewise, the crime is described only once (vv. 1b–2a) rather than being repeated in v. 8—the latter is part of the conversation with Peter.

Form. O'Toole identifies the form of the story as a rule miracle of punishment, following Theissen, who defines this form as follows: "Rule miracles seek to reinforce sacred prescriptions. They may . . . punish behaviour contrary to the rules."[124] Others consider the form to be an excommunication (of rather extreme form, it must be said!), e.g., Havelaar cites the expulsion in Iamblichus, *Vit. Pyth.* 17.72.8–73.3; 74.11–16, which includes the erection of a tomb for one who leaves the community.[125]

Setting. As noted on Acts 4:32–35, this story is a companion piece to that of Barnabas (4:36–37), and both are "worked examples" of the principle of sharing possessions in 4:32–35. Here, Ananias and Sapphira provide a negative example of giving gone wrong when people present their gift as being a greater contribution than it actually is. Key words and themes are echoed from ch. 4, making the link clear: καρδία, "heart" (5:3, 4; cf. 4:32); πληρόω, "fill" (5:3; cf. 4:31 πίμπλημι); φέρω, "bring" (5:2; cf. 4:34, 37); παρὰ τοὺς πόδας τῶν ἀποστόλων ἔθηκεν, "laying at the apostles' feet" (5:2; cf. 4:35 and feet in 5:9, 10); τιμή, "proceeds" (v. 2; cf. 4:34); πιπράσκω, "sell" (5:4; cf. 4:34); the sharing of possessions (5:2; cf. 4:32, 34–35); χωρίον, "field" (5:3, 9; cf. 4:34); ὑπάρχω "be/were" (5:4; cf. 4:34); the unity of the couple (συνεφωνήθη ὑμῖν, "you agreed together," 5:9) versus the unity of the community (καρδία καὶ ψυχὴ μία, "one heart and soul," 4:32).[126] The following paragraph (5:12–16) closes the section by further underlining the quality of the community's life and its outflows and impact on the people of Jerusalem. The mention of Solomon's Portico as the believers' regular meeting place (v. 12) and as the place where they go after the healing of the man at the Beautiful Gate (3:11) may suggest that the intervening stories are located in the temple courts too, although it is impossible to be sure.[127]

Comment

5:1 Ἀνὴρ . . . τις, "A certain man," introduces a new character (also 8:9; 10:1), Ananias, married to Sapphira. Luke says nothing of Ananias and

123 "Lie," 185–97.
124 Theissen, *Stories,* 106 (see 109 on 5:1–11); O'Toole, "Lie."
125 "Parallels," 77–78.
126 Cf. Thompson, *One,* 72; Pesch, *Apostelgeschichte,* 1:196; Marguerat, *Historian,* 158n12.
127 Le Donne, "Offering," 359–60.

Sapphira's prehistory, although we may assume they were members of the Jesus-community who had therefore gone through water baptism (2:38 makes this an entry requirement). σὺν Σαπφίρῃ τῇ γυναικὶ αὐτοῦ, "together with Sapphira his wife," is the first of a sequence of uses of σύν, "together with," which place the two together and thus distance them from the believing community (see vv. 2, 9, and the compound verbs σύνοιδα, "share knowledge," v. 2, and συμφωνέω, "agree together").[128]

ἐπώλησεν κτῆμα, "sold a piece of property." Ananias and Sapphira dispose of an asset, which is thereby presented as belonging to them both or as a part of the husband's property that was earmarked for his wife's *ketubah* (see *Comment* on v. 2).[129] There is no clarity over what proportion of their property this represented and no necessary implication that it represents all of their property. Acts 4:34, similarly, does not imply that all believers sold all of their possessions or that they gave the whole proceeds of each sale to the community, hence Peter's response in v. 4.[130] There is no indication here that the community could instruct an individual or couple within the community to sell property, or that the commitment to join the community necessarily involved readiness to be so instructed.[131]

2 ἐνοσφίσατο, "he kept back for himself." This verb is found only here and Titus 2:10 in NT. The echo of this verb in Josh 7:1 LXX assists in understanding this passage (it is the only LXX use other than 2 Macc 4:32: in 2 Maccabees it refers to stealing from the temple). Luke's reading of Josh 7 may have affected his (or his source's) presentation of this story.[132] Some Israelites pilfered (ἐνοσφίσαντο) some of the "devoted things" that belonged to YHWH for themselves, and God was angry with the Israelites for this (cf. Josh 7:11–13, stressing that "*Israel* [LXX 'the people'] has sinned"), ultimately resulting in Achan and his family being killed as a particular example of one who acted in this way (Josh 7:16–26). Hellenistic use of νοσφίζω is fairly common:[133] it is found in co-texts where the appropriation of the goods or money is secret; generally only part of the money is taken (ἀπό here indicates this); and the verb is most often used for theft from a trust rather than an individual, e.g., a guardian misappropriating funds held in trust for a minor (Plutarch, *Dem.* 4.2 [847D]) or an individual taking property considered communal among the Vaccaei, (Diodorus Siculus, 5.34.3[134]). Here, the offence is not against humans but against God.[135] In sum, this is a term describing insiders to the group

128 Hume, *Community*, 145, with Marguerat, *Historian*, 174.
129 For evidence of married women's property rights, see Reimer, *Women*, 2–6.
130 Contra Witherington, *Acts*, 236.
131 As Reimer, *Women*, 12–14 speculates.
132 With, e.g., Bruce, *Book (1988)*, 102; Johnson, *Acts*, 88, 91–92; Roloff, *Apostelgeschichte*, 95; Park, *Herem*, 131–45.
133 *BegC*, 4:50, provides full and helpful discussion with references; see also "νοσφίζω," MM 430.
134 See Hays, *Ethics*, 214 with n50.
135 Haenchen, *Acts*, 237n4.

keeping something back for themselves rather than the action of thieves from outside breaking in to take something.[136] It would be "illegitimate totality transfer" to assume that the senses of this word found elsewhere are all found here,[137] so there is no necessary sense of embezzling something that belongs to the community in keeping back part of the sale proceeds.[138]

συνειδυίης καὶ τῆς γυναικός, "with his wife's full knowledge." This genitive absolute places husband and wife in parallel, which is how the story will develop (see *Form/Structure/Setting*). The clause's location in the middle of the sentence probably marks it as an aside.[139] Sapphira is as culpable as Ananias for this action (also v. 9); there is no expectation that she should submit to her husband's plans when they go against godly behavior.[140] The involvement of a couple here could cause readers who know Scripture to think of the first couple's falling into sin and then hiding from God (Gen 3, esp. vv. 8–10).[141] Derrett speculates, unverifiably, that the text should be read through the lens of an extra-textual perspective: that the portion kept back was a kind of "insurance" against the failure of the early Christian community, and specifically that it represented Sapphira's *ketubah*, an amount the husband must pay on divorce, agreed in a prenuptial contract (m. Ketub. passim).[142]

καὶ ἐνέγκας μέρος τι παρὰ τοὺς πόδας τῶν ἀποστόλων ἔθηκεν, "and brought only a part, which he laid at the apostles' feet." As in 4:35, 37, the presentation to the apostles involves a humble gesture of bowing at the apostles' feet. Capper suggests that this presentation makes a claim to present the whole of the proceeds of the sale, but the text is silent on this issue.[143] Rather, the lie (5:3, 4) was to present part of the price while claiming it to be the whole amount.[144] Ascough interprets this gift within the framework of Greco-Roman associations being supported by benefaction.[145] Benefactors would expect appropriate public honor as a result of their gift, perhaps through an inscription or statue or a ceremony to honor them.[146] Ananias and Sapphira (on this reading) would expect appropriate honor—and honor on earth rather than in heaven (contrast Luke 12:33–34). However, the believers could not easily erect inscriptions or offer the kinds of honor typical in Greco-Roman associations. Ascough's analysis, though helpful in indicating some of the cultural resonances of gift

136 Reimer, *Women*, 7–8.
137 Famously, Barr, *Semantics*, 218.
138 "νοσφίζω," BDAG 679; contra Reimer, *Women*, 8–9.
139 Culy and Parsons, Acts, 85.
140 Blomberg, *Neither*, 166n34.
141 Forbes and Harrower, *Raised*, 158–59, suggest that Adam and Eve's sin is parallel to this sin in "God's newly created community."
142 "Ananias," 195–96.
143 "Interpretation," 119, 120; cf. Jeremias *Jerusalem*, 130.
144 With Barrett, *Acts*, 1:266.
145 "Benefaction," 96–105; cf. Bartchy, "Community," 315–18.
146 Ascough, "Benefaction," 98–101, gives examples.

giving, is too imprecise to provide a full explanation of the stunning results of Ananias and Sapphira's deed.[147]

3 Peter speaks to Ananias and confronts him in a rapid-fire series of rhetorical questions (vv. 3–4), after the manner of prophetic accusations expressed in questions (e.g., 1 Sam 15:14, 17, 19; 2 Sam 12:9; 2 Kgs 1:3, 6, 16; Isa 39:3).[148] Unlike Sapphira, Ananias receives no opportunity to tell the truth about his deeds, in similar manner to the Israelites who died in the battle at Ai following the pilfering of material devoted to God who were given no chance to repent (Josh 7:3–5).[149]

διὰ τί ἐπλήρωσεν ὁ σατανᾶς τὴν καρδίαν σου, "Why has Satan filled your heart?," sinisterly echoes the believers' experience of being filled with the Spirit (4:31, although using the synonym πίμπλημι, rather than πληρόω found here):

> The reason "why" the *Satan*, God's opponent . . . filled the heart of Ananias and made it the instrument of an evil plan . . . lies open: because Ananias had not given his whole heart to God (and God's people, the community), but had kept part of it for mammon—because Ananias had not given his *whole* confidence to the community and the apostles in their midst.[150]

There is thus a contrast between the single heart of the believers (4:32) and Ananias's separate heart here.[151] "Satan has taken over the territory that should be the Spirit's: the heart of the believer"[152] (cf. Luke 11:24–26). So the story should be seen as part of the cosmic battle between God, represented by the Spirit, and Satan, who seeks to corrupt the believing community, a battle signaled as far back as Luke 4:1–13.[153] Earlier, Judas has been characterized as one in the grip of Satan (Luke 22:3): his sin was expressed using a purchase of a field rather than its sale (Acts 1:18)[154]—money and property continue to be emblematic of a person's spiritual state. Jesus warns Peter himself of Satan's desire to sift the disciples (Luke 22:31–33).[155] This incident mirrors the Spirit's transformation of the believers' identity that prompted earlier generous sharing of possessions, a significant ethical transformation (2:44–45; 4:34–35).[156] There is no evidence in the text for the speculation

147 With McCabe, *Kill,* 62–64.
148 Discussion: McCabe, *Kill,* 125–27.
149 Park, *Herem,* 132–33, notes the parallel development of the two stories.
150 Pesch, *Apostelgeschichte,* 1:198–99 (my translation; his italics).
151 Thompson, *Keeping,* 79–80.
152 Marguerat, *Historian,* 170.
153 McCabe, *Kill,* 26–27; Marguerat, *Historian,* 170–71; Garrett, *Demise,* 57; Thomas, *Devil,* 235–36.
154 Shepherd, *Function,* 172; cf. Brown, *Apostasy,* 106–7.
155 Hume, *Community,* 143.
156 Turner, *Power,* 406; Kuecker, "Spirit"; Wenk, *Power,* 305–6.

that Peter "ups the ante" on a threat to his own authority, through Ananias and Sapphira's lying to him, by interpreting their lies as directed to the Spirit and as evidence of Satanic influence.[157] Wenk notes that this passage is evidence against Menzies's thesis that the Spirit's role in Acts is purely empowerment for witness.[158] The paradise-like unity of the community's life is harmed by Satan's intervention, successfully tempting a husband and wife to give in to sin and to lie to God; the Genesis creation and fall story (Gen 1–3) may form a template for Luke's theological reflection on this story.[159] Accordingly, the restoration of Israel in process among the believers and by the Spirit is a restoration to God's original creational intention for humanity.

ψεύσασθαί σε τὸ πνεῦμα τὸ ἅγιον, "so that you attempted to deceive the Holy Spirit." The holiness of the community stems from the holiness of the Spirit who indwells it: the Spirit is the presence of God in the believing community, as God was considered to be present in the temple.[160] Truth telling is a feature of the community's holy character; cf. Pliny, *Ep.* 10.96, writing ca. AD 110, observing that the Christians bind themselves by an oath never "to falsify their word." So Ananias is guilty of bearing false witness.[161] Indeed, the somewhat surprising lack of a preposition connecting the infinitive ψεύσασθαι, "to deceive," with its object τὸ πνεῦμα τὸ ἅγιον, "the Holy Spirit," suggests that the Spirit is being injured by the deception.[162] Luke characterizes the Spirit here by contrast with Satan: Satan causes lies, whereas the Spirit brings the truth to light.[163] It is the purity of the believing community which is at stake here.[164] Peter's reference to the Spirit here, and to lying to God (Acts 5:4), suggest that Peter is exercising charismatic knowledge and discernment given by the Spirit, after the manner of Jesus (Luke 5:22; 6:8; 9:46–47).[165] Is this blasphemy against the Holy Spirit (Luke 12:10)? It is possible, if such blasphemy is considered to be rejection of the apostolic gospel[166] or if lying to God is de facto blasphemy.[167] The latter suggestion is strengthened by noting that Luke 12:13–21 goes on to focus on possessions and tells the story of the rich fool who hoards possessions for himself. However, this story contains no statement

157 Contra King, "Pointing," esp. 29–33.
158 Menzies, *Empowered*, passim.
159 Marguerat, *Historian*, 174–76, noting a parallel example of using the Genesis fall story as a template in the second-century document *Acts Andr.* B 5 (translation: Schneemelcher, 2:129–30); contra O'Toole, "Lie," esp. 201–2.
160 Le Donne, "Offering," 351–59, although his claim (362) that the Spirit's presence is an extension of God's temple presence is less persuasive; on that, see Oh, "Name," 158–76.
161 Havelaar, "Parallels," 79.
162 Johnson, *Function*, 207–8.
163 Hur, *Reading*, 234, 175–78.
164 Forbes and Harrower, *Raised*, 158.
165 Turner, *Power*, 407.
166 Brown, *Apostasy*, 107–8.
167 Havelaar, "Parallels," 80.

about Ananias and Sapphira's "eternal destiny," as we might say, whereas Luke 12:10 plainly states that a blasphemer against the Spirit will not be forgiven.

καὶ νοσφίσασθαι ἀπὸ τῆς τιμῆς τοῦ χωρίου, "by keeping something back for yourself from the proceeds of the field." This second infinitive clause expresses the means by which Ananias sought to deceive the Holy Spirit; καί, "by," is epexegetical.[168] The means by which Satan works is through appealing to human greed,[169] which leads to this deceit. This deceit is the symptom of a wrong attitude to the Spirit and the Spirit-filled community.[170]

4 οὐχί, translated "wasn't it?," signals that Peter's question expects a positive answer.

μένον σοὶ ἔμενεν, lit., "remaining yours it remained," clarifies that it was entirely Ananias and Sapphira's choice what to do with the property and the money it produced (contrast the "devoted things" in the Achan story, Josh 6:17–19, 24). This goes against any suggestion that the sharing of possessions was mandatory in the community; e.g., Capper suggests that this phrase shows that the couple were in a "novitiate" like that at Qumran, where their property had been given to the community but was not fully part of the common pool until they entered full membership of the community[171]—but we lack evidence for such a probationary period, and in Barnabas's case (4:36–37) no such "probation" seems to happen (thus he speedily rises to prominence, 9:27; 11:22–26; 13:1).[172] This phrase also goes against the suggestion that believers were required to give the entire proceeds of a particular sale to the community[173]—the most we can say is that *in this case* it appears that Ananias and Sapphira represented what they gave as the whole amount from the sale, perhaps in advance of the sale.[174] Leviticus 27:28–29; Num 18:14 speak of voluntary gifts to God which could not then be redeemed, and thus the sin here was to offer a voluntary gift but then (secretly) to keep part of it.[175] In such a situation, people who sought to withdraw or hide voluntary gifts to God were to be destroyed in the same way as things mandated by God to be given to him were to be destroyed—as Achan and his family were (Josh 7:24–26).[176]

τὸ πρᾶγμα τοῦτο, "this deed." The only other Lukan use of πρᾶγμα, "deed," in Luke 1:1 is in the context of something carefully planned. This use in collocation with ἔθου ἐν τῇ καρδίᾳ σου, "contrive . . . in your heart," underlines

168 With Barrett, *Acts*, 1:266; Thomas, *Devil*, 236n23.
169 Spencer, *Acts*, 56–57, helpfully comparing Satan's temptation of Jesus (Luke 4:5–8) and of Judas (Luke 22:3–6; Acts 1:18–19).
170 Kuecker, "Spirit," 98.
171 Capper, "Interpretation," 124–28; Capper, "Context," 339. For fuller critique of Capper's proposal, see Walton, "Communism," 106–8.
172 Ascough, "Benefaction," 95.
173 Contra Brown, *Apostasy*, 106; Haenchen, *Acts*, 237.
174 Seccombe, *Possessions*, 212.
175 With Park, *Herem*, 50, 132.
176 Park, *Herem*, 136–37.

that Ananias (and Sapphira) have deliberately acted this way (see also vv. 1–2).[177] The heart is a key location—as Jesus has said, God knows people's hearts in a way that humans do not (Luke 16:15) (see *Note* oo on 7:23 and *Comment* on 7:54).[178]

οὐκ ἐψεύσω ἀνθρώποις ἀλλὰ τῷ θεῷ, "You have not lied to human beings but to God." Ananias's lie to Peter is treated as a lie to God himself, for God indwells the life of the community. The parallel use of the verb ψεύδομαι, "lie," here and in v. 3 implies that Luke presents the presence of the Spirit in the community (cf. 4:31) as the very presence of YHWH himself.[179] To lie to the renewed people of God is to counterfeit the work of the Spirit, who indwells the community, and to stand with Satan, who opposes God's work and God's people (v. 3): "whoever fights against her [sc. the church], fights against God."[180] Ananias and Sapphira thereby practise unbelief, well defined by D. Otto Dibelius, "Unbelief consists in the fact that a person does not take the holy and merciful God seriously, that they acknowledge him, but do not want to completely surrender to him, but try to claim a limit on the area of their life and being on which God should have his influence."[181] Such partial faith is poisoned and poisonous to a believing community.[182] Satan's involvement (v. 3) does not annul Ananias's culpability for his actions.

5 Levinsohn observes that the use of the full noun phrase ὁ Ἁνανίας, "Ananias," where the article alone would express the subject clearly, highlights this action as the narrative climax of vv. 1–6.[183]

ἀκούων . . . τοὺς λόγους τούτους, "On hearing these words." The present participle ἀκούων, "hearing," is fronted, suggesting some emphasis; the words of Peter are powerful weapons in the hands of God. The participle's tense suggests that the hearing coincided with Ananias's falling over and dying,[184] a dramatic portrait.

ἐξέψυξεν, "he died," is an unusual word for dying (the more regular NT words are ἀποθνῄσκω and θανατόω), connoting "lose one's life energy completely."[185] It is used for the death of Sisera (Judg 4:21a LXX) and in Acts for the death of those experiencing divine punishment (here, v. 10, and Herod

177 Thomas, *Devil*, 237.

178 Mitchell, "Function," 270–71.

179 Shepherd, *Function*, 172; Turner, *Power*, 406. Harrill, "Judgement," 357, draws a series of interesting parallels with oaths in ancient comedies, which were sometimes taken by people who did not believe in the reality of the gods by whom they swore—and which did not result in their deaths (by contrast with this story). Harrill proposes that Ananias and Sapphira's lies imply they do not believe in divine judgment.

180 Lohfink, *Sammlung*, 87 (my translation); cf. Saul's experience, Acts 9:4–5; 26:14; and Thomas, *Devil*, 237; Reimer, *Miracle*, 109–10; Brawley, *Centering*, 178.

181 Dibelius, *Kirche*, 63 (my translation).

182 Dibelius, *Kirche*, 64.

183 *DFNTG*², 140.

184 Haenchen, *Acts*, 237n9; Thomas, *Devil*, 238n33.

185 "ἐκψύχω," BDAG 110; "ἐκψύχω," MM 200.

in 12:23—the only NT uses). It is predominantly used by medical writers, although not often,[186] but it is also found in Herondas 4:29 (third century BC). It contrasts with the refreshing promised to those who repent: in 3:20, "refreshing" is ἀνάψυξις, whose cognate verb is ἀναψύχω, an antonym of ἐκψύχω used here.[187] The believing community is life-giving; to step outside this community is death-dealing.

The medical mechanism of Ananias's death is unstated but could be a heart attack on the part of one who has been confronted with sin against the Holy Spirit.[188] His death should, however, be seen principally in the light of Peter's words (5:4) and so understood as an action of the Spirit in conjunction with and through Peter's words. Ananias sadly models one who does not submit to the prophet like Moses and is cut off from the community (cf. 3:22–23).[189] Origen writes that Peter killed them "with the sword of his mouth" (*Philoc.* 27.8). McCabe similarly proposes that Peter's words in Acts 5:3–4 have a performative function and cause Ananias's death.[190] Nevertheless Peter is not an executioner but a divine agent who reveals the lie, and "in the face of this revelation the lie cannot go on living."[191] This contrasts with both Achan (Josh 7) and the Vaccaei (Diodorus Siculus, 5.34.3), where the community executed the deviant individual—here, it is God's deed without human stoning being interposed. There are some echoes of direct killing by God of those who inappropriately approach God and thus attempt to pollute his holiness, e.g., Nadab and Abihu (Lev 10:1–3), the rebellion of Korah (Num 16, esp. vv. 23–35), and Uzzah (2 Sam 6:6–7).[192] The Spirit's role in judgment is as God's agent and representative acting to preserve the community's holiness,[193] and the appropriate response is ἐγένετο φόβος μέγας ἐπὶ πάντας τοὺς ἀκούοντας"ἐκψύχω," "great fear came up all who heard," a phrase that echoes and contrasts with the "great grace" (χάρις . . . μεγάλη, Acts 4:33) on the community. It probably includes both insiders and outsiders to the community (cf. 5:11). The stark choice for those who hear is between life and death, between being part of the restored Israel or opposing God's work.

6 συνέστειλαν αὐτὸν καὶ ἐξενέγκαντες ἔθαψαν, "they wrapped him up, carried him out, and buried him." The response of the young men (see *Note* 1 for the idiom ἀναστάντες, "having arisen") was to prepare the body for burial, and that as quickly as possible—not only because of the Middle Eastern preference for speedy burial because of decay in the heat[194] but also because

186 Cf. Hobart, *Language*, 37.
187 Kuecker, "Spirit," 99.
188 Derrett, "Ananias," 197.
189 Kuecker, "Spirit," 99; Brawley, *Centering*, 177–78.
190 McCabe, *Kill*, passim; cf. Strelan, *Strange Acts*, 208.
191 Wieser, "Community," 88; cf. Reimer, *Women*, 19.
192 Le Donne, "Offering," 361.
193 Cf. Marguerat, *Historian*, 167.
194 Bruce, *Book* (1988), 106.

one struck down by God would be buried quickly and without ceremony.[195] Cf. Sem. 2, listing those denied mourning rites, the lack of delay in Achan's burning and burial (Josh 7:25b–26), and the denial of traditional burial and mourning to the sons of Aaron who offered "strange fire" (Lev 10:1–6). συνέστειλαν, "they wrapped," here has the sense of "wrap up" in the sense of covering the body for burial,[196] perhaps with a shroud[197] or a "winding sheet."[198] Haenchen notes that medical usage was for bandaging but does not think that this would happen in a room where the apostles sat "enthroned"; he thus prefers "cover up"[199]—but why would they not prepare the body for burial there, particularly if haste was necessary? ἐξενέγκαντες, "carrying out," is a Lukanism (five of eight NT uses are in Luke-Acts), here used in a technical sense of "carry out for burial"[200] (cf. the more usual sense of "carry out" in v. 15). ἔθαψαν, "[they] buried," is another Lukanism (seven of eleven NT uses in Luke-Acts), meaning "they buried."[201]

The burial rite may be seen as a final act of love by the community, even toward a disobedient member, leaving open the question of the "eschatological resurrection" of the one buried.[202] It also has the effect of removing a polluting dead body from the community, both physically (from the place where they were gathered) and socio-religiously (restoring purity by removing the body of the sinful member) (cf. Num 19:11–22).[203]

7 Ἐγένετο δὲ ὡς ὡρῶν τριῶν διάστημα, "There was an interval of about three hours," may signal that the next incident occurred at the next set time of prayer (cf. 2:46; 3:1).[204]

Sapphira's state is μὴ εἰδυῖα τὸ γεγονός, "not being aware of what had happened," contrasting with her knowledge of the deceptive plan (v. 2 συνειδυίης, a compound of the verb εἰδυῖα used here). She is ignorant both of Ananias's fate and, more significantly, of God's purposes.[205]

8 By contrast with the conversation with Ananias, Peter gives Sapphira opportunity to tell the truth, in similar manner to Joshua's words to Achan (Josh 7:19).[206] As with his conversation with Ananias, there is no indication of the tone of Peter's question, whether sorrow or anger.[207] However, the

195 Derrett, "Ananias," 198, 201; McCane, *Roll,* 95–96, 99, 102–4.
196 "συστέλλω," BDAG 978.
197 Barrett, *Acts,* 1:269; cf. Hobart, *Language,* 38.
198 Bruce, *Acts* (1990), 164.
199 *Acts,* 238n4.
200 "ἐκφέρω," BDAG 311, §1.
201 "θάπτω," BDAG 444.
202 Reimer, *Women,* 22.
203 McCabe, *Kill,* 216–17; on Jewish understanding of the pollution caused by a dead body, and thus concern for proper funeral rites, see McCane, *Roll,* esp. 50–51, 55–56, 70–72, 112–15.
204 Marguerat, *Historian,* 166.
205 Thomas, *Devil,* 240.
206 Park, *Herem,* 132–33.
207 Contra Reimer, *Women,* 17.

content of Peter's question is significant. He does not ask, "Did you give the full price of the field?," but rather, "Did you sell the field for such and such a price [τοσούτου]?" Peter does not assume that it is necessary to give the whole price of the field to the community—the issue is rather that she and her husband have attempted to deceive the community and God the Spirit who indwells the community.[208]

ἀπέδοσθε, "you sold," is plural: Peter's question is asking about what Sapphira and her husband did.

ναί, τοσούτου, "Yes, for such and such a price." Sapphira's answer echoes the precise wording of Peter's question: she answers positively, lying deliberately and culpably.

9 τί ὅτι συνεφωνήθη ὑμῖν, "Why did you agree," contrasts the unity of the believing community in the Spirit (1:14; 2:42–43; 4:32) with Ananias and Sapphira's Satan-inspired unity (see also v. 2).[209] The aim of Satan's attack is to divide the believing community.[210]

πειράσαι τὸ πνεῦμα κυρίου, "to test the Spirit of the Lord," parallels Satan's testing of Jesus in the wilderness (Luke 4:1–14), which Luke sums up using the cognate noun συντελέσας πάντα *πειρασμὸν* ὁ διάβολος, "the devil having finished every *test*" (Luke 4:13).[211] The devil's tests of Jesus seek to stretch the boundaries of his devotion to God's purposes: what can Jesus get away with and still be within God's purposes?[212] By contrast with Jesus, who passed the test, Sapphira fails (in common with Eve, Gen 3:1–6; see *Comment* on Acts 5:3). More than that, to test God is a mark of Israel's disobedient response to God in Scripture (e.g., Exod 17:2, 7; Num 14:22; Deut 33:8; Ps 95:8–9 [LXX 94:8–9]), and thus Sapphira is part of disobedient Israel[213] and thereby faces God's wrath, as Peter goes on to announce. Testing God will also be a danger in the debates over the admission of gentiles to the believing community (15:10, τί *πειράζετε* τὸν θεόν, "Why are you *testing* God?").

ἰδοὺ οἱ πόδες τῶν θαψάντων τὸν ἄνδρα σου ἐπὶ τῇ θύρᾳ καὶ ἐξοίσουσίν σε, "Look, the feet of those who buried your husband are at the door and they will carry you out." Peter's prophetic announcement[214] implies that the feet of the young men could be heard, and thus that they were wearing sandals, rather than being barefoot, as was the custom for a normal burial, reinforcing the sense that Ananias's death was understood as divine judgment (see *Comment* on v. 5; Sem. 6:1; 10:5. Semaḥot 5:12 allows mourners to wear sandals on the highway but specifies that they must remove them in a town).[215] The combination

208 Cf. Theissen, "Liebeskommunismus," 694–95.
209 Cf. Thomas, *Devil*, 241; Thompson, *Keeping*, 80–81.
210 Thompson, *One*, 72–74.
211 Shepherd, *Function*, 172.
212 Thomas, *Devil*, 241; Barrett, *Acts*, 1:270.
213 McCabe, *Kill*, 139–40.
214 So Schneider, *Apostelgeschichte*, 1:377; Johnson, *Function*, 209.
215 Shulam and Le Cornu, *Acts*, 1:269.

of the news of Ananias's death and the implied failure to observe normal burial ritual would have been deeply shocking to Sapphira: "Small wonder she collapsed!"[216]

10 ἔπεσεν δὲ παραχρῆμα πρὸς τοὺς πόδας αὐτοῦ, "Immediately she fell at his feet." Sapphira collapses suddenly, although (as with Ananias) without the medical mechanism being specified. It is ironic that she falls at Peter's *feet*, for the gift was laid at the apostles' feet (v. 2), symbolizing submission to the apostles' authority[217]—and, further, Luke has mentioned the feet of those who will carry her out (v. 9) in like manner to Ananias being carried out.

ἐξέψυξεν, "she died," echoes the verb used of Ananias's death (v. 5; see *Comment*), further reinforcing the parallelism of the two deaths as resulting from serious sin.

11 The response of φόβος μέγας, "great fear," is repeated from v. 5 (and cf. 2:43) and again contrasts with the "great grace" (χάρις . . . μεγάλη) the believers experienced in their community life (4:33). Such fear would arise from two deaths within a short period, especially in the knowledge that they had conspired to deceive the community. This is fear of God, not of the apostles or the community,[218] and is experienced by the believers—ὅλην τὴν ἐκκλησίαν, "the whole congregation"—as well as outsiders—πάντας τοὺς ἀκούοντας, "all who heard." "All who heard" now includes Luke's readers as they hear the story; Luke seeks to inculcate holy fear, which is a realistic and humble assessment of the place and power of God (through the Spirit) and the word in the community and the world that results in an appropriate lifestyle.[219]

ἐκκλησίαν, "assembly," is the first use of this term for the Jesus-community in Acts (19x in total, although it is unevenly spread; it is used 15x for the community in Acts 1–15 and 4x in Acts 16–28). It seems unlikely that Luke has accidentally introduced it here,[220] so we should ask the significance of its use at this point. It is a biblical term, used for the assembly (Heb. קהל [*qhl*]) of Israel (e.g., LXX Deut 4:10; 18:16; 31:30; Josh 8:35; Judg 20:2; 1 Kgs 8:14, 22, 55; 1 Chr 13:2, 4; 29:1, 10, 20; 2 Chr 6:3, 12, 13; 1 Macc 4:59; Joel 2:16), as well as being used for the citizen-assembly of a Greek city (e.g., Acts 19:39).[221] Its use here entails a claim not only that the believing community is the true assembly of God,[222] the true Israel, but also that this community models what it is to be a believing community: it is "a prototype of the eschatological com-

216 Derrett, "Ananias," 198.

217 O'Toole, "Lie," 194, suggests that she fell on their money laid at Peter's feet. This is not impossible, but the text is not explicit about it.

218 Derrett, "Ananias," 198.

219 Cf. Marguerat, *Historian*, 171.

220 Marguerat, *Historian*, 163; contra Jervell, *Apostelgeschichte*, 198.

221 "ἐκκλησία," MM 195, note inscriptions found in the theatre at Ephesus using this term; see also "ἐκκλησία," BDAG 303, §1; "ἐκκλησία," *TDNT* 3:504–5.

222 Thomas, *Devil*, 243.

munity of salvation."[223] This label given at this point in the narrative indicates that the believing community has responded rightly to impurity introduced by deceit and disunity.[224] Luke uses ἐκκλησία mainly of individual assemblies in particular places (8:1; 11:22, 26; 12:5; 13:1; 14:23, 27; 15:3, 41; 16:5; 18:22; 20:17), in common with Paul (e.g., Rom 16:1, 4, 5, 16, 23; 1 Cor 1:2; 4:17), but also occasionally for the wider "catholic" (i.e. universal) assembly (20:28; 9:31—see *Note* and *Comment* on the latter; cf. 1 Cor 10:32; Eph 1:22; 3:10, 21; Phil 3:6; Col 1:18, 24). It may be that its origins are among the Hellenists, as an alternative to συναγωγή, "synagogue," since that was in use by Jewish groups already.[225]

Explanation

For those educated to think of God through the lens of Scripture this story—while shocking—is in genuine continuity with the portrait of God and his ways found in the OT and, indeed, with the teaching of Jesus. Five key features of this story show its contribution to the narrative of Acts.[226]

First, we meet a radical view of the holiness of the community. This united community (4:32–35), filled with the Spirit (4:31) and therefore possessed by God and experiencing his "great grace" (4:33), meets disunity from Ananias and Sapphira, who are united against the Spirit (v. 9a) and filled by Satan (v. 3), and therefore experience great judgment (vv. 5, 10). The Spirit, whom Ananias and Sapphira are both seeking to deceive and testing (vv. 3, 9), preserves the holiness of the community by enabling Peter to speak prophetically to bring their deeds and inner intentions to light (vv. 3–4, 8–9), and then by their deaths, which are stressed as immediately following Peter's words ("On hearing these words," v. 5; "Immediately," v. 10). The appropriate response is holy fear (vv. 5, 11; cf. 2:43), that is, fear of God, which touches both the congregation and those outside who hear of these dramatic events.

Secondly, Luke underlines the leadership role of the apostles and continues the contrast already established with the Jerusalem Jewish leadership. As with other gifts, Ananias lays the money at the apostles' feet (5:2; cf. 4:35, 37), a posture of humility and submission that is belied by the pretence that this is the whole amount received from the sale (v. 2a). Peter's prophetic insight and discernment show that he is in tune with God and enabled by the Spirit (cf. 2:17–18). The contrast with the Jerusalem leadership is clear, for they have sought to prevent the apostles speaking in Jesus's name (4:16–18) and have approached what God is now doing in Jesus and through the Spirit from the perspective of expediency, rather than openness to God (see on 4:5–22). This

---

223 Marguerat, *Historian*, 163.

224 Marguerat, *Historian*, 164.

225 Trebilco, *Self-designations*, 185–98. See also the valuable discussion of the term in O'Brien, "Church," esp. 91–98.

226 McCabe, *Kill*, 20–29 offers a slightly different list.

is why the Jerusalem leadership is powerless in the face of what the believing community is doing and saying (note 4:16) and why Luke will go on to record the great regard in which the community is held (5:13), the great power seen in "signs and wonders," healing and deliverance (5:12, 16), and the growth of the community (5:14).

Thirdly, a dimension of cosmic conflict between the Spirit and Satan is made explicit for the first time in Acts. Luke introduces this conflict in Jesus's own ministry (Luke 4:1–13). Behind human actions stand greater powers: Satan, the arch-deceiver (Acts 5:3; cf. Rev 12:9; 20:10) and tester of God and his people (Acts 5:9; cf. Job 1:6–12; 2:1–7; Luke 22:31; 1 Cor 7:5), and the Holy Spirit, who brings the truth to light (Acts 5:3, 9; cf. Isa 11:2; Dan 5:11–14; Mic 3:8) and is grieved at human rebellion (cf. Isa 63:10; Eph 4:30).

Fourthly, the nature of the community as other-oriented is further clarified. To belong to the believing community means having an identity formed by the generosity of God seen in giving Jesus (2:23) and in giving new life by the Spirit to those who believe (2:38–39). This identity entails generosity and openness, and though Ananias and Sapphira appear to enact the first, they fail to enact the second. "Ananias and Sapphira were pretending to act as insiders; Peter exposed them as dangerous, satanic outsiders."[227] Luke's readers are being educated about the nature of the community to which they belong and thereby encouraged to embody their Christian identity in such generosity and openness to others, as well as to God.

Fifthly, there is a strong warning against "[t]he destructive power of greed."[228] Why do Ananias and Sapphira die as a result of their actions? It is difficult to account for the severity of their punishment other than as violating the holiness of the community and thus violating the holiness of God. As often in Luke-Acts, how possessions and money are handled is a crucial index of spirituality. A key parallel is Achan's sin in keeping for himself things devoted to God (Josh 7), signaled by the key verb "kept back for himself" (v. 2; Josh 7:1 LXX). Achan's sin resulted in his family's stoning, for the Israelite community could not make progress in conquering the land unless and until the one who kept back devoted things for himself was removed.

How are Luke's readers invited to respond to this story? In two principal ways, I suggest. First, by self-examination, to ensure that they are not allowing possessions, possessiveness, or deceptive outward appearance houseroom in their lives. "Spirit and money go hand in hand in Luke . . . money can kill one who is attached to it."[229] Secondly, by openness to God and their sisters and brothers in the believing community, to ensure that they are instantiating the generous love of God by sharing what they have.

227 McCabe, *Kill*, 59.
228 Seccombe, *Possessions*, 214.
229 Marguerat, *Historian*, 177.

4. God Acts through the Assembly's Shared Life (5:12–16)

Bibliography

Black, A. "Sons." **Burchard, C.** "Fussnoten." **Dawsey, J. M.** "Unity." **Dunn, J. D. G.** "ΚΥΡΙΟΣ." ———. *Jesus*, 255–56. **Hume, D. A.** *Community*, 129–30. **McCabe, D. R.** *Kill.* **Pervo, R. I.** *Dating*, 36–38. **Rackham, R. B.** "Acts II." **Reimer, I. R.** *Women*, 233–34. **Schwartz, D. R.** "Sympathisers." **Thomas, J. C.** *Devil*, 244–49. **van der Horst, P. W.** "Shadow." **Walton, S.** "Ὁμοθυμαδόν." **Wenk, M.** *Power*, 268–70.

Translation

12 Through the apostles' hands many signs and wonders were being done among the people. They all used to meet together in unity in Solomon's Portico, 13 but none of the rest dared to join them; nevertheless, the people spoke highly of them. 14 More than ever[a] believers were added to the Lord, large numbers of both men and women, 15 so that they even carried their sick people[b] into the streets and placed them on beds and mats, that as Peter came by[c] at least[d] his shadow might fall[e] on them.[f] 16 A great number of those from the towns surrounding Jerusalem kept gathering, bringing sick people and those troubled by unclean spirits, and they[g] were all healed.

Notes

a. δέ signals switch of subject rather than contrast of content and so is untranslated; Levinsohn, *Connections*, 87–89, 166; Barrett, *Acts*, 1:275.

b. D reads τοὺς ἀσθενεῖς αὐτῶν, "their sick people," implying that the sick people are believers (or perhaps believers' family members); Rius-Camps and Read-Heimerdinger, *Message*, 1:323.

c. ἐρχομένου Πέτρου, "as Peter came by," temporal (pres.) gen. abs.

d. κἂν crasis of καί + ἄν, "at least." Moule, 138, sees an implied conditional clause here and Mark 6:56, the only other collocation of ἵνα . . . κἂν in the NT, rendering "even if it were . . . no more than the shadow."

e. ἐπισκιάσῃ, "might overshadow" (translated "fall on"), is cognate with σκιά, "shadow."

f. D also has ἀπηλλάσσοντο γὰρ ἀπὸ πάσης ἀσθενείας ὡς εἶχεν ἕκαστος αὐτῶν, "for they were set free from all the sicknesses according to what each one had" (translation: Rius-Camps and Read-Heimerdinger, *Message*, 1:317). This looks like a clarifying addition; it is unlikely that such a clause would be removed if already present (Comfort, 347).

g. οἵτινες, "they," masc. denoting people. Haenchen, *Acts*, 243n5, notes that in the Hellenistic period there was no longer the classical distinction made between the definite rel. pn. ὅς, "who," and the indefinite rel. pn. ὅστις, "whoever." On the whole, Acts uses the latter form where to use the article might confuse, e.g., 8:15.

Form/Structure/Setting

Delimitation of pericope. Luke uses imperfect and present verbs here to give a general portrait of the ongoing life of the community—these features are presented as typical of their life. Every main verb in this passage is imperfect, picturing events as ongoing and typical,[230] reflecting Luke's practice in other summaries (e.g., 2:42–47; 4:32–35). Further, all the participles and infinitives are present, again portraying events as in process; only the subjunctive ἐπισκιάσῃ, "might fall," is another tense (aorist, v. 15; see *Comment*). These tenses mark this section off from the particularities of the previous two paragraphs (4:36–37; 5:1–11), where aorists predominate (thirty-eight aorists; two imperfects; seven presents; one future; three perfects).

Sources/historicity. Pervo suggests that "Luke composed vv. 15–16 on the basis of Mark, especially Mark 6:55–56,"[231] a section of Mark unparalleled in Luke.[232] Certainly this paragraph, in common with other summaries, has the marks of Lukan phrasing and vocabulary, but Pervo concedes that the parallels are "more thematic than verbal";[233] for example, Jesus is touched by those he heals (Mark 6:56), but here there is no contact (v. 15). Direct dependence of Acts on Mark seems unlikely. Certainly, Luke is portraying the apostolic "signs and wonders" in similar colors to those of Jesus in Luke's Gospel (see *Comment* on v. 12), and probably drawing on tradition about the life of the early community in doing so.

The wider question of the historicity of "signs and wonders" such as healings depends on the reader's view of the general possibility of such events.[234] Luke certainly believes that such events happened among the early believers.

Structure. The passage begins with a general statement (v. 12a) that appears to be expanded in vv. 15–16. Verses 12b–14 concern the meetings of the believers and their evangelistic effectiveness, and some see the transition from v. 14 to v. 15 as awkward and thus regard vv. 12b–14 as an interruption.[235] However, v. 12a can be seen as a summary echoing previous passages (notably 4:29–31), developing from the Petrine event of Ananias and Sapphira's death to show that the apostles in general did such things. The tension between the people's hesitancy about joining the believers in Solomon's Portico (5:13 echoes φόβος μέγας, "great fear," in vv. 5, 11) and the evangelistic success (v. 14) is there in the events which took place. Luke's development is thus from the apostles (v. 12a) to the congregation (v. 12b) to the congregation's relationship with the Jerusalemites at large (vv. 13–14).[236] Luke then returns to the "signs and wonders" and reports healings (vv. 15–16). These healings echo and multiply the healing of the man at the Beautiful Gate, which provoked the ire of the

230 Wallace, 541.
231 *Acts*, 136; *Dating*, 36–38.
232 Lüdemann, *Early Christianity*, 67; also *BegC*, 4:54–55, more cautiously.
233 *Dating*, 38.
234 See the defense of this possibility in Keener, *Miracles*.
235 Summary: Haenchen, *Acts*, 243–44.
236 Cf. Haenchen, *Acts*, 244–45.

temple leadership and will provoke further persecution by the temple leadership (vv. 17–42).

Setting. This paragraph partners with 4:32–35, which focused on the internal life of the community and led into two examples (4:36–5:11). Here the focus is on the believers' relations with outsiders, particularly the witness of the community's life.[237] Unlike other summaries so far (2:42–27; 4:32–35), there is no explicit mention of sharing possessions or the work of the Spirit here, although the setting of 5:1–11 contains both themes. The unity of the believers and their high regard among the Jerusalem populace contrasts sharply with the following action of the temple leadership against the believers (5:17–40).

Comment

12 Διά . . . τῶν χειρῶν τῶν ἀποστόλων, "Through . . . the apostles' hands," is fronted, suggesting some emphasis. As the apostles' feet (symbolizing their authority) were crucial in the previous sequence of passages (note 4:35, 37; 5:2, 10), here their hands symbolize the gracious generosity and effective power of God (cf. their prayer for action by God's *hand*, 4:30).[238] Διά expresses "by means of."[239] Luke's stories of Jesus healing by laying on hands (see above) suggest that the apostles laying on hands is in view here,[240] contra Barrett, who thinks the expression τῶν χειρῶν τῶν ἀποστόλων, "the hands of the apostles," is simply equivalent to τῶν ἀποστόλων, "the apostles," as in 2:43, but with a more Semitic cast, although Barrett concedes that LXX usage is mainly with singular χειρός, "hand."[241]

ἐγίνετο σημεῖα καὶ τέρατα πολλά, "many signs and wonders were being done." Luke repeats this characteristic phrase, which links this story back to 4:30 and identifies God's present activity through the apostles with both the mighty deeds of the exodus and Joel's prophecy (see *Comment* on 2:19, 22, 43; 4:30). Acts 5:13–16 elucidate this statement through people's responses: there is unity among the believers (v. 12b); others hesitate to join them (v. 13); yet many new believers are added (v. 14); and people from the surrounding countryside experience healings and deliverance from unclean spirits (vv. 15–16).[242]

τῷ λαῷ, "the people," here and in v. 13 denotes the general population of Jerusalem (as in 2:47; 3:9, 11, 12; 4:1, 2, etc.): the believers are in good standing

237 Wenk, *Power*, 269.

238 Cf. also 8:17; 9:17; 11:21; 14:3; 19:6, 11; 28:8; Mark 6:2; Luke 1:66; 4:40; 5:13; 13:13; LXX Pss 94:7 (MT 95:7); 103:28 (MT 104:28); 143:7 (MT 144:7); 144:16 (MT 145:16).

239 "διά," BDAG 224, §A.3.a; Moule, 57.

240 With Stählin, *Apostelgeschichte*, 86.

241 *Acts*, 1:273–74.

242 Hume, *Community*, 129–30.

with the populace, by contrast with the opposition of the temple leadership (4:1–21; 5:17–40).

ἦσαν ὁμοθυμαδὸν ἅπαντες ἐν τῇ στοᾷ Σολομῶντος, "They all used to meet together in unity in Solomon's Portico," identifies both the ethos and the location of the believers' meetings. "They" is unspecified and could indicate the apostles alone[243] but seems more likely to denote a large group of believers given the size of this portico, the use of ἅπαντες, "all," and the presence of the qualifying adverb ὁμοθυμαδόν, "in unity" (previously used for the whole believing community in 1:14; 2:46; 4:24); none of these features would be necessary for the Twelve alone.[244]

τῇ στοᾷ Σολομῶντος, "Solomon's Portico," is a large building with a roof supported by colonnades, located in the temple complex (see *Comment* on 3:11). The large size of this meeting place and the use of ἅπαντες, "all," indicates that the believers met as a larger group in public as well as in households, most probably here for the apostles' teaching[245] (cf. 2:46, 5:42 which portray household and temple meetings).

To the φόβος μέγας, "great fear," of v. 11 is now added the great unity of the believers, expressed by ὁμοθυμαδόν, "in unity" (see *Comment* on 1:14); here, the presence of ἅπαντες, "all," already shows that the believers were in one location, and thus ὁμοθυμαδόν adds a further element of description, stressing the unity of the meetings, rather than simply being locative.[246] The deaths of Ananias and Sapphira result in the reinforcement and restoration of the believing community's oneness (see *Comment* on 5:9).

13 τῶν δὲ λοιπῶν οὐδεὶς ἐτόλμα κολλᾶσθαι αὐτοῖς, "none of the rest dared join them." τῶν . . . λοιπῶν, "the rest," indicates the rest of the people of Jerusalem, not the other believers,[247] since this term distinguishes "the rest" from a group already mentioned (as it does elsewhere in Luke-Acts: Luke 8:10; 12:26; 18:9, 11; 24:9, 10; Acts 2:37; 17:9; 27:44; 28:9[248]). It comes in the context of the believers' meetings in Solomon's Portico. In the wake of Ananias and Sapphira's deaths, people went on being hesitant (imperfect ἐτόλμα, "dared") to be present with the believers when they met publicly (as 5:11b). κολλᾶσθαι, "to join," generally indicates intimate association, including sexual intimacy (e.g., Matt 19:5; 1 Cor 6:16);[249] it has a sense of intimate involvement here, in line with Luke's usage (Luke 10:11; 15:15; Acts 8:29; 9:26; 10:28; 17:34),[250] picturing "an

243 So Johnson, *Acts*, 92; Witherington, *Acts*, 225.
244 With Jervell, *Apostelgeschichte*, 200–201; Thomas, *Devil*, 245.
245 Schneider, *Apostelgeschichte*, 1:380.
246 Walton, "Ὁμοθυμαδόν," 102; contra Culy and Parsons, *Acts*, 90.
247 Contra Witherington, *Acts*, 225–26. Williams, *Acts*, 88, rightly observes, "nowhere else are the apostles regarded as objects of fear to their fellow believers."
248 Schwartz, "Sympathisers," 551.
249 "κολλάω," BDAG 555, §2.b.α; Burchard, "Fussnoten," 159–60.
250 Schwartz, "Sympathisers," 552–53.

invisible cordon"[251] around the group that gave others pause about becoming closely involved with the group in the temple courts. Perhaps being present at the group's meetings in Solomon's Portico was seen as indicating acceptance of Jesus's claims as Messiah.[252] With τῶν . . . λοιπῶν, "the rest," κολλᾶσθαι signals that the believers are now seen as a distinct community within Judaism.[253]

ἐμεγάλυνεν αὐτοὺς ὁ λαός, "the people spoke highly of them." There is a striking contrast between the high esteem in which the people held the believers and the Jerusalem temple leadership's fear of the people (4:21; 5:26).[254] The people's verdict echoes that of God, for God acts in signs and wonders to confirm the validity of the believers' lives and faith (cf. 4:29–31).

14 appears to be in tension with v. 13,[255] but v. 14 speaks of the wider ministry of the believers (cf. 2:47; 6:7). The proclamation and lifestyle of the new community were attractive to many (4:31) who moved from admiration to joining the community. The imperfect προσετίθεντο, "were added," again expresses the continuing nature of the numerical growth, and its passive voice signals that God is the actor who adds.[256]

τῷ κυρίῳ could be taken: (i) with πιστεύοντες, "believers," to give "believers in the Lord," since πιστεύω "believe" takes dative of the one believed (cf. 18:8);[257] (ii) with προσετίθεντο, "were added," to give "were added to the Lord" (cf. 11:24);[258] or (iii) with προσετίθεντο, "were added," as expressing agency, "by the Lord."[259] Acts 11:24 presents the closest parallel, and the absence here of another expression indicating to what the believers were added supports sense (ii), "to the Lord" (contrast 2:47[260]). That said, sense (iii) "by the Lord" might also be present, and we may not need to choose between (ii) and (iii). This reading indicates that the new community was indwelt by the Lord, which is most probably Jesus rather than God.[261]

ἀνδρῶν τε καὶ γυναικῶν, "both men and women," highlights the inclusiveness of the sexes in the new community,[262] developing the male/female parallels elsewhere in Luke-Acts.[263] This phrase is characteristic of Acts, particularly with τε καί, "both . . . and," but is not found in Luke's Gospel;[264] it echoes

251 Burchard, "Fussnoten," 159 (my translation).
252 Barrett, *Acts,* 1:274.
253 Cf. Barrett, *Acts,* 1:274.
254 McCabe, *Kill,* 197.
255 BDF, §465(1) dubs v. 14 a "parenthesis."
256 Fitzmyer, *Acts,* 329.
257 "πιστεύω," BDAG 817, §2.a.α; Rackham, "Acts II," 68.
258 Bruce, *Acts* (1990), 168; Barrett, *Acts,* 1:275; Haenchen, *Acts,* 243n3.
259 Jervell, *Apostelgeschichte,* 201.
260 Note the textual variant at 2:47, τῇ ἐκκλησίᾳ, "to the community," whose presence suggests that scribes felt the need of a specific dative for the body to which people were added; see *Note* h on 2:47.
261 Dunn, "ΚΥΡΙΟΣ," 250; Fitzmyer, *Acts,* 329.
262 Black, "Sons," 202.
263 See Black, "Sons," esp. 194–95, 203.
264 Dawsey, "Unity," 63–65.

the mention of both male and female slaves in the Joel quotation in Peter's Pentecost speech (2:18). Three key passages in Isaiah speak of YHWH acting in blessing for his sons and daughters (Isa 43:6–7; 49:22; 60:4) and form a part of the Isaianic hope for Israel's restoration which Luke appropriates.[265] Thus Luke's focus is not only inclusiveness of the sexes: the involvement of both women and men in the new community is evidence that God is acting to fulfill Isaianic promises of the restoration of Israel.

15 ὥστε, "so that," introduces a result clause with present infinitives ἐκφέρειν, "carried," and τιθέναι, "placed." It would be a natural result of the new believers' faith (v. 14) that they would bring sick family and friends for healing (cf. D's reading, *Note* b) and that others would hear of the healings and bring their family and friends; v. 15 flows naturally from v. 14.[266] Bauernfeind further suggests that ὥστε looks back to the whole paragraph, especially v. 12a, so that this result flows from the whole of the believers' life together;[267] this has merit.

πλατείας denotes a broad road or street, leading to Latin *platea*, Italian *piazza*, French *place*, German *Platz*.[268] This word denotes the main streets rather than narrow side streets (which are usually ῥύμη, e.g., 9:11; 12:10[269]). Certainly, κλιναρίων καὶ κραβάττων, "beds and mats," would require wide streets if any number at all were brought.

ἐρχομένου Πέτρου κἂν ἡ σκιὰ ἐπισκιάσῃ τινὶ αὐτῶν, "as Peter came by at least his shadow might fall on them," is unique in Scripture in portraying such a means of healing (although cf. healing by Paul's handkerchiefs and aprons, 19:12). The aorist subjunctive ἐπισκιάσῃ, "might fall," portrays a snapshot of Peter's shadow falling on one person at a time. Some take this practice to indicate "primitive superstition,"[270] and think Luke did not agree with such events. However, the next verse goes on to affirm that people *were* healed, so this seems unlikely. Shadows in Scripture are more often symbolic of darkness, transience, and God's absence,[271] although the phrase "the shadow of [God's] wings" denotes protection and care (Ps 57:1 [LXX 56:2, MT 57:2]), and the verb σκιάζω, "overshadow" (and its compounds), is used for the cloud of God's presence "overshadowing" the tabernacle (LXX Exod 40:35; Num 9:18, 22; 10:34). This latter parallel may suggest that the significance of Peter's shadow is that God is overshadowing the sick people.[272] Bede takes overshadowing as an image for the church moving like a shadow in the world bringing renewal.[273]

265 Black, "Sons," esp. 203–6; cf. Mallen, *Reading*, passim.
266 Cf. Reimer, *Women*, 234.
267 *Apostelgeschichte*, 89.
268 "πλατεία," BDAG 823; L&N §1.103. Bruce, *Acts* (1990), 168, notes the derived words.
269 L&N §1.104; Barrett, *Acts*, 1:276.
270 E.g., Dunn, *Jesus*, 165–66.
271 E.g., Pss 23:4 (LXX 22:4); 88:6 (LXX 87:7, MT 88:7); 102:11 (LXX 101:12, MT 102:12); Matt 4:16; Luke 1:79; Col 2:17; Heb 8:5; 10:1.
272 Barrett, *Acts*, 1:276–77; Thomas, *Devil*, 248.
273 *Acts*, 58.

Van der Horst seeks to argue that the shadow stands for the soul of a person, and thus contact with Peter's shadow was intimate contact with him.[274] While he gathers a fascinating range of Greco-Roman material, he is unable to find Jewish evidence for such a belief in this period,[275] and it is thus impossible to be confident of his interesting conjecture.

16 The unity of the group in faith issues in powerful deeds of healing. The crowds from the surrounding countryside show that Jesus's prediction of 1:8 continues to be carried out as people from Judea come and are healed. οἵτινες . . . ἅπαντες, "they . . . all," as subject of ἐθεραπεύοντο, "were healed," indicates that whoever was brought was healed. Luke maintains a distinction between two kinds of healing: from illness (ἀσθενεῖς, "sick people") and from demonization (ὀχλουμένους ὑπὸ πνευμάτων ἀκαθάρτων, "those troubled by unclean spirits"; cf. Luke 6:18).[276]

Explanation

This further paragraph on the believing community's life adds to Luke's earlier focus on the community's internal life (4:32–35) by portraying the believers' impact on outsiders.

As before, Luke stresses the unity of the community, which is a unity of heart and mind and not merely of shared location (5:12b; cf. 2:44–45; 4:32). Luke also underlines God's work in "signs and wonders" through the apostles (5:12a; cf. 2:43; 4:33). This is a community that manifestly demonstrates God's blessing in its life and deeds.

Luke goes on to draw attention to how others respond, and there is some tension between some people's hesitancy to join the community (5:13a), the high regard in which the Jerusalem populace hold them (v. 13b), and the numerical growth of the community (v. 14). The high regard stems from the quality of their shared life (2:43–47; 4:32–35)—this community, as we saw (on 4:34), fulfills the biblical hope that God's people will provide and care for those in need. This commitment to one another's welfare would be naturally attractive and thought well of, while also giving outsiders pause about joining the group, for they would see the potential cost of membership in being open to share their goods and provide for those in need. The temple leadership's earlier attempt at silencing the apostles (4:1–22) would add to the people's hesitancy about being seen to be part of the believing community—"private faith" was simply not an option in the ancient world, for to identify with the believers was necessarily to identify publicly with them. In addition, the widespread knowledge of the dangers of being a member of the group

274 "Shadow."
275 "Shadow," 210.
276 Thomas, *Devil*, 249.

following the deaths of Ananias and Sapphira (5:5, 11) would put off all but the very convinced from associating closely with the community.

Nevertheless, there are people—in significant numbers—who join the believing community (v. 14), and Luke draws attention to the mix of men and women (v. 14b). This inclusion of both sexes echoes the Isaianic future hope when YHWH will bring blessing for his sons and daughters (Isa 43:6–7; 49:22; 60:4). Each of the Isaianic texts comes in the setting of Israel's restoration, and thus the sexual inclusiveness, of interest in its own right, is also a sign that God is acting to restore Israel. It is striking that the community's growth is people being "added to the Lord": the renewed Israel is a community in which Jesus himself is the "container," a thought similar to Paul's "in Christ" language (e.g., Rom 12:5; 15:17; 16:3, 7; 1 Cor 1:2, 30; 2 Cor 5:17). The Lord Jesus is portrayed as suprapersonal, a being who can incorporate others into himself, a fascinating contribution to Luke's Christology.

The "signs and wonders" are exemplified by healing and deliverance from unclean spirits, and these are good things done for people without (it appears) any limitation to the believing community—the community is generous to the same extent as God himself. Remarkably, some of the healing happens through Peter's shadow passing over people (Acts 5:15), a distinctive form of healing that demonstrates that God dwells among the believers and indwells Peter in particular. The effectiveness of this healing is also remarkable, for "all" are healed (v. 16b). This "Jerusalem springtime" of the Jesus-believing community starts to have ripple effects wider than the city, as people from the Judean countryside bring people to be healed (v. 16a), and Luke thereby signals that Jesus's promise of 1:8 is continuing to be fulfilled: from Jerusalem, the Spirit is now impacting Judea. Further expansion of the mission will follow.

C. God Comes First: The Apostles before the Sanhedrin (5:17–42)

Bibliography

Barnett, P. *Birth,* 199–200. ———. "Prophets." **Black, M.** "Judas." **Bock, D. L.** *Proclamation,* 208–9. **Brawley, R. L.** *Luke-Acts,* 97–100. **Bruce, F. F.** "Church." **Chapman, D. W.** *Perceptions.* **Cohen, S. J. D.** *Josephus.* **Crabbe, K.** "Being Found." ———. *Luke/Acts,* 197–200. **Cunningham, S.** *Tribulations,* 190–203. **Darr, J. A.** "Irenic." ———. *Character,* 85–126, esp. 116–20. **Dibelius, M.** *Studies,* 186–91. **Dupont, J.** *Salvation,* 61–84. ———. *Sources,* 33–50, esp. 43–45. **Elliott, J. K.** "Text of Acts." **Elliott, M.** *Faithful Feelings,* 165–81. **Goldingay, J.** "Comic," 102–4. **Gowler, D. B.** *Host,* 274–80. **Green, J. B.** "Happiness" [= *Narrative Theologian,* 233–47]. **Hyytiäinen, P.** "Gamaliel Tradition." **Jeremias, J.** "Untersuchungen," 208–13. **Johnson, L. T.** *Function,* 196–98. **Jones, D. L.** "Title," esp. 632–34. **Lee, D.** *Luke-Acts,* 205–7. **Lyons, W. J.** "Words." **MacDonald, D. R.** *Gospels and Homer,* 279–81. **MacDonald, W. G.** "Christology." **Marshall, M.** *Portrayals,* 142–45. **Mason, S.** "Chief Priests." ———. *Josephus,* 251–95. **Morrice, W. G.** *Joy,* 91–99. **Neusner, J.** *Traditions,* 1:341–76. **Ovey, M. J.** *Feasts,* 45–48. **Pervo, R. I.** *Dating,* 152–58. **Peterson, D.** "Motif." **Ravens, D.** *Luke,* 139–69. **Reardon, T. W.** "Hanging." **Reicke, B. I.** *Glaube,* 108–14. **Rese, M.** *Motive,* 115–16. **Sanders, J. T.** *Jews,* 241–43. **Sleeman, M.** *Geography,* 125–30. **Smalley, S. S.** "Christology." **Sterling, G. E.** *Historiography,* esp. 281–82. **Strelan, R.** "Gamaliel's Hunch." ———. *Strange,* 261–63. **Swain, J. W.** "Gamaliel's Speech." **Tannehill, R. C.** "Functions," esp. 408–10. ———. *Shape,* 84–101. **Tomson, P. J.** "Gamaliel's Counsel." **Trites, A. A.** *Concept,* 151–53. **Trumbower, J. A.** "Historical Jesus." **Vöegli, A.** "Lukas." **Volf, M.** *Free,* 127–224. **Weatherly, J. A.** "Jews." ———. *Responsibility,* 69–70. **Weaver, J. B.** *Plots,* 93–148. **Wilcox, M.** "Tree." **Williams, M. H.** "Names," 86, 99–100. **Ziesler, J. A.** "Luke."

Translation

17 In reaction,[a] the high priest and all those with him—the local[b] party of the Sadducees—were filled with jealousy 18 and arrested[c] the apostles and put them in the public prison. 19 However, during the night the angel of the Lord opened the prison doors and led them out and said, 20 "Go and stand[d] in the temple and speak to the people all the words of this life." 21 When they heard [this], they went at dawn[e] into the temple and got on with teaching.[f] When the high priest arrived, and those with him, they summoned the Sanhedrin—the whole Council[g] of the sons of Israel—and sent to the prison in order to have them brought. 22 However, when the [Sanhedrin's] attendants arrived, they did not find them in the prison. So they returned and reported, 23 "We found the prison well and truly locked[h] and the guards standing[i] at the doors, but when we opened them, we found no one inside!" 24 When the captain of the temple guard and the chief priests heard these words, they were perplexed about them, wondering what this might mean.[j] 25 But someone arrived and reported to them, "Amazing![k] The men you put in the prison are standing in the temple and teaching[l]

the people!" 26 Then the captain went with the attendants and brought them without using force, for they were afraid that the people might stone[m] them.

27 They brought them and stood them before the Sanhedrin. The high priest interrogated[n] them, 28[o] "We expressly forbade you to teach in this name, but, see—you have filled Jerusalem with your teaching and you want to bring this man's blood upon us!" 29 Peter and the apostles[p] responded,[q] "We must obey God rather than mere humans. 30 The God of our ancestors raised up Jesus, whom you yourselves murdered by hanging on a tree. 31 This is the one God exalted to[r] his right side to be leader and savior[s] in order to give[t] repentance to Israel and forgiveness of sins. 32 We ourselves are witnesses[u] of these things, along with the Holy Spirit,[v] whom[w] God gives to those who obey him." 33 Those who heard were beside themselves with rage and began to want[x] to kill them.

34 However, a certain Pharisee, Gamaliel by name, a teacher of the law respected by all the people, rose in the Sanhedrin and ordered the people to be put[y] outside for a short time. 35 Then he said to them, "People of Israel,[z] be very careful concerning what you are about to do to these people. 36 For some time ago Theudas rose up claiming to be someone important, and about four hundred men attached themselves to him. He was executed, every single one of those who were won over by him was scattered, and they came to nothing. 37 After him, Judas the Galilean rose up at the time of the census and stirred up people[aa] to follow him in revolt.[bb] That man perished too, and every single one of those won over by him was scattered. 38 Now, concerning the present situation,[cc] I say to you, keep away from these people and give them space; for if this plan or this work turns out to be[dd] of human origin, it will come to nothing; 39 but if it is from God, you will not be able to stop them[ee]—you may even be found fighting against God!" They were won over by him.[ff] 40 So, after they summoned the apostles and beat them, they commanded them not to speak in the name of Jesus and released them. 41 So then, they left the Sanhedrin[gg] rejoicing that they were considered worthy to be shamed for the sake of the name. 42 Indeed, every day,[hh] both in the temple and in homes, they did not cease teaching and proclaiming the good news that the Messiah was Jesus.

Notes

a. Ἀναστάς, aor. ptc. of ἀνίστημι, is a Lukan favorite (the verb is found: 26x Luke; 45x Acts; 107x NT in total), and so the reading Ἄννας, "Annas," found in it^{p} mae, is unlikely; *TCGNT*^{2}, 288; Barrett, *Acts*, 1:282.

b. οὖσα, ptc. of εἰμί, meaning "local"; so MHT, 3:151–52, citing this verse and Acts 13:1; 14:13 D. The construction is also found at 28:17; cf. Barrett, *Acts*, 1:283; Bruce, "Church," 641n2.

c. ἐπέβαλον τὰς χεῖρας ἐπί, "they laid hands upon," denoting arrest as in 4:3 (see *Note* z there).

d. σταθέντες, aor. pass. ptc. of ἵστημι, perhaps "stand up to make a speech" (Haenchen, *Acts*, 249; "ἵστημι," BDAG 472, §2) or connoting "in public" (Culy and Parsons, *Acts*, 94).

e. ὄρθρον, "at dawn" ("ὄρθρος," BDAG 722), found only 3x in NT (here; Luke 24:1; John 8:2).

f. inceptive impf. of ἐδίδασκον: they began and continued teaching.

g. καί is epexegetical = "namely"; Bruce, *Acts* (1990), 170–71; Barrett, *Acts*, 1:285; Schürer, 2:206n17.

h. ἐν πάσῃ ἀσφαλείᾳ, lit., "in all safety"; cf. ἐν ἀσφαλίᾳ, "in safe custody," in *NewDocs* 3:149, 154 §101 line 22, early 4th century AD.

i. ἑστῶτας, "standing," pf. act. ptc. of ἵστημι intransitive, so functioning as pres. ptc.; "ἵστημι," BDAG 483, §C.2.b.

j. τί ἂν γένοιτο τοῦτο, lit., "what this might be"; aor. opt. γένοιτο with ἄν for indirect question. This potential opt. is the apodosis of an incomplete fourth-class condition, used to indicate a future consequence of an unlikely condition (Wallace, 483–84, 699–700). The implicit protasis is something like, "If these bizarre words proved to be true. . . ." A rare construction in NT; Barrett, *Acts*, 1:286; Bruce, *Acts* (1990), 171; Wallace, 699–701.

k. ἰδού, lit., "See!" The word draws attention to the startling nature of the remainder of the speech.

l. εἰσὶν . . . ἑστῶτες καὶ διδάσκοντες, "are . . . standing and teaching," pres. periph.

m. μὴ λιθασθῶσιν, "lest they be stoned," aor. pass. subj. with μή following verb of fearing ἐφοβοῦντο, "they were afraid," to express the danger they feared; Wallace, 477.

n. ἐπηρώτησεν, "interrogated"; "ἐπερωτάω," BDAG 362, §1.b.

o. א[2] D E 1739 𝔐 and many versions include οὐ at the beginning of this speech, which would make the speech a question expecting the answer, "Yes"; it is absent from 𝔓[74] א* A B 1175 most Latin MSS, some Sahidic MSS, Boharic, Lucifer (a strong combination of witnesses). NA[27, 28]/UBS[4, 5] place it in square brackets, indicating doubt about its presence (it is omitted in NA[25]). If οὐ were original, the omission could result from copyists transforming the question into a rebuke by the high priest. The translation agrees with Metzger, who enters a dissentient note on the grounds of the strength of the MS support and the probability that the use of ἐπηρώτησεν, "he asked/interrogated," suggested to copyists that a question followed rather than a statement, leading them to transform a rebuke into a question by inserting οὐ; *TCGNT*[2], 289; with THGNT; NET; Barrett, *Acts*, 1:288; Bruce, *Acts* (1990), 171.

p. D reads ὁ δὲ Πέτρος εἶπεν πρὸς αὐτούς, "and Peter said to them," heightening his role and smoothing the syntax (see next *Note*).

q. m. sg. ptc. ἀποκριθείς, "answering," with 3 pl. ind. εἶπαν, "they said." The sg. ptc. may be treating "Peter and the apostles" as a collective character or as indicating that Peter spoke on behalf of the group, Wallace, 401–2.

r. τῇ δεξιᾷ may mean "*by* the right [hand]." See *Note* t on 2:33 (the only other use of dat. δεξιᾷ without prep. in the NT).

s. τοῦτον . . . ἀρχηγὸν καὶ σωτῆρα double acc. of object-complement (Wallace, 182–89; Barrett, *Acts*, 1:290) = "this one . . . *to be* leader and savior."

t. δοῦναι, aor. inf. of δίδωμι expressing purpose. א* B read τοῦ before the inf.; this gen. art. would mark the inf. more clearly as of purpose.

u. D[2] E *Byz*, etc. read αὐτοῦ, "his," echoing 1:8; 945 1739 bo[mss] Irenaeus[lat] read ἐν αὐτῷ, "in him," perhaps echoing a similar Western reading at the end of v. 31; NA[28]/UBS[5] and THGNT include neither, which has strong MS support, including 𝔓[74vid] א (A) D*; *TCGNT*[2], 290. ECM, 1.1:161 has a split line, allowing the possibility of either αὐτοῦ or nothing, but Wachtel's commentary observes that the genitive αὐτοῦ may have been added under the influence of 1:8; ECM, 3:11.

v. τὸ πνεῦμα τὸ ἅγιον, "the Holy Spirit": "hanging" nom., thus emphasized; Wallace, 51.

w. ὅ, neut. sg. pn. agreeing with n. sg. πνεῦμα, "Spirit"; v.l. ὅν (m. sg. pn.) in D*, probably *ad sensum,* although not correctly so (Elliott, "Text of Acts", 251). *TCGNT*^{2}, 290, sees omission in B and a few others as accidental.

x. ἐβούλοντο, inceptive impf. of βούλομαι, "they began to wish," portraying a desire arising from their rage. ἐβουλεύοντο, impf. from βουλεύομαι, "they were planning," is read by ℵ D various minuscules including 1739 *Byz* some lectionaries some it vg arm slav Lucifer; also ἐβουλεύσαντο ("they planned," aor.) in 1175 1409 geo. However, βουλεύομαι is only found elsewhere in Acts at 27:39, whereas βούλομαι is found 13x in Acts (5:28; 12:4; 15:37; 17:20; 18:15, 27; 19:30; 22:30; 23:28; 25:20, 22; 27:43; 28:18), including in the near co-text (v. 28). Contextually, too, "the Sanhedrin . . . were scarcely in a mood quietly to take counsel" (*TCGNT*^{2}, 291), and so ἐβουλεύοντο is probably a copyist's error.

y. Unusual use of ποιέω with adv. of place ἔξω, "outside," in the sense "to put/send outside"; "ποιέω," BDAG 840, §2.h.γ.

z. ἄνδρες Ἰσραηλῖται, "People of Israel," see *Comment* on 2:22. Here the audience is entirely masculine, but this translation is appropriate because their ethnicity rather than their sex is in focus.

aa. A^{c} 0140 1739 *Byz* read ἱκανόν, "a considerable"; C D it read πολύ(ν) "many." These seem clear examples of copyists strengthening the narrative; so *TCGNT*^{2}, 292, noting that, unusually, the Latin text of Codex Bezae [it^{d}] lacks an additional word.

bb. ἀπέστησεν, aor. of ἀφίστημι in transitive sense of "altering allegiance" ("ἀφίστημι," BDAG 157, §1), as in Josephus *Ant.* 8.7.5 §198; 20.5.2 §102.

cc. See *Note* m on 4:29.

dd. ᾖ, pres. subj. of εἰμί, "be," following ἐάν, "if," in second-class conditional sentence; it is unusual to find pres. in this construction concerning the present, but it may well be equivalent to "if it turns out to be . . ."; Bruce, *Acts* (1990), 178.

ee. αὐτούς, "them," read by NA^{28}/UBS^{5}, *THGNT,* and ECM. There are a number of variant readings: (i) αὐτό, "it," C^{*vid} some minuscules *Byz l*156 *l*422 *l*617 it$^{c,\ dem,\ w}$ vg^{cl} syr^{p} cop$^{sa\ (mss),\ bo\ (mss)}$ Chrysostom; (ii) αὐτοὺς οὔτε ὑμεῖς οὔτε οἱ ἄρχοντες ὑμῶν, "them, neither you nor your rulers," E it$^{ar,\ e,\ gig}$ Bede (citing otherwise unknown Greek MSS); (iii) αὐτοὺς οὔτε ὑμεῖς οὔτε βασιλεῖς οὔτε τύραννοι· ἀπέχεσθε οὖν ἀπὸ τῶν ἀνθρώπων τούτων, "them, not you nor kings nor tyrants; therefore keep away from these people," D it$^{d,\ h}$ (syr$^{h\ with}$ *) (cop^{meg}); (iv) αὐτούς· ἀπέχεσθε οὖν ἀπὸ τῶν ἀνθρώπων τούτων, "them, therefore keep away from these people," 614. (iii) seems to arise from the influence of Wis 12:13–14 οὔτε γὰρ θεός ἐστιν πλὴν σοῦ ᾧ μέλει περὶ πάντων ἵνα δείξῃς ὅτι οὐκ ἀδίκως ἔκρινας οὔτε βασιλεὺς ἢ τύραννος ἀντοφθαλμῆσαι δυνήσεταί σοι περὶ ὧν ἐκόλασας, "For neither is there any god besides you whose care is for all people, to whom you should prove that you have not judged unjustly, nor can any king or monarch confront you about those whom you have punished" (NRSVue). The Wisdom passage is addressing the same issue, whether one can safely oppose God (*TCGNT*^{2}, 293–94; Barrett, *Acts,* 1:297). (ii) is effectively (iii) with τύραννοι replaced by οἱ ἄρχοντες, but this now introduces a second reference to the Sanhedrin and thus creates less clarity. (iii) and (iv) add ἀπέχεσθε οὖν ἀπὸ τῶν ἀνθρώπων τούτων, repeating the contents of v. 38 unnecessarily, but they prepare for the following clause more smoothly than αὐτούς. All are easily seen as arising from the bare αὐτούς; Haenchen, *Acts,* 253n3; Hyytiäinen, "Gamaliel Tradition," 12–17. For discussion of the wider series of variants found in D in vv. 38–39, see Hyytiäinen, "Gamaliel Tradition," esp. 7–21, arguing that the readings of D here represent different layers of text rather than one coherent tradition.

ff. αὐτῷ, "by him," is an unusual dat. use, expressing either agency with ἐπείσθησαν, "they were persuaded" ("πείθω," BDAG 792, §3.c), or the dat. is used because of the idea "they believed," which normally takes dat. (I owe the latter suggestion to Daniel B. Wallace.)

gg. ἀπὸ προσώπου τοῦ συνεδρίου, lit., "from the face of the Sanhedrin"; synecdoche, probably a Semitism, in the style of LXX (Bruce, *Acts* (1990), 143; Barrett, *Acts*, 1:300, noting Gen 4:16 as parallel). "πρόσωπον," BDAG 887, §1.b.β.a, also notes (a few) parallels in classical sources.

hh. πᾶσάν τε ἡμέραν, acc. of time, denoting extent of time, is fronted, suggesting emphasis on the fact that they spoke every day, hence "Indeed. . . ."

Form/Structure/Setting

Delimitation of pericope. Luke transitions from the preceding summary (vv. 12–16) by introducing the Jewish authorities' reaction to the believing community's activities (v. 17). The following sequence portrays different facets of this reaction and the divine and apostolic responses. The whole comes to a climax in the rejoicing and continuing teaching and proclamation of the gospel by the apostles (v. 42), the latter in a summary with an imperfect main verb (οὐκ ἐπαύοντο, "they did not cease"). This closing summary echoes the themes of vv. 12–16 and demonstrates that the divine purpose will not be frustrated by human opposition, which is the central theme of Gamaliel's speech (vv. 38–39).

Sources/historicity. "The angel of the Lord" appears in Luke-Acts to act on YHWH's behalf (e.g., Luke 1:11; 2:9; Acts 8:26; 12:7, 23), as in the OT (e.g., Gen 16:7–11; 21:9–19, esp. 17; 22:10–18; 31:11–13; Exod 3:1–6; Judg 2:1–5). Similar stories about divine or semi-divine beings appearing in order to to free people occur in Greco-Roman literature.[1] E.g., the god Bacchus frees his followers from prison and in process the chains fall off αὐτόματα, "of their own accord" (Euripides, *Bacch.* 447; cf. Acts 12:10), and the keys in the doors turn without human hands doing so (*Bacch.* 447–48; in full, see *Bacch.* 434–50); cf. the story of Dionysius's own escape, which involves him leaping over a wall (*Bacch.* 610–55). The use of such stories in ancient culture is not evidence for the historicity or non-historicity of any particular event, since larger worldview questions are in play in that debate.[2]

Verses 33–39 portray a closed session of the Sanhedrin; it is possible that Saul of Tarsus may be Luke's source for the discussion here—his presence in the Sanhedrin is suggested by 26:10 (see *Comment* there).

MacDonald suggests some verbal and content parallels with Homer, *Od.* 16.394, 397–408, including use of two different Greek conditionals (see *Comment* on vv. 38–39).[3] The parallel of the situations is interesting, for the result of the Homeric story is that Telemachus is freed rather than killed and that Zeus is invoked by Amphinomos. However, to suggest that Luke is imitating Homer falls foul of "parallelomania."[4]

1 Cf. Johnson, *Acts*, 97; for a full account of ancient sources, see Weaver, *Plots*, 29–91.
2 Bock, *Acts*, 239; see discussion of ancient and modern stories of this kind in Keener, *Miracles*, 1:585–87; 2:1209–12.
3 MacDonald, *Gospels and Homer*, 279–81.
4 Sandmel, "Parallelomania."

There are a number of similarities with the earlier Sanhedrin meeting in Acts 4: (i) arrest and imprisonment (4:3; 5:18); (ii) a Sanhedrin hearing with an apostle speaking—probably Peter in both cases (4:5–12; 5:27–33); (iii) the Sanhedrin conferring in the absence of the accused apostles (4:15–17; 5:34–39); (iv) the apostles freed but forbidden to speak in Jesus's name (4:18; 5:40); (v) the apostles continuing to speak in Jesus's name (4:19–20; 5:42). Such similarities lead some to see this story as a "doublet" of Acts 4.[5] However, there is a stepping up of tension in ch. 5, which begins where the previous story ends, with the Sanhedrin's charge not to speak or teach in Jesus's name (4:18; 5:28). The significance of this is that in rabbinic law a person could only be punished if conscious of the outcome(s) of an act; thus, the first hearing in Acts 4:1–22 had provided the required legal warning, and this hearing was the formal follow-up (see *Comment* on 4:21)—Jeremias rightly argues that this sequence makes perfect sense of Luke's story.[6] In addition: (a) "the apostles" are arrested, not just Peter and John (4:1, 3; 5:18); (b) rather than the apostles being brought from prison to the hearing (4:3, 5–7), an angel facilitates their escape from prison, so that the Sanhedrin have to bring them less violently to a hearing (5:17–26); (c) the Sanhedrin move from being deeply offended (4:2) to jealousy (5:17) and rage leading to a desire to kill the apostles (5:33); (d) the Sanhedrin seek to suppress not only what is taught about Jesus (4:9–12) but now their responsibility for Jesus's death (5:28, 30; cf. 4:10, 11); (e) rather than the Sanhedrin finding no way to punish Peter and John (4:21), even though Gamaliel persuades the Sanhedrin to release the apostles, they are beaten (5:40).[7] Jeremias's argument and these escalations suggest there is a real development of events rather than the two stories being mere doublets.

Structure. The story develops by a series of switches of actants (expressed as grammatical subjects), mostly marked by δέ (which I have generally left untranslated). These switches and changes of location combine to produce a series of "scenes":

vv. 17–21a The temple authorities imprison the apostles for their teaching about Jesus, the angel of the Lord frees the apostles, and they continue speaking.
- vv. 17–18 [δέ] The high priest and his colleagues react to the believers' conduct by imprisoning the apostles.
- vv. 19–20 [δέ] The angel of the Lord frees the apostles and instructs them to continue speaking in the temple.
- v. 21a [δέ] The apostles enter the temple and continue teaching.

5 E.g., Harnack, *Acts,* 179–86; *BegC,* 2:137–47; Reicke, *Glaube,* 108–14; for critique of Reicke, see Dupont, *Sources,* 47–49.
6 Jeremias, "Untersuchungen," 208–13; Dupont, *Sources,* 44.
7 On the similarities and differences, see Tannehill, *Unity,* 2:59–79; Gowler, *Host,* 275–76; Cunningham, *Tribulations,* 192–94; Weaver, *Plots,* 126–32.

vv. 21b–26 The authorities discover the apostles' absence from prison and respond by rearresting them.

- v. 21b [δέ] The high priest and his colleagues call a Sanhedrin meeting and send for the apostles to be brought from prison.
- vv. 22–23 [δέ] The Sanhedrin's attendants discover that the apostles are not in prison and report this to the Sanhedrin.
- v. 24 [δέ] The captain of the temple and the chief priests are puzzled by this news.
- v. 25 [δέ] An anonymous person (τις "someone") tells them that the apostles are teaching in the temple.
- v. 26 [marked by τότε "then"] The captain and the temple police go to the temple and rearrest the apostles, but without violence.

vv. 27–40 The Sanhedrin conduct a hearing concerning the apostles.

- v. 27a [δέ] The apostles are placed before the Sanhedrin.
- vv. 27b–28 The high priest questions the apostles on the basis of their failure to keep the Sanhedrin's earlier order not to speak in Jesus's name.
- vv. 29–32 [δέ] Peter responds to the charges.
- v. 33 [δέ] First reaction: the hearers (the Sanhedrin) wish to kill the apostles.
- vv. 34–39a [δέ] Second reaction: Gamaliel orders the apostles to be put outside and urges caution.
- vv. 39b–40 [δέ] The Sanhedrin are convinced by Gamaliel and again order the apostles not to speak in Jesus's name.

vv. 41–42 [marked by μὲν οὖν "so then," introducing the key outcome of the story] The apostles respond by rejoicing that they suffer dishonor for Jesus's sake and by continuing to teach and proclaim Jesus.

Setting. This episode is a further fulfillment of the promises of Jesus concerning the help he/the Spirit will give to his followers when persecuted (Luke 12:4–12; 21:12–19).[8] The language here also echoes the language of Luke's passion narrative, portraying the apostles as suffering the same persecution as their Lord (cf. Acts 9:4; John 15:20):[9] (i) the opponents are the same: ὁ στρατηγὸς τοῦ ἱεροῦ, "the captain of the temple guard" (Luke 22:4, 52; Acts 5:24, 26; cf. 4:1), οἱ Σαδδουκαίοι, "the Sadducees" (Luke 20:27; Acts 5:17; cf. 4:1), ὁ ἀρχιερεύς, "the high priest" (Luke 19:47; 20:1, 19; 22:2, 4, 50, 52, 54, 66; 23:4, 10, 13; 24:40; Acts 5:17, 21, 24, 27; cf. 4:6, 23), and τὸ συνέδριον, "the Sanhedrin" (Luke 22:66; Acts 5:21, 27, 34, 41; cf. 4:15); (ii) both are teaching the people in the temple (Luke 20:1; Acts 5:25; see *Comment* below); (iii) the people's support

8 See Cunningham, *Tribulations*, 194–95, for a full enumeration of parallels.
9 For what follows, see Cunningham, *Tribulations*, 195–96.

prevents the authorities from taking precipitate action against them (Luke 19:48; 20:6, 19, 26; 22:2; Acts 5:26); the authorities "lay hands on" (ἐπιβάλλω τὰς χεῖρας = "arrest") the apostles and attempt to do so with Jesus (Luke 20:19; Acts 5:18; cf. 4:33); (iv) both are beaten (Luke 22:63; Acts 5:40, using δέρω "beat" in both cases); (v) the Sanhedrin hearings happen on the day following arrest (Luke 22:66; Acts 5:18–21; cf. 4:5).

This story flows on from the summary of the external impact of the community's life (5:12–16) and presents further opposition and persecution by the temple authorities, echoing Peter and John's appearance before the Sanhedrin (4:5–22), the prayerful response that follows (4:23–30; cf. 5:41), and the believers' continuing testimony to Jesus (4:31; cf. 5:42). Peter's final speech in Jerusalem to not-yet-believers (5:31–32) closes with a similar emphasis to his first such speech, at Pentecost, linking Jesus's exaltation to his pouring out of gifts (2:33) for the blessing of Israel (2:14, 22, 29, 36).[10] The speech climaxes Peter's proclamation in Jerusalem.

The following section (6:1–7) returns to the internal life of the community (cf. 4:32–35), showing how they responded to a particular issue of need (cf. 4:34–35) and underlining their continuing outreach (6:7; cf. 5:12–16).

Comment

17–18 The aorist participle Ἀναστάς (lit., "standing up") connotes that the high priest and his associates' reaction to the previous event(s) was speedy and immediate, hence the translation "In reaction" (see *Note* 1 on 5:6, ἀναστάντες).

Luke identifies the driver of their reaction as ζήλου, which could mean "jealousy/envy,"[11] here a negative response to others taking an interest in the gospel message,[12] or "zeal," i.e., being positively zealous for their traditions and opposing those who appear to reject those traditions (cf. 13:45)[13]—or perhaps a combination of both ideas. It is notable that ἐπλήσθησαν, "they were filled," with ζήλου, contrasting with the believers, who ἐπλήσθησαν ἅπαντες τοῦ ἁγίου πνεύματος, "were all filled with the Holy Spirit" (4:31; cf. the same phrase concerning the Antiochene Jews, 13:45 with *Comment*). This negative emotion leads them to seek to suppress the apostles' testimony by causing them to be imprisoned. "If the Church remains faithful to its mission, persecution becomes an integral element in its story."[14]

ἐπέβαλον τὰς χεῖρας ἐπὶ τοὺς ἀποστόλους, "[they] arrested the apostles," precisely echoes Jesus's warning that this will happen to his followers (Luke 21:12), both confirming Jesus's prophetic powers and indicating that his promise that

10 Tannehill, "Functions," 408–10.
11 Discussion: Malina and Pilch, *Acts*, 50–51.
12 "ζῆλος," BDAG 427, §2.
13 Reardon, "Hanging," 423–24.
14 Cunningham, *Tribulations*, 198.

he will enable them to testify for him in this situation will be fulfilled (Luke 21:13–16).

τηρήσει δημοσίᾳ, "the public prison," is equivalent to τὸ δεσμωτήριον, "the prison" (vv. 21, 23), and is probably the same location as in 4:3. Lake proposes that this prison was probably either in the temple courts or below the Hall of Hewn Stones (*Lishkat ha-Gazith*) where the Sanhedrin met.[15] δημοσία can be used as an adverb meaning "publicly," which would give the translation "*publicly* put them in prison."[16] δημοσία can also be used in an adjectival sense, "the *public* prison."[17] Because of its equivalence with τὸ δεσμωτήριον and v. 19 showing that they were out of public view,[18] the latter sense seems most likely here, although the former is not impossible.

19 Ἄγγελος . . . κυρίου, "the angel . . . of the Lord." The force of this expression is that YHWH is acting to free the apostles,[19] in similar manner to other prison escape stories in 12:6–10; 16:25–26 (the former specifies that "the angel of the Lord" was present; the latter does not). God continues to answer the prayer of 4:29[20] and thereby undoes the injustice of their imprisonment after the manner in which he undid the injustice of Jesus's crucifixion in the resurrection (cf. 2:23–24). Not only that, but by freeing them God legitimates their preaching and leadership: the question of who truly speaks for God is being answered with clarity by God's actions here. The anarthrous Ἄγγελος . . . κυρίου is regularly used in LXX for "*the* angel of the Lord" (*ml'ḵ YHWH*, e.g., Gen 16:7, 8; 22:11, 15; Exod 3:2; Num 22:31), an expression that can be interchangeable with YHWH in the Pentateuch (Gen 16:7–14; 21:14–19, etc.).[21] The angel is a supernatural agent, not merely a human sympathizer.[22] Apollonius's canon and corollary strengthen this point, for they suggest that both nouns being anarthrous need not mean they are indefinite and that where both nouns are anarthrous, they have equivalent semantic force: thus this expression means either "*an* angel of *a* Lord" or "*the* angel of *the* Lord"[23]—and the latter is much more likely in biblical Greek.[24] Luke uses the anarthrous singular expression in Luke 1:11; 2:9; Acts 8:26; 12:7, 23. (On angels, see further *Comment* on 1:10.)

The switch to φυλακή for "prison" (here, vv. 22, 25; contrast v. 18) perhaps recalls Luke 21:12, Jesus's statement that the authorities will deliver his followers to prisons (φυλακάς).[25]

---

15 *BegC*, 5:479; Schürer, 2:223–25.
16 "δημοσία," BDAG 223, §2; *BegC*, 4:57; Barrett, *Acts*, 1:283.
17 "δημοσία," BDAG 223, §1; Haenchen, *Acts*, 249n1; Pesch, *Apostelgeschichte*, 1:213n16.
18 "δημοσία," BDAG 223, §2.
19 Fitzmyer, *Acts*, 335.
20 Sleeman, *Geography*, 125.
21 Cf. Bruce, *Acts* (1990), 170.
22 Strelan, *Strange Acts*, 262, contra Dunn, *Acts*, 68.
23 Wallace, 239–40, 250–52; cf. Culy and Parsons, *Acts*, 94.
24 Contra MacDonald, "Christology," who argues that in both Testaments the expression should be translated "*an* angel of *the* Lord."
25 Cunningham, *Tribulations*, 195.

ἐξαγαγών τε αὐτούς, "[the angel] led them out," echoes descriptions from the exodus of both God (Exod 6:7 LXX) and the angel who led the people of Israel out (Num 20:16 LXX). The verb ἐξάγω, "lead out," is frequently used in LXX with ἐξ Αἰγύπτου, "out of Egypt."[26] Luke is using language that has resonances with Israel's liberation and thereby encouraging his readers to see that the God who thus delivers the apostles is the same God who delivered Israel from Egypt.[27]

20 The angel instructs the apostles to return to the temple and continue speaking (the present imperative λαλεῖτε, "speak," implies "go on speaking") πάντα τὰ ῥήματα τῆς ζωῆς ταύτης, "all the words of this life." The apostles are to hold nothing back but are to speak πάντα τὰ ῥήματα, "*all* the words," again answering the prayer of 4:29 to speak the word with boldness[28] and also in similar manner to Paul's claim not to have held anything back (20:20, 27). Their release from prison is purposeful: to enable continued gospel proclamation.[29] The genitive τῆς ζωῆς ταύτης, "of this life," suggests that the words produce "this life." "Life" has been a theme in earlier speeches (2:28; 3:15) and is the result of gentile repentance later (11:18); the parallels to 11:18 in 13:46, 48 suggest that ζωή, "life," denotes ζωή αἰώνιος, "eternal life." The temple is not only an appropriate place for such proclamation, it is being claimed for the gospel message, recalling that the believers have been meeting there (5:12).[30] The apostles' return to the temple after their removal at the Sanhedrin's behest indicates that "God has completely reversed the scheme of the Jewish leaders."[31]

21 Luke stresses that the apostles are entirely obedient, matching the present imperative command λαλεῖτε, "speak," with the ingressive imperfect ἐδίδασκον, "[they] got on with teaching." Not only that, but they do this ὑπὸ τὸν ὄρθρον, "at dawn," taking the earliest possible opportunity to speak the gospel.

The apostles' obedience contrasts with the Sanhedrin's preparations to try the apostles, for they consider the apostles to be disobedient to God. Luke identifies τὸ συνέδριον, "the Sanhedrin," as τὴν γερουσίαν, "the Council," of Israel (see *Note* g and *Comment* on 4:5, 15). Haenchen suggests Luke is comparing the Sanhedrin to the Roman Senate;[32] if so, Luke is explaining an unfamiliar term for a Greco-Roman readership.

22–24 The scene unfolds in a somewhat comical manner, inviting readers to see the Sanhedrin and their associates as foolish and mistaken.[33] The

26 E.g., Exod 12:17, 42, 51; 20:2; 29:46; 33:1; Lev 19:36; 22:33; 23:43; Num 15:41; 20:16; 23:22; Deut 1:27; 4:20, 37. Strelan, *Strange Acts*, 263, estimates fifty uses in the Pentateuch.
27 Strelan, *Strange Acts*, 262–63; Weaver, *Plots*, 101–2.
28 Sleeman, *Geography*, 125.
29 Weaver, *Plots*, 286, commenting on all three prison escapes in Acts 5, 12, and 16.
30 Cf. Barrett, *Acts*, 1:284; Roloff, *Apostelgeschichte*, 102; Weaver, *Plots*, 112.
31 Weaver, *Plots*, 108.
32 *Acts*, 249–50.
33 Goldingay, "Comic," 102.

powerlessness of the Sanhedrin in the face of God's actions will be articulated by Gamaliel, one of their own, later (vv. 38–39).[34]

The Sanhedrin's ὑπηρέται, "attendants," are a group of priests or Levites whose usual job is providing a security guard for the temple at night (m. Mid. 1:2). Luke presents them as overseen by ὁ στρατηγός, "the captain" (v. 26; see *Comment* on 4:1). They do not find the apostles in prison, in spite of the prison being secure. The doors, by contrast with their earlier opening by the angel (v. 19), are now κεκλεισμένον ἐν πάσῃ ἀσφαλείᾳ, "well and truly locked," the perfect participle κεκλεισμένον connoting this security (cf. the locked doors in the upper room, John 20:19, 26). Further, the guards are standing there: ἑστῶτας, Acts 5:23, ironically echoing the angel's command to the apostles to stand in the temple, σταθέντες, v. 20 (both participles are from ἵστημι, "stand"). Their presence leads the reader to wonder what the guards were doing when the angel released the apostles the previous night. On opening the doors (ἀνοίξαντες, v. 23, again echoing the angel's action, ἀνοίξας, v. 19), instead of finding the apostles, they find no one—the threefold repetition of εὑρίσκω, "find," in vv. 22–23 adds to the comedy.

διηπόρουν, "[they] were perplexed." The captain of the temple guard (see *Comment* on 4:1) and the chief priests are "baffled" (CSB) by this event: something strange has clearly happened, and they need to understand it. Their perplexity echoes the reaction of the Pentecost crowds (2:12; cf. Peter after his rooftop vision, 10:17) and, as at Pentecost, is resolved by a voice of explanation (5:25; cf. 2:14–36).

25 τις ἀπήγγειλεν αὐτοῖς, "someone . . . reported to them." An anonymous individual reports the consequences of the jailbreak. There is some irony in the echo of the combination of a participle of παραγίνομαι, "go," and the main verb ἀπαγγέλλω, "report," from v. 22: what the Sanhedrin's attendants entered not knowing and thus reporting the apostles' absence, an unknown individual knows and thus reports the apostles' location—Luke portrays the Sanhedrin's ignorance as comical and laughable, for they do not know something that is public knowledge.

ἐν τῷ ἱερῷ ἑστῶτες καὶ διδάσκοντες τὸν λαόν, "standing in the temple and teaching the people." The apostles are doing exactly what the angel commanded: Luke echoes ἵστημι (σταθέντες "stand") from v. 20 and the command λαλεῖτε ἐν τῷ ἱερῷ τῷ λαῷ, "speak in the temple to the people," which is explained as ἐδίδασκον, "they got on with teaching." The apostles' obedience to God echoes the actions of Jesus: the key terms found here, διδάσκω, "teach," τὸν λαόν, "the people," and ἐν τῷ ἱερῷ, "in the temple," are also collocated in Luke 20:1, where Jesus teaches in the temple. Their obedience contrasts starkly with the Sanhedrin's opposition (cf. Acts 4:19–20) and prepares for the following scene, esp. 5:28–29.

---

34 Cunningham, *Tribulations*, 190n8.

26 οὐ μετὰ βίας, "without force." The captain and the attendants are more cautious on this occasion. βία, "force, violence,"[35] is found only in Acts in the NT (here; 21:35; 27:41). οὐ μετὰ βίας is emphatically located at the end of its clause and is further emphasized by its nature as a negative statement chosen to express the idea.[36]

Luke's choice of imperfect verbs ἦγεν . . . ἐφοβοῦντο, "[they] brought . . . they were afraid," portrays the event as if a video is showing before his readers, and the captain and his attendants' fear of the people stoning them is going on for some time. This further highlights the division between the people at large (cf. 5:12–16) and the temple leadership over the believing community.

27 ἔστησαν, "stood," echoes uses of ἵστημι in vv. 20, 23, 25, and 4:7; standing appears to be the normal posture of one being interrogated (cf. 22:30; 24:20; 26:6, 22; Matt 27:11).

The setting is ἐν τῷ συνεδρίῳ, "before the Sanhedrin"; this is a formal hearing to determine what steps should follow, similar to that in 4:5–21 (see *Comment* on 4:9 for the hearing's nature). The apostles, standing at the focal point of the semicircle of Sanhedrin members, are the center of attention (see *Comment* on 4:7).

28 παραγγελίᾳ παρηγγείλαμεν ὑμῖν μὴ διδάσκειν ἐπὶ τῷ ὀνόματι τούτῳ, "we expressly forbade you to teach in this name," points back to the Sanhedrin's instruction in 4:17, 18. παραγγελίᾳ παρηγγείλαμεν, combining the verb with its cognate noun in the dative, is forceful: "with a command we commanded."[37]

ἰδοὺ πεπληρώκατε τὴν Ἰερουσαλὴμ τῆς διδαχῆς ὑμῶν, "see—you have filled Jerusalem with your teaching." Luke again highlights the contrast of the apostles' obedient teaching and the Sanhedrin's opposition with the high priest's overstated accusation. The perfect πεπληρώκατε, "you have filled," pictures their teaching as having filled and now filling the city.[38] This earthly space is being claimed by the gospel message, which is the agent of Jesus's claim as ascended Lord of the world (cf. 6:7).

ἐπαγαγεῖν ἐφ' ἡμᾶς τὸ αἷμα τοῦ ἀνθρώπου τούτου, "you want to bring this man's blood upon us!," is an idiom meaning "to make us responsible for his death" (cf. Luke 11:50–51; Acts 18:6; 20:26; Matt 27:4, 24–25). The high priest's perception is that the temple leadership are being named as responsible for Jesus's death, and Peter will confirm this point in Acts 5:30 (cf. 4:10).[39] However, the temple leadership are not held solely responsible for Jesus's

35 "βία," BDAG 175.
36 Bruce, *Acts* (1990), 171.
37 An uncommon construction in the NT; Wallace, 168–69.
38 As often, πληρόω, "fill," takes genitive of the thing filling, here διδαχῆς, "teaching."
39 Weatherly, *Responsibility*, 69; contra Sanders, *Jews*, 241–42, who wishes to read this verse through the lens of his interpretation of other verses that, he believes, charge the whole Jewish race with the death of Jesus. For fuller critique of Sanders, see Weatherly, "Jews"; Weatherly, *Responsibility*.

death in Acts: the wider Jerusalem community are also implicated (2:36; 3:15), as well as Pilate and the Romans (4:27).

29 ἀποκριθεὶς δὲ Πέτρος καὶ οἱ ἀπόστολοι εἶπαν, "Peter and the apostles responded," combines a singular participle ἀποκριθείς, "responding," describing Peter, with a plural verb εἶπαν, "they said," describing an action of Peter and the apostles. Presumably Luke means us to think either of Peter as the apostles' spokesman (as D considers, see *Note* p) or of Peter as the leading speaker among a number of apostles.

πειθαρχεῖν δεῖ θεῷ μᾶλλον ἢ ἀνθρώποις, "We must obey God rather than mere humans," introduces the keynote of the speech, obedience to God, and the verb πειθαρχέω, "obey," will be repeated at the end of the speech (v. 32). In the immediate co-text, the apostles were commanded by an angel, a divine agent, to speak in the temple (v. 20): the rest of the speech will explain the grounds of this assertion, which are rooted in God's exaltation of Jesus. As elsewhere in NT (Acts 5:32; 27:21; Titus 3:1), πειθαρχέω takes dative:[40] θεῷ, "God," is contrasted with ἀνθρώποις, "human beings," hence "*mere* humans."

30 ὁ θεὸς τῶν πατέρων ἡμῶν ἤγειρεν Ἰησοῦν, "The God of our ancestors raised up Jesus." Peter goes on to testify about Jesus, fulfilling Luke 12:8, but stressing the continuity with the ancestral faith: it is "[t]he God of our (ἡμῶν) ancestors" who has acted this way (cf. Acts 22:14)—Israel is being renewed and restored through Jesus. This phrase has been understood two ways: (i) bringing Jesus "onto the human scene" in his public ministry (cf. 3:26);[41] or (ii) "raised" refers to Jesus's resurrection.[42] In favor of (i), Bruce suggests that ὕψωσεν, "exalted" (5:31), may concern resurrection, and so that idea is likely excluded here. In favor of (ii), the parallel in 13:22 reads ἤγειρεν τὸν Δαυὶδ αὐτοῖς εἰς βασιλέα, "[God] raised up David for them as king." Similarly, uses of ἐγείρω, "raise," with God as subject and Jesus as object in Luke-Acts suggest that, unless there is a prepositional phrase or other co-textual signal to the contrary, ἐγείρω concerns Jesus's resurrection.[43] Elsewhere in Acts, the contrast of Jesus's death—here through the murderous action of the Sanhedrin (v. 30b)—and God's action in raising Jesus (v. 30a) are strongly indicative of the "raising" being Jesus's resurrection (2:23–24; 3:15; 4:10; 10:39–40; 13:28–30; 17:3).

ὃν ὑμεῖς διεχειρίσασθε, "whom you yourselves murdered." The emphatic personal pronoun ὑμεῖς, "you yourselves," underlines that Peter and the apostles are holding the Sanhedrin responsible, at least in part, for Jesus's death (see *Comment* on 5:28). διεχειρίσασθε is forceful, with the sense "kill forcibly and

40 *NewDocs* 2:105 cites a second-century BC example of this construction.
41 Bruce, *Acts* (1990), 172.
42 Barrett, *Acts*, 1:28.
43 With prepositional phrase: Luke 7:16; with an expression clarifying that it is Jesus's resurrection: Acts 4:10; 10:40; 13:30; without prepositional phrase: Luke 9:22; 24:6, 34; Acts 13:37. See also n40 above.

with malicious intent";[44] it is found only here and 26:21 in NT. This accusation is shocking and offensive, asserting that the Sanhedrin's actions were deeply shameful,[45] as the Sanhedrin's reaction in 5:33 shows: they consider that they rightly did away with a messianic pretender who claimed a unique relationship of sonship to God (Luke 22:66–71; 23:2).

κρεμάσαντες ἐπὶ ξύλου, "by hanging on a tree," denotes the means of Jesus's murder. ξύλον, "tree," here is the cross:[46] six of twenty NT uses are in Luke-Acts (Luke 22:52; 23:31; Acts 5:30; 10:39; 13:29; 16:24; Revelation has seven uses, also of the cross). This expression echoes Deut 21:22–23 LXX:

> Now if sin is found in someone [which would lead to] a judgment of death, and he dies and *you hang him on a tree* (κρεμάσητε αὐτὸν ἐπὶ ξύλου), his body shall not remain overnight upon the tree, but you shall bury him that same day, for *anyone hanging on a tree is cursed by God* (κεκατηραμένος ὑπὸ θεοῦ πᾶς κρεμάμενος ἐπὶ ξύλου). (my translation)

The practice is that the bodies of those stoned to death were then publicly exposed by hanging, shamefully demonstrating God's curse on them.[47] By the first century, 4QpNah [= 4Q169] frg. 3–4 I, 7–8, "for anyone hanging alive on the tree" (Wise, Abegg, and Cook), interprets the hanging as crucifixion rather than only post mortem (so also 11QT [= 11Q19] LXIV, 7–13; see n47).[48] 11QT LXIV, 10–12 echoes Deut 21:23 and instructs that the body should not be left hanging overnight but must be buried on the same day, as required by Deuteronomy. Similarly, Josephus, *Ant.* 4.8.6 §202, echoes the process of stoning and hanging from Deut 21:23. This phrase in Acts evokes the whole of Deut 21:22–23 and thereby indicates both that the Jewish leaders' (mistaken) judgment was that Jesus was cursed by God (cf. 1 Cor 1:23) and that their error was anticipated in Scripture (cf. Gal 3:13).[49] This use probably reflects a widespread early Christian tradition of seeing the death of Jesus through the lens of Deut 21:22–23, recognizing and responding to the disgrace involved in such a death[50]—and quite possibly in response to Jewish opponents citing Deut 21:22–23 against believers.[51]

---

44 "διαχειρίζω," BDAG 240.

45 Gowler, *Host*, 279–80.

46 "ξύλον," BDAG 685, §2.c.

47 Marshall, "Acts," 555; Reardon, "Hanging," 409–10.

48 Reardon, "Hanging," 412–14.

49 Bock, *Proclamation*, 208–9; Barrett, *Acts*, 1:289–90; Bruce, *Acts* (1990), 172; cf. full discussion of Jewish interpretation of Deut 21:22–23 in Chapman, *Perceptions*, 117–49.

50 Peterson, "Motif," 100–101.

51 E.g., Trypho, Justin's Jewish interlocutor in the second century, Justin Martyr, *Dial.* 32. See also Hengel and Deines, *Pre-Christian*, 83–84; Wilcox, "Tree," esp. 90–94; contrast Chapman, *Perceptions*, 241–44, who argues that "hanging on a tree" represents a "standard Semitism of the age."

31 τοῦτον, "This is the one." In similar manner to Acts 2:23, 32, 36, this fronted demonstrative pronoun moves the focus to Jesus[52] and shifts attention from the mistaken human verdict on him to God's verdict in exalting him.

ὁ θεὸς ἀρχηγὸν καὶ σωτῆρα ὕψωσεν τῇ δεξιᾷ αὐτοῦ, "God exalted to his right side to be leader and savior," echoes the themes and words of 2:33–35 (see *Comment* there), and it is therefore likely that the ascension is in view here as well as there. Jesus's exaltation in the ascension by God's power to the place of honor at God's right side now establishes his authority, expressed as that of ἀρχηγὸν καὶ σωτῆρα, "leader and savior."

ἀρχηγός, "leader," echoes 3:15 (see *Comment* there),[53] although this is a unique NT use without a qualifying genitive; it stresses Jesus's primacy, perhaps by contrast with Moses[54] or any other human leader of the Jewish people—Jesus is now the one who leads the people of God.

σωτήρ, "savior," points back to the christologically rich description of Jesus in Luke 2:11, σωτὴρ ὅς ἐστιν χριστὸς κύριος, "a savior, who is the Messiah, the Lord." This term, not heard in Luke-Acts since Luke 2:11, signals that Jesus saves; what follows indicates what it is from which he saves, and the means by which people enter into that salvation. Strikingly, σωτήρ is a biblical designation of God[55] as well as (less frequently) of human deliverers sent by God (e.g., Jdg 3:9, 15; Neh 9:27). It may have become a messianic designation by NT times (1 En. 48:7; 51:5a).[56] The Hebrew name "Jesus/Joshua" means "YHWH is salvation" (cf. Matt 1:21), and so the use of "savior" for Jesus would be natural.

[τοῦ] δοῦναι μετάνοιαν τῷ Ἰσραὴλ καὶ ἄφεσιν ἁμαρτιῶν, "in order to give repentance to Israel and forgiveness of sins." "Despite the gravity of the offenses committed against him, God is ready to forgive, but this requires repentance."[57] This purpose clause (signaled by the infinitive δοῦναι, "to give") explains that Jesus saves from sins and does this through people's repentance. It is notable that three of Acts's five uses of "forgiveness of sins" are collocated with the mistaken judgment of those who hang Jesus on a tree in disgrace (here with Acts 5:30; 10:39, 43; 13:29, 38),[58] showing that Jesus's shameful death brings the offer of forgiveness.[59] μετάνοιαν τῷ Ἰσραήλ, "repentance to Israel," renews attention on Jesus's mission of restoring Israel (see *Comment* on 1:4–8; 2:36;

52 Culy and Parsons, *Acts*, 100.

53 Cf. Soards, *Speeches*, 52.

54 So Jones, "Title," 633.

55 E.g., LXX Deut 32:15; 1 Sam 10:19; Pss 23:5 (MT 24:5); 24:5 (MT 25:5); 26:1 (MT 27:1); 61:3 (MT 62:3, EVV 62:2); 94:1 (MT 95:1); Isa 12:2; 17:10; 45:15, 21; 62:11; Bar 4:22; Jdt 9:11; 1 Macc 4:30; 3 Macc 6:29, 32; 7:16; cf. Luke 1:47.

56 O'Neill, *Theology* (1970), 144; Smalley, "Christology," 362.

57 Dupont, *Salvation*, 68.

58 So Reardon, "Hanging," 419. The other uses of ἄφεσις ἁμαρτιῶν, "forgiveness of sins," in Acts are 2:38; 26:18.

59 Contra Rese, *Motive*, 116, who does not notice the connection of forgiveness and hanging on a tree and thus claims that, for Luke, Jesus's death is "only the antithesis of God's saving action" (my translation).

3:19–21; 4:10); Israel is called to reject its leaders' actions in murdering Jesus and change to a new view of Jesus as exalted by God (see *Comment* on 2:38). The location here is significant: Peter is speaking to the Sanhedrin, the leaders of Israel, who bear responsibility for Jesus's death (5:28, 30), and thus there is a particular focus on that sin and therefore a continuing opportunity for these Jewish leaders to repent, although—strikingly—there is no call to the Sanhedrin to repent here[60] (cf. *Comment* on 2:38). The reference to "Israel" also includes a broader turning back to God, in tune with John the baptizer's call to repent and offer of forgiveness (Luke 3:3, 7–9). In what sense does Jesus (not God here) give (δοῦναι) repentance? Acts 11:18 uses a similar phrase (τοῖς ἔθνεσιν ὁ θεὸς τὴν μετάνοιαν εἰς ζωὴν ἔδωκεν, "to the gentiles God has given the repentance that leads to life"), and cf. 3:26 (with *Comment* there). Barrett reads both passages as indicating that God himself *enables* the repentance,[61] whereas Conzelmann considers that God simply gives the *opportunity* for repentance.[62] More probably, both elements are present: "God's gift of repentance refers to a new opportunity to repent, but it also refers to God's dynamic action in people's lives to bring them to repent."[63] This has the benefit of understanding "to give" (δοῦναι) in the same sense in relation to the two objects, repentance and forgiveness—both are offered through Jesus and both are enabled and empowered by Jesus (and, as 5:32 will show, by the Spirit). Forgiveness on the side of the forgiver entails both a recognition that there has been offence and wrongdoing and the readiness to set this aside and not allow it to affect the future of the relationship. On the side of the one forgiven, repentance involves the open admission of offence and wrongdoing against the other and the request for forgiveness and a restored relationship.[64]

32 ἡμεῖς ἐσμεν μάρτυρες τῶν ῥημάτων τούτων, "We ourselves are witnesses of these things." The emphatic personal pronoun ἡμεῖς, "we ourselves," contrasts sharply with the emphatic ὑμεῖς, "you yourselves" (v. 30)—i.e., "you who crucified Jesus"—and highlights both that the speakers are eyewitnesses of God's actions for and through Jesus and—because it is the apostles speaking (v. 29)—the particular role of the apostolic band as witnesses (see *Comment* on 1:8, 22; cf. Luke 21:13, in the context of Jesus's warning of persecution). Luke is claiming to convey eyewitness testimony of the central events of Jesus's death, resurrection, and ascension to his readers.

καὶ τὸ πνεῦμα τὸ ἅγιον ὃ ἔδωκεν ὁ θεὸς τοῖς πειθαρχοῦσιν αὐτῷ, "along with the Holy Spirit, whom God gives to those who obey him." The conjunction of human testimony and the Spirit is found in 1:8 and recalls the Pentecost

60 Ovey, *Feasts*, 47.
61 *Acts*, 1:291; also Dupont, *Salvation*, 75.
62 *Acts*, 42; also Fitzmyer, *Acts*, 338.
63 Tannehill, *Shape*, 93; Stenschke, *Portrait*, 160–61; cf. Ravens, *Luke*, 152–53; Calvin, *Acts*, 1:149.
64 On forgiveness, see the superb discussion in Volf, *Free*, 127–224, esp. 165–91.

event and speech (cf. 2:38). Given the Jewish understanding of the Spirit as speaking of God in action, Peter is claiming that God co-testifies with the apostles concerning Jesus (cf. Isa 43:10 LXX γένεσθέ μοι μάρτυρες, κἀγὼ μάρτυς, λέγει κύριος ὁ θεός, "Be my witnesses, and I too am a witness, says the Lord God"; John 15:26–27), not only by God's actions in raising and exalting Jesus but in enabling and empowering their testimony to be both bold (cf. 4:13, 29, 31, all in the sequence around the previous Sanhedrin hearing) and effective—a testimony expressed in both words and in the life of the believing community (e.g., 4:32–35).[65] The added witness of the Spirit demonstrates that there is the required dual testimony to Jesus (Deut 19:15).[66] The growing portrait of the Spirit in personal terms is reinforced here by the activity of testimony, which is inherently personal. Peter's further claim that God gives the Spirit to those who obey God "bookends" his speech with uses of πειθαρχέω, "obey" (Acts 5:29), signaling that this is the central issue: will the Sanhedrin's actions show obedience to God, or are their decision-making processes merely human? There is an implicit invitation throughout Peter's speech to the Sanhedrin to change their view and thus become part of the renewed Israel of the Spirit—the door to repentance is open to them. However, the parallel thus far with the previous hearing before the Sanhedrin, where Peter and John speak of God and the Sanhedrin do not even mention God, is very striking (4:5–22; see *Explanation there*). What follows will present a significant alternative voice in the Sanhedrin.

33 sketches the first response to Peter's speech: διεπρίοντο, "[they] were beside themselves with rage." The imperfect of this verb and ἐβούλοντο, "began to want," portray the Sanhedrin's immediate reaction. Both imperfects are inceptive, indicating entering into a state that continued; the rage leads to the desire to kill (ἀνελεῖν). διαπρίω derives from πρίω, "saw through, saw asunder," and portrays the Sanhedrin being (as we would say) "cut to the quick" (cf. the Pentecost crowd's reaction, 2:37). It denotes "strong emotion of any kind" and can denote grinding teeth.[67] It need not be negative but is so here and in 7:54 (the only other NT use), where it is collocated with grinding teeth.

34 introduces the second, more measured, reaction to Peter's words. ἀναστὰς δέ τις ἐν τῷ συνεδρίῳ, "However, a certain [one] . . . rose in the Sanhedrin." ἀναστάς, "rose," echoes the beginning of v. 17, and thus contrasts the Pharisee Gamaliel's response with that of the Sadducees and the high priest and his companions. Here, the qualifying phrase ἐν τῷ συνεδρίῳ, "in the Sanhedrin," indicates a literal rising (to stand up), in addition to a speedy response (as in v. 17)—for the likelihood is that Gamaliel's response was rapid in order to avoid the kind of mob reaction that leads to Stephen's death (7:57–58).

65 Cf. Peterson, *Acts*, 223; Jervell, *Apostelgeschichte*, 208–9.
66 See Trites, *Concept*, 152–53.
67 "διαπρίω," LSJ, §II; Barrett, *Acts*, 1:291.

τις . . . Φαρισαῖος ὀνόματι Γαμαλιήλ, νομοδιδάσκαλος τίμιος παντὶ τῷ λαῷ, "a certain Pharisee, Gamaliel by name, a teacher of the law respected by all the people." The great respect in which Gamaliel is held explains why the Sanhedrin listen to him and accept his advice.[68] We know from rabbinic writings of a famous first-century Jewish teacher called Gamaliel, sometimes called "the Elder" (e.g., m. ʿOr. 2:12; m. Roš Haš. 2:5; m. Yebam. 16:7) to distinguish him from a later Gamaliel, who appears to be the earlier Gamaliel's grandson. The rabbinic sources call him Rabban (= "my master"), a title normally given to presidents of the Sanhedrin, although it is historically unlikely that Gamaliel presided, since prior to AD 70 the high priest presided over the Sanhedrin (and Pharisees were a lay movement, not priests).[69] In tune with Luke's τίμιος παντὶ τῷ λαῷ, "respected by all the people," m. Soṭah 9:15 records, "When Rabban Gamaliel the Elder died, the glory of the Torah came to an end, and cleanness and separateness (*pərîšût*) perished." Bruce notes the use of *pərîšût* as a pun suggesting "that he was the last of the true Pharisees."[70] It may be that the people's respect is somewhat ironic, for "the people" are a fickle character in Luke's Gospel, switching from favoring Jesus (Luke 18:43; 19:47–48; 20:19; 21:38; 22:2; cf. Acts 2:47) to rejecting him (Luke 23:13–25). Further, Jesus warns against the Pharisees who seek honor from people rather than God (Luke 16:15). "Gamaliel may well be respected by the λαός, but the λαός are not respected by the reader."[71] Some see this Gamaliel as Hillel's grandson, although the evidence is late and debated (b. Šabb. 15a).[72] It is likely that this is the Gamaliel mentioned here in Acts and named as Paul's teacher (Acts 22:3). His name means "my reward is God" and, although an ancient name (Num 2:20; 7:54), it was not widely used until the first century AD.[73]

The Pharisees, mentioned for the first time in Acts here, are known to readers of Luke's Gospel as teachers of the law of whom Jewish people think highly and with whom Jesus at times disputes.[74] Nevertheless, Pharisees—including their leaders—offer Jesus hospitality (Luke 7:36; 11:37; 14:1) and warn Jesus of Herod's plot to kill him (13:31). Although Luke's portrait of the Pharisees seems superficially more mixed than those of Mark or Matthew, in fact Luke consistently characterizes the Pharisees as imperceptive, both of Jesus and of what God is now doing in and through Jesus.[75] Until now

68 Darr, *Character*, 116–18.
69 More fully on Gamaliel, see Neusner, *Traditions*, 1:341–76; Schürer, 1:367–68; see also Josephus, *J.W.* 4.3.9 §159; *Life* 38 §190. 60 §309.
70 *Acts* (1990), 175.
71 Darr, "Irenic," 135.
72 See Schürer, 1:367n47.
73 Williams, "Names," 86.
74 Luke 5:17, 21, 30, 33; 6:2, 7; 7:39; 11 38–39, 42–43, 53; 12:1; 14:3; 16:14; 17:20; 18:10–11; 19:39.
75 Luke 7:30; cf. 5:21, 30, 33; 6:2, 7, 11; 7:39, 44–47; 11:37–44, 53–54; 12:1; 14:12–14; 15:2;

Luke has not mentioned that there are Pharisees in the Sanhedrin but has portrayed the Sanhedrin as consisting of the high priest and his associates, including Sadducees (4:1; 5:17). Luke's passion narrative does not mention Pharisees among the Sanhedrin (Luke 22:66; 23:13; contrast Matt 27:62; John 18:3), although their presence and beliefs will be important in Paul's later hearing (Acts 23:6–9; cf. 26:5). Pharisaic membership of the Sanhedrin in the first century is highly probable.[76] The Pharisees, although a lay (rather than priestly) group, were considered the supreme experts in interpreting Jewish tradition, especially oral tradition (Josephus, *J.W.* 1.5.1 §110; 2.8.12 §162; *Ant.* 17.2.4 §41; *Life* 38 §191). Paul's own Pharisaic training allows him to claim strong loyalty to ancestral Jewish traditions (Acts 26:5; cf. Phil 3:5). It is this strong adherence to Jewish tradition that causes a dispute begun by Pharisaic believers concerning the place of circumcision and the Jewish law for gentile believers (Acts 15:5).[77]

ἐκέλευσεν ἔξω βραχὺ τοὺς ἀνθρώπους ποιῆσαι, "[he] ordered the people to be put outside for a short time," demonstrates the regard which Gamaliel had, for he could instruct such action to be taken.

35 προσέχετε ἑαυτοῖς, "be very careful" (lit., "watch out for yourselves"). Gamaliel warns against an unwise course of action. This expression is used by Luke alone in the NT (Luke 12:1; 17:3; 21:34; Acts 20:28), although προσέχω + ἑαυτοῦ/σεαυτοῦ is quite common in LXX (19x), notably in warning against a bad idea (Gen 24:6; Exod 19:12; 34:12) or godless behavior (Deut 4:9, 23; 6:12; 8:11; 11:16; 12:19, 30; Tob 4:12, 12, etc.). Warning against a bad idea and unwise action are present here, for Gamaliel goes on to argue that acting against the apostles is a bad idea because there is the possibility that their mission is of divine origin (Acts 5:38–39), enunciating a principle found in Deut 18:21–22; m. 'Abot 4:11 (see *Comment* on 5:38–39); Acts 5:17.[78]

36–37 Gamaliel turns to cite two historical precedents in support of his argument that the Sanhedrin should leave the apostles alone: the rebellions of Theudas and Judas. It may be that the presence of these parallels implies that others were identifying Jesus as such a "sign-prophet."[79] In both cases, Gamaliel stresses that the rebellions dissipated after the death of their leader, and thus he argues that the Sanhedrin should be circumspect in their treatment of the apostles (v. 38). It is interesting that he only offers negative examples,

16:14; 18:9–14; 19:39; see discussion in Darr, *Character,* 86, 92–115; Darr, "Irenic," 126–34; contra Ziesler, "Luke." For valuable overviews of the Pharisees in Luke, see Mason, "Chief Priests," 134–42; Gowler, *Host,* 177–274.

76 Schürer, 2:213.

77 On the Pharisees more generally, see Schürer, 2:388–403; S. Mason, "Pharisees," *DNTB* 782–87; A. J. Saldarini, "Pharisees," *ABD* 5:289–303.

78 Hyytiäinen, "Gamaliel Tradition," 12.

79 Trumbower, "Historical Jesus," 509, 516–17; cf. Barnett, "Prophets," who argues that those after Jesus may have been influenced by Jesus himself in their style and actions.

thus implying that the believers will go the same way[80]—Luke clearly thinks otherwise! There are severe difficulties in understanding Gamaliel's account of Theudas (v. 36) and Judas (v. 37) (see below); the Theudas reference is "quite intractable,"[81] leading Swain to propose that Gamaliel's speech is misplaced and should be in Acts 12.[82] Swain's suggestion, however, leaves the same problem of anachronism, as well as creating misplacement of a number of details, as he recognizes.[83]

36 Gamaliel's speech gives little detail about Theudas: he was "claiming to be someone important," λέγων εἶναί τινα ἑαυτόν; cf. the description of Simon, 8:9, the only other biblical Greek passage using this expression: 8:9 adds μέγαν, "great"; contrast Peter's pointing away from himself to Jesus, 3:12–16.[84] About four hundred men followed Theudas, he was executed (ἀνηρέθη), and his followers disappeared. The parallel with Jesus is clear: he is dead, and so (Gamaliel implies) the likelihood is that his followers will disperse.

Who was Theudas? We know a Theudas from Josephus (*Ant.* 20.5.1 §§97–99) as the leader of a rebellion. Josephus calls him γόης, "a magician," which connotes "swindler, cheat,"[85] and says Theudas claimed to be προφήτης "a prophet," able to part the waters of the river, a claim to replicate Israel's entry into the land under Joshua (cf. Josh 3) or the feats of Elijah and Elisha (2 Kgs 2:1–18). Josephus states that τὸν πλεῖστον ὄχλον, "a great part of the people," followed Theudas (by contrast with four hundred here). Fadus, the procurator, sent mounted troops against them, killing many and capturing others. Theudas was decapitated (ἀποτέμνουσι τὴν κεφαλήν) and his head taken to Jerusalem (presumably for public display). Josephus states these events happened while Fadus was procurator of Judea, which dates this event to ca. AD 44–46.[86] These events took place well after both the ostensible date of Gamaliel's speech (early-to-mid-30s AD) and the time of Judas the Galilean's rebellion (Acts 5:37, ca. AD 6; see below). Three main explanations have been offered: (i) Luke makes an error: Luke intends to refer to the same person as Josephus (so Eusebius, *Hist. eccl.* 2.11.1–3), but makes an historical error[87] from inadequate use of Josephus, an erroneous source, or a simple mistake.[88] In particular, Pervo suggests Luke knew Josephus's writings and erred in his use of them.[89] However, if Luke were using Josephus, it is a little surprising that he does not mention Theudas's claim to be a prophet,

80 Darr, "Irenic," 136.
81 Hemer, *Book*, 175.
82 Swain, "Gamaliel's Speech."
83 Swain, "Gamaliel's Speech," 342.
84 So Sleeman, *Geography*, 129.
85 "γόης," BDAG 204.
86 On this Theudas, see further Barnett, "Prophets," 680–81.
87 E.g., Haenchen, *Acts*, 252; Schneider, *Apostelgeschichte*, 1:400–401.
88 Barrett, *Acts*, 1:296.
89 *Acts*, 148; *Dating*, 158–59.

for in Luke's presentation that would contrast nicely with Jesus as the true prophet like Moses (Acts 3:22–23; 7:37).[90] For this and other reasons, it is unlikely that Luke knew Josephus's writings.[91] (ii) Josephus makes an error by dating Theudas wrongly to the time of Fadus. Josephus does make errors in places; e.g., Cohen identifies a number of inconsistencies between *J.W.* and *Life*, including six chronological differences.[92] (iii) Our information is incomplete: Luke and Josephus refer to different men of the same name.[93] Josephus reports a large number of uprisings around the turn of the eras (*Ant.* 17.10.4–8 §§269–85; *J. W.* 2.4.1–3 §§55–65) and gives few of the names of their leaders. Theudas was a fairly common Greek name[94] and was also used as a familiar form (hypocorism) of Theodotus, Theodorus, Theodotion, etc.[95] Knowling notes that Josephus mentions four Simons as leaders of rebellions within a forty-year period and similarly three Judases in a ten-year period.[96] It is thus debatable whether Luke's Theudas is the same as Josephus's Theudas.[97] In my judgment, (iii) is most likely, given Luke's general accuracy with details of names and places, although (i) and, less likely, (ii) are also possible. The paucity of evidence makes certainty impossible.[98]

37 μετὰ τοῦτον, "After him," places Judas later than Theudas. Judas the Galilean also led a rebellion ταῖς ἡμέραις τῆς ἀπογραφῆς, "at the time of the census," most probably the census under Quirinius (Luke 2:2)[99] and, like Theudas, was killed (with similar vagueness about the means) and his followers were scattered. Again, the parallel Gamaliel implies with Jesus is clear. Judas here is very probably to be identified with the Judas in Josephus (*Ant.* 20.5.2 §102). Both Josephus and Luke have a Judas leading a rebellion at the time of a census (Josephus has Judas collaborate with a Pharisee, Sadduk [= Zadok?]), and Josephus identifies the uprising's cause as the taxation associated with the census (*Ant.* 18.1.1 §§1–4; *J.W.* 2.8.1 §§117–18; 2.17.8 §433; 7.8.1 §253); it is highly likely this is the same man.[100] Josephus claims Judas as the ἡγεμών, "cofounder," with the Pharisee Sadduk, of the "fourth philosophy" (*Ant.* 18.1.1 §9; 18.1.6 §23), a group generally recognized as

---

90 Cf. Witherington, *Acts*, 238.
91 With Sterling, *Historiography*, esp. 281–82; contra Mason, *Josephus*, 251–95.
92 Cohen, *Josephus*, 3–8, 233–34.
93 E.g., Barnett, *Birth*, 199–200; Bruce, *Acts* (1990), 176–77.
94 *NewDocs*, 4:183–85 §101, cites some thirty examples; Hemer, *Book*, 162n5, 225, adds a number of others.
95 Barrett, *Acts*, 1:293; Williams, "Names," 99–100.
96 "Acts," 158.
97 Cf. Barnett, "Prophets," 294n2; Hemer, *Book*, 162–63n5.
98 With Johnson, *Acts*, 99.
99 For helpful analysis and response to the claim that Luke has mis-dated this census, see Nolland, *Luke*, 1:99–102; Wright, *Who*, 88–89; and cf. Huebner, *Papyri*, 31–50.
100 Barrett, *Acts*, 1:294; Hemer, *Book*, 163.

the revolutionaries later known as the Zealots. Josephus tells us nothing of Judas's demise.[101]

38–39 There is great irony in Gamaliel, a Pharisee—and thus one of a group who "rejected God's purpose for themselves" (Luke 7:30)—offering advice on how not to oppose God's will.[102] The Sanhedrin—presumably including Gamaliel—had an earlier opportunity to repent of their mistaken view of Jesus but declined to do so (Acts 4:4–22) and continued to pursue the apostles and imprison them (5:17–18). The Pharisaic members—who, ironically, believe in the resurrection of the dead! (26:8)—reject the apostles' testimony to Jesus's resurrection (5:30–32) and thus continue to show the lack of perception they displayed in Luke's Gospel (see *Comment* on v. 34). Luke's readers know that the apostles' ministry and message are ἐκ θεοῦ, "from God," and thus can see that Gamaliel's attempted "neutrality" is not only impossible but deeply mistaken and dangerous—he himself gives no sign of accepting the apostolic testimony to Jesus's resurrection[103] and thus should not be seen as sympathetic to the believers or an "almost Christian."[104] Gamaliel's advice has a partial parallel in m. 'Abot 4:11: "R. Yohanan Hassandelar [= sandal maker] says, 'Any gathering which is for the sake of Heaven is going to endure. And any which is not for the sake of Heaven is not going to endure'" [Neusner]. Gamaliel's speech prevents the Sanhedrin stoning the believers—at least for now (it is Saul, taught by this same Gamaliel, who persecutes and kills believers, 22:3–5; 9:1–2)—but it does not prevent the Sanhedrin from publicly shaming the apostles by beating them (vv. 40, 41). The Sanhedrin act in a way that shows they are θεομάχοι, "fighting against God."[105] The cognate verb is used in Euripides for people who oppose new gods and usually suggests that the gods will punish those people for their actions (*Bacch.* 45, 325, 541, 1255–56; cf. Lucian, *Jupp. Trag.* 45).[106] Cf. Josephus, *Ant.* 18.8.1 §§259–60, reporting Philo as telling Jewish people in Alexandria that Gaius ἤδη τὸν θεὸν ἀντιπαρεξάγοντος, "was now bringing God into action against himself" (my translation), and *J.W.* 5 §378, ἀκούετε δ' ὅμως, ἵνα γνῶτε μὴ μόνον Ῥωμαίοις πολεμοῦντες ἀλλὰ καὶ τῷ θεῷ, "listen to me, so that you may understand that you are not only waging war against the Romans, but against God" (my translation).[107] Although it is unlikely that Luke is influenced by

101 For full discussion of Judas, see Black, "Judas."
102 Darr, *Character*, 119.
103 Sleeman, *Geography*, 129.
104 Contra Chrysostom, *Hom. Act.* 14; Brawley, *Luke-Acts*, 97–98; Tomson, "Gamaliel's Counsel," 592–96. The phrase "almost Christian" echoes Acts 26:28 and is the title of a John Wesley sermon based on that verse, preached at St Mary the Virgin, Oxford, as a University Sermon on 25 July 1741.
105 Johnson, *Function*, 197–98. On the use of this term in Josephus and 2 Maccabees, see Crabbe, *Luke/Acts*, 231–34.
106 Weaver, *Plots*, 136–39.
107 See the valuable discussion of the latter Josephus passage in conversation with this part of Acts, Crabbe, "Being Found."

Euripides,[108] the implication that danger from the gods followed from fighting against them would have been recognized by at least some Greco-Roman readers of Acts, who would thus have perceived the Sanhedrin as placing themselves in great danger from Israel's God.

ἐὰν ᾖ ἐξ ἀνθρώπων ἡ βουλὴ αὕτη ἢ τὸ ἔργον τοῦτο . . . εἰ δὲ ἐκ θεοῦ ἐστιν, "if this plan or this work turns out to be of human origin . . . if it is from God." Gamaliel presents two possible scenarios using two different conditional constructions. The first uses ἐάν + subjunctive (Acts 5:38, a third-class condition, usually considered more tentative[109]) and the second εἰ + indicative (a first-class condition, v. 39). Some see the first as implying less confidence in its protasis than the second.[110] However, the distinction need not imply that Gamaliel thought that the second was more likely than the first, since the second is still conditional.[111] Gamaliel's second conditional may use the construction with an indicative because this was the apostles' contention, "and so the concrete supposition to be discussed."[112] In addition, the second is "a more actual and pressing" issue:[113] if the first proves to be true, then it does not matter much, whereas if the work is truly of God, then it matters a great deal. The distinction, whatever it may be, is in Luke's presentation in Greek, since Gamaliel would speak in Aramaic.[114]

ἄφετε αὐτούς, "give them space." The verb conveys a call both to release the apostles from custody and to allow them to carry on with what they are doing.[115]

ἐπείσθησαν δὲ αὐτῷ, "They were won over by him," ironically echoes the uses of πείθω, "win over," in vv. 36, 37, for here Gamaliel wins over the Sanhedrin to the right course of action—allowing the apostles space—whereas the examples Gamaliel gave earlier were of leaders who won people over to mistaken and lost causes. Hearers of Acts already know that the apostles have been freed by an angel (vv. 19–20), showing that their proclamation is truly God's plan at work (cf. v. 38), and yet Gamaliel does not recognize this. Ironically, his words, as a nonbeliever, confirm that the Jesus movement is unstoppable.[116] Further, God works through his words to save the apostles from punishment

---

108 See Vögeli, "Lukas"; Lee, *Luke-Acts*, 205–7; cf. Dibelius, *Studies*, 189–91.

109 Moule, 150.

110 E.g., Gowler, *Host*, 278 wrongly sees εἰ, "if," as having the force of "since"; see n112 below.

111 Zerwick, §308.

112 Zerwick, §307; also cited by Darr, "Irenic," 137n42. Cf. BDF, §372.1; Wallace, 690: "The first-class condition indicates *the assumption of truth for the sake of argument*" (his italics). For example, Jesus states, "If I cast out (εἰ + indicative ἐκβάλλω) demons by Beelzebul . . ." (Luke 11:19), not implying that he actually does so but accepting the premise of his opponents (Luke 11:18b) in order to show that it leads to nonsense; cf. Zerwick, §306.

113 Zerwick, §307.

114 Bruce, *Acts* (1990), 178. Radermacher, 176, asserts too strongly that the distinction implied by the conditional represents Luke's own view; see critique by Zerwick, §308.

115 "ἀφίημι," BDAG 156, §5.a.

116 With Crabbe, "Being Found," 34. Kurz, *Reading*, 146, compares the irony of Caiaphas as high priest announcing the efficacy of Jesus's death for the nation (John 11:49–53).

and perhaps death—even opponents of the gospel can carry forward the gospel's advance. Gamaliel's problem is "fence-sitting."[117]

Hence, Luke suggests, faithful Judaism should not oppose the believing community[118]—thus, Luke is communicating to his (predominantly gentile) audience that Judaism itself is not to be condemned but only Jewish people who reject the messengers of the gospel. The issue of who speaks for God, raised in the earlier Sanhedrin hearing, rumbles on, and it is clear from God's action in freeing the apostles by sending an angel (vv. 19–25), the apostles' desire to obey God (v. 29), and God's action in exalting Jesus (v. 30) that Luke presents the apostles as the true divine spokespeople: they are "witnesses of these things" (v. 32).[119] However, Luke does not regard Gamaliel's approach as a "principle" to use more widely: for example, when it comes to the Jerusalem conference (15:6–29), James does not argue that the believers should "wait and see" whether God's blessing is on the gentile mission but is clear that a decision is being made to admit gentiles to the believing community without requiring circumcision (15:13–21).[120]

40 δείραντες, "beat." In this physical punishment and the following command not to speak, the authorities fulfill Luke 21:12. The punishment was probably thirty-nine lashes (2 Cor 11:24; cf. Acts 22:19), a punishment Jewish authorities could inflict (cf. m. Mak. 3:1–14 on various kinds of beating; a person could die from such a beating, 3:14). Such a treatment was designed as a warning against further unacceptable conduct.

παρήγγειλαν μὴ λαλεῖν ἐπὶ τῷ ὀνόματι τοῦ Ἰησοῦ, "they commanded them not to speak in the name of Jesus," echoes the Sanhedrin's earlier instruction (Acts 4:18; see *Comment* there), as well as Jesus's warning that they will be persecuted ἕνεκεν τοῦ ὀνόματός μου, "because of my name" (Luke 21:12). However, this does not look like Gamaliel's proposal to "give them space" (Acts 5:39); the Sanhedrin continues to work to suppress the apostolic proclamation. The apostles' response to the earlier instruction—defiance and continuing proclamation—signals that this instruction will not be obeyed either. Readiness to take risks to proclaim Jesus, even in the face of threats, is characteristic of the believing community in Acts (cf. 15:26; 21:13).

41–42 are transitional, closing this story by summarizing its outcome and also closing this section of the book, which describes the initial stages of the believing community's life. They parallel 28:30–31 in the continuing open gospel proclamation.[121]

---

117 Crabbe, "Being Found," 35.

118 Cf. Schille, *Apostelgeschichte*, 164; Marshall, *Portrayals*, 145.

119 See Strelan, "Gamaliel's Hunch," for a good discussion of the ways Luke shows Peter and Paul to be "of God," vindicating Gamaliel's "hunch."

120 See further the fascinating discussion in Lyons, "Words," critiquing the contrasting approaches of Gowler, *Host*, 274–80; Darr, *Character*, 116–20.

121 Barrett, *Acts*, 1:299.

41 μὲν οὖν, "so then," denotes "continuation": Luke is presenting the consequences which flow from the apostles' commitment in vv. 29–32.[122]

χαίροντες, "rejoicing," is a Lukan keynote for the life Jesus brings (most typically at the reception of the gospel or of Jesus himself[123]). Here, remarkably, the apostles do not merely rejoice *in* suffering but rejoice *at* suffering,[124] acting as Jesus calls them to do when they suffer for his sake (Luke 6:22–23).[125] This is the first of a number of uses of χαίρω, "rejoice," in Acts,[126] and the word group appears twenty times in Luke (see *Comment* on 2:46).[127]

κατηξιώθησαν ὑπὲρ τοῦ ὀνόματος ἀτιμασθῆναι, "they were considered worthy to be shamed for the sake of the name." The apostles rejoice because their suffering confirms that they are true followers of Jesus, identified with the suffering Messiah, as his own warnings and promises of persecution are fulfilled (Luke 12:4–15; 21:12–19).[128] καταξιόω is found only here and Luke 20:35; 2 Thess 1:5 in the NT, always in the aorist passive, suggesting that the implied actor is God (or perhaps the Lord Jesus).[129] The collocation with ἀτιμασθῆναι, "be shamed," seems an oxymoron,[130] for public punishment was considered shameful in the ancient world. Green paraphrases aptly, "they were counted worthy enough to have their honor deprived of them."[131] The combination is also another example of Luke's reversal motif, by which the disciples are honored, for they are thereby marked as truly belonging to their Lord[132] (cf. Luke 21:12–19; 10:16; John 15:18 for the close identification of Jesus and his disciples). Hence the suffering is marked as ὑπὲρ τοῦ ὀνόματος, "for the name," ironically echoing the Sanhedrin's prohibition to speak in Jesus's name (v. 40).

42 πᾶσάν τε ἡμέραν ἐν τῷ ἱερῷ καὶ κατ᾽ οἶκον οὐκ ἐπαύοντο διδάσκοντες καὶ εὐαγγελιζόμενοι, "Indeed every day, both in the temple and in homes, they did not cease teaching and proclaiming the good news." Luke stresses the comprehensive commitment of the apostles to their ministry: they do it "every day"; they do it in public ("in the temple") and in private ("in homes"; see *Comment* on κατ᾽ οἶκον in 2:46); they persist ("they did not cease," litotes); and they both teach and proclaim the good news. This is in continuity with their actions before the Sanhedrin hearing (v. 21): "it is as though nothing

122 Levinsohn, *Connections*, 142.

123 E.g., Luke 19:6, 37, 40; 24:41, 52–53; Acts 2:46; 8:8, 39; 13:48, 52; 16:34.

124 Conzelmann, *TDNT* 9:368.

125 I owe this connection to Brian Tabb. Elliott, *Faithful Feelings*, 167 observes the cognitive basis of joy.

126 See also 8:8, 39; 11:23; 12:14; 13:48, 52; 15:3, 23, 31; 23:26; and cf. the ἀγαλλιάω, "rejoice greatly," word group in 2:46; 16:34.

127 See also the helpful overview in Morrice, *Joy*, 91–99, esp. 96–99.

128 Cunningham, *Tribulations*, 198.

129 "καταξιόω," BDAG 523.

130 Bruce, *Acts* (1990), 179.

131 Green, "Happiness," 169.

132 So Barrett, *Acts*, 1:300.

had happened in between."[133] A greater contrast to the prohibition to speak in Jesus's name could hardly be found. This is the first use of εὐαγγελίζομαι, "proclaim good news," or its cognate noun εὐαγγέλιον, "good news, gospel," in Acts (see *Comment* on 10:36 for probable backgrounds to its use).

τὸν χριστόν Ἰησοῦν, "the Messiah was Jesus," is most probably a double accusative of object-complement[134] with an implied equative verb (cf. 18:5, 28).[135] Since χριστόν, "Messiah," has the article τόν, it should be identified as the object in the object-complement construction,[136] hence "the Messiah was Jesus."[137] Such a translation makes good sense in a Jewish context, as here, where the apostles proclaim the identity of the Messiah.

Explanation

As persecution of the believers intensifies—and of the apostles in particular as leaders of the community—so does God's action to ensure that their testimony continues unhindered. This section picks up from the previous Sanhedrin hearing (4:5–22), which resulted in Peter and John being told not to speak or teach in Jesus's name, by echoing that prohibition (5:28). By contrast with the previous hearing, the Sanhedrin are in a murderous mood (v. 33) and Luke's hearers wait to see how the apostles—and God—will respond.

The story alternates between the apostles suffering and speaking: imprisonment (vv. 17–18) is followed by the angel freeing them to speak of "this life" (vv. 19–21); the apostles are brought before the authorities (vv. 26–27) and speak freely of Jesus to them (vv. 29–32) in spite of the threat of danger (v. 33); the apostles are beaten (v. 40), which they see as an honor for the sake of "the name" (v. 41); and they are then free to persist in speaking freely of Jesus (v. 42).

Throughout this sequence of events, it is God who is the focus of what is happening. While human authorities seek to suppress testimony to Jesus, God acts so that the word is able to be heard and received: God frees his witnesses from prison (vv. 17–26); answering to God is far more important than to human—even religious—authorities (vv. 27–33); and God enables his witnesses to go on speaking (vv. 34–42).

So who is this God? What has this God done and what is this God now doing? He is the ancestral Jewish God (v. 30), now known as the one who raised Jesus from the dead (v. 30). This God exalted Jesus to the highest place, at his right side (v. 31), and now gives the Spirit to enable testimony to Jesus to those who obey him (v. 32). Jesus's ascended status, through which the

133 Cunningham, *Tribulations*, 199.
134 Wallace, 182–89.
135 See Barrett, *Acts*, 1:301; Bruce, *Acts* (1990), 179.
136 Cf. John 20:31 with the discussion of Carson, "Purpose," 639–51, esp. 642–45.
137 Contra Wallace, 184n32.

Spirit is poured out (2:33–36), again comes into focus, for his resurrection and exaltation show that he is the one marked by God as leader and savior (v. 31). Through Jesus, God remarkably offers and gives forgiveness to Israel, even to the apostles' audience, the Sanhedrin, who murdered Jesus (vv. 28, 30). Not only that, but through Jesus God enables people to turn back to God in repentance (v. 31), a theme that goes beyond what Peter has said earlier. God's work and actions are focused in and through Jesus and by the Spirit (vv. 30–32), although the Sanhedrin themselves do not even speak the name of Jesus: they only speak of "this name . . . this man's blood" (v. 28). By contrast, the apostles testify that Jesus now works from heaven to transform people, and potentially nations, on earth.

Who speaks for this God? The Sanhedrin represent the Jewish leadership, those who should speak for YHWH, Israel's ancestral God; Luke stresses their role here (vv. 21, 35; cf. 4:5–6). Now that God's purposes are focused in Jesus, however, the Sanhedrin are disobeying God, for they both murdered Jesus (5:30) and now seek to suppress the apostles' testimony to Jesus (vv. 28, 33, 40). Their disobedience means they forfeit their place as Israel's leaders and contrasts with the apostles' ready obedience to God (v. 29), an obedience that means that they receive the power of the Spirit promised by Jesus to enable them to respond to their accusers (v. 31; Luke 12:11–12). The leadership of the renewed and restored Israel is passing—indeed, has passed—from the disobedient Sanhedrin to the obedient apostles. The response YHWH seeks is obedience to Jesus. The door is still open; there is still a way back, if the Sanhedrin will repent (5:31) and obey (vv. 29, 32), for then God will give them the Spirit, who co-testifies with the apostles to the death, resurrection, and exaltation of Jesus and makes their meaning understood (v. 32; cf. 2:38).

And what of Gamaliel (5:34–39)? This elder statesman of the Sanhedrin superficially appears to speak positively of the apostles and their actions, but further investigation shows that he is hedging his bets and failing to commit himself. He seeks to stand on neutral ground, neither arguing for nor against the apostolic message, but there is no neutral ground, for people must decide whether they are with the Messiah and his people or against them. Gamaliel ironically speaks some truth, for the apostolic testimony to Jesus will be unstoppable (v. 39)—Acts will end with the message being "unhindered" (28:31)—but Gamaliel does not offer a reliable voice. He and the Sanhedrin are to be numbered among those "fighting against God" (5:39), and that is a highly dangerous place to be.

The story ends with a transition showing that the apparent dishonor of suffering is actually true honor (v. 41), for it is following in the footsteps of the suffering Messiah (v. 30; cf. Luke 6:22–23) and by implication accepting such dishonor will lead his people, like the suffering of the Messiah, to receiving honor from God. The apostles go on testifying to Jesus as Messiah in every situation where and at every time when they can (Acts 5:42)—that is the activity that honors Jesus and that is enabled by the Spirit (v. 32) and is the activity to which Luke calls his readers in their day.

D. Growth and Conflict (6:1–7)

Bibliography

Biggar, N. "Showing." **Blackman, E. C.** "Hellenists." **Blomberg, C. L.** *Neither,* 167–69. **Brehm, H. A.** "Meaning." **Brinkhof, J. H. A.** "Philip." **Bruce, F. F.** "Church." **Bultmann, R.** *Theology,* 1:54–56. **Cadbury, H. J.** "Hellenists," *BegC,* 5:59–74. **Capper, B. J.** "Community." ———. "Context," 350–55. **Catto, S. K.** *Synagogue,* 165–68. **Collins, J. N.** *Diakonia.* ———. *Diakonia Studies,* 152–61. **Coppens, J.** "L'imposition." **Daube, D.** "Reform." ———. *Testament,* 224–46. **Domagalski, B.** "Sieben." **Dunn, J. D. G.** *Beginning,* 241–57. **Dupont, J.** *Sources,* 62–72, 166. **Esler, P. F.** *Community,* 135–61. **Ferguson, E.** "Hellenists." ———. "Laying." **Finger, R. H.** "'Mary." ———. *Widows.* **Fiorenza, E. S.** *Memory,* 162–68. **Forbes, G. W. and S. D. Harrower.** *Raised,* 160–70. **Fraser, R.** "Office." **González, J. L.** "Reading." **Green, J. B.** *Practicing,* 43–70. **Hays, C. M.** *Ethics,* 225–32. ———. "Place." **Hengel, M.** *Acts,* 73–75. ———. *Between,* 1–29, 54–58. **Hill, C. C.** *Hellenists.* **Jeremias, J.** *Jerusalem,* 100–108. **Johnson, L. T.** *Function,* 211–13. **Johnson, S. E.** "Manual." **Kodell, J.** "Word." **Koet, B. J.** "Luke 10:38–42." **Koperski, V.** "Luke 10,38–42." **Larsson, E.** "Hellenisten." **Lee, S.-I.** *Jesus,* 175–208. **Lienhard, J. T.** "Acts 6:1–6." **Marshall, H.** "Palestinian." **McCaughey, J. D.** "Intention." **Moore, G. F.** *Judaism,* 2:174–75. **Moule, C. F. D.** "Once More." **Nagel, N. E.** "Twelve." **Pao, D. W.** "Waiters." **Penner, T. C.** *Praise.* **Pervo, R. I.** "ΠΑΝΤΑ," esp. 170–72. **Price, R. M.** *Widow,* 210–16. **Reicke, B. I.** *Glaube,* 115–17. **Reimer, I. R.** *Women,* 234–37. **Schnabel, E. J.** *Mission,* 1:653–68. **Schweizer, E.** *Order,* 63–76. **Seccombe, D. P.** "Charity." **Seim, T. K.** *Message,* 108–12. **Sell, P.** "Seven." **Smith, T. C.** "Significance." **Spencer, F. S.** *Portrait,* 189–211. ———. "Widows." **Strange, W. A.** *Problem,* 122–26. **Talbert, C. H.** *Reading Luke-Acts,* 47. **Theissen, G.** "Hellenisten." ———. "Liebeskommunismus," 707–9. **Thompson, A. J.** *One,* 93–96. ———. "Unity." **Trebilco, P. R.** *Self-designations,* 208–46. **Turner, M.** *Power,* 165–69, 408–12. **Tyson, J. B.** "Acts 6:1–7." **Walter, N.** "Apostelgeschichte 6.1." **Walton, S.** "Calling." ———. "Communism." ———. "Minority." **Weatherly, J. A.** *Responsibility,* 176–94.

Translation

1 In these days, that is, when the disciples were increasing in number,[a] grumbling
arose among the Greek speakers against the Hebrew speakers because[b] their widows
kept being neglected[c] in the daily distribution.[d] 2 So the Twelve called a meeting[e] of
the whole group of the disciples and said, "It is not right for us to neglect[f] God's word
to serve at tables.[g] 3 Instead, brothers and sisters, look for seven men from among you
who are well spoken of,[h] full of the Spirit and wisdom. We will put them in charge of
this matter; 4 but, as for us, we will devote ourselves to prayer and serving the word."
5 This idea pleased the whole group, and they selected Stephen, a man full of faith and
the Holy Spirit, Philip, Procorus, Nicanor, Timon, Parmenas, and Nicolaus, a proselyte
from Antioch. 6 They presented them[i] to the apostles and they prayed[j] and laid hands
on them. 7 God's word continued growing and the number of disciples in Jerusalem
continued to multiply, and a large group of priests became obedient[k] to the faith.

Notes

a. πληθυνόντων τῶν μαθητῶν, "when the disciples were increasing in number," temporal (pres.) gen. abs.

b. ὅτι, "because" (NRSVue; Culy and Parsons, *Acts,* 107); could be "that," introducing the content of their complaint (REB).

c. παρεθεωροῦντο, "[they] kept being neglected," impf., implying ongoing action.

d. διακονίᾳ, here "distribution," is more usually "service" (cf. uses in vv. 2, 4; "διακονία," BDAG 230, §4); it denotes the "service" of food to community members as part of their daily communal meals. See *Comment* on v. 1; cf. Finger, *Widows,* 256–57; Collins, *Diakonia,* 230–31. D* reads ἐν τῇ διακονίᾳ τῶν Ἑβραίων, "by the ministry of the Hebrews"; d and cop^{G67} have equivalents. This locates the problem in the hands of "Hebrews" who were carrying out the distribution. Although it may accurately represent what happened, it is difficult to see why all other witnesses would remove such a phrase if it were original; see Strange, *Problem,* 122–24.

e. προσκαλεσάμενοι, "having summoned"; "προσκαλεω," BDAG 881, §1.a.

f. καταλείψαντας, "to neglect," m. pl. acc. aor. ptc., adj., describing ἡμᾶς, "us" (see also next *Note*).

g. ἡμᾶς . . . διακονεῖν τραπέζαις, "for us . . . to serve at tables"; acc. + inf. following οὐκ ἀρεστόν ἐστιν, "it is not right"; "ἀρεστός," BDAG 130; BDF, §408.

h. μαρτυρουμένους, "well spoken of," aor. pass. ptcp.; the pass. voice here means "be well spoken of, be approved"; "μαρτυρέω," BDAG 617, §2.b.

i. D begins a new sentence οὗτοι ἐστάθησαν, "These were presented," clearly intending "these" to be the seven, and τῶν ἀποστόλων, οἵτινες προσυεξάμενοι, "the apostles, who prayed," by contrast with the reading found in the rest of the MS tradition, οὓς ἔστησαν ἐνώπιον τῶν ἀποστόλων, "whom they presented . . . before the apostles, and having prayed" (Rius-Camps and Read-Heimerdinger, *Message,* 2:17). The mainstream reading suggests that the whole group prayed and laid on hands, whereas D isolates the apostles as the ones who prayed and laid on hands, reflecting the practice of bishops in later Christian orthodoxy; with McCaughey, "Intention," 30–31.

j. Taking προσευξάμενοι, "prayed," as ptc. of attendant circumstances; Culy and Parsons, *Acts,* 110; cf. NEB, REB.

k. ὑπήκουον, "became obedient," inceptive impf.; 3 pl. verb with collective sg. subject πολύς . . . ὄχλος, "a large crowd"; Wallace, 400–401.

Form/Structure/Setting

Delimitation of pericope. This section's beginning is signaled by a temporal note (Ἐν . . . ταῖς ἡμέραις ταύταις, "In those days," v. 1) combined with a marker of switch of subject (δέ, untranslated) that locates this incident during the period of the church's growth and persecution. The dating is thus vague.

The ending is a summary (v. 7), which uses only imperfect main verbs to signal its summary character. Verse 7 echoes the growing number of disciples from v. 1, thus "bookending" the section: πληθυνόντων τῶν μαθητῶν, "the disciples were increasing in number," v. 1; ἐπληθύνετο ὁ ἀριθμὸς τῶν μαθητῶν, "the number of disciples continued to increase," v. 7.[1]

1 Penner, *Praise,* 64.

Sources/historicity. The difference between the task of table service for which the seven are ostensibly commissioned (v. 3) and the fact that at least two of them are proclaimers of the gospel (Stephen, 6:8–8:4; Philip, 8:5–40) has led some to suggest that Luke developed this story from other traditions to introduce the following stories. Lienhard, who is typical, reconstructs Luke's source as consisting of parts of vv. 1, 5–6 on the basis of peculiarly Lukan vocabulary (considered only against other NT books, rather than the wider world of ancient Greek) and the presence of rhetorical elements (which he also takes to be Lukan).[2] These criteria are inadequate for this conclusion: the presence of Lukan vocabulary and rhetorical features shows that Luke has told the story in his own words and style but not that he has invented it.

An influential historical reconstruction of the growth and development of the gentile mission among the earliest believers is rooted in a particular view of the groups designated Ἑλληνιστῶν, "Greek speakers," and Ἑβραίους, "Hebrew speakers" (v. 1; see *Comment* there). F. C. Baur claims that earliest Christianity divided into a Peter party and a Paul party,[3] and this scenario finds clear expression in Hengel[4] and Dunn.[5] These scholars see the Greek speakers and Aramaic speakers as representing (respectively) more liberal and more conservative forms of both Judaism and Jewish Christianity. The division among believers arose, on this view, from the need for Greek speakers and Aramaic speakers to meet for worship and teaching separately. These separate gatherings generated theological differences,[6] as well as the dispute over provision for widows, and led to a split after Stephen's murder.[7] The Greek speakers thus pioneered the gentile mission, rather than Peter (10:1–11:18), for they were the only group persecuted in 8:1b; they thus fled Jerusalem and began to evangelize gentiles (11:20).[8]

However, it is unlikely that Greek-speaking Jews who lived in Jerusalem spoke *no* Aramaic—they would need some Aramaic to manage daily life in the city[9]—and this suggests that there were communal meetings of the believers, as Acts portrays (7:2, cf. 5:12, 42), and/or that there were bilingual believers who moved between meetings of the two groups.[10] Luke's emphasis on the unity of the Jerusalem believers fits with this portrait (e.g., 1:14; 2:46; 4:24; 5:12), and this picture is plausible in a time of persecution, for a persecuted group unites for mutual support against its persecutors.[11] Thompson notes

2 "Acts 6:1–6."
3 *Christentum*, esp. 42–43.
4 *Acts*, 71–81; *Between*, 1–29, 54–58.
5 *Beginning*, 241–57.
6 Roloff, *Apostelgeschichte*, 117.
7 Cf. Esler, *Community*, 141–45.
8 Hengel, *Acts*, 73–75; cf. Bultmann, *Theology*, 1:54–56.
9 Schnabel, *Mission*, 1:654.
10 Marshall, "Palestinian," 277–80.
11 Schnabel, *Mission*, 1:655.

the widespread discussion of issues of unity in the ancient world, a discussion that "draws on historical realities" and infers that we cannot assume that Acts's emphasis on the believers' unity is necessarily an idealization.[12] Acts 6:1–7 paints a "warts and all" picture of tensions in the early believing community (see also the disagreements described in 15:36–41; 19:30–31; 21:1–14[13]), so the picture is not of unalloyed unity. Further, and significantly, we lack evidence for a "Hebrew" theological stance that differs in any recognizable way from that of the "Greek speakers."[14] (See also on Stephen's speech, 7:2–53, often taken as typifying "Greek-speaker" theology.) Moreover, the claim that the Hellenists' view was more "liberal" is improbable, for diaspora Jews who went to Jerusalem were intrinsically likely to hold "conservative" views (note the strong commitment of such people to temple and torah in 6:8–15; 21:27–29!).[15] Rather than Greek-speaking believers being persecuted for (e.g.) their anti-temple "liberal" views, it is Aramaic-speaking believers who are persecuted (4:1–22; 5:17–40; 12:1–3; 1 Thess 2:14–16).[16]

Hengel, following others going back to Harnack, suggests an Antiochene source may underly this story while conceding that Luke has here, as elsewhere, woven his sources so well into his cloth that they are impossible to identify with precision.[17] Dunn identifies the following features as suggesting that Luke used a source:[18] (i) the introduction of the terms Ἑλληνιστής, "Greek speaker," and Ἑβραῖος, "Hebrew speaker," without explanation; (ii) the contrast between the believers' unity in Acts 1–5 and the dispute in 6:1; (iii) the election of the seven as a "decline" from the theocracy portrayed earlier; (iv) the names of the seven, especially since five are not mentioned elsewhere in Acts; (v) Stephen and Philip's subsequent roles suggest that Luke is not inventing their origins as "waiters" at table; (vi) the mention of a synagogue in Jerusalem (6:9) is surprising, given the focus of the city on the temple; (vii) it is fellow Greek speakers who oppose Stephen, not the priests; (viii) the accusations against Stephen (6:14) bespeak a tradition of Jesus speaking against the temple (cf. Mark 14:57–58; John 2:19); (ix) the uniqueness of Stephen's speech in Acts, which is thus likely to draw on source material; (x) the temple motif running through the Greek speakers' stories; (xi) Stephen does not experience God's protection in the way Peter and John did (Acts 5:19–21;

---

12 "Unity," esp. 528–34 (quotation from 528); more fully, *One*.

13 Discussed in Thompson, "Unity," 537–41.

14 Marshall, "Palestinian," 279–81; Theissen, "Hellenisten; Walton, "Minority," 317–20; Hill, *Hellenists*, passim; contra Dunn, *Beginning*, 248–51.

15 With Esler, *Community*, 145–48.

16 Cf. Hill, *Hellenists*, 194; on the authenticity of 1 Thess 2:14–16, see Walton, *Leadership*, 163n124; Weatherly, *Responsibility*, 176–94. For fuller analysis, see Walton, "Minority"; Penner, *Praise*, 1–78; Hill, *Hellenists*, 5–17; Witherington, *Acts*, 240–47.

17 *Between*, 3–4; with Dupont, *Sources*, 166; Fitzmyer, *Acts*, 85. Helpful discussion: Dupont, *Sources*, 62–72.

18 *Beginning*, 242–44.

contrast 7:57–60); (xii) Paul confirms that he was a key persecutor of the early Christians in Jerusalem (1 Cor 15:9; Gal 1:13, 23; Phil 3:6); (xiii) "linguistic peculiarities" are found in these stories, such as the phrase πλήρης πνεύματος, "full of the Spirit."[19] The cumulative force of these arguments is strong, and they suggest that Luke is not creating this story *ex nihilo.*

Structure. This section is straightforwardly organized into five sentences with switches of subject marked by δέ (vv. 1, 2, 3) followed by continuations marked by καί (vv. 5, 7) and a final statement introduced by τέ (v. 7c). The first sentence sets the scene by introducing the situation of dispute and its cause (v. 1).[20] The next two sentences lay out the apostles' intervention, calling the disciples together and inviting them to choose suitable men to resolve the situation (vv. 2–4). The following sentence portrays the community's response to the apostles' words, accepting what they recommend and then choosing seven men for this task who are commissioned with prayer and the laying on of hands (vv. 5–6). A final sentence closes the section and transitions to the next by underlining the continuing success of the gospel among the people of Jerusalem (v. 7).

Levinsohn considers that the structure of vv. 5–7, using a series of continuative καί and final τέ, indicates that this story is part of a larger complex of stories concerning a Christian leader—here, Stephen—who will be the focus of what follows.[21] Thus Levinsohn argues that 6:7 should not be seen as the marker of the end of the first major section of Acts. Certainly, there is continuity into the following material (6:8–8:1a), but (see *Setting* below) there are also links back to earlier parts of the story. This means that, as often, Luke is not providing sharply divided and clear-cut sections but that sections have fuzzy boundaries.

Setting. This story adds to the picture of the earliest believers by showing them continuing to deal with difficulties, following the internal difficulty over Ananias and Sapphira (5:1–11) and the external threat from the Sanhedrin (5:17–42).[22] Here the issue is an internal dispute about care for those in need (6:1), which builds on the earlier picture of community meals but contrasts with the earlier positive picture of the community's life (2:42–27; 4:32–35, esp. 34; 5:12–16). This issue leads to a new feature, a group of seven given responsibility for supervising the sharing of food among needy believers (vv. 4–6). In naming the group, Luke introduces his readers to two key figures who will be in focus in the next sections of the story: Stephen (6:8–8:1a) and

19 Bruce, "Church," 645n15, adds the transitional formula Ἐν δὲ ταῖς ἡμέραις ταύταις, "In those days," as evidence of a new source, but Luke's quite wide use of this or a very similar phrase suggests we cannot be confident of this (Luke 1:39; 6:12; 19:42; 23:7; 24:18; Acts 1:15; 11:27).

20 Tyson, "Acts 6:1–7," 152, divides this into two stages according to his fourfold schema: v. 1a representing a statement of peace in the community, and v. 1b a threat. Stages three and four are (respectively) resolution, vv. 2–6, and restoration, v. 7.

21 *Connections,* 113–16.

22 Forbes and Harrower, *Raised,* 160.

Philip (8:4–40), thus transitioning into the explicit expansion of the gospel among non-Palestinian Jews (through Stephen) and outside Jerusalem and to an uncircumcised person (through Philip: note the implicit statement of this expansion in 5:16).

Koet[23] draws a fascinating parallel with Jesus's encounter with Martha and Mary (Luke 10:38–42), observing that Martha's role, which she desires her sister to share, is διακονεῖν, "to serve" (v. 40).[24] By contrast Mary is engaged in learning from Jesus, sitting at his feet (v. 39). Martha is invited by Jesus to participate in learning (v. 42), which is better, but not the *only* thing to do—people do need to eat! Koet argues that to read these stories together is to recognize the complementarity of learning and doing, of serving tables and serving the word. "The apostles stress that the διακονία of the Word takes precedence, but not at the expenses of the ministry of tables."[25] He thus rejects Collins's argument that the issue is that the Greek-speaking widows are not able to learn (see *Comment* on v. 1), and argues rather that the seven are people who embrace both doing (serving tables) and responsibility for the word, as Stephen and Philip demonstrate. The exegesis below agrees that Luke presents two forms of service which are complementary, not competitive, within the life of the community, while particular people may focus on one or other form of service.

Comment

1 Ἐν δὲ ταῖς ἡμέραις ταύταις, "In those days," marks the transition to this story, locating these events in the setting of the initial growth of the believing community in Jerusalem (5:42). Collins speculates that this co-text indicates that the lack in the daily distribution the Greek-speaking widows experienced was a lack of preaching.[26] This is very unlikely given the mention of τραπέζαις, "tables," which indicate the serving of food (6:2, see *Comment* there). Collins suggests that the "tables" signify meetings in homes, but that is not Luke's term for home meetings (2:46; 5:42; 20:20).

πληθυνόντων τῶν μαθητῶν ἐγένετο, "when the disciples were increasing in number." This is the first use of "disciples" for the believers in Acts, and Luke sets the context for this story as a time of growth (see also 5:42). The designation μαθηταί, "disciples," is found twenty-seven times in Acts and almost exclusively used for believers (the main possible exception is 19:1; see *Comment* there).[27] Uses in Acts are mainly plural, particularly groups of believers in

23 Koet, "Luke 10:38–42," esp. 52–63; see also Koperski, "Luke 10,38–42."

24 Koperski, "Luke 10,38–42," 517, notes other linguistic parallels between the passages, καταλείπω, "leave," and λόγος, "word." Her essay offers a nuanced analysis of a number of readings of these two passages in feminist scholarship.

25 Koet, "Luke 10:38–42," 58.

26 Collins, *Diakonia Studies*, 160.

27 For what follows, see Walton, "Calling," 226–29; Trebilco, *Self-designations*, 208–46.

Jerusalem, Damascus, Joppa, Syrian Antioch, Pisidian Antioch, Lystra, Galatia and Phrygia, Achaia, Ephesus, Tyre, and Caesarea[28] (the exceptions are 9:1; 16:1; 21:16, each of named individuals, and the feminine form μαθήτρια used for Dorcas, 9:36). It is found only in the Gospels and Acts in the NT, and twenty-one times in the apostolic fathers. In Luke's Gospel it is used for the group who traveled with Jesus, a group wider than the Twelve (Luke 6:13, 17; 7:11), as well as specifically for the Twelve (Luke 8:22; 9:14, 16). All those so designated are itinerant, leaving family loyalties to travel with Jesus (Luke 14:26), and thus sit light to possessions and depend on God's provision (Luke 12:22; 14:33). It is rare in the Greek OT (only 1 Chr 25:8), the Greek Pseudepigrapha, Philo, and Josephus. The Heb. equivalent, *talmîd*, is not found in the Dead Sea Scrolls, although here, as in these other Jewish sources, the idea of following a master is present.[29] Greco-Roman authors use the term for those learning a trade or being taught, or of being devotees of a particular lifestyle (e.g., Plato, *Prot.* 343A, "disciples of Spartan culture"). By the first century AD, the sense of learning from a teacher or master predominates. The absence of the term in the NT outside the Gospels and Acts may bespeak its particular use for *itinerant* followers of Jesus during his earthly ministry, a situation that changed after Jesus's resurrection.[30] Further, other than 15:10, μαθητής is found only in the author's voice, which Trebilco takes to indicate that this is a Lukan term not used by the Jesus followers themselves, but used by Luke to signal continuity with the earthly Jesus's disciple group. The later use for gentile Jesus followers (11:26, 29; 14:20, 21, 22, 28) thus highlights their continuity with, and incorporation into, the Jesus-following community. In Acts, disciples suffer for their faith (14:22; 19:9) in continuity with Jesus's words about suffering for his followers (e.g., Luke 12:4–12; 21:12–19).

Luke here contrasts "the Greek speakers," τῶν Ἑλληνιστῶν, with "the Hebrew speakers," τοὺς Ἑβραίους. These rare terms in the NT have provoked much discussion.[31] Ἑλληνισταί, traditionally translated "Hellenists," is found only here and 9:29; 11:20 in the NT, and is unattested prior to Acts.[32] Ἑβραῖοι, traditionally translated "Hebrews," is found only here and 2 Cor 11:22; Phil 3:5 in the NT. The uses in Acts vary: here τῶν Ἑλληνιστῶν denotes members of the believing community; in Acts 9:29 τοὺς Ἑλληνιστάς are unbelieving (probably Jewish) opponents of Paul; in 11:20 τοὺς Ἑλληνιστάς (assuming this is the correct reading—see *Note* there) are non-Jews, for some believers speak "*also* (adverbial καί) to the Ἑλληνιστάς," contrasted with speaking "*only* (μόνον) to Jews" (11:19). Brehm shows that the verb ἑλληνίζω was used from

28 Acts 6:1–2, 7; 9:1, 10, 19, 26, 38; 11:26, 29; 14:20–22, 28; 18:23, 27; 19:9, 30; 20:1, 30; 21:4, 16 (twice).

29 For examples, see Trebilco, *Self-designations*, 210–12.

30 See Trebilco, *Self-designations*, 220–23, for a cogent case that the term was used by Jesus.

31 Good summaries: Hengel, *Between*, 4–6; Ferguson, "Hellenists."

32 "Ἑλληνιστής," BDAG 319.

the fifth century BC in two senses: to speak Greek (often with emphasis on correct grammar) and to adopt Greek understanding and lifestyle.[33] Hengel wrongly denies the latter;[34] contrast the importance of speaking Aramaic/Hebrew in 2 Macc 7:8, 21; 12:37; 15:29.[35] However, such a synchronic analysis alone does not allow us to decide between these possibilities: we also need to consider the words with which the terms are collocated and contrasted.[36] Ἑβραῖος, "Hebrew," in Paul denotes *opponents* of the believing community who observe the torah with particular strictness, whereas here it denotes *members* of the believing community. Acts uses other terms for ethnic Greeks, especially Ἕλλην, "Greek" (14:1; 16:1, 3; 17:4; 18:4; 19:10, 17; 20:21; 21:28; cf. 17:12), and once uses Ἑλληνιστί, "in the Greek language" (21:37). All of this implies that the people described as Ἑλληνιστής here are not ethnically Greek, but Jewish, and that they were known by their predominant language being Greek and/or by their adoption of a Greek lifestyle—although these options cannot easily be divided, since the latter would necessarily involve the former. A significant proportion of first-century ossuaries in Jerusalem are inscribed with Greek names, strongly suggesting that a number of diaspora (and thus predominantly Greek-speaking) Jews moved to the city toward the end of their lives in order to be buried there.[37] There were also Greek-speaking synagogues in the city (6:9).[38] Barnabas appears to be a "Greek speaker" too (4:36–37). It is unlikely that these people spoke *only* Greek if they lived in Jerusalem, since they would need to have at least some Aramaic to manage life in such a strongly Aramaic-speaking context.[39] Hence these "Greek speakers" were probably Jesus-following Jews who had originally lived in the diaspora and had at some point migrated to Palestine.[40] In that case, Ἑβραῖος refers to believers whose predominant language was Aramaic (see p. 152n86) and/or whose lifestyle was traditionally Jewish. They, too, would be likely to know at least some Greek, since that was the *lingua franca* of the Roman Empire. Ἑβραῖος thus designates Jesus-following Jews born in Palestine.[41] For clarity and simplicity, I have translated the two terms as "Greek speakers" and "Hebrew speakers," while recognizing the complications above.[42]

---

33 "Meaning," 185–92.
34 *Between*, 8–9.
35 With Green, *Practicing*, 64–65.
36 Brehm, "Meaning," 193–98. Tyson's failure to consider this leads him to see the "Hellenists" here as gentile; Tyson, "Acts 6:1–7," 156–58, following Cadbury, "Hellenists." This misleads Tyson to see a dietary issue here, as gentile widows would not require kosher food.
37 Fitzmyer, *Acts*, 347; Haenchen, *Acts*, 261.
38 See Catto, *Synagogue*, 165–68.
39 Moule, "Once More."
40 For a stimulating theological reading of the significance of their migrant status, see Hays, "Place."
41 Brehm, "Meaning," 195–99.
42 See discussion in Lee, *Jesus*, 182–96, arguing cogently that we must speak of the predominant (matrix) language of each group rather than seeing them each as entirely monolingual.

γογγυσμός, "grumbling," among the Greek-speaking believers belies the claim that Luke is seeking to suppress a significant dispute, for it states clearly that there was a problem, and it was serious.[43] This grumbling shows that there was contact and communication between the two groups, for otherwise how would the Greek speakers know how the Hebrew speakers were treated? That necessitates some members of the believing community in Jerusalem being bilingual, even if most were primarily monolingual (see *Form/Structure/Setting*). González observes that this problem is ultimately created by the Spirit, for it is through the Spirit that both language groups have been drawn into the believing community.[44] γογγυσμός echoes biblical grumbling against Moses, especially when food was short (LXX Num 11:1; cf. Exod 16:7–9, 12; 17:3; Num 14:27, 29; 17:5, 10): in Num 11 it led to the appointment of seventy elders to assist Moses. πλῆθος, "whole group" (v. 2), echoes a description of the Israelites' growth (LXX Deut 1:10, 22; 26:5) and, again, Deut 1:10 is in the context of Moses needing to delegate some of his leadership responsibility to others because of this numerical growth (Deut 1:9–18). Luke has already written of "grumbling" in the setting of Jesus eating at Levi's home, where the Pharisees and scribes complain that Jesus eats with tax collectors and sinners (Luke 5:30), a group whose outsider status may parallel that of the Greek-speaking widows here.[45]

παρεθεωροῦντο ἐν τῇ διακονίᾳ τῇ καθημερινῇ αἱ χῆραι αὐτῶν, "their widows were habitually being neglected in the daily distribution." The cause of the grumbling is a critical issue for the believing community: the imperfect παρεθεωροῦντο, "[they] were habitually being neglected," portrays this as an ongoing issue.[46] Widows were generally a vulnerable group, lacking a husband to provide for them—hence others from their community speak on their behalf.[47] If widows did not remarry, they could be drawn to prostitution to support themselves.[48] There was a small number of wealthy widows, but these were rare among the general population in Palestine, where most people lived around or below subsistence level. The Greek-speaking widows were particularly vulnerable, for they had probably moved to Jerusalem from the diaspora with their husbands and then had been widowed in a place where they lacked an extended family to support them (their adult children would probably have remained in the diaspora[49]). Widows are also a particular object of YHWH's affection in Scripture, and thus the way God's people treat them—and others in need—is a key index of faithfulness to YHWH.[50] In Luke's

43 Contra Fiorenza, *Memory*, 164–65.
44 González, "Reading," 144.
45 Pao, "Waiters," 137–38.
46 Theissen, "Liebeskommunismus," 708.
47 Green, *Practicing*, 60.
48 On widows more generally, see Stählin, "Bild"; Finger, *Widows*, 194–214.
49 Spencer, "Widows," 728.
50 Deut 10:18; 14:29; 16:11, 14; 24:17, 19–21; 26:12–13; 27:19; Pss 68:5 [MT 69:5, EVV 69:4];

Gospel, widows are generally presented positively regarding their relationship with God and Jesus (Luke 2:37; 4:25–26; 7:12; 18:3–5; 21:2–3). Luke presents the early community as having no needy person (4:34; see *Comment* there), thus fulfilling YHWH's purpose for Israel (Deut 15:4), so this dispute is a key test of the renewed Israel's ability to fulfill the torah. Moreover, Luke's Gospel contains several distinctive passages where widows receive Jesus's approval or act as God's mouthpiece,[51] so whether the believers carry out Jesus's own concern for widows is at stake too (cf. Peter's actions in revivifying Dorcas, who provides for widows, Acts 9:39, 41; and commands to care for widows, 1 Tim 5:3–5, 9, 16; Jas 1:27). Can the believers overcome a language-based division within Judaism in dealing with this issue? Will the nature of the believing community as a "family" or "fictive kinship group" issue in providing for the neediest members of the community?

τῇ διακονίᾳ τῇ καθημερινῇ, "the daily distribution," echoes the daily (καθ' ἡμέραν) fellowship meals (2:46; see *Comment* there).[52] That parallel suggest that the distribution here was of food being shared to meet needs among the believers at communal gatherings in the temple and in homes,[53] rather than distribution of money (see *Comment* on v. 2). The communal setting (especially in the temple) would highlight the situation of one group being treated inequitably. Fiorenza's speculation that the conflict was about the role and participation of women in the Eucharist is groundless and involves the assumption of a separation of communal meals from the Eucharist that is anachronistic for this period.[54] The shared-meals context, providing for unmet needs at a daily gathering, suggests that the sense of διακονία is unspecific, "provision for taking care of, arrangement for support."[55] διακονία is here translated "distribution," denoting the provision and serving of food[56] (or perhaps money[57]), and the choice of διακονία, echoed in the Twelve's "serving the word" (τῇ διακονίᾳ τοῦ λόγου, v. 4; cf. 1:25) and the task of "serv[ing] at table" (διακονεῖν τραπέζαις, v. 2), is no accident: Luke points readers to see this issue within the valuing of humble service that characterized Jesus (see *Comment* on v. 2). Jeremias sees this "daily distribution" as paralleling provision for poor people in rabbinic Judaism, where a weekly synagogue collection known

94:1–7, esp. 6 [MT 95:1–7, esp. v. 6]; 146:9 [MT 147:9]; Prov 15:25; Isa 1:17, 23; Jer 7:6; 22:3; Ezek 22:7; Zech 7:10; Mal 3:5; 2 Macc 8:28, 30; 2 Esd 2:20; cf. Spencer, "Widows," 721.

51 Luke 2:36–38; 4:25–27; 7:11–17; 18:1–8 (all distinctive Luke material); cf. (paralleled in Mark) 20:47; 21:1–4; discussion: Spencer, "Widows," 721–28.

52 Spencer, *Portrait*, 201.

53 Cf. Finger, *Widows*, 257; Pao, "Waiters," 136–37.

54 Fiorenza, *Memory*, 164–66.

55 L&N §35.38; contrast §57.110.

56 Cf. the cognate verb διακονέω, "serve," and this noun concerning food in Luke 4:39; 10:40; 17:8; 22:27; with Tyson, "Acts 6:1–7," 153.

57 Bruce, *Acts* (1990), 182. If so, τράπεζα, "table" has a financial sense, as in Luke 19:23 ("τράπεζα," BDAG 1013, §1.c), and the seven were being appointed, at least in part, to oversee financial arrangements.

as the "basket" (*quppāh*) provided money for a week's food for poor people, and a daily "tray" (*tamḥūy*) collection provided for those in immediate need.[58] However, the evidence for such a system before AD 70 is slim, and the fact that begging in the Gospels and Acts was not seen as dishonorable (e.g., Luke 18:35; cf. Acts 3:2) makes it likely that the rabbinic system was not current at this date, for if the rabbinic system had been current, people would have been unlikely to give alms to beggars.[59] Thus the believers did not model their solution on the Jewish provision.[60] Moreover, the distribution mentioned here happens in the context of believers' daily meetings, in similar manner to the Essenes, where those working brought to the evening gathering their wages and these were pooled to buy food for all at a common meal (Philo, *Hypoth.* 11.10–11).[61] "Care for the poor of the community was always associated with table-fellowship in early Christianity; a continuation of Jesus's characteristic meal-fellowship with 'tax-collectors and sinners.'"[62]

Finger proposes an alternative view, that the issue concerns widows not as recipients of food but as contributors to the cooking and serving of the food.[63] She postulates that the Greek-speaking widows were involved with other Hebrew-speaking women in the kitchen and that the Greek speakers were not being permitted to take their part in preparing and serving food for the communal meals. However, it would be surprising if only widows were engaged in the preparation of community meals, and the apostles speak of the possibility of *themselves* serving tables (v. 2); therefore, it is much more likely that the issue was unfair distribution of food among different groups of widows.

2 προσκαλεσάμενοι δὲ οἱ δώδεκα τὸ πλῆθος τῶν μαθητῶν, "So the Twelve called a meeting of the whole group of the disciples." The whole community is called together to address the issue, rather than negotiations between two separate groups happening,[64] and this presumably includes the widows.[65] τὸ πλῆθος τῶν μαθητῶν, "the whole group of the disciples," echoes the summary in 4:32, and thus underlines the believers' united response to this issue. This approach signals how seriously the apostles take the issue, for it is tied up with a central community activity, the believers' shared meals.[66] There seems little ground for seeing the apostles as directly culpable for the failure causing this division:[67] rather, they are seeking to address the issue presented to them. The

58 *Jerusalem*, 126–34.
59 Hays, *Ethics*, 226.
60 Seccombe, "Charity"; Moore, *Judaism*, 2:174–75; Capper, "Community," 351.
61 Cf. Walton, "Communism," 108–9.
62 Capper, "Context," 351.
63 *Widows*, esp. 246–75; cf. Fiorenza, *Memory*, 166; Reimer, *Women*, 234–37.
64 Penner, *Praise*, 273.
65 Forbes and Harrower, *Raised*, 162.
66 Finger, *Widows*, 265, 267; Finger, "Mary."
67 So Green, *Practicing*, 65–66.

meeting's membership makes clear that the dispute is an inner-group dispute among believers rather than among the wider Jewish community.[68] This is the only use in Acts of οἱ δώδεκα, "the Twelve," although it is an established term in Luke's Gospel (Luke 6:13; 8:1; 9:1, 12; 18:31; 22:3, 30, 47). Luke may be using it here to signal again, by their number, that the body of believers is the renewed and restored Israel. Acts 4:4 pictures the group as more than five thousand at this point, so if the whole community met, Luke must envisage a meeting in the temple courts (cf. 5:12), the only place capable of easily holding such a crowd—the believers are thus dealing with their dirty washing in public.

οὐκ ἀρεστόν ἐστιν ἡμᾶς καταλείψαντας τὸν λόγον τοῦ θεοῦ διακονεῖν τραπέζαις, "It is not right for us to neglect God's word and serve at table." In tune with the earlier focus on "the apostles' teaching" (2:42) and their testimony to Jesus (1:8, 22; 2:32; 3:15; 4:33; 5:32), the Twelve propose that they should retain that focus (on τὸν λόγον τοῦ θεοῦ, "God's word," see *Comment* on 4:31). τράπεζα most frequently denotes meal tables in Luke-Acts (Luke 16:21; 22:21, 30; Acts 16:34; although it can denote a bank, Luke 19:23) and, given that Luke frequently uses the διακονέω word group in the co-text of meals and hospitality (Luke 4:39; 8:3; 10:40; 12:37; 17:8; 22:26–27), the issue is probably about how meals were provided.[69] Traditionally, women were the primary servers at table (cf. Luke 4:39; 8:1–3; 10:38–42).[70] It is not necessary to suppose that the Twelve were directly involved in the daily distribution of food.[71] 4:35 does not state that the apostles did the distributing to the needy themselves;[72] rather, they step aside from their regular activity of proclamation (5:42) for a time and intervene in this dispute in order to resolve it—and thus Talbert is mistaken in assuming this is as a *transfer* of "serving tables" from the apostles to the seven.[73] οὐκ ἀρεστόν ἐστιν, "it is not right," may imply "in God's eyes": ἀρεστός "right" is often found with a dative of reference (e.g., 12:3; John 8:29), and τῷ θεῷ, "with reference to God," may be implied here. If so, the focus is on the apostles' divine commission (cf. 1:24–25). Resolving how the table service (διακονεῖν τραπέζαις) takes place is the task for the seven, i.e., τῆς χρείας ταύτης, "this matter" (v. 3). It could be suggested that the apostles dealt with this issue only because it was a distraction from their "serving the word," but the portrait of the believing community in the earlier chapters of Acts is one where care is taken to ensure that all are provided for (2:42, 44; 4:33–34; see *Comment* on v. 1); thus this issue of social justice within the community is

68 *Pace* Larsson, "Hellenisten," 209–11; cf. Walter, "Apostelgeschichte 6.1," 377–83, who argues that the issue is the exclusion of the Greek-speaking widows from *Jewish* provision for the needy.

69 Pao, "Waiters," 135–36; Blomberg, *Neither,* 168–69.

70 Fiorenza, *Memory,* 165–66; Finger, *Widows,* 205–10.

71 With Haenchen, *Acts,* 262; Seim, *Message,* 109–10; Strange, *Problem,* 124–25; contra (e.g.) Nagel, "Twelve," 118; Fraser, "Office," 15.

72 Contra Hays, *Ethics,* 277.

73 *Reading Luke-Acts,* 47.

both crucial to the believers' credibility among the Jerusalemites, and "the formation of just community is . . . a manifestation of the power of the Spirit in its own right."[74] Further, the use of the same word group for this task as for the apostolic ministry of διακονία, "serving," the word (v. 4), read with Jesus's saying about the greatness of serving at table (Luke 22:24–27), indicates that Luke is identifying both tasks as honorable.[75] The apostles are not avoiding a "socially demeaning action";[76] rather, the seven may rightly be seen as Jesus's honored successors in serving in this way.[77]

3 ἐπισκέψασθε δέ, ἀδελφοί, ἄνδρας ἐξ ὑμῶν . . . ἑπτά, "Instead, brothers and sisters, look for seven men from among you." The choice is placed in the hands of the community rather than the apostles making the selection: the solution to a communal problem is made through a communal process. The number seven may reflect town councils of seven, which are known in first-century Israel (Josephus, *Ant.* 4.8.14 §214; 4.8.38 §287; *J.W.* 2.20.5 §§569–71).[78] The choice of men to oversee a traditionally female task perhaps reflects Jesus's call to humble servant leadership (Luke 22:24–27),[79] for it shows men serving at tables, traditionally a women's task. Luke's theme of reversal is at work here, this time indicating that social expectations for women may be fulfilled by men.[80] Of course, this move could create some tension because of men entering traditionally female space in the kitchen.

Those chosen are to be μαρτυρουμένους . . . πλήρεις πνεύματος καὶ σοφίας, "well spoken of . . . full of the Spirit and wisdom." μαρτυρουμένους, "well spoken of," indicates an ability to relate well to others,[81] as well as trustworthiness, perhaps among outsiders as well as believers (cf. 1 Tim 3:7). "Full of the Spirit," πλήρεις πνεύματος, echoes the apostles' experience (2:4; 4:8, 31; cf. Luke 1:41, 67; 4:1) and that of Joshua (Num 27:18; cf. Deut 34:9). This is the first use in Acts of the construction with the adjective πλήρης, "full."[82] This spatial metaphor using πλήρης indicates that the genitive is a "*quality* [which] *clearly marks the person's life or comes to visible expression in his or her activity*," with the implication that it is a "long-term state of affairs" (by contrast with the construction with a verb).[83] σοφίας, "wisdom," forms a hendiadys with πνεύματος, "Spirit," indicating wisdom given by the Spirit, reflecting the Second Temple Jewish perspective that one mark of the work of "the Spirit of prophecy" is

74 Biggar, "Showing," 14.
75 Spencer, *Portrait*, 201–6; Biggar, "Showing," 14–15; contra Spencer, "Widows," 729–30; Spencer, *Acts*, 65–67; Green, *Practicing*, 66–68.
76 Pervo, "ΠΑΝΤΑ," 170n34, comparing Luke 17:7–10.
77 Pao, "Waiters," 141–42.
78 Hengel, *Between*, 15–16; Haenchen, *Acts*, 263.
79 Finger, *Widows*, 268–69.
80 Forbes and Harrower, *Raised*, 163.
81 Finger, *Widows*, 269.
82 πλήρης + genitive of what fills is found in LXX and Philo, although not with πνεύματος "Spirit," e.g., Gen 25:8; Lev 16:12; Judg 6:38; 1 Sam 2:5; Philo, *Alleg. Interp.* 3.7; *Posterity* 43.
83 So Turner, *Power*, 167 (his italics); his discussion of "full of the Spirit" (164–69) is illuminating.

giving charismatic wisdom.[84] The practical wisdom to resolve this dispute echoes biblical ideals of practical wisdom.[85] The task of resolving a dispute by Spirit-given wisdom is one of a number of examples of the Spirit working in ways that are not directly empowerment for witness.[86]

οὓς καταστήσομεν ἐπὶ τῆς χρείας ταύτης, "We will put them in charge of this matter," states the chosen seven's task: to resolve the dispute rather than to serve only the Greek-speaking widows.[87] There is no statement that the seven will *only* handle the dispute[88] or that they will do the table service themselves, rather than being responsible for facilitating it happening fairly—or, indeed, what they have been doing previously. Their qualifications suggest that they are already people of some standing: Stephen will exercise "wisdom," σοφία, in his speaking ministry (6:10). We should not necessarily be surprised when Stephen and Philip are proclaimers of the faith (6:8–8:40)—again, there is no suggestion that they did this to the exclusion of their responsibility for overseeing the provision for needy people in the believing community. Their service prior to their appointment here, which could include teaching, may well have been one reason the group identified them as having the community's trust to carry out this task.[89] Indeed, Jesus's own teaching ministry takes place in Luke at meals with outcasts (Luke 5:30; 7:34; 15:1).[90] Stephen and Philip's subsequent ministries, with the use of the cognate terms διακονία, "service," and διακονέω, "serve," for both the apostolic word service and the seven's table service (see *Comment* on Acts 6:4), undermine any attempt to subordinate the seven to the Twelve.[91] Luke himself designates apostolic ministry as διακονία elsewhere (Acts 1:17, 25; 20:24; 21:19).[92] Johnson considers the apostles to delegate responsibility for material goods—food—as a proxy for delegating spiritual authority to preach.[93] He concedes that this is "awkward," since their responsibility for enabling a just distribution of food is not mentioned after this passage; we simply see Stephen and Philip exercising spiritual authority as preachers of the word. However, it is not necessary to choose between responsibility for distribution of food and distribution of the word in the tasks carried out by the seven; Johnson dichotomizes unnecessarily.

4 ἡμεῖς δὲ τῇ προσευχῇ καὶ τῇ διακονίᾳ τοῦ λόγου προσκαρτερήσομεν, "but, as for us, we will devote ourselves to prayer and serving the word." The

84 Turner, *Power,* 95–97, 350.
85 E.g., LXX Exod 31:3; 35:31, 33, 55; 2 Sam 14:20; 1 Kgs 2:35a (MT 4:29); Ezra 7:25; Jdt 8:29; 11:8, 20; 4 Macc 1:15–16; Ps 110:10; Prov 1:7; 8:1, 11–12; 10:31.
86 *Pace* Menzies, *Empowered,* passim; for other examples, see Turner, *Power,* 408–12, 431–33.
87 With Penner, *Praise,* 64–65; contra Capper, "Community," 353–54.
88 Price, *Widow,* 212.
89 Spencer, *Acts,* 67.
90 Cf. Pao, "Waiters," 138–39.
91 *Contra,* e.g., Walter, "Apostelgeschichte 6.1," esp. 370, 372–73.
92 With Collins, *Diakonia Studies,* 157–58.
93 Johnson, *Function,* 213.

juxtaposition of the emphatic personal pronoun ἡμεῖς, "as for us," with the dative complement τῇ προσευχῇ καὶ τῇ διακονίᾳ, "to prayer and serving," of προσκαρτερήσομεν, "we will devote ourselves," highlights the connection between διακονεῖν τραπέζαις, "serve at table" (v. 2), and τῇ διακονίᾳ τοῦ λόγου, "serving the word." This echo underlines the unity of the ministries of the Twelve and the seven (see *Comment* on v. 2).[94] The seven are not appointed to serve *under* the authority of the Twelve, for the Twelve "serve" too.[95] Collins claims that διακονία, "service," implies acting as an intermediary;[96] if so, the Twelve's role in "serving the word" is focused on passing on the message to others (cf. 2 Tim 2:2). The Twelve are qualified for this task by their eye- and ear-witness experience of Jesus (cf. Acts 1:21–22; 2:32; 3:15; 4:33; 5:32), and so their focus on it needs to be preserved (see *Comment* on 6:2). This should not be taken to imply, of course, that the Twelve are to be the *only* ministers of the word or that they seek to restrict that ministry to themselves,[97] and thus when Philip and Stephen emerge as evangelists no improper boundary is crossed.[98]

5 ἤρεσεν ὁ λόγος ἐνώπιον παντὸς τοῦ πλήθους, "This idea pleased the whole group," echoes τὸ πλῆθος, "the whole group" (v. 2), and continues the focus on the unity of the believers, here in acceptance of the apostles' proposal. παντὸς τοῦ πλήθους, "the whole group," must include the widows themselves (v. 1) and other women disciples. Luke (frustratingly) does not describe the means by which their choice was made. A process engaging the whole group is in view, for the whole group is the subject of ἐξελέξαντο, "they selected"; its middle voice suggests "they chose for themselves" (cf. Exod 18:25 LXX, using the active of ἐπιλέγω for Moses's selection of the judges).[99]

Στέφανον . . . καὶ Φίλιππον καὶ Πρόχορον καὶ Νικάνορα καὶ Τίμωνα καὶ Παρμενᾶν καὶ Νικόλαον, "Stephen . . . Philip, Procorus, Nicanor, Timon, Parmenas, and Nicolaus." The names are all Greek, and so they may be chosen from the migrant Greek-speaking community, although three of the Twelve (who are undoubtedly "Hebrew speakers") bear Greek names—Andrew, Philip, and Bartholomew (1:13)—so we cannot be certain that they were all migrants.[100] (On Stephen as a Greek speaker, see *Comment* on 6:9.) Luke does not identify any of the seven as leaders of the Greek speakers, although that is possible; Luke does not identify the leaders of the Hebrew-speaking group, either, although they were presumably the Twelve. Lee plausibly suggests that the seven may have been bilingual, enabling them to mediate between the two

94 Thompson, *One*, 95–96.

95 Spencer, *Portrait*, 201.

96 *Diakonia*, 213.

97 Contra González, "Reading," 145. Note, e.g., the planting of Jesus-communities by unnamed disciples in 8:4; 11:19–21.

98 Neagoe, *Trial*, 159.

99 "ἐκλέγομαι," BDAG 305, §2. Johnson, "Manual," 112, suggests that πλῆθος denotes "majority," but there is no reason in the text to think so.

100 Spencer, *Portrait*, 191; Barrett, *Acts*, 1:314; cf. Hays, *Ethics*, 230.

primary-language groups.[101] Other than Stephen (6:8–8:1a) and Philip (8:4–40), Acts says nothing more of these men, as for almost all the Twelve; the parallel silence with most of the Twelve shows that there need not be "suspicion as to [the list of the seven's] accuracy."[102]

Stephen is singled out as ἄνδρα πλήρης πίστεως καὶ πνεύματος ἁγίου, "a man full of faith and the Holy Spirit." We read more of his exploits shortly; in addition to being full of the required wisdom, he is also πλήρης πίστεως, "full of faith." The mention of "faith" suggests a different quality of faith to other believers, the kind of faith that could see signs and wonders done (v. 8;[103] see *Comment* on 3:16 concerning "faith" in Luke-Acts). Philip is unlikely to be the same person as the apostle (1:13) (see *Comment* on 8:5).[104] Nicolaus is προσήλυτον Ἀντιοχέα, "a proselyte from Antioch," a convert to Judaism (the term is used only in Judaism[105]); the process of conversion generally involved circumcision (Jdt 14:10) and perhaps a ritual bath and offering sacrifice.[106] It does not necessarily follow that the others are all converts; Nicolaus being identified this way may imply that he is distinctive as a proselyte.[107] Nicolaus's origins in Antioch point us toward the significant developments that will happen there through believers going to gentiles (11:19–20). Irenaeus, *Adv. Haer.* 1.26.3 (among others), claims that Nicolaus became the leader of the Nicolatians, who are condemned in Rev 2:6, but this suggestion lacks firm evidence.[108]

6 It is most natural to take the same group as the subject of ἔστησαν, "presented," and προσευξάμενοι ἐπέθηκαν, "they prayed and laid," namely the whole group.[109] The reading in D demonstrates that one scribe found this surprising (see *Note* i above). The whole group not only chooses the seven but also commissions them for the task in collaboration with the Twelve authorizing them (note καταστήσομεν, "*we* will place," v. 3).[110] This process parallels similar processes elsewhere in Acts:[111] (i) the appointment of Matthias, where the believers address the issue collectively: the congregation propose the

101 Lee, *Jesus*, 197–208.

102 Esler, *Community*, 141.

103 *Pace* Pervo, *Acts*, 161, who sees the difference as merely "stylistic."

104 *Contra*, e.g., Theissen, "Hellenisten," 331–32.

105 P. F. Stührenberg, "Proselyte," *ABD* 5:503.

106 Although the evidence for the latter two in this period is thin; S. McKnight, "Proselytism and Godfearers," *DNTB* 835–47, esp. 844–46.

107 Spencer, *Portrait*, 194n3; contra Blackman, "Hellenists"; Reicke, *Glaube*, 115–17.

108 Aune, *Revelation*, 1:148–49.

109 Spencer, *Portrait*, 196; Barrett, *Acts*, 1:315–16; Culy and Parsons, *Acts*, 110; Daube, *Testament*, 237–38; contra Fitzmyer, *Acts*, 351. Peter Mansell suggests to me that καί may indicate the change of subject where "the person who experiences an event . . . becomes the subject of the next sentence" (Levinsohn, *Connections*, 89), similar to the use of καί in 8:26. This is not impossible, but the community (even representatively) laying on hands fits better with the corporate decision making taking place here.

110 With Fraser, "Office," 15.

111 Spencer, *Portrait*, 197–98.

candidates (1:23), pray (1:24), and cast lots (1:26); (ii) Barnabas and Saul's sending out from Antioch, where the Spirit calls (through a prophetic word, 13:2) and the whole group commissions (13:3, taking those meeting in 13:2 to be the whole community; see *Comment* there); (iii) the assembly of a large group to confer concerning the admission of gentiles, including τῆς ἐκκλησίας καὶ τῶν ἀποστόλων καὶ τῶν πρεσβυτέρων, "the congregation and the apostles and the elders," (15:4)—πᾶν τὸ πλῆθος, "the whole group," listened to the speeches (15:12), and chose those who would take the letter (15:22–23). Biblical examples of Moses appointing assistants are germane too: Moses chooses his own assistants on Jethro's advice (Exod 18:25), or Moses asks the people to choose suitable individuals and he then appoints them (Deut 1:13–15), or Moses chooses suitable people on YHWH's instruction (Num 11:16–17, 24–25; cf. Chrysostom, *Hom. Act.* 14).[112] Note also that the Israelites as a whole laid hands on the Levites when they were commissioned (Num 8:10). The process seen here, where the community choose the seven and then take part in commissioning them, is similar to and different from the Mosaic examples in interesting ways, and the involvement of the whole community throughout the process reflects the universal gift of the Spirit to the community (Acts 2:17, 38; cf. Num 11:29). The laying on of hands does not, therefore, imply any "hierarchical relationship" between the Twelve and the seven.[113]

προσευξάμενοι ἐπέθηκαν αὐτοῖς τὰς χεῖρας, "they prayed and laid hands on them." Laying on hands by the Israelite community is a feature of the Levites' commissioning (Num 8:10),[114] whereas Moses alone lays hands on Joshua to commission him (Num 27:18, 23; Deut 34:9).[115] Daube notes an OT distinction between "leaning" hands (*samakh*), which involved physical pressure, and "placing" hands (*śim* or *shith*)—the former is used in the passages noted above—and proposes that a similar distinction must be in use in the NT.[116] He claims that "leaning" involves identifying people as substitutes for those doing the "leaning," with those receiving laying on of hands having qualities poured into them by the layers on of hands. However, LXX and NT use only ἐπιτίθημι (predominantly) or τίθημι for laying on hands, and so the distinction Daube claims in Hebrew cannot be reproduced in the NT.[117] The use of the hands for this activity suggests interaction with the environment; the people laying on hands are engaging with the seven in this activity, which also symbolizes prayer for them.[118] In the light of the OT parallels, it denotes authorizing the seven for their task, and the prayer invokes God to equip and strengthen

112 See discussion Daube, "Reform," 154; Spencer, *Portrait,* 206–11.
113 Contra Brinkhof, "Philip," 81.
114 See McCaughey, "Intention," 32; Ferguson, "Laying," 251.
115 Ferguson, "Laying," 250.
116 *Testament,* 224–28, 233.
117 Schweizer, *Order,* 74n285.
118 Cf. Malina and Pilch, *Acts,* 56, 234.

the seven for that task.[119] Luke does not say that Matthias had hands laid on him (1:26),[120] perhaps reflecting that Matthias was chosen before the Spirit's coming at Pentecost, in similar manner to the change of requirements from Matthias to the seven—here the Spirit's evident presence is crucial (6:3, 5), by contrast with silence about the Spirit in Matthias's election (1:21–22).

From Irenaeus (*Adv. Haer.* 1.26.3) onwards this passage has been seen as a precedent for the ordination of deacons, and the seven have been identified as such.[121] This identification is anachronistic and often reads this passage through the lens of Phil 1:1 and 1 Tim 3:8–13. Although the cognate verb διακονέω, "serve," and noun διακονία, "service," are used here (vv. 1, 2, 4) and elsewhere in Luke's writings, the noun διάκονος, "servant/deacon," is not used at all in Luke-Acts. "[B]eyond the act of commissioning, there is nothing in the narrative to suggest that Luke is here providing the reader with an intentional account of the origin of the office of deacon."[122] Nevertheless, it is possible that by Luke's time Christians recognized this passage as a precedent for later development of the office of deacon.[123]

7 This verse transitions from the resolution of this dispute, indicating that one outcome is the continuing growth of the church, into the next scenes, where the focus switches to Stephen (6:8–8:1a) and Philip (8:4–25). It appears that the growth of the community is a consequence of well-fed widows! Certainly, to care for the needy (whom widows exemplify, see *Comment* on v. 1) would underline the credibility of the believing community's claim to be Israel renewed and restored, for they thereby fulfill the biblical vision of Israel's life (cf. *Comment* on 4:34). In addition, 6:2, 4 imply that the seven's ministry enables the apostles to continue their ministry of proclamation, a ministry of God's word that was effective in the multiplication of disciples. Stephen's death and the departure of Philip and others (8:1b) may suggest that the issue concerning the widows was resolved before those later events.[124]

Καὶ ὁ λόγος τοῦ θεοῦ ηὔξανεν καὶ ἐπληθύνετο ὁ ἀριθμὸς τῶν μαθητῶν ἐν Ἰερουσαλὴμ σφόδρα, "God's word continued growing and the number of disciples in Jerusalem continued to multiply." This is the third mention of ὁ λόγος τοῦ θεοῦ, "God's word," in Acts (see *Comment* on 4:31) and the first that personifies the word as an active agent in the story (cf. 12:24; 19:20). Here the word is said to grow (ηὔξανεν), an image Luke elsewhere applies only to living things, whether people (e.g., Luke 1:80; 2:40) or plants (e.g., Luke 12:17; 13:19).[125] The image of growth signals the power inherent in the word, a power

119 For other uses, see *Comment* on 8:17.
120 Cf. Domagalski, "Sieben," 28–29.
121 E.g., Pelikan, *Acts*, 91; Lightfoot, *Acts*, 105–6; Fraser, "Office," 14–16. See the summary of developments in Nagel, "Twelve," 121–25.
122 Penner, *Praise*, 269.
123 Blomberg, *Neither*, 169, with Coppens, "L'imposition," 421.
124 I owe this suggestion to Conrad Gempf.
125 Pao, *Acts*, 160.

that effects real change, in similar manner to the power of the word of YHWH in the OT (e.g., Isa 55:10–11). "It is not just a report of God's activities but the way in which God continues to act in fulfilling the divine purpose."[126] It may echo the parable of the sower, where the seed represents the word (Luke 8:4–15). The growth of the word is seen in the multiplication of the number of disciples (the second καί is epexegetical) in Jerusalem—the word has conquered the city. Pao notes that ὁ λόγος does not again appear in Jerusalem in Acts and infers that its [initial] work there is complete.[127] Thus, "the church is a creature of the word."[128] In LXX, αὐξάνω, "grow," and πληθύνω, "multiply," are also collocated in both the instruction to the animals and the first human pair to "increase and multiply" (Gen 1:22, 28), an instruction renewed after the flood (Gen 9:1, 7), and the promises of Israel's restoration after exile (Jer 3:16; 23:3).[129] In particular, Pao suggests that the echo of Exod 1:7 LXX, where the two verbs are also collocated, implies that what is now happening is "the creation of a new people by an act of God":[130] "But the sons of Israel increased and multiplied [ηὐξήθησαν καὶ ἐπληθύνθησαν] and became common and were growing very, very strong. Now the land kept multiplying [ἐπλήθυνεν] them" (NETS; cf. Acts 7:17). Paul also uses "grow" as an image for the church's increase in number and maturity (1 Cor 3:6; 2 Cor 9:10; Eph 4:15); the closest Pauline parallel is Col 1:6, which speaks of the gospel (τοῦ εὐαγγελίου) bearing fruit and growing (αὐξανόμενον). Luke thus uses ὁ λόγος τοῦ θεοῦ, "God's word," as equivalent to the Pauline τὸ εὐαγγέλιον, "the gospel."

πολύς τε ὄχλος τῶν ἱερέων ὑπήκουον τῇ πίστει, "and a large group of priests became obedient to the faith." Luke continues to stress the way the gospel is transforming the mainstream Jewish community by showing that a significant number of priests—from the heart of that community—became believers, thus further underlining the nature of the believing community as the restored true Israel.[131] Priests often lived outside Jerusalem (e.g., Luke 1:39) and, other than the major festivals, when all priests were "on duty," spent two separate weeks each year serving at the temple, and so they would come into contact with the believing community (cf. Acts 5:12). Many were poor, for the priestly tithe for their support was often not paid.[132] Their joining the believing community is described as ὑπήκουον τῇ πίστει, "[they] became obedient to the faith"; the closest NT parallels to this unusual expression are Rom 1:5 ὑπακοὴν πίστεως, "the obedience that consists in faith"; 6:17, ὑπηκούσατε . . . εἰς . . . τύπον διδαχῆς, "you became obedient . . . to . . . the form of teaching";

126 Tannehill, *Unity*, 2:82.
127 Pao, *Acts*, 152.
128 Marguerat, *Actes*, 1:213 (my translation); cf. Roloff, *Apostelgeschichte*, 110.
129 Kodell, "Word," 510–11.
130 *Acts*, 168–69, quoting 169.
131 Cf. Jervell, *Apostelgeschichte*, 221.
132 Jeremias, *Jerusalem*, 108.

and 2 Thess 1:8 τοῖς μὴ ὑπακούουσιν τῷ εὐαγγελίῳ, "those who do not obey the gospel." These Pauline texts lead Bruce to suggest that "the faith" here is "almost equivalent" to "the gospel."[133] There are similar "absolute" uses of "the faith" as summing up the Christian message in Acts 13:8; 14:22; 16:5. Some see this as presenting an "early catholic" view in which "the faith" is now a formula (cf. Jude 3, 20; 1 Tim 1:19; 4:6; 6:10), but Rom 6:17 (which is certainly not "early catholic") expresses a similar idea, and "the faith" may be equivalent to "the community of faith."[134]

Explanation

This section continues the theme of the community's growth, focused on how the believers resolve a major internal conflict. This is not the first conflict among believers, and it will not be the last. Ananias and Sapphira's deceitful actions (5:1–11) did not prevent the community's growth (5:12–16), and similar growth follows this conflict (v. 7).

The conflict centers on provision for widows, a needy group, for they lack a family to support them. In Scripture, the people's provision for the needy, including widows, is an important index of their faithfulness to YHWH and of the extent to which they share YHWH's compassion (e.g., Deut 10:18; 14:29; 24:17, 19–21; 26:12–13; 27:19; Ps 68:5 [MT 68:6, LXX 67:6]). The community is a mixture of those who predominantly speak Aramaic, largely native Palestinian Jews, and those who predominantly speak Greek, largely diaspora Jews who had relocated to Palestine (and the wider subcultural differences of those groups). The Greek-speaking widows are not being treated justly in the sharing of food at community gathering, which is a key feature of the community's life (Acts 2:42–47; 4:32–35; 5:12). While it is not impossible that the languages people speak lead to some separate meetings, 5:12 implies that the believers regularly meet all together—perhaps some interpret for those in the opposite language group to the speaker. The dispute is potentially very damaging for the life of the community, and not only internally, for the testimony of their life together is crucial to their claim to be the true, restored Israel (note, e.g., the echo of Deut 15:4 in 4:34–35). The credibility of the believing community is here at stake.

This communal issue is resolved by a communal process, initiated by the Twelve, who call the believers together: the whole community meets to deal with the conflict rather than representatives of the two groups negotiating. As in the Mosaic exodus stories, dispute leads to delegation (note the echo of "grumbling" from Num 11:1; 14:27, 29; 17:5, 10; Deut 1:10, 22;

133 Bruce, *Acts* (1990), 185.

134 Johnson, *Acts*, 108, citing 13:8; 14:22; cf. *BegC*, 5:391.

26:5). The Twelve's proposal is that a special group of seven should resolve the conflict and that the apostles themselves should continue to focus on their testimony to Jesus (vv. 2–4). The apostles are clear over the seven's purpose (equitable distribution of food), roles (vis-à-vis the apostles), required character and gifts (full of Spirit and wisdom), and authority to act (public commissioning).[135]

This is not a case of the apostles handing off an uncongenial, lower task, for the apostles know the example and teaching of Jesus, that service *is* true greatness (Luke 22:24–27)—thus the language of "serving" is attached to both the apostolic testimony and teaching ("serving the word," Acts 6:4) and the seven's role ("serve at table," v. 2). The Twelve and the seven are colleagues, and there is no hierarchy of role signaled here—rather the reverse, echoing the communal engagement in Matthias's appointment (1:15–26), Barnabas and Saul's commissioning (13:1–3), and the Jerusalem council (15:4, 22–23). "The interplay of a proposal by the Twelve, the choice of seven by 'the whole group', the presentation of the Seven to the apostles and the final ratification of the decision by the apostles is a model of harmonious cooperation."[136]

The communal process continues with the selection of the seven by "the whole group" (6:5). Although their names are all Greek, they need not all be Greek speakers, for some of the apostles had Greek names too. However, some certainly were Greek speakers, notably Nicolaus, a convert to Judaism. This communal selection leads to a communal commissioning, for the natural reading of v. 6 is that the whole community commissions them by praying and laying hands on the seven.

The chosen seven were men of high character, "well spoken of, full of the Spirit and wisdom" (v. 3), and thus may well already have been leaders, formally or informally. Luke does not present them as *only* engaging in resolving the conflict or say anything about their previous activities. It should not necessarily be a surprise, then, when Stephen and Philip act as evangelists in the following chapters (6:8–8:40). Indeed, at one level, the dispute about the Greek-speaking widows paves the way for the expansion of the believing communities to include Samaritans and, ultimately, gentiles through Greek-speaking evangelists.

The communal nature of the whole process resonates with the universal gift of the Spirit to believers (2:17–18, 38). The whole community now possesses—is possessed by—the Spirit, and thus there is no élite who make decisions for the body of believers, but the community is engaged in this process. While some have particular gifts from the Spirit for particular tasks (6:3, 5), the Spirit of prophecy's gift of charismatic wisdom is in principle and in practice given to all.

---

135 Sell, "Seven," 65–67.

136 Thompson, *One*, 96.

The communal solution to this communal issue leads to communal growth (v. 7), strongly implying that God is pleased with this outcome—not only does the community grow, but some of their natural opponents, the priests (cf. 4:1), become believers. This is a remarkable example of handling and resolving conflict in a way that enables the community to move forward together rather than the community's energies being absorbed by internal conflict. This story prepares the way for further growth of the community, as Luke now moves to focus on two of the seven, Stephen and Philip.

E. The Ministry of Stephen and Its Consequences (6:8–8:3)

1. God Works in and through Stephen (6:8–8:1a)

Bibliography

Aarflot, C. H. *God,* 94–118. **Alexander, P. S.** "Retelling." **Bachmann, M.** "Stephanusepisode." **Barclay, J. M. G.** "Manipulating." **Barrett, C. K.** "Attitudes." ———. "OT History." ———. "Stephen." **Beale, G. K.** *Temple,* 216–29. **Bihler, J.** *Stephanusgeschichte.* **Blinzer, J.** "Jewish Punishment." **Bock, D. L.** *Proclamation,* 215–25. **Boesenberg, D.** "Retelling." **Bowker, J. W.** "Speeches." **Brawley, R. L.** "Covenant." **Brehm, H. A.** "Vindicating." **Callan, T.** "Pauline Midrash," 550–54. **Carleton Paget, J.** "Jewish Christianity," *CHJ* 3:731–75. **Catto, S. K.** *Synagogue.* **Coggins, R. J.** "Samaritans." **Crump, D.** *Jesus,* 178–203. **Cunningham, S.** *Tribulations,* 203–14. **Dahl, N. A.** "Story." **Dibelius, M.** *Studies,* 167–70. **Dinkler, M. B.** "Politics." **Doble, P.** *Paradox,* 132–45. ———. "Saying." **Donaldson, T. L.** "Moses." **Dunn, J. D. G.** *Beginning,* 257–73. ———. *Partings,* 23–31. **Dupont, J.** "Structure." **Edwards, J. R.** "Parallels," 488–89. **Evans, C. A.** "Prophecy." ———. "Rewritten Bible." **Fletcher-Louis, C. H. T.** *Luke-Acts,* 96–98. **Garrett, S. R.** "Meaning." **Gempf, C. H.** "Speaking." **Glombitza, O.** "Charakterisierung." **Green, J. B.** *Narrative Theologian,* 161–69. **Hall, R. G.** *Revealed Histories,* 195–200. **Hamm, D.** "Tamid," 227–31. **Hays, C. M.** "What is the Place." **Hemer, C. J.** *Book,* 418–27. **Hirzel, R.** *Strafe.* **Horbury, W.** "Conceptions." **Hötzinger, H.** "Schriftgebrauch." **Hübner, H.** *Biblische Theologie,* 3:139–51. **Humphrey, E. M.** *And I Turned,* 48–54. **Hurtado, L. W.** *Lord,* 29–48, 197–200, 618. **Jantsch, T.** "God of Glory." **Jeremias, J.** "Gebetsleben." ———. *Heiligengräber,* 37–38. **Jeska, J.** *Geschichte.* **Johnson, L. T.** *Midrash,* 24–29. **Jones, B. C.** "Meaning." **Katz, P.** "ἐν πυρί." **Keener, C. S.** "Marriages," 30–33. ———. "Three Notes," 42–45. **Kennedy, G. A.** *Interpretation,* 121–22. **Kilgallen, J. J.** "Function." ———. *Stephen Speech.* **Kilpatrick, G. D.** "Quotations," 83–84. **Kim, J.-W.** "Quotations." **Klijn, A. F. J.** "Speech." **Koet, B. J.** "Isaiah," 89–90. **Koivisto, R. A.** "A Theology." **Levine, L. I.** *Ancient Synagogue,* 53–54. **Longenecker, B. W.** *Rhetoric,* 192–94. **Lyall, F.** *Slaves,* 39–45. **MacDonald, D. R.** *Gospels and Homer,* 77–79. **Malina, B. J.** *World* (3rd ed.), 27–57. **Mare, W. H.** "Acts 7." **Martín Asensio, G.** "Reference." **Matthews, S.** *Perfect Martyr.* **Maxwell, K. R.** *Hearing,* 159–60. **Miller, J. B. F.** *Convinced,* 178–81. **Mittelstadt, M. W.** *Spirit,* 103–16. **Moessner, D. P.** "Christ." ———. "Suffering." **Moule, C. F. D.** *Origin,* 11–22. ———. *Phenomenon,* 90–91. ———. "Sanctuary." **Mundle, W.** "Stephanusrede." **Naiden, F. S.** *Supplication.* **Neagoe, A.** *Trial,* 152–74. **Neudorfer, H.-W.** "Speech." **O'Neill, J. C.** *Theology* (1961), 71–93. **O'Toole, R. F., SJ.** "Parallels." **Owen, H. P.** "Vision." **Pao, D. W.** *Acts,* 206–8. **Paschke, B.** "Prayer." **Penner, T. C.** "Narrative." ———. *Praise.* **Pesch, R.** *Vision.* **Peterson, B. K.** "Stephen's Speech." **Peterson, D.** *Engaging,* 139–42. **Pilch, J. J.** *Visions,* 57–59. **Pulleyn, S.** *Prayer,* 188–94. **Ravens, D.** *Luke,* 50–72, 87–91. **Richard, E. J.** *Acts 6:1–8:4.* ———. "Acts 7." ———. "Character." ———. "Use," 38–44, 52–53. **Riesner, R.** *Period,* 59–74. ———. "Synagogues." **Robb, J. E.** "Prophet," 104–21. **Rostovtzeff, M. I., and P. M. Fraser.** *Social,* 1:67–68. **Safrai, S.** "Synagogue." **Sanders, E. P.** *Jewish Law,* 97–130. **Scharlemann, M. H.** *Stephen.* **Schneider, G.** "Stephanus." **Schwemer, A. M.** "Lukas." **Scobie, C. H. H.** "Origins." ———. "Use." **Scroggs, R.** "Earliest." **Seland, T.** *Violence,* 245–50. **Shin, W. G.** "Stories." **Simon, M.** "Saint Stephen." ———. *St Stephen.* **Skinner,**

M. L. *Trial Narratives,* 117–20. **Sleeman, M.** *Geography,* 139–73. **Smith, A.** “Full.” **Smith, S.** *Fate,* 140–89. **Smith, T. C.** “Significance.” **Soards, M. L.** *Speeches,* 57–70. **Sparks, H. F. D.** “Semitisms,” 24–25. **Spencer, F. S.** *Portrait,* 70–81. **Stanton, G. N.** “Stephen.” **Stemberger, G.** “Stephanusrede.” **Sterling, G. E.** “‘Opening.” **Strelan, R.** *Strange Acts,* 149–53. **Sweeney, J. P.** “Speech.” **Sylva, D. D.** “Meaning.” **Tabb, B. J.** “Lucan Jesus.” ———. *Suffering,* 129–42. **Tabb, B. J. and S. Walton.** “Exodus.” **Taylor, N. H.** “Luke-Acts.” **Thompson, R.** “Diaspora.” **Thornton, T. C. G.** “Stephen’s Use.” **Tov, E.** “Texts.” **Trites, A. A.** *Concept,* 128–53. **Trudinger, P.** “Stephen.” **Turner, M.** *Power.* **Twelftree, G. H.** “Prayer,” 273–74. **van den Eynde, S.** “Children.” **Via, E. J.** “Interpretation.” **Walton, S.** “Acts, Book of.” ———. “Acts of God” ———. “Anthropology.” ———. “Calling.” ———. “Tale,” 138–43. ———. “Ὁμοθυμαδόν,” 102–3. **Weinert, F. D.** “Luke.” **Wendel, S. J.** *Scriptural Interpretation,* 218–22. **White, A. W.** *Prophets,* 101–41. ———. “Revisiting.” **Whitenton, M. R.** “Rewriting.” **Wiens, D.** *Stephen’s Sermon.* **Wilcox, M.** *Semitisms.* **Wilson, B. E.** “Hearing,” 464–69. ———. *Unmanly Men,* 201–35. **Wright, N. T.** *Resurrection,* 109–15. **Zehnle, R. F.** *Discourse,* 76–89.

Translation

68 Stephen, full of grace and power, was performing great wonders and signs among the people. 9 Certain men[a] came forward from the synagogue of the Freedmen (as it was known), both Cyrenians and Alexandrians, as well as men from Cilicia and Asia, in order to debate with Stephen, 10 but they were unable to resist the wisdom and the Spirit[b] with which he was speaking. 11 Then they secretly prompted men who said, “We have heard him speaking blasphemous words against Moses and God.” 12 They stirred up the people, the elders, and the scribes, and they came upon Stephen, seized him, and brought him to the Sanhedrin, 13 where they presented false witnesses who said, “This person does not cease speaking words against the[c] holy place and the law; 14 for we have heard him say that this Jesus the Nazarene will destroy this place and will change the customs which Moses handed down to us.” 15 As everyone sitting in the Sanhedrin fixed their attention on him, they saw his face was like the face of an angel.

71 The chief priest said, “Are these things true?”[d]

2 Stephen[e] replied, “Men, brothers and fathers, listen! The God of glory[f] appeared to our ancestor Abraham while he was in Mesopotamia before he lived in Haran, 3 and he said to him, ‘Leave your land and[g] your relatives, and come away to the land that I will show you.’ 4 Then he left the land of the Chaldeans and settled in Haran. After his father’s death, God[h] moved him out from there into this land in which you yourselves now live, 5 and he did not give him any inheritance whatsoever[i] in it, but promised to give it as a possession to him and to his descendants[j] after him, even though he was childless.[k] 6 God spoke in this way, that his descendants[l] would be aliens[m] in a land not their own where the people[n] would enslave and ill-treat them[o] for four hundred years.[p] 7 ‘Yet I myself will judge the nation that enslaves[q] them,’ God said, ‘And after these things they will come out and they will worship me in this place.’ 8 God[r] gave him the covenant of circumcision; and so he fathered Isaac and circumcised him on the eighth day, and Isaac Jacob, and Jacob the twelve patriarchs.

9 The patriarchs, because they became jealous[s] of Joseph, sold[t] him into Egypt. Yet God was with him, 10 and delivered[u] him from all his sufferings, and gave to him favor

and wisdom before Pharaoh, king of Egypt; he[v] put him in charge of Egypt and his whole household. 11 A famine came upon the whole of Egypt and Canaan, with great suffering, and our ancestors could not find[w] food. 12 When Jacob heard there was[x] grain in Egypt, he sent our ancestors to begin with.[y] 13 On the second time, Joseph made himself known[z] to his brothers, and Joseph's racial origin[aa] became known to Pharaoh. 14 Joseph sent a message inviting his father Jacob to join him,[bb] with the whole extended family of seventy-five people.[cc] 15 Jacob went down to Egypt and he died, as well as our ancestors, 16 and they were brought back to Shechem and placed in the tomb that Abraham bought for a sum[dd] of money from the sons of Hamor in Shechem.

17 Now as the time of the promise that[ee] God made to Abraham was drawing near, the people multiplied greatly[ff] in Egypt 18 until the time when[gg] another king who had not known Joseph came to power.[hh] 19 This man outwitted our race by trickery and ill-treated our[ii] ancestors by compelling[jj] them to expose[kk] their infants so that they would not live. 20 At that very time, Moses was born, and he was good-looking as far as God was concerned.[ll] He was brought up for three months in his father's house, 21 but when he was exposed, Pharaoh's daughter claimed him for herself[mm] and brought him up as her own son. 22 Moses was educated in all the wisdom of the Egyptians, and he was powerful in his words and deeds. 23 When he was forty years old,[nn] it came into his mind[oo] to visit his compatriots,[pp] the descendants[qq] of Israel. 24 When he saw a certain one in the process of being treated wrongly, he came to his defense and took vengeance on the oppressor by striking the Egyptian. 25 He supposed that his compatriots would understand[rr] that God, through his hand, was giving salvation to them; but they did not understand. 26 The next day he appeared as some[ss] were fighting and he tried to reconcile[tt] them by saying, 'Men, you are brothers: why are you harming each other?' 27 The one who was harming his neighbor pushed him aside, saying, 'Who put you in charge as a judge and ruler over us? 28 You surely don't want to kill me in the same way as you killed the Egyptian, do you?' 29 Moses fled because he said this[uu] and became an alien in the land of Midian, where he fathered two sons.

30 When forty years had passed[vv] an angel appeared to him in the wilderness of Mount Sinai in flaming[ww] fire in a bush. 31 When Moses saw this, he was amazed at the sight. As he was approaching[xx] to look more closely, the voice of the Lord came: 32 'I am the God of your ancestors, the God of Abraham and Isaac and Jacob.' Moses began to tremble[yy] and did not dare to look more closely. 33 Then the Lord said to him, 'Take the sandals off your feet, for the place where you are standing is holy ground. 34 I have indeed seen[zz] the oppression of my people in Egypt and I have heard their groaning, and I have come down in order to deliver them. So now, come, let me send[aaa] you to Egypt.' 35 This Moses[bbb]—the one they rejected,[ccc] saying, 'Who put you in charge as a ruler and judge?'—this is the one[ddd] God sent as ruler and deliverer through[eee] the hand of an angel who appeared to him in the bush. 36 This is the one[fff] who led them out by doing wonders and signs in the land of Egypt and at the Red Sea—as well as[ggg] in the wilderness for forty years. 37 This is the Moses who said to the descendants[hhh] of Israel, 'God will raise up a prophet like me for you from among your compatriots.'

38 This is the one who was in the congregation in the wilderness with the angel who spoke to him on Mount Sinai—and with our ancestors. He received living words to give to us, 39 and it was him that our ancestors were not willing to obey; instead, they pushed him aside and turned back in their hearts to Egypt, 40 when they said to Aaron, 'Make for us gods who will go before us; for this Moses,[iii] who led us out from Egypt—we don't know what has happened to him!' 41 At that time they made a calf, offered sacrifice to the idol, and began celebrating what their hands had made. 42 But God turned away[jjj] and handed them over to worship the army of heaven, just as it is written in the book of the prophets:

You did not bring offerings and sacrifices to me
  for forty years in the wilderness, O house of Israel, did you?
43 You took along the tent of Moloch
  and the star of the god[kkk] Rephan,
  the images which you made in order to worship them,
and so I will deport you beyond Babylon.

44 The tent of witness was with our ancestors in the wilderness just as the one who spoke instructed Moses to make it according to the pattern that he had seen. 45 Our ancestors, who received it in turn, also brought it in with Joshua when they took possession of the land of the nations[lll] whom God drove out before the face of our ancestors until the time of David. 46 He [sc. David] found favor before God and asked that he might find a dwelling place for the house[mmm] of Jacob. 47 However, it was Solomon who built a house for it, 48 though[nnn] the Most High does not live in hand made things, as the prophet says:

49 Heaven is my throne,
  and earth the footstool for my feet;
What kind of house will you build for me,
  says the Lord,
  or what is my place of rest?
50 Didn't my hand made all these things?[ooo]

51 Stiff-necked and uncircumcised in hearts and ears—that's you,[ppp] constantly resisting the Holy Spirit; you are just like your ancestors![qqq] 52 Which of the prophets did your ancestors not persecute? Indeed, they killed those who announced in advance the coming of the righteous one, and you yourselves have become his betrayers and murderers; 53 you people, who[rrr] received the law by angels acting under God's direction[sss] and you did not keep it."

54 On hearing these things, they became infuriated in their hearts and began grinding their teeth at him. 55 He, however, being full of the Holy Spirit and looking intently into heaven, saw the glory of God and Jesus standing at the right side of God 56 and said, "Look! I see the heavens open and the Son of Man standing at the right

side of God." 57 Shouting at the tops of their voices, they closed their ears and rushed
as one person upon him. 58 They threw him out of the city and began stoning him.
The witnesses placed their cloaks at the feet of a young man called Saul. 59 As they
were stoning Stephen he called upon the Lord[ttt] and said, "Lord Jesus, receive my
spirit!" 60 He knelt down and shouted at the top of his voice, "Lord, do not hold this
sin against them!" After he said this, he fell asleep.

8:1 And Saul approved[uuu] of killing him.[vvv]

Notes

a. τινες, "certain," m. could denote "men" or "people"; the setting, speaking in a synagogue, makes "men" virtually certain.

b. inf. ἀντιστῆναι, "to resist," + dat. of what/who is being resisted ("ἀνθίστημι," BDAG 80, §1.b). It is possible that τῇ σοφίᾳ καὶ τῷ πνεύματι forms a hendiadys meaning "spiritual wisdom" (Culy and Parsons, *Acts*, 111–12)—within Luke's worldview, that nevertheless suggests wisdom given by the Holy Spirit (with Calvin, *Acts*, 1:166).

c. v.l. τούτου, "this," omitted in 𝔓[74] א A D E H P Ψ 049 056 066 0175 614 1175 1241 1505 𝔐 it[d] arm eth; included in B C 33 36 69 323 945 1739 *al* it[h, p, t] vg[mss] syr cop[sa, bo]; Gregory-Nyssa. The MS support is finely balanced. τούτου was probably introduced from v. 14, where it is secure. It is thus likely that it was originally absent (with Barrett, *Acts*, 1:327; cf. *TCGNT*[2], 298).

d. εἰ introduces a direct question (BDF, §440[3]). ταῦτα οὕτως ἔχει is an impersonal idiom, ἔχω + adverb, here meaning, "Is this the situation?"; Barrett, *Acts*, 1:340; "ἔχω," BDAG 422, §10.a; see Acts 12:15; 15:36; 17:11; 21:13; 24:9, 25; Rev 2:15.

e. ὁ δέ signals a switch of subject to Stephen.

f. Perhaps "the glorious God," if gen. τῆς δόξης, "of glory," is attributive; Wallace, 86–88, §c.3.

g. NA[28] places the second ἐκ in square brackets; ECM includes it in its main text. Its presence or absence makes little difference to the sense; it is absent from B D, but present in 𝔓[74] א A C E Ψ, plus minuscules, 𝔐 and versions. It is textually secure in Gen 12:1 LXX (the passage being quoted here), reflecting the repetition of מן (*mn*), "from," in MT; perhaps it was absent in Acts and supplied by scribes who knew its presence in LXX.

h. μετῴκισεν αὐτόν, lit., "he moved him out"; the object αὐτόν is Abraham, and so the implied subject is God; Culy and Parsons, *Acts*, 116; L&N §85.83.

i. κληρονομίαν ἐν αὐτῇ οὐδὲ βῆμα ποδός, lit., "an inheritance in it, not a step of a foot"; cf. Deut 2:5 LXX.

j. τῷ σπέρματι αὐτοῦ, "his seed," used for "descendants"; "σπέρμα," BDAG 937, §2.a.

k. οὐκ ὄντος αὐτῷ τέκνου, "there not being to him a child," gen. abs.: impersonal expression, with concessive force; Culy and Parsons, *Acts*, 117; NET.

l. τὸ σπέρμα αὐτοῦ, lit., "his seed"; cf. v. 5.

m. πάροικον, sg., "an alien," agreeing in number with τὸ σπέρμα, "the seed"; because I translated the latter as "descendants," the former needs to be translated as pl. too.

n. καὶ δουλώσουσιν, "and they will enslave," implying the people of the land as subject.

o. αὐτό, neut. sg. rel. pron., refers back to the sg. τὸ σπέρμα, "the seed," and is the direct obj. of δουλώσουσιν, "they will enslave."

p. ἔτη τετρακόσια, acc. expressing extent of time, "for four hundred years."

q. ECM reads aor. subj. δουλεύσωσιν, "would enslave," different from NA[28] fut. ind. δουλεύσουσιν, "will enslave." The lack of coherence in the attestation of the fut.

ind. reading, as well as the possibility that later scribes might assume this was more appropriate, support ECM's decision. See ECM, 3:12.

r. The subject of ἔδωκεν, "he gave," is God, the subject of εἶπεν, "said," in the previous sentence.

s. ζηλώσαντες, aor. ptc., "having become jealous," causal; Culy and Parsons, *Acts*, 119; NET.

t. ἀπέδοντο, aor. mid. ἀποδίδωμι; mid. has sense "sell"; "ἀποδίδωμι," BDAG 110, §5.a; "ἀποδίδωμι," LSJ 197, §III.

u. ἐξείλατο, aor. mid. of ἐξαιρέω; mid. has sense "deliver"; "ἐξαιρέω," BDAG 344, §2.

v. See *Comment* on 7:9: the subject could be God or Pharaoh.

w. οὐχ ηὕρισκον, negated impf., has sense "could not find"; McKay, 43, 44–45.

x. Acc. anarthrous ptc. ὄντα, "being," with acc. noun σιτία, "grain," is in indirect discourse following the verb of perception ἀκούσας, "hearing"; Wallace, 645–46; Robertson, 1041–42, 1122–24; contra Culy and Parsons, *Acts*, 120.

y. πρῶτον, "to begin with"; "πρῶτος," BDAG 893, §1.a.β. This sense is clear because of the following ἐν τῷ δευτέρῳ, "on the second time," (v. 13).

z. ἀνεγνωρίσθη, aor. pass. of ἀναγνωρίζω, with reflexive mid. sense "made *himself* known"; Fitzmyer, *Acts*, 373.

aa. τὸ γένος, "racial origin": use in 7:19 suggests ethnicity is in view here; with Barrett, *Acts*, 1:350.

bb. μετεκαλέσατο, aor. mid., with reflexive sense "inviting . . . to join him"; "μετακαλέω," BDAG 639.

cc. ἐν ψυχαῖς ἑβδομήκοντα πέντε, "amounting to seventy-five lives." For the sense of ἐν see MHT, 3:265; "ἐν," BDAG 330, §12; Barrett, *Acts*, 1:350; contra Culy and Parsons, *Acts*, 121.

dd. τιμῆς, gen. of price "for a sum"; BDF, §179(1); Wallace, 122.

ee. ἧς, "which," fem. sg. rel. pn., attracted into gen. by gen. ἐπαγγελίας "promise"; it would usually be acc. direct obj. of ὡμολόγησεν.

ff. ηὔξησεν ὁ λαὸς καὶ ἐπληθύνθη, hendiadys: "the people grew and multiplied"; cf. 6:7; 12:24.

gg. ἄχρι οὗ, "until the time when"; rel. attraction: see *Note* d on ἄχρι ἧς ἡμέρας in 1:2.

hh. NA^{28} includes ἐπ' Αἴγυπτον, "over Egypt," in square brackets, and ECM has a split guiding line, both indicating uncertainty. It is absent from 𝔓$^{45\text{vid}}$ D E 81 614 1241 𝔐 it^{gig} syr^{h}, and present in 𝔓$^{33\text{vid}, 74}$ א A B C Ψ 104 323 945 1175 1505 1739 2818 vg syr$^{\text{p, hmg}}$ cop D E it $^{\text{gig, p}}$ also read ἐμνήσθη, "remember," rather than ᾔδει, "had . . . known." This verse quotes Exod 1:8 LXX, which includes ἐπ' Αἴγυπτον and ᾔδει; the majority readings could be assimilation to LXX, or the other witnesses could have omitted ἐπ' Αἴγυπτον, since "in Egypt," ἐν Αἰγύπτῳ, is already present in 7:17, and chosen a different verb; *TCGNT*^{2}, 302–3.

ii. I read ἡμῶν, "our," which NA^{28} places in square brackets, and where ECM has a split guiding line, both indicating uncertainty. It is present in A C E Ψ 81 323 614 945 1241 1739 𝔐 it vg^{cl} syr, and absent from 𝔓^{74} א B D 1175 1505 vg$^{\text{st ww}}$, both strong and coherent attestations. If originally absent, it could have been inserted under the influence of the phrase τὸ γένος ἡμῶν, "our race," earlier in the sentence. If originally present, it may well have been deleted in error or as redundant (B is known for doing this), and this seems more likely. Discussion: ECM, 3:12; *TCGNT*^{2}, 303.

jj. Epexegetical inf. ποιεῖν, showing how Pharaoh "ill-treated" the Israelites, "by making (them)."

kk. τοῦ ποιεῖν τὰ βρέφη ἔκθετα αὐτῶν, "by compelling them to expose their infants," gen. inf. clause, epexegetical, expressing the way in which the king ill-treated the ancestors; Culy and Parsons, *Acts*, 124; Barrett, *Acts*, 1:352–53; contra Wallace, 592.

ll. τῷ θεῷ, ethical dat. = "as far as God was concerned"; Wallace, 146–47; "θεός," BDAG 451, §3.g.β.

mm. ἀνείλατο, aor. mid. with sense, "claimed for herself"; "ἀναιρέω," BDAG 64, §3; contrast act., which can mean "kill," §2.

nn. ἐπληροῦτο αὐτῷ τεσσερακονταετὴς χρόνος, lit., "was fulfilled for him a time of forty years"; rare idiomatic expression (cf. 13:18) focusing on length of time.

oo. τὴν καρδίαν, generally "heart," here denotes the place of thought, hence "mind"; "καρδία," BDAG 509, §1.b.β; cf. Paul's use in 1 Cor 2:9.

pp. ἀδελφούς, "compatriots"; "ἀδελφός," BDAG 18–19, §2.b (also v. 25).

qq. υἱούς "descendants"; "υἱός," BDAG 1024, §1.c.

rr. συνιέναι τοὺς ἀδελφοὺς αὐτοῦ, "his compatriots would understand," inf. + acc. in indirect discourse; contra Barrett, *Acts*, 1:357, who takes pres. tense of inf. συνιέναι as suggesting that Moses supposed that they *already* understood.

ss. αὐτοῖς, unspecific "they."

tt. συνήλλασσεν, conative impf., "he tried to reconcile"; Wallace, 550–51; MHT, 1:128–9; Bruce, *Acts* (1990), 199. εἰς εἰρήνην, "in peace," is redundant, perhaps adding emphasis, and is omitted in translation.

uu. ἐν τῷ λόγῳ τούτῳ, "at this word/saying"; ἐν introduces causal dat., a Semitic usage; BDF, §219(2); "ἐν," BDAG 329, §9.a; MHT, 2:463.

vv. πληρωθέντων ἐτῶν τεσσεράκοντα, temporal gen. abs., "forty years having been fulfilled."

ww. Treating πυρός, "of fire," as gen. modifying φλογί, "a flame," as in LXX Isa 66:16; Dan 7:9; Sir 21:9; Pss. Sol. 15:4; 2 Thess 1:8; Heb 1:7 (quoting Ps 103:4 LXX [MT 104:4]); Rev 2:18; 19:12; with Barrett, *Acts*, 1:360; Bruce, *Acts* (1990), 200; contra Culy and Parsons, *Acts*, 132. On the variant reading πυρὶ φλογός, "a fire of flame," see ECM, 3:13; Katz, "ἐν πυρί."

xx. προσερχομένου . . . αὐτοῦ, temporal gen. abs., "as he was approaching."

yy. Treating γενόμενος, "came," as inceptive aor.; ἔντρομος . . . γενόμενος Μωϋσῆς = "trembling came upon Moses."

zz. ἰδὼν εἶδον, lit., "seeing, I have seen," a Semitic idiom intensifying the main verb; Bruce, *Acts* (1990), 200.

aaa. ἀποστείλω, 1 sg. aor. subj. of ἀποστέλλω, "send" = "let me send," hortatory, as is usual in NT for subj. with δεῦρο, "come!"; Wallace, 464; Robertson, 931–32.

bbb. Τοῦτον τὸν Μωϋσῆν, thematic acc., "this Moses," is fronted to focus on him; cf. 2:32, 36.

ccc. ἠρνήσαντο, "they refused to follow"; L&N §36.43.

ddd. τοῦτον, "this one," is emphatic (by being fronted) and resumptive, refocusing on Moses.

eee. This is the only clear use of σύν in the instrumental sense "through" in the NT; Price, *Lexicology*, 122.

fff. See n. ddd.

ggg. In the book of Exodus (as well as logically), the wonders and signs in the wilderness (and perhaps those at the Red Sea) *follow* Moses leading the people out, and this does not sit comfortably with the most natural reading of the aor. ptc. ποιήσας, "having done." I have translated as a kind of anacoluthon; cf. Bruce, *Acts* (1990), 201; Barrett, *Acts*, 1:364–65. A plausible alternative is to see ἐξήγαγεν, "[he] led them out," as constative aor., describing the exodus and wilderness period as a whole; MHT, 1:133.

hhh. See n. qq.

iii. ὁ . . . Μωϋσῆς οὗτος, "this Moses," hanging nom. to introduce main focus of clause; MHT, 1:69.

jjj. Intransitive use of ἔστρεψεν, "he turned"; "στρέφω," BDAG 948, §4; Bruce, *Acts* (1990), 203; Barrett, *Acts*, 1:367–68; contra Johnson, *Acts*, 131.

kkk. 𝔓⁷⁴ ℵ A C E Ψ 33 (614 1505) 1739 𝔐 it$^{h\ p}$ vg syr^{h} cop$^{mae,\ bo}$; Cyr read τοῦ θεοῦ ὑμῶν, "your god," found also in Amos 5:26 LXX, which is being quoted here (and thus probably a harmonizing addition); ὑμῶν, "your," is absent from B D 36 453 it$^{d,\ gig}$ syr^{p} cop^{sa}; Ir^{lat} Origen.

lll. ἐν τῇ κατασχέσει τῶν ἐθνῶν, "when they took possession of the nations"; τῶν ἐθνῶν, "the nations," stands for the territory they occupy.

mmm. θεῷ, "for the God," ℵ^{2} A C E Ψ 33 1739 𝔐 lat syr cop (read by NIV); οἴκῳ, "for the house," 𝔓⁷⁴ ℵ* B D H 049 *pc* sa^{ms} (read by NRSVue). ECM places the two in parallel, suggesting the decision is not straightforward; see discussion, ECM, 3:13, and *Comment*.

nnn. ἀλλ' introduces a qualification to the previous statement; "ἀλλά," BDAG, §2.

ooo. οὐχί, "not," implies a positive answer to the question; Culy and Parsons, *Acts*, 142.

ppp. ὑμεῖς, "you," fronted for emphasis, focusing Stephen's charge against his hearers.

qqq. ὡς οἱ πατέρες ὑμῶν καὶ ὑμεῖς, "just like your ancestors, you too."

rrr. οἵτινες, "people who," referring back to ὑμεῖς, "you" (v. 52); indef. rel. pn. BDF, §293(2).

sss. εἰς διαταγὰς ἀγγέλων, "by directions of angels"; "διαταγή," BDAG 237: "by angels under God's direction [to transmit it]." Cf. Fitzmyer, *Acts*, 386.

ttt. "the Lord," absent in the Greek, is the implied object of ἐπικαλούμενον, "calling upon," seen by the vocative κύριε, "Lord."

uuu. ἦν συνευδοκῶν, "approved," periph. impf., highlighting that this was an ongoing state more strongly than the simple impf.; cf. Porter, *Aspects*, 460; Fanning, *Aspect*, 314–15.

vvv. αὐτοῦ, "him," obj. gen.

Form/Structure/Setting

Delimitation of pericope. This long section, including the longest speech in Acts, is held together by its focus on Stephen, the first Christian martyr, a figure briefly introduced as one of the seven to "serve at table" in 6:5 and whose direct presence in the narrative ends with his death at 7:60, although that death indirectly provokes growth among the believing communities as believers are scattered geographically (8:1b; 11:19).

Sources/historicity. These events are now widely seen as historically rooted,[1] particularly because of their explanatory power in contributing further to the gradual division of the believing community from the Jewish leadership, as well as to the historical development of persecution that led to the scattering of believers and the planting of churches in other places. Some doubt that the speech can be from the occasion where Luke locates it.

The dating of the event is not straightforward. Some church tradition from fourth to fourteenth centuries dates it to seven years after the death and

---

1 E.g., Lüdemann, *Early Christianity*, 85, 93; Haenchen, *Acts*, 273; Fitzmyer, *Acts*, 355; Dunn, *Beginning*, 264–65; Schwemer, "Lukas," 304; contra earlier work, such as Mundle, "Stephanusrede."

resurrection of Jesus.[2] However, this is difficult to square with Paul's assertion that he "persecuted the church of God" (Gal 1:13), for the only substantial persecution for which we have evidence is that of Acts 8:1b, 3, which Luke links chronologically with Stephen's death (ἐν ἐκείνῃ τῇ ἡμέρᾳ, "on that day" or "at that time," 8:1) and in which he presents Paul (named as Saul) as a ringleader (8:3). There are bigger issues than can be considered here, notably the correlation with Pauline chronology, but this link suggests a date around AD 31–32.[3]

Stephen's speech is deeply rooted in Scripture (see *Comment*),[4] and in this way is similar to other reviews of biblical and Jewish history. However, it differs from other such reviews in, for example, its strong focus on Moses (vv. 17–42).[5] Bowker suggests that the speech has the form of a proem homily, known from synagogues, based on Gen 12:1 with engagement with Exod 23:12–24:9 (from the Pentateuch, a Seder reading) and Isa 65:22–66:5 (from the Prophets, a haftarah reading).[6] Such a sermon typically touched on a number of biblical texts (a process called *ḥaruzin*). If so, early Christian communication here utilizes forms known from synagogue preaching. However, there are so many OT texts woven into this discourse that it is hard to be as precise as Bowker—and the speech's form reads more like a legal refutation (and counter accusation) than a homily.[7] The citations from Scripture are from the Greek OT, which would be appropriate for a "Hellenist" such as Stephen, and naturally reflects Luke's use of Scripture in Greek. The speech is certainly expressed through Luke's own words. The language spoken by Stephen to the Sanhedrin may have been Greek and, if so, would have been translated: it is a gratuitous assumption that Stephen could not have spoken Greek in this setting.[8] Further, to suggest that because these events are told in Lukan diction and with echoes of the trial and death of Jesus in Luke's Gospel (see *Comment* on 7:54–60), we should doubt this account, is to make a false assumption.[9] It is, of course, highly unlikely that the speech was written down at the time: at most, this passage offers a précis of what was said.[10]

Jeska studies numerous reviews of Israel's history;[11] he calls them "summaries of the history of Israel" and distinguishes them from "rewritten Bible"

---

2 References and discussion: Riesner, *Period*, 59–60.

3 See full discussion in Riesner, *Period*, 59–74; so also Neudorfer, "Speech," 277.

4 For detailed analysis, see Smith, *Fate*, 140–89. For a fascinating consideration of how other Jewish writers read and retell the Abraham and Joseph stories, see Whitenton, "Rewriting," 151–61.

5 Richard, *Acts 6:1–8:4*, 143; Robb, "Prophet," 108.

6 Bowker, "Speeches," 107.

7 Cf. Marshall, "Acts," 556.

8 Contra Dunn, *Beginning*, 266.

9 E.g., Simon, *St. Stephen*, 20–25. He qualifies this by saying that the speech "in its essentials" is pre-Lukan (39).

10 Cf. Hemer, *Book*, 418–27; Lightfoot, *Acts*, 131–33.

11 Notably Pss 105:7–44 (LXX 104:7–44); 106:6–46 (LXX 105:6–46); Josh 24:2–13; Neh 9:7–31; Jdt 5:6–19. See Jeska's full list: Jeska, *Geschichte*, 21. See also Neudorfer, "Speech," 281–83.

on the basis that these summaries appear as sections in longer works (rather than being full works in their own right, such as LAB or Jubilees) and are generally more concise.[12]

There are also parallels with how Greco-Roman authors consider history's importance in establishing the nature and values of their community or nation (e.g., Cicero, *Inv.* 1.30.49; *De or.* 1.18; 2.36; Livy, *Ab urbe cond.* 22.60.14; Thucydides, *P.W.* 1.22.4; Polybius, *Hist.* 1.1.2).[13] Dibelius considers that the speech is a general Hellenistic-Jewish review of Israel's history with vv. 51–53 added to relate it to the setting.[14] The comparison with other reviews of Israel's history suggests the speech is coherent, focused on critiquing the Jewish leadership's rejection of Jesus, and thus the conclusion belongs with the rest of the speech—other reviews are similarly slanted to speak to their contemporary situation.[15] Nevertheless, it is likely that this, the first martyrdom, was highly memorable—not least to Saul—and thus Saul remembered what Stephen said, at least in outline.[16]

There is substantial discussion of the extent to which the speech actually answers the charges against Stephen in 6:13–14.[17] Much of the speech establishes common ground with his accusers and the Sanhedrin while offering a critique of their localization of God's presence in the Jerusalem temple by showing that YHWH regularly meets with people outside the land and the temple (see *Comment* on 7:2, 9–15, 20–22, 25, 30–34, and *Explanation*; cf. Paul's similar tactics of establishing common ground and offering critique in Athens, 17:16–31). Peterson, arguing that the speech is a modified form of the prophetic lawsuit (Heb. רִיב [*rîb*]),[18] suggests that Stephen is responding to the injustice of the false charges more than answering the charges themselves and thus speaks as plaintiff rather than defendant.[19] This is plausible, particularly when Stephen directly addresses charges against the Sanhedrin (7:51–53).

12 Jeska, *Geschichte*, 19–22. Vermes defines "rewritten Bible" as "[A] narrative that follows Scripture but includes a substantial amount of supplements and interpretative developments" (Schürer, 3.1:326). On "rewritten Bible," see Alexander, "Retelling," esp. 116–18. For a contrary view to Jeska, see Evans, "Rewritten Bible," esp. 175–79.

13 I owe these references to Dinkler, "Politics," 41; see her helpful discussion there.

14 Dibelius, *Studies*, 167.

15 Brehm, "Vindicating," 273–77, with table on 298–99, noting parallels (LXX versification added in brackets where it differs from MT) with Josh 24:2–15; Neh 9:6–37 [2 Esd 19:6–37]; Pss 78 [77]; 105 [104]; 106 [105]; Ezek 20; Wis 10–19; Sir 44–50; Jdt 5:6–21. So also Hall, *Revealed Histories*, 197–98.

16 Kennedy, *NT Interpretation*, 122. Sparks, "Semitisms," 25, suggests that the best explanation is that Luke "was writing up the story as he had heard it," although he does not specify from whom Luke heard it.

17 Dibelius, *Studies*, 167–69, and Haenchen, *Acts*, 286, consider the speech irrelevant to the charges against Stephen by contrast with (e.g.) Holladay, *Acts*, 159–62, and Hall, *Revealed Histories*, 198, who show how well it fits the rhetorical situation.

18 E.g., Deut 32:1–25; Ps 50 [LXX 49]; Isa 1:2–20; 3:13–15; Jer 2:2–37; Mic 6:1–8; Amos 3:1–4:13. Examples where historical review is part of the lawsuit include Deut 32:7–14; Isa 1:2; Jer 2:6–7a; Amos 4:6–11; Mic 6:4–5. I owe these references to Peterson, "Stephen's Speech," 357.

19 Peterson, "Stephen's Speech," 359.

It also has the benefit of locating the genre in a lawcourt setting where the human setting is turned on its head: Stephen is the plaintiff, rather than the defendant; the Sanhedrin are the defendant rather than judge; and God is the judge to whom the Sanhedrin must answer.

Some suggest that there are Samaritan influences evident in this speech.[20] As Spencer notes, there are significant difficulties in this claim:[21] (i) the comparison is from documents of different periods: other than the Samaritan Pentateuch (first century BC), the only extant Samaritan sources date from the fourth century AD onwards, whereas Acts is much earlier; (ii) it is difficult to identify traditions that are *distinctively* Samaritan rather than shared with other sources—thus it is impossible to claim that themes shared by this speech, Samaritan traditions, and other traditions are due to specifically *Samaritan* influence.[22] The attempt by some to make a cumulative case, claiming that multiple small pieces of evidence that could point to Samaritan influence add up to evidence of considerable Samaritan influence, depends on the strength of the small pieces of evidence, and Richard shows how weak these pieces of evidence are.[23] Further, Stephen's references to David and Solomon (vv. 45–47), quotations from the prophets (vv. 42b–43, 49–50), and apparent opposition to any specific place of worship (v. 48) would not fit easily with Samaritan thought.[24]

That said, we know that the Samaritans worshiped at a different sanctuary in the first century AD: Shechem (note 7:16) rather than Jerusalem (see *Comment* on 8:5). However, the only clear reference to Shechem in the speech is as the burial place of Jewish ancestors (see *Comment* on 7:16); other claimed references are tenuous at best.[25]

Strikingly, there is no evidence in the speech of a later gentile Christian perspective.[26] Gentiles are not mentioned, and the argument of the speech only makes sense in a Jewish setting. It would certainly benefit Jewish believers by connecting them to Abraham, Joseph, Moses, and David as their ancestors in faith and in showing that Jesus's experience was in continuity with that of these ancestors. The Jewish law is seen positively, as God's "living words" (v. 38). There is a challenge to the present idolatry of the temple but no

20 E.g., Scobie, "Use," 409; Munck, Albright and Mann, *Acts,* 285–301, esp. 286 (representing the research of A. Spiro); Trudinger, "Stephen," esp. 22; Ravens, *Luke,* 87–91. Fuller references: Spencer, *Portrait,* 70–71.

21 Spencer, *Portrait,* 72–73; also Coggins, "Samaritans," 423–29; cf. Mare, "Acts 7," critiquing Spiro's work.

22 As examples with parallels in Jewish literature besides Samaritan writings, Spencer, *Portrait,* 72, cites the example discussed below in 7:4 concerning the date of Abraham leaving Haran and in 7:37 concerning the prophet like Moses.

23 Richard, "Acts 7," 193–94, critiquing Scharlemann, *Stephen,* 50–51; Scroggs, "Earliest," 189–95; Scobie, "Origins," 393–96.

24 Donaldson, "Moses," 33.

25 Scobie, "Use," 406–7, 408–10; critique: Spencer, *Portrait,* 75–77.

26 With Ravens, *Luke,* 67–68.

rejection of the temple as always outside God's purposes (see *Comment* on vv. 46–50). These features suggest that the speech fits well into a context of a "sectarian" group within Judaism defining itself against the majority (similar in some ways to the Qumran rejection of the Jerusalem temple)—exactly the literary setting of the speech.[27]

Structure. After sketching Stephen's activities (6:8), the grammatical subject switches to his opponents, highlighting their perception of Stephen and the actions they take against him (vv. 9–14), including the charges they present to the Sanhedrin (vv. 13–14). The Sanhedrin's (and the accusers') perception of Stephen develops as they see his angelic face (v. 15).

As is proper in a legal setting, the high priest invites Stephen to respond (7:1), and the long speech that follows details Stephen's response (7:2–53, 55–56—the hearers do not interrupt Stephen in v. 54[28]). Luke contrasts Stephen's Spirit-filled state with the anger of the hearers, who rush on him and murder him by stoning (vv. 57–58a). Thus, the speech seems incomplete, ended by the hearers (v. 57).[29] Luke now introduces Saul for the first time as one who looks after the cloaks of the stoners (v. 58b)—Saul is a character who will be highly significant for the continuing narrative. The focus then moves back to Stephen, who now prays to Jesus as he is being killed, and then dies (vv. 59–60). The story ends with a further brief note on Saul, which prepares for his campaign of persecution (8:1a; cf. 9:1–2).

The speech itself is the longest in Acts, signaling its importance for Luke. It is a selective review of Israel's history along similar lines to "rewritten Bible," a genre familiar from other Jewish writings—some as long, or longer, than this speech (see above).[30] This genre makes Greco-Roman rhetorical analysis less relevant, and the quasi-judicial setting speaks against the speech or the whole scene being epideictic.[31] After an opening call to be heard (7:2a), the choice of key figures in Jewish history is significant: Abraham (and the patriarchs) (vv. 2b–8); Joseph and Jacob (7:9–16); Moses (7:17–43, split into three periods of forty years: vv. 17–22, 23–29, 30–43);[32] David and Solomon,

27 On this paragraph, see the fuller discussion of Donaldson, "Moses."

28 Schnabel, *Acts*, 362.

29 Kennedy, *NT Interpretation*, 122.

30 E.g., Deut 6:20–24; 26:5–10; Josh 24:2–13; 1 Sam 12:6–13; Neh 9:6–31; Pss 78:5–72 [LXX 77:5–72]; 105:7–44 [LXX 104:7–44]; 106:7–46 [LXX 105:7–46]; 135:5–12 [LXX 134:5–12]; 136:4–25 [LXX 135:4–25]; Ezek 20:5–9; Jdt 5:6–19; 1 Macc 2:52–60; Wis 10:1–11:26; Sir 44:3–50:21; 3 Macc 2:4–12; 6:4–8; 1 En. 85:3–90:38; 93:3–10; 91:11–17; 2 Bar. 56:2–74:4; 4 Ezra 5:4–8; Sib. Or. 3:248–294; LAB 32:1–12; CD 2.14–4.12a; Josephus, *J.W.* 5.9.4 §§375–412; *Ant.* 3.5.3 §§86–87. Discussion: Alexander, "Retelling"; Doble, *Paradox*, 135–37.

31 *Contra*, e.g., Penner, "Narrative as Persuasion," 354–58. Witherington, *Acts*, 260, is closer to the mark in identifying the speech as judicial, although it is doubtful that the form is that of classical Greek rhetoric.

32 Dupont, "Structure," 157–60, identifies v. 35 as a transition, and Witherington, *Acts*, 260, takes it as the main proposition of the speech, even though it is indirectly stated. Both see vv. 36–30 as the main argument of the speech. It seems more likely that we should read the

particularly their project to build the temple (vv. 44–50). The speech climaxes with Stephen's indictment of his hearers that they resist the Spirit after the pattern set by their ancestors (vv. 51–53). Stephen here turns the tables on his accusers, arguing that *they* are the ones failing God (having hinted at this in vv. 25, 39)—the core issue, as in earlier hearings, is who speaks for God, and (thus) who rightly understands what God has done in history and is doing now (cf. 4:7, 19–20, 29–31; 5:29, 32, 38–39). Hence, when Stephen relates his vision of the exalted Jesus, he is presenting his credentials for the claim that he, as a member of the believing community, speaks for God, now known in and through Jesus (7:55–56).[33] There is considerable engagement with Scripture, particularly the Greek OT, in the speech, often staying quite close to the scriptural wording (see *Comment*).[34] Alongside this, there is use of extrabiblical tradition concerning Moses in particular (see *Comment* on 7:20, 21, 22).

The speech's flow centers on the interplay between God's actions and self-revelation and people's responses.[35] In the Abraham story, God is the subject of most main verbs (vv. 2b, 3c, 4b, 6a, 7b, c, 8a): God initiates events and makes promises to Abraham.[36] Similarly, it is crucial for Joseph that "God was with him" (v. 9); this is why his wrongful rejection by his brothers is not the final word, for God delivers him and gives him a favorable reception from Pharaoh (v. 10). God's promise to Abraham (v. 17) is key to the next phase, under Moses. It is God's view of Moses which is crucial (v. 20), and it is God who will deliver the people by Moses's hand (v. 25). It is God who initiates Moses's call to lead the people (vv. 31–34) and who chooses Moses to lead (v. 35). God's promise is that another prophet like Moses will appear (v. 36). God continues to oversee history in not allowing the idolatrous Israelites to enter the promised land—indeed, YHWH hands them over to false gods (vv. 42–43). God drives out the other nations (v. 45) and, in due time, favors David (v. 46). It is God who gave the law through angelic intermediaries (v. 53).[37]

People's responses to God vary. For named characters, the responses are generally positive: Abraham, told to "leave" (ἔξελθε, v. 3), "left" (ἐξελθών, v. 4);

---

section on Moses as a unity (vv. 17–43) and, indeed, that the theme of the rejected leader is already present in the Joseph section (vv. 9–16).

33 For other views of the structure, see Soards, *Speeches*, 59 with 58n138.

34 With Johnson, *Midrash*, 26; Richard, *Acts 6:1–8:4*, 33–155.

35 Brawley, "Covenant," 127n62, and Dinkler, "Politics," 57–58, rightly assert that the speech is theocentric, and thus Brawley criticizes readings that focus on Israel's unbelief. He is correct that, in Stephen's telling of Israel's story, the initiative lies with God. However, the elements of *both* divine initiative *and* human response are significant in the speech, as Dinkler, "Politics," 59, observes.

36 van den Eynde, "Children," 476; Koivisto, "A Theology," 105.

37 Parsons, *Acts*, 91, observes the use of θεός, "God," in different cases throughout the speech: nominative 12x (vv. 2, 6, 7, 9, 17, 25, 32 [twice], 35, 37, 42, 45), genitive 3x (vv. 43, 46, 56), and once each in accusative (v. 40) and dative (v. 20) and suggests this represents the rhetorical device of "inflection" (κλίσις or πολύπτωτον), which puts the focus on God. See Quintilian, *Inst.* 9.34; Theon, *Prog.* 74.24–35; 85.29–31.

Abraham is given the covenant of circumcision (περιτομῆς, v. 8a), and so he obediently circumcises Isaac (περιέτεμεν, v. 8b), and Isaac in turn circumcises his sons (v. 8c); Moses, after the error of killing the Egyptian (vv. 24–28), accepts God's call at the bush to go to Pharaoh and to lead the Israelites out of Egypt (vv. 35–36). By contrast, the Israelites reject God's gift of Moses's leadership and turn to idolatry (vv. 27–28, 35a, 39–41), and they are models of the present Jewish leadership's rejection of Jesus and his messengers (vv. 51–53).[38] This rejection may also mirror the situation of Luke's own day, where the rejection of Jesus by the Jewish leaders—and many of the people—required explanation and comment.[39] Luke's use of this story to help provide such explanation need not imply that he created it to do so (see *Comment* on 7:24–25 with n193); the resonances of the story with the later situation would be clear.

Setting. Scholars have identified a number of parallels between Luke's accounts of the deaths of Jesus and Stephen.[40] Both are tried by the Sanhedrin (Luke 22:66; Acts 6:12, 15), both cry aloud at their death (Luke 23:46; Acts 7:60), and Stephen's last three sayings echo sayings of Jesus (Luke 22:69// Acts 7:56; Luke 23:46//Acts 7:59; Luke 7:60//Luke 23:34[41]). The continuity between Jesus and Stephen is considerable, for Jesus has said that his disciples will be hated for his name's sake (Luke 21:17) and will testify while suffering (Luke 21:12–13)—both features are seen in Stephen's death. Further, Jesus has acted to critique the temple's present use in his "cleansing" (Luke 19:45–46), focusing (as Stephen does) on the actions of the leaders that have corrupted the place of prayer into a "den of robbers" rather than critiquing the temple itself.[42] Jesus appears to Stephen as he testifies while suffering (Acts 7:56) and identifies himself as suffering with his people (9:4). Stephen's link to Jesus goes beyond imitation to instantiation—in Stephen's testimony and suffering, Jesus continues his work (cf. 1:1).[43] Smith suggests that there is also a parallel in the self-mastery of Jesus and Stephen in the face of suffering, designed to offer assurance to believers facing persecution.[44] The two men both show some control in the face of suffering, for sure, but that they suffer in the way they do places them outside elite Greco-Roman expectations of masculinity, which included self-control and avoiding being under others' control. So, the parallelism is certainly there but probably points away from self-mastery to submission to God's will that believers suffer, following in the path of Jesus.[45]

---

38 Ravens, *Luke,* 61–63, notes the theme of division within Israel within the speech.

39 Barclay, "Manipulating," 43; O'Neill, *Theology* (1961), 71–93.

40 This paragraph draws on Tabb, *Suffering,* 138–39; Cunningham, *Tribulations,* 209–12. See also Moessner, "Christ," 223–34.

41 If Luke 23:34 is part of the original text; see *Comment* on 7:60.

42 Brehm, "Vindicating," 292–95. Dunn, *Beginning,* 260, is thus mistaken in asserting that Stephen is the first to mount a "full-blown attack" on the temple.

43 Cunningham, *Tribulations,* 212.

44 Smith, "Full."

45 See the discussion of Jesus in Wilson, *Unmanly Men,* 190–242.

Acts 6:8–8:1a appears relatively isolated in the overall story of Acts because of its focus on Stephen, a character only briefly introduced earlier (6:5) and mentioned little later (only 8:2; 11:19; 22:20). However, his activities and description echo the portrait of the faithful proclamation of the apostles (see *Comment* on 6:8), and his martyrdom moves the story of the suffering of the early believers forward in four ways. First, it is a development of the trials, and specifically the threats and violence against the believers made by the Sanhedrin (4:18, 21; 5:28, 33, 40).[46] Secondly, the speech provides an interpretation of Israel's history through the lens of the coming of Jesus, and through it Luke communicates to his readers that God's action in Jesus is the fulfillment of long-standing purposes—and that believers are part of the true, renewed people of God.[47] Thirdly, this story introduces Saul, who will be a key figure in the story of the believing community's growth (7:58; 8:1a). Fourthly, the persecution arising from Stephen leads to a geographical and ethnic expansion of the community of faith (8:1b, 4; 11:19–21).

There are significant parallels between the portrayals of Moses and Jesus in Stephen's speech and Peter's speech in the temple courts (3:12–26):[48] (i) both identify Jesus as the prophet like Moses (3:22; 7:37; Deut 18:15); (ii) God is identified as "the God of Abraham, Isaac, and Jacob" in both, echoing Exod 3:6 (Acts 3:13; 7:32); (iii) ἀρνέομαι, "reject," concerning a person sent by God is found only in these two speeches in Acts (3:13, 14; 7:35);[49] (iv) both Moses and Jesus are described as "leader" (ἀρχηγός [3:15]; ἄρχων [7:27, 35]) and "righteous one/judge" (δίκαιος [3:14; 7:52]; δικαστής, [7:27, 35]); (v) Jesus's return is explicitly mentioned at 3:20–21 and alluded to in Moses's return (7:34); (vi) these are the only two Acts speeches that parallel Moses and Jesus; and (vii) there is reference to God's covenant with Abraham in both speeches (3:25; 7:2–8, 17). The presence of this parallelism only in these two speeches is striking, for both are located in the earliest period in Jerusalem, and thus this is likely to be primitive material.[50]

After the mention of Saul here (with 8:1, 4), he disappears from the story until the Damascus Road event (9:1–22) and his first visit to Jerusalem (9:23–30), before disappearing again until his engagement with the church in Antioch, at Barnabas's invitation (11:25–26), and then reappears there after a gap (13:1–3). Thereafter, he is constantly present in Acts. The brief introduction here, followed by the more extensive material later, forms a chain-link connection, whereby the major unit of 1:1–8:3 transitions to 8:4–12:25.[51]

---

46 Skinner, *Trial Narratives*, 117–18.

47 Cf. Hötzinger, "Schriftgebrauch," 339–40, suggesting that the Stephen episode contributes to the "self-assurance of religious identity" of believers that is in continuity with God's historic people Israel (quoting 339; my translation).

48 What follows expands Zehnle, *Discourse*, 76–77; Bihler, *Stephanusgeschichte*, 104–11.

49 The use in 4:16 concerns the rejection of a claim.

50 Zehnle, *Discourse*, 78.

51 Longenecker, *Rhetoric*, 192–94; see *Form/Structure/Setting* on 8:1b–3.

Sterling helpfully identifies four streams of mission that flow from the death of Stephen and the subsequent scattering of believers (8:1b):[52] (i) Philip's ministry in Samaria, as one of those scattered (8:4–25) and also a member of the Seven (6:5); (ii) Saul's conversion, as one pursuing believers to arrest them (8:4; 9:1; 22:20) and yet turned around by his encounter with Jesus on the Damascus Road (9:1–31); (iii) Peter's mission in Palestine (9:32–11:18), based on his travelling from Jerusalem after the initial persecution (8:4; 9:32); and (iv) the nameless missionaries who plant the church in Antioch (11:19, 26).

Comment

6:8 Στέφανος δὲ πλήρης χάριτος καὶ δυνάμεως ἐποίει τέρατα καὶ σημεῖα μεγάλα ἐν τῷ λαῷ, "Stephen, full of grace and power, was performing great wonders and signs among the people." This description echoes key features of the apostles' role as witnesses and thereby identifies Stephen as another faithful witness. Stephen is πλήρης πίστεως καὶ πνεύματος ἁγίου, "full of faith and the Holy Spirit" (6:5), echoing the Pentecost story (2:2, 4, using the cognate verbs for "fill," πληρόω and πίμπλημι) and Peter's ministry (πλησθεὶς πνεύματος ἁγίου, "filled with the Holy Spirit" 4:8; cf. 4:31). Τέρατα καὶ σημεῖα, "wonders and signs," are a feature of the apostles' ministry (2:43; 4:30, 31; cf. 2:19 with *Comment* there), as they were of the ministry of Jesus (2:22) and will be of the ministry of Paul and Barnabas (15:4). Stephen's actions are similar to those of Moses (7:36; cf. Exod 7:3; Deut 6:22; 26:8; 34:11; Neh 9:10; Jer 32:20–21) and prepare for the Moses section of his speech (Acts 7:17–44).[53] The public nature of Stephen's actions, ἐν τῷ λαῷ, "among the people," i.e., the people of Israel (see 2:47 with *Comment* there), is also an important mark of the community's life.[54] It is therefore no surprise when Stephen faces opposition and is hauled before the Sanhedrin.[55]

9 τινες τῶν ἐκ τῆς συναγωγῆς τῆς λεγομένης Λιβερτίνων καὶ Κυρηναίων καὶ Ἀλεξανδρέων καὶ τῶν ἀπὸ Κιλικίας καὶ Ἀσίας, "Certain men came forward from the synagogue of the Freedmen (as it was known), both Cyrenians and Alexandrians, as well as men from Cilicia and Asia." Συναγωγή, "synagogue," denotes both the group of people and the building where they meet (rather like today's use of "church").[56] The named locations are places from which these diaspora Jews relocated to Jerusalem. Diaspora Jews in Jerusalem[57] would

52 Sterling, "Opening," 216.
53 Green, *Narrative Theologian*, 161.
54 2:47; 3:9, 11, 12; 4:1, 10, 21; 5:12, 20, 25, 26; cf. 26:26.
55 Mittelstadt, *Spirit*, 111.
56 Cf. εἰς ἱεροὺς ἀφικνούμενοι τόπους, οἳ καλοῦνται συναγωγαί, "they go to the sacred places, which they called synagogues," Philo, *Good Person* 81, writing ca. AD 40. This demonstrates that Luke is not anachronistic in his use of συναγωγή for buildings; Riesner, "Synagogues," 182; Catto, *Synagogue*, 23–24.
57 See *Comment* on 2:5; cf. Mark 15:21; Luke 23:26; Acts 11:20 with Levine, *Ancient Synagogue*, 53.

naturally form synagogues where Greek was spoken, since many diaspora Jews knew little, if any, Aramaic or Hebrew.[58] As well as places for weekly meetings on the Sabbath, such synagogues provided hospitality for Jews on pilgrimage to the feasts. The first-century Theodotus inscription provides evidence for assembly halls where such groups met; that particular building was also "an inn for those in need from foreign parts."[59]

The fact that opposition came from a Greek-speaking synagogue suggests that it is with such people that Stephen debates, and thus that he himself may well have been a Hellenistic Jew.[60]

Λιβερτίνων, "Freedmen," is a Latin loanword (from *libertinus*);[61] such men and women are manumitted slaves, for the children of manumitted slaves were considered simply "free."[62] Thus they may be descendants of Jews taken as prisoners to Rome by Pompey.[63] Because they may not have been free to ractice Judaism as slaves—depending on the view of their master—their devotion to the temple and the law after being manumitted may have been all the greater, and thus their opposition to Stephen very vigorous.[64] The number of synagogues intended here is not clear: it could be one, two, or five.[65] The view that there are two is attractive, since it would explain the repetition of τῶν: the groups would be (i) the synagogue of the Freedmen, consisting of Cyrenians and Alexandrians (both from North Africa), and (ii) the synagogue of the Cilcians and Asians (areas close together in Asia Minor). If both pairs of geographical locations are epexegetical of Λιβερτίνων, "Freedmen," then one synagogue is meant.[66] The compatibility of the latter view with the singular articular use of συναγωγή suggests the "one synagogue" view is more likely. If there is one synagogue, it is plausible that Saul of Tarsus (who came from Tarsus in Cilicia) and Stephen (who engages with the members of this synagogue) both belong to this synagogue.[67]

ἀνέστησαν, "they came forward." The intransitive use of ἀνίστημι signals that the men of the synagogue(s) enter the scene to carry out a role or function,[68]

58 Safrai, "Synagogue," 192–94; see *Comment* on 7:1.

59 *CIJ* II §1404. Greek text and English translation with judicious discussions in Catto, *Synagogue*, 82–85; Riesner, "Synagogues," 192–200. Cf. Levine, *Ancient Synagogue*, 54; Thompson, "Diaspora," 171–73 (with further references).

60 With Tabb, *Suffering*, 130; Neagoe, *Trial*, 159–60.

61 The use of a foreign loanword may explain the presence of λεγομένης, "as it was known"; Bruce, *Acts* (1990), 187.

62 See helpful discussion in Lyall, *Slaves*, 39–45; Thompson, "Diaspora," 177–78; cf. Barclay, *Jews*, 290 with n24.

63 Schürer, 2:428n8, citing Philo, *Embassy* 155.

64 Thompson, "Diaspora," 179–80.

65 One: Hemer, *Book*, 176; Bruce, *Acts* (1990), 187; Riesner, "Synagogues," 204–5; Culy and Parsons, *Acts*, 111. Two: *BegC*, 4:66; Catto, *Synagogue*, 165–66; Barrett, *Acts*, 1:323 (tentatively); Jervell, *Apostelgeschichte*, 225. Five: Schürer, 2:248; Levine, *Ancient Synagogue*, 53.

66 Bruce, *Acts* (1990), 187.

67 Keener, *Acts*, 2:1309.

68 "ἀνίστημι," BDAG 83, §9.

which is expressed by the participle συζητοῦντες, "in order to debate." The substance of debate is indicated in vv. 13–14.

10 οὐκ ἴσχυον ἀντιστῆναι τῇ σοφίᾳ καὶ τῷ πνεύματι ᾧ ἐλάλει, "they were unable to resist the wisdom and the Spirit with which he was speaking." Stephen's superior wisdom is attributed to the Holy Spirit's empowerment, in line with Jewish expectation that the Spirit of prophecy would give charismatic wisdom.[69] "The Spirit is the God who cannot be gagged,"[70] for the Spirit's power continually overcomes Stephen's critics—both οὐκ ἴσχυον, "they were unable," and ἐλάλει, "he was speaking," are imperfect, portraying events as in progress: Luke portrays Stephen's success as taking place over some time (cf. v. 13). That Luke attributes his effective speech to the Spirit is in line with Jesus's promise that the Spirit will enable his followers to speak when opposed and on trial (Luke 12:11–12: see *Comment* on 4:8, 13, 16–17; 5:31)—and his speech which follows is further fulfillment of Jesus's words.

11–14 τότε ὑπέβαλον ἄνδρας, "Then they secretly prompted men." A shift occurs (τότε, "then"), and cultural values of honor/shame probably underlie this reaction. Stephen's irresistible speaking results in his opponents being shamed. In turn, this generates an "honor challenge": the opponents attempt to shame Stephen by desperate and unethical measures in prompting men (whose testimony would be recognized in a legal setting[71]) to make untrue claims about Stephen (as v. 13 makes clear).[72] Luke does not mention use of this tactic by Jesus's accusers (cf. Mark 14:56–59), although Jesus is declared innocent on numerous occasions in Luke's passion narrative (Luke 23:4, 14, 15, 22, 41, 47).

The claims are that Stephen speaks blasphemously against Moses and God (Acts 6:11), which summarizes the effect of the two misdeeds alleged, that Jesus will destroy the temple and change Mosaic customs (vv. 13–14). βλάσφημα, "blasphemous," indicates that the words abused God's power and greatness, that Stephen spoke falsely of God and Moses (cf. Jesus's being accused of blasphemy, Mark 14:64, unparalleled in Luke, although cf. Luke 5:21).[73] Ironically, as false witnesses (Acts 6:13) these men are the real blasphemers (cf. Exod 20:16; Deut 19:16–19)—they are necessarily false witnesses because they speak against God's true spokesman, Jesus.[74] Because their testimony is false, it is

69 Turner, *Power*, 350.

70 Turner, *Power*, 439.

71 Cf. Josephus, *Ant.* 4.8.15 §219. Seim, *Message*, 156, notes that female testimony was at least thought less believable than male and that generally female testimony was less valid in legal contexts; see further Bauckham, *Women*, 268–77 (who mis-cites Josephus, *Ant.* as 2:219).

72 On the honor and shame dimension, see Pilch, *Visions*, 58; Malina, *World* (3rd ed.), 27–57.

73 *TDNT* 1:621–23. Moule, "Sanctuary," 30–31 expresses confidence that Jesus did announce the destruction and replacement of the temple on the basis of Mark 14:58 and parallels—although note that Mark labels this claim, like that of Stephen's critics, "false testimony" (Mark 14:57).

74 Bruce, *Acts* (1990), 188.

not necessary to see Stephen's speech as a direct answer to their accusations.[75] Acts thus far presents a major debate over who speaks for Israel's God in the wake of Jesus's exaltation.[76] We lack evidence that Stephen's proclamation was different from that of the apostles—readers of Acts so far are led to presume that Stephen said similar things to the apostles, for he had been commissioned by the apostles (Acts 6:5–6). Luke directs readers to see the central issue in Stephen's debating as concerning Jesus, his identity, and the implications of his deeds for Israel's present (v. 14).

At this time, Jewish people held the temple in very high regard as the location of YHWH's presence,[77] hence its description as τοῦ τόπου τοῦ ἁγίου, "the holy place" (v. 13). Although strictly only a small part of the temple was called "the holy place," the whole temple area was seen as holy—hence the (unholy) Roman fortress of Antonia (παρεμβολή, "the barracks," 22:24) was just outside the temple precincts. It is notable that no Jesus-following speaker in Acts describes the temple as "holy": this expression is only found in accusations against believers.[78] Believers prefer ἱερόν, "temple."[79] However, believers do not disregard the temple: they pray there,[80] they habitually preach there,[81] they regularly meet there,[82] and God reveals himself in the temple.[83] To be seen to attack or criticize the temple led to punishment.[84] Nevertheless, there has been no criticism of the temple per se by the apostles at this stage. Stephen, likewise, does not say that the temple was a mistake but rather asserts that its day is over (see especially on 7:48–50 below).[85] Luke roundly asserts that it is "false witnesses," μάρτυρας ψευδεῖς (v. 13), who claim that Stephen says that Jesus will destroy the temple (v. 14). The witnesses' bias is also hinted at in the pejorative Ἰησοῦς ὁ Ναζωραῖος *οὗτος*, "*this* Jesus the Nazarene"[86]—the label "the Nazarene" may suggest that the believers are an unwelcome sect.[87]

The placement of the alleged attack on the temple comes first; καί, "and" (in both vv. 13, 14), may be epexegetical with the force "that is," indicating that the attack on the temple is seen as an attack on the law and oral

75 Weinert, "Luke, Stephen," 89.
76 See 2:32–33, 36, 38–39; 3:13–14, 17, 22–23, 26; 4:7–12, 16–21, 29–31; 5:4, 17–20, 27–32, 38–42 with *Comment*.
77 Cf. 1QS V, 4–7; VIII, 4–7, 8–10; IX, 3–6.
78 Acts 6:13–14; 21:28.
79 Acts 22:17; 24:12, 18; 25:8; 26:21.
80 Acts 2:46; 3:1; 21:21.
81 Acts 3:11–26; 5:21; see *Comment* on the latter.
82 Acts 5:12.
83 Acts 3:1–10; 22:17–21.
84 E.g., Jesus ben Ananus, ca. AD 62, was flogged for his criticisms, Josephus, *J.W.* 6.5.3 §§300–309.
85 More fully, see Walton, "Tale," esp. 148–53.
86 Barrett, *Acts*, 1:330.
87 Doble, "Saying," 73.

traditions themselves.[88] The "law" (νόμος [v. 13]) denotes the Pentateuch, which contains the regulations for the tent of meeting. The associated "customs" (ἔθη [v. 14]) are oral traditions expounding and applying the Torah to specific situations and issues.[89] The Pharisees (and perhaps other Jews) understood these traditions to go back to Moses himself: hence the traditions were considered to have the same authority as the Pentateuch.[90] The Torah and the customs were key pillars of Judaism,[91] so to present Stephen as attacking them or claiming that Jesus would change them would incite a hostile and violent response.[92]

In reaction to Stephen's repeated claims (οὐ παύεται λαλῶν, "does not cease speaking" [v. 13]), either the false witnesses or the opponents of Stephen (the grammatical subject in v. 12 could be either) stirred the people's emotions (συνεκίνησαν [v. 12][93]), as easily happens concerning deeply felt religious claims. The elders and scribes are groups within the Sanhedrin (4:5, 8, 23) who earlier held hearings with the apostles: the articles τοὺς . . . τούς (v. 12) may have anaphoric force, i.e., they refer to previous mentions of the scribes and elders, signaling that the same Jewish authorities are intended. That said, the Sanhedrin is not presented as initiating the hearing with Stephen:[94] rather, they are reacting to popular sentiment, stirred up by the Hellenistic synagogue members.

15 καὶ ἀτενίσαντες εἰς αὐτὸν πάντες οἱ καθεζόμενοι ἐν τῷ συνεδρίῳ, "As everyone sitting in the Sanhedrin fixed their attention on him," increases the tension in the story in preparation for Stephen's speech. The focused attention (ἀτενίσαντες) of the Sanhedrin is understandable in light of the accusations against him: can he really have said what the witnesses say? Pilch's suggestion that Stephen "entrances" the Sanhedrin (based on the view that ἀτενίζω "often

---

88 J. Carleton Paget, "Jewish Christianity," *CHJ*, 3:743, suggests that the epexegetical force may be that the claim is that Stephen wishes to change only the laws and customs concerning the temple. This seems less likely than seeing Stephen's claimed attack on the temple as a particular case of attacking Jewish law and customs.

89 E.g., the calendar, some parts of the structure of the temple courts, rules about washing, the correct handling of food for priests and their families; Sanders, *Jewish Law*, 103–6. Cf. Jesus's controversies over Qorban (Mark 7:9–13), and handwashing (Mark 7:1–8, esp. vv. 3, 5; cf. Luke 11:37–41), in which he criticises both as human traditions.

90 E.g., 2 Macc 12:38; cf. Josephus, *Ant.* 13.10.6 §297; 13.16.2 §408; cf. m. ʾAbot 1:1; the whole tractate traces a chain of transmission of the oral traditions from Moses to first- and second-century rabbis. It is debated how widely such oral traditions were accepted in the first century; see: Schürer, 2:339–46, esp. 340–41; W. D. Davies, "Law in First-century Judaism," *IDB* 2:89–95, esp. 91–93; Sanders, *Jewish Law*, 97–130.

91 Dunn, *Partings*, 23–31; Schürer, 2:330–36, 339–55, esp. 343.

92 Cf. 21:21; 26:3; 28:17. Luke will later portray similar violently emotional reactions to Paul, e.g., from Jews in Lystra (14:19) and from Artemis worshipers in Ephesus (19:23–34).

93 "συγκινέω," BDAG 952.

94 Nor does Luke here present the Sanhedrin as "vigorously oppose[d]" to Stephen (so Peterson, *Acts*, 238); they are reacting to Stephen rather than actively seeking to pursue Stephen—to this extent, they appear to be following Gamaliel's advice to wait and see (5:34–39). I owe this observation to Peter Mansell.

signals that a person is in a trance"[95]) is speculative at best: we lack evidence for such a connotation for this verb.[96]

Εἶδον τὸ πρόσωπον αὐτοῦ ὡσεὶ πρόσωπον ἀγγέλου, "they saw his face was like the face of an angel." Various echoes and parallels illuminate this statement, which itself underlines that the Spirit is transforming Stephen (6:3, 5, 10; 7:55).[97] In combination with the role of an angel as a divine messenger,[98] Luke creates the expectation that Stephen's speech will be divinely inspired, as we see by echoes of other stories involving similar physical changes.[99] First, there is an echo of Jesus's transfigured face (Luke 9:29), which is connected closely with Jesus's forthcoming death (his "exodus," ἔξοδος [Luke 9:31]).[100] It is noteworthy that Stephen dies shortly afterwards (the vision of Acts 7:55 precipitates Stephen's stoning). This is a new phenomenon, for such "proleptic and eschatological angelization" is not found in pre-Christian sources.[101] Secondly, Moses is transformed, so that his face shines when he meets with YHWH (Exod 34:29–35), as is Abraham according to Philo (*Virtues* 217).[102] The Moses parallel is striking, for Stephen goes on to (re-)Interpret the Mosaic law: "Stephen is not *opposed* to Moses, but *cast as* Moses."[103] The later Tg. Song 1:5 portrays the Israelites after repenting and being forgiven for their sin with the golden calf at Sinai with "the radiance of their faces . . . as great as the angels" because of their obedience in making curtains for the tent of meeting. Further, Jewish tradition suggests that prophets sent by God could appear "awe-inspiring" because "the Holy Spirit . . . rested upon them" (Num. Rab. 10.5), to the extent that a prophet could not be distinguished from an angel.[104]

7:1 Εἶπεν δὲ ὁ ἀρχιερεύς· εἰ ταῦτα οὕτως ἔχει;, "The chief priest said, 'Are these things true?'" This question reflects the dissonance between Luke's characterization of Stephen (6:8, 10) and the accusations against him (6:11, 13–14). It sets the stage for Stephen's lengthy response (vv. 2–56), which fulfills Jesus's promises that he or the Spirit would enable believers to respond when on trial (Luke 12:11–12; 21:12–15).[105]

2 Ἄνδρες ἀδελφοὶ καὶ πατέρες, ἀκούσατε, "Men, brothers and fathers, listen!," is a formal call to be heard. "Men" is an appropriate translation of Ἄνδρες in the setting of the all-male Sanhedrin (6:12; contrast 1:16 with *Comment*; cf.

95 Pilch, *Visions*, 59.
96 See *Comment* on 1:20; contra Strelan, *Strange Acts*, 127; Pilch, *Visions*, 59.
97 Strelan, *Strange Acts*, 128, provides references beyond those cited below.
98 Acts 7:38, 53; 8:26; 10:3–7, 22; 11:13; 27:23–24. On angels, see *Comment* on 1:10.
99 Cf. 2:4, 14; 4:8–13, 19–20; with Haenchen, *Acts*, 272; cf. Glombitza, "Charakterisierung."
100 Strelan, *Strange Acts*, 127; Fletcher-Louis, *Luke-Acts*, 96–98.
101 Fletcher-Louis, *Luke-Acts*, 97.
102 Indeed, the rabbis believe that Moses ascended into heaven to receive the torah; Alexander, ed., *Targum Canticles*, 82n42, gives full references; cf. 2 Cor 3:7–18.
103 Tabb, *Suffering*, 132 (his italics).
104 Freedman and Simon, eds., *Midrash Rabbah*, 5:367; cf. Str-B, 2:665–66; Kittel, "ἄγγελος," *TDNT* 1:83.
105 With Doble, "Saying," 72. See *Comment* on 6:10.

Comment on 4:5). The imperative ἀκούσατε, "listen!," signals the importance of what Stephen will say (see *Comment* on 2:22), as well as being the verb used in prophetic lawsuits in LXX Jer 2:4; Mic 6:1; Amos 3:13.[106]

2b–8 The first section of the speech focuses on Abraham, especially God's encounters with him. Stephen focuses on God's call to Abraham to migrate to the land and characterizes God as one who makes and keeps promises, a theme central to the whole speech.

2 Ὁ θεὸς τῆς δόξης ὤφθη τῷ πατρὶ ἡμῶν Ἀβραάμ, "The God of glory appeared to our ancestor Abraham." Stephen's speech immediately focuses on God and will continue to do so (see *Form/Structure/Setting*).[107] His defense of the Jesus believers is through interpreting the way(s) Israel's God has made himself known and acted in the distant past (God's actions in the history of Israel, vv. 2b–52), the recent past (the ministry of Jesus, 6:9–10; 7:52b–53, 55–56), and the present (the believing community's life and testimony, empowered by the Spirit, 6:8–10, 15). The God whom the believers worship and proclaim is the God of Abraham and Israel.[108] The description "the God of glory (τῆς δόξης)" is both distinctive and striking. Although "of glory" highlights the distance between God and his creation, for "glory" frequently points to the honor and reverence God deserves,[109] the collocation with ὤφθη, "appeared," portrays the invisible and inaccessible God making himself known to Abraham, and later with Moses, for "the glory of God/YHWH" came on Mount Sinai in a cloud at the revelation of the law (Exod 24:16, 17; see *Comment* on v. 38 below). That God has, gives, or is due glory is frequently stated or assumed in the NT,[110] but the only exact parallel to this phrase is Ps 28:3 LXX (MT 29:3), which has God speaking powerfully through loud thunder (implicitly critiquing Baal, the Canaanite weather god).[111] The genitive τῆς δόξης, "of glory," may be attributive, "the glorious God," or more broadly descriptive, presenting God as one who has and gives glory. Although δόξα, "glory," originally denotes what a person thinks or seems to be,[112] a transition occurs, seen in Josephus, Philo,

---

106 Peterson, "Stephen's Speech," 361.

107 Martín-Asensio, "Participant," 244, observes that Abraham is only present as non-explicit subject or non-subject participant, rather than as grammatical subject (either explicit or not). Abraham is thus not the driver of narrative events, but "the God of glory."

108 With Jantsch, "God of Glory," 211.

109 Heb. כבוד (*kbwd*) denotes riches, honor, splendor and derives from a sense of "weight"; "כָּבוֹד," BDB 458.

110 In addition to v. 55, note Luke 2:14; 17:18; John 5:44; 8:54; 11:4, 40; 12:43; Rom 1:23; 3:23; 4:20; 5:2; 8:21; 15:7; 16:27; 1 Cor 10:31; 2 Cor 1:20; 4:4, 6, 15; Eph 1:17; Phil 1:11; 2:11; 4:19; Col 1:27; 1 Thess 2:12; 1 Tim 1:17; Titus 2:13; Heb 2:9; 1 Pet 1:21; 4:11, 14; 5:10; 2 Pet 1:17; Jude 25; Rev 1:6; 4:11; 7:12; 11:13; 14:7; 15:8; 16:9; 19:1; 21:11, 23.

111 Craigie, *Psalms 1–50*, 247. Andrew Angel observes that Ps 28 LXX (MT 29) is a classic "divine warrior" theophany, in line with Second Temple Jewish writings (LAB 11.5; 23.10; 32.7–8; Josephus, *Ant* 3.5.2 §80; 4 Ezra 3:17–19—in the first two with angels); see Angel, *Chaos*, 162–90.

112 G. Kittel, "δόξα," *TDNT* 2:233–36.

and some LXX usage, to "glory" as reputation or splendor.[113] God's glory is frequently portrayed as bright light (cf. Acts 22:11; Luke 2:9, 32) and marks the distinction between YHWH and the created order. The phrase "bookends" the speech, for Stephen sees the glory of God at its end too (Acts 7:55). The bookending suggests that what comes between shows how God's glory is seen.[114]

ὄντι ἐν τῇ Μεσοποταμίᾳ πρὶν ἢ κατοικῆσαι αὐτὸν ἐν Χαρράν, "while he was in Mesopotamia before he lived in Haran." Not only does YHWH make himself known to Abraham; Stephen signals that this encounter took place away from the land of Israel. Genesis 11:26–12:4 seems to place God's call of Abram in Haran rather than Chaldea (= Mesopotamia). Stephen is not alone among first-century Jews in his reading of Genesis, for both Philo, *Abr.* 62, 67, and Josephus, *Ant.* 1.7.1 §154, understand Abraham's call to happen in Chaldea.[115] It is possible that Luke's Stephen has the vision of Gen 15:7 in mind, where YHWH says that he "brought you from Ur of the Chaldeans," which suggests that God called Abraham in Ur.[116] That YHWH is not confined by space (cf. Acts 7:48), but is active in places away from Palestinian soil (and, especially, the temple), is a crucial theme of this speech (vv. 4, 6, 9–10, 15, 17, 30, 36, 42, 44).[117] Implicitly, this shows YHWH is the God of the whole world, a theme whose importance is growing in Acts, ultimately leading to the inclusion of gentiles in the people of God. Mesopotamia ("between the rivers") is the LXX version of Aram-naharaim ("Aram of Mesopotamia," ארם נהרים [*ʾrm nhrym*], Gen 24:10); in the Genesis Abraham narrative it is called "Ur of the Chaldeans" (Gen 11:31 מאור כשׂדים [*mʾwr kśdym*]; LXX τῆς χώρας τῶν Χαλδαίων, "the country of the Chaldeans"). In Luke's day, it denotes the area from Haran in the north down to Ur in the south, near the Persian Gulf.[118]

3 ἔξελθε ἐκ τῆς γῆς σου καὶ ἐκ τῆς συγγενείας σου, καὶ δεῦρο εἰς τὴν γῆν ἣν ἄν σοι δείξω, "Leave your land and your relatives, and come away to the land that I will show you," is a quotation of Gen 12:1 LXX, with the omission of καὶ ἐκ τοῦ οἴκου τοῦ πατρός σου, "and from your father's house," and the addition of καὶ δεῦρο, "come away." These differences are not greatly significant, for the quotation's purpose is to underline that God spoke to Abraham to promise him a new home at a time before he lived in the land God promised to him. This promise is fundamental to the rest of the speech, which will keep returning to the question of land (vv. 6, 19, 33, 36, 40, 49).[119] God's call necessitates faith on Abraham's part, expressed in active obedience. Luke does not anachronisti-

113 E.g., Josephus, *Life* 53 §274; *Ant.* 2.12.1 §268; 5.1.28 §115; 6.10.2 §200; 8.6.5 §166; 11.6.6 §217; 13.3.1 §63; 16.5.4 §158; *J.W.* 6.4.8 §267; Philo, *Creation* 79; *Spec. Laws* 1.45; for LXX usage, see "δόξα," *GELS* 175, §§1, 2.

114 Aarflot, *God*, 94–118; summary: 117–138.

115 Whitenton, "Rewriting," 163–64.

116 So Pervo, *Acts*, 180n63; Koivisto, "A Theology," 111; Kilgallen, *Stephen Speech*, 42–43.

117 With Ravens, *Luke*, 60–61; Green, *Narrative Theologian*, 163–64, among others.

118 Marshall, "Acts," 556–57.

119 With Hall, *Revealed Histories*, 197.

cally quote the rest of the passage, which promises blessing through Abraham to "all the families of the earth" (Gen 12:3), although God's meeting Abraham outside the promised land without the classic Jewish markers of circumcision, Torah, or temple hints in that direction.

4 τότε ἐξελθὼν ἐκ γῆς Χαλδαίων κατῴκησεν ἐν Χαρράν, "Then he left the land of the Chaldeans and settled in Haran." Abraham's obedience to God's call is central—ἐξελθών, "he left," uses the same verb as for God's call, ἔξελθε, "Leave" (v. 3)—and will contrast with the disobedience of the Sanhedrin and their Israelite ancestors (vv. 51–53). The speech here draws on LXX Gen 11:31; 12:4–5, without precise quotation.

κἀκεῖθεν μετὰ τὸ ἀποθανεῖν τὸν πατέρα αὐτοῦ, "After his father's death." Stephen, like Philo, *Migration* 177, reads Gen 11:32–12:5 as narrating an historical sequence and assumes that Terah, Abraham's father, was dead before Abraham travelled to Haran. Genesis 11:26 indicates that Terah *began* having children at 70. Terah died at 205 (Gen 11:32), so, on this reading, Abraham could have been as old as 145 when he left for Haran. However, Gen 12:4 and Philo, *Migration* 176, record that Abraham was 75 years old when he *left* Haran, so he must have been younger when he arrived in Haran. Genesis 12:5 suggests that Abraham lived in Haran long enough to acquire people and possessions. Two main ways of resolving this tension have been proposed. (i) Luke (or Stephen) uses a Greek version of an alternative tradition to MT Genesis, echoed in the Samaritan Pentateuch and the Samaritan Pentateuch Targum of Gen 11:32, which state that that Terah was 145 when he died. This argument is attractive to scholars who consider that Stephen's speech reflects Samaritan thinking and theology.[120] However, the similar timing of events in Philo shows that this is not a *distinctively* Samaritan tradition, which weakens the argument for Samaritan influence.[121] Further, Stephen's speech does not generally reflect the traditions found in Samaritan texts.[122] (ii) More probably, Gen 11:26–12:5 is not providing a sequential record of events: Terah's death (11:32) happened after Abraham's departure for Haran (12:1). This speech and Philo, however, both read Gen 11:26–12:5 as a sequential account.[123] Why mention Terah's death? One Jewish reading of the story has Terah as an idolator and maker of idols (Gen. Rab. 38:13), perhaps building on Josh 24:2, which states that the ancestors, including Terah, "worshiped/served other gods." If this tradition were current in Stephen's (or Luke's) day, the mention of Terah's death would clarify that the land God promised would not be

---

120 E.g., Scobie, "Origins," 393, summarizing others' research (with which he agrees). Cf. Lightfoot, *Acts,* 109, suggesting that the text of Genesis may be corrupt.

121 Spencer, *Portrait,* 72; Emerton, review of Wilcox, *Semitisms,* 284. Richard, "Acts 7," 196–97, plausibly posits a "common textual tradition" used by Acts, Philo, and the Samaritan Pentateuch.

122 Bruce, *Acts* (1990), 193; see *Form/Structure/Setting.*

123 Barrett, *Acts,* 1:342–43.

polluted by Terah's idolatry.[124] If so, this gives poignancy to Stephen's identification of the Sanhedrin's sin with that of "your fathers" (Acts 7:51): note the separation of Joseph from his family, vv. 9–16, and in particular that God was with Joseph rather than the patriarchs (v. 9); and note that "our fathers" rejected Moses (v. 39).[125]

μετῴκισεν αὐτὸν εἰς τὴν γῆν ταύτην, "[God] moved him out from there into this land." God is the implied subject of the verb μετῴκισεν, "moved . . . out": Stephen continues to focus on divine action as the driver of Abraham's story (cf. the use of the same verb in v. 43, with *Comment* there). Stephen goes on to state that this is the land εἰς ἣν ὑμεῖς νῦν κατοικεῖτε, "in which you yourselves now live," showing that YHWH is faithful to his promise (vv. 3, 5), now fulfilled in the Jewish people's experience.

5 οὐκ ἔδωκεν αὐτῷ κληρονομίαν ἐν αὐτῇ οὐδὲ βῆμα ποδός, "he did not give him any inheritance whatsoever in it." It is somewhat surprising that Stephen states that Abraham did not receive the promise YHWH made, for God's words in v. 3 imply that Abraham will inhabit this land. "Inheritance," κληρονομία, echoes the parable of the wicked tenants (Luke 20:14), in which the tenants desire the inheritance for themselves, and will be used by Paul for what God gives to the multiracial believing community (Acts 20:32). This use stands between those two: (i) Stephen's Sanhedrin audience embody the wicked tenants of the parable, wanting to hold onto the inheritance of the land promised by God to Abraham—and the relationship with YHWH that the land embodied and made tangible—for themselves, rather than recognizing that God is handing it over to the believing community under the leadership of the exalted Jesus; (ii) Stephen is a prototype of the worldwide community of believers, unrestricted by race and by location; Abraham's engagement with God by trusting and obeying God's promise outside the land models such inclusive engagement with God as now known in Jesus. οὐδὲ βῆμα ποδός, "whatsoever," literally "not one step of the foot," is a verbatim echo of Deut 2:5, where God instructs the people after the exodus that he will give them "not one step of the foot" of the Edomites' land because he has the promised land for them.[126] This scriptural phrase thus further evokes God's promise of the land.

ἐπηγγείλατο δοῦναι αὐτῷ εἰς κατάσχεσιν αὐτὴν καὶ τῷ σπέρματι αὐτοῦ μετ᾽ αὐτόν, "[God] promised to give it as a possession to him and to his descendants after him." The surprise of the earlier part of the verse is resolved by clarification of God's promise: although the promise was made to Abraham, the divine promise includes Abraham's descendants (including those to whom Stephen speaks). Although σπέρμα, "descendants," is singular, it commonly refers to

124 Koivisto, "A Theology," 112.
125 With Koivisto, "A Theology," 112–13.
126 Schwemer, "Lukas," 308.

a body of descendants (e.g., Acts 3:25 with *Comment* there; Luke 1:55; 20:28). The term, and the promise, echoes Gen 12:7; 13:15; 17:8; 24:7; 48:4 LXX; the wording here is particularly close to 17:8; 48:4.[127]

οὐκ ὄντος αὐτῷ τέκνου, "even though he was childless." This concessive genitive absolute clause stresses God's action in spite of outward circumstances; it is in an emphatic position at the end of the sentence.[128] Luke does not put Abraham's childlessness under the spotlight using main verbs, for he continues to reserve main verbs for God's action—this childlessness is a challenge to God's promise, but Luke focuses readers' attention on the promise. Abraham and Sarah's childlessness echoes Gen 15:2 LXX (or perhaps Gen 16:1 LXX), where Abraham reminds God that he is ἄτεκνος, "childless."

6–7 This sentence prepares the way for the story that follows in much of the rest of this speech, acting as a preview.[129] Here is the last quotation from God in Stephen's Abraham story (the only subsequent direct speech from God in Stephen's speech is to Moses, vv. 32–34): God's final and climactic word to him is of promise.[130] Stephen combines quotations from LXX Gen 15:13–14 and Exod 3:12 (with minor variations, none of which affect the substance of what God said).[131] God's word to Abraham is that his descendants (singular σπέρμα, as Acts 7:5) will be enslaved and ill-treated for a long time, presenting a further challenge to God's promise of the land. To speak of Abraham's descendants in juxtaposition with the statement that he was childless (v. 5) itself conveys that God keeps his promises. Stephen builds up tension in this retelling of Israel's history by adding to the list of obstacles to fulfillment. Egypt is not named at this point but soon will be (v. 9). However, Stephen goes on to show that God's promise to Abraham is powerfully effective, for it finds fulfillment in the exodus (vv. 17, 34, 36, 37–39).

καὶ τὸ ἔθνος ᾧ ἐὰν δουλεύσουσιν κρινῶ ἐγώ, "Yet I myself will judge the nation that enslaves them." With God as subject, κρίνω, "judge," highlights "the condemnation or punishment" that follows God's verdict.[132] The allusion is probably to the series of plagues and the Egyptian army's drowning in the Red Sea (Exod 7–12; 14:21–31; note God's motivation in 14:4, "so that I will gain glory for myself over Pharaoh and all his army; and the Egyptians shall know that I am YHWH"; cf. "the God of glory," Acts 7:2). The emphatic ἐγώ,

127 With Smith, *Fate*, 148.

128 *DFNTG*², 183, notes that gen. abs. clauses preceding their main verb clause generally convey background information; here the location following the main clause(s) conveys significant information, preparing for the mention of the children who fulfill YHWH's promise (v. 8). This may be an example of "tail-head" linkage, used to introduce the new characters Isaac, Jacob, and the patriarchs; Runge, *Grammar*, 304–7.

129 Keener, *Acts*, 2:1358; Dahl, "Story," 143–44.

130 Kilgallen, *Stephen Speech*, 37.

131 Marshall, "Acts," 558; Kilgallen, *Stephen Speech*, 37–38. For a full discussion of the variations, see Kim, "Quotations," 345–51.

132 "κρίνω," BDAG 568, §5.b.α.

"I myself," shifts readers' attention from the obstacle of oppression onto God's actions to bring about his promise to Abraham. The next phrase μετὰ ταῦτα ἐξελεύσονται, "after these things they shall come out," is God's positive action to liberate the Israelites—YHWH keeps his word.

λατρεύσουσίν μοι ἐν τῷ τόπῳ τούτῳ, "they will worship me in this place." The goal of the exodus is worship of YHWH.[133] Exodus 3:12 LXX is the probable source of this final phrase, although it has ἐν τῷ *ὄρει* τούτῳ, "on this *mountain*," identifying the "place" as Mt Horeb (Exod 3:1).[134] If so, the "place" where the people worship is outside the land of Israel.[135] Alternatively, τούτῳ, "this," may indicate the place where Stephen is now standing, i.e., the land of Israel, and the temple in particular (since that is where the Sanhedrin meet). If so, Stephen's point is that the land and the temple are proper places of worship,[136] and Stephen is not rejecting the temple per se.[137] There is irony in the contrast of the uses of "this place" in 6:13 and here, for the (false) accusation is that Stephen claims Jesus will destroy "this place," and yet God's promise is of worship in "this place." Kilgallen helpfully proposes that the focus is not on a particular place, for the phrase "this place" is imprecise; rather, the freedom to worship is the focus.[138] This highlights the further irony that proper worship did not, in fact, occur after the exodus, for at the mountain where the people were meant to worship YHWH, they worshiped the golden calf (vv. 39–43). Luke's presentation of Moses as a type of Jesus in his Gospel (esp. 4:16–20) shows Jesus as bringing a new exodus (note ἔξοδος, "departure" [Luke 9:31]) that will result in deliverance from Satan, necessary because the first exodus did not produce proper worship.[139]

8 καὶ ἔδωκεν αὐτῷ διαθήκην περιτομῆς, "God gave him the covenant of circumcision." The theme of divine initiative continues: now God gives his covenant promise characterized by circumcision (referring to Gen 17:10, 13).[140] This, one of only two mentions of διαθήκη, "covenant," in Acts (cf. 3:25 with *Comment* there), continues Stephen's focus on God's promise-commitment to Abraham's family, expressed by περιτομή, "circumcision," which baby boys

---

133 Shin, "Stories," 499.

134 Contra Schille, *Apostelgeschichte*, 181, who sees the "place" as Canaan, and Barrett, *Acts*, 1:345, who prefers Jerusalem, specifically the temple (cf. 6:13–14). However, Stephen goes on to speak of the temple's limitation and passing, since Jesus has taken over its role (vv. 48–50, 55–56); Walton, "Tale," 138–43, 44–46.

135 Spencer, *Portrait*, 71.

136 Keener, *Acts*, 2:1359–60; Schneider, *Apostelgeschichte*, 1:455; Barrett, *Acts*, 1:345.

137 Aarflot, *God*, 101.

138 Kilgallen, *Stephen Speech*, 38–39.

139 Garrett, "Meaning," esp. 12, 16; on the broader "new exodus" theme in Acts, see Pao, *Acts*, passim.

140 Smith, *Fate*, 156; cf. John 7:22, where Moses is said to give circumcision, immediately qualified by, "not that it is from Moses, but from the ancestors (i.e., the patriarchs)." Nevertheless, John 7:22 points to circumcision as a human gift, by contrast with Stephen's highlighting it as a divine gift.

received "on the eighth day," τῇ ἡμέρᾳ τῇ ὀγδόῃ. Circumcision was thus a regular reminder of YHWH's firm covenantal commitment both to individual men (in their own bodies) and to the community (through the performance of the ritual on baby boys), much as baptism is in the new covenant (although baptism is performed on both women and men).[141] As with the mention of "descendants" (7:6), the institution of circumcision presupposes the existence of male children, again signaling God's fulfillment of his promise.

καὶ οὕτως ἐγέννησεν τὸν Ἰσαὰκ καὶ περιέτεμεν αὐτὸν τῇ ἡμέρᾳ τῇ ὀγδόῃ, καὶ Ἰσαὰκ τὸν Ἰακώβ, καὶ Ἰακὼβ τοὺς δώδεκα πατριάρχας, "and so he fathered Isaac and circumcised him on the eighth day, and Isaac Jacob, and Jacob the twelve patriarchs." οὕτως, "so," points back to "the covenant of circumcision" and signals that what follows fulfills what went before: Abraham and his descendants continue to do what God asks, as in vv. 2–4. Such obedience to God is foundational for Israel: hence Jacob's twelve sons are called πατριάρχαι, "patriarchs," a word that indicates their status as founders.[142] In the two clauses καὶ Ἰσαὰκ τὸν Ἰακώβ, καὶ Ἰακὼβ τοὺς δώδεκα πατριάρχας, "and Isaac Jacob, and Jacob the twelve patriarchs," no verb is present; the verb could be ἐγέννησεν, "fathered" (NRSV [contra NRSVue, which retains vagueness with "did"], NIV, ESV, RSV), or περιέτεμεν, "circumcised" (CEB), or, most likely, both (HCSB, CSB), since it is not only fathering boys that shows obedience but also circumcising them.

Looking back so far in the speech, Stephen has established that his retelling of Israel's history focuses on God's promise to Abraham and its fulfillment in spite of obstacles.[143] God's promise is of a place for free worship, but it is vital to Stephen's thrust that God is not limited to particular locations, whether the temple (v. 48) or the land (for throughout the speech God encounters his people outside the land). The promise and fulfillment theme will develop through Joseph (vv. 9–16), Moses (vv. 17–44), Joshua (v. 45a), David, and Solomon (vv. 45b–47) before Stephen brings his review of history to a climax in Jesus, "the righteous one" (v. 52).

9–10 transition to the Joseph stories: vv. 9–16 summarize Gen 37; 39–50.

Verse 9 very briefly summarizes the story of the jealousy of Joseph's brothers (here designated πατριάρχαι, "patriarchs") and their action to sell him as a slave (Gen 37), thus highlighting his status as a victim.[144] καὶ ἦν ὁ θεὸς μετ᾽ αὐτοῦ, "Yet God was with him" (v. 9; cf. Gen 39:2, 3, 21, 23), is a keynote to Acts 7:9–16 (cf. this theme's application to Jesus in 10:38). καί, "yet," is

141 See *Comment* on 2:38, and cf. the interchange between baptism and circumcision in Col 2:11–16.

142 "πατριάρχης," BDAG 788. This word is rare in the NT; cf. 2:29; 7:9; Heb 7:4, referring to Abraham, David, or Jacob's twelve sons.

143 Bihler, *Stephanusgeschichte*, 38–46, sees the theme of promise and fulfillment as central to the whole speech. However, Stephen's consideration of Joseph and Moses stresses their rejection by God's people in spite of their being agents of God's purposes, and this emphasis is also significant; cf. Brehm, "Vindicating," 278n24.

144 With Richard, "Character," 258–62.

adversative and highlights the presence of God as "noteworthy."[145] Stephen continues to center his history of Israel on YHWH and his actions. He interprets what Reuben does in delivering (ἐξείλατο, as Gen 37:21 LXX) Joseph as God's action (cf. Gen 39:2, 3) and portrays God as the one who gives Joseph favor in Pharaoh's eyes (cf. Gen 39:4, concerning Joseph finding favor with Potiphar; 41:37–45, concerning Joseph's appointment as Pharaoh's governor). Luke thereby identifies Stephen as in continuity with Joseph, as a suffering righteous person with whom God stands.

Joseph's positive reception by Pharaoh with χάριν καὶ σοφίαν, "favor and wisdom," plays on the meaning of χάρις, which can denote human or divine favor.[146] ἐναντίον Φαραὼ βασιλέως Αἰγύπτου, "before Pharaoh the king of Egypt," is a verbatim quotation of Gen 41:46 LXX;[147] Joseph "standing before" Pharaoh denotes entering the king's service. Joseph's wisdom is seen in his ability to interpret dreams (Gen 40–41, esp. 41:33, 39), although Genesis does not mention σοφία, "wisdom." Jewish authors see Joseph as an example of a good person who suffers and is vindicated by God, and some use σοφία or an equivalent (e.g., Jub. 40:5; T. Jos. 1:2–7; 18:2; T. Reu. 4:8, 10; T. Sim.; Jos. Asen. 4:7; Philo, *Joseph* 106).[148] Stephen himself exhibits both qualities (Acts 6:8, 10), and he will characterize David as finding "favor (χάριν) with God" (7:46). A double reference to human and divine favor and wisdom seems likely here, adding to the picture of God's work in Israel's story and suggesting that Joseph is a "type" of Stephen[149]—as Joseph suffered at the hands of his brothers, so will Stephen suffer at the hands of those he addresses as "brothers," ἀδελφοί (v. 2). In turn, of course, Stephen is being modeled on Jesus as the ultimate rejected servant of God (vv. 51–53), one who also experienced and displayed God's "favor and wisdom" (Luke 2:40, 52).[150]

κατέστησεν αὐτὸν ἡγούμενον ἐπ᾽ Αἴγυπτον, "he put him in charge of Egypt." The following reference to ὅλον τὸν οἶκον αὐτοῦ, "the whole of his household," could suggest that Pharaoh is the grammatical subject. Nevertheless, αὐτοῦ, "his," most likely refers back to Φαραώ, "Pharaoh," and if so, the (implied) subject of κατέστησεν could be the same as that of ἐξείλατο, "he delivered," and ἔδωκεν, "he gave"—in both cases, clearly God.[151] Genesis 45:8 LXX strengthens this possibility: "Now therefore it is not you who have sent me here, but rather God, and *he* made (ἐποίησεν) me like a father to Pharaoh and lord of all his household (κύριον παντὸς τοῦ οἴκου αὐτοῦ) and ruler of the whole land of Egypt" (NETS, my italics). There, God is undoubtedly

145 "καί," BDAG 494, §1.b.η; Culy and Parsons, *Acts*, 119.
146 Human favor: Acts 2:47; divine favor: Luke 1:30; 2:40, 52; Acts 4:33.
147 Schwemer, "Lukas," 311.
148 Discussion: Brehm, "Vindicating," 279–82. Whitenton, "Rewriting," 165, cites other sources, but the word σοφία is not present for the places he cites.
149 Eckey, *Apostelgeschichte*, 1:170.
150 On the Christology implicit in the speech, see Kilgallen, "Function," 185–87.
151 Culy and Parsons, *Acts*, 119–20.

the subject of the main verb ἐποίησεν, "he made," and αὐτοῦ, "his," refers to Pharaoh.[152] Stephen himself was "put in charge" (6:3, also καθίστημι), and Stephen will present Moses as rejected from being "put . . . in charge" by his own people (7:27, 35, again καθίστημι). Here is a long chain of divinely appointed leaders who are rejected by their own,[153] a chain that culminates in Jesus (v. 52).

11–15a summarize the dramatic story of Gen 42–47. Egypt's suffering and Joseph's action to save the Egyptian people are peripheral to Stephen's summary (as they largely are in Genesis), which aims to demonstrate God's provision for his own people through Joseph. Thus the speech mentions only: the *ancestors'* need of food (Acts 7:11; cf. Gen 42:2); their first visit to Egypt (Acts 7:12; cf. Gen 42:1–38); their second visit, when Joseph made his identity known (Acts 7:13; cf. Gen 43:1–45:15); Joseph's invitation to his father to bring the family to Egypt (Acts 7:14; cf. Gen 45:16–28; 46:8–27); and Jacob and his family's move to Egypt (Acts 7:15a; cf. Gen 45:28–47:12). These events illustrate God's presence with Joseph (Acts 7:9), a presence—significantly—not limited to Joseph's homeland but also known in Egypt.

11 χορτάσματα, "food," is an unusual term: it is used mainly for *animal* fodder in LXX[154] and appears only here in NT. βρώματα is the commoner term for human food: it appears in Gen 42:2 LXX when Jacob sends his sons to buy food in Egypt, and seventeen times in NT. This lexical choice perhaps indicates the famine's severity[155]—they had to eat animal fodder.[156]

12–13 are Stephen's brief retelling of the Joseph stories. It is unlikely that the two visits are symbolic, either of the first and second comings of Jesus,[157] or of the second occasion showing that God's people are now without excuse,[158] since the visits are by Joseph's *brothers*, not Joseph himself (if he is considered as a christological prototype).

14 Stephen states the number of Jacob's family who lived in Egypt is seventy-five, which agrees with LXX Gen 46:27; Exod 1:5 (and 4QExod[b] frg. 1; 4QGen-Exod[a] frgs 17–18[159]), and contrasts with MT Gen 46:27; Exod 1:5; Deut 10:22 (and LXX); Jub. 44:33, which count the total as seventy (= the

152 With *BegC*, 4:72; Barrett, *Acts*, 1:348; cf. also Ps 104:21 LXX (MT 105:21).

153 Cf. Pervo, *Acts*, 182.

154 E.g., Gen 24:32; 42:27; Judg 19:19; see "χόρτασμα," *GELS* 734.

155 Schnabel, *Acts*, 370–71.

156 The cognate verb χορτάζω, "feed, fill," is used sixteen times in the NT, mainly in the passive for "be filled, satisfied," including in Luke 6:21; 9:17; 15:16 (of the prodigal son longing to fill his stomach with the pigs' food); 16:21, all for humans being filled.

157 Contra *BegC*, 4:73; with Barrett, *Acts*, 1:349. Bock, *Proclamation*, 217–18, criticizes any attempt at making Joseph in the speech a type of Jesus.

158 Contra Witherington, *Acts*, 268.

159 Fitzmyer, *Essays*, 87, with n75, gives 4QGen-Exod[a] (which he refers to as 4QEx[a]) as an example of traditions found in Qumran texts influencing the NT. The Qumran texts are available in Ulrich, ed. *Biblical Qumran Scrolls*, 27–28: ET: Abegg, Flint and Ulrich, *DSS Bible*.

sixty-six who traveled to Egypt plus Jacob, Joseph, and Joseph's two sons).[160] The difference is that LXX includes nine sons of Joseph born in Egypt and appears to reckon the sixty-six as including Jacob and Joseph, whereas MT has only two sons and does not include Jacob and Joseph in the sixty-six. The Qumran texts and LXX show that seventy-five was known at the time of Stephen and may suggest that this is the older form (especially if LXX translates a Heb. text earlier than MT, as the Dead Sea Scrolls might suggest).

15b–16 summarize Gen 47:29–50:26; Exod 1:6. Shechem, Συχέμ (near to Mount Gerizim), was the site of the Samaritan temple (see *Comment* on 8:5), and some see Shechem's mention as evidence of Samaritan influence on Stephen.[161] To address this possibility, we need to consider the traditions in the background here.

Stephen locates the tomb Abraham purchased in Shechem, whereas the OT locates it in Hebron (Gen 23:17–19); Hebron is also where Jacob was buried (Gen 49:29–30; 50:13). According to Gen 33:18–19, Jacob bought a burial plot in Shechem, and this was the burial place of Joseph (Josh 24:32)—the OT does not specify where Joseph's brothers were buried, although other sources suggest they were buried in Hebron.[162] The text of Acts is a little ambiguous: αὐτός, "he," referring to Jacob, is the subject of the singular verb ἐτελεύτησεν, "was buried"; but the subject of μετετέθησαν, "they were brought back," and ἐτέθησαν, "they were placed," could refer either to both Jacob and the ancestors (implying that they were all buried at Shechem)[163] or to the ancestors alone (leaving open the possibility that Jacob was buried in a different place to the ancestors).[164] The evidence of Jewish tradition is that the inclusive view—that both Jacob and the ancestors were buried in the same place—was the usual reading of Scripture.[165] Stephen's speech blends the two traditions of burial places by having Abraham purchase the site in Shechem that Genesis has Jacob purchase. The blending of the Abraham and Jacob burial-site purchase stories might be accidental or deliberate and might be from Luke's source or Luke's own handiwork—it could well be based on extrabiblical tradition.[166] It seems unlikely that Luke, whose knowledge of Scripture is considerable, would not correct a source that he perceived to contain such an error.[167] If the blending of traditions is deliberate, on the part of Luke or his source, it

160 Cf. Philo, *Migration* 198–200 (seeking to reconcile the two figures by allegorizing the difference of five as concerning the five senses), with Bruce, *Acts* (1990), 196; Josephus, *Ant.* 2.7.4 §276; 6.5.6 §89 (giving 70).

161 See n20.

162 All: Jub. 46:9; Josephus, *J.W.* 4.9.7 §432; *Ant.* 2.8.2. §199. See also n165.

163 E.g., Scobie, "Use," 407; Spencer, *Portrait*, 77.

164 E.g., Barrett, "OT History," 62; Kilgallen, *Stephen Speech*, 57.

165 As frequently in T. 12 Patr.: T. Reu. 7:2; T. Sim. 8:2; T. Levi 19:5; T. Jud. 26:3; T. Iss. 7:8; T. Zeb. 10:7; T. Naph. 9:1; T. Gad 8:5; T. Ash. 8:1–2; T. Jos. 20:6–7; T. Benj. 12:3.

166 Bovon, *Luke 1950–2005*, 109; contra Wilcox, *Semitisms*, 61, who speculates that Luke uses a non-extant Greek OT text different from LXX.

167 Spencer, *Portrait*, 77–78.

is comparable to that practice elsewhere in the speech[168] (e.g., Acts 7:9–13), although its purpose is unclear.[169]

The location in Shechem—a place outside Judea—continues the speech's theme of the relativization of the land, and underlines that Abraham and his descendants did not have a place in the land (v. 5), even for their grave(s).[170] Indeed, the local people welcomed Israelite ancestors by making a burial place available, by contrast with Israelites who "drove the prophets to their grave" (v. 51).[171]

Some see the mention of Shechem as an allusion to the Samaritan belief that their temple there, on Mount Gerizim, was the true temple. Scobie proposes that Luke is dependent on a local Samaritan tradition,[172] a claim lacking contemporary evidence—the only extant support is third-century AD and later Christian sources.[173] The most that might be suggested is that Luke, with this mention of Shechemite hospitality for Abraham's family, hints at a prefiguring of the Samaritan welcome of the gospel in Philip's ministry (8:5–13).[174]

17–19 transition to the time of Moses and the exodus, which runs through to v. 43 in three forty-year periods (vv. 17–22, 23–29, 30–43). Verse 17a is Stephen's commentary on what follows, for he knows that the day of Moses was the time when God's promise to Abraham (vv. 5–7; Gen 15:13–16) was fulfilled—the speech's emphasis is on God's activity on behalf of his people, again set outside the land (although it will lead to their restoration to the land). Verse 17b sets the scene by portraying the growth in number of the Israelites and the rise of the Pharaoh who was threatened by this, to the extent that he caused their newborns to be exposed (Acts 7:19). ηὔξησεν ὁ λαὸς καὶ ἐπληθύνθη ἐν Αἰγύπτῳ, "the people multiplied greatly in Egypt" (v. 17b), echoes Exod 1:7 LXX; ἀνέστη βασιλεὺς ἕτερος ὃς οὐκ ᾔδει τὸν Ἰωσήφ, "another king, who had not known Joseph, came to power" (Acts 7:18), reproduces Exod 1:8 LXX almost verbatim[175] (see *Note* hh for textual variants here); and

168 Bruce, *Acts* (1990), 196; cf. Bede, *Acts*, 71–72, who suggests Stephen is using "popular opinion" in this conflation of events, and that he focuses on "the point with which he is concerned."

169 See the exhaustive, but inconclusive, discussion of possibilities in Kilgallen, *Stephen Speech*, 58–59.

170 Stemberger, "Stephanusrede," 164–65, 173.

171 Spencer, *Portrait*, 81.

172 Scobie, "Use," 407–8; Jeremias, *Heiligengräber*, 37–38; cf. Stemberger, "Stephanusrede," 162–63, 73.

173 Jeremias, *Heiligengräber*, 37–38, refers to Jerome, *Epist.* 57.10; 108.11 (mis-cited as 13); Georgius Syncellus 176 (cited by Jeremias as S[eite]. 284; ninth century). Jeremias also notes that although Jewish traditions of the first and second centuries BC locate the grave of Jacob's sons (excluding Joseph) in Hebron, rabbinic and Christian sources do not speak of this; however, our sources for the rabbis and Christian authors are not from the first century AD, so not much weight can be placed on this argument.

174 Spencer, *Portrait*, 81.

175 With Smith, *Fate*, 152.

Acts 7:19 echoes Exod 1:10. Stephen refers to βασιλεὺς ἕτερος, "another king," rather than "another Pharaoh," since Acts 7:9 clarifies that the Pharaoh is the Egyptian king.

19 ποιεῖν τὰ βρέφη ἔκθετα αὐτῶν εἰς τὸ μὴ ζῳογονεῖσθαι, "by compelling them to expose their infants so that they would not live," denotes the widespread ancient practice of abandoning unwelcome infants—often girls—to the elements, which resulted in the death of up to 10% of infants in ancient Rome.[176] In Egypt exposure was used as a means for controlling the burgeoning population of Israelites (Exod 1:10, 15–16, 22).

20–22 Moses comes onto the scene (cf. Exod 2:1–10). ἦν ἀστεῖος τῷ θεῷ, "he was good-looking as far as God was concerned." ἀστεῖος, "good-looking," originally denoted a person as well-bred, refined; in time, its sense expanded to a general term of approbation (cf. Heb 11:23, the only other NT use).[177] The speech qualifies ἀστεῖος by the ethical dative τῷ θεῷ, "as far as God was concerned,"[178] in order to signal that the statement is not merely about human qualifications but about divine acceptance. Like God's choice of David, human characteristics are not irrelevant—for David was good-looking too[179]—but they are not the determining factor: that is God's decision (1 Sam 16:6–7, 11–12). Exodus 2:2 LXX suggests that Moses's looks were a cause of his parents' decision to hide him (MT has his mother alone hide him), while other Jewish tradition explicitly links Moses's pleasing appearance to his parents' decision to hide him.[180]

20 ὃς ἀνετράφη μῆνας τρεῖς ἐν τῷ οἴκῳ τοῦ πατρός, "He was brought up for three months in his father's house," goes a little beyond Exod 2:3–4 LXX, which merely says that his family ἐσκέπασαν, "sheltered," Moses (cf. the fuller elaborations in Jub. 47:3; Josephus, *Ant.* 2.9.4 §218; Philo, *Moses* 1:9).[181]

21 δέ, "but" (v. 21), introduces a new and contrasting event: divine intervention may be implied in Pharaoh's daughter taking Moses. The consequences of this action are played out in v. 22, where Moses is being equipped—ironically, by the Egyptians—to lead the Israelites out of Egypt.

ἀνείλατο, "took for herself" (v. 21), is unlikely to be as precise as "adopt."[182]

---

176 Toner, *Culture*, 47, with further detail on exposure, 17–18, 62–63; more briefly, J. R. Sallares, "Infanticide" in *OCD*³ 757; more fully, with documentation, Keener, *Acts*, 2:1376–81.

177 "ἀστεῖος," LSJ; "ἀστεῖος," *GELS* 98.

178 τῷ θεῷ may be an idiomatic expression derived from Heb. expressing greatness. cf. Jonah 3:3 where Heb. עיר גדולה לאלהים (*ʿyr gdwlh lʾlhym*), "a great city to God," has the sense "an extremely large city" (LXX πόλις μεγάλη τῷ θεῷ, "a great city to God" [NETS]); Culy and Parsons, *Acts*, 125. Either way, the focus on God's engagement with the story is clear.

179 1 Sam 16:12 LXX describes David as ἀγαθὸς ὁράσει κυρίῳ, "good in appearance as far as the Lord was concerned," also using an ethical dat. MT lacks the Heb. equivalent.

180 Philo, *Moses* 1.9 (where Moses is called ἀστειοτέραν, "good-looking"), 18; Josephus, *Ant.* 2.9.6 §§230–32 (using κάλλος and χάρις to denote Moses's "beauty").

181 On Stephen's use of extrabiblical traditions here and in vv. 21, 22, see Johnson, *Midrash*, 27–28.

182 With "ἀναιρέω," BDAG 64, §3; contra Barrett, *Acts*, 1:355; "ἀναιρέω," BAGD 55, §2.

Rather, it simply describes picking up a child left exposed,[183] and the next phrase, ἀνεθρέψατο αὐτὸν ἑαυτῇ εἰς υἱόν, more clearly suggests adoption: "she brought him up him as her own son" (cf. Exod 1:10a LXX ἐγενήθη αὐτῇ εἰς υἱόν, "he became as a son to her" [my translation]). As in v. 20, other Jewish writers elaborate the story more fully, such as by providing a name for Pharaoh's daughter or identifying her as childless (e.g., Josephus, *Ant.* 2.9.5 §224; Jub. 47:5; Philo, *Moses* 1:12–15).

22 lacks a basis in Exodus, although it reflects other accounts of Moses's upbringing.[184] Luke continues to paint his characters using colors from his portrait of Jesus:[185] δυνατὸς ἐν λόγοις καὶ ἔργοις αὐτοῦ, "powerful in his words and deeds," gives a comprehensive picture of Moses's competence and echoes Luke's description (on the lips of Cleopas and his companion) of Jesus as δυνατὸς ἐν ἔργῳ καὶ λόγῳ, "powerful in deed and word" (Luke 24:19).[186] Exodus 4:10 presents Moses as hesitant in speech, which some take as Moses seeking to evade a difficult task;[187] God's willingness to appoint Aaron as his spokesman (Exod 4:14–16) suggests this is not false modesty on Moses's part. Alternatively, it may be that Stephen's speech presumes the power of Moses's words to be in their *content* rather than in Moses's own articulation of them, or it may be that the written form of Moses's words is implied.[188]

23–29 describe the second forty-year period of Moses's life, his entrance into public life, which goes badly wrong when he kills the Egyptian (v. 24) and leads to Moses fleeing to Midian. Stephen here selectively retells Exod 2:11–22.

23 ἀνέβη ἐπὶ τὴν καρδίαν αὐτοῦ ἐπισκέψασθαι τοὺς ἀδελφοὺς αὐτοῦ, "it came into his mind to visit his compatriots." Exodus 2:11 lacks a specific mention of the idea either of visiting entering Moses's mind or of his age.[189] The expression is a Semitism, found in LXX as well as NT.[190] Its use elsewhere with God as subject (Jer 51:21 LXX [MT 44:21]) suggests the passive voice here is not

183 "ἀναιρέω," BDAG 64, §3, citing papyri speaking of exposed children taken up and brought up as slaves, by contrast with Moses, who is brought up as a son.

184 Philo, *Moses* 1:22–24; cf. Ezekiel the Tragedian *apud* Eusebius *Praep. ev.* 9.28. cf. Josephus, *Ant.* 2.9.2–7 §§205, 210, 215–16, 224, 228–31, 232–34, 236. More fully on Jewish views of Moses, see "Μωυσῆς," *TDNT* 4:848–55.

185 See, e.g., *Comment* on 3:8, 10; *Form/Structure/Setting* on 4:5–22; with O'Toole, "Parallels"; Praeder, "Jesus-Paul."

186 For the combination "deed and word," see Rom 15:18; 2 Cor 10:11; Col 3:17; 2 Thess 2:17; cf. the contrast of word and deed in 1 John 3:18.

187 Marshall, *Acts* (TNTC), 140. Josephus, *Ant.* 3.1.4 §§13–23, portrays Moses as pacifying the people at Elim by his words, although this stands alone in Jewish tradition as a portrait of Moses speaking effectively.

188 The latter suggested by Barrett, *Acts*, 1:356.

189 Deut 34:7 records Moses's death at the age of 120. Sipre Deut 357 (on Deut 34:7) divides Moses's life into three forty-year periods in similar manner to Stephen's speech; cf. Gen. Rab. 100.10, which uses Moses as template for a 3 x 40-year life-structure for Hillel, R. Johannan ben Zakkai, and R. Akiba.

190 LXX 2 Kgs 12:5 (EVV 12:4); Isa 65:15; Jer 3:16; 28:50 (MT 51:50); 39:35 (MT 32:35); 51:21 (MT 44:21); cf. "ἀναβαίνω," BDAG 58, §2, with Wilcox, *Semitisms*, 63, on the idiom.

a "divine passive"—Stephen is not attributing divine prompting to Moses's visit—but is simply a way to speak of an idea arising in the mind.

24–25 combine Exod 2:11b–12 (v. 24) with an attribution of motive to Moses not found in Exodus: that he considered himself to be acting as God's agent to save the people (v. 25). Luke's use of σωτηρία, "salvation" (v. 25), would cause sensitive readers to recognize that Jesus is now the one who brings salvation (Luke 1:69, 71, 77; 2:11; 19:19; Acts 4:12; 5:31). Stephen's claim that Moses "came to his defense," ἠμύνατο, suggests that he considers Moses's action justified. Philo similarly asserts that Moses considered his action εὐαγής, "holy, right" (*Moses* 1.44). The late-third- to early-first-century BC Egyptian writer Artapanus radically rewrites the story to have Moses killing an Egyptian called Chanethotes who has been instructed by Pharoah to kill Moses (Eusebius, *Praep. ev.* 9.27.1–19).[191] Neither Artapanus nor Philo presents Moses as thinking that he was acting as God's agent to save the Israelites or hoping his compatriots would recognize this, as Stephen does here. Indeed, Exodus locates Moses's call to deliver Israel later, at the burning bush (see Acts 7:30–34); the fact that the speech locates that sense of call here underlines the parallel with Jesus.[192] As with Joseph (vv. 9–14), Stephen speaks of one chosen by God as God's agent to deliver his people but whom the people reject, continuing the build up toward the accusation of the Jewish leaders' rejection of Jesus as Messiah (v. 52).[193]

26–29 retell Exod 2:13–15 (Acts 7:26–29a), including verbatim agreement with much of 2:14 LXX (Acts 7:27–28),[194] plus a hint of Exod 2:16–22 (Acts 7:29b). Stephen in places goes beyond what Exodus says, drawing out the (appropriate) implication that Moses sought reconciliation (συνήλλασσεν, "he tried to reconcile," Acts 7:26; cf. Exod 2:13 "Why do you strike your fellow [sc. Hebrew]?") and emphasizing their relationship as "brothers," ἀδελφοί (Acts 7:26).

27–28 The initiator of the attack responds with violence in deed and word: he pushes Moses aside (ἀπώσατο, v. 27[195]) and replies aggressively. The attacker's reply agrees with Exod 2:13b–14a LXX. His questions are rhetorical, with the second marked as expecting the answer, "No."[196] However, Luke/

191 On Artapanus's interpretation of Moses more broadly, see Barclay, "Manipulating," 31–34.

192 Barclay, "Manipulating," 42; Kilgallen, *Stephen Speech*, 69–70.

193 Boesenberg, "Retelling," who, after discussing the Philo and Artapanus parallels with Stephen's interpretation (149–53), suggests that CD evinces a similar approach to dividing Israel (153–55), although the lack of retelling of this story makes the parallel less compelling. Nevertheless, Boesenberg does demonstrate that the biblical interpretation here fits well into first-century Judaism.

194 Smith, *Fate*, 151.

195 Culy and Parsons, *Acts*, 129–30, note that other uses of ἀπωθέω in the NT are metaphorical (Acts 7:39; 13:46; Rom 11:1, 2; 1 Tim 1:19). However, as they also note, the story from Exod 2 fits with physical pushing.

196 It begins with μή. Culy and Parsons, *Acts*, 130, suggest it "carries a taunting tone."

Stephen would answer the first question (v. 27b), "God!"[197]—Moses is God's chosen agent for redemption and reconciliation, but the people reject him, as they will Jesus.

29a ἔφυγεν δὲ Μωϋσῆς ἐν τῷ λόγῳ τούτῳ, "Moses fled because he said this," telescopes the fuller account in Exod 2:14–15; there, Moses becomes afraid because others know he has murdered the Egyptian, and the immediate cause of Moses's migration to Midian is a threat from Pharaoh after he learns of the murder.

29b provides a very brief account of Moses's time in Midian, since this period is not directly Stephen's concern. Instead of being at home among God's people, Moses becomes an alien (πάροικος connotes "resident alien," implying temporary residence[198]) in a land some distance away, on the eastern coast of the Gulf of Aqabah, beyond the Sinai Peninsula. The location outside the promised land is significant, for here God blesses Moses with children and will meet with Moses at Mount Sinai (vv. 30–34). Moses's marriage to a non-Israelite, the daughter of a gentile priest, is implied in the fathering of two sons (Exod 2:15b–22; 18:3–4), a development which hints at God's concern for gentiles.[199]

30–43 cover the third forty-year period of Moses's life, beginning with the burning bush episode and its consequences. Moses is a miracle worker (v. 36), deliverer (v. 35), prophet (v. 37), and divine mouthpiece (v. 38)—and yet the people reject him (vv. 35, 39–40), with the result that God rejects them (vv. 42–43). While Stephen's words center on Moses (see especially on vv. 35–39), God's appearance and speech are crucial to what now happens.

30–34 retell the story of the burning bush (Exod 3:1–10) but without the extended conversation between God and Moses (Exod 3:11–4:17), since Stephen's focus is on God's commission of Moses and the people's negative reaction to Moses as leader. There are small differences from LXX/MT (which are substantially the same as each other), none of which affect the sense of Stephen's key points.[200]

The character and activity of God are central to this part of the speech (as they are to the story in Exodus). Stephen does not mention that the bush is not consumed by the fire (Exod 3:2)—the bush's burning is sufficient to attract Moses's attention. Once God has gained Moses's attention through the burning bush (Acts 7:30–31a), God speaks (v. 31b).

30 Καὶ πληρωθέντων ἐτῶν τεσσεράκοντα, "When forty years had passed." Exodus 3 does not explicitly state the period of Moses living in Midian as forty years; Exod 7:7 gives Moses's age as eighty when he spoke to Pharaoh and

---

197 Stählin, *Apostelgeschichte*, 108.

198 Cf. LXX Gen 15:13; 23:3; Exod 2:22; 12:43; Lev 25:45, 47; etc.; Barrett, *Acts*, 1:359.

199 Keener, "Marriages," 30–33.

200 For detail, see Marshall, "Acts," 562–63; Tabb and Walton, "Exodus," 92–99.

Acts 7:23 records Moses's age as forty when he went to Midian (see *Comment* on v. 23 above). Moses's shepherding of Jethro's flock takes him into the Sinai Peninsula. Exodus 3:1 identifies the mountain as Horeb; the two names are used with the same referent in Scripture.[201]

32 ἐγὼ ὁ θεὸς τῶν πατέρων σου, ὁ θεὸς Ἀβραὰμ καὶ Ἰσαὰκ καὶ Ἰακώβ, "I am the God of your ancestors, the God of Abraham and Isaac and Jacob," echoes Exod 3:6 LXX but with the plural τῶν πατέρων, "ancestors," found in Exod 3:15, 16 LXX instead of the singular τοῦ πατρός, "father," found in 3:6 LXX.[202] By this self-identification God characterizes himself as in covenant with the Israelites and continues to do so by calling them τοῦ λαοῦ μου, "my people" (Acts 7:34).

ἔντρομος δὲ γενόμενος Μωϋσῆς, "Moses began to tremble," echoes Exod 3:6b LXX. The God of whom Stephen speaks is awesome and must be treated with proper reverence; this God is to be listened to and obeyed rather than taken lightly. Moses's reaction to God's presence is fear, an appropriate and widespread biblical reaction to God appearing.[203]

Μωϋσῆς οὐκ ἐτόλμα κατανοῆσαι, "Moses did not dare to look more closely," points to the biblical theme that no human can encounter God and live—hence the safeguards around Mount Sinai at the giving of the law, including the specification that the people should not "break through to YHWH to look" (LXX κατανοῆσαι, "to look more closely," as here; Exod 19:21, 12–13; cf. Exod 3:6b; Deut 5:24).

33 blends Exod 3:7a LXX and the command to Moses to remove his sandals in Exod 3:5 LXX, omitted earlier in this speech. The phrase τὸ ὑπόδημα τῶν ποδῶν λῦσαι, "Take the sandals off your feet," will recur in Paul's Antioch speech (Acts 13:25).

ὁ γὰρ τόπος, ἐν ᾧ σὺ ἕστηκας, γῆ ἁγία ἐστίν, "for the place where you are standing is holy ground," is significant in the context of Stephen's speech, for it identifies a place outside the promised land as holy and thus contributes to Stephen's relativization of the temple (which Stephen's opponents call "the holy place," τοῦ τόπου τοῦ ἁγίου [6:14]). Stephen's point is not that the

---

201 E.g., Horeb: Exod 3:1; Deut 1:6, 19; 4:10, 15; 1 Kgs 8:9; Ps 106:19; Mal 4:4; Sinai: Exod 19:11, 18, 20, 23; 24:16; 31:18; 34:29; Lev 25:1; 26:46; 27:34. NT authors consistently use Σινά, "Sinai": here, v. 38; Gal 4:24, 25.

202 The plural "the God of (y)our/the ancestors (τῶν πατέρων)" is found three other times in Acts, at 3:13; 5:30; 22:14, and thus could represent Lukan redaction; see Richard, "Acts 7," 199–200, although Richard (200–202) prefers the view that "textual fluidity" is a more likely explanation. Wilcox, *Semitisms*, 29–30, 33–34 suggests a Samaritan influence since the Samaritan Pentateuch and Pentateuch Targum both read "your ancestors." However, the presence of the plural in Exod 3:15, 16 LXX, and Stephen's focus on God's activity throughout the history of Israel, are sufficient to explain the use of the plural; with Barrett, *Acts*, 1:361.

203 ירא (*yr'*), "fear" (Exod 3:6), originally meant "tremble" (Günter Wanke, "φόβος and φοβέομαι in the Old Testament," *TDNT* 9:199), as v. 32 renders it here, differently from LXX. For fear on meeting God, see e.g., Gen 3:10; 28:17; Exod 19:16; 20:20; Dan 10:7–8; Tob 12:16.

temple is not holy but that the holiness of God's presence is not confined to the temple precincts;[204] rather, "'Holy' . . . is where the presence of God is."[205] In other words, "[a]ny ground can be holy ground."[206] "Is this anti-Judaism? Hardly!"[207] The strong contrast with Barn. 16:1–10, where the Jerusalem temple is regarded as disastrous, shows that Luke's Stephen is not anti-Jewish.

34–35 Stephen sharply contrasts God's commission of Moses and the people's rejection of Moses. As in Exod 3:7–10, on which these verses draw, divine initiative drives the narrative. God's speech expresses his concern in the first person: "I have seen (εἶδον)" . . . "I have heard (ἤκουσα)" . . . "I have come down (κατέβην)" . . . "I will send (ἀποστείλω)." God's appointment of Moses comes as the last of this sequence, signaling that human action follows and is responsive to God's desires and concerns; indeed, Moses's earlier error was to act on his own initiative, mistakenly supposing that he was acting in tune with God's will (Acts 7:24–25). Here is the tip of an iceberg of a Lukan theme: that God's people need to be attentive to God and respond appropriately to him rather than pursuing their own concerns.[208]

The people's response to Moses is expressed through the earlier rejection of him: v. 35 quotes from Exod 2:13b LXX, using the same words as in Acts 7:27. Stephen goes on to provide direct commentary on the story rather than the interpretive retelling that he has been doing up to now.

Τοῦτον τὸν Μωϋσῆν, "This Moses." This thematic fronted accusative initiates a series of statements (vv. 35–40) about what God did through Moses to deliver and speak to the people, bookended by statements of their rejection of Moses (vv. 35a, 39–40). The statements maintain the focus on God's action through Moses by referring to Moses using accusatives (v. 35 ὃν "the one," τοῦτον, "this is the one") and demonstrative pronouns (οὗτος "this/this is the one," vv. 36, 37, 38).[209] God remains the grammatical subject and (thus) the driver of events, for ὁ θεὸς . . . ἀπέσταλκεν, "God sent," Moses (v. 35). God chooses the migrant Moses to lead Israel's migration from Egypt.[210]

ὃν ἠρνήσαντο εἰπόντες· τίς σε κατέστησεν ἄρχοντα καὶ δικαστήν; τοῦτον ὁ θεὸς ἄρχοντα καὶ λυτρωτὴν ἀπέσταλκεν, "the one they rejected, saying, 'Who put you in charge as a ruler and judge?'—this is the one God sent as ruler and deliverer." Stephen contrasts the people's rejection of Moses as "ruler and *judge* (δικαστήν)" with God's choice of him as their "ruler and *deliverer* (λυτρωτήν)."

---

204 Walton, "Tale," 141–43.
205 Johnson, *Acts*, 128.
206 Hays, "Place," 156–57.
207 Bachmann, "Stephanusepisode," 561–62 (quoting 561; my translation).
208 E.g., the repeated "all that God had done" (14:27; 15:4, 12) and the stress in Peter's speech at the Jerusalem meeting on God's actions (15:7, 8, 10, 11). More fully, see Walton, "Acts, Book of"; Walton, "Acts of God."
209 Cf. Peter's series of statements about Jesus using thematic fronted accusative and resumptive accusatives in 2:22, 24, 32, 36, with *Comment* there.
210 Hays, "Place," 155.

Rather than sending Moses with a rule exercised to condemn, as the people suppose, God sends him with a rule exercised to deliver.[211] The source of the idea may be Exod 6:6 LXX, where YHWH announces his purpose to deliver the people (using the cognate verb λυτρώσομαι, "I will deliver"). Λυτρωτής, usually "redeemer," occurs only here in the NT (and only four times in LXX[212]), although cognate words occur in the NT.[213] Moses is not strictly the redeemer himself but YHWH's *agent* in redeeming. Common use of the word group suggests redemption by paying a price, but in redemption through Moses no payment is involved, so the thought here is simply of deliverance.[214] Strikingly, Luke has Zechariah and Anna announce that what Jesus comes to do is redemption (λύτρωσις, Luke 1:68; 2:38) and "bookends" his Gospel by the announcement that the pair walking to Emmaus had hoped that Jesus would redeem Israel (λυτροῦσθαι, Luke 24:21). Moses in Stephen's speech is in some respects a "type" of Jesus, the one who has now redeemed Israel, not unlike Peter's comparison of Moses and Jesus (3:22–23),[215] although in Jesus's case with the payment of a price (cf. 20:28). In this connection, Moule sees the perfect verb ἀπέσταλκεν, "sent," as the "perfect of allegory," that is, as highlighting the contemporary significance of an OT event.[216]

σὺν χειρὶ ἀγγέλου τοῦ ὀφθέντος αὐτῷ ἐν τῇ βάτῳ, "through the hand of an angel who appeared to him in the bush." Here χείρ, "hand," is metonymy for the power or help the angel—a divine agent—gives,[217] an LXX turn of phrase.[218]

36 οὗτος ἐξήγαγεν αὐτοὺς ποιήσας τέρατα καὶ σημεῖα ἐν γῇ Αἰγύπτῳ καὶ ἐν ἐρυθρᾷ θαλάσσῃ καὶ ἐν τῇ ἐρήμῳ ἔτη τεσσεράκοντα, "This is the one who led them out by doing wonders and signs in the land of Egypt and at the Red Sea—as well as in the wilderness for forty years." The "wonders and signs," τέρατα καὶ σημεῖα, echo Peter's description of Jesus (2:22), Luke's descriptions of the life of the early community (2:43; 4:30; 5:12), and Stephen's (6:8) and Paul's ministry (14:3; 15:12), thus continuing the typological connection from Moses to Jesus and also to his followers. Paul will use the same verb, ἐξήγαγεν, "led out," for the exodus, but with God as the subject (13:17).

ποιήσας, "by doing" (aorist participle of means), relates to τέρατα καὶ

---

211 Horbury, "Conceptions," 8, notes that vv. 35–38 portray "the congregation of Israel . . . united around a ruler," namely Moses, and sees the Christian community as utilizing this idea, with Jesus as the uniting ruler.

212 Lev 25:31, 32; Pss 18:15 (MT 19:15, EVV 19:14); 77:35 (MT 78:35).

213 λύτρον, "ransom," Matt 20:26; Mark 10:45; λυτρόω, "ransom," Luke 24:21; Titus 2:14; 1 Pet 1:18; λύτρωσις, "redemption," Luke 1:68; 2:38; Heb 9:12.

214 Barrett, *Acts*, 1:364.

215 With Brehm, "Vindicating," 284–87.

216 Moule, 14–15; cf. MHT, 1:144; contrast Wallace, 578; BDF, §343(2), who treat it as "aoristic," that is, as having no focus on the present consequences of the past event depicted by the verb.

217 "χείρ," BDAG 1082, §2.b.δ; Culy and Parsons, *Acts*, 134.

218 "χείρ," *NIDNTTE* 4:662–64, JL, §§1, 2, and NT, §1.

σημεῖα, "wonders and signs," performed in three locations: in Egypt, at the Red Sea, and in the wilderness.[219] Those in Egypt are the signs commanded by Moses, including the plagues (Exod 4:21; 7–12), and *precede* Moses leading them out (ἐξήγαγεν), a natural use of the aorist participle ποιήσας, "by doing." The wonders and signs in the wilderness, such as the provision of manna and drinkable water (Exod 15:22–16:36), and perhaps those at the Red Sea (Exod 14), *follow* Moses leading the people out, which sits less comfortably with the aorist participle ποιήσας—I have thus translated the second clause as an anacoluthon.[220] A possible alternative is to see ἐξήγαγεν, "[he] led them out," as a constative aorist describing the whole period of the exodus and the wilderness wanderings.[221]

37 προφήτην ὑμῖν ἀναστήσει ὁ θεὸς ἐκ τῶν ἀδελφῶν ὑμῶν ὡς ἐμέ, "God will raise up a prophet like me for you from among your compatriots," is a quotation from Deut 18:15,[222] although not precisely LXX: the word order differs, and the group addressed is plural here (ὑμῖν) by contrast with LXX singular σοι (reflecting the Heb. singular לְךָ [lᵉḵā], "for you")—although in both languages "you" singular here is a collective singular, for both Hebrew and Greek have plural verbs for "you shall listen to him" later in Deut 18:15.[223] A similar change to the plural is made in the quotation of Deut 18:15 in Acts 3:22, reflecting (as here) that an appeal is being made to the nation—in 3:22 this change is because of the strategic location in the temple, and here the change is because Stephen is addressing the whole Sanhedrin, the national leadership.[224]

On the "prophet like Moses," see *Comment* on 3:22. Stephen is identifying Jesus as the one announced by Moses; here, the key resemblance between Moses and Jesus (whom Luke identifies as a prophet, Luke 4:24; 7:16; 13:33; 24:19) is their rejection by God's people (Acts 7:35, 39, 51–52).[225] Stephen does not attribute "wonders and signs" (v. 36) to Jesus, although Luke attributes them to both Jesus (2:22) and Stephen (6:8).

The Samaritan Pentateuch (SP; first century AD) inserts Deut 5:28–29, followed by Deut 18:15–22 and then Deut 5:30–31, into the account of the giving of the law in Exod 20, following the tenth commandment (v. 21). 4Q158 frg. 6 also commingles Deut 5:28–31; 18:18–22 and Exod 20, but not identically with

219 Cf. T. Mos. 3.11 "Moses, who suffered many things *in Egypt and at the Red Sea and in the wilderness* for forty years" (*OTP*, my italics). The parallel is not exact, for Acts speaks of the wonders and signs which Moses did in those locations, whereas T. Mos. speaks of Moses's suffering.

220 Cf. Bruce, *Acts* (1990), 201; Barrett, *Acts*, 1:364–65.

221 MHT, 1:133.

222 Contra Wilcox, *Semitisms*, 33, who sees Deut 18:18 as the source; for critique of Wilcox, see Bock, *Proclamation*, 218–19; Robb, "Prophet," 111, noting that only Deut 18:15 includes ὁ θεός, "God," and ὡς ἐμέ, "like me."

223 תִּשְׁמָעוּן [*tišmāʿûn*] and ἀκούσεσθε.

224 Bock, *Proclamation*, 119.

225 With Keener, *Acts*, 2:1402; on wider resonances of Moses and Jesus in vv. 35–37, see Via, "Interpretation."

SP.[226] While SP and 4Q158 agree against MT in places, none are in the citation of Deut 18:15–22. Thus, the association of the Deuteronomy texts with Exod 20 seen in Stephen's speech probably exists at a "proto-Samaritan," Palestinian stage of the textual traditions and does not point to Samaritan influence on this part of Stephen's speech.[227] What Luke presents here is historically and exegetically plausible as coming from a first-century Jew like Stephen.

The Samaritans saw Moses as the one and only prophet and expected a messianic prophet-like-Moses figure known as the *Taḥeb*, although references are found first only in third and fourth century AD sources. It thus seems most likely that the expectation of the *Taḥeb* developed after the first-century SP, and the association with the prophet like Moses was independent of SP's textual insertions into Exod 20.[228] Again, then, it is unlikely that we should see Samaritan influence at this point in Stephen's speech.

38 τῇ ἐκκλησίᾳ ἐν τῇ ἐρήμῳ, "in the congregation in the wilderness." Luke has only recently used ἐκκλησία for the first time, there of the believing community (Acts 5:11), and here qualifies it by ἐν τῇ ἐρήμῳ, "in the wilderness," clarifying that the reference is to the people in the wilderness period. LXX frequently uses this term for the congregation of Israel (see *Comment* on 5:11), notably in Deut 18:16, part of the passage concerning the prophet like Moses echoed in Acts 7:37. This suggests Stephen is making a typological point about the believing community as in continuity with the congregation of Israel.[229]

ὃς ἐδέξατο λόγια ζῶντα δοῦναι ἡμῖν, "He received living words to give to us," characterizes Moses in prophetic terms, passing on what he receives from God (here, via an angel, cf. v. 53 with *Comment*). The description of the law as λόγια ζῶντα, "living words," is unique in NT and striking. The nearest phrases in LXX are τὸ λόγιόν σου ἔζησέν με ("your word gives me life") . . . ἀντιλαβοῦ μου κατὰ τὸ λόγιόν σου, καὶ ζήσομαι ("support me according to your word, and I shall live") (Ps 118:50, 116 [MT 119:50, 116]). In Scripture, God is designated "the living God,"[230] reflecting belief in God's life-giving and sustaining power. The livingness of the words thus consists in their ability to *give* life by directing people along YHWH's path.[231] Stephen sees Moses giving these living words to "us," ἡμῖν, as he will do in

226 See discussion in Tov, "Texts," 125–26; Robb, "Prophet," 69–73. Cf. also 4Q175, which quotes Exod 20:21 with Deut 5:28b–29 and then Deut 18:18–19 (and goes on to quote Num 24:15–17; Deut 33:8–11; Josh 6:26; 4Q379), discussed by Richard, "Acts 7," 204.

227 Richard, "Acts 7," 206, considers it most likely that direct use of Deut is the more likely solution, either by Luke or the tradition he uses.

228 Robb, "Prophet," 73; see further *Comment* on 8:5.

229 Marshall, "Acts," 563–64.

230 E.g., Deut 5:26; 1 Sam 17:36; 2 Kgs 19:16; Esth 16:16 (EVV with Deuterocanonical books) [LXX 8:12q]; Tob 13:2; 3 Macc 6:28; Pss 41:3 [MT 42:3, EVV 42:2]; 83:4 [MT 84:4, EVV 84:3]; Hos 2:1 [EVV 1:10] (quoted Rom 9:26); Isa 37:4, 17; Dan 4:19 LXX; 6:21 MT [EVV 6:20]; 6:26; cf. Matt 16:16; 22:32; 26:63; Mark 12:27; Acts 14:15; 2 Cor 3:2; 6:16; 1 Thess 1:9; 1 Tim 3:14; 4:10; Heb 3:12; 10:31; 12:22; Rev 7:2.

231 Cf. τὰ ῥήματα ἃ ἐγὼ λελάληκα ὑμῖν πνεῦμά ἐστιν καὶ ζωή ἐστιν, "the words that I have spoken to you are spirit and life" (John 6:63); also Deut 8:3, quoted in Matt 4:4; 1 Pet 2:23.

Acts 7:53. Thus, the law is presented not only as an historical gift for the people of past generations but also as a present gift to those listening to Stephen; the claim against Stephen that he speaks against the law (6:13) is thus shown to be manifestly false—rather, Stephen's criticism is that his hearers fail to keep the law (7:53). In thus interpreting the Moses stories, Stephen turns on its head the accusation that he speaks blasphemously against Moses (6:11).[232]

39–41 refer to the incident with the golden calf (Exod 32–34) when the people become impatient for Moses's return from Sinai and call on Aaron to make gods for them (Acts 7:40; Exod 32:1).[233] The story is told in summary rather than by quotations from Exodus.

39 ᾧ, "[it was] him" (i.e., Moses), is fronted in its clause to signal that the people reject Moses by calling on Aaron to make gods, and thus they have rejected the God whose messenger Moses is. That wrong action "begins the downward spiral into idolatry."[234]

ἐστράφησαν ἐν ταῖς καρδίαις αὐτῶν εἰς Αἴγυπτον, "[they] turned back in their hearts to Egypt," cf. Num 14:3. Stephen expresses the people's turning back toward Egypt using στρέφω, whose compound ἐπιστρέφω is used to describe the response to the apostolic preaching, turning from sin and to God (Acts 3:19, 26; 14:15; 15:19; 26:18, see *Comment* on 3:19). The quotation from Isa 6:10 in 28:26 provides a valuable parallel, for it is Luke's commentary on failure of the Roman Jews to respond by turning (ἐπιστρέψωσιν, sc. back to God).

40–41 The people ask for θεούς, "gods" (echoing LXX Exod 32:1, 23[235]), but Stephen designates the calf Aaron constructs as τῷ εἰδώλῳ . . . τοῖς ἔργοις τῶν χειρῶν αὐτῶν, "the idol . . . the works of their hands." ἐμοσχοποίησαν, "they made," with τῶν χειρῶν *αὐτῶν*, "*their* hands," identifies the people as a whole as responsible for the calf's construction (although Exod 32:4 identifies Aaron himself as the maker of the calf), and thereby underlines the people's rejection of Moses.[236]

ἀνήγαγον θυσίαν τῷ εἰδώλῳ, "[they] offered a sacrifice to the idol." Stephen builds common ground with his audience, who would share his horror at idolatry, the worship of human-made objects, while also preparing the way for the implication that the temple has become an idol—it is described as χειροποιήτοις, "hand-made things," shortly afterwards (Acts 7:48). Simon's claim that this, the only mention of sacrifice in the speech, shows that Stephen rejects sacrifices and regards them as rooted in idolatry involves considerable over-reading.[237]

42–43 ἔστρεψεν . . . ὁ θεός, "God turned away," picks up the verb στρέφω

---

232 With Simon, *St Stephen*, 44–46.
233 On the story in Exod 32–34, see the excellent work of Moberly, *Mountain*.
234 Robb, "Prophet," 116.
235 With Smith, *Fate*, 152.
236 Green, *Narrative Theologian*, 164.
237 Simon, "Saint Stephen," 134.

from v. 39, where it expresses the people's "turning away" from Moses, now to state that God turns away from the idolatrous people (Exod 32:7–10). The form of God's rejection is to permit the people to follow the path of idolatry (cf. Rom 1:20–23): τὴν σκηνὴν τοῦ Μόλοχ, "the tent of Moloch" (Acts 7:43), a place of idolatrous worship, ironically prepares for Ἡ σκηνὴ τοῦ μαρτυρίου, "the tent of meeting" (v. 44), and points to the way the audience are now treating the temple as an idol.[238] Stephen interprets that path as worshiping "the army of heaven," the sun, moon, and stars (so NIV), something condemned in Scripture (2 Chr 33:3, 5; Zeph 1:5; Jer 7:18 LXX; 8:2; 19:13). Their error is to worship created things rather than the Creator (cf. Hos 13:4 LXX; Rom 1:25). "It becomes God to rejoice in the works of His own hands: and it becomes us to rejoice in the works of His hands. Men (*sic*) are idolaters who rejoice in the works of their own hands."[239]

καθὼς γέγραπται ἐν βίβλῳ τῶν προφητῶν, "as it is written in the book of the prophets." God's verdict is clinched by a biblical quotation from Amos 5:25–27 (Acts 7:42b–43), a component of the Book of the Twelve (Prophets) in Scripture, considered one book in the Jewish canon (hence the plural, "prophets"). The text follows LXX with mainly small differences, which make the main change from Damascus to Babylon stand out.[240] Amos's rhetorical question beginning with μή (v. 42b; Amos 5:25) implies the answer, "No, there were no sacrifices offered during the wilderness wanderings." The reason could be that no sacrifices were offered in this period, which is hard to prove;[241] or that the people offered sacrifice to other gods during the forty years wandering in the wilderness, such as the golden calf; or that, although they offered sacrifices, they did not obey God (cf. Jer 7:21–26). It could be that Amos is portraying the period of the exodus as ideal, when the people were focused on the relationship with YHWH rather than the sacrifices that became central to that relationship,[242] but this is unlikely to be Stephen's understanding, for he places this quotation from Amos in the context of the people's idolatry with the golden calf (Acts 7:39–41). Amos

---

238 Peterson, "Stephen's Speech," 364.

239 Bengel, *Gnomon*, 2:578.

240 MT and LXX/Acts differ rather more: LXX/Acts slant the question in Acts 7:42b (= Amos 5:25) with μή, whereas the Heb. uses only an interrogative particle, which makes the question more neutral in tone; ἀνελάβετε, "You took" (v. 43), is נשׂאתם (*nśʾṯm*), "You shall take" (MT); MT has סכות מלככם (*sḵwṯ mlḵḵm*), naming the Akkadian god Sakkut as king, whereas LXX/Acts reads the Heb. consonants differently to give τὴν σκηνὴν τοῦ Μόλοχ, "the tent of Moloch" (v. 43); MT names the second god as כיון (*ḵywn*, "Kiyyun"), whereas LXX/Acts has Ῥαιφάν, "Rephan." Both Sakkut and Kiyyun seem to be names for an Assyrian god Kaiwanu, and may be names for the planet Saturn, which symbolized the god Molech; Wolff, *Joel and Amos*, 265; Lightfoot, *Acts*, 112.

241 Wolff, *Joel and Amos*, 264–65.

242 White, *Prophets*, 105–6. Jantsch, "God of Glory," 212, argues that this means the original worship of Israel was without sacrifices but fails to recognize that the Amos quotation refers specifically to the wilderness period and thus need not imply that *all* sacrifice is mistaken.

portrays the people in the future carrying around images of other gods in order προσκυνεῖν αὐτοῖς, "to worship them," words not found in MT or LXX, but echoing the false worship of the golden calf (where their sacrifice is worship, and the people are handed over by YHWH λατρεύειν, "to worship/serve," other gods.[243] This adds a parody of carrying the ark of the covenant (5:26; cf. 7:44–45) and points toward the idolatry of the temple in which the leaders now engage (see *Comment* on 7:48a). The prophet warns on God's behalf that God will take them into exile beyond Damascus, to the north—in that historical context, a reference to the Assyrian exile of the northern kingdom Israel in 722 BC (2 Kgs 15:29). μετοικιῶ, "I will remove," echoes Acts 7:4, where God causes Abraham to remove from Haran, but here the removal is *from* the promised land, whereas in v. 4 the removal was *to* that land (these are the only uses of this verb in the NT).[244] The co-text in Amos is God's rejection of the Israelites' sacrifices and temple worship (Amos 5:21–23): God is criticizing the people's behavior, not the temple itself. Stephen interprets Amos in the light of the later, Babylonian, exile of the southern kingdom Judah in 587 BC (2 Kgs 24–25) and substitutes "Babylon" for "Damascus."[245] White plausibly proposes that Luke uses this Amos citation and the citation of Amos 9:11–12 in 15:16–18 to delimit the section of Acts that introduces Saul and the gentile mission.[246]

44–50 focus on the tent of witness and then the temple, both significant as places where God was thought to dwell ("a house," v. 47). This section covers several hundred years quickly, moving from the wilderness period (v. 44), through the conquest of the land under Joshua (v. 45), on to the united monarchy under David and Solomon (vv. 45b–47), and ending with a quotation from Isa 66:1–2.[247]

Sylva draws attention to four elements found in the same sequence in both vv. 46–50 and the dedication of the temple in 1 Kgs 8:14–30,[248] which suggests that a similar array of theological claims are involved: (i) David's desire to find a place for God (1 Kgs 8:17; Acts 7:46); (ii) an immediately following statement that Solomon will build the temple (1 Kgs 8:17–21; Acts 7:47); (iii) the question whether God will dwell with humans on earth (1 Kgs 8:27a; Acts 7:48); (iv) an assertion of God's transcendence of the temple by reference to God's

243 Kilpatrick, "Quotations," 83. Richard, "Creative Use," 40, suggests echoes in vv. 41–42 of the prohibition of worship of idols in the Ten Commandments (Exod 20:4–5; Deut 5:8–9), although there is little overlapping language.

244 Richard, "Creative Use," 42, considers this use "structural," marking the beginning and end of Stephen's recital of Israel's history; however, vv. 44–50 go on to further (much more abbreviated) historical review.

245 Kilpatrick, "Quotations," 83.

246 White, "Revisiting"; see also *Comment* on 15:16–18.

247 On this section, see Walton, "Tale," 138–43.

248 Sylva, "Meaning," 266–67; cf. Beale, *Temple*, 222–23, suggesting that the appeal to Isa 66:1 here draws on Isaiah's echo of 1 Kgs 8:27.

relation to the heavens, the earth, and a house (1 Kgs 8:27b; Acts 7:49–50, quoting Isa 66:1–2a). The two passages thus offer a perspective that combines God's transcendence of the temple, or any other earthly location, with the appropriateness of the temple for Solomon's day. (See further in *Comment* on vv. 46–50 below.)

44 Ἡ σκηνὴ τοῦ μαρτυρίου, "The tent of witness," is introduced in Exod 25:8 as a direct command of YHWH (25:1), and detailed instructions for its construction are given in Exod 26–27. Hebrew has "the tent of meeting" (אֹהֶל מוֹעֵד [*ʾōhel môʿēd*] Exod 27:21), whereas LXX has "the tent of witness," as here. The Greek name fits well with Stephen's theme, that God is a God who has made himself known and accessible and who is not tied down to one particular physical location: the mobile tent held the ark, which contained the Ten Commandments written on stone (Deut 10:1–5), along with Aaron's staff and a jar of manna (Exod 16:32–34; Num 17:8–10; cf. Heb 9:4–5). The tent was a key sign of God's presence with the people, and it was there that God met with Moses (Exod 30:36).

καθὼς διετάξατο ὁ λαλῶν τῷ Μωϋσῇ ποιῆσαι αὐτὴν κατὰ τὸν τύπον ὃν ἑωράκει, "just as the one who spoke instructed Moses to make it according to the pattern he had seen," makes clear that the tent of witness's design originates with YHWH—indeed, the tent was God's initiative and Moses was simply "instructed" what to do, as the echo of Exod 25:40 LXX, κατὰ τὸν τύπον, "according to the pattern," shows (cf. Heb 8:5). It was a place where God met with Moses and the priests who followed him.

45 Joshua 3:4 describes the priests carrying the ark (and, by implication, the tent and its equipment) as the people crossed the River Jordan. After the battles to occupy the land, the tent was then set up at Shiloh (Josh 18:1; 19:51). God ἐξῶσεν, "drove out," powerful nations before the Israelites (echoing Josh 23:9; 24:18) to give them the land—again, the focus is on God's action and his decision, and at this point the Sanhedrin would be nodding in agreement with Stephen.

ἕως τῶν ἡμερῶν Δαυίδ, "until the days of David," indicates a period of some three hundred years. It is not obvious whether this expression should be taken: (i) with ἐξῶσεν, "drove out," implying either that the nations were expelled until the time of David (something the OT suggests was not the case, e.g., Judg 1:19, 21, 27–35); (ii) as indicating that it was not until the time of David that the land was fully ruled by Israel (not the most natural understanding of ἕως, "until");[249] or (iii) with διαδεξάμενοι, "received," indicating that the tent was in use up to and including the time of David.[250] The latter fits most naturally with Acts 7:46–47.

46 ὃς εὗρεν χάριν ἐνώπιον τοῦ θεοῦ, "He [sc. David] found favor before God,"

249 Bruce, *Acts* (1990), 206.

250 Culy and Parsons, *Acts*, 140–41; Barrett, *Acts*, 1:372.

employs LXX language without citing a specific passage,[251] although the fact that the exact parallel is in Moses's intercession after the golden calf episode (Exod 34:9) is suggestive, for that story is echoed earlier in the speech (Acts 7:39–42) and Stephen shortly uses a key term from that story (σκληροτράχηλος, "stiff-necked," v. 51), applied to his hearers (see below). David and Solomon were seen as the high point of the monarchy, for they reigned over the united nation, even though both committed serious sins.[252]

καὶ ᾐτήσατο εὑρεῖν σκήνωμα τῷ οἴκῳ Ἰακώβ, "and asked that he might find a dwelling place for the house of Jacob." David arranged for the ark to be transported to Jerusalem after it became his capital (2 Sam 6) and wanted to provide a suitable place to hold it (2 Sam 7:1–2). The story of 2 Sam 7 is the implicit background to Acts 7:46–47, where in both LXX and Heb. there is play on the word "house" (Heb. בַּיִת [*bayit*]) as referring to the temple (which Nathan says Solomon will build) and a dynasty for David (which Nathan says God will build).[253] This is Luke's only use of σκήνωμα, "dwelling place," a term used in LXX to refer to both the temple and the tent of meeting.[254] Thus there may also be an allusion to 2 Sam 6:17, where David places the ark in a tent in Jerusalem as its dwelling place.[255] The speech here echoes Ps 131:5 LXX (MT 132:5), a psalm of ascents sung on pilgrimage to the Jerusalem temple: ἕως οὗ εὕρω τόπον τῷ κυρίῳ, σκήνωμα τῷ θεῷ Ιακωβ, "until I find a place for the Lord, a dwelling place for the God of Jacob." Both here and in the psalm εὑρίσκω, "find," has the sense "obtain" or "provide."[256]

σκήνωμα τῷ οἴκῳ Ἰακώβ, "a dwelling place for the house of Jacob." To speak of the temple as "for the house of Jacob" is unusual, for "the house of Jacob" is the people of Israel.[257] The sense is thus that the temple is a meeting place for the descendants of Jacob,[258] which is rare, but not unique, among Jewish writers.[259] Probably because this is surprising, the textual tradition divides over whether to read θεῷ, "for God," or οἴκῳ, "for the house" (see *Note* mmm).

---

251 See 2 Sam 15:25 (concerning David); Gen 6:8; 18:3; 30:27; 33:10, 15; Exod 34:9; Sir 3:18.

252 See David M. Howard Jr, "David," *ABD* 2:46–47, §F; Tomoo Ishida, "Solomon," *ABD* 6:105–13, esp. §L.

253 Walton, "Tale," 141.

254 Temple: LXX Psa 14:1 (MT 15:1); 45:5 (MT 46:5, EVV 46:4); 73:7 (MT 74:7). Tent: 1 Kgs 2:28; 8:4. See Sylva, "Meaning," 264; contra Haenchen, *Acts*, 285, who asserts that David seeks to find a place for the tent in Jerusalem but does not recognize the breadth of OT usage of σκήνωμα, "dwelling place."

255 Evans, "Prophecy," 197.

256 "εὑρίσκω," BDAG 412, §3.

257 E.g., Gen 46:27; Exod 19:3; Ps 114:1 [LXX 113:1]; Isa 8:7; 48:1; 58:1; Jer 2:4; Ezek 20:5; Amos 7:16; Obad 17; Mic 1:5.

258 *BegC*, 4:81.

259 Klijn, "Speech," 30, identifies Josephus, *Ant.* 8.4.2 §107 as showing that the temple was conceived as "for the benefit of Israel," as well as 1QS VIII, 5–6, 8–9 which present the community's council as a holy house or abode, and 1QS IX, 3–6, which presents the whole community as a temple (specifically, as a holy of holies).

It would be more expected to speak of the temple as "for God,"[260] and thus scribes might naturally substitute θεῷ for οἴκῳ, especially given the echo of Ps 131:5 LXX noted above. By contrast, it is not easy to suggest why scribes might replace an original θεῷ by οἴκῳ. Further, the reading οἴκῳ has strong MS support (𝔓[74] א* B D) and is in tune with Luke's temple theology.[261]

47 Σολομὼν δὲ οἰκοδόμησεν αὐτῷ οἶκον, "However, it was Solomon who built a house for it." The implied narrative of 2 Sam 7 continues, for there David is told that it is his son who will build a house for God's name (vv. 12–13). Scripture tells the story of this building in stages under Solomon's oversight (2 Kgs 5–7; 2 Chr 2–4) and its dedication by Solomon (1 Kgs 8; 2 Chr 5–7). Solomon is given credit for the work (e.g., 1 Kgs 6:2; 8:20; 1 Chr 22:6; 2 Chr 2:1 [MT 1:18]; 3:1). The terms οἰκοδόμησεν . . . οἶκον, "built a house," imply permanence, rather than the σκηνή, "tent" (Acts 7:44; 2 Sam 7:6 LXX). δέ, "However," does not imply that Solomon was disobedient to God in building the temple. This conjunction is not a strong adversative, and the shift it marks is simply from one person to another.[262]

The antecedent of αὐτῷ is most likely οἴκῳ Ἰακώβ, "the house of Jacob" (hence αὐτῷ means "it"), continuing the thought that the temple was a meeting place for the people and thus implicitly critiquing the idea that the temple was a container for God—indeed, to take the latter view would be to set up the temple as an idol.[263] That said, the antecedent could be θεοῦ, "God" (which implies that αὐτῷ means "him"; so NRSVue, NIV), although its greater distance away in the text makes this less natural. The presence of αὐτῷ may well have led scribes to write θεῷ, "God," in v. 46 instead of οἴκῳ, "house" (see above).

48a ἀλλ' οὐχ ὁ ὕψιστος ἐν χειροποιήτοις κατοικεῖ, "though the Most High does not live in hand-made things," brings us to the crux of Stephen's speech. The adversative ἀλλά, "however," introduces a qualification to the previous statement that Solomon built a house to make clear that Israel's God is not limited to a temple. The reading οἴκῳ, "house," in v. 46 reinforces the contrast, for Stephen has asserted that the temple was built for the *people*. Barrett takes the adversative as indicating that building the temple at all was an error;[264] however, that is not the point of the contrast. Rather, Stephen's observation reflects an ambivalence about the temple that dates back to its dedication, where Solomon recognizes the transcendence of God in similar terms to here

---

260 E.g., 2 Sam 12:20; 1 Chr 9:11, 13; 23:28 26:27; 29:2, 3; 2 Chr 3:3; Ezra 4:24; 5:16; Neh 12:40; 13:9; Ps 42:4 (LXX 41:5); 134:1 (LXX 133:1); Mic 4:2; Jdt 9:1; Tob 14:4, 5.

261 With *TCGNT*², 308–9; Barrett, *Acts*, 1:372; Bruce, *Acts* (1990), 206; Schwemer, "Lukas," 319–20; ECM, 3:13 (Strutwolf minority vote). THGNT reads θεῷ, although the apparatus notes that the editors were in doubt.

262 Levinsohn, *Connections*, 87–89; "δέ," BDAG 213; contra Simon, *St Stephen*, 51–52.

263 Jervell, *Theology*, 21.

264 Barrett, "Attitudes," 352. For critique, see Smith, *Fate*, 169–70.

(see further below on "the Most High" and vv. 48b–50) and asks whether God can live (κατοικήσει, the same verb as here) with humans on earth (1 Kgs 8:27 LXX). In both its original dedication and Stephen's speech, the temple is relativized by God's transcendence: "the issue is not 'tent' versus 'house' but rather true and false thinking about God's presence."[265]

The principle enunciated here is not controversial in first-century Judaism, by contrast with the widespread pantheism of the Greco-Roman world,[266] a world Stephen probably knew, assuming he grew up in the diaspora.[267] Further, although there is no explicit mention of tent or temple in this verse, χειροποίητος, "hand-made," signals that the temple is now being treated as an idol (note the echo of v. 41 τοῖς ἔργοις τῶν χειρῶν αὐτῶν, "the works of their hands," referring to the golden calf), a shocking claim that would be deeply offensive to those present.[268] χειροποίητος, "hand-made," only occurs elsewhere in Acts at 17:24, in a pagan context in Athens where Paul asserts that the creator God does not live (κατοικεῖ, as here) in hand-made shrines (cf. Mark 14:58, a saying without parallel in Luke; Heb 9:11, 24[269]). LXX use of χειροποίητος, "hand-made," is exclusively for idols (e.g., Lev 26:1, 30; Isa 46:6); notably, Isa 16:12 uses τὰ χειροποίητα αὐτῆς, "her hand-made things," for the sanctuary where the Moabites pray to their god.[270] By contrast, and relatively unusually, Philo understands that the tent (Acts 7:44) was made by human hands too; he calls it ἱερὸν χειροποίητον, "a temple made with hands," and that is no criticism (*Moses* 2.88). Thus, the atmosphere of χειροποίητος for Jewish hearers is generally negative. These statements about the temple chime in with Jesus's warning of the temple's destruction because of the people's sin (Luke 19:44 with 21:6), and it is striking that Stephen goes on to highlight the Sanhedrin's sin in killing Jesus (vv. 51–52).[271]

God is ὁ ὕψιστος, "the Most High," for the only time in this speech, stressing God's transcendence and supremacy.[272] The juxtaposition with οὐχ, "not," is striking, for "the position of οὐχ puts *the Most High* in relief,"[273] further

265 Witherington, *Acts*, 263; so also Peterson, *Engaging*, 141; Taylor, "Luke-Acts," 719–21.

266 Notably in Stoicism; see Koester, *Introduction 1*, 143–44. There were some Greeks who considered Stephen's principle to hold; references in Barrett, *Acts*, 1:374.

267 Schneider, "Stephanus," 219, notes the diaspora synagogues as evidence that Jewish former inhabitants of pagan cities now live in Jerusalem (6:9).

268 Pao, *Acts*, 207; Skinner, *Trial Narratives*, 118–19.

269 Beale, *Temple*, 223–24.

270 For a fuller list, see Beale, *Temple*, 224n45.

271 I thus agree with Shin, "Stories," 510, interacting with Walton, "Tale," 140, that there is ambivalence about the temple in its origins and in Stephen's speech, while still thinking that v. 48a offers a qualification, rather than a contradiction, of what goes before.

272 Cf., e.g., LXX Gen 14:18, 19, 20, 22; Num 24:16; Deut 32:8; 2 Sam 22:14; Pss 7:18 [EVV 17]; 9:3 [EVV 2]; 17:14 [MT 18:14, EVV 18:13]; 20:8 [MT 21:8, EVV 21:7]; Job 31:28; Isa 14:14; Dan 2:18, 19; Mic 6:6; 1 Esd 2:3; 6:30; 8:19, 21; 9:46; Luke 8:28; Acts 16:17; Heb 7:1. Interestingly, the vast majority of uses of this designation for God in the Greek Bible are in non-Israelite settings. Greeks used ὕψιστος of Zeus; "ὕψιστος," LSJ, §2; see *Comment* on 16:17.

273 MHT, 3:287 (italics original).

contrasting the greatness of YHWH with a humanly constructed temple. God's true living place is heaven (1 Kgs 8:30, 32, 34, 36, 39, 43, 45, 49), not earth, but God can and does make himself known on earth, as he appeared in the cloud at the temple's dedication (1 Kgs 8:10–11) and has now made himself known in Jesus and among Jesus's followers.

48b–50 Stephen clinches his claims concerning the temple which a quotation from Isa 66:1–2, introduced by the formula καθὼς ὁ προφήτης λέγει, "as the prophet says." The choice of the present tense λέγει, "says," evinces Stephen's/Luke's view that Scripture is not a "dead letter" but continues to speak.[274]

The quotation follows LXX Isa 66:1–2 quite closely, only relocating λέγει κύριος, "says the Lord," from the beginning to midway through, turning Isaiah's statement πάντα γὰρ ταῦτα ἐποίησεν ἡ χείρ μου, "for my hand made all these things," into a question expecting the answer "yes" introduced by οὐχί, and abbreviating repetitive clauses that reflect Hebrew poetry.[275] Stephen contrasts the work of God's hand in creation with the work of human hands in constructing a temple (Acts 7:48a)—God is worthy of worship as creator and by implication is accessible in his creation rather than being confined to a temple.[276] It is interesting that Isa 66 continues, καὶ ἐπὶ τίνα ἐπιβλέψω ἀλλ' ἢ ἐπὶ τὸν ταπεινὸν καὶ ἡσύχιον καὶ τρέμοντα τοὺς λόγους μου;, "and to whom will I look but to the one who is humble and quiet and who trembles at my words?" (v. 2, NETS), and will go on to encourage such people who are opposed by their own (v. 5), for both points are highly pertinent to this setting, where Stephen represents such a "humble and quiet" person, by contrast with the Sanhedrin, who refuse to listen—they have "uncircumcised . . . ears" (Acts 7:51) and will "close their ears" (v. 57) before stoning Stephen. Ironically, too, the Isaiah quotation comes from a section where God is speaking *from the temple* (66:6). The prophecy is being quoted, thus, not to reject the temple per se[277] but to critique *the people* by underlining Stephen's claim that the creator God is not limited to such places, in similar manner to Solomon's recognizing that YHWH can hear his people's prayers in exile (1 Kgs 8:46–53). The temple is inadequate to contain the living God.[278] Thornton draws attention to an Aramaic midrash commenting on Isa 66:1–2, which says that after Isaiah spoke these words King Manasseh had him killed, a striking parallel to Stephen's murder following his citation of that passage.[279]

---

274 Cf. John 19:37; Rom 4:3; 10:11; 11:2; Gal 4:30; 1 Tim 5:18; Jas 4:5.
275 Smith, *Fate*, 153–54.
276 Contrast the use of Isa 66:1 alone, without v. 2, in Barn. 16:2, where it is part of an anti-temple polemic (Barn. 16); with Stanton, "Stephen," 352, countering *BegC*, 4:81–82.
277 *Contra*, e.g., Hübner, *Biblische Theologie*, 3:150–51.
278 Koet, "Isaiah," 90.
279 Thornton, "Stephen's Use," 432–33 (quoting the passage). The midrash is found in marginal comments in Codex Reuchlinianus (a codex of Tg. Ps-J.) and Codex Vaticanus Ebr. Urbin. 1, f. 616. He concedes that the date of the midrash is unknown but suggests that it is possible that that it was known in the first century AD (434).

51–53 hammer home Stephen's points in counteraccusation against the Sanhedrin.[280] Bruce labels this section "Personal application."[281] It should be noted that Stephen does not criticise the law (recall that that accusation was false, 6:13) but the failure of his audience and their ancestors to live consistently with the law.[282]

51 Σκληροτράχηλοι καὶ ἀπερίτμητοι καρδίαις καὶ τοῖς ὠσίν, "Stiff-necked and uncircumcised in hearts and ears" links Stephen's hearers to the rebellious people of Moses's generation. σκληροτράχηλος, "stiff-necked," is an NT *hapax legomenon*; uses in LXX predominantly focus on the people's attitudes in the golden calf story (see *Comment* on vv. 39–42).[283] ἀπερίτμητοι καρδίαις καὶ τοῖς ὠσίν, "uncircumcised in hearts and ears," echoes biblical language about disobedience and rejection of God, for it was the men of other nations who were physically uncircumcised, and for Israel to act like them was to adopt their attitudes and decisions (καρδίαις, "in hearts,"[284] e.g., LXX Lev 26:41; Jer 9:26), and to be openly disobedient to God by refusing to listen (τοῖς ὠσίν, "in ears," Jer 6:10 LXX, the only place where ears are "uncircumcised" in LXX).[285] The refusal to listen is present in the co-text of the Isa 66:1–2 quotation (Acts 7:49–50) in Isa 66:4–6 and ties Stephen's direct criticism here to the preceding quotation.[286] Stephen thus parallels the present Jewish leadership with the rebellious people of Moses's and Jeremiah's days, as he earlier paralleled Jesus with the obedient Moses and will parallel Jesus with "the prophets" (Acts 7:52).

ὑμεῖς ἀεὶ τῷ πνεύματι τῷ ἁγίῳ ἀντιπίπτετε ὡς οἱ πατέρες ὑμῶν καὶ ὑμεῖς, "that's you, constantly resisting the Holy Spirit; you are just like your ancestors." The fronting of ὑμεῖς, "you," is emphatic, as is its presence at the end of the Greek sentence. Stephen distances himself from his audience for the first time: up to now he has spoken consistently of "our (ἡμῶν) ancestor(s)" (vv. 2, 11, 12, 15, 19, 38, 39, 44, 45 [twice]), but now he shifts to a direct accusation of, effectively, blaspheming against the Holy Spirit (cf. Luke 12:10; see *Comment* on 4:17). "This is more than a simple shift in possessive pronouns; it is . . . a mechanism of disowning."[287] The move is from implicit criticism of his hearers earlier in the speech to explicit. Such a shift is typical of summaries of Israel's history, for the retelling of this history is done with the purpose of changing the audience.[288] His claim that they are ἀεὶ τῷ πνεύματι τῷ ἁγίῳ ἀντιπίπτετε,

280 Moessner, "Suffering," 218–19, argues that Stephen's speech presents the counteraccusation that Israel's temple worship is idolatrous, paralleling a similar argument in T. Mos.

281 Bruce, *Acts* (1990), 207.

282 Dunn, *Beginning*, 272.

283 LXX Exod 33:3, 5; 34:9; Deut 9:6, 13; other LXX uses are Prov 29:1; Sir 16:11; Bar 2:30; Baruch sees the people as exiled because they are stiff-necked.

284 As most commonly in OT and NT, the heart is the seat of the will and decision making.

285 Both terms were also in use at Qumran (1QS 5.5; 1QpHab 11.13) and in Jub. 1:7, 23.

286 Smith, *Fate*, 171.

287 Dinkler, "Politics," 60.

288 Jeska, *Geschichte*, 94–98. Sweeney, "Speech," esp. 210, observes that Stephen's speech is not

"constantly resisting the Holy Spirit," is striking, for Isa 63:10 speaks of people who provoked τὸ πνεῦμα τὸ ἅγιον αὐτοῦ, "his Holy Spirit" (a rare phrase in OT[289]), which God himself had put within them (63:11). The Isaianic context is the exodus (63:9), which strengthens the probability that Stephen echoes Isa 63:10 and again points Stephen's hearers to the parallel between their actions and those who rebelled against Moses (cf. also Num 27:14 LXX, where ἀντιπίπτω "resist, oppose" is used concerning the Israelites' rebellion against YHWH in the wilderness). The point is underlined by the shift here to "*your* (ὑμῶν) ancestors" from "*our* (ἡμῶν) ancestor(s)" earlier in the speech (Acts 7:2, 11, 12, 15, 19, 38, 39, 44, 45 [twice]; cf. 3:13; 5:30; 13:17, 32; 15:10; 22:14; 22:6; and note a similar shift in 28:25)—Stephen is now distancing himself from his audience.[290] Far from Stephen being the one who blasphemes Moses (6:11), the Sanhedrin are themselves like those who rejected Moses in his day.

52 τίνα τῶν προφητῶν οὐκ ἐδίωξαν οἱ πατέρες ὑμῶν;, "Which of the prophets did your ancestors not persecute?" Stephen makes an accusation in the form of a question and in effect invokes the prophets as witnesses on his behalf.[291] He also echoes words of Jesus criticizing the scribes' hypocrisy in building tombs for the prophets whom their ancestors killed (Luke 11:47), which lead into Jesus declaring that "this generation," τῆς γενεᾶς ταύτης, will be held responsible for all the prophets from Abel to Zechariah—the first and last people murdered in the Hebrew canon (Luke 11:50–51; Gen 4:10; 2 Chr 24:20–22).[292] Jesus goes on to weep over Jerusalem and state that it is the destiny of prophets, including him, to die there (Luke 13:33–34).

καὶ ἀπέκτειναν τοὺς προκαταγγείλαντας περὶ τῆς ἐλεύσεως τοῦ δικαίου, οὗ νῦν ὑμεῖς προδόται καὶ φονεῖς ἐγένεσθε, "Indeed, they killed those who announced in advance the coming of the righteous one, and you yourselves have become his betrayers and murderers." Stephen develops the thought by answering his rhetorical question positively and then applying the answer to his hearers: just as their ancestors killed those who announced Jesus's coming,[293] so they have dealt with Jesus. Peterson rightly sees this as incisive "lawsuit rhetoric" that refutes his opponents' potential response, that they are defending the temple

"anti-temple" but locates the temple as a stage in salvation history, a stage that is now at an end with the coming, death, resurrection, and exaltation of Jesus.

289 The only other use of "the/your *Holy* Spirit" in OT is Ps 51:10–11 (LXX 50:12–13, MT 51:12–13); when referring to the divine Spirit, OT authors usually write of "the Spirit of God/the Lord," πνεῦμα θεοῦ/κυρίου, e.g., Gen 1:2; 1 Sam 10:10; 19:20, 23; Isa 11:2; 61:1; Ezek 11:5; or "my Spirit," τὸ πνεῦμά μου, e.g., Ezek 36:26–27; 37:14.

290 Pao, *Acts*, 208, suggests that this shift signals separation of the early Christian community from "the Jewish community"; at the stage of history being portrayed, that seems premature, since all believers are still Jewish, although Luke may be writing up the speech, consciously or unconsciously, in the light of the situation in his day.

291 Peterson, "Stephen's Speech," 365.

292 An interesting hint that by Luke's day Chronicles was the last book in the Hebrew canon.

293 The OT records little of the prophets' deaths, but cf. Mart. Isa 5.1–14; Tertullian, *Scorp.* 8; Jerome, *Jov.* 2.37; with Bruce, *Acts* (1990), 208; see further *BegC*, 4:82.

and the law from a false prophet such as Stephen.[294] Jesus is τοῦ δικαίου, "the righteous one," a rare designation used only in Jewish settings in Acts (only here and 3:14; see *Comment* there). προκαταγγέλλω, "announce in advance," is also rare in NT (only here; 3:18 [see *Comment* there]; 22:14—again, all Jewish settings),[295] increasing the sense of the appropriateness of the lexical choices to this (Jewish) situation.[296] Scripture testifies to Jesus as the one to come, as frequently in Luke-Acts.[297] The thought that Scripture announces Jesus's suffering is implied, although not explicit, as elsewhere in Acts (e.g., 3:18, 24; 4:10–11, 25–28; 8:32–35; 13:27).

53 οἵτινες ἐλάβετε τὸν νόμον εἰς διαταγὰς ἀγγέλων καὶ οὐκ ἐφυλάξατε, "you people, who received the law by angels acting under God's direction and you did not keep it." Stephen continues to press the point that the Jewish leaders disobeyed the law. It is likely that he is focused on the killing of Jesus, since that is the salient point in the previous part of this Greek sentence.[298] Stephen turns the tables on the claim that he attacks the law (6:11, 13) by retorting that in fact his accusers did not keep it.[299]

εἰς διαταγὰς ἀγγέλων, "by angels acting under God's direction." There is no mention of angelic mediation of the law in the OT,[300] although YHWH is said to be accompanied by angels at Sinai (ἄγγελοι μετ᾽ αὐτοῦ, "angels with him," Deut 33:2 LXX; also Mek. on Exod 20:18 [text and translation: Lauterbach, 2:269]; Sifre Num 102 on Num 12:5). Paul and Hebrews equally assume without argument that angels delivered the law (Gal 3:19; Heb 2:2), which suggests that this belief was quite widely known when Luke wrote.[301] Stephen's point in citing the angelic mediation is positive: the law's value and importance is shown by the engagement of these figures who are messengers of God (so also Heb 2:2), and thus his accusers are all the more culpable—the angels are witnesses against them. That positive view of angelic mediation is underlined by the role angels have elsewhere in Luke-Acts.[302]

54–8:1a The story climaxes in Stephen's stoning, finally provoked by his vision of Jesus, named as "the Son of Man," standing at God's right side

294 Peterson, "Stephen's Speech," 365.

295 It is never found in LXX. Josephus uses it six times: *Ant.* 1.12.3 §219; 2.5.2 §68; 2.5.6 §85; 2.9.4 §218; 10.4.4 §67; 10.11.3 §243. LSJ s.v. cites no other sources.

296 See Gempf, "Speaking," for valuable discussion of historical and literary appropriateness in ancient historians and the speeches in Acts.

297 See *Comment* on (e.g.) 2:14–36; 3:12–26; 4:23–31; 8:29–35; 13:16–41; 17:1–4, 10–12; 18:27–28; with Marshall, "Acts," on those passages.

298 Paul makes a wider point about Jewish people not keeping the whole law in Rom 2, esp. vv. 17–25.

299 Penner, *Praise*, 293.

300 That is the implication of διαταγή here, "διαταγή," BDAG 237.

301 Dunn, *Galatians*, 191, cites Jub. 1:29–2:1; Philo, *Dreams* 1.143; Josephus, *Ant.* 15.5.2 §136; Apoc. Mos., preface, as evidence for "the *association* of angels in the giving of the law" (my italics), but that is not the same as angels *mediating* the law. See discussion of these references in Bruce, *Galatians*, 176–78; Callan, "Pauline Midrash," 550–54.

302 See *Comment* on 5:19.

(7:55–56). The presence of Saul is mentioned twice (7:58; 8:1), introducing one of the most significant characters of Acts.

54 partially echoes the Sanhedrin's reaction to the apostles in 5:33, where the Sanhedrin's hearing them produces rage, and also prepares for their violent response to Stephen. ταῖς καρδίαις αὐτῶν, "in their hearts," locates the anger, pictured using a verb whose original sense was sawing (διαπρίω),[303] followed by a clause describing the outward manifestation of the anger: ἔβρυχον τοὺς ὀδόντας ἐπ' αὐτόν, "they ground their teeth against him." Both are unusual images in the Greek Bible. The heart is typically the location of will, attitudes, and decision making (e.g., Gen 6:5; 20:5; Exod 8:32; Deut 8:17) and can also be the location (as here) of emotions produced by attitudes (e.g., Pss 27:3 [LXX 26:3]; 28:7 [LXX 27:7]; Neh 2:2); notably Ps 39:3 [LXX 38:4, MT 39:4] portrays anger as the heart growing hot.[304] Grinding or gnashing (βρύχω) the teeth expresses hostility or disdain to a foe (Pss 35:16 [LXX 34:16]; 37:12 [LXX 36:12]; 112:10 [LXX 111:10]; Job 16:9; Lam 2:16).[305] This rage and the subsequent murder of Stephen echo similar rage in the Nazareth synagogue at Jesus's telling of scriptural stories to indicate God's love and welcome for gentiles, and the (frustrated) attempt to murder Jesus (Luke 4:25–29).[306]

55–56 Luke's focus switches (marked by δέ, "however") back to Stephen, who is (re-)filled with the Holy Spirit (cf. 6:3, 5, 10) and thereby enabled to pierce the barrier between earth and the heavenly sphere and see the reality of Jesus's present position—a widespread function of visions is to pull aside the curtain to show how things really are.[307] Luke describes the event in his authorial voice (Acts 7:55) and then presents Stephen's explanation (v. 56), which suggests that this is a private vision given only to Stephen, who interprets for others what he sees.

θεωρῶ τοὺς οὐρανοὺς διηνοιγμένους, "I see the heavens opened," is standard language for a revelation from the heavenly realm (cf. 10:11; Luke 3:21; John 1:51; Rev 4:1). Readers would naturally recall the description of Stephen as having a face like an angel (6:15).[308] This expanded spatiality, opening up the invisible heavenly world, shows both Stephen and Luke's readers what is truly going on: events are under the control of Jesus, exercising executive authority from his place at God's right side. The God of glory who appeared to Abraham (7:2) shows himself to Stephen from heaven—for where God's glory is seen, there God is seen.[309] However, this glorious God is now seen

303 *GE* 504 s.v.
304 See "Heart," *DBIm* 368–69.
305 "βρύχω," *GELS* 123; the image is found in non-Christian sources too: "βρύχω," LSJ 332, §II.
306 Dinkler, "Politics," 63, highlights the storytelling elements in both events.
307 Doble, "Saying," 74. Visions can be a feature of martyr stories, e.g., Mart. Isa. 5:7; 4 Macc 6:6. For a helpful discussion of the relationship of Luke's use of verbal and visual, see Wilson, "Hearing," esp. 464–69.
308 Humphrey, *And I Turned*, 49.
309 See Exod 16:10; 24:16–17; Lev 9:23; Ps 26:8 (LXX 25:8); Isa 4:5; Ezek 10:18.

with Jesus, who is standing for Stephen: "to see the glory of God is now to see Jesus at the same time."[310] The place where heaven and earth meet, which Stephen's opponents considered to be the temple, is now the exalted Jesus, who is not "hand-made" and is the one in whom the God of Israel uniquely dwells (cf. v. 48).[311] The focus of the vision is thus christological,[312] as Stephen is given visual, charismatic revelation of Jesus's present place and power by the Spirit.[313]

This vision bookends the story of Stephen's trial, which began with the Sanhedrin fixing their attention (ἀτενίσαντες) on Stephen's appearance as like that of an angel, which probably signals his experience of the Spirit (6:15, see *Comment* there), and now ends with the Spirit giving him revelation as he looks intently (ἀτενίσας) into heaven. Indeed, this vision continues a theophanic theme that runs through the speech (7:2–8, 30–34, 38, 44, 53).[314]

Stephen not only reports the vision but interprets it by identifying Jesus as τὸν υἱὸν τοῦ ἀνθρώπου, "the Son of Man," the only NT use of this phrase outside the Gospels.[315] Luke uses this term extensively in his Gospel on the lips of Jesus as a self-designation.[316] Its widespread use throughout the Gospels by Jesus, combined with its relative lack of use by the early churches as a designation for Jesus, make it highly likely to originate with Jesus.[317] There is a strong likelihood that Dan 7:13–14 is echoed here, for both passages are in martyr contexts.[318] In combination with Luke 22:69, which also echoes Dan 7, the use of "the Son of Man" signals Jesus's present rule and authority, the universal reign given to the Son of Man by the Ancient of Days. Jesus now rules, as he had said before the Sanhedrin that he would,[319] and his rejection as the Son of Man will result in the fall of Jerusalem (Luke 21:20–28).[320]

---

310 Aarflot, *God*, 115.

311 See Walton, "Tale," 144–46.

312 With Sleeman, *Geography*, 165–69.

313 On charismatic revelation as a manifestation of the Spirit, see Turner, *Power*, 92–95, 349.

314 Miller, *Convinced*, 178–81.

315 It is found without articles in Heb 2:6 (quoting Ps 8:5 LXX [EVV 8:4]); Rev 1:13; 14:14. On the term, see I. H. Marshall, "Son of Man," *DJG* 775–81; D. L. Bock, "Son of Man," *DJG2* 894–900; Nolland, *Luke*, 2:468–75.

316 Twenty-five times in Luke, of which nine are paralleled in Mark (5:24; 6:5; 9:22, 26, 44; 18:31; 21:27; 22:22, 69), ten are shared with Matthew alone (6:22; 7:34; 9:58; 11:30; 12:8, 10, 40; 17:24, 26, 30), and six are found in Luke alone (17:22; 18:8; 19:10; 21:36; 22:48; 24:7).

317 This does not necessarily mean that every use in the Gospels comes from Jesus; it is impossible to prove or disprove whether the evangelists or others added the term to traditional material or replaced it with a personal pronoun.

318 Moule, *Origin*, 17.

319 Smith, *Fate*, 184–85 connects Luke 22:69 with Luke 21:27, another "Son of Man" passage, and suggests that Jesus's standing posture here in Acts reflects the Son of Man coming on the clouds, standing "in preparation for action." However, the Son of Man in Luke 21:27 is not said to be standing.

320 It is notable that the speech does not anachronistically betray knowledge of the city's fall, further suggesting that Luke is working with primitive material in writing up the speech; Smith, "Significance," 20.

Why is Jesus ἑστῶτα, "standing," when his usual position at God's right side is sitting (Luke 22:69; Acts 2:33–34; cf. Mark 16:19; Eph 1:20; Col 3:1; Heb 1:13; 8:1; 10:12; 12:2)? His posture is repeated, so it is evidently meant to be noticed by readers. A number of proposals have been suggested,[321] including that Jesus stands: to welcome (and thus, vindicate) his first martyr;[322] to indicate that he is ready to return;[323] to give a private *parousia* to Stephen;[324] to intercede for Stephen, perhaps after the manner of Moses interceding for the people;[325] or as witness for Stephen, thus parodying the improper judicial process going on.[326] The normal position of witnesses in Jewish/OT judicial processes was standing, whereas the judge sat to hear the case and stands only to give the verdict.[327] Given the judicial process happening on earth, this is a probable context for understanding Jesus's standing posture and suggests that he is either acting as a witness for Stephen (whom Paul describes as Jesus's μάρτυς, "witness," 22:20) against the false witnesses (6:13) or as judge, now standing as judge to give his not-guilty verdict on Stephen. Jesus promises in Luke that those who acknowledge him before others, *the Son of Man* will acknowledge before the angels (Luke 12:8), and this chimes in with understanding Jesus's posture as witness or judge—indeed, it echoes the way Jesus, the rejected righteous one (Acts 7:52; 3:14), is vindicated and now sits at God's right side (2:34–35; 5:31).[328] Thus the vision fills the gap the incomplete speech leaves: the speech lacks a clear conclusion, inviting the audience to repent or calling them to give a just verdict of innocence (cf. 2:38–39; 3:19–26)—Jesus is standing to vindicate his servant Stephen.[329]

57 κράξαντες δὲ φωνῇ μεγάλῃ συνέσχον τὰ ὦτα αὐτῶν, "Shouting at the tops of their voices, they closed their ears." Both actions portray the Sanhedrin's[330]

321 For lists with assessments, see Barrett, "Stephen"; Barrett, *Acts*, 1:384–85; Bruce, *Acts* (1990), 210; Crump, *Jesus*, 179–90.

322 Johnson, *Acts*, 139; Bengel, *Gnomon*, 2:583.

323 Owen, "Vision."

324 Barrett, "Stephen," 35–37.

325 Pesch, *Apostelgeschichte*, 264; Schneider, *Apostelgeschichte*, 1:475; Scobie, "Origins," 397; Crump, *Jesus*, 197–99.

326 Cullmann, *Christology*, 183; Moule, *Phenomenon*, 90–91; Trites, *Concept*, 132; C. Blendinger, "δεξιά," *NIDNTT* 2:147–48; Crump, *Jesus*, 190–97.

327 Trites, *Concept*, 132; Peterson, "Stephen's Speech," 367. Witnesses standing: 1 Kgs 3:16; Jer 26:16–19 [LXX 33:16–19]. Judge sitting to hear a case: Exod 18:13–14; Judg 4:5; Dan 7:10; cf. Acts 6:15; 23:3. Judge standing to give verdict: Isa 3:13; 2:19, 21; Amos 9:1; As. Mos. 10.3. Pesch, *Vision*, 27–28, 30, 32, 38–39, 58, argues that Jesus is standing as judge to judge the Jewish people and that this moment marks a turning point in Acts as the mission moves to the gentiles; this seems unlikely, given that mission to the gentiles does not immediately follow but rather mission to the Jewish diaspora (8:1b) and the Samaritans (8:4–25), who are not outright gentiles.

328 Talbert, *Reading Acts*, 65, notes the parallel story of the righteous one who dies and is vindicated to live forever in Wis 4:16–5:16.

329 Humphrey, *And I Turned*, 49–50, sees the vision as the conclusion to the speech. On the gap, see Maxwell, *Hearing*, 159–60.

330 The grammatical subject is the same as v. 54. Seland, *Violence*, 245–50, argues that the diaspora Jews from the synagogue (6:9) took the lead in accusing Stephen and, ultimately,

rejection of Stephen and his testimony as blasphemous: loud shouting drowns Stephen's voice and expresses anger (already seen in v. 54), and closing ears (συνέσχον τὰ ὦτα, a phrase unique in the Greek Bible[331]) indicates refusal to listen further, ironically fulfilling Gamaliel's words that warned the Sanhedrin against finding themselves fighting against God (5:33–39; see *Comment* there). Jervell justly writes, "Because of the words of Stephen, a storm breaks loose."[332] It is only after the vision report that they react thus, rather than after Stephen's direct accusation (7:51–53), for that report (to their minds) blasphemously identifies Jesus as the Son of Man who exercises universal power and authority alongside God.

ὥρμησαν ὁμοθυμαδὸν ἐπ' αὐτόν, "[they] rushed as one person upon him." The relatively uncommon ὥρμησαν, "they rushed," indicates the "mob" nature of event, for it portrays a mass acting in an uncontrolled way.[333] Such "vigilante" action in response to Stephen's christological claim was contrary to the orderly process for stoning envisaged in Jewish law (cf. m. Sanh. 6.1–4), although it is unlikely that the law recorded was in operation before AD 70.[334] ὁμοθυμαδόν, "as one person," indicates the unity of their action as their shared passion leads to shared action.[335]

58 ἔξω τῆς πόλεως, "outside the city," echoes stoning "outside the camp" (Num 15:35) as well as the attempt to kill Jesus by throwing him off the hill outside Nazareth (ἐξέβαλον αὐτὸν ἔξω τῆς πόλεως, "they threw him out of the city" [Luke 4:29])[336] and the murder of the son (who stands for Jesus) outside the vineyard by the wicked tenants (ἐκβαλόντες αὐτὸν ἔξω τοῦ ἀμπελῶνος ἀπέκτειναν, "they threw him out of the vineyard and killed [him]" [Luke 20:15]). To cast someone out of a Jewish city in Scripture denotes eliminating a cause of defilement (e.g., plague, Lev 14:40–41, 45; foreign gods, 2 Chr 33:15; people understood to be evil, 1 Kgs 21:13—see below on the latter).[337] Echoes of Jesus continue in Acts 7:59–60.

ἐλιθοβόλουν, "they began stoning [him]." Among the offences punishable by stoning in the Old Testament is blasphemy (Lev 24:11–16, 23; Deut 17:2–7), which is the charge against Stephen (6:11). The lynch-mob action here recalls

---

in stoning him, which fits well with the "proper" procedure, that the witnesses against the defendant should be the first to cast stones.

331 The nearest is βαρύνων τὰ ὦτα, "weighing down the ears," Isa 33:15 LXX, an image for refusing to hear of evil deeds. Cf. "When a man hears a word which is not right to him, he should put his fingers in his ears" (Str-B, 2:684, my translation). More typically, the metaphor for refusal to listen to God is closing eyes: Acts 28:27 (quoting Isa 6:10 LXX); Isa 29:10.

332 Jervell, *Apostelgeschichte*, 252 (my translation).

333 Cf. the pigs, Luke 8:33; the mob in Ephesus, Acts 19:29; also, e.g., LXX Judg 20:37; Nah 3:16; Hab 1:8; Isa 5:29; 2 Macc 9:2; 10:16.

334 Blinzer, "Jewish Punishment," 151–61.

335 Johnson, *Acts*, 140, sees an ironic echo of the unity of the early believing community (e.g. Acts 1:14; 2:46); on the word, see Walton, "Ὁμοθυμαδόν," esp. 102–3.

336 Edwards, "Parallels," 489.

337 Edwards, "Parallels," 489.

the stoning of Naboth at Jezebel's behest (1 Kgs 21:13 [LXX 20:13])[338] and perhaps Phinehas's action to purify Israel during a time of idolatry (Num 25:1–15).[339] (Jesus has already spoken with sadness of Jerusalem as the city that "stones (λιθοβολοῦσα) those sent to it" (Luke 13:34), suggesting that this event is a tragic fulfillment of his words. Stoning was an utter rejection of the criminal by the community (cf. Acts 14:19),[340] which is exactly what is happening here.

οἱ μάρτυρες ἀπέθεντο τὰ ἱμάτια αὐτῶν παρὰ τοὺς πόδας νεανίου καλουμένου Σαύλου, "The witnesses placed their cloaks at the feet of a young man called Saul." Here proper judicial procedure is followed, as the witnesses against Stephen take the lead in stoning (Deut 17:7; m. Sanh. 6:4), for their testimony has led to the verdict of blasphemy. This removal of cloaks (τὰ ἱμάτια), an outer garment, for the act of stoning is a unique event in the whole Bible. Other examples of removing cloaks generally foreshadow the intent to violence, freeing a man's body for such action (cf. 21:30).[341] That said, typically the one being executed would have their clothes removed, highlighting the inversion of the accusations against Stephen: they are guilty, not he.[342]

Saul's guarding the cloaks (later mentioned in Saul's voice in 22:20) introduces him as a persecutor of the believers (cf. 8:3 with *Comment*),[343] and he becomes a major character in the remainder of Acts. Luke identifies him as νεανίου, "a young man," which could place him between twenty-five and thirty-five.[344] Placing the cloaks at Saul's feet may suggest that Saul is a ringleader in the stoning of Stephen, in parallel with the placing of gifts at the apostles' feet (4:35, 37; 5:1).[345] It is plausible that Saul debated with Stephen in the synagogue and participated in Stephen's accusation and trial (see *Comment* on 6:9). (On the literary effect of this brief introduction of Saul followed by a gap until 9:1, see *Form/Structure/Setting*: *Setting* above.)

59–60 ἐπικαλούμενον καὶ λέγοντα· κύριε Ἰησοῦ, δέξαι τὸ πνεῦμά μου, "he called upon the Lord and said, 'Lord Jesus, receive my spirit!'" Stephen's prayers as he is being stoned come in two parts: first, he asks κύριε Ἰησοῦ, "Lord Jesus," that he might be received (v. 59), and secondly, he prays for his killers (v. 60).

338 The resemblance is striking: καὶ ἐξήγαγον αὐτὸν ἔξω τῆς πόλεως καὶ ἐλιθοβόλησαν αὐτὸν λίθοις, "and they took him out of the city and they stoned him with stones" (1 Kgs 20:13 LXX); with Marguerat, *Actes*, 1:275.

339 Seland, *Violence*, 243.

340 On stoning, see the full discussion of Hirzel, *Strafe*.

341 The excellent discussion of Jones, "Meaning," 116–17, notes Theophrastus, *Char.* 27.5; Hipponax, fr. 70; Plutarch, *Alc.* 39.3; Plato, *Resp.* 5.473–74. The latter is particularly relevant, for there Socrates is told that because of his offensive words, he must expect to be attacked by men who "throw off their cloaks" (ῥίψαντας τὰ ἱμάτια), in similar manner to Stephen's words leading to violence here.

342 Keener, "Three Notes," 43–44 with n9.

343 On his names, see *Excursus: The Names Saul and Paul* at *Comment* on 13:9–10.

344 Hengel and Deines, *Pre-Christian*, 67; "νεανίας," BDAG 667, suggests between 24 and 40.

345 Jones, "Meaning," 117; Johnson, *Acts*, 140.

The verb ἐπικαλούμενον, "called upon," here has a semi-technical use for prayer (as in 2:21; 9:14, 21; 15:17; 22:16).[346] Although ἐπικαλούμενον has no object, the following vocative κύριε Ἰησοῦ, "Lord Jesus," clarifies that "the Lord" is the one addressed.[347] This address to Jesus in prayer is remarkable in the context of Second Temple Judaism, for faithful Jews would address only YHWH (in LXX, typically κύριος, "Lord") in prayer—daily recital of the Shema (Deut 6:4–6) and the introduction to the Ten Commandments (Exod 20:2–6) both reinforce the requirement that YHWH alone may be worshiped.[348] To pray to Jesus bespeaks a "pattern of devotion" that places him alongside the Father as a proper object of prayer and worship.[349] "[T]rue worship of the God of Israel is worship of God and of Jesus with him."[350]

δέξαι τὸ πνεῦμά μου, "receive my spirit." Also remarkable is the content of the prayer, for Stephen assumes that Jesus has decisive power over who is (and is not) received into God's realm after death. δέχομαι, "receive," has the sense of "welcome" or "accept," as one would welcome a person (e.g., Luke 2:28; 9:5, 48, 53; 16:4, 9; Heb 13:11). τὸ πνεῦμά μου, "my spirit," should not be understood through Greek thinking that regarded the body as evil and the soul or spirit as the "real person" separable from the body: in common with other NT (and OT) writers, Luke assumes a holistic view of being human, and here uses πνεῦμα, "spirit," to stand for the whole person.[351] To invite the Lord Jesus to act in this way also makes clear that *his* decision is crucial, not that of the Sanhedrin: Jesus acts as the true judge.[352] To pray in this way at the time of death echoes Jesus's prayer: πάτερ, εἰς χεῖράς σου παρατίθεμαι τὸ πνεῦμά μου, "Father, into your hands I commit my spirit" (Luke 23:46), which itself echoes Ps 30:6 (MT 31:6; EVV 31:5), a passage used in Jewish evening prayers[353]—although Jesus's prayer is addressed to the Father. Stephen's prayer also becomes a pattern for Christian martyrs (e.g., Mart. Pol. 14; cf. 9:3).[354]

θεὶς δὲ τὰ γόνατα ἔκραξεν φωνῇ μεγάλῃ, "He knelt down and shouted at the top of his voice." Kneeling is not the usual posture for prayer in first-century Judaism: more typically, Jews or Israelites stand to pray (e.g., Gen 19:27; Job 30:20; 2 Chr 20:5–6; Ps 133:1 [MT 134:1]; Jer 7:10; 15:1; 18:20; m. Ber. 3:5;

346 "ἐπικαλέω," BDAG 373, §1; Hurtado, *Lord*, 197–200.
347 Cf. Paul's usage μαράνα θά, "Our Lord, come!" (1 Cor 16:22); τρὶς τὸν κύριον παρεκάλεσα, "three times I called upon the Lord" (2 Cor 12:8).
348 Bauckham, *God*, 6. More fully, see Hurtado, *Lord*, 29–48 (on first-century Jewish monotheism), 140–43 (on early Christian invocation of Jesus in prayer).
349 Hurtado, *Lord*, passim. For a valuable discussion of the influence of this prayer on prayers in the apocryphal Acts, see Paschke, "Prayer," esp. 53–71.
350 Hamm, "Tamid," 230.
351 "πνεῦμα," *NIDNTTE* 3:807, NT §2 "The Human Spirit"; Hermann Kleinknecht, "πνεῦμα," *TDNT* 6:357–58. On Luke's anthropology, see Walton, "Anthropology."
352 With Aarflot, *God*, 115–17. Cf. biblical pictures of YHWH standing to judge: Isa 3:13; 2:19, 21; Amos 9:1. Kennedy, *NT Interpretation*, 122, considers that God is the true judge.
353 Str-B, 2:269; Jeremias, "Gebetsleben," 126n3.
354 Hurtado, *Lord*, 618.

5:1; m. Yebam. 7:6). Kneeling[355] before another human expresses submission (e.g., 2 Kgs 1:13; Mark 1:40–45; Luke 5:8) and/or request (Josephus, *Ant.* 19.3.4 §234; *J.W.* 2.2.7 §37); thus in Greco-Roman cultures, slaves kneel before a magistrate when seeking manumission,[356] and suppliants grasp the knees of the one they approach,[357] or in Roman settings, non-Romans would kneel to supplicate.[358] Kneeling thus is a natural way of expressing submission or request to a god, such as Baal (1 Kgs 19:18; Rom 11:4) or YHWH (Isa 45:23), although Greco-Roman prayer was most often offered standing with arms directed either upward to the god or forward toward the god's statue.[359] In Scripture, kneeling in prayer expresses both this humble attitude[360] and often the intensity of the request, such as the prayers of Solomon, Ezra, and Daniel in extreme situations (2 Chr 6:13–14; Ezra 9:5–6; Dan 6:10): it is in such settings—including here—that kneeling to pray is found in the NT (Luke 22:41; Acts 9:40; 20:36; 21:5; Eph 3:14—in the NT, primarily a Lukan idiom).[361] This is also true of the relatively rare occasions when Greeks and Romans kneel to pray.[362] Bede observes, "For himself he [sc. Stephen] prayed standing up, for his enemies he prayed kneeling down. Because their iniquity was so great it called out for the greater remedy of falling to his knees."[363] Luke's echo of Jesus praying in Gethsemane again portrays Jesus as Stephen's model. Kneeling is also found when under intense attack (e.g., Josephus, *Ant.* 19.1.14 §110; *J.W.* 6.1.6 §§64–65), as Stephen is here, although the expression θεὶς . . . τὰ γόνατα, "placing . . . the knees," is more commonly used in prayer settings—the verb when under attack is different. That said, the attack may explain Stephen's shouting (which ironically echoes the Sanhedrin's shouting, v. 57), for Stephen prays aloud, as was usual in antiquity in order that others might hear and join in the "Amen"—he may not expect his murderers to say, "Amen," but he may well hope they will hear what he prays for them. Stephen's loud cry also echoes Jesus's loud cry at his death (Luke 23:46), underlining that he follows his Master in faithfulness to death.[364]

---

355 On this posture, see H. Schönweiss, "γονυπετέω," *NIDNTT* 2:859–60; "Knee, Kneel," *DBIm* 483.

356 Rostovtzeff and Fraser, *Social*, 1:67–68, has a photograph of a carving of this posture, dated to the first century AD.

357 E.g., Homer, *Od.* 22. 333–54, where Phemius approaches Odysseus; see discussion in Naiden, *Supplication*, 3, 29, 43–47.

358 Naiden, *Supplication*, 50.

359 E.g., Homer, *Il.* 1.445; 3.275; 5.174. See BNP 11:792; H. S. Versnel, "Prayer and Curse," *OHAGR* 450; Pulleyn, *Prayer*, 188–90.

360 *NIDNTTE* 1:593, NT§2.

361 Hermas later writes of kneeling in prayer: Herm. Vis. 1.3 (1.1); 5.2 (2.1); 9.5 (3.1).

362 Pulleyn, *Prayer*, 190–91, 194.

363 Bede, *Acts*, 76 (on 7:60), echoing Augustine, *Serm.* 319.4.

364 In a conference paper, Jaimie Gunderson argues that Stephen's loud cry represents loss of control, a trait subversive of Greco-Roman expectations of elite masculinity as exemplifying self-control; Gunderson, "Stones." The parallel with Jesus's loud cry at his death suggests

κύριε, μὴ στήσῃς αὐτοῖς ταύτην τὴν ἁμαρτίαν, "Lord, do not hold this sin against them!" Stephen's second request focuses on his assailants, asking forgiveness for them rather than asking anything for himself; he further underlines that his killers are guilty of sin, not him (see *Comment* on v. 58).[365] He again uses κύριε, "Lord," to address Jesus[366] and now assumes that Jesus can forgive sins. Luke presents the earthly Jesus as having this ability as part of his authority as "the Son of Man" (Luke 5:20–24; cf. v. 56) and proclaiming and offering forgiveness of sins is part of the believers' role (Luke 24:47; Acts 2:38; 3:19; 5:31; 10:43; 13:38; 22:16; 26:18; see *Comment* on 2:38). Zechariah's prayer as he is being stoned is a striking contrast, for he prays, "May the Lord see and avenge!" (2 Chr 24:22),[367] as is the contrast with the Maccabean martyrs' statements that those who kill them will suffer divine retribution (e.g., 2 Macc 7:14, 16, 19, 31, 35, 36).[368] Stephen is being portrayed as far more generous in spirit than these martyrs, for in line with the teaching of Jesus, he prays for his enemies.[369] The Lukan parallel (πάτερ, ἄφες αὐτοῖς, οὐ γὰρ οἴδασιν τί ποιοῦσιν, "Father, forgive them, for they do not know what they are doing" [Luke 23:34a]) is textually uncertain—NA[28] places it in double square brackets, indicating near certainty that it is not original, although Nolland considers it original.[370] If original, it provides a further feature that portrays Stephen's death as modeled on that of Jesus. Matthews considers that the prayer is unanswered;[371] but the stress on the presence of Saul here (Acts 7:58; 8:1a) and his later transformative encounter with Jesus on the Damascus Road (9:1–9) rather suggest that Saul is one in whose life Stephen's prayer is answered positively.

καὶ τοῦτο εἰπὼν ἐκοιμήθη, "After he said this, he fell asleep." This is the first of two uses of κοιμάω "fall asleep" for "die" in Acts (the other is 13:36, concerning David). The parallel uses elsewhere in the NT are primarily in Paul and mainly in the context of discussing believers' resurrection at the end (1 Cor 7:39; 11:30; 15:6, 18, 20, 51; 1 Thess 4:13, 14, 15; 2 Pet 3:4). The term reflects early Christian confidence in "waking up" at the return of Jesus,

---

that masculinity is being remodeled; more fully, see Wilson, *Unmanly Men*, esp. 201–35, although she does not discuss the loudness of Jesus's death cry.

365 Keener, "Three Notes," 44.

366 For critique of the suggestion that κύριε is God rather than Jesus, in v. 60, see Paschke, "Prayer," 51.

367 Bruce, *Acts* (1990), 213.

368 Carter, *Forgiveness*, 230, provides a good discussion of a claimed parallel between Jesus's death in Luke and that of the Macabbean martyrs, showing that Luke does not portray Jesus as dying the death of a martyr. More fully, see Tabb, "Lucan Jesus."

369 As Matthews, *Perfect Martyr*, 11, 110, recognizes.

370 Nolland, *Luke*, 3:1141–42, 44; so also Matthews, *Perfect Martyr*, 101–3; contra *TCGNT*[2], 154; Comfort, ad loc. Comfort suggests the words were included later as an inspiration for Christian martyrs (e.g., Eusebius, *Hist. eccl.* 2.23.16 reports James the Just as saying, "I beseech thee, O Lord, God and Father, forgive them for they know not what they do" [Lake, LCL]).

371 Matthews, *Perfect Martyr*, 99, 100.

rooted in the Jewish hope of the bodily resurrection of righteous sleepers to shine like stars (Dan 12:2–3).[372] It is in tune with the physicality of Jewish and Christian hope of resurrection at the last day, by contrast with Greek ideas of the immortality of the soul.[373]

8:1 Σαῦλος . . . ἦν συνευδοκῶν, "Saul . . . approved," uses a periphrastic imperfect for "offline" information, here comment on the main events in the narrative that describes Saul's settled attitude.[374] The fronted Σαῦλος with δέ, "and," marking switch of subject, also indicates some focus on Saul, who will become a key character in Acts.[375] ἀναίρεσις, "murder," is an NT *hapax legomenon* and is not simply "death" (KJV) but "killing."[376]

Explanation

Stephen entered the Acts narrative as a man with a Greek name called by the believers to be part of a group administering care for widows (6:5), and this section fills out his portrait, presents a lengthy speech, and describes him being stoned to death. Luke does not say whether Stephen was already a leader among Greek-speaking believers ("Hellenists," 6:1), although this is certainly possible on the basis of his prior reputation as a godly man ("full of faith and the Holy Spirit," 6:5)—and that is an implied factor in the group's choice of him and the public ministry he now undertakes. His ministry echoes that of the apostles (and Jesus before them): he performs wonders and signs and speaks with power and effectiveness (6:8–10). His success, like theirs, derives from God, particularly in his exercising wisdom given by the Holy Spirit (6:6, 8; cf. 6:5) in fulfillment of Jesus's promise (Luke 12:11–12).

As with the apostles, Stephen's proclamation and deeds lead to opposition, particularly among those culturally and religiously close to him—other diaspora Jews (Acts 6:9). Greek-speaking Jews living in Jerusalem founded and joined Greek-speaking synagogues, of which the synagogue of the Freedmen is an example. Such people were strongly committed to their ancestral Judaism and thereby motivated to move to the city (frequently toward the end of their lives, in order to be buried there). They were likely to be more conservative in their views of the law and the temple. It would be predictable that Stephen would meet staunch opposition from these people in the Greek-speaking synagogue as he engaged them in conversation and debate about Jesus and what it meant to follow Jesus. It may be that Saul of Tarsus was among Stephen's interlocutors, for Tarsus is located in Cilicia (6:9).

---

372 See the excellent discussion of Dan 12 in Wright, *Resurrection*, 109–15.

373 Wright, *Resurrection*, passim.

374 Campbell, *Indicative*, 91–96; Haenchen, *Acts*, 293.

375 Culy and Parsons, *Acts*, 148.

376 Field, *Notes*, 116; "ἀναίρεσις," BDAG 64. The cognate verb ἀναιρέω, "kill," is a Lukanism (2x Luke; 20x Acts; 3x rest of NT); Barrett, *Acts*, 1:388. In this passage it occurs in vv. 21, 28; cf. 22:20; 26:10, both on the lips of Paul describing his pre-Christian persecuting activities.

Stephen's critics attack him by secretly and unethically agitating people to speak against him, thus challenging his honored status (6:11). The initial accusation is blasphemy, in speaking against Moses and God, i.e., speaking falsely about, or on behalf, of God. This accusation becomes public criticism and leads to Stephen's arrest and presentation to the Sanhedrin (6:12), the legal authority charged with dealing with such claims (recall that Jesus was similarly accused before the Sanhedrin, Luke 22:66–71; cf. Mark 14:55–64, esp. v. 64, which identifies Jesus's crime as blasphemy). Stephen follows his Master and the apostles in being called to answer for his proclamation (Acts 4:5–22; 5:17–41). Luke makes no suggestion that the content of Stephen's proclamation is different from that of the apostles; that silence, and the debate's focus on Jesus (6:14), strongly suggest that readers should understand that Stephen spoke in similar ways to the apostles.

The accusation before the Sanhedrin is more precise than the initial one: Stephen is alleged to be attacking the temple ("the holy place") and the "law" (i.e., the Pentateuch, understood to derive from Moses) and claiming that Jesus will both destroy the temple and change the oral traditions ("customs"), which were understood to go back to Moses (6:13–14). These are very serious charges—even though they are false (v. 13)—for they attack key pillars of first-century Judaism, and hence lead to the emotional heat of the situation ("stirred up," 6:12; anger and rejection, 7:54, 57).

The contrast between Luke's characterization of Stephen and of Stephen's opponents is total. The Sanhedrin, at this stage, stand in the middle, for Luke has not yet mentioned their attitude, and readers may be wondering if the Sanhedrin's view has changed in the light of Gamaliel's advice to treat the believers with caution (5:34–39). The Sanhedrin's members are on tiptoe to hear Stephen's response, fixing attention on him and seeing his face shining (6:15)—the latter marks him as a divine messenger. The chief priest's question is phrased neutrally rather than being slanted to imply a positive answer (7:1).

Stephen's speech is the longest in Acts and thus highly significant for Luke's developing story and message. He responds indirectly to the charges against him but does not avoid those charges: rather, he turns them back on his accusers—they are the ones who are undermining Moses, rejecting God's law, and regarding the temple improperly by *de facto* treating it as an idol. He develops his response by a selective retelling of Israel's history, a genre also used by other contemporary Jews to re-express their understanding of Judaism for their time and place. He interprets Scripture in some fresh and creative ways that show how the revelation of YHWH in Scripture leads to Jesus and why the accusations against Stephen are mistaken, providing a window into early Christian evangelism and apologetic among Jewish people.

The speech is strongly theocentric, highlighting God's actions and self-revelation and the people's responses to God. God's choice of and promises to Abraham (7:2–8) are the springboard and basis of Stephen's story of Israel.

The second focus is Joseph, whose main role is to explain how the Israelites were in Egypt for Moses to lead them out from there (vv. 9–16). The story of Moses then receives the most "airtime," beginning with his birth and upbringing by Pharaoh's daughter (vv. 20–22), moving to his need to leave the land after killing an Egyptian and emigrate to Midian (vv. 23–29), and then describing his divine call at the burning bush, his leadership in taking the people out of Egypt, and his reception of the law (vv. 30–38). By contrast, the people's rejection of Moses and their subsequent construction and worship of the golden calf at the very time Moses is receiving the law on Mount Sinai repeat the error of the two Israelites who years earlier rejected Moses and worshiped other gods (vv. 39–43, 25–28). Stephen then moves rapidly from the tent in the wilderness (v. 44), through the conquest of the land under Joshua (v. 45), to the time of David and Solomon, when the temple was built (vv. 46–47). Stephen quotes Isa 66:1–2 (vv. 49–50) to the effect that God does not live in hand-made things, thus relativizing the (hand-made) temple. Stephen's theocentricity continues in his peroration, where he highlights his response to the accusations against him (vv. 51–53): it is not he who rejects the revelation God has given but his hearers; their attack on him is like their ancestors' murderous attacks on the prophets, God's messengers; and, most ironic of all, although they claim loyalty to the divine law, they fail to keep it.

Reviewing the whole speech, four major themes come through. First, *Stephen relativizes the land and the temple* by highlighting that YHWH made himself known outside the land: to Abraham in Mesopotamia (v. 2); by blessing Joseph and his family in Egypt (vv. 9–15); by protecting Moses as a child (vv. 20–22: God's motivation is signaled by "he was good-looking *as far as God was concerned*" [v. 20b]); by leading Moses to deliver the Israelites (v. 25, an interpretation of the story of Moses's killing the Egyptian not found previously in Judaism); by calling Moses at the burning bush at a site outside the land and calling that place "holy" (vv. 30–34; note the echo of "the *holy* place" as a description of the temple, 6:13); by giving Moses the law at Mount Sinai, outside the land (7:38); and by reminding his hearers that the impermanent tent was the place where God met his people in the wilderness (v. 44), long before the building of the temple (v. 47). Stephen focuses on the migrant status of these characters: Abraham, who travels from Ur and Haran to the land; Joseph, trafficked by his brothers to Egypt; Jacob, migrating away from the brother he deceived; and Moses, who flees Egypt after murdering an Egyptian. Each of them meets God outside the land. Further, Stephen highlights the Jewish and biblical principle that God does not dwell in hand-made things, citing Isa 66:1–2 and echoing Solomon's ambivalence concerning the temple at its dedication (1 Kgs 8:14–30, esp. v. 27). Thus, his accusers are the ones in error about the temple: the temple was valid in its time, but now that God has made himself known in and through Jesus and the Spirit, the way of access to God is no longer through a building and the priestly system of mediation which it represents and never was restricted to the land. Rather, as Stephen's vision conveys, the way the barrier between earth and heaven is pierced is through Jesus, the Danielic Son of Man, who now stands in the place of authority, at God's right side (Acts 7:55–56; Dan 7:13–14). That is why Stephen can take the revolutionary step of praying to Jesus and assuming Jesus's power over his own and his killers' destiny (Acts 7:59–60).

Secondly, *the people consistently reject divinely appointed spokespeople and deliverers,* and that extends to the Sanhedrin's rejection of Jesus. This theme relates to the choice of characters from Israel's history in the speech: the patriarchs rejected Joseph, and he turned out to be their deliverer during the famine (vv. 9–16); Israelites rejected Moses after he killed the Egyptian (vv. 24–29), and yet Moses became the deliverer who took Israel out of Egypt (vv. 35–36); the people's worship of the golden calf amounted to rejection of Moses, at the very time he was receiving the law on Mount Sinai (vv. 38–42a); this same Moses obediently constructed the tent of witness exactly as YHWH instructed (v. 44), and yet the people in Stephen's day did not understand that God's presence was not restricted there (vv. 48–50); and the prophets of Israel spoke for God and yet were persecuted and killed (v. 52). This pattern of the people rejecting those who speak and act for God is repeated in the Sanhedrin's rejection of Jesus (v. 52b), which bespeaks their resistance to the Holy Spirit (v. 51b) and means that they are like uncircumcised men (v. 51a)—the latter is a huge insult to men who considered themselves true Jews par excellence! The pattern of rejecting God's messengers is further fulfilled in their stoning of Stephen (vv. 54–60).

Thirdly, *Stephen invokes the "luminaries of Israel's legacy"*[377] *as his witnesses in order to claim that Jesus believers are the true Israel,* in line with God's purposes and self-revelation in the law, by contrast with Stephen's accusers and the Sanhedrin, who want to fossilize God in the past. The prophets announced the coming of Jesus (v. 51b), who is typologically seen in Joseph, rejected by his brothers and yet "raised" by God to power in Egypt (vv. 9–16), and also in Moses, similarly rejected by his own people and yet the one whom God chose to lead the people out of Egypt (vv. 24–36) and the one through whom God revealed the law even while the people were rejecting his leadership (vv. 38–42a). The prophet Amos witnesses to God's reaction to idolatry (vv. 42b–43, citing Amos 5:25–27), an idolatry now being racticed by the Sanhedrin in their mistaken devotion to the temple as the dwelling place of YHWH. Stephen invokes the prophet Isaiah to underline this point: Israel's God is the God of the whole earth and therefore cannot be contained within human houses or temples (Acts 7:49–50, citing Isa 66:1–2).

Fourthly, *God's glory* bookends the speech, and much of the speech then shows how and where God's glory is known. Stephen's angelic face (Acts 6:15)

377 Skinner, *Trial Narratives*, 120.

and his characterization of YHWH as "the God of glory" (7:2) open the speech, and the appearance of Jesus, the Son of Man, accompanied by "the glory of God" (7:55–56) closes it. Both features attract focused attention: the Sanhedrin "fixed their attention" on Stephen (6:15), and Stephen is "looking intently" into heaven (7:55, the same Greek verb). God's glory is known through his deeds in Israel's history, in promising and fulfilling his promise to Abraham (7:2–8, 17), in guarding the nascent nation through Joseph (vv. 9–16), in bringing the people out of Egypt under Moses (vv. 34–37), in revealing the law to the people through Moses (v. 38), and through the tent of witness in the wilderness (v. 44) and the temple in Jerusalem (v. 47).

Stephen's answer to the accusations is thus threefold. First, *he is not the lawbreaker, but his accusers, in line with their ancestors, are,* for they resist God's self-revelation and the deliverer whom God has sent (vv. 51–53). While they acknowledge the divine origin of the law, they failed to keep it—Stephen may have their condemnation of Jesus and their connivance in his execution by the Romans specifically in mind here (v. 52b).

Secondly, *the Jesus whom they rejected and his followers whom they oppose are the true Israel and the true fulfillers of the law.* To that extent, the charge that "Jesus the Nazarene . . . will change the customs that Moses handed down to us" (6:14) is accurate, for it is now through Jesus and by the Spirit that God is available to be known and experienced. Jesus is the "prophet like Moses" (7:37, echoing 3:22 and Deut 18:15); he is the one who brings the new exodus as God's chosen deliverer (Acts 7:36; see Luke 4:4–6, quoting Isa 40:3–5); he is the one who did wonders and signs (Acts 7:36; see 2:22), as his followers, including Stephen, now do (6:8; see 2:43; 4:30, 31); he is the one who speaks for God as prophet and divine revealer (7:37, 38b; see Luke 4:24; 7:16; 13:33; 24:19); and, supremely, he is the one now at God's right side as the glorified Son of Man in the place of rule and authority in the universe (Acts 7:55–56). As a result, Israel is "*re-interpreted* and *reunderstood* through the lens of Jesus as Messiah."[378]

Thirdly, the temple had a valid role as the successor of the tent of testimony in the wilderness once the people settled in the land. However, *the temple is not the sole meeting place of heaven and earth,* for God met with and acted for key people in Israel's history outside the land: Abraham was in Mesopotamia (7:2); Joseph was in Egypt (v. 9); and Moses was in Egypt (vv. 20–22, 34, 36), the Sinai peninsula (vv. 30–34), and the wilderness at Mount Sinai (v. 38). Not only that, but God does not inhabit human structures (vv. 48–50, quoting Isa 66:1–2) and thus should not be thought to be constricted by the temple. Stephen does not suggest that the temple was mistaken from its inception but that its day is now over, particularly because it is now being treated as an idol (Acts 7:48–50), and those who treat it thus are like pagans, uncircumcised

378 Walton, "Calling," 241 (italics original).

men (v. 51). Instead, Jesus, the glorified Son of Man, is the means of access to God, and that is demonstrated by Stephen praying to Jesus, both for himself and for his murderers (vv. 59–60).

The upshot of all of this is that the Sanhedrin are now ironically fulfilling Gamaliel's warning (5:33–39): they are fighting against God by rejecting his chosen one, Jesus, and refusing to listen to those who speak for God, including Stephen. The debate over who speaks for God, which has been running through the earlier chapters of Acts, continues, and Luke points his readers to the reality of God's glory, seen in his fulfillment of the promise to Abraham and in the vision of the heavenly Jesus as the Son of Man, to show that the believers are now the true Israel, the obedient followers of the one true God now known in Jesus and by the Spirit.

This passage is highly significant christologically, especially the latter part (7:55–60). Jesus is revealed as standing at God's right side (v. 55b), located in heaven at the place of authority and power. It is the Spirit who makes this revelation known to Stephen (v. 55a), and that divine source means it is a trustworthy vision (see 2:17). Stephen's description of the vision (7:56) highlights three points: the heavens are open, signaling that this is a divine revelation (see 10:11; Luke 3:21; John 1:51; Rev 4:1); Jesus is identified as the (Danielic) Son of Man at God's right side, now given his rightful place of authority and universal rule (see Dan 7:13–14); and Jesus is standing, portraying him as either witness or judge in the real, heavenly trial of Stephen, of which the earthly trial that is going on is a travesty—Jesus, as the Son of Man, has the power to overturn the erroneous verdict of this human court.

Stephen's two prayers (Acts 7:59–60) also make big christological claims. The exalted Jesus is an appropriate person to be addressed in prayer (twice with the vocative, "Lord"), whereas first-century Jews regarded YHWH alone as one who should be the object of prayer. To pray to Jesus places him in a category in which only YHWH belongs and thus leads to fresh ways of engaging with God in and through Jesus. Stephen further assumes that this Jesus has authority to settle the destiny of his spirit (which stands for his whole person), and thus requests to be received (v. 59), and that Jesus the glorified Son of Man has authority to forgive sins, even of his murderers (v. 60; see Luke 5:20–24, and contrast the approach of Zechariah and the Maccabean martyrs, 2 Chr 24:22; 2 Macc 7:14, 16, 19, 31, 35, 36). Both of these are divine prerogatives in first-century Judaism and reinforce the extraordinary readiness of the early believers to place Jesus alongside YHWH as a proper and appropriate object of prayer and worship.

Finally, Luke introduces his readers to the young Saul as the one who guards the cloaks of the stoners and approves of them killing Stephen (Acts 7:58b; 8:1a). Saul's action and Luke's description of his attitude will be played out in his persecution of the believers (8:3; 9:1–2) before his surprising meeting with Jesus on the Damascus Road (9:3–9).

2. Persecution: The Believers Are Scattered (8:1b–3)

Bibliography

Bauckham, R. "James," 427–29. **Baur, F. C.** *Paul.* **Cunningham, S.** *Tribulations,* 215–18. **Dana, H. E.** "Where." **Hengel, M.** *Acts,* 71–77. **Hengel, M., and R. Deines.** *Pre-Christian,* 23–34, 72–79. **Hill, C. C.** *Hellenists,* 19–40. **Hultgren, A. J.** "Persecutions." **Kurz, W. S.** *Reading,* 144–45. **Longenecker, B. W.** *Rhetoric,* 192–98. **Moule, C. F. D.** "Once Again." **Petterson, C.** *Acts* (2nd ed.), 40–45. **Reimer, I. R.** *Women,* 237–39. **Richard, E.** *Acts 6:1–8:4,* 224–29, 239–41, 301–4, 338–46. **Seim, T. K.** *Message.* **Wilson, S. G.** *Gentiles,* 137–53.

Translation

[1b] At that time[a] a great persecution arose against the Jerusalem assembly, and all except the apostles[b] were scattered throughout[c] the countryside of Judea and Samaria. [2] Devout men buried Stephen and lamented greatly for him. [3] Saul, however,[d] set out to destroy the assembly by entering[e] house after house, dragging both men and women away and handing them over to prison.

Notes

a. ἐν ἐκείνῃ τῇ ἡμέρᾳ, "at that time," dat. Of time; ἡμέρα here denotes a period of time rather than a specific twenty-four-hour period; "ἡμέρα," BDAG 438, §4.a; Barrett, *Acts,* 1:390.

b. D* 1175 it sa[mss] mae also read οἳ ἔμειναν ἐν Ἰερουσαλήμ, "who stayed in Jerusalem," which Rius-Camps and Read-Heimerdinger, *Message,* 2:116, see as implying that the apostles are attached to the "old religious order" on the grounds that this spelling of Jerusalem represents the city as "the Jewish religious institution" (see *Comment* on 1:7–8).

c. κατά is here "throughout"; "κατά," BDAG 511, §B.1.a.

d. δέ, "however," indicates a switch of subject to Saul.

e. εἰσπορευόμενος, "by entering," ptcp. of means.

Form/Structure/Setting

Delimitation of pericope. The paragraph begins with ἐγένετο δέ, a typical Lukan beginning of a new section (e.g., 4:5). The next paragraph (v. 4) begins with οἱ μὲν οὖν, also a common Lukan new-section marker,[379] and v. 4 resumes the story of οἱ . . . διασπαρέντες, "those who were scattered," from v. 1.

Sources/historicity. A number of scholars express surprise that the apostles were not persecuted (v. 1),[380] although the text does not actually say this (see *Comment*). However, this reading, in combination with the appearance that the scattering of "all" (v. 1) was only some (for they were still there to be persecuted in v. 3), has led many to consider that it was only the Hellenists, or their leaders, who were scattered.[381] But if the Hebrews and Hellenists were

379 Levinsohn, *Connections,* 141–50; Longenecker, *Rhetoric,* 198.
380 E.g., Dunn, *Acts,* 104.
381 E.g., Wilson, *Gentiles,* 137–53.

divided linguistically rather than theologically (see *Comment* on 6:1), there is no reason to think that it was only Hellenists who fled Jerusalem. A careful reading of the next chapters of Acts shows that the Greek-speaking believers were at the vanguard of new outreach: Philip went to Samaria (8:5–25) and met the Ethiopian eunuch (8:26–40), and others spoke to gentiles (11:19–21). This would be natural as the gospel spread into areas where Aramaic was not widely spoken.

Some suggest that Paul's statement that he was ἀγνοούμενος τῷ προσώπῳ ταῖς ἐκκλησίαις τῆς Ἰουδαίας, "unknown by face to the church of Judea" (Gal 1:21), precludes the historicity of persecution by Saul in Jerusalem at this time (which Acts 9:21 clearly implies).[382] Dunn also observes that Paul presents himself as a persecutor motivated by "zeal" (e.g., Phil 3:6; Gal 1:13–14), which Dunn understands to be opposition to those who compromised Israel's separation to God and from other nations.[383] Since there was no gentile mission yet, Dunn argues that the events of Acts 8:3 could not have taken place at this time and that there is some "telescoping of events" by Luke.

However, Gal 1:21–23 needs to be read with 1:13, which speaks of Paul's pre-Christian persecution of "the church of God" and naturally refers to the believers in Jerusalem.[384] One way of reading Gal 1 as a whole is to treat "Judea" (v. 21) as excluding Jerusalem.[385] On this view, Paul states that he persecuted the Jerusalem church but was not known by sight to the churches in wider Judea; they only heard about his change of allegiance (v. 22). However, it seems more likely that Gal 1:22 refers to the Roman province of Judea, which included Jerusalem.[386] Nevertheless, Paul's claim is that he was not known "by sight" by the Judean believers, although he was known by his reputation as a persecutor.

An alternative solution begins by noticing that Paul's point in Gal 1 is that after the Damascus Road experience he was not under human authority, including that of the Jerusalem apostles (vv. 11–12, 15–17).[387] Thus Paul is asserting that *after he became a believer* the Judean churches did not see him but only heard about him.[388] On this reading, there is no incompatibility between Gal 1:21–23 and Acts 8:3. In any case, while Saul is presented in Acts 8:3 as the leader of the persecution, this verse should probably not be read as presenting Saul as the immediate agent of every act of entering houses and dragging people away—given the size of the task, Saul probably supervises others who carried out these acts.[389] Indeed, in a city the size of Jerusalem at the time

---

382 E.g., Hill, *Hellenists*, 35; Haenchen, *Acts*, 297–98.
383 *Acts*, 105.
384 Witherington, *Acts*, 245; Caird, *Apostolic Age*, 87; Hengel and Deines, *Pre-Christian*, 72–79.
385 So Lightfoot, *Galatians*, 86; Dunn, *Galatians*, 81.
386 Burton, *Galatians*, 63–64.
387 Hengel and Deines, *Pre-Christian*, 74–75.
388 Hultgren, "Persecutions," 105–7; Fung, *Galatians*, 81–82.
389 Bruce, *Galatians*, 104.

(perhaps thirty-two thousand to eighty thousand people), it is not necessarily likely that Saul would be personally known to the believers.[390]

Structure. Structurally, δέ is used to mark transitions: in v. 1b a temporal transition takes place; in v. 1c the subject switches from the great persecution to all the believers; in v. 2a to devout men; in v. 3 to Saul (also echoing Σαῦλος δέ from v. 1). Thus, δέ mostly should not be translated as adversative. The switching has the effect of strongly connecting Stephen's martyrdom and Saul's persecution[391] and demonstrates how effectively Luke has organised the material in this summary, drawn from traditions he has gathered.[392] When seen in a wider literary context, this paragraph forms a transition from Stephen's death to Acts 8–12, which focus on the spreading of the gospel community into Judea and Samaria, and does so by the device of introducing the new theme (v. 1b), closing off the previous narrative (v. 2) and then going on to resume the new theme (v. 3).[393]

Setting. Thus, this transitional paragraph moves from Stephen (7:60) to Philip (8:5) by way of briefly introducing Saul (8:1a, 3), who will return to the picture more fully in 9:1, where his story resumes with an anaphoric definite article and ἔτι, "still." The mention of persecution (v. 1) prepares for the next steps in the story:[394] Luke reintroduces Saul (from 7:58; 8:1a) as a major protagonist in the persecution of believers (v. 3); this persecution ironically enables the spread of the gospel outside Jerusalem (v. 4); and it means hearers of Acts know Saul before he encounters the exalted Jesus on the Damascus Road (9:3–22). Thematically, the scattering of the believers (v. 4) is the first stage of the fulfillment of the program of 1:8, taking in Judea and Samaria, and then including Philip's mission in Samaria (8:5–25). Arguably, the persecution and scattering theme continues to the end of Acts 12; notably, the dispersion of the witnesses in vv. 1b, 4 is clearly echoed in 11:19: Οἱ μὲν οὖν διασπαρέντες ἀπὸ τῆς θλίψεως τῆς γενομένης ἐπὶ Στεφάνῳ, "So then, those who were scatted because of the persecution which happened on account of Stephen."[395]

Comment

1b The Semitic idiom Ἐγένετο . . . ἐν ἐκείνῃ τῇ ἡμέρᾳ, "arose . . . at that time," both marks the transition to a new scene and connects the persecution to Stephen's death. It is a natural development from the earlier attacks on Peter and John (4:1–22; 5:17–40). The persecution leads to the scattering of the community and the spread of the gospel message to the second and third

390 Hengel and Deines, *Pre-Christian*, 24.
391 Cunningham, *Tribulations*, 215–16.
392 Barrett, *Acts*, 1:390; Roloff, *Apostelgeschichte*, 129.
393 Longenecker, *Rhetoric*, 195–97.
394 For what follows, see Hill, *Hellenists*, 39.
395 See Longenecker, *Rhetoric*, 194–97, and *Explanation* for fuller discussion.

areas mentioned in 1:8, Judea and Samaria. Luke for the second time calls the community ἐκκλησία, "assembly" (see *Comment* on 5:11).

Luke's contrast πάντες . . . διεσπάρησαν . . . πλὴν τῶν ἀποστόλων, "all . . . were scattered . . . except the apostles," when combined with the continuing persecution (v. 3), suggests that the hyperbolic "all" focuses on the contrast rather than precise description—for if there were believers still in the city to be dragged out by Saul, "all" could not have left (cf. πᾶς in Luke 3:15; Acts 1:1; 3:9; 9:35).[396] The apostles remaining in Jerusalem chimes in with Luke's portrait of them as the core and leadership of the renewed Israel (2:42–43; 4:33, 35, 37; 5:2, 18, 29, 40; 6:6; cf. Luke 22:28–30). However, Luke is silent over whether the apostles are persecuted, which appears surprising—if the leaders of the movement are in the city, then they would be the natural target for persecution. A common explanation is that the persecution was focused on the Hellenists, whereas the Hebrews, including the apostles, escape persecution.[397] This explanation fits with the persecution arising at the time of Stephen's death, if he was a Hellenist (see *Form/Structure/Setting*: *Sources/historicity* for 6:1–7 and *Comment* at 6:1, rejecting the view that the Hellenists had a theology distinct from that of the Hebrews). However, Luke does not claim that the apostles escaped persecution;[398] the assertion here would still be true if the apostles are imprisoned (v. 3) and later freed. Alternatively, Witherington suggests that respect for the apostles as "holy persons of power" among the general populace might allow them to stay in Jerusalem.[399] Thus it is most likely that this persecution includes both Hebrew and Hellenist believers[400] and contrasts with later persecution that results in James's death (12:2) and Peter fleeing the city (12:17).

διεσπάρησαν κατὰ τὰς χώρας τῆς Ἰουδαίας καὶ Σαμαρείας, "they were scattered throughout the countryside of Judea and Samaria," implies the establishment of (doubtless, initially small) believing communities in rural areas of Judea and Samaria, for χώρα denotes "country," by contrast with πόλις, "city, town."[401] These may be some of the groups Peter later visits (9:32). διεσπάρησαν, "they were scattered," is the cognate verb of διασπορά, the word used for the Jewish dispersion around the Mediterranean basin (cf. Isa 49:6 LXX, which speaks of τὴν διασπορὰν τοῦ Ισραηλ, "the dispersion of Israel"). It is possible that these scattered believers are being presented as a "new diaspora" (a phrase I owe to my student Dr Will Loescher). It is ironic that Acts 8:4 and 11:19–21 will go on to note that this scattering leads to the growth of the believing community.

---

396 Calvin, *Acts*, 1:225.

397 This view dates back at least to Baur, *Paul*, 39; more recently see, e.g., Hengel, *Acts*, 74–75; Moule, "Once More," 101. Moule suggests that the apostles, as Galileans, were not members of a Jerusalem synagogue and therefore escaped the persecutors' reaction against synagogue members who became believers. For literature on this topic, see Hill, *Hellenists*, 7–15.

398 Bauckham, "Jerusalem Church," 428–29; so also Schnabel, *Mission*, 1:671.

399 *Acts*, 278n330.

400 Richard, *Acts 6:1–8:4*, 333–34.

401 See Petterson, *Acts of Empire* (2nd ed.), 40–45, drawing on de Ste. Croix, *Class Struggle*.

2 ἄνδρες εὐλαβεῖς, "devout men," is a Lukan phrase, see *Comment* on 2:5. There is an echo here of Joseph of Arimathea, ἀνὴρ ἀγαθὸς καὶ δίκαιος, "a good and righteous man" (Luke 23:50), who arranged the burial of Jesus (Luke 23:50–53), underlining that Stephen, like his Master, dies innocently. Jesus's body was prepared for burial by women (Luke 23:55–24:1), whereas Luke specifies that "men" arrange Stephen's burial, in similar manner to the young men who carry out the bodies of Ananias and Sapphira (5:6, 10). Assuming that "all" (v. 1) is hyperbole, these men are probably Jewish believers rather than simply Jewish sympathisers with Stephen, in similar vein to Ananias, a Jesus follower, who is described as ἀνὴρ εὐλαβής, "a devout man" (22:12).[402]

ἐποίησαν κοπετὸν μέγαν, lit., "made great lamentation," an LXX expression; cf. Mic 1:8 LXX ποιήσεται κοπετόν, "I will make lamentation." κοπετός, "lamentation," is an NT *hapax legomenon*. Mishnah Sanh. 6:5–6 forbids burying felons in their ancestral grave and mourning openly for them; if a similar law is in force in the first century, those burying Stephen and "lamenting greatly" are taking a significant risk.

3 Saul reappears, portrayed in violent and angry colors. Σαῦλος δὲ ἐλυμαίνετο τὴν ἐκκλησίαν, "Saul, however, set out to destroy the assembly," uses an NT *hapax legomenon* for Saul's actions—ἐλυμαίνετο, "he sets out to destroy" (conative imperfect[403]), i.e., to bring the congregation's life to an end. The imperfect need not imply that Saul only now begins to do this—his prior action in guarding the cloaks of Stephen's murderers suggests otherwise. The verb is used in LXX Ps 79:14 (MT 80:14; EVV 80:13) for a boar raging destructively around, a suggestive parallel (cf. LXX Isa 65:25; Sir 28:13).[404] MESSAGE thus renders, "Saul just went wild, devastating the church." σύρων, "dragging," expands the portrait of Saul's violent actions (cf. 4 Macc 6:1); it is ironic that he himself will be subject to such treatment at a later date (Acts 14:19). The portrait of Saul here is very much in tune with his own comments (e.g., Gal 1:13–14; 1 Cor 15:9; Phil 3:6) and the way Luke's Paul later tells his story (Acts 22:4–5; 26:9–11). Saul's leading role as "the persecution in person"[405] prepares for the statement of 9:31, that the church was at peace "throughout Judea, Galilee and Samaria," for by that time Saul himself had become a believer. Ironically, he would later suffer similar things to those which he meted out here (e.g., 9:23–35, 29–30; 14:2, 4–6, 19–20; 16:19–24; cf. 2 Cor 11:24–26).

Why did Saul persecute believers? It is most likely that he despised and rejected the believers' claims about Jesus as Messiah and Lord.[406] A crucified

---

402 With Fitzmyer, *Acts*, 397; Marshall, *Acts* (TNTC), 151–52; contra Barrett, *Acts*, 1:392; Haenchen, *Acts*, 294.

403 Jervell, *Apostelgeschichte*, 255.

404 Good discussion of usage in *BegC*, 4:88.

405 Schneider, *Apostelgeschichte*, 1:480 (my translation).

406 For discussion of alternative explanations, such as that Saul rejected believers' practice of sharing meals with gentiles or that Jewish believers were espousing politically disastrous

Messiah would be a foolish contradiction in terms to a devout Pharisee (cf. Gal 3:13; 1 Cor 1:22–25). The believers' view of Jesus meant, of course, that what devout Jews most valued, the temple, was now downgraded, for access to God was through Jesus rather than the sacrificial system.[407] Thus the believers were both "accursed lawbreakers, and followers and proclaimers of an accursed deceiver."[408] (See also *Comment* on 9:1.)

κατὰ τοὺς οἴκους εἰσπορευόμενος, "entering house after house," and τε ἄνδρας καὶ γυναῖκας, "both men and women," stress the universality of persecution. The former phrase describes the believers' meetings κατ' οἶκον, "in homes" (2:46; 5:42), and so may suggest that Saul's people entered while they were meeting. The latter phrase indicates that women were significant enough in the new community to be persecuted[409] and later underlines response by both sexes in Samaria (8:12) and Saul's continuing persecution of believers of both sexes (9:2). It is most natural to see these events as taking place in Jerusalem and its environs (note 9:21), particularly in the light of Paul's own statement that the Judean believers were hearing of his persecuting activity (Gal 1:22–23; see further *Form/Structure/Setting: Sources/historicity*).[410]

παρεδίδου εἰς φυλακήν, "handing over to prison," echoes Luke 21:12, showing that these actions are not outside God's control but rather were predicted by Jesus. Ironically, Saul himself will later be imprisoned for his faith; he spends about the last quarter of Acts as a prisoner (16:23–24; 22:24–28:31). παρεδίδου, "he was handing them over" (imperfect), denotes a customary activity, corresponding to the imperfect ἐλυμαίνετο, "he set out to destroy." Saul is thus portrayed as dedicating his life to destroying the believing community.

Explanation

This transitional paragraph plays a key role in Luke's developing story and serves several functions.

First, it closes the chapter of the Jerusalem focus in Acts 1–7 while indicating that God's work continues in the city. The continuing presence of the apostles (8:1b) and the "devout men" who bury Stephen (v. 2) and the believers whom Saul attacks (v. 3) shows that God has not abandoned the city. The missionary growth that will follow is not the founding of a new "religion" but builds on the restored and renewed messianic Israel now established, to include others who were previously outsiders to the people of God.

Secondly, it moves the story on to the next stages of the agenda set in 1:8, Judea and Samaria (8:1b). Luke thus indicates that Jesus's words in 1:8 are

---

stances—each unlikely because they depend on later issues and events—see Schnabel, *Mission*, 2:927–28.

407 Hengel and Deines, *Pre-Christian*, 80–84.

408 Hengel and Deines, *Pre-Christian*, 84.

409 Spencer, *Acts*, 83; Seim, *Message*, 51; Reimer, *Women*, 238.

410 With Dana, "Where," esp. 22–23.

being carried out and that even persecution is subject to his authority; the clear echo of Jesus's earlier warnings about imprisonment (8:3; Luke 21:12) underlines this point. The theme of inclusive growth amidst persecution, and even caused by persecution, is developed in Philip's ministry among Samaritans (Acts 8:5–25), with the Ethiopian eunuch (8:26–40), Peter's travels to Lydda and Joppa (9:32–43), his visit to Cornelius (10:1–11:18), the expansion to Phoenicia, Cyprus, and Antioch (11:19), the establishment of an assembly including "Greeks" (11:20–30), and Herod's persecution of the believers in Jerusalem (12:1–19), which ultimately leads to his death (12:20–23). Acts 8–12 thus forms a unit delineating the contours of this growth.

Thirdly, Luke introduces Saul in preparation for his role in the rest of Acts. The persecutor par excellence is painted in violent colors (8:3) that agree with the impression we receive from Paul's letters (e.g., Gal 1:13–14; 1 Cor 15:9; Phil 3:6). Calvin justly observes on Acts 8:3: "Two things are to be noted here; how great the savagery of their enemies was; and how wonderful the goodness of God was in honoring Paul by making a pastor out of so cruel a wolf."[411]

411 Calvin, *Acts*, 1:228.

III. Mission in Samaria and Syria-Palestine (8:4–12:25)

A. Philip's Divinely Guided Ministry (8:4–40)

1. God Acts through Philip in Samaria (8:4–25)

Bibliography

Adler, N. *Taufe*. **Avemarie, F.** *Tauferzählungen*, 214–66. **Barrett, C. K.** "Light." **Bauckham, R.** "Restoration," 435–87. **Beasley-Murray, G. R.** *Baptism*, 112–20. **Bergmeier, R.** "Gestalt." **Beyschlag, K.** *Simon*. **Blomberg, C. L.** *Neither*, 169–70. **Böhm, M.** *Samarien*, esp. 279–308. **Bowman, J.** *Samaritan Problem*. ———. *Samaritan Documents*. **Brinkhof, Joke H. A.** "Philip," 84–90. **Brodie, T. L.** "Rhetorical Imitation." **Casey, R. P.** "Simon Magus," *BegC*, 5:151–63. **Coggins, R. J.** "Samaritans," esp. 429–32. **Coppens, J.** "L'imposition." **Crown, A. D.**, ed. *Samaritans*. **Cullmann, O.** *Early Church*, 185–92. **Derrett, J. D. M.** "Simon." **Dickerson, P. L.** "Sources." **Drane, J.** "Simon." **Dunn, J. D. G.** *Baptism*, 55–72. ———. "Response" [= *Christ*, 2:222–42]. **Edwards, M.** "Simon." **Ehrhardt, A.** *Acts*, 36–46. **Eisen, U. E.** *Poetik*. **Garrett, S. R.** *Demise*, 61–78. **Gourgues, M.** "Esprit." **Green, J. B.** "Good News to Whom?" ———. "John's Baptism." **Griffiths, J. D.** "Spirit." **Haar, S.** *Simon*. **Haenchen, E.** "Simon." **Hartman, L.** *Name*, 37–50, 136–37. **Hays, C. M.** *Ethics*, 244–45. **Heintz, F.** *Simon*, 102–48. **Heitmüller, W.** *Namen*. **Hengel, M.** "Geography," 67–76 [= *Between*, 121–28]. **Hertig, P.** "Tour." **Hjelm, I.** "Simon." **Hovenden, G.** *Speaking*, 96. **Hull, J. H. E.** *Spirit*, 104–9. **Hur, J.** *Reading*, 239–41. **Janowitz, N.** *Magic*. **Jervell, J.** *Luke*, 113–32. **Johnson, L. T.** *Function*, 213–17. **Klauck, H.-J.** *Magic*, 13–23. **Koch, D. A.** "Geistbesitz." **Kurz, W. S.** *Reading*, 84–86, 144–45. **Lampe, G. W. H.** *Seal*, 66–69. **Lüdemann, G.** "Beginnings." ———. *Untersuchungen*, esp. 39–55. **MacDonald, J.** *Theology*. **MacDonald, W. G.** "Glossolalia," 131–32. **Mansell, P. W.** "Rise," esp. 220–21. **Marguerat, D.** "Magic," 115–23. **Matthews, C. R.** "Philip and Simon." ———. *Philip*, esp. 35–70. **McCabe, D. R.** *Kill*, 148–53. **McCollough, D. J.** *Ritual*, 137–71. **Meeks, W. A.** "Simon." **Menzies, R. P.** *Empowered*, 204–13. **Oulton, J. E. L.** "Spirit." **Ovey, M. J.** *Feasts*, 48–49. **Park, H. D.** *Herem*, 141. **Penney, J. M.** *Emphasis*, 106–7. **Pfitzner, V. C.** "Pneumatic Apostleship," 222–26. **Porter, S. E.** "Magic," 116–17. **Pummer, R.** "State I." ———. "State II." ———. *Samaritans*. ———. *Authors*. ———. *Profile*. **Quesnel, M.** *Baptisés*. **Ravens, D.** *Luke*, 72–106. **Reimer, A. M.** *Miracle*. **Rudolph, K.** "Simon." **Samkutty, V. J.** *Mission*. **Sanders, J. T.** *Jews*, 142–51, 250–2. **Schnabel, E. J.** *Mission*, 1:674–82, 765–79. **Shepherd, W. H., Jr.** *Function*, 179–84. **Skeat, T. C.** "Codex." **Smith, M.** "Account." **Spencer, F. S.** *Portrait*, 26–127, 211–41. **Squires, J. T.** "Plan." **Stenschke, C. W.** *Portrait*, 64–71. **Strelan, R.** "Bar Jesus." ———. *Strange Acts*, esp. 85–89. **Talbert, C. H.** *Gnostics*. **Thiering, B.** "Qumran Initiation," esp. 625. **Thomas, J. C.** *Devil*, 249–54. **Turner, M.** "Interpreting." ———. *Power*, 360–75. ———. *Spirit*, 44–55. **Twelftree, G. H.** "Prayer," 274. **van Unnik, W. C.** "Apostelgeschichte." **Walton, S.** "Ὁμοθυμαδόν." **Wilcox, M.** *Semitisms*, 102–5, 142–43, 155–56, 174. **Wilson, R. McL.** "Simon." **Witherington, B., III.** "Salvation." **Zangenberg, J.** *Frühes Christentum*.

Translation

4 So then, those who had been scattered went from place to place proclaiming the word. 5 Philip went down to the[a] city of Samaria[b] and began preaching[c] the Messiah

to them. 6 The crowds, with one accord, kept paying close attention[d] to the things that Philip was saying as they listened and observed[e] the signs that he was doing. 7 For many of those who had unclean spirits—as they cried out with a loud voice[f] they came out, and many who had been paralyzed or had disabilities[g] were healed, 8 and there was much joy in that city.

9 A certain man, Simon by name,[h] had previously been practising magic[i] in the city and astounding the people of Samaria,[j] claiming that he himself was someone great. 10 All the people, from the least to the greatest, used to pay close attention to him, saying, "This is the power of God that is called[k] great." 11 They paid close attention to him because he had astounded them over a considerable time[l] by deeds of magic. 12 However, when they believed Philip as he proclaimed the good news concerning the kingdom of God and the name of Jesus the Messiah, they were baptized,[m] both men and[n] women. 13 Even Simon himself[o] believed and, after he was baptized, continued to stay in Philip's company; as he saw both signs and great deeds of power taking place, he was astounded.

14 Now when the apostles in Jerusalem heard that Samaria had accepted the word of God, they sent Peter and John to them. 15 Peter and John[p] went down and prayed for them to receive[q] the Holy Spirit; 16 for the Holy Spirit[r] had not as yet fallen upon any of them—they had only been baptized[s] into the name of the Lord Jesus. 17 Then Peter and John[t] laid hands on each of them[u] and they received the Holy Spirit. 18 When Simon saw that the Spirit was given through the laying on of the apostles' hands, he offered them money, 19 saying, "Give this authority to me too, so that, if I lay hands on someone, they will receive the Holy Spirit." 20 Peter said to him, "May your money[v] go with you to destruction,[w] because you supposed[x] you could acquire God's gift with money. 21 You have neither part nor share in this matter,[y] because your heart is not right before God. 22 So repent from this wickedness of yours and humbly pray[z] to the Lord, whether perhaps[aa] the intention of your heart might be forgiven, 23 for I see that you are in[bb] the gall of bitterness and bound to wickedness."[cc] 24 Simon answered, "You yourselves humbly pray to the Lord for me, that[dd] nothing of what you have said may come upon me."[ee]

25 So then, those who had testified and spoken the word of the Lord returned to Jerusalem, proclaiming the good news as they went[ff] to many Samaritan villages.

Notes

a. τήν, "the," is found in 𝔓74 ℵ A B 181 1175 2344 but omitted in C D E Ψ, most minuscules, lectionaries, Coptic MSS and Chrysostom; τήν is missing in the Byzantine tradition; see *Comment* on v. 5.

b. Σαμαρείας, "Samaria," v.l. in ℵ only Καισάρεια, "Caesarea", which Skeat sees as evidence that that ℵ was written in Caesarea ("Codex", 584–85)—a doubtful argument; it is more likely that "Caesarea" appears because that is where Philip is from (8:40; 21:8) (I owe this point to Dirk Jongkind).

c. ἐκήρυσσεν, inceptive impf., "he began (and continued) preaching."

d. προσεῖχον, "[they] kept paying close attention," iterative impf. For translation, see "προσέχω," BDAG 879–80, §2.b.

e. ἐν τῷ ἀκούειν αὐτοὺς καὶ βλέπειν, "as [they] listened and observed," art. infs.

following prep. ἐν suggesting that these events are contemporaneous with προσεῖχον, "[they] kept paying close attention"; Wallace, 595, 611.

f. The confusing syntax here (see *Comment* on v. 7) has led to a number of variant readings: (i) 𝔓[74] ℵ A B C D[c] E 81 1175 *pc* read πολλοί, "many" (nom. pl., a "hanging" nom.), the NA[28]/UBS[5] text, translated above; (ii) H P Ψ 049 056 1 33 a bo; Chr read πολλῶν "of many" (gen. pl.); (iii) D* has πολλοῖς, "many" (dat. pl.), with a blot or erasure allowing space for three or four letters preceding it; there is probably a prep. covered, which could be παρά, "from" (Scrivener, *Bezae*, 442), or ἀπό, "from" (Boismard, *Texte occidental* [2nd ed.], 147, based on the Latin *a multis*, "from many," found in d)—although ἀπό would really require πολλῶν (gen. pl.). Either (ii) or (iii) would lead to treating πνεύματα ἀκάθαρτα, "unclean spirits," as the subject of ἐξήρχοντο, "[they] came out"; indeed, many of the witnesses for (ii) have the sg. ἐξήρχετο, "[it] came out," which would be appropriate in classical usage with the neut. pl. πνεύματα ἀκάθαρτα. The strength of MS support for (i), along with the improbability of scribes creating this reading from the other, smoother, readings, strongly supports (i) (*TCGNT*[2], 312–13; *BegC*, 4:90; ECM, 1:257).

g. χωλοί, "disabilities," denotes various physical disabilities, usually of the legs; cf. 3:2; 14:8.

h. ὀνόματι Σίμων, "by name Simon"; see *Note* b on 5:1.

i. προϋπῆρχεν, "he had previously been" (impf.), functions as an auxiliary verb with μαγεύων (pres. ptc.), "practising magic," to form a periph. impf. (Culy and Parsons, *Acts*, 153, contra BDF, §414[1]). Cf. Luke 23:12 προϋπῆρχον γὰρ ἐν ἔχθρᾳ ὄντες πρὸς αὐτούς, "for previously they had been enemies," the only other NT use of this verb.

j. Heintz, *Simon*, 105–6, suggests that the two ptcs. μαγεύων καὶ ἐξιστάνων, "practising magic and astounding," may share the object τὸ ἔθνος τῆς Σαμαρείας, "the people of Samaria," and thus that μαγεύων should be translated "casting a spell on" or "bewitching." μαγεύων can be transitive or intransitive (LSJ s.v.), so this is not impossible, although the sense of καί, "and," is most likely simply coordinating the ptcs. and thereby denoting what followed from his practice of magic ("καί," BDAG 495, §1.a.ε). That is certainly the sense in v. 11, where instrumental dat. ταῖς μαγείαις denotes "by deeds of magic"; with Culy and Parsons, *Acts*, 154.

k. v.l. (i) καλουμένη, "called," is read by 𝔓[74] ℵ A B C D E 33 81 323 945 1175 *al l*1178 it[ar, c, d, dem, e, gig, p p, r, ro, w] vg cop[bo] arm geo Irenaeus[lat] Origen; (ii) λεγομένη, "said to be," is read by only 614 *pc*; (iii) nothing is read by Ψ 36 307 453 1678 a *Lect* syr[p] cop[sa, meg] eth slav Chrysostom. It is hard to see why the strongly supported and more awkward reading (i) would be introduced if (ii) or (iii) was original; *TCGNT*[2], 313–14; ECM, 1:259.

l. ἱκανῷ χρόνῳ, "over a considerable time," dat. of time, when we would expect acc. for extent of time; Barrett, *Acts*, 1:408; Wallace, 156 with n44.

m. ἐβαπτίζοντο, distributive impf. with the sense, "*each of them* was baptized."

n. τε καί, "both . . . and," is Lukan diction; see *Comment* on 5:14.

o. αὐτός, "himself," emphatic pers. pn. implies a certain amount of surprise hence "even," as RSV, NRSVue.

p. οἵτινες, masc. nom. pl. indef. rel. pron., "who" (a Lukan favorite), referring to Πέτρον καὶ Ἰωάννην, "Peter and John" (v. 14). The translation breaks up a long Gk. sentence which runs from v. 14 to v. 16 and clarifies the grammatical subject.

q. ὅπως, "so that," + subj. λάβωσιν, "they might receive," expresses the purpose of the prayer and thus its content.

r. Gk. has no explicit subject for periph. plpf. ἦν . . . ἐπιπεπτωκός, "had . . . fallen," but the Spirit is clearly in view; so, e.g., NIV, TNIV.

s. βεβαπτισμένοι ὑπῆρχον, periph. plpf., "they had been baptized."

t. Gk. has no explicit subject for ἐπετίθεσαν, "they laid," but clearly refers to Peter and John.

u. ἐπετίθεσαν, "they laid hands," and ἐλάμβανον, "they received," both distributive impf.—each one had hands laid on them and each one received the Holy Spirit. Culy and Parsons, *Acts*, 156, see the impf. as foregrounding these actions.

v. ἀργύριον, lit., "silver money," a different word from v. 18 and later in this verse (there χρήματα) but with no significant difference in meaning; "ἀργύριον," BDAG 128, §2.b.

w. εἴη, lit., "may it be," pres. opt. εἰμί; the opt. here expresses a wish (Wallace, 481–83). The preposition εἰς, "to, into," gives the sense of movement "may it go."

x. or "you are accustomed to," a possible sense of νομίζω + inf. (here κτᾶσθαι, "to obtain"); Park, *Herem*, 141; "νομίζω," LSJ 1179, §I.4.

y. λόγῳ, "matter"; "λόγος," BDAG 600, §1.a.ε; cf. L&N §13.115.

z. δεήθητι, aor. impv. of δέομαι, "ask pleadingly," taking gen. of person asked, here τοῦ κυρίου, "the Lord"; "δέομαι," BDAG 208.

aa. εἰ ἄρα, "whether perhaps"; "εἰ," BDAG 278, §6.a.

bb. εἰς, "in," is used where we would normally expect ἐν, "in," but note the interchangeability of the two prepns in Hellenistic use; BDF, §205; Moule, 67, 70 §1v with note on p. 204.

cc. Taking ἀδικίας as obj. gen., functioning as obj. of the verbal idea in σύνδεσμον, "bound to," contra "σύνδεσμος," BDAG 966, §3, which takes the gen. as epexegetical, "the bond *that consists of* wickedness."

dd. ὅπως + subj. ἐπέλθῃ, "that . . . may come," expressing content of the request, as equivalent of inf. after verb of asking; "ὅπως," BDAG 718, §2.b; contra Culy and Parsons, *Acts*, 159, who treat it as expressing purpose. However, if it expresses a request's content, it necessarily expresses the request's purpose.

ee. D cop^{G67} syr^{hmg} Tertullian Ephraem also read ὃς πολλὰ κλαίων οὐ διελίμπανεν, "who with many tears did not stop weeping," strongly suggesting that Simon does repent (Rius-Camps and Read-Heimerdinger, *Message*, 139, 146–47), thus making explicit a point that is probably implicit in the Alexandrian text.

ff. εὐηγγελίζοντο, "proclaiming the good news," and ὑπέστρεφον, "they returned," both impf., portraying the events as simultaneous.

Form/Structure/Setting[1]

Delimitation of pericope. This story is "bookended" by two uses of εὐαγγελίζομαι, "proclaim the gospel," and τὸν λόγον, "the word," denoting the message proclaimed (vv. 4, 25), both generalized descriptions of proclaiming the gospel.[2] Both are in transitional sentences beginning Οἱ μὲν οὖν, "So then, they/those." Verse 4 picks up from πάντες . . . διεσπάρησαν, "all . . . were scattered," from Jerusalem (v. 1) and completes the geographical change of scene, and μέν is answered by δέ (v. 5), introducing Philip as a specific example of those scattered. Verse 25 closes the Samaritan phase of the story with a change of location as Peter and John return to Jerusalem via the Samaritan villages, and μέν is answered by δέ (v. 26), specifying the different path Philip took

1 This pericope is much discussed; for an excellent literature survey, see Samkutty, *Mission*, 18–53.

2 Spencer, *Portrait*, 26–27.

toward his meeting with the Ethiopian eunuch.[3] Thus the story begins by those scattered moving away from Jerusalem and ends by Peter and John moving toward that city.

Sources/historicity. A range of source hypotheses have been proposed for this story.[4] Because Philip disappears from the narrative after v. 13, and v. 14 clearly begins a new scene, some propose that Peter's or Philip's involvement is a Lukan invention or that one part or other of the story is a Lukan construct.[5] However, it is unlikely that vv. 14–25 existed as a freestanding narrative, since the events there are dependent on those of vv. 4–13.[6] Given the groundbreaking nature of Philip's ministry in Samaria (vv. 4–13), it is unlikely that such a minor character's name would later be attached to a tradition without there being an historical basis for that connection.[7] Indeed, Acts 21:8–9 provides a plausible situation in which the author (or his "we" source) might learn of at least the part of the story in vv. 4–13, for there "we" visit Philip and his family in Caesarea.[8]

Others suggest that the two parts of the story were drawn from different sources, one focused on Philip and one on Peter.[9] However, if so, the narrative as it now stands is so well integrated and presented in thoroughly Lukan diction and style that it is impossible to reconstruct Luke's sources with any confidence.[10] Further, as Samkutty notes, both the Samaritan believers and Simon feature in both parts of the story: it is not Simon alone who connects the two parts.[11]

Haenchen proposes that Simon was originally a gnostic redeemer figure but suggests that Luke "demoted" him to a mere magician.[12] However, Beyschlag argues cogently that one should not simply read back the later portrait of Simon and his disciple Menander as heresiarchs found in Justin (*1 Apol.* 26.2, 4; 56.1, 2; *Dial.* 100.4; 106.3; 120.6) and Irenaeus (*Haer.* 1.23)—the latter calls him "the father of all kinds of heresies."[13] Lüdemann similarly notes that we cannot get beyond the knowledge that Justin and Irenaeus have foisted gnostic beliefs on Simon, for which we lack any reliable first-century evidence.[14]

---

3 Spencer, *Portrait,* 131.
4 See Samkutty, *Mission,* 18–29, summary 26; Turner, *Power,* 361–62; Barrett, *Acts,* 1:51.
5 E.g., Bauernfeind, *Apostelgeschichte,* 124–25; see Samkutty, *Mission,* 18–20, for details.
6 Witherington, *Acts,* 281n10.
7 Matthews, "Philip and Simon," 145–46.
8 With Barrett, *Acts,* 1:51; Witherington, *Acts,* 280n7.
9 E.g., Koch, "Geistbesitz."
10 Contra Dickerson, "Sources," 219–32; see Avemarie, *Tauferzählungen,* 222–24, for a very full list of Lukanisms.
11 *Mission,* 28–29; contra Barrett, "Light," 285.
12 Haenchen, "Simon."
13 Beyschlag, *Simon,* passim. For useful accounts of later portraits of Simon, see Edwards, "Simon"; Hjelm, "Simon."
14 Lüdemann, *Untersuchungen,* 29, although see *Comment* on v. 22. See also Wilson, "Simon";

Heintz regards the story as polemical and convicts Luke of propaganda against Simon by portraying Simon negatively. He doubts that events took place in detail as Luke describes them, although his reconstruction is close to the overall story Luke tells.[15] Certainly Luke does not approve of Simon's prior magical activities or of his attempt to purchase the power to give the Spirit, but Luke's disapproval does not mean he is falsifying events to a substantial degree. Postmodern questions about whose interests are being served by a text do not rule out that what the text reports is substantially historical.

Structure. The story falls into two parts. Verses 4–13 focus on the response to Philip's ministry in Samaria; vv. 14–25 focus on Peter and John's ministry there. Simon is a common factor in both parts (vv. 9–11, 13, 18–24): in the first part he is an outsider who becomes an insider; in the second he is an insider in danger of returning to be an outsider. The Samaritans who respond to Philip are also a common factor in the two parts (vv. 6–8, 11–12, 15–17): in the first, their response to Philip's message and experience of deliverance from spirits and disease is contrasted with their former response to Simon; in the second, the Samaritan believers are (implicitly) recognized as true believers by Peter and John and receive the Holy Spirit, thus completing their initiation according to the pattern of 2:38–39.

While the first part of this story (8:4–13) is ostensibly about Philip's ministry, he is rarely in the spotlight: he is the subject of only two main verbs, ἐκήρυσσεν, "he began preaching" (v. 5), and ἐποίει, "he was doing" (v. 6). Otherwise, he appears only in oblique cases (vv. 6a, 12, 13) and is thus not the focus of the narrative. The people's and Simon's reactions form the heart of the story, for the stress is on the strength and depth of positive response: the crowds unitedly pay close attention (προσεῖχον . . . οἱ ὄχλοι . . . ὁμοθυμαδόν, v. 6); many are delivered from unclean spirits (πολλοί, v. 7a) and many are healed (πολλοί, v. 7b); there is great joy in the city (πολλὴ χαρά, v. 8); the crowds come to faith and are baptized, both men and women (ἄνδρες τε καὶ γυναῖκες, v. 12); and Simon likewise believes and is baptized, then stays close to Philip (v. 13).

That said, there is a fascinating contrast of Philip and Simon through the use of similar terms in relation to both.[16] Luke uses these terms to show that Philip's gospel ministry of word and deed has greater power and effect than Simon's work and that the focus of Philip's ministry is not promoting himself, by contrast with Simon: (i) προσεῖχον, "they kept paying close attention," is used in relation to the crowd's reaction to both (vv. 6, 10, 11), although only in the case of Philip is this attention said to be ὁμοθυμαδόν, "with one accord" (v. 6); (ii) ἐξίστημι, "be astounded," is used for the crowd's reaction to Simon

Meeks, "Simon"; Drane, "Simon" (critiquing Talbert, *Gnostics*, who argues that Luke-Acts was written to defend Christianity against Gnosticism), each coming to similar conclusions.

15 Heintz, *Simon*, 143–48.

16 Samkutty, *Mission*, 134–35; Klauck, *Magic*, 18; Beyschlag, *Simon*, 101.

(vv. 9, 11) and for Simon's reaction to Philip's ministry (v. 13)—but the crowd is not "astounded" by Philip, for he does not draw attention to himself; rather, they believe and are baptized; (iii) μέγας, "great," is used regarding results of Philip's ministry (vv. 7, 13) and concerning Simon himself and his actions (vv. 9, 10)—but Philip himself has no pretensions to greatness; it is his gospel proclamation that has great results; (iv) δύναμις, "power/deed of power," is used concerning Simon himself (v. 10) and of the results of Philip's ministry (v. 13); (v) in v. 13 Philip's success over Simon is described using the three key words ἐξίστημι, μέγας, and δύναμις in quick succession, and Simon begins by astounding people (v. 9) but finishes by being astounded (v. 13).

The second part (vv. 14–25) focuses on the Holy Spirit falling on the Samaritan believers (v. 17) and consequences that flow from that event in relation to Simon. Here Simon offers money to gain authority (τὴν ἐξουσίαν ταύτην, v. 19) to be able to convey the Spirit. Peter's response (vv. 20–23) echoes his dialogue with Ananias and Sapphira (5:3–4, 8–9); like his dialogue with Sapphira, Peter offers Simon chance to tell the truth and repent (v. 22). Simon's response (v. 24)—and the fact that he is not struck down in the same manner as Ananias and Sapphira—suggests that he recognizes his error. Although this part is *prima facie* about Peter and Simon, the spotlight actually falls on what God is doing.

It is the divine focus of the story which also explains why Philip appears tangential: he is God's agent in this new initiative, but at the deepest level, the initiative is truly God's and the various actors in the story are responding to God rather than his human agents alone.[17] Throughout the story, language about God and his actions are prominent. The message proclaimed is τοῦ θεοῦ, "of God" (vv. 12, 14, 25), centers on Jesus the Messiah, into whose name the new believers are baptized (vv. 5, 12, 16), and results in God giving them the Holy Spirit (vv. 15, 17, 18, 19, 20). The proclamation is accompanied by divine activity, both in "much joy" (v. 8, a marker of divine activity: see *Comment* there) and in "signs and great deeds of power" (vv. 6–7, 13, cf. 2:22). Simon's sin is to fail to recognize that God's Spirit is pure gift (v. 20) and to seek to obtain the Spirit by his own efforts—here, financial; thus, Simon's heart is out of tune with God's (v. 21) and he is in danger of divine judgment (vv. 20, 23).

Setting. This story clearly marks an important stage in the fulfillment of the program of 1:8, with the first gospel proclamation outside Judea. However, the roots of this story are found further back, in Luke's Gospel, where Samaritans are significant characters at key points.[18] Most notably, Samaritan villagers reject Jesus because his face is set to go to Jerusalem, producing James and John's request to call fire from heaven down on the village (Luke 9:51–56). That story reflects the hostility between Samaritans and Judeans during

17 Cf. Tannehill, *Unity*, 2:102–3.

18 Samkutty, *Mission*, 102–16, 121, 141–49; Jervell, *Luke*, 113–32.

this period (see *Comment* on v. 5). It is therefore a great reversal that John is one of the two apostles who are involved in the Holy Spirit (imaged as fire in 2:3) falling from heaven on the Samaritan converts, bringing blessing from God rather than judgment,[19] and shows that this story is significant in the drawing together of Jew and Samaritan in the restored Israel. This reopening of relationships through the gospel and the Spirit's coming can be seen as fulfilling the hope for the reunification of the lost northern tribes with the Judean southern tribes (e.g., Ezek 37:15–24).[20] More positively, the good Samaritan (Luke 10:29–37) and the grateful Samaritan among the ten people with leprosy (Luke 17:11–19) suggest that Jesus anticipates Samaritans becoming members of God's people.[21]

It is debated whether the Samaritans should be seen as Jews, gentiles, or a third entity (see *Comment* on v. 5). Whatever our conclusion on this, it is clear from Acts 1:8 that Samaria is an important staging post on the way to "the end of the earth," that is, the gentile mission.[22] This story forms the first step in that direction and will be followed rapidly by the conversions of an African outsider (8:26–40) and Saul, who is to be a prime agent of the gentile mission (9:1–30), Peter's ministry in the Hellenistic cities of Lydda and Joppa (9:32–42), and then the conversion of Cornelius the centurion (10:1–11:18) and the proclamation among "Greeks" in Antioch that produces the first Jew-plus-gentile congregation (11:19–30).

Hearers of Acts next meet Samaritan believers in the summary in 9:31, which draws this section of Acts to a close. After that, we find Barnabas and Saul encouraging Samaritan believers as they travel through on way to Jerusalem (15:3, the last mention of Samaritans in Acts).

Comment

4 μὲν οὖν, "so then," both resumes discussion of those scattered from v. 1b and marks v. 4 as background information to the events of v. 5, where δέ (untranslated) "answers" μέν.[23] It thus links vv. 1b–3 with vv. 5–25 and shifts the narrative to a new location.[24]

Οἱ . . . διασπαρέντες, "those who had been scattered," excluding the apostles (v. 1). It is ironic that Philip, a man rejected by the unbelieving Jewish leadership in Jerusalem (v. 5), will now go to the Samaritans, a people rejected by Jerusalem.[25] It is further divine irony that human attack on the gospel

---

19 Samkutty, *Mission*, 147.

20 Samkutty, *Mission*, 208–10; Bauckham, "Restoration," 470–71; cf. Bowman, *Samaritan Problem*, 61.

21 Samkutty, *Mission*, 107–13.

22 Sanders, *Jews*, 251; Cullmann, *Early Church*, 191.

23 *DFNTG*², 171.

24 E.g., as 1:6; 2:41; 5:41; 8:4. 25; 9:31; 11:19; 12:5; 13:4; 15:3, 30; 16:5; Bruce, *Acts* (1990), 216; Barrett, *Acts*, 1:400; Haenchen, *Acts*, 301.

25 Ravens, *Luke*, 92.

community becomes the means by which God works out his expansive purposes and the next stage of the fulfillment of the program of 1:8, as the gospel goes to Samaria.[26]

διῆλθον, "they went about from place to place,"[27] portrays the scattered believers as not settling in one place but traveling around, since they are εὐαγγελιζόμενοι τὸν λόγον, "proclaiming the word," a phrase used of both the apostles' work (5:42) and the proclamation of both Jesus (Luke 4:18, 43; 7:22; 20:1) and the apostles (v. 25; Luke 9:6), as well as for godly, divinely appointed spokespeople in Luke's Gospel.[28] διέρχομαι, "go about," itself is widely used later in Acts for Jesus's own ministry (Acts 10:38) and itinerant Christian missionary activity.[29] The scattered believers, including Philip, are thus being portrayed as acting in the same way and conveying the same message as Jesus and his followers (see *Comment* on vv. 5, 12), underlining Luke's portrait of the earliest believers as united in their central message and in tune with their Master.

5 Φίλιππος, "Philip," is mentioned without further specification. It seems natural to take him to be the Philip who was one of the seven along with Stephen (6:5), rather than the apostle (1:13), given that this story follows the Stephen stories (6:8–8:1a) and that the apostles remain in Jerusalem (v. 1).[30] The later Acts of Philip assumes that there is only one Philip who has the features of Luke's two Philips, as does Matthews, on the doubtful basis that the second-century sources (especially Polycrates and Papias) are more reliable than Luke.[31] δέ (untranslated) is correlative to μὲν οὖν, "So then" (v. 4), making Philip a specific example of the activity of the scattered believers.[32]

κατελθών, "went down," has three nuances, all of which contribute to its sense here: first, it is used because Samaria is nearer sea level than Jerusalem and thus "down"; secondly, it may be used because to go to Jerusalem was to "go up" because the latter was the capital;[33] thirdly, with εἰς, "to," and a location it suggests a purposeful going,[34] expressed by the main verb on which this participle depends, ἐκήρυσσεν, "he began preaching."

Σαμάρεια, "Samaria," is mentioned without introduction (contrast John 4:9), assuming that readers recognize the significance of the gospel's journey to this location. Luke has mentioned Samaritans at key points in his Gospel (Luke 9:51–56; 10:29–37; 17:11–19; see *Form/Structure/Setting*: *Setting*), and 1:8 has prepared for Philip's mission there. Samaritans are monotheists who

---

26 On this irony, see Kurz, *Reading*, 144–45.
27 "διέρχομαι," BDAG 244, §1.a.
28 Luke 1:19; 2:10; 3:18; 4:18, 23; 7:22; 8:1; 9:6; 16:16; 20:1.
29 Acts 8:40; 9:32; 13:6, 14; 14:24; 15:3, 41; 18:23, 27; 19:1, 21; 20:2; see "διέρχομαι," *EDNT* 1:323.
30 Spencer, *Portrait*, 34.
31 Matthews, *Philip*, esp. 64–70.
32 With Kurz, *Reading*, 144.
33 E.g., Acts 11:2; 15:2; 21:12, 15; 25:1, 9; Luke 18:31; 19:28; John 5:1; 11:55; Gal 1:17, 18; 2:1.
34 Cf. Acts 9:32; 11:27; 13:4; 15:30; 19:1; "κατέρχομαι," BDAG 531, §2.

see themselves as faithful descendants of Israel: they observe circumcision and keep the food laws and other provisions of the Torah. While there are other significant differences in belief between Judean Jews and Samaritans, notably over the canonical status of books outside the Pentateuch (which the Samaritans reject but most Judeans accept[35]), the Samaritan temple on Mount Gerizim is the focus of this hostility, for Judeans believe it to be heretical, whereas Samaritans regard the Jerusalem temple as degenerate and corrupt (cf. Luke 9:53; John 4:20; Josephus, *Ant.* 18.2.2 §30; 20.6.1–2 §§118–30).[36] Thus from a mainstream Judean perspective, Samaritans are seen as outsiders to the people of God, even hated. Sirach 50:25–26 characterizes the Samaritans as οὐκ . . . ἔθνος . . . ὁ λαὸς ὁ μωρὸς ὁ κατοικῶν ἐν Σικιμοις, "not . . . a nation . . . the foolish people who live at Shechem," and Josephus as τῶν ἀποστατῶν τοῦ Ἰουδαίων ἔθνους, "apostates from the Jewish nation" (*Ant.* 11.8.6 §340; cf. John 4:9). Hence Luke can refer to a Samaritan as ἀλλογενής, "a foreigner" (Luke 17:18). However, Samaritans are not seen by Luke as outright gentiles or as syncretistic deviants from Judaism but more like estranged distant cousins of the Jews.[37] They may be seen as the heirs of the ten lost northern tribes (Ezek 37:15–24).[38] It is sometimes not noticed that the Samaritans continue to this day.[39]

Should we read "*a* city (πόλιν) of Samaria" or "*the* city (τὴν πόλιν) of Samaria," and to which city is Luke referring? While the presence of the article has strong support (see *Note* a above), and its absence lacks early Alexandrian support, the decision also hinges on how the genitive τῆς Σαμαρείας, "of Samaria," is taken. Four possibilities are proposed: (i) a city belonging to Samaria (possessive genitive, no article); (ii) the city that is Samaria (epexegetical genitive, with article); (iii) the city of Samaria, i.e., Luke supposed there was only one city (possessive genitive, with article);[40] (iv) a particular city of Samaria (possessive genitive, with article, taking the article as indicating an important city of the region). The strength of manuscript support for the article rules out (i).[41] Each rendering including the article (ii, iii, and iv above) has problems attached,

35 However, the Sadducees shared the Samaritans' view on this, Schürer, 2:407–9.

36 For overviews of the Samaritans, see R. T. Anderson, "Samaritan Literature," and H. G. M. Williamson and C. A. Evans, "Samaritans," *DNTB* 1052–61; Samkutty, *Mission*, 188–89 (summarizing 57–98); Pummer, "State I"; Pummer, "State II"; Pummer, *Samaritans*, 1–25; or the major treatments in Crown, ed. *Samaritans*; Pummer, *Profile*; Böhm, *Samarien* (the latter in relation to Luke-Acts). See also the valuable primary sources for the first five Christian centuries (with English translations) collected in Pummer, *Authors*, with summary of issues: 6–10; and Bowman, *Samaritan Documents*.

37 Pummer, *Profile*, 40–41; Jervell, *Luke*, 117–23; Ravens, *Luke*, 93; Sanders, *Jews*, 250; Stenschke, *Portrait*, 64–69; contra Bowman, *Samaritan Problem*, 69–70.

38 Ravens, *Luke*, 97–105; cf. Coggins, "Samaritans," 432–33.

39 See Pummer, *Profile*, 289–301. In 1987 Pummer estimated there were only slightly over five hundred people; Pummer, *Samaritans*, 1.

40 Barrett, *Acts*, 1:402.

41 Contra Böhm, *Samarien*, 281–89.

in spite of its strong external support—and this causes the NA[28]/UBS[5] editors to include τήν, "the," in square brackets and rate the reading including it as C, expressing significant hesitation about including it.[42] (iv) seems the most likely of these options, since (ii) and (iii) would require Luke's knowledge of geography to be sketchier than it seems to be; if Luke's source for this story is Philip himself (at first or second hand), they seem more unlikely.

Assuming (iv) to be most likely, some identify the city as Shechem (cf. 8:16), the Samaritan religious center.[43] However, Shechem was destroyed in 128 BC and we lack evidence of its repopulation prior to AD 72, when it was rebuilt as Flavius Neapolis.[44] Others suggest Gitta, Simon Magus's birthplace according to Justin (*1 Apol.* 26),[45] but we lack any early evidence for this identification. The capital of Samaria was generally known as Sebaste (rather than Samaria) by NT times and was strongly Hellenized,[46] whereas Philip's preaching of τὸν Χριστόν, "the Messiah," suggests a mission focused on ethnic Samaritans.[47] The difficulties lead Hengel, among others, to conclude that Luke envisages a prominent city that is not Sebaste.[48] However, there is no reason to think that Sebaste did not have *any* ethnic Samaritan population,[49] and thus it seems most likely that Luke refers here to Sebaste and Philip's audience includes Samaritans and other ethnic groups. Josephus can use Σαμάρεια, "Samaria," when he means the city (e.g., *Ant.* 17.10.9 §289), and on one occasion writes Σαμαρείᾳ τῇ κληθείσῃ Σεβαστῇ, "Samaria, which is called Sebaste" (*Ant.* 15.7.7. §246),[50] suggesting that the older name "Samaria" may have continued to be used. For Luke to use "Samaria" suits his purpose in showing the fulfillment of 1:8.[51] Overall, to regard the city as being Sebaste is the solution with least problems.

ἐκήρυσσεν αὐτοῖς τὸν Χριστόν, "he began preaching the Messiah to them." Luke continues to describe Philip's preaching in terms used for John the baptizer, Jesus, the apostles,[52] and later Paul[53] (see *Comment* on v. 4 above). These echoes suggest that Luke wishes his hearers to understand that Philip's preaching was similar to the fuller summaries of Peter's preaching (2:14–36; 3:12–26).[54] Philip preaches τὸν Χριστόν, "the Messiah," whereas he will proclaim

---

42 *TCGNT*², 311. ECM, 1:255, has a split-line reading, also indicating hesitation; see discussion, ECM, 3.3:11–12.
43 E.g., Pesch, *Apostelgeschichte*, 1:272.
44 Hengel, "Geography," 73; Samkutty, *Mission*, 74–76; Zangenberg, *Frühes Christentum*, 29–31.
45 *BegC*, 4:89.
46 Hengel, "Geography," 71.
47 Bruce, *Acts* (1990), 216.
48 Hengel, "Geography," 76.
49 See the cogent arguments of Samkutty, *Mission*, 88–97.
50 Hemer, *Book*, 225–26.
51 Gaventa, *Acts*, 136.
52 Luke 3:3; 4:18, 19, 44; 8:1; 9:2; 24:47; Acts 10:37.
53 Acts 9:20; 10:42; 19:13; 20:25; 28:31.
54 With Gaventa, *Acts*, 135.

τὸν Ἰησοῦν, "Jesus," to the African eunuch (8:35). This underlines that his audience are already monotheists (contrast 17:16–31, where Paul argues for monotheism in Athens) and that his preaching focuses on Jesus as the fulfillment of messianic hopes. Τὸν Χριστόν *simpliciter* is also used in summaries of central themes of the gospel (cf. 2:31; 3:18; 9:22; 17:3; 26:23), so this term should not be understood to limit Philip's preaching to messianic themes alone. Through the gospel, the Samaritans are being restored to Israel, an Israel which is being reconstituted around Jesus as Messiah. Significantly later sources attest the Samaritans' expectation of a messianic figure later called the *Taḥeb*, a Moses redivivus figure, based on Deut 18:18–22 (cf. John 4:25).[55] Josephus (*Ant.* 18.4.1 §§85–87) reports an incident from AD 36 where a Samaritan announced that he would show the people the sacred vessels hidden by Moses on Mount Gerizim. Dunn suggests that Philip's preaching was misheard as announcing the imminent arrival of the *Taḥeb* and thus interpreted in nationalistic terms—hence Peter and John needed to come (Acts 8:14) to correct this wrong impression.[56] However, Luke gives no hint that the Samaritans misunderstood Philip's preaching. Further, the choice of verbs for Philip's preaching in vv. 4, 5 parallels the preaching of other believers, suggesting that Philip delivers the same message as them.[57]

6 προσεῖχον, "they kept paying close attention." The imperfect portrays ongoing action. Bruce suggests it includes the idea of a favorable response,[58] whereas Johnson considers that it here has the sense of "mental attentiveness" by contrast with the uses in vv. 10, 11, where he sees it as denoting "commitment of the heart."[59] However, there are no co-textual clues to suggest differing senses in these uses, and Luke reserves πιστεύω (v. 12) for "commitment of the heart," so it is likely that προσέχω simply denotes "pay close attention" in all its uses in this story. Nevertheless, there is a clear contrast between their former close attention to Simon (vv. 10, 11) and their present close attention to Philip (v. 6): in both cases the individuals make claims (vv. 5, 9), and signs and deeds of power are significant (vv. 6, 11). Philip's message is about another, "the Messiah" (v. 5), whereas Simon's is about himself (v. 10). As in Luke's Gospel, people considered marginal by those holding power in the Jewish world (here, the Samaritans) respond positively to the proclamation (e.g., people in poverty, those who are ill or have disabilities, demonized people, those regarded as unclean).[60]

τὰ σημεῖα, "the signs," are here, as earlier in Acts, signs of the new age of the

---

55 See MacDonald, *Theology*, 359–71.
56 *Baptism*, 63–64.
57 Turner, *Power*, 363; Menzies, *Empowered*, 208.
58 *Acts* (1990), 217.
59 Johnson, *Acts*, 145.
60 See, e.g., Green, "Good News to Whom?"; Roth, *Blind*; Dawson, *Healing*; Witherington, "Salvation; Klutz, *Exorcism*; Walton, "Heavens."

Spirit (2:19, 43; 4:16, 22, 20; 5:12; 6:8), and Philip's ministry is thus portrayed as Spirit-enabled.[61] There is a power encounter going on here between the forces of Satan and those of God, which may also underlie the reference to the "kingdom of God and the name of Jesus the Messiah" as a key part of the content of Philip's preaching. God's rule is challenging that of Satan, and God's Messiah is greater than Satan.[62]

ὁμοθυμαδόν, "with one accord," highlights the unity of the crowds' attitude and action[63] and echoes the description of the Jerusalem believers' unity (1:14; 2:46; 4:24; 5:12). Barrett observes, "[T]hey began to be united with one another as they accepted the Christian message."[64]

ἐν τῷ ἀκούειν αὐτοὺς καὶ βλέπειν, "as [they] listened and observed." These present infinitives suggest ongoing action, in tune with the imperfects of the main verbs προσεῖχον, "[they] were paying close attention," and ἐποίει, "he was doing." Hearing about God and seeing what God does through Philip are both components in the Samaritans coming to faith in Jesus as Messiah—Philip's message alone is not persuasive; 8:7 (introduced by γάρ, "for") goes on to explain the nature of the things they saw.

7 πολλοὶ γὰρ τῶν ἐχόντων πνεύματα ἀκάθαρτα βοῶντα φωνῇ μεγάλῃ ἐξήρχοντο, "For many of those who had unclean spirits—as they cried out with a loud voice they came out." This is the first explicit mention of deliverance from evil spirits in Acts (although cf. 5:16), echoing Jesus's ministry (Luke 4:18–19, 31–44; 7:21–22; 8:1–2; 9:37–43; 11:14–26). The further connection that Philip also proclaims the kingdom of God (Acts 8:12) underlines that Philip is from the same mold as Jesus (Luke 11:22).

The syntax here is somewhat unclear and gives rise to a number of alternative readings (see *Note* f): the natural subject for ἐξήρχοντο, "they came out," is πολλοί, "many," but this refers syntactically to the people who had the spirits rather than the spirits who came out. This may be "mental telescoping," treating the accusative πνεύματα ἀκάθαρτα, "unclean spirits," as if it were the nominative subject of the verb, and thus a mark of incomplete revision of the text.[65] Haenchen considers that this way of speaking confuses the people with the spirits,[66] but it is natural, even if not grammatically correct.[67]

βοῶντα φωνῇ μεγάλῃ, "as they cried out with a loud voice," echoes the experience of Jesus's deliverance ministry (Luke 4:33; 8:28) and again presents Philip's ministry as in proper succession to his Master and the apostles

61 With Strelan, *Strange Acts*, 85; contra Matthews, *Philip*, 78.
62 Garrett, *Demise*, 63–65.
63 Walton, "Ὁμοθυμαδόν," 100.
64 Barrett, *Acts*, 1:403.
65 *BegC*, 4:90.
66 Haenchen, *Acts*, 302.
67 Cf. Fitzmyer, *Acts*, 403, who considers this to be Luke's way of speaking of mental illness.

(Acts 5:16). Μέγας, "great," occurs seven times in this story (8:7, 9, 10 [twice], 13), suggesting that Luke highlights the issue of true and false greatness.

As Jesus healed those with a disability of the lower limbs (Luke 7:22) and Peter and John were the agents of healing such a man (χωλός, Acts 3:2), so Philip is the agent of healing πολλοὶ . . . παραλελυμένοι καὶ χωλοί, "many who were paralyzed or lame." Philip's actions also recall the summary of the Jerusalem assembly's effectiveness (5:16).[68] Again, Philip is painted in apostolic colors (cf. 9:33; 14:8). Thomas notes that Luke distinguishes healing and deliverance from spirits and thus does not attribute all illness to direct demonic or satanic influence.[69]

The healing and deliverance ministry are not merely signs extrinsic to the message Philip proclaims but intrinsic demonstrations of the reality of which the gospel speaks.[70] Thus it is both through these "signs" (8:6) and Philip's interpretive words (v. 5) that God's rule/kingdom invades enemy territory in Samaria (v. 12).

8 πολλὴ χαρά, "much joy," is a common sign of God's saving action in Luke-Acts, brought by the Holy Spirit (Luke 2:10; 24:52; Acts 13:52; 15:3).[71] The positive and glad response of the Samaritans stands in ironic contrast to the Judeans who recently rejected the believers (8:1b). Here, Luke makes a striking contrast: Simon's magic produced astonishment and acclaim (vv. 9–11), but Philip's preaching produced joy.

9–11 introduce Simon, although mainly in terms of others' response to him, which is unusual for a new character.[72] About Simon himself we learn three main things.

(i) Simon previously μαγεύων, "practised magic" (v. 9; an NT *hapax legomenon*), and performed μαγείαις, "deeds of magic" (v. 11); the latter probably included passing spells for payment to clients who could use them.[73] The cognate nouns μαγεία, "magic," and μάγος, "magician," are found in the NT (13:6, 8; Matt 2:1, 7, 16), although LXX only has three uses of the word group (Wis 17:7; Dan 2:2, 10). The meaning—even the use—of the term "magic" is contested in recent scholarship,[74] but it is clear that, by the contrast with Philip, Luke uses the term pejoratively, as others did (e.g., the Greeks identified "magicians," μάγους, as "wizards," γόητας, Dio Chrysostom, *Or.* 36.41[75]).

68 Ehrhardt, *Acts*, 42.
69 Thomas, *Devil*, 253–54.
70 For this distinction, see Turner, *Holy Spirit*, 247, 251.
71 With Jervell, *Apostelgeschichte*, 260, contra Pesch, *Apostelgeschichte*, 1:273.
72 Dickerson, "Sources," 218–19.
73 Heintz, *Simon*, 106: Lucian of Samosata criticizes a disciple of Apollonius of Tyana who does such things as a γόης, "a quack," Lucian, *Alex.* 5 [LCL Harmon]. Heintz's article provides many helpful sources on ancient perceptions of magicians.
74 See Porter, "Magic," 109–15; Janowitz, *Magic*, 2–26; Garrett, *Demise*, 13–36, esp. 22–36; Marguerat, "Magic," 115–18.
75 Strelan, "Bar Jesus," 66, unintentionally mis-cites this as 39.41. I am grateful to Dr. Strelan for giving me the correct reference.

Indeed, it is possible that Simon had performed actions similar to Philip's, but Luke's labeling of Simon's actions as "magic" shows that his evaluation of Simon was negative.[76]

(ii) Simon draws attention to himself, claiming to be τινα . . . μέγαν, "someone . . . great" (v. 9); λέγων εἶναί τινα ἑαυτόν, "claiming himself to be someone," echoes the description of Theudas, who led a failed rebellion (5:36). Others identify Simon as ἡ δύναμις τοῦ θεοῦ ἡ καλουμένη μεγάλη, "the power of God that is called great" (v. 10). Two inscriptions and a magical papyrus provide interesting parallels to this phrase:[77] "one god, ruler of all things, great [μεγάλη] Kore, the unconquered" (late-third/fourth century AD, Samaria);[78] "one god in the heavens, great [μέγας] heavenly Mên, great power [μεγάλη δύναμις] of the immortal god" (no date, Lydia);[79] "I call upon you, the great power [τὴν μεγίστην δύναμιν], who is in the heaven, appointed from god" (*PGM* IV.1275–79). In Luke's usage elsewhere, ἐκ δεξιῶν τῆς δυνάμεως τοῦ θεοῦ, "at the right side of the power of God" (Luke 22:69), and ἐκ δεξιῶν τοῦ θεοῦ, "at the right side of God" (Acts 7:55–56), suggest that "the power" here is likely a synonym for "God";[80] Haenchen sees the title as a claim to be "the highest divinity itself."[81] More broadly, Garrett compares Luke's use of δύναμις, "power," in the Gospel, where it designates divine power (1:35; 4:14, 36; 5:17; 6:19; 8:46; 9:1; 10:13, 19; 19:37; 21:27; 22:69; 24:49).[82] Thus, Simon's claim is usurping the place of God, in similar manner to Satan's inviting Jesus to worship him (Luke 4:6–7), and may well have resulted in Simon being worshiped by the crowds.[83] Inevitably, this would lead to conflict with Philip's message, which presents Jesus as exercising sovereignty over the universe, and thus draws attention away from Philip and onto Jesus (cf. Acts 3:12–13; 10:26, 36–43; 14:14–15).[84] In Luke's narrative, to draw glory to oneself rather than give it to God will inevitably result in judgment (cf. Herod in 12:23, and contrast Barnabas and Saul in 14:14–17).

(iii) The people respond to Simon with astonishment and acclaim: ἐξίστημι, "be astonished," is used in 8:9, 11; cf. this verb as reaction to God's action in 2:7, 12; 9:21; 10:45; 12:6. Their close attention (προσεῖχον) to Philip (8:6) mirrors their previous close attention to Simon (same verb, vv. 10, 11). Their universal acclaim of Simon by πάντες ἀπὸ μικροῦ ἕως μεγάλου, "all from least

76 Reimer, *Miracle*, 76–77; Klauck, *Magic*, 15. Cf. Philo, *Spec. Leg.* 3:100–101, distinguishing true and counterfeit magic.

77 Porter, "Magic," 116–17.

78 *NewDocs* 1, §68.

79 *NewDocs* 3, §7.

80 Spencer, *Portrait*, 92.

81 Haenchen, *Acts*, 303.

82 Garrett, *Demise*, 65–67.

83 Smith, "Account," presents evidence that someone might make such a claim in the first century. A common accusation against magicians is arrogance; Heintz, *Simon*, 116.

84 So Tannehill, *Unity*, 2:106.

to great" (v. 10), is replaced by the crowds' united (ὁμοθυμαδόν, "with one accord" [v. 6]) response to Philip's proclamation and deeds. In highlighting the people's response to Simon, Luke prepares for the inevitability of conflict.

12 ἐπίστευσαν τῷ Φιλίππῳ, "they believed Philip." πιστεύω + dative has the sense "believe a person."[85] Dunn claims that this shows the response was defective, since the Samaritans merely assented mentally to Philip's message rather than trusting in Jesus.[86] However, Lydia's (genuine) response to Paul's preaching is portrayed in very similar terms (16:14; cf. 18:8; Luke 10:16). Further, the participial clause εὐαγγελιζομένῳ περὶ τῆς βασιλείας τοῦ θεοῦ καὶ τοῦ ὀνόματος Ἰησοῦ Χριστοῦ, "as he proclaimed the good news concerning the kingdom of God and the name of Jesus the Messiah," indicates both that the response was to the message Philip preached and that the message was the apostolic gospel (see below). Moreover, ἐπίστευσαν suggests a decisive coming to believe (inceptive aorist), and the response in baptism is the same as at Pentecost (2:41). The report of v. 14 gives no hint that the Samaritans' response was other than complete, echoing phrases from indubitably genuine conversions in 2:41; 11:1, 18, and Peter and John make no effort to correct Philip's teaching as faulty—they assume the Samaritans are genuine believers and pray for them to receive the Spirit.[87]

εὐαγγελιζομένῳ περὶ τῆς βασιλείας τοῦ θεοῦ καὶ τοῦ ὀνόματος Ἰησοῦ Χριστοῦ, "as he proclaimed the good news concerning the kingdom of God and the name of Jesus the Messiah," continues to portray Philip in apostolic colors (see *Comment* on vv. 4, 5). περὶ τῆς βασιλείας τοῦ θεοῦ, "concerning the kingdom of God," recalls the summary of Jesus's post-resurrection teaching (1:3; see *Comment* there). Philip follows Jesus and the apostles in proclaiming the good news of the kingdom (Luke 4:43; 8:1; 9:2; 10:9, 11; 16:16); Paul will be portrayed in similar terms (Acts 14:22; 19:8; 20:25; 28:23, 31). As here, the name of Jesus or the Lord or simply Jesus has been the theme of apostolic proclamation (2:21; 4:17–18; 5:28, 40, 42; 8:35; 11:20), functioning both as a summary of the apostolic gospel and denoting the power brought by the message: this name is also the power of healing (3:6; 4:10, 29), the object of faith (3:16; 4:12), and invoked in baptism (2:38; 8:16).[88]

ἐβαπτίζοντο, "they were baptized." The proper response to proclamation of the gospel message is baptism, as in 2:38 (see *Comment* there). Little is said of the content of this baptism other than that it is εἰς τὸ ὄνομα τοῦ κυρίου Ἰησοῦ, "in the name of the Lord Jesus" (v. 16), for two reasons. First, Luke expects

85 "πιστεύω," BDAG 816–18, §1.b; it is unusual to find the dative of the preacher, Barrett, *Acts*, 1:408.

86 Dunn, *Baptism*, 65. He later modifies this view: Dunn, "Response," 24–25 [= Dunn, *Christ*, 2:222–42].

87 For these points, see Turner, *Power*, 365–66; Samkutty, *Mission*, 158–59; Menzies, *Empowered*, 208–10.

88 On "the name," see *Comment* on 2:38, with Spencer, *Portrait*, 42–44.

his hearers to treat this baptism as following the 2:38 model—and v. 16 will highlight the surprise that the 2:38 model has not been fully completed by the coming of the Spirit (see *Comment* on 8:15–17). Secondly, Luke has already spoken of the content of the proclamation in the previous phrase τῆς βασιλείας τοῦ θεοῦ καὶ τοῦ ὀνόματος Ἰησοῦ Χριστοῦ, "the kingdom of God and the name of Jesus the Messiah": this is the message to which baptism is an appropriate response. Since no other believers are mentioned, Philip is the likely baptizer, as in 8:38—both 8:12–13 and 8:38 are unusual in Acts in naming the (human) baptizer.[89] Luke does not use "salvation" language in this story, and Turner rightly (and roundly) criticizes Menzies for an inadequate understanding of salvation according to Luke. Turner rightly sees "salvation" as much more than receiving forgiveness of sins and entering into justification.[90]

ἄνδρες τε καὶ γυναῖκες, "both men and women," respond to Philip's message; Luke again parallels male and female responsiveness (cf. 5:14; 17:12, 34), as he parallels the persecution of both sexes (8:3; 22:4).[91]

13 This is the only sentence in the passage where Philip and Simon coincide, and Conzelmann therefore suspects it to be a Lukan creation.[92] However, Beyschlag shows that there is a strong parallelism between Simon and Philip in this whole story and that v. 13 is essential to this parallel.[93] Further, it seems unlikely that Luke would create a link between Simon and Philip in this way, since he would be more interested in moving directly to the clash between Simon and Peter; it is thus likely that this verse is based on traditional information.[94]

ὁ δὲ Σίμων καὶ αὐτὸς ἐπίστευσεν καὶ βαπτισθείς, "Even Simon himself believed, and afterwards he was baptized." While καί, "even," and the emphatic personal pronoun αὐτός, "himself," suggest a certain amount of surprise on the narrator's part, there is no reason to doubt the genuineness of Simon's conversion: readers will naturally regard the content of what he believes as being the same as others who believed and were baptized in v. 12.[95] That said, his faith is "not yet so firm as it ought to be,"[96] as the clash with Peter will show (vv. 18–24), perhaps because Simon's faith depends too much on miraculous phenomena rather than the message about Jesus.

ἦν προσκαρτερῶν τῷ Φιλίππῳ, θεωρῶν τε σημεῖα καὶ δυνάμεις μεγάλας γινομένας ἐξίστατο, "[he] continued to stay in Philip's company; as he saw both signs and

89 Brinkhof, "Philip," 85.

90 Menzies, *Empowered*, 204–13, esp. 204, 211; similarly, Chrysostom, *Hom. Act.* 18; critique: Turner, "Interpreting," 268–71, 272–73, 275.

91 On Luke's pairing of men and women, see Seim, *Message*, 11–24.

92 *Acts*, 64; so also Barrett, *Acts*, 1:409.

93 Beyschlag, *Simon*, 101; summary in English in Samkutty, *Mission*, 161.

94 With Lüdemann, *Early Christianity*, 98.

95 Turner, *Power*, 366–67; Menzies, *Empowered*, 208–10; contra Dunn, *Baptism*, 55–68; Witherington, *Acts*, 285.

96 Klauck, *Magic*, 18.

great deeds of power taking place, he was astounded," summarizes Simon's continuing reaction to Philip's ministry using imperfect verbs.[97] Simon's reaction mirrors that of the crowds to him: ἐξίστημι, "be amazed," is also used in v. 11. It also echoes the Pentecost crowds' reaction to Spirit-produced phenomena (2:7, 12), and thus this lexical choice should not be seen as denoting mere admiration for a fellow magician.

τε σημεῖα καὶ δυνάμεις μεγάλας, "both signs and great deeds of power," echo two of the terms used concerning Jesus's ministry in 2:22 and once again underline that Philip (like Stephen in 8:6) faithfully instantiates his Master's example and exercises the same power. The terms chosen equally echo Philip's performing σημεῖα, "signs," (v. 6), and, ironically, Simon's claims to be δύναμις . . . μεγάλη, "power . . . great" (v. 10). The terms chosen also echo the miracles done by Moses as Stephen reports them (7:36).[98] These miracles involve a clash between Moses and Pharaoh's magicians (Exod 7–11), and it may be that Philip is being painted in the colors of a prophet like Moses, in succession to Jesus (cf. Acts 7:37, 39).[99]

14 The focus switches to the apostles who are confined to Jerusalem (v. 1), and the report they receive suggests that the response in Samaria is genuine, for Luke uses a favorite phrase for the authentic gospel message, τὸν λόγον τοῦ θεοῦ, "the word of God" (see *Comment* on 4:31), and combines it with δέδεκται, "[they] had received," to echo other authentic responses (2:41; 11:1; 17:11)[100]—this verb contrasts with the refusal of the Samaritans to receive Jesus, using the same verb as here: οὐκ ἐδέξαντο αὐτόν, "they did not receive him" (Luke 9:53). The perfect δέδεκται suggests that they received the word and continued to hold to it.

ἀπέστειλαν πρὸς αὐτοὺς Πέτρον καὶ Ἰωάννην, "they sent Peter and John to them," expresses no explicit motive for the visit. Peter and John appear as a pair, as earlier in Acts 3:1, 3, 11; 4:13, 19; this will be the last mention of John in Acts. The parallel with Barnabas's visit to Antioch (11:22) suggests that the two apostles were a delegation to assess what was happening in Samaria[101] (cf. the use of ἀποστέλλω in Luke 9:2, 52; 10:1; 22:8 for Jesus sending people) and to encourage the new believers. Some regard this as the visit of a supervisory team[102] and, because the Spirit comes through the apostles' ministry, a visit that minimizes the success of Philip.[103] However, nothing in Acts "measures" the quality of ministers of the gospel by whether the Spirit comes through their ministry or not.[104] Indeed, nothing in this sentence and the following

97 Hence Squires, "Plan," 31, regards it as a "summary statement."
98 Spencer, *Portrait*, 47–48.
99 Spencer, *Portrait*, 103–22, assembles a case for this.
100 So also Penney, *Emphasis*, 107.
101 Barrett, *Acts*, 1:410.
102 Bruce, *Acts* (1990), 220.
103 Haenchen, *Acts*, 304; full discussion: Samkutty, *Mission*, 33–42.
104 Samkutty, *Mission*, 35.

one indicates that Peter and John knew that the Spirit had not yet fallen on the new believers before they traveled from Jerusalem.[105] The apostles' readiness to pray for the Spirit to come recognizes the validity of Philip's evangelism, and Peter and John join in evangelizing Samaria afterwards (8:25).[106] The Jerusalem delegation's visit has the effect of recognizing the Samaritan believers as genuine and reverses the antagonism Peter and John had toward the Samaritans who rejected Jesus (Luke 9:51–56).[107] Given the general antagonism between Judeans and Samaritans, it is remarkable that the apostles sent a delegation to Samaria at all.[108]

15–17 Peter and John meet a striking situation in Samaria, οὐδέπω γὰρ ἦν ἐπ' οὐδενὶ αὐτῶν ἐπιπεπτωκός, "for [the Holy Spirit] had not as yet fallen upon any of them" (v. 16a). There is evident surprise in the authorial voice here, expressed by the strong double negative οὐδέπω . . . οὐδενί, "not yet . . . no one," and the intensive periphrastic pluperfect ἦν . . . ἐπιπεπτωκός, "had fallen," which highlights the continuing state of the Spirit not having fallen, by contrast with the norm of 2:38. If it were normal for the Spirit's coming to be separate from water baptism, 8:16 would be redundant.[109] This phrasing suggests that there were expected clear signals that the Spirit had come (see *Comment* on v. 18 and cf. Gal 3:1–5). Oulton seems to argue that it was the Spirit's outward manifestation that was missing, whereas the "inner life which is the gift of the Spirit" was already manifest.[110] Cf. Beasley-Murray's tentative suggestion that the Samaritan believers lacked the spiritual gifts rather than the Spirit.[111] Both suggestions fail to hear the surprise in Luke's voice here that πνεῦμα ἅγιον, "the Holy Spirit" (v. 15)—rather than the Spirit's gifts—had not fallen. The fact that Philip is from the Hellenistic group of seven who are πλήρεις πνεύματος, "full of the Spirit" (6:3), and thus fully conversant with experience of the Spirit, supports the historicity of this statement, for it goes against the grain of Luke's overall story.[112] The metaphor of the Spirit falling is used for the first time in Acts and recurs at 10:44; 11:15.

By contrast with the Samaritan believers' (non-)reception of the Spirit, the periphrastic pluperfect βεβαπτισμένοι ὑπῆρχον "they had been baptized" emphasizes that their baptism is a completed action in past time. They were

105 Hull, *Spirit*, 104–5.
106 Tannehill, *Unity*, 2:105.
107 Samkutty, *Mission*, 139–43, 212.
108 Gaventa, *Acts*, 137.
109 Turner, *Power*, 360–75; Turner, "Interpreting," 267. The evident surprise in Luke's voice at the abnormal separation of water baptism from receiving the Spirit means Thiering's claim that this separation is similar to initiation at Qumran is mistaken; Thiering, "Qumran Initiation," 625.
110 "Spirit," 238.
111 *Baptism*, 118–19.
112 Avemarie, *Tauferzählungen*, 259; his further proposal that Philip therefore practised a baptism like John's, purely denoting repentance for forgiveness of sins, runs beyond the evidence of 9:12, 16, which specify the content of this baptism as in the name of Jesus.

baptized εἰς, "into," the name of the Lord Jesus, clarifying that this is *Christian* baptism, as in 19:5 (cf. *Comment* on 2:38, where ἐπί is used with no significant difference in meaning). This is the first use of εἰς τὸ ὄνομα, "into the name," in a baptismal setting in Acts, a formula that may represent a rather literal translation into Greek of a Hebrew or Aramaic idiom meaning "with regard to," expressing the framework within which the action of baptism took place (cf. m. Zeb. 4:6).[113] Heitmüller's older view is that the phrase parallels usage found in ancient banking, where to put money εἰς τὸ ὄνομα, "into the name," denotes that the money enters the possession of the one named.[114] Hartman rejects this view on the ground that baptism and banking come from very different worlds.[115] However, Hartman's rejection is premature, for images from a wide range of Greco-Roman life are plundered by Christians in attempts to express their faith. It is notable that the formula here is baptism into the name τοῦ *κυρίου* Ἰησοῦ, "of the *Lord* Jesus," and that echoes the early Christian confession that Jesus is Lord (Rom 10:9; 1 Cor 12:3; Phil 2:11)[116] and thus implies submission to his authority, an idea not far from Heitmüller's proposal for the phrase's content, if not its derivation.

The apostles pray (Acts 8:15a) and lay hands (v. 17a) on the Samaritan believers so that they might receive the Holy Spirit. Both features are important: prayer marks dependence on God to give the Spirit, and hand-laying identifies the one being prayed for. For Jews to touch Samaritans, whom they considered unclean, is notable.[117] Since the exalted Jesus is the one who pours out the Spirit (2:33), it is likely that the prayer should be understood to be addressed to Jesus. Laying on hands is mentioned three times in this passage (8:17, 18 [twice]), in each case with the consequence of the Spirit being received. Barrett argues that these verses do not imply that the gift of the Spirit is contingent on laying on of hands—this is a special case, not regular practice,[118] contra Quesnel, who suggests that there are two separate rites: water baptism representing repentance, and laying on of hands, which mediates the Spirit.[119] Thus 10:44 has the Spirit fall prior to water baptism without any human agency at all, although Heb 6:2 shows that laying on hands could be juxtaposed with baptism (cf. Tertullian, *Bapt.* 8.1–2). Indeed, "The Spirit is given in answer to prayer . . . but always and only *given*."[120] God's initiative and power lie at the heart of apostolic (indeed, Christian) ministry according to Luke. Laying on hands generally has three main significances in

113 So Hartman, *Name,* 41–50.
114 Heitmüller, *Namen.*
115 Hartman, *Name,* 39–40.
116 See J. A. Fitzmyer, "κύριος," *EDNT* 2:328–30.
117 Hertig, "Tour," 110.
118 Barrett, *Acts,* 1:412; so also Twelftree, "Prayer," 274; cf. Hur, *Reading,* 240, observing that laying on of hands is not "a necessary means of receiving the Spirit."
119 Quesnel, *Baptisés,* 177, 194.
120 Barrett, "Light," 295 (my italics).

the NT: (i) transfer of power, especially for healing (e.g., 9:12, 17); (ii) prayer or blessing for a person (e.g., 28:8; cf. Gen 48:14; Mark 10:16);[121] (iii) commissioning for a task (e.g., Acts 6:6;[122] 13:3; 14:23).[123] Recall that Ananias lays hands on Saul (9:17–18), which clarifies that this activity is not solely an apostolic prerogative.[124] Bruce proposes that laying on hands is about incorporating Samaritans into the believing community and assuring them of their membership, as does Samkutty, noting that this happens with the Hellenistic seven (6:3, 6).[125] Lampe agrees but goes on to suggest that the laying on of hands constitutes a commissioning for mission.[126] But if this were so, why is there no mention of any evangelistic work by the Samaritan believers? In 8:25 it is Peter and John who evangelize other Samaritan villages.

Samkutty suggests that the descent of the Spirit here, symbolized by "fire" elsewhere in Luke-Acts (e.g., Luke 3:15–17; Acts 2:1–4), fulfills an unfulfilled "contract" from Luke 9:54, where James and John wish to call down fire from heaven on Samaritans but are not allowed to do so by Jesus.[127] On the part of the Samaritans, the hostility to Jesus, who was traveling to Jerusalem (Luke 9:53), is now gone, and they have welcomed Philip's message and Peter and John's prayer ministry, which both came from Jerusalem (Acts 8:4–5, 14–15).

Why did the Samaritans not receive the Spirit until the apostles came from Jerusalem? Four main explanations have been proposed. (i) Their faith was inadequate and not yet Christian.[128] However, there is no evidence that Peter and John saw need to correct Philip's inadequate preaching. (ii) They did in fact receive the Spirit when they were baptized but lacked experience of spiritual gifts.[129] However, v. 16 specifically says that the Spirit had not yet ἐπιπεπτωκός, "fallen," on them, and other uses of this verb in Acts are about the Spirit himself, not spiritual gifts (10:44; 11:15). (iii) Luke presents two different baptismal paradigms in Acts 8, one ἐν τῷ ὀνόματι Ἰησοῦ Χριστοῦ, "in the name of Jesus the Messiah," for forgiveness of sins (2:38; 10:48), associated with Spirit reception, and another from Hellenistic-Pauline circles εἰς τὸ ὄνομα τοῦ κυρίου Ἰησοῦ, "into the name of the Lord Jesus" (v. 16), associated with union with the death of Jesus.[130] However, this reads a Pauline theology into v. 17 and falsely separates Philip's baptism from that of 2:38. (iv) The separation ensured that the Samaritan believers were recognized by Jerusalem believers as genuine, since two leading apostles had had a hand in their initiation into

121 Cf. "What else is [the laying on of hands] but prayer over a person?" Augustine, *Bapt.* 3.16.
122 See *Comment* there.
123 Turner, *Power,* 372; cf. Adler, *Taufe,* 62–81; Coppens, "L'imposition," 406–7, 412–32.
124 Pfitzner, "Pneumatic Apostleship," 223.
125 Bruce, *Acts* (1990), 221; Samkutty, *Mission,* 162.
126 *Seal,* 69–72.
127 *Mission,* 126.
128 Dunn, *Baptism,* 55–68, esp. 65.
129 Beasley-Murray, *Baptism,* 118–19; Oulton, "Spirit"; Gourgues, "Espirit."
130 Quesnel, *Baptisés,* 48–53, 92–98; Dickerson, "Sources," 228; cf. Turner, *Power,* 369–70.

the community of Jesus and had seen God act in sending the Spirit on the Samaritans:[131] "[T]he presence of the Spirit assures the reader that the plan of God is working as promised."[132] Samkutty observes that the long-standing mutual hostility between Samaritans and Judeans meant that acceptance by the Jerusalem leadership of the believers was vital to the inclusion of the Samaritan believers—Luke is thus legitimating the Samaritan mission and the Samaritan believing community.[133] It is unlikely, given that Luke regards the exalted Jesus as the believing community's center,[134] that Jerusalem is being seen as a "mother church" to which new communities must relate.[135] Green notes that when water and Spirit baptism are separated in Acts, the believing community needs particular conviction that it is appropriate to incorporate the new people, for their incorporation leads to a metamorphosis of the believing community.[136] This principle applies both here and with Cornelius (10:44–48). The comparison with the twelve "disciples" in Ephesus (19:1–7) is also instructive, for there is no significant interval between water and Spirit baptism there since those Jewish people's incorporation as believers is not in question (see *Comment* on 19:1–7).

18–19 The story now refocuses on Simon. *ἰδὼν δὲ ὁ Σίμων*, "when Simon *saw*" (v. 18), suggests that there was some tangible manifestation of the Spirit's coming, and it is natural to think of similar phenomena from other occasions when the Spirit comes in Acts, such as speaking in tongues and/or prophesying (2:4; 10:46; 19:6), since this event appears to be a "Samaritan Pentecost."[137] Simon may himself received the Spirit in this manner, since he had been baptized along with others (8:13) and is now in conversation with Peter, through whom the Spirit comes on the Samaritan believers (v. 15).

προσήνεγκεν αὐτοῖς χρήματα, "he offered them money." Simon's offer is to purchase the ability to give the Spirit rather than to purchase the Spirit himself. It is wrongheaded and displays at least three misunderstandings; it shows that, although he may profess faith in Jesus, his worldview is not yet transformed into that of the believing community. He is thus not a reliable character.[138] The Jewish exorcists of Ephesus make a similar mistake in treating the name of Jesus like a spell (19:13–16).[139]

First, Simon assumes that Peter and John are in control of the Spirit in a

131 Hur, *Reading*, 241.
132 Shepherd, *Function*, 182.
133 *Mission*, 175.
134 Walton, "Tale," 144–46.
135 Contra Pfitzner, "Pneumatic Apostleship," 225.
136 Green, "John's Baptism," 172.
137 Hovenden, *Speaking*, 96; Dunn, *Acts*, 111; Jervell, *Apostelgeschichte*, 264; MacDonald, "Glossolalia," 131–32.
138 With Hur, *Reading*, 135.
139 Heintz, *Simon*, 126–27.

similar way to Simon's own control of spiritual forces through magic.[140] Rather, the reality is that the Spirit comes (or not) at God's behest, for that is why the apostles need to *pray* for the Spirit to fall (8:15). This error causes Simon to desire to have the same authority himself; he is continuing to make the mistake of wanting to have himself at the center of his "world" rather than realizing that believers have God-in-Jesus at the center of their world. The presence of κἀμοί, "to *me* too," signals this self-focused world. Believers' generous handling of possessions in giving them away and sharing with others demonstrates their response to God visiting them (2:44–45; 4:32–35), whereas Simon's desire to put himself at the center shows a basic and sinful misunderstanding.

Secondly, Simon believes that the authority Peter and John seem to have can be bought and sold: the aorist imperative δότε perhaps suggests, "here and now, give."[141] He is impressed by τὴν ἐξουσίαν ταύτην, "this authority," which he sees Peter and John exercising and wants this, for it is greater than mere δύναμις, "power," even Simon's claim to be "the great power of God" (vv. 10, 13). In this he assumes a model of control of spirits similar to that followed by priests of pagan idols[142] and may reflect his previous magical practice if we translate ἐνόμισας διὰ χρημάτων κτᾶσθαι as "you are accustomed to obtain with money" (v. 20, see *Note* x). ἐξουσία, "authority," may connote that Simon seeks leadership in the community comparable to that which he had previously.[143] However, the Spirit is given *freely*. The lexical choices are notable here, for χρήματα, "money," is regularly used negatively in Acts, of money offered for bad reasons (see *Comment* on 4:37), and δωρεάν, "gift" (8:20) is characteristically used in classical and biblical sources for divine gifts.[144] Simon's attitude here contrasts sharply with believers who share possessions earlier in Acts (2:44–45; 4:32–35); Simon's evil heart is shown by his handling of possessions—a Lukan theme.

Thirdly, Simon's request suggests that he hopes to make money by charging people who wish to receive the Holy Spirit from him.[145] A standard criticism of magicians in antiquity is that they were in it to make money.[146] Brodie thus suggests that Simon is modeled on Gehazi, Elijah's avaricious servant (2 Kgs 5:19b–27),[147] but there are few contacts in wording between this account and LXX 2 Kgs 5: the similarity seems to end with this one point. It is remarkable,

---

140 Casey, "Simon," *BegC*, 5:151; Eisen, *Poetik*, 116–17.

141 As van Unnik notes, this is clearly a different issue to the later responses to Gnotics, such as by Justin Martyr; van Unnik, "Apostelgeschichte," 404. Thus, van Unnik concludes that Acts was written in a context "where the conflict with Judaism and certain expressions were the dominant problem" (409, my translation).

142 Derrett, "Simon," 63.

143 Wall, "Acts," 139; cf. W. Foerster, "ἐξουσία," *TDNT* 2:569–70.

144 "δωρεά," BDAG 266; Lindars, *John*, 181–82.

145 Samkutty, *Mission*, 163; Garrett, *Demise*, 70.

146 Plato, *Leg.* 909B; Philo, *Spec. Laws* 3:100–1; Lucian, *Philops.* 14–16; Celsus *apud* Origen, *Cels.* 1.68; Juvenal, *Sat.* 6.542–47; Philostratus, *Vit. Apoll.* 8.7; with Hays, *Ethics*, 244.

147 Brodie, "Rhetorical Imitation," 59–63.

by contrast with Simon's hopes for financial gain, that the Spirit is given without price through the apostles; money provides an index of spirituality, as frequently in Luke-Acts, for the apostles give freely and Simon wishes to use money to acquire authority for himself.[148]

20 Peter treats Simon as an insider, rather as Peter did Ananias and Sapphira (5:1–11),[149] and presents him with the dangerous reality of his situation; cf. Lev 19:17, which states that a person should warn a neighbour who sins.[150] Philip is not mentioned here, which suggests there is no implied rebuke of Philip for having baptized Simon: the rebuke is focused on Simon himself.[151]

τὸ ἀργύριόν σου, "your money," is fronted in Peter's speech for emphasis: the offensive thing Simon does is to offer money for something God gives freely. Just as Simon's offer of money symbolizes his attitude of wrongly wanting authority for himself, so here the potential destiny of his money symbolizes Simon's potential destiny.[152] The situation is so serious that Peter wishes εἴη εἰς ἀπώλειαν, "may [it] go to destruction," echoing Nebuchadnezzar's dire threats of physical destruction in Theodotion's rendering of Dan 2:5c; 3:96 (MT 3:29). ἀπώλεια is also used in magical papyri for casting out of demons to go εἰς τὸ μέλαν χάος ἐν ταῖς ἀπωλείαις, "into the black chaos in perdition" (*PGM* IV:1247–48[153]). Although found only here in Luke-Acts, other NT authors use ἀπώλεια for eternal destruction,[154] and that is the probable sense here since repentance is always focused on the final day of judgment (e.g., 17:30–31).[155] The link with the Ananias and Sapphira story suggests that Peter is using a technical *ḥerem* formula that places Simon under God's curse unless he repents.[156] By contrast with the amoral world of the magical papyri, where people seek to use power from the spiritual world without any court sitting in judgment on their actions, Luke's symbolic universe has God as righteous judge in a central place.

τὴν δωρεὰν τοῦ θεοῦ, "God's gift," is also fronted within its clause, thus highlighting a twofold contrast with Simon's offer of money. Magic seeks to gain control, whereas the Spirit, who is God's gift, is given freely—but *God* is in control of the process of giving, not his human servants (as in 10:45; Luke 11:13).[157] Simon's focus is entirely in the wrong place.

21 οὐκ ἔστιν σοι μερὶς οὐδὲ κλῆρος ἐν τῷ λόγῳ τούτῳ, "You have neither part

---

148 Johnson, *Function*, 215.
149 Samkutty, *Mission*, 167.
150 Haar, *Simon*, 185.
151 Brinkhof, "Philip," 88.
152 Johnson, *Function*, 216.
153 Translation: Betz, ed. *Papyri*, 62.
154 Matt 7:13; Rom 9:22; Phil 1:28; 3:19; 2 Thess 2:3; 1 Tim 6:9; Heb 10:39; 2 Pet 2:1, 3; 3:7, 16; Rev 17:8, 11; cf. LXX Prov 27:20; Sir 51:2; Isa 33:2; 34:12; Ezek 26:19–21.
155 Garrett, *Demise*, 71.
156 Park, *Herem*, 141.
157 On the Spirit as gift, see further Griffiths, "Spirit," arguing that Luke sees the Spirit as a gift bringing social consequences and effects in building community among believers.

nor share in this matter," warns Simon that he is in real and present danger of exclusion. Cf. Deut 12:12; 14:27, 29 LXX, where the Levites are said οὐκ ἔστιν αὐτῷ μερὶς οὐδὲ μεθ' ὑμῶν, "they have neither part not lot with you," and note the echo of κλῆρος, "share," from the story of Judas's replacement (Acts 1:17, 26).[158] τῷ λόγῳ τούτῳ, "this matter," recalls λόγος in 8:4, 14, where it denotes the gospel message, and that perhaps suggests that Luke regards the gospel itself as the thing Simon has no part in.[159] Alternatively, it may denote the apostolic ministry more broadly[160] or specifically the giving of the Spirit.

ἡ γὰρ καρδία σου οὐκ ἔστιν εὐθεῖα ἔναντι τοῦ θεοῦ, "because your heart is not right before God." καρδία, "heart," denotes the seat of the will, for it is Simon's actions that show he is in a bad state. The key to the situation is his standing ἔναντι τοῦ θεοῦ, "before God," a characteristically Septuagintal phrase found almost two hundred times to denote life with God (e.g., Lev 5:19; Deut 1:41; Judg 3:7, 12; Prov 3:32; Sir 3:18; Isa 23:18; Bar 1:17). The whole phrase echoes Ps 77:37 LXX (MT 78:37), ἡ δὲ καρδία αὐτῶν οὐκ εὐθεῖα μετ' αὐτοῦ, "their heart was not right with him," and it is notable that the psalm continues with an assurance of God's readiness to forgive and turn away his wrath (Ps 77:38 LXX [MT 78:38]), as Peter will continue here. Simon's heart is where his true treasure is (Luke 12:34).[161]

22 μετανόησον οὖν ἀπὸ τῆς κακίας σου ταύτης καὶ δεήθητι τοῦ κυρίου, "So repent from this wickedness of yours and humbly pray to the Lord." Because the central issue is Simon's standing before God, Peter calls him to change his attitude to God and call upon God. The aorist imperative μετανόησον, "repent," suggests, "here and now, repent!" The unusual combination with ἀπὸ τῆς κακίας σου ταύτης, "from this wickedness of yours," highlights a particular sin from which to repent, as in Jer 8:6 LXX; 1 Clem 8:3,[162] and may reflect a Semitic idiom, for the combination of μετανοέω and ἀπό is rare in LXX, but equivalent expressions are found in Targumic renderings of Gen 18:21; 19:24; Exod 10:28; 14:29; Job 36:10b; Jer 18:8; Ezek 33:12, and in the Dead Sea Scrolls (1QS V, 1; CD XV, 7).[163] δεήθητι, "humbly pray," echoes the way the believers pray in Acts 4:31; Cornelius is characterized as praying this way too (10:1), and the eunuch will speak to Philip similarly (8:34). Two important pastoral implications for Luke's hearers follow: that sin can and does persist in those who profess faith in Jesus and that repentance and forgiveness are available in that situation.[164]

εἰ ἄρα ἀφεθήσεταί σοι ἡ ἐπίνοια τῆς καρδίας σου, "whether perhaps the

158 See McCabe, *Kill*, 151; Hays, *Ethics*, 245.
159 Barrett, "Light," 294.
160 Johnson, *Acts*, 149.
161 Hays, *Ethics*, 245.
162 Samkutty, *Mission*, 165.
163 Wilcox, *Semitisms*, 103–4.
164 With Ovey, *Feasts*, 49; cf. Hertig, "Tour," 107.

intention of your heart might be forgiven," here has an implied protasis "if God wills." The combination εἰ ἄρα, "whether perhaps," suggests some doubt about whether Simon will be forgiven,[165] but this hinges on Simon's readiness to repent and pray (or not!), not on God's willingness to forgive a sinner who repents (cf. Neh 9:17). ἡ ἐπίνοια τῆς καρδίας σου, "the intention of your heart," expands on the reference to "heart" in v. 21 using the NT *hapax legomenon* ἐπίνοια, "intention, thought," which can denote positive or negative thoughts (cf. 2 Macc 12:45; 4 Macc 17:2; Wis 6:16; 9:14; 14:12; 15:4). Although this word is later used for Helen, Simon Magus's supposed consort (Hippolytus, *Haer.* 6.19; cf. Justin, *1 Apol.* 26, who calls her πρώτη ἔννοια, "the first idea," which Simon generated), there is no evidence for Lüdemann's conjecture that there was originally a reference to Helen here and Luke amended the tradition to refer ironically to her.[166] Lüdemann's claim illustrates the danger of reading this story through the lens of later speculation about Simon. As Barrett suggests, Luke's use of a gnostic-sounding term here is more likely to have given rise to the use of the term in later (orthodox) believers' criticisms of gnostics.[167]

23 ὁρῶ, "I see," echoes the use of this verb in v. 18, ἰδών, "when he saw," but Peter's perception is deeper than Simon's purely outward sight, for he sees into Simon's inner bondage.

Simon's situation is expanded using two metaphors. χολὴν πικρίας, "the gall of bitterness," denotes that Simon is in a state of sin; χολή, "gall," is a bitter-tasting herb (Matt 27:34). For the combination, cf. Deut 29:17 LXX, MT (EVV 18), ἐν χολῇ καὶ πικρίᾳ, "with gall and bitterness" (echoed in Heb 12:15), and that in the co-text of a condemnation of idolatry that is particularly apposite to Simon, who claimed to be great and was recognized as such (Acts 8:9, 10). The expression πικρότερον χολῆς, "bitter as gall," is also found in Prov 5:4 LXX, warning against breaking covenant with God (there, by pursuing a loose woman), again paralleling Simon's situation. σύνδεσμον ἀδικίας, "bound to wickedness," portrays Simon as chained to sin, treating the genitive ἀδικίας as objective rather than epexegetical.[168] Cf. Isa 58:6 LXX λῦε πάντα σύνδεσμον ἀδικίας, "loose every bond of wickedness," a verse quoted in Luke 4:18–19, which states Jesus's program for his ministry. Simon is in a state of helplessness from which God alone can free him; this is why he needs to turn to God and cry out for mercy from God (Acts 8:22).

24 Simon now recognizes that it is God who does things, not human beings, and so he asks Peter and John δεήθητε, to "pray humbly," echoing v. 22, that God will not harm him. The man who had been known as "the

165 Moule, 158n1.

166 Lüdemann, "Beginnings," 424; Lüdemann, *Early Christianity*, 100–101. For cogent critique in detail, see Bergmeier, "Gestalt."

167 Barrett, *Acts*, 1:416. For a comprehensive overview of discussion up to 1977 of whether Simon was a magician or a gnostic, see Rudolph, "Simon."

168 Contra "σύνδεσμος," BDAG 966, §3.

great power of God" will not even consider approaching Peter's God to pray for himself.[169] Luke leaves the ending of the story open, not saying explicitly whether Simon did truly repent or not. Garrett sees Simon's reaction as that of a "cornered criminal" rather than as expressing genuine penitence, and as resembling Pharaoh, who asked Moses to intercede for him (Exod 8:8, 28; 9:18; 10:17).[170] However, there are other occasions in Acts where impenitent people are struck down and killed by God, notably Ananias and Sapphira (5:1–11) and Herod Agrippa I (12:20–23), and Simon is not said to die. Luke's silence concerning such judgment of Simon is thus compatible with the view that Simon's request may be evidence of genuine repentance and turning back to God that was carried through, although Simon's fate is not Luke's focus.[171] Alternatively, Luke may simply have lacked information concerning Simon's ultimate response.[172] The implication of the open ending for Luke's hearers, somewhat like the ending of Jesus's parable of the two sons (Luke 15:25–32), is to portray two incompatible ways to live, in submission to Jesus or focused on oneself, and to call them to follow Jesus.[173]

25 μὲν οὖν, "so then," signals that Luke draws the threads of this story together and moves the action on with this succinct summary.[174] Thrall notes that most NT uses fit classical usage "as a particle of transition, and adverbially, chiefly in answers in dialogue."[175] This may connect with δέ ("Now," v. 26, see *Comment* there) and (if so) contrasts Peter and John's return to Jerusalem with Philip's trip into the desert.[176]

Οἱ . . . διαμαρτυράμενοι καὶ λαλήσαντες τὸν λόγον τοῦ κυρίου, "those who . . . had testified and spoken the word of the Lord." First, Luke draws this episode to a close by summarizing their activities and suggests that they stayed for a little time in the city, as Peter will with Cornelius (10:48). The articular participle Οἱ . . . διαμαρτυράμενοι καὶ λαλήσαντες, "those who . . . had testified and spoken," in combination with μὲν οὖν, "so then," suggests that the grammatical subject is the whole group who have been testifying and speaking, which certainly includes Peter and John, and perhaps Philip (see above on μὲν οὖν); it may have wider reference to the group mentioned in 8:4, Οἱ . . . διασπαρέντες, "those who . . . were scattered."[177] This summary echoes the

169 Spencer, *Acts*, 89.
170 Garrett, *Demise*, 72.
171 Calvin, *Acts*, 1:242; Fitzmyer, *Acts*, 407; Barrett, *Acts*, 1:417–18; Johnson, *Acts*, 153.
172 Garrett, *Demise*, 73. Blomberg, *Neither*, 170, suggests that the setting, with later church tradition, implies that Simon does not repent. The use of later tradition is not a strong argument.
173 Cf. Hertig, "Tour," 110.
174 "μέν," BDAG 630, §2.e; cf. Spencer, *Portrait*, 131.
175 Thrall, *Particles*, 34–36, quoting 34.
176 See *Form/Structure/Setting*: *Delimitation of pericope* on 8:26–40, commenting on δέ (v. 26).
177 With Mansell, "Rise," 220–21; contra NRSVue, which mistakenly inserts "Peter and John" as the subject.

devotion of the earliest believers in Jerusalem following Pentecost to the apostolic teaching (2:42).

Luke then moves his characters off stage in order to prepare for Philip's return to center stage in 8:26. In v. 25 ὑπέστρεφον is inceptive: "they set off to return." Wallace notes that inceptive use of the imperfect often denotes a topic shift, underlining the transitional nature of μὲν οὖν, "so then."[178]

The distributive imperfect εὐηγγελίζοντο, "they proclaimed good news," portrays the group evangelizing each of the villages they visited as they traveled to Jerusalem.[179] Peter and John do not merely approve Philip's mission but actively participate in it,[180] since they have been convinced that God is at work among the Samaritans by God sending the Spirit. There is no mention of the Samaritan believers evangelizing; this makes problematic Menzies's view that the Spirit's role is only empowerment for mission, and the appeal to the rather vague and distant summary in 9:31 as the sole evidence for the Samaritan believers evangelizing is unlikely.[181]

Explanation

Philip is the second of the seven (6:5), following Stephen (6:8–7:60), to move in an evangelistic direction. As one of those scattered by persecution in Jerusalem (8:4) he goes to Samaria (v. 5), which Luke has signaled as a key destination on the journey of the gospel to "the end of the earth" (1:8). Luke seems to locate him in Sebaste, the principal city of Samaria ("*the* city of Samaria," 8:5) and a strongly Hellenized city, but a city that probably has a "native" Samaritan population too.

The Samaritans share many beliefs with Judean Jews, but not all: they regard the Pentateuch alone as authoritative Scripture (in common with the Judean Sadducees) and see their temple on Mount Gerizim as a valid place for worship (by contrast with the Judeans' exclusive focus on the Jerusalem temple). They are looking forward to a messianic figure, known later (and perhaps at this time) as the *Taḥeb*. Philip's proclamation of Jesus as Messiah (v. 5) suggests that he builds upon the Samaritans' existing monotheistic beliefs and messianic expectations and engages with Scripture in similar manner to the sermons given in Jerusalem (e.g., 2:14–36; 3:12–26). Philip's proclamation is presented in similar terms to that of John the baptizer, Jesus, and the apostles (Luke 3:3; 4:18, 19, 44; 8:1; 9:2; 24:47; Acts 10:37), implying there is no inadequacy in it. This proclamation, in combination with God acting in healing and deliverance from unclean spirits (8:6–7, a further sign that Philip's work is

178 Wallace, 544–45.

179 Schnabel, *Mission*, 1:765–69, lists a wide range of Samaritan settlements which may have been visited by the apostles.

180 Johnson, *Acts*, 150.

181 Menzies, *Empowered*, 212–13, following Lampe, *Seal*, 69–72. Critique: Turner, *Power*, 372–73.

in similar vein to that of the apostles), leads to a widespread positive response by the people expressed in baptism (v. 12), similar to that seen in Judea (cf. 2:43; 3:1–10; 4:16–17, 22; 5:12; 6:8). Luke stresses that what they both hear and see is significant in their response (8:6).

Luke's introductory portrait of Simon contrasts sharply with Philip (vv. 9–11): (i) Simon practises magic, whereas Philip serves God and proclaims God's word (vv. 4–5); (ii) Simon draws attention to himself, seeking divine honors and worship as "the great power of God," whereas Philip preaches a message about another, the Messiah (v. 5), and seeks a response of faith to him; (iii) universal acclaim of, and close attention to Simon is replaced by a united response of faith in Jesus, baptism, and close attention to Philip's message (vv. 6, 12). However, Simon—"Even Simon"! (the surprise in Luke's voice is clear)—responds to Philip's proclamation; he has met a power greater than his and is amazed (v. 13). There is no suggestion here that Simon's response is not genuine. His later wrong actions show that his mindset needs further change but do not suggest that he is pretending or merely impressed in accepting baptism.

Luke continues to emphasize that the response to the gospel in Samaria is genuine by stating (with understandable hyperbole) that "Samaria had accepted the word of God" (v. 14), thus portraying this response in similar terms to others that are indubitably genuine (4:31 with 2:41; 11:1; 17:11) and contrasting with the Samaritans who refused to accept Jesus (Luke 9:52–53). This news leads the Jerusalem apostles to send Peter and John, a remarkable decision given the antagonism between Judeans and Samaritans. Luke does not explicitly say why Peter and John are sent, but the parallel with Barnabas's visit to Antioch (Acts 11:22–24) suggests that at least part of the purpose is to support and encourage the new believers. John's involvement is particularly striking, for he and James had asked Jesus about calling down fire on a Samaritan village that rejected him (Luke 9:52–54). A great reversal of attitude is going on here among Jesus's disciples, suggesting that the legitimacy of acceptance of the Samaritans is being underlined as a fruit of the gospel of Jesus. The further contrast with Jesus forbidding the disciples to go to Samaritans (Matt 10:5–6) underlines that such a change did not happen before Jesus's death and resurrection and the gift of the Spirit.

The surprise for Luke's hearers is that the Spirit has not yet fallen on the Samaritan believers (Acts 8:16), breaking the pattern of Christian initiation set in 2:38. Peter and John respond to this eventuality by prayer and laying on hands, here signifying prayer for the Spirit (cf. 9:17; 19:6). Since the Spirit is sent at the behest of the exalted Jesus (2:33), the apostles have no control over the Spirit's coming and can only ask. Acts 2:33 rather suggests that they pray to Jesus for this, a striking development. "The church possesses the inestimable privilege of having the Spirit as its guide and defender, but it has the privilege as a gift which it may depend on but cannot control, and never possesses in its own right."[182]

The coming of the Spirit has visible manifestation, for Simon can see that it has happened (8:18). This "new Pentecost" provides strong evidence that the Samaritan believers are genuine (cf. 10:44–48; 11:15–18) and leads to Peter and John evangelizing Samaritan villages as they return to Jerusalem (8:25). There is no suggestion that Philip's earlier ministry was inadequate: his deeds of power (vv. 6–7) are works of the Spirit, as earlier in Acts (cf. 2:43; 5:12).

Luke now portrays how far Simon has yet to travel in his journey of faith. Simon's offer of money to gain the authority to lay hands and thereby give the Spirit (8:18–19) shows three serious errors: (i) he assumes Peter and John control the Spirit in the way that he sought to control spiritual forces through magic, whereas the Spirit comes on God's initiative; (ii) he believes that the authority Peter and John have can be bought and sold, whereas the Spirit is "the *gift* of God" (v. 20), given freely; (iii) by implication, Simon considers that he can make money by charging people who wish to receive the Spirit, as magicians were paid for casting spells, whereas the Spirit is given without price.

Peter's response treats Simon as a believer, in similar manner to Ananias and Sapphira (5:1–11), and confronts him with the serious danger he is in. Simon's approach to money, as often in Acts, is emblematic of his standing with God—he is in mortal danger of perdition (8:20). The way back is to change direction from this evil path and make earnest request of God, for it is against God he has offended (v. 22). Simon in return asks Peter to pray for him, for he now dare not approach God whom he has so offended (v. 24). The close of the story leaves open whether Simon repents, but the contrast with Ananias and Sapphira, who collapse dead when confronted with their misdeeds, suggests that he does.

The role of this story in the flow of Acts focuses on God's purpose to restore Israel, which has been partially achieved in Judeans responding to the gospel of Jesus. The response of Samaritans to Philip's proclamation of Jesus as Messiah begins to enlarge the believers' understanding of the nature of God's action and represents a wider circle of inclusion within God's purposes.

A comparison with the later story of the gentile Cornelius's conversion shows that Samaritans are included in the restored Israel: (i) when Peter and John visit (vv. 14–24) it is because Samaria has received the word of God (v. 14), whereas when Cornelius becomes a believer, there are doubts in Jerusalem (11:2–3); (ii) when the Jerusalem meeting concerning gentile inclusion takes place (15:6–29), there is no suggestion that Samaritan inclusion is under debate. Indeed, Paul and Barnabas visit believers in Samaria en route to Jerusalem to tell them of gentile conversions (15:3). While Luke does not present the Samaritans as Jews, he does not regard them as gentiles: they are

182 Barrett, "Light," 295.

those being *restored* to Israel, as heirs of the lost ten northern tribes being joined to the southern tribes to form a reunited Israel. This reunification takes place before the gentile mission begins—indeed, this reunification needs to take place before the gentile mission *can* begin.

Throughout the story is driven by God's action. It is striking how few of the main verbs are actions performed by Philip; rather, divine signs (8:6–7) and the message that is God's word about the Messiah Jesus (vv. 5, 12) open the Samaritans to respond in baptism. God pours out the Spirit on the new believers, confirming his acceptance of them (vv. 15–17; cf. vv. 18–19). Peter meets Simon's wrong thinking by calling him back to God (vv. 21b, 22). The apostles' time in Samaria is then spent teaching the Lord's word (v. 25a).

There is therefore here a critique of magic and the hope to control the divine or to make money from such control. The gospel is greater, since the God of the gospel is greater, and believers serve God rather than seeking to control him. "The dazzling and powerful Simon is rendered dazzled and powerless in the face of the gospel."[183] This theme will develop and return: in each of Paul's three "journeys," there is a confrontation between the gospel's messenger and magic (13:6–12; 16:16–18; 19:11–20),[184] and thus Philip and Paul are presented in parallel as faithful servants of the living God and faithful gospel ministers.

2. God Arranges for Philip to Meet an Ethiopian Eunuch (8:26–40)

Bibliography

Argyle, A. W. "Cullmann's Theory." **Avemarie, F.** *Tauferzählungen*, 267–94. **Baban, O. D.** *Road*, 207–71. **Bock, D. L.** *Proclamation*, 225–30. **Brinkhof, J. H. A.** "Philip." **Brodie, T. L.** "Rhetorical Imitation." **Bruce, F. F.** "Philip." **Burke, S. D.** "Queering." **Byron, G. L.** *Blackness*, esp. 108–21. **Carson, C. R.** "Acts 8:37." ———. "Understand." **Cullmann, O.** *Baptism*, 71–80. **Das, A. A.** "Acts 8," esp. 119–20. **Decock, P. B.** "Understanding." **Dinkler, E.** "Philippus." **Dodd, C. H.** *According*, 288–94. **Edwards, J. R.** "Parallels," 489–90. **Esler, P. F.** *Community*, esp. 149, 160. **Gaventa, B. R.** *Darkness*, 98–107, 123–25. **Grassi, J. A.** "Emmaus." **Green, J. B.** "Witnesses," esp. 233–35. **Harnack, A. v.** *Date*, esp. 156. **Hengel, M.** "Geography," 51–58. ———. *Peter*, 116–20. **Hengel, M., and D. P. Bailey** "History." **Hengel, M., and A. M. Schwemer.** *Between*, 110–16. **Hooker, M. D.** *Jesus*, 113–14, 137–39, 150–51. **Jeremias, J.** *Jerusalem*, 343–44. ———. παῖς θεοῦ, *TDNT* 5:677–717. **Juel, D.** *Exegesis*, 127–31. **Koet, B. J.** "Isaiah," 87–89. **Lee, J. J.** "Distracting." **Leivestad, R.** "ταπεινός." **Lindars, B.** *Apologetic*, 77–88, esp. 83–84. **Lindemann, A.** "Eunuch." **Lindjier, C. H.** "Encounters." **MacDonald, D. R.** *Gospels and Homer*, 113–17. **Malina, B. J.** *World* (3rd ed.), 174–76. **Mallen, P.** *Reading*, 108–13. **Marshall, I. H.** "Place." **Martin, C. J.** "Journey." **Matthews, C. R.** *Philip*, esp. 71–94. **McCollough, D. J.** *Ritual*, 164–66. **Melbourne, B. L.** "Acts 1:8." **Metzger, B. M.** *Studies*, 111–22. **Myllykowski, M.** "Being." **O'Toole, R. F.** "Philip." **Pao, D. W.** *Acts*, 140–42. **Parsons, M. C.** "Isaiah 53." ———. *Body*, 123–41. **Pervo, R. I.** *Profit*, 70–72. **Porter,**

183 Gaventa, *Acts*, 139–40.
184 Spencer, *Portrait*, 95–98.

R. J. "What." **Rhamie, G. C. A.** "Whiteness." **Robinson, B. P.** "Place." **Rosica, T. M.** "Road." **Sanders, J. T.** *Jews,* 151–53. **Schnabel, E. J.** *Mission,* 1:682–87. **Schröter, J.** "Taufe," 572–76. **Smith, A.** "Step." **Snowden, F. M., Jr.** *Before.* ———. *Blacks.* **Spencer, F. S.** "Eunuch." ———. *Portrait,* 128–87. **Stenschke, C. W.** *Portrait,* 147–48. **Strange, W. A.** *Problem,* 65–77. **Strelan, R.** "Prophet." ———. *Strange,* 85–89. **Stuhlmacher, P.** "Isaiah 53." **Thornton, T. C. G.** "End." **Trocmé, É.** *Livre,* 179–81. **Tyson, J. B.** "Gentile Mission," esp. 622–23. **van Unnik, W. C.** "Befehl." **von Dobbeler, A.** *Philippus,* 107–80, 211–15. **Walton, S.** "Rhetorical Criticism." **Wanke, J.** "Brotbrechen." **Weissenrieder, A.** "Searching." **Wilcox, M.** *Semitisms.* **Wilson, B. E.** *Unmanly Men,* 113–49. **Wilson, S. G.** *Gentiles,* 171–72. **Yamauchi, E. M.** "Eunuch."

Translation

26 Now an angel of the Lord spoke to Philip, "Get up and go at noon on the road which goes down from Jerusalem to Gaza"—this is a desert road.[a] 27 So[b] he got up and went. And (notice this!)[c] there was a man who was an Ethiopian eunuch, a court official of the Candace,[d] the queen of the Ethiopians, who was in charge of her whole entire treasury. He had been to Jerusalem to worship;[e] 28 while he was on his way back, sitting[f] in his chariot, he was reading the prophet Isaiah. 29 The Spirit said to Philip, "Go over and stay close to this chariot." 30 When he ran up, Philip heard him reading Isaiah the prophet, and said, "Excuse me: do you really understand what you are reading?"[g] 31 He replied, "How can I[h] unless someone will guide[i] me?" So he invited Philip to come up and sit[j] with him. 32 The passage of Scripture which he was reading was this:

> As a sheep he was led[k] to the slaughter
> and as a lamb before its shearer without a voice,
> so also he did[l] not open his mouth.
> 33 In[m] [his] humiliation, justice was denied him.[n]
> Who will tell of his descendants,[o]
> for his life is taken[p] away from the earth?

34 The eunuch responded[q] to Philip, "Please tell me, who is the prophet saying this about—himself or someone else? 35 Philip opened his mouth and, beginning from this Scripture, told him the good news about Jesus.[r] 36 As they were going along the road, they came to some water, and the eunuch said, "Look: water! What is preventing me from being baptized?"[s] 38 He commanded the chariot to stop,[t] and they went down together into the water, both Philip and the eunuch, and Philip[u] baptized him. 39 When they came out of the water, the Spirit of the Lord[v] snatched Philip away and the eunuch did not see him any longer, but[w] continued on his way rejoicing. 40 Meanwhile,[x] Philip was found[y] at Azotus and, as he traveled around, he continued to proclaim the good news to all the cities until he came[z] to Caesarea.

Notes

a. Taking the referent of αὕτη, "this," as τὴν ὁδόν, "the road," rather than Γάζαν, "Gaza"; both nouns are fem.; MHT, 3:44.

b. Treating καί, "so," as continuative; Wallace, 671.

c. ἰδού, lit., "see!," functions as a signal to the reader that something significant or surprising is happening; see *Comment* on 1:10.

d. Κανδάκης lacks a definite article but seems to be the title of the Ethiopian queen rather than a personal name, hence "*the* Candace" (Strabo, 17.1.54 τῆς Κανδάκης, misunderstood in LCL as a personal name; Pliny, *Nat.* 6.35 §186; Barrett, *Acts*, 1:425; "Κανδάκη," BDAG 507). Deissmann, *Light*, 352, cites a 13 BC inscription calling the Candace τὴν κυρίαν βασίλισσαν, "the lady queen."

e. προσκυνήσων, "to worship," fut. ptc. expressing purpose; Wallace, 635–37; BDF, §351. Fut. ptc. is rare in NT: Luke-Acts has 6 of 13 NT uses.

f. ἦν . . . ὑποστρέφων καὶ καθήμενος, "he was returning and sitting," periph. impfs (Wallace, 647–50) or descriptive ptcs (Barrett, *Acts*, 1:427). No significant difference in meaning hinges on this choice.

g. γινώσκεις ἃ ἀναγινώσκεις; "Do you understand what you are reading?": paronomasia, impossible to reproduce in English; cf. 2 Cor 3:2.

h. πῶς . . . ἂν δυναίμην, "how can I?," opt. δυναίμην: see *Comment* on v. 31.

i. ὁδηγήσει, "will guide," fut. with ἐάν in conditional sentence, suggesting greater certainty about the protasis than a subj.; Porter, 45.

j. Inf. καθίσαι, "to sit," follows παρεκάλεσεν, "he invited," expressing the content of indirect discourse (Wallace, 603–5) and representing an impv. in what the eunuch said.

k. The parallel between this line and the following two lines requires that we treat "he" as the subject of ἤχθη, "was led," with KJV, NIV, TNIV, NASB, NLT, ESV, CEV, NRSVue, contra RSV.

l. ἀνοίγει, historic pres. in co-text of predominantly past verbs, hence "he did [not] open."

m. C E Ψ 33^{vid} 𝔐 vg^{mss} syr read αὐτοῦ, "his," and LXX Isa 53:8 lacks αὐτοῦ, and this causes some hesitation by the NA^{28}/UBS^{5} editors, since copyists generally seem to conform the NT text to LXX; *TCGNT*^{2}, 315. However, the weight of witnesses lacking αὐτοῦ is overwhelming: 𝔓^{74} ℵ A B 103 629 1642* 1739^{c} *pc* lat; Ir^{lat} (Bock, *Proclamation*, 228); D lacks this verse.

n. ἡ κρίσις αὐτοῦ ἤρθη, lit., "justice was taken away from him" ("αἴρω," BDAG 28–29, §3); the gen. pn. αὐτοῦ has ablative force implying separation, a typical classical usage; Wallace, 107–8; BDF, §180.

o. γενεάν "family history" ("γενεά," BDAG 191–92, §4), rather than the more usual senses "age, generation." The fut. tense of διηγήσεται, "will tell," shows that descendants yet to come must be in view; L&N §10.28.

p. αἴρεται, historic pres., adding vividness; Culy and Parsons, *Acts*, 165.

q. ἀποκριθείς, lit., "answering," an LXX idiom (cf. Dan 5:13; there are at least 30 LXX uses) is formulaic here, since what the eunuch says is not really an answer.

r. εὐηγγελίσατο . . . τὸν Ἰησοῦν, "he told the good news . . . about Jesus"; for this use of acc. for the content of the proclamation; "εὐηγγελίζω," BDAG 402, §2.a.α. Cf. Acts 5:42 εὐαγγελιζόμενοι τὸν χριστόν Ἰησοῦν, "they were proclaiming good news about the Messiah Jesus."

s. v.l. (i) adding v. 37 Εἶπεν δὲ αὐτῷ ὁ Φίλιππος· ἐὰν πιστεύεις ἐξ ὅλης τῆς καρδίας σου σωθήσει. Ἀποκριθεὶς δὲ εἶπεν· πιστεύω εἰς τὸν Χριστὸν τὸν υἱὸν τοῦ θεοῦ, "And Philip said to him, 'If you believe with all your heart, you will be saved.' And he answered, 'I believe in the Messiah the son of God,'" in E some old Latin, Greek MSS according to Bede; (ii) adding v. 37 Εἶπεν δὲ αὐτῷ· εἰ πιστεύεις ἐξ ὅλης τῆς καρδίας σου ἔξεστιν. Ἀποκριθεὶς δὲ εἶπεν· πιστεύω τὸν υἱὸν τοῦ θεοῦ εἶναι τὸν Ιησοῦν Χριστόν, "And he said to him, 'If you believe with your whole heart, it is lawful.' And he said, 'I believe the son of God to be

Jesus the Messiah,'" in 36 307 453 610 945 1678 1739 (Western) 1891 some lectionaries, many old Latin MSS and some other versions, most fathers; (iii) omit v. 37 in 𝔓[45, 74] ℵ A B C Ψ 33[vid] 81 181 614 1175 1409 2344, Byzantine MSS, most lectionaries, some versions, Chrysostom, Ambrose. See *Comment.*

t. Taking τὸ ἅρμα, "the chariot," as the subject of the inf. στῆναι, "to stop"; Culy and Parsons, *Acts,* 167.

u. ἐβάπτισεν αὐτόν, "he baptized him"; it is clear that Philip is the subject. Burke, "Queering," 184, gratuitously asserts that the grammatical subject and object are ambiguous, while making the accurate observation that "the baptism represents Philip's conversion as much as it does the eunuch's."

v. v.l. πνεῦμα ἅγιον ἐπέπεσεν ἐπὶ τὸν εὐνοῦχον. ἄγγελος δὲ κυριοῦ, "the Holy Spirit fell upon the eunuch. And the angel of the Lord" (thus making the angel the one who takes Philip away), found in A[c] 36 307 453 610 945 1678 1739 (Western) 1891 *l*1178 some old Latin, Vulgate, Syriac, Coptic, etc., plus one MS of Jerome; πνεῦμα κυριοῦ, "(the) Spirit of the Lord," alone in 𝔓[45, 74] ℵ A* B C E Ψ 33[vid] 81 181 614 1175 1409 2344, Byzantine MSS, most lectionaries, some versions, Didymus[lat] Chrysostom; Rebaptism, one MS of Jerome. See *Comment* on v. 39.

w. Taking γάρ as "but" (coordinate) rather than "for" (explanatory); "γάρ," BDAG 189, §2. Alternatively, γάρ introduces an ellipsis, which would read in full: "The eunuch saw no more of Philip, for he, unlike Philip, was not supernaturally removed but simply continued on his journey"; Barrett, *Acts,* 1:434–45; cf. Culy and Parsons, *Acts,* 168. See also *Note* v.

x. δέ, "meanwhile," marks the switch of subject to Philip and contrasts Philip's and the eunuch's onward journeys.

y. Taking εὑρέθη, "was found," as aor. pass., "(he) was found," rather than mid., "(he) found himself"; cf. "εὑρίσκω," BDAG 411, §1.b. Wilcox, *Semitisms,* 100, proposes an Aramaic original אשתכחב "to arrive in"; cf. Wensinck, reported in Black, *Aramaic,* 303. However, LXX combines the pass. of εὑρίσκω, "find," with ἐν, "in," and Luke frequently uses εἰς, "into," in place of ἐν (in Hellenistic writers this is especially common with town names, with Bruce, *Acts* [1990], 230), so Wilcox's hypothesis is unnecessary; Avemarie, *Tauferzählungen,* 275–76; Barrett, *Acts,* 1:435.

z. ἕως τοῦ ἐλθεῖν αὐτόν, "until he came": art. inf. with acc. pn. as "subject."

Form/Structure/Setting

Delimitation of pericope. δέ, "now" (v. 26), functions in three ways to introduce a new section; (i) it answers μέν, "then" (v. 25), contrasting the return of the proclaimers to Jerusalem with Philip's journey toward the road to Gaza (and thus links this section to the preceding one);[185] (ii) it switches the narrative's focus, from the proclaimers (v. 25) to Philip; (iii) it marks a change of grammatical subject, from the proclaimers to the angel of the Lord.[186]

The section closes (v. 40) with Philip's travels, which parallel those of Peter and John (v. 25), echoing the imperfect of εὐαγγελίζομαι, "proclaim the gospel," noticing that proclamation happened en route in many places and signaling the destination with εἰς, "to." The new section is then signaled at 9:1 by a switch of subject (to Saul) and of geographical and temporal setting.

185 Spencer, *Portrait,* 131; van Unnik, "Befehl," 185–86.
186 Levinsohn, *Connections,* 26–27.

Sources/historicity. Harnack considers that Philip and his daughters were one of Luke's sources.[187] Given that the "we" character met Philip and his family (Acts 21:8–9), it is very possible that that meeting was the means by which Luke obtained this story. Haenchen proposes, rather, that the story emerged from Hellenistic Christian circles;[188] his view is of a piece with the doubtful claim that the Hellenistic believers held significantly different beliefs to the "Hebrews" (see *Form/Structure/Setting* and *Comment* on 6:1). Lüdemann concludes that there is a "historical fact" of the conversion of an Ethiopian eunuch behind this story.[189] Matthews sees two different portraits of Philip in this story and the preceding one: in the former he is a miracle worker and preacher, whereas here he is the Spirit's envoy and a biblical interpreter; but this is a false dichotomy—both Peter and Paul display this range of characteristics in the rest of Acts.[190] Whatever Luke's source, the story is told in Lukan diction with a number of Lukanisms.[191]

Readers have noticed parallels between this story and the experiences of Elijah (1 Kgs 18) and Elisha (2 Kgs 5). Luke mentions the two prophets in Luke 4:25–27, a passage that prepares for the gentile mission by its portrayal of prophets engaging with foreigners as well as explicitly modeling John the baptizer on Elijah (Luke 1:17) and relating the appearance of Elijah at the transfiguration (Luke 9:30, 33).[192]

Spencer builds on the work of Trocmé to identify eleven parallels with 1 Kgs 18. Like Elijah, Philip:[193] (i) goes in response to a divine command (Acts 8:26; 1 Kgs 18:1); (ii) goes to a wilderness (Acts 8:26; 1 Kgs 18:2, 5); (iii) meets a pious royal official (Acts 8:27–28; 1 Kgs 18:3–4); (iv) outruns a chariot (Acts 8:30; 1 Kgs 18:46); (v) speaks with the official (Acts 8:30–35; 1 Kgs 18:7–15); (vi) has sacrifice at the heart of the narrative (Acts 8:32–35; 1 Kgs 18:20–40); (vii) has necessary water provided (Acts 8:36; 1 Kgs 18:41–45); (viii) leaves through divine intervention (Acts 8:39; 1 Kgs 18:46); (ix) moves about through the Spirit (Acts 8:39; 1 Kgs 18:12); (x) finds that the royal official attends to the prophet(s) (Acts 8:30–34; 1 Kgs 18:4, 13); (xi) meets the official at noon (Acts 8:26; 1 Kgs 18:26–29).

Similarly, Brodie sees a number of themes in this story and the preceding one as influenced by 2 Kgs 5, the story of Elisha's meeting with Naaman, the Syrian general who had leprosy.[194] The strongest connections with this story

187 *Date*, 156; so also Barrett, *Acts*, 1:51, 421.

188 Haenchen, *Acts*, 314–16.

189 Lüdemann, *Early Christianity*, 105.

190 Matthews, *Philip*, 74–75.

191 For details, see Avemarie, *Tauferzählungen*, 274–75. MacDonald, *Gospels and Homer*, 113–17, identifies structural parallels with Hermes's encounter with Priam in Homer, *Il.* 24, although he concedes that the biblical parallels identified below are strong. However, MacDonald's parallels are at such a general level, with little contact of vocabulary, that they are unpersuasive as evidence that Luke draws on Homer here.

192 Nolland, *Luke*, 1:201, 321–22; Green, *Luke*, 218.

193 Spencer, *Portrait*, 135–36; Trocmé, *Livre*, 180.

194 Brodie, "Rhetorical Imitation," 47–64.

are: (i) Naaman and the eunuch are both foreign royal officials who supervise money and ride in chariots (Acts 8:27; 2 Kgs 5:1, 5, 9); (ii) providential guidance is central to both stories (Acts 8:26, 29; 2 Kgs 5: 8–10, 14); (iii) the prophetic word needs explanation (Acts 8:30–38; 2 Kgs 5:10–13, although the explainer is not parallel in the two stories); (iv) the use of water as the instrument of cleansing (Acts 8:36–38; 2 Kgs 5:10, 14). Spencer adds: (v) both Naaman and the eunuch suffer from physical afflictions that exclude them from Israel's assembly, castration (Acts 8:27) and leprosy (2 Kgs 5:1); (vi) the contrast of Naaman's reluctance to comply (2 Kgs 5:11–12) and the eunuch's ready compliance (Acts 8:36).[195]

Both OT stories may have influenced Luke's portraits of Philip and the receptive foreigner, although it is hard to assess how far Luke has deliberately modeled this story on them. It is noticeable that the narrative sequence is not the same in the three stories, and some parallels are more persuasive than others. How far we should see specific dependence on a particular story, and how far general dependence on story patterns from the OT,[196] is a matter of fine judgment; overall, it seems probable that Luke to some extent echoes elements from both stories.

Others propose links between this story and the Emmaus narrative (Luke 24:13–35).[197] There are some parallels in structure: (i) people on a journey encounter a stranger (Acts 8:29–30; Luke 24:13–16); (ii) conversation begins with a sharp question (Acts 8:30; Luke 24:17); (iii) discussion centers on the death of Jesus, seen through the lens of Scripture (Acts 8:32–35; Luke 24:18–27); (iv) "sacred acts" (baptism and breaking bread) form the climax of the narratives (Acts 8:36–39; Luke 24:28–30); (v) Jesus and Philip both vanish and reappear elsewhere (Acts 8:39–40; Luke 24:31, 36–43); (vi) the travelers are emotionally moved by the encounter (Acts 8:39; Luke 24:32). Although these parallels are rather general, Spencer argues that they show Philip in continuity with Jesus. He goes on to suggest that the following scenes in Luke point to the key link between Jesus and Philip, which is that they read Scripture christologically and, in particular, they see the inclusion of gentiles as foretold in Scripture understood christologically. Thus, Jesus opens the disciples' minds to the Scriptures (Luke 24:44–46) and states that Scripture shows that repentance and forgiveness will be proclaimed "to all nations" (24:47), echoing the Emmaus scene's emphasis on Jesus interpreting Scripture as about himself (24:25–27).[198]

Structure. Acts 8:26–40 oscillates between Philip and the eunuch:

---

195 Spencer, *Portrait,* 138–39.

196 So Matthews, *Philip,* 82.

197 Baban, *Road,* 201–70; Grassi, "Emmaus"; Lindjier, "Encounters"; Wanke, "Brotbrechen"; Robinson, "Place"; Edwards, "Parallels," 489–90; Rosica, "Road"; O'Toole, "Philip," 31–32; Spencer, *Portrait,* 141–45 (with further references).

198 Cf. Wanke, "Brotbrechen," 192.

vv. 26–27a In response to the angel, Philip goes to the desert road

vv. 27b–28 Luke's readers and Philip are introduced to the eunuch

vv. 29–30 In response to the Spirit, Philip asks the eunuch a question

vv. 31–34 The eunuch explains and asks for help

v. 35 Philip explains the gospel of Jesus to the eunuch

v. 36 The eunuch responds and wants to be baptized

v. 38 They go together into the water and Philip baptizes the eunuch

v. 39a Philip is snatched away by God, his work completed

v. 39b The eunuch goes on his way in joy

v. 40 Philip then carries on sharing the gospel in the places he visits

Some have seen a chiastic structure in the passage,[199] although this requires taking v. 25 with this section rather than the preceding one. While echoes of language within the passage speak of Luke's artful design (see *Comment*), the chiastic structures proposed are somewhat arbitrary in the echoes they choose; for example, Spencer notes the uses of πορεύομαι, "go," in vv. 26, 39 but omits the uses of this verb in vv. 27, 36.

Central to this meeting is God's initiative, expressed in key imperatives (vv. 26, 29) and key actions (v. 39), and also God's provision—the repetition of ἰδού, "see!," signals key moments when God's providence has organised events so that the right people are in the right place at the right time (vv. 27, 36). Luke's design shows how God first orchestrates the meeting, leading to the two men finally standing in the baptismal water together (v. 38), and then separates the two when the divine purpose for their meeting is accomplished.

Von Dobbeler identifies parallels with the structure of Peter's encounter with Cornelius (10:1–11:18): the message of an angel initiating the encounter (8:26–27a; 10:1–8); the switch to the other person (the eunuch, 8:27b–28; Peter, 10:9–16); the Spirit's direction that leads the believer to the not-yet-believer (8:29; 10:17–23); dialog (8:30–31; 10:24–33) followed by proclamation (8:32–35; 10:34–43) and baptism (8:36–38; 10:44–48); and the departure of the believer (8:39–40; 11:1–18).[200] Some of these parallels are more general (and thus, less cogent) than others, but that there is a parallel of divine initiative leading to inclusion of gentiles is clear.

Setting This story forms a natural partner to the preceding story about Philip (8:5–25), and this explains its location here.[201] Apart from Philip, there are at least three links between the two: (i) the eunuch and the Samaritans are both outsiders and not admitted to the Jerusalem temple;[202] (ii) the eunuch contrasts with Simon, for the eunuch accepts the message of a humble servant

199 E.g., Spencer, *Portrait*, 131–34; O'Toole, "Philip," 25–29.

200 von Dobbeler, *Philippus*, 119–20; so also Matthews, *Philip*, 86–90.

201 Barrett, *Acts*, 1:426.

202 Esler, *Community*, 149, 160; see *Comment* on 8:4.

and does not seek to use his money or position to win favor;[203] (iii) a similar closing (see *Comment* on v. 40).

This story also prepares for moves toward gentile mission in Acts 9–11:[204] Saul becomes a believer and will be a missionary to gentiles (9:1–31, esp. 15); Peter stays with Simon the tanner, an impure trade (9:43); Peter speaks the gospel to the Godfearing Roman centurion Cornelius and his household and stays there (10:1–48), and then he successfully explains and defends his actions in Jerusalem (11:1–18); and some believers speak to "Greeks" who join the community in Antioch and are taught by Barnabas and Saul (11:19–26). The theme of divine guidance links this story particularly with the Cornelius story; Luke particularly highlights God's intervention to direct believers to evangelize non-Jews and include them within the renewed and restored Israel.[205]

Comment

26 Ἄγγελος . . . κυρίου, "an angel . . . of the Lord"; see *Comment* on 5:19. It is important for Luke's overall plot that God initiates this encounter, for it is to be a step toward gentile mission.[206] Within most Jewish circles, the idea of an angel speaking was accepted (23:8–9), and the angelic intervention echoes Stephen's speech (7:30, 35, 38, 53). (On angels, see *Comment* on 1:10.)

πρὸς Φίλιππον, "to Philip." Pesch regards Philip here as the apostle rather than the table server appointed in 6:5.[207] Thus Pesch treats the journey as originating in Jerusalem, where the apostles remained (8:1b). The latter point is not impossible, but without some textual signal otherwise, Luke's readers would naturally assume that this is the same Philip as in the immediately preceding story (8:5–25).[208] Thus, if the journey was from Jerusalem, because the proclaimers, including Philip of the seven, returned there (v. 25), the same is meant here.

ἀνάστηθι καὶ πορεύου, "Get up and go," is a combination found only in Luke-Acts in the NT (Luke 1:39; 15:18; 17:19; Acts 8:27; 9:11; 10:20; 22:10) and probably reflects a Semitic idiom that connotes, "Go at once!"[209] The travel motif provided by πορεύομαι, "go," runs as a thread through the passage (Acts 8:27, 36, 39).

203 Spencer, *Portrait*, 159–60; Rackham, *Acts*, 120.

204 With Spencer, *Portrait*, 129; Tannehill, *Unity*, 2:107–11; Lindemann, "Eunuch."

205 See Tannehill, *Unity*, 2:110–11.

206 Marshall, *Acts* (TNTC), 161.

207 Pesch, *Apostelgeschichte*, 1:287–90. Hengel, *Peter*, 116–20, sees Philip here as one of the twelve who became one of the seven.

208 Fitzmyer, *Acts*, 411.

209 Culy and Parsons, *Acts*, 161; MHT, 2:453; the combination of the two verbs in the imperative is found in LXX 1 Sam 9:3; 2 Sam 13:15; 1 Kgs 12:24γ; 17:19; Mic 2:10; Jonah 1:2; 3:2; see discussion, van Unnik, "Befehl," 187–88.

κατὰ μεσημβρίαν could mean "toward the south" or "at noon";[210] either could fit in this co-text. The only other NT use of μεσημβρία is Acts 22:6, where it clearly carries a temporal sense, although the preposition there is περί, "about." LXX usage is generally also temporal (e.g., 1 Kgs 18:26; Job 11:17; Sir 34:16; Zeph 2:4), although none of these has either of the prepositions used in Acts, and Dan 8:4, 9 are clear uses in the directional sense. Culy and Parsons over-press their translation of ἀνάστηθι καὶ πορεύου as "Go at once!" to imply that the temporal sense cannot be relevant here.[211] For God to send Philip at the hottest time of day—and to a wilderness area—is remarkable, for noon is normally a time for rest under shade, not travel (Sir 43:3; Gen 18:1–8; 43:16; 2 Sam 4:5; Song 1:7; although note Gen 18:1; Jer 6:4). Thus, Philip's expectation would be to meet no one. However, noon is also a time of divine revelation, particularly to or concerning non-Jews (e.g., 10:9; 22:6; 26:13; cf. John 4:6).[212]

ἐπὶ τὴν ὁδὸν τὴν καταβαίνουσαν ἀπὸ Ἰερουσαλὴμ εἰς Γάζαν, "on the road that goes down from Jerusalem to Gaza." Given that Philip was previously in Samaria (8:5–13), if he did not return to Jerusalem (see *Comment* on 8:25), it is unlikely that hearers are to picture him traveling to Jerusalem and then on to Gaza—that would be a roundabout route. Rather, he would travel on a shorter route either south from Samaria to meet a road that runs from Jerusalem to Gaza or southwest through Antipatris and Lydda to the coast road to Gaza.[213] Either way, the road would go "down," as Gaza lies on the coast some 670 metres (0.4 miles) lower than Jerusalem.

αὕτη ἐστὶν ἔρημος, lit., "this is desert," is ambiguous; both ὁδός, "road," and Γάζα, "Gaza," in the previous phrase are feminine, so either could be the antecedent of αὕτη, "this." Given that the action of the story takes place on the road and not in Gaza, and that the town does not otherwise feature in the story, it seems more likely that the road is the referent.[214] While the area may not be "desert" in the literal sense (Arrian, *Anab.* 2.26, notes that the desert begins at Gaza[215]), the term denotes that the area is deserted and uninhabited, especially at the hottest time of day.[216] The atmosphere of a wilderness setting is of desolation, and space and time for reflection (cf. uses of ἔρημος, "wilderness," in Stephen's speech, 7:30, 36, 38, 42, 44).[217] The encounter that takes place with the Ethiopian takes place in a liminal space, with a man characterized as liminal to standard expectations of masculinity.[218]

210 "μεσημβρία," BDAG 634.
211 Culy and Parsons, *Acts*, 162.
212 So Strelan, "Prophet," 33–34.
213 Spencer, *Portrait*, 148n3.
214 Bauernfeind, *Apostelgeschichte*, 128.
215 Cf. Smith, *Geography*, 183–84.
216 Hengel, *Between*, 111.
217 Spencer, *Acts*, 90–91.
218 So also Wilson, *Unmanly Men*, 132.

27–28 καὶ ἀναστὰς ἐπορεύθη, "And he got up and went." The combination of God commanding an individual using imperatives followed by the statement that they got up and went (v. 27) paints Philip in the colors of obedient servants of God in Scripture, notably Elijah (1 Kgs 17:9, 10) and the eventually obedient Jonah (Jonah 3:2, 3; cf. 1:2!). Like Elijah, Philip will later be transported by the Spirit (see *Comment* on v. 39). Philip contrasts with Ananias and Peter, who will shortly be presented as hesitant to follow divine instructions that also lead to other surprising people coming to faith in Jesus (Acts 9:13–14; 10:10–17).

ἰδού, "notice this!," signals to readers that something remarkable is happening, as divine guidance leads to Philip's encounter with a man in this liminal place at a liminal time (see *Comment* on 1:10).[219]

ἀνήρ, "a man." The man Philip meets is introduced very fully, making clear his ambiguous and liminal status.[220] Although he is a "non-man" as a eunuch (see below), Luke introduces him first as ἀνήρ, a masculine person.[221] His portrait parallels that of Ebed-melech, an Ethiopian eunuch serving as a servant and confidant of King Zedekiah (Jer 38:7–13), who receives a word from the Lord through the prophet Jeremiah (Jer 39:15–18).[222] Nevertheless, even though the eunuch is characterized ambiguously here, he emerges as a model of a powerful person responding to the gospel.[223]

He is Αἰθίοψ, "an Ethiopian," from the area known as Cush in the OT (כוש [*kwš*], e.g., Gen 2:13; 2 Kgs 19:9; Isa 11:11; 43:3; Ezek 38:5); the capital was Meroë (modern Bagrawiya). Today it is part of the Sudan.[224] Ethiopia was described as "the ends of the earth" (Homer, *Od.* 1.23; Herodotus, *Hist.* 3.25.1; Strabo 17.1.3; 17.2.1; cf. Ezek 29:10; Esth 1:1; 8:9, which portray it as remote);[225] this man is from far, far away.[226] It is notable that no Jews from Ethiopia are said to be present at Pentecost (Acts 2:9–11). In the setting of Acts, the gospel's journey "to the end of the earth" (1:8) and to πᾶσιν τοῖς εἰς μακράν, "all those far away" (2:38), this story follows on the gospel's arrival in Samaria. The juxtaposition of this story, where Philip meets a man from "the ends of the earth," with Philip's ministry in Samaria underlines that the words of Jesus are being fulfilled and that "the end of the earth" in 1:8 is not Rome.[227] Philip is thus the "trailblazer" for this mission, although he clearly does not complete

219 Spencer, *Portrait,* 157; van Unnik, "Befehl," 183.
220 Lee, "Distracting," 66–68; more fully, Spencer, "Eunuch."
221 "ἀνήρ," BDAG 79, §1.c.
222 Carson, "Understand," 115–18.
223 Wilson, *Unmanly Men,* 114–15.
224 See further Yamauchi, "Eunuch"; Barrett, *Acts,* 1:424; Bruce, *Acts* (1990), 225; Spencer, *Portrait,* 149–52; Schnabel, *Mission,* 1:682–83; Dinkler, "Philippus."
225 See Byron, *Blackness,* 111; Thornton, "End"; Wilson, *Unmanly Men,* 126–27.
226 Cf. Weissenrieder, "Searching," 138.
227 Spencer, *Portrait,* 151; and see *Comment* on 1:8. Melbourne, "Acts 1:8," 9–11, argues the nuanced view that 1:8 is being fulfilled here but that this is not the *only* fulfillment of 1:8; contra Thornton, "End," 374.

the task.[228] Somewhat ironically, the gospel's journey to the end of the earth in Ethiopia begins on Judean soil, for that is where Philip meets this man. OT references suggesting an expectation that Ethiopians would meet God prepare for this man's story: Ps 67:32 LXX (MT 68:2; EVV 68:31), Αἰθιοπία προφθάσει χεῖρα αὐτῆς τῷ θεῷ, "let Ethiopia open her hands to God" (noted as early as Bede[229]); Zeph 3:10 ἐκ περάτων ποταμῶν Αἰθιοπίας οἴσουσιν θυσίας μοι, "from beyond the rivers of Ethiopia they shall bring offerings to me" (also Isa 45:14). These Scriptures are in tune with the way Luke portrays this man as an "included outsider."[230]

As an Ethiopian, the man is dark-skinned (αἰθίοψ means "burnt-face,"[231] note Jer 13:23); in the ancient world black people were regarded as exotic and unusual,[232] and modern forms of racism on the basis of skin color seem to have been uncommon.[233] Thus Homer writes of "blameless Ethiopians" (*Il.* 1.423–24), and Herodotus praises Ethiopians as the tallest and most handsome of humankind (*Hist.* 3.20; cf. Diodorus Siculus 3.3.1). The picture is not entirely positive, for Herodotus also cites the view in relation to the Persians that those living at great distance from the center of the inhabited world are held in least honor (*Hist.* 1.134), and Pseudo-Aristotle comments, "Those who are too dark-skinned are cowardly; this applies to Egyptians and Ethiopians" (*Physiogn.* 812a12–13); although he also there makes the same observation about people who are too fair-skinned.[234]

He is εὐνοῦχος, "a eunuch," and δυνάστης Κανδάκης βασιλίσσης Αἰθιόπων, "a court official of the Candace, the Queen of the Ethiopians." A eunuch was castrated and at least partially dismembered.[235] While εὐνοῦχος was occasionally used for a court official without this implication (e.g., LXX Gen 39:1 uses εὐνοῦχος of the married Potiphar[236]), it seems unlikely that the apposition with δυνάστης is merely repeating the same point using a different word.[237] High officials in the ancient world were frequently eunuchs,

---

228 Spencer, *Portrait*, 152.

229 Bede, *Acts*, 81, commenting on v. 26a. Eusebius, *Hist. eccl.* 2.1.13, sees the eunuch's conversion as fulfilling Ps 67:32 LXX.

230 I owe this phrase to Wilson, *Unmanly Men*, 130.

231 "Αἰθίοψ," LSJ 37.

232 Pervo, *Profit*, 70–71.

233 Snowden, *Blacks*, esp. 169–95; Snowden, *Before*, esp. 46–59.

234 Thus Wilson, *Unmanly Men*, 126–27, argues that Greco-Roman authors "tend to either demonize or idealize those who live in 'far-away' lands."

235 Weissenrieder, "Searching," 135, implausibly suggests that the juxtaposition of Αἰθίοψ, "Ethiopian," and εὐνοῦχος, "eunuch," connects his homeland to his castrated state and thus that Luke is implicitly characterizing Ethiopians as foreign bodies.

236 Surprisingly not noted in "εὐνοῦχος," BDAG 409. G. H. Johnston, "סָרִיס (sārîs)," *NIDOTTE* 3:290, OT §4, observes that there is no evidence of (literal) eunuchs as officials in Egypt.

237 Wilson, *Unmanly Men*, 118, although Rhamie, "Whiteness," 290, proposes that δυνάστης, "a court official," specifies the specific role the eunuch has; this is not impossible, but the wider usage of εὐνοῦχος, "a eunuch," implies that he was most likely a physical eunuch. Thus Burke, "Queering," 178, claims that uses of εὐνοῦχος, "a eunuch," in Greek sources from

particularly if they had regular contact with female members of the ruling family, so that they could not become sexually involved with those women (e.g., Esth 2:14; in the court of Herod, Josephus, *Ant.* 16.8.1 §230; 15.7.4 §226; *J.W.* 1.24.7 §488). Since the ruler of Ethiopia was female,[238] the likelihood increases that this man was a literal eunuch. Ethiopia was regarded with some disdain by Greeks and Romans because it had a female ruler; female rulers indicate the nation to be barbaric (e.g., Cleopatra).[239] Strabo thus characterizes the Candace as "a masculine sort of woman" (ἀνδρική τις γυνή, *Geog.* 17.1.54). Therefore, the eunuch's status was highly ambiguous in the world at large: Philo has Pharaoh's butler, a eunuch, describe himself as "neither male nor female" (οὔτ' ἄρρεν οὔτε θῆλυ, *Dreams* 2:184), Lucian of Samosata regards a eunuch as "neither man nor woman, but something composite, hybrid and monstrous, alien to human nature" (*Eunuch.* 6), and eunuchs were actively despised in Judaism (Josephus, *Ant.* 4.8.40 §§290–91; Philo, *Spec. Laws* 1:324–25).[240] Even though he is powerful and wealthy, he falls short of how masculinity was understood in the Greco-Roman world.[241] Luke designates him as ὁ εὐνοῦχος, "the eunuch," without further qualification throughout the rest of the story (Acts 8:34, 36, 38, 39), thereby focusing on this ambiguous sexual status.[242]

The eunuch would be excluded from full participation in temple worship (Deut 23:1 EVV [23:2 MT, LXX]; cf. 1QSa II, 5–6[243]), and hence his visit to Jerusalem προσκυνήσων, "to worship," would have had limited results (cf. the Greeks of John 12:20 and the gentile visitors to the temple who offered sacrifices but could not partake of them, Josephus, *Ant.* 3.15.3 §§318–19[244]). As a eunuch, he could not become a proselyte and thus at most would have similar status to the Godfearers found elsewhere in Acts (e.g., Acts 13:16 with *Comment* there).[245] The eunuch joins the Lukan catalog of people with physical impairments whom God meets, notably Naaman the Syrian with leprosy (Luke 4:27),

---

the fifth century BC to the second century AD all evoke a castrated male, as do Spencer, *Portrait*, 166–67; Parsons, *Body*, 133–34; "εὐνοῦχος," *EDNT* 2:80–81; Matthews, *Philip*, 79n24; Weissenrieder, "Searching," 134–35; contra Wilson, *Gentiles*, 171; Longenecker, "Acts," 363.

238 Discussion of the Candace, the title of the Ethiopian Queen: Dinkler, "Philippus," 92–94; Bruce, *Acts* (1990), 226.

239 Wilson, *Unmanly Men*, 128–29.

240 Malina, *World* (3rd ed.), 174–76.

241 Wilson, *Unmanly Men*, 115. She also observes that eunuchs were regarded as "foreign," for most eunuchs were not Romans (121). Indeed, Domitian (late first century AD) made castration illegal for Romans (Suetonius, *Dom.* 7.1). Her whole chapter is a valuable discussion of this point.

242 So also Wilson, *Unmanly Men*, 117.

243 Jeremias, *Jerusalem*, 343–44.

244 Discussion: Schürer, 2:309–13.

245 Full discussion: Spencer, *Portrait*, 160–72; *pace* Wilson, *Gentiles*, 171–72; Sanders, *Jews*, 151–53; Fitzmyer, *Acts*, 410. For a review of how the church fathers predominantly read the eunuch's identity as not Jewish in the light of their anti-Jewish sentiments, see Rhamie, "Whiteness," 116–86.

as well as those concerned for them, such as the centurion (Luke 7:2–3), Jairus (Luke 8:41–42), or Publius (Acts 28:7–8).[246]

The Ethiopians are regular opponents of Rome in the imperial period, from Gaius Petronius's attack (Cassius Dio 54.5.4; Strabo 17.1.54; Pliny, *Nat.* 6.35 §§181–82) to Nero's unexecuted plan to attack Meroë (Seneca, *Nat.* 6.8.3; Pliny, *Nat.* 6.35 §181; Tacitus, *Ann.* 15.36; Cassius Dio 57.8.1).[247] Thus the eunuch represents at least a potential enemy of Rome, and there may be political overtones to his presence in this story.[248]

His role as δυνάστης, "a court official," is explained by ὃς ἦν ἐπὶ πάσης τῆς γάζης αὐτῆς, "who was in charge of her entire treasury." Note the stylish punning assonance of γάζης, "treasury," and Γάζαν, "Gaza" (v. 26; cf. Zeph 2:4). Plutarch, *Demetrius* 25.5, comments, "They [sc. the Greeks] were accustomed . . . to have mostly eunuchs as treasurers." The eunuch is the chief finance minister of the Queen, and thus a man of significant social standing: he travels in a chariot (Acts 8:28) with a driver (vv. 28–31 have him read and converse while in the chariot, which imply a driver's presence, and see *Comment* on v. 38) and was probably dressed in suitable clothing for a man of power, wealth, and influence. Yamauchi suggests that he may have been on a mission to Agrippa's court to establish links for trade and diplomacy.[249]

ὃς ἐληλύθει προσκυνήσων εἰς Ἰερουσαλήμ, ἦν τε ὑποστρέφων, "He had been to Jerusalem to worship; while he was on his way back." The long journey of well over 1300 miles/2100 km to Jerusalem shows the eunuch's earnest desire to know God.[250] The mention of Jerusalem is ironic in two ways: first, it was the place par excellence where Jews expected to meet God, and the Ethiopian appears to have failed to do so, for he has not been able to participate fully in worship (see above); moreover, he still has major questions that he will pose to Philip (v. 34). Secondly, it is ἦν τε ὑποστρέφων, "while he was on his way back," that he encounters the person who enables him to meet God: the gospel message is continuing to be scattered *from* Jerusalem and Philip continues to be a key agent of the gospel's broadcasting (cf. 8:1b, 4–5).

καθήμενος ἐπὶ τοῦ ἅρματος αὐτοῦ, "sitting in his chariot." We know little of the vehicles of this period, but it would not be a war chariot pulled by horses (cf. Rev 9:9 and many LXX uses, e.g., Exod 14:6, 7, 9, etc.), for the eunuch was a civil, rather than a military, official. It was probably pulled by oxen, may have been covered to protect from the elements, and was large enough at least for the eunuch, his driver, and Philip (Acts 8:31).

ἀνεγίνωσκεν τὸν προφήτην Ἠσαΐαν, "he was reading the prophet Isaiah,"

---

246 See, more fully, helpful discussions of eunuchs in the ancient world in Parsons, *Body*, 133–35; Carson, "Understand," 94–124.

247 See Yamauchi, "Eunuch," 357–60.

248 Byron, *Blackness*, 111–12.

249 Yamauchi, "Eunuch," 361.

250 Stenschke, *Portrait*, 147.

introduces two keynotes. First, the man is reading (repeated in vv. 30, 34), which marks him as educated. As was usual in the ancient world, he would be reading aloud (see v. 30, Philip could hear him; see Augustine, *Conf.* 6.3).[251] Reading was a customary way of whiling away a journey.[252] Secondly, he is reading Isaiah, the book being referred to by its assumed author, who is a prophet (also Acts 8:29, 34). He is thus portrayed in similar colors to the Bereans, as eager to engage with Scripture (17:11). Isaiah appears to be widely read among first-century Jews; for example, there are numerous copies among the Dead Sea Scrolls.[253] This is a rare NT instance of the source of an OT quotation being given (cf. 2:16; 3:22; 7:37, 42; 28:25; contrast Heb 2:6), and the designation of Isaiah as a prophet suggests that Luke wishes his readers to see Isaiah's words as fulfilled in Jesus, as Philip will go on to explain to the eunuch (v. 35). The scroll of Isaiah would be a relatively expensive item, further highlighting this man's wealth.[254] It is more likely that the scroll was written in Greek than Hebrew, given that it was usual in the diaspora for Scripture to be read in Greek.[255] He may have purchased it in Jerusalem.[256]

29 εἶπεν δὲ τὸ πνεῦμα τῷ Φιλίππῳ, "The Spirit said to Philip." Haenchen notes that the aorist εἶπεν, "said," introduces "the real action" after the scene setting has been done using imperfects in v. 28.[257] The theme of divine initiative continues here, for Philip understandably does not go unprompted up to this powerful man, whose position and wealth would be all too apparent from his clothes and mode of travel. For Luke's storyline in Acts 8–12, it is crucial that the approach to this outsider, who is not only gentile but also a eunuch, is prompted by God, to continue the theme that God initiates mission among such outsiders.

30 προσδραμών, "when he ran up," portrays Philip approaching the ox wagon of the eunuch. Given the typical speed of such a vehicle, it would not be difficult to catch up and keep up with it.[258] It may be that Philip's running adds a little to his portrayal as a divine messenger, for Strelan assembles a number of texts on running to propose that it is an activity typical of prophets (notably Elijah, 1 Kgs 18:46; Jer 23:21; see *Form/Structure/Setting*: *Sources/historicity*) and those on sacred duty as priests (e.g., LXX Num 17:12; 1 Sam 20:6).[259]

ἆρά γε is a polite, highly literary form of address[260] and also expresses some

251 Walton, "Rhetorical Criticism," 6 with n52, for further ancient references and bibliography.
252 Hock, *Context*, 28, 79n24.
253 Fitzmyer, *Acts*, 413.
254 Millard, *Reading*, 164–65, estimates six to ten denarii (a denarius was roughly a day's wage) to copy a scroll of Isaiah; cf. calculations in Richards, *Paul*, 165–69.
255 Hengel and Deines, *Septuagint*, 80–81; Barclay, *Jews*, 424–26; Bruce, "Philip," 379.
256 Schnabel, *Mission*, 1:685; Hengel and Deines, *Septuagint*, 89–90n41.
257 Haenchen, *Acts*, 311n1.
258 Contra Pervo, *Acts*, 224.
259 Strelan, "Prophet."
260 MHT, 3:330; Bruce, *Acts* (1990), 226.

doubt, hence, "*Excuse me*, do you *really* understand . . . ?"[261] Meeting a powerful stranger, Philip would be most likely to address him in Greek as the *lingua franca* of the day.

31 The eunuch's reply is in highly literary Greek. The protasis of the conditional question follows the apodosis, by contrast with the commoner sequence. πῶς γὰρ ἂν δυναίμην, "How can I," combines ἄν with the optative δυναίμην, normally the apodosis of a fourth-class condition. ἐὰν μή τις ὁδηγήσει με, "unless someone will show me," combines ἐὰν μή, "unless," with the future ὁδηγήσει, "will show," normally the protasis of a third-class condition.

γάρ ("for," but untranslated here) implies a protasis to the conditional along the lines of "*Of course I do not understand*, for how . . . ?"[262] As with Cleopas and his companion (Luke 24:25–27), this man needs the Scriptures interpreted in order to make sense of them. He epitomises a person with a visual impairment who needs a sighted person as guide (cf. Luke 6:39, using ὁδηγέω, "guide," as here; cf. 1QpHab II, 1–6, where the Teacher of Righteousness claims to be a reliable biblical interpreter). The key that unlocks the Scriptures is Jesus, to whom they bear witness (v. 35).[263] Nevertheless, this man is a very sympathetic outsider to Judaism, and his openness to Philip and desire to understand Scripture prepare him well to hear the gospel—hence his astute question (v. 34).[264] He models the openness and teachableness called for by Jesus: "Ask, and it will be given you; search, and you will find; knock, and the door will be opened for you. For everyone who asks receives, and everyone who searches finds, and for everyone who knocks, the door will be opened" (Luke 11:9–10 NRSVue; cf. Chrysostom, *Hom. Act.* 19).

32–33 περιοχή, "portion," is a NT *hapax legomenon*;[265] ἡ . . . περιοχὴ τῆς γραφῆς, "the portion of Scripture," is equivalent to τῆς γραφῆς ταύτης, "this Scripture" (v. 35). This is the only passage of Scripture in Acts presented in the narrator's voice.[266]

The passage the eunuch is reading is Isa 53:7–8a, corresponding almost verbatim to LXX; the only differences are that αὐτοῦ, "his" (Acts 8:33), is added (see *Note* m for the textual question) and κείραντος (aor. ptc.) substitutes for κείροντος (pres. ptc.), both meaning "shearer" (v. 32). LXX of Isa 53:7–8a here varies from MT; the Hebrew is difficult to translate.[267]

The citation does not include explicit "atonement" language but focuses on the humiliating treatment the servant receives. Hooker thus proposes that the citation is used to show "the necessity for Christ's Passion, and not as

261 "ἆρα," BDAG 127 (N.B. accent); Moule, 158; Barrett, *Acts*, 1:427–28.
262 Barrett, *Acts*, 1:428; Culy and Parsons, *Acts*, 164.
263 So also Roloff, *Apostelgeschichte*, 140.
264 Stenschke, *Portrait*, 148; cf. Rhamie, "Whiteness," 292–93 (the latter reads the eunuch as Jewish).
265 BDAG 803 s.v., §2.
266 Pao, *Acts*, 142.
267 Bock, *Proclamation*, 226–27.

a theological exposition of its meaning."[268] If we understand the subject of ἤχθη, "was led," as the servant, his destiny is clearly stated as death. Moreover, the theme of his demise is implicit in much of the quotation: the ταπείνωσις, "humiliation," of the servant is his death;[269] and the likely reason he lacks descendants is that he is killed before fathering them—both humiliation and not having children were considered negative in the ancient world (e.g., Epictetus, *Discourses* 4.1.2;[270] Gen 11:30; 25:21; 29:31; Exod 23:26). Further, Baban helpfully observes that the precise quotation chosen follows and precedes phrases specifying Israel as the recipients of the benefits of the servant's death (Isa 53:6, 8b LXX), and thus the delimitation of the quotation fits well with the focus on the eunuch as a gentile.[271]

We lack any detail from Luke of Philip's interpretation of this passage, other than the general claim that Jesus is the fulfillment of the servant prophecy.[272] It is probable that the eunuch would read more than two verses in a long journey, so we may reasonably suppose that at least the whole of Isa 52:13–53:12 is in view. Jesus quotes Isa 53:12 in Luke 22:37 concerning his forthcoming suffering and death, which underlines the significance of this passage for Luke's understanding of Jesus's death.[273] Furthermore, as Dodd argues, a particular phrase may be cited in order to point to the whole of an OT passage.[274] We may therefore reasonably assume that Luke is suggesting that Philip's exposition of Jesus "*beginning* from this Scripture" (Acts 8:35) includes the "atoning" parts of the Isaiah passage as well as ranging more widely.[275] Luke, then, here makes explicit the link between Jesus and Isaiah's suffering servant toward which Luke 22:37 gestures.[276] It is also probable that the choice of the Isaiah passage may not have been Luke's own; if he received this story orally from Philip (directly or indirectly), the passage the eunuch was reading would have been embedded in the story already at that stage. Luke would have had no reason to change this feature of the story.[277]

These verses from Isaiah resonate in interesting ways with the eunuch's situation and Luke's description of the passion, and that may help to understand the choice of the particular section quoted from Isaiah.[278] The knife

268 Hooker, *Jesus*, 114.
269 Haenchen, *Acts*, 312.
270 Cf. H. H. Esser, "ταπεινός," *NIDNTT* 2:259–64.
271 Baban, *Road*, 244.
272 Bock, *Proclamation*, 229–30.
273 Koet, "Isaiah," 87–88.
274 Dodd, *According*, esp. 126, 92–94; Lindars, *Apologetic*, 83–84, argues exactly this here.
275 *Contra*, e.g., Schmithals, *Apostelgeschichte*, 85, who sees this passage as evidence of Luke deliberately eliminating traces of Pauline atonement theology from his sources.
276 Koet, "Isaiah," 89.
277 On "atonement" theology in Luke-Acts, cf. 20:28, and see Marshall, *Historian*, 169–75; Marshall, "Place."
278 Parsons, "Isaiah 53," 113–15; Lee, "Distracting," 68; Mallen, *Reading*, 122; Jervell, *Apostelgeschichte*, 273; Wilson, *Unmanly Men*, 143.

applied to the sheep (Acts 8:32) is suggestive of the knife used to castrate the eunuch.[279] The ταπείνωσις, "humiliation," of the servant reflects the lowly status of the eunuch in relation to Judaism,[280] as well as the characterization of sheep as timid, lowly creatures among ancient writers (Pseudo-Aristotle, *Physiogn.* 806b8; Sir 13:17).[281] Both Jesus and the eunuch, in common with Isaiah's servant, have things done to them, a mark of not meeting elite expectations of masculinity.[282] Jesus gives little response to his accusers (Luke 22:67–70; 23:3, 9–10); Jesus is an innocent man who is humilated (Luke 22:63–65; 23:11, 36–38; cf. 1:52b) and unjustly executed (Luke 23:2–4, 14–15, 22–25). The quotation communicates that humility is a quality of people whom God loves, exemplified by Jesus, and so acts as an invitation to a man whose status is regarded as lowly and humble (cf. Luke's wider "reversal" theme, noted below).

ἡ κρίσις αὐτοῦ ἤρθη could be translated "justice was denied him" (implying that he was treated unjustly) or "judgment was taken away from him" (implying that he was vindicated from judgment). The former seems more likely in the co-text of ἐν τῇ ταπεινώσει, "in humiliation," but Luke may be exploiting this ambiguity, in conjunction with other ambiguities (see below), to hint at Jesus's vindication.

τὴν γενεὰν αὐτοῦ τίς διηγήσεται;, "who will tell of his descendants?," is another *double entendre*: it could mean that the servant will have no descendants—a sense that echoes both the eunuch's inability to have children and that Jesus did not father children—or it could mean that the servant's descendants are so numerous that they are uncountable.[283] The latter sense would function as an invitation to the eunuch to join Jesus the servant's growing family, a family brought into being through his suffering.[284] It may also point to the possibility for the eunuch to have "spiritual children" of his own through sharing the good news of Jesus with his compatriots.[285] Given its relevance when read each of these ways, it seems unnecessary to choose between them. There are parallel ideas elsewhere in the NT, notably adoption language in Paul (e.g., Gal 3:16, 26–29; Rom 8:14–17).

The final phrase of the quotation, αἴρεται ἀπὸ τῆς γῆς ἡ ζωὴ αὐτοῦ, could be translated "his life was *taken away* from the earth" or "his life was *lifted up* from the earth," which creates an ambiguity as to whether it refers to the death of Jesus (Luke 23:33, 44–46)[286] or his exaltation.[287] The Hebrew clearly means "his life is *cut off* from the earth," whereas LXX, cited here, is ambiguous,

279 So also Wilson, *Unmanly Men*, 141.
280 Leivestad, "ταπεινός."
281 Parsons, *Body*, 137–38.
282 Wilson, *Unmanly Men*, 143.
283 Spencer, *Portrait*, 178–80.
284 Spencer, *Portrait*, 159–61; cf. Barrett, *Acts*, 1:431; Decock, "Understanding," 123.
285 Spencer, *Portrait*, 182.
286 So Fitzmyer, *Acts*, 413.
287 Spencer, *Portrait*, 176–77; Juel, *Exegesis*, 128.

uniquely translating גזר (*gzr*), "cut off," with αἴρω, "lift up." Isaiah 53:9 goes on to speak of the burial of the servant and thus with that co-text this phrase refers to the servant's life being taken away, the former translation. If we translate "lifted up" in the sense of exaltation, there is a natural conclusion to the quotation here, as the whole quotation maps the death and exaltation of Jesus.[288] If so, Luke is reading this phrase differently from its most natural sense in Isa 53 and interpreting it through the lens of the exaltation of Jesus after his suffering (cf. Jesus interpreting the Scriptures as showing "that the Messiah must suffer . . . and then enter his glory," Luke 24:25–27). Such a reading is in tune with Luke's emphasis on raising up the lowly in his Gospel (e.g., Luke 1:52; 14:11; 18:14)[289] and hints that the exaltation of Jesus is the route to the exaltation of other lowly ones, such as the eunuch.[290] Pauline echoes are obvious (e.g., Phil 2:5–11) and illustrate the pervasiveness of the reversal theme in connection with Jesus's death and resurrection in earliest Christianity.

34 δέομαί σου, lit., "please allow me to ask you," is a very courteous phrase preparing for a question (cf. 2 Cor 8:4).[291] The eunuch, Philip's social superior, continues to display great courtesy toward Philip.

τίνος ὁ προφήτης λέγει τοῦτο;, "who is the prophet saying this about?" Given that Jeremiah could speak of his own sufferings in a similar manner (Jer 11:18–20) and that there was a Jewish tradition of Isaiah's martyrdom, the question whether the prophet spoke about himself is natural (cf. Isa 49:5; 50:10). Equally, given that the servant figure is identified as Israel (Isa 44:1–2; 49:3), he could be identified as embodying the nation or a faithful remnant of it, although it is interesting that there is no evidence in rabbinic literature for interpretation of Isa 53 as a reference to Israel.[292] Thirdly, the servant was sometimes seen as Elijah *redivivus* (Sir 48:1–10) or a messianic figure (phrases from Isa 52:13; 53:11 are echoed in 1 En. 37–71; Tg. Isa.).[293] All three views seem to have been current in Judaism at the time.[294] The christological interpretation of this passage was clearly crucial to the earliest Jesus followers, building on Jesus's own use of the servant texts to interpret his own mission.[295]

35 ἀνοίξας δὲ ὁ Φίλιππος τὸ στόμα αὐτοῦ, "Philip opened his mouth," prepares for a significant speech or explanation. It has a biblical ring (e.g., LXX

288 Parsons, *Body*, 139–40; Pervo, *Acts*, 225–26.
289 More fully, see Decock, "Understanding," 115–22; York, *Last*.
290 Green, "Witnesses," 235.
291 "δέομαι," BDAG 218; Bruce, *Acts* (1990), 227.
292 J. Jeremias, "παῖς θεοῦ," *TDNT* 5:685.
293 Cf. Stuhlmacher, "Isaiah 53," 161.
294 Jeremias, "παῖς θεοῦ," *TDNT* 5:684–89; Hengel and Bailey, "History"; Stuhlmacher, "Isaiah 53," 157.
295 E.g., France, "Servant"; contra Hooker, *Jesus*, who denies that the servant concept was influential on Jesus. See the debate between Hooker and Parsons in Bellinger and Farmer, eds., *Jesus*, 88–124. See further, *Comment* on 3:13.

Judg 11:35, 36; Job 3:1; Sir 51:25; Ezek 3:27; Dan 10:16). It parallels Matt 5:2 (at the beginning of the Sermon on the Mount), where it signals that something important is about to be said (cf. also Acts 10:34). In place of the servant who οὐκ ἀνοίγει τὸ στόμα αὐτοῦ, "did not open his mouth," Philip speaks freely both for and about Jesus and thus exemplifies in his own person the role and mission of Isaiah's servant in bringing good news to the nations (Isa 49:6, alluded to in Acts 1:8 and quoted in 13:47).[296]

ἀρξάμενος ἀπὸ τῆς γραφῆς ταύτης εὐηγγελίσατο αὐτῷ τὸν Ἰησοῦν, "beginning from this Scripture, [he] told him the good news about Jesus." What does Philip say to the eunuch? Luke places the focus on Jesus as the fulfillment of prophetic Scripture, in tune with both the speeches earlier in Acts and Jesus's own interpretation of Scripture, especially after the resurrection (Luke 24:25–27).[297] In particular here, Luke intends his readers to see Jesus as the servant figure of Isaiah (cf. Acts 3:13, 26; 4:27, 30 with *Comment*; Luke 22:37 quotes Isa 53:12), and thus, while the passage quoted is not understood to authorize the gentile mission directly, "its interpretation makes it possible."[298]

In addition, however, Isa 56:3–8 follows soon after the portion Luke quotes, and it speaks of welcome from God for foreigners and eunuchs:

> Do not let the *foreigner* joined to the LORD say, "The LORD will surely separate me from his people"; and do not let the *eunuch* say, "I am just a dry tree." For thus says the LORD: To the *eunuchs* who keep my sabbaths, who choose the things that please me and hold fast my covenant, I will give, in my house and within my walls, a monument and a name better than sons and daughters; *I will give them an everlasting name that shall not be cut off.* And the *foreigners* who join themselves to the LORD, to minister to him, to love the name of the LORD, and to be his servants, all who keep the sabbath, and do not profane it, and hold fast my covenant—*these I will bring to my holy mountain, and make them joyful in my house of prayer; their burnt offerings and their sacrifices will be accepted on my altar; for my house shall be called a house of prayer for all peoples.* (NRSVue, my italics)

Isaiah 56:3–8 offers hope to foreigners and eunuchs who keep the Jewish law, and Philip's companion is both. Luke echoes ἔσται ὁ οἶκός μου οἶκος προσευχῆς, "my house shall be a house of prayer" (v. 7), in justifying Jesus's action in the temple that presages its downfall (Luke 19:46),[299] for the gospel expounded by Philip is more generous than even Isaiah's vision. The eunuch has traveled to Jerusalem, God's "holy mountain," but has been excluded

296 Cf. Tannehill, *Unity*, 2:112.
297 Cf. Rosica, "Road," 129–31; Weiser, *Apostelgeschichte*, 1:213. For a suggestive outline of how Luke sees Jesus as fulfilling Scripture, see Talbert, *Reading Acts*, 77–78.
298 Tyson, "Gentile Mission," 623.
299 Mallen, *Reading*, 109.

from the "house of prayer" by the law's demands. He now discovers from Philip that, as a member of the renewed people of God marked by faith in Jesus expressed in water baptism, he has full and unhindered access to God. The Isaianic vision is fulfilled with a generosity that could not have been envisaged.[300] Pao suggests that the use of Isa 53 evokes the Isaianic program of Israel's restoration,[301] but it seems more likely that Israel's *expansion* to include gentiles is primarily in view here. Cf. also Wis 3:14, which calls God's blessing on "the eunuch who has not done wickedness"; this eunuch will receive χάρις, "grace," and "an inheritance (κλῆρος) in the temple (ναῷ) of the Lord" (my translation).[302] Wisdom 3:14 may be drawing on Isa 56, but nevertheless, the statement about access to the temple in relation to the eunuch's probable lack of such access is striking.

Porter offers the intriguing proposal that Isa 54:9–10 (cf. 1 Pet 3:21) and/or 55:1 (cf. John 4:10, 13–14; 6:35; 7:37–38; Rev 7:16–17; 21:6; 22:17) could have been used by Philip, as passages intervening between Isa 53 and 56, as the basis for teaching about baptism, and thus as giving rise to the eunuch's question (Acts 8:36).[303] Porter suggests this on the basis that Philip might offer a continuous exposition of Isaiah from 53:7–8 (vv. 32–33) up to at least 56:3–8 and thus that ἀρξάμενος ἀπὸ τῆς γραφῆς ταύτης, "beginning from this Scripture," indicates the starting point *within Isaiah* of Philip's teaching.

36 φησιν ὁ εὐνοῦχος· ἰδοὺ ὕδωρ, "The eunuch said, 'Look: water!,'" expresses surprise and (to the reader) a further evidence of God's provision (cf. ἰδού, v. 27) as water is provided in the wilderness.[304]

τί κωλύει με βαπτισθῆναι;, "what is to prevent me from being baptized?," implies two thoughts. First, Philip's explanation of the gospel included the response of baptism (cf. 2:38), and this man is eager to respond this way. Secondly, there may be something that might prevent his baptism;[305] note also the use of κωλύω, "hinder," in the setting of questions about baptizing gentiles (10:47; 11:17) and in Jesus's response to his disciples' attempt to prevent children being brought to him (Luke 18:16 pars).[306] Such hesitation would be understandable, given his experience of being shut out from full participation in temple worship in Jerusalem as a eunuch and a foreigner and the ambiguity of his status within the Greco-Roman world (see *Comment* on v. 27).[307] Argyle notes the interesting parallel with Isa 43:2–3 LXX: "I will say to the north,

300 Mallen, *Reading*, 111–13; cf. Porter, "What."
301 Pao, *Acts*, 141–42.
302 von Dobbeler, *Philippus*, 116–17.
303 Porter, "What."
304 Barrett, *Acts*, 1:412; Plümacher, *Lukas*, 91.
305 Spencer, *Portrait*, 183–85.
306 Contra Schröter, "Taufe," 574, who thinks the question has the sense "Why should I not be baptized?" This might be likely if the question began with μή, implying either a negative or hesitant answer, but that is not so.
307 Burke, "Queering," 184; Wilson, *Unmanly Men*, 124.

'Bring!' and to the south, 'Do not prevent (μὴ κώλυε)! Bring my sons from a land far off, and my daughters from the ends of the earth (ἄκρων τῆς γῆς)!'" (my translation).[308] Ethiopia is in the south and was reckoned as "the ends of the earth" (see *Comment* on v. 27). And here, water is now available at just the right moment! Thus, the baptism which follows demonstrates that barriers of ethnicity and physical non-conformity that formerly prevented membership in the people of God are now being overcome in Jesus's community, for a eunuch can be baptized.[309] Cf. Jesus's comment that no one should prevent the children coming to him expands the horizons of the people of God (Luke 18:16, also using κωλύω, "prevent"). There is an implicit critique of the temple, which imposed limitations on access to Israel's God.[310] Cullmann's suggestion that this question echoes primitive baptismal liturgy is highly speculative.[311]

37 Some (mainly Western) scribes added a fuller explanation of the eunuch's baptism, spelling out the basis on which he was baptized as his confession of faith in Jesus as Messiah and son of God (see *Note* s). The oldest Greek manuscript containing this reading is E (sixth century), although Irenaeus, *Haer.* 3.12.8 (second century) attests it. It is highly unlikely that, if it had been originally present, such an exchange would be omitted by later scribes,[312] and 16:31 may provide a source for this addition. Irenaeus's citation may provide insight into baptismal practices in the late second century, *pace* Strange, who argues that secrecy among second-century Christians about sacramental practices would make it natural to remove v. 37.[313]

38 ἐκέλευσεν στῆναι τὸ ἅρμα, "he commanded the chariot to stop," implies the presence of a driver. The eunuch's ability to command contrasts sharply with his humble submission to baptism, which follows immediately. Yet humble submission is characteristic of the Isaianic servant in the quotation in vv. 32–33; the powerful eunuch imitates Jesus's humility by learning from Philip and by being baptized.[314] The Lukan theme of reversal is once again played out.

κατέβησαν ἀμφότεροι εἰς τὸ ὕδωρ . . . καὶ ἐβάπτισεν αὐτόν, "they went down together into the water . . . and Philip baptized him." This is the first description of the process of baptism in Acts; it is compatible with immersion, aspersion, or affusion,[315] although the contrast of κατέβησαν, "they went down," and ἀνέβησαν,

308 Argyle, "Cullmann's Theory."
309 Rosica, "Road," 124; Lee, "Distracting," 70.
310 Parsons, "Isaiah 53," 113.
311 Cullmann, *Baptism*, 71–80; critique: Argyle, "Cullmann's Theory."
312 *TCGNT*², 315–16; Pervo, *Acts*, 217; for an alternative view, see Carson, "Acts 8:37"; Rius-Camps and Read-Heimerdinger, *Message*, 2:152, 161–63; Bede, *Acts*, 84–85. McCollough, *Ritual*, 164–66, views the two readings as "equally plausible."
313 Strange, *Problem*, 69–77. ECM wisely places v. 37 in double square brackets, indicating the editors' confidence that it is not part of the initial text of Acts.
314 Smith, "Step."
315 Calvin, *Acts*, 1:254 considers the mode of baptism a "trifling difference." Schröter, "Taufe,"

"they came up" (v. 39), implies they both entered the water. In the absence of an explicit baptismal formula, it seems likely that we are to presume that a phrase such as "in the name of Jesus the Messiah" (2:38) was used, for Philip told the eunuch the good news *about Jesus* (v. 35).[316] The eunuch is a further example of "everyone who (πᾶς ὃς ἄν) calls on the name of the Lord" being saved (2:21).[317]

The baptism of the eunuch is one of a series of baptisms running through Acts 8–12, including the Samaritans (8:12–13, 16), Saul (9:18), and Cornelius and his household (10:47–48; 11:16). In each story, verbal proclamation and response in water baptism are present, often linked with the gift of the Spirit (8:14–17; 9:17; 10:44–45; 11:15–16), thus presenting in narrative form the pattern set in 2:38 (see *Comment* there). This story is unusual in identifying the baptizer (since no one else was available) as Philip—generally people become believers by being baptized (using a passive voice verb) without the baptizer being named (e.g., 2:41; 10:47–48; 18:8).[318]

The eunuch's willing—indeed, eager—baptism in the pool contrasts in an interesting way another foreigner's reluctance to bathe in the Jordan, Naaman the Syrian leper (2 Kgs 5:10–12); the similarity of the LXX wording *καὶ κατέβη* Ναιμαν καὶ *ἐβαπτίσατο*, "Naaman *went down* and *dipped himself*," to this verse sharpens the contrast, for the two men do the same thing, but after expressing very different attitudes. Brodie notes the similarity but not the contrast.[319] This contrast highlights the eunuch's humility, which is itself one of the marks of Isaiah's servant (ταπείνωσις, "humilation," Acts 8:33). To become a follower of Jesus, who himself exemplifies the servant's role, is to become humble like Jesus, even for those who have the trappings of power like the eunuch.

39 πνεῦμα κυρίου ἥρπασεν τὸν Φίλιππον, "the Spirit of the Lord snatched Philip away," just as he had prompted Philip to approach the chariot (v. 29). Luke seems to mean that Philip was physically transported by the Spirit[320] rather than ἁρπάζω, "snatch up," having the same force here as in 2 Cor 12:2 and referring to an ecstatic experience.[321] In this case there is no indication of "heavenly" phenomena other than the transportation, whereas in 2 Cor 12:2 the co-text ἕως τρίτου οὐρανοῦ, "into the third heaven," clearly signals the ecstatic nature of the experience.[322]

οὐκ εἶδεν αὐτὸν οὐκέτι, "he saw him no more," echoes 2 Kgs 2:12 LXX almost verbatim, regarding Elisha seeing Elijah no more after he was taken up by

---

573–74, noting this as the first description of a baptism, thinks it is assumed that the mode was immersion.

316 Avemarie, *Tauferzählungen*, 270, 292.

317 Burke, "Queering," 185.

318 Brinkhof, "Philip," 85.

319 Brodie, "Rhetorical Imitation," 58–59.

320 Haenchen, *Acts*, 313.

321 So Friedrich, "Gegner," 200–201.

322 Spencer, *Portrait*, 155n1; Martin, *2 Corinthians*, 201.

God. Divine guidance—indeed, divine direction and control[323]—continues to be a major theme in this story; Philip's transportation by the Spirit echoes the experiences of Elijah (1 Kgs 18:12) and Ezekiel (Ezek 3:12, 14; 8:3; 11:1, 24; cf. the angel of the Lord transporting Habakkuk, Dan 14:36 LXX = Bel 36) and thus identifies Philip as the same calibre of godly person as these prophets. Pesch plausibly suggests that the Spirit snatching Philip away shows God's approval of his ministry to this gentile.[324]

Some manuscripts present the angel of the Lord as the agent of Philip's snatching away and the Spirit as falling on the eunuch (see *Note* v). The manuscript support for this reading is not strong, and it would be natural for later scribes both to make the Spirit's coming on the eunuch explicit, to maintain the pattern of Christian initiation set in Acts 2:38 and also to make the angel the agent both of Philip's coming and his going. Had these words been present originally, it is difficult to see why they might have been removed.[325]

The eunuch travels τὴν ὁδὸν αὐτοῦ χαίρων, "on his way rejoicing," returning to Ethiopia and thus symbolically taking the gospel with him "to the end of the earth" (1:8).[326] The eunuch contrasts with the reaction of the sons of the prophets to Elijah's departure, for (against Elisha's advice) they arrange search parties, on the supposition that Elijah has been transported by the Spirit elsewhere (2 Kgs 2:16–18). His rejoicing reflects a Lukan theme that Jesus brings joy (see *Comment* at 5:41) and links this story with Philip's ministry in Samaria, where there was also πολλὴ χαρά, "great joy" (8:8).[327] Further, his rejoicing connotes that he received the Spirit[328] rather than this being another example of a "Spirit-less" baptism by Philip (8:16). Later writers see this man as the origin of the church in Ethiopia (cf. Eusebius, *Hist. eccl.* 2.2.13; Irenaeus, *Adv. Haer.* 3.12.8); otherwise, our earliest accounts of the church in that region date only to the fourth century.[329]

40 καὶ διερχόμενος εὐηγγελίζετο τὰς πόλεις πάσας, "as he traveled around, he continued to proclaim the good news to all the cities," highlights Philip's continuing work of evangelism. It is as though, having completed his internship as a gospel midwife,[330] he now takes up wider responsibilities with alacrity. The phrasing parallels the closing of the previous episode, where Peter and John, perhaps with others, were εὐηγγελίζοντο, "proclaiming the good news"

323 Strelan, *Strange Acts*, 89.
324 Pesch, *Apostelgeschichte*, 1:294.
325 Thus, ECM omits them from the main text. See also *TCGNT*², 316; contra Strange, *Problem*, 66–68; Marshall, *Acts* (TNTC), 165.
326 Martin, "Journey," 119–20; Spencer, *Acts*, 91; Gaventa, *Darkness*, 106; Myllykoski, "Being," 171.
327 Lee, "Distracting," 72–73, translates γάρ, "for," suggesting that the eunuch's great joy is the cause for his not noticing Philip's disappearance.
328 Das, "Acts 8," 119–20.
329 Metzger, *Studies*, 111–22.
330 Cf. Spencer, *Portrait*, 182.

(8:25), and the beginning of the Philip stories, where those who were scattered διῆλθον εὐαγγελιζόμενοι, "went about proclaiming the good news" (8:4).

εἰς Ἄζωτον . . . τὰς πόλεις πάσας . . . εἰς Καισάρειαν, "in Azotus . . . all the cities . . . to Caesarea," sketches the route which Philip took for the about 90 km/56 miles journey from Azotus (modern Ashdod) to Caesarea Maritima. It is notable that Azotus and Caesarea were Hellenistic towns and had major gentile populations at this time.[331] Luke differentiates Caesarea from Judea in speaking of Herod journeying ἀπὸ τῆς Ἰουδαίας εἰς Καισάρειαν, "from Judea to Caesarea" (12:19). The implication is that Philip continues his outreach among gentiles over the years he resides in Caesarea[332] until we next meet him in 21:8–9, when he has four daughters and welcomes Paul as the missionary to the gentiles *par excellence* into his home. Further, Philip's journey along the coast parallels that of Peter (9:32–10:48), both ending in Caesarea, but Peter visits Lydda and Joppa, two prominent Jewish towns (see *Comment* on 9:32–35; 9:36–10:48). Spencer proposes that Philip may have ministered in the Jewish believing communities prior to Peter's visits, and thus, as in Samaria, Peter builds on the work Philip has done.[333] This is possible, but we lack evidence to be sure, not least because many anonymous believers contributed to the planting of new gospel communities (8:4; 11:19).

διερχόμενος εὐηγγελίζετο τὰς πόλεις πάσας, "as he traveled around, he continued to proclaim the good news to all the cities." Philip is transported elsewhere by the Spirit in order to engage in further gospel ministry; he has been faithful in a little with one person, the eunuch, and so his Lord gives him greater responsibility, even for numerous cities (Luke 19:17, 19).

Explanation

The second main Philip story also presents him as an agent of the gospel's journey through Samaria "to the end of the earth" (1:8). This story is a first fruit of the mission "to the end of the earth," whether or not Luke (and his readers) knows that Ethiopia was specifically called "the ends of the earth," for this powerful black African man is culturally and ethnically "other" than Jewish, and yet he is included in the renewed people of God which fulfills God's promise to Abraham that "through you all the families of the earth shall be blessed" (Gen 12:3, quoted in Acts 3:25). This story thus prepares for the conversions of Cornelius and Peter (Acts 10:1–11:18), climaxed by Peter recognizing that "God shows no partiality" (10:34). "The Spirit blows where it wills, sweeping the gospel across standard zones of time, space, and society."[334]

The initiative throughout this story lies with God, who sends Philip to the

331 Hengel, *Between*, 112–16; Fitzmyer, *Acts*, 415.
332 With Hengel and Schwemer, *Paul between*, 153.
333 Spencer, *Portrait*, 153.
334 Spencer, *Acts*, 94.

wilderness (Acts 8:26), instructs him to move so that he will hear the eunuch reading Isaiah (v. 29), provides water for baptism (v. 36) and then snatches Philip away to his next assignment (vv. 39–40). Philip's responsiveness to God echoes that of Jesus (Luke 4:1–2, 14–15, 18), contrasts with Ananias's and Peter's initial cautious responses to divine instruction (9:13–14; 10:9–17), and prepares for Paul's responsiveness to the Spirit (13:2–4; 16:6–10; 19:21; 20:22–23). "From start to finish the events in the eunuch story unfold according to a divinely ordered agenda."[335]

Philip's baptism of the eunuch demonstrates the inclusive nature of the believing community both in telling the story of a gentile coming to faith and in showing that barriers of physical deformity that shut people out from full participation in Jewish worship (LXX Deut 23:1 [MT 23:2]) are overcome in belonging to the people of Jesus. The symbolic world of first-century Judaism is reordered to include this outsider: a man considered unclean is now clean through baptism. "The book of Acts is not only the story of how a small community converted multitudes to faith in Jesus, but it is also simultaneously the story of how that community itself was converted by its own mission."[336]

But in order to be accepted, the eunuch must respond to Jesus, for there is no other route to membership in God's people except through Jesus (4:12). The eunuch needs both to hear the good news about Jesus (8:35) and to submit humbly to baptism, marking him as repentant and accepting of Jesus (2:38). He models what it is to respond, for he recognizes his need of enlightenment and asks for help (8:31), responds in humble obedience to baptism (vv. 36–38), and goes away praising God (v. 39).

This story complements that of Philip's evangelism in Samaria by portraying evangelism with an individual rather than a group. This incident does not have the impact on the storyline of Acts that Peter's meeting with the Godfearer Cornelius and his household does, for the eunuch returns to his own country and there is no indication that his conversion was reported more widely. Nevertheless, it is a key symbolic step along the road to gentile inclusion in the people of God: "[t]he scene is important for what it anticipates and symbolizes rather than for its consequences. It is prophetic of the gospel's reach."[337] God works through many to that end, not through the apostles alone—and Philip will continue to be God's agent to that end as he moves through gentile towns continuing to proclaim the gospel (v. 40).

335 Spencer, *Portrait*, 154.
336 Burke, "Queering," 186.
337 Tannehill, *Unity*, 2:108.

B. Saul Meets the Exalted Jesus (9:1–31)

Bibliography

Allison, D. C., Jr. "Acts 9:1–9." **Aune, D. E.** *Environment,* 134–35. **Avemarie, F.** *Tafuerzählungen,* 295–339. **Baban, O. D.** *Encounters,* 207–17. **Bauckham, R.** *Jewish World,* 325–70 [= "Restoration"]. **Béchard, D. P.** *Paul,* 162–63. **Berger, P. L. and T. Luckmann.** *Construction,* 166–80. **Bolt, P.** "Mission." **Bowker, J. W.** "Merkabah," esp. 167–73. **Bratcher, R. G.** "ἀκούω." **Buitenwerf, R.** "Acts 9:1–25." **Bunine, A.** "La date." **Campbell, D. A.** "Anchor." **Churchill, T. W. R.** *Divine Initiative,* 36–41, 192–204. **Clark, A. C.** *Parallel Lives,* 150–208. ———. "Role." **Coggins, R. J.** "Samaritans." **Collins, R. F.** "Damascus Experience." **Cosgrove, C. H.** "Divine." **Cunningham, S.** *Tribulations,* 216, 219–33. **Czechesz, I.** "Exegesis." ———. *Narratives,* 61–70. **Dodd, C. H.** "Psychological." **Dunn, J. D. G.** *Baptism,* 73–78. ———. "ΚΥΡΙΟΣ." **Ervin, H. M.** *Conversion-initiation,* 41–50. **Ferguson, E.** *Baptism,* 173–75. **Gaventa, B. R.** *Darkness,* 54–67. ———. "Enemy." **Gen, R. M.** "Phenomena." **Giles, K. N.** "Use." **Gill, D. H.** "Structure." **Gill, D. W. J.** "Behind." **Goguel, M.** "Réalisations." **Green, J. B.** *Conversion.* **Hamm, D.** "Blindness." **Hanson, J. S.** "Dreams." **Haya-Prats, G.** *Believers.* **Hedrick, C. W.** "Paul's Conversion/Call." **Hemer, C. J.** *Book,* esp. 244–307. ———. "Reconsidered." **Hengel, M.** *Acts,* 81–91. **Hengel, M., and A. M. Schwemer.** *Paul between,* 24–90. **Hobart, W. K.** *Language,* 30–31. **Hubbard, B. J.** "Commissioning Stories." **Hultgren, A. J.** "Persecutions." **Humphrey, E. M.** *And I Turned,* 82–101. **Jervell, J.** *Luke,* 153–83. **Kern, P. H.** "Conversion." **Kim, S.** *Origin* (2nd ed.). **Klein, G.** *Apostel.* **Kollmann, B.** *Joseph Barnabas,* 27–28. **Kurz, W. S.** "Effects." ———. *Reading,* 125–31. **Lamoreaux, J. T.** "Social Identity." **Lang, M.** *Kunst,* 226–43. **Lohfink, G.** *Conversion.* **Longenecker, B. W.** *Rhetoric,* 193–94. **Longenecker, R. N.,** ed. *Road.* **Löning, K.** *Saulustradition.* **Lyons, G.** *Autobiography,* 146–52. **Macnamara, L.** *Instrument,* 71–182. **Marguerat, D.** *Historian,* 179–204. **McCollough, D. J.** *Ritual,* 172–77. **Menoud, P. H.** *Jesus,* 47–60. **Menzies, R. P.** *Empowered,* 213–15. **Miller, J. B. F.** *Convinced,* 189–93. **Moehring, H. R.** "Verb." **Murphy, S. J.** "Role," 322–24. **Myllykowski, M.** "Being." 171–72. **O'Neill, J. C.** "Connection." **Öhler, M.** *Barnabas,* 188–201. **Parker, P.** "Once More." **Peace, R. V.** *Conversion,* 21–29. **Pilch, J. J.** "Trance." ———. *Visions,* 68–82. **Rapske, B. M.** "Acts," 3–21. **Riesner, R.** *Period,* esp. 64–74. **Røsæg, N. A.** "Blinding." **Sanders, E. P.** *Judaism,* 319–27. **Sanders, J. T.** *Jews,* 75–76. **Schnabel, E. J.** *Mission,* passim. **Schröter, J.** "Taufe," 576–78. **Segal, A. F.** *Paul.* **Seim, T. K.** *Message,* 11–24. **Sleeman, M.** *Geography,* 198–217. **Squires, J. T.** "Function." **Stanley, D. M.** "Conversion." **Stendahl, K.** *Paul,* 1–77. **Strelan, R.** *Strange,* 153–55. **Taylor, J. E.** "Paul's Caesarea." **Thompson, M. B.** "Internet." **Townsend, J. T.** "Acts 9:1–29." **Trebilco, P. R.** *Self-designations,* passim. **Trites, A. A.** *Concept,* 136–39. **Trocmé, É.** *Livre.* **Turner, M.** *Power,* 375–78. **Twelftree, G. H.** "Prayer," 274–75. **Walton, S.** "Calling." **Wenham, D.** "Acts II," esp. 218–26. **Wikenhauser, A.** "Doppelträume." **Wilson, B. E.** "Blinding." **Witherington, B., III.** "Editing," 335–44. **Witherup, R. D.** "Redundancy." **Wright, T.** *Biography,* 27–39.

Translation

1 Now Saul, still breathing[a] threat and murder against the Lord's disciples, went
to the high priest 2 and asked letters from him for the synagogues of Damascus, so
that, if he should find any belonging to the Way, whether men or women,[b] he might
bring them bound[c] to Jerusalem.

3 As he was traveling[d] and getting near[e] to Damascus, suddenly there was a light
from heaven shining around him. 4 He fell to the ground and heard a voice saying to
him, "Saul, Saul, why do you keep persecuting[f] me?" 5 He said, "Who are you, Lord?"
The speaker[g] replied, "I am Jesus, whom you keep persecuting;[h] 6 instead, get up now
and enter the city and you will be told[i] what you must do." 7 The men who were traveling with him had been standing[j] speechless because,[k] as they heard the voice, they
saw no one. 8 Saul got to his feet,[l] but when he opened his eyes he could see nothing;
so, leading him by the hand, they entered Damascus. 9 And Saul was sightless[m] for
three days, and he neither ate nor drank.

10 Now,[n] there was a certain disciple in Damascus named Ananias, and the Lord
said to him in a vision, "Ananias!" He said, "Here I am,[o] Lord." 11 The Lord said[p] to
him, "Get up and go to the street called Straight and look[q] in a house belonging to
Judas for a Tarsian named Saul[r]—notice this,[s] he is praying. 12 And he has seen in a
vision[t] a man called Ananias enter and lay hands on him in order that[u] he may recover
his sight." 13 Ananias answered, "Lord, I heard[v] from many people concerning this man
how many evil deeds he did to your holy ones in Jerusalem; 14 and he has authority
in this place from the chief priests to bind all who call upon your name." 15 The Lord
said to him, "Go, for[w] this man is my[x] chosen[y] vessel to carry my name before gentiles[z]
and kings and sons of Israel; 16 for I will show him[aa] how much he must suffer for my
name." 17 Ananias went and entered the house; laying hands on him, he said, "Brother
Saul, the Lord has sent me, Jesus, who appeared to you on the road by which you were
coming, so that you might see again and be filled[bb] with the Holy Spirit." [cc] 18 And
immediately something like scales fell from his eyes, and[dd] he both recovered his sight
and got up,[ee] and was baptized. 19 He then took food and became strong.[ff]

He spent time[gg] with the disciples in Damascus for some days 20 and immediately
began proclaiming Jesus in the synagogues: "This one is the son of God." 21 All who
heard were astonished and kept saying, "Surely this is the one who destroyed those in
Jerusalem who call on this name, and came here in order to take them bound to the
chief priests?"[hh] 22 But Saul was growing stronger and stronger[ii] and kept confounding[jj]
the Jews who lived in Damascus by demonstrating that this [Jesus][kk] was[ll] the Messiah.

23 When[mm] many days had gone by, the Jews plotted together to kill him; 24 however,
their plot became known[nn] to Saul. They were also watching[oo] the [city] gates both day
and night[pp] in order to[qq] kill him; 25 but his disciples took him by night[rr] and let him
down through an opening in the wall[ss] by lowering[tt] him in a basket.

26 When he arrived in Jerusalem, he began trying[uu] to join the disciples; and
they were all in fear[vv] of him, because they did not believe[ww] that he was[xx] a disciple.

27 However, Barnabas took and brought him to the apostles and explained to them
how he had seen the Lord on the road, that[yy] the Lord had spoken[zz] to him, and how
Saul[aaa] had spoken boldly in the name of Jesus in Damascus. 28 And so Saul moved
freely among them in[bbb] Jerusalem while he was speaking boldly[ccc] in the name of the
Lord; 29 he kept both speaking and debating[ddd] with the Greek speakers,[eee] but they
kept attempting to kill him. 30 When the brothers and sisters learned, they took him
down to Caesarea and sent him away to Tarsus.

31 So then, the assembly[fff] throughout Judea, Galilee, and Samaria went on having
peace; as it was being built up and walking[ggg] in the fear of the Lord and encouragement given by the Holy Spirit,[hhh] it kept being multiplied.

Notes

a. ἐμπνέων, "breathing out," pres. ptc. NT *hapax legomenon,* here figurative ("ἐμπνέω," BDAG 324, §1), takes obj. in gen., ἀπειλῆς καὶ φόνου, "threat and murder."

b. ἄνδρας τε καὶ γυναῖκας, "both men and women"; cf. 5:14; 8:12.

c. δεδεμένους, perf. ptc., "having been bound" to denote action prior to ἀγάγῃ, "he might bring," but with continuing results at the time of the main verb—they would still be bound when they were brought to Jerusalem.

d. Ἐν . . . τῷ πορεύεσθαι, pn. + dat. art. inf., expressing contemporaneous time, "as he was going."

e. ἐγγίζειν, pres. act. inf., "to come near," following ἐγένετο, "it came to pass," is Lukan style, possibly imitating LXX (McKay, §6.1.5; Burton, §§357, 360; MHT, 1:15–17; 2:425–28; Barrett, *Acts,* 1:448); cf. Luke 16:22; Acts 9:43.

f. διώκεις, 2 sg pres. indic. act.; pres. implies, "Why are you *in the process of* persecuting me?"

g. ὁ δέ, "he replied."

h. See *Note* f above.

i. λαληθήσεταί (fut. pass.) σοι, "it will be told to you."

j. εἱστήκεισαν, plpf. intransitive of ἵστημι, "they had been standing" referring to prior action in the midst of a story told in aor.; "ἵστημι," BDAG 482–83, §C.2.c.

k. ἀκούοντες . . . θεωροῦντες, "hearing . . . seeing," causal ptcs. that, unusually, follow their main verb; Wallace, 631–32.

l. ἠγέρθη . . . ἀπὸ τῆς γῆς, "he got up . . . from the ground." ἠγέρθη, aor. pass. ind., ἐγείρω, "raise": intrans. pass. for "move to a standing position"; "ἐγείρω," BDAG 271–72, §4.

m. ἦν . . . μὴ βλέπων, "he was . . . not seeing"; the ptc. βλέπων, "seeing," negated by μή, is adjectival rather than this being a periph. verb.

n. δέ, marking switch of subj. to "a certain disciple."

o. ἰδοὺ ἐγώ, "Lo, I."

p. "Said" is absent in Gk.

q. ζήτησον, aor. impv. of ζητέω, "seek," in the sense "look for"; "ζητέω," BDAG 428, §1.c.

r. Or "Saul, who is a Tarsian": Σαῦλον, "Saul," and Ταρσέα, "Tarsian," are both acc. and in simple apposition.

s. ἰδού, "see!": a signal to readers or Ananias (or both) that something worthy of note is about to be mentioned.

t. ἐν ὁράματι, "in a vision," is absent from 𝔓[74] א A 81 1646. Other MSS have variations in word order, some (B C 1175) having ἄνδρα ἐν ὁράματι, "a man in a vision," and others (E H L P 049 056 1 33 69 88[c] 1739 and many other minuscules) ἐν ὁράματι ἄνδρα, "in a vision a man," with no significant difference in meaning. *TCGNT*², 319–20, notes that ἐν ὁράματι could be an explanatory gloss introduced to explain εἶδεν, "he saw," or, if originally present, may have been removed because ἐν ὁράματι is already in v. 10, or in confusion with ὀνόματι, "by name" (v. 11); for such reasons ECM, 1:296; 3:14–15 omits the expression from its guiding line. *Per contra*, Barrett, *Acts*, 1:354 considers ἐν ὁράματι original; so also THGNT.

u. ὅπως + subj. expressing purpose; with Barrett, *Acts*, 1:454.

v. Ψ 33[vid] 1739 𝔐 read perf. ἀκηκόα "I have heard," which would be a natural substitution for aor. ἤκουσα, "I heard," found in 𝔓[74] ℵ A B C E 36 81 453 1175 *pc*.

w. NIV (1984 and 2011) do not translate ὅτι, and so the linkage is unclear in their translations.

x. μοι, "by me," dat. identifies the one performing the action of ἐκλογῆς, "chosen."

y. ἐκλογῆς, attributive gen., "a chosen vessel"; with Barrett, *Acts*, 1:456; Bruce, *Acts* (1990), 238; the latter calls this a "Hebraic gen."

z. B C* *pc* read τῶν ἐθνῶν, "*the* gentiles," but the art. is scarcely necessary (so ECM), since Acts frequently has the inart. form in the sense "the gentiles," e.g., 2:5; 4:25, 27; 15:14, 23; 21:11; 22:21; contra Barrett, *Acts*, 1:456.

aa. αὐτῷ, dat. "object" of ὑποδείκνυμι; "ὑποδείκνυμι," BDAG 1037, §2.

bb. ἀναβλέψῃς καὶ πλησθῇς, "see again and be filled," subj. verbs in purpose clause with ὅπως "so that."

cc. πνεύματος ἁγίου, gen. of what or who fills; "πίμπλημι," BDAG 813, §§1.a.α, β: this verb is transitive in pres. and impf., whereas πληρόω—also "fill"—is intransitive in those tenses.

dd. C² E L 33 323 614 945 1241 1739 *pm*, Latin MSS (h) p; syr[h] mae read παραχρῆμα, "immediately," which increases the drama of this moment but lacks strong MS support; with ECM.

ee. The participle ἀναστάς, "he got up," used widely in Luke-Acts to indicate the beginning of a state (viz., inchoatively) echoes LXX style (e.g., Gen 19:15; 22:3; Exod 24:13; Num 24:25), where it renders Heb. קום (*qwm*); Fitzmyer, *Luke*, 1:114.

ff. v.l. ἐνισχύθη, aor. ind. pass., "he was strengthened," in (𝔓[45]) B C* 323 945 1175 1739 *pc*; ἐνίσχυσεν, aor. ind. act., "he became strong," in 𝔓[74] ℵ A C² E L Ψ 33 81 614 1241 1505 𝔐; read with ECM.

gg. Ἐγένετο, "he was."

hh. The questions form one sentence in Gk. and expect the answer "Yes," since they begin with οὐχ.

ii. ἐνεδυναμοῦτο, impf. mid./pass., with active sense, "he was growing stronger" ("ἐνδυναμόω," BDAG 333, §2); v.l. ἐν τῷ λόγῳ, "in the word," read by C (lacks ἐν) E 467 it[h, p] cop[G67] (not strong support, with ECM) focusing the growth in strength on preaching (*TCGNT*², 321).

jj. συνέχυννεν, iterative impf. (Wallace, 546–47) = on a number of occasions he was confounding.

kk. οὗτος, "this one," referring back to οὗτος (v. 20), referring to Jesus.

ll. ἐστιν, "is," in indirect speech, preserving the words spoken (Wallace, 537–39).

mm. Ὡς = "when," signaled by impf. verb ἐπληροῦντο, "had been fulfilled," and time notice ἡμέραι ἱκαναί, "many days"; "ὡς," BDAG 1105, §8.b.

nn. ἐγνώσθη, aor. ind. pass.: in pass. "become known to someone" usu. with dat. of person to whom it becomes known, here τῷ Σαύλῳ, "to Saul"; "γινώσκω," BDAG 200, §2.a.

oo. παρετηροῦντο, impf. mid., "they were watching"; v.l. impf. act. παρετήρουν, with no difference in meaning; "παρατηρέω," BDAG 771.

pp. ἡμέρας τε καὶ νυκτός, "both day and night," gen. expressing time during which they watched the gates; Wallace, 122–24.

qq. ὅπως, expressing purpose, "in order that" (Wallace, 676, citing this verse), with subj. ἀνέλωσιν, "they might kill him."

rr. gen. νυκτός expressing time during which: "by night," as v. 24.

ss. διὰ τοῦ τείχους, "through the wall"; see *Comment* on v. 25.

tt. χαλάσαντες, ptc. of means, "by means of lowering"; Wallace, 628–30.

uu. ἐπείραζεν, ingressive impf.: he began and continued to try, with pres. pass. inf. κολλᾶσθαι, "to join"—pres. inf. also suggests ongoing attempts.

vv. ἐφοβοῦντο, "they were in fear," impf. suggests ongoing fear, echoing Saul's ongoing attempts to join.

ww. μὴ πιστεύοντες, pres. act. ptc. causal: "because they did not believe"; unusually, causal ptc. follows main verb, ἐφοβοῦντο, "they feared"; Wallace, 631–32.

xx. See *Note* ll above.

yy. ὅτι, "that," introducing further content of what Barnabas told them. Bruce, *Acts* (1990), 243 (with Barrett, *Acts*, 1:469) follows 945 1704 *et al.* in reading ὅ τι, "what thing" [he had said], producing two clauses governed by πῶς, "how."

zz. ἐλάλησεν, "he had spoken," recycling τὸν κύριον, "the Lord," from the previous clause, now as subj.

aaa. ἐπαρρησιάσατο, "he had spoken boldly": "he" is clearly Saul; for clarity, I have made the subj. explicit.

bbb. εἰς equivalent to ἐν, "in," as frequently in Hellenistic Gk.; Moule, 69.

ccc. παρρησιαζόμενος, temporal (pres.) ptc., "while he was speaking boldly," cf. v. 27.

ddd. ἐλάλει, "he was speaking," and συνεζήτει, "he was debating," both iterative impf., i.e., on a number of occasions, regularly.

eee. πρὸς τοὺς Ἑλληνιστάς, "with the Greek speakers"; v.l. Ἕλληνας, "Greeks," in A arm slav; unlikely to be original because of overwhelming weight of external evidence for Ἑλληνιστάς, including 𝔓[74] ℵ B C E 1739 and most other MSS; *TCGNT*[2], 322, rates the reading as A; Barrett, *Acts*, 1:470; ECM. On the translation, see *Comment* on 6:1.

fff. ἐκκλησία, "assembly" (so ECM); v.l. pl. ἐκκλησίαι, "assemblies," (and consequent changes to verbs to pl.) in various forms in E 614 1409 2344 Byz Lect it syr[h] bo[mss] geo slav Chrysostom (Augustine) Bede[1/4]. Bruce, *Acts* (1990), 245–46, notes that pl. accords with Pauline and other NT usage (e.g., 1 Thess 2:14; Gal 1:22). Giles, "Use", 137–40, prefers a conjectural reading of the singular ἐκκλησία with plural verbs, based on Ψ, which reads Ἡ . . . ἐκκλησία . . . εἶχον . . . οἰκοδομουμένοι καὶ πορευομένοι . . . ἐπληθύνετο, "the assembly . . . were having . . . were being built up and walking . . . it kept being multiplied," where the first three verbs are plural, but the last singular, but conjecture is a last resort. *TCGNT*[2], 322–23, notes that the weight and range of MSS reading sg. is vastly superior to pl., and it is hard to see why scribes should modify pl. to sg. here and not do so at 15:41; 16:5, where it is clear the pl. is the original. It seems most likely that this passage has been amended to harmonize with pl. use in 15:41; 16:5; with Barrett, *Acts*, 1:474–75.

ggg. Taking ptcs. οἰκοδομουμένη καὶ πορευομένη, "being built up and walking," as temporal, qualifying ἐπληθύνετο, "it kept being multiplied"; with Culy and Parsons, *Acts*, 184.

hhh. τοῦ ἁγίου πνεύματος, subj. gen., "given by the Holy Spirit"; with Bruce, *Acts* (1990), 246; Barrett, *Acts*, 1:474; Culy and Parsons, *Acts*, 184.

Form/Structure/Setting

Delimitation of pericope. The section opens with a switch of subject from Philip (8:26–40) to Saul (9:1), marked by the anaphoric article Ὁ with δέ. The article is resumptive, by pointing back to previous references to Saul, especially 8:3 (where Σαῦλος is anarthrous; see *Comment* on 9:1). The section is held together by its focus on Saul's transformation from persecutor of Jesus's followers to advocate of Jesus: Saul is the subject or object of most main verbs in this section. The opening and closing of the section form an inclusio signaling reversal: the journey from Jerusalem to Damascus is reversed (vv. 1–2, 25–26); the persecutor becomes the persecuted (vv. 1, 29); the believers' enemy speaks in the Lord's name (vv. 2, 27–29); and Saul's murderous intent is replaced by brotherly love (vv. 1, 28, 30).[1] The section closes with Saul's departure from Jerusalem to Tarsus, via Caesarea Maritima (v. 30); at this point Saul disappears from the narrative until 11:25–26. The shift to Peter (9:32) after a summary (9:31) opens the next section.[2]

Sources/historicity. That Saul of Tarsus was transformed into a follower of Jesus is beyond dispute; the story Luke tells, and Paul's letters too, makes good sense as the basis of this transformation. The most likely source is Saul himself, suggested by the fact that many of the details are paralleled in the Pauline letters (see below).[3] Luke has undoubtedly adapted the story, for the vocabulary is Lukan, based on his source.[4]

On the dating of this event, see *Dating* below.

Pauline parallels. This section has two interesting sets of parallels, in the two retellings of the story in Acts (22:3–21; 26:2–23) and in the Pauline letters (notably Gal 1:13–20, but also 1 Cor 9:1; 15:18; 2 Cor 11:32–33; 1 Thess 2:15), and the relationships of the information in these different accounts is much debated.[5] The Pauline parallels show that Paul spoke about the Damascus Road encounter, and the allusive nature of many of them suggests that Paul spoke at greater length when present with his communities, perhaps particularly in his evangelism and apologetics (as Luke portrays him in Acts 22 and 26).[6] See the *Excursus* below on the Acts accounts; here we consider the Pauline parallels.

---

1 Marguerat, *Historian*, 185n19; it is thus inappropriate to regard the middle of v. 19 as a break, as does Johnson, *Acts*, 161.

2 Czachesz, "Exegesis," 63, notes the bracketing of this story between the Philip and Peter stories.

3 With Fitzmyer, *Acts*, 420.

4 For a list of Lukanisms, see Avemarie, *Tauferzählungen*, 301–2. For discussion of Luke's relationship to Paul, see the closing section of vol. 2 of this commentary.

5 See the helpful summaries in Wenham, "Acts II," 218–26. Buitenwerf, "Acts 9:1–25," 67–82, uses the agreements with the Pauline letters to propose that Luke has constructed this story based on information in the letters, which is not a necessary conclusion.

6 See Kim, *Origin* (2nd. ed.), esp. 55–66, on key passages in the Pauline letters concerning Paul's vision and commission.

There are several agreements between Acts and Paul:[7] (i) Paul persecutes the church (1 Cor 15:9; Gal 1:13; Acts 9:1–2, 21; 22:3–4; 26:9–11); (ii) the exalted Jesus appears to Paul (1 Cor 9:1; 15:8; Acts 9:4–6; 22:7–8; 26:14–15), and that produces a sudden, dramatic change in his behaviour (Gal 1:13, 23; Phil 3:7; Acts 9:20–22; 26:19–20);[8] (iii) a strong light shines (2 Cor 4:6;[9] Acts 9:3–4; 22:6–7; 22:13–14); (iv) God revealing his Son to Paul is closely linked to Paul's call to be apostle to the gentiles (Gal 1:16; Acts 26:16); and (v) the incident is near Damascus (Gal 1:17; Acts 9:3; 22:6; 26:12–13).

There are also a number of apparent differences between Acts and Paul:[10] (i) Paul does not tell the story of his calling as in Acts 22; 26 but mentions it only briefly and in passing. This raises the question whether Paul reported the details of his experience to others; (ii) "I have seen the Lord" (1 Cor 9:1) contrasts with Acts 22:14; 9:17, 27; 26:13–16, which focus on Paul *seeing* light and *hearing* the Lord; (iii) for Paul the Damascus Road encounter is part of the sequence of Easter resurrection appearances (1 Cor 15:3–9), but Luke's description (Acts 1:3, 9–11) suggests that those appearances last for forty days and end with Jesus's ascension. Further, Acts 13:31–33 seems to place Paul outside the circle of "witnesses"—he simply brings the good news; (iv) Paul considered himself an apostle on the basis of the Damascus Road encounter (1 Cor 9:1), but Luke reserves the designation "apostle" for the Twelve.[11] On this view, Acts 14:4, 14 are non-specific uses of "apostles," identifying Barnabas and Paul as sent (by the church in Antioch, Acts 13:1–3); (v) Paul is sure he received his call and gospel directly from God (Gal 1:1–2, 11–12), whereas in Acts, Paul learns what he is to do through Ananias;[12] (vi) after Saul's time in Damascus, he spends time in "Arabia" (Gal 1:17), whereas Luke has him travel to Jerusalem (Acts 9:26)—indeed, Paul denies that he visited Jerusalem until "after three years" (1:18); (vii) Barnabas plays no role as intermediary in Paul's account in Gal 1, whereas his intercession is vital to Saul's acceptance (Acts 9:27);[13] (viii) Acts 9:27–29 gives the impression that Saul becomes well-known among the Jerusalem believers, whereas Paul himself says he met only

---

7 Cf. Lohfink, *Conversion*, 21–24.

8 Lyons, *Autobiography*, 146–52.

9 Lohfink, *Conversion*, 22–23, does not think this passage refers to the Damascus Road encounter, but see the persuasive discussion of Kim, *Origin* (2nd. ed.), 5–8.

10 Cf. Lohfink, *Conversion*, 24–30; Townsend, "Acts 9:1–29." Townsend considers that Luke has composed much of this story by adding information from Paul's opponents to a small historical core that identified Paul as a Jewish persecutor of believers who was transformed near Damascus, escaped the city in a basket, and became an evangelist. The wide agreements between Acts and the Pauline accounts noted above suggest otherwise, and Townsend's view faces the further difficulty that Luke is so sympathetic to Paul throughout Acts (with Witherington, *Acts*, 322n66).

11 Haenchen, *Acts*, 114–15.

12 Conzelmann, *Acts*, 71; Klein, *Apostel*, 146.

13 Öhler, *Barnabas*, 197–201, regards Barnabas's role as unhistorical because of his absence in Gal 1. However, Paul's rhetorical aim in Galatians is to establish his own apostleship and message as having come directly to him through his meeting with the exalted Jesus

Cephas (Peter) and James the Lord's brother (Gal 1:18–19), and was unknown in person (τῷ προσώπῳ, "by face") to the believers in Judea, even though they heard what he was doing (Gal 1:22–23).

However, each of the apparent differences have alternative explanations, particularly bearing in mind the different purposes of Acts and the Pauline letters. (i) Kim has shown that there are clear allusions to the Damascus Road encounter in Paul's letters. Paul is relatively brief in his letters about his personal experience of Jesus (e.g., 2 Cor 12:1–4, assuming that to be Paul's own experience). He would not need to write at length if he had previously told the story of the Damascus Road encounter orally; rather, he could briefly allude to the story to evoke the memory of his converts. (ii) See the discussion of the key verses in Acts, ad loc., but note that 9:17 has Ananias speak of "the Lord Jesus who *appeared* (ὀφθείς, "was seen") to you on the road," 9:27 has Barnabas reporting that on the journey Saul "*had seen* (εἶδεν) the Lord," 22:14 has Ananias say that God appointed Saul "*to see* (ἰδεῖν) the righteous one," and 26:16 has the Lord himself telling Saul that he is to be a witness "of the events in which *you saw* (εἶδες) [me]." In each retelling of the story there is a clear signal that Saul saw the exalted Jesus. (iii) Paul's reporting of the resurrection appearances is not as straightforward as may appear, for it is widely recognized that he is passing on a traditional summary in 1 Cor 15:3–7[14]—the uses of the "language of tradition" (παρέδωκα, "I passed on," παρέλαβον, "you received" [v. 3]) imply this, as does the way Paul demarcates his experience as ὡσπερεὶ τῷ ἐκτρώματι, "as to one born in an untimely way" (v. 8), suggesting that it is not straightforwardly part of the same series as the appearances in vv. 5–7. Further, Luke uses "witness" (both verb and noun) as a semi-technical term for those who are eye- and ear-witnesses to Jesus's resurrection (note Acts 1:21–22)[15]—thus, according to Luke, Paul is a witness (Acts 22:14–15; 26:16). By contrast, Paul both uses this language less and treats as witnesses the broad group who presently give testimony to Jesus as witnesses (e.g., 1 Cor 15:15) or who speak in Jesus's name (e.g., Gal 5:3; 2 Thess 1:10—the latter includes Silas and Timothy, the co-senders of the letter). Thus, Luke's usage is consistent with that found in Acts 13:31–33 and is compatible with Paul's less technical usage. (iv) Luke does generally reserve "apostles" for the Twelve (28x in Acts, always plural), and 14:4, 14 is a significant exception. The quotation of Isa 49:6 applied to Paul and Barnabas's work is nearby (13:47), and that quotation echoes Acts 1:8 (which itself alludes to Isa 49:6—see *Comment* on 1:8). Thus, Paul and Barnabas are participating in the same mission promised originally to the Eleven. Further, they perform "signs and wonders done through their

---

(1:11–12), and thus Paul would have reason to omit mention of any intermediary role played by Barnabas in order not to fuel his opponents' claims; so also Witherington, *Acts*, 324n85.

14 E.g., Thiselton, *1 Corinthians*, 1186–89.

15 On this theme, see Bolt, "Mission"; Trites, *Concept*, 136–39.

hands" (σημεῖα καὶ τέρατα γίνεσθαι διὰ τῶν χειρῶν αὐτῶν, 14:3), a strong parallel to the work of the apostles: "through the hands of the apostles were done signs and wonders" (Διὰ δὲ τῶν χειρῶν τῶν ἀποστόλων ἐγίνετο σημεῖα καὶ τέρατα, 5:12). These features suggest that Luke saw Paul and Barnabas as fulfilling a role like that of the Twelve.[16] Clark argues further that the parallels of Peter and Paul in Acts reinforce this identification.[17] (v) Reading Acts 9 alone, one could gain the impression that Saul received his commission secondhand through Ananias, but reading the sequence of the three accounts of the Damascus Road encounter in Acts, there is a buildup of information about Saul's commission.[18] Acts 9:6 provides the answer to an implied question: "What must I do?" Acts 22:10 provides this missing question: "What shall I do, Lord?" (τί ποιήσω, κύριε;), but no answer other than the instruction to go to Damascus and await further instructions. Acts 26:16–18 has Jesus answer Paul's unposed question by telling him that he will testify to what he has seen and will experience, including to gentiles. Reading all three accounts, Luke has built up the body of information in such a way that he maintains suspense and then breaks that suspense in the final account. The careful buildup suggests that Luke wishes readers to recognize this and thus to see Paul receiving his commission to mission among gentiles on the Damascus Road, in tune with Paul's own description (Gal 1:1–2, 11–12). (vi) The time notices in Acts 9 are vague: Saul spends "some days" (ἡμέρας τινάς, v. 19) with the Damascene disciples; and it was after "many days" (ἡμέραι ἱκαναί, v. 23) that Saul's Jewish opponents plotted against him. This certainly allows for a period between the two points sufficient to cover a period in "Arabia" (which could have been fairly brief—see *Comment* on v. 23) followed by a return to Damascus (Gal 1:17). (vii) The impression of reading Acts 9 alone is certainly that Saul would have met more "apostles" than Peter and James (Gal 1:18–19) on his visit to Jerusalem and that he became quite well-known among the believers (Acts 9:27–29). However, the Acts account is compatible with Paul's words in Galatians, for Luke is making a general, rather than precise, statement and is not aiming to offer exact information (as Paul is) in defense of the independence of Paul's call. During this visit, Luke makes no suggestion that Saul left Jerusalem, and so Paul's statement that he was unknown among the "churches of Judea" (Gal 1:22) may mean "Judea outside Jerusalem" or simply that he was not well-known among Judean believers.[19] Paul indicates that this visit to Jerusalem was brief—fifteen days (Gal 1:18)—which would have limited how much Saul could get to know the Jerusalem believers, let alone those in wider Judea. In sum, while Luke does not give us all the information we

---

16 In what precedes, I draw on Clark, "Role," esp. 182–85.

17 Clark, "Role," 185–89.

18 On this sequence, and the wider buildup among the three accounts, see Churchill, *Initiative*, 225–29.

19 Wenham, "Acts II," 224–25.

can glean from Paul's letters about this period, Luke's summarized account, which focuses on essentials, is compatible with the extra information which we have from Paul, even though in places if we read Acts 9 alone, we might gain a less-than-complete impression.

Conversion or call? Since Krister Stendahl's "Paul among Jews and Gentiles,"[20] there has been discussion of whether this event should be considered as a "conversion," as it has been traditional known, or is better seen as a "call" analogous to those received by OT prophets.[21] As often, the debate turns on definitions: Stendahl understands "conversion" to entail a change of religion and criticizes the view that Saul underwent a conversion since "religion" is an anachronistic category in the first century. Rather, Saul himself remained a Jew, and the focus of the event is on Saul's call to a specific mission.[22] To understand the event as a conversion is to read Paul through the eyes of Luther and Calvin, and that makes the error of attributing to Paul the "introspective conscience of the West," focused on how God is working in an individual's "soul," and seeing the pre-conversion Saul as racked by guilt, rather than recognizing Paul's "robust conscience."[23] Many of these points are well taken.

Specifically, there are clear parallels between Saul's Damascus Road experience and OT prophetic call stories:[24] "chosen instrument," σκεῦος ἐκλογῆς (Acts 9:15), echoes the calls of Jeremiah and the Isaianic servant (Jer 1:5; Isa 49:1); the shining light parallels that in Ezekiel's call vision (Ezek 1:28; 2:1; Acts 9:3); the task of engaging with gentiles echoes the calling of Isaiah's servant (Isa 49:6; Acts 9:15; cf. Acts 1:8; 13:47), opening blind (gentile) eyes (Isa 35:5; 42:7, 16; cf Acts 9:9, 18); and the coming of the Spirit who brings salvation to equip for the task (Isa 61 1; Acts 9:17; cf. Luke 4:18). The account in Galatians has similar echoes (Gal 1:13–16 alludes to Isa 49:1, 6; Jer 1:5). Further, the focus of the Acts 9 account is on Saul's calling to proclaim Jesus, including among gentiles (vv. 15, 20, 27–28). This certainly makes the language of call appropriate for the Damascus Road experience.

By contrast with "change of religion" accounts, sociological approaches to conversion focus on a person's change of the community to which they belong and their resocialization to the new community.[25] This necessarily involves the convert's reinterpretation of their pre-conversion life, and Phil 3:4b–11 represents such a reinterpretation. Paul either left or was rejected

20 Stendahl, *Paul,* 1–77, esp. 7–23.

21 For a helpful survey of this debate, see J. M. Everts, "Conversion and Call of Paul," *DPL* 157–63; on the wider debate about "conversion," see Rambo and Farhadian, eds., *Oxford Handbook of Religious Conversion,* esp. 1–22; Green, *Conversion,* esp. 1–43.

22 Stendahl, *Paul,* 11–12; for critique, see Peace, *Conversion,* 27–29.

23 Stendahl, *Paul,* 12–15, 17, 78–96.

24 Stendahl, *Paul,* 8–10.

25 E.g., Berger and Luckmann, *Construction,* 166–80, esp. 177–80; Segal, *Paul,* 20–30.

by the Pharisaic community to which he belonged and joined a messianic community that soon embraced gentiles alongside Jews.[26]

The understanding of "conversion" has been highly influenced by psychological studies,[27] and in relation to Saul these are frequently criticized for projecting categories onto an ancient character and ancient texts that are inappropriate. By contrast, Joel Green, who engages with cognitive science, shows that the language of conversion and repentance in the NT (respectively, ἐπιστρέφω/ἐπιστροφή and μετανοέω/μετάνοια) focuses on metamorphosis from one life orientation to another, including Paul's missions among Jews and gentiles (Acts 9:35; 28:27; 14:15; 15:3, 19; 26:17–18).[28] Moreover, a number of gentiles in Acts already worship Israel's God (e.g., Cornelius, 10:1–2) and thus need no conversion from one god to another. Further, in the OT it is most frequently God's people who are called to "turn" (Heb. שׁוב [*šwb*], generally translated ἐπιστρέφω in LXX), and thus it is wise to regard both "[m]oving from one religious affiliation to another *or transformations in one's understanding of one's long-held religious commitments*" as forms of conversion.[29] Green closes his study with this valuable definition drawn from his work on Luke-Acts:

> Converts are those who, enabled by God, have undergone a redirectional shift and now persist along the Way with the community of those faithfully serving God's eschatological purpose as this is evident in the life, death, and exaltation of the Lord Jesus Christ, and who lives are continually being formed through the Spirit at work in and through practices constitutive of this community.[30]

Scholars in recent times have rightly stressed the way that the believing Paul sees himself as in continuity with Judaism—he is a messianic Jew who believes that Jesus is Israel's Messiah, and that understanding has produced a radical reorientation and transformation of his worldview and theology. Paul's reinterpretation of Judaism through a messianic lens produces a worldview centered on God as now known in and through Jesus and by the Spirit. Scholarship since Stendahl has recognized the huge impact the Damascus Road experience has on Paul's thought and life.[31] Philippians 3:4a–6 demonstrates that Saul's pre-Damascus Road life is not one of being racked by guilt but of real satisfaction and contentment in his Jewish heritage—Paul's transformation is thus not about "inner peace" but the proper object of worship

26 Segal, *Paul*, 117–25, 14–30; Kern, "Conversion," 72–73.

27 Notably James, *Varieties*, and (strongly influenced by James) Nock, *Conversion*; for summary and critique of James, see Green, *Conversion*, 6–10.

28 Green, *Conversion*, 49–53.

29 Green, *Conversion*, 53 (my italics).

30 Green, *Conversion*, 163.

31 E.g., Kim, *Origin* (2nd. ed.); Longenecker, ed., *Road*.

and service, and thus generates a change of group membership. Hence, the language of conversion, carefully defined (as by Green, above), is also appropriate to describe the radical reorientation concerning the identity and intentions of Israel's God that happens through Saul's Damascus Road experience and its aftermath—we do not, in other words, need to choose between "call" and "conversion" as descriptions of Saul's transformation; both represent important aspects of what happens to him.

Dating. Dating this event is complicated by debates over the dates of Galatians and the events Gal 1–2 describe, the death and resurrection of Jesus, and Paul's escape from Damascus during the rule of Aretas as ethnarch (2 Cor 11:32–33; he probably took office in AD 37 and died ca. AD 40).[32] Many of the arguments are finely balanced, and so we must be cautious how much we build on the detail of our reconstruction. These issues are too large to be resolved here, so I simply indicate the basis on which I proceed.[33] The main dates proposed for the death and resurrection of Jesus are AD 30 and 33, and I am inclined to the former.[34] The Jerusalem "council" (Acts 15) took place early in AD 49,[35] and I am persuaded that Galatians is Paul's earliest letter, written in the throes of the debates prior to the "council," ca. AD 48.[36] To fit in the periods of time involved, the period of "three years" before Paul visited Jerusalem must be included in the "fourteen years" before his second visit (Gal 1:18; 2:1). If Paul's second visit to Jerusalem (Acts 11:27–30; Gal 2:1–10) fell in AD 46–47,[37] counting backwards places the Damascus Road encounter in AD 33–34.

Structure. The two key factors in the organisation of this section are the protagonist Saul, usually marked as the main grammatical subject, and the location where events take place. Regarding the protagonist, Luke initially uses an alternating pattern: he focuses first on Saul in Jerusalem and on the way to Damascus (Acts 9:1–9), and then on Ananias in Damascus (vv. 10–16), each encountering the exalted Jesus, before they meet (vv. 17–19a). Each of these three scenes has one or more visions at its heart: Saul's vision of Jesus (vv. 4–6, identified as a vision in vv. 17, 27); Ananias's vision (v. 10) and the Lord's report of Saul's vision of Ananias (v. 12); and Ananias's report of Saul's vision on the road (v. 17). These visions place the focus firmly on the Lord Jesus, who appears to both Saul and Ananias, as the one who drives the story

32 See, e.g., the discussions of L. Alexander, "Chronology of Paul," *DPL* 115–23; Wenham and Walton, *Exploring, vol. 1* (2nd ed.), 302–6; Hemer, *Book*, 244–307. For the death of Aretas, see Hemer, *Book*, 164n7.

33 I largely follow Hemer, *Book*.

34 Hemer, *Book*, 261–63.

35 A widely accepted date, based on confidence about the date of Paul's first visit to Corinth as AD 50–52 (Acts 18; see discussion, ad loc.).

36 Hemer, "Reconsidered"; Longenecker, *Galatians*, lxxii–lxxxviii; see *Excursus: Acts 11:27–30 and Gal 2:1–10* following *Comment* on 11:30.

37 See *Comment* on 11:28.

forward.[38] Thereafter, the focus is on Saul's exploits in Damascus (vv. 19b–25) and Jerusalem (vv. 26–30). This alternating pattern echoes the meeting of Philip and the Ethiopian eunuch (8:26–40: see *Form/Structure/Setting* there) and prepares for a similar series in Peter's meeting with Cornelius (10:1–48; see *Form/Structure/Setting* there). Verse 31 then summarizes and marks a transition to a Peter-focused section of Acts.

In greater detail, in vv. 1–9 we first (re-)meet Saul, earlier encountered at Stephen's death (7:58; 8:1a). He is the subject of most main verbs until the voice speaks (vv. 5b–6) and we learn of his fellow-travelers' experience (v. 7). Thereafter, Saul resumes his primary place (vv. 8–9). This section follows the classic five-part pattern of an epiphany:[39] (a) introduction (vv. 1–3a); (b) appearance (vv. 3b–4); (c) message (vv. 5–6), including the complication of Saul's question and Jesus's answer;[40] (d) departure (here, as frequently, implied rather than described[41]); and (e) conclusion (vv. 7–9). The story is told from an external (extradiegetic) perspective, in the narrator's voice, by contrast with the other accounts of this event in Acts (22:3–11; 26:4–20), which are told from an internal (intradiegetic) perspective, in the character Paul's voice.

Acts 9:10–19a repeats the fivefold epiphany pattern, as Ananias encounters "the Lord" (v. 10), who is identified as Jesus (v. 17): (a) introduction (v. 10a); (b) appearance (v. 10b); (c) message (vv. 11–16); (d) departure (again, implied); (e) conclusion (vv. 17–19a).[42] As with Saul's encounter with the Lord, there is a complication: Ananias objects to the Lord's instructions (vv. 13–14). The second account also tells of Ananias's part in the story (22:12–16), although the third does not. This account continues the extradiegetic perspective from vv. 1–9, again contrasting with the later intradiegetic accounts in Acts 22 and 26. Saul and Ananias meet together in the latter part of this section, as Saul recovers sight, is baptized, and is strengthened (9:17–19a).

The focus shifts to Saul in vv. 19b–25, still in Damascus, as Saul first spends time with the Damascene believers (v. 19b) and then proclaims a new and effective message, centered on the identity of Jesus (vv. 20, 22). Those who hear share Ananias's surprised reaction (v. 21; cf. vv. 13–14); as with the Ananias section, this surprise is sandwiched between statements about Saul and his ministry (vv. 20, 22; cf. vv. 11–12, 15–16). A hostile reaction follows from Saul's fellow Jews, and they plot to kill him (vv. 23–24), providing a

---

38 With Humphrey, *And I Turned*, 90–91. Cf. Czachesz, "Exegesis," 6–8, who provides a helpful chart showing how pervasive language of sight and (divine) verbal communication is in this section.

39 For this pattern, see Churchill, *Initiative*, 36–41; cf. the analyses of Hubbard, "Commissioning Stories," 117; Czachesz, "Exegesis," 19–20.

40 Churchill, *Initiative*, 38, notes that question and answer is often a feature of the "message" part of an epiphany.

41 Churchill, *Initiative*, 39.

42 Cf. Hubbard, "Commissioning Stories," 117–18.

speedy fulfillment of Jesus's words (v. 16). A flurry of imperfective verbs (imperfects and present participles) in vv. 19b–24 suggests Luke is portraying a period of time in summary, followed by the decisive action of Saul's escape in the basket, portrayed using perfective verbs (aorists).

Saul's time in Jerusalem (vv. 26–30) goes through three phases. Initially, he finds it hard to be accepted by the disciples because of their understandable concern that he may not really have changed (v. 26; cf. vv. 13–14[43]). The second phase is introduced by Barnabas's decisive intervention to vouch for Saul (v. 27), portrayed primarily using perfective verbs (aorists). Saul is then accepted and continues his proclamation of Jesus (v. 28; cf. v. 19b), especially among Greek-speaking Jews (v. 29a; cf. vv. 20–22). His activities are portrayed in imperfectives (imperfects and present participles), suggesting a summary of a longer period. The third phase of events begins with a reaction to Saul that echoes that in Damascus, as these Jews seek to kill him (v. 29b; cf. vv. 23–24), further fulfilling Jesus's words to Ananias (v. 16). When the believers learn of these hostile plans, they take Saul to the coast and then on to Tarsus (v. 30; cf. v. 25); as with Barnabas's intervention, perfective verbs naturally portray this change of situation and scene.

Excursus: The Three Acts Accounts of the Damascus Road Experience

Acts contains three accounts of this story: 9:1–31; 22:3–21; and 26:2–23. The similarities and differences among them require consideration. The voice speaking the story differs: 9:1–31 is in Luke's authorial third-person voice, whereas the others are both spoken by the character Paul. The setting of the stories differs: 9:1–31 is in the narrative flow of Acts, following Saul's participation in persecution of believers (7:58; 8:1a, 3); 22:3–21 is Paul speaking under the protection of the Romans to the riotous mob in the Jerusalem temple; and 26:2–23 is Paul addressing Agrippa and Festus in a quasi-judicial setting while imprisoned at Caesarea Maritima. These factors suggest that we ought to expect differences between the stories, as well as a common core, as the telling of each version is slanted to its literary and narrative context.

The *common core* is clear: Saul's persecution of believers (9:1; 22:3–4; 26:4–5, 9–11); Saul's authority from the high priest to seek and arrest believers (9:1b–2; 22:5a; 26:10, 12); the journey to Damascus for this purpose (9:2; 22:5b; 26:11–12); en route, close to Damascus, a bright light shining (9:3–4a; 22:6–7a; 26:13–14a); a voice heard

43 Gill, "Structure," 547–48, identifies parallelism between Saul's activities in Damascus and Jerusalem; see the following references.

by Saul that is identified as that of Jesus (9:4b–5; 22:7b–8; 26:14b–15) and tells Saul he is persecuting Jesus (9:5b; 22:8b; 16:25b); Saul is given further instructions (9:6; 22:10; 26:16–18); Saul was unable to see (9:8–9; 22:11; not mentioned in ch. 26); the role of Ananias (9:10–19; 22:12–16); and Saul's proclamation of Jesus in Damascus (9:20–22; 26:19–20a; absent in 22) and in Jerusalem (9:26–20; 22:17–21; 26:20b).

In each version, particular features are *distinctive.* In *9:1–31*: the dialogue between Ananias and the Lord (vv. 11–16), unsurprisingly absent from the other two versions, which are told from Saul's perspective; the Jewish conspiracy in Damascus to kill Saul and his escape through the wall (vv. 23–25); and Saul's journey to Tarsus (v. 31). In *22:3–21*: Paul's zeal and study under Gamaliel (v. 3; cf. 26:4–5), stressing his loyalty to Judaism, appropriately in the setting; the stress on Ananias's Jewish devotion (9:12), also natural in the temple setting among a hostile crowd who were told that Paul was not a loyal Jew (21:28); Paul's encounter with Ananias is told from Paul's perspective (22:13–16); and Paul's vision of the Lord in the temple telling him to leave and sending him to the gentiles (vv. 17–21). In *26:2–23*: Paul casting his vote against believers (v. 10), which may suggest that he was a member of the Sanhedrin; Jesus's call to Paul to mission among the gentiles as part of the Damascus Road experience (vv. 16–18); and a stress on the resurrection of Jesus (vv. 8, 23), which is (from the character Paul's perspective) the major issue at dispute in the trial, for it bespeaks the exalted status of Jesus.

There are a small number of *apparent inconsistencies,* notably: whether Saul learned of his call to gentile mission from Ananias or from Jesus (9:15–16; 22:13–16; 26:16–18); and what Saul's companions saw and heard and their bodily reaction (9:7; 22:9; 26:14a). In considering these, it is important to remember that ancient historians did not have the same concern for small points of detail that moderns do.[44]

A variety of explanations for the similarities and variations have been offered.[45] Source critics mostly regard the three stories as deriving from different sources and treat each as containing information different from the others.[46] Redaction critics attribute variations to

44 Witherington, *Acts,* 311.

45 For summaries, see Marguerat, *Historian,* 180–83; Lohfink, *Conversion,* 40–46; Collins, "Damascus Experience."

46 E.g., Jervell, *Luke,* 166, who considers that Luke wishes to preserve different traditions he has received. Witherington, "Editing," 335–44, regards the three versions as having different traditional origins: Acts 9 is based on Paul's reminiscences; Acts 22 is Luke's composition based on an oral report by Paul (he notes that the speech is given in Aramaic, 22:2); Acts 26 is Luke's eyewitness account.

Luke's literary creativity, regarding Acts 9 as the traditional narrative, with Acts 22 and 26 as edited versions.[47] Form critically, Hedrick argues that the three accounts differ in form: Acts 9 is a healing story and chs. 22 and 26 are commissioning stories.[48] Acts 26 is the most compressed and "schematic" narrative.[49] Hedrick considers that the accounts in chs. 22, 26 are "correcting the earlier legend"[50]—however, that raises the question why Luke would leave the stories with apparent contradictions, since that would be likely to confuse his readers and seems out of character with a writer who both declares and models care in making his account "orderly" (καθεξῆς, Luke 1:3).[51] Nothing in the three accounts indicates that readers should disbelieve elements of the story in Acts 9 and see chs. 22 and 26 as more accurate.

More recently, the three tellings are seen as each rooted in their narrative setting and displaying progression and development among themselves.[52] These approaches prove fruitful for understanding how Luke invites his readers to understand the story. Marguerat notices amplifications (Paul's life as a Pharisee is first mentioned in 26:4–8; Paul's persecution of believers grows from 9:1–2 to 22:3–5; 26:9–11), suppressions (Ananias is a key character in 9:10–17, is mentioned more briefly in 22:12–16, and disappears in ch. 26; Saul is persecuted in 9:23–25, 29–30, but this is not mentioned in chs. 22 and 26), and an interpolation (Paul's call to mission among gentiles is part of his meeting with Jesus in 26:16–18 but appears to be later in 9:15–16, where readers might gain the impression that Ananias relayed this call to Saul, and 22:17–21, where Saul hears this call in a vision in the temple).[53] Likewise, the portrayal of Saul's companions goes through suppression (their role decreases from 9:6–8 through 22:9, 11 to 26:14), interpolation (Luke writes of them before the conversation between Jesus and Saul, 26:14, during that conversation, 22:9–10, and afterwards, 9:7–8), and transformation (they hear without seeing in 9:7, they see without hearing in 22:9; they stand speechless

47 Notably Dibelius, *Studies*, 110, 111, 158–61; cf. Pervo, *Acts*, 233, who considers that Luke is editing a hypothetical source that stands behind Acts 9:1–19a.

48 Hedrick, "Paul's Conversion/Call."

49 Hedrick, "Paul's Conversion/Call," 427.

50 Hedrick, "Paul's Conversion/Call," 431; Aune, *Environment*, 135, suggests that Luke may be presenting the three versions and inviting readers to choose, as some Greek historians did; however, Luke does not signal that he is doing that, as the ancient historians generally do; Keener, *Acts*, 2:1601.

51 This also speaks against the view that Luke has edited his three versions derived from one brief source rather carelessly; e.g., Conzelmann, *Acts*, 72.

52 Gaventa, *Darkness*, 95; Marguerat, *Historian*, 179–204; Churchill, *Initiative*, 191–249; Witherup, "Redundancy." The first to pursue such an approach seems to be Stanley, "Conversion."

53 Marguerat, *Historian*, 185.

in 9:7, they fall to the ground with Paul in 26:14, and their posture is not mentioned in ch. 22).[54] Marguerat draws on Kurz's work to argue that what we are seeing are different perspectives based on different narrators and situations (technically, different filtrations of the story). Hence, we should read the later accounts as "retrospective readings" of the event.[55]

Seen from this perspective, Acts 9 tells the story, surrounded by other surprising conversions (see *Setting* below). Acts 22 has Paul present himself to fellow Jews as a godly, traditional Jew whose mind has been changed by his encounter with Jesus—he is defending himself against the charge of "teaching everyone everywhere against our people, our law, and this place [sc. the temple]" (21:28). Acts 26 has Paul present himself to gentiles, and he there focuses on the resurrection of Jesus as a matter of internal Jewish controversy and thus a matter that need not concern Festus and Agrippa (esp. vv. 19–23).[56]

In light of these settings, the focus on Jewish matters in the temple (Acts 22) makes good sense: it is here that Jesus is "the Nazarene," ὁ Ναζωραῖος (22:8), a phrase Luke uses of Jesus only with Jewish audiences (Luke 18:36; Acts 2:2; 3:6; 4:10; 6:14; 22:8; 24:5; 26:9).

These settings are also suggestive for the variations concerning the experience of Saul's companions: 22:9 is reporting what happened in the midst of Saul conversing with Jesus (22:7–8, 10), whereas 9:7 describes the companions' response after the conversation (9:4–6) is over.[57] Thus the focus of the two accounts is different: 22:9 draws attention afresh to the light, already mentioned in 22:6, and indicates that Saul alone hears what Jesus said. While the argument from the case following ἀκούω, "hear," is impossible to prove (see *Comment* on 9:7), the explanation that the companions hear a noise but not the content of what is said offers a plausible explanation of this difference between the two accounts, as is also the case in John 12:29, where the crowd hear the voice from heaven but do not understand. The apparent difference in posture of the companions (9:7; 26:14) is not significant—Paul himself is staring into a blinding light at this point, so he could be forgiven for not knowing the precise details[58]—and εἱστήκεισαν, "they had been standing" (9:7), highlights their presence rather than their precise posture (see *Comment* on 9:7).

Similarly, the compression involved in Acts 26 makes good sense

54 Marguerat, *Historian*, 186.

55 Marguerat, *Historian*, 187, drawing on Kurz, *Reading*, 125–31.

56 With Marguerat, *Historian*, 189–91.

57 Thus Churchill, *Initiative*, 230, suggests that the companions may not have heard the voice at first (22:9) but did so a little later (9:7).

58 So also Kurz, "Effects," 573–74; Witherington, *Acts*, 312.

of Paul saying that Jesus told him on the Damascus Road that he would go to the gentiles (26:26–18, see *Comment* there), for it allows Paul to avoid unnecessary detail and focus on the heart of his testimony to Agrippa: the resurrection of Jesus as the fulfillment of Scripture (26:8, 22–23). In this setting, Paul cuts down the story of his encounters with Jesus to the minimum—and Luke/Paul does not state in Acts 9 or 22 that Jesus did *not* call Saul to gentile mission on the Damascus Road. It is possible that Paul did receive his call to go to the gentiles on the Damascus Road, something Luke reveals only at the climax of the three tellings.[59] Paul himself implies this (Gal 1:1, 15–16). On this reading, Ananias's role in telling Paul of his vision of Jesus (22:14–15) is to confirm what had already been said in the Damascus Road encounter. Alternatively, Luke/Paul may be telescoping events for the setting before Agrippa.[60]

The broader "increasing sequence" among the three tellings is worth noticing:[61] Paul's persecuting efforts grow (9:1; 22:4; 26:9–11); the light is ever brighter (9:3; 22:6; 26:13) and spreads more widely (9:3; 22:6; 26:13); and the response to the light is more marked (9:7; 22:7; 26:14). Most notably, the conversation between Jesus and Paul develops: Jesus's message begins as a directive to wait to learn what to do, in response to an unspoken but implied question that is not answered (9:6; see *Comment* there); in the temple, Paul makes the question explicit (22:10), but Jesus does not answer it explicitly, telling Paul that he will be told in Damascus what he must do; finally, on trial, Jesus tells Paul explicitly about his calling without Paul asking the question at all (26:16–18).[62] Luke here uses literary techniques to engage readers by: (i) suspense, gradually opening readers' eyes to the nature of Paul's call through the three accounts; (ii) curiosity, provoking readers to reflect by the relation of (unasked) question and answer in the accounts; and (iii) reversal of reader expectations (peripateia), as the initial impression of Paul's call to gentile mission is that Ananias was its vehicle (9:15–16) is shifted to the temple vision as its means (22:17–21), and finally the Damascus Road encounter itself is the time when this call occurred (26:16–18).[63] Ananias's conversation with Jesus (9:15–16) thus functions as a key signal to *readers* at that point that Saul is called to gentile mission.[64]

---

59 Churchill, *Initiative*, 227–28; Witherington, *Acts*, 743–44.

60 Witherington, *Acts*, 312; Marshall, *Acts* (TNTC), 396, compares the condensed Matt 9:18 with the fuller Mark 5:22–23, 25.

61 Churchill, *Initiative*, 226; Clark, *Parallel Lives*, 157–58.

62 Churchill, *Initiative*, 226–27.

63 Churchill, *Initiative*, 228, drawing on Lodge, "Analysis," 7; similarly, Hedrick, "Paul's Conversion/Call," 427.

64 Churchill, *Initiative*, 228–29.

Setting. This story comes amidst a series of surprising conversion stories: the Samaritans, including Simon (8:4–25), the Ethiopian eunuch (8:26–4), and Cornelius's household (10:1–48). Each of the people here is transformed by their encounter with Jesus. Luke is portraying the gospel's growing embrace of those considered outsiders to the people of God (Samaritans, a magician, a eunuch, gentiles), initiated and carried forward by God (8:4–8, 26; 9:3–12; 10:1–23). Saul's story is similarly surprising, for he persecutes the believers (8:3; 9:1–2), and characters within the story express their surprise or hesitation about Saul (9:13–14, 21, 26)—he is a Jew at the greatest distance from the gospel, and thus this story fits well in this sequence of outsiders to the gospel becoming insiders.[65]

There are clear verbal and thematic echoes of the Stephen story:[66] διώκω, "persecute" (7:52; 9:4, 5); φόνος/φονεύς, "murder/murderer" (7:52; 9:1); Stephen's resistance to the accusations of his critics and Saul's resistance to the believers (8:3; 9:1–2); Saul's presence at Stephen's death (7:58; 8:1); and God's response to Stephen's dying prayer for forgiveness for his murderers (7:60) in Saul's conversion expressed in baptism (9:19).

In the wider context of Acts, the parallels between this account and the second and third accounts of Saul's Damascus Road encounter contain significant echoes of the disciples' commissioning in Luke 24:44–49 and Acts 1:3–8:[67] (i) Saul learns Jesus's true identity (9:4–5; 22:8; 26:15; Luke 24:44–46; Acts 1:3, 6–7); (ii) Saul is instructed about his role (9:15; 22:14–15; 26:16; Luke 24:48; Acts 1:8); (iii) Saul is empowered by the Spirit (9:17–18; 22:16, 17–18;[68] 26:17–18; Luke 24:49; Acts 1:4b–5, 8a); and (iv) the mission is to all nations (9:15; 22:15, 21; 26:15b–17; Luke 24:47; Acts 1:8). These common factors place Saul firmly in the same purposes of God as the first disciples, including the Jerusalem apostles.[69]

Comment

1 reintroduces Saul, the main protagonist in this section. Luke's focus is less on the persecution than on the persecutor, for that emphasizes the transformation of Saul (see also 22:4–5; 26:9–11).[70] Ὁ δὲ Σαῦλος ἔτι ἐμπνέων ἀπειλῆς καὶ φόνου εἰς τοὺς μαθητὰς τοῦ κυρίου, "Now Saul, still breathing threat and murder

65 Gaventa, *Darkness*, 67. Kern, "Conversion," argues that Saul's portrait prior to the Damascus Road event is as an outsider because of parallels with the pre-believing state of the Ethiopian eunuch (8:26–40), Cornelius (10:1–11:18), Bar Jesus (13:11), and the Philippian jailer (16:25–34).

66 Gaventa, *Darkness*, 55–56.

67 For these points, see Béchard, *Paul*, 162–63.

68 The Spirit is not explicitly mentioned here; the presence of water baptism (cf. 2:38) and a trance (ἔκστασις) (cf. 2:17b) implies the Spirit's engagement.

69 For broader parallels between Saul and the twelve, see Clark, *Parallel Lives*, 169–77.

70 Cunningham, *Tribulations*, 216–17.

against the Lord's disciples," is resumptive from 8:3. The anaphoric article Ὁ indicates that this is the Saul previously mentioned there (and 7:58; 8:1—all three earlier use are anarthrous), and ἔτι, "still," signals a continuation of his earlier actions,[71] as does the echo of ἄνδρας τε καὶ γυναῖκας, "both men and women" (9:2; 8:3).[72] Saul progresses from bystander (7:58) to approver of persecution (8:1) to persecutor (9:1–2; 8:3), a journey that contrasts with his humbling by Jesus (9:8–9), leading to his submission to Jesus (vv. 11–12, 17–19a), and active (and effective) proclamation of Jesus (vv. 19b–22).[73] The contrast of Saul's rage (cf. 8:3) with the eunuch's joy (8:39) is considerable and portrays Saul as strongly opposed to the gospel as the eunuch is strongly immersed in the gospel.[74] Saul is "fighting against God" (5:39) in opposing the Jesus movement.[75] ἀπειλῆς, "threat," recalls the threats made by the Sanhedrin against the apostles (4:29; the only other NT use is Eph 6:9).[76] φόνου, "murder," echoes Stephen's description of the Sanhedrin as φονεῖς, "murderers" (7:52; there, of Jesus).[77] Luke does not make Saul's motivation explicit,[78] although it seems likely that he saw biblical actions against those who broke the Jewish law as precedents, such as Phinehas killing an Israelite man having sex with a Midianite woman (Num 25:6–15),[79] or Moses killing Israelites who took Midianite wives and thus apostatized (Num 25:1–5), or Mattathias and the Hasideans killing unfaithful Jews (1 Macc 2:23–26, 42–48).[80] (See also *Comment* on 8:3.) The repetition of μαθητής, "disciple," throughout this section is notable (vv. 1, 10, 19, 25, 26), signaling an interest in discipleship in Luke's telling of the story. To call the believers τοὺς μαθητὰς τοῦ κυρίου, "the Lord's disciples," stresses Jesus's engagement with his followers in their suffering, a

---

71 With Bruce, *Acts* (1990), 232. Longenecker, *Rhetoric*, 193–94, considers 9:1–31 to be part of a "chain-link construction" with 8:1b–3, where the earlier passage anticipates the later, fuller one.

72 Cunningham, *Tribulations*, 216.

73 Similarly, Gaventa, "Enemy," 443. Lamoreaux, "Social Identity," 130–32, working with a model of social identity theory, characterizes Saul's movement as transfer from near the center of one in-group to near the center of another (see his summary diagram, 132).

74 Gaventa, *Darkness*, 56.

75 Lang, *Kunst*, 228–29. He nicely summarizes that "the phenomenological God-fighter is now the phenomenological God-lover (Theophilus)!" (241, my translation).

76 With Clark, *Parallel Lives*, 154.

77 Gaventa, *Darkness*, 55.

78 A former generation of scholars attempted to psychoanalyze Saul and suggested that he was attempting to externalize his own doubts about his opposition to the believers (e.g., Dodd, "Psychological," 100–101; Goguel, "Réalisations," 224), but such a speculative reading is highly unlikely, not least in the light of Phil 3:4b–6, which indicates Paul's considerable satisfaction with his standing with God prior to the Damascus Road experience. For summary of views and cogent critique, see Peace, *Conversion*, 43–50.

79 "[I]t is clear that the imagery of the priestly story is meant to be explicitly sexual"; Dozeman, "Numbers," 199.

80 With Longenecker, "Acts (2007)," 851–52, who also cites possible precedents from the Dead Sea Scrolls: 1QS IX, 3–4, 20–22; 1QH[a] XIV, 13–15. See the imaginative narrative reconstruction of Saul's mindset in Wright, *Biography*, 27–39.

point underlined in Jesus's identification with the believers' suffering (vv. 4–5; see *Comment* on v. 5), suffering Saul himself will experience as a disciple (v. 16).

This passage is dense with references to Jesus as κύριος, "Lord" (vv. 1, 5, 10 [twice], 11, 13, 15, 17, 29), highlighting Jesus's sovereign power, breaking into Saul's life and orchestrating Ananias's visit to Saul, and implying his place alongside YHWH as deserving worship and obedience (cf. 2:36 with *Comment* there).[81] With the identification of Jesus as ὁ υἱὸς τοῦ θεοῦ, "the son of God," and ὁ χριστός, "the Messiah" (9:20, 22), this passage is christologically significant—in becoming a disciple, Saul is accepting Jesus as identified in this constellation of ways.

προσελθὼν τῷ ἀρχιερεῖ ᾐτήσατο παρ' αὐτοῦ ἐπιστολὰς εἰς Δαμασκὸν πρὸς τὰς συναγωγάς, "went to the high priest and asked letters from him for the synagogues of Damascus." Saul initiates the new phase of persecution, which appears remarkable for a relatively young man. However, Paul himself speaks of his persecution of the believers and observes that he was "advancing in Judaism beyond many among my peers" (Gal 1:13–14), something he would scarcely write if it were untrue, for it was deeply embarrassing to him as a believer. Indeed, he claims that it was well-known (Gal 1:13).[82]

2 The nature of the ἐπιστολάς, "letters," which Saul sought from the high priest is unclear. They are addressed εἰς Δαμασκὸν πρὸς τὰς συναγωγάς, "to the synagogues of Damascus," rather than the civil authorities,[83] and thus may be simply letters of recommendation of Saul that requested the synagogues' cooperation in his task. The high priest is highly regarded in Jewish communities, even outside Judea, where he does not have legal jurisdiction, and such a request would be likely to be accepted and acted upon—hence v. 14 presents Ananias as believing that Saul has ἐξουσίαν παρὰ τῶν ἀρχιερέων, "authority from the chief priests" (see further on v. 14). The high priest has some power of extradition, according to evidence from the previous two centuries: (i) the Egyptian ruler, Ptolemy VIII, was instructed by the Roman ambassador to hand over offenders to Simon the high priest (138 BC; 1 Macc 15:21); (ii) Julius Caesar in 47 BC confirmed to Hyrcanus and his descendants the powers previously granted to the high priest, including that he might determine "any question about the Jewish customs" (τις ζήτησις περὶ τῆς Ἰουδαίων ἀγωγῆς, Josephus, *Ant.* 14.10.2 §§192–95, quoting 195).[84] However, these examples are of letters from Romans to civil authorities, whereas Saul's letters are from the high priest to the synagogues, and it is thus unlikely that they carried legal force with the Roman authorities.

εἰς Δαμασκὸν πρὸς τὰς συναγωγάς, "for the synagogues of Damascus." The

81 With Clark, *Parallel Lives*, 166–67.
82 See the judicious discussion in Longenecker, *Galatians*, 27–30.
83 Unless we should translate "to Damascus, concerning the synagogues," in which case the letters may be to the civil authorities; so Schnabel, *Acts*, 442.
84 On the role and powers of the high priest, see Sanders, *Judaism*, 319–27.

city of Damascus is located in southern Syria (it is the capital of Syria today), some 241 km/150 miles by road north-northeast of Jerusalem. Saul travels on Roman roads available for this journey. His journey would have taken six to seven days on foot;[85] that seems his probable means of travel because of his falling to the ground (v. 4), getting to his feet, and being led by the hand (v. 8).[86] Damascus is a very ancient city, dating at least to the fifteenth century BC,[87] and a prosperous trading center with a multicultural population, including a substantial Jewish community in the first century AD.[88] Luke's plural συναγωγάς, "synagogues," is consistent with Josephus's report that 10,500 Jews are killed by the gentile population in AD 66;[89] Josephus also notes that some (many?) gentile women convert to Judaism (*J.W.* 2.20.2 §§559–61). Philo mentions Cilicia, whose capital Tarsus is, as a province where Jews live (*Legat.* 281), and in ca. AD 80, Philostratus implies that there are Jewish Tarsian citizens (*Vit. Apoll.* 6.34). Saul's long journey implies that he has good information of significant numbers of believers in Damascus at this time (cf. Acts 9:19b). There is also an Essene community in or near the city (CD VI, 5, 19; VIII, 21; XIX, 34; XX, 12); they probably chose to relocate there because of the expectation of the messianic age beginning there, prompted by reading Isa 8:23–9:1 (EVV 9:1–2) as prophesying God's shining light into the region of Naphtali, within which Damascus is located (Josephus, *Ant.* 5.1.22 §86).[90]

ὅπως ἐάν τινας εὕρῃ τῆς ὁδοῦ ὄντας . . . δεδεμένους ἀγάγῃ εἰς Ἰερουσαλήμ, "so that if he should find any belonging to the Way . . . he might bring them bound to Jerusalem," nests a third-class condition within a ὅπως, "so that," purpose clause. Saul's purpose in obtaining letters of recommendation from the high priest is to find and take believers into custody and take them to Jerusalem (presumably to stand trial for apostasy). Luke presupposes that there are such people in Damascus, although he has not given any account of how the gospel reached the city: at most 8:1b, 4, and 11:19 hint at this. In particular, 11:19 is resumptive from 8:4 and may well cover the same time period as the stories of Philip, Peter, and this story in Acts 8–11.

The believers whom Saul seeks are characterized as τῆς ὁδοῦ ὄντας, "belonging to the Way," and include ἄνδρας τε καὶ γυναῖκας, "both men and women." This is Luke's first use of the designation "the Way" for the believers (also in 18:25–26; 19:9, 23; 22:4; 24:14, 22), a term that identifies them as a group

---

85 Compare Peter's two-day journey from Joppa to Caesarea, a distance of about 40 miles/64 km (10:23–24, 30). On land travel in the ancient world, see Thompson, "Internet," 60–65; Rapske, "Acts," 3–21, esp. 6–7.

86 Generations of NT students have been misled by Caravaggio's 1601 painting "The Conversion of Saul on the Way to Damascus," which shows Saul having fallen from a horse.

87 On the city's history, see J. McRay, "Damascus," *ABD* 2:5–8.

88 Gill, "Behind," 100, notes numismatic evidence from Damascus for cults of various gods.

89 The larger figure of eighteen thousand in *J.W.* 7.8.7 §368 includes women and children.

90 Cf. Paul's use of this image in 2 Cor 4:6 Riesner, *Period*, 237–38.

within Judaism[91]—a group Saul sees as heterodox.[92] Saul intends not only to persecute Hellenistic believers but τινας, "any," who were members of this group.[93] "The Way" is used at Qumran[94] to indicate the community's strict observation of the Torah (1QS VIII, 12–15), rooted in Isa 40:3, "A voice cries out, 'In the wilderness, prepare the way of the Lord (LXX τὴν ὁδὸν κυρίου), make straight in the desert a highway for our God.'" Acts's use of this term is located in contexts of opposition and found on the lips of outsiders to the believing community, or those speaking of their life when outsiders, although the use here suggests that the term was a self-designation. It is used only in Palestine (Acts 9:2; 22:4; 24:12, 22) and Ephesus (18:25–26; 19:9, 23) and thus may not be widely used by the believers—this clustering indicates the term's origins in a Jewish, Palestinian matrix and signals that the believing community saw themselves as the heirs of Israel's role, as the promised restored people of God (see *Comment* on 15:13–18). This designation may well echo John's call to prepare the way of the Lord (itself drawn from Isa 40:3; see Luke 3:4) and thus contribute to our recognition of the strong influence of Isa 40–55 on Luke. ἄνδρας τε καὶ γυναῖκας, "both men and women," echoes other uses of this phrase (Acts 5:14—see *Comment* there; 8:3, 12; 22:14) and, as in 8:3 and 22:14, indicates the thoroughness of Saul's persecuting activity.[95] The mix of the sexes in the believing community contrasts with the all-male group of persecutors traveling with Saul (9:7).

3 Ἐν δὲ τῷ πορεύεσθαι ἐγένετο αὐτὸν ἐγγίζειν τῇ Δαμασκῷ, "As he was traveling and getting near to Damascus," locates the event not far from the city. ἐγένετο + infinitive echoes LXX, where it translates Heb. וַיְהִי וְ (*wayyəhî wə*), "it came to pass that."[96] Luke's style here may be because he is describing a theophany;[97] it may also be that he is drawing on a Semitic source, whether oral or written, although the frequency of this construction in Acts (17x; 5x in Luke) suggests caution about the latter.

ἐξαίφνης τε αὐτὸν περιήστραψεν φῶς ἐκ τοῦ οὐρανοῦ, "suddenly there was a light from heaven shining around him," portrays Saul in the middle of a pool of light, somewhat like a spotlight on a theatre stage (as 22:6). The focus is entirely on Saul here—we only learn in 9:7 that he has companions traveling with him.[98]

91 On "the Way," see Walton, "Calling," 236–38; Trebilco, *Self-designations*, 247–71.

92 I.e., Luke does not anachronistically separate believers from Jews; with Hultgren, "Persecutions," 100.

93 *Contra*, e.g., Hengel and Schwemer, *Paul between*, 88–89; Haenchen, "Book," 263–65, speculating without basis that Saul lived in Damascus. For critique of the wider view of the Hellenists presupposed by such scholars, see Walton, "Minority."

94 E.g., CD I, 13; II, 6; XX, 18; 1QS IX, 17, 18; X, 21; XI, 13.

95 With Seim, *Message*, 21.

96 E.g., Gen 19:29, among many others.

97 Barrett, *Acts*, 1:448.

98 The singular focus on Saul differs from Xenophon, *Cyr.* 4.2.15, where a light from heaven

Light is a regular symbol for God's presence in Scripture,[99] and thus when we learn that the one who appears is Jesus (9:17), the implication is that Jesus now shares the divine light and is thus appropriately designated "Lord" (see *Comment* on vv. 5, 10, 17). This heavenly opening echoes both Stephen's death (7:55–56), which suggests that what is now happening is an answer to Stephen's dying prayer (7:60), and Jesus's ascension, with its threefold εἰς τὸν οὐρανόν, "into heaven" (1:9–11). Both echoes bespeak the christological reality that Jesus the Lord invades earthly space from heaven to make himself known to Saul in order to commission him for service.[100] Paul himself draws on this experience in speaking of τὸν φωτισμὸν τοῦ εὐαγγελίου τῆς δόξης τοῦ Χριστοῦ, ὅς ἐστιν εἰκὼν τοῦ θεοῦ . . . ἔλαμψεν ἐν ταῖς καρδίαις ἡμῶν πρὸς φωτισμὸν τῆς γνώσεως τῆς δόξης τοῦ θεοῦ ἐν προσώπῳ Ἰησοῦ Χριστοῦ, "the light of the glorious gospel of the Messiah, who is the image of God . . . [God] has shone in our hearts to give the light of the knowledge of God's glory in the face of Jesus the Messiah" (2 Cor 4:4, 6).[101] There he treats the message about Jesus as enlightening people and in both clauses highlights Jesus's exalted status—God is now known through Jesus.

4 καὶ πεσὼν ἐπὶ τὴν γῆν, "He fell to the ground." Saul is overpowered by the experience; his fall expresses submission before the powerful experience he is having[102] and echoes the reaction of others to a theophany (e.g., Gen 17:3; Num 22:31; Josh 5:14; Ezek 1:28; Tob 12:16).[103] In the Gospels prostration expresses reverence for Jesus, often in combination with προσκυνέω, "worship, do obeisance" (e.g., Matt 2:11; Mark 7:25; John 11:32), and Revelation portrays the elders bowing to the ground in worship before God as ruler of all (Rev 4:10). Saul is not yet consciously submitting to Jesus, for he does not know who is speaking (9:5),[104] although Luke's audience will realise that prostration is appropriate as a response to Jesus's appearance. Saul's loss of self-control contrasts with ancient expectations of elite masculinity, that a true man is in control.[105] Saul's posture of submission echoes and parodies

---

(φῶς . . . ἐκ τοῦ οὐρανοῦ) is said to shine upon (προφανές) Cyrus and his army, giving them courage for the battle to come against the Hyrcanians.

99 E.g., Exod 10:23b; Ps 42:3 (LXX; MT 43:3); 88:16 (LXX; MT 89:15, EVV 89:14); 103:1–2 (LXX; MT 104:1–2); Isa 2:5; 60:1; Wis 7:26. See the helpful discussion "Light," *DBIm* 509–11.

100 Sleeman, *Geography*, 199–200; see also *Comment* on 1:9–11; 7:55–56, 60. Luke (unsurprisingly as an ancient author) shows no interest in psychologizing interpretations of Paul's experience; for speculation about such things drawing on anthropological research, see Pilch, *Visions*, 69–77; Pilch, "Trance," esp. 697–703, postulating that Paul's "ecstatic trance" arose from travel (in heat) and intense concentration. Pilch acknowledges that Paul's (and Luke's) interpretation of these events is as God's actions and initiative (*Visions*, 73), thus avoiding the error of "nothing-buttery" (MacKay, *Clockwork Image*, 40–47).

101 With Kim, *Origin* (2nd ed.), 5–11.

102 Acts 22:7 maintains the focus on Saul whereas 26:14 indicates that Saul's companions also fell to the ground—see *Comment* there.

103 Churchill, *Initiative*, 38.

104 With Schnabel, *Acts*, 444.

105 Wilson, "Blinding," 370–71.

kneeling before the emperor or his representative, and implicitly places Jesus above the emperor (cf. 10:36; 17:7). Contrast Peter's rejection of Cornelius's falling upon his knees in obeisance before Peter (10:25).

ἤκουσεν φωνὴν λέγουσαν αὐτῷ, "[he] heard a voice saying to him." The experience is first portrayed as auditory: the focus is on the message.[106] There is no indication of Saul's seeing Jesus yet (nor in 22:14; 26:14), although 9:7 may hint that Saul sees something (see *Comment* there), v. 17 speaks of Jesus as ὁ ὀφθείς σοι, "the one who appeared to you," v. 27 has Barnabas explain that Saul εἶδεν τὸν κύριον, "had seen the Lord," and the experience is called ὀπτασία, "a vision," in 26:19.[107]

Σαοὺλ Σαούλ, τί με διώκεις;, "Saul, Saul, why do you keep persecuting me?" The vocative "Saul" is repeated, suggesting some intensity in the address[108] as well as echoing biblical commissioning stories (and thereby hinting that this encounter is a commissioning, which vv. 15–16 make clear).[109] "Saul" is in the LXX spelling Σαούλ, used for King Saul (the more regular spelling in Acts is Σαῦλος).[110] This spelling is appropriate given that Luke later narrates Paul saying that Jesus spoke to him "in the Hebrew language," τῇ Ἑβραΐδι διαλέκτῳ (26:14). The question identifies Jesus with his followers, as "whom you keep persecuting" (v. 5) confirms, echoing Jesus's prediction that his followers will be persecuted because they are his people (Luke 10:16),[111] and Stephen's observation that the Sanhedrin's ancestors persecuted the prophets (7:52). Indeed, other than Stephen's words, Luke reserves διώκω, "persecute," for versions of this story in Acts (9:4, 5; 22:4, 7, 8; 26:11, 14, 15).[112] Paul's letters also present his pre-Damascus-Road life as one of persecuting believers (see *Comment* on 8:3).

5 τίς εἶ, κύριε;, "Who are you, Lord?" Saul, tutored by the Jewish Scriptures, would expect that he was encountering God or an angel: a voice following a display of light echoes Moses's experiences at the burning bush (Exod 3:2–4, also with a double vocative) and at Sinai (Exod 19:16–20). Thus, it is

---

106 In tune with other epiphanies; Churchill, *Initiative*, 38.

107 Cf. 1 Cor 9:1: οὐχὶ Ἰησοῦν τὸν κύριον ἡμῶν ἑόρακα;, "I have seen Jesus our Lord, haven't I?" Lohfink, *Conversion*, 25, treats this verse as contradicting Acts 9:4, but the indications noted above suggest that Luke understands that Saul did see Jesus here; with Churchill, *Initiative*, 199, 203.

108 Cf. LXX Gen 22:1; 46:2; Exod 3:4; 1 Sam 3:4; 2 Sam 19:1, 5; Luke 10:41; 13:34; 22:31

109 Gen 22:11; 46:2; Exod 3:4; 1 Sam 3:4, 10; with Cunningham, *Tribulations*, 224.

110 See *Excursus: The Names of Saul/Paul* at *Comment* on 13:9–10.

111 Cunningham, *Tribulations*, 221.

112 Gaventa, *Darkness*, 58, suggests that Saul is "the *one* who deserves that title [sc. persecutor]" in Luke-Acts (her italics). Rius-Camps and Read-Heimerdinger, *Message*, 2:200–201, note the use of the compound verb καταδιώκω, "pursue (with a view to persecuting)," concerning King Saul's pursuit of David (LXX 1 Sam 20:20; 27:1) and plausibly suggest there are other parallels with Samuel's spirit appearing to Saul in 1 Sam 28:8–25. The major difference is that King Saul called for Samuel's spirit to appear and was wrong to do so, whereas the initiative here lies with Jesus.

appropriate to translate κύριε as "Lord" rather than the polite address "Sir."[113] This question is not simply about the identity of the speaker; it is also, implicitly, asking for deeper knowledge of that person.[114]

ὁ δέ· ἐγώ εἰμι Ἰησοῦς ὃν σὺ διώκεις, "The speaker replied, 'I am Jesus, whom you keep persecuting.'" Now Saul learns the astonishing truth that the one whom he had assumed to be dead is alive and present with God. Bowker makes the intriguing suggestion that Saul may be engaging in a *merkabah* meditation on the chariot vision of Ezek 1 and is amazed to discover that the figure in the chariot throne is the exalted Jesus rather than YHWH (Ezek 1:26–28).[115] If so, Ezekiel's commission (Ezek 2) takes on a new meaning as Saul's commission to be an advocate for Jesus. This latter possibility is strengthened by noticing the quotations from Ezek 2:1, 3 in Acts 26:16 (see *Comment* there). For Saul to attack Jesus's followers is to attack him, and that implies that Jesus is present with the believers in different locations where Saul has been persecuting them, at least in Jerusalem (8:1b–3) and Damascus (9:2). Thus, the exalted Jesus is to be seen as able to be present in more than one location and as identified with his people—both divine characteristics (e.g., Ps 139:10 [LXX 138:10]; Gen 28:15; Exod 29:45–46; Isa 41:10; 43:5; 57:15). The vast ontological distance between Jesus and Saul is emphasized by the emphatic personal pronouns ἐγώ, "I," and σύ, "you."[116] This saying is "entirely congruous with the Pauline conception" of the relationship of Christ and believers,[117] for Paul's "in Christ" language evokes a similar identification of Jesus with the believers.[118] However, it is less likely that ἐγώ εἰμί, "I am," is a deliberate echo of the divine name YHWH (Exod 3:13–15), for Luke uses the phrase elsewhere without such reference (Luke 1:9; 22:70; 24:39; Acts 10:21; 18:10; 22:3).[119]

6 ἀλλ', "instead," introduces a sharp contrast between Saul's former persecution of Jesus and his people and the obedience to Jesus that he will now exhibit. Rather than Saul doing the decision-making in planning to persecute the believers, Jesus now instructs Saul what to do.

ἀνάστηθι καὶ εἴσελθε εἰς τὴν πόλιν καὶ λαληθήσεταί σοι ὅ τί σε δεῖ ποιεῖν, "get up and enter the city and you will be told what you must do." Jesus instructs Saul what he must do, and the instructions create further dependence by Saul on Jesus, as well as introducing an element of suspense for the reader—what will the instructions be?[120] The first of a cluster of passive verbs follow, opening a sequence running through to v. 9, marking Saul as a submissive "unmanly

113 With most EVV (not NLT); Bruce, *Book* (1988), 182–83; Dunn, "ΚΥΡΙΟΣ," 248; Tabb, *Suffering*, 144n163; contra Gaventa, *Acts*, 149; Macnamara, *Instrument*, 78.

114 Batibuka, "Baptism," 90.

115 Bowker, "Merkabah," 171–72; cf. Allison, "Acts 9:1–9."

116 Sleeman, *Geography*, 201.

117 Moule, *Origin*, 87; cf. Campbell, *Paul*, 420.

118 On this language, see the full discussion of Campbell, *Paul*, 67–199.

119 With Churchill, *Initiative*, 247.

120 Miller, *Convinced*, 190, notes that this suspense is unusual.

man":[121] ἀνάστηθι καὶ εἴσελθε, "get up now and enter," uses a pair of aorist passive imperatives to signal a here-and-now action—Saul is to obey without delay (cf. Philip, 8:26–27 with *Comment*). λαληθήσεταί σοι uses a future passive indicative that could be translated "it will be told to you"—the instruction comes from an outside source, as in this experience. ὅ τί, "what," introduces the answer to an indirect (and thus unspoken but implied) question, "What must I do?"[122] ὅ τί σε δεῖ ποιεῖν, "what you must do," uses the Lukanism δεῖ + infinitive, "it is necessary," to signal a divine necessity—this is what God intends for Saul, by contrast with Saul's earlier conviction that he must (δεῖν) oppose Jesus (26:9).[123] The time of this further revelation of Saul's future life is his meeting with Ananias, who relays to Saul what Jesus tells him (vv. 15–16).

7 οἱ δὲ ἄνδρες οἱ συνοδεύοντες αὐτῷ εἱστήκεισαν ἐνεοί, "The men who were traveling with him had been standing speechless." Only now does Luke introduce Saul's companions, who are most likely men who hold the same view of Jesus and his followers as Saul himself, since Saul would hardly be capable of pursing the believers to arrest them alone.[124] εἱστήκεισαν, "[they] had been standing," here focuses on their presence rather than their posture[125] and is compatible with Saul's later statement that all of them fell to the ground (26:14).[126]

ἀκούοντες μὲν τῆς φωνῆς μηδένα δὲ θεωροῦντες, "because, as they heard the voice, they saw no one," reinforces the sense that the message is central to Saul's experience. Acts 22:9 reports that the companions did not hear the voice, and some scholars appeal to Greek case use to resolve this apparent contradiction. Here, the voice is genitive τῆς φωνῆς—in classical use the more usual case for the *person* heard without reference to understanding; 22:9 states τὴν δὲ φωνὴν οὐκ ἤκουσαν τοῦ λαλοῦντός μοι, "but they did not hear the voice which spoke to me," using the accusative τὴν . . . φωνήν—in classical use the more usual case for the *content* of what is heard and indicating understanding.[127] However, Luke does not consistently observe this classical "rule," particularly when the object of ἀκούω, "hear," is φωνή, "voice."[128] Haenchen observes regarding this issue, "it is only the means of expression [sc. between 9:7 and 22:9] that has changed, not the sense of the statement,"[129] i.e., the apparent

121 Wilson, "Blinding," 372n16.

122 BDF, §300(1); Robertson, 731.

123 Cosgrove, "Divine," 176–77.

124 Rather than simply fellow-travelers who banded together for safety; so Roloff, *Apostelgeschichte*, 150. They may have been members of the temple police; so Schnabel, *Acts*, 445.

125 "ἵστημι," BDAG 482, §C.2.c.

126 Contra the rather sweeping dismissal of this view by Lohfink, *Conversion*, 39.

127 MHT, 1:66; Robertson, 506, both regard this as explaining the difference between the two uses.

128 Bratcher, "ἀκούω"; Moehring, "Verb." Wallace, 133–34, cites examples of ἀκούω + gen. as indicating understanding of the content of what is heard (e.g., Acts 3:23; 11:7) and of ἀκούω + acc. where little understanding is present (e.g., Luke 21:9; Acts 5:24).

129 Haenchen, *Acts*, 322.

contradiction is not real—Luke is varying his style,[130] perhaps in tune with different sources for the stories[131] (although this is impossible to establish with confidence). Luke himself sees no difficulty in having these two different expressions within his book, a book he would edit and revise before allowing public access to it,[132] and so he probably thinks this minor difference is appropriate within the tradition of ancient historiography and thus not to be pressed in the way modern scholars are inclined to do.[133] Putting 9:7 and 22:9 together produces a coherent picture: the companions heard something but did not hear the conversation between Jesus and Saul. The implied contrast μηδένα δὲ θεωροῦντες, "but they saw no one," suggests that Saul sees the exalted Jesus and thus contributes to the emerging picture of the experience, a picture that will be expanded further (9:17, 27).

8–9 ἀνεῳγμένων δὲ τῶν ὀφθαλμῶν αὐτοῦ οὐδὲν ἔβλεπεν, "but when he opened his eyes, he could see nothing." Saul's visual impairment humbles him (in Greco-Roman terms, he loses honor[134]), in parallel with the magician Elymas being blinded at Saul's hands and thus prevented from opposing Saul's gospel proclamation to Sergius Paulus (13:6–12). In Scripture, God blinds people for a time to stop their intended erroneous action (Gen 19:11; 2 Kgs 6:18), as here.[135] Notably, a man from a priestly family who had impaired sight (among other disabilities) could not function as a priest (Lev 21:18, 20). Metaphorically, blindness is widespread as an image for lack of spiritual discernment or an inability and/or unwillingness to recognize the truth (e.g., Exod 23:8; Job 9:24; Isa 44:9–10; Jas 1:23–24; Rev 3:17), and both leads to and is itself an expression of God's judgment (Deut 28:28–29; Isa 6:9–10; 29:2–10; Rom 1:21).[136] Paradoxically, Isaiah's servant of YHWH is blind (Isa 42:19; cf. 43:8) and yet is commissioned to open blind people's eyes (Isa 42:7; cf. 61:1). Thus, "[b]efore Paul can embody the vocation of Israel to be a light to the nations he must be converted from his condition of embodying Israel's blind resistance to the straight way of God."[137] In Luke's Gospel, Jesus heals people with visual impairments (7:21; 18:35–43) and declares this as part of his mission in reading Isa 61:1–2 in the Nazareth synagogue (Luke 4:18). Jesus will go on to heal Saul through Ananias (Acts 9:17–18). Hamm observes that ἀνεῳγμένων could be passive voice (which is identical in form to the middle

130 Keener, *Acts*, 3:3231.

131 Wenham, "Acts II," 219.

132 See the valuable discussion of editing of books in antiquity applied to Acts in Strange, *Problem*, 167–89.

133 With Keener, *Acts*, 3:3231.

134 Czachesz, "Exegesis," 25–26, hints at the double reversal of Saul's honor: he first loses his honor and then is given the honored role of Jesus's messenger. On Greco-Roman and Jewish views of the unmanliness of blindness, see Wilson, "Blinding," 375–83.

135 It is notable that the language of "punishment" is not used, and thus humbling is a better way to understand this episode, contra Buitenwerf, "Acts 9:1–25," 65–66.

136 More fully, see "Blind, Blindness," *DBIm* 99; Røsæg, "Blinding," 159–70.

137 Hamm, "Blindness," 70.

voice), and thus the phrase means "when his eyes *were opened*, he could see nothing."[138] The opening in view is then Jesus opening Saul's eyes both to see Jesus and to recognize him as Lord (cf. 9:27). This is possible: Luke may be playing on the ambiguity of the verb voice here. If so, it continues the stream of passive verbs concerning Saul begun in v. 6 (see *Comment* there).

χειραγωγοῦντες δὲ αὐτὸν εἰσήγαγον εἰς Δαμασκόν. καὶ ἦν ἡμέρας τρεῖς μὴ βλέπων, "so, leading him by the hand, they entered Damascus. And he [sc. Saul] was sightless for three days." There is considerable irony in the man who was coming to Damascus to bring (ἀγάγῃ from ἄγω) men and women believers bound (v. 2)—and thus leading *them* by the hand—now finding himself entering Damascus (εἰσήγαγον from the compound εἰσάγω) in that condition (cf. also ἤγαγεν, v. 27). The verb χειραγωγέω, "lead by the hand," another compound of ἄγω, is found only here and in the parallel 22:11 in the NT; the cognate adjective χειραγωγός, "one who leads by the hand," is used of Elymas's response to being blinded (13:11), further underlining the parallel stories of two rebels against Jesus who are blinded. Although the participle is active voice, Saul is the recipient of the leading by hand, thus continuing the theme of his "unmanly" lack of self-control (see *Comment* on 9:6).[139]

καὶ οὐκ ἔφαγεν οὐδὲ ἔπιεν, "and he neither ate nor drank." Saul's blindness becomes the occasion for seeking God earnestly (also 9:11). "Ironically, it is in being blinded that Saul really begins to see."[140] Fasting was, and is, a widely practised Jewish discipline, used when seeking God (e.g., Pss 35:13 [LXX 34:13]; 69:10 [LXX 68:11, MT 69:11]; Acts 13:2; 14:23), particularly in repentance (e.g., on the Day of Atonement, Lev 16:29, 31; 23:27, 29, 32).[141] The prophet Anna exemplifies this attitude (Luke 2:37), and the disciples of John and the Pharisees fast regularly (Luke 5:33; 18:12). Saul's fasting connotes praying.[142]

10 Ἦν δέ τις μαθητὴς ἐν Δαμασκῷ ὀνόματι Ἁνανίας, "Now, there was a certain disciple in Damascus named Ananias," introduces Jesus's agent in restoring Saul's sight and inducting him into the believing community, the first stage of his resocialization as a Jesus follower (see *Comment* on vv. 19, 27).[143] Ananias is characterised as μαθητής, "a disciple," the first use of this term since 6:1, 2, 7 (see *Comment* there), marking him as a follower of Jesus. The term is ubiquitous in this passage, used six times (9:1, 10, 19, 25, 26), but elsewhere in the plural to denote the body of believers. The name Ananias was not uncommon (notoriously in 5:1, 3, 5).[144]

138 Hamm, "Blindness," 64; Witherup, "Redundancy," 75–76.
139 Wilson, "Blinding," 373–74.
140 Humphrey, *And I Turned*, 87.
141 More fully, see "Fasting," *DBIm* 273; J. Muddiman, "Fast, Fasting," *ABD* 2:773–76.
142 Twelftree, "Prayer," 275.
143 Czachesz, *Narratives*, 63–64, identifies these three stages but anachronistically identifies Luke's presentation as a "bureaucratic machine." The earliest believers do not appear so organized at this time!
144 Cf. the high priest Ananias (23:2; 24:1). See also Josephus, *Ant.* 20.5.2 §103; 20.6.2 §131;

καὶ εἶπεν πρὸς αὐτὸν ἐν ὁράματι ὁ κύριος, "and the Lord said to him in a vision." As with Jesus's appearance to Saul, the message is central: the verb of speech εἶπεν, "he said," is fronted in this clause;[145] the means by which the voice was heard and the speaker follow. The authority of the one appearing is clear, as "the Lord," ὁ κύριος—indeed, κύριος appears six times in this story (vv. 10–17). This appearance is described as ὅραμα, "a vision," a visual phenomenon, and can be used for physical sight as well as non-physical visual experiences while a person is awake, often called visions.[146] Visions are a means of God speaking in the Jewish Scriptures and other Second Temple Jewish writings.[147] Significantly, by experiencing this vision Ananias is marked as one on whom the Spirit has been poured out (2:17). It is notable that Luke has not yet called Jesus's appearance to Saul a vision (see 9:17)—that seems to be the same kind of event as Jesus's post-resurrection appearances to the disciples (Luke 24).[148] Ananias's vision includes a description of a vision Saul has seen (Acts 9:12), and such "double dream-visions" are known in ancient literature and used by Luke also in Acts 9–12.[149] Such double visions link two characters tightly together.[150] A further vision is reported in 9:12. Readers are naturally expecting ὁ κύριος, "the Lord," here to be the same as in v. 5, and v. 17 confirms this.

ἰδοὺ ἐγώ, κύριε, "Here I am, Lord." Ananias's response expresses readiness to listen and respond, echoing Abraham's similar response to God speaking (Gen 22:1 LXX)[151] and contrasting with Saul's (at best) puzzled response (Acts 9:5). He is not only a disciple but a godly and responsive one. The scene as a whole has similarities to biblical prophetic call accounts.[152]

11 ἀναστὰς πορεύθητι ἐπὶ τὴν ῥύμην τὴν καλουμένην Εὐθεῖαν, "Get up and go to

---

20.9.2 §205; 20.9.3 §§208–10; 20.9.4 §213, *J.W.* 2.12.6 §243; 2.17.6 §§426, 429; 2.17.9 §§441–42. LXX Dan 3:24 calls Azarias (Heb.) Ananias.

145 I here follow Porter's analysis: he sees the place of prominence as the front of the clause (Porter, 290–97) and rejects the view that "standard" Greek word order is verb-subject-object, contra BDF, §471(1), although note the qualification in §472(2).

146 "ὅραμα," BDAG; for fuller discussion of this category, see Miller, *Convinced*, 8–9 (who prefers the designation "dream-vision"); Hanson, "Dreams." Malina and Pilch, *Acts*, 185–87, consider visions to be an example of "alternate states of consciousness," a category from modern anthropology.

147 E.g., Gen 15:1; 46:2; Num 12:6; Job 7:4; Isa 21:1–2, 11; 23:1; Dan 2:1; 7:13; 8:2; 10:1; T. Levi 9:3; 11:5; T. Jud. 3:10; Apoc. Ab. 4:8, 11.

148 Strelan, *Strange Acts*, 133–34. Baban, *Road*, 215, distinguishes Ananias's vision from Saul's Christophany.

149 Miller, *Convinced*, 191 with n92; Wikenhauser, "Doppelträume," provides a helpful survey.

150 Wikenhauser, "Doppelträume," 111.

151 Bruce, *Acts* (1990), 237, suggests that ἰδοὺ ἐγώ is equivalent to Heb. הִנֵּנִי [*hinnenî*], used in Gen 22:1; cf. 1 Sam 3:4, 6, 8. Moule, 183, observes that ἰδοὺ ἐγώ is a "literal" translation of the Heb.

152 Marguerat, *Actes*, 1:331–32, and Macnamara, *Instrument*, 108, note: divine appearance to the prophet (v. 10a); the prophet's response (v. 10b); the prophet's mandate (vv. 11–12); objection (vv. 13–14); and divine reassurance (vv. 15–16). This pattern is found in, e.g., 1 Sam 3:4–14; Jer 1:5–98; Amos 7:14–15; Jonah 1:1–3; 3:1–3; Ezek 2:3–10.

the street called Straight." A pair of imperatives direct Ananias's movements in similar terms to Philip (8:26–27). τὴν ῥύμην τὴν καλουμένην Εὐθεῖαν, "the street called Straight," is probably the 50 ft.-/15 m-wide street with colonnades that ran east-west in the ancient city and that has been partially excavated in modern times.[153] The modern thoroughfare *Derb al-Mustaqim* is generally identified as this street.[154]

ζήτησον ἐν οἰκίᾳ Ἰούδα Σαῦλον ὀνόματι Ταρσέα, "look in a house belonging to Judas for a Tarsian named Saul." This is the first indication in Acts of Saul's place of origin (repeated 21:39; 22:3; note also 9:30; 11:25). Paul's letters give no indication of his birthplace: this is a detail Luke would scarcely invent, for Luke stresses Saul's connection with Jerusalem rather than Tarsus (9:26–29).[155] Tarsus was the capital of the Roman province of Cilicia in the southeast of modern Turkey, a prosperous city whose major industry was textiles.[156] Strabo writes of a strong interest in philosophy and education in Tarsus, including schools of rhetoric (*Geog.* 14.4.12–15).

ἰδοὺ γὰρ προσεύχεται, "notice this, he is praying." Jesus informs Ananias that Saul's response to his encounter with Jesus is to engage with God in prayer as well as fasting (Acts 9:9). Rather than exhaling "threat and murder" (v. 1), he now prays.[157] This response, as well as being natural for a deeply devout Jew, is in tune with the early community's prayers (1:14; 2:42) and the emphasis on Jesus's prayer life in the Third Gospel (see *Comment* on 1:14).

12 καὶ εἶδεν ἄνδρα ἐν ὁράματι Ἁνανίαν ὀνόματι εἰσελθόντα καὶ ἐπιθέντα αὐτῷ [τὰς] χεῖρας ὅπως ἀναβλέψῃ, "And he has seen in a vision a man called Ananias enter and lay hands on him in order that he may recover his sight." Jesus further informs Ananias that his visit will be expected, perhaps anticipating the objection Ananias will bring (vv. 13–14). Jesus's description of Saul's vision of Ananias's visit calls Ananias to go and lay hands on Saul. Saul's "unmanliness" is underlined by his need of Ananias to pray for him.[158]

13 ἤκουσα ἀπὸ πολλῶν περὶ τοῦ ἀνδρὸς τούτου, "I have heard from many people concerning this man." Saul's reputation goes before him. The fact that Ananias has only "heard" implies that Ananias has at least lived for some time in Damascus and has not experienced the Jerusalem persecution (8:1b–3) firsthand. It also implies that there is communication between believers in Damascus and Jerusalem, against some scholars who see each believing community as essentially isolated.[159] It further suggests that Ananias is far from alone in knowing Saul's past actions and his purpose in coming to Damascus,

153 McRay, "Damascus," *ABD* 2:7.
154 For good discussion, with further references, see Keener, *Acts*, 2:1652–53.
155 Schmithals, *Apostelgeschichte*, 89.
156 On Tarsus, see Schnabel, *Mission*, 2:1056–58.
157 McCollough, *Ritual*, 173.
158 Wilson, "Blinding," 374.
159 See further Thompson, "Internet"; Bauckham, "For Whom," 30–44.

and thus Ananias is in some sense a spokesman for the believers in the city.[160] Ananias's reluctance will be echoed in the Jerusalem believers' initial fear of Saul (9:26). From the perspective of Luke's hearers, Ananias's objection repeats information from vv. 1–2, and thereby underlines the magnitude of Jesus's transformation of Saul from enemy to advocate.[161]

τοῖς ἁγίοις σου, "your holy ones."[162] This is the first use of this expression for Christians in Acts (it is found again in only 9:32, 41; 26:10; cf. the articular participle ἡγιασμένοις, "having been sanctified," 20:32; 26:18—almost all these occasions are on Palestinian soil). This is the only place in Acts where the possessive σου, "your," is collocated with οἱ ἅγιοι, "the holy ones," and it is notable that Jesus's possession of the church is mentioned only in this setting of persecution (cf. ἐγώ εἰμι Ἰησοῦς ὃν σὺ διώκεις, "I am Jesus, whom you are persecuting" [9:5]). The general sense of ἅγιος, "holy," is "separated" or "dedicated," specifically to God.[163] It is found consistently in the plural in the NT.[164] The adjective ἅγιος, "holy," with reference to people is not common among Greco-Roman writers, and it is relatively infrequent even in LXX.[165] Second Temple Jewish writers use the term quite rarely, but when they do use "the holy ones," it refers to people in eschatological contexts, notably in 1 Enoch.[166] For example, in 1 En. 100:5 "the holy ones" are guarded by holy angels, thus making it clear that "the holy ones" are human. The Qumran community, by contrast, use "the holy ones" for angelic beings whom the covenanters believe live among them (e.g., 1QSa II, 8–9; 1QM I, 16; X, 9–11; XII, 1, 7–8) rather than for humans. Prior to NT use, then, τοῖς ἁγίοις, "the holy ones," is used rarely of humans and, when used, it is in eschatological settings. Luke's use this term of the believing communities consequently signals an inaugurated eschatology: history has been changed irrevocably by the coming, life, death, resurrection, and exaltation of Jesus, and believers now live in the age to come. This probability is strengthened by Trebilco's proposal that a key inspiration for this use is Dan 7:13–14, where "the holy ones" are associated with the exalted son of man, a passage in a clear eschatological setting.[167] Daniel

160 Johnson, *Acts*, 169.

161 Witherup, "Redundancy," 80–81. This approach enables us to make sense of Luke's writing, rather than a redaction-critical approach that assumes that Luke simply combines traditions without an overall rhetorical purpose, e.g., Löning, *Saulustradition*, 26–32.

162 On this expression in Acts, see Walton, "Calling," 239–40; Trebilco, *Self-designations*, 122–63, esp. 137–40.

163 "ἅγιος," BDAG 11, §2.d.β; Trebilco, *Self-designations*, 122.

164 The only exception is Phil 4:21, but Ἀσπάσασθε πάντα ἅγιον, "Greet *every* holy one," is hardly a real exception.

165 "ἅγιος," BDAG 11; "ἅγιος," LSJ. In MT, the Heb. equivalent is found only in Ps 34:10 [EVV 34:9] for humans and in Dan 7:18, 21, 22, 25, 27; 8:24 for celestial beings; with Collins, *Daniel*, 312–19. In LXX it is similarly found in Exod 15:11 (although anarthrous); Pss 73:3; 82:4; Wis 18:9.

166 First Enoch 43:4; 51:12; cf. 39:1, 4–5; 41:2; 47:2, 4; 48:7, 9; 50:1; 58:3, 5; 61:8, 10; 61:12; 62:8; 65:12; 69:13; 71:4.

167 Trebilco, *Self-designations*, 143–46.

7:13, 18, 22, 25, 27 interpret the son of man as embodying "the holy ones of the Most High," and thus the early believers' understanding that Jesus is the exalted Son of Man underlines that the Messiah's people saw themselves as Israel restored under the reign of Jesus (cf. Acts 7:56 with *Comment* there). Paul's use is similar, for he portrays οἱ ἅγιοι, "the holy ones," as those who will judge the world (1 Cor 6:2).

14 ἔχει ἐξουσίαν παρὰ τῶν ἀρχιερέων δῆσαι πάντας τοὺς ἐπικαλουμένους τὸ ὄνομά σου, "he has authority from the chief priests to bind all who call upon your name." Ananias's comment elucidates the authoritative nature of the letters Saul had sought and received (v. 2; see *Comment* there on the regard in which the high priest was held in diaspora Jewish communities).

Believers are characterised as those τοὺς ἐπικαλουμένους τὸ ὄνομά σου, "who call upon your name," a phrase that implies both submission and worship to Jesus, in LXX to YHWH (see *Comment* on 2:21; 7:59), as does the similar phrase in 1 Cor 1:2.[168] The verb is also used when Paul appeals to Caesar (Καίσαρα ἐπικαλοῦμαι, "I appeal to Caesar" [Acts 25:11], also vv. 12, 25; see *Comment* there). Although the use there is as a legal technical term,[169] the echo would be striking to Luke's readers, for it implicitly locates Jesus as a challenge to Caesar's authority. ὄνομα, "name," is used three times in 9:14, 15, 16, indicating the importance of Jesus's name (see *Comment* on 2:21 on the potency of Jesus's name).

15–16 are programmatic for Saul's life and service hereafter: he is chosen by the exalted Jesus to carry his name to gentiles and Jewish rulers, and this will necessarily involve suffering for the sake of Jesus. In response to Ananias focusing on Saul's past, Jesus focuses on his future.[170] Each element is important, and each element is fulfilled and developed in the rest of Acts, as well as being echoed in the Pauline letters.

15 Jesus repeats his instruction to Ananias πορεύου, "Go," and then gives an explanation introduced by ὅτι, "for." The conversation here is shorter, but the echo of Moses's reluctance to act as YHWH calls him to do at the burning bush, including repeated calls by YHWH to "Go," is noticeable (Exod 3:10, 16; 4:12: in LXX, the last uses the same imperative as here).

σκεῦος ἐκλογῆς . . . μοι, "my chosen vessel." σκεῦος, "vessel," is used metaphorically for a person carrying out a role or function.[171] The explanatory clause shows that ἐκλογῆς, "chosen," is about Saul's role rather than his transformed relationship with Jesus.[172] Saul is presented as having been selected by Jesus

168 With Hurtado, *Lord*, 143.
169 "ἐπικαλέω," BDAG 37, §3.
170 With Macnamara, *Instrument*, 102.
171 Its more mundane use is for an inanimate object used for a purpose, e.g., 10:11, 16; 11:5; 27:17. 2 Cor 4:7 combines the mundane and the metaphorical uses. BDAG 927 s.v.
172 Cf. uses of the cognate verb ἐκλέγομαι in 1:2, 24; 6:5; 15:22, 25, with Tabb, *Suffering*, 145; contra Collins, "Damascus Experience," 113; Lohfink, *Conversion*, 94, who see the choice

for a particular role, which the purpose clause that follows will elucidate. In particular, σκεῦος is used for a human body that can be a container for God's Spirit (1 Thess 4:4; Herm. Mand. 5.1.2 [33:2])—this overtone may be present in the light of Saul's filling with the Spirit (Acts 9:17). μοι, "my," is the first of a series of first-person pronouns that emphasize Saul's new relationship of belonging to Jesus: Saul will carry "my (μου) name," "I myself (ἐγώ)" will show him, and he will suffer "for my (μου) name."[173]

τοῦ βαστάσαι τὸ ὄνομά μου ἐνώπιον ἐθνῶν τε καὶ βασιλέων υἱῶν τε Ἰσραήλ, "to carry my name before gentiles and kings and sons of Israel," is an unusual expression without clear parallel in the NT. Given that Saul is being commissioned for a role, τοῦ βαστάσαι τὸ ὄνομά μου, "to carry my name," is not focused on the confession of his faith as a Jesus follower but on being an announcer of the message about Jesus.[174] This is signaled by Saul's immediate actions (vv. 20, 22) as well as the interpretation of this phrase in the second and third tellings of this story (22:15; 26:16–17).[175] Saul will announce Jesus to three groups, a statement worked out in the rest of the narrative:[176] gentiles (11:20–22, 25–26; 13:6–12, 44–48; 14:8–18; 16:25–34; 17:17b–18; 18:6–8; 19:9–10, 18–19), kings (i.e., rulers: 13:6–12; 17:19–34; 18:12–18; 23:11; 24:1–26; 25:13–14, 23–27; 26:32; 28:7–8), and Jewish people (v. 20; 13:5, 14–43; 14:1; 16:13–15; 17:1–4, 10–12, 17a; 18:4–5; 19:1–7, 8; 22:3–21). It is particularly salient that the retellings of this story on Paul's lips occur in such situations: before the Jewish people in Jerusalem (22:3–21) and before a gentile ruler, Agrippa (26:2–23).[177] Typically, Saul's first destination in a new city is a synagogue (where there is one), where he speaks to Jews and Godfearing gentiles; when he is no longer welcome there he turns to gentiles outside the synagogue (for this pattern, see Pisidian Antioch, 13:14–48). Saul's ministry will thus model the movement "to the end of the earth" (1:8).

16 γάρ, "for," defines the relationship between the Lord's two statements about Saul, that he will bear the Lord's name and that he will suffer. It probably introduces a second ground for the Lord's command πορεύου, "Go" (v. 15): Ananias must go to Saul because of the Lord's choice of Saul as a messenger and because the Lord will show Saul how much he must suffer. This fits with typical use of γάρ as providing the basis of the preceding statement[178] and is consistent with usage in Acts 10:45–46a, the only other passage in Acts where a ὅτι clause is followed by a γάρ clause—there it is clear that the γάρ

---

as being his call to be a believer. For critique of Lohfink, see Cunningham, *Tribulations*, 222–24.

173 With Gaventa, *Darkness*, 62.

174 Contra Roloff, *Apostelgeschichte*, 151; Weiser, *Apostelgeschichte*, 1:226.

175 Tabb, *Suffering*, 146.

176 Tannehill, *Unity*, 2:118, calls this statement a "preview," and helpfully tabulates the way it plays out in Acts (119–20).

177 Cf. Myllykoski, "Being," 171.

178 "γάρ," BDAG 189, §1.a.

clause introduces a second reason for the Jewish believers' amazement (see *Comment* there).[179] There may also be an explanatory connection between these two clauses, giving the sense that Saul's service of Jesus will necessarily and integrally entail suffering.[180]

ὅσα δεῖ αὐτὸν ὑπὲρ τοῦ ὀνόματός μου παθεῖν, "how much he must suffer for my name," echoes and reverses Ananias's understanding of Saul: from being one who has done "how many (ὅσα) evil deeds" (9:14) to one who will learn "how much" (ὅσα) he must suffer for Jesus.[181] The combination of [ἔ]δει, "it is necessary," with παθεῖν, "to suffer," is used elsewhere only in relation to the suffering of Jesus (Luke 9:22; 17:25; 24:26; Acts 17:3; cf. Matt 16:21; Mark 8:31; Heb 9:26), implying that Saul will instantiate in his own life the suffering of Jesus (cf. Col 1:24).[182] Just as Jesus's suffering was not an accident but God's purpose, the same is true for Saul as Jesus's messenger.[183] Indeed, Haenchen nicely observes the irony that one who came to make followers of Jesus suffer (Acts 9:13–14) will himself suffer for the sake of Jesus.[184] The suffering is ὑπὲρ τοῦ ὀνόματός μου, "for my name," recalling Jesus's words (Luke 21:12, 17) and earlier experience of the Jerusalem believers (Acts 5:41). Thus, Gaventa rightly characterizes the story as a whole as the overthrow of an enemy: Saul is transformed from an enemy of Jesus to one who serves him.[185]

Tabb observes that five functions of δεῖ, "it is necessary," can be seen at work here: Saul's ministry is part of God's plan; Saul is called by Jesus to obedience (cf. 9:5b–6; 26:19); Jesus's plan for Saul will certainly be carried out; there is a comedic divine reversal taking place in Saul's life; and this divine δεῖ provides credibility to Saul's turnaround from persecutor to proclaimer.[186]

17 *Ἀπῆλθεν* δὲ Ἁνανίας καὶ *εἰσῆλθεν* εἰς τὴν οἰκίαν καὶ *ἐπιθεὶς ἐπ᾽ αὐτὸν τὰς χεῖρας*, "Ananias *went* and *entered* the house; *laying hands on him.*" The italicised words and phrases echo v. 12, where the Lord tells Ananias what Saul has seen in his dream. Now, after the Lord's explanation and repeated command, Ananias is obedient, echoing Philip's quicker obedience (8:26–27) and prefiguring Peter's debate with the heavenly voice about the animals on the sheet (10:10–16). Peter's vision leads to his obedient going to Cornelius (10:19–20), as Peter eventually understands his vision to apply to gentile people (10:28–29). Luke stresses that the mission to gentiles—in which Saul will be a significant protagonist—is not something undertaken through human plans or understanding; here and with Peter, the Lord has to persuade and cajole

179 See the helpful discussion of this and alternative views in Tabb, *Suffering*, 147–49.
180 Cunningham, *Tribulations*, 224–25, 228.
181 Haenchen, *Acts*, 325.
182 Cunningham, *Tribulations*, 224.
183 On δεῖ, see the illuminating discussion of Tabb, *Suffering*, 146–47.
184 Haenchen, *Acts*, 325.
185 Gaventa, *Darkness*, 65.
186 Tabb, *Suffering*, 146–47, drawing on Cosgrove, "Divine."

his reluctant followers to pursue this path—and that applies to the call of the apostle to gentiles here (cf. Gal 2:9).

ἐπιθεὶς ἐπ' αὐτὸν τὰς χεῖρας, "laying hands on him." Earlier references to laying on hands were for commissioning for a task (Acts 6:6; cf. 13:3; 14:23) or prayer for the coming of the Spirit (8:17, 18, 19), whereas the focus here is Saul's healing (9:12; cf. 28:8; Jas 5:14). The common factor is calling upon God on behalf of the person on whom hands are laid.[187] There is irony in Saul, who planned to lay hands on believers to imprison them (Acts 8:3; 9:13), having hands laid on him by the believer Ananias.[188]

For Ananias to address Saul as Σαοὺλ ἀδελφέ, "Brother Saul," represents a jaw-dropping change, both for Ananias (vv. 13–14) and, most remarkably, Saul (vv. 1–2). The use of the believers' familial language portrays Saul as now an insider through the heavenly intervention of Jesus rather than simply reflecting his and Ananias's shared Jewish heritage.[189] Ananias's address to Saul implies that his allegiance is now to Jesus.[190]

ὁ κύριος ἀπέσταλκέν με, Ἰησοῦς ὁ ὀφθείς σοι ἐν τῇ ὁδῷ ᾗ ἤρχου, "the Lord who sent me, Jesus, the one who appeared to you on the road by which you were coming." Ananias clarifies his divine commission[191] and confirms the identity of the one Saul met on the road (Acts 9:5), thus assuring Saul that his vision of Ananias (v. 12) is indeed being fulfilled. Saul is learning that his life from here on will be in submission to and service of the exalted Lord Jesus. ὁ ὀφθείς σοι, "who appeared to you," indicates that Saul's experience was visual as well as auditory (so also v. 27, and cf. 1 Cor 9:1; 15:8), although the narrative (Acts 9:3–6) only mentions auditory elements.

ὅπως ἀναβλέψῃς καὶ πλησθῇς πνεύματος ἁγίου, "so that you might see again and be filled with the Holy Spirit." Saul's healing, while clearly significant, is "old news" (v. 12), but Luke has held back until now the information that Saul will be filled with the Holy Spirit. That said, Saul's physical recovery of sight reflects both his own fresh spiritual sight of who Jesus now is and prepares for his participation in Jesus's mission of opening eyes (26:18, itself part of a report of this event).[192] This story removes any possible misunderstanding of the Samaritan story that an apostle's hands are required for people to

187 See *Comment* on 6:6; 8:17 for fuller discussion.

188 So Clark, *Parallel Lives*, 160–61. There is not an exact echo of χεῖρ, "hand," in 8:3; 9:13, although cf. 4:3; 5:18; 12:1, 11; 21:27, where "placing hands" indicates arrest or violent attack.

189 With Haenchen, *Acts*, 325; Lamoreaux, "Social Identity," 132; contra Dunn, *Baptism*, 74, who sees it as language to make Saul comfortable, along the lines of similar address to bodies of Jewish people earlier in Acts (e.g., 2:29, 37; 3:17). On ἀδελφός in Acts, see Trebilco, *Self-designations*, 50–53; Walton, "Calling," 225–26.

190 McCollough, *Ritual*, 173.

191 κύριος + ἀποστέλλω + με, "(the) Lord + send + me," is used regularly for a divinely commissioned messenger in LXX, e.g., Num 15:28, 29; 1 Sam 15:1, 20; 2 Kgs 2:2, 4, 6; Isa 48:16; Jer 32:17 (MT 25:17); 33:12, 15 (MT 26:12, 15); Zech 6:12, 15.

192 Røsæg, "Blinding," 183.

receive the Spirit, for Ananias is certainly not an apostle.[193] Luke does not explicitly state that Saul is filled with the Spirit at this point, and it may be that he had this experience during or after water baptism (v. 18).[194] Macnamara is an example of those who consider that Saul is filled with the Spirit later (13:4–12), and that is when he becomes effective in fulfilling Jesus's plans for him.[195] This seems unlikely given: the paradigm of initiation into the believing community (2:38–39), which gives no reason to expect any delay in the Spirit's coming; Luke's evident surprise when the Spirit does not come closely associated with baptism (see *Comment* on 8:16); and Saul's effective speaking for Jesus here (9:20, 22, 28–29), for bold speech for Jesus is evidence of the Spirit's filling (e.g., 4:31).[196] Earlier in Acts, the Pentecostal gathering were filled (ἐπλήσθησαν) with the Spirit (2:4), and Peter and the Jerusalem community were similarly filled (πλησθείς, ἐπλήσθησαν) in order to proclaim the truth under pressure (4:8, 31; cf. Luke 12:11–12). Saul's experience of the Spirit provides an example of the untidy fulfillment of the paradigm of Christian initiation in 2:38 (see *Comment* there).[197] All of these uses of πίμπλημι are in the passive voice, here clearly a "divine passive"—they are filled with the Spirit *by God as known in Jesus*. By contrast, those who join the community at Pentecost are told they will *receive* (λήμψεσθε) the Holy Spirit (2:38), and Luke does not record that those believers bore witness. Thus, the choice of πλησθῇς, "[you may] be filled," indicates that Saul will have a similar divinely empowered witnessing role to the apostolic band and the believers.[198] It is very unlikely that Saul's experience represents a two-stage process of conversion separate from "baptism in the Spirit" (the conversion being considered complete with the Damascus Road experience and the baptism in the Spirit to happen now), for Saul's "conversion" is incomplete until his subsequent water baptism (v. 18).[199] It is better, with Dunn, to see Saul's transformation as involving a three-day process that culminated in his water baptism.[200]

18 ἀπέπεσαν αὐτοῦ ἀπὸ τῶν ὀφθαλμῶν ὡς λεπίδες, "something like scales fell from his eyes." The description of Saul's healing uses language used in medical contexts (although not exclusively by medical writers),[201] including a close par-

193 With McCollough, *Ritual*, 172.
194 So Turner, *Power*, 377.
195 Macnamara, *Instrument*, 114–17, 246–47; similarly Haya-Prats, *Believers*, 149.
196 Miller, *Convinced*, 193.
197 O'Neill, "Connection," 94, is confident of this sequence of events.
198 To that extent the Spirit's work is focused on empowering Saul for witness (Menzies, *Empowered*, 214), although it is considerably less likely that this episode also represents Saul's commissioning for that task. Cf. Turner, *Power*, 377–78.
199 See Ervin, *Conversion-initiation*, 41–50, with response by Turner, *Power*, 375.
200 Dunn, *Baptism*, 74–78.
201 "λεπίς," BDAG 592, §2; for other examples of λεπίς with ἀποπίπτω in medical writings from Hippocrates, Dioscorides, and Galen, see Hobart, *Language*, 30–31, although these are examples of scabs and the like falling off skin rather than of coverings of the eyes; with Bruce, *Acts* (1990), 239. Cf. also Tob 11:12–13, where Tobit's son peels (ἐλεπίσθη) white

allel in Galen: οἷον λεπὶς ἀπέπιπτε, "something like a scale fell off" (*Atr. Bil.* 4.1.1), perhaps referring to a cataract. This brings the healing part of the story to completion, having described the physical problem and its duration (Acts 9:8–9), the coming of the agent of healing (v. 17a), the means of healing: laying on of hands (v. 17b), and now Saul's instantaneous healing (v. 18).[202]

ἀναστὰς ἐβαπτίσθη, "[he] got up[203] and was baptized." Saul now completes his initiation into the messianic community by being baptized (22:16 adds that Ananias calls on him to do this).[204] Of the initiation elements in 2:38, repentance is implied by Saul's fasting and prayer (9:9, 11), and the gift of the Spirit is explicit (v. 17). Forgiveness of sins may be implied here and is explicit in Ananias's exhortation in 22:16 (see *Comment* there).[205] Luke does not state who baptizes Saul—the fact that he is baptized is more important than who does it (which is Paul's own view in 1 Cor 1:12–17)—although we may reasonably presume it is Ananias.[206] Hengel and Schwemer suggest that some instruction precedes this baptism, although it could only be rudimentary (as in other baptisms in Acts, e.g., 2:38–39, 41; 8:36, 38; 16:30–34)—Luke does not anachronistically include a catechumenate.[207] Indeed, Saul was already well aware of the believers' claims about Jesus; the change is that he now knows them to be true, and thus only minimal instruction would be required before baptism.

19 καὶ λαβὼν τροφὴν ἐνίσχυσεν, "He then took food and became strong," marks the end of Saul's period of fasting (v. 9). The compound verb ἐνισχύω, "become strong," is used elsewhere in NT only at Luke 22:43, which is textually insecure.[208] It is possible, although unverifiable, that Luke here alludes to Saul taking the eucharistic bread and wine, although that would be more likely if Luke's signature phrase "break bread" (κλάω + ἄρτος) were included.[209] Saul's renewed strength is certainly physical, after fasting for three days, and what

---

films from his father's eyes; Pliny, *NH* 29.21 where Pliny criticizes money-hungry doctors because they direct that a film (Lat. *squama* = "scale") on the eyes should be moved rather than removed, which then requires a further operation on the patient and a further fee for the doctor.

202 Trocmé, *Livre*, 176–77, identifies this sequence, followed by Hedrick, "Paul's Conversion/Call," 422.

203 Ferguson, *Baptism*, 174, suggests that this verb implies that Saul had to go elsewhere to be baptized. This is not impossible, but Luke's general use of ἀνασάς, "stood up," as a prelude to further action in in the same location or in conjunction with a verb of movement suggests otherwise (e.g., Acts 1:15; 5:6, 34; 8:27; 9:11).

204 Dunn, *Baptism*, 74–75.

205 With Schröter, "Taufe," 576.

206 Ferguson, *Baptism*, 174; Hengel and Schwemer, *Paul between*, 46; Barrett, *Acts*, 1:458.

207 Hengel and Schwemer, *Paul between*, 44–45.

208 NA[28]/UBS[5] place Luke 22:43–44 in square brackets to indicate the uncertainty; see discussion *TCGNT*[2], ad loc., and the commentaries. The simple verb ἰσχύω, "be strong," is much more frequent, twenty-eight times in the NT, of which eight occur in Luke and six in Acts.

209 As in Luke 22:19; 24:30; Acts 2:46; 20:7; cf. 1 Cor 10:16. Barrett, *Acts*, 1:458 thinks a eucharistic reference unlikely.

follows (Acts 9:20) suggests it is also spiritual and moral, enabling him to confess his new understanding of Jesus.

Ἐγένετο δὲ μετὰ τῶν ἐν Δαμασκῷ μαθητῶν ἡμέρας τινάς, "He spent time with the disciples in Damascus for some days." "The narrator adroitly shows Saul switching sides by the company he keeps."[210] Saul would need time and conversation to come more fully to terms with his dramatic experiences of the previous days, and his understanding must have grown through discussion, worship, and prayer with the Damascene believers—we can expect that the believing community in Damascus has a similar pattern of life to the Jerusalem community (2:42–47). Here is the second stage of Saul's resocialization as a Jesus follower (see *Comment* on 9:10, 27), as he is integrated into the local assembly of believers: "this Saul can now be looked in the eye without fear."[211] Luke implies this is a relatively short period: ἡμέρας τινάς, "for some days," contrasts with ἡμέραι ἱκαναί, "many days" (v. 23). Paul's denial that he consulted with people (Gal 1:16) is specifically addressing the source of his message, and engagement with the Damascene believers would not be of the order of being told the gospel message by the Jerusalem apostles;[212] v. 20 will go on to show that he rapidly became a proclaimer of the gospel.

20 καὶ εὐθέως ἐν ταῖς συναγωγαῖς ἐκήρυσσεν τὸν Ἰησοῦν, "and immediately [he] began proclaiming Jesus in the synagogues." Saul's proclamation follows spending time with the Damascene disciples; it seems most likely that καὶ εὐθέως, "and immediately," denotes events after those in the earlier part of the sentence. The ingressive imperfect ἐκήρυσσεν, "he began to proclaim," implies that he continued to do so. The plural ἐν ταῖς συναγωγαῖς, "in the synagogues," implies the presence of several synagogues in Damascus, which fits with this large city's substantial Jewish population (see *Comment* on v. 2). Saul's immediate proclamation suggests that Ananias shares his vision with Saul, although it is not explicitly stated here, by contrast with Paul's own account (22:14–15).

οὗτός ἐστιν ὁ υἱὸς τοῦ θεοῦ, "This one is the son of God," summarizes Saul's synagogue message, focused—like his experience on the road—on the identity of Jesus. If Jesus truly is God's son, then everything in Saul's world and symbolic universe looks different as a result. This is the only use of ὁ υἱὸς τοῦ θεοῦ, "the son of God," in Acts and is paralleled by Saul's demonstration that Jesus is ὁ χριστός, "the Messiah" (9:22). These two descriptions are mutually interpreting, for the Messiah, in common with Israel's king, was considered God's son (e.g., 13:33, quoting Ps 2:7 in a synagogue setting). Luke's use of ὁ υἱὸς τοῦ θεοῦ in his Gospel expresses this understanding (Luke 1:35; 4:3, 9, 41; 8:28; 22:70), as well as the heavenly words at Jesus's baptism declaring him to

210 Macnamara, *Instrument*, 131.
211 Lang, *Kunst*, 242 (my translation).
212 In this regard, see discussion of the role of Ananias in Bruce, *Book* (1988), 188–89.

be God's beloved son (ὁ υἱός μου ὁ ἀγαπητός, Luke 3:22).[213] Luke may reflect the Jewish connotations of the expression by its absence in evangelism among gentiles (where to be "son of god" could easily be misunderstood as implying birth from sex between a god and a human woman).[214] Paul, describing the same period, speaks of God revealing τὸν υἱὸν αὐτοῦ, "his son" (Gal 1:16)—a striking parallel.[215] Indeed, Paul's usual use of "the son of God" is in contexts where he emphasizes the closeness of relationship between Jesus and God in the work of saving humanity—and this verse is summarizing the believer Saul's proclamation of that saving message.[216]

21 ἐξίσταντο δὲ πάντες οἱ ἀκούοντες, "All who heard were astonished." The forward position of ἐξίσταντο, "[they] were astonished," focuses attention on their reaction; the imperfect tense matches the tense for Saul's proclamation, ἐκήρυσσεν, "he began proclaiming" (v. 20). Luke uses ἐξίστημι, "be astonished," intransitively in response to God's actions here (see *Comment* on 2:7). It combines reactions of "astonishment mingled with fear"[217]—what God has done with Saul is awesome. This reaction and their being confounded echo the responses of the Pentecost crowd using the same words (ἐξίσταντο 2:7, 12; συνεχύθη 2:6).[218]

οὐχ οὗτός ἐστιν ὁ πορθήσας εἰς Ἰερουσαλὴμ τοὺς ἐπικαλουμένους τὸ ὄνομα τοῦτο, καὶ ὧδε εἰς τοῦτο ἐληλύθει ἵνα δεδεμένους αὐτοὺς ἀγάγῃ ἐπὶ τοὺς ἀρχιερεῖς;, "Surely this is the one who destroyed those in Jerusalem who call on this name, and came here to take them bound to the high priests?" This double question expresses considerable surprise, marked by οὐχ as expecting the answer "yes," echoing Ananias's reaction, which also contains the two elements of Saul's actions in Jerusalem and his intentions in Damascus (vv. 13–14). Luke thereby underlines Saul's past in order to shine a light on the transformation brought about by Saul's encounter with Jesus. The thread of suspicion will continue in Jerusalem (v. 26). The language used is violent: πορθέω, "destroy," is used for plundering and pillaging (e.g., 4 Macc 4:23; Josephus, *Ant.* 10.8.2 §135; *J.W.* 4.7.2. §405),[219] as well as for murderous persecution (e.g., 4 Macc 11:4) and is found only here and Gal 1:13, 23 in the NT; moreover, the uses in Galatians are also in connection with Paul's actions before he was a believer.[220] τοὺς ἐπικαλουμένους τὸ ὄνομα τοῦτο, "those who call upon this name," echoes the

---

213 On Luke 3:21–22, see Dennison, "How," 21–22; Turner, *Power,* 197–201.

214 See Hengel and Schwemer, *Paul between,* 46 with n214.

215 Hengel and Schwemer, *Paul between,* 46; Lüdemann, *Early Christianity,* 116.

216 Hengel, *Son of God,* 10, agreeing with Bousset, *Kyrios,* 206.

217 "ἐξίστημι," BDAG 350, §2.b.

218 Gen, "Phenomena," proposes that responses to healings and divine afflictions in Luke-Acts are similar: amazement, which can lead to faith in Jesus, and fear, although the words for amazement are not always those used here.

219 See Menoud, *Jesus,* 47–60; he implausibly argues that Saul's persecution was simply "theological," viz., that Saul publicly argued against the believers' views of Jesus (50–56)—but the language of physical violence here and in Galatians suggests otherwise.

220 It is unlikely that Luke is drawing these verbs from Galatians (with Marguerat, *Actes,* 1:339).

description of believers in the prayers of Ananias (Acts 9:14). ἐληλύθει, "came," is pluperfect of ἔρχομαι, "come," and is used to speak of action prior to the present of the story, with results that are now completed, since his original purpose of destroying the church no longer existed.[221] We are hearing Luke's omniscient narrator's perspective in this verb tense rather than that of the characters at the time of the story.

22 Σαῦλος δὲ μᾶλλον ἐνεδυναμοῦτο, "But Saul was growing more and more powerful," again uses imperfect to portray his powerful proclamation as a continuing process. The verb is different from ἐνισχύω, "become strong" (v. 19), although both verbs can refer to physical and spiritual strength.[222]

καὶ συνέχυννεν τοὺς Ἰουδαίους τοὺς κατοικοῦντας ἐν Δαμασκῷ συμβιβάζων ὅτι οὗτός ἐστιν ὁ χριστός, "and [he] kept confounding the Jews who lived in Damascus by demonstrating that this [Jesus] was the Messiah." Luke explains the way in which Saul grew more powerful, i.e., in his proclamation,[223] and continues to use verbs that portray continuing action, here imperfect συνέχυννεν, "[he] kept confounding," and present participle συμβιβάζων, "by demonstrating."[224] Saul's prior education combines with his experience of Jesus (vv. 3–6) and the empowerment of the Spirit (v. 17) to produce mightily effective speaking and argument—doubtless including both personal testimony and proof from Scripture (cf. 13:32–39)—which reduce his opponents to disarray (cf. Stephen's similar effectiveness, also attributed to the Spirit, 6:18–10). Luke alone uses συγχέω/συγχύννω,[225] "confound," in the NT, for crowds that were bewildered or in confusion, and thus chaos, as here among the Jewish population (2:6; 19:31; 21:27, 31). This and the following verse are the first occasion in Acts where οἱ Ἰουδαῖοι, "the Jews," are opponents of believers. Luke portrays Saul as causing division among the Jewish population, as will characteristically happen in numerous other places (13:44–51; 14:1–2; 17:4–5; 18:5–6; 19:8–9) and as happened earlier in Jerusalem (4:1–4; 5:12–18, 29–33; 6:8–14). Luke is not portraying *all* Jews in Damascus with this expression, since some respond to Saul's message (οἱ μαθηταὶ αὐτοῦ, "his disciples" [9:25]), but rather those Jews who reject Saul's message.[226] Luke is also not anachronistically implying a contrast between Jewish unbelief and gentile faith, for no gentiles have yet come to faith.

οὗτός ἐστιν ὁ χριστός, "This [Jesus] was the Messiah." οὗτος, "this one," points back to οὗτος (v. 20), where it refers to Jesus. The subject is οὗτος, "this

221 Bruce, *Acts* (1990), 241; Barrett, *Acts,* 1:464.
222 "ἐνδυναμόω," BDAG 333, §§2.a, b; "ἐνισχύω," BDAG 337; "ἐνισχύω," LSJ.
223 καί, "and," is explicative, "καί," BDAG 495, §1.c.
224 συμβιβάζω can portray *logical* demonstration, but that need not be the sense here (contra "συμβιβάζω," BDAG 956, §3), as I suggest above.
225 The latter is a Hellenistic form, "συγχέω," BDAG 953; BDF, §73.
226 Contra Sanders, *Jews,* 75.

one," and the claim is that Jesus is the Messiah,[227] by contrast with other places where ὁ χριστός is the subject and Ἰησοῦς the complement—in the latter, the claim is that the Messiah is Jesus (5:42; 18:5, 28; cf. John 20:31). Thus, the discussion here is about who Jesus is, and Saul is claiming that Jesus matches the biblical messianic portrait; in other places, the understanding of "Messiah" is the given, and the question is how this understanding was fulfilled in Jesus. In other words, here the question being answered is, "Who is Jesus?," arising from Saul's proclaiming Jesus (v. 20); in the other places, the question is, "Who is the Messiah?"[228] (See *Comment* on v. 20 for discussion of "Messiah" and "son of God"; on χριστός, "Messiah," see *Comment* on 2:36.)[229]

23 Ὡς δὲ ἐπληροῦντο ἡμέραι ἱκαναί, "When many days had gone by," includes the imprecise time reference ἡμέραι ἱκαναί, "many days" (cf. 14:3; 18:18; 27:7). Luke uses πληρόω, "fill, fulfill," for the completion of longer periods (e.g., 7:23, 30; 19:21; 24:27) without always being precise about their length. The plot to kill Saul leads to him fleeing to Jerusalem (9:26), and Gal 1:18 states that at least two years elapsed before Saul visited Jerusalem (reckoning ἔτη τρία, "three years," inclusively to mean "during the third year"[230]). This period is thus much longer than ἡμέρας τινάς, "some days" (Acts 9:19), and may be the time of Paul's visit to "Arabia" before returning to Damascus (Gal 1:17).[231] However, Acts gives no hint of a visit to Arabia, and it is thus possible—perhaps likely—that this was only a relatively short visit and that Saul spent most of the "three years" in Damascus.[232] Luke portrays Saul's initial proclamation in Damascus as taking a significant amount of time; the Galatians parallel suggests it could be comparable in length with his residencies to Corinth (Acts 18:11) and Ephesus (19:8, 10).

συνεβουλεύσαντο οἱ Ἰουδαῖοι ἀνελεῖν αὐτόν, "the Jews plotted together to kill him." Luke switches the focus to Saul's opponents by making οἱ Ἰουδαῖοι, "the Jews," the grammatical subject.[233] They consult together (the force of the middle voice of συνεβουλεύσαντο[234]) in order to plan to kill Saul, prefiguring other plots actively to dispose of him (9:29; 13:50; 14:5, 19; 16:19–24; 17:5–7, 13; 18:6; 19:23–34; 21:27–31). Throughout Acts, S/Paul's primary opponents are Jewish, not least in gentile areas.[235] Jesus's words through Ananias about Saul are being fulfilled (9:16): "The cycle is complete: The persecutor has

227 Wallace, 42–43.
228 With Holladay, *Acts,* 199 n. a.
229 Hurtado, *Lord,* 178, observes that the uses of ὁ χριστός and ὁ υἱὸς τοῦ θεοῦ are historically plausible for the ostensible date of this story, since they echo Pauline passages that are understood as traditional (Rom 1:4, etc.).
230 Bruce, *Acts* (1990), 241; Longenecker, *Galatians,* 37.
231 See discussion in Longenecker, *Galatians,* 34. On Arabia, see Schnabel, *Mission,* 2:1033–34.
232 Hengel, *Acts,* 84; Wenham, "Acts II," 223.
233 Levinsohn, *Connections,* 72.
234 "συμβουλεύω," BDAG 957, §2.
235 Cunningham, *Tribulations,* 230n151, cites 9:29; 13:6, 45, 50; 14:2, 5, 19; 17:5, 13; 18:6, 12; 20:3; 21:11, 27; 22:22; 23:2, 10, 12, 20–21, 27; 24:1, 9, 27; 25:2–3, 7, 15, 24; 26:2, 7, 21; 28:19.

become the persecuted."[236] Some suggest that Luke is mistaken here because 2 Cor 11:32–33 portrays the ethnarch under King Aretas as the prime mover in guarding the city to capture Saul,[237] but it is entirely plausible that the Jewish population make common cause with the ethnarch over this, particularly if the Damascene Jewish community leaders portrayed Saul as source of civil unrest; cf. the action of Jewish community leaders in Thessalonica (Acts 17:5–9), Corinth (18:12–13), and Caesarea (24:1).

24 ἐγνώσθη δὲ τῷ Σαύλῳ ἡ ἐπιβουλὴ αὐτῶν, "however, their plot became known to Saul." Luke does not specify how Saul learns of the plot, using a passive verb ἐγνώσθη, "[it] became known." We may reasonably suspect that a sympathetic person told Saul because Luke generally specifies when divinely revealed knowledge is involved (e.g., 18:9–10; 20:22–23; 27:23–24; contrast 23:16).

παρετηροῦντο δὲ καὶ τὰς πύλας ἡμέρας τε καὶ νυκτὸς ὅπως αὐτὸν ἀνέλωσιν, "They were also watching the [city] gates both day and night in order to kill him." The danger Saul faces is real and present. The customary imerfect. παρετηροῦντο, "they were watching," reinforced by ἡμέρας τε καὶ νυκτός, "both day and night," portrays constant vigilance in order to capture and kill Saul.

25 λαβόντες δὲ οἱ μαθηταὶ αὐτοῦ νυκτὸς διὰ τοῦ τείχους καθῆκαν αὐτὸν χαλάσαντες ἐν σπυρίδι, "but his disciples took him by night and let him down through an opening in the wall by lowering him in a basket." Saul's means of escape involves secrecy (νυκτός, "by night") and imagination (the use of the basket and the gap in the wall) and is the work of others—he is the object of the verbs here. Paul's own description of this escape specifies that he escaped διὰ θυρίδος ἐν σαργάνῃ . . . διὰ τοῦ τείχους, "through a window in a rope-basket . . . through the wall" (2 Cor 11:33;[238] cf. Josephus, *Ant.* 5.1.2 §15), filling out Luke's generic term for "basket";[239] Luke also does not state that the escape was through a window. Both of these points are compatible with Luke's account. It was οἱ μαθηταὶ αὐτοῦ, "his disciples," who facilitated Saul's escape—the only occasion in the NT where a Christian leader is said to have his own disciples; elsewhere in Acts (including 9:19, 26 nearby), they are always disciples of Jesus.[240] The sense is most likely to be that they were Saul's

---

236 Gaventa, *Darkness*, 65.

237 E.g., Lüdemann, *Early Christianity*, 119.

238 Pauline scholars debate this event in the light of Paul's mentioning an ethnarch under King Aretas who sought to arrest him (2 Cor 11:32), on which Acts is silent. For the main views, see Campbell, "Anchor," 280–81; Bunine, "Date," 441–50. This has implications for the dating of Paul's escape here: Campbell, "Anchor," 287–98, with summary 297–98, argues for dating Paul's escape to late AD 36 to early 37; Bunine, "Date," 612–19, with summary 618–19, proposes late AD 37. Martin, *2 Corinthians* (2nd ed.), 574–75, gives only Aretas's death in AD 40 as *terminus ad quem* for Paul's escape from Damascus. Hemer, *Book*, 163–64, 264; Schnabel, *Mission*, 2:1037, similarly express caution about dogmatism over the date of Nabatean control over Damascus given our very limited evidence.

239 σπυρίς, "basket," is found only here in Luke-Acts; the other NT uses are in the feeding stories at Matt 15:37; 10:10; Mark 8:8, 20.

240 Some MSS read οἱ μαθηταὶ αὐτόν, "the disciples him," making αὐτόν the object of ptc. λαβόντες,

converts, people who had come to faith through his ministry in Damascus (cf. 1 Cor 4:15; 1 Tim 1:2; Titus 1:4).[241]

26–30 The scene shifts to Jerusalem, where Saul encounters the same suspicion that Ananias (vv. 13–14) and the Damascenes (v. 21) showed. This visit is most probably that referred to in Gal 1:17–24, even though there are variations between the stories.[242]

Acts 9:26–30	Galatians 1:17–24
vv. 25–26 Saul travels from Damascus to Jerusalem	vv. 17–18 Paul travels from Damascus to Jerusalem
vv. 26–27 Barnabas facilitates Saul's welcome by the apostles	not explicitly mentioned, but Barnabas is prominent in the Pauline letters, e.g., Gal 2:1
v. 27 Saul meets "the apostles"	vv. 18, 19 Paul meets only Cephas and James
v. 28 Saul continues to be involved with the apostles	v. 18 Paul stays with Cephas fifteen days
vv. 29–30 Saul's stay seems brief	v. 18 Paul's stay was brief
v. 30 Saul goes to Tarsus via Caesarea Maritima	v. 21 Paul travels to Cilicia via Syria

See *Comment* below on points of detail in these passages.

26 Παραγενόμενος δὲ εἰς Ἰερουσαλὴμ ἐπείραζεν κολλᾶσθαι τοῖς μαθηταῖς, "When he arrived in Jerusalem, he began trying (ingressive imperfect ἐπείραζεν) to join the disciples." Saul's response to his experience over the previous two to three years is to seek to engage with the believing community in Jerusalem. His encounter with the exalted Jesus led to his engaging with Jesus's people, initially through Ananias and the Damascene community, and now he seeks out believers in Jerusalem. The implication of what follows (v. 27) and Paul's own account (Gal 1:18–19) is that he sought out the apostles, as leaders of the community.

"they took," a natural error for scribes who knew the "normal" use of μαθηταί, "disciples," in Acts. Haenchen, *Acts*, 332, with n3, postulates an early corruption of the text, but αὐτοῦ is hard to explain as such.

241 Trebilco, *Self-designations*, 227–28, proposing this view, observes that Paul himself does not write of people as "my disciples" but plausibly suggests that Luke uses the term to make their imitation of Paul clear.

242 With, e.g., Fitzmyer, *Acts*, 438; Bruce, *Acts* (1990), 242–43; Schnabel, *Mission*, 2:1045–46; Keener, *Acts*, 2:1687–88 (the table is based on Keener's); Johnson, *Acts*, 173–74; contra Parker, "Once More," 179–82, who denies that this visit took place.

καὶ πάντες ἐφοβοῦντο αὐτὸν μὴ πιστεύοντες ὅτι ἐστὶν μαθητής, "and[243] they were all in fear of him, because they did not believe that he was a disciple." Word spread that Saul was looking for the community's leaders, and the believers at large responded in similar manner to Ananias (vv. 13–14) and the Damascene believers (v. 21), persistently fearing that Saul was not genuine (ἐφοβοῦντο, imperfect, matching Saul's ongoing attempts to join).

27 Βαρναβᾶς δὲ ἐπιλαβόμενος αὐτὸν ἤγαγεν πρὸς τοὺς ἀποστόλους, "However, Barnabas took and brought him to the apostles." Barnabas's decisive intervention is marked by both the lack of an article, making him prominent and signaling his reintroduction into the narrative after a substantial absence (since 4:36–37),[244] and the contrasting δέ, "However," which has more than its usual "switch of subject" role, seen by the contrast with the reaction of other believers (v. 26). ἤγαγεν, "he brought," echoes uses of this verb and its compounds in vv. 2, 8 (see *Comment* there). Luke's "the apostles" is a generalizing summary: Gal 1:18, 19 record that Saul met only Cephas (Peter) and James the Lord's brother at this point, in Paul's mind a subgroup of "the apostles." For Saul to meet such a limited group, and to require Barnabas's intercession, makes sense in a time of persecution.[245] This event ultimately leads to a partnership between Barnabas and Saul (11:25–26; 13:1–14:28; 15:1–4, 12).[246]

διηγήσατο αὐτοῖς πῶς ἐν τῇ ὁδῷ εἶδεν τὸν κύριον καὶ ὅτι ἐλάλησεν αὐτῷ καὶ πῶς ἐν Δαμασκῷ ἐπαρρησιάσατο ἐν τῷ ὀνόματι τοῦ Ἰησοῦ, "[Barnabas] explained to them how he [Saul] had seen the Lord on the road, that the Lord had spoken to him, and how he [Saul] had spoken boldly in the name of Jesus in Damascus." Barnabas's intervention involves a third telling of the Damascus Road encounter, here in miniature, since readers know the story from 9:3–9, 17. Barnabas here exemplifies his nickname υἱὸς παρακλήσεως, "son of encouragement" (4:36), as he takes a positive initiative to support Saul and thus integrates him into the Jerusalem community. Barnabas's intercession for Saul builds a bridge for Saul into the Jerusalem community.[247] "The apostles trust Paul only because they trust Barnabas."[248] Barnabas's narrative (διηγήσατο, "explained," is cognate with διήγησις, "orderly account" [Luke 1:1; cf. Acts 12:17]) identifies three significant moments, each introduced by key words: πῶς, "how," Saul saw Jesus (9:17), καὶ ὅτι, "and that," Jesus spoke to Saul (vv. 5–6, 15–17), καὶ πῶς, "and how," Saul spoke boldly in Jesus's name in Damascus (vv. 20, 22). Neither

---

243 Levinsohn, *Connections*, 102–3, notes that καί, "and," here associates two events that together issue in Barnabas's action (v. 27).

244 Read-Heimerdinger, *Bezan Text*, 119, 123–28; she does not discuss this passage because it is absent from D.

245 Hengel and Schwemer, *Paul between*, 136, 140; Hemer, *Book*, 248–49; contra Kollmann, *Joseph Barnabas*, 27–28, who finds Luke's account of Barnabas's role implausible.

246 Öhler, *Barnabas*, 195, identifies Barnabas as a patron of Saul here and in fetching him to Antioch (11:26–26).

247 Murphy, "Role," 323.

248 Öhler, *Barnabas*, 196 (my translation).

Luke nor Paul explain how Barnabas knew these things about Saul—perhaps he was a member of the Damascene community or had heard from someone there. Jesus's ὄνομα, "name," is again prominent (cf. vv. 14, 15, 16, 21) and will be repeated in v. 28, indicating Jesus's authorization and empowerment of Saul to speak for him and perhaps also the content of what Saul says (see *Comment* on 4:18).[249] This third stage of Saul's resocialization as a Jesus follower integrates him with the Jerusalem leadership (see *Comment* on vv. 10, 19).

28 ἦν μετ' αὐτῶν εἰσπορευόμενος καὶ ἐκπορευόμενος εἰς Ἰερουσαλήμ, "And so Saul moved freely among them in Jerusalem," uses a Semitic idiom εἰσπορευόμενος καὶ ἐκπορευόμενος, "coming in and going out" (cf. 1:21),[250] to indicate intimate involvement. Paul himself says that he stayed with Cephas at this time for fifteen days (Gal 1:18), which fits well with Luke's portrait. It would be a mistake to see this engagement with "the apostles" as Luke's flat-footed attempt to bring Saul under the authority of Jerusalem, in contradiction to Paul's own vehement claims of his independence from the Jerusalem apostles in Galatians.[251] Luke's narrative says nothing about the apostles authorizing Saul, for he comes to Jerusalem as one who already proclaims Jesus (Acts 9:20, 22). Further, Paul's claim in Galatians is about the source of his message (Gal 1:11–12), which Luke makes equally clear is Jesus's appearance to him (thus Saul speaks publicly about Jesus εὐθέως, "immediately," Acts 9:20).

παρρησιαζόμενος ἐν τῷ ὀνόματι τοῦ κυρίου, "while he was speaking boldly in the name of the Lord," echoes v. 27 ἐπαρρησιάσατο ἐν τῷ ὀνόματι τοῦ Ἰησοῦ, "he had spoken boldly in the name of Jesus": as Saul acted in Damascus, so he acts in Jerusalem (see *Comment* on 2:29; 13:46). In Acts, the period seems short, confirmed by the "fifteen days" of Gal 1:18. The short period could well account for Paul's claim that he was not yet known to the assemblies of Judea (Gal 1:22), especially if "Judea" means the province outside Jerusalem.[252] ἐν τῷ ὀνόματι τοῦ κυρίου, "in the name of the Lord," again signals both Jesus's authorization and empowerment (see *Comment* on 9:27 and 4:18).

29 ἐλάλει τε καὶ συνεζήτει πρὸς τοὺς Ἑλληνιστάς, "he kept both speaking and debating with the Hellenists." Saul regularly seeks to persuade Greek-speaking Jews of the truth concerning Jesus. (On the identity of τοὺς Ἑλληνιστάς, "the Hellenists," see *Comment* on 6:1.) The location(s) where they meet is not specified; it is possible that it is in a Greek-speaking synagogue. It is deeply ironic that Saul debates with a similar—perhaps the same—group as Stephen (6:9–10), whose murder he supported (7:58; 8:1). Saul not only shares

249 Macnamara, *Instrument*, 156–57, taking ἐν as introducing the content of what Saul said, since the verb ἐπαρρησιάσατο, "he had spoken boldly," already indicates the manner of Saul's speaking.

250 Found frequently in LXX: Deut 28:6, 19; 31:2; 1 Sam 18:13, 16; 2 Kgs 11:8; 1 Chr 27:1; 2 Chr 15:5; 23:7; Zech 8:10; Tob 5:18; 1 Macc 3:45.

251 As Conzelmann, *Acts*, 75, asserts.

252 With Haenchen, *Acts*, 332n5.

Stephen's ministry among the Hellenists but also himself meets with the same murderous response.[253] Paul's later claim that he proclaimed the gospel in Jerusalem (Rom 15:19) may well be a reference to this period.[254]

οἱ δὲ ἐπεχείρουν ἀνελεῖν αὐτόν, "but they were attempting to kill him." Luke further underlines the integral nature of suffering to Saul's commission (9:15–16) by the Jerusalem Hellenists' ongoing attempts to kill him (ἐπεχείρουν, "they were attempting," iterative imperfect, echoing imperfect for Saul's speaking and preaching). Just as the Damascenes wanted to do away with Saul (vv. 23–24; see *Comment* on v. 23 on other such attempts in Acts), so also the Hellenists of Jerusalem. Cf. 6:10–11 concerning the Jerusalem Hellenists' action against Stephen. Paul may refer to this occasion in speaking of "the Jews [in Judea, 1 Thess 2:14], who killed both the Lord Jesus and the prophets and drove us out (ἡμᾶς ἐκδιωξάντων)" (v. 15).[255]

30 ἐπιγνόντες δὲ οἱ ἀδελφοὶ κατήγαγον αὐτὸν εἰς Καισάρειαν καὶ ἐξαπέστειλαν αὐτὸν εἰς Ταρσόν, "When the brothers and sisters learned, they took him down to Caesarea and sent him away to Tarsus." As in Damascus (vv. 24–25), the believing community hear about the plans to dispose of Saul and facilitate his safe departure. κατήγαγον αὐτὸν εἰς Καισάρειαν, "they took him down to Caesarea," connotes two forms of "going down": Caesarea Maritima, at the coast, was lower in altitude than Jerusalem, and the verb is a natural choice to speak of travel there (so also 22:30; 23:15, 20); in addition, people "go up" (ἀναβαίνω) to Jerusalem as the capital and the location of the temple,[256] and so it was usual to speak of "going down" from that city. Καισάρειαν, "Caesarea" (= Caesarea Maritima), was both the headquarters of the Roman administration (from AD 6; Paul will later be held there for two years, 24:27) and a major port of some thirty thousand people, physically dominated by statues and buildings promoting and expressing the imperial cult.[257] This city, known to Paul, Herod the Great built between 22 and 10 BC (Josephus, *Ant.* 15.9.6 §§331–41) and named it after Caesar Augustus to show his loyalty. Luke's readers would recognize that Saul takes a ship from Caesarea, probably to Rhegma, a lagoon and the port of Tarsus, about 7 km/4.3 miles south of Tarsus on the River Kydnos.[258]

εἰς Ταρσόν, "to Tarsus." The city was Saul's hometown (Acts 9:11, see *Comment* there) and thus a wise place for him to retreat. It is in Cilicia (cf. Gal 1:21), in the south of modern Turkey. This sentence presages a long silence concerning Saul, lasting some six to ten years, until his reappearance when Barnabas takes

253 With Tannehill, *Unity*, 2:114.
254 Hengel, *Acts*, 87.
255 Wenham, "Acts II," 225.
256 E.g., 2 Sam 19:35 LXX [MT 19:34]; 1 Kgs 12:27; Ezra 1:3, 5; 7:9, 28; Ps 121:4 LXX [MT 122:4]; Isa 2:3; Luke 18:31.
257 On the city, see Taylor, "Paul's Caesarea," esp. 57–62; Schnabel, *Mission*, 1:688–90; R. L. Hohlfelder, "Caesarea," *ABD* 1:798–803.
258 Schnabel, *Mission*, 2:1056.

him to Antioch (Acts 11:25–26; see *Comment* there). Paul's own account has a similar gap, between the "after three years" visit to Jerusalem (Gal 1:18–20), his time in Syria and Cilicia (Gal 1:21), and a further "after fourteen years" visit to the city (Gal 2:1–10). It is possible that Saul evangelized in and from Tarsus, for it would provide a good base for travel into the double province of Syria-Cilicia, and his citizenship of Tarsus and Rome would provide some protection; however, we lack evidence for other believers in Tarsus until the third century.[259]

31 This transitional summary statement,[260] as usual with such summaries, uses imperfective verbs (imperfects and present participles), portraying events as in process over a period of time. It functions to draw a section of the book to an end (8:4–9:30) and marks a transition to the section that is the hinge of the book's story, focused on Peter's ministry outside Jerusalem which features the introduction of outright gentiles into the believing community (9:32–12:25).

μὲν οὖν, "so then," denotes continuation: μέν looks forward and οὖν looks backward (as 8:25).[261] Here, the events of v. 31 develop from what goes before—Saul's departure (v. 30) removes the source of danger to the believers, and the wider mission of the believers is built on their success in Judea[262]—and the time of peace prepares for Peter's ministry outside Jerusalem (9:32–10:48).[263]

Ἡ . . . ἐκκλησία καθ' ὅλης τῆς Ἰουδαίας καὶ Γαλιλαίας καὶ Σαμαρείας, "the assembly throughout Judea, Galilee and Samaria," takes up the locations πάσῃ τῇ Ἰουδαίᾳ καὶ Σαμαρείᾳ, "in all Judea and Samaria," in 1:8, and signals that the evangelization of those areas has been initiated to the extent that the remainder of the book will focus on "to the end of the earth."[264] This sentence distinctively uses the singular ἐκκλησία, "assembly," to denote believers and their local groups spread throughout Judea, Galilee, and Samaria (on the variant plural reading, see *Note* fff). The inclusion of Σαμαρείας, "Samaria," indicates that Samaritans were included in this network (8:5–25);[265] the likelihood, following Philip's evangelism on the coastal plain from Azotus to Caesarea, is that gentiles were included too, under τῆς Ἰουδαίας, "Judea" (see *Comment* on 8:40). Luke more frequently uses the plural for assemblies in different places, in common with Paul (15:41; 16:5; cf. Rom 16:4, 16; 1 Cor 7:17; 11:16; 14:33–34; 16:1; 2 Cor 8:1, 18–19, 23–24; 11:8, 28; 12:13; Gal 1:22; 1 Thess

259 Schnabel, *Mission*, 2:1058; Riesner, *Period*, 266. Hengel and Schwemer, *Paul between*, 151–61, suggest that Saul planted a church in Tarsus.

260 Squires, "Function," 31; Bruce, *Acts* (1990), 245; Barrett, *Acts*, 1:472.

261 "μέν," BDAG 629–30, §2.e; Levinsohn, *Connections*, 141–50; Rius-Camps and Read-Heimerdinger, *Message*, 2:208–9; and *Comment* on 8:25.

262 Barrett, *Acts*, 1:472.

263 Barrett, *Acts*, 1:472.

264 Cf. Clark, *Parallel Lives*, 152, although I doubt that Luke regards the mission to Judea and Samaria as "basically accomplished."

265 Jervell, *Luke*, 113–32, who reads this verse as indicating that Luke regards Samaritans as Jews. However, Coggins, "Samaritans," 431, rightly observes that this sentence is about Ἡ . . . ἐκκλησία, "The . . . assembly," rather than the Jewish people.

2:14; 2 Thess 1:4), although note the singular use in 20:28 (and see *Comment* there). Hort observes, "it was no longer the Ecclesia of a single city, and yet it was *one*";[266] others see this as an (anachronistic) use of the whole church.[267] However, Paul can use the singular for the whole church (Gal 1:13; Phil 3:6), so Luke's use here need not be anachronistic; rather, it represents a conscious sense of the interconnectedness of the groups of believers in individual towns and villages. This inclusive usage is no more "early catholicism" than is the understanding of diaspora Jews that they and their synagogues are members of an international community, "Israel."

Much of the language of this summary connotes Israel's restoration.[268] εἰρήνην, "peace," denotes lack of harassment by human authorities, contrasting with the rough passage of earlier times in Jerusalem. It is also used for eschatological blessing from God (e.g., 10:36; Luke 1:79; 2:14, 29; 19:38) and locates the assembly as inhabiting God's eschatological future now.

οἰκοδομουμένη, "being built up." Luke uses οἰκοδομέω, "build up," metaphorically for building up the assembly only here and 20:32. Behind the verb may lie an understanding of the assembly as an eschatological temple, and that connection offers a further nuance to the singular use of ἐκκλησία, "assembly," earlier in the sentence.[269] The passive participle οἰκοδομουμένη, "being built up," portrays God's action in building the church up; this understanding is reinforced by the following two phrases.

πορευομένη τῷ φόβῳ τοῦ κυρίου, "walking in the fear of the Lord," suggests that the believers' characteristic (metaphorical) journeying place is reverence of the Lord (dative of sphere) and/or that they live with constant attention to revering the Lord (dative of reference), in similar manner to Zechariah and Elizabeth (Luke 1:6, which also uses πορεύομαι, "walk," in Jewish idiom for lifestyle).[270] This Lukan language echoes the requirement of Israel in Deut 10:12 LXX φοβεῖσθαι κύριον τὸν θεόν σου πορεύεσθαι ἐν πάσαις ταῖς ὁδοῖς αὐτοῦ, "to fear the Lord your God, to walk in all his ways" (cf. Deut 8:6 LXX), set on the brink of the promised land.[271] Fear has overcome the believers earlier in Acts in response to the deaths of Ananias and Sapphira (Acts 5:5, 11); now it is a normal characteristic of their life, in tune with the wider biblical

266 Hort, *Ecclesia*, 56 (his italics).

267 E.g., Conzelmann, *Acts*, 75.

268 Bauckham, *Jewish World*, 366–67.

269 Luke uses the compound ἀνοικοδομέω, "rebuild," in the quotation from Amos in Acts 15:16, for an eschatological "tent of David." Cf. Matt 16:18; Rom 15:20; 1 Cor 3:9–17; Eph 2:20–22; 1 Pet 2:5; with Bauckham, *Jewish World*, 366.

270 Eighty-eight of one hundred fifty NT uses of πορεύομαι are found in Luke-Acts, although most are for physical walking. Cf. Paul's use of περιπατέω, "walk," for lifestyle, e.g., Rom 6:4; 8:4; 13:13; 14:15; 1 Cor 3:3; 7:17; 2 Cor 4:2; 5:7; 10:2, 3; Gal 5:16; Eph 2:2, 10; 4:1, 17; 5:2, 8, 15; Phil 3:17, 18. Luke largely reserves περιπατέω for physical walking: Luke 5:23; 7:22; 11:44; 20:46; 24:17; Acts 3:6, 8, 12; 14:8, 10; the only metaphorical use is in Acts 21:21, notably in a Jewish setting.

271 See further "πορεύομαι," *NIDNTTE* 4:107, JL §2.c.

understanding of the respect and awe due to God.[272] τοῦ κυρίου, "of the Lord," identifies the one they fear (objective genitive). Given Ananias's clarification that the "Lord" who appeared to Saul is Jesus (v. 17), it is likely that "the Lord" here is also Jesus.[273] Jesus continues to receive honors formerly understood to be appropriate to YHWH alone (cf., e.g., 2:33, 36; 7:59–60).

τῇ παρακλήσει τοῦ ἁγίου πνεύματος. "the encouragement given by the Holy Spirit." Luke uses παράκλησιν τοῦ Ἰσραήλ, usually translated "consolation of Israel," for Simeon's desire (Luke 2:25). παράκλησις, "encouragement," is a restoration-of-Israel term echoing Isa 40:1 LXX (where the cognate verb παρακαλέω, "encourage," is used) and further underlines the restoration eschatology in play here—God is acting to re-create Israel around its Messiah, and the characteristics of peace, being built up, walking in the fear of the Lord, and the encouragement of the Holy Spirit show this to be the case.

ἐπληθύνετο, "[it] kept being multiplied," is a further imperfect and a further indication of divine action: God gives the assembly's growth (cf. 1 Cor 3:6). The assembly's engagement with God is producing growth in multiple dimensions, including numerically. In terms of OT "mission theology" and eschatology, the lifestyle of the assembly displays divinely enabled attractiveness, and God uses this to draw others into its circle (cf., e.g., Zech 8:20–23).

Explanation

Saul's encounter with the exalted Lord Jesus near Damascus (v. 3) is pivotal in Acts, for through it a ferocious opponent of the believing community (7:58; 8:1, 3) becomes one of its greatest advocates. Within Acts, Saul's earlier introduction (8:1b–3) is "chain linked" with this fuller story, and Saul then disappears from the narrative for some time (until 11:25–26, some ten years later). From 13:1–3 onwards, Saul will become the major human protagonist of Acts. By this means Luke gradually introduces first-time readers to Saul as a key figure in the Jesus movement—although the majority of Luke's readers would already be well aware of Saul in this role. At this point we hear the story from the narrator's perspective; later in Acts we shall twice hear this story on Saul's lips (22:3–21; 26:2–23).

As with the story so far, it is Jesus's intervention that is critical in transforming Saul from persecutor to proclaimer. Luke gives no opening for a psychological reading of Saul as a man opposing a faith to which he was secretly attracted; from Paul's own writings, the opposite is likely (e.g., Phil 3:4b–6).

272 E.g., Deut 5:29; 1 Sam 12:14; Pss 25:14 (LXX 24:14); 33:8 (LXX 32:8); 111:10 (LXX 110:10); Prov 2:5; 8:13; 9:10; see "Fear of God," *DBIm* 277–78.

273 Contra Dunn, "ΚΥΡΙΟΣ," 249, who sees the biblical echo of "the fear of the Lord" as pointing to God as "the Lord"; it is more likely that biblical language used for God is now being used for Jesus, as with the pouring out of the Spirit in 2:33 (see *Comment* there).

Through encountering Jesus, Saul changes from a man who knows his own mind (Acts 9:1–2) to one who must await instructions (v. 6), and from a man who intends to lead believers away from Damascus (v. 2) to one who is himself led by the hand in dependence because of his temporary blindness (vv. 8–9). From being one who controls others by imprisoning them, Saul becomes one under the control of Jesus and in the hands of Jesus's people. The light of the encounter floods Saul's life with fresh discovery as he realizes that he has been persecuting not merely a group of apostate Jews, but a heavenly figure who is properly called "Lord" (vv. 4–5).

Not only is Saul transformed from persecutor to proclaimer, he himself becomes persecuted. Ananias is told that programmatically Saul will suffer for Jesus's name (v. 15), and this is played out in Damascus, as Jews who were expecting to welcome his campaign against the believers turn against Saul and seek his life (vv. 21, 23). It is further seen in Jerusalem as Hellenistic Jews seek to kill him (v. 29). In both places, his new sisters and brothers ensure his safe escape (vv. 25, 30)—Saul's family allegiance has changed through his baptism (v. 18); it is striking how widely Paul's letters use family imagery for the believing communities (e.g., Rom 1:13; 12:1; 1 Cor 1:10, 26; 2 Cor 1:8; 8:1; Gal 1:11; Phil 1:14; 3:1; 1 Thess 1:4; 2:1, 9, 17; Phlm 16, 20). The suffering Saul experiences in these two cities is the precursor of many events later in Acts, where Saul's ministry is rarely received without controversy, debate, and often physical attack (e.g., 13:45; 14:2, 5, 19–20; 16:19–24; 17:5–7, 32; 18:6, 12–13; 19:23–29; 20:18–23; 21:27–31).

At the heart of the encounter is the Lord Jesus whom Saul subsequently proclaims. In this story Jesus is located in heaven (9:3; cf. 1:9–11; 3:21) and appropriately addressed as "Lord" (9:5, 10, 13). Both of these features sit comfortably with Acts's emerging picture of Jesus as one who properly receives devotion alongside YHWH, echoing Peter's Pentecost declaration that he is "Lord and Messiah" (2:36), the dying Stephen's vision of Jesus alongside God (7:55), and his prayer to Jesus as Lord (7:59). Luke is portraying a remarkable transformation in the Jewish believers' symbolic universe, for now an exalted human, Jesus, rightly receives the accolades and attitudes that properly belong to God alone. This Jesus acts from heaven to transform Saul. Although Saul's encounter with Jesus is personal, it is not privatized or individual, for it leads to engagement with a single believer, Ananias (9:17–19a), the Damascus believers (vv. 19b, 25), and later (after "many days," v. 23) Barnabas and the Jerusalem apostles (vv. 26–27).

Ananias emerges as a minor character who exemplifies early Jewish Christian devotion to Jesus. By contrast with Saul, his response to being addressed is to offer himself ready to act (v. 10; contrast v. 5a). Ananias then has a feisty conversation with the Lord Jesus about what he is to do, for Ananias has doubts about Saul (vv. 13–14). Jesus's reassurance to Ananias is sufficient to persuade him (vv. 15–16), and Ananias then does as Jesus asks

(v. 17). Such a conversation echoes psalms where the psalmist asks questions of God and sometimes challenges God (e.g., Pss 10:1, 13; 13:3; 22:1, 2; 42:9; 43:2; 44:23–24; 69:16; 74:1, 11; 86:1; 88:14; 102:2; 120:1; 143:7)—Jesus as Lord shares the characteristics of YHWH in that he is big enough to face and respond to human questioning and challenge.

Saul expresses his transformed understanding of Jesus quickly (Acts 9:20). Saul already knows the claims the believers make and has assessed them as blasphemous prior to the Damascus Road encounter—as a highly intelligent and educated Jew, he would quickly recognize how his worldview was reorientated around his fresh understanding of Jesus and thus proclaim him as Messiah and the son of God (vv. 20, 22). The latter is strikingly the same name used in Paul's account of his early days as a believer: "God . . . was pleased to reveal *his son* to me" (Gal 1:15–16). Saul presumably makes the same set of connections that Peter had made at Pentecost: because of Jesus's resurrection and exaltation to God's right side, he is now Lord and Messiah of Israel and the world (2:22–36). Saul's conversations with the Damascene believers would help firm up his thinking (v. 19b), and the evidence of Galatians is that he also goes for a period in "Arabia," where he would reflect further on how his transformed view of Jesus affected his reading of Scripture and his understanding of YHWH's purposes for Israel and the world, before returning to Damascus (Gal 1:17). Luke is thus giving a compressed account of a longer period by focusing on key events for his own communicative purposes.

Saul leaves the Acts narrative quietly at this point, traveling to his home city of Tarsus (Acts 9:11, 30), and Luke tells us nothing of what he did for the next ten years until Barnabas goes to fetch him to help with the new community in Antioch (11:25–26). At this stage, Luke wants readers to know simply about Saul's radical change and that this happens through encountering Jesus.

The section transitions to the next story with a summary statement (9:31) that characterizes the believers as "assembly" (traditionally "church") for only the fourth time in Acts—previous uses were 5:11; 8:1b, 3, all notably in the setting of persecution (the latter two by Saul himself). By contrast, the assembly, which embraces a wide geographical region, now has "peace." This peace is rooted in two key characteristics that produce continuing numerical growth: fearing the Lord and being encouraged by the Holy Spirit. The former echoes Scripture (e.g., Deut 8:6; 10:12; 1 Sam 12:24; Neh 5:15; Pss 22:23 [MT 22:24, LXX 21:24]; 25:12 [LXX 24:12]; 34:9 [MT 34:10, LXX 33:10]; 111:10 [LXX 110:10]; Prov 1:7; 19:23; Isa 8:13; Hag 1:12; Sir 1:8, 11, 12, 13, 14); the latter is a fresh feature because of the universal gift of the Spirit to believers at and following Pentecost (cf. 2:17–28, 38).

C. God Continues to Act in Syria-Palestine (9:32–12:24)

1. God Works through Peter in Western Palestine (9:32–42)

Bibliography

Dawson, A. *Healing,* 79. **Edwards, J. R.** "Parallels," 488. **Erichsen-Wendt, F.** "Tabitha." **Finger, R. H.** *Widows,* 260–61. **Forbes, G. W., and S. D. Harrower.** *Raised,* 171–75. **Hays, C. M.** *Ethics,* 233–34. **Helingenthal, R.** "Werke." **Hemer, C. J.** *Book,* 226. **Hengel, M.** *Between,* 116–18. ———. *Peter.* **Karmon, Y.** "Influences." **Kochenash, M.** "Aeneas." ———. "Correction." **MacDonald, D. R.** *Gospels and Homer,* 47–49, 138–40. **Myllykowski, M.** "Being," 172–73. **Read-Heimerdinger, J.** *Bezan Text,* 124–25. **Reece, S.** "Jesus as Healer." **Reimer, I. R.** *Women,* 31–69. **Schnabel, E. J.** *Mission,* 1:687–88. **Schwartz, J.** "Peter." **Seim, T. K.** *Message,* 11–24, 241–42. **Sleeman, M.** *Geography,* 219–22. **Sparks, H. F. D.** "Semitisms," 25–26. **Spencer, F. S.** *Portrait,* 152–54. ———. "Widows," 731–32. **Strelan, R.** "Tabitha." **Thiede, C. P.** *Simon Peter,* 139–40. **Wilcox, M.** *Semitisms,* 109–11. **Williams, M. H.** "Names," 96, 103, 110.

Translation

32 Now, it came about that, as Peter was going around among all these areas,[a] he came down[b] to the holy ones living in Lydda. 33 There he found a certain person, Aeneas by name, who had been bedridden for eight years[c] and who was paralyzed.[d] 34 Peter said to him, "Aeneas, Jesus the Messiah heals you; get up and make your bed!"[e] Immediately he got up. 35 All those who lived in Lydda and the Sharon saw him and[f] turned to the Lord.

36 Now in Joppa there was a certain female disciple, Tabitha by name, which translates as Dorcas. She was full of good works and habitually gave alms.[g] 37 At that time that she became ill and died. After they had washed[h] her, they laid her out in an upstairs room. 38 Because Lydda was near Joppa,[i] when the disciples heard that Peter was[j] there,[k] they sent two men to him to urge[l] him, "Come to[m] us—don't delay!"[n] 39 So Peter got up and went with them. When he arrived,[o] they took him into the upstairs room, and all the widows came to him weeping and showing tunics and clothes that Dorcas used to make[p] while she was[q] with them. 40 Peter sent everyone out and knelt down and prayed. Then he turned to the body and said, "Tabitha, get up!" She opened her eyes and, on seeing Peter,[r] she sat up. 41 He held out his hand[s] to her and helped her up; calling the holy ones and widows, he presented[t] her alive. 42 This became known throughout the whole[u] of Joppa, and many people came to believe[v] in the Lord.

Notes

a. Taking πάντων as denoting "all the areas" mentioned in v. 31.

b. κατελθεῖν, aor. inf., "to go down," with Ἐγένετο, "it happened," taking acc. "subject" Πέτρον, "Peter" (see 9:3 and *Note* e there).

c. ἐξ ἐτῶν ὀκτώ probably means "for eight years"; it could mean "from the age of eight." ἐκ with a temporal expression can denote the time from which something began, which causes the slight ambiguity here; "ἐκ," BDAG 297–98, §5.a; Robertson, 597; Culy and Parsons, *Acts*, 186; Barrett, *Acts*, 1:480.

d. ἦν παραλελυμένος, periph. plpf., "[he] was paralyzed," portraying a result in past time of an earlier past event.

e. στρῶσον σεαυτῷ; verb is aor. impv. of στρωννύω/στρώννυμι, "spread, furnish"; 5x NT, only use in Acts. "στρωννύω/στρώννυμι," BDAG 949, §1, "make your own bed"; L&N §46.10, "to make one's bed," citing this verse.

f. οἵτινες, "who," functions as equivalent of rel. pn. οἵ, "who" ("ὅστις," BDAG 729, §3), referring back to those living in the two places earlier in the verse.

g. ἐλεημοσυνῶν ὧν ἐποίει, lit., "alms which she habitually gave." The rel. pn. ὧν has been attracted from acc. ἅ into gen. by ἐλεημοσυνῶν (which is gen. to express what she was full of).

h. λούσαντες, temporal aor. ptc., "after they had washed."

i. οὔσης Λύδδας, causal pres. ptc., εἰμί, "because Lydda was"; gen. abs., here explaining why the event in the rest of the sentence naturally occurs; Levinsohn, *Connections*, 75.

j. ἐστίν pres. in reported (indirect) discourse.

k. i.e., in Lydda (v. 32).

l. παρακαλοῦντες, pres. ptc., "urging," expressing purpose of ἀπέστειλαν, "they sent"; with Culy and Parsons, *Acts*, 188.

m. ἕως, "to," with διέρχομαι is Lukan (*VL* 267); Acts frequently uses this prep. spatially (1:8; 11:19, 22; 13:47; 17:14, 15; 21:5; 23:23; 26:11).

n. μὴ ὀκνήσῃς, aor. subj., with μή expressing prohibition. ὀκνέω, "delay," "ὀκνέω," BDAG 702 (NT *hapax legomenon*).

o. παραγενόμενον, adjectival aor. ptc., "having arrived," acc., agreeing with rel. pn. ὅν, which is the object of the main verb ἀνήγαγον, "they took." The combination of acc. rel. pn. and acc. ptcp. is rare (in NT, only here and 28:4), functioning to identify when they took Peter to the upstairs room; Culy and Parsons, *Acts*, 189.

p. ἐποίει, "used to make"; "pluperfective" impf., describing repeated action in time prior to the main storyline, which is in aor.; Wallace, 549; McKay, 45 §4.3.5.

q. οὖσα, temporal ptc., "while she was."

r. ἰδοῦσα, "on seeing," temporal aor. ptc.

s. δοὺς . . . αὐτῇ χεῖρα, "giving her [a] hand," idiomatic expression for "holding out his hand to her"; "δίδωμι," BDAG 243, §16.

t. παρέστησεν, 1 aor. (transitive) of παρίστημι; "παρίστημι," BDAG 778–9, §1.b.β, "he presented."

u. καθ' ὅλης, "throughout the whole of"; "ὅλος," BDAG 511, §A.1.c.

v. ἐπίστευσαν, inceptive aor., "came to believe."

Form/Structure/Setting

Delimitation of pericope. This passage shifts the focus of Acts from Saul (9:1–31) to Peter, who will be at the heart of the narrative until his near-final appearance in Acts in 12:1–17 (his final appearance is the cameo in 15:7–11). Peter is named six times in this pair of stories, signaling that in the story he is the key agent for the exalted Jesus (9:32, 34, 28, 39, 40 [twice]). Only 11:19–30 does not include Peter, and that section continues the story of the inclusion of gentiles in which Peter's meeting with Cornelius is crucial. Two ἐγένετο + infinitive constructions ("it happened that . . .") begin the individual stories (vv. 32, 37), and a third such construction opens a new story (v. 43, see *Comment* there).

Sources/historicity. These Petrine stories bear marks of local traditions in the inclusion of specific details: the names of the people (Aeneas, Tabitha/Dorcas), the use of Tabitha, an Aramaic name, explained for Luke's Greek-speaking audience as Dorcas,[1] Jewish customs of funeral preparation (v. 37), and knowledge of Palestinian geography (v. 38a).[2] The believers as οἱ ἅγιοι, "the holy ones" (vv. 32, 41), and μαθήτρια, μαθηταί, "disciples" (vv. 36, 38), use designations found only or first in Jewish settings, which are thus likely to be primitive.[3] Peter's engagement with Jewish communities at this stage foreshadows the Jerusalem agreement (Gal 2:7). The lack of parallelism with Paul's later church-planting exploits—Peter is not said to start any congregation other than the Jerusalem one—speaks for the veracity of this account of his visiting assemblies founded (presumably) by others.[4] Beyond this, it is difficult to discuss the historicity of these specific events, for readers' assessment of healings and raisings will largely flow from their worldview, that is, whether such events can take place at all.[5]

Structure. As often, Luke "pairs" stories with central male and female characters, here Aeneas and Tabitha/Dorcas.[6] Aeneas is healed by Jesus, and Dorcas is raised from death. The stories share a typical healing story form:[7] setting the scene geographically (vv. 32, 36), introducing the person and their need (vv. 33, 37), Peter's intervention (vv. 34a, 38–40a), the outcome (vv. 34b, 40b–41), and the response of faith from others (vv. 35, 42). By contrast with Jesus's healings, Peter is not the one who performs the healing: in each case the active healer is Jesus, acting from heaven. Thus, Peter informs Aeneas that Jesus is healing him (v. 34), and Peter prays before calling Tabitha to get up (v. 40). The Tabitha story is fuller than that concerning Aeneas, making her more prominent.[8]

Two sets of parallel passages help in hearing Luke's stories here: the biblical stories of raisings by Elijah and Elisha and Jesus's raisings in Luke's Gospel.

---

1 With Pervo, *Acts*, 252n6. Sparks, "Semitisms," 25–26, suggests that this and other Aramaisms in the story imply that Luke heard, rather than read, the story and then wrote it in Greek; similarly, Wilcox, *Semitisms*, 109–11.

2 Hengel, *Between*, 116–18, provides details, and observes that if Luke is a gentile and non-Palestinian, it is most likely that the geographical accuracy implies that Luke has early traditions to draw on here.

3 Trebilco, *Self-designations*, 137–39, 228; he notes that "disciples" is used twenty-eight times in Acts but never for gentiles before 11:26.

4 Cf. Hengel, *Peter*, 91.

5 For carefully documented evidence for modern healings and raisings, see Keener, *Miracles Today*. For a cogent defense of the plausibility of biblical miracle stories, see Keener, *Miracles*, including modern examples (e.g., 1:523–56; 2:737–38).

6 Cf. Luke 1:5–25 (Zechariah), 26–38 (Mary); Acts 1:13–14; 2:27–28; 5:14; 5:1–11; 17:34; 18:1–28; 24:1–27; 25:23–27. Tannehill, *Unity*, 1:132–36; Seim, *Message*, 11–24; and Marguerat, *Actes*, 348n2 provide lists.

7 Classically described in Bultmann, *History*, 220–26.

8 Forbes and Harrower, *Raised*, 172.

Between them, they point to the power of the gospel community, represented by Peter, as no less than that of the great prophets, although the believers' power derives from the exalted Jesus who acts from heaven to restore people to health and life (note v. 34).

The Tabitha story shows similarities to two biblical stories: the raising of the widow's son at Zarephath through Elijah (1 Kgs 17:17–24) and the raising of the Shunammite woman's son through Elisha (2 Kgs 4:18–37). Like Tabitha, both include: prayer by the "man of God" for the dead person (Acts 9:40; 1 Kgs 17:20–21; 2 Kgs 4:33); the widow's son located in an upstairs room (Acts 9:37, 39; 1 Kgs 17:19); the Shunammite's son's recovery being seen by his eyes opening (Acts 9:40; 2 Kgs 4:35); and the revived person being presented to others (Acts 9:41; 1 Kgs 17:23; 2 Kgs 4:36). Unlike with Tabitha: both prophets lie on the body of the dead person (1 Kgs 17 21; 2 Kgs 4:34), which would have been inappropriate for Peter with a woman's body; and both mothers honor the prophet (1 Kgs 17:24; 2 Kgs 4:37), whereas Luke reports the propagation of the story leading to the response of faith (Acts 9:42). Second- and early fourth-century AD rabbis are reported as seeing the Shunammite's son's raising as "the resurrection of the dead . . . come before its time" (Midr. Song 2.5.3 = 98a [Simon]), which suggests they saw it as emblematic of the final resurrection of the dead.[9] Tabitha's story invites a similar interpretation.

Careful readers of Luke-Acts also hear echoes of Jesus's actions:[10] his healing of the centurion's slave (Luke 7:2–10); his raising the widow's son at Nain (Luke 7:11–17); and his raising of Jairus's daughter (Luke 8:40–42a, 49–56//Mark 5:21–24, 35–43). The centurion's slave story has some closeness of structure to the present passage: people sent to request Jesus/Peter to come speedily (Luke 7:4; Acts 9:38), followed by Jesus/Peter going and restoring the sick/dead person (Luke 7:6; Acts 9:39). That story is juxtaposed with Jesus's raising of the widow's son at Nain, a public event—indeed, in the midst of the funeral procession! Both of the stories in Luke 7 bear some resemblances to the Elijah and Elisha stories discussed above. Jesus's raising of Jairus's daughter is more similar in location and timing to this story: a separate room, from which Jesus excludes others, and shortly after death. However, there is little precisely parallel language—the nearest is with Mark 5:41 (see *Comment* on v. 40); the contrast with Jesus is more notable.[11] See *Comment* on 9:40 for wording which parallels or contrasts with the Gospel stories.

Setting. These two stories prepare for Peter's crucial role in the mission

9 Contra Reimer, *Women*, 53, cf. 62, who cites this passage as evidence that the Shunammite's son's raising is merely "a dead person . . . come to life again" and "is not the same as resurrection." On Second Temple Jewish resurrection hopes, see Wright, *Resurrection*, 146–206 (summary: 202–6).

10 On the stories from Luke 7, see Edwards, "Parallels," 488.

11 Edwards, "Parallels," 499–501, argues cogently that such parallels between Luke and Acts both point to Jesus as the model for his disciples to follow and show that Jesus is preeminent, above his disciples.

to gentiles (9:43–11:18), both by locating him in the coastal plain near to Cornelius's home in Caesarea Maritima (10:1) and by showing his role as a divine agent. Peter is a key spokesman of God and Jesus: he informs Aeneas that Jesus heals him (9:34) and calls Tabitha to get up (v. 40). The name Tabitha/Dorcas ("gazelle") can be seen as preparing for Peter's vision of the animals on the sheet (10:10–16),[12] although there is little hint here that gentiles may be included in God's people. Tabitha's character and deeds parallel those of Cornelius, particularly because both do ἐλεημοσύνη, "almsgiving" (9:36; 10:2), and thus the two stories are linked—both of these merciful people receive God's mercy.[13]

Later in Acts, Paul will be the agent of similar events—the healing of the man with a congenital disability of his feet in Lystra (14:8–10) and the raising of Eutychus (20:9–12). See *Comment* on those passages for discussion.

Comment

32 δέ, "now," marks a shift to a new grammatical subject and may "answer" μέν, "so," in the preceding summary (v. 31). The narrative resumes from 8:25, where the those who were on mission in Samaria returned to Jerusalem after evangelizing Samaritan villages.

Πέτρον διερχόμενον διὰ πάντων, "as Peter was going around in all these areas," refers back to 9:31, so denoting Judea, Galilee, and Samaria. It is likely that he visits some of the rural believing groups first established through the persecution that caused believers to flee from Jerusalem (8:1 with *Comment* there). Like the visit to Lydda that follows, his visits probably combined pastoral care and encouragement for the believers with further evangelism.[14]

Ἐγένετο . . . Πέτρον . . . κατελθεῖν, "it came about that . . . Peter . . . came down." Peter is reintroduced with an anarthrous accusative Πέτρον and Luke's characteristic ἐγένετο + infinitive construction (see *Note* e on 9:3). The anarthrous use is usual for a character's reentry into the narrative and makes Peter prominent.[15] κατελθεῖν, "went down," is a characteristic verb for travel to a coastal plain or lake, which is normally lower than inland areas, although it can also denote travel from Jerusalem as the capital city (and Jerusalem was also known for its relative height).[16] The believing communities he visits could well have been founded by Philip during his travels from Azotus to Caesarea (8:40).[17]

12 Strelan, "Tabitha," 84, arguing that she is a proselyte.

13 With Spencer, "Widows," 731; he also thinks a transformation of Peter's attitudes, to widows here and gentiles in the Cornelius story, links the two stories. See *Comment* on 6:2 for reasons that Peter's attitude to his serving widows in 6:1–6 is not negative.

14 So Pesch, *Apostelgeschichte*, 318; Jervell, *Apostelgeschichte*, 295.

15 Read-Heimerdinger, *Bezan Text*, 124–25; she notes 3:1; 4:8; 5:3 (D), 15; 8:14; 11:2; 12:3; 15:7. She does not mention this verse, presumably because D lacks 9:30–10:13.

16 For travel to sea/lake, see 12:19; 13:4; 18:22; Luke 4:31. "Normally" because of exceptions such as the Dead Sea, which is well below sea level.

17 Spencer, *Portrait*, 153.

τοὺς ἁγίους τοὺς κατοικοῦντας Λύδδα, "the holy ones living in Lydda." On τοὺς ἁγίους, "the holy ones," see *Comment* on 9:13. These holy ones were κατοικοῦντας, "living," in Lydda already—and thus Peter is not the founder of this (or any other) believing community (e.g., in Joppa, v. 36), by contrast with Paul.[18] Peter's visit may be for "inspection," like Barnabas's later visit to Syrian Antioch (11:22–23). Some in Lydda may have become believers at Pentecost and returned home (Lydda is in Judea, 2:9), or be among those who fled Jerusalem during persecution (8:1), or be believers who had fled Jerusalem and evangelized in Lydda (8:4)—or the community might have been founded or established by Philip as he traveled through the coastal towns (8:40). Lydda,[19] also known as Lod (modern Lud), is on the road from Jerusalem to Joppa, about 44 km/27.3 miles northwest of Jerusalem and 17 km/10.6 miles southeast of Joppa. It had come under Jewish control ca. 145 BC (1 Macc 11:34; Josephus, *Ant.* 13.4.9 §127) and so probably has at least a substantial Jewish population at the time of Peter's visit. Jews and gentiles would regularly encounter each other there. It became capital of one of the eleven subregions (toparchies) of Judea under the Romans (Josephus, *J.W.* 2.20.4 §567; 3.3.5 §55), although Luke does not use Roman administration terms to describe Lydda and its location. It is substantial, although not formally a "city," πόλις ("a village [κώμην] that was in size not inferior to a city [πόλεως]," Josephus, *Ant.* 20.6.2 §130 [Feldman, LCL]). In the second century AD and later, it is known as a place where anti-Christian rabbis lived.[20]

33 εὗρεν δὲ ἐκεῖ ἄνθρωπόν τινα, "There he found a certain person." Luke is vague about how, where and when Peter meets Aeneas, perhaps because his source only included that they meet and Aeneas's name—understandably, since the focus of the story is the healing and its effects.

ὀνόματι Αἰνέαν ἐξ ἐτῶν ὀκτὼ κατακείμενον ἐπὶ κραβάττου, ὃς ἦν παραλελυμένος, "Aeneas by name, who had been bedridden for eight years and who was paralyzed." It is unusual in Luke's double-work to name people who are healed: none are named in the Gospel, and in Acts only Saul (9:17–18; 22:12–13), Tabitha/Dorcas (9:36–43), and Eutychus (20:9–12). The name "Aeneas" is Greek rather than Jewish and is known among Greek writers, including Josephus (*Ant.* 14.10.22 §248; 16.9.4 §294; *J.W.* 5.7.4 §327).[21] He is probably Jewish, for, if not, Luke would

---

18 Hengel, *Peter*, 91.

19 On Lydda/Lod, see Schnabel, *Mission* 1:687–88; M. Hunt and J. Kaplan, "Lod," *ABD* 4:345–46; Schürer, 2:190–98.

20 Schwartz, "Peter," 413, although his wider claim that the tradition of Ben Stada in Lod as a "deceiver" was derived from Peter's ministry lacks clear evidence.

21 Williams, "Names," 110, cites examples from the second century BC to the fourth century AD from within and outside Palestine. See also K. Dowden, "Aeneas," *DDD* 11–12, who notes that *LGPN* (1:19) cites thirty-five uses prior to AD 1. Kochenash, "Aeneas," 671–72, adds that later published volumes of *LGPN* provide few examples in the first two centuries AD, with the exception of coastal Asia Minor (202 examples), and that he is informed by the *LGPN* staff that Syria, Palestine, and Trans-Euphrates offer only seven examples including Acts 9:33–35 (this volume is as yet unpublished).

surely mention it,[22] but it is unclear whether he was a believer.[23] Readers who knew Virgil's *Aeneid* or Homer's *Iliad* would hear an echo of Aeneas the traveler and might reflect on the irony of Luke's Aeneas being unable even to get out of bed.[24] Luke portrays Aeneas's condition as severe, and thus healing as difficult, by indicating its length, effect, and nature. παραλελυμένος, "paralyzed," denotes its nature as inability to move limbs, here the legs.[25] The periphrastic pluperfect ἦν παραλελυμένος, "he was paralyzed," indicates a state resulting from a past event (here, eight years previously—the length of the illness) that persisted for a time but is over at the time of Luke's writing (since Aeneas was healed). The effect was that Aeneas was κατακείμενον ἐπὶ κραβάττου, "bedridden" (= "lying on a bed"), unable to move independently, for this long period.

34 Αἰνέα, ἰᾶταί σε Ἰησοῦς Χριστός, "Aeneas, Jesus the Messiah heals you." Peter's words announce Aeneas's healing, echoing Peter's words to the man at the Beautiful Gate (3:6). However, it is not by Jesus's *name* that the man is healed, but Ἰησοῦς Χριστός, "Jesus the Messiah," is the subject who accomplishes the healing. The word play of ἰᾶται, "heals," and Ἰησοῦς, "Jesus," underlines this point (cf. 4:30), particularly as it comes in a setting where meanings of names are significant: Aeneas has a Greek name (9:33); Tabitha is also known as Dorcas (v. 36); Simon is identified as a tanner, a dubious trade (v. 43); and Cornelius the Roman centurion is introduced by name (10:1).[26] This shows the exalted Jesus (1:9–11) acting directly from heaven (as in his appearances in 7:55–56; 9:3–6). Although Jesus is physically absent, he is reordering any understanding of space that regards earth and heaven as completely distinct;[27] that barrier is now overcome in part, as heaven invades earth (cf. the various comings of the Spirit, 2:1–4, etc.), and will be overcome in full at Jesus's return (1:11; 3:21).[28] Jesus is not an "absentee" but an active character in events.[29]

---

22 With Barrett, *Acts*, 1:480.

23 Weiser, *Apostelgeschichte*, 1:242, thinks he is a believer, since otherwise Luke would have recorded him becoming a believer. However, others in Acts who are not believers are healed without a statement that they became believers, e.g., Publius's father 28:8.

24 With Holladay, *Acts*, 223. Kochenash, "Aeneas" (followed by MacDonald, *Gospels and Homer*, 47–49), suggests that "Aeneas" connotes "Rome" because of his association with that city, the destination of the book of Acts, and that "Joppa" (9:36) connotes gentile inclusion in the believing community. He speculates that these names are metonyms bridging from the Jewish mission (summarized in 9:31) to the gentile mission begun with Cornelius (10:1–11:18) and open a narrative arc that ends in Rome (28:16–31). It is unclear whether he considers these links to exist in Luke's mind or the minds of his readers/hearers. That 9:32–42 is a bridge to the inclusion of gentiles in the Cornelius story is plausible; Kochenash's basis for that claim is far less so.

25 Luke prefers the verb παραλύω (Luke 5:18, 24; Acts 8:7); the other Synoptics prefer the adjective παραλυτικός (Mark 2:9, 10; Matt 8:6; 9:2, 6). Both denote the same form of illness. For suggestions of the medical condition, see Dawson, *Healing*, 79n77.

26 Reece, "Jesus as Healer," 194–95.

27 Sleeman, *Geography*, 220.

28 More fully, see Walton, "Heavens," 65–68.

29 More fully, see Walton, "Jesus"; Walton, "Identity," 140–46; Gaventa, "Acts," 42–43; contra Conzelmann, *Theology*, 170–206.

ἀνάστηθι καὶ στρῶσον σεαυτῷ . . . εὐθέως ἀνέστη, "get up and make your bed! . . . immediately he got up." Peter's instruction, ἀνάστηθι, "get up" (aorist imperative), is exactly what happens: Aeneas ἀνέστη, "got up" (aorist indicative of the same verb, ἀνίστημι "get up"). στρῶσον σεαυτῷ, "make your bed," seems to be an idiom:[30] the verb στρωννύω means "spread, furnish" (5x NT; this is the only Acts use), and the dative reflexive possessive pronoun σεαυτῷ has the force "for yourself" (dative of advantage). These actions demonstrate that the healing has taken place (cf. Luke 5:17–26, where the successful healing of the man with paralysis confirms Jesus's words of forgiveness).

35 εἶδαν αὐτὸν πάντες οἱ κατοικοῦντες Λύδδα καὶ τὸν Σαρῶνα, "All those living in Lydda and the Sharon saw him." As with the man at the Beautiful Gate, Aeneas's healing becomes well-known as people see him (3:9–10; 4:14, 21–22), presumably because Aeneas's disability was well-known, not just in the town of Lydda but also in the wider region τὸν Σαρῶνα, "the Sharon." This coastal region stretched inland about 17.7 km/11 miles. It changed from being proverbially desolate (Isa 33:9; 35:2) to widely occupied and urbanized as a result of Herod and the Romans' construction of Caesarea Maritima and a network of roads and bridges in the region (ca. 22–10/9 BC), in tune with Luke's implication here.[31]

οἵτινες ἐπέστρεψαν ἐπὶ τὸν κύριον, "and they turned to the Lord." Luke's greatest interest, here and elsewhere, is in the progress of the mission, seen in the response of people in Lydda and the Sharon whose lives were changed as they turned ἐπὶ τὸν κύριον, "to the Lord." In this predominantly Jewish setting, "the Lord" is Jesus, for Jews do not need to turn to YHWH.[32] This is Luke's first use of ἐπιστρέφω, "turn," with an object; in 3:19 the object is implicitly "God,"[33] and that use in Peter's speech in the temple informs this use, suggesting that the turning involves the reorientation of life to center on Jesus as the exalted Lord. The implication that (at least) a large number responded in this way is plausible in the spread of a new movement.[34] (See also *Comment* on v. 42.)

36 Ἐν Ἰόππῃ, "in Joppa." Joppa (modern Jaffa) is an ancient port dating to at least 1500 BC, 18 km/11.2 miles northwest of Lydda (hence v. 38a) and 60 km/37.3 miles west of Jerusalem.[35] In this period it belongs to the Roman province of Judea and is thus under the procurator's authority, mediated by the puppet Archelaus (Josephus, *Ant.* 14.4.4. §76; 17.11.4. §320). Joppa has a substantial Jewish population: during the Jewish war of AD 66–73 it is a center for the Jewish rebels: Cestius's troops killed 8,400 there (Josephus, *J.W.*

---

30 "στρωννύω," BDAG 949, §1; L&N §46.10.

31 On the Sharon, see H. R. Weeks, "Sharon," *ABD* 5:1161–63; Karmon, "Influences," 53–57.

32 So also (with some hesitation) Dunn, "ΚΥΡΙΟΣ," 250.

33 cf. 11:21; 14:15; 15:19; 26:18, 20, where the stated or implied object of ἐπιστρέφω is God in each case.

34 Keener, *Acts*, 2:1709n49, cites a number of examples from Christian history.

35 On Joppa, see Schnabel, *Mission*, 1:688; J. & H. R. Kaplan, "Joppa," *ABD* 3:946–49.

2.8.10 §§507–9; 3.9.2–3 §§414–26). Tensions between the Jewish and gentile populations are attested in the Maccabean period (2 Macc 12:3–9) and may well have persisted to this time. Luke's repeated naming of the city[36] highlights its significance for the progress of the gospel, symbolically marking the edge (and completion?) of "all Judea" (πάσῃ τῇ Ἰουδαίᾳ, 1:8).[37]

τις ἦν μαθήτρια ὀνόματι Ταβιθά, ἣ διερμηνευομένη λέγεται Δορκάς, "there was a certain female disciple, Tabitha by name, which translates as Dorcas," introduces a new character. She is identified as μαθήτρια, "a female disciple" (a NT *hapax legomenon*, the feminine form of μαθητής, "disciple"), and thus is a believer.[38] Both names mean "gazelle"; "Tabitha" is Aramaic, and "Dorcas" Greek.[39] She may be known by both names, by Aramaic speakers and Greek speakers, or Luke may give the Greek equivalent for his Greek-speaking audience,[40] or she may be a proselyte who received the Aramaic name on conversion.[41] Peter addresses her only as "Tabitha" (9:40), whereas in the narrative later, Luke calls her "Dorcas" (v. 39). Luke's lack of mention of her family—a surprising gap in the context of mourning—suggests she may well be a widow.

αὕτη ἦν πλήρης ἔργων ἀγαθῶν καὶ ἐλεημοσυνῶν ὧν ἐποίει, "She was full of good works and habitually gave alms." Tabitha exhibits godly generosity, expressed in making garments for widows (v. 39)—and thus ἐλεημοσυνῶν, "alms," embraces a larger range of activities than simply giving money.[42] Cornelius, whose piety is

---

36 9:36, 38, 42, 43; 10:5, 8, 23, 32; 11:5, 13; see *Comment* on 9:43.

37 Hengel, *Between*, 117.

38 μαθήτρια, "female disciple," is found in some of the apocryphal Acts, and Gos. Pet. I.12.50; as well as concerning women in philosophical schools, e.g., Diog. Laert. 4.2; 8.42. See "μαθήτρια," LSJ; "μαθήτρια," BDAG 610. Forbes and Harrower, *Raised*, 173, suggest a parallel of response to Jesus with Mary (Luke 10:39–42), which portrays Tabitha as an "ideal convert."

39 "Tabitha" is the only known specific Jewish example, although it appears later to be a generic slave name in Gamaliel II's household (Williams, "Names," 96). "Dorcas" is well-known in the Greco-Roman world, although not attested among Palestinian Jews (Williams, "Names," 103, with references in n256; Hemer, *Book*, 226); cf. Josephus, *J.W.* 4.3.5 §145, which speaks of a man as "called 'the son of Dorcas' in the language of our country," probably bar Tabitha. The small Dorcas gazelle is still known in Israel and North Africa (Strelan, "Tabitha," 78); gazelles were considered clean animals by Jews (Deut 12:15, 22–23; 14:4–6). Erichsen-Wendt, "Tabitha," 75–78, suggests that Luke's explanation *could* (his italics, 78) echo ancient authors who saw gazelles as industrious like Tabitha.

40 Reimer, *Women*, 35. Pervo, *Acts*, 252n6, considers the Greek translation to signal that the Aramaic form comes from tradition. Jervell, *Apostelgeschichte*, 296, sees the Aramaic name as derived from local tradition.

41 Strelan, "Tabitha," 78–84. Kochenash, "Correction," speculates that Tabitha/Dorcas is an echo of Dido, Aeneas's wife who dreams that she is being hunted by her husband and later commits suicide with Aeneas's sword. He proposes that "deer" imagery is used in Virgil's *Aeneid* 4 for Dido (pp 2–6) and that Luke plays on the name in order to contrast the death-delivering Roman Empire with the life-restoring kingdom of God. The most that can be said is that it is (remotely) possible that a reader of Acts who knew Virgil's stories would make this connection.

42 Cf. 3:2, 3, 10; 10:2, 4, 31; 24:17; Luke 11:41; 12:33–34, where ἐλεημοσύνη denotes giving money. For discussion of the range of referents of ἐλεημοσύνη, see Heiligenthal, "Werke," contra Bultmann, "ἐλεημοσύνη," *TDNT* 2:486, who claims that the NT uses always portray almsgiving.

painted in Jewish colors, also gives alms (ποιῶν ἐλεημοσύνας, 10:2 with *Comment* there). That she was known by Jewish and Greek names may suggest that she engaged with both Jewish and Hellenistic communities.[43] The lack of a man being named with her as overseeing her work or helping her heightens her personal standing.[44] Jesus himself went around εὐεργετῶν, "doing good" (10:38),[45] and ἔργων ἀγαθῶν, "good works," mark widows and other women in 1 Timothy (2:10; 5:10), as well as believers more generally elsewhere in the Pauline corpus (Rom 2:7; 2 Cor 9:8; Eph 2:10; Col 1:10; 2 Thess 2:17; 2 Tim 2:21; 3:17; Titus 3:1).[46]

37 ἐγένετο δὲ ἐν ταῖς ἡμέραις ἐκείναις ἀσθενήσασαν αὐτὴν ἀποθανεῖν· λούσαντες δὲ ἔθηκαν αὐτὴν ἐν ὑπερῴῳ, "At that time she became ill and died. After they had washed her, they laid her out in an upstairs room." Luke names Tabitha's need: she is dead. Not only that, but funeral preparations have begun by washing her body[47] and laying it out for mourners to visit. Funerals in Palestine normally take place within a day (e.g., 5:6–10), for bodies begin to decompose in the hot climate (this continues to be the custom among Jews and Muslims today). The "upstairs room" may have been in Tabitha's home and could have been a meeting place of the Joppa believers.[48] This location echoes the stories of Elijah and Elisha raising dead people (1 Kgs 17:19, 23; 2 Kgs 4:10, 20–21), and Luke may well mention it to highlight this echo—the followers of Jesus are agents in similar raisings to the great prophets of Scripture (cf. Luke 4:25–26, where Jesus speaks of Elijah raising the widow's son).[49]

38 ἐγγὺς δὲ οὔσης Λύδδας τῇ Ἰόππῃ, "Because Lydda was near Joppa." See *Comment* on v. 36.

οἱ μαθηταὶ ἀκούσαντες ὅτι Πέτρος ἐστὶν ἐν αὐτῇ ἀπέστειλαν δύο ἄνδρας πρὸς αὐτὸν παρακαλοῦντες· μὴ ὀκνήσῃς διελθεῖν ἕως ἡμῶν, "when the disciples heard that Peter was there, they sent two men to him to urge him, 'Come to us—don't delay!'" The Joppa disciples' learning of Peter's presence in Lydda shows that there was communication between the believing communities, here presumably by believers from Lydda traveling to Joppa. The Joppa disciples' sending for Peter shows that they greatly value Tabitha—perhaps because of her prominence in their assembly—and that they think Peter could change things,[50] a hope (i.e., confidence, as usually in biblical usage[51]) based on Peter's

---

43 Forbes and Harrower, *Raised*, 173.

44 Cf. Forbes and Harrower, *Raised*, 174.

45 Forbes and Harrower, *Raised*, 174, suggests that Tabitha also liberates "widows from their socio-economic affliction," which may be over-paralleling.

46 On "good works," esp. in the Pauline corpus, see Marshall and Towner, *Pastoral Epistles*, 227–29.

47 Washing was often combined with anointing with fragrant ointment, which would stave off the smell of decomposition. References: Barrett, *Acts*, 1:483; Keener, *Acts*, 2:1716nn117–20.

48 Spencer, *Acts*, 107–8.

49 These events are hardly examples of the "greater works" promised in John 14:12—note Luke 7:11–17; Barrett, *Acts*, 1:478; contra Haenchen, *Acts*, 341.

50 Pesch, *Apostelgeschichte*, 1:323.

51 "ἐλπίς," *NIDNTTE* 2:186, NT, §1.

known healing ministry (3:1–10; 5:15), most recently in Lydda (9:32–35). Their hope may also be indicated by Tabitha not yet being buried,[52] although Luke's ordering of events in this sentence implies that they send for Peter only after learning that he was nearby.

39 ἀναστὰς δὲ Πέτρος συνῆλθεν αὐτοῖς, "So Peter got up and went with them." Luke does not say that this happened immediately, suggesting that the two from Joppa stay overnight in Lydda before setting out with Peter next day. They would be unlikely to travel at the hottest time of day, in the afternoon, and would be equally cautious of traveling after dark because of bandits; so they may well stay in Lydda overnight. If so, Tabitha would have been dead for at least two days—perhaps three—by the time Peter arrives. The challenge of raising her from death is thus enormous (cf. John 11:17).

παραγενόμενον ἀνήγαγον εἰς τὸ ὑπερῷον καὶ παρέστησαν αὐτῷ πᾶσαι αἱ χῆραι κλαίουσαι καὶ ἐπιδεικνύμεναι χιτῶνας καὶ ἱμάτια ὅσα ἐποίει μετ᾽ αὐτῶν οὖσα ἡ Δορκάς, "When he arrived, they took him into the upstairs room, and all the widows came to him weeping and showing tunics and cloaks that Dorcas used to make while she was with them." Widows were proverbially poor and (thus) under God's care (see *Comment* on 6:1). These widows probably washed Dorcas's body (9:37) in preparation for burial. Their attachment to Dorcas is strong, and thus their grief is great: as well as weeping, they show the garments Dorcas regularly made (see *Note* p). These include undergarments (χιτῶνας, "tunics," shirts worn next to the skin by women and men) and outer garments (ἱμάτια, "cloaks").[53] ἐπιδεικνύμεναι, "showing," is middle (the only such use of this verb in the NT) and may have the nuance "showing on themselves," i.e., they were actually wearing the clothes Dorcas had made.[54]

40 ἐκβαλὼν δὲ ἔξω πάντας, "[Peter] sent everyone out." As when Jesus raises Jairus's daughter (Luke 8:51–52), Peter removes the mourners, perhaps in order to avoid distraction as he prays. πάντας, "everyone" (masculine), indicates that more than the widows were present, probably including the two male messengers from Joppa (Acts 9:38).

ὁ Πέτρος καὶ θεὶς τὰ γόνατα προσηύξατο, "and Peter knelt down and prayed." Kneeling is an unusual posture for prayer in Judaism; more commonly prayer is standing. Kneeling suggests intensity of prayer, as in other uses in Luke-Acts (see *Comment* on 7:60), and thus the aorist προσηύξατο, "[Peter] prayed"

---

52 Thiede, *Simon Peter*, 139.

53 "ἱμάτιον," BDAG 475, §2; "χιτών," BDAG 1085.

54 Zerwick, §234; "ἐπιδείκνυμι," BDAG 370, §1; Bruce, *Acts* (1990), 249. Finger, *Widows*, 260–61, suggests that we should translate ἱμάτια ὅσα ἐποίει μετ᾽ αὐτῶν οὖσα ἡ Δορκάς as "clothes that Dorcas made while she was with them [sc. the widows]" and thus proposes that Dorcas employed the widows to make clothes with her. However, the presence of the (probably temporal) participle οὖσα, "being," more naturally suggests that Dorcas made the clothes at a time when she was with the widows. If Luke had intended to state that Dorcas and the widows collaborated in making the clothes, it would have been more natural to omit this participle and to use a plural verb.

probably denotes a period of prayer. The parallels with Elijah and Elisha, who pray alone for a dead person to be raised (1 Kgs 17:20–21; 2 Kgs 4:33), are as striking as the contrast with Jesus, who does not pray for Jairus's dead daughter but simply issues a word of command (Luke 8:54). Luke thus makes clear that the power experienced by the earliest believers does not lie with them—even as great a leader as Peter—but with the One whom they serve.

καὶ ἐπιστρέψας πρὸς τὸ σῶμα εἶπεν· Ταβιθά, ἀνάστηθι, "Then he turned to the body and said, 'Tabitha, get up!'" As with the man at the Beautiful Gate (Acts 3:6), Peter instructs Tabitha to get up, using her Aramaic name. Luke may intend readers to see Peter's instruction as expressing a divine conviction, after his time of prayer, that the Lord would raise Tabitha. Certainly, "[h]is power in relationship to Tabitha is a sign of his power in relationship to God."[55] Heavenly spatiality invades earth as the Lord acts from heaven to raise her (cf. v. 34) and does so away from the Jewish "heavenly space" of the temple in which God's presence was traditionally located.[56] If, as Luke hints by using her Aramaic name, Peter spoke Aramaic here, he would say *Tabitha kum(i)*, only one letter different from Jesus's words to Jairus's daughter, *Talitha kum(i)* (Mark 4:51; absent from the Lukan parallel).[57]

ἡ δὲ ἤνοιξεν τοὺς ὀφθαλμοὺς αὐτῆς, καὶ ἰδοῦσα τὸν Πέτρον ἀνεκάθισεν, "She opened her eyes and, on seeing Peter, she sat up." Luke continues his dual echo of Elisha and Jesus. In the raising of the Shunammite's son through Elisha, the boy opens his eyes as a key indication that he is alive (ἤνοιξεν τὸ παιδάριον τοὺς ὀφθαλμοὺς αὐτοῦ, "the child opened his eyes," 2 Kgs 4:35 LXX). Like the widow's son whom Jesus raises from death, she then ἀνεκάθισεν, "sat up" (Luke 7:15, the only other use of ἀνακαθίζω,"sit up," in the NT). Peter's ministry is as effective as those of Elisha and Jesus because it is empowered by the exalted Lord.

41 δοὺς δὲ αὐτῇ χεῖρα ἀνέστησεν αὐτήν· φωνήσας δὲ τοὺς ἁγίους καὶ τὰς χήρας παρέστησεν αὐτὴν ζῶσαν, "He held out his hand to her and helped her up; calling the holy ones and widows, he presented her alive." Peter's practical help in raising Tabitha to her feet is followed by his presenting her to the believers. The specific mention of τὰς χήρας, "the widows," picks them out as a subgroup of τοὺς ἁγίους, "the holy ones." The raisings of only children of widows by Elijah (1 Kgs 17:9, 10, 12—the latter suggests that he was an only child) and Jesus (Luke 7:12) may suggest that the need of the widows in each story is a factor in their dead being raised.[58] The semipublic nature of this event is significant: it was not "done in a corner" (Acts 26:26), and was thus open to falsification.

55 Reimer, *Women*, 62.
56 More fully, see Walton, "Tale," 145–48.
57 Thiede, *Simon Peter*, 139–40.
58 Hays, *Ethics*, 234; Seim, *Message*, 241–42.

42 γνωστὸν δὲ ἐγένετο καθ' ὅλης τῆς Ἰόππης καὶ ἐπίστευσαν πολλοὶ ἐπὶ τὸν κύριον, "This became known throughout the whole of Joppa, and many people came to believe in the Lord." The news spreads, for Tabitha would be seen around Joppa. People's response is not wonder or amazement, as is common with Jesus's healings, deliverances, and raisings (e.g., Luke 5:26; 7:16; 9:43; 11:14), but coming to faith (ἐπίστευσαν, inceptive aorist), echoing the response to Aeneas's healing in Lydda (v. 35). This faith is ἐπὶ τὸν κύριον, "in the Lord," which in this predominantly Jewish setting is faith in *Jesus* as Lord.[59] As in v. 35, Luke's primary interest here, as throughout Acts, is the mission of God seen in the growth of the believing community rather than the marvel of Tabitha's raising.[60]

Explanation

This typically Lukan pairing of stories about a man and a woman (see *Structure*) continues the story of the gospel's spread in Judea (1:8), as Peter travels to the coastal plain west of Jerusalem. His purpose is to visit believing communities in Judea, Galilee, and Samaria (9:31 = "all these areas," v. 32), probably to "inspect" and encourage them. Peter is prominent, named some six times in these stories, and his actions here will parallel those of Paul at a later time. The pairing of the stories continues Luke's emphasis on the inclusion of women and men in what God is now doing.

In calling Aeneas to get up, Peter makes it clear that it is Jesus the Messiah who is doing the healing, as with the man at the Beautiful Gate (3:6, 12–13; 4:10). Peter acts in similar manner to Elijah and Elisha in raising Tabitha by praying alone and with particular intensity—unusually for Jews, Peter kneels to pray (9:40; see *Comment* there, and cf. 1 Kgs 17:20–21; 2 Kgs 4:33). The contrast with Jesus's raising of Jairus's daughter is striking, for Jesus does not pray but simply issues a command to her to get up (Luke 8:54). This contrast underlines that the power at work in Tabitha's raising is that of Jesus, not Peter. Like the great prophets, Peter is the agent of divine power but not its source.

Peter's words to Aeneas (Acts 9:34) further expand readers' understanding of ascension geography, for Jesus is not unavailable (see *Comment* and *Explanation* on 1:9–11). Jesus continues to engage with people (cf. 1:1), but now he acts from heaven. Following his exaltation, Jesus sends "times of refreshing" (3:20), including healings and raisings from the dead. His actions from heaven now reshape "believer space," where Jesus followers live, as a place where the corruption and damage of the present creation begin to be reversed, proleptically anticipating the "restoration of all things" (3:21) that will happen on Jesus's return to earth.

59 With Dunn, "ΚΥΡΙΟΣ," 250; Cheng, *Characterisation*, 89.
60 Myllykoski, "Being," 173.

Jesus's identification as Messiah (9:34), raised from the dead, and as Lord (vv. 35, 42), exalted to heaven, results in these remarkable deeds. Even more, it results in people responding to the exalted Lord Jesus by "turning" to him (v. 35) and believing in him (v. 42). Both verbs portray aspects of conversion in Acts by echoing features of the programmatic 2:38, namely repentance (turning) and faith, expressed elsewhere in baptism in the name of Jesus the Messiah (see *Comment* on 2:38).

Luke's eye is, as ever, on mission, as this shows. 1:8 sets the direction and agenda of Acts, and these stories set in Lydda and Joppa take us to the edge of Judea, the second destination after Jerusalem in Jesus's words. God's mission is being carried forward through his agents—although the Lord has got to Lydda and Joppa before Peter, for there are already believing communities in those cities (see *Comment* on 9:32). In this story, too, Luke prepares for Peter evangelizing the Roman Cornelius (10:1–48). Although no gentiles are said to become believers here, these stories are located at the edges of Jewish territory in places where Jews and gentiles rub shoulders as fellow inhabitants of these cities, and not always in friendly ways. The gospel is coming to this territory as an announcement of Jesus's claim on it, as on the whole planet, to the "end of the earth" (1:8).

Scripture and Extrabiblical Index

Old Testament

Genesis

Leviticus

Numbers

Deuteronomy

Joshua

2 Kings

1 Chronicles

2 Chronicles

Ezra

Jeremiah

Lamentations

Ezekiel

Daniel

Hosea

Joel

New Testament

Mark

Luke

John

Acts

Romans

Ephesians

Philippians

Colossians

1 Thessalonians

2 Thessalonians

1 Timothy

2 Timothy

Deuterocanonical

Pseudepigrapha

Dead Sea Scrolls

Ancient Jewish Writers

Apostolic Fathers

New Testament Apocrypha and Pseudepigrapha

Rabbinic Works

Ancient Christian and Classical Writings

Subject Index

Author Index